Best Wishes
Bob

Happy 21st Mike - Neil

↑ Pretty original eh! - Martin

THROUGH THE AGES

THROUGH THE AGES

An Illustrated Chronicle of Events from 2000 BC to the Present

ALF HENRIKSON

Galley Press

First published in Great Britain by Orbis Publishing Limited,
London, 1983

Edited by Lesley Bernstein Editorial Services, London

Published in this edition 1986 by Galley Press,
an imprint of W.H. Smith and Son Limited,
Registered No. 237811 England
Trading as WHS Distributors, St John's House,
East Street, Leicester, LE1 6NE

Printed in Singapore

ISBN 0–86136–650–6
92847 N

Introduction

The fact that kingdoms perish and political power is transient emerges clearly from the charts in this book, in which with implacable regularity the generations succeed each other page by page for four thousand years.

While in Spain during the 1960s, I tried to understand the history of this country by preparing a chart of events that took place simultaneously. These involved Visigoths, Swabians, Moors, Aragonians, Castilians, not to mention Celtiberi, Roman proconsuls, Sicilians, Neapolitans and Milanese – since for several centuries, large portions of Italy belonged to the Spanish Empire. To one accustomed to thinking about the history of a country in terms of kings and queens, it all seemed very complex and disjointed. Since then I have learned that the history of all Mediterranean countries is similar to that of Spain. The famous pronouncement that the history of Sweden is its kings is both true and wise; indeed the political events of Sweden and other Scandinavian countries can be seen from the viewpoint of central power, whether or not one approves of this central power. The same could be said of countries such as France, England and the United States of America, where the power of the state is permanent and continuous, even if the central character often changes. But in the case of a country like Italy, with a history, incidentally, twice as long as that of any of the other countries mentioned above, one has to take into account the Greeks, Etruscans, Goths, Lombards, Franks, Saracens, Byzantines and Spaniards, almost as much as the Romans.

I enjoyed playing about with the parallel Spanish dynasties and thought it would be amusing to assemble a more extensive chart, to include other countries as well and to extend the time spans. It was relaxing to draw charts on graph paper, as a break from my usual writing routine. Soon I realized this pastime brought me another kind of joy, that of discovery. The two revolutionaries, Joan of Arc and Jan Hus turned out to be more or less contemporary with one another, which may not seem particularly remarkable. What appeared extraordinary, though, was that Buddha, Confucius, Pythagoras and Isaiah all lived at about the same time. It has never occurred to me before that while Genghis Khan was conquering Asia, the Magna Carta was being drawn up in England, or that Vivaldi was perfecting the form of the violin concerto while the slave trade still flourished between the European powers and their particular colonies.

Many younger people for whom history began in the twentieth century AD may protest at the endless succession of kings who from the twentieth century BC follow on one another's heels. This procession does not imply any special royalist fervour on the part of the author. Individually, most of them are uninteresting, often almost anonymous figures, only in rare instances are they worth recalling for their achievements. On the other hand, their names and reigns constitute milestones in the histories of almost every nation; in fact, these are virtually the only perceptible factors whereby the past can conveniently be surveyed. Kings are usually better suited for this purpose than presidents with shorter terms of office. The history of ancient republics, with their rulers and consuls, is difficult to treat in this way; thus the republic of Switzerland, which elects a new president every year is the only modern European state that has had to be omitted for reasons of space from this account. The oldest compilers of chronological tables seeking to present the destinies and affairs of peoples and princes by this method had no doubts as to where to begin. Their outline of all world events commenced with Adam or, at any event, Noah, accepted as universal forefathers. The creation of the world and the emergence of languages and nations were long regarded as concrete historical events, the dates of which could be determined from biblical texts. On these terms world history is conveniently short. Reckoning backwards according to the genealogy of the Old Testament, the conclusion must be that the Creation occurred around 4000 BC, while the Flood took place in approximately 2000 BC. Thus the time-span back to the origins of the world seemed quite modest, and easily embraced by a known succession of rulers.

Geologists, anthropologists, archaeologists and philologists have since taught us otherwise. Nowadays, almost every child has heard of the Stone Age and has been taught that even this long, obscure period must have been preceded by unimaginable stretches of time when there was no semblance of human life. A mere list of historical names cannot possibly cover any really vast period of world history. At most, with many century-long gaps, it might be carried back some six thousand years, to an era of obscure figures and inscriptions that archaeologists have dug up along the Nile and the Euphrates.

Fairly exact data on Egyptian and Mesopotamian people and events can be produced from about the 28th century BC. It was then that the Sumerian conqueror Lugal-Zaggisi was defeated by the even more bellicose Sargon from Akkad; and this was the period when the brilliant Imhotep helped Pharaoh Zoser to found the Old Kingdom in the early days of the 3rd Egyptian dynasty. The pyramid builders Cheops, Chefren and Mycerinus belonged to the next dynasty and lived about a century later. After yet another one and a half millennia the Greeks asserted themselves and, in their era of political greatness, when Alexander had just seized for them the whole of the ancient world, the Egyptian priest Manetho drew up in Greek a list of all the ancient Pharaohs. Manetho introduced the division into dynasties which is still valid in Egyptology. But prior to the 1st dynasty, which recent scientists date to the close of the 4th millennium BC, Manetho inserted four dynasties of demigods embracing a total period of 5212 years. This figure is by no means unreasonable, for there are numerous archaeological indications of an Egyptian civilization dating back tens of thousands of years.

The annals of the Mesopotamian peoples, meanwhile, extend much further back in time, even though the Flood is the fixed point in their chronology. The Babylonian priest Berusos, who was more or less contemporary with Manetho and who also drew up a table of rulers in Greek, reckoned on a basis of 432,000 years before the Flood and some 36,000 years between the Flood and his own period. In his list of rulers after the Flood the first dynasty contains eighty-six kings, the last of whom lived about 2000 BC. Thus the Babylonian Flood is dated almost 1000 years earlier than the Biblical Flood.

The ancient Chinese historical accounts are also very definite in their early figures and dates. They list twelve celestial emperors who managed the newly created world between them for a total of no less than 18,000 years, after which they were succeeded by twelve mortal emperors who reigned for the same stretch of time. After this came yet another nine superhuman emperors who ruled the world for a span of 45,600 years. Of the nineteen subsequent named potentates, the last three were known as Fu Xi, Shen Nung and Huang Di. These were the inventors of all manner of arts and activities, later to be handed down to mankind by the great emperors of antiquity Zhuan Xiu, Ku, Yao, Shun and Yu. Yu founded the Xia dynasty, dated at 2205-1557 BC. This is followed by the Shang dynasty, the latter era of which is called Yin. This dynasty is genuinely historic, although Chinese annals do not actually begin before the long-lived Zhou dynasty which, according to the chronicles, originated in 1122 BC.

For other nations history starts later. In Scandinavia, where the people were erecting cairns (dolmens) at the time of the Pharaohs, no names would emerge for yet another 2000 years. The recorded history of countries such as Britain, Denmark, Russia, Poland and Sweden embraces little more than thirty generations, which is about one-quarter of the time back to Cheops.

With respect to the very earliest times, and certain other periods as well, the dates given in this book should be treated as only approximate. The dating of the Babylonian kings, for example, differs greatly among various experts; it is not easy to decide which is right, but we have to settle for one or another. Certain figures of antiquity, although probably legendary, have been included intentionally because they are still of some chronological significance. Thus those singularly dubious characters, the kings of Rome, occupy their traditional position after the founding of the city, along with Hezekiah, Nebuchadrezzar, Psamtik and others whose historical existence can hardly be disputed. A number of legendary emperors in Japanese antiquity have similarly been included at the times when they are suppposed to have appeared. Any such liberties, merely for literary guidance, are always pointed out in the text above the relevant tables.

The table of monarchs is to be read horizontally at the bottom of each double spread. At the top of each page is a frieze drawn with scientific exactitude and artistic skill by Björn Berg. These friezes constitute a kind of fashion cavalcade through the ages. This space shrinks towards the end of the book, by which time there are so many sovereign states that their rulers ultimately take up the whole page.

As far as is practical, the tables use forms of name as given in the 15th edition of The New Encyclopaedia Britannica. In the case of Chinese names the Pinyin system of transcription has been used, rather than that of Wade-Giles. Pinyin was developed in 1958 by the Chinese themselves and used within the People's Republic, but only in 1979 was it accepted by most nations as the system to be employed officially for romanized Chinese names. An exception has therefore been made in the case of the historical maps on China in this book apart from the dynastic titles where the Wade-Giles system has been retained (or English as in the case of Yellow River or R. Yangtze). This also applies to any map references which appear in the text. We feel that this will facilitate cross-reference with other works.

In the text where there are well-known names which may still be unfamiliar to the reader in the Pinyin form (eg Mao Zedong for Mao Tse-tung, Beijing for Peking) the Wade-Giles form is given in brackets at first mention and in the index. Where there are Chinese names in the Tables, the first word is usually the name of the dynasty, which for the reader's convenience is included for each emperor. From the Ming dynasty onwards, the emperors are not listed under their individual names but under the name of their reign or *nien-hao*, since it is invariably these which appear in history books and in marks on works of art, porcelain etc.

The sign '&' between two or more names implies a

joint reign between them. The plus sign (+) in the same place means that the country in question was divided by two or more rulers each reigning over his own portion.

I have worked on this book for a number of years, both in Scandinavia and in southern Europe. Facts and figures have been checked several times, and in this work I have received invaluable help from Ove Dybkaer, Copenhagen, and especially from Gil Dahlström, Höganäs, the editor-in-chief of *Bra Böckers Lexikon*, whose clear judgment, wide general knowledge, stamina and scientific exactitude I greatly admire. A considerable portion of our joint effort has been given over to making sure that each decade contains the right amount of text and that the sequences of events are given fair treatment.

I know by experience that every book has its fair share of mistakes, and I would not be so foolish as to believe that this particular book, with its mass of facts and figures, is an exception to the rule – in spite of scrupulously careful checking of both manuscript and proofs. I can only hope that the mistakes are few and far between, and that the book itself will prove useful and enjoyable. Four thousand years of global history are covered in this book. It involved a great deal of work, but work which was enjoyable.

Alf Henrikson

BABYLONIA

At the beginning of the 20th century BC Shulgi, King of the Sumerians in Ur, had reigned for fifty-eight years over Elam, Assyria and Mesopotamia. His vassals included King Gudea of Lagash to whom posterity owes much for his records of Sumerian affairs. They had a numerical system based on 60, they devised mathematical tables with square and cubic roots, and they used Pythagorean numbers fifteen centuries before Pythagoras.

King Shulgi also left his own inscriptions. In one day he travelled from Ur to Nippur and back again, about 160 kilometres (100 miles), despite hailstorms en route: 'I widened the paths and straightened the roads in this land'.

The provincial officer Ishbi-Erra established an independent monarchy in the northern town of Isin; in the south the Elamites conquered Ur and demolished the city for ever. King Ibbi-Sin of Ur was taken prisoner and transported to Elam.

The dynasty in Isin and nearby Larsa reasserted Sumerian power for another few generations, but by the mid-19th century BC Babylon had won its independence and soon seized political control of that region.

During the reign of the Babylonian King Ishme-Dagan, the Assyrians made their grand entry onto the stage of political history. Led by King Ilu-shuma, they ravaged Babylon and destroyed the religious centre and holy city of Nippur.

By the close of the 18th century BC King Hammurabi of Babylon ruled over a reunited Mesopotamian empire. The Sumerian language was now dying out while the Semitic Akkadian was developing into a world language. Tens of thousands of clay tablets with cuneiform characters relate to Hammurabi's victories, correspondence and legislation. The last comprises 282 criminal and civil law paragraphs, though these lack any apparent internal order.

In the 1530s BC Babylon was razed to the ground by the Hittite King Mursilis I. Then a people known as the Kassites streamed in from the Iranian hill-country. They deposed Hammurabi's dynasty but quickly absorbed the local culture, and their long period of power in the restored Babylon was a time of peace with neither political nor cultural disruptions.

The Hurrians came out of the Caucasian regions with their horses and wagons. Their aristocracy had Indo-European names but they used both the Akkadian language and the cuneiform letters even before they established their kingdom between Syria and Assyria around 1500 BC. This was called Mitanni and it became a major power.

The Hittites also spoke Indo-European languages: Nesian and Luwian. They had settled in Asia Minor, assembling great collections of documents in their capital which one day was to be called Bogazkoy. They derived their religion and much else too from a people who used a language so difficult for posterity to grasp that it is simply referred to as proto-Hittite.

EGYPT

In 2000 BC the pyramids at Gizeh were already 500 years old. The Old Kingdom had long since disintegrated and the country had been divided into small squabbling states for the best part of two centuries. A new era began with Pharaoh Mentuhotep II, who came from Thebes in upper Egypt. In the 1990s he defeated a more democratic regime from northern Egypt and united the nation under his dynasty. This was the advent of the Middle Kingdom.

Sesostris III led a campaign into Palestine, and during his reign the Egyptian empire was extended to Semneh beyond the second cataract of the Nile in Nubia.

The story of Sinuhe probably derives from the time of Amenemhet III. His reign was a period of economic expansion, the national irrigation system was expanded and mining flourished in Sinai.

The Egyptian 15th dynasty was of alien origin, associated with an invasion by a people known as the Hyksos. They came from Syria or Palestine and had Semitic names. The Hyksos appear to have brought horses and wagons into Egypt. Generally speaking, they controlled only the Nile delta. The Biblical narrative of Joseph in Egypt may well be related to the Hyksos era.

The history of Egypt from the 18th to the 16th centuries BC is confused and indeterminate. The 16th dynasty, which controlled only part of the nation, probably coexisted with other neighbouring dynasties for a considerable period. However, the chronological order of the Pharaohs is most likely to be correct.

Egypt's Late Kingdom began with Pharaoh Ahmose and his son Amenhotep I. The 18th dynasty, introduced by these two Pharaohs was perhaps the most renowned of all the Egyptian dynasties, and included both Akhenaton and Tutankhamen.

CHINA

The Xia (Hsia) dynasty may be legendary, but classical Chinese historians are very specific concerning the dates involved here. According to them, the dynasty was founded by the Emperor Yu, to whom they attribute many achievements, the greatest of which was to save the Chinese people from perishing in a century-long, world-wide flood. Yu is reputed to have died in about 2205 BC and to have been succeeded by a series of emperors, each one worse than the previous one. In 1766 BC the last of these, Zhie, ended a life totally devoted to self-indulgence and such curious pastimes as disturbing the peace with the aid of 30,000 female musicians, releasing tigers in the public market-place, tearing up silks belonging to the state depositories, and so on. Finally he was deposed by a pure-hearted individual named Tang who in 1783 BC founded the Shang dynasty. This dynasty has been historically established, though there is great doubt as to the accuracy of its dates.

Many archaeological finds have been made in China from the period traditionally known as Shang. Among the most remarkable of these are the oracle bones, mainly the shoulder blades of mammals, which are covered in Chinese ideograms. These inscriptions were originally used for soothsaying and were then placed in archives, furnishing posterity with a great deal of information on contemporary social conditions, thoughts and ideas, besides throwing much light on the development of the written as well as the spoken word in China.

20th century BC

Shulgi (Ur) | Bur-Sin (Ur) — Babylonia
Mentuhotep II (dyn. XI) - - - - - - | — Egypt
Xia dyn. — China

2000	1999	1998	1997	1996	1995	1994	1993	1992	1991

Bur-Sin | Shu-Sin (Ur) — Babylonia
Amenemhet I (XII dyn.) — Egypt
Xia dyn. — China

1990	1989	1988	1987	1986	1985	1984	1983	1982	1981

Shu-Sin (Ur) | Ibbi-Sin (Ur) — Babylonia
Amenemhet I (XII dyn.) — Egypt
Xia dyn. — China

1980	1979	1978	1977	1976	1975	1974	1973	1972	1971

Ibbi-Sin (Ur) — Babylonia
Amenemhet I (XII dyn.) | — Egypt
Xia dyn. — China

1970	1969	1968	1967	1966	1965	1964	1963	1962	1961

Ibbi-Sin (Ur) | — Babylonia
Sesostris I (XII dyn.) — Egypt
Xia dyn. — China

1960	1959	1958	1957	1956	1955	1954	1953	1952	1951

Ishbi-Erra (Isin) — Babylonia
Sesostris I (XII dyn.) — Egypt
Xia dyn. — China

1950	1949	1948	1947	1946	1945	1944	1943	1942	1941

Ishbi-Erra (Isin) — Babylonia
Sesostris I (XII dyn.) — Egypt
Xia dyn. — China

1940	1939	1938	1937	1936	1935	1934	1933	1932	1931

Ishbi-Erra (Isin) | Babylonia
Sesostris I (XII dyn.) | Amenemhet II (XII dyn.) — Egypt
Xia dyn. — China

1930	1929	1928	1927	1926	1925	1924	1923	1922	1921

Shu-ilishu (Isin) | Babylonia
Amenemhet II (XII dyn.) — Egypt
Xia dyn. — China

1920	1919	1918	1917	1916	1915	1914	1913	1912	1911

| Iddin-Dagan (Isin) — Babylonia
Amenemhet II (XII dyn.) — Egypt
Xia dyn. — China

1910	1909	1908	1907	1906	1905	1904	1903	1902	1901

19th-18th century BC

Babylonia — Iddin-Dagan (Isin)
Egypt — Amenemhet II (XII dyn.) — Sesostris II (XII dyn.)
China — Xia dyn.

1900	1899	1898	1897	1896	1895	1894	1893	1892	1891

Babylonia — Ishme-Dagan (Isin)
Egypt — Sesostris II — Sesostris III (XII dyn.)
China — Xia dyn.

1880	1879	1878	1877	1876	1875	1874	1873	1872	1871

Babylonia — Ur-Ninurta (Isin)
Egypt — Sesostris III (XII dyn.)
China — Xia dyn.

1860	1859	1858	1857	1856	1855	1854	1853	1852	1851

Babylonia — Ur-Ninurta (Isin)
Egypt — Amenemhet III (XII dyn.)
China — Xia dyn.

1840	1839	1838	1837	1836	1835	1834	1833	1832	1831

Babylonia — Sumu'abum — Sumulael
Egypt — Amenemhet III (XII dyn.)
China — Xia dyn.

1820	1819	1818	1817	1816	1815	1814	1813	1812	1811

Babylonia — Sumulael
Egypt — Amenemhet IV (XIII dyn.)
China — Xia dyn.

1800	1799	1798	1797	1796	1795	1794	1793	1792	1791

Babylonia — Sabium
Egypt — Sekemkheres (XII dyn.)
China — Shang dyn.

1780	1779	1778	1777	1776	1775	1774	1773	1772	1771

Babylonia — Apilsin
Egypt — Neferhotep (XIV dyn.)
China — Shang dyn.

1760	1759	1758	1757	1756	1755	1754	1753	1752	1751

Babylonia — Sinnuballit
Egypt — Sebekhotep (XIV dyn.)
China — Shang dyn.

1740	1739	1738	1737	1736	1735	1734	1733	1732	1731

Babylonia — Hammurabi
Egypt — Apopi I (XVI dyn. Hyksos)
China — Shang dyn.

1720	1719	1718	1717	1716	1715	1714	1713	1712	1711

Ishme-Dagan (Isin) — Babylonia
Sesostris II (XII dyn.) — Egypt
Xia dyn. — China

1890	1889	1888	1887	1886	1885	1884	1883	1882	1881

Lipit-Ishtar (Isin) — Babylonia
Sesostris III (XII dyn.) — Egypt
Xia dyn. — China

1870	1869	1868	1867	1866	1865	1864	1863	1862	1861

Ur-Ninurta (Isin) — Babylonia
Amenemhet III (XII dyn.) — Egypt
Xia dyn. — China

1850	1849	1848	1847	1846	1845	1844	1843	1842	1841

Sumu'abum (Babylon) — Babylonia
Amenemhet III (XII dyn.) — Egypt
Xia dyn. — China

1830	1829	1828	1827	1826	1825	1824	1823	1822	1821

Sumulael — Babylonia
Amenemhet III (XII dyn.) — Egypt
Xia dyn. — China

1810	1809	1808	1807	1806	1805	1804	1803	1802	1801

Sumulael — Babylonia
Sebeknefru (XII dyn.) — Chatauire Ugafa (XIII dyn.) — Egypt
Xia dyn. — Shang dyn. — China

1790	1789	1788	1787	1786	1785	1784	1783	1782	1781

Sabium — Apilsin — Babylonia
Neferhotep (XIV dyn.) — Egypt
Shang dyn. — China

1770	1769	1768	1767	1766	1765	1764	1763	1762	1761

Apilsin — Sinnuballit — Babylonia
Sebekhotep (XIV dyn.) — Egypt
Shang dyn. — China

1750	1749	1748	1747	1746	1745	1744	1743	1742	1741

Sinnuballit — Hammurabi — Babylonia
Salitis (XV dyn.) — Egypt
Shang dyn. — China

1730	1729	1728	1727	1726	1725	1724	1723	1722	1721

Hammurabi — Babylonia
Apopi II (XVI dyn. Hyksos) — Egypt
Shang dyn. — China

1710	1709	1708	1707	1706	1705	1704	1703	1702	1701

17th-16th century BC

Babylonia — Hammurabi
Egypt — Apopi III (XVI dyn. Hyksos)
China — Shang dyn.

1700	1699	1698	1697	1696	1695	1694	1693	1692	1691

Babylonia — Samsuiluna
Egypt — Seqenenre I (XVII dyn.)
China — Shang dyn.

1680	1679	1678	1677	1676	1675	1674	1673	1672	1671

Babylonia — Samsuiluna
Egypt — Seqenenre II (XVII dyn.)
China — Shang dyn.

1660	1659	1658	1657	1656	1655	1654	1653	1652	1651

Babylonia — Abieshu
Egypt — Seqenenre III (XVII dyn.)
China — Shang dyn.

1640	1639	1638	1637	1636	1635	1634	1633	1632	1631

Babylonia — Ammiditana
Egypt — Kamose (XVII dyn.)
China — Shang dyn.

1620	1619	1618	1617	1616	1615	1614	1613	1612	1611

Babylonia — Ammiditana
Egypt — Kamose (XVII dyn.)
China — Shang dyn.

1600	1599	1598	1597	1596	1595	1594	1593	1592	1591

Babylonia — Ammisaduqa
Egypt — Ahmose (XVIII dyn.)
China — Shang dyn.

1580	1579	1578	1577	1576	1575	1574	1573	1572	1571

Babylonia — Shamshuditana
Egypt — Ahmose (XVIII dyn.) — Amenhotep I (XVII dyn.)
China — Shang dyn.

1560	1559	1558	1557	1556	1555	1554	1553	1552	1551

Babylonia — Shamshuditana
Egypt — Amenhotep I (XVIII dyn.)
China — Shang dyn.

1540	1539	1538	1537	1536	1535	1534	1533	1532	1531

Babylonia — Agum I
Egypt — Thutmose II, III & Hatshepsut (XVIII dyn.)
China — Shang dyn.

1520	1519	1518	1517	1516	1515	1514	1513	1512	1511

Hammurabi | Samsuluna — Babylonia
Apopi III (XVI dyn. Hyksos) — Egypt
Shang dyn. — China

1690	1689	1688	1687	1686	1685	1684	1683	1682	1681

Samsuiluna — Babylonia
Seqenenre I (XVII dyn.) — Egypt
Shang dyn. — China

1670	1669	1668	1667	1666	1665	1664	1663	1662	1661

Samsuiluna | Abieshu — Babylonia
Seqenenre II (XVII dyn.) — Egypt
Shang dyn. — China

1650	1649	1648	1647	1646	1645	1644	1643	1642	1641

Abieshu — Babylonia
Seqenenre III (XVIII dyn.) — Egypt
Shang dyn. — China

1630	1629	1628	1627	1626	1625	1624	1623	1622	1621

Ammiditana — Babylonia
Kamose (XVII dyn.) — Egypt
Shang dyn. — China

1610	1609	1608	1607	1606	1605	1604	1603	1602	1601

Ammiditana | Ammisaduqa — Babylonia
Senechtenre (XVII dyn.) — Egypt
Shang dyn. — China

1590	1589	1588	1587	1586	1585	1584	1583	1582	1581

Ammisaduqa | — Babylonia
Ahmose (XVIII dyn.) — Egypt
Shang dyn. — China

1570	1569	1568	1567	1566	1565	1564	1563	1562	1561

Shamshuditana — Babylonia
Amenhotep I (XVIII dyn.) — Egypt
Shang dyn. — China

1550	1549	1548	1547	1546	1545	1544	1543	1542	1541

Gandza (Kassite) — Babylonia
| Thutmose I (XVIII dyn.) — Egypt
Shang dyn. — China

1530	1529	1528	1527	1526	1525	1524	1523	1522	1521

Kashtiliash I | Usshi — Babylonia
Thutmose II, III & Hatshepsut (XVIII dyn.) — Egypt
Shang dyn. — China

1510	1509	1508	1507	1506	1505	1504	1503	1502	1501

15th century BC

Mitanni	Shuttarna I
Khatti	Alluwamnas
Assyria	Enlil-nasir
Babylonia	Abirattash
Egypt	Hatshepsut & Thutmose III (XVIII dyn.)
China	Shang dyn.

1500	1499	1498	1497	1496	1495	1494	1493	1492	1491

The Egyptian queen Hatshepsut was the daughter of Thutmose I and at first reigned jointly with her brother and husband Thutmose II. He died young; when her

Mitanni	Saustatar
Khatti	Zidantas II
Assyria	Ashur-rabi
Babylonia	Harbashipak
Egypt	Thutmose III (XVIII dyn.)
China	Shang dyn.

1480	1479	1478	1477	1476	1475	1474	1473	1472	1471

The Mitanni kingdom was invaded by Thutmose III in 1475 BC, but he failed to subjugate it. Mitanni remained a major power for yet another century.

Mitanni	Saustatar
Khatti	Tudhaliyas II
Assyria	Ashur-nirari II
Babylonia	Agum II
Egypt	Thutmose III (XVIII dyn.)
China	Shang dyn.

1460	1459	1458	1457	1456	1455	1454	1453	1452	1451

Mitanni	
Khatti	Arnuwandas I
Assyria	Ashur-bel-nisheshu
Babylonia	Burnaburiash I
Egypt	Amenhotep II (XVIII dyn.)
China	Shang dyn.

1440	1439	1438	1437	1436	1435	1434	1433	1432	1431

Amenhotep III was a successful diplomat who retained Egypt's control over Syria throughout his reign: to this end he married the daughters of Shuttarna II and Tushretta of Mitanni. He was also a great builder and during his reign the temple of Amon and the colossi of Memnon, two statues of himself, were built at Luxor.

Mitanni	Artatama I
Khatti	Hattusilis II
Assyria	Ashur-rim-nisheshu
Babylonia	Ulamburiash
Egypt	Thutmose IV (XVIII dyn.)
China	Shang dyn.

1420	1419	1418	1417	1416	1415	1414	1413	1412	1411

Hautilis II — Khatti
Enlil-nasir — Assyrla
Tashigurumash — Babylonia
Hatshepsut & Thutmose III (XVIII dyn.) | Thutmose III — Egypt
Shang dyn. — China

1490	1489	1488	1487	1486	1485	1484	1483	1482	1481

son Thutmose III came of age, he deposed his mother and embarked successfully upon a major military campaign, directed mainly at Mitanni.

During his reign Egypt reached its greatest extent, embracing both Syria and Palestine and extending from the Euphrates to the fourth cataract of the Nile in Nubia.

Saustatar — Mitanni
Huzziyas II — Khatti
Ashur-rabi — Assyria
Tiptakzi — Babylonia
Thutmose III (XVIII dyn.) — Egypt
Shang dyn. — China

1470	1469	1468	1467	1466	1465	1464	1463	1462	1461

Saustatac — Mitanni
Arnuwandas I — Khatti
Ashur-bel-nisheshu — Assyria
Agum II — Babylonia
Thutmose III (XVII dyn.) | Amenhotep II (XVIII dyn.) — Egypt
Shang dyn. — China

1450	1449	1448	1447	1446	1445	1444	1443	1442	1441

Posterity knows very little about the Assyrian, Babylonian, Hurrian and Hittite kings of this century. The successions are probably correct but only occasionally can the length of their reigns be determined.

Artatama I — Mitanni
Arnuwandas I — Khatti
Ashur-rim-nisheshu — Assyria
Kashtiliash II — Babylonia
Amenhotep II (XVIII dyn.) — Egypt
Shang dyn. — China

1430	1429	1428	1427	1426	1425	1424	1423	1422	1421

The Shang dynasty changed its capital in the 15th century BC and at the same time assumed the name Yin. It moved its place of residence several times without altering its name, and its influence expanded.

Shuttarna II — Mitanni
Hattusilis II | — Khatti
Ashur-nadin-akhe — Assyria
Kurigalzu I — Babylonia
Amenhotep III (XVIII dyn.) — Egypt
Shang dyn. | Yin — China

1410	1409	1408	1407	1406	1405	1404	1403	1402	1401

14th century BC

Mitanni — Shuttarna II ---------- Artasumara ---------- Tushratta —
Khatti — Tudhaliyas III —
Assyria — Ashur-nadin-akhe — | — Eriba-Adad I —
Babylonia — Kurigalzu I ----------
Egypt — Amenhotep III (XVIII dyn.) —
China — Yin dyn. —

1400	1399	1398	1397	1396	1395	1394	1393	1392	1391

Kurigalzu I was probably the most bellicose of the Kassite kings in Babylon, who reigned quite peacefully. He conquered Susa.

Mitanni — Tushratta ---------- Shuttarna III ----------
Khatti — Arnuwandas II — | — Suppiluliumas —
Assyria | — Ashur-uballit I —
Babylonia ---------- Kurigalzu II ---------- Kadashman-Enlil I ----------
Egypt — Amenhotep III — | — Amenhotep IV alias Akhenaton (XVIII dyn.) —
China — Yin dyn. —

1380	1379	1378	1377	1376	1375	1374	1373	1372	1371

Amenhotep IV was a religious reformer who sought to replace the cult of Amon with that of the Sun god Aton. For this reason he changed his name to Akhenaton. His queen was Nefertite. A more naturalistic art emerged during their reign. At the same time Egypt began to lose its position as a major power, relinquishing part of Syria.

Khatti — Suppiluliumas —
Assyria — Ashur-uballit I —
Babylonia — Burnaburiash II —
Egypt — Tutankhamen (XVIII dyn.) — |
China — Yin dyn. —

1360	1359	1358	1357	1356	1355	1354	1353	1352	1351

Tutankhamen came to the throne in 1361 BC.

Khatti — | — Arnuwandas III — | — Mursilis II —
Assyria — Ashur-uballit I — | —
Babylonia — Kurigalzu III —
Egypt — Horemheb (XIX dyn.) —
China — Yin dyn. —

1340	1339	1338	1337	1336	1335	1334	1333	1332	1331

During Ashur-uballit I's reign Assyria was a great military power. Enlil-nirari I defeated Kurigalzu III, and Arik-den-ili extended the kingdom over former Mitanni territory.

Khatti — Mursilis II —
Assyria — Arik-den-ili —
Babylonia ---------- Nazima-ruttash —
Egypt ----- Horemheb ---------- Ramses I ---------- Seti I (XIX dyn.) —
China — Yin dyn. —

1320	1319	1318	1317	1316	1315	1314	1313	1312	1311

Tushratta — Mitanni
Tudhaliyas III | Arnuwandas II — Khatti
Eriba-Adad I — Assyria
Melishipak I --- Karaindash --- Kadashman-Harbe I Babylonia
Amenhotep III (XVIII dyn.) — Egypt
Yin dyn. — China

1390	1389	1388	1387	1386	1385	1384	1383	1382	1381

A diplomatic correspondence between kings Kurigalzu I and Burnaburiash II of Babylonia with the Pharaohs Amenhotep III and IV of Egypt has survived.

Mattiwaza — Mitanni
Suppiluliumas — Khatti
Ashur-uballit I — Assyria
Burnaburiash II — Babylonia
Amenhotep IV alias Akhenaton (XVIII dyn.) | Smenkhkare — Egypt
Yin dyn. — China

1370	1369	1368	1367	1366	1365	1364	1363	1362	1361

Suppiluliumas, greatest of the Hittite kings, intervened in a fraternal dispute in the Mitanni kingdom and appropriated a large part of this area. As a result, King Tushratta was assassinated. After the death of Suppiluliumas, Ashur-uballit I of Assyria attacked and wholly destroyed Mitanni.

Suppiluliumas — Khatti
Ashur-uballit I — Assyria
Burnaburiash II --- Kurigalzu III — Babylonia
Ay | Horemheb (XIX dyn.) — Egypt
Yin dyn. — China

1350	1349	1348	1347	1346	1345	1344	1343	1342	1341

Horemheb, a general by profession, re-established the cult of Amon in Egypt.

Mursilis II — Khatti
Enlil-nirari I | Arik-den-ili — Assyria
Kurigalzu III — Babylonia
Horemheb (XIX dyn.) — Egypt
Yin dyn. — China

1330	1329	1328	1327	1326	1325	1324	1323	1322	1321

The Exodus from Egypt, vividly described in the Bible, is thought by the experts to have taken place in the days of Ramses II, of whom Moses would therefore have been a contemporary.

Moses — Israel
Mursilis II | Muwatallis — Khatti
| Adad-nirari I — Assyria
Nazima-ruttash — Babylonia
Seti I (XIX dyn.) | Ramses II (XIX dyn.) — Egypt
Yin dyn. — China

1310	1309	1308	1307	1306	1305	1304	1303	1302	1301

13th century BC

Israel	Moses
Khatti	Muwatallis
Assyria	Adad-nirari I
Babylonia	Nazima-ruttash | Kadashman-Turgu
Egypt	Ramses II (XIX dyn.)
China	Yin dyn.

1300	1299	1298	1297	1296	1295	1294	1293	1292	1291

In 1298 the Hittites engaged the Egyptians in battle at Kadesh in Syria. Ramses II boasted in his writings of having avoided an ambush and winning the battle, but Muwatallis rightly claimed the victory, for under the peace terms the Egyptians drew back slightly from their Syrian frontier, though still retaining Palestine.

Israel	Moses
Khatti	Urhi-Teshub | Hattusilis III
Assyria	Shalmaneser I
Babylonia	Kadashman-Turgu | Kadashman-Enlil II |
Egypt	Ramses II (XIX dyn.)
China	Yin dyn.

1280	1279	1278	1277	1276	1275	1274	1273	1272	1271

Ramses II made a memorial to his victories over the sea-peoples – Pelesets, Thekels, Danunae, Sherdens and Achaeans – who had threatened Egypt's existence ever since they first occupied the Syrian and Palestinian coastlines. The Pelesets correspond to the Bible's Philistines. The Thekels and Sherdens are possibly from Sicily and Sardinia, while the Danunae are probably the Danaou-na of the Iliad.

Israel	Moses
Khatti	Hattusilis III
Assyria	| Tukulti-ninurta I
Babylonia	Shagerakhti-Shuriash
Egypt	Ramses II (XIX dyn.)
China	Yin dyn.

1260	1259	1258	1257	1256	1255	1254	1253	1252	1251

Merneptah claimed in 1232 to have inflicted a great defeat on the Israelites in Palestine. The Bible makes no mention of this. Merneptah's inscription indicates, nevertheless, that Israel had now reached Canaan.

Israel	Joshua
Khatti	Tudhaliyas IV
Assyria	Tukulti-ninurta I |
Babylonia	Adad-shum-iddin (Tukulti-ninurta) | Adad-shum-nasir
Egypt	Ramses II (XIX dyn.) | Merneptah
China	Yin dyn.

1240	1239	1238	1237	1236	1235	1234	1233	1232	1231

The Egyptian 19th dynasty ended in a confusion of short reigns followed by an interregnum.

Israel	
Khatti	| Arnuwandas IV
Assyria	Ashur-nadin-apli | Ashur-nirari III
Babylonia	Adad-shum-nasir
Egypt	| Siptah
China	Yin dyn.

1220	1219	1218	1217	1216	1215	1214	1213	1212	1211

Moses	**Israel**
Muwatallis — Urhi-Teshub	**Khatti**
Adad-nirari I	**Assyria**
Kadashman-Turgu	**Babylonia**
Ramses II (XIX dyn.)	**Egypt**
Yin dyn.	**China**

1290	1289	1288	1287	1286	1285	1284	1283	1282	1281

The long reign of Ramses II witnessed numerous building projects. Huge statues of him abound in Egypt from Abu Simbel to the Nile delta.

Moses	**Israel**
Hattusilis III	**Khatti**
Shalmaneser I	**Assyria**
Kudur-Enlil — Shagerakhti-Shuriash	**Babylonia**
Ramses II (XIX dyn.)	**Egypt**
Yin dyn.	**China**

1270	1269	1268	1267	1266	1265	1264	1263	1262	1261

Tukulti-ninurta I attacked and subjugated Babylonia which remained a vassal state throughout his reign. Toward the close of this century, however, the Assyrian empire underwent a period of weakness.

Moses	**Israel**
Tudhaliyas IV	**Khatti**
Tukulti-ninurta I	**Assyria**
Kadashman-Harbe II (Tukulti-ninurta)	**Babylonia**
Ramses II (XIX dyn.)	**Egypt**
Yin dyn.	**China**

1250	1249	1248	1247	1246	1245	1244	1243	1242	1241

Biblical information on Israel's political leaders prior to David cannot be dated accurately. The order of names in the tables is somewhat arbitrary and there may be errors of a decade or more.

Joshua	**Israel**
Tudhaliyas IV	**Khatti**
Ashur-nadin-apli	**Assyria**
Adad-shum-nasir	**Babylonia**
Merneptah (XIX dyn.)	**Egypt**
Yin dyn.	**China**

1230	1229	1228	1227	1226	1225	1224	1223	1222	1221

Around 1210 the Hittite empire was destroyed by invading barbarians from the European side of the Bosporus. These were presumably Phrygians.

	Israel
Arnuwandas IV	**Khatti**
Ashur-nirari III — Enlil-kudur-usur	**Assyria**
Adad-shum-nasir — Melishipak II	**Babylonia**
Seti II	**Egypt**
Yin dyn.	**China**

1210	1209	1208	1207	1206	1205	1204	1203	1202	1201

12th century BC

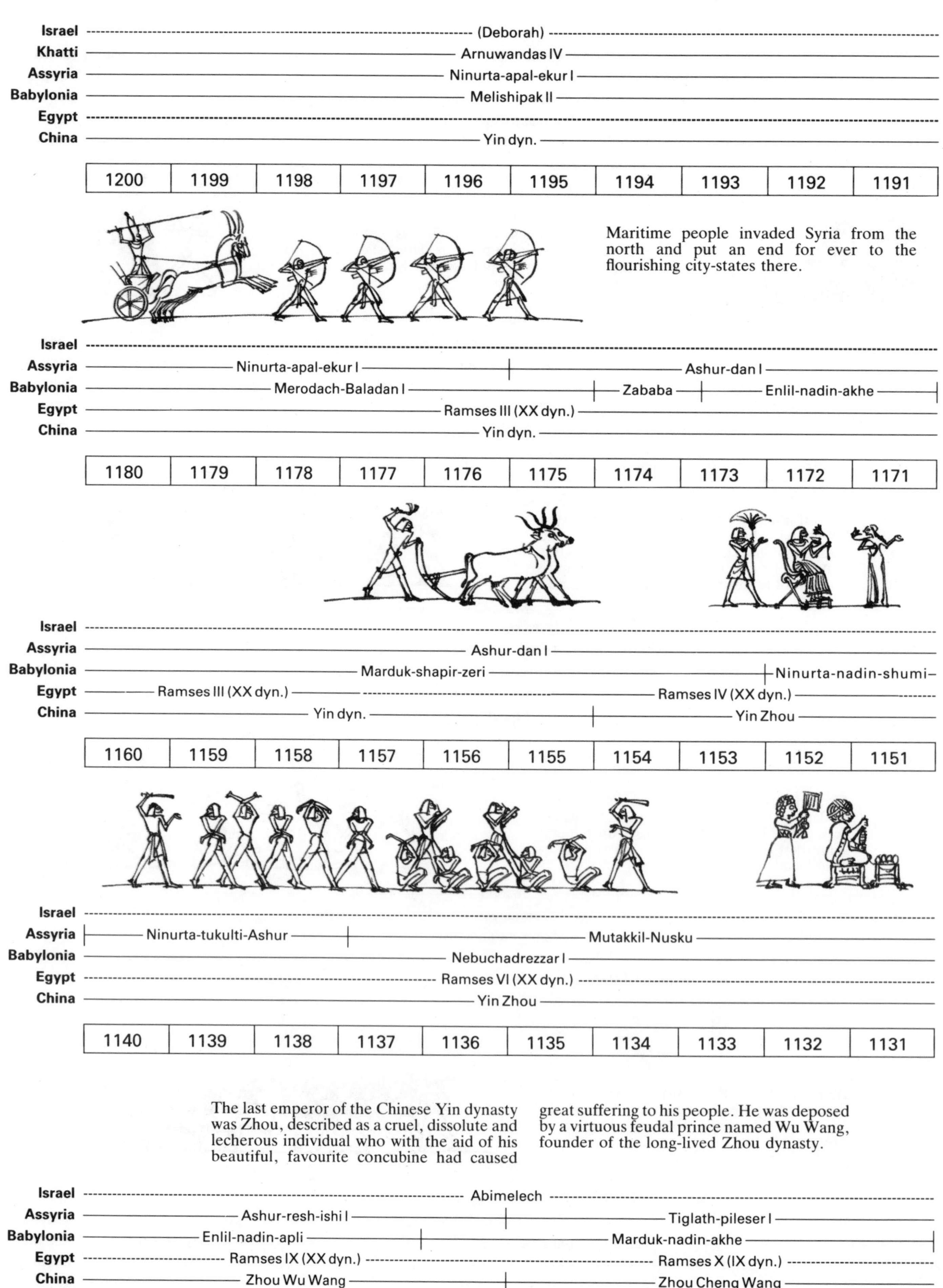

Israel (Deborah)
Khatti Arnuwandas IV
Assyria Ninurta-apal-ekur I
Babylonia Melishipak II
Egypt
China Yin dyn.

1200	1199	1198	1197	1196	1195	1194	1193	1192	1191

Maritime people invaded Syria from the north and put an end for ever to the flourishing city-states there.

Israel
Assyria Ninurta-apal-ekur I | Ashur-dan I
Babylonia Merodach-Baladan I | Zababa | Enlil-nadin-akhe
Egypt Ramses III (XX dyn.)
China Yin dyn.

1180	1179	1178	1177	1176	1175	1174	1173	1172	1171

Israel
Assyria Ashur-dan I
Babylonia Marduk-shapir-zeri | Ninurta-nadin-shumi
Egypt Ramses III (XX dyn.) | Ramses IV (XX dyn.)
China Yin dyn. | Yin Zhou

1160	1159	1158	1157	1156	1155	1154	1153	1152	1151

Israel
Assyria Ninurta-tukulti-Ashur | Mutakkil-Nusku
Babylonia Nebuchadrezzar I
Egypt Ramses VI (XX dyn.)
China Yin Zhou

1140	1139	1138	1137	1136	1135	1134	1133	1132	1131

The last emperor of the Chinese Yin dynasty was Zhou, described as a cruel, dissolute and lecherous individual who with the aid of his beautiful, favourite concubine had caused great suffering to his people. He was deposed by a virtuous feudal prince named Wu Wang, founder of the long-lived Zhou dynasty.

Israel Abimelech
Assyria Ashur-resh-ishi I | Tiglath-pileser I
Babylonia Enlil-nadin-apli | Marduk-nadin-akhe
Egypt Ramses IX (XX dyn.) | Ramses X (IX dyn.)
China Zhou Wu Wang | Zhou Cheng Wang

1120	1119	1118	1117	1116	1115	1114	1113	1112	1111

Israel

Suppiluliumas II — Khatti

Ninurta-apal-ekur I — Assyria

Melishipak II | Merodach-Baladan I — Babylonia

Ramses III (XX dyn.) — Egypt

Yin dyn. — China

1190	1189	1188	1187	1186	1185	1184	1183	1182	1181

The Hittites, who, following the attacks by the maritime people, had moved south to Syria, where they established new city-states, were now hard pressed by the Aramaeans, and were subsequently attacked by the Assyrians.

Israel

Ashur-dan I — Assyria

Marduk-shapir-zeri — Babylonia

Ramses III (XX dyn.) — Egypt

Yin dyn. — China

1170	1169	1168	1167	1166	1165	1164	1163	1162	1161

In Babylon, in about 1170, the degenerate Kassite dynasty was succeeded by the Isin dynasty, whose most remarkable ruler was Nebuchadrezzar I. In his reign Babylonia enjoyed a political renaissance, though this was short-lived; Ashur-resh-ishi restored Assyrian hegemony and Tiglath-pileser I again subjugated Babylonia, after first defeating the invading hordes of Aramaeans in Syria and Phrygians from Anatolia.

Gideon — Israel

Ashur-dan I — Assyria

Ninurta-nadin-shumi | Nebuchadrezzar I — Babylonia

Ramses V (XX dyn.) — Egypt

Yin Zhou — China

1150	1149	1148	1147	1146	1145	1144	1143	1142	1141

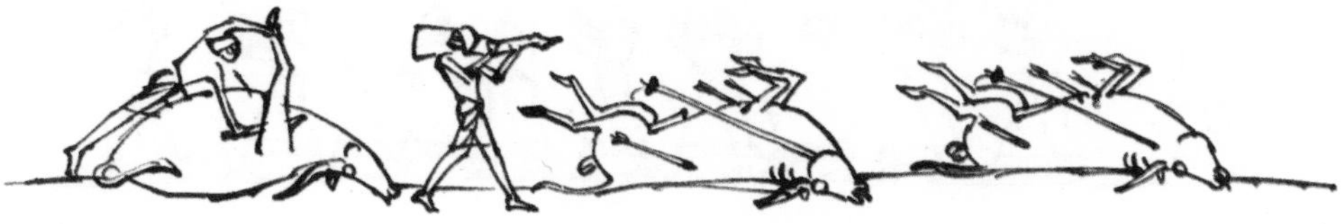

Israel

Mutakkil-Nusku | Ashur-resh-ishi I — Assyria

Nebuchadrezzar I | Enlil-nadin-apli — Babylonia

Ramses VII (XX dyn.) — Ramses VIII (XX dyn.) — Egypt

Yin Zhou | Zhou Wu Wang — China

1130	1129	1128	1127	1126	1125	1124	1123	1122	1121

Jephthah — Israel

Tiglath-pileser I | Ninurta-apal-ekur II — Assyria

Marduk-nadin-akhe | — Babylonia

Ramses XI (XX dyn.) — Egypt

Zhou Cheng Wang — China

1110	1109	1108	1107	1106	1105	1104	1103	1102	1101

11th century BC

Israel	Izban
Assyria	Ninurta-apal-ekur II — Ashur-bel-kala I
Babylonia	Itti-Marduk-balatu
Egypt	Ramses XI (XX dyn.)
China	Zhou Cheng Wang

1100	1099	1098	1097	1096	1095	1094	1093	1092	1091

Around 1100 China was ruled by a man usually referred to as the Duke of Zhou, guardian of the boy emperor Cheng Wang. The Duke of Zhou appears in Confucian literature as a political and moral paragon. However, China was at that point divided into 1800 small feudal states, and earlier there had been even more.

Israel	Abdon
Assyria	Ashur-bel-kala I — Enlil-rabi
Babylonia	Adad-apal-iddin
Egypt	Herihor (XXI dyn.)
China	Zhou Cheng Wang — Zhou Kang Wang

1080	1079	1078	1077	1076	1075	1074	1073	1072	1071

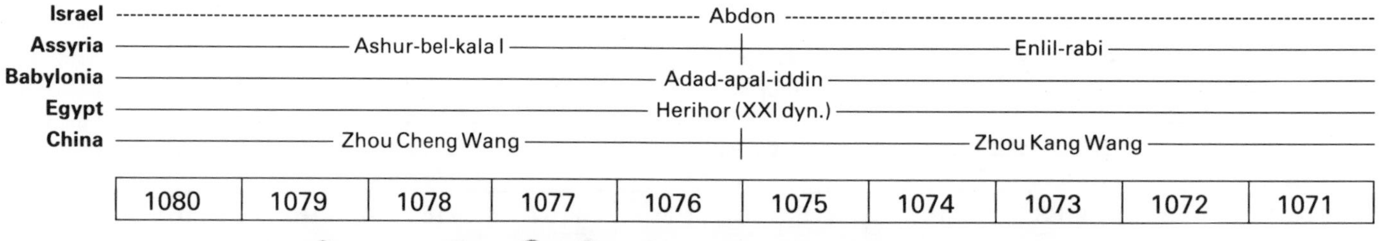

Israel	Eli
Assyria	Eriba Adad II — Shamshi-Adad IV
Babylonia	Nabu-shum-libur
Egypt	Piankh
China	Zhou Kang Wang — Zhou Zhao Wang

1060	1059	1058	1057	1056	1055	1054	1053	1052	1051

Israel	Samuel
Assyria	Ashurnasirpal I
Babylonia	Nabu-shum-libur — Shimmash-Shipak
Egypt	Psusennes I (XXI dyn.)
China	Zhou Zhao Wang

1040	1039	1038	1037	1036	1035	1034	1033	1032	1031

An anonymous Elamite and his three sons made up the Babylonian dynasty of Bazi.

Israel	Saul
Assyria	Shalmeneser II — Ashur-nirari IV — Ashur-rabi II
Babylonia	Kashu-nadin-akhe — Bazi dyn.
Egypt	Psusennes I (XXI dyn.)
China	Zhou Zhao Wang

1020	1019	1018	1017	1016	1015	1014	1013	1012	1011

Elon — Israel
Ashur-bel-kala I — Assyria
Marduk-shapik-zeri | Adad-apal-iddin — Babylonia
Herihor (XXI dyn.) — Egypt
Zhou Cheng Wang — China

1090	1089	1088	1087	1086	1085	1084	1083	1082	1081

In this century both Assyria and Babylonia were harried by invading Aramaeans and Chaldeans. Little more than the names of the rulers here are known to us today.

Samson — Israel
Enlil-rabi | Ashur-bel-kala II | Eriba-Adad II — Assyria
Adad-apal-iddin | — Babylonia
Herihor (XXI dyn.) — Egypt
Zhou Kang Wang — China

1070	1069	1068	1067	1066	1065	1064	1063	1062	1061

Egypt's power over Syria had dissolved and in about 1070 Nubia also won its freedom. A prince named Smendes, alias Nesbenebded, founded a dynasty which ruled at Tanis in the Nile delta, while the high priest Herihor resided as Pharaoh in Thebes, claiming to represent the god Amon on earth. Thus at home, too, Egyptian unity was crumbling.

Eli — Israel
| Ashurnasirpal I — Assyria
Nabu-shum-libur — Babylonia
Smendes (XXI dyn.) — Egypt
Zhou Zhao Wang — China

1050	1049	1048	1047	1046	1045	1044	1043	1042	1041

Samuel — Israel
| Shalmaneser II — Assyria
| Ea-mukin-shum | — Babylonia
Psusennes I (XXI dyn.) — Egypt
Zhou Zhao Wang — China

1030	1029	1028	1027	1026	1025	1024	1023	1022	1021

The weakness of Egypt and the Mesopotamian countries offered scope for the formation of new states in Syria and Palestine. The latter derived its name from the Philistines. The Philistines were constantly at war with the Israelites, whose king, Saul, suffered defeat and was himself killed in battle. Not until David's time did the Israelites gain the upper hand over the Philistines.

Saul | | David — Israel
Ashur-rabi II — Assyria
Bazi dyn. — Babylonia
Psusennes I (XXI dyn.) — Egypt
Zhou Zhao Wang | Mu Wang — China

1010	1009	1008	1007	1006	1005	1004	1003	1002	1001

1000-991 BC

PHILISTINES
EGYPT
IRAN

Tombs of individuals who have established societies and patronized art exist on every continent. America had been inhabited for 20,000 or 30,000 years and Australia for at least 10,000 years. The earliest traces of human activity in Asia, Europe and Africa are perhaps 500,000 years old. On this scale, King David and his contemporaries are comparatively recent.

In Egypt, which teems with hieroglyphs and monuments, papyrus had also been used at least since the time of the pyramid builders. The stalks of the papyrus plant were cut longitudinally into thin strips and then plaited together and pressed into sheets. No other glue than that in the plant itself was needed.

At the beginning of the first millennium BC the pyramids of Egypt were already fifteen centuries old. Thus as much time elapsed between Pharaoh Cheops and the biblical King David as between Attila the Hun and Mao Zedong (Mao tse-tung).

Egyptian scripts date back to the fourth millennium BC, but Sumerian scripts of the Mesopotamian countries, mainly in the form of clay or stone tablets, are even older.

The Northern peoples, central Europeans, South Africans, Indians and central Asians were presumably still illiterate. Chinese script is of ancient date. In the ruined capital of the ancient Shang dynasty there is an archive containing innumerable oracle questions and answers, inscribed on tortoiseshell and animal bones. These exhibit more than 2000 different characters which to all intents and purposes, contain every element and idea that characterize the later development of writing in China. To some extent, these characters are straightforward, unmistakable depictions of the things they are intended to represent, but there are also many with abstract connotations. Chinese literature has thus existed since at least the 12th century BC, which is the date attributable to the earliest poems in the classical Shijing anthology. Some of these are lucid, tender songs about love, a motif which subsequently disappeared in Chinese lyric poetry until this century.

The Zhou (Chou) dynasty, originating in the westerly (Shaanxi) (Shensi) province, ruled over a feudal state which principally embraced the great plains around the Yellow River. The first sovereigns appear to have been energetic politicians and warriors. It is said of Mu Wang, who incidentally is reputed to have visited a legendary queen in a fabulous country far to the west, that his influence extended as far as the Yangtze valley where there lived a barbarian, amply bearded people who bore no resemblance to any Chinese. Mu Wang also asserted his authority over the many feudal princes who conformed to a social system with a rigid order of precedence.

In Babylonia and Assyria practically nothing is known about the duration of reigns, events, or names of rulers from the mid-12th century through until 890 BC. The Mesopotamian countries had entered a period of political stagnation.

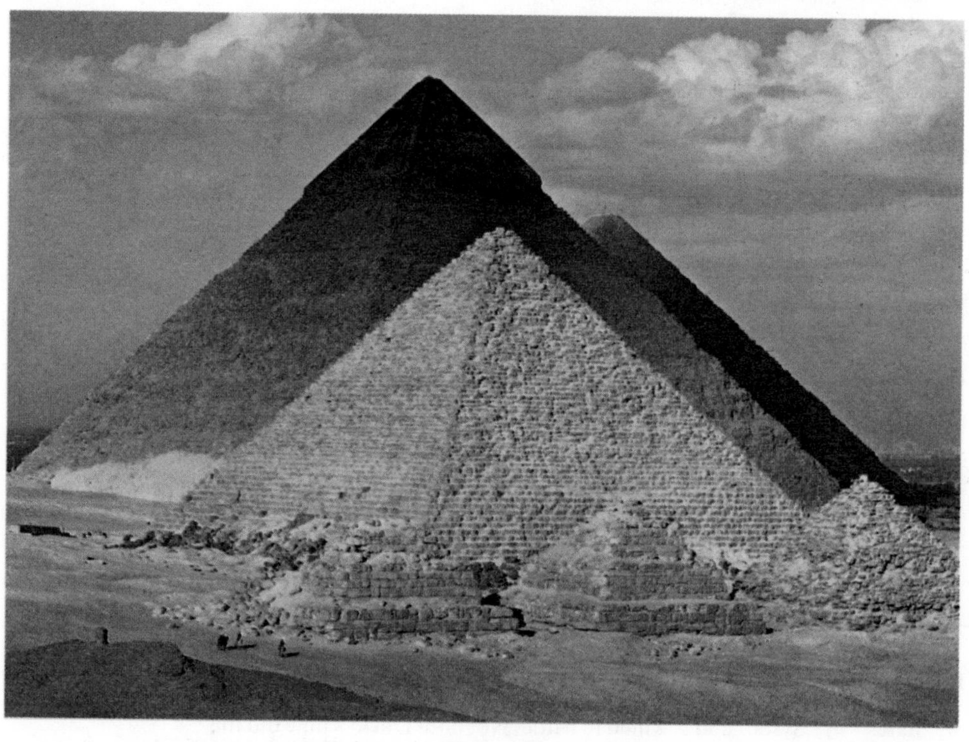

The pyramids at Gizeh had long been in existence by this time. They contain graves of the Pharaohs Cheops, Chefren and Mycerinus. The pyramid of Mycerinus at the front was probably once the most ornate, while the Cheops pyramid is the largest of the three.

Israel	David
Assyria	Ashur-rabi II — Ashur-resh-ishi II
Babylonia	Bazi dyn. — Marbiti-apal-usur
Egypt	Psusennes I (XXI dyn.)
China	Zhou Mu Wang

1000	999	998	997	996	995	994	993	992	991

EGYPT
IRAN
LURISTAN

The Zhou dynasty could hardly be described as a major power. According to the records, China was divided into 1800 small feudal states, the most celebrated of which were Chin, Wu and Lu. These were ruled over by members of the house of Zhou, who enjoyed hereditary rights to their principalities but were seldom at peace among themselves. The Emperor's capital was called Feng and was inland in the region of the Yellow River.

A city which later excavators were to call Troy VIIb flourished on the hill of Hissarlik in Asia, some miles from where the Hellespont empties into the Aegean Sea. The inhabitants were comparative new-comers who had built their homes on the site of a war-devastated settlement known to modern archaeologists as Troy VIIa. Troy VIIa had been destroyed a few centuries earlier—a local incident that was to become known world-wide since it served as the theme of the *Iliad*. The people of Troy VIIb appear to have come from the Balkan peninsula and the Danube region, judging from the cracked urns and similar implements unearthed by archaeologists.

Students of the ancient world believe they can establish the date of Troy's destruction very accurately—attributing it to the year 1184 BC. For them this represents the starting point of world history, because from this time onwards the gods of Olympus ceased, visibly at least, to intervene personally in human affairs. The *Iliad* was a sacred record for the people of antiquity who, incidentally, were unaware that Troy had been destroyed on several occasions in the course of several thousands of years.

The Egyptian 21st dynasty consisted of priests. According to the list made by Manetho, its last rulers were Psusennes I, Nefelkheres, Amenemope, Osokhor, Siamon and Psusennes II. Psusennes I was probably reigning at this particular time. Little or nothing is known of their political activities, but they left certain objects behind them, and inscribed their Egyptian names on mummy wrappings and the like.

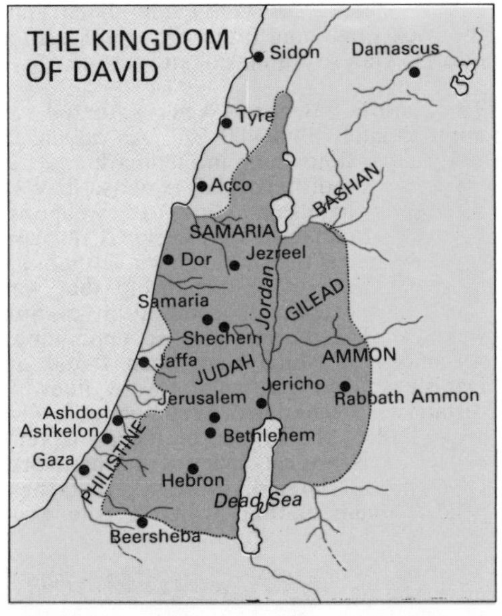
THE KINGDOM OF DAVID
Sidon
Damascus
Tyre
Acco
BASHAN
SAMARIA
Dor
Jezreel
Samaria
Jordan
GILEAD
Shechem
Jaffa
JUDAH
AMMON
Jericho
Rabbath Ammon
Ashdod
Ashkelon
Jerusalem
Bethlehem
Gaza
PHILISTINE
Hebron
Dead Sea
Beersheba

In the Greek world the Doric incursion was taking place—a prolonged process that began a century and a half earlier. By this time the Minoan and Mycenaean cultures of Crete and Peleponnesus had run their course and their cities and palaces were in ruins. It is by no means certain that the Dorians were entirely responsible, but in any event they were now settled in these regions and were apparently also established on Rhodes, whose inhabitants later spoke a Doric dialect, like the Spartans, Corinthians and Cretans.

Nabu-mukin-apli originated a new Babylonian dynasty which survived for two and a half centuries. Although he called himself 'king of kings', he evidently had problems that compelled him to wage campaigns against plundering Aramaeans. His predecessor was an Elamite, though he had a Semitic name. No details are known of the circumstances leading to this change of rule.

The Judaean King David, who seems to have reigned at Hebron since 1003, seized Jerusalem in 996 and subsequently lived there. All the information we possess about David is to be found in the Bible, specifically in the two Books of Samuel, I Kings and I Chronicles, each of which contain narratives concerning this unscrupulous politician.

After the preliminary spadework of his predecessor Saul, David defeated and subjugated the Philistines on the Mediterranean coast. He also successfully fought the Aramaeans, the Ammonites and other tribes in establishing an extensive Israelite empire in the political vacuum arising from the temporary debility of the Egyptian and Mesopotamian powers.

Ruins of Troy, the southern entrance to the excavated area.

David — **Israel**
Ashur-resh-ishi II — **Assyria**
Nabu-mukin-apli — **Babylonia**
Nefelkheres (XXI dyn.) ---- Amen. (XXI dyn.) — **Egypt**
Zhou Mu Wang — **China**

990	989	988	987	986	985	984	983	982	981

NORDIC BRONZE AGE
EGYPT

In northern Europe an anonymous Bronze Age culture prevailed. Magnificent barrows and burial mounds had existed in Scandinavia for a thousand years or more. The climate was pleasantly temperate; 10,000 years had elapsed since the inland ice receded. A new religion seems to have emerged, for people had begun cremating their dead. Petroglyphs (rock-carvings) of a symbolic and, (for us) obscure significance were being fashioned at the Kivik barrow in southernmost Sweden, at Tanum in western Sweden and at numerous places in Norway and Denmark.

The Scandinavian petroglyphs mostly lacked composition; one seldom encounters a coherent scene. The pictures quite certainly relate to the cult activities of a Bronze Age farming people, but at the same time the religious significance appears to be more closely associated with technique than content: the figures were evidently cut into the rock singly and often on top of earlier efforts. They are unmistakenly exotic.

The Nordic Bronze Age is dated at approximately 1400-400 BC. An advanced culture was flourishing in Denmark and the southern Swedish coastal regions, leaving behind it handsome finds of weapons, helmets, ornamented horns, etc. A remarkable example is the chariot from Trundholm Mose, a piece of craftsmanship that was surely connected with some form of Sun worship. The bronze horns, euphonious specimens of which have been found on Danish soil in particular, were likewise certainly associated with a religious cult. The great skill of the bronze craftsmen is very evident, as is the proficiency of the engravers. It might be claimed, however, that their helical ornamentation, which a couple of centuries earlier had culminated in a splendid stylistic achievement, had passed its peak.

In northern Scandinavia, too, petroglyphs have been found, though these have little in common with the Tanum works. The former are grandiose, naturalistic line drawings of animals, mostly on a large scale, and their dating is uncertain. They probably relate to a type of art created tens of thousands of years ago by Ice Age people living farther south in Europe when reindeer and mammoths were indigenous game. The petroglyphs found on rock faces in Tröndelagen, Jämtland, Härjedalen and Ångermanland were probably the work of primitive hunters who remained at the Stone Age level.

The Sun chariot, from Trundholm Mose, Denmark.

Israel	David
Assyria	Ashur-resh-ishi II
Babylonia	Nabu-mukin-apli
Egypt	Amenemope (XXI dyn) ---- Osokhor
China	Zhou Mu Wang

980	979	978	977	976	975	974	973	972	971

NORDIC
BRONZE
AGE

The Littorina period, an important phase in the evolutionary history of the Baltic Sea area, began sometime around 5000 BC when a strip of land between Scandinavia and the continent was flooded by the waters of the Danish sound. It is not altogether clear how long the Littorina period lasted, though by the 960s BC it was probably drawing to a close.

The water was still fairly salty and covered a large area of what in time became Östergötland, Sörmland, Uppland and the Norrland coastal regions.

The Hittite empire disintegrated in the 13th century BC, but a number of Hittite city-states appear still to have existed in northern Syria. At this time a Phrygian empire was established to the west in Asia Minor and possibly a Lydian empire as well, though there is little record of early events in the history of these peoples. We are somewhat better informed about a state known as Urartu, which is synonymous with Ararat. This was located between Caucasia and Lake Van and was subject to continual attacks from its Assyrian neighbours. In their records, almost all the principal kings of Assyria reported victories against Urartu.

The Bible, almost the only source of information on people and events at this time, has a great deal to tell of King David and his son Solomon. The last chapter of 2 Samuel relates the unfortunate consequences of a population census that David ill-advisedly conducted in the new empire of his creation. This invoked the wrath of God who sent a pestilence on Israel, leading David to acknowledge his error and to erect an altar for sacrificial atonement. The Scriptures do not state whether he subsequently destroyed his census figures and register of taxpayers. 1 Kings continues the narrative, beginning with the story of the beautiful Abishag the Shunammite, who was brought in to attend the old king, while intrigues over the succession were pursued within his court and harem. The victor was Solomon who took the life of his older half-brother Adonijah and at the same time appropriated Abishag. Solomon also married the Egyptian Pharaoh's daughter, in addition to numerous other foreign ladies. 'He had seven hundred wives, princesses, and three hundred concubines', states 1 Kings.

The capital of the 21st Egyptian dynasty was the town of Tanis in the Nile delta; its sovereignty virtually covered lower Egypt only, while another high priesthood dynasty ruled in Thebes. At this period, however, the whole nation was apparently united under one sceptre. The rule of the Tanite Pharaohs lacked forcefulness and initiative, their finances were disrupted and their cities and institutions were in decline. There was, meanwhile, a considerable immigration of Libyans to the Nile delta, and this was of historic significance, for it pacified Egypt's western frontier: the Libyans no longer saw any reason to attempt the seizure of this region by armed force. Many of them acquired influential posts in the Egyptian administration, especially in the army.

The capital of the Hittite empire was situated in the middle of the Anatolian plateau, in the place now known as Bogazkoy. The ruins are extensive and impressive. A considerable amount of literature in cuneiform writing has been found, enabling archaeologists to become familiar with Hittite religion and politics, and also to reconstruct the grammar of their long extinct Indo-European language.

David ———— Solomon — **Israel**
Asur-resh-ishi II ——|—— Tiglath-pileser II — **Assyria**
Nabu-mukin-apli — **Babylonia**
Osokhor (XXI dyn) ---- Siamon (XXI dyn) — **Egypt**
Zhou Mu Wang — **China**

970	969	968	967	966	965	964	963	962	961

PHOENICIA
EGYPT

The west coast of Asia Minor was colonized at this time by Greek immigrants who established a number of cities there, including Miletus and Ephesus. This colonization was probably connected with what the authors of antiquity term the return of the Herclidae, i.e. the entry of the Dorians into Greece proper. But the Dorians were by now already established on Peloponnesus and the southerly islands, including Rhodes and Crete. The Ionians had set up a twelve-city union to the north which included Smyrna, Samos and Chios: a sanctuary on Delos kept them united with kinsfolk in Euboea and Attica. Farther still to the north the Aeolians had settled on Lesbos and in the country beyond. Their dialect was also spoken in Thessalia and Boeotia on the European side of the Aegean. But we know nothing whatsoever of the actual Dorian immigration or of the reasons why the Greek tribes were divided in this manner.

Phoenician Tyre enjoyed a period of greatness. There are frequent allusions in the Bible to King Hiram of Tyre because he was allied with Israel, which enabled him to keep a fleet in the Red Sea as well. Phoenician ships were also probing even farther west across the Mediterranean.

Unlike the Greeks, the seafaring Phoenicians set up practically no colonies in the true sense of the term. There are accounts of Phoenician trading sites on the west coast of Morocco and of voyages in quest of tin as far afield as the Scilly Isles, off Cornwall, but there was apparently no question of any permanent settlements in these distant places. By the time Carthage was founded and flourishing, a century and a half later, the golden age of the Phoenicians had already passed. Although the Phoenicians made many long voyages, these seamen preferred not to stray too far from land. Neither did the Greeks venture out into open waters unless compelled to do so. Their ships were still small, the compass still to be discovered. But when necessary, the Greeks found the North Star by extending a line through the hind part of the Great Bear, while the Phoenicians looked directly at the Little Bear.

A new discovery was the colouring of cloth by means of purple shell dye. The Phoenicians in particular were renowned for their skill in this field.

In Jerusalem a water conduit was built in the form of a 537 m. long brick tunnel.

A limestone tablet calendar from Tel Gezer in Palestine lists the names of the months and describes the seasonal activities of the farmers.

The relationship between Solomon and Hiram is not clear. According to the Bible they were friends, yet in fact Solomon was probably Hiram's vassal. Otherwise there seems no reason why he should have handed over to Hiram twenty Galilean towns and 120 gold talents.

Phoenician votive statues from Byblos, now in the archaeological museum of Beirut. The Phoenicians often may have felt impelled to make vows to their cruel gods—the sea was immense, their ships fairly small.

Israel	Solomon
Assyria	Tiglath-pileser II
Babylonia	Nabu-mukin-apli — Ninurta-kudur-usur — Marbiti-akhe-iddin
Egypt	Psusennes II (XXI dyn)
China	Zhou Mu Wang

960	959	958	957	956	955	954	953	952	951

PHOENICIA
EGYPT

In Egypt royal tombs were systematically plundered over a long period, even though the authorities had endeavoured to mislead the thieves by constantly shifting the mummies from place to place. Under Psusennes II the mummies were finally collected together and all the 18th and 19th dynasty Pharaohs and their precious accoutrements were deposited in an ancient tomb which was once intended for Amenhotep I, but for some reason was never used for him. This was located in a practically inaccessible corrie and here the Pharaohs were left in peace until 1871 when they were discovered by modern tomb plunderers.

India, with very early vestiges of human habitation, has no history in the European and Chinese sense of the word. Before and during the 11th century there flourished an advanced civilization which archaeologists have termed the Indus culture: it was an enlightened society notable for its hygienic accomplishments (including a complicated drainage system and a bathroom in every house), and diverse technical skills. By King Solomon's time this culture had disappeared, probably extinguished by the invasion of Arian barbarians from the north. Instead there emerged a literature in the Arian language, though this cannot be dated accurately. The era of the Veda books with their hymns and other forms of sacred text admittedly covered several centuries, but the oldest of these Rig-Veda could have originated at about this time.

Gong Wang and many successors in this and the following century are shadowy figures. Dating from this time, however, is a document entitled Yukung, a kind of Chinese national geography. It describes nine provinces and embraces almost the entire region of northern China down to the Yangtze, though this does not necessarily imply that the Zhou dynasty ruled the whole area. Its contacts with inhabitants of the neighbouring provinces were doubtless transient and superficial.

Little was heard of the countries along the great river valleys of the Euphrates and the Tigris. The great days of the Sumerians had long since passed.

A Stone Age civilization, now known as the Jomon culture, had been flourishing in Japan for several thousand years. Japan's Bronze Age did not begin until the 3rd century BC.

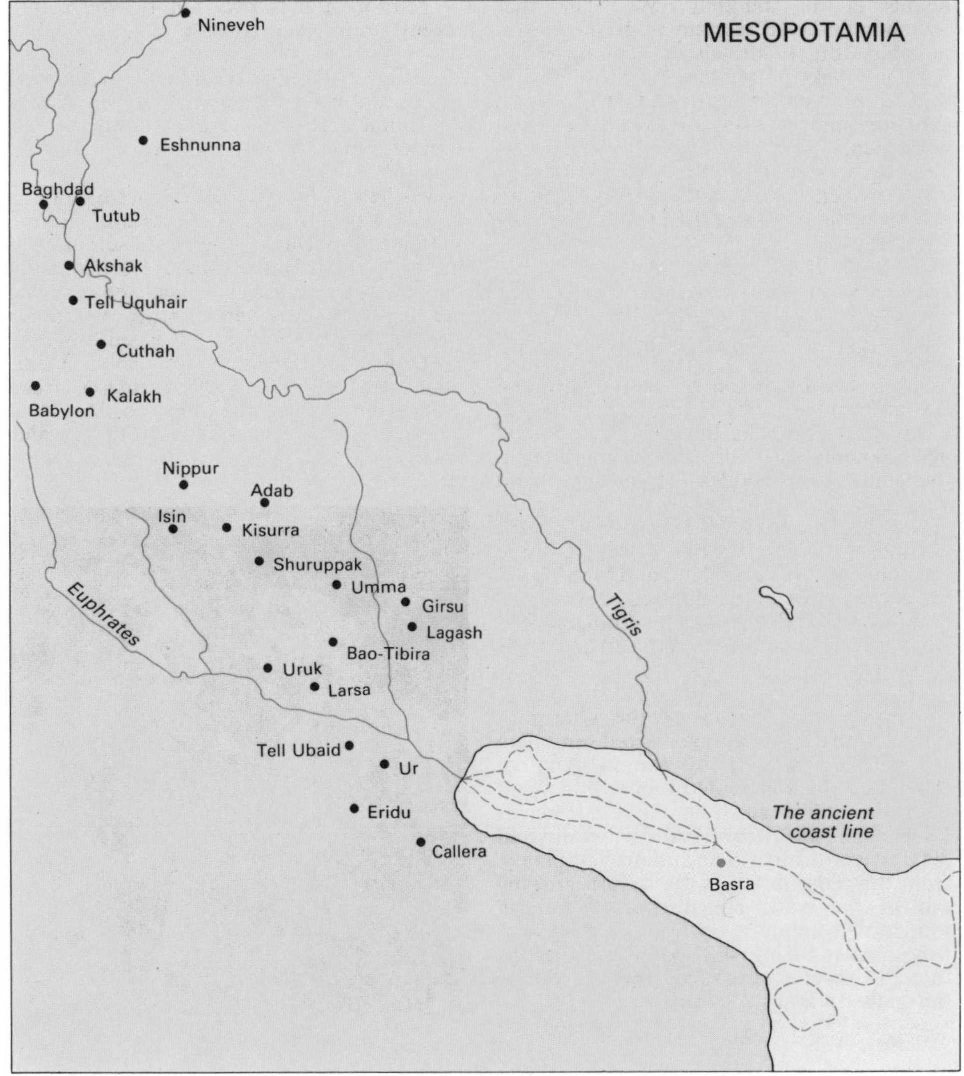
MESOPOTAMIA
Nineveh
Eshnunna
Baghdad
Tutub
Akshak
Tell Uquhair
Cuthah
Babylon
Kalakh
Nippur
Adab
Isin
Kisurra
Shuruppak
Umma
Girsu
Lagash
Bao-Tibira
Uruk
Larsa
Tell Ubaid
Ur
Eridu
Callera
Euphrates
Tigris
The ancient coast line
Basra

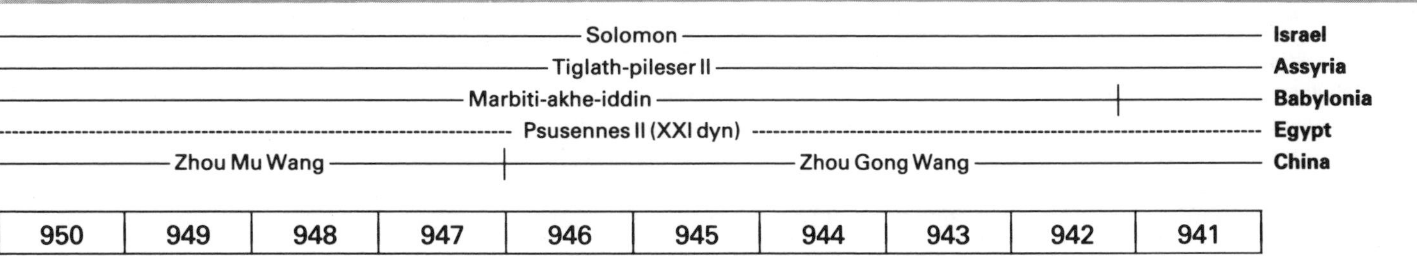
Solomon — Israel
Tiglath-pileser II — Assyria
Marbiti-akhe-iddin — Babylonia
Psusennes II (XXI dyn) — Egypt
Zhou Mu Wang — Zhou Gong Wang — China
950
949
948
947
946
945
944
943
942
941

EGYPT

Four chapters in the I Kings and some ten chapters in the I and II Chronicles are devoted to Solomon's temple in Jerusalem. Consequently we are well informed concerning the origins, the design and the interior details of this building. We learn that Solomon enslaved as many non-Israelites as possible. 'But of the children of Israel did Solomon make no servants for his work; but they *were* men of war, and chief of his captains, and captains of his chariots and horsemen.'
'And these *were* the chief of king Solomon's officers, even two hundred and fifty that bare rule over the people.' (II Chronicles 8:9-10)

Solomon's history was written by the priesthood in Jerusalem, who owed their very existence to him. But the Bible also has a good deal to tell of Solomon's religious deviations:
'And he had seven hundred wives, princesses, and three hundred concubines: and his wives turned away his heart.' Thus in his old age Solomon began also to worship Astarte, the Phoenician goddess from Sidon and various other deities as well:
'Then did Solomon build an high place for Chemosh, the abomination of Moab, in the hill that *is* before Jerusalem, and for Molech, the abomination of the children of Ammon.'
'And likewise did he for all his strange wives, which burnt incense and sacrificed unto their gods'. (I Kings 11:3, 7-8).

According to 2 Chron. 9, the Queen of Sheba, with a large retinue, visited Jerusalem to convince herself of the wisdom of Solomon. She confronted him with difficult questions, all of which he answered, for his knowledge was proverbial: he composed 3000 proverbs and was an authority on plants, from the cedar down to the hyssop growing out of the wall. He discoursed too on four-footed animals, on birds, reptiles and fishes, states I Kings 4:32-33. The Bible says that this meeting produced trading results: the allied kings Solomon and Hiram subsequently obtained their gold, algum wood and precious stones from the Sheba region. According to Abyssinian tradition, Solomon became the lover of the Queen of Sheba who gave birth to a son, Menelik, progenitor of the royal family which until recently reigned in Abyssinia.

The story of the Queen of Sheba has always captivated the popular imagination. There are innumerable pictures relating to the subject, particularly in folk art.

Nevertheless, Solomon's conduct of foreign affairs was not always successful. Edom, subjugated by David, liberated itself under a prince named Hadad who returned from political asylum in Egypt. But Solomon did manage to retain a narrow strip of territory down towards the Bay of Elam, thereby keeping a route open to Eshon-Geber. Simultaneously in the north, Damascus freed itself from Solomon's dominion. An Aramaean kingdom was established there which later became a serious harassment to Israel.

China was still divided up into innumerable small feudal states, though the emperor possessed central power which had more substance than the mere lip-service of his vassals. He maintained fourteen standing armies and evidently interfered often in the affairs of the different regions. Most of the vassal princes were members of his own dynasty.

Comparatively advanced cultures which developed in various parts of Central and South America, later received such names as Qaluyu, Chiripa, Barrancas, Saladero and Chavin. The Qaluyu culture had flourished for a long time around Lake Titicaca though it still made no use of metals. But the Chavin culture which emerged at about this time on Peru's north coast, grew maize, manioc and cotton, built pyramid temples and irrigation systems, made copper and golden alloys and kept tame llamas.

In the Greek world the Dorians continued their immigration. They appear to have occupied Sparta and to have driven the Acharians and Ionians out of Peloponnesus. The tribes that moved into Epirus and other areas west of Pindus had interbred with Illyrians and ever after the latter were regarded as semi-barbarians by the inhabitants of Attica and the Aegean islanders.

In the Baltic region the shoreline contours slowly but surely changed. The Danish sound which had long been broad and deep, became shallower, the water less salty; the *Littorina* snail was no longer at home here. The pine forests moved southward over Scandinavia, though oaks were as yet predominant. The climate was still mild.

Solomon's encounter with the Queen of Sheba; detail from one of Piero della Francesca's frescoes in Arezzo, painted 1452-66 in the San Francesco church.

Israel — Solomon

Assyria — Tiglath-pileser II | Ashur-dan II

Babylonia — Shamash-mudammiq

Egypt — Sheshonk I (XXII dyn)

China — Zhou Gong Wang | Zhou Yi Wang I

940	939	938	937	936	935	934	933	932	931

EGYPT
BYBLOS, PHOENICIA

Solomon's Jewish kingdom and Hiram's Phoenician state had gained power because of a period of political weakness in Egypt and among the countries around the Euphrates. But there were indications that this situation might change. In Egypt the clerical 21st dynasty was succeeded by the more extrovert 22nd dynasty, whose first Pharaoh was Sheshonk. This was not an Egyptian name: the family appears to have originated in Libya, whence the Egyptians had long imported mercenaries. We possess no details of this change of dynasty. Sheshonk established himself as Pharaoh in the city of Bubastis to the east in the Nile delta and sought to legitimize his family by marrying his son Osorkon to a daughter of Psusennes II. He appointed another of his sons as high priest of Amon in Thebes, but it failed to have the desired effect: Thebes retained its independence and, so far as can be ascertained, paid no taxes whatsoever to Sheshonk. The Pharaoh also had problems with his Libyan kinsmen who were prepared to lend him troops only in return for large grants of land. Sheshonk had to agree and thereby paved the way for the division of Egypt into countless small principalities. In other respects, Sheshonk's policies were quite successful. Like all the great Pharaohs before him, he extended his power southward to Nubia.

In the Bible Sheshonk I is referred to as Shishak. At the very beginning of his reign an Israelite named Jeroboam came to Egypt as a fugitive and was well received. He had supervised the labour force of Solomon's building projects in Jerusalem, where he attempted unsuccessfully to organize a revolt. He remained in Egypt for a couple of decades, biding his time. Relations between Egypt's new dynasty and powerful Israel were poor; both sides were arming. Solomon fortified a place called Tamar on the southern frontier of his kingdom and assembled a large force of war-chariots and cavalry.

The death of Solomon terminated Israel's era of power. In order to be recognized, his son Rehoboam had to meet a representative popular assembly in Shechem, the city from which the Jewish tribes had been governed before David made himself king and moved to Jerusalem. The people resented the compulsory labour and other impositions connected with Solomon's building activities, which Rehoboam wished to perpetuate. 2 Chron. 11:6-12, names fifteen towns that he fortified, including Bethlehem, Tekoa, Aijalon, and Hebron. At this meeting Rehoboam was urged to reduce the burden of work but refused to do so. The result was a public outcry: 'Every man to your tent, O Israel, and now, David, see to thine own house.' Kings relates that Jeroboam was present at this meeting in Shechem; at any rate he was shortly afterwards hailed as king of all the Israelite tribes except that of Judah, which remained loyal to Rehoboam. In the inevitable war that followed Jeroboam was immediately assisted by Sheshonk, who sent a strong Egyptian army against Jerusalem: 1200 chariots, 60,000 cavalry and limitless numbers of Libyans, Sacae and Ethiopians. They won an easy victory, seized and plundered Jerusalem, and removed the treasures of Solomon to the treasure chamber of their own Pharaohs. We learn from 2 Chron. that King Rehoboam resided in Jerusalem with eighteen wives and sixty concubines who bore him twenty-eight sons and sixty daughters.

After a century and a half of silence, the annals of Assyria reopen with the reign of King Ashur-dan II. Ashur-dan and his successor restored Assyrian power and built up a centralized bureaucracy.

Rehoboam, according to 1 Kings 12, said to the people: 'And now whereas my father did lade you with a heavy yoke, I will add to your yoke: my father hath chastised you with whips, but I will chastise you with scorpions.' Fresco (detail) by Holbein the younger.

Solomon	Rehoboam	**Judaea**
	Jeroboam	**Israel**
Ashur-dan II		**Assyria**
Shamash-mudammiq		**Babylonia**
Sheshonk I (XXII dyn)		**Egypt**
Zhou Yi Wang I		**China**

930	929	928	927	926	925	924	923	922	921

EGYPT
HITTITES

The First Book of Kings and the Second Book of Chronicles recount extraordinary details of the fates of Rehoboam and Jeroboam. Both kings were berated by prophets, particularly the latter who, nevertheless, is more charitably described than his enemy and rival. Thus one fearsome man of God known as Ahijah informed Jeroboam's wife that her ailing son would die and that their entire household would be demolished because the head of their family had made a graven image. Jeroboam, ruling from Shechem, had erected two golden calves in different parts of the country, one in the village of Bethel some miles north of Jerusalem. These biblical golden calves, which were to fascinate and counfound Christians through the centuries, were probably not calves at all. 'Calf' was a disparaging term used by the Jewish scribes to deprecate the bull cults of the Egyptians and Middle East peoples. Nor was it even a question of an alien god in Israel, despite the contrary allegations of the Old Testament prophets. Yahweh himself had been worshipped in the form of a bull symbol even in Jerusalem, but in northern Israel this type of Yahweh cult was of considerably greater significance. Bethel itself was an ancient Canaan cult site, and in the account of the patriarch Jacob's visit to this place (Genesis 28 : 10-12 & 35 : 1-7) the bull god was specifically identified with Yahweh. The bull cult had been widespread for a millennium or more. It had a fertility aspect, but also a divine connotation. The golden calves of the Bible assume a relationship both with the Egyptian Apis and with the bull symbols of Aegean Crete, and they also have a counterpart in the Mesopotamian countries where in remote times the Sumerians had sculpted golden bulls.

When considering the ancient cultures of the East, it is worth bearing in mind time spans in other parts of the world as well. Agamemnon's palace in Mycenae, built 500 years beforehand, was already a ruin when the earliest prophets of the Old Testament were raging against golden calves and other abominations, while Scandinavian stone cairns had by this time existed for 2000 years or more, and were thus almost as ancient as the pyramids.

Pharaoh Sheshonk's successors left little of consequence and their obituaries relate mainly to temple gifts, Apis bulls and similar non-political matters. Egypt no longer had much impact on major political events.

This golden bull's head adorns a harp from Ur in Chaldaea. Philadelphia University Museum, USA. The object dates from approximately 2500 BC. The Sumerians and other ancient peoples often adorned their liturgical instruments with the image of a bull.

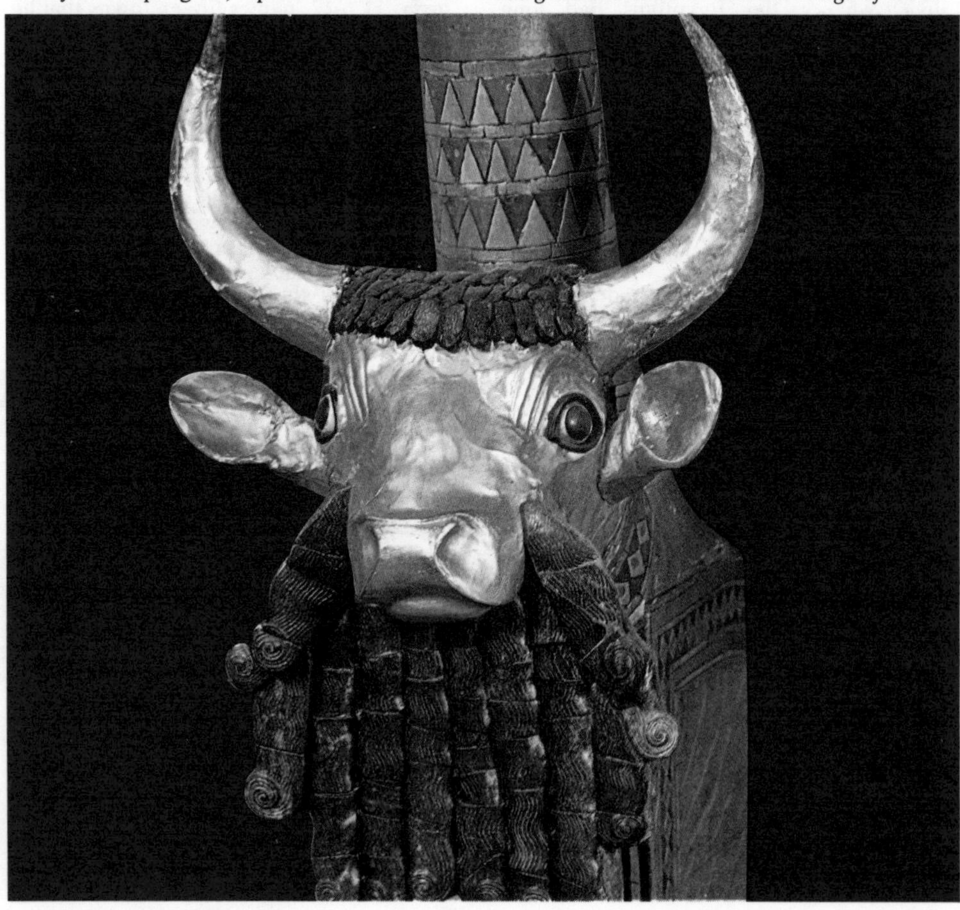

Judaea	Rehoboam
Israel	Jeroboam
Assyria	Ashur-dan II
Babylonia	Shamash-mudammiq
Egypt	Sheshonk I (XXII dyn) — Osorkon I (XXII dyn)
China	Zhou Yi Wang I

920	919	918	917	916	915	914	913	912	911

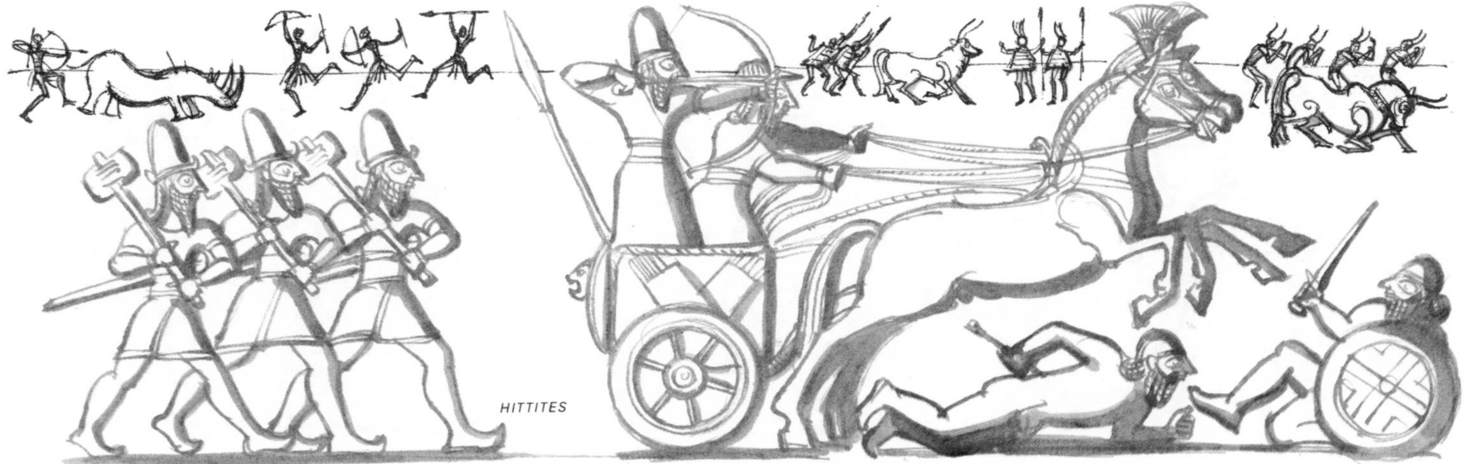
HITTITES

The Bible tells no more of Abijah than that he won a victory over Jeroboam and that he had fourteen wives and thirty-eight children, which was remarkable enough. Asa, meanwhile, is described as an orthodox potentate busily dismantling abominations throughout the country. His puritanical rampaging and in particular his propaganda against the leaders in Israel where there was greater tolerance in matters of worship, was historically significant in that it received mention in the Bible and thereby influenced the course of later Judaism and Christianity.
Asa, predictably, went to war with the Israelite king, Baasha, a brutal military dictator who deposed Jeroboam's son and successor and swiftly exterminated his entire family.

As from the reign of Adad-nirari II, the history of Assyria has a chronologically dependable basis. A list has survived in numerous fragments recording the high officials who from now on were appointed for periods of one year at a time and who thereby each gave a name to their year of service, and the appointment was usually taken up by the king himself during the second year of his reign. This list records a solar eclipse which can be dated 15 June 763 BC, and by reckoning backwards in the list from this point it is possible to determine the year of Adad-nirari's death. Historically, this monarch was a great warrior who, among other things, seized a large part of Babylonia, which led to a revolt in that land; the vanquished king, Shamash-mudammiq, was assassinated, but Nabu-shum-ukin, who succeeded him was likewise defeated by Adad-nirari II.

Arians for the last 500 years in the process of conquering India, had now reached the river Ganges.

Italy had already entered its Iron Age, later known as the Villanovan culture. This was probably associated to some extent with the arrival of the Etruscans.

In southern Spain, according to the Bible and other ancient sources, there was a flourishing and wealthy city named Tarshish or Tartessus. King Hiram of Tyre and the Judaean King David sent ships to this city, but the site has never been located.

The Scandinavian cairns are nearly as ancient as the Egyptian pyramids, so by 900 BC they had been in existence for a long time. The picture shows a cairn in Luttra in Västergötland, Sweden. There are many Stone Age relics in the province of Västergötland, whereas the Bronze Age, now prevailing, was to leave fewer traces.

Rehoboam — Abijah — Asa	**Judaea**
Jeroboam — Nadab — Baasha	**Israel**
Adad-nirari II	**Assyria**
Shamash-mudammiq	**Babylonia**
Osorkon I (XXII dyn)	**Egypt**
Zhou Xiao Wang	**China**

910	909	908	907	906	905	904	903	902	901

HITTITES

At about this time the Phoenician alphabet was adopted by the Greeks, following the sensible introduction of symbols for vowels as well. Some form of phonetic alphabet had long existed in the Orient. The inventors were probably the Sumerians who had lived in southern Mesopotamia some 2000 years earlier and who had taught it to the Babylonians. The Babylonians immediately adopted the Sumerian cuneiform characters and passed it on to the Egyptians, who now used their hieroglyphs to denote language sounds. Both nations adopted a form of syllable script, but the Phoenicians created a consonant alphabet, but with no vowel symbols. Semitic languages such as Hebrew and Arabic continued without vowels.

The Greek alphabet, containing both vowels and consonants, was the basis for both Latin and Russian script, even though the appearance of the letters changed.

Chinese writing was differently constructed. The characters were basically ideograms, independent of dialect and of progressive linguistic changes. For this reason, far more than twenty-eight characters were needed in Chinese writing.

The characters in the blue field represent the entire Western alphabet. The four first alphabets are northern Semitic: the vertical lines show from the left an archaic Phoenician, an archaic Hebraic, a Moabite and a later Phoenician alphabet. The four following lines are Greek characters, first archaic, then eastern and western forms, and finally the classical line of capital letters. The ninth and tenth lines from the left show Etruscan characters from an earlier period and from the Roman time. These are followed by three varieties of Latin characters: two archaic, the right-hand one of which is usually found in inscriptions, then classical characters: capitalis quadrata. *On the right-hand side are three alphabets of capital letters of more recent origin: Gothic, italic Roman and straight Roman.*

NORTHERN SEMITIC				GREEK				ETRUSCAN		LATIN			MODERN		
archaic Phoenician	archaic Hebrew (italic)	Moabite	Phoenician	archaic	eastern	western	classic	archaic	classic	archaic	archaic Epigraphic	classic	Gothic	italic Roman	straight Roman
							A					A	𝔄	*A*	A
							B					B	𝔅	*B*	B
							Γ					C	ℭ	*C*	C
							Δ					D	𝔇	*D*	D
							E					E	𝔈	*E*	E
					see letter U							F	𝔉	*F*	F
	see letter C											G	𝔊	*G*	G
							Z								
							H					H	ℌ	*H*	H
							Θ								
							I					I	ℑ	*I*	I
	see letter I												𝔍	*J*	J
							K					K	𝔎	*K*	K
							Λ					L	𝔏	*L*	L
							M					M	𝔐	*M*	M
							N					N	𝔑	*N*	N
							Ξ								
							O					O	𝔒	*O*	O
							Π					P	𝔓	*P*	P
												Q	𝔔	*Q*	Q
							P					R	ℜ	*R*	R
							Σ					S	𝔖	*S*	S
							T					T	𝔗	*T*	T
							Y					V	𝔘	*U*	U
													𝔙	*V*	V
													𝔚	*W*	W
					X	X+	X				X	X	𝔛	*X*	X
												Y	𝔜	*Y*	Y
												Z	ℨ	*Z*	Z

Judaea	Asa
Israel	Baasha
Assyria	Asad-nirari II
Babylonia	Nabu-shun-ukin
Egypt	Osorkon I (XXII dyn)
China	Zhou Xiao Wang (900–895); Zhou Yi Wang II (894–891)

900	899	898	897	896	895	894	893	892	891

ATTICA
HITTITES

There is a great wealth of hieroglyphic and cuneiform literature. The Egyptians, scarcely an heroic people, were not history writers, but were excellent tellers of tales, and of these the stories of Sinuhe were already about 1000 years old. There was a large collection of religious hymns, love poems and legends, and, in addition, many medical and mathematical texts. Even more extensive was the literature in the Sumerian and Babylonian-Assyrian languages, written on stone and, in particular, on clay tablets. At least a quarter of a million of these tablets long survived in the royal library at Nineveh and elsewhere in Mesopotamia, as in the Hittites' former capital Bogaskoy, on Cyprus and in the ancient Syrian metropolis Ugarit. In Adad-nirari II's time there were probably many more. Almost without exception these had a religious connotation, a large proportion consisting of hymns, prayers, myths and ritual texts; but there were also laws, medical prescriptions, multiplication tables and lexicons, as well as historical accounts and chronicles. One of the better known cuneiform texts was undoubtedly the Gilgamesh epic containing, among other tales, the story of Ut-Napishtim the Babylonian Noah.

The art of casting bronze was flourishing in China. Among the articles produced in this epoch were large numbers of sacrificial vessels for meat, wine, etc., superbly executed with many inscriptions and rich ornamentation in which a stylized bird with long feathers often recurred. Shape and decoration varied considerably. China clearly possessed a sophisticated social order with a rigid class system. Writing was highly developed and there was a complex religious organization.

Chinese bronzes are greatly superior to all other relics of artistic creation in China, but there are many jade, marble and bone objects that have also survived in good condition. The potter's craft had long been practised too, and there are numerous examples of fine, black ceramic from this period. Silk production was already flourishing; only the Chinese would know the art of silk-making for another 1000 years or more.

In his old age the Jewish king, Asa, was comforted by the news that the Israelite King Baasha was dead and that his son and successor Elah had been assassinated. The assassin himself, Zimri, seized power in the country but failed to retain it for more than a week. When the entire army marched upon his capital, he perished in the flames of his palace.

A cuneiform text of 147 lines describes the achievements of Tukulti-Ninurta II: his campaigns in Mesopotamia and neighbouring countries. He conquered many states and cities but his operations were more in the nature of forays and therefore produced no lasting political results. Tributes and taxes poured in wherever he happened to be with his army, but as soon as he left his sovereignty ceased to be recognized. Tukulti-Ninurta II and his successor Ashurnasirpal II were fully engaged in continual reconquest of foreign territory.

Nabu-shum-ukin had murdered the former Babylonian king because the latter had allowed himself to be defeated by the Assyrians. But he himself fared no better when he was severely defeated by Adad-nirari II. Evidently, however, he was not completely vanquished, for in time the two kings made peace, married each other's daughters and drew up definite borders between the two kingdoms.

A sacrificial vessel in the shape of a bronze tiger. Freer Gallery, Washington D.C.

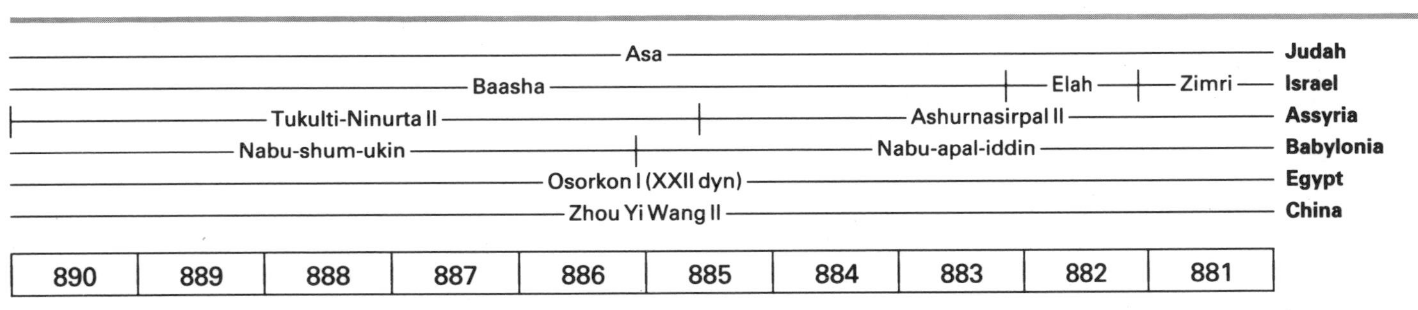
Asa
Judah
Baasha
Elah
Zimri
Israel
Tukulti-Ninurta II
Ashurnasirpal II
Assyria
Nabu-shum-ukin
Nabu-apal-iddin
Babylonia
Osorkon I (XXII dyn)
Egypt
Zhou Yi Wang II
China
890
889
888
887
886
885
884
883
882
881

880–871 BC

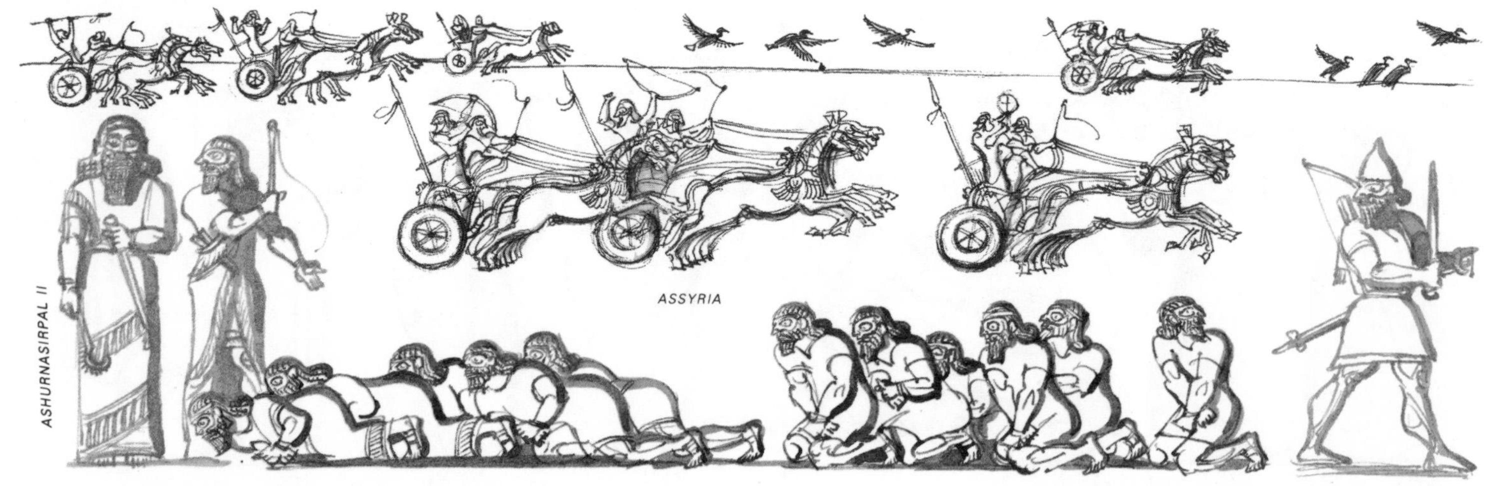
ASHURNASIRPAL II
ASSYRIA

Ashurnasirpal II capturing a city. This relief originally came from the king's palace in Nimrud and is now kept in the British Museum, London. In contemporary documents the king is depicted as belligerent and bloodthirsty. However, he was a builder as well as a destroyer. Nimrud was a large city at this time, and the palace there was splendidly decorated.

Amber statuette of King Ashurnasirpal, now in the Museum of Fine Art, Boston. The statuette measures 24 centimetres, unusually large for an amber object.

Judah	Asa
Israel	Omri
Assyria	Ashurnasirpal II
Babylonia	Nabu-apal-iddin
Egypt	Osorkon I (XXII dyn)
China	Zhou Yi Wang II — Zhou Li Wang

880	879	878	877	876	875	874	873	872	871

ASSYRIANS
PHOENICIA

Ashur-nasir-apli II, alias Ashurnasirpal II, emerges as an indescribably cruel king, which in Assyrian history is saying a great deal. He waged war continuously, executed his conquered enemies and ruthlessly deported whole populations. He often boasted in writing of his own atrocities, and reliefs illustrating his ravages reveal, among other things, how his prisoners were flayed alive.

Many cuneiform records exist from Ashurnasirpal II's reign. The longest of these are his own annals, comprising 356 lines, and including an account of his westward march to the Mediterranean where he demanded tribute from the Phoenician cities. He also rebuilt the ancient Assyrian capital, Kalakh, the ruins of which are known as Nimrud. His palace there was guarded by two immense bull figures with human heads, one on each side of the entrance, and the walls, handsomely decorated in blue, yellow and white enamelled tiles, were also covered with countless reliefs and inscriptions.

King Ahab, who succeeded his father Omri in a fairly consolidated Israel, was closely allied with Tyre and was married to Jezebel, a Phoenician princess who had religious interests and promoted the cult of the Phoenician divinities Astarte and Baal. Consequently, in I Kings, she plays a nefarious role in the splendid account of the prophet Elijah, who performs miracles with an oil jar at the house of a widow in Zarephath and finally calls down rain over Mount Carmel after the prophets of Baal have failed to end the divinely instigated drought. According to I Kings 17-21, Ahab was a fairly able and, for a time, successful politician. After the death of the old king, Asa, he brought about a reconciliation and an alliance with Asa's successor in Jerusalem. Furthermore, according to the Bible, Ahab won several victories against the Aramaeans, built cities and also constructed an ivory tower.

Omri, who seized power in Israel after a long struggle with a rival, is mentioned in the Bible and also on the famous Mesha Stone (Louvre). Omri fought a war, among other places, in Moab east of the Dead Sea, and also built a new capital, Samaria.

In the North the Bronze Age was in progress and petroglyphs were still being produced. The religious symbols contained in these are difficult to interpret. This rock engraving is on the shore of Råvarpen lake in Dalsland, Sweden, near several other petroglyphs.

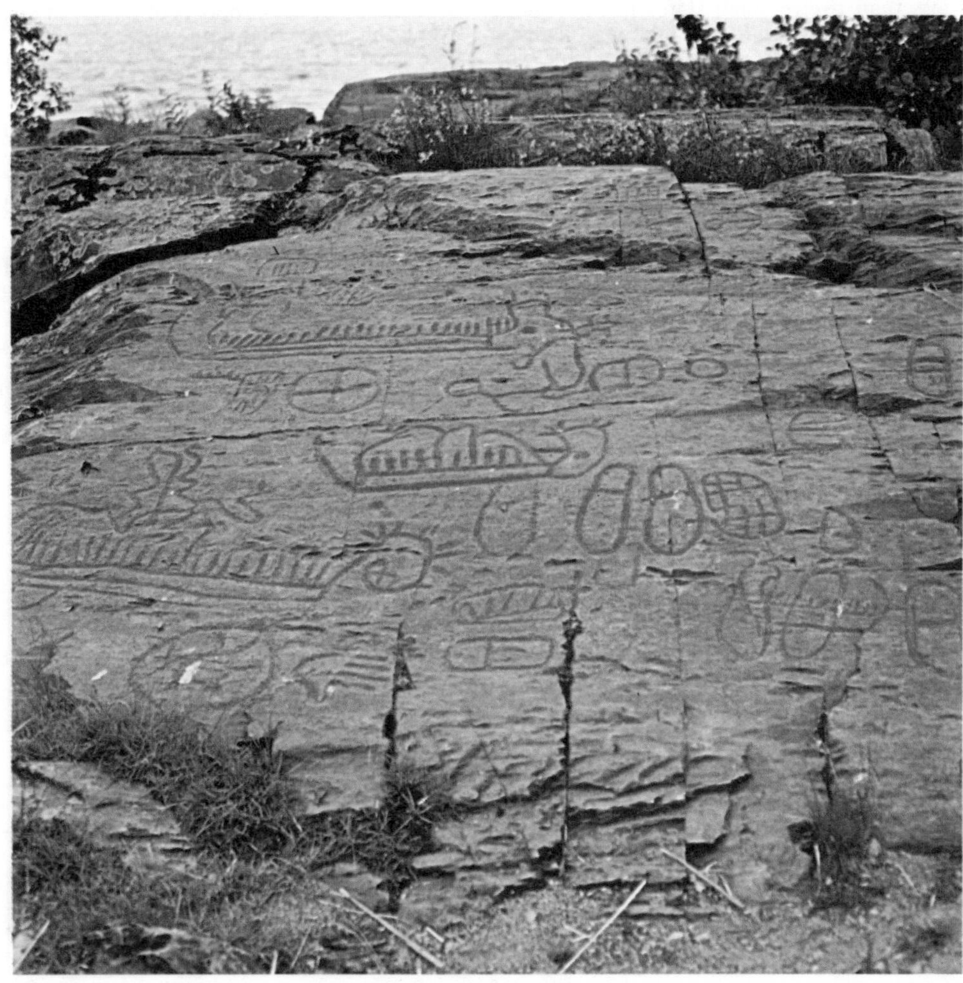

Asa — Jehoshaphat	Judah
Ahab	Israel
Ashurnasirpal II	Assyria
Nabu-apal-iddin	Babylonia
Takelot I (XXII dyn)	Egypt
Zhou Li Wang	China

870	869	868	867	866	865	864	863	862	861

AFRICA
ASSYRIA
MARDUK-
ZAKIR-
SHUMI
BABYLON

During the very first year of his reign Shalmaneser III moved westward with the Assyrian armies, crossed the Euphrates and Orontes, and after a series of easy victories reached the Mediterranean coast where he levied tributes on the Phoenician cities. After his departure a coalition was formed of no less than twelve small states in the region, including Israel and the kingdom of Damascus where King Ben-Hadad II reigned. The purpose of this coalition was to prevent a recurrence of the onslaught. But a few years later, in 853 BC, Shalmaneser returned and at Qarqar on the Orontes defeated the armies of the coalition, which then dissolved. Again, for some reason, the Assyrians withdrew, but instead war now erupted between Israel and Damascus. The Damascene king, Ben-Hadad, after a number of initial successes, was defeated and taken prisoner. King Ahab did not put him to death, but demanded certain territorial and trade concessions, a course of action which was vociferously condemned by the prophets of Israel. In any event, the peace conditions were not fulfilled, and in an attempt to enforce them by arms Ahab was killed.

Shalmaneser also meddled in the internal affairs of Babylon by supporting King Marduk-zakir-shumi against the latter's rebellious brother. The brother was defeated and killed, but it was Shalmaneser who now became master of Babylon.

Three of Shalmaneser's military expeditions were directed at Urartu and its king, Arame. Arame was defeated and his capital north of Lake Van ravaged and burned. Shalmaneser continued north into almost inaccessible mountainous terrain, building pyramids of enemy heads wherever he went. All this he described himself. Inscriptions on a black obelisk in his palace at Kalakh (Nimrud) recount in chronological order his military atrocities.

The Bible's account of the prophet Elijah makes exciting reading. He called fire down from heaven, not only on the heads of Baal's prophets, but also on the Jewish royal contingents sent out to arrest him. In his old age he was carried up to heaven. His followers seemed to have had prior warning of the event, for they watched the proceedings from a safe distance, while Elijah and his disciple Elisha miraculously wandered dryshod to the other side of Jordan. Then, according to II Kings 2: 'Behold, there appeared a chariot of fire, and horses of fire, and parted them both asunder; and Elijah went up by a whirlwind into heaven.' Elisha picked up the mantle that had fallen off Elijah, whereupon he, too, was able to perform miracles. 'And when the sons of the prophets which were to view at Jericho saw him, they said, The spirit of Elijah doth rest on Elisha.'

Elijah goes up into heaven. Wall painting from Dalarna, Sweden, 1861. Scandinavian folk art of this kind is often based on 18th-century illustrated Bibles, which in turn refer back to the so-called Gustavus Adolphus Bible from 1618, containing woodcuts of German origin. The stories of Elijah have been a frequent source of inspiration in folk art and literature.

Judah	Jehoshaphat
Israel	Ahab
Assyria	Shalmaneser III
Babylonia	Nabu-apal-iddin
Egypt	Osorkon II (XXII dyn)
China	Zhou Li Wang

860	859	858	857	856	855	854	853	852	851

ASSYRIA
SHALMANESER III

The prophet Elisha continued to exert considerable influence on the history of Israel. As the successor of Elijah, of whom the first six chapters of II Kings have so much to tell, Elisha performed all manner of tricks and miracles: the inexhaustible oil vessel in the widow's house, the floating axe, death in the pot, and so on. But from time to time he also intervened in military and political affairs.

Jehoram of Israel and Jehoram of Judah were two different persons, although brothers-in-law. The two Ahaziahs were cousins. The Israelite Ahaziah, son of Ahab and Jezebel, fell from a gallery in the palace in Samaria and was killed; he was succeeded as king by Jehoram. The latter had previously held a command in the Aramaean war, in which he was wounded and temporarily invalided out of the army. During his convalescence he was visited by his nephew Ahaziah from Jerusalem; the author of II Kings regarded this as being decreed by fate since it facilitated the swift dispatch of his entire family. Chapters 9 and 10 of I Kings tell the terrible story of Jehu who, with the blessing of the prophet Elisha, murdered not only Jehoram and Ahaziah but also the dowager queen Jezebel and seventy minor princes whose heads were stacked in baskets in Samaria. He then had the good fortune to overtake the murdered Ahaziah's younger brothers, (forty-seven of them) and slaughtered them as well. After this he was ready to set about the priests of Baal who were duped into attending a service.

Apart from the eastern Mediterranean countries, Mesopotamia and China, there are no historical records of happenings elsewhere in the world, even though important events were obviously taking place. A group of people from the Pyrenean peninsula appears to have invaded England around 2000 BC and if that were so, they were probably the builders of Stonehenge. It is impossible to date Stonehenge accurately, but it could have been 1000 years old or more at the time of Jezebel, Jehu and Elijah. These enormous monoliths had been dragged to the site from remote places and arranged in a U-shape around a central 'altar stone'. Standing at the centre and looking towards the entrance, one sees another stone that marks the point where the sun rises at the dawn of midsummer day.

In 842 the Moabite king, Mesha, inscribed on a stone that he had erected a place of sacrifice to the god Chemosh, who had visited his wrath on the Moabites by allowing them to be oppressed by the Israelite king, Omri. But now, with the aid of Chemosh, Mesha had freed his people from the Israelites and slain 7000 of them.

The Mesha Stone was discovered in AD 1868 by a German and its text was copied by a Frenchman. While their compatriots argued over right of ownership, the Arabs broke up the stone, hoping to get more for it if they sold it piece by piece. Most of these fragments were reassembled, however, and the partially restored stone was placed in the Louvre, Paris. The text is the only example of the Moabite language in existence, but the writing itself is a unique record since it shows a very early form of the Phoenician alphabet, which is the basis for the one subsequently adopted in the West.

There are several references in the Bible to King Mesha and his war of liberation. According to II Kings 3, he had 'rendered unto the king of Israel an hundred thousand lambs, and an hundred thousand rams with the wool', and when this came to an end, King Jehoram and King Jehoshaphat took the field against Moab, after first consulting the prophet Elisha, who instructed the monarchs to destroy all trees, fields and sources of water (having first conjured up a private water supply for them). Despite the Israelite destruction, King Mesha triumphed in the following way. When he realized he could not hold his own in battle, 'he took his eldest son that should have reigned in his stead, and offered him for a burnt offering upon the wall. And there was great indignation against Israel: and they departed from him, and returned to their own land.'

The Mesha Stone, Louvre, Paris. The Moabite language is closely related to Hebrew, and King Mesha's inscription is reminiscent of the Old Testament. He tells of his battles against the kings of Israel and of his building work. He also praises the Moabite god Chemosh.

— | — Jehoram — | — Ahaziah — | — Athaliah — **Judah**

Ahaziah | — Jehoram — | — Jehu — **Israel**

— Shalmaneser III — **Assyria**

— Marduk-zakir-shumi — **Babylonia**

— Osorkon I (XXII dyn) — **Egypt**

— Zhou Li Wang — **China**

850	849	848	847	846	845	844	843	842	841

ASSYRIA

Xuan Wang was involved in fierce battles with a Hun people who had advanced to the gates of his capital, Hoa. They plundered the city and only with great difficulty could Xuan Wang repel them, for they had taken up a position in the hilly regions on the south bend of the Yellow River. They were finally dislodged, however, and decisively defeated in Shansi.

The large Bronze Age gravefield, Bredarör, at Kivik in Sweden, contains interesting religious-historical details in the form of petroglyphs. One shows a procession led by four men, followed by a ritual carriage, the wheels of which are also Sun symbols. In the centre of the stone the sacrificial animals can be seen, and in the lower part is a row of marching priests wearing beak-shaped head-dresses. On another stone these figures are grouped around a sacrificial vessel. There are also pictures of horn-blowers and a type of percussion instrument, in addition to symbolic signs probably unconnected with the Sun cult. The pairs of stylized horses are similar to patterns that reappear frequently many centuries later.

Shalmaneser, who had made several expeditions to Syria in the 840s and 830s in vain attempts to seize Damascus, faced other problems in 827. A revolt led by his own son deprived him of many Assyrian towns and fortifications, so that in his remaining years he reigned over only part of his formerly vast kingdom. But Shalmaneser's second son, Shamshi-Adad, who succeeded him, managed to restore the kingdom and also quelled a revolt in Babylonia; this had been an Assyrian tributary since Shalmaneser had conquered the territory in 856.

In the neighbourhood of Persia's Lake Urmia the Assyrian armies encountered for the first time a newly arrived people known as Medes.

King Sarduri I of Urartu, having recently succeeded Arame, had assumed the defiant title of 'King of kings', as a result of which king Shalmaneser despatched an army to punish him; but Shalmaneser's general was unable to achieve a decisive victory.

Some 3000 stone blocks are laid out in straight lines and circles at Carnac in Brittany. These date from the Stone Age and early Bronze Age. The significance of these arrangements, which were to puzzle later archaeologists, was presumably quite clear to the local population of the period.

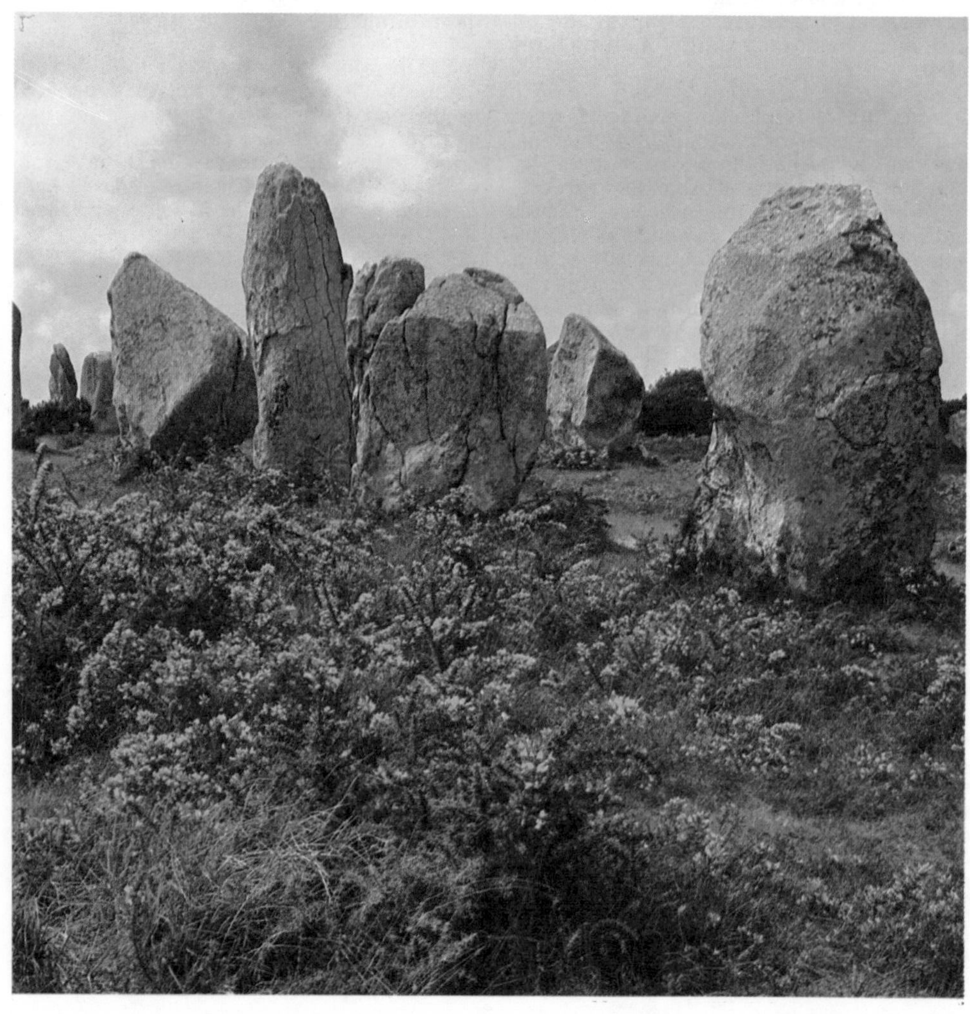

Judah	Athaliah				Joash					
Israel	Jehu									
Assyria	Shalmaneser III									
Babylonia	Marduk-zakir-shumi									
Egypt	Osorkon II (XXII dyn)							Takelot II (XXII dyn)		
China	Zhou Li Wang									
	840	839	838	837	836	835	834	833	832	831

ASSYRIA

When the dowager Queen Athaliah in Jerusalem heard of the assassination of all her close relatives, she had the entire royal family put to death; but, as related in II Kings, her small grandson Joash was rescued by a courageous aunt and taken into the safety of a temple. This sounds improbable, and modern historians take the view that the child was given refuge as protection against the agents of Jehu, who had already liquidated so many of the line of David. It is certain, nevertheless, that the boy Joash was brought up in the temple. His grandmother, Athaliah, seized power and governed the Jewish nation for six years. Then the high priest Jehoiada organized a revolt, slew Athaliah and swore allegiance to the seven-year old Joash as head of the nation in Athaliah's place.

This revolution in Jerusalem was significant because it left the priesthood in sole control for a long time to come; it also had its influence on the text of the Bible, parts of which were probably completed at about this time.

In Italy the Etruscans made their first appearance. Their origins are uncertain, and the authors of antiquity were equally divided in their views. Herodotus believed they were emigrants from Lydia, while others claimed they came from Etruria. Dionysius of Halicarnassus argued that the Etruscans were the original inhabitants of Italy – a verdict generally accepted by modern scholars. Thus the Etruscan language would be a remnant of early south European tongues.

Shamshi-Adad was married to a Babylonian princess named Sammu-ramat, better known as Semiramis, the name employed by Greek scribes who referred, for example, to her hanging gardens in Babylon.

The Urartu people developed a considerable culture, built large houses and left magnificent works of sculpture. They had adopted the Assyrian cuneiform and had initially used Akkadian as a written language. Now, however, they had exchanged this for their own tongue which was known as Churritic and makes difficult reading today. Culturally they had learned much from the ancient Hittites. Thus they worshipped the Hittite weather god Theshub, though they called him Teisbas. Some of their other gods may well have been Indian: Indra, Mithra, etc.

The north was undoubtedly very sparsely populated and the forests largely virgin. Land levels were rising around the coasts, and inland too the landscape was gradually changing shape. Lakes became shallower or were completely overgrown. Fortunately, however, there was still sufficient water to last for several more millennia.

Approximately 6000 years have passed since the last Ice Age ended in northern Europe, but its visible traces are likely to be permanent. These are particularly noticeable in Finland, where some 70,000 lakes testify to the great thaw when spring eventually arrived. Lake Pielinen, illustrated here, is situated near the Soviet border, and is one of the largest. Sweden, too, is rich in freshwater lakes of this type, which rise even higher above sea-level as a result of progressive land elevation, which continues to drain bays and straits on the Baltic coast.

Joash	**Judah**
Jehu	**Israel**
Shalmaneser III — Shamshi-Adad V	**Assyria**
Marduk-zakir-shumi — Marduk-balassu-iqbi	**Babylonia**
Takelot II (XXII dyn) — Sheshonk III	**Egypt**
Zhou Li Wang — Zhou Xuan Wang	**China**

830	829	828	827	826	825	824	823	822	821

820–811 BC

HITTITES.
ASSYRIA

Since 820 Phoenician Tyre had been ruled by a king named Pu'myaton, better known by his Greek name Pygmalion. According to the classical legend, in the seventh year of his reign Pygmalion slew his rich brother-in-law, but his sister Dido – or Elissa, according to the version – put her dead husband's treasures on board a ship and set sail with a group of followers. Landing in Cyprus, she secured some fifty young women as wives for her followers; continuing westward, they eventually reached the Tunisian coast where they founded the city of Carthage. In the Aeneid Virgil recounts the subsequent destiny of Dido, though this is an epic written by a poet and thus not a dependable historic source. According to the Aeneid, Dido took her own life when, by order of the gods, her Trojan lover Aeneas deserted her, sailing off to found a Latin realm in Italy, later to be the site of Rome. Thus Rome's future enmity with Carthage was fated.

The story of Dido is of major literary and historical significance. Although the event is likely to have occurred several decades later than stated in the legend, there seems little doubt that the city of Carthage was founded by Phoenicians from Tyre.

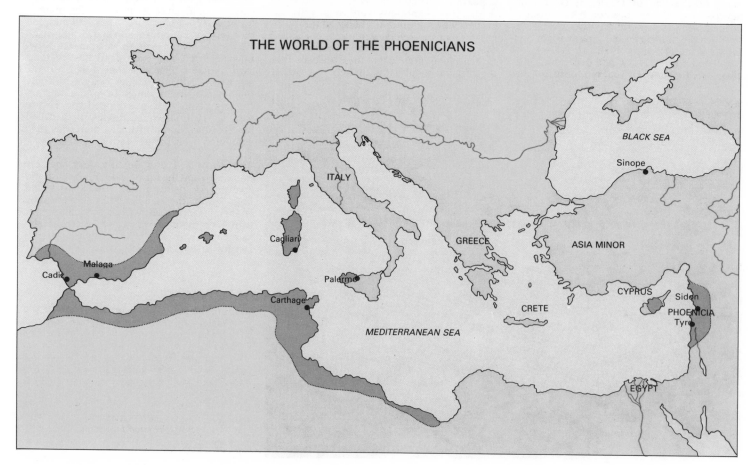

THE WORLD OF THE PHOENICIANS

BLACK SEA
Sinope
ITALY
Cagliari
GREECE
ASIA MINOR
Malaga
Cadiz
Palermo
CYPRUS
Sidon
PHOENICIA
Tyre
Carthage
CRETE
MEDITERRANEAN SEA
EGYPT

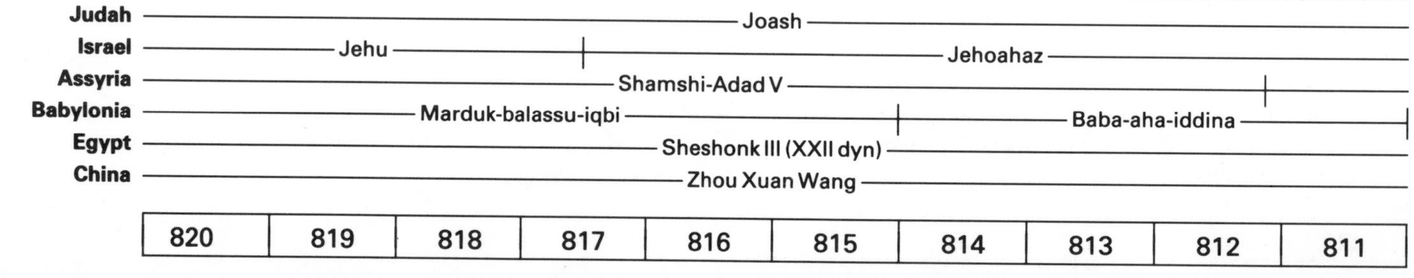
Judah
Israel
Assyria
Babylonia
Egypt
China
Joash
Jehu
Jehoahaz
Shamshi-Adad V
Marduk-balassu-iqbi
Baba-aha-iddina
Sheshonk III (XXII dyn)
Zhou Xuan Wang
820
819
818
817
816
815
814
813
812
811

SCYTHIANS
KING
HAZAEL
ASSYRIANS
DAMASCUS

The Babylonian king, Baba-aha-iddina, attempted to free himself from the Assyrian yoke, but was defeated and imprisoned. This was followed by eight years of political chaos in Babylonia where a series of rulers quickly succeeded one another. Adad-nirari III was still a child when his father died and for some time the regency was in the hands of the dowager queen Sammu-ramat.

An Armenian prince named Hazael, having recovered from a defeat by the Assyrian Shalmaneser, now ruled Damascus. Hazael conquered Transjordan in Jehu's day and made Israel a tribute-paying vassal state under Jehoahaz. When Hazael died in 806 and was succeeded by Ben Hadad II, Armenia was attacked by Adad-nirari III. The kingdom was not totally destroyed but its power was undermined and its empire broken up. Shortly after the turn of the century, Israel re-established its independence and regained the territories lost in Joash's time. Joash of Judah and Joash of Israel were two different individuals.

Outside pressure on the small biblical kingdoms around Jerusalem and Samaria had momentarily eased. The Judaean king, Joash, became involved in a conflict with the priesthood that had earlier put him in power. At the beginning of the following decade he was removed.

The last of the Pharaohs in the 22nd dynasty had little authority: their power seems not to have extended far beyond the capital Bubastis in the eastern Nile delta. Almost every city in the west of the delta and southward along the Nile had its own ruler.

Adad-nirari III organized several campaigns northward towards Urartu, which had grown stronger and now emerged as a major power that threatened the existence of Assyria. However, his forestalling operations had little lasting effect.

In Europe, this period saw the beginning of a culture, later named Hallstatt after a place in Germany. The Hallstatt style was fairly uniform, with elaborate pottery utensils, the handles of which were often in the shape of animal heads.

The seven-branched candlestick, the menorah, was used to light the Holy of Holies in the Temple of Jerusalem. The first known representation of the menorah is now in the Jerusalem Museum.

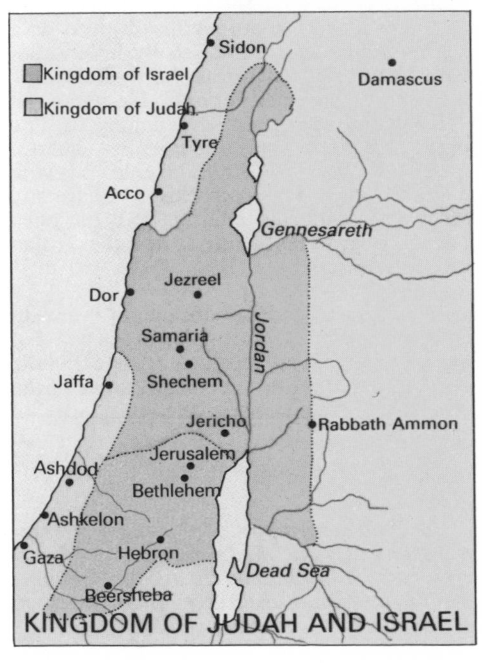
Kingdom of Israel
Kingdom of Judah
Sidon
Damascus
Tyre
Acco
Gennesareth
Jezreel
Dor
Samaria
Jordan
Jaffa
Shechem
Jericho
Rabbath Ammon
Jerusalem
Ashdod
Bethlehem
Ashkelon
Gaza
Hebron
Dead Sea
Beersheba
KINGDOM OF JUDAH AND ISRAEL

Joash	**Judah**
Jehoahaz — Joash	**Israel**
Adad-nirari III	**Assyria**
Eriba-Marduk	**Babylonia**
Sheshonk III (XXII dyn)	**Egypt**
Zhou Xuan Wang	**China**

810	809	808	807	806	805	804	803	802	801

CHINA
BABYLON
SYRIA
CANAANITE KING
ASSYRIANS
NUBIANS

A blind poet named Homer was reported to be travelling around various Greek cities on the west coast of Asia, reciting two long poems written by himself. This has somewhat baffled later scholars. The epics in question, the *Iliad* and the *Odyssey*, have survived down the centuries and continue to be read widely, but since they differ so in style and content, it seems unlikely that they could have been written by one and the same poet. Some suggest that the *Iliad*, at least, was not composed by a single person but was a collective creative effort which emerged gradually through the ages. The enigma of Homer will probably never be solved.

In any event, the two poems almost certainly date from the 8th century BC. The *Iliad*, which was the earlier, is the longer and the more dramatic; it relates to the battles around the city of Troy which, according to many ancient historians, fell in 1184 BC. This, for them, was the point at which history really began, for the Olympian deities played a major part in the struggle for Troy; never again would they intervene directly in human affairs.

Seven cities claim the honour of having been Homer's birthplace: Smyrna, Rhodes, Colophon, Salamis, Chios, Argos and Athens. Of these, three lie to the west of the Aegean Sea, and from the linguistic evidence, it is improbable that the poet grew up there. The poems were written in Greek, with traces of Ionian and Aeolian dialects, and may thus be assumed to have originated in the borderland between these two dialects. Of the places mentioned, Smyrna and Chios are perhaps the most likely.

The theme of the 16,000 lines of the *Iliad* is the anger of Achilles and the fateful consequences arising from this. A girl named Chryseis has been abducted and handed over to the Greek general Agamemnon. Her father, a local priest of Apollo, seeks to free her, but when his appeals are haughtily rejected, he turns to his god for help. Apollo descends to earth and fires plague-infested arrows into the Greek camp. Achilles then consults the priest Chalchas and learns what has happened. Agamemnon is furious when Achilles urges him to restore Chryseis to her father, and demands in return Achilles' beautiful mistress Briseïs. Achilles consents to this but is filled with bitter despair and appeals to his mother, the sea-goddess Thetis, for retribution. He then retreats into his tent and refuses to take any further part in the war. Through Zeus, Thetis now ensures that the Trojans continue to have the upper hand in the war until Agamemnon is reconciled with Achilles.

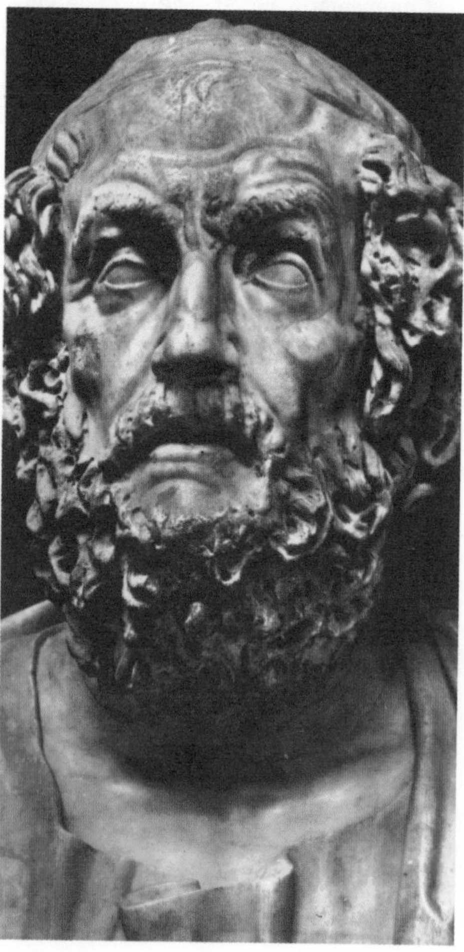

The story of Achilles' anger is the main thread of the war-like episodes that make up the *Iliad*. The principal character, however, is not Achilles but Hector, the Trojan, who gains the reader's sympathy. Under Hector's leadership the Trojans are highly successful, and when the Greeks are hard-pressed Patroclus begs his friend Achilles to lend him his arms and equipment. Achilles agrees and Patroclus performs many heroic deeds until finally he meets and is slain by Hector himself. Grief over the death of his friend causes Achilles to forget his dispute with Agamemnon and, equipped by his mother with wonderful new arms, he re-enters the war with heightened fervour. He seeks out and kills Hector; then in avenging fury he drags Hector's body behind his chariot around the walls of Troy. The epic ends with a description of Patroclus' burial and Hector's last journey after his body has been handed over to his ageing father, the Trojan king, Priam.

Other sources describe subsequent events in the Trojan War. The accounts of the wooden horse and the fall of Troy do not appear in the *Iliad*, and neither do preceding stories of the beautiful Helen and the sacrifice of Iphigenia.

There is no contemporary portrait of Homer, as there was some doubt as to his existence. However, a traditional image of the poet evolved in Classical Greece. Bust in Museo Archeologico Nazionale, Naples.

Judah	Joash	Amaziah
Israel		Joash
Assyria		Adad-nirari III
Babylonia		Eriba-Marduk
Egypt		Sheshonk III (XXII dyn)
China		Zhou Xuan Wang

800	799	798	797	796	795	794	793	792	791

ASSYRIANS

Eriba-Marduk claimed to have ended the anarchy that had prevailed in Babylonia and to have obtained the assent of Marduk to be king of all that country. His authority, however, appears to have been limited. The inhabitants of Babylon, Borsippa and Dilbat, as well as the Chaldeans and the Aramaeans, were engaged in a form of civil war, and at one point the city of Borsippa even went so far as to declare its independence.

After his successful war of liberation against Ben Hadad II in Damascus, the Israelite king, Joash, turned his attention to the Jewish kingdom in the south, captured Jerusalem and made King Amaziah his vassal. Thus during the long reign of Joash and his son Jeroboam II, Israel was a comparatively powerful state. According to II Kings, it was remarkable that Amaziah refrained from slaying the children of those persons who had murdered his father. Amaziah himself was later assassinated, after being defeated in a war with Israel.

Although it is evident that the story of the Trojan War is legendary, the German Archaeologist Heinrich Schliemann, who made remarkable discoveries on the site of Troy in the AD 1870s, would hardly have begun his excavations had he not believed there were some elements of truth in the tale.

The other Homeric epic, the *Odyssey*, is more complex in structure. It describes Odysseus' long journey home from Troy to Ithaca, though not as a straightforward narrative. The poem begins in Olympus where the goddess Athene entreats Zeus to allow the sorely tried hero to return home at last. She then descends in person to Ithaca where Odysseus' faithful wife Penelope is besieged by a houseful of insistent suitors, all of whom assume that Odysseus will never come back. Penelope nevertheless persuades her son Telemachus to go out and seek his father; he visits Odysseus' former comrades-in-arms, old Nestor of Pylos and Menelaus in Sparta. The story then moves back again to Ithaca where the suitors resolve to pursue and kill Telemachus. Now for the first time Odysseus appears. He is being held captive by a nymph named Calypso. When the gods order her to release him, she permits him to build a vessel and depart; but the sea-god Poseidon, who has long persecuted Odysseus, causes him to be shipwrecked yet again. Naked and destitute, Odysseus comes ashore in the country of the Phaeacians, and in the splendid sixth book of the epic, the princess Nausicaa, urged by the gods, goes down to the seashore and meets Odysseus. In her father's palace he describes, in the following six books, his previous adventures. In the thirteenth book the Phaeacians row Odysseus over to Ithaca where he first makes a cautious approach to his loyal steward, the old swineherd Eumaeus, and then makes himself known to his son Telemachus who, unobserved, has meanwhile returned home. Father and son lead the attack on the suitors inside the palace, and kill them with arrows and spears. Odysseus is reunited with Penelope, and the poem ends in Hades where the souls of the dead are received by Agamemnon and other heroes from Troy, and the conclusion of peace is announced by the goddess Athene at Ithaca.

The adventures of Odysseus during his wanderings are presented as episodes recounted by himself to the Phaeacians. He is first blown ashore in the land of the Lotus-eaters – people who live on the fruit of the lotus which induces a state of bliss and forgetfulness. Odysseus' Greek companions quickly succumb to these pleasures and dream away their days in indolent voluptuousness, until with a supreme effort Odysseus rouses himself and forces his men to return on board. They then reach a land inhabited by Cyclops, a race of one-eyed giants. They are captured by the Cyclops Polyphemus, who confines them in a cave and plans to devour them one at a time. But Odysseus manages to intoxicate Polyphemus, then blinds him with a burning stake and escapes with his men. The god Aeolus causes the west wind to blow the Greek ships on their way, imprisoning all the other winds in a sack. Ithaca is already in sight when the seamen decide to open the sack. The ships are then blown ashore in the land of the man-eating Laestrygones. Odysseus' ship is the only one to escape. On an island inhabited by the beautiful witch Circe, several of his men are turned by her into swine, but although she cannot administer her potion to Odysseus, she detains him for one year. The eleventh book describes a visit to Hades by Odysseus seeking further instructions for his journey home. This is a valuable source of information regarding Greek belief in a future life. Later episodes tell of the voyage between the lairs of the female monsters Scylla and Charybdis, the Sirens who with their irresistible songs lured seafarers to their ruin, and the oxen of the Sun god which are slaughtered by Odysseus's companions, who, in punishment, are struck down by lightning.

Achilles and Ajax playing a game of dice. Figures in black on an amphora from Etruscan Vulci, signed by Exekias, now in the Vatican in Rome. The Etruscans were familiar with Homer's epics, judging by the frequency with which they were depicted.

Amaziah	**Judah**
Jeroboam II	**Israel**
Adad-nirari III; Shalmaneser IV	**Assyria**
Eriba-Marduk	**Babylonia**
Sheshonk III (XXII dyn)	**Egypt**
Zhou Xuan Wang	**China**

790	789	788	787	786	785	784	783	782	781

SYRIA
HELLENES

The first Greek lists of victors in the Olympic Games date from the year 776 BC. These lists, which continued until AD 221 , were subsequently used as a chronological reference by the Sicilian historian Timaeus, who utilized the Olympic four-year periods as a basis for his catalogue of the ephors of Sparta, the archons of Sparta and other leading officials in the Greek world. In this way he provided fairly accurate dates for his history, this being his sole intention. Such a chronology, based upon the fact that the Olympic Games were held unerringly every fourth year throughout antiquity until they were prohibited in Christian times, hardly served as a calendar, but was useful for determining particular dates in the past. For almost 1000 years the Olympic Games remained an important all-Greek event, not restricted to athletics. Prominent authors, for example, often appeared there to discuss their works—an effective form of publicity in the absence of any organized book production.

The River Alpheus has from time to time flooded its banks and gradually changed the landscape around Olympia. Probably the best early description is found in the travelogue by Pausanias who was active in the 2nd century AD. Yet later archaeologists achieved wonders here. The entrance to the Stadium is magnificent, even in its restored state.

The ruins of ancient Olympia are extensive and impressive. The picture shows what is left of Hera's temple, which originated in archaic times but appears to have been erected in stages. The Olympic temple of Zeus was built after Hera's temple.

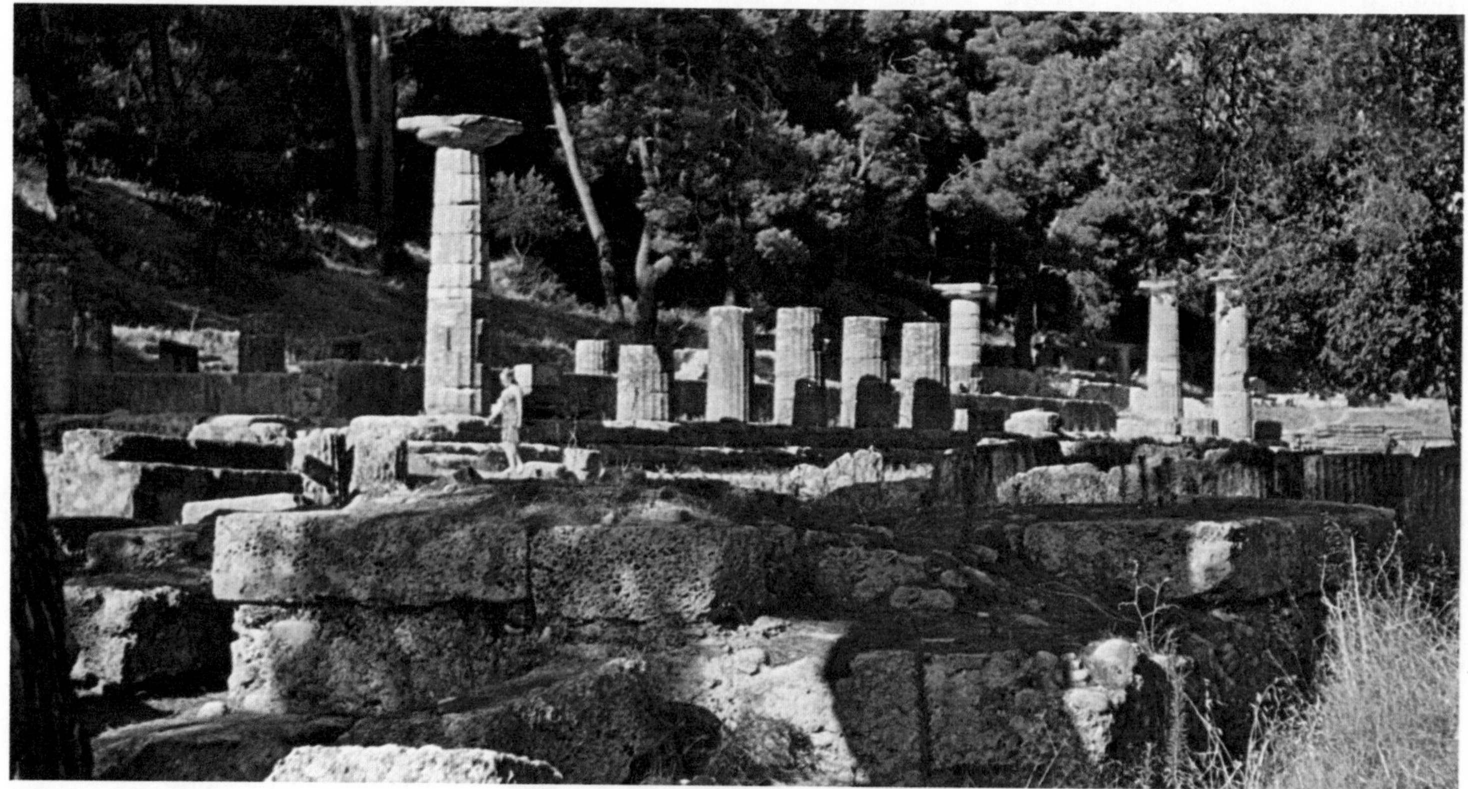

Judah — Uzziah
Israel — Jeroboam II
Assyria — Shalmaneser IV —|
Babylonia — Eriba-Marduk
Egypt — Sheshonk III (XXII dyn)
China — Zhou You Wang —|

780	779	778	777	776	775	774	773	772	771

770–761 BC

HELLENES

A Phrygian state had been flourishing for several centuries and now embraced the greater part of Asia Minor. The capital, Gordium, was strongly fortified, but practically all that is known of the kings who resided there is that they were successively called either Gordius or Midas. Herodotus tells us, however, that the first Gordius was a simple peasant whom the Phrygians appointed their king by decree of an oracle. He entered the town in his cart, the yoke of which was attached to the pole by an intricate knot. Whoever untied it would be conqueror of Asia. This knot remained in Gordium until the 4th century BC when Alexander the Great cut it through with his sword.

The Phrygians, who spoke an Indo-European language, appear to have invaded the country at the time of the Hittite fall from power in the 13th century BC. They had also adopted Hittite traditions of art and handicrafts. Their religion was remarkable. They had a mother-goddess known as Cybele, and worshipped the image of a small, black meteoric stone kept in the city of Pessinus, under the direction of a priesthood dressed in female attire, with oiled, unbound hair. The priests performed wild dances to the accompaniment of flutes, cymbals and hand drums, and then entered a state of ecstacy during which they castrated themselves in honour of their goddess, allowing their blood to flow on to her altar. There was also a male god named Attis – the son, or lover, or possibly both, of Cybele.

In the kingdom of Judah there appeared at this time Amos from Tekoa, the first biblical prophet whose writings have survived. Amos was patently a great writer. His entire text of nine chapters vibrates with religious wrath and social fervour.

The Scythians ruled north of the Black Sea. Generally they were still nomads, although gradually becoming settled. They were a gifted people; although they did not leave any written literature, some of their art remains.

Shalmaneser IV, Ashur-dan III and Adad-nirari IV were all weak rulers presiding over a decline of Assyrian power. An energetic military figure, Argishti I, had reigned in Urartu since 780. Certain Syrian towns were seized during this time.

In 771 the Emperor You Wang was killed in his palace at Shensi and was succeeded by one of his sons. But a second son, who lived in a town later to be called Loyang, in eastern China, was also proclaimed emperor. China was thus divided between two branches of the Zhou (Chou) dynasty, but within twenty years the country was reunited under the eastern emperor, known as Ping Wang. He remained in Loyang, which was from then on virtually the capital of China. The year 770 was thus a milestone in China's historical records; the eastern Zhou dynasty was to last about 550 years.

On 6 September 775 there was an eclipse of the sun in China, which provides a chronological point of reference in China's history.

Azariah, known by that name in II Kings, is referred to as Uzziah in Chronicles II. It is clear that this is one and the same person; both accounts mention that he was stricken with leprosy. Kings II claims that this was not his fault, but Chronicles II insists that he had brought it upon himself by quarrelling with the priests in the temple over who should light the incense there. After this he lived alone in a separate house until his death, while his son Jotham ruled the country. Chronicles II are appreciative of his past poliltical deeds. He had fought and won battles against Philistines and Arabs, fortified Jerusalem against attack and recruited an army of 306,500 men. Furthermore, he had dug wells in the desert for his cattle and planted vineyards and orchards in the mountains, 'for he loved husbandry'.

An increasing number of cities and cultures that once flourished in Asia Minor are being excavated, including Greek cities on the west coast and Hittite and Syro-Hittite cities to the east. The picture shows the recent excavation of the Phrygian city Gordium.

Uzziah	**Judah**
Jeroboam II	**Israel**
Ashur-dan III – Adad-nirari IV	**Assyria**
Eriba-Marduk – ----	**Babylonia**
Pimai (XXII dyn) – Sheshonk IV (XXII dyn)	**Egypt**
Zhou Ping Wang	**China**

770	769	768	767	766	765	764	763	762	761

760–751 BC

ASSYRIA
AFRICA
SYRO-HITTITES

The year 753 BC is the official date for the foundation of Rome and provides the basis for the antique and medieval chronology *ab urbe condita*, (from the founding of the city). The founder's name was Romulus and he was the son of a god and a vestal virgin, as was his brother Remus. Romulus staked out the future walls of the city and killed Remus for leaping over them. The Romulus and Remus legend also features a she-wolf which suckles the two abandoned infants.

Obviously there is no historical basis for Romulus. He and his legendary successors are included here simply as guide-lines, for whether or not they actually existed, the ancient Roman kings have a certain chronological significance.

This Roman she-wolf is an Etruscan bronze sculpture from the 5th century BC. Musei Capitolini, Rome. The Romulus and Remus figures beneath her in the museum were added during the Italian Renaissance.

Rome	Romulus (from 753)
Judah	Uzziah
Israel	Jeroboam II
Assyria	Adad-nirari IV (to 755) — Ashur-nirari V
Babylonia	- - -
Egypt	Sheshonk IV (XXII dyn)
China	Zhou Ping Wang

760	759	758	757	756	755	754	753	752	751

OLMECS, MEXICO
CHAVIN, PERU
CHAVIN, PERU
HELLENES
MESOPOTAMIA

In the kingdom of Israel the son and successor of Jeroboam II was murdered, having reigned for a few months only. The assassin was in turn killed by a Samaritan called Menahem. In Menahem's time there were Assyrian military units at large in Israel, the presence of which generated anxiety and dissent; some argued that Israel should ally herself with Egypt. The general feeling was to some extent reflected by the prophet Hosea whose writings, however, are mainly concerned with the punishment in store for Israel on account of the Samaritans' golden calf and other such abominations:

> 'For they have sown the wind, and they
> shall reap the whirlwind: it hath no stalk:
> the bud shall yield no meal: if so be it yield,
> the strangers shall swallow it up.
> Israel is swallowed up....'

The Eastern Zhou dynasty established in Loyang was greatly dependent upon the neighbouring feudal princes. Their states, lying on either side of the Yellow River, professed loyalty to the Emperor, but were united with one another by a common language and various political and economic ties. Despite constant internal conflicts, however, the Chinese culture developed swiftly.

A king named Nabonassar ascended the throne in Babylon in 747 BC and for some time to come the years were reckoned from this date in the ancient world. Nabonassar himself achieved nothing of consequence, but his Assyrian neighbour Tiglath-pileser III marched into Babylonia and made Nabonassar his vassal.

Afterwards Tiglath-pileser moved northwards and destroyed Urartu; then he turned west and seized Damascus, for centuries a prime objective of the Assyrian kings. Tiglath-pileser III restored Assyria to her position as a major power. In Israel the Assyrians occupied numerous cities and many people were deported to the east. The Jewish king, Ahaz, became in effect a vassal prince, and hastened to Damascus to pay tribute.

In the 740s Grecian Sparta was involved in a bloody enterprise known as the First Messenian War. This ended with the Spartan occupation and enslavement of Messenia on Peloponnesus. The Messenians henceforth worked the land for the Spartans, who spent their entire time in encampments under continuous threat of rebellion. Sparta's remarkable constitution is said to have been introduced by a legislator named Lycurgus. There were two kings who were army commanders but with no civil powers. Political affairs were handled by five ephors who were elected for a year at a time and whose first measure was to urge men to shave off their moustaches and obey the laws. At seven years old all boys were put into government boarding schools to learn gymnastics and choral music; they were given the minimum of food and clothing and were severely birched whether or not they had transgressed. Adult men ate daily at common messes and were fed a soup made from pork, blood, vinegar, and salt. Buildings were of the simplest possible form; no extravagance whatever was permitted. Roof timbers were adzed, doors sawn, and by law no seats were permitted in the lavatories. Only short swords were carried, and hair was worn long, so making good-looking men more handsome and ugly men more repulsive.

The Egyptian 23rd dynasty, established by Petubastis in the city of Bubastis, was probably fairly local and of short duration. A prince in Sais, Tefnakhte, competed with Petubastis for the Nile delta, and a Nubian general named Piankhi seized the Nile valley.

As expected, the Spartans left very few works of art. Archaeological finds on the site of the city were few and far between. Illustrated here, however, is a Spartan stela, now in the local museum in Sparta. The figures are said to represent Agamemnon and Clytemnestra, whereas the two figures at the back of the stela may represent Menelaus and Helen, the king and queen of Sparta at the time of the Trojan war.

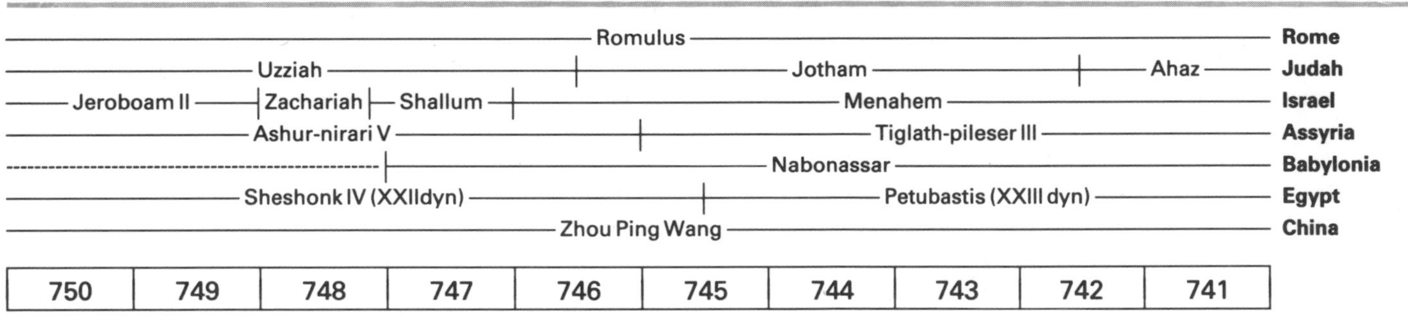
Romulus
Rome
Uzziah
Jotham
Ahaz
Judah
Jeroboam II
Zachariah
Shallum
Menahem
Israel
Ashur-nirari V
Tiglath-pileser III
Assyria
Nabonassar
Babylonia
Sheshonk IV (XXIIdyn)
Petubastis (XXIII dyn)
Egypt
Zhou Ping Wang
China
750
749
748
747
746
745
744
743
742
741

740–731 BC

AFRICA
ATTICA
HITTITES
MARAS
KING BARACUB
SYRO-HITTITE

One day when King Ahaz was inspecting the military defence installations north of Jerusalem, he met the prophet Isaiah who, holding the hand of his small son, spoke encouragingly to the king about the current war with Damascus. So far this had gone badly; the enemy had occupied a large area of the country and now aimed to depose David's dynasty and appoint the son of a certain Tabal king of Judah. But Isaiah prophesied that this would not happen. 'Behold, a virgin shall conceive and bear a son, and shall call his name Emmanuel. For before the child shall have knowledge to cry, My father and my mother, the riches of Damascus and the spoil of Samaria shall be taken away before the king of Assyria.' That is to say: Assyria will defeat the enemies of Ahaz from Damascus, but also invade the kingdom of Judah, where hard times can be expected. 'Nevertheless the dimness shall not be such as was.... The people that walked in darkness have seen a great light, they that dwell in the land of the shadow of death, upon them hath the light shined. Thou hast multiplied the nation and not increased the joy, they joy before thee according to the joy in harvest, and as men rejoice when they divided the spoil. For thou hast broken the yoke of his burden, and the staff of his shoulder, and the rod of his oppressor, as in the day of Midian. For every battle of the warrior is with confused noise, and garments rolled in blood; but this shall be with burning and fuel of fire. For unto us a child is born, unto us a son is given; and the government shall be upon his shoulder; and his name shall be called Wonderful, Counsellor, the mighty God, the everlasting Father, the Prince of Peace. Of the increase of his government and peace there shall be no end, upon the throne of David and upon his kingdom.' This magnificent biblical text, which was to reverberate down the centuries, is found in the ninth chapter of the Book of Isaiah. Those interested in history should also read the adjoining chapters, all composed by one of the great poets of world literature.

The prophet Isaiah has been portrayed innumerable times through the ages. This is a sculpture in the church doorway in Suillac, France.

The prophecy of Isaiah on the imminent downfall of Damascus was in fact a warning to King Ahaz not to involve Assyria in the war; but the latter paid no heed. He despatched a message to Tiglath-pileser, sent him all the gold and silver in the temple and treasury, and requested military assistance. Tiglath-pileser did not hesitate: 'And the king of Assyria hearkened unto him; for the king of Assyria went up against Damascus and took it, and carried the people of it captive to Kir, and slew Rezin.' (II Kings 16:9)

In Egypt the 23rd dynasty was drawing to a close. The Nubian Piankhi had settled in Heliopolis, where the Sun god Ra had his sanctuary; he proclaimed himself son of Ra and received homage from local Egyptian princes, including the official Pharaoh in Bubastis. Tefnakhte of Sais, however, continued to assert his independence.

The last King Midas of Phrygia appeared around 738 and reigned until about 695 BC. He is, therefore, in a sense, historically palpable, though we are likely to remember him mainly for the tales relating to his ass's ears and his greed for gold. According to the former tale, King Midas acquired a cap in order to conceal his ass's ears, but he was unable to; keep this from his barber, who was ordered never to divulge the secret and dared not gossip about it. Finally, however, unable to contain himself, the barber dug a hollow in the ground and whispered his secret into it, after which he refilled the hole. But the underground roots of the reeds absorbed his words, and soon afterwards the people of Phrygia heard to their astonishment how the reeds whispered again and again: 'King Midas has ass's ears - King Midas has ass's ears.....' The other tale relates how Midas captured the satyr Silenus and demanded that the latter should fulfil one wish for him - that all should be transformed into gold. Silenus agreed and was granted his freedom. But Midas soon realised his folly, for his very food turned to gold the moment he put it in his mouth.

In the 730s the first Greek colonists reached Sicily. In 735 Naxos was founded by a group from Chalcis, while another group from Corinth founded Syracuse the following year. The Greeks quite clearly regarded themselves as superior to the native Sicilians, many of whom were made slaves.

Rome	Romulus
Judah	Ahaz
Israel	Menahem | Pekahiah | Pekah | Hoshea
Assyria	Tiglath-pileser III
Babylonia	Nabonassar | Nadinu ---- Ukin-zer
Egypt	Petubastis (XXIII dyn)
China	Zhou Ping Wang

740	739	738	737	736	735	734	733	732	731

ASSYRIA

Having made Syria an Assyrian province, Tiglath-pileser III turned south against Ukin-zer, an Aramaean intruder who had seized the throne in Babylon. After a battle Ukin-zer was slain, and in 729 Tiglath-pileser ceremonially embraced the hand of the god Marduk, thereby signifying that he was now king not only of Assyria but also of Babylonia. In Babylonia he was known as Pulu, and the Bible also refers to him by that name. This union created a formidable consolidated power which was inherited by Tiglath-pileser's son Shalmaneser V, known in Babylonia as Ululai. But hardly had Ululai begun his rule before there was trouble in the west where the Israelite king, Hoshea, rebelled by refusing to pay his tributes. Shalmaneser himself led a campaign against Israel, took Hoshea prisoner and laid siege to the capital, Samaria, which nevertheless held out throughout Shalmaneser's lifetime. His successor, a general named Sargon, established a new dynasty which in many respects sought to change Assyrian policy, though for Israel's part this was hardly discernible. Samaria fell in 722, and Sargon's records reveal that 27,290 of its citizens were removed in captivity. To replace them, the Assyrians moved in people from the east. The prophet Hosea, (not to be confused with King Hoshea) was in fact a republican who detested the line of Jehu; he appears to have written his prophesies while Samaria was still under siege: 'Where now is your king who shall ensure your salvation in all your cities? The Samarians have suffered as they deserve through defying their God'. Thus in traditional prophetic style, Hosea, though apparently critical of official policy, blamed the people for what had occurred, rebuking them for their sins and heretical faith.

Tiglath-pileser was expert in the technique of removing inhabitants from captured cities and countries; this shifting of population was an important feature of his policy. Assyrian administration was immediately introduced in the Damascus region. King Ahaz went to pay homage to his conqueror and, seeing an altar, ordered a copy of it to be installed at once in the temple at Jerusalem, to the gratification of Tiglath-pileser and with the approval of the high priest.

Sargon was unsuccessful in asserting his authority in Babylonia where a Chaldean named Merodach-Baladan ascended the throne.

On the River Yangtze there was a barbarian state, Ch'u, which had been ruled since 740 by a prince named Wu. He greatly expanded his territory to the north, making many minor princes in Honan his vassals. His own country soon became every bit as Chinese as the settlements around the Yellow River. The Chinese chronicle Qun Qui, Spring and Autumn, covers the period 722-481 BC, and these years are therefore also referred to as the spring and autumn period. The chronicle, describing events in the feudal state of Lu, where a century or so later Confucius was to be born, is brusque, and dry, but it is the first chronologically accurate account to be found among Chinese historical records.

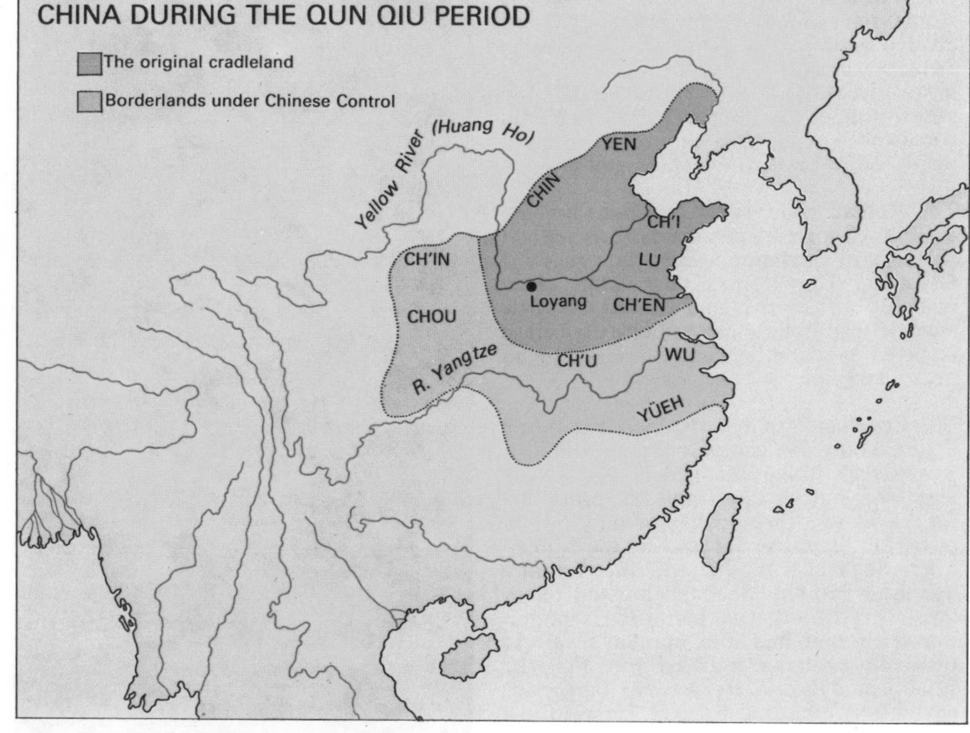
CHINA DURING THE QUN QIU PERIOD
The original cradleland
Borderlands under Chinese Control
Yellow River (Huang Ho)
YEN
CHIN
CH'I
LU
CH'IN
CHOU
Loyang
CH'EN
R. Yangtze
CH'U
WU
YÜEH

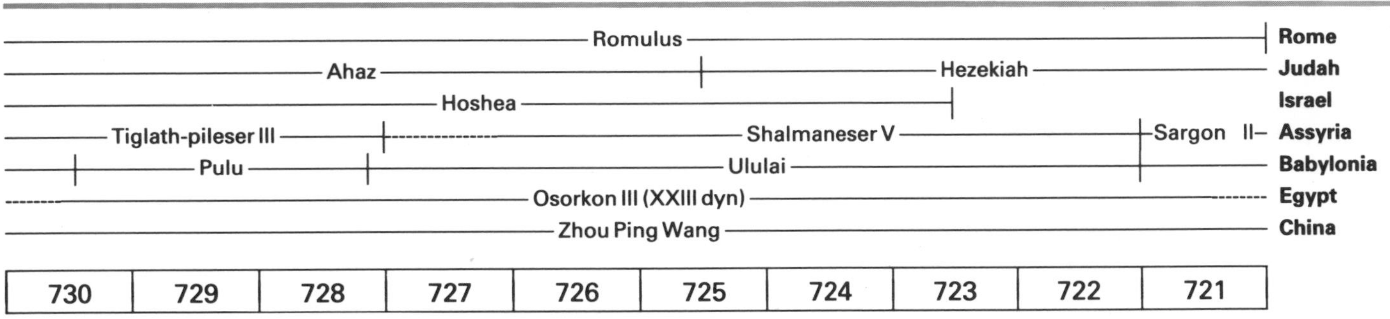
Romulus
Rome
Ahaz
Hezekiah
Judah
Hoshea
Israel
Tiglath-pileser III
Shalmaneser V
Sargon II
Assyria
Pulu
Ululai
Babylonia
Osorkon III (XXIII dyn)
Egypt
Zhou Ping Wang
China
730
729
728
727
726
725
724
723
722
721

720–711 BC

ASSYRIA
EGYPT

The Roman king, Numa Pompilius, is about as legendary as his predecessor Romulus. Numa organized legislation and religion in Rome on the basis of frequent deliberations with the nymph Egeria and regular negotiations with the nation's gods concerning sacrifices to be made and assistance to be expected in return. Rome's newly erected Janus temple, the doors of which were to stand wide open during war, remained closed throughout Numa's reign.

Ancient authors claimed that the twelve months of the Roman calendar derived from Numa — Romulus is supposed to have reckoned with ten months only and discounted altogether the worst of winter. Numa reinstated the missing season and created the months of January and February. January was named after the god Janus with his two faces, the one looking ahead and the other turned to the past. The year still commenced with the month of March, dedicated to Mars, the Roman god of war.

The Roman gods, some of whom became established for ever in calendars, as yet had nothing in common with the gods of Olympus. The Romans were still unacquainted with Homer and Hesiod and their legends. The Italic gods were obscure beings involved in adventures and burdened by no ties of kinship.

The Egyptian 24th dynasty consisted of one Pharaoh only: Bocchoris son of Tefnakhte in Sais. Greek scribes claimed he was a wise legislator, but he faced political problems, for Egypt was threatened not only by the powerful Assyrians but also by the Nubian ruler Shabaka, brother of the recently deceased Piankhi. Shabaka pressed relentlessly northward with his army, captured Bocchoris and had him burned alive. As Pharaoh, Shabaka initiated the 25th, or Ethiopian dynasty. He was no barbarian, having been educated in Egypt. He was also a practical man who abolished capital punishment and introduced hard labour instead, thereby utilizing the physical potentialities of his captives for the good of the community.

This image of the Italic god Janus, who gave his name to one of the months in King Numa's calendar, eventually ended up in the cathedral of Ferrara.

The authors of antiquity, Thucydides in particular, provide a great deal of precise information on the founding of various Greek cities. Sybaris is said to have been founded in 720, Croton in 710, and Taras, Tarentum or Taranto in 707. It is related that Taras was founded by youngsters from Sparta after the Messenian war, when the Spartan soldiers imprudently swore an oath not to return home until they were victorious. But this was long delayed, and there was soon an acute shortage of males in Sparta. The birth-rate fell alarmingly and the ephors felt compelled to advocate uninhibited relations between the women and such men as remained in Sparta. The result was an abundant crop of children who had grown up by the time the old Spartans finally won their war and came home. The returning warriors poured scorn on these young people who, in frustration, left Sparta altogether and founded Taranto. The Greek immigrants appear to have met little resistance. The pioneers fought more among themselves than against the native inhabitants, who were evidently poorly organized and belonged to different tribes: Messapii, Oenotrii, Lucani and Itali. The Itali grazed their cattle in this virgin country.

Greek expansion proceeded in other directions, too. The various tribes were seldom at peace among themselves and their colonies elsewhere maintained this tradition, being constantly at war with one another. For the time being, emigration was first and foremost from Chalcis in Euboea, whose pioneers on the north coast of the Aegean had already made this Hellenic territory.

Rome	Numa Pompilius
Judah	Hezekiah
Assyria	Sargon II
Babylonia	Merodach-Baladan II
Egypt	Bocchoris (XXIV dyn) — Shabaka (XXV dyn)
China	Zhou Huan Wang

720	719	718	717	716	715	714	713	712	711

HELLAS
SARGON II'S PALACE
CANAAN
CANAANITES
GILGAMESH
ASSYRIANS
ASSYRIANS

The reign of the Assyrian Sargon appears to have comprised an endless succession of military campaigns. Sargon was victorious in all directions and collected tributes from Chaldeans, Hittites, Syrians, Churrites, Cypriots and others. But this was of no avail; revolts and hostilities continued. Even in the insignificant border states such as Judah there were conspiracies against Assyria, whose possessions extended as far as Gaza and the Egyptian frontier. In Judah, however, there were some who felt that this was a hazardous policy. The prophet Isaiah had gone in sackcloth and ashes for three years on account of Egypt and Ethiopia, insisting that the alliance with Egypt could only result in calamity for Judah. When the authorities in the town of Ashdod gave up paying tribute and were consequently attacked by an Assyrian army, the prophet, according to the 20th chapter of the Book of Isaiah, demonstrated his disapproval by appearing naked and barefoot.

Isaiah was also critical of the Jewish king, Hezekiah, even though other biblical scribes praised him warmly. II Chronicles, in particular, has much to say of the orthodoxy and devout deeds of Hezekiah. This king had dared defy the Assyrians who were ravaging his country and compelling him to pay large tributes in gold and silver, some of which had to come from the temple in Jerusalem. King Sennacherib's cuneiform account of this is confirmed in II Kings, l8: 13-16 .Despite the tribute, Sennacherib marched on Jerusalem, but never succeeded in taking the city. This failure is explained in II Chronicles 32:21: 'And the Lord sent an angel which cut off all the mighty men of valour, and the leaders and captains in the camp of the king of Assyria.' For the Jews this unexpected deliverance of the city of Jerusalem was of great political and religious significance.

Dorian Sparta, which in recent decades had achieved a position of considerable local power, having seized the neighbouring cities of Amyclae and Messene, was adapting to its new constitution, whereby the city was to have two kings who commanded the army during wartime and who acted virtually as high priests when the nation was at peace. Government was conducted by a council of twenty-eight elders, all above sixty years of age, but the supreme power (in theory, at least) rested with the popular assembly. By drawing lots, five overseers from the principal landowning families were selected from the elders' council. The land was worked by an enslaved proletariat—helots, who were singularly ill-treated by the nobility, the Spartiates. The latter lived in constant fear of revolution. Up to the age of thirty they were accommodated in barracks and maintained a permanent state of military readiness. After that age they were permitted to live at home, though even then they continued to eat their daily meal of black soup communally until they reached the age of sixty.

Lycurgus, the man reputed to have drawn up the constitution was by now dead. Having completed his legislation, he made his kinsmen solemnly promise to honour his laws until he returned from a journey he proposed to make. He then went to Crete and killed himself. His law book consisted of rhetoric, the first injunction of which was that none of the decrees would be written down, but should be passed on orally. Boxing matches were prohibited on the grounds that people should not be encouraged to sit and stare. Newborn children were inspected by the elders and were bathed in wine; if this caused them to faint they were to be put out to die.

Sargon II on a relief from Khorsabad, once this king's capital under the name of Dur Sharrukin. Khorsabad was extensively excavated in the l9th century AD, as well as between the world wars. Winged bulls with human heads are among the more remarkable finds. The relief pictured here is now in the Louvre, Paris.

Numa Pompilius — **Rome**
Hezekiah — **Judah**
Sargon II — Sennacherib — **Assyria**
Sargon II — Merodach-Baladan II — **Babylonia**
Shabaka — **Egypt**
Zhou Huan Wang — **China**

710	709	708	707	706	705	704	703	702	701

700–691 BC

EGYPTIANS
ASSYRIANS

Biblical authors were boundless in their praise for Hezekiah, notably for destroying the altars of alien gods and for performing massive sacrificial rites in the temple at Jerusalem: 'And the number of the burnt offerings which the congregation brought was threescore and ten bullocks, an hundred rams and two hundred lambs: all these were for a burnt offering to the Lord. And the consecrated things were six hundred oxen and three thousand sheep. But the priests were too few, so that they could not flay all the burnt offerings; wherefore their brethren the Levites did help them'. (II Chronicles 29: 32-34). Hezekiah also listened obediently to Isaiah who prolonged his life by fifteen years, but also prophesied terrible misfortunes for the royal family. 'Then said Hezekiah to Isaiah: Good is the word of the Lord which thou hath spoken. He said moreover, For there shall be peace and truth in my days'.

Hezekiah's son, Manasseh, was only twelve years old when he became king of Judah and consequently his reign was a long one. In his day Assyrian power was at its peak, there was no political liberty for small nations, and Manasseh had to pay tribute to Esarhaddon and provide troops to take part in the latter's campaign against Egypt. Even more damning to Manasseh's posthumous reputation was the fact that he was responsible for ensuring that the Assyrian religion be properly honoured in Israel. Horrified prophets and chroniclers regarded Manasseh as a traitor and apostate. He was virtually compelled to persecute his critics; this proved a bloody process and the prophet Isaiah is reputed to have been one of the victims.

A ruler whom Assyrian sources refer to as Kashtariti created a large coalition of warrior tribes who moved southward against the Mesopotamian countries. These tribesmen were Cimmerians, Mannians, and Medes. The Cimmerians were closely related to the Scythians in the regions north of the Black Sea. According to Herodotus, they had lived in the Crimea and later scholars claimed to have found a connection between the name of the peninsula and the name of the tribe. Presumably oppressed by their kinsmen, the Scythians, the Cimmerians retreated southward; if we are to believe the Greek scribes, one group journeyed through the Balkans, but most of them probably crossed Caucasia. This march provoked universal fear and confusion in the eastern Mediterranean world; and in distant Judah news of them even reached the ears of Isaiah:
'None shall be weary nor stumble among them; none shall slumber nor sleep; neither shall the girdle of their loins be loosed....'
'Whose arrows are sharp and all their bows bent, their horses' hooves shall be counted like flint, and their wheel like a whirlwind.'
'Their roaring shall be like a lion, they shall roar like young lions; yea, they shall roar and lay hold of the prey and shall carry it away safe, and none shall deliver it'. Isaiah 5:27-29.

The Mannians or manna people were a Median tribe under the suzerainty of the Scythians. Their ruler had confirmed this officially and a Scythian force had occupied the Caucasian pass of Khubushkia. In Nineveh there was justifiable anxiety and King Esarhaddon decided to despatch an embassy to Kashtariti. The ambassador Shanabushumma met the leader of the coalition in the latter's camp. Unfortunately, we know nothing of the outcome of these negotiations.

Esarhaddon was either a skilled statesman or he was simply fortunate, for one day the Scythian King Partatua asked Esarhaddon's daughter to marry him and she immediately agreed. This broke up the coalition since the Scythians now ordered the Mannians to keep the peace with Assyria. The Cimmerians attempted in vain to seize the pass at Khubushkia but their assault was repelled.

How this affected the other Medes is not very clear, presumably only a few of them were involved in Kashtariti's coalition, for the Median folk were now split into several tribes. For a brief period in the 680s they were united under a ruler named Mamitiarshu but this did not last.

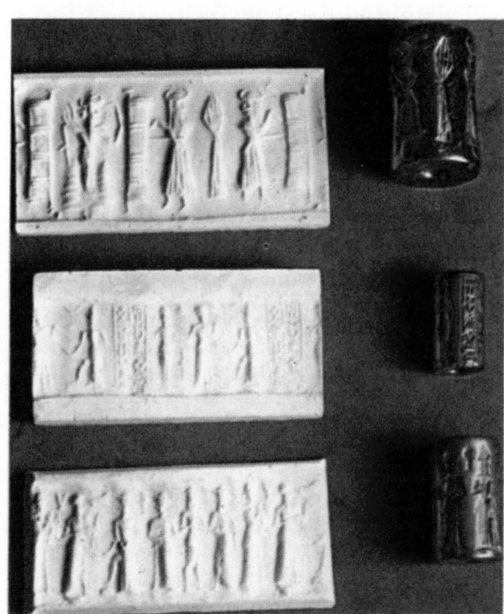

Seals were useful implements for printing signs and symbols into soft clay. Cylindrical seals which were rolled across the flat surface of the clay had been common in Mesopotamia for some time and were used to sign documents and to denote ownership of private property. These three cylindrical seals come from the Sumerian city of Uruk and are 1000 years older than Manasseh and his Assyrian contemporaries. German archaeologists who excavated a temple in Uruk found not only the seals illustrated above but also trade accounts with signs for words and numbers, i.e. the beginnings of writing, which over the years were to develop into a syllabic alphabet with about 2000 cuneiform characters.

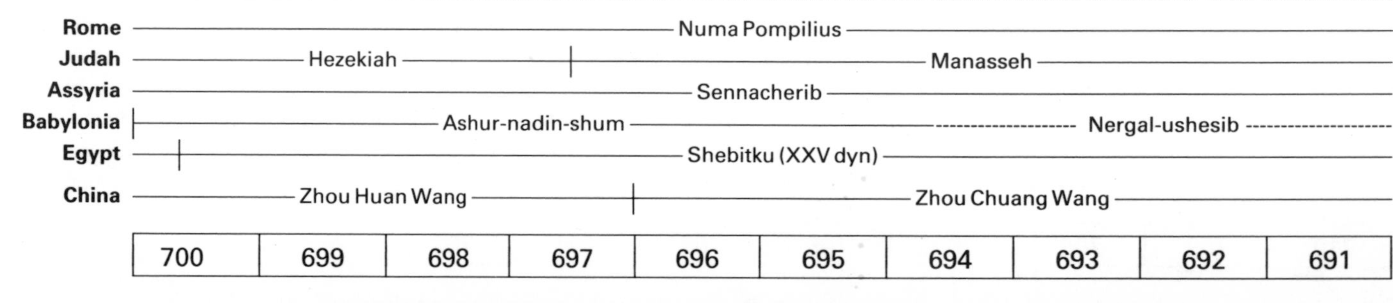
Rome
Numa Pompilius
Judah
Hezekiah
Manasseh
Assyria
Sennacherib
Babylonia
Ashur-nadin-shum
Nergal-ushesib
Egypt
Shebitku (XXV dyn)
China
Zhou Huan Wang
Zhou Chuang Wang
700
699
698
697
696
695
694
693
692
691

ASSYRIANS
HEBREWS
ASSYRIANS

Phoenician Tyre, which had also attempted to escape Babylonian domination, was under siege from 685 by King Nebuchadrezzar who, however, was unable to seize the colonies in the western Mediterranean. Political leadership there was assumed by Carthage.

Chalcis became involved in a long war with the neighbouring city of Eretrea and thereafter never regained its leading role in the coalition, which was taken over by Megara, Corinth and Miletus.

Emigration from Greece was frequent in the 7th century. Those who left generally made for Sicily and southern Italy, but some also travelled north toward the Hellespont and the Black Sea. Among the cities founded around this time were Trapezus, Chalcedon, Cumae, Messina, Sybaris, Croton and Taras.

Many Greek cities and regions, however, were unaffected by such shifts of population. No colony-founding expeditions departed from Attica, Argos, Arcadia or Thessalia. Aegina, then the wealthiest of all Greek trading centres, did not establish a single Italian subsidiary. Chalcis, Miletus and Megara, on the other hand, continuously sent out new groups, though it is possible that the towns they established were no more than exporting settlements. Those who set out from Chalcis were not only native citizens, but doubtless included land-hungry farmers, from Boeotia, for example, not far away.

In 689, after severe fighting, Sennacherib succeeded in taking Babylon, where the Chaldeans under Meredach-Baladan, expelled by Sargon, had re-established power. In order to end once and for all the Babylonians' persistent endeavours to achieve independence, Sennacherib decided to destroy the city. So thorough was this destruction that practically nothing of ancient Babylon was left for archaeologists. Babylon remained an Assyrian vassal for a very long time to come. Sennacherib, who between wars built up Nineveh into a handsome capital city, was murdered by Esarhaddon, one of his sons, just as he apparently murdered his own father, Sargon. Esarhaddon was likewise a great warrior and city builder and he re-erected the temple of Marduk in Babylon.

In 683 BC, so it is said, the monarchy was abolished in Athens. The city had been ruled by a score or more of kings following the reign of its founder Cecrops, who is reputed to have arrived there from Egypt. These kings included Aegeus and his son Theseus who fought the Minotaur in the Labyrinth on Crete and abandoned Ariadne on Naxos. The last of these kings was named Codrus, who allowed himself to be killed in a battle with the Dorians after an oracle had foretold that victory would go to the side whose commander was slain. The Athenians expressed their gratitude to Codrus by resolving to appoint no successor. In the new republic two officials were elected as heads of state for a period of one year. These were called archons, one of whom was a military leader, the other a civil functionary.

To the west in Asia Minor were Phrygia and Lydia, two states of great importance to the Greeks. Phrygia, with its capital Gordium (of Gordian knot fame) had been invaded by homeless Cimmerians, who also challenged the mighty Assyrian empire. King Midas of Phyrgia – he of the legendary ass's ears and golden touch – had offered some resistance to the Assyrian Sargon, but the Cimmerian invasion so weakened Phrygia that it was overrun by the neighbouring state of Lydia. Lydia was ruled by Gyges, central figure of a Greek tale which later was to interest the Baroque painters. According to this story, a certain King Candaules, who had a very beautiful wife, insisted that Gyges should spy on her and admire her nakedness. But the queen discovered the voyeur and took revenge by giving Gyges the choice of assassinating Candaules and marrying her, or else being murdered himself.

The 7th century heralded the golden age of the Etruscans. Theirs was an urban culture, similar to that of the Greeks, and there was considerable interchange between the two countries. Politically, the Etruscans were organized into three federations, each consisting of twelve cities.

Theseus was a mythical figure linked with Athens, a city that was still of fairly minor importance. Theseus' battle with the Minotaur in the Cretan Labyrinth is the best known of all his feats. This story is frequently encountered in art and literature from the classical period onwards. Painting by an unknown artist. Louvre, Paris.

Numa Pompilius — **Rome**
Manasseh — **Judah**
Sennacherib | Esarhaddon — **Assyria**
Suzubu | — **Babylonia**
Shebitku (XXV dyn) | Taharqa (XXV dyn) — **Egypt**
Zhou Chuang Wang | — **China**

690	689	688	687	686	685	684	683	682	681

680–671 BC

CYPRUS
HELLAS

Literary endeavours in the Greek world were not restricted to the Homeric poems. The morose poet Hesiod lived and worked somewhere in Boeotia and he left posterity not only his *Theogony,* a long account in hexameters of the origins and relationships of the gods, but also a shorter work entitled *Works and Days*, comprising a collection of rural maxims and mythological tales. A much younger writer lived on the island of Paros. This was Archilochus, a satiric and lyrical poet who created the renowned Archilochian verse form. Archilochus was a bitter and vindictive individual; when a man refused him the hand of his daughter in marriage, Archilochus composed such a defamatory lampoon on the issue that the entire family went out and hanged themselves.

In 673, having sought the advice of various oracles, Esarhaddon attacked the Cimmerians on the Upper Tigris and thoroughly defeated them. At the same time a Scythian leader named Ishpakai, who clearly did not support King Partatua's marriage plans, was defeated. This definitely ended Kashtariti's coalition, and Esarhaddon could now feel secure in this direction. However, he was himself an ill man and died young.

King Pheidon reigned in Argos around 680 and enjoyed the honour of having introduced the coin into the Greek world. bringing this innovation from his native Lydia.

The little city of Rome was squabbling with its neighbours, and it was during the legendary reign of King Tullus Hostilius that the combat of the Horatii and Curiatii triplets was said to have occurred. The sole survivor of this feud was one of the Horatii. When he returned home in victorious possession of the armour of the Curiatii, his sister burst into tears for she was betrothed to one of the victims. This so enraged her brother that he cut her down too; he was sentenced to death and spared only through the intervention of his elderly father. Naive stories of this nature abound throughout the royal era of Rome's history.

After long preparations, Esarhaddon marched against Egypt. Two year-long campaigns around the middle of the decade failed to achieve the desired result, but in 671 the Assyrian army took Memphis and seized the crown prince, the Pharaoh's harem, and his court and administration. Pharaoh Taharqa himself escaped to his dynastic homeland to the south in the Nile valley. Egypt was now ruled by Esarhaddon who received oaths of allegiance from a dozen or more of the local princes in the Nile delta and then marched victoriously homeward, hailed en route by no less than twenty-five kings from Judah, Tyre, Byblus, Cyprus and other small states.

The tale of the Horatii and the Curiatii has attracted many poets and artists. The most famous and admired work of art on the subject is the great painting by Jacques Louis David, The Oath of the Horatii. This was painted in l785, immediately purchased by Louis XVI and placed in the Louvre. It concentrated on the patriotic aspect of this Roman tale and within a few years it proved an inspiration to patriots of the French Revolution. The artist became a member of the revolutionary convention, voted for the execution of the king, later became Napoleon I's court artist and was forced into exile after Napoleon's downfall.

Rome — Numa Pompilius — | — Tullus Hostilius
Judah — Manasseh
Assyria — Esarhaddon
Egypt — Taharqa (XXV dyn)
China — Zhou Yi Wang III — | — Zhou Hui Wang

680	679	678	677	676	675	674	673	672	671

LION OF NIMRUD
EGYPTIANS
HELLENES
ESARHADDON

Locri, in southern Italy, had been founded twenty years earlier by a rabble of bandits and runaway slaves accompanied by a group of well-born young ladies from Locris in Greece. In 664 a man named Zaleucus set about establishing law and order in the city; anyone wishing to change his laws was to appear before a popular assembly with a rope about his throat, and if he failed to gain the support of the majority would have the noose tightened.

Pharaoh Taharqa continued to oppose the Assyrian invaders and organized a number of uprisings, though the only outcome was that the captive Egyptian princes involved were hauled away to Nineveh. When Taharqa died in 663, the young co-regent he had appointed failed to assert himself and quickly disappeared from the records. This signalled the end of the Ethiopian dynasty, which was succeeded by a princely line from Memphis. The first of these Pharaohs was known as Psamtik I, so named because of his Greek connections. With the aid of Ionian mercenaries he gained control over the other local princes and then set about liberating Egypt from the Assyrians. This task was facilitated by the fact that King Ashurbanipal had enemies to contend with in other quarters and therefore withdrew some of his occupation troops from Egypt.

In 680 BC a coalition was formed in China known as the Zhongguo: the Middle Kingdom. This was set up to protect original Chinese states around the Yellow River against the semi-barbaric Ch'u people in the Yangtze valley, and also as defence against barbarians from the north. The leading state in this coalition was located at Shantung on the coast. The king here was Huan, who was the real ruler of China since he collected tribute from the other princes in the alliance and sent his troops to help them whenever this seemed necessary.

In Central America an advanced culture was flourishing which archaeologists call La Venta and ascribe to the Olmec people. These left behind them a a variety of sculptures, and their religious emblem was the jaguar which appears to have symbolized heaven, earth and the underworld.

A Bronze Age culture, now known as Tung-son, existed on the Malacca peninsula and in Sumatra. From this were left axes, drums and other objects with geometric ornamentation and different configurations.

Literature and art were evidently flourishing in Assyria, producing magnificent reliefs and large quantities of cuneiform tablets. The artistic skill, whereby scenes like those below were infused with movement by purely sculptural means, has never since been bettered. This relief is from Ashurbanipal's palace at Nineveh. It is interesting for the information it provides concerning the outfitting of the hunters and their horses.

Tullus Hostilius — **Rome**
Manasseh — **Judah**
Esarhaddon | Ashurbanipal — **Assyria**
Taharqa (XXV dyn) | ------------ XXVI dynasty — **Egypt**
Zhou Hui Wang — **China**

670	669	668	667	666	665	664	663	662	661

660–651 BC

ASSYRIA
HELLENES

The Lydian King Gyges was killed in 652 while fighting the Cimmerians, after having broken his alliance with Ashurbanipal of Assyria. Prior to his death, he had made war, with varying success, on the Greek cities along the Asian coast; he also took Colophon. Gyges' son Ardys captured vantage points on the west coast and re-established the Lydian empire.

According to ancient, official mythology, in 660 a Japanese body politic was formed known as Yamato, the history of which contains accounts of battles with Korean tribes, possibly Ainu people.

The little Judaean kingdom virtually formed part of the Assyrian empire, even though it claimed to be independent having never actually been occupied by Ashurbanipal's troops. The biblical scribes spoke scathingly of King Manasseh, although he must have been under some pressure. In the words of II Kings:
'And he built altars for all the host of heaven in the two courts of the house of the Lord'.
'And he made his son pass through the fire, and observed times, and used enchantments and dealt with familiar spirits and wizards...'
'And he set a graven image in the house...'
The implication is that he was obliged to tolerate the religious practices of the ruling power. According to II Chronicles, however, this was of no avail. Manasseh is said to have been imprisoned and taken to Babylon: 'And when he was in affliction he besought his God.....And prayed unto Him; and He was intreated of him, and heard his supplication and brought him again to Jerusalem in to His kingdom. Then Manasseh knew that the Lord, he was God'.

Ashurbanipal went out to do battle with the Elamites in Iran. He inflicted a crushing defeat upon them and put his foes to death with frightful cruelty during his triumphal procession to Nineveh. A few years later he suppressed a revolt led by his own brother in Babylon. The brother was burned to death in the palace while his associates were taken to Nineveh and sacrificed to the spirit of Sennacherib. Ashurbanipal's own writings and reliefs tell a terrible story. In 656, however, Egypt freed herself from the Assyrian yoke and this was the signal for a general insurrection in the western part of Ashurbanipal's empire. This was subdued fairly easily in the Phoenician cities whose leaders were then compelled to send their wives and daughters to Ashurbanipal's harem. A number of Arab sheiks also fared badly and were so heavily penalized that the price of camels in Nineveh fell to half a shekel each. But elsewhere in the Assyrian empire the unrest continued.

In Greece the oppressed people of Messenia rose against Sparta and it took a decade to put down the revolt, known as the Second Messenian War and notable because the poet Tyrtaeus took part in it. He was a small, weak, misshapen man, incapable of bearing arms, yet his battle songs inspired the Spartans to victory. One of these begins roughly as follows: 'Glorious is death when courageously in the front line you fall fighting for your country, for your city and for your home...'

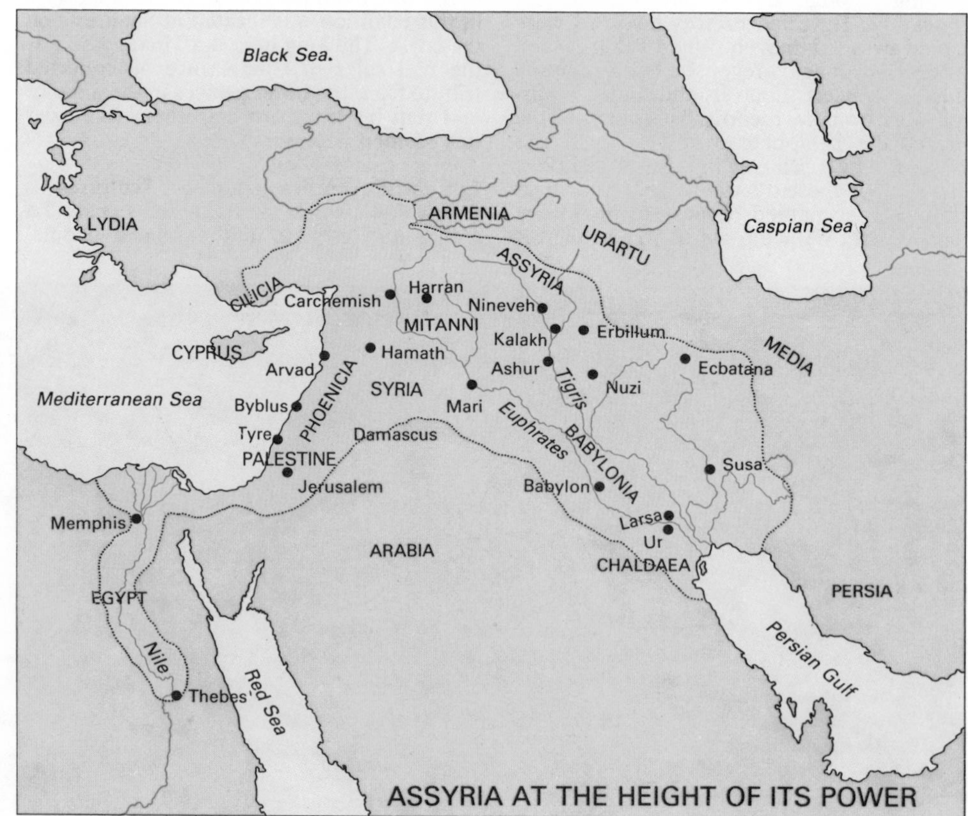
Black Sea.
LYDIA
ARMENIA
URARTU
Caspian Sea
ASSYRIA
CILICIA
Carchemish
Harran
Nineveh
MITANNI
Kalakh
Erbillum
MEDIA
CYPRUS
Arvad
Hamath
Ashur
Tigris
Nuzi
Ecbatana
Mediterranean Sea
Byblus
PHOENICIA
SYRIA
Mari
Euphrates
Tyre
Damascus
BABYLONIA
PALESTINE
Susa
Jerusalem
Babylon
Memphis
Larsa
Ur
ARABIA
CHALDAEA
PERSIA
EGYPT
Nile
Thebes
Red Sea
Persian Gulf
ASSYRIA AT THE HEIGHT OF ITS POWER

Rome	Tullus Hostilius
Judah	Manasseh
Assyria	Ashurbanipal
Egypt	Psamtik I (XXVI dyn)
China	Zhou Hui Wang

660	659	658	657	656	655	654	653	652	651

ASSYRIANS
ASHURBANIPAL

A Cimmerian horde invaded Lydia and ravaged the country right through to the capital, Sardes. King Gyges died fighting these intruders who continued eastwards, and posed a threat to Assyria as well.

King Ashurbanipal, an educated and cultured man, built a big new palace in Nineveh and assembled a vast library. Thousands of years later this was excavated by archaeologists, who found in it the key to the alphabet and the dead language of cuneiform. The library contained historical annals, moral maxims and ordinary tales.

The Japanese national calendar is said to date from 11 February 660 BC, the day the first emperor, Jimmu-Tenno, ascended the throne. Unfortunately he is a purely imaginary figure who failed to found any dynasty.

In China King Huan of Ch'i died in 643, and with him the political structure collapsed. A prince from Song (Sung) named Xiang attempted to take control of the Middle Kingdom alliance, but was unsuccessful. The outside state of Ch'u, led by an able young man named Cheng, recruited some of the other states to his side.

During this decade the city of Byzantium was founded by Greek colonists from Megara. The northern Grecian city of Abdera, was also refounded, after having earlier been destroyed.

A large Median kingdom had emerged at about this time. Greek scribes claimed that its founder was Deioces and said that the kingdom survived for a century and a half, until 550. Later sources show this to be incorrect, though otherwise little is known about the Medes. They certainly spoke an Indo-European language and fought the Assyrians on a number of occasions. In 719 King Sargon had put an end to a Median state in Mannai, but this was quickly re-established. Median possessions farther eastward were called Parsua and Illi, and the latter was also quelled for a brief period by Sargon.

A Median king named Phraortes ruled from 646 the next after Deioces on the Greeks' list. He was busy consolidating his kingdom after the defeat in which his predecessor had perished.

Sybaris was the wealthiest of the Greek states in southern Italy. It occupied an area that extended from coast to coast across the Calabrian peninsula and even farther, since a little to the north on the west coast a subsidiary town was founded: Poseidonia, later Paestum. In order to check the competition from expanding Taras, the Sybarites also encouraged the foundation of Achaean Metapontium. There were continual minor wars in progress between the different cities both in Sicily and on the mainland.

The location of Sybaris long remained a mystery. However, recent excavations have brought the city to light. The picture shows the part of the city called Horse's Park.

Tullus Hostilius	Rome
Manasseh — Amon	Judah
Ashurbanipal	Assyria
Psamtik I (XXVI dyn)	Egypt
Zhou Xiang Wang	China

650	649	648	647	646	645	644	643	642	641

ASSYRIA
HELLENES

No information is available concerning the last twenty years of Ashurbanipal's reign, though clearly Assyria was no longer as powerful as it had once been. This famous king appears to have died in 633 and was succeeded by his son Ashur-etel-ilani, who had to deal with another pretender. There were evidently no outstanding events in Ashur-etel-ilani's reign, and the ruins of his palace are in no way comparable with those of Ashurbanipal's.

In the little Judaean vassal state, the signs of the times were interpreted by the prophet Nahum who foretold the approaching downfall of the Assyrian oppressor: 'Behold upon the mountains the feet of him that bringeth good tidings,that publisheth peace! O Judah, keep thy solemn feasts, perform thy vows: for the wicked shall no more pass through thee; he is utterly cut off.' The prophet Zephaniah, who was probably somewhat earlier than Nahum, also foresaw the end of the foreign rulers and their local accomplices: 'And it shall come to pass in the day of the Lord's sacrifice, that I will punish the princes, and the king's children, and all such as are clothed with strange apparel.'

The manoeuvering and fighting between the feudal states in China continued. During the years immediately after 640 BC Ch'u was still predominant, but to the northwest, in Shansi, there was another ambitious state named Ch'in and in 632 there was a tremendous battle between the two armies at Chengbu, involving a hundred thousand men. Ch'u suffered a ruinous defeat and sued for peace. The Emperor Zhou Xiang Wang came in person to the victor's camp and proclaimed him Prince Wen – leader of all the feudal states.

In Corinth, then the world's principal trading city, an individual named Cypselus had made himself absolute ruler. He was succeeded in 627 by his son Periander in whose time Corinth enjoyed a period of commercial greatness, illustrated by the fact that Corinthian vases have since been found in large numbers throughout the Mediterranean region. Periander was counted by the antique scribes as a member of an illustrious company known as the Seven Wise Men of Greece, which also included a number of tyrants. Periander's political ideology was summed up in his assertion that every ear of grain that raised itself above the majority should be clipped off.

The Seven Wise Men of Greece likewise included Thales from Miletus. He was a scientist, celebrated, among other things, for discovering that important branch of mathematics relating to the equilateral triangle.

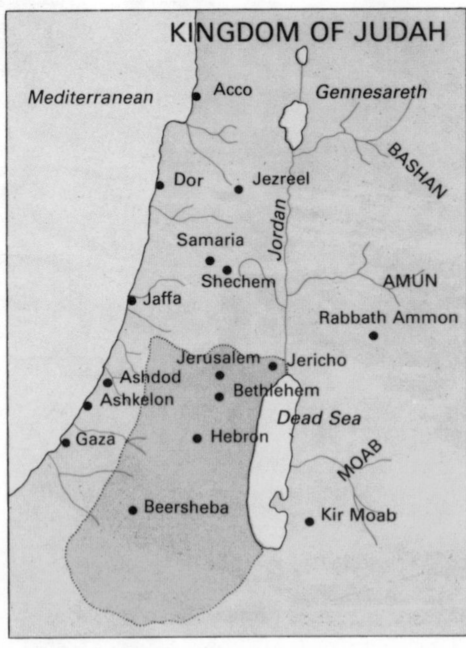
KINGDOM OF JUDAH
Mediterranean
Acco
Gennesareth
BASHAN
Dor
Jezreel
Jordan
Samaria
Shechem
AMUN
Jaffa
Rabbath Ammon
Jerusalem
Jericho
Ashdod
Ashkelon
Bethlehem
Dead Sea
Gaza
Hebron
MOAB
Beersheba
Kir Moab

In Athens a conservative lawyer named Draco codified the laws he had inherited from his father. He attempted to abolish vendettas between families by asserting the right of the community to punish severely all acts of violence. His name has become proverbial thanks to his biographer Plutarch. The Draconian laws were so strict that they were said to have been written in blood rather than ink, and since every type of offence was punished in the same way, even those guilty of trivial crimes were liable to be put to death. Draco himself was a very upright man who enjoyed public respect and admiration - so much so that on one occasion when he attended the theatre he was applauded by the entire audience who began showering him with articles of clothing in token of their admiration. As a result Draco was suffocated.

632 is given as the year when the Greek colony of Cyrene was founded on the African coast by a group from the island of Thera led by a young man named Battus. Battus had consulted the oracle at Delphi concerning a cure for his hopeless stammer and was told that he would go to Libya to raise cattle and found a city. The oracle directed him to a place that did indeed offer excellent grazing. Furthermore, a herb named *Silphium*, not to be found anywhere else, grew freely here; the plant was edible and was eaten both by humans and animals in Cyrene, while a desirable spice was extracted from its root. The people of Cyrene had an export monopoly of this plant.

Judah was not a big country, but its historic significance was overwhelming. In the Bible, II Kings 22-23 recounts the fortunes of the land at this time. As a result of King Josiah's religious zeal and cruel reforms, sacrificial altars were torn down, the idolatrous priests were slain, and divine worship was restricted to the temple of Jerusalem.

Rome	Ancus Marcius
Judah	Amon — Josiah
Assyria	Ashurbanipal — Ashur-etel-ilani
Egypt	Psamtik I (XXVI dyn)
China	Zhou Xiang Wang

640	639	638	637	636	635	634	633	632	631

EGYPT
SARDINIA

The reign of Psamtik I was fortuitous for Egypt: foreign trade expanded and the economy flourished. This engendered a cultural and religious revival. As foreigners passed into the country and business prospered, the Egyptian priesthood jealously clung to its own traditions and history. The priests did what they could to recall the glories of the past, assiduously observing ancient customs and ceremonies, especially in matters pertaining to death and burial. They were no longer able to build pyramids but the ancient rituals were revived. The Book of Death, which in places dates back to the pyramid builders, was re-edited in a papyrus scroll twenty metres in length.

By 627 the Assyrian hold on Egypt seems to have relaxed completely, so that the Judaean King Josiah entered the former kingdom of Israel and annexed the provinces of Samaria, Galilee and Gilead. Josiah also stationed garrisons along the coast road in the former land of the Philistines. At an appropriate moment the high priest Hilkiah discovered an old law book in the temple, whereupon Josiah proceeded to eliminate all alien cults, especially those of the Assyrians, and introduced a reform that unified religion and politics. In 622 a magnificent Passover festival was celebrated in Jerusalem – the sole-prescribed place of sacrifice. Josiah's reformation was the basis for re-establishing the kingdom of David and created a foundation for the ensuing religious and national unity of Judaism.

In Media, south of the Caspian Sea, an energetic politician named Cyaxares ruled. He repelled a Scythian invasion which apparently had the support of the Assyrian leaders in Nineveh.

The Persian religious innovator Zoroaster may possibly have lived at this time, though he would by now have been an old man. There are widely differing views on his place in history, and some modern historians assert quite flatly that he is legendary. But Mazdaism, the religion that he is credited with having founded, did exist at this time in Persia and Media.

Detail from the Egyptian Book of Death, a kind of guide book, in which the deceased was told what gods and adventures he was likely to encounter.

------------------ Phraortes ——|—— Cyaxares —— **Media**
—— Ancus Marcius —— **Rome**
—— Josiah —— **Judah**
—— Ashur-etel-ilani ------------------ Sin-shar-ishkun —— **Assyria**
|—— Nabopolassar —— **Babylonia**
—— Psamtik I (XXVI dyn) —— **Egypt**
—— Zhou Xiang Wang —— **China**

630	629	628	627	626	625	624	623	622	621

620–611 BC

PHOENICIA
HELLAS
HALLSTATT,
CENTRAL EUROPE
ARABS

The advent of Tarquinius Priscus undoubtedly placed Rome under Etruscan rule. This was admitted indirectly by the ancient Latin scribes when they said that Tarquinius was actually a Greek from Corinth, though married to an Etruscan woman named Tanaquil who possessed the gift of prophecy. Tarquinius came to power after bypassing the sons of his predecessor Ancus Martius. In due course, however, they were to assassinate him. He built the Forum Romanum, the Jupiter Temple on the Capitoline Hill and the Cloaca Maxima. He also introduced the fasces, the bundle of rods and axehead, as the symbol of power.

Babylon, a city of a million people, was now the centre of a great empire. In 616 the Babylonian viceroy Nabopolassar revolted against the Assyrian rule in Nineveh and two years later the Median king, Cyaxares, attacked Assyria from the north. In 612 Nineveh was taken and destroyed and King Sin-shar-ishkun burned to death in his palace. From then on the Assyrian kingdom virtually ceased to exist. The Judaean prophet Nahum left a singularly expressive description of the fall of Nineveh. Nahum certainly lived at this time, though the modern scholars are not in agreement as to whether or not his book in the Old Testament is of later date. His prose, nonetheless, is magnificent:

'But Nineveh is of old like a pool of water; yet they shall flee away. Stand, stand, shall they cry; but none shall look back'.

'Take ye the spoil of silver, take the spoil of gold; for there is no end of the store and glory out of all the pleasant furniture'.

'She is empty and void and waste; and the heart melteth, and the knees smite together, and much pain is in all loins, and the faces of them are all blackness....'

'Woe to the bloody city. It is all full of lies and robbery; the prey departeth not....'

'And it shall come to pass, that all that look upon thee shall flee from thee, and say, Nineveh is laid waste: who will bemoan her?'

After the fall of Nineveh Media became the leading power in this part of the world and Cyaxares could deploy all his might in another direction. For some decades his relations with the Scythians had been strained and he had even been severely defeated by them on the north western frontier of his kingdom. Now he marched against them again and won a great victory at Zela in Pontus, after which the Scythians were progressively expelled from Asia Minor. New peoples speaking an Indo-European language moved in; they were mainly Armenians and Cappadocians.

Cyaxares made over the Assyrian regions west and south of the Tigris to Nabopolassar, while Elam was placed under Median rule. But this arrangement was not accepted by the Elamites who fought bravely for their liberty. The prophet Ezekiel, who commented on the subject some twenty years after the Elamites had lost their cause, was clearly in sympathy with the Medians:

'There is Elam and all her multitude round about her grave, all of them slain, fallen by the sword, which are gone down uncircumcized into the nether parts of the earth, which caused their terror in the land of the living; yet have they borne their shame with them that go down to the pit.'

The Cloaca Maxima in Rome was built to drain a marsh which in the reign of Tarquinius Priscus was to become the Forum Romanum. It was under the protection of a deity named Venus Cloacina and remained in use for many years. It discharged into the river Tiber under a vault which can still be seen by visitors.

Lictors on a relief in Museo Nazionale, Pontegruario. Their accoutrements and other Roman emblems were a legacy from Etruscan times.

Media	Cyaxares
Rome	Ancus Marcius (to 617) / Tarquinius Priscus
Judah	Josiah
Assyria	Sin-shar-ishkun (to 612)
Babylonia	Nabopolassar
Egypt	Psamtik I (XXVI dyn)
China	Zhou Xiang Wang (to 619) / Zhou Qiong Wang (to 613) / Zhou Guang Wang

620	619	618	617	616	615	614	613	612	611

HELLENE
EGYPT
HELLENES
NECHO II

Egypt, whose restored power stemmed from the weakness of the Assyrian empire, was alarmed by events in Mesopotamia, where a new major power was emerging. Pharaoh Necho therefore resolved to send troops to assist the Assyrians who were still holding out against the Babylonians and Medians. The Judaean king, Josiah, in an attempt to halt the passage of the Egyptians, was killed in a battle at Megiddo, not far from Mount Carmel in the year 609. The Egyptian army then moved on towards the Euphrates but at Carchemish it was checked by the Babylonian crown prince, Nebuchadrezzar and defeated. Both politically and culturally, the outcome of the battle at Carchemish was an event of immense historical importance. Egypt was compelled to withdraw from both Syria and Palestine; these regions now formed part of the Babylonian sphere of interest.

Pharaoh Necho, devoting himself instead to peaceful affairs, ordered a canal to be dug between the Nile and the Red Sea. This project employed a hundred thousand workers, though it was never completed. Meanwhile he dispatched a Phoenician expedition to circumnavigate the continent of Africa. This voyage took three years and brought back important information on conditions elsewhere in the world.

Jehoahaz, son of the late Judaean king Josiah, succeeded his father but was soon deposed by Necho, who found his brother Jehoiakim more amenable. Yet this did not prevent Jehoiakim paying his respects to Nebuchadrezzar after the latter's victory at Carchemish. A few years later, however, when Jehoiakim felt that the danger had receded, he stopped sending tribute to Babylon, despite warnings of the prophet Jeremiah. In fact, according to Jeremiah 36, he personally burned the prophet's manuscripts. Nebuchadrezzar promptly advanced on Jerusalem to demand taxes. He seized the city, confiscated some of its treasures and deported several thousand Jews. Jehoiakim, however, was allowed to retain his throne. The poet Aesop, who composed many celebrated animal fables, lived at this time as a slave on the island of Samos. He was of Thracian origin, but probably wrote in Greek.

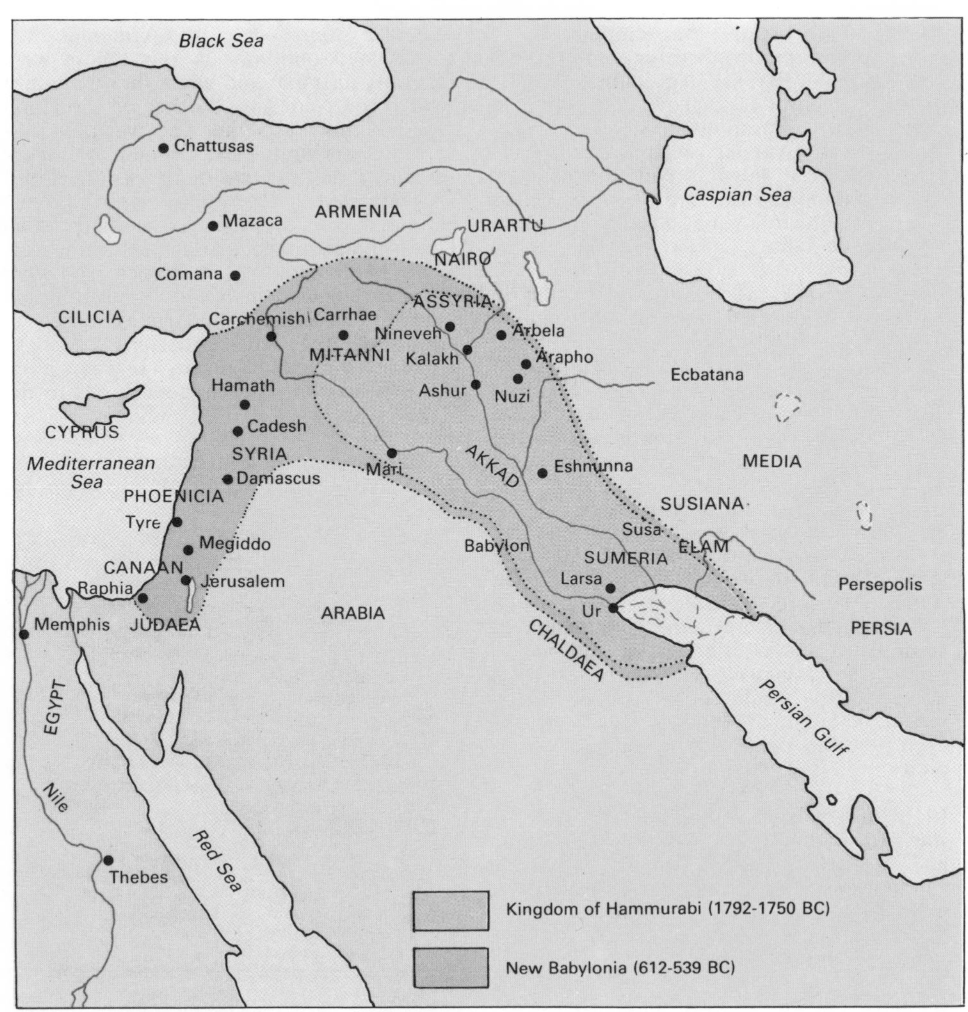
Black Sea
Chattusas
Caspian Sea
Mazaca
ARMENIA
URARTU
NAIRO
Comana
ASSYRIA
CILICIA
Carchemish
Carrhae
Nineveh
Arbela
MITANNI
Kalakh
Arapho
Hamath
Ashur
Nuzi
Ecbatana
Cadesh
CYPRUS
SYRIA
Mari
Mediterranean Sea
AKKAD
Eshnunna
MEDIA
Damascus
PHOENICIA
SUSIANA
Tyre
Susa
Megiddo
Babylon
ELAM
CANAAN
SUMERIA
Jerusalem
Larsa
Persepolis
Raphia
ARABIA
Ur
Memphis
JUDAEA
PERSIA
CHALDAEA
EGYPT
Persian Gulf
Nile
Red Sea
Thebes
Kingdom of Hammurabi (1792-1750 BC)
New Babylonia (612-539 BC)

Cyaxares										**Media**
Tarquinius Priscus										**Rome**
Josiah	Jehoahaz	Jehoiakim								**Judah**
Nabopolassar					Nebuchadrezzar II					**Babylonia**
	Necho (XXVI dyn)									**Egypt**
Zhou Guang Wang				Zhou Ding Wang						**China**
610	609	608	607	606	605	604	603	602	601	

CHINA
HELLAS
ETRUSCANS
PHRYGIA

At about this time the temperature in northern Europe dropped for some reason, and the mild, Bronze Age climate of the preceding centuries changed and within a couple of generations conditions were unendurable. Annual precipitation greatly increased, peat bogs spread and conifers began to dominate the forest lands. Ancient fossils from the following 500 years are sparse and of little value.

In 594 the laws of Solon were issued in Athens, providing a foundation for Athenian democracy. Solon set up a council of 400 which in time assumed the political powers of the more exclusive Areopagus. He also issued a number of economic decrees aimed at limiting the sizes of estates, preventing the enslavement of destitute citizens, reducing debts and promoting the national economy. He was acting quite legally in his capacity as an archon, since it was evident to almost everyone that the former political and social system could no longer be tolerated. An original feature of Solon's laws was a paragraph that decreed the confiscation of possessions and banishment of any person disassociating himself with party conflicts. Some 500 years later the author Aulus Gellius stated that Solon had tried to compel even sensible people to become active in politics.

In the mid-590s Media became involved in a war with Lydia. The Lydian king, Alyattes, had destroyed what was left of the Cimmerian hordes and had extended his frontiers to the Aegean Sea in the west and to the Halys river in the east, bordering on the Median sphere of power.

Immediately before this time, large-scale migrations appear to have taken place in Asia Minor. The ancient Alarodoi, Tibareni and Moschi were scarcely heard of anymore, while the Cappadocians and Armenians had moved in. Conditions in this region were generally unstable and when the two major powers confronted each other on the Halys both had much at stake. This war raged for sixteen years until it was ended by mutual agreement on the occasion of a solar eclipse. This occurred on 28 May, 585, having been predicted by the Greek mathematician Thales. It had not been anticipated,however, by the Median and Lydian forces, who were that day engaged in battle. When the sun suddenly darkened, the armies halted in astonishment. Peace negotiations began and produced immediate results. It was agreed that the frontier between them should be the Halys river.

The Pharaohs of the 26th dynasty were Greek influenced. After Necho II had won his Asiatic war—at the battle of Megiddo where Josiah of Judaea was slain—he offered up his campaign armour in the temple of Apollo at Miletus. When Psamtik attempted to regain Nubia, he had his campaign recorded in Greek writing on the Ramses II statue at Abu Simbel.

The 18-year old Jehoiachin in Jerusalem was taken into custody for safety's sake by Nebuchadrezzar and interned in Babylon with all his household and many prominent subjects, including the prophet Ezekiel. In 597 Jehoiachin's uncle Zedekiah was put on the Judaean throne in his place.

Zedekiah gradually succumbed to the temptation of throwing off Babylonian rule by forming an alliance instead with Egypt. The prophet Isaiah earnestly warned Zedekiah against this course of action. Isaiah had also urged the deported Jews in Babylonia to accept their situation; for this advice he was condemned as a collaborator. When he openly declared that the Babylonians would destroy Jerusalem, he was thrown into prison. Nebuchadrezzar meanwhile laid siege to Jerusalem, which surrendered two years later. Zedekiah was apprehended and punished: after being compelled to witness the execution of his sons and some seventy of his followers, his eyes were put out and he was taken in captivity to Babylon. Jerusalem as Isaiah rightly predicted, was destroyed, the royal palace and the temple were burned down, the city walls were demolished and 745 citizens were deported. The kingdom of Judaea no longer existed.

This Babylonian account in cuneiform of the fall and destruction of Jerusalem is now to be found in Berlin. This event was understandably described in King Nebuchadrezzar's annals as a glorious victory.

	600	599	598	597	596	595	594	593	592	591
Media	Cyaxares									
Rome	Tarquinius Priscus									
Judah	Jehoiakim		Jehoiachin	Zedekiah						
Babylonia	Nebuchadrezzar II									
Egypt	Necho (XXVI dyn)						Psamtik II			
China	Zhou Ding Wang									

HELLAS
MEDES
MEDIA
SYRACUSE

The Amphictyonic council which governed the oracle at Delphi and consisted of delegates from twelve Greek tribes, proclaimed a holy war against the city of Crisa which owned the land where the oracle was located. Crisa fell in 590 and was completely destroyed. The site was appropriated by the Delphi priesthood who decreed that the land might no longer be cultivated or fertilized but that trees should be planted and it should become pasture.

The oracle was the mouthpiece of Apollo. His temple in Delphi contained a conical white stone which was considered to mark the centre point of the earth and was therefore called Omphallos, 'navel'. It was built over an opening in the rock from which issued a magical vapour that was wafted to Phythia, his divine medium, who murmured proclamations which were interpreted by the priests. Usually she was a young girl from the neighbourhood who was methodically prepared for her task by fasting, mortification and ritual bathing. Closely supervised by theological specialists, she was constantly subjected to carefully composed suggestions.

The oracle at Delphi enjoyed an international reputation and played an important political role both in and beyond Greece: Phrygian, Lydian and other Asiatic kings sought its advice. The answers to questions were always equivocal, which was vital to the oracle's reputation since it had always to be right. There could never be any question about the oracle's infallibility, even though sceptics might have found it odd that Apollo, the god of lucidity , tended to express himself so ambiguously. For several centuries new buildings continued to be added to the temple area at Delphi and extant illustrations show mainly buildings that were erected a long time after the holy war against Crisa. The topography of Delphi, however, is such that its general character remains largely unchanged.

The amphitheatre and Apollo's temple at Delphi. To the right, the Hyampeia rock can be seen beside the narrow passage .

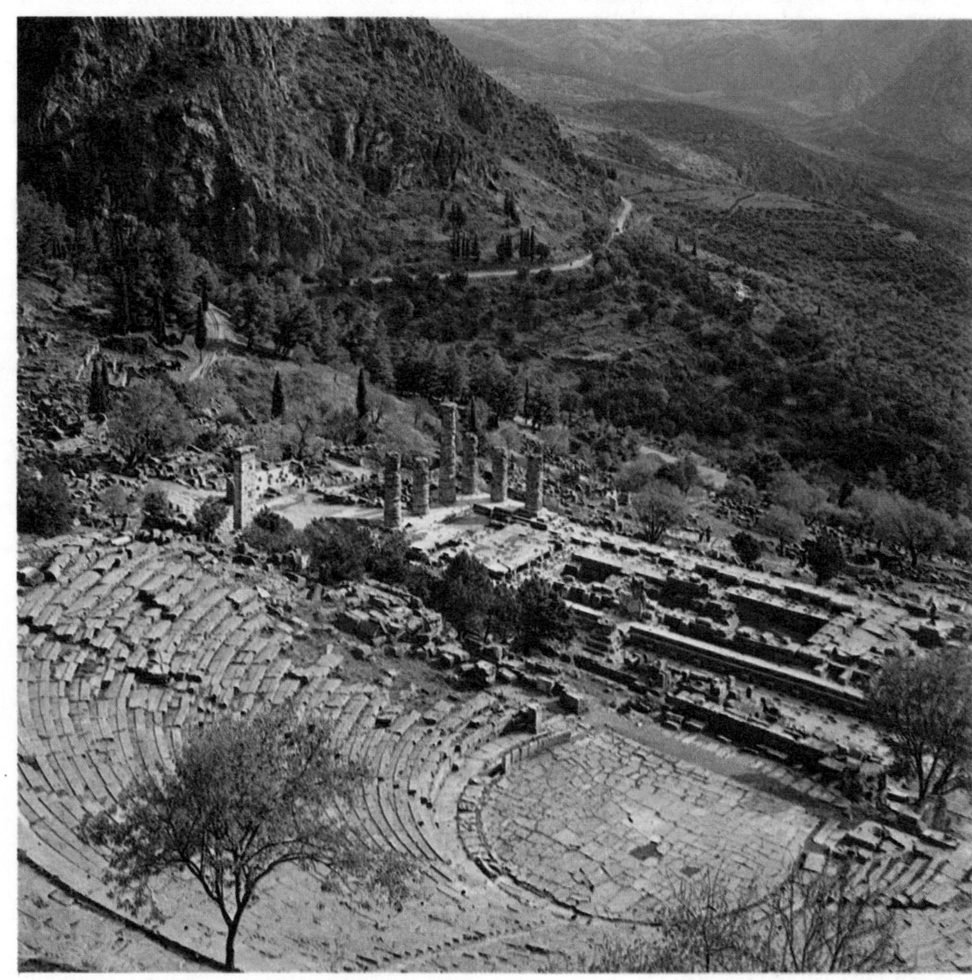

Bimbisāra	**India**
Alyattes	**Lydia**
Cyaxares — Astyages	**Media**
Tarquinius Priscus	**Rome**
Zedekiah	**Judah**
Nebuchadrezzar II	**Babylonia**
Psamtik II — Apries (XXVI dyn)	**Egypt**
Zhou Ding Wang — Zhou Jian Wang	**China**

590	589	588	587	586	585	584	583	582	581

580–571 BC

CENTRAL EUROPE
HELLAS
SICILY
ETRUSCANS

In Italy the Etruscans were prospering. We are familiar with their art and their burial forms, but know little of their language and political life, though it is evident that they had commercial and cultural relations with Corinth, Rhodes, Crete and, increasingly, with Athens. Their influence was also of fundamental significance to emergent Rome. For many generations Rome was ruled by kings of Etruscan stock.

Tarquinius Priscus was assassinated by Marcius's sons whom he had tricked out of their royal birthright. They derived no benefit from the deed for his widow Tanaquil promptly settled one of her protegés on the vacant throne. This was Servius Tullius, a wise and gentle king who surrounded Rome with a wall and organized its citizens according to wealth and neighbourhood.

The Etruscans were on good terms with the Phoenicians in Carthage, who were constantly at war with the Greeks in Sicily. The Carthaginians had occupied the western corner of Sicily and established a number of towns such as Motya, Solus, and Zizmen, which the Greeks called Panormus, later known as Palermo. By far the largest of these Grecian towns was Syracuse, founded by an aristocratic villain from Corinth who had expelled the Sicilian inhabitants from the island of Ortygia. The Greeks regarded themselves as rightful rulers of the Sicilians and also of other tribes whom they encountered.

They made contact with the Etruscans in Cyme or Cumae, said to be the oldest of their colonies in Italy, and the latter could hardly have remained indifferent when around 597 BC the Greek town of Massilia, today's Marseilles, was founded by groups from Ionian Phocaea in Asia Minor.

The names of many tribes and peoples in southern Italy featured in Greek and later also in Latin literature. We know little about their languages and mutual relationships, though in many instances there would appear to have been practically no connections at all between them. Archaeologists have demonstrated that the Sicilian ceramics prior to the Greeks' arrival on the island had not the slightest affinity with corresponding products from the other side of the Messina Straits.

The Greek immigrants were determined and active; pioneer towns grew up rapidly and soon became quite large. The last of these to be founded on Sicily was Acragas, today's Agrigento, dating from 581 BC.

In China the feudal state of Ch'u suffered a decisive defeat in 578 at the hands of a coalition led by the north-western state of Ch'in. After this Ch'in retained its supremacy for fifty years or more.

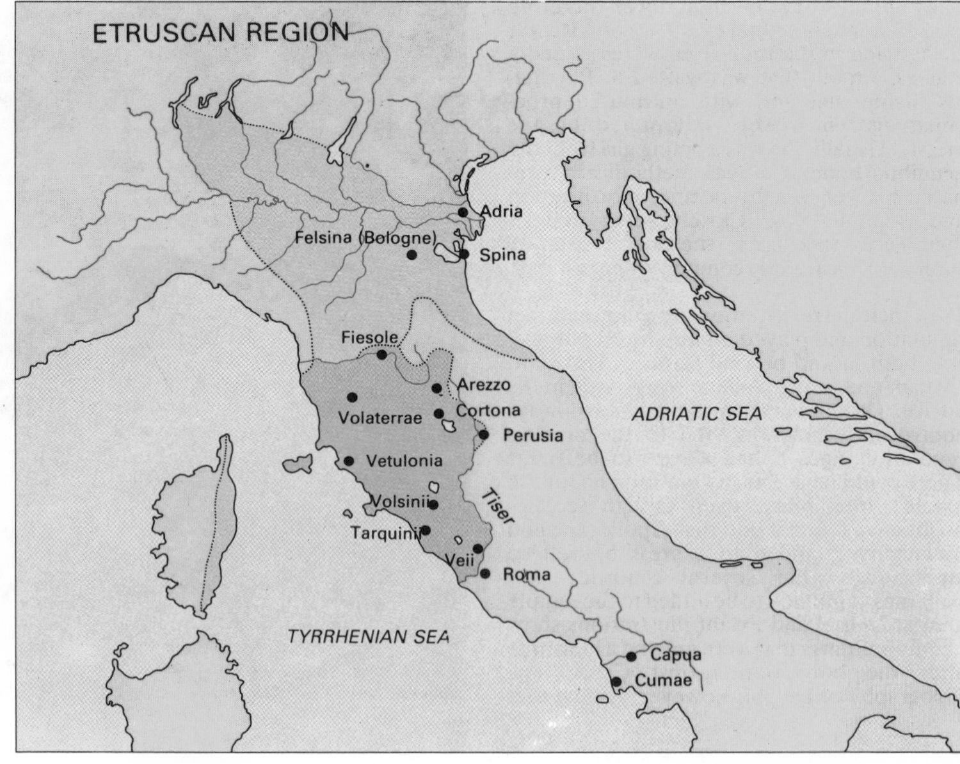

ETRUSCAN REGION
Adria
Felsina (Bologne)
Spina
Fiesole
Arezzo
Volaterrae
Cortona
Perusia
ADRIATIC SEA
Vetulonia
Volsinii
Tiser
Tarquinii
Veii
Roma
TYRRHENIAN SEA
Capua
Cumae

India	Bimbisára
Lydia	Alyattes
Media	Astyages
Rome	Tarquinius Priscus — Servius Tullius
Babylonia	Nebuchadrezzar II
Egypt	Apries (XXVI dyn)
China	Zhou Jian Wang

580	579	578	577	576	575	574	573	572	571

HELLAS
CHAVIN, PERU
ITALY

In the Middle East there was a balance of power between Media, Babylonia and Lydia. They had their differences, but the governments took pains, nevertheless, to keep the peace, partly by means of inter-dynastic unions. Astyages was married to a Lydian princess and Nebuchadrezzar to a Median princess named Amytis. It was she who furnished Babylon with its renowned hanging gardens; nostalgic for her homeland, she resolved to make the mighty walls of Babylon bloom like her native meadows and mountainsides.

The literary activities of the Jewish elite who had been deported after the fall of Jerusalem exerted considerable influence. The prophet Jeremiah was apparently still alive at the beginning of the 570s; his kinsmen had fled with them despite his protests, to Egypt, a country for which he had no sympathy, since his loyalties had always been to Babylonia. And he persisted in this during his exile in Egypt:

'Then came the word of the Lord unto Jeremiah in Tähpanhes, saying:

Take great stones in thine hand, and hide them in the clay in the brick kiln, which is at the entry of Pharaoh's house in Täpanhes, in the sight of the men of Judah.'

'And say unto them, thus saith the Lord of hosts, the God of Israel; Behold I will send and take Nebuchadrezzar, the king of Babylon, my servant, and I will set his throne upon these stones that I have hid; and he shall spread his royal pavilion over them.'

'And when he cometh he shall smite the land of Egypt, and deliver such as are for death to death; and such as are for captivity to captivity; and such as are for the sword to the sword.'

'And I will kindle a fire in the houses of the gods of Egypt; and he shall burn them, and carry them away captives: and he shall array himself with the land of Egypt, as a shepherd putteth on his garment; and he shall go forth from thence in peace.' But things did not work out this way. The gods of Egypt survived for some time.

In Egypt Pharaoh Apries reigned long in peace and prosperity, but there was unrest among the mercenaries he had sent to aid the Libyans against the Greek colonizers in Cyrene. After the defeat of the mercenaries, they revolted, causing Apries to send out an individual named Amasis or Ahmose, who performed his task so effectively that he was proclaimed Pharaoh by the insurrectionists. It is not clear what happened after this, except that for some years there were two Pharaohs. Finally they went to war with each other and Apries was defeated and put to death.

A dynasty known as Saisunaga in eastern India had established a powerful kingdom called Magadha. This survived for a number of generations and is notable for the fact that, during the reigns of Bimbisāra and Ajátaŝatru, both Mahavira, the founder of Jainism, and Siddharta Buddha lived there (see 520s BC).

Alyattes of Lydia was finally killed in a campaign against the Greek city of Miletus. Year by year he had probed more deeply into the land of the Milesians, but had refrained from pillaging or burning so that he could eventually reap the maximum profit from the people and the land they continued to farm.

In 556 the first festival was held at the Acropolis, in Athens in honour of Pallas Athene. A temple to the goddess had been completed some years earlier. This was embellished with limestone statues, some of which have survived. As the years passed this festival achieved increasing renown and importance, for it was associated with the birth of drama and the development of art in the Western world. This and the following decade constituted the great age of the Greek lyric. On Lesbos the poets Sappho and Alcaeus sang the praises of love and wine respectively. Alcaeus also developed an interest in politics, so displeasing the tyrant Pittacus who ruled the island despotically. Alcaeus was driven into exile several times while Sappho, too, spent some fifteen years in the new colony of Sicily.

Traces of the long Phoenician rule in western Sicily are few and far between. One of the largest cities was Motye, situated on a small island off the west coast, from which some ruins have been excavated.

Bimbisāra	**India**
Alyattes	**Lydia**
Astyages	**Media**
Servius Tullius	**Rome**
Nebuchadrezzar II — Awil-Marduk	**Babylonia**
Apries — Apries & Ahmose — Ahmose (XXVI dyn)	**Egypt**
Zhou Ling Wang	**China**

570	569	568	567	566	565	564	563	562	561

560–551 BC

ETRURIA
CAPESTRANO, ITALY
ETRUSCANS
HELLENES

In the west of the Nile delta Pharaoh Ahmose founded the city of Naucratis. This was totally Grecian and became in time Egypt's most important harbour. Ahmose had strong Greek sympathies, so much so that he contributed funds for a new building at Delphi and made gifts to various Greek temples, acts, however, that scarcely increased his popularity at home.

Nebuchadrezzar's son and successor, Awil-Marduk, known in the Bible as Evil Merodach, who liberated the Judaean king Jehoiachin from captivity, was murdered by his brother-in-law Neriglissar. He was succeeded by his young son, who in turn was assassinated a couple of months later. The court now appointed in his place a pious individual known as Nabonidus who devoted himself to temple restoration, astrology and archaeological studies. Many inscriptions relating to these activities came to light some 2500 years later.

By the rivers of Babylon, or possibly in Judaea, the prophet Jeremiah sat lamenting the fate of his people.
'We gat our bread with the peril of our lives, because of the sword of the wilderness.'
'Our skin was black like an oven because of the terrible famine.'
'They ravished the women in Zion, and the maids in the cities of Judah.'
'They took the young men to grind, and the children fell under the wood.'
'The elders have ceased from the gate, the young men from their music.' (Lamentations 5: 9-14)

A tale is told of Cyrus, or Koresh as the Bible calls him, which in certain details resembles those told of such historic figures as Moses, Romulus, etc. Cyrus was the nephew of King Astyages of Media, who had dreamed that a son of his daughter would overthrow Media. To prevent this dream becoming a reality, the king put the child out to die; but a shepherd found and raised him, and in time the boy began to show distinctly royal qualities of leadership in games with his companions. These qualities came to the notice of the cruel grandfather, who was unable to prevent Cyrus gaining such a position of power in his Persian province that he was able to instigate a revolt against Astyages. Thus, in 559, the Persians came to rule Media.

The name Kroisos, Croesus in its Latin form, has become a descriptive noun in European languages, and the reputed wealth of this Lydian king appears to have been founded on fact. The oldest known coins today are believed to be Lydian and are inscribed with the name of Alyattes. Croesus, who succeeded him, is said to have deposited large sums in metal coins abroad, specifically in the great temple of Apollo at Didyma. In ancient times, it should be noted, temples also often served as banks.

Various enterprising individuals proclaimed themselves tyrants in many Greek city-states, especially on Sicily where their rule survived far longer than anywhere else. Acragas, later Agrigento, was ruled by a tyrant only ten years after being founded by Phalaris, notorious for the hollow, bronze bull in which he is reputed to have roasted criminals. This had been invented by a man named Perillos, and when Phalaris saw it he immediately tried it out on the unfortunate inventor himself. Peisistratus, who made himself tyrant of Athens in 560 BC, left behind a good reputation. 'He ruled more like a citizen than a tyrant', commented Aristotle 200 years later. Peisistratus authorized the continuation of Solon's constitution but reorganized the taxation system and the state finances. Athens progressed both commercially and culturally during Peisistratus's reign.

In northern Europe the mean temperature had fallen and precipitation had increased over a few decades, and the areas of peat bogs and lakes were expanding. The Bronze Age had given way to the Iron Age. The vegetation changed as warmth-loving species died out, to be replaced by those thriving in damp, cool conditions. Although there was plenty of fresh water, there were few human settlements on the shores.

Carriage decoration in chased silver, found in the Etruscan town of Perugia, but almost certainly made by an Ionian artist. Trade between Greeks and Etruscans was brisk, and Greek influence on Etruscan art and ideology was unmistakable. This was not mere imitation; it is almost always possible to distinguish between Greek and Etruscan artefacts.

Athens	Peisistratus
India	Bimbisāra — Ajātaśatru
Lydia	Croesus
Persia	Cyrus
Rome	Servius Tullius
Babylonia	Awil-Marduk — Neriglissar — Nabonidus
Egypt	Ahmose (XXVI dyn)
China	Zhou Ling Wang

560	559	558	557	556	555	554	553	552	551

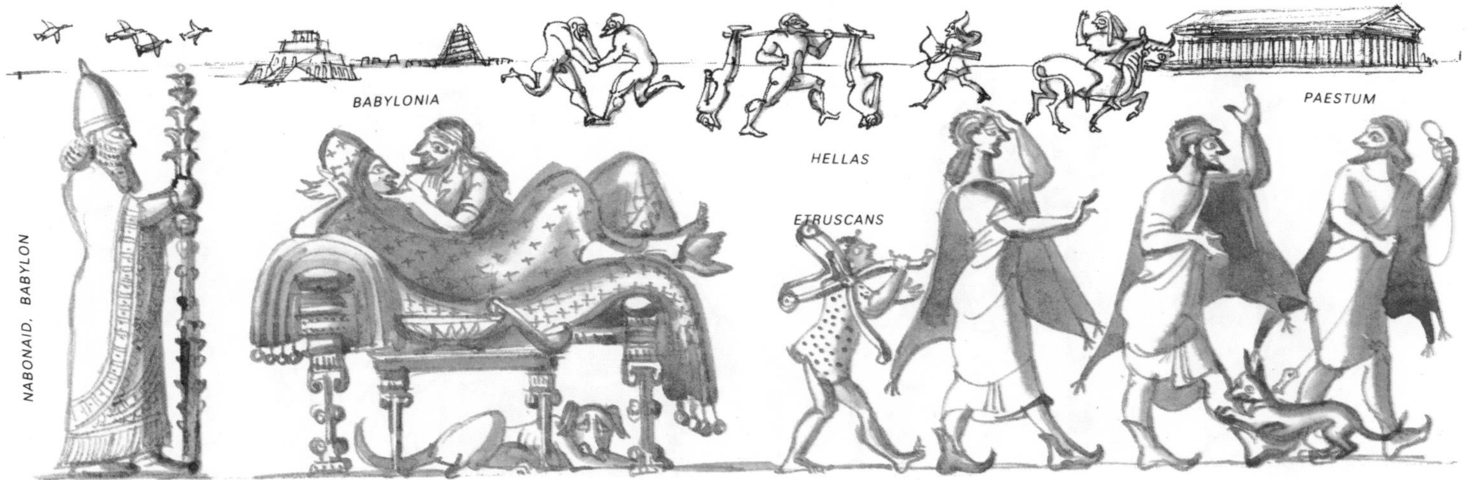
BABYLONIA
HELLAS
ETRUSCANS
PAESTUM
NABONAID, BABYLON

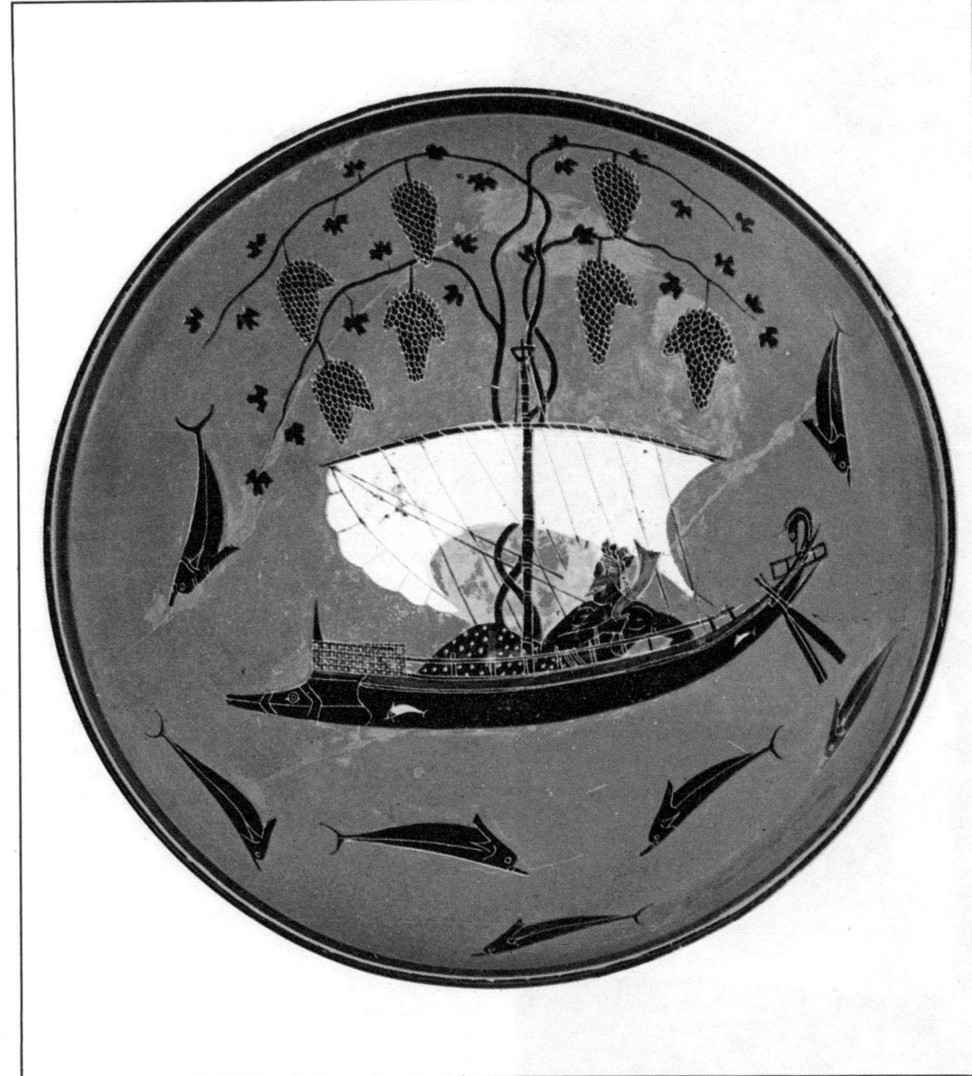

Cyrus's conquest of the great Median empire caused general anxiety in the west and led to a defensive coalition in 547 between Lydia, Egypt, the Babylonian empire and Grecian Sparta. But before the allies had time to co-ordinate their forces Cyrus struck again.

In 547 he seized the Lydian capital of Sardes after defeating Croesus and taking him captive. The entertaining Greek historian, Herodotus, embroidered these facts in several memorable anecdotes, relating that Croesus consulted the oracle in Delphi as to whether he should initiate the war, receiving the ambiguous answer from the oracle that if he were to overstep the boundary river of Halys a great kingdom would fall.

After conquering Lydia, Cyrus immediately attacked the Greek cities on the west coast of Asia Minor, all of which came under Persian rule. Many were important centres in their time, particularly the Ionian city of Miletus, which continued to flourish economically together with its many colonies on the Black Sea coast: Sinope, Trapezus, Panticapaeum, Olbia, Odessus and others. Other cities which also prospered included Ephesus, Mytilene in Lesbos, Samos, Halicarnassus and Lindus on Rhodes, although they lost their former political freedom.

Great artists lived and worked in the Hellenic world, (ceramics have survived best), but most of them did not sign their work. One of the few known by name is Exedias, responsible for this painting of Dionysus, who, bearing the gift of wine, travels from country to country, having probably arrived in Greece from Lydia. The chalice is now in Staatliche Antikensammlungen und Glyptotek, Munich.

Peisistratus	Athens
Ajātaŝatru	India
Croesus (to 547)	Lydia
Cyrus	Persia
Servius Tullius	Rome
Nabonidus	Babylonia
Ahmose (XXVI dyn)	Egypt
Zhou Ling Wang (to 545) / Zhou Jing Wang I	China

550	549	548	547	546	545	544	543	542	541

540–531 BC

ETRURIA
HELLENES
HELLAS
ETRUSCANS

This was a decade of tremendous political upheaval. In the year 539 Babylon was taken by Cyrus who thereby incorporated Mesopotamia and Syria in the Persian empire. This extended, theoretically at least, from the Aegean Sea to the frontiers of India, and was the largest body politic the world had yet known.

The fall of Babylon was a sensational biblical event which was immediately important for the return home of 42,360 deported Jewish citizens. This was described not only by Ezra and Nehemiah but also by the prophets Ezekiel and Isaiah (Isaiah 44 and below) both of whom were great poets whose words have echoed down the centuries.

'Come down, and sit in the dust, O virgin daughter of Babylon, sit on the ground: there is no throne, O daughter of the Chaldeans: for thou shalt no more be called tender and delicate.

Take the millstones, and grind meal: uncover thy locks, make bare thy leg, uncover the thigh, pass over the rivers.

Thy nakedness shall be uncovered, yea, thy shame shall be seen.' (Isaiah, 47: 1-3.)

In the Greek towns on the Asian coast there was less satisfaction with the Persian advance, and the inhabitants of maritime Phocis emigrated rather than wait to be subjugated. The Phocians had long been engaged in colonizing the western Mediterranean. Now they set sail with their women, children and chattels for Corsica, but this alarmed both the Phoenicians in Carthage and the Etruscans on the nearby mainland of Italy. A coalition was formed and in a great sea battle off Alalia in 535 the Phocians suffered a severe defeat and had to return eastward - the survivors eventually settling at Elea on the southern Italian coast. Greek expansion westward had been thwarted.

In Athens Peisistratus appointed a literary committee to edit the *Iliad* and the *Odyssey*.

The results were the texts that have survived to this day.

Tarquinius Superbus, last of the kings of Rome, went down in history as an impious man who, among much else, usurped the Campus Martius and grew grain on divine land. One day the Cumaean sibyl came to him with nine books containing all the facts on the future destiny of Rome. She offered to sell them to Tarquinius for a specific price. When he refused, the sibyl burned three of the books and offered the king the remaining six books for the same price as for the original nine. When he again refused, she burned three more books and once more quoted the same sum for the three that were left. By now Tarquinius was unable to restrain his curiosity any longer and paid the original sum for the remaining volumes which were deposited in Jupiter's temple on the Capitoline Hill. Here they were kept for several centuries, to be consulted intermittently by the Romans in times of pestilence and other periods of crisis.

Peisistratus built the first water conduit in Athens. He had found a rich source of income from the mine at Pangaion on the Thracian coast. He also consolidated the trading route to the Black Sea by erecting the Sigeum fortress on the Asiatic side of the entrance to the Hellespont. On the European side an Athenian nobleman named Miltiades set himself up as the ruling prince in a vassal state.

There are many caves and grottoes in Cumae, but the large one where the sibyl is believed to have hidden was forgotten and not rediscovered until the present century when an amateur archaeologist removed an old baking oven which had blocked the entrance.

Athens — Peisistratus —
India — Ajātaŝatru —
Persia — Cyrus —
Rome — Servius Tullius —| — Tarquinius Superbus —
Babylonia — Nabonidus —|
Egypt — Ahmose (XXVI dyn) —
China — Zhou Jing Wang I —

540	539	538	537	536	535	534	533	532	531

HELLAS
PERSIANS
HELLENES

In the summer of 530 Cyrus was killed fighting a northern people known as the Massagetae. He was succeeded by his son Cambyses who also achieved historical significance by incorporating Egypt in the Persian empire. There are some gruesome details concerning the decisive battle, after which many young Egyptians of both sexes were either executed or enslaved. Psamtik III, the last of his dynasty, was murdered in an original manner, with a goblet of poisoned ox-blood.

Another figure involved in Cambyses' Egyptian campaign was the tyrant Polycrates of Samos. He had long been allied with the Egyptian Ahmose but had suddenly changed sides and sent auxiliary forces to Cambyses. In due course, however, he was seized and crucified by a Persian satrap. According to a typical Greek anecdote, Polycrates had luck with him in everything he undertook. This was unlikely to last under the watchful eye of Nemesis, goddess of retribution. Consequently he was advised to dispose of something he valued, thereby appeasing her. He threw a precious ring into the sea, but the next day this was returned to him by a fisherman who had found it in the belly of a fish he had caught. Thus the fate of Polycrates was ordained.

All that we know about Buddha is legendary. His earthly family name was Siddharta Gautama. He is said to have been of princely birth but, surrounded by his disciples, he abandoned worldly things in the pursuit of enlightenment. His doctrine was introduced by the sermon of Benares and he performed many miracles. He died in old age, widely revered and respected, in the town of Kusinagara. According to Buddhist doctrine, a buddha appears on earth from time to time and there is always one, a bodhisattva, in heaven.

The prince of Ch'u usurped the leadership of the Chinese federation at the expense of the prince of Ch'in.

The Egyptian 27th dynasty was identical with the Persian list of rulers from Cambyses through to Darius II. The 28th dynasty, a domestic one, commenced in the year 408.

Darius I, was not attached to the line of Cyrus, but was the great organizer of the Persian empire, which was divided up into administrative districts known as satrapies.

Towards the close of the century the Indus valley was included in the empire, while the Magadhari kingdom in eastern India went into decline.

A journeyman actor named Thespis ran a one-man theatre and toured the Greek cities. He dyed his face with grape skins and performed songs.

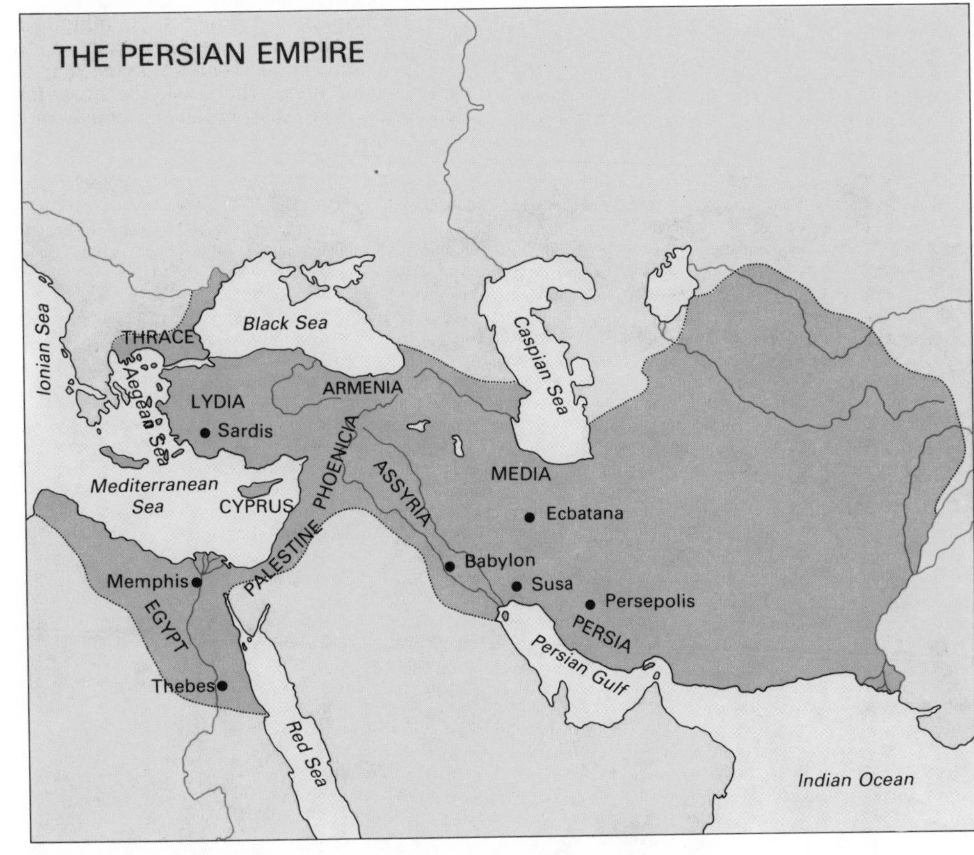
THE PERSIAN EMPIRE
Black Sea
THRACE
Ionian Sea
Aegean Sea
LYDIA
Sardis
ARMENIA
Caspian Sea
MEDIA
Ecbatana
Mediterranean Sea
CYPRUS
PHOENICIA
ASSYRIA
PALESTINE
Babylon
Susa
Persepolis
PERSIA
Persian Gulf
Memphis
EGYPT
Thebes
Red Sea
Indian Ocean

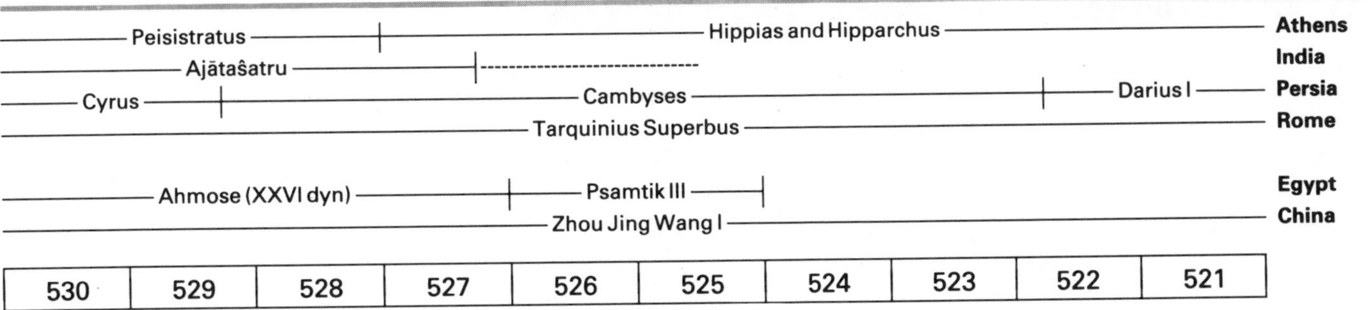
Peisistratus
Hippias and Hipparchus
Athens
Ajātaśatru
India
Cyrus
Cambyses
Darius I
Persia
Tarquinius Superbus
Rome
Ahmose (XXVI dyn)
Psamtik III
Egypt
Zhou Jing Wang I
China
530
529
528
527
526
525
524
523
522
521

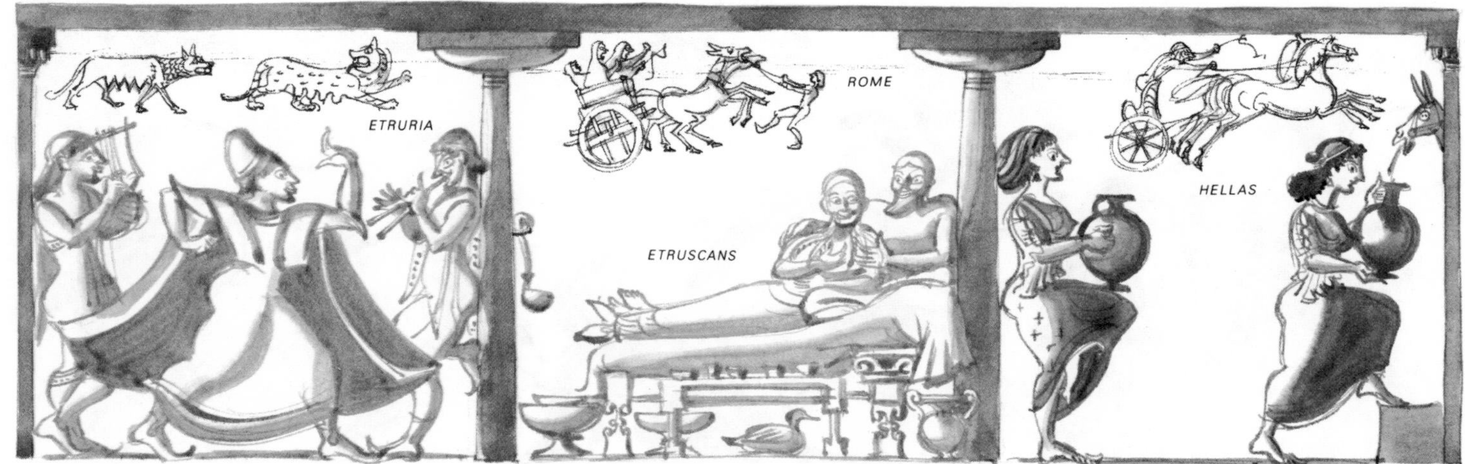
ETRURIA
ROME
ETRUSCANS
HELLAS

The earthly life of Siddharta Buddha, said to have spanned 560-477, was almost exactly contemporaneous with that of Kongfuzu, or Confucius, 551-479. The author of the Book of Job is also believed to have lived at this time; and in the Greek cities intellectual aristocrats sat contemplating the purpose and meaning of life. Thus there was considerable religious activity in different parts of the world.

In Ephesus the old philosopher Heraclitus deplored the madness of mankind while comforting himself with the thought that everything is transient. When we step down into the river for a second time, it is no longer the same river as it was before.

Pythagoras was an unusual type of religious innovator. He was now living in the southern Italian city of Croton, having left Samos after the tyrant Polycrates seized power there. In Croton Pythagoras formed an aristocratic brotherhood with a doctrine of mystical salvation that had a mathematical basis. He claimed that the elements of numbers were the elements of the world and that number one was the ultimate structure of matter and the fundamental factor in creation. The Pythagoreans believed in metempsychosis and Pythagoras himself recalled several of his former incarnations. They were vegetarians who also refused to eat beans, claiming that these were in some manner related to mankind, and they also had a divine fear of irrational numbers, the existence of which Pythagoras had discovered in connection with his studies into right-angled triangles, where the square on the hypotenuse is always equal to the sum of the squares of the other two sides.

There is an interesting story about the final encounter between Croton and Sybaris. The former city was governed by the Pythagorean mathematicians and aesthetes, the latter by the luxury-loving Sybarites who issued dinner invitations a year in advance so that their womenfolk would have plenty of time to plan what to wear. Sybaris and Croton had long been at each other's throats and in 510 the Sybarites were defeated in battle when the enemy's military bands played music which caused their parade-trained cavalry horses to dance in step. Sybaris was razed to the ground and never rebuilt.

The pronouncements of Confucius in an early work entitled Lunyu, were largely concerned with politics and complained about existing conditions in China. The many feudal states were badly governed; everything had been better in the past.

The temple of Jerusalem, plundered and demolished after the Babylonian victory in Nebuchadrezzar's day, was now rebuilt as a result of encouraging exhortations from the prophets Haggai and Zachariah, and with funds contributed by the Persian treasury. The work began in 520 and by 516 the temple was ready for reconsecration. It was by no means as splendid as that of Solomon, nor was it properly completed until a couple of decades later.

Siddharta Buddha, the Indian religious leader and founder of Buddhism, was born from his mother's hip. Siddharta was of a Hindu princely race in north-east India, near the Nepal border. When he was still a young man he left his family, to seek enlightenment. This relief, depicting his birth, can be found in Gandhara in India.

	520	519	518	517	516	515	514	513	512	511
Athens	Hippias & Hipparchus						Hippias			
Persia	Darius I									
Rome	Tarquinius Superbus									
China		Zhou Jing Wang II								

HELLENES
LYDIANS
MEDES
PERSIANS
HELLENES

The tyrant Hipparchus of Athens was assassinated in 514 by two young men named Harmodius and Aristogiton. This apparently insignificant incident was nevertheless interesting for having sparked off discussions through the centuries on the legitimacy of murdering tyrants.

Darius I suppressed a number of uprisings in his vast Persian empire and it was not until 517 that he became undisputed ruler there. After this he divided his realm up into administrative districts.

The tyrannic rule in Athens was destroyed with Spartan assistance, but the democratic Athenian Cleisthenes was soon involved in conflicts with the land-owning nobles and also with Sparta. After fierce military clashes, he managed to introduce a democratic system in Athens. Cleisthenes supplemented the laws of Solon - these had failed to do away with the power of the few over the many - with a new division of districts which split the power of the influential families and enabled a large number of citizens to have a voice in government decisions. Political democracy in ancient Athens was due principally to the work of Cleisthenes.

Curiously, a revolution occurred in Rome at almost the same time. The last of the kings, Tarquinius, presumably an Etruscan, was expelled and the history of the Roman republic began. In both Athens and Rome chronological events were indicated by the names of various senior officials and since these were elected for only a year at a time this has left historians with a very long, cumbersome and fairly meaningless register. For this reason, neither the archons of Athens nor the consuls of Rome are listed below and mention is only made of prominent politicians whose actions helped to make history.

Junius Brutus, leader of the Roman revolution against Tarquinius Superbus, was killed shortly afterwards doing battle with a son of Tarquinius, and the city was governed by his colleague Publius Valerius, known as Publicola on account of his democratic views. At this time Rome was severely defeated by an Etruscan ruler named Lars Porsena, an event that Latin historians attempted to skirt over by relating instead the heroic deeds of Horatius Cocles and Mucius Scaevola. The former defended a bridge over the Tiber against the entire enemy force, while the latter thrust his hand into burning coals to prove that no torture could ever make him divulge the secrets of the fatherland.

The two Ying Wangs are written with different symbols in Chinese, but the only way to distinguish effectively between them is to number them I and II according to Western practice.

Confucius, known in Chinese as Kongfuzu, or the master Kong, instructs his disciples. The illustration shows a painting on silk which is part of the Palace collection, now in Taiwan. There are many conflicting references to events in Confucius's life in Chinese literature. He was born in the province of Lu to a distinguished but poor family, and is said to have spent the early part of his earthly life in the employment of a noble family as a granary manager, earning praise for the exceptional justice with which he weighed the grain. Later he was involved in research into ancient rituals and ceremonies in the city of Loyang, but in his old age he returned to Lu where he devoted himself to teaching, as well as editing the original documents that he considered the basis of his doctrine.

(Cleisthenes) — Athens
Darius I — Persia
Tarquinius Superbus | (Junius Brutus) — (Publius Valerius) — Rome
Zhou Jing Wang II — China

510	509	508	507	506	505	504	503	502	501

ETRUSCANS
OLMECS, MEXICO
PERSIANS
MEDES
PERSIANS

The historian Herodotus, who gave the Hellenic viewpoint of the Persians' wars with the Greeks, was very impressed by King Darius I's administrative genius. Herodotus noticed, among other things, that there never appeared to be any empty bottles in Egypt, despite the fact that large quantities of wine were imported. Investigation revealed that every Egyptian village headman had been ordered to collect all the empty wine vessels and send them to Memphis where they were filled with water and forwarded to the Syrian desert. This was one of the minor details of organization that Darius had introduced in the vast Persian empire, where the administration was highly centralized yet due consideration given to the peculiarities and traditions of the different regions.

The empire was divided into twenty satrapies, each governed by a satrap whose position was clearly exalted since he represented the emperor and held all the civil and military power in his province. In fact, however, he was held in check by a royal control commission whose representatives were constantly on the move, hearing the people's wishes and problems. They travelled at a remarkable rate, for the road network was well developed with regular hostels along the way for changes of horse, and for board and lodging. The equestrian post couriers also used these roads and likewise moved very fast. The public, too, was allowed to use this mail service, though only official despatches went uncensored. Much of this road system in the Persian empire had been taken over from the Assyrians, Egyptians and other vanquished peoples, but many routes were new, as was the co-ordination of communications.

The Prince of Ch'u who, like his predecessors, had led the Chinese federation, was heavily defeated in 506 by the Prince of Wu, but the latter in his turn was attacked by the barbarian coastal state of Yüeh a considerable distance south of the Yangtze. The Prince of Wu managed for the time being to repel Yüeh, then turned north to subjugate a number of smaller feudal states. During the 490s and 480s Wu ruled supreme in China.

In the South Pacific the Polynesian islands were being colonized from the west by new tribes whose Stone Age culture overlapped an earlier culture of the same type. The older inhabitants were probably enslaved. The social strata were very distinct and there was some form of divine royal family. Sizeable temples and fortifications were built.

The people's tribunes are said to have been introduced in Rome in the year 494, with the object of safeguarding the plebeians against arbitrary patrician authority. Only plebeians were permitted to sit in the assembly and those elected were regarded as inviolable. The people's tribunes had the power to veto the judgements and measures of the authorities, and the decisions of the senate. Initially there were only two tribunes, but this figure was soon doubled and forty years later there were to be no less than ten.

The tyrant Aristagoras of Miletus, which like the other Greek cities on the Asian coast was under Persian suzerainty, instigated a revolt in 499 and obtained military assistance from Athens. The Greeks captured and burned Sardis, where the Persian satrap resided, but this did not go unpunished. In 494 a Persian army surrounded and took Miletus, the inhabitants were deported to the mouth of the Tigris, their city was destroyed and the area was handed over to Carian and Persian colonists. Miletus had been one of the largest and wealthiest cities in the Greek world and its fate was mourned above all in Athens, where a writer named Phrynicus was fined for distressing the people by referring to the tragic subject in a drama.

A Persian army, accompanied by the exiled tyrant Hippias, landed in Greece in the spring of 490. This was met at Marathon in Attica by ten thousand Athenians under the command of an aristocrat named Miltiades. The Athenians won a great victory here, Hippias was killed, and the Greek runner Pheidippides raced almost 23 miles in record time to bring the news to Athens. Reaching the city, he was only able to announce the victory before he collapsed and died.

The tomb of Darius I near Persepolis. It has been cut into the rock face, the surface of which has been carved to resemble the front elevation of a palace. There are also many remains of the actual palace of Darius. Xerxes, too, built himself a palace, the reliefs of which are equally impressive.

Athens	(Themistocles)
Persia	Darius I
Rome	(Appius Claudius)
China	Zhou Jing Wang II

500	499	498	497	496	495	494	493	492	491

CENTRAL ASIAN
PERSIANS
ETRUSCANS
MEDES
LYDIANS
HELLENES

In Italy, Etruscan culture was flourishing. A large number of the Tarquinian grave paintings, later to be seen reproduced in art books, originate in this decade.

The tyrant Gelon in Sicilian Gela seized power in Syracuse too and moved there. Realizing that he could win popularity through sport, in 488 he sent a team to the Olympic games and the chariot race.

In 486 a change in the constitution was introduced in Athens whereby the archons were no longer elected by vote but were appointed instead by drawing lots among 500 candidates. This meant that the leading officials in Athens were usually fairly average individuals without any special political knowledge or talents. From now on, instead of the archons ruling Athens, the popular assembly made the decisions in consultation with the politician who was currently in favour. The professional military men, who were still elected by vote, were also given more political power.

Aristides, the leader of the aristocratic party in Athens, was according to an ancient biographer, such an upright man that he never paid a debt without first satisfying himself that the recipient would put the money to good use. The leader of the democratic party, Themistocles, rid himself of the admirable Aristides by means of a curious institution in Athenian law known as ostracism. According to this, the popular assembly, by written ballot, could banish any individual who was adjudged a threat to the constitution. It was thus an effective way of nipping potential dictators in the bud. The names of suspected usurpers were written on earthenware fragments, and those nominated by a stipulated number of assembly delegates were banished for ten years.

Having sent Aristides into exile, Themistocles introduced his military programme, putting an emphasis on the navy. Plato observed later that he removed the spears and shields of the Athenians and chained them instead to galley-seat and oar.

King Xerxes went out to do battle with the Greeks. With a fleet and a huge army, he advanced westward to the Hellespont and crossed the strait on a bridge of anchored ships, logs and planks. The crossing took seven days and seven nights.

By modern standards the battle of Marathon was not a major encounter, though many soldiers were involved. The grave mounds on the battlefield are said to be genuine. An Englishman who visited the place in the 19th century sketched the picture on the left, depicting the resting place of the dead Athenians.

(485–) Gelon I	**Syracuse**
(Miltiades) — (Aristides) — (Themistocles)	**Athens**
Darius I (–486) — Xerxes I (486–)	**Persia**
(Coriolanus)	**Rome**
Zhou Jing Wang II	**China**

490	489	488	487	486	485	484	483	482	481

HELLENES

Four famous battles were fought in the Greek world between 480 and 479: Thermopylae, Salamis, Himera and Plataea. Led by Xerxes himself, the Persians invaded Greece by land and sea, seized Macedonia and Thessaly without encountering resistance, forced the pass at Thermopylae where the Spartan king, Leonidas, and his small force, fighting heroically, were destroyed to the last man, and burned Athens. However, the assembled Greek fleets defeated the Persian fleet at Salamis, Xerxes departed for home and the Persian army met its fate some months later at Plataea.

The Persians had advanced from the east, but the Greeks on Sicily were attacked from the west by the Carthaginians who occupied the western tip of the big island, doubtless in collusion with their Phoenician kinsmen in the Persian empire. But at the town of Himera the Carthaginians suffered a severe defeat and their general, Hamilcar, committed suicide. The tyrants Gelon of Syracuse and Theron of Acragas, victors in the battle, were astonished to learn that the battle of Salamis had been won on that same day.

The name of Hieron I is remembered in literature because he provided poets and dramatists with commissions and entertained them as his guests at his court in Syracuse. The poet Pindar lived for years at the court of Hieron. He sang the tyrant's praises in one Olympic and two Pythian odes, for Hieron had sent winning teams to the races at the Olympic Games and also to the Pythian Games in Delphi. He also founded the city of Aetna and celebrated this with the premiere of a drama by Aeschylus, who personally attended the performance and, in fact, remained in Sicily until his death in the following decade.

In Rome Spurius Cassius submitted a law for the redistribution of land seized by the city on a more equitable class basis. This was opposed by the existing landowners who accused Spurius Cassius of treason and subversion and had him condemned to death. In 479 Confucius died. At the same time major changes occurred in China's political geography when the feudal state of Ch'en was annexed by the feudal state of Ch'u. This event marks the transition, in classical Chinese history,from the Spring and Autumn period to the Warring States period. During the 470s, too, the prince of Wu was defeated and his country seized by the barbaric prince of Yüeh. The significance of this event was that it heralded the disintegration of the feudal system, now past its peak. None of the Chinese states, least of all Yüeh, which was still underdeveloped, was sufficiently strong to lead and govern the Central Kingdom federation, which dissolved into a multitude of provincial states where vassals ruled as they pleased.

The Spartan warrior Pausanias who had been in command at Plataea and in the following year conquered Cyprus as admiral of the Greek fleets, fell foul both of his Ionian allies and the authorities in Sparta. The Athenians thus took over command at sea and this marked the beginning of Athens' era of political greatness.The young aristocrat, Cimon, son of Miltiades the victor of Marathon, seized all the places still held by the Persians along the Aegean coasts. The liberated cities sent their squadrons to join the Athenian fleet and become part of a confederation led by Athens. With its headquarters on Delos, it became known as the Delian League.

Domestic affairs remained troubled . Themistocles was expelled from Athens by ostracism in 471. In the same year the Spartans executed Pausanias by bricking him up in a temple where he starved to death. In 461 it was the turn of Cimon to be banished, following the victory of the democratic party in Athens.

The island of Siphnos contributed to the victory at Salamis, and commemorated it at Delphi. This fresco depicts the gigantomachia *or battle of the giants, Museum at Delphi.*

Syracuse	Gelon I			Hieron I						
Athens	(Themistocles)						(Cimon)			
Persia	Xerxes I									
Rome	(Spurius Cassius)									
China	Zhou Jing Wang II					Zhou Yuan Wang				
	480	479	478	477	476	475	474	473	472	471

ETRUSCANS

The marble lions lining the road to Apollo's temple on Delos were the guardians of Athenian interests exclusively. Athens prescribed and collected tributes from its allies and determined the use to which such revenue should be put. The other members of the federation were no more than tax-paying vassal states awaiting the opportunity to secure their freedom. Only by continual wars and massacres could the Athenians contrive to keep their allies in line.

In the Sicilian cities, long notorious for their dictatorial systems, the days of the tyrants were almost at an end. In Acragas the tyrant Hieron died in 471 and his son and successor opened his career by losing a war against Syracuse. In Syracuse, five years previously, the townspeople had risen in revolt against Hieron's younger brother and won a great victory over his professional army.

A Sicilian chieftain named Doucetius attempted to rally his countrymen against the Greek colonists on the island. He was initially successful and tore down the town of Aetna that had been founded by Hieron.

An old Roman legend describes how the good Cincinnatus was once tilling his land peacefully when suddenly informed by the senate that the fatherland was in peril and that he had been appointed dictator to conduct the inevitable war ahead. Greatly distressed, Cincinnatus abandoned his fields, donned his toga, accepted the insignia of his office, mustered his divisions in the Forum and set out for battle. Having roundly defeated the enemy and exacted advantageous peace terms, he made his offerings of gratitude to the gods, relinquished his dictatorship and returned to his rural life.

Lions guarding the sacred path to the sanctuary of Apollo on the small island of Delos.

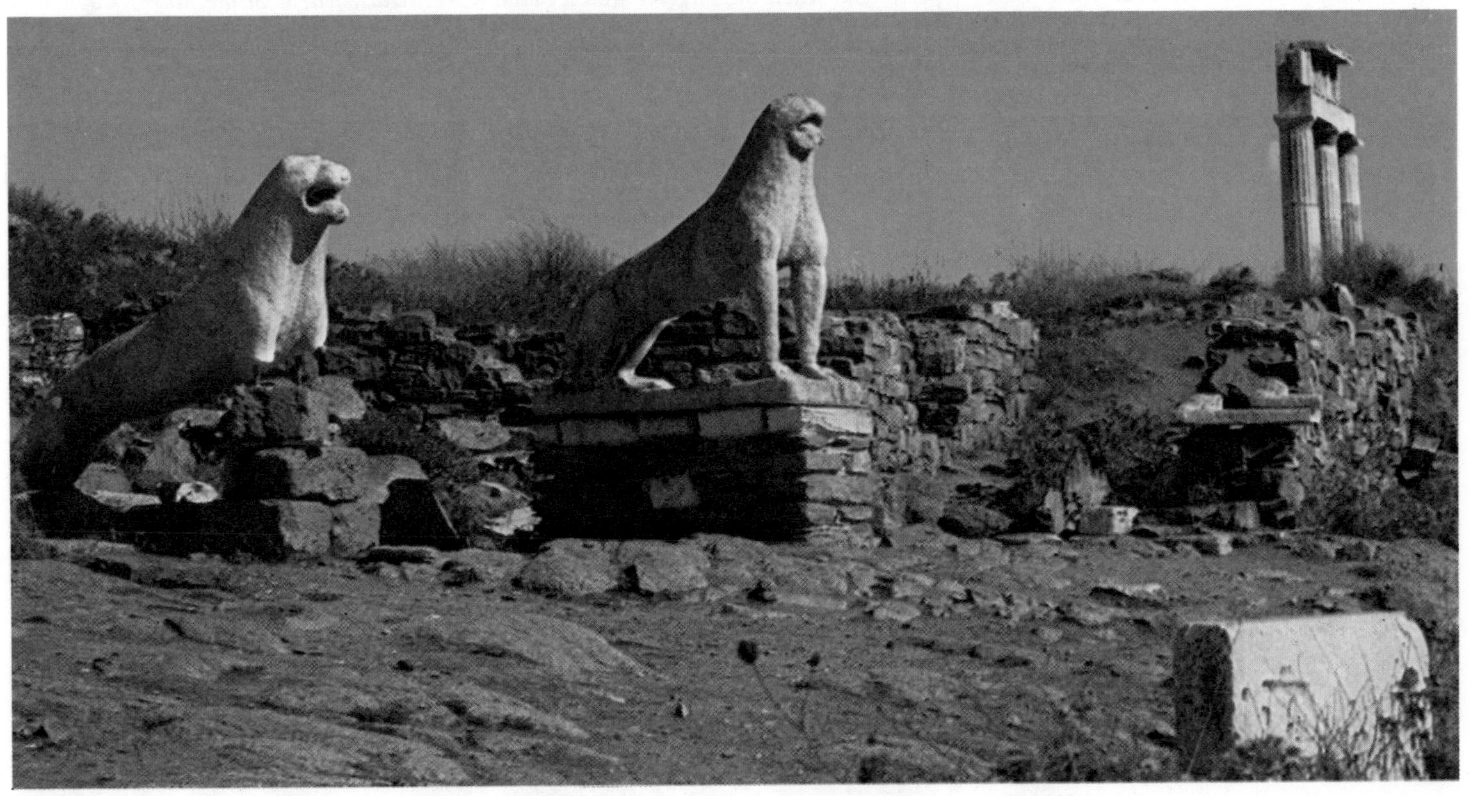

Hieron I	**Syracuse**
(Cimon) — Pericles	**Athens**
Xerxes I — Artaxerxes I	**Persia**
(Cincinnatus)	**Rome**
Zhou Zhen Ding Wang	**China**

470	469	468	467	466	465	464	463	462	461

460–451 BC

HELLENES

Athens, now a major power to which all the Ionian cities and islands paid taxes, was ruled for more than forty years by the popular aristocratic leader Pericles, who provided employment with his large-scale building operations at the Acropolis. Among the prominent men who set high cultural standards for Athens during his reign were Aeschylus, Sophocles, Euripides, Herodotus, Phidias and Socrates. Aeschylus was by now an old man living in Sicily and died in 456, allegedly in a somewhat original fashion: an eagle dropped a tortoise from a great height directly onto his bald pate. Sophocles, then forty years old, was still to write most of his great dramas, and the same was of course true of Euripides, barely twenty-five. The philosopher Socrates was only in his teens, but the sculptor Phidias, about the same age as Pericles, was busy on a huge gold and ivory statue of Athene for the new Parthenon temple. The historian Herodotus was likewise in his prime.

In the modest little city of Rome, a ten-man committee, the decemvirate, was appointed to arrange and codify legislation. The outcome was ten bronze tablets inscribed with laws that were to remain in force for some time.

The Greeks' war with the Persians came to a standstill of its own accord, but a series of minor conflicts erupted among the various Greek states. The Athenians allied themselves with their former enemy Argos against Sparta, and when the Argives won a battle this was commemorated by sculptures and battle-scene paintings by the leading Athenian artists. Athens also made war on Aegina and Thebes, and was engaged, furthermore, in an immense military campaign in Egypt, against the occupying Persians. The Persian general Megabyzus defeated the Athenians at Memphis and forced them to retreat to an island in the Nile delta; he then diverted one of the branches of the river, stranded the Athenian fleet and attacked with his entire army. Only a few Athenians escaped this trap. A few days later, an unsuspecting squadron of some fifty Athenian ships arrived on the scene, and was almost totally destroyed by the Phoenician fleet.

Portraits of the Greek tragedians date from the Roman period and may not be true to life. The Aeschylus, left, is in the Museo Capitolino, Rome; Sophocles, centre, is in the Museo del Laterano, Rome; and Euripides, right, is in the Museo Nazionale, Naples.

Athens — Pericles —
Persia — Artaxerxes I —
Rome - - - - (Decemvirate) - - -
China — Zhou Zhen Ding Wang —

460	459	458	457	456	455	454	453	452	451

HELLENES
HELLENES
PERSIANS
IBERIAN GENTLEWOMAN
AMAZON

In Mexico there were already large cities, some of which were religious centres with their own priesthoods. There appears to have been a strict social system. Extensive agriculture sometimes produced a surplus of foodstuffs.

Opinions varied as to the qualities of the Roman decemvirate. Their laws were praised yet their principal magistrate was described as a rascal. This was Appius Claudius, who was protagonist of the tale concerning the virtuous Virginia, a plebeian girl whom he had abducted on the grounds that she was the daughter of one of his slaves. The girl's father and suitor took the matter to a court of law, but Appius Claudius was the magistrate and acquitted himself. Virginia's father, seeing no moral alternative but to slay his daughter, thrust a knife into her breast with the words,'Thus do I grant thee thy freedom!' The deed caused a public outcry and Appius Claudius was duly brought again before the court; he was sentenced and died in gaol.

In 450 the Sicilian chieftain Doucetius suffered a decisive defeat and was forced into exile. This confirmed Greek control over the island, and Greek culture was predominant in all the Sicilian towns which now surrendered to Syracuse.

In Jerusalem the temple had been rebuilt with Persian financial support. The priest Ezra was in authority here and did all in his power to contain Judaism. Enquiries were made into mixed marriages and Ezra himself named over a hundred Jews who were made to renounce their wives: 'All these had taken strange wives; and some of them had wives by whom they had children', states Ezra smugly in the Old Testament (Ezra 10:44).

At about this time an anonymous scholar was at work in China. He was known as Laozi, which simply means the Old Master, and he was regarded as the author of an obscure but profound work entitled Daodejing, his earliest and most significant document and one of the great achievements in world literature. The creed as expressed here is in sharp contrast to the sober, political-type wisdom of Confucius, and asserts, briefly, that existence is mystical and that it is futile and foolish to attempt to improve or even concern oneself with worldly things.

Left: Laozi leaves his official post one day and makes his way westward on a black ox. At the frontier he meets the guard Yin Xi and spends an edifying evening with him in conversation. Next day Yin Xi asks Laozi to record some of his thoughts before he goes on his way. He does so, and this is the origin of the Daodejing. Below: In AD 1945 at a place called Tenochtitlan (Mexico City) this huge basalt head was discovered and eighteen years later it was placed in the anthropological museum in Mexico City.

Pericles	**Athens**
Artaxerxes I	**Persia**
(Decemvirate)	**Rome**
Zhou Zhen Ding Wang	**China**

450	449	448	447	446	445	444	443	442	441

HELLENES

Athens' era of greatness had been far from peaceful. The war in Egypt had brought enormous losses in men and ships. More successful, however, was the campaign against Aegina, which for several generations had been one of the largest trading centres in Greece and which had only reluctantly relinquished this position. Neither was Athens popular within its own maritime federation.

In Athens, in 433, the astronomer Meton presented a heliotrope and a parapegm - a device for showing the time of the equinoxes and solstices, and a form of perpetual calendar inscribed on stone. He also taught an important chronological system known as Meton's cycle. This comprised nineteen years, twelve of which had twelve lunar months and seven of which had thirteen. After this nineteen-year cycle the seasons would revert to their original times and the phases of the moon to the same dates. The Metonic cycle was to remain an important factor in chronology for thousands of years.

The Peloponnesian War, between Athens and a coalition of Doric states, broke out in 431. This developed into a tremendous trial of strength that soon involved the entire Mediterranean world and it continued with only brief interruptions for a quarter of a century.

431 was also the year of the premiere of Euripides' *Medea*. Sophocles' *Oedipus* was first performed in 427.

Events in the Peloponnesian War led to a series of appalling massacres of prisoners and political opponents in all the Greek cities. In many places, such as Corcyra and Megara, there was full-scale civil war between aristocrats and democrats, the former mostly sympathetic to Sparta, the latter to Athens. Murder of a neighbour or fellow citizen was a daily occurrence.

In 438 the Parthenon temple on the Acropolis was inaugurated . This had taken ten years to build - a remarkably short time considering the enormous precision of the work involved. Phidias' enormous statue of Athene was merely representational, since the true patron deity of Athens was an ancient creation in olive wood which on a certain day each year was adorned in a splendid mantle and jewellery and taken out to be dipped in the sea.

Some Athenian cities were founded outside Greece in the time of Pericles. Thus Thurii in southern Italy was founded in 440, and Amphipolis, in Thrace, in 437.

Apollo's temple in Rome was built in 431. The Etruscans, whose influence on Roman religion was considerable, also worshipped this Asiatic and Greek god under the name of Apulu.

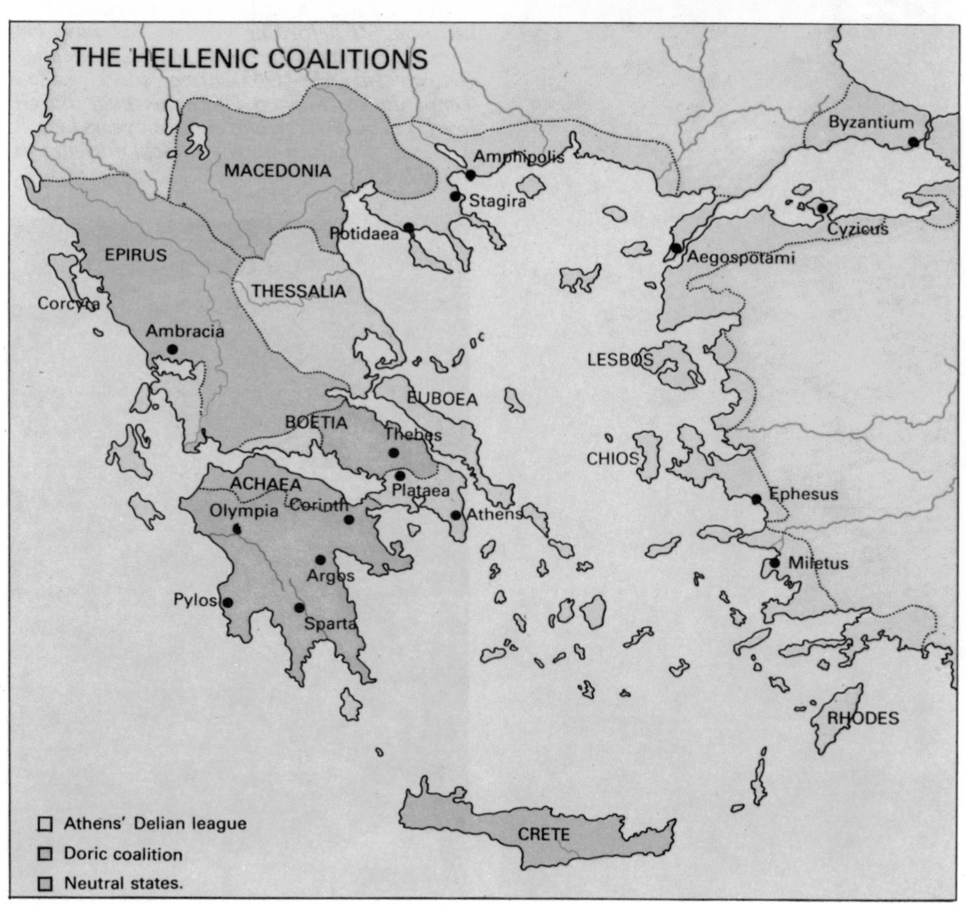
THE HELLENIC COALITIONS
Byzantium
Amphipolis
MACEDONIA
Stagira
Potidaea
Cyzicus
Aegospotami
EPIRUS
THESSALIA
Corcyra
Ambracia
LESBOS
EUBOEA
BOETIA
Thebes
CHIOS
ACHAEA
Plataea
Olympia
Corinth
Athens
Ephesus
Miletus
Argos
Pylos
Sparta
RHODES
CRETE
Athens' Delian league
Doric coalition
Neutral states.

Athens — Pericles

Persia — Artaxerxes I

Rome - - - - -

China — Zhou Kao Wang

440	439	438	437	436	435	434	433	432	431

SCYTHIAN
FROM
ALTAI
HELLENE
HELLENES

In 430 the plague struck Athens. The rural population of Attica huddled within the city walls while outside the Spartans pillaged and burned. Pericles, whose authority was declining, lost both his sons in the epidemic and shortly afterwards followed them to the grave.His successor, the tanner Cleon, was unfavourably portrayed both by the playwright Aristophanes, and by the historian Thucydides who has left us the outstanding account of the Peloponnesian War. Cleon suffered this harsh judgment even though he had won a great victory against the Spartans in 425 and died in another campaign against them in 422.

After his failure as an admiral in the initial stage of the Peloponnesian War, Thucydides was exiled by the Athenian popular assembly and settled down to observe the progress of the war from a distance. As a writer he was composed, sensible, critical and objective; possibly one of the greatest journalists of all time.

The pacifist and religious founder Mo Zu is said to have been born in 480 and was thus probably active at this time in China. He left behind him a creed that preached contentment, all embracing love and the repudiation of war. He believed implicitly in a supreme being and a supernatural world capable of intervening in matters of good and evil. Mo Zu's disciples formed a society that exerted considerable influence for several centuries but which then declined into obscurity. The writings of the society have survived, however, until the present day.

Artaxerxes I died a natural death, a privilege enjoyed by only a few of the Persian kings. He is known in history as Macrocheir or Longimanus because one of his hands was larger than the other. Very little of importance was achieved in his reign. His son Darius, who succeeded him after an orgy of fratricide, married his own aunt, Parysatis. She was described as a terrifying creature who specialized in poisoning and having people skinned alive.

There was nothing of significance to record from rural Rome, though there must have been social conflicts. The consul in the year 439 was Menenius Agrippa, of whom the historian Livy tells the story of a group of plebeians who fled Rome and entrenched themselves on the Sacred Mountain where they debated whether to make an armed attack on the patrician governors or to found their own town. The patricians despatched Menenius Agrippa to negotiate with the plebeians. He told them the fable of rebellious limbs, which refused to sustain the belly so that the entire body withered and died. The plebeians, astonishingly, bowed to this moral tale and obediently returned to Rome. As history it is hardly convincing.

The philosopher Anaxagoras, a close friend of Pericles, upset the Athenians with his views on the universe. He claimed that matter was eternal and indestructible, that the celestial bodies were made of the same substances as the earth, that the moon might be inhabited and that the sun was a molten mass at least the size of Peloponnesus. For these blasphemous teachings he was condemned to death, though Pericles contrived to have the sentence reduced to exile.

The good-humoured philosopher Democritus, originator of the atomic doctrine, lived and worked in the ill-reputed town of Abdera on the Aegean coast. He is said to have been friendly with the physician Hippocrates of Cos, who now lived in Larissa. Hippocrates believed that the first duty of the doctor was to do no harm and apparently coined the familiar aphorism: 'Life is short, art is long, opportunity fugitive, experiment dangerous, reasoning difficult.....'

The kingdom of Bosporus on the north coast of the Black Sea was a state of some commercial importance. Named after the Cimmerian Bosporus, the strait between the Black Sea and the Sea of Azov, it was a federation of the Greek colonies of Apollonia, Callatis, Odessus, Tomi, Istrus, Olbia, Chersonesus and Panticapaeum. The last two of these were in the Crimea,(the latter became Kerch) and they traded extensively with the Scythian tribes. The archon Spartacus of Particapaeum actually established a dynasty. He ruled from 438 to 433 and was succeeded by his son Satyrus I who ruled the kingdom for more than forty years.

In the mid-430s the Jewish governor Nehemiah, who appears to have been granted exceptional powers by King Artaxerxes, energetically implemented the religious laws proclaimed by Ezra some decades earlier. In so doing he assured the power of the priesthood in Jerusalem for centuries to come.

Pericles is reputed to have had a disproportionately long head, and is invariably portrayed wearing a helmet. This sculpture is in the British Museum.

Cleon — (Nicias) — **Athens**

Artaxerxes I — **Persia**

---------- **Rome**

Zhou Kao Wang — Zhou Wei Lie Wang — **China**

430	429	428	427	426	425	424	423	422	421

HELLAS

The Peloponnesian War continued with increasing fury and changing fortune. In 420 the Athenians appointed the young Alcibiades commanding general along with the older and more cautious Nicias. Alcibiades successfully advocated a military invasion of Sicily but was recalled almost at once to answer charges of sacrilege, and fled to Sparta. This left Nicias as sole leader of the Sicilian expedition which lasted two years and culminated in disaster. The surviving Athenians were imprisoned in a quarry in Syracuse and were subsequently sold as slaves. In 411 Alcibiades was restored as supreme commander of the Athenians. The war was now conducted mostly at sea along the coast of Asia where the Persian satraps had a decisive influence.

Aristophanes' political comedy *Lysistrata* was performed in Athens in 411, in the midst of the war. Sophocles died in 405, Euripides, much younger, had passed away the year before. During their lifetime theatre had developed from oratorio-type choral works to psychological drama with exciting plots. As the centuries passed, innumerable works were to be written on the art of tragedy in Athens. The very word 'tragedy' is something of an enigma, though presumably it is connected with *tragos* meaning 'goat', and is said either to have derived from the fact that originally the chorus was clad in goatskins, or that the cast danced around a sacrificial animal as part of the performance. Certainly the tragedies were connected with religious cults.

They were not performed at random but only on the occasion of certain festivals, in particular that of Dionysus in the early spring, when three poets were invited to compete, each with three tragedies and a satire. So there were many other tragedians in Athens besides the three great dramatists whose works are the only ones to have survived.

The first of these, Aeschylus, who had died half a century earlier, wrote some ninety tragedies, seven of which have survived. The most famous of these relates to the events associated with the assassination of King Agamemnon by his wife and her lover. His son Orestes, an early Hamlet, feels compelled to take the life of his mother and is finally exonerated by a divine tribunal. Sophocles was even more productive than Aeschylus. He is said to have written over 120 tragedies, again only seven of which have come down to us. These deal mainly with the hapless ruling family of Oedipus at Thebes. Sophocles introduced a third character into the cast, as opposed to the two of Aeschylus (prior to Aeschylus there had been only one actor plus the chorus), and he also made certain scenic improvements. The stage settings of the period were probably primitive, even though by this time they included the *periactori* – three-sided revolving devices with painted scenery on either side of the stage. Costume had also been introduced for the actors. Sophocles is reputed to have said of his younger colleague Euripides that he presented people as they were while he himself showed them as they ought to be. Euripides was clearly less compliant than his predecessors concerning the official religion and moral code. His dramas, eighteen of which have been preserved, present a remarkable series of heroic or evil female characters.

Some of the Athenian prisoners languishing in the Syracuse quarry secured their freedom when it was learned that they were capable of performing Euripidean scenes, and when Athens fell in 404 and the victors contemplated destroying the entire city and all its inhabitants, one Phocian moved the Spartan generals to compassion by reciting the chorus lines from Euripides' *Electra*:

"Break up, tis time, spur your feet
To work, to work with tears."

The Celts were inhabitants of central Europe. The authors of ancient Greece knew very little about them. Herodotus mentions merely that the Danube rose in their land. Archaeologists are better informed and have discovered much about the so-called Hallstatt and La Tène cultures. The former, in the Danube region, lasted until about 400 BC when it was succeeded by the latter.

For the Nordic peoples, the establishment of the Celts in central Europe meant a severance of the direct route to the Mediterranean world. Instead, Celtic culture began to influence the North, though broadly speaking these people were still mainly engaged in eking out the bare necessities of life in the rigid winter of the early Iron Age. Archaeological finds from this time are simple, and few.

Greek theatrical masks denoted the sex and personality of the character. This miniature of a tragic mask depicts a quarrelsome woman.

Athens ---------- (Alcibiades) ---------- (Nicias) ----------
Persia —————— Darius II ——————
Rome --------------------
China —————— Zhou Wei Lie Wang ——————

420	419	418	417	416	415	414	413	412	411

HELLAS

The Spartan admiral Lysander seized almost the entire Athenian fleet off Aegospotami on the Gallipoli peninsula in 406. The war dragged on for a few more years but Athens was by now defeated and the lyre-maker Cleophon, who had recently held political responsibility, was deposed, sentenced to death and executed. The peace settlement that followed implied the dissolution of the Athenian empire. The long walls down to Piraeus were torn down to the accompaniment of flute music, and thirty aristocrats who enjoyed the confidence of the Spartans took over the government in Athens. For a time they conducted a rule of terror but were soon ejected. The Peloponnesian War had involved monstrous massacres on both sides, involving prisoners-of-war and civilians alike. The Athenian Thucydides, who in the early stages participated in this carnage, described it in a memorable volume.

For about a half century to come Egypt contrived to avoid Persian dominance. The 28th dynasty comprised a single Pharaoh who gained the throne with the assistance of Greek mercenaries; but the latter quickly disposed of him again. After two unstable decades, the 29th dynasty emerged, though little is known about this or the 30th dynasty apart from the names of the Pharaohs.

A major orthographic reform took place in the Greek world in 403 when the Athenians abolished the old and unnecessary letters digamma and koppa, and introduced instead epsilon, phi, chi, psi and omega.

In China, Ch'in, which had long aimed to lead the other feudal states, dissolved into three small independent states each with their own dynasty. This was confirmed officially by the Zhou emperor in 403 BC. This historical period in China was aptly described by a contemporary chronicle as the 'era of the warring states'.

Nike statue from the temple of Zeus, Olympia, commemorating the great Athenian victory at Sphacteria in 425. This statue is the work of the Thracian artist Paenius. Olympia Museum.

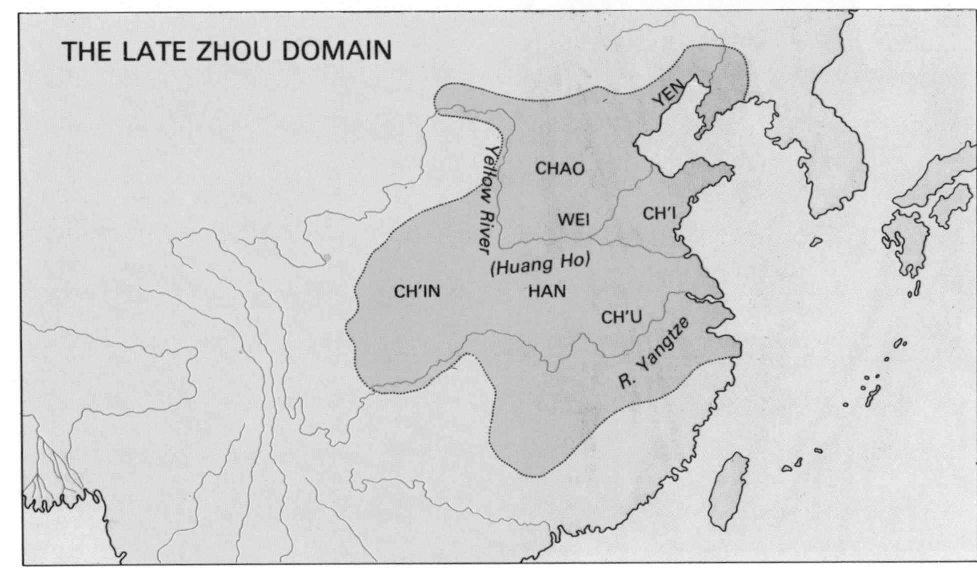
THE LATE ZHOU DOMAIN
YEN
CHAO
Yellow River
WEI
CH'I
(Huang Ho)
CH'IN
HAN
CH'U
R. Yangtze

Dionysius I — Syracuse
Amyrtaeus (XXVIII dyn.) — Egypt
(Alcibiades) — (Cleophon) — (30 tyrants) — Athens
Darius II — Artaxerxes II — Persia
Rome
Zhou Wei Lie Wang — China

410	409	408	407	406	405	404	403	402	401

400-391 BC

OLMECS MEXICO
ETRUSCANS
HELLENES
PARACAS PERU

The democrat Thrasybus, with seventy followers, captured the harbour at Piraeus, after which the terrorist regime of the thirty tyrants in Athens quickly collapsed. King Pausanias of Sparta now made honest attempts to mediate between the parties in Athens and actually succeeded in bringing about some form of atonement. But war soon broke out again, for the Athenian popular assembly had apparently learned nothing and leading politicians in other quarters were little wiser.

The Persians in Asia Minor had watched the course of the Peloponnesian War with great interest and the Spartan victory was partly the result of powerful support by the Persian prince Cyrus, who was the governor in Sardis. Cyrus had hoped to become king, but when his father died his elder brother Artaxerxes quickly succeeded him. Cyrus assembled an army of Greek mercenaries, led by a Spartan officer, and in the spring of 401 moved eastward against his brother. Their forces met at Cunaxa near Babylon where Cyrus was defeated and slain. The Greeks, despite a flank victory, were in a desperate position deep inside enemy territory. There is a good account of their long retreat over the Armenian mountains by Xenophon, an Athenian officer who was present. This work, *Anabasis* (Journey Upward), is a classic Greek text book. Xenophon was the author of other works as well, including a continuation of Thucydides' account of the Peloponnesian War, the latter having died before its conclusion.

In Palestine the Samaritans built their own Mosaic cult site on Mount Gerizim in deliberate defiance of the priesthood in Jerusalem.

The Carthaginians were in the process of occupying Malta.

At the climax of the Peloponnesian War, in an atmosphere of gloom and depression, the philosopher Socrates was working in Athens. Nobody reading Socrates today is aware of this political background. He writes of other matters and this may be one reason why upright, patriotic citizens accused him of perverting youth. In their view his behaviour was criminal.

A central idea in Socrates' philosophy is that knowledge is virtue; no person is consciously and willingly wicked, for happiness consists in doing right, so that it is simply a matter of determining what is right and of encouraging appropriate action. His method is to dispose of all false knowledge by feigning ignorance, demanding instruction of those who are deemed to know better, and then tearing their words and arguments to shreds.

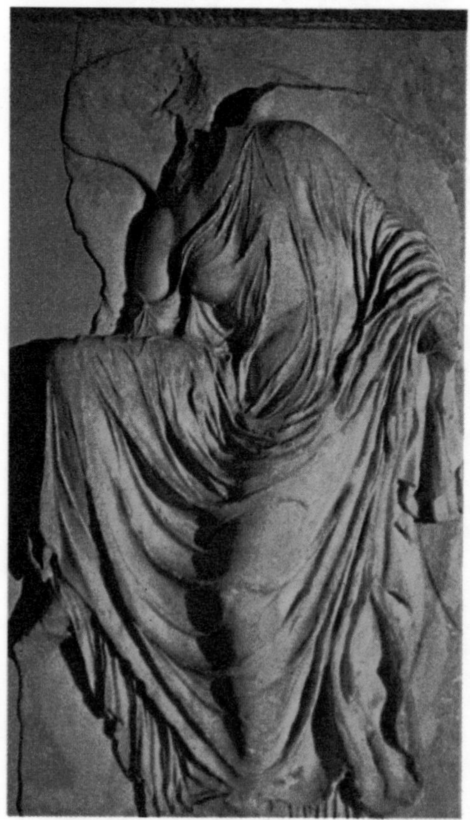

Socrates himself wrote nothing; what we know of him is conveyed to us by his disciples Plato and Xenophon, particularly the former. The account of Socrates' trial and death can be found in Plato's two dialogues *Crito* and *Phaedo*, while there are two quite different versions of Socrates's defence address, one of which is by Xenophon. It was certainly not the intention of the authorities to take the life of Socrates, but he brought the death sentence on himself by refusing to compromise or to show humility before the court.

The so-called 'Hopewell culture' was flourishing in the distant region later known as Ohio. Evidence of this comes from monumental tombs containing technically and artistically advanced artefacts. These objects were often made of raw materials taken from remote parts of the North American continent.

In 396 the Romans, under their general Camillus, conquered and destroyed the Etruscan city of Veii and this was a significant milestone in Roman history. They entered the city through a tunnel, having first drained the Alban lake by means of another tunnel.

Nike unfastens her sandal: relief from her temple at the Acropolis, Athens. Here there is also a cult portrait of her, known as Nike Apteros, because she is depicted, untypically, without wings. Nike figures are very common in Greek art. There was no mythology associated with her, nor was she worshipped with any religious fervour, but simply as a patriotic symbol.

Syracuse ———— Dionysius I ————
Egypt ----------|---------- Nepherites I ---------- Psammuthis ---------- Achoris ————
Athens (Thrasybulus) ---------- (Iphicrates) ----------
Persia ———— Artaxerxes II ————
Rome ---------- (Camillus) ----------
China ———— Zhou An Wang ————

400	399	398	397	396	395	394	393	392	391

HELLENES
SCYTHIANS

The Gauls, who had recently overrun central and western Europe, crossed the Po valley and pressed on southward. They defeated the Romans decisively on the River Allia and took Rome itself, although one army dug in and held a fortified position on the Capitoline Hill. A nocturnal attempt by the enemy to storm the heights was foiled by the sacred geese in the temple of Juno, the cackling of which alarmed the defenders. When the Gauls demanded a thousand marks of gold to abandon the siege, the Romans agreed and sent the gold to the Gallic chieftain Brennus. Brennus claimed it was short. When the Roman delegates protested, Brennus tossed his sword in with the gold crying: *Vae victis* (Woe to the defeated!).

After the departure of the Gauls, there were social conflicts in Rome where the victorious general, Camillus, championed the aristocracy while the valiant defender of the Capitoline hill, Marcus Manlius, took up the people's cause. Camillus had Manlius tried and condemned for high treason and he was sentenced to be thrown from the Tarpeian rock on the Capitoline hill.

In 390 BC the Athenian general Iphicrates routed a Spartan hoplite regiment with the aid of lightly-armed professional soldiers, peltasts. This was considered an event of major military significance. The heavily armed citizen units had seen their best days. Iphicrates was himself a career soldier and when on one occasion he was accused of violating democracy, he appeared in court surrounded by his soldiers, at which the plaintiff abandoned the case.

There are various memorable stories about Dionysius, the tyrant of Syracuse. He lived in constant fear of being assassinated and would never go to a barber; instead he had his daughter trim his beard, using a heated nut-shell instead of a razor. The courtier Damocles, extravanant in his flattery of the tyrant's lot, was given an object-lesson: he was seated at a table loaded with food and drink beneath a sword suspended point downwards by a single hair. The account of Dionysius's taxation policy is also of interest. Whenever people complained of the taxes, he increased them and continued doing so until he heard the citizens laughing and joking in the square. At this point, when they no longer had any money left to complain about, he knew it was time to ease the level. Dionysius left behind in Syracuse an immense fortification system known as Euryalus which provided employment for a great many Sicilians throughout his reign. It was shrewd policy and ensured that he remained fairly popular with the broad majority. In Syracuse there was also a cave with such remarkable acoustics that it registered even the faintest whisper. It was called Dionysius' ear and the tyrant is said to have had a monitoring tube leading from it up to his private room. Suspected individuals were imprisoned in the cave, so that every chance remark was overheard.

A celebrated land law proposed in Rome by the plebeian politician Caius Licinius sought to fix an upper limit to the area of arable land that a man might own or inherit, and it remained a bone of contention for a long time to come. The patricians naturally opposed it, and went so far as to make the elderly general Camillus dictator in order to get it rejected. The threated civil war was avoided at the last moment and Camillus celebrated the settlement by founding a temple to Concordia.

According to legend, Romulus marked his city limits with a plough drawn by a pure white cow; and Servius Tullius, who enlarged Rome, is said to have used the same method. His name is associated with the city's oldest existing wall erected after the conquest of Gaul. The photograph above shows a section of the Servian Wall. The arch, intended as a vantage point for a catapult, is of later date. Below: Dionysius' ear in Syracuse.

Dionysius I	**Syracuse**
Achoris (XXIX dyn)	**Egypt**
	Athens
Artaxerxes II	**Persia**
(Marcus Manlius Capitolinus) ---- (Camillus)	**Rome**
Zhou An Wang	**China**

390	389	388	387	386	385	384	383	382	381

CHINA
EGYPTIANS
ETRUSCANS

The Greek colonies on the Italian mainland had seen their best days. They had fought among themselves and with the native inhabitants of the country and some had already disappeared, including Sybaris. But during their time of prosperity the Sybarites had founded a daughter city, Poseidonia, which had flourished a century or two earlier but which was now assaulted and occupied by a Lucanian tribe. In the next century Poseidonia was to be seized by the Romans who made it a military colony and re-named it Paestum. The most interesting relic of Paestum is the Greek temple which is estimated to date from the 6th century BC.

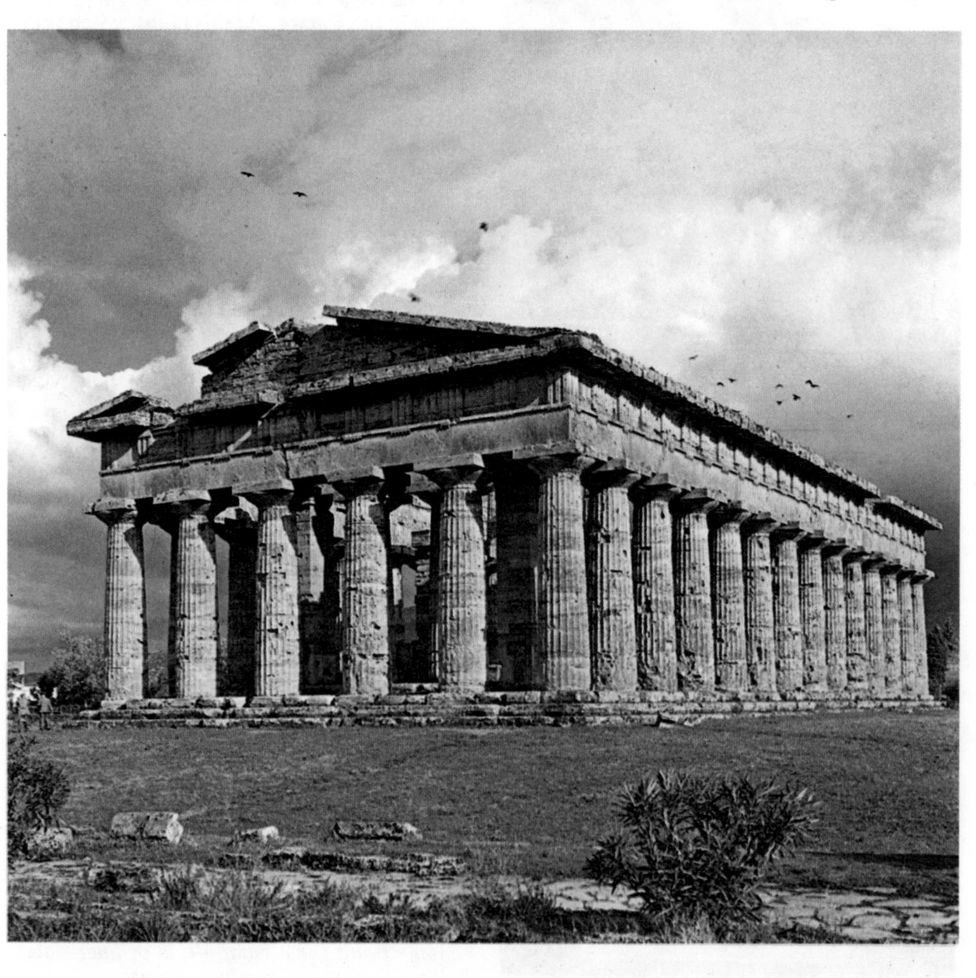

Athens was now of little political importance; instead Boeotian Thebes enjoyed a brief period of greatness. This city, occupied by the Spartans for a number of years, was liberated in 378 by a coup by returning emigrants, and now Epaminondas the Pythagorean assumed leadership. He defeated the Spartans in 371 at the remarkable battle of Leuctra and this marked the end of Spartan power. In the ascendant, however, was Macedonia, which now began to intervene in the squabbles among the small Greek city republics.

The Persian empire, too, encountered a crisis. Egypt asserted its independence, and the Asiatic vassal princes likewise exercised a fair measure of autonomy in Babylon and Susa. One such independent ruler was Mausolus in Halicarnassus who incorporated in his kingdom the islands of Rhodes, Cos and Chios. In due course his queen, Artemisia, who was also his sister, had the greatest building of the day erected as a memorial to him: the Mausoleum–one of the seven wonders of the world.

The plague visited Rome while Caius Licinius was consul. Everything possible was done to placate the wrath of the gods, including dramatic performances known as *ludi scenici.* Actors known locally as histrios or histrions were brought in from Etruria. They danced a kind of pantomime to flute music. Unfortunately, theatrical performances had little effect on the course of the epidemic.

The so-called Poseidon temple in Paestum is probably a temple to Hera; but the building is, in any event, one of the most beautiful monuments of the classical period. Paestum, which also contains other ancient buildings, remained abandoned and forgotten for nearly a thousand years.

Macedonia	Amyntas III
Thebes	(Pelopidas) — Epaminondas
Syracuse	Dionysius I
Egypt	Nectanebo I (XXX dyn)
Persia	Artaxerxes II
Rome	(C. Licinius)
China	Zhou An Wang — Zhou Lei Wang

380	379	378	377	376	375	374	373	372	371

HELLAS

In the kingdom of Bosporus, north of the Black Sea, Leucon I reigned long and contentedly (389-349).

The cultural heyday of Hellas was by no means over. Plato was now at work in Athens; his early dialogues are believed to have been written in the 370s. His school of philosophy, named after an olive grove called Academia, became highly successful and counted politicians and princes among its pupils.

Plato's writings have survived in fairly good order and without any major gaps in the texts. They are in the form of dialogues in which Socrates is usually the protagonist, though to what degree the thoughts expressed are those of Socrates or Plato it is difficult to say. Modern scholars usually divide the dialogues into three groups: one in which Socrates himself speaks, one in which he serves partly as Plato's mouthpiece, and a third in which Plato alone is involved. The last group includes, in particular, the *Republic*, later to have immense influence on political theorists.

The famous account of Atlantis derives from Plato: an island in the sea to the west of the Pillars of Hercules and inhabited by a people who remained the most powerful in the world only so long as they regarded virtue as greater than wealth or luxury. In time, however, their morals deteriorated and likewise their blissful existence, until finally Atlantis was torn apart by a mighty earthquake and sank beneath the ocean. Plato also invented the hell of Christianity by evolving a doctrine of judgment and eternal damnation; a concept that can be studied in the *Gorgias* dialogue.

The political greatness of Thebes failed to survive Epaminondas who was killed fighting a coalition of Athenians and Spartans in 363. The battle was named after the Peloponnesian city Mantineia. This hastened the disruption of Greece, with recurrent massacres even among parties and communities.

At length the plebeians were victorious in the Roman estates system. The first plebeian consul was Lucius Sextius, an unmemorable figure.

Below: Plato's School of Philosophy in a Roman mosaic. The figure on the right is the master himself. His Academy survived him only by a couple of generations, but his teachings were to endure through the centuries.

Alexander II — Ptolemaeus — Perdiccas III	**Macedonia**
Epaminondas	**Thebes**
Dionysius I — Dionysius II	**Syracuse**
Nectanebo I (XXX dyn) — Tachos (XXX dyn)	**Egypt**
Artaxerxes II	**Persia**
(Lucius Sextius)	**Rome**
Zhou Lei Wang — Zhou Xian Wang	**China**

370	369	368	367	366	365	364	363	362	361

360-351 BC

HELLENES

THEBES' GOLDEN AGE
(AFTER THE BATTLE OF MANTINEIA)

ILLYRIA
MACEDONIA
EPIRUS
THESSALY
Thebes
Athens
Olympia
Corinth
Mantineia
Sparta
Ephesus

Athenian Empire
Theban Empire
Spartan Empire

Aristotle, the disciple of Plato who had continued on his own course, was responsible for categorizing knowledge and science into different sectors: physics, zoology, ethics, poetry, and so forth. Aristotle came from the town of Stagira in Thrace, but most of his life's work was done in Athens.

In the land of Qin, (Ch'in), which was a sort of oriental Macedonia on the outskirts of Chinese civilization, the feudal system was gradually giving way to national authority. A resolute statesman named Shang Yang introduced a new land distribution system which freed the peasants yet at the same time left them wholly dependent upon the central authorities who exercised firm control over the irrigation system. He also introduced written legislation and equality before the law, which was considered a shocking innovation in China. Shang Yang's dictatorship was followed by growing prosperity and a sharp population increase in Qin.

352 a certain Herostratus achieved notoriety by setting fire to the temple of Artemis in Ephesus.

A vassal king, Tennes of Sidon, led a revolt in the Persian empire in the middle of this century, but this was an imprudent undertaking. Artaxerxes seized Sidon and destroyed it in a terrible bloodbath.

In Syracuse the tyrant Dionysius II was driven out and succeeded by his uncle Dion who was a devoted disciple of Plato, though he never had the opportunity to put the latter's political theories into practice. Dion was soon assassinated and this heralded ten years of anarchy in Syracuse, until Dionysius II returned. A couple of years later, however, Dionysius was again expelled, by the republican aristocrat Timoleon.

Sparta evidently having recovered from the disaster at Leuctra, dared to give a harsh, laconic reply to notes from King Philip of Macedonia. When the king enquired in a letter if he should visit them as friend or foe, the Spartans replied succinctly: "Neither." As a result, Philip II led a military expedition in the following decade to Peloponnesus, and captured most of Sparta. The city itself retained its independence for a few more generations, until the Romans arrived; but its military power was gone, and the population was declining.

Aristotle, (above left) bust in Museo Capitolino, Rome. This protrait hardly tallies, however, with the description of the philosopher's appearance in classical literature.

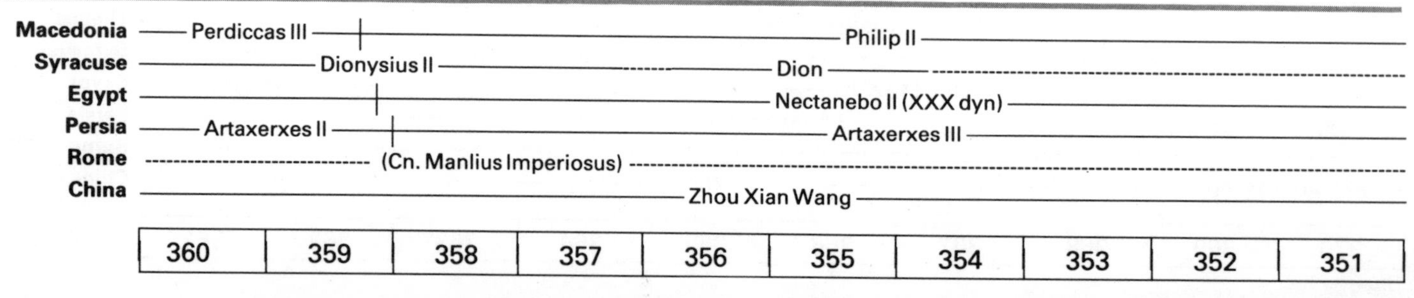
Macedonia — Perdiccas III — Philip II
Syracuse — Dionysius II — Dion
Egypt — Nectanebo II (XXX dyn)
Persia — Artaxerxes II — Artaxerxes III
Rome — (Cn. Manlius Imperiosus)
China — Zhou Xian Wang
360 | 359 | 358 | 357 | 356 | 355 | 354 | 353 | 352 | 351

HELLAS
MONGOL
THRACIAN WARRIOR
MONGOL

There is a somewhat improbable story relating to the Roman consuls Manlius; father and son. As an antidote to the plague the Romans proposed hammering a ritual nail into the wall of Jupiter's temple. Only a dictator could be entrusted with this sacred undertaking and Cnaeus Manlius Imperiosus was thus invested with dictatorial powers. Having hammered in the nail to general satisfaction, however, he refused to give up the dictatorship until he had mobilized an army. In due course he was brought before a people's tribunal and charged with inhuman conduct, even to his own family and in particular his son Titus, whom he allegedly treated like a slave. Next day the young Titus visited the tribunal and asked to speak alone with his father. No sooner did he close the door behind him than his father seized him, held a dagger to his throat and made him promise to have the charges withdrawn. The public account of this event made Titus Manlius Torquatus a popular figure in Rome.

The Persian king, Artaxerxes III, once more suppressed Egyptian independence, with great cruelty. Nectanebo II, the last Egyptian in a long line of Pharaohs, was not, however, made captive. In 343 Egypt became a Persian province.

Philip II had lived in Thebes, when still a prince, as a Macedonian hostage; he was therefore as experienced in the political affairs of a small Greek state as he was in the strategic skills of Epaminondas. Having now become regent during his nephew's minority, he refused to stand down in the latter's favour. He was already prospering, for he had seized a gold mine in the mountains to the west, and had wrested the important town of Amphipolis from the Athenians.

In Greece itself Thebes became involved in a dispute with the neighbouring Phocians. The Thebans brought charges against them before the amphictyonic council and had them fined for various offences. The Phocians retaliated by occupying Delphi, appropriating the temple treasures and using this wealth to recruit an army. The army was deployed with great success against the Thebans and their allies, who appealed for assistance. Philip II, seeing his chance, proclaimed a holy war against the temple-desecrating Phocians, who were allied to Athens. The Phocians were defeated and Athens lost its remaining influence on the Aegean north coast when the town of Olynthus fell. A young lawyer named Demosthenes won repute by unflaggingly urging the Athenians to continue the fight against Philip. Demosthenes is probably best remembered as the orator who managed to cure his own stammer and poor diction by practising to speak with pebbles in his mouth, strengthening his lungs by outshouting the roar of the surf, and overcoming his shyness by shaving only one side of his head.

In 343-341 the Romans fought their first battle with the Samnites in southern Italy. This occurred because the Romans had now extended their territories down to Capua.

A mural from a tomb in Paestum, now in the Museo Archeologico Nazionale there, shows the weapons and protective armour of a Lucanian warrior. The Lucanians were the southernmost tribe on the Italian mainland.

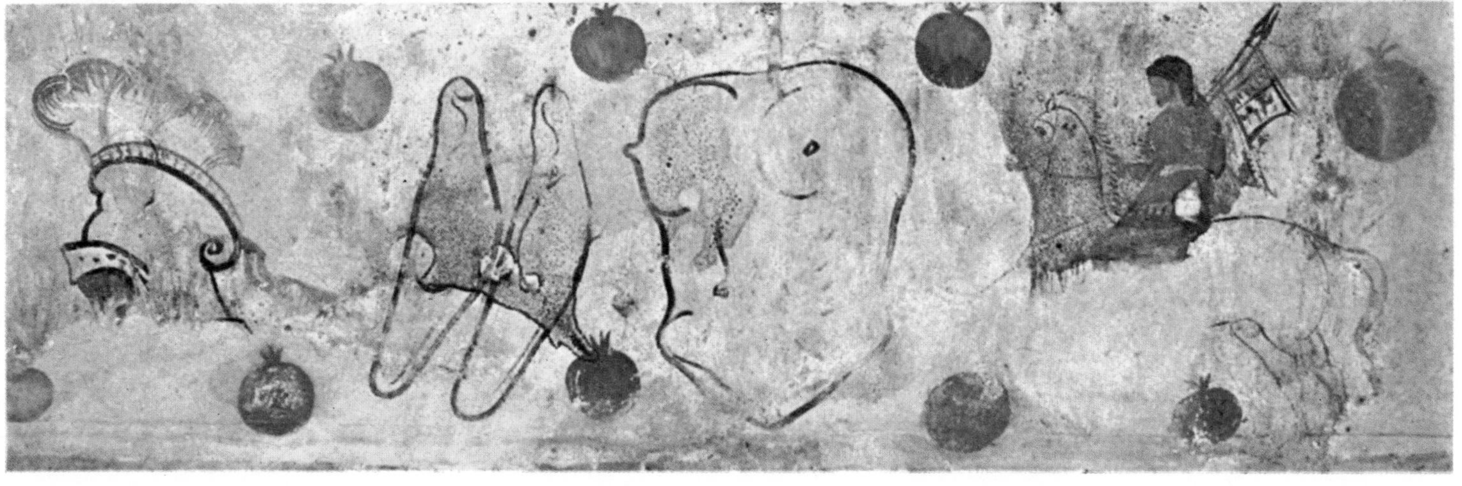

Philip II	**Macedonia**
Dionysius II — Timoleon	**Syracuse**
Nectanebo II (XXX dyn)	**Egypt**
Artaxerxes III	**Persia**
(Titus Manlius Torquatus)	**Rome**
Zhou Xian Wang	**China**

350	349	348	347	346	345	344	343	342	341

AFTER THE BATTLE
OF ISSUS

The philosopher Aristotle, who since the previous decade had been the tutor of Alexander at the Macedonian court of Philip II, returned to Athens and founded the Lyceum school in 335.

Of all the uningratiating rulers in the Roman republic, one of the most inflexible was surely Titus Manlius Torquatus, now an army commander in his capacity as consul. His own son, a cavalry officer, performed a courageous deed in battle under explicit orders, yet without hesitation the consul had him executed for disobedience.

Alexander in the battle of Issus. Detail of mosaic in Pompeii, from a lost Greek mural.

The Romans continued to wage war incessantly. Now that they had extended the domains to embrace Campania and seized the Greek city of Naples, they came to grips with the Samnites, not always with success. The Roman consul Spurius Postumius was trapped by the Samnites in a pass with his army, and was forced to surrender and sign a peace treaty. Afterwards the consul urged the senate not to recognize the treaty but instead to allow him to deliver himself to the enemy and claim sole responsibility for the signature. The senate agreed to this, but the Samnite commander who received the captive raised his arms to heaven and called on the gods to witness Roman faithlessness and contempt for contracts. The consul was then freed and sent on his way.

338 was the year of the battle of Chaeronea; a memorable event. Philip II's defeat of a coalition of Greek republics marked the end of the period of small Hellenic states. Thebes and Sparta had played their part and were finished. But the cultural inheritance of Athens survived, since Greek was also the language of the victorious Macedonians.

Hardly had Philip II made himself master of the Hellenic world than he was assassinated in his palace. This murder was followed by a bloodbath within the family, and eventually Philip's son, the young Alexander, was pronounced king of Macedonia. He had no difficulty in quelling a Greek revolt and it was on this occasion that he is said to have encountered the cynical philisopher Diogenes. Alexander made an effort to be gracious to him and was promptly asked to move a little to one side, for he was blocking the philosopher's sunlight.

In only a few years Alexander the Great conquered the entire civilized world of antiquity, from Italy in the west to the Indus in the east. In 334 he crossed the Hellespont; in 333 he defeated the Persian armies at the Granicus River and Issus; in 332 he dealt with Egypt and founded Alexandria; in 331 he routed the last of the Persian armies at Arbela near Nineveh and put Darius III to flight eastward. During the following years he overran Persia itself and also Bactria and Sogdiana, later known as West Turkestan and Afghanistan. Continuing his advance, he reached the Hydaspes and the Hyphasis, which were tributaries of the Indus. Here he had to turn back, receiving ambassadors from all corners of the world in Babylon. He then set about consolidating his immense empire.

Persia	Artaxerxes III (340–338) | Arses (338–336) | Darius III (336–331)
Syracuse	Timoleon
Macedonia	Philip II (340–336) | Alexander III the Great (336–331)
Rome	(Titus Manlius Torquatus)
China	Zhou Xian Wang

340	339	338	337	336	335	334	333	332	331

HELLENE
SAMNITES
HELLENE

Alexander introduced a uniform monetary system throughout his great empire, since this was a sector where there had been widespread confusion. But when he released the gold and silver of the Persian kings in the form of coins, the result was inflation.

From the Greek viewpoint, Alexander's expeditions were not only brilliant military achievements, they were also voyages of discovery. While Alexander himself marched home from India by land his admiral, Nearchus, made his way along the Indus with a newly built fleet and found the sea route to the lands of the ancient civilizations of Asia.

Alexander the Great died in Babylon in the year 323, a mere thirty-two years old. He was succeeded officially by his somewhat irresolute brother Philip Arrhidaeus, but the Macedonian generals, who were all masters of newly acquired provinces, immediately set about strengthening their own positions of power. Thus Alexander the Great's empire began to disintegrate immediately; and in the course of incessant war, all against all, there emerged instead a series of sovereign monarchies each with its own dynasty. The most stable of these was Ptolemaic Egypt. The names of some of the blood-sullied sovereigns wielding power in other parts are shown in the table of rulers below.

The greatest by far of the kingdoms set up by the successors of Alexander is usually called the Seleucid after the dynasty established there. Initially this embraced all the Persian empire's provinces and vassal states eastward: Syria, Mesopotamia, Media, Persia, certain zones of India, Bactria and Sogdiana in central Asia. But the Seleucids soon lost most of this.

Pairisades I, with his brothers, ruled the country of Crimea in the Bosporus (349-311), which traded profitably with the Scythians and other peoples around the Dnieper, the Don and the Volga. Large numbers of Attic vases were imported via the capital Panticapaeum.

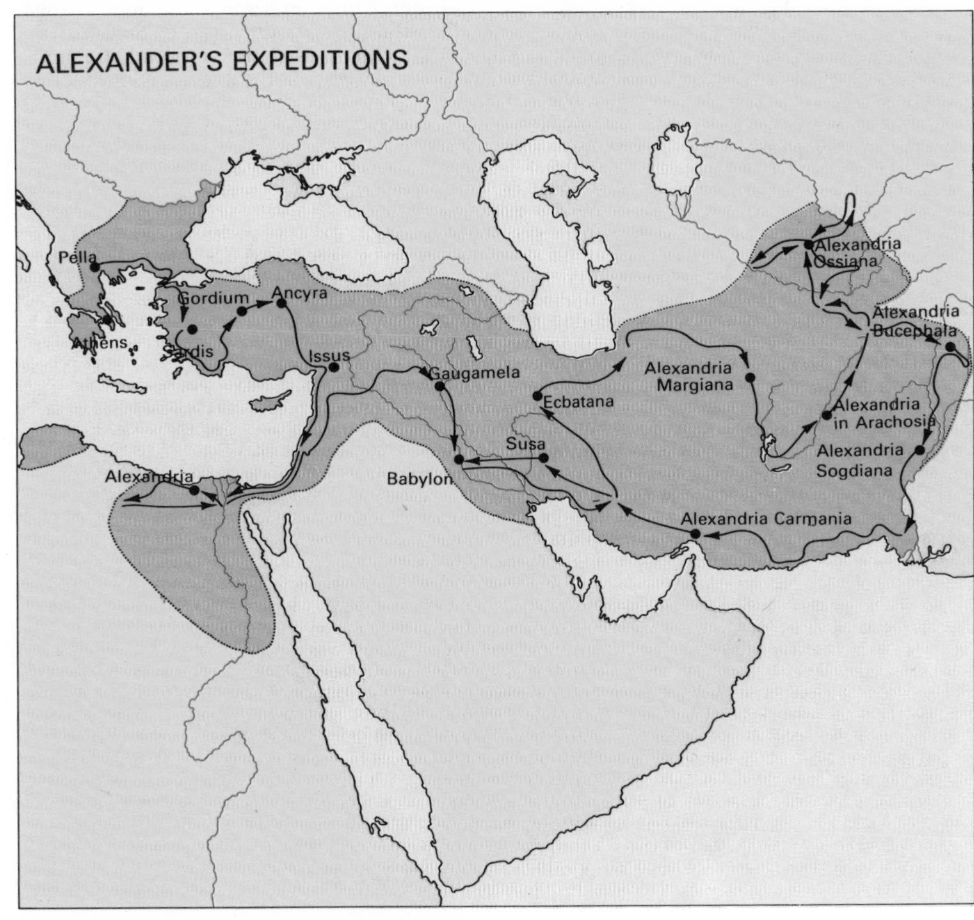
ALEXANDER'S EXPEDITIONS
Pella
Gordium
Ancyra
Athens
Sardis
Issus
Gaugamela
Ecbatana
Susa
Babylon
Alexandria
Alexandria Margiana
Alexandria Ossiana
Alexandria Bucephala
Alexandria in Arachosia
Alexandria Sogdiana
Alexandria Carmania

Chandra Gupta Maurya	**India**
Perdiccas	**Babylon/Persia**
Antigonus	**Phrygia**
Eumenes	**Cappadocia**
Lysimachus	**Thrace**
Ptolemy I	**Egypt**
	Syracuse
Alexander — Antipater	**Macedonia**
(Spurius Postumius)	**Rome**
Zhou Xian Wang	**China**

330	329	328	327	326	325	324	323	322	321

320-311 BC

EGYPT
ROMANS

Alexander the Great's generals and inheritors, (the Diadochi) fought constantly among themselves in different combinations. The first to succumb was Eumenes whose kingdom was taken over by Antigonus. Antigonus now ruled all Asia from the Hellespont to the Indus, and his former colleagues refused to accept this. At the head of a small army, Seleucus occupied Babylon, Persia and Media. In Macedonia Antipater had appointed a certain Polyperchon his successor, but after much bloodshed and murder Antipater's son Cassander changed this situation. In due course Seleucus and Lysimachus ended the imperial dreams of Antigonus who, at the age of eighty-one, was killed in the decisive battle. His son Demetrius survived and within twenty years made himself king of Macedonia and Greece, succeeding Cassander who, remarkably, died a natural death. The course these events is very complicated, but the fates of these potentates can be broadly traced in the tables on this and the following pages.

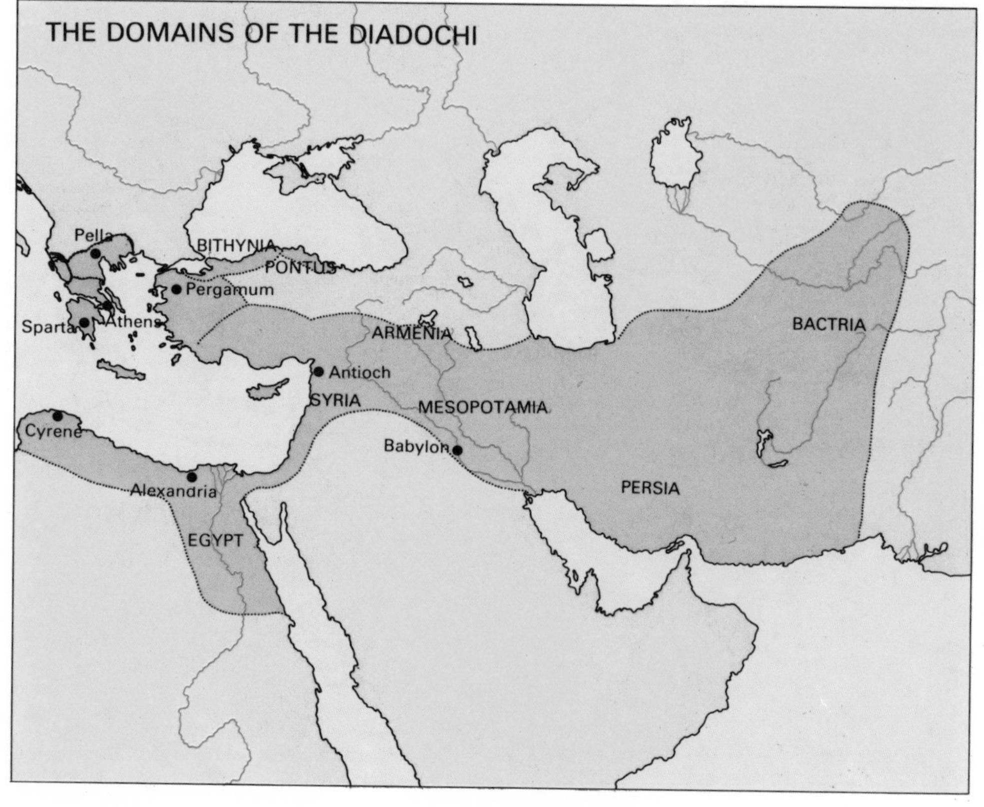

THE DOMAINS OF THE DIADOCHI
Pella
BITHYNIA
PONTUS
Pergamum
Athens
Sparta
ARMENIA
BACTRIA
Antioch
SYRIA
MESOPOTAMIA
Cyrene
Babylon
Alexandria
PERSIA
EGYPT

The Bosporan kingdom north of the Black Sea began to encounter problems; the neighbouring Scythians were becoming increasingly insolent and the archon Eumelus, successor to Pairisades I, was by no means as prudent as his predecessor. He exterminated almost the entire dynasty, though his rule was brief. In 304 he was succeeded by Spartacus III who assumed the title of king according to the Hellenic pattern: but the Greek character of the kingdom gradually disappeared.

On 1 October 312 Seleucus entered Babylon. This date marked the starting point for the Seleucid era – a chronology that was widely used in the Orient and was adopted, for example, in the biblical books of the Maccabees.

The Macedonian conquerers never really controlled the eastern part of the great empire. Seleucus was eventually assassinated on his way home to Macedonia. His dynasty resided mainly in Syrian Antiochia, not in Babylon.

Alexander the Great's brief sojourn in India had given rise to new political activity. A prince named Chandra Gupta Maurya gathered the northern parts of the country into a large empire and built his capital on the Ganges. Seleucus ceded the Macedonian possessions in India to Chandra Gupta Maurya in exchange for 500 elephants which he needed for his war against Antigonus.

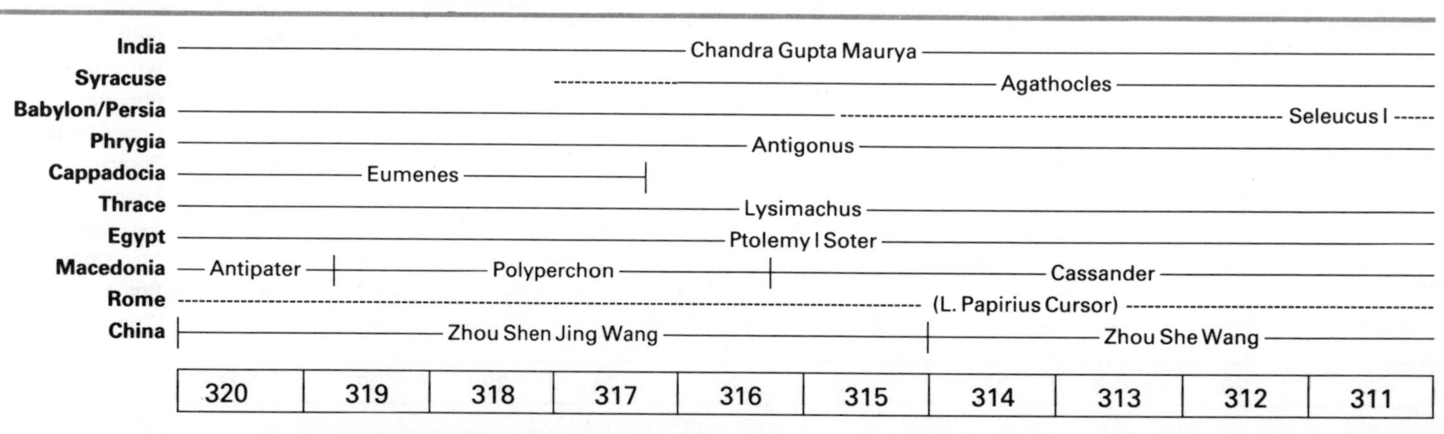

India — Chandra Gupta Maurya
Syracuse — Agathocles
Babylon/Persia — Seleucus I
Phrygia — Antigonus
Cappadocia — Eumenes
Thrace — Lysimachus
Egypt — Ptolemy I Soter
Macedonia — Antipater — Polyperchon — Cassander
Rome — (L. Papirius Cursor)
China — Zhou Shen Jing Wang — Zhou She Wang
320 319 318 317 316 315 314 313 312 311

PERSIANS
HELLENES
HELLENES, TANAGRA

A Greek named Euclid had studied mathematics in Athens and settled in Alexandria where he worked as a teacher and was granted the privilege of giving lessons to King Ptolemy Soter. The king, however, found his studies oppressive and asked for the subject to be revised and simplified; to which Euclid replied: "There is no royal road to mathematics". Instead he methodically and painstakingly produced a step by step presentation in thirteen volumes of all that was known on the science. This work is called the *Stoicheia* (in Latin the *Elementa*), and is constructed with logical consistency, piece by piece, from a mass of definitions, axioms and postulates. The arithmetical parts of the *Elements* have since become outdated, but the geometrical side remains surprisingly sound. The twelfth of his axioms, that only one line parallel with another given line can be drawn through a given point, proved in due course to be a weak link in his method; but the system does not fail altogether on account of this.

We are indebted to Euclid not only for such things as the case of equality in all respects, and the art of constructing figures where the dimensions are the same as figures of an entirely different nature, but also for our entire terminology in geometry – triangle, rectangle, base, cyclinder, cone, circle, sphere, etc.

A new culture which was to be named after the city of Teotihuacán appears to have reached central Mexico. No written evidence has been left, however, of the identity or language of those who originated this culture.

Numerous Greek towns had been founded by Alexander and his successors and some of these developed into important trading and cultural centres: Alexandria in Egypt, Herat and Kandahar in Afghanistan, Antiochia in Syria and Thessalonica in Macedonia.

For Greece itself, this universal expansion in due course led to poverty, depopulation and decline. The situation was particularly difficult in Sparta because of the curious property system there, but inflation raged everywhere. In addition war once more broke out among the small states as a result of disputes between the royal houses of the Diadochi.

Pytheas of Massilia undertook a journey to northern Europe, where the sea froze in the winter and the midnight sun shone in the summer. It would be interesting to know more about the journey. All we have are some extracts quoted by classical Greek authors, who cast doubt on his descriptions of the land of Thule.

There were reports from China in 307 that King Wu Ling of Zhao, a land in western China on the Mongolian border, was replacing his war chariots with cavalry, an improvement in military tactics.

The land of Ch'u was the homeland of Qu Yuan, the first of the great Chinese poets. He had been an adviser to the king of Ch'u but had fallen out of favour, and spent the long years of exile writing poems full of melancholy and nostalgia. Finally he lashed himself to a large stone, extemporized a prose poem called 'Thoughts of the Sand' and drowned himself in the river Miluo. This was to be commemorated for the next 2 000 years in an annual Chinese folk festival. The land of Ch'u, whose ruler did not heed Qu Yuan's advice, soon fell victim to the state of Qin (Ch'in).

Lucius Papirius Cursor was elected Roman dictator twice during the Samnite wars. A law-abiding and conscientious man, he resigned his dictatorship as soon as his time of office had passed. This was not unusual among the generals of Rome.

Appius Claudius Caecus, censor of Rome, built the first Roman aqueduct, and also Via Appia (the Appian Way) which ran southwards to Capua and which immortalized his name.

Via Appia, by far the most important Roman road, was barely three metres at its widest, hardly allowing two carts to pass each other, but it was usable in all weathers. It was built by soldiers for soldiers.

Chandra Gupta Maurya	**India**
Agathocles	**Syracuse**
Seleucus I Nicator	**Babylon/Persia**
Antigonus (to 301)	**Phrygia**
Lysimachus	**Thrace**
Ptolemy I Soter	**Egypt**
Cassander	**Macedonia**
(Appius Claudius Caecus)	**Rome**
Zhou She Wang	**China**

310	309	308	307	306	305	304	303	302	301

300-291 BC

CHINA
TANAGRA
HELLENES

Demetrius was a prominent officer, an indefatigable libertine and a cunning though hardly persevering politician. He was the son of Antigonus and was his father's brave and loyal aide until the latter's death in his Asiatic domains. Demetrius then conducted numerous military campaigns, succeeded in becoming ruler of Macedonia, lost a battle against a superior coalition and ended his days in comfortable captivity under his son-in-law Seleucus. Earlier he had resided luxuriously for some time in the Parthenon and had enjoyed the divine worship of the courteous Athenians. His family continued to rule in Macedonia until it died out.

The philosopher Mencius, or Mengzi, lived and worked in China. He was the most talented and wittiest of the Confucian writers, believing in the good nature of mankind and claiming that the difference between saint and rascal was merely superficial. A good prince ruled his land justly and benevolently; failure to do so was unmannerly and base, deserving deposition. The Taoist philosopher Zhuangzi was probably contemporary with Mengzi, and he too left an entertaining and memorable work. He was a mystic who cheerfully opposed the Confucian intellectual ideals and advocated an irresponsible and indifferent attitude to worldy matters.

Culture survived in the Hellenic world despite the many political paroxysms. The philosophers Epicurus and Zeno were in Athens, each preaching their own creed in the art of living. The former recommended full enjoyment of the good things of life since he did not believe in a future life. The latter, whose doctrine is called Stoicism, claimed that virtue was the will of providence: man should dismiss extrinsic values and pursue the cause of duty, the sole bringer of happiness.

Alexandria had become a new centre of culture. The mathematician Euclid worked here and scholarly Jews translated his sacred writings into Greek. This was the origin of the Septuagint or Greek version of the Old Testament. Manetho, the Egyptian priest, composed his register of the Pharaohs at this time.

The realm of Chandra Gupta Maurya appears to have extended over large areas of India, and information about this ruler derives mainly from fragmentary writings left by the Seleucid ambassador, Megasthenes. Practically nothing is known of Chandra Gupta's son and successor.

History records two more Indian rulers named Chandra Gupta. These lived in the 4th and 5th centuries AD and their kingdoms were quite certainly not identical with the above. It is convenient to designate them Chandra Gupta I and II.

A certain Zipoetes unobtrusively detached Asiatic Bithynia from the empire of Lysimachus and established a dynasty there. Zipoetes himself ruled in Bithynia 297-280.

Massilia, subsequently Marseilles, was an old Greek colony though by now the population was doubtless quite mixed. But its trade and shipping flourished and various Massilian subsidiary towns were founded on the Gallic and Iberian coasts. These included the settlements that later became Antibes and Nice. An outpost known as Hemeroscopium formed the foundation for the future Denia.

In Egypt Ptolemy I dedicated temples to Sarapis, a synthetic national god of both Greek and Egyptian character. The first Sarapeum was erected in Saqqarah where Apis bull mummies had been deposited for a thousand years or more. Another Sarapeum was built in Alexandria.

The era of the Olympian gods had by now vanished everywhere. There was widespread interest not only in the mystic religions of the Orient but also in the universal interpretations and practical wisdom of the Greek philosophers.

In Africa the capital of a prosperous Ethiopian realm was the ancient Egyptian Meroë. Skilled iron workers probably exported tools and other artefacts to the south and west.

In the land that later became Guatemala, talented artists from Izapa, Miraflores and Chicanel produced works that included reliefs showing a rain-god associated with the jaguar of the Olmecs.

The Chinese emperors of the Zhou (Chou) dynasty did not have much authority, but in the feudal state of Qin, a line of decisive rulers had formed a strong central government, popular among the commoners. A land reform had created peasant proprietors. Ditches and canals had been constructed between the fields. This irrigation system certainly benefitted the farmers, but above all it enabled the state to control the whole economy. The standard of living was rising in Qin, and the population was fast increasing.

India	Chandra Gupta Maurya
Syracuse	Agathocles
Babylon/Persia	Seleucus I Nicator
Thrace	Lysimachus
Egypt	Ptolemy II Soter
Macedonia	Cassander — Demetrius I
Rome	(Publius Decius Mus)
China	Zhou She Wang

300	299	298	297	296	295	294	293	292	291

HELLENES
HELLENES
CHINESE

In Italy the Roman republic continued to make war, year after year. In 298-290 the Third Samnite War was fought, involving Etruscans and Umbrians as well. This ended with a Roman victory and direct contact with the Greek towns in southern Italy which adjoined the territories of the defeated Samnites.

The historian Livy has a weird story to tell of the decisive battle of Sentinum in the Third Samnite War. Consul Publius Decius Mus, commanding the Roman army, decided, when facing defeat, to commit himself to the powers of the underworld, just as his father had once done. Dressed in ritual attire, he hurled himself into the fray, invoking death both on the enemy and himself. He claimed to be driving ahead of him fear and flight, murder and blood, and the enemy would follow in his wake.

Another moral story from the period of the Samnite wars concerns the consul, Marcus Curius Dentatus. He was sitting in his tent, preparing a pot of mashed turnips, when a Samnite delegation of negotiators arrived with presents. The consul calmly went on stirring his brew, informing the delegation that he preferred his earthenware pot to all their golden vessels, choosing to remain poor himself and rule instead over those who were wealthy.

While fighting Seleucus and rebellious subjects, the elderly Lysimachus was finally killed after a long and tumultuous life, and his empire, which had encompassed both Thrace and Asia Minor, fell with him. Seleucus now assumed supreme power and thereby became master of all the domains of Alexander the Great, excepting Egypt, Greece and the Indian territories. But when he was about to advance into Greece he was assassinated.
The death of Lysimachus resulted in the emergence of a number of new states in Asia Minor: Bythinia, Pontus and Pergamum. The most important of these was to be Pergamum, founded by the eunuch Philetaerus who had controlled state finances in the reign of Lysimachus and was therefore able to hand down a prosperous kingdom to his nephew Eumenes.

Demetrius I Poliorcetes made himself master of Macedonia and all Greece. Sparta, too, was put in a position where it had to surrender its formal independence.

Agathocles, who became tyrant of Syracuse, was an adventurous figure. There was a war in progress with Carthage whose brilliant general, Hamilcar, won great victories and finally surrounded Syracuse. Agathocles escaped, however, to Africa where with a few ships and a small force he plundered at liberty. The Carthaginian forces were recalled from Italy, after which Agathocles prudently returned home as well.

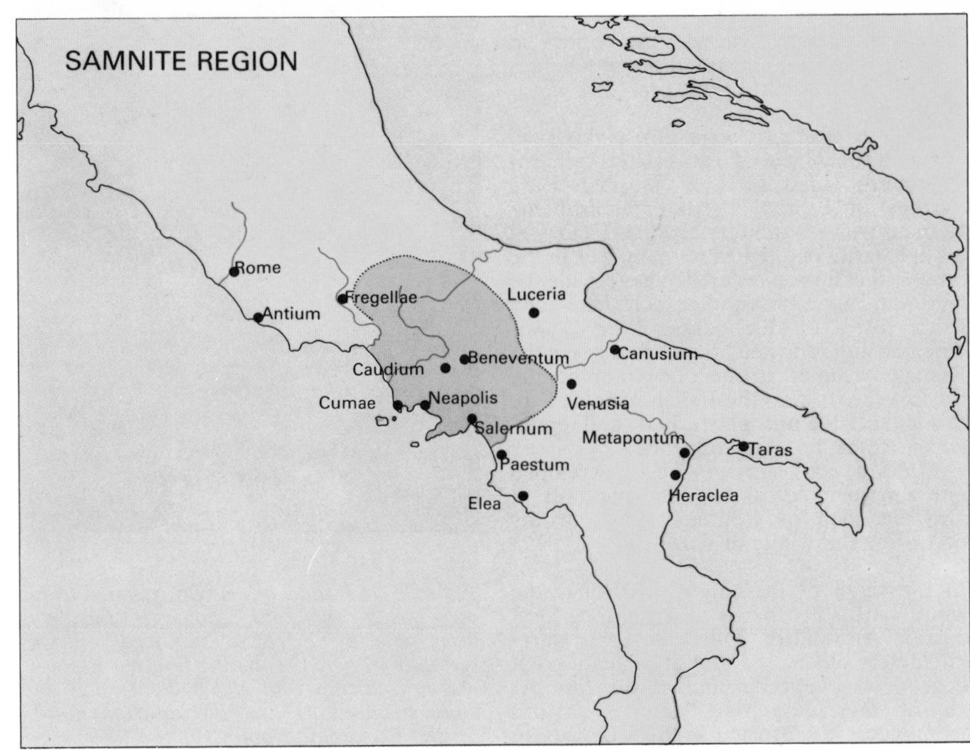
SAMNITE REGION
Rome
Antium
Fregellae
Luceria
Caudium
Beneventum
Canusium
Cumae
Neapolis
Venusia
Salernum
Metapontum
Taras
Paestum
Heraclea
Elea

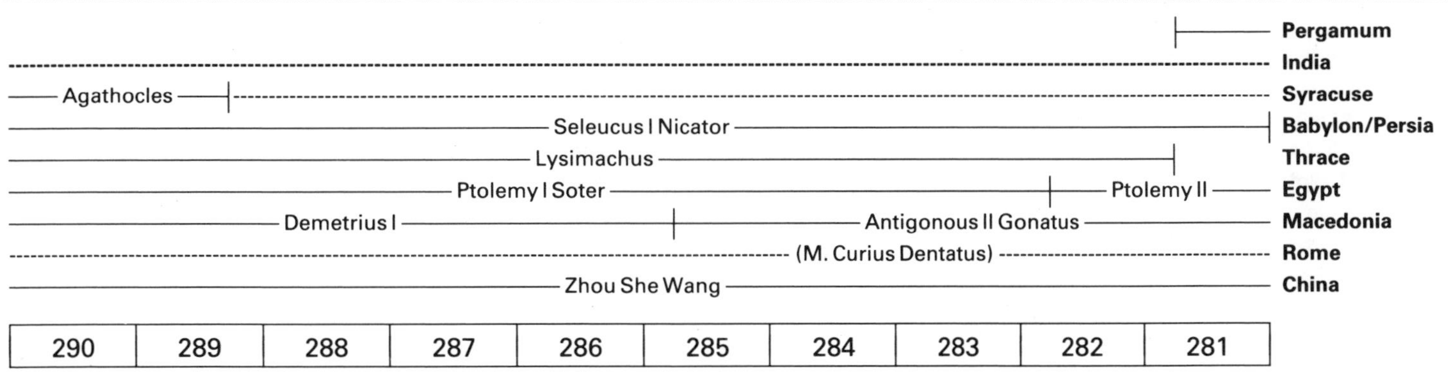
Pergamum
India
Agathocles
Syracuse
Seleucus I Nicator
Babylon/Persia
Lysimachus
Thrace
Ptolemy I Soter
Ptolemy II
Egypt
Demetrius I
Antigonous II Gonatus
Macedonia
(M. Curius Dentatus)
Rome
Zhou She Wang
China
290
289
288
287
286
285
284
283
282
281

INDIANS, PATNA
GREEK PHILOSOPHERS

The Balkan peninsula and Asia Minor were overrun by Celtic migrants in the 270s. The Macedonian king, Ptolemaeus Ceruanus, died fighting the Celts and the latter then swung around Thermopylae and attempted to take Delphi. They were repulsed, however, and withdrew north again. But other forces which crossed over into Asia by way of the Hellespont refused to be expelled; after pillaging and plundering at will, they finally settled in Phrygia in an area named after them–Galatia. This lawless, belligerent state long constituted a threat to all neighbouring countries.

An Hellenic kingdom was established in Bactria. It was administered on Greek lines and lasted for several centuries.

In Italy the Romans were now involved in war with the people of Taras (later Taranto) who were aided by their kinsman King Pyrrhus of Epirus. Pyrrhus terrified the Romans with his military elephants and won his first battle but he lost so many men in the process that he was reputed to have made the famous comment: "Another such victory and I am lost". In due course Pyrrhus was defeated and returned home, after which the Romans occupied, in one form or another, all the Greek cities on the Italian mainland. In this manner the unsophisticated rural republic of Rome became influenced by Greek civilization, and simultaneously developed into a major political and military power. It also extended its frontiers northward by occupying the whole of Etruria.

In the reign of Ptolemy Philadelphus the white marble lighthouse of Pharos was built outside Alexandria. This was visible thirty kilometres out to sea and at nights a great beacon was kept burning at the top. At almost the same time another famous monument was erected – the Colossus of Rhodes, a vast bronze statue straddling the harbour entrance and giving adequate clearance for the masts of ships passing below. Rhodes enjoyed a period of great economic expansion during the 3rd century BC, though the Colossus failed to last: it was destroyed by an earthquake in 224. The ruins of the Colossus remained where they fell for almost a millennium, until AD 672 when a Jewish merchant bought the bronze for scrap and transported it on 900 camels to Edessa.

Ptolemy II Philadelphus was married to his own sister Arsinoë. Although this was acceptable by Egyptian standards, it was certainly frowned on by the Greeks. Ptolemy was a politician who also built temples and cities. Bronze bust from Herculaneum, now in Museo Nazionale Naples.

Pharos and the Colossus of Rhodes are both included in the Seven Wonders of the World; making such lists was popular during the Hellenic era. The other wonders included Apollo's altar at Delos, (or, alternatively, Phidias' Zeus Statue at Olympia), the Egyptian pyramids, the hanging gardens of Semiramis in Babylon, the temple of Artemis at Ephesus, and the tomb of Mausolos at Halicarnassus. The Colosseum in Rome, often in later lists, had not yet been built.

Viksubuu or Veksuna, which was the Etruscans' religious centre, was taken by a Roman force in 280. The city was plundered and the victors took away an enormous booty, including 2000 statues which were to adorn the squares and gardens of Rome. The great age of the Etruscans had now passed, their cities became latinized and their language gradually declined into oblivion. It survived longest in the religious context (since Etruscan gods and rites were still venerated) and was used as a cultured language in Rome itself until the Christian era.

The Etruscan religion, manifested by a prophet named Tages and later also by a nymph named Vegoia, had a multitude of gods. Their Uni appears to be closely related to the Roman Juno, while Menerva, Maris, Nethuns and Artumas are easily identified with Minerva, Mars, Neptune and Artemis. Others were more obscure, and the Etruscan world also abounded in nameless griffins, sphinxes, furies and demons.

India	----- Aśoka -----
Syracuse	-----
Pergamum	----- Philetaerus -----
Syria	----- Antiochus I Soter -----
Egypt	----- Ptolemy II Philadelphus -----
Macedonia	----- Antigonus II Gonatus -----
Rome	----- (Caius Fabricius) -----
China	----- Zhou She Wang -----

280	279	278	277	276	275	274	273	272	271

HELLENES

The Seleucid empire. which still embraced Persia, Mesopotamia, Syria and Palestine, had already seen its best days. The Seleucid hold over its territories in the east and north continued to decline. The principal country in the area was now Syria and the capital Antiochia.

The year 264 saw the First Punic War, a massive and bloody contest between the two major powers, Rome and Carthage. The war lasted twenty-three years. First and foremost, it involved control of Sicily where King Hieron of Syracuse afforded the Romans firm support. In the fourth year of the war Consul Caius Duilius won the first naval battle for the Romans, giving rise to great rejoicing in Rome where prows from the captured Carthaginian vessels henceforth adorned the rostrum at the Forum.

The fact that the maritime Phoenicians could be defeated at sea by the Roman landlubbers is said to have been due to a simple combat device which the Romans had invented. Their ships were fitted with a sort of collapsible platform, known as a crow on account of the sharp iron "beak" on the underside of the front end. Normally the crow was kept raised but when the ship closed with an enemy vessel the hoist was released and the platform fell by its own weight so that the "beak" fastened into the enemy's deck. The Roman soldiers then crossed the platform and attacked as regular infantry.

The astronomer Aristarchus was working on Samos. He was not only aware that the Earth is round – many ancient thinkers had already realized this – but he also maintained that it rotates about its own axis and moves in orbit around the Sun.

The Indian king, Aśoka, grandson of Chandra Gupta, is notable for important records he left concerning his religion and language. He despatched Buddhist missionaries in all directions.

A military man named Hieron seized power in Syracuse. There were confrontations with Rome during the early part of his reign, but relations improved later.

Theocritus of Syracuse, now a young poet in his best years, founded the influential bucolic school in poetry.

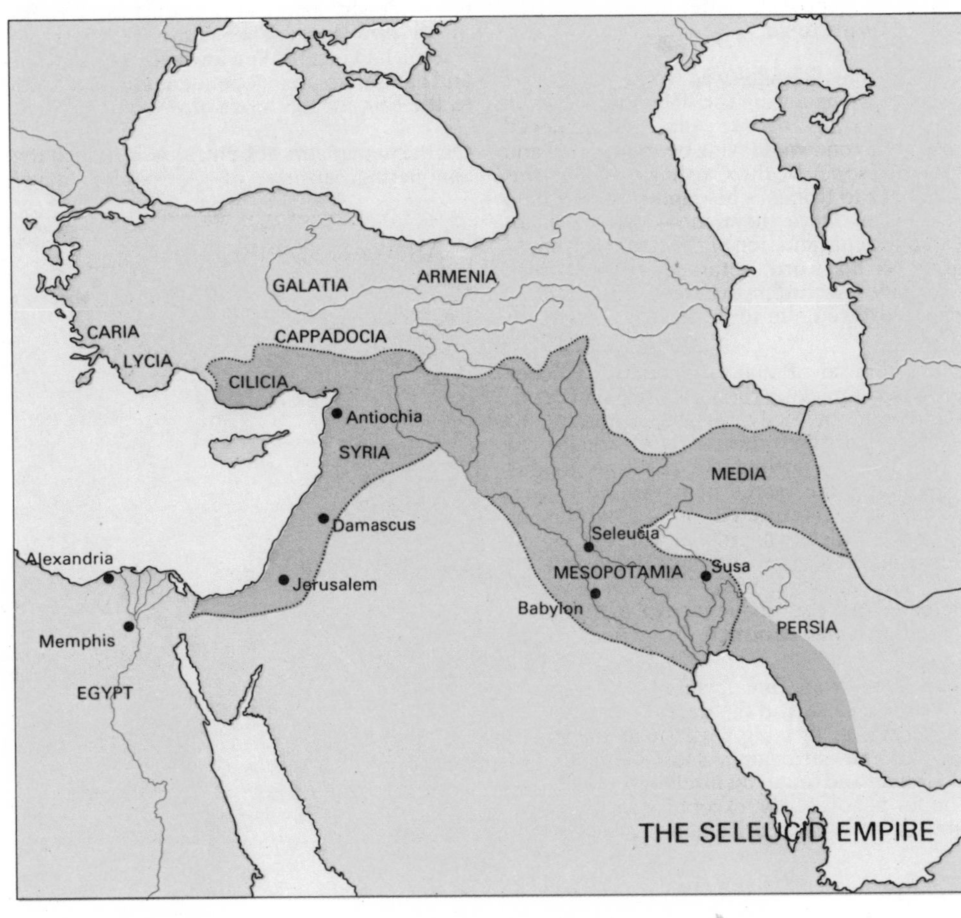
GALATIA
ARMENIA
CARIA
CAPPADOCIA
LYCIA
CILICIA
Antiochia
SYRIA
MEDIA
Damascus
Seleucia
Alexandria
MESOPOTAMIA
Susa
Jerusalem
Babylon
PERSIA
Memphis
EGYPT
THE SELEUCID EMPIRE

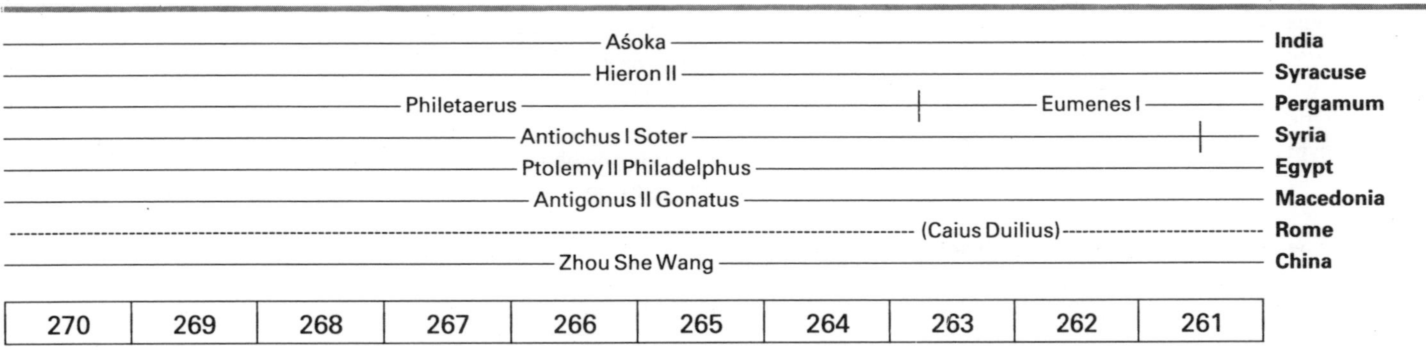
Aśoka — India
Hieron II — Syracuse
Philetaerus — Eumenes I — Pergamum
Antiochus I Soter — Syria
Ptolemy II Philadelphus — Egypt
Antigonus II Gonatus — Macedonia
(Caius Duilius) — Rome
Zhou She Wang — China
270
269
268
267
266
265
264
263
262
261

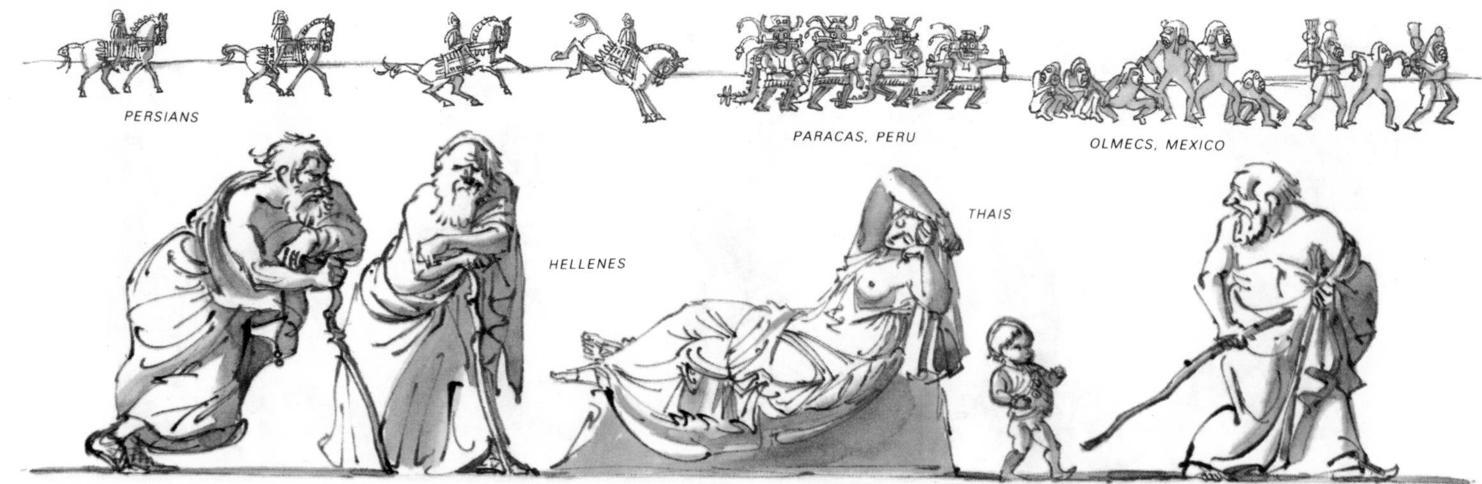
PERSIANS
PARACAS, PERU
OLMECS, MEXICO
THAIS
HELLENES

Aśoka was a very pious man who summoned a Buddhist meeting in his capital Pataliputra and issued remarkable edicts related to good deeds, claiming that he himself showed his subjects the best of examples. His inscriptions mention a number of notable contemporaries in the Hellenistic world and this makes it somewhat easier to establish the period of his reign.

Caius Atilius Regulus was Roman consul on two occasions during the 250s, but it was in the following decade that he achieved historical renown. Having been defeated and taken prisoner by the Carthaginians, he was sent back to Rome by his captors to negotiate for peace. Once there, however, he advocated the continuation of the war and then, as good as his word, returned voluntarily to Carthage. According to Cicero, the Carthaginians tortured him to death.

The admiral Publius Claudius Pulcher proposed attacking the Carthaginian fleet at Drepanum in Sicily. When, according to Roman custom, the Augurs sought to determine the attitude of the gods to this expedition, the sacred hens refused to eat, which was interpreted as a bad omen. Claudius Pulcher angrily kicked the sacred hens into the sea, exclaiming: "If they will not eat then let them drink." He was severely defeated in the subsequent naval battle and in due course was punished.

The long war, meanwhile, was moving towards a close and the decisive action took place at sea. In a big battle near the Lipari Islands, the Carthaginians lost a large part of their fleet and found themselves compelled to sue for peace. Sicily, except for the Syracuse area, now became a Roman province.

The Ptolemies and the Seleucids were constantly at war with each other, which strained the resources of both sides. The Seleucids were certainly unaware that dangerous neighbours were looming up in the east. The Parthians, who lived to the south-east of the Caspian Sea, were conducting successful campaigns against the Greeks in all directions. The satrap Diodotus of Bactria had just broken away from Antiochia and had set up an independent Hellenic state to the east, in the heart of Asia.

On the high plains of Central Asia, which the conquering armies of Alexander never entered, the independent kingdom of Cappadocia was established around the year 260. Here Ariarathes Eusebes made himself king over a people who were probably for the most part of Median origin.

In the middle of the 3rd century an equestrian people, the Sarmatians, marched westward, crossed the Don, established themselves along the Dnieper and soon gained control of the entire fertile region north of the Black Sea. The small Scythian principalities here were transformed into vassal states, though the Greek federation in the Crimea, the Bosporus kingdom, continued to hold out.

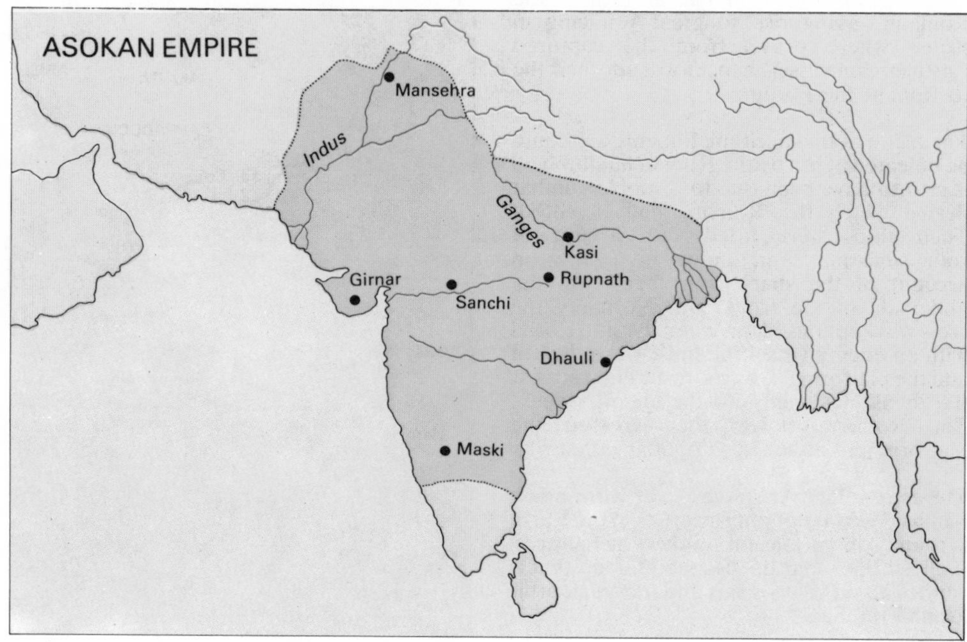
ASOKAN EMPIRE
Mansehra
Indus
Ganges
Kasi
Girnar
Rupnath
Sanchi
Dhauli
Maski

	260	259	258	257	256	255	254	253	252	251
India	Aśoka									
Syracuse	Hieron II									
Pergamum	Eumenes I									
Syria	Antiochus II Theos									
Egypt	Ptolemy II Philadelphus									
Macedonia	Antigonus II Gonatus									
Rome	(C. Atilius Regulus)									
China	Zhou She Wang					Zhou Jun				

HELLENES
INDIANS,
BIHAR

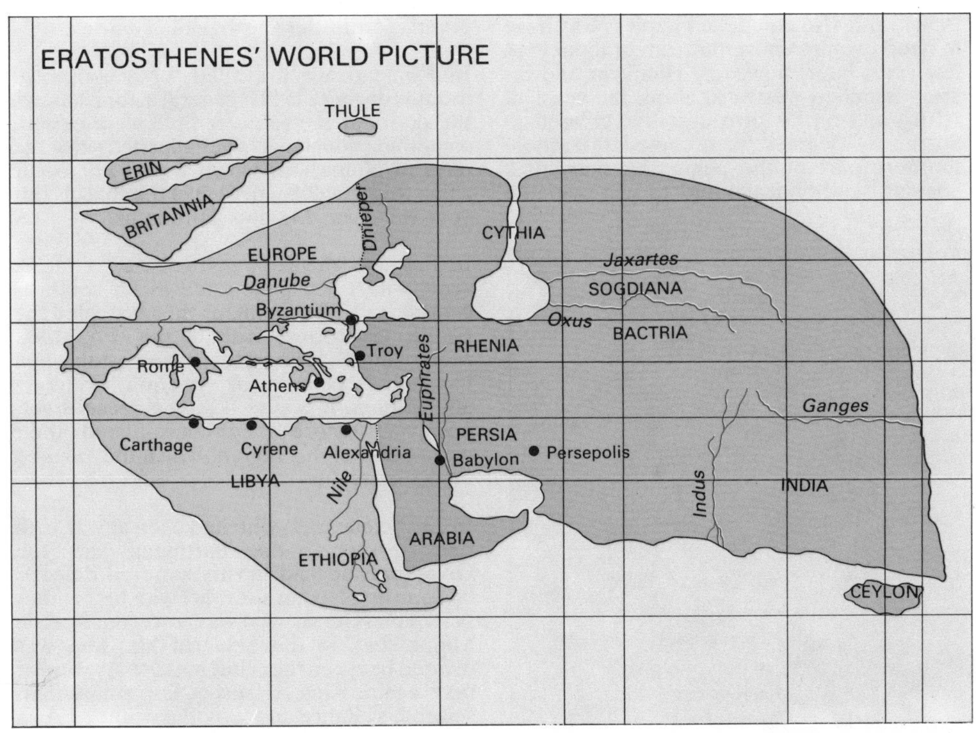
ERATOSTHENES' WORLD PICTURE
THULE
ERIN
BRITANNIA
EUROPE
Dnieper
CYTHIA
Danube
Jaxartes
SOGDIANA
Byzantium
Oxus
BACTRIA
Troy
Euphrates
RHENIA
Rome
Athens
Ganges
Carthage
Cyrene
Alexandria
PERSIA
Babylon
Persepolis
LIBYA
Nile
Indus
INDIA
ARABIA
ETHIOPIA
CEYLON

Eratosthenes' map of the world looks fairly unimpressive today. The American continent is missing and so are the East Asian and Australian islands. He was, nevertheless, a pioneer, and made a major contribution to geography.

Among the many scientists residing and working in Ptolemaic Alexandria was the geographer Eratosthenes. He was the first man to have made a realistic calculation of the Earth's circumference. Having determined that on midsummer day the sun was at its zenith in Egyptian Syene, or Aswan, on the following midsummer day he measured the altitude of the sun in Alexandria and found that the angle was one-fiftieth of a circle arc. Since he knew that the distance between Alexandria and Syene was 5000 stadia, he was able to determine that the circumference of the Earth must be fifty times 5000 stadia, i.e. 250,000 stadia. This figure is correct to within a mere 300 km.

Eratosthenes was also the originator of our grid system of longitude and latitude. His angles were right-angles, so that his projection was cylindrical; and his maps left much more to be desired as well. In the context of the Mediterranean region, however, which was the only part of the world he really knew, his notions were relatively sound. His latitudes were more accurate than the longitudes, for the latter were difficult to calculate in the absence of a reliable chronometer.

In China the long-lived Zhou dynasty finally died out and was succeeded by a dynasty known as Qin (Ch'in). Although this name was hardly Chinese, it was to give rise to the name China. Qin far to the west, had long been expanding its power; one feudal state after another had been annexed and when the last of the Zhous lost his final domains and retreated into obscurity, the prince of Qin assumed the title of emperor. He went down in history as Qin Shi Huang Di, which means quite simply first Emperor of Qin. He was the first ruler of a united China and as emperor he set about reorganizing and centralizing the government. The political influence of the feudal lords was systematically eliminated, a standard written language was prescribed and enforced, and coins, measures, weights and even road widths were standardized. The first emperor of Qin also began construction of the Great Wall of China for a distance of 2400 km. Yet despite these achievements Qin Shi Huang Di left behind an unfavourable reputation for his numerous nation-wide projects involved large-scale shifts of population and much incidental suffering. Individual liberty was curtailed and strict censorship introduced.

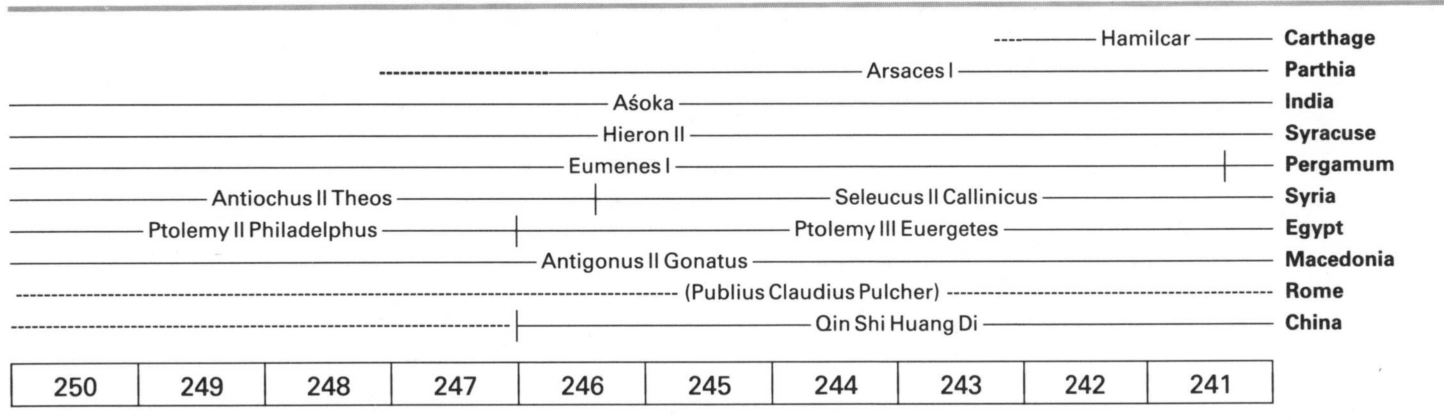
Hamilcar — Carthage
Arsaces I — Parthia
Aśoka — India
Hieron II — Syracuse
Eumenes I — Pergamum
Antiochus II Theos — Seleucus II Callinicus — Syria
Ptolemy II Philadelphus — Ptolemy III Euergetes — Egypt
Antigonus II Gonatus — Macedonia
(Publius Claudius Pulcher) — Rome
Qin Shi Huang Di — China
250 249 248 247 246 245 244 243 242 241

CHINA

HELLENES
SCYTHIAN SLAVES

Defeat by Rome was followed in Carthage by revolt among the mercenary troops. General Hamilcar Barca re-established Carthaginian authority in Africa, but not on Sardinia and Corsica where the insurgents placed themselves under Roman protection. The Romans promptly appropriated these islands, which had not been surrendered in the peace treaty, and also compelled hapless Carthage to hand over an enormous sum of money. A few years later, however, Hamilcar and his army marched westward along the coast of Africa and on his own initiative crossed to Spain. By degrees he occupied the whole southern part of the peninsula, married a Spaniard and endeavoured to win over the population to the Carthaginian cause.

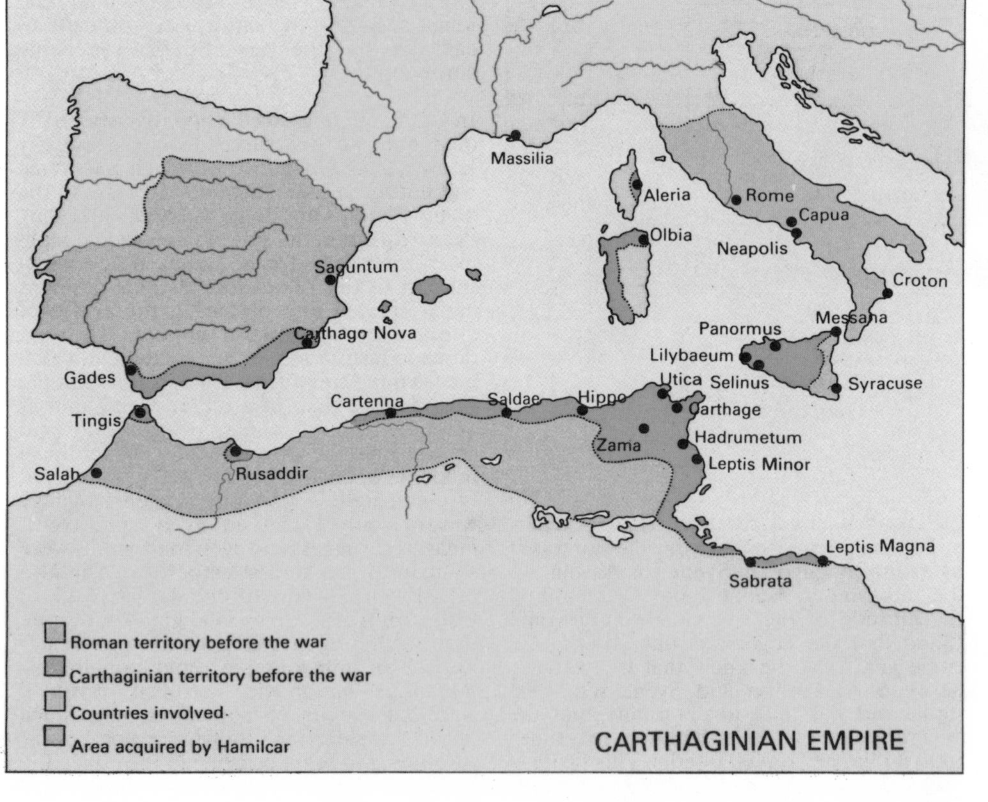
Massilia
Aleria
Rome
Capua
Olbia
Neapolis
Saguntum
Croton
Carthago Nova
Panormus
Messana
Lilybaeum
Gades
Utica
Selinus
Syracuse
Cartenna
Saldae
Hippo
Carthage
Tingis
Zama
Hadrumetum
Salah
Rusaddir
Leptis Minor
Leptis Magna
Sabrata
Roman territory before the war
Carthaginian territory before the war
Countries involved
Area acquired by Hamilcar
CARTHAGINIAN EMPIRE

In Rome peace prevailed for a couple of months during 235. To general astonishment, the doors of the Janus temple were closed, something which had not happened since the days of Numa and which would not occur again for a generation. One of the consuls this year was Titus Manlius Torquatus.

In the 220s the Romans defeated a Gallic army which had penetrated as far south as central Italy. The Romans then occupied the Gallic territories around the Po, took Mediolanum (future Milan), and established the military colonies of Placentia, Cremona and Mutina. It was to be some decades yet, however, before they consolidated their occupation of this region, which they named Gallia Cisalpina.

In 239 Seleucus II, who had been at war with the Egyptians, the Parthians and the Galatians and had mostly suffered defeats, became involved in a conflict with his brother Antiochus Hierax who was co-regent in Asia Minor. In 234 the Seleucid kingdom was divided between them but by 228 they were at odds again. King Attalus of Pergamum then seized his chance and took the whole of Asia Minor from Antiochus Hierax.

In 238 the Egyptians produced a calendar which set the duration of the solar year at 365 days and 6 hours, and they put the odd hours together to form one intercalary day every four years.

Little is known about the origins and early history of the Parthian kingdom. King Arsaces I, who is regarded as its founder, appears to have lived and ruled at this time.

India	Aśoka
Carthage	Hamilcar
Parthia	Arsaces I
Syracuse	Hieron II
Pergamum	Attalus I Soter
Syria	Seleucus II Callinicus
Egypt	Ptolemy III Euergetes
Macedonia	Antigonus II — Demetrius II
Rome	(Titus Manlius Torquatus)
China	Qin Shi Huang Di

240	239	238	237	236	235	234	233	232	231

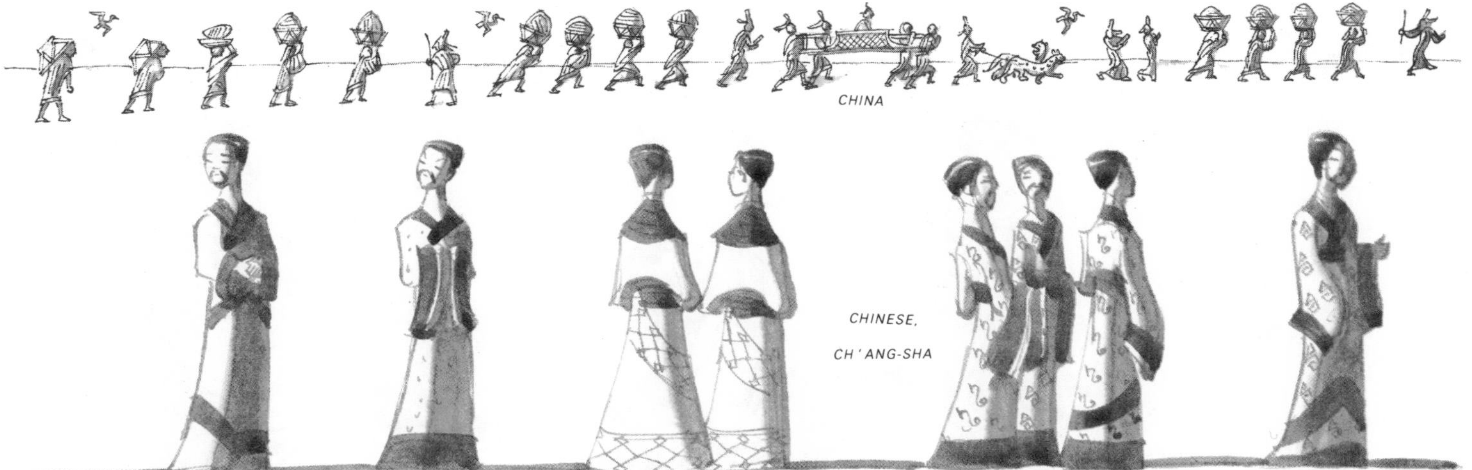
CHINA
CHINESE,
CH'ANG-SHA

Hamilcar died in a battle in Spain and was succeeded by his son-in-law Hasdrubal who energetically pursued his father's work and founded the provincial capital of Carthagena (Carthago Nova). Here in due course Hasdrubal was assassinated and the army proclaimed Hamilcar's twenty-four year-old son Hannibal his father's political heir.

Aśoka, for all his Buddhist piety, had hardly been popular with the Brahmans in India and a Brahman counter-reformation appears to have begun immediately after Aśoka's death. This doubtless contributed to the disintegration of his large empire. Nothing is known of the subsequent fate of this dynasty.

From this decade the name Scipio often occurred in the list of Roman consuls; Cnaeus and Publius Scipio were brothers.

King Cleomenes III of Sparta enjoyed great military success at this period and defeated various coalitions in the local wars among small states. In 226 he tried to implement a major social reform which would have liberated the helots and introduced some form of democratic order in the city. But the landowners called on the Achaean federation and Macedonia for assistance. Cleomenes was defeated at Sellasia in 222 and a couple of years later he died in Egypt.

The last of the independent states in China was crushed by Shi Huang Di in 221. The demarcation point between the dynasties of Zhou and Qin is therefore sometimes set at this year which, in fact, brought to an end the period of the Warring States.

Generations continued to work on the Great Wall of China. Shi Huang Di, who initiated the project, sent out tens of thousands of labourers, and their condemnation of him echoed through the annals of Chinese literature. Nothing complimentary was ever said in Chinese literature about the first emperor of Qin, who was evidently a despot who tightened up the penal code and even extended capital punishment to include the relations of the condemned person.

A series of forts and earthworks along China's western frontier had long been strongpoints against Turkic tribes known as Xiongnu; the Huns. This system was now developed into a defence line which was continuously extended. When completed, the Great Wall of China was about 5000 kilometres in length and had 24,000 fortified towers.

------	**India**
Hamilcar | Hasdrubal |	**Carthage**
Arsaces I	**Parthia**
Hieron II	**Syracuse**
Attalus I Soter	**Pergamum**
Seleucus II Callinicus | Seleucus III Soter | Antiochus III	**Syria**
Ptolemy III Euergetes | Ptolemy IV	**Egypt**
Demetrius II | Antigonus III Doson |	**Macedonia**
(Cn. & P. Cornelius Scipio)	**Rome**
Qin Shi Huang Di	**China**

230	229	228	227	226	225	224	223	222	221

220-211 BC

CHINA
CARTHAGE
HELLENES
EGYPTIAN
GENTLEWOMAN

The Second Punic War was fought from 218 to 201 BC. This was another trial of strength between Rome and Carthage, though it affected the whole of the western civilized world. Carthaginian policy was being determined for the moment by the aristocratic Barca family which, contrary to the council's approval, had created an empire for itself in Spain. The Romans, no less imperialistic in outlook, attempted to halt this expansion by forming an alliance with the half-Greek town of Saguntum, the only place south of the Ebro on the Spanish coast that was still resisting. Even so, the young Carthaginian general, Hannibal, captured Saguntum. A Roman mission was then despatched to Carthage with the demand that Hannibal should be handed over - a gesture that was tantamount to a declaration of war. In the autumn of 218 Hannibal marched on Rome from Spain. The Romans managed to block the coastal road by landing an army at Massilia, but Hannibal took another route up the Rhone to the Alps and then crossed to the Italian side with his foot soldiers and his elephants; a remarkable achievement which took him fifteen days. He formed an alliance with the Gauls in the Po valley and then continued southward. At Lake Trasimenus he encountered a Roman army under Consul Caius Flaminius, who had recently been responsible for building the Via Flaminia. Flaminius was killed and his army destroyed or captured. Instead of making straight for Rome, Hannibal marched south to Campania where in 216 he won the great Battle of Cannae. The following year he entered into an alliance with Macedonia; Syracuse, whose king, Hieron, had recently died, also joined the campaign against Rome.

The Romans acted very resolutely towards Syracuse. An army under Marcus Claudius Marcelius briskly occupied its territories and took the town itself after a long siege. As a citizen of Syracuse Archimedes produced a number of military devices which helped to hold off the enemy. But in the course of certain religious festivities which dulled the alertness of the defenders, the city was stormed and Archimedes, engrossed in a mathematical problem, was killed.

Meanwhile Hannibal's movements in southern Italy were being watched by another Roman army under Consul Quintus Fabius Maximus. He was careful not to confront Hannibal in open battle and concentrated instead upon strangling the latter's communications. This earned the cautious consul the title of Cunctator, the Delayer.

A large number of anonymous communities and cultures were at this time flourishing on the American continent, though they left no written word behind them; only a miscellaneous selection of pots, tools and textiles. Modern archaeologists have designated these finds, from widely differing periods, according to their provenance: Hopewell, Cochise, Teotihuacán, La Venta, Izapa, San Augustin, Barrancas, Tocuyano, etc. Tocuyano was located in what is now Venezuela, and here the people appear already to have been growing potatoes.

Antiochus III opened his career by quelling a rebellious satrap on the Tigris and then attempted to extend his authority over all the territories that Alexander the Great had at one time conquered and united. This single-minded policy of reconquest was designed primarily to compel the various princes who had replaced the former satraps to recognize his sovereignty. He met with varying success. In a major battle at Raphia in 217 he lost Palestine and certain Lebanese regions, but by making concessions to his royal colleagues in Pergamum and to Bythinia's Nicomedes he succeeded subsequently in retaking an area in Asia Minor. Between 212 and 203 he conducted major campaigns in Armenia, Mesopotamia, Media, Parthia, Hyrcania, Bactria and India. In 205 he assumed the title of "great king", according to the custom of Alexander and the early Persian rulers.

When crossing the Alps, Hannibal had with him a number of elephants, but by the time he reached Lake Trasimenus he had only one left, which he rode himself. It is said that back in Carthage even civilians knew the names of the army's elephants and, as this illustration shows, these animals even appeared on Carthaginian coins.

Carthage	Hannibal
Parthia	Arsaces I — Arsaces II
Syracuse	Hieron II — -----------
Pergamum	Attalus I Soter
Syria	Antiochus III
Egypt	Ptolemy IV Philopator
Macedonia	Philip V
Rome	---- (C. Flaminius) ---- (Q. Fabius Maximus) ----
China	Qin Shi Huang Di

220	219	218	217	216	215	214	213	212	211

CHINA
INDIANS,
MATHURA
HELLENES
CHINESE

While Hannibal was threatening the Romans in Italy the Carthaginian possessions in Spain were being attacked by the Scipio brothers. They both died in this fateful campaign and the son of one of them, Publius Cornelius, took command in their place. He proved to be a great soldier who immediately took Carthagena and remorselessly expelled the Carthaginians from the country. He then crossed to Africa, compelling Hannibal's army to leave Italy and be shipped home to defend Carthage itself. The armies met at Zama where Hannibal was roundly defeated and fled into exile. Carthage was now disarmed and lost its status as a major power.

Mathematics and technology were flourishing in the large Greek cities, especially Alexandria where the Ptolemies had established an institute, known as the Museion, with a large central library and scholarships for artists and researchers. Euclid had been dead for a generation now, but his geometry was not forgotten. The *Elements* was of enormous practical value to Roman engineers. Until his death Archimedes of Syracuse had been a close friend of some of the Alexandrian scholars. Not only had he calculated the value of pi with great exactitude, he had also discovered the physical law to the effect that the volume of a body immersed in fluid is equal to the volume of fluid it displaces.

Motivated by his animosity towards the doctrines of Confucius, the emperor, Qin Shi Huang Di had all books in the kingdom of China confiscated and burned. This measure, taken in 213, destroyed practically the entire body of Chinese literature. In time, however, the Confucians were able to reconstruct some of the most important writings.

In 210 the empire builder Shi Huang Di died and his dynasty was quickly dissolved. A general named Liu Bang emerged victorious from the subsequent power intrigues and went down in history as Han Gao Zu; the founder of the Han dynasty. This marked the end of the political system of small feudal states. Under the Han dynasty China grew into a vast empire based on the Qin dynasty's brutal policy of unification.

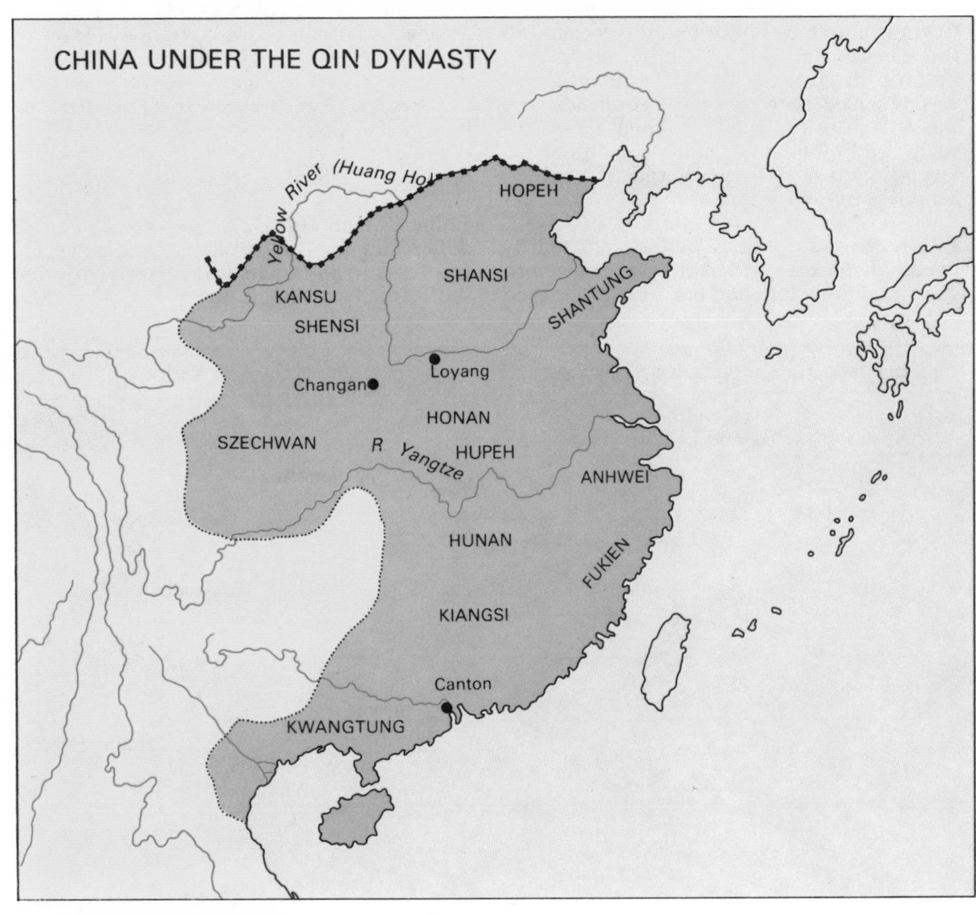
CHINA UNDER THE QIN DYNASTY
Yellow River (Huang Ho)
HOPEH
SHANSI
SHANTUNG
KANSU
SHENSI
Loyang
Changan
HONAN
SZECHWAN
R Yangtze
HUPEH
ANHWEI
HUNAN
FUKIEN
KIANGSI
Canton
KWANGTUNG

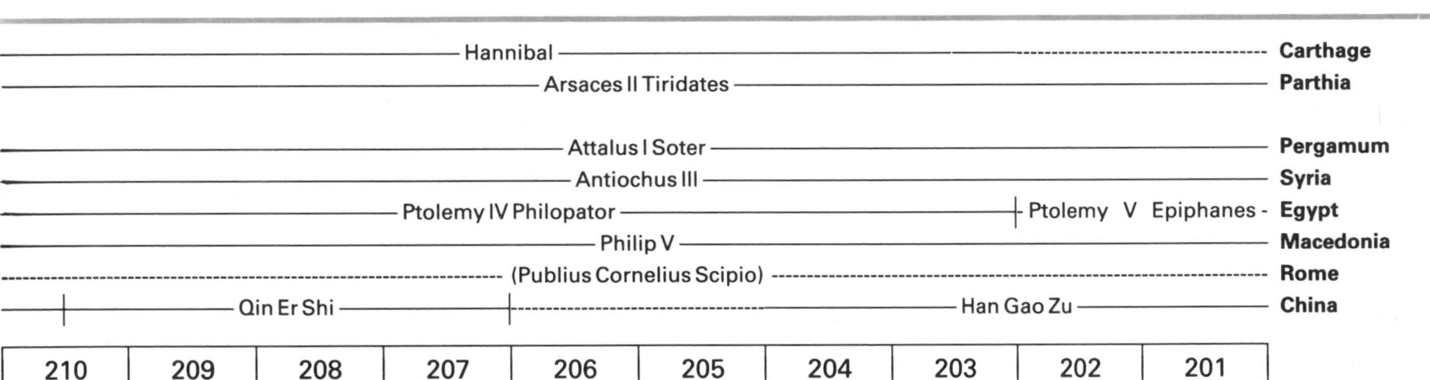
Hannibal — Carthage
Arsaces II Tiridates — Parthia
Attalus I Soter — Pergamum
Antiochus III — Syria
Ptolemy IV Philopator — Ptolemy V Epiphanes - Egypt
Philip V — Macedonia
(Publius Cornelius Scipio) — Rome
Qin Er Shi — Han Gao Zu — China
210 209 208 207 206 205 204 203 202 201

HELLENES

After the fall of Carthage, the Romans turned on Macedonia with a large army and the battle of Cynoscephalae took place in 198. Consul Titus Quinctius Flaminius was victorious and the subsequent peace settlement cost the Macedonian king his dominion over Greece. At the Isthmian games in Corinth Flaminus had a herald proclaim all the Greek states, free, independent and absolved from taxation. The announcement was received with incredulous silence and was therefore repeated, at which there was such wild jubilation that, according to legend, crows flying overhead tumbled senseless into the arena.

In Greece itself politics were dominated by two confederacies: the Aetolian league with its capital in Delphi and the Achaean league which held Peloponnesus. The latter had a general named Philopoemen and was allied with Rome. Philopoemen captured Sparta where, after the fall of Cleomenes, constitutional monarchy had been abolished and two tyrants were building a new and powerful city wall. Philopoemen sold 3000 Spartan citizens as slaves when they refused to obey his order to emigrate. But in 183 the city of Messene defected from the league, took Philopoemen prisoner and forced him to swallow a cup of poison. The politics of the small Greek states continued to vacillate. Thus for a while, Sparta was forced into the Achaean league.

Emperor Han Hui Di allowed himself to be dominated by his mother, the dowager-empress Lu; and when he died at an early age she formally assumed power in China. She attempted to replace her late husband's other sons by another woman, but they were on their guard and when Lu died they exterminated her entire family, whereupon the eldest son of her rival became emperor.

At last a Latin literature began to emerge. In 184 the playwright Plautus died, having written over a hundred comedies, twenty of which have survived. The same year Marcus Porcius Cato was appointed consul in Rome and fulfilled his duties with zealous severity, attacking luxury, affluence and foreign customs. He was also a writer whose works included a book on agriculture and a number of succinct maxims, as, for example, his advice to would-be speechmakers: *"Rem tene, verba sequenter"*– "stick to the point; the words will follow".

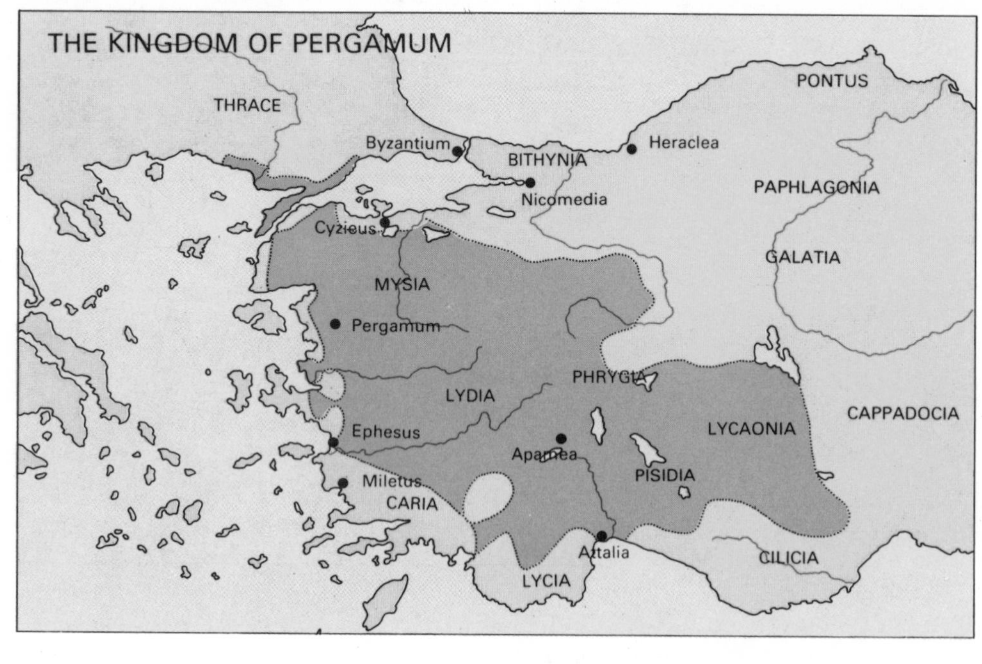
THE KINGDOM OF PERGAMUM
THRACE
PONTUS
Byzantium
BITHYNIA
Heraclea
Nicomedia
PAPHLAGONIA
Cyzicus
GALATIA
MYSIA
Pergamum
PHRYGIA
LYDIA
CAPPADOCIA
Ephesus
LYCAONIA
Apamea
PISIDIA
Miletus
CARIA
Attalia
CILICIA
LYCIA

The Roman consul Titus Quinctius Flaminius, depicted on a gold coin. British Museum, London. Flaminius, like many other Roman generals, had received a Greek education. In this way Hellenic culture was promoted in Rome.

Parthia	Arsaces II Tiridates
Pergamum	Attalus I Soter (200–197); Eumenes II Soter (197–191)
Syria	Antiochus III
Egypt	Ptolemy V Epiphanes
Macedonia	Philip V
Rome	(T. Quinctius Flaminius)
China	Han Gao Zu (200–195); Han Hui Di (195–191)

200	199	198	197	196	195	194	193	192	191

HELLENES

The royal library in Pergamum contained perhaps a quarter of a million manuscripts. Some of these were on parchment, an excellent material said to have been introduced when for some reason the Egyptians stopped exporting papyrus to Pergamum.

In Central Asia the Hellenic kingdom of Bactria was still prospering. During his Oriental expedition, Antiochus III had formally recognized Euthydemus of Magnesia as king there and had even promised to marry his daughter to the latter's son. But Euthydemus was not really the vassal of Antiochus; Bactria was fully independent. The crown prince, Demetrius, was an able general who during this reign conquered the Kabul region and the Punjab in India. But Demetrius was soon ejected by an even more formidable warrior named Eucratides. the latter was probably the most powerful ruler in Bactria's history, and was also the last to reign over both Bactria and the Indian territories. Arriving home from a successful campaign in India, he was murdered by his son who detested him so much that he would not even grant him a decent burial.

Egypt remained neutral in the conflict between Antiochus, Macedonia and Rome, but this was a costly decision. It lost Egypt various possessions on the Aegean Sea and the south coast of Asia Minor, which were seized uncompromisingly by the victors. All that Egypt managed to retain was Thera, a few parts of Crete and Arsinoë on Peloponnesus. Cyprus remained under Ptolemaean rule, as did Cyrene in Africa.

Ptolemy Epiphanes was still a boy, whose principal interests were sports and falconry and who for the most part left government to others. Yet he possessed sufficient authority to instruct an able minister who had been his tutor to poison himself and tortured to death some rebels who had objected to paying taxes. As a reaction against foreign influence, Greek was abolished as the official language in the Egyptian administration, and later, too, in the courts. The text of the Rosetta Stone, which some 2000 years later was to solve the riddle of hieroglyphics, relates mainly to these language reforms.

King Antiochus III, who at the last moment had entered the fray on the side of the Macedonians, was immediately defeated and expelled. The Romans then invaded Asia where their steadfast ally Eumenes II of Pergamum profited greatly from their successes. In the peace settlement Antiochus III had to cede half of Asia Minor to Eumenes.

All the kings of Pergamum were patrons of the arts and sciences. Their wealth was fabulous and their cultural influence extended beyond the frontiers of their own kingdom. Thus on the square in Athens they erected a magnificent building known as Attalus' stoa, which was subsequently restored and converted into a museum for the many treasures excavated locally. The capital of Pergamum is also of archaeological interest since it was one of the most magnificent cities of the Greek world, and still a wonder even after it had fallen into ruin and been deprived of most of its treasures.

The altar of Zeus from Pergamum was taken to Berlin by German archaeologists and can be seen there in a museum. In the course of time much else was also removed from Pergamum and yet this city, with its extensive ruins, is an impressive sight.

Arsaces III Priapatius	Parthia
Eumenes II Soter	Pergamum
Antiochus III – Seleucus IV Philopator	Syria
Ptolemy V Epiphanes	Egypt
Philip V	Macedonia
(Marcus Percius Cato)	Rome
Han Hui Di – Lü Hou	China

190	189	188	187	186	185	184	183	182	181

180-171 BC

CHINA
HELLENES

The central Asian people whom the Chinese called Xiongnu, were later known in the West as the Huns. They were nomads, though politically quite well organized, and by now they were consolidated as a major power under a chieftain named Mao Dun. The Huns had long harassed the Chinese; twenty years earlier they had surrounded the Emperor Gao Zu and his entire army which had scarcely managed to fight its way out. Since then they had made war continuously on China, with varying success. In 176 Mao Dun suddenly turned westward from the Ordos plateau outside the Great Wall and attacked a people living in that region. In Chinese these were known as the Yuechi though, oddly enough, they spoke an Indo-European language known as Tocharian. The Huns slew their king, made a goblet out of his skull and drove the whole race westward, first into the Ili valley, then to the Jaxartes river and the Tashkent region. Here it was the turn of the Tochari to expel a tribe called the Sakas who moved south into Bactria (Afghanistan) and there destroyed an Hellenic kingdom that had flourished in these parts since the expedition of Alexander the Great. The Tochari pursued the Sakas to this region and eventually created the so-called Indo-Scythian empire, which had a very advanced culture.

Parthia was also affected by these events. Two Parthian kings were killed fighting the Sakas during the subsequent decades.

The mathematician Apollonius from Perga was now an old man. He had issued a work on the conic section and made familiar such Greek terms as ellipse, parabola and hyperbole.

Philometor means "he who loves his mother", and Ptolemy VI received this title because he was under the guardianship of his mother Cleopatra. At the age of twenty he made war on Antiochus Epiphanes in Syria and was imprisoned, enabling his brother Ptolemy Physcon to become king of Egypt instead. But Antiochus helped Ptolemy Philometor to reclaim his throne. The relationship between them remained hostile and Ptolemy Physcon sought the aid of Rome. The Romans then made him ruler of Libya and Cyrene while Ptolemy Philometor continued to reign over Egypt and Cyprus. Physcon, incidentally, means 'stomach'. It seems unlikely that in most cases the Ptolemies chose their own surnames.

The Roman consuls and generals of the 170s were not very popular with the historians and appear to have been insignificant individuals mainly bent on self-interest. Roman victories led to vast economic expansion. Treasure flowed in and there was a lucrative trade in slaves collected from Sardinia, Spain, Epirus, Galatia and Africa.

The Chinese emperor Wen Di introduced a form of military-tenure system by providing his troops along the northern frontier with small-holdings so that they could be self-sufficient. He also permitted anyone who so wished to make his own coins, provided the denomination corresponded to the value of the metal; this soon proved an imprudent reform.

The face of Nordic landscape was gradually changing. More parts of Finland and Svealand were exposed by the sea as the process of land elevation continued. On the other hand, in the south-west coastal region of Denmark the terrain was sinking and producing more fenland.

Far left: the Swedish Baltic Sea coast was rising as a result of land elevation at the rate of about 50 centimetres a century. Left: Han Chinese grave figure. Metropolitan Museum, New York.

Parthia — Arsaces III Priapatius — Phraates I
Pergamum — Eumenes II Soter
Syria — Seleucus IV Philopator — Antiochus IV Epiphanes
Egypt — Cleopatra I & Ptolemy VI Philometor — Ptolemy VI Philometor & Cleopatra II
Macedonia — Philip V — Perseus
Rome — (Lucius Fulvius Nobilior)
China — Lü Hou — Han Wen Di

180	179	178	177	176	175	174	173	172	171

PERSIANS
CHINA
INDIANS,
BHARHUT

Rome, which preserved its somewhat rural atmosphere, now acquired its first large public buildings, mainly through the efforts of the general Lucius Fulvius Nobilior, noted by historians exclusively for his municipal philanthropy. A more remarkable figure was Lucius Aemilius Paullus who not only won a major war but also originated a proverb. He was married to a beautiful lady named Papiria and they had attractive children. There was consternation among his friends when he suddenly left her. When they reproached him for this, he pointed to his shoes and observed that they were both new and good looking; bet, he added, nobody but he knew where they pinched.

Rome went to war once again with Macedonia and other Greek states, and this culminated in 168 at the battle of Pydna where the elderly general, Lucius Aemilius Paullus, defeated King Perseus of Persia, taking him and his entire family prisoners. The spoils were so immense that the citizens of Rome were absolved from taxes for several centuries to come. Macedonia was divided up into four separate republics. Epirus was methodically sacked and 150,000 of its citizens were made slaves. Rhodes was ruined economically when the Romans established a free port at Delos where for centuries to come countless numbers of slaves were sold and resold.

Since 198 Palestine, long ruled by the Ptolemies of Egypt, had formed part of the cosmopolitan Seleucid kingdom, which Antiochus Ephipanes endeavoured to Hellenize. This was opposed, of course, by members of the Jewish priesthood; so Antiochus embarked on a policy of relentless persecution to stamp out Jewish dissension. Led by the priest's son, Judas Maccabeus, the Jews defeated two stronger armies, reconsecrated the temple in Jerusalem in 164 and made Judas Maccabeus high priest. He established an alliance with Rome, but this resulted in a swift offensive by the Seleucids.

The Ponte Rotto in Rome is now all that remains of the classical Pons Aemelius at the Forum Boarium, built in two stages, beginning in 179 BC. Earlier still there was a wooden bridge, Pons Sublicius, which crossed to the Etruscan side at about the same place.

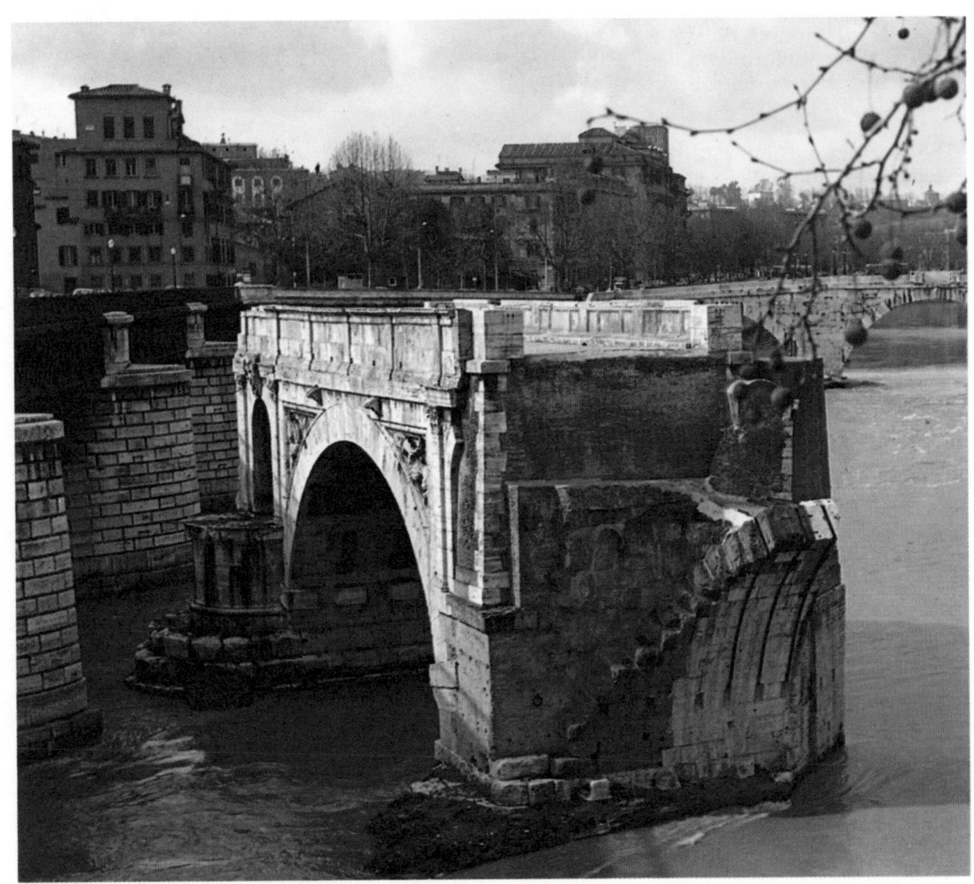

Judas Maccabeus	Israel
Mithradates I	Parthia
Eumenes II Soter	Pergamum
Antiochus IV Epiphanes — Antiochus V — Demetrius I	Syria
Ptolemy VI Philometor & Cleopatra II — Ptol. VIII — Ptolemy VI & Cleopatra II	Egypt
Perseus	Macedonia
(L. Aemilius Paullus)	Rome
Han Wen Di	China

170	169	168	167	166	165	164	163	162	161

INDIANS,
BHARHUT

Of all the powerful aristocratic Roman consuls in this decade, Caius Popillius Laenas was the most memorable, notably for the famous anecdote relating to him. He was despatched by the senate to the Syrian king, Antiochus Epiphanes, who had invaded Egypt in 168, to demand his withdrawal. When Antiochus asked for time to consider the matter, Popillius Laenas drew a circle on the ground around the king saying: "You shall answer before you leave this ring." Antiochus had no choice but to obey, and withdrew his troops.

The Parthians, under Mithradates I, took Media from the Seleucids in 160.

Judas Maccabeus died sword in hand, but his brother continued the struggle and upheld the independence and autonomy of the Jewish state.

The Roman New Year, reckoned since time immemorial from 1 March, was moved backwards two months in 153 BC. The reason was that the consuls, each elected for one calendar year, needed more time to plan the summer's military campaigns now that foreign policy embraced a much wider area, with much greater distances to be covered. This calendar reform had the desired effect and became permanent. In time it was also adopted by other, more peaceable nations who likewise reckoned their calendar year from 1 January.

In 160, *Adelphi*, the new play by the comic dramatist Terence, was performed in Rome, to mark the funeral of the great general, Aemilius Paullus. The plot is highly contrived, involving abduction, seduction and other such wanton frivolities - clearly the Romans had their own views as to what entertainment was suitable for such sombre occasions.

Publius Terentius Afer was of Carthaginian origin. He had been sold as a slave after the Second Punic War but had been freed by his Roman master on account of his literary talent. Yet he was by no means highly regarded. Plautus, the other Roman comic dramatist, who had died twenty years or more ago, was far more popular than Terence.

Alexander the Great had never reached Arabia, although it was thanks to him that the local tribes who had been subject to Persia were liberated. The kingdom of the Nabataeans now emerged here, with its capital of Petra. The first known Nabataean king was Aretas I.

The Ptolemaic system of numbering is in retrospect somewhat confusing. Ptolemy VI and Ptolemy VIII, for example, were brothers while Ptolemy VII was the former's small son by Cleopatra II who was also Ptolemy VI's sister. Ptolemy VI was expelled for some years by Ptolemy VIII who, when VI returned, ruled over Cyrenaica; and when VI died there was a co-regency for a while between VII and VIII and the dowager queen Cleopatra. Cleopatra was then forced into marriage with VIII who, on his wedding day, had VII murdered. He then married his new spouse's daughter Cleopatra III, which infuriated Cleopatra II, who plotted against the couple and succeeded in deposing them. Then it was her turn to be overthrown. But she soon reappeared and when Ptolemy VIII finally died she apparently reassumed power. This royal merry-go-round, not untypical of its period, lasted several decades.

In India Buddhism flourished in the aftermath of King Aśoka and magnificent temples continued to be built. This sculpture is from a renowned stupa in Barhat. Indian Museum, Calcutta.

Israel	Jonathan Maccabeus
Parthia	Mithradates I
Pergamum	Attalus II
Syria	Demetrius I Soter
Egypt	Ptolemy VI Philometor & Cleopatra II
Rome	(Publius Pompillius Laenas)
China	Han Wen Di — Han Jing Di

160	159	158	157	156	155	154	153	152	151

INDIANS, BHARHUT

There was a continuous power struggle in the Seleucid kingdom and the pretenders could always reckon on the support of Rome, which pursued a consistent policy, namely to undermine the authority of Seleucia. One such pretender held the capital from 145-142 and was afterwards known as Antiochus VI.

The Hellenic kingdom of Bactria collapsed at about this time. Heliocles was the name of its last ruler, as is evident from his coins. Otherwise there is no record either of him personally or of the fate of his kingdom. It does appear that Tochari invaders from China ransacked the land. Yet when a Chinese explorer looked for the Tochari in 127, he found no trace of them.

In 146 the Romans cold-bloodedly destroyed two of the world's largest cities. One of these was Corinth, scene of an anti-Roman rising that was immediately suppressed. Directly afterwards Consul Lucius Mummius enslaved all the citizens, plundered their temples, stores and homes, set fire to everything burnable and demolished what was left.

The other city was Carthage, which had made a fair economic recovery since Hannibal's defeat. Marcus Porcius Cato undoubtedly had Rome's financial interests in mind when he concluded his address to the senate with the famous words: *"Praeterea censeo Carthaginem esse delendam"* "In addition, I consider Carthage should be destroyed." Cato died, however, in 149, and so failed to see his wish fulfilled.

The manner in which the Romans treated the defenceless Carthaginians was as treacherous as anything in history. Having devised an excuse for war, they landed an army and ordered the Carthaginians to surrender all their weapons and war machines. After this had been done, the Romans ordered that the city be evacuated and destroyed. This, of course, so enraged the Carthaginians that they barricaded their gates and attempted to rearm. This struggle, known as the Third Punic War, lasted several years, but the outcome was inevitable. The young Consul Publius Cornelius Scipio Aemilianus razed Carthage to the ground, then strewed salt over the entire site.

Servius Sulpicius Galba was a great speaker and a very rich man. He had acquired much of his fortune in Spain where a revolt had been raging for some years and where he had served Rome as praetor. He had then come to an agreement with the Lusitanians on the distribution of certain areas of land. Trusting him, they allowed themselves to be divided up into three groups, whereupon he ordered his soldiers to kill the men and to seize the women and children for sale as slaves. He was brought before the courts in Rome but was acquitted by his kinsmen. He was also made an augur.

Below: the ruins of Carthage. The scene today is very different from that in Scipio's day, for a Roman city grew up here and in its turn crumbled to ruins. Not much remains of the Punic settlement with its six-storey buildings and its triple city wall. There are traces, however, of the two harbours from the classical period.

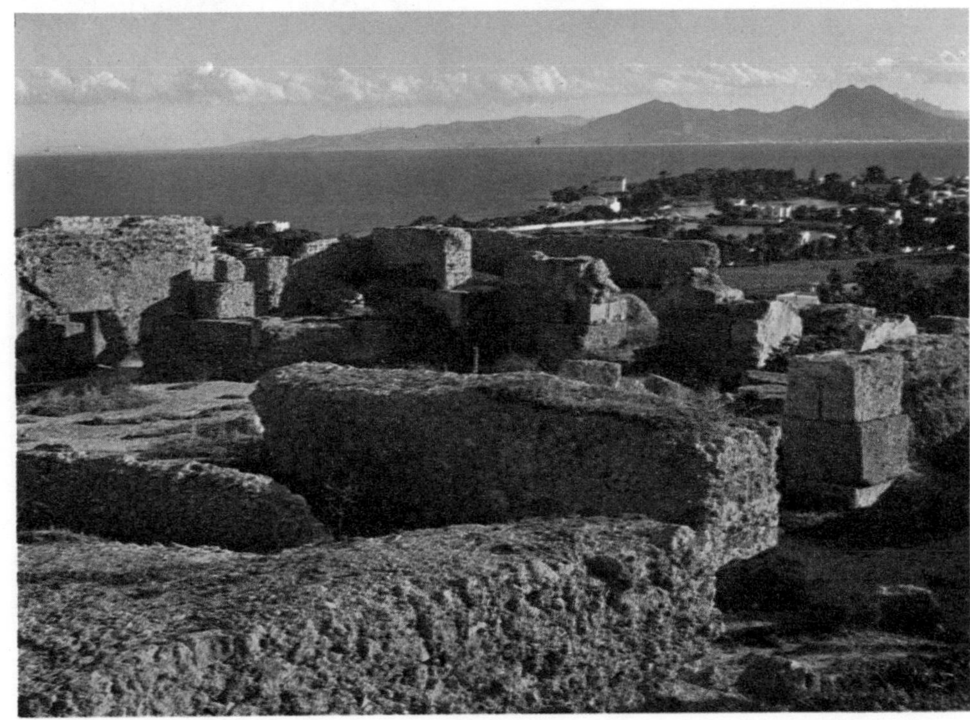

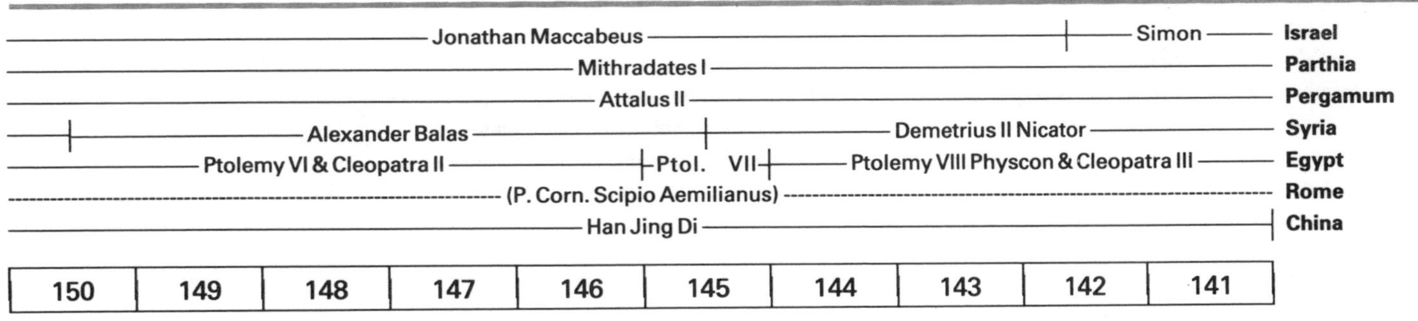
Jonathan Maccabeus
Simon
Israel
Mithradates I
Parthia
Attalus II
Pergamum
Alexander Balas
Demetrius II Nicator
Syria
Ptolemy VI & Cleopatra II
Ptol. VII
Ptolemy VIII Physcon & Cleopatra III
Egypt
(P. Corn. Scipio Aemilianus)
Rome
Han Jing Di
China
150
149
148
147
146
145
144
143
142
141

CHINA
INDIANS, BHARUT
PERSIANS, SHAMI

Attalus III of Pergamum died without issue and willed his lands and wealth to the Roman people. His half-brother Aristonicus attempted to stop this being implemented but was prevented and put to death. The tribune, Tiberius Gracchus, raised the question of what should be done with this money; he was a great public speaker and, though the brother-in-law of Scipio Aemilianus, a revolutionary politician. Recently, bypassing the senate, he had persuaded the popular assembly to approve a reform that would deprive the rich of their land monopolies for the benefit of the common people; and he now proposed using the Attalus inheritance to provide livestock and other requisites for the new smallholders. His mandate expired, however, and when, contrary to custom and procedure, he stood for re-election, he was beaten to death by his conservative kinsmen.

In a battle with the Parthians, Demetrius II was defeated and imprisoned by Mithradates I. This lost Seleucia Persia and Babylon as well, leaving only Syria. Parthia emerged as a major power, though this threw little light on its history. Practically nothing is known about its rulers, beyond their names.

Having won the Punic and Macedonian wars, the Romans now controlled practically the entire Mediterranean area. Syria and Egypt were independent, however, and appear individually to have been considerable powers.

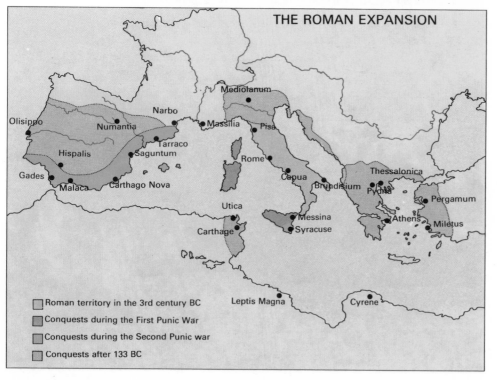

THE ROMAN EXPANSION

Mediolanum
Narbo
Olisippo
Numantia
Massilia
Pisa
Tarraco
Hispalis
Saguntum
Rome
Gades
Malaca
Carthago Nova
Capua
Brundisium
Thessalonica
Pydna
Pergamum
Utica
Messina
Athens
Miletus
Carthage
Syracuse
Leptis Magna
Cyrene

Roman territory in the 3rd century BC
Conquests during the First Punic War
Conquests during the Second Punic war
Conquests after 133 BC

In Sicily, Greece and Asia Minor the slaves' war was raging, though now approaching its close. In 135 the slaves had rebelled against their masters, initially with great success. But they lacked internal discipline and competent leaders and now, confronted by regular Roman troops, they were facing defeat.

The Spanish revolt continued under an able leader named Viriatus. One Roman legion after another was defeated and a peace settlement was reached which caused joy throughout the country. But no sooner was peace restored than the Romans returned; after several years of aimless compaigning supreme command was assumed by Scipio Aemilianus. In 133 Numantia, the last stronghold of the Celtiberians, fell. The starving citizens had evidently got drunk on beer and attempted an attack. When this failed they set fire to their own city and cremated themselves. The fall and destruction of Numantia ended all resistance to Roman domination. The inhabitants learned Latin and Spain rapidly became the most Romanized of all the imperial provinces.

In Israel closed societies were being formed, involving what the Bible calls *farisairoi*, Pharisees, from a Hebrew verb meaning 'to separate'. The Pharisees set a high ethical standard for themselves and others, and prospective members were subjected to a month's trial to prove they could live in accordance with the Law of Moses. The Pharisees became a people's party to which the ruling powers had to pay heed. They were convinced that a moral life and good deeds were vital to the salvation of the soul and the order of the world.

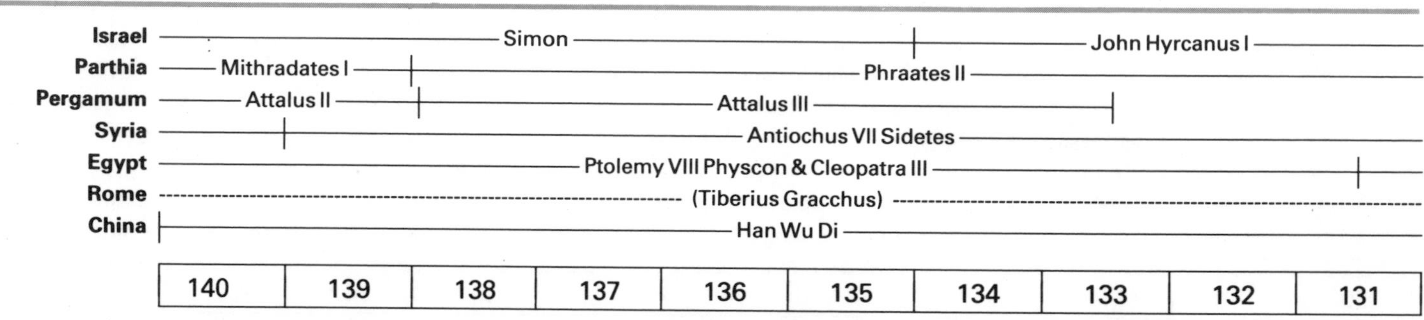
Israel
Simon
John Hyrcanus I
Parthia
Mithradates I
Phraates II
Pergamum
Attalus II
Attalus III
Syria
Antiochus VII Sidetes
Egypt
Ptolemy VIII Physcon & Cleopatra III
Rome
(Tiberius Gracchus)
China
Han Wu Di
140
139
138
137
136
135
134
133
132
131

CHINA
CHINESE
INDIANS,
BATANMARA

To seek contact with possible allies behind the backs of the Huns, Emperor Wu Di despatched an officer named Zhang Xian to West Turkestan and Bactria, to which country the nomadic Yuechi had retreated some twenty years previously. Zhang Xian located them, though only to find they had settled well in their new environment and had little interest in moving back east to fight the Huns. But this expedition was still of some value, for when Zhang Xian returned to his master a full twelve years later he had wondrous things to tell of the distant lands in the west. He brought with him grape vines and the European forage herb lucerne or alfalfa. More important still were his geographic discoveries, which were shortly to have important economic and cultural consequences. China now opened a caravan route to the West, so that the Chinese soon learned of such things as beds and tables, fire-eating and sword-swallowing! In return they introduced delicacies like the peach and the apricot to the West; and, incidentally, the crossbow, recently invented in China.

To ensure the safe passage of these caravans the Huns had to be crushed. In 121, after a cavalry battle lasting seven days, the Huns were driven out of the former lands of the Yuechi and in an even greater battle at the beginning of the next decade the Khan of the Huns was killed, while 19,000 of his men were taken prisoner. This left the caravan route open and unmolested for a long time to come.

Emperor Wu Di was famous for his currency manipulations. He had notes of very high values made from unreproducible white deer hide, while the nominal value of his metal coins far exceeded that of the metal itself. The coin-producing industry reaped huge profits and led rapidly to inflation.

The islands of Mallorca and Menorca were included in the Spanish province of the Roman Empire in 122 BC.

Caius Gracchus, tribune like his brother Tiberius, though a more radical politician, was successful in altering the obsolescent administration and disgraceful property system in Rome. He instituted a series of laws reviving and extending his brother's land laws, and also statutes whereby Rome was to provide grain for its citizens at greatly subsidized prices. All this made him very popular with the common people. He courted the new, proletarian capitalists by introducing an arrangement whereby tax collecting in Asia was conducted by contract, and also by barring the senators from belonging to the courts that supervised provincial administration. He then endeavoured to acquire land for the inhabitants of rural Italy. But the conservative landowners quickly undermined his position by out-bidding him, and when he proposed that the Latinians affected by the land reforms should be granted full rights of Roman citizenship, the city dwellers became exceedingly indignant and he was not re-elected the following year. When he attempted to vindicate his actions he was proscribed by the senate and committed suicide. His supporters, moreover, were massacred, and their widows and children prohibited from wearing mourning.

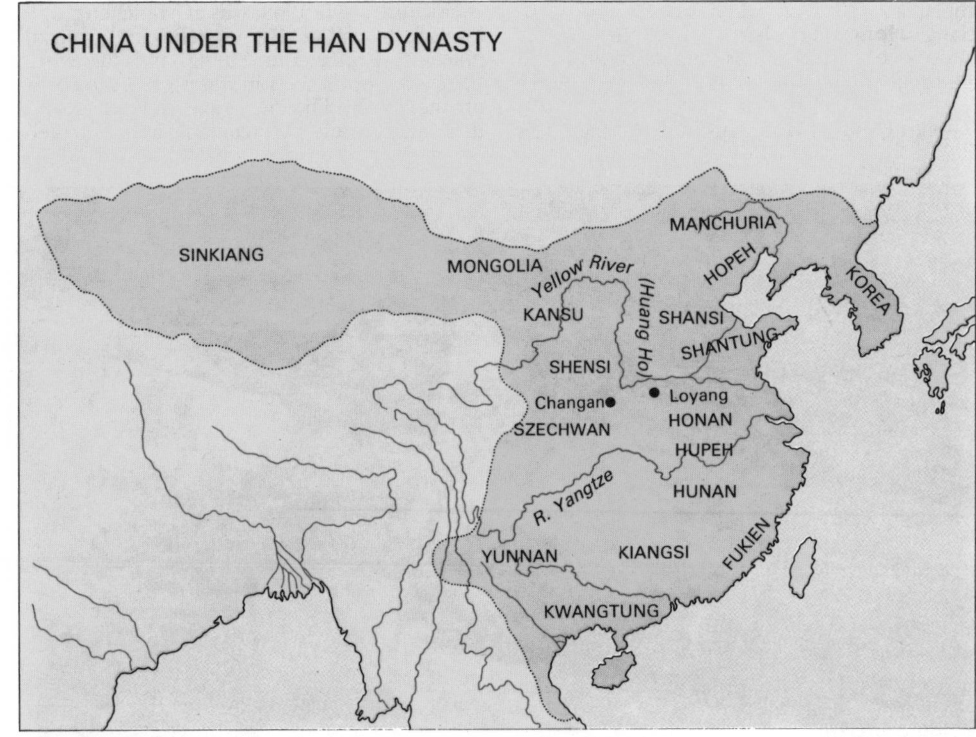
CHINA UNDER THE HAN DYNASTY
SINKIANG
MONGOLIA
MANCHURIA
HOPEH
KOREA
Yellow River
(Huang Ho)
KANSU
SHANSI
SHANTUNG
SHENSI
Changan
Loyang
HONAN
SZECHWAN
HUPEH
R. Yangtze
HUNAN
YUNNAN
KIANGSI
FUKIEN
KWANGTUNG

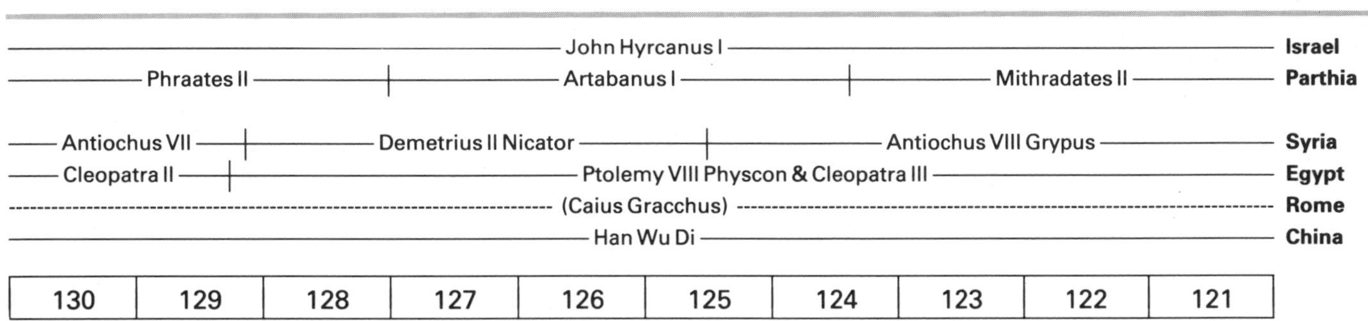
John Hyrcanus I — Israel
Phraates II — Artabanus I — Mithradates II — Parthia
Antiochus VII — Demetrius II Nicator — Antiochus VIII Grypus — Syria
Cleopatra II — Ptolemy VIII Physcon & Cleopatra III — Egypt
(Caius Gracchus) — Rome
Han Wu Di — China
130 129 128 127 126 125 124 123 122 121

ROMAN EMPIRE
HELLENES

After various attempts to make money that could not be counterfeited, Wu Di found himself compelled to start minting coins with the denomination more or less corresponding to the value of the metal. He also granted a pardon to all the counterfeiters who had been apprehended and as a result more than a million people were released from Chinese prisons. Once more, observance of the currency laws was restored.

Sang Hongyang, Emperor Wu Di's minister of finance since 119, successfully introduced a system for maintaining fixed price levels. The state stepped in to support purchases of key products when prices declined, and to release these goods again when prices improved. Sang Hongyang also assured the steady supply of vital goods by introducing a national transport system.

The kingdom of Bosporus in the Crimea was vanquished in 107 when King Mithradates VI of Pontus sent in an army led by the general Diophantus, ostensibly to give aid to the Scythians. The inhabitants resisted but were heavily defeated; and since King Pairisades V had been assassinated in the previous year, Mithradates was able to add this country to his own dominions without difficulty.

In 111 Canton was taken by Emperor Wu Di, under whose long reign North Korea, North Vietnam and a large part of central Asia were also added to the Chinese empire.

Recent grave finds indicate that the arts were very advanced in China. One such site, excavated in AD 1968, was at Mancheng, 150 km southwest of Beijing (Peking), burial place of Prince Liu Sheng and his wife, Princess Dou Wan. Liu Sheng was the older brother of Wu Di. The grave yielded several thousand finely conceived and worked objects, the most remarkable of which was the jade burial attire of the princess.

The Taurini were a people who established a state on the Danube. Their kings lived in Noreia, close to modern Klagenfurt, and the name of their city soon displaced their tribal name so that the country became known as Noricum. Silver coins, modelled on those from Macedonia, were minted here.

In 118 a force of Roman war veterans marched into southern Gaul and established a colony known as Narbo. This soon developed into the capital of a province: Gallia Narbonensis, and later Narbonne.

A new equestrian horde known as the Alani were moving towards Europe from the east. On the steppes to the east of the Caspian Sea they joined up with a Sarmatian tribe and also with a Caucasian tribe called Siraks.

From the Roman viewpoint the great event of this decade was the war against Jugurtha, an African prince who had become master of Numidia after murdering his cousin and rival. According to the historian Sallust, he managed to bribe the Roman generals into agreeing an armistice and peace terms. Some of these senior officers were subsequently judged and sentenced by a Roman commission. But the noble family of Metellus, four different members of which had been consuls during this decade, had not been involved in these dealings with Jugurtha, and the war against him was thus entrusted to a fifth member of the family, Quintus Caecilius.

The leaders of the ruling Jewish family of the Hasmoneans, to which the Maccabees belonged, were high priests. It would appear however, that their rule was hardly exemplary: palace revolutions, fratricide and political violence were evidently common occurrences in their circles.

Princess Dou Wan's jade burial attire.

Israel	John Hyrcanus I
Parthia	Mithradates II
Syria	Antiochus VIII Grypus
Egypt	Ptolemy VIII Physcon & Cleopatra III — Cleopatra III & Ptolemy IX Lathyrus
Rome	(Quintus Caecilius Metellus)
China	Han Wu Di

120	119	118	117	116	115	114	113	112	111

ROMAN BOXERS
SICILY

The military tribune Caius Marius, who was of low birth, was disliked by Metellus, his superior in the war against Jugurtha, but obtained permission to stand in the consul elections. He secured a majority in the popular assembly and was thus able to take over the command from Metellus. Caius Marius proved an equally able commander, and soon brought the campaign to a victorious conclusion.

Meanwhile, a more extensive war awaited him. Two nomadic Germanic tribes, the Cimbri and the Teutones, had destroyed two Roman armies in the Alps and then wandered down separately through the Brenner pass and the Rhône valley.

Marius met the Teutones in southern Gaul, halted his legions momentarily so that they could accustom themselves to the howls of their opponents, and then annihilated the entire tribe. The inhabitants of nearby Massilia were later able to fence off their vineyards with the whitened bones of the defeated Teutones. Marius then turned his attention to the Cimbri and destroyed them on the plain of the Po.

The wanderings of the Cimbri were of particular interest to Nordic historians. Ancient geographers mention Cimbrian Chersonesus, namely the Jutland peninsula. So the Cimbrians seem to have come originally from what was later to become Danish territory. The Swede Olaus Rudbeck believes that the Cimbri lived both in the north where the winters are long and dark, and in the south where Cimershafwen, (modern Simrishamn) is located.

John Hyrcanus I was the only member of the Maccabee family in Israel to die a natural death, most of the others having been stabbed, executed or poisoned. Unlike his predecessors and successors, he maintained good relations in Jerusalem with the clerical nobles, the Sadducees.

There were fraternal conflicts among the rulers (and their families) of both Syria and Egypt. The little that remained of the Seleucid state was divided for a time into two separate spheres of power. Judea was probably able to retain its independence as a result of these upheavals in neighbouring states. But, as is reflected in the palace revolutions and killings, Judea was by no means politically united.

The numbering of the Syrian kings inevitably seems confusing. Antiochus VIII and Antiochus IX ruled jointly from 111 to 96, having fought each other for some years. In 96 Antiochus VIII was assassinated whereupon one of his sons murdered Antiochus IX and established himself as Seleucus VI. A son of Antiochus IX slew Seleucus and himself became Antiochus X. But Seleucus had a brother who called himself Antiochus XI until he was defeated and killed by Antiochus X. Antiochus X died in a battle with the Parthians in 93, and in 88 Demetrius III was himself defeated and taken prisoner by the Parthians. His brother Antiochus XII was killed in another minor war in 84. The last remaining son of Antiochus VIII was Philip I, but he was expelled from Antiochia by a revolutionary force, leaving Tigranes of Armenia to become master of Syria. Antiochus XIII, who appeared in the 70s, was the son of Antiochus X and had to fight Philip II, son of Philip I.

Marius, below left, and Sulla, according to contemporary busts in Rome and Munich respectively. Politically these two were irreconcilable, and this was later to be a significant factor in Roman history. But in the war against the Numidian king Jugurtha, where Sulla was a cavalry officer under Marius, they collaborated effectively.

John Hyrcanus I — Alexander Jannaeus	Israel
Mithradates II	Parthia
Antiochus VIII Grypus + Antiochus IX Cyzicenos	Syria
Cleopatra III & Ptolemy IX — Cleopatra III & Ptolemy X Alexander	Egypt
(Caius Marius)	Rome
Han Wu Di	China

110	109	108	107	106	105	104	103	102	101

100-91 BC

BUDDHIST INDIANS, SANCHI

The social and domestic policy conflicts in Italy resounded throughout the entire Mediterranean world. At the beginning of the decade the democrat Marius was consul in Rome, but he was persuaded, for the sake of restoring law and order, to suppress the activities of those whose sentiments he in fact shared. This made his position as a politician momentarily untenable, and the conservative and plutocratic elements seized power. In 91 the young tribune Marcus Livius Drusus, himself a wealthy aristocrat, proposed a number of laws intended to mitigate the social tension and bring about a more just relationship between the classes and between Roman citizens and rural Italians. He was in close touch with leading figures outside Rome, but this was fatal to his popularity in the city and one day he was murdered in his own house.

As a result of Rome's selfish and restrictive municipal policy, a general state of revolt developed throughout central Italy. The Romans attempted to suppress this by armed force but they merely suffered one defeat after another until they seized upon the idea of guaranteeing Roman citizenship rights to all those communities laying down their arms within sixty days. Although the formal purpose of the rebellion was thus achieved, the Romans were not wholly trusted. The Samnite and Campanian towns in particular, continued to fight; they were defeated in turn, and retribution was cruel.

Cyrenaica in Africa, previously under the Ptolemies, became a Roman province in 88.

The census, or tax count, was conducted in Rome every fifth year and the inhabitants were divided up into five categories. Adult male citizens and wealthy widows were subject to taxation and paid various dues, known as *aes hordearium, aes equestre,* etc. The census is interesting inasmuch as the figures constitute a form of population count, albeit very incomplete. Rome may have had about 900,000 inhabitants at this time. The populations of other ancient cities can similarly be assessed. Alexandria and Syrian Antiochia each had more than a half million inhabitants at this time. Athens was now no longer a major city, though in 432, in Pericles' day, there had probably been a quarter of a million inhabitants, a third of them slaves.

In central Asia the Huns prevailed; not even the Great Wall could restrain them. Their dominions extended throughout Mongolia to the region around the Altai mountains and Lake Baikal, and their cavalry often swept into Chinese territory and had to be expelled by imperial troops. They also disrupted communications, until finally Emperor Wu Di lost patience and resolved to devote all his resources to opening trade routes to the West. About 10,000 Chinese horsemen attacked the Huns at Kansu and put them to flight after a week-long battle. A few years later another general with 50,000 cavalry won a second major victory against the Huns outside the Great Wall. This ultimately enabled the Chinese to open a caravan route - the famous silk route - to the West.

In China Confucianism was becoming re-established. A university had recently been founded in Changan where fifty specially selected students were instructed exclusively in the Confucian writings, which had by now been reconstructed after Qin Shi Huang's notorious bonfire. A literary examination system was instituted, which would dominate Chinese society for a couple of thousand years to come. Personally, however, Emperor Wu Di was not a genuine Confucian, for he was too superstitious. A certain Huai Nan Zi transformed the philosophical Taoist mysticism into a regular religion which featured spirits and various other strange pheonomena. The great historian Sima Qian, mentions the emperor's interest in wizards and elixirs. Sima Qian was Wu Di's contemporary but by no means his friend; when he intervened on behalf of an individual who had offended the emperor, the latter flew into a rage and had Sima Qian castrated.

Sima Qian's history was a remarkable work. He had very carefully studied many earlier writings and numerous documents in the imperial archives, including travel accounts and reports from all corners of the empire. He copied all painstakingly and compiled it without commentary. The style thus varies constantly and the total effect is somewhat bizzare; nevertheless it possesses a certain authenticity that is seldom evident in early historical accounts from the West.

There are no reliable Japanese historical records before the 6th century AD, but there does exist a traditional table of rulers whose first representatives belong to this period. Probably imaginary, but they have much the same right to inclusion as the Roman kings.

A draper's shop according to a Roman relief, now in the British Museum, London. Mediterranean culture was becoming increasingly international and the mutual effects were far-reaching. The photograph on the opposite page shows how Greek and Egyptian architectural styles could be harmonized.

Israel	Alexander Jannaeus
Parthia	Mithradates II
Syria	Antiochus VIII + Antiochus IX — Demetrius III Philopator
Egypt	Ptolemy X Alexander & Cleopatra Berenice
Rome	(C. Marius) ---- (Marcus Livius Drusus)
Japan	Shujin-Tenno
China	Han Wu Di

100	99	98	97	96	95	94	93	92	91

THE SILK ROUTE
BUDDHIST INDIANS, SANCHI
CHINESE

While the Romans were fully occupied with their war in Italy, their Asiatic subjects seized the chance to free themselves. King Mithradates of Pontus, absolute ruler of a kingdom to the south and east of the Black Sea and protector of the Greek cities on the Black Sea's north coast, launched an offensive and was hailed everywhere as a liberator. Some 80,000 Roman officials and businessmen in Asia Minor were killed, and the island of Delos, where vast numbers of prisoners-of-war had been sold as slaves, was razed to the ground and never recovered. Mithradates now established himself in Pergamum and despatched an army to Greece.

Having brought their Italian campaign to an end, the Romans, under Consul Lucius Cornelius Sulla, prepared to move out to meet Mithradates. But the democratic party in Rome persuaded the popular assembly to relieve him of his command and give it instead to Marius, now back in favour. Sulla, confident that he could depend upon his army, refused to comply, however, marched on Rome with his six legions, asserted his authority and departed for Greece to deal with Mithradates. No sooner had he left than Marius seized power and embarked on an unparalleled reign of terror, executing every one of his political opponents.

Sulla initially paid his legions out of the plunder he obtained in Greece and western Asia, including the temple treasures of Ephesus, Epidaurus and Olympia. After this he routed the army of Mithradates and returned home with his veterans, mercilessly suppressing all opposition. To give a semblance of legality to his position he had himself proclaimed dictator perpetuus. Now, with calculated thoroughness, he proceeded to eliminate every inconvenient individual in the city and secured mass support by distributing the gains from property confiscation. Sulla introduced proscription, whereby lists of names were posted of all those who had forfeited their property and the right to live; such individuals were now beyond the law and anyone killing them was rewarded.

In 83 Syria was overrun by the Armenian king, Tigranes.

The mathematician Hero, who appears to have lived in Ptolemaic Alexandria, left records of many technical inventions. His name is associated, among other things, with steam power and the first reaction turbine. His writings also describe a distance recorder, a fire hose, an angle-measuring instrument for land surveying and an automatic water device. Another Alexandrian mathematician, Ctesibius, invented the antique water clock, the Clepsydra, which consisted of a water-filled container with a float carrying a sort of indicator. The water gradually dripped out through a hole at the bottom and the float indicator moved downward, showing the passage of time on a scale. In Ctesibius' apparatus the drops of water turned a wheel and his invention was widely acclaimed. Subsequent inventors made this more accurate and dependable simply by bending down the indicator and marking the scale on the outside of the container.

Temple of Horus at Edfu, built at the time of Ptolemy X.

Alexander Jannaeus — **Israel**

Mithradates II — Gotarzes — **Parthia**

Demetrius III — Antiochus XII — Philip I — **Syria**

Ptol. X & Cleop. Ber. — Ptolemy IX Lathyrus — **Egypt**

Sulla — C. Marius — Lucius Cornelius Sulla — **Rome**

Shujin-Tenno — **Japan**

Han Wu Di — Han Zhao Di — **China**

90	89	88	87	86	85	84	83	82	81

CELTS

One result of the Chinese expansion in central Asia was the introduction into China of a new breed of horse. Emperor Wu Di's emissaries had brought home wondrous reports of the existence of these large animals, and after a victory over the Prince of Fergana the Chinese had succeeded some twenty years earlier in bringing back a few specimens, superior in almost every way to the small steppe horses of the Chinese. These had proved a great success and there was already quite a large stock in the country. Chinese artists loved to portray these splendid creatures.

In Rome Sulla relinquished his dictatorship after having introduced great changes. One of the two consuls who succeeded him, Marcus Aemilius Lepidus, emerged unexpectedly as a democrat, however, and proposed that most of Sulla's innovations should be abolished. This led to a conflict among the consuls and unrest in many parts of Italy. In some places people reclaimed the lands that had been confiscated for Sulla's veterans. Lepidus was banished, but the senate found it wise nevertheless to adopt one of his demands; the resumption of the public distribution of grain in Rome. This created a breach in Sulla's constitution and in the next few years it was dissolved altogether, mainly because of a number of court cases which revealed the cupidity and brutality of the leaders. The first of these became universally celebrated, for the prosecutor was Marcus Tullius Cicero, who in due course published his records of the case; these are as readable today as they were almost 2000 years ago. The accused in Cicero's case was a certain Verres, who as Roman governor in Sicily had been guilty of the most appalling excesses.

China, too, was ruled by a general because Emperor Zhao Di died young and Emperor Xuan Di was still a child. The general's name was Ho Guang and he ruthlessly suppressed the revolts that shook the country from time to time. The Chinese empire now extended from North Korea to the Caspian Sea.

In southernmost Arabia the country known as Saba, or Sheba, still existed, now peopled by a tribe called the Himyarites. The capital was Timnah and Saba was on a good footing with Ptolemaic Egypt. The gods had assumed Hellenic forms; there was a monumental Sun temple at Hureidha and a magnificent Moon temple at el-Huqqa.

Israel during the time of Alexander Jannaeus and his dowager queen Salma Alexandra (Salome) was just as large as was the kingdom of David. The Hasmoneans had been more efficient in the political arena than in religious matters. One day when Alexander Jannaeus was performing his priestly duties, he incurred the anger of the people and was bombarded with lemons. When he eventually repressed this popular outbreak, he took a dreadful revenge crucifying 800 of the leaders outside Jerusalem; and from their crosses they were forced to witness the slaughter of their wives and children, while Jannaeus and his concubines sat at table and viewed the spectacle from a suitable distance.

In southern Italy there was a great slave rebellion in 73 led by a gladiator named Spartacus. The slaves defeated several Roman armies, though their discipline grew increasingly lax. In 71 they met a greatly superior force under the command of the consul Marcus Licinius Crassus. Crassus was Rome's wealthiest citizen, who remarked that no man should call himself rich unless able to afford, as he could, to maintain a private army. Spartacus and most of his men were killed in this battle, but Crassus seized 6000 slaves and had them crucified.

Gladiators in training. Relief in Museo della Civita Romana, Rome. Below; *Bronze horseman of Wu-wei, Kansu.*

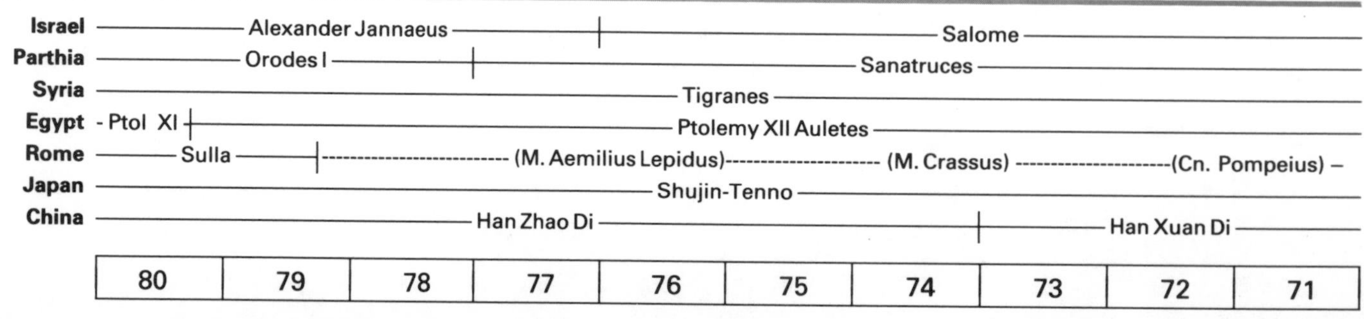
Israel — Alexander Jannaeus — Salome
Parthia — Orodes I — Sanatruces
Syria — Tigranes
Egypt - Ptol XI — Ptolemy XII Auletes
Rome — Sulla — (M. Aemilius Lepidus) — (M. Crassus) — (Cn. Pompeius) –
Japan — Shujin-Tenno
China — Han Zhao Di — Han Xuan Di
80 79 78 77 76 75 74 73 72 71

INDIANS, CHAITYA
ROMANS

The cost of food in Italy was sky-high because hordes of Cilicean pirates were operating in the Mediterranean and intercepting the grain vessels coming up from the south. A people's tribune had Cnaeus Pompeius (Pompey) appointed imperator for a three-year period and he was given exceptional powers to redress the situation. He stationed thirteen guard squadrons each in their own sea district and then made a sweep from west to east with his main fleet. In forty days he cleared the entire western Mediterranean of freebooters, assured a secure passage for the grain vessels from Sardinia and Africa, and made his famous pronouncement to seamen who were unwilling to risk their lives in bad weather: *"Navigare necesse est, vivere non est necesse."* (Sailing is necessary, living is not essential.) Three months later Pompey landed in Cilicia and dealt with the remaining pirates' base. The prisoners were treated surprisingly leniently, however, being neither hanged nor enslaved.

In Spain a democratic officer named Quintus Sertorius had established an independent state. He was murdered a few years later by a rival in his own camp and General Cnaeus Pompeius, sent by the senate with an army to Spain, had no difficulty in retaking the peninsula for Rome.

When the last king of Bithynia died, it was found that he had willed his country to the Roman people, but King Mithradates of Pontus moved into Bithynia himself. Consequently Rome sent an army against Mithradates; it was led by Lucius Licinius Lucullus, renowned for his love of food and other worldly pleasures. But Lucullus was also a very able general and he repulsed Mithradates, besides defeating the latter's ally, Tigranes of Armenia.

In 66 Pompey had finished with the pirates and was in need of a new command. Lucullus was ousted by skilfully directed popular opinion in Rome, and Pompey succeeded him. He brought the campaign against Mithradates to a swift conclusion, driving him to the Crimea, where he committed suicide; Tigranes, too, was forced to surrender his conquests in Syria. Representatives of both fighting branches of the Seleucid dynasty approached Pompey and presented their cases, but he decided neither was worth retaining and he thus made Syria a Roman province. He then marched into Palestine, captured Jerusalem where two brothers were quarrelling over the priesthood, and made the younger one Judaean regent. He then visited the temple where, to the anger of the pious Jews, he entered the Holy of Holies, permitted only once a year to the high priests.

Pompey subsequently made a political settlement in Asia Minor, created new Roman provinces and fixed the frontiers for such small kingdoms as Galatia, Cappadocia and others.

A young man named Caius Julius Caesar began to assert himself in the political world. In 63, to the general surprise, he was elected to the important office of pontifex maximus of Rome.

A Germanic chieftain whom the Romans called Ariovistus crossed the Rhine in 72 and pushed into Gaul with his Suebian people, causing great alarm among the local tribes.

In 62 an attempted revolution was checked by Cicero, who was consul for that year. The leader of the revolt was Catilina whose name was remembered thanks mainly to Cicero's famous exclamations, for example: *"Quosque tandem", "Dum tacent clamant", "O tempora, o mores".*

A Celtic people known as Boii had established a kingdom to which they gave the name Boiohaemum or Bohemia. They minted gold coins and did considerable trade to the west, but politically they were hard-pressed by a Vandal tribe in the west and a Dacian horde in the east, the latter being led by a certain Burebistas. A few generations earlier the Romans had defeated the Boii in the plain of the Po, where they had settled as early as the 5th century BC.

Returning from his victorious expedition, Pompey celebrated his triumphs, but soon found he had over-estimated his authority in Rome. Bust in the Museo Nazionale, Naples.

Salome ---- Hyrcanus II — **Israel**

Phraates III — **Parthia**

Tigranes — Antiochus XIII Asiaticus ---- — **Syria**

Ptolemy XII Auletes — **Egypt**

---- (L. Licinius Lucullus) ---- (Cn. Pompeius) ---- (M. Tullius Cicero) ---- **Rome**

Shujin-Tenno — **Japan**

Han Xuan Di — **China**

70	69	68	67	66	65	64	63	62	61

ROMAN EMPIRE

The year 60 was the date of the First Triumvirate in Rome, a political partnership between a general, Pompey, a plutocrat, Crassus, and a hostile politician, Julius Caesar. Between them they overrode the senate and divided the power between them. The leaders of the senate party, Cicero and Marcus Cato, were expelled from Rome.

Caesar, apparently the least significant of the triumvirate, set himself up as governor and military commandant of the Roman provinces to the north and during the course of this decade incorporated the greater part of Gaul in the Roman empire. Crassus, seeking similar honour, set out against the Parthians in Mesopotamia, but was defeated and killed. Pompey, who had already won glory, remained in Rome. Towards the close of the decade his friendship with Caesar began to wane as Caesar rose in prominence.

The Roman conquest of Gaul, an event of major significance in world history, was described by Caesar in his literary masterpiece: *De bello gallico* (*The Gallic War*). It contains all we know of this decisive campaign. Caesar met the Germanic Suebi whom he drove out of Gaul and went on pursuing on the other side of the Rhine. He also made two military expeditions into Britain, though he was unable to consolidate his foothold there.

In Egypt a revolution expelled Ptolemy XII Auletes who was replaced by his daughter. He returned two years later, however, with Roman assistance.

In 59, Caesar, then a consul, issued an edict on the publication of *Acta Diurna*, (*The Events of the Day*). Later it was assumed that this was a type of newspaper and that Caesar therefore was the founder of journalism in Europe. It is more likely, however, to have consisted of notes taken at the meetings of the senate and democratic party and made available for reference.

Of contemporary events in other parts of the world, there are few written accounts.

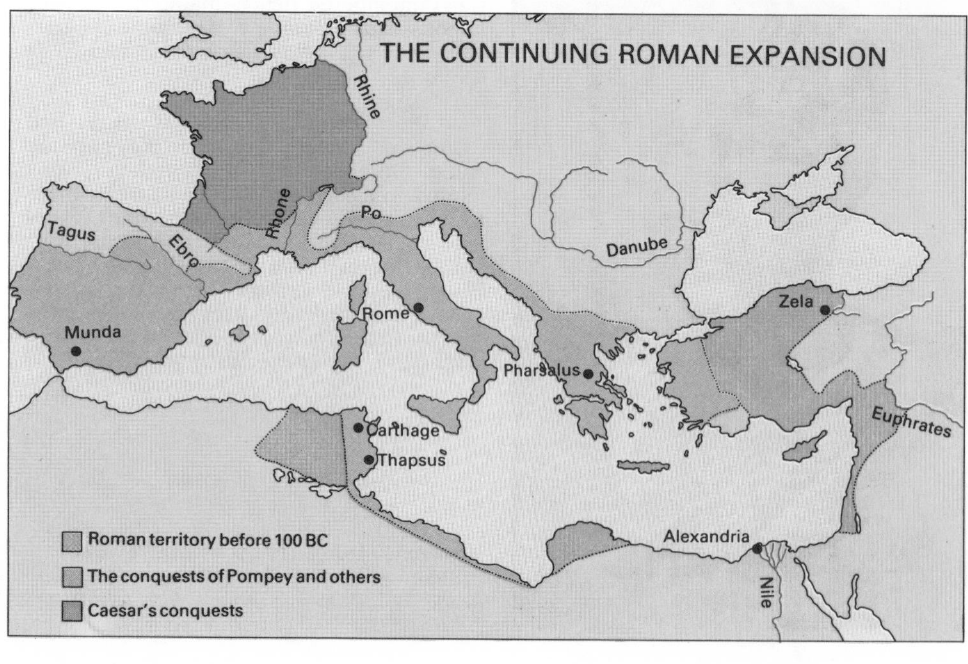
THE CONTINUING ROMAN EXPANSION
Rhine
Rhone
Po
Tagus
Ebro
Danube
Zela
Rome
Munda
Pharsalus
Euphrates
Carthage
Thapsus
Alexandria
Nile
Roman territory before 100 BC
The conquests of Pompey and others
Caesar's conquests

Cicero wrote copiously, greatly influencing the prose style and vocabulary of the Latin language and hence in due course, of all Western languages. His many letters provide fascinating information about his thoughts and daily activities. Bust in the Uffizi, Florence.

Israel	Hyrcanus II
Parthia	Phraates III — Orodes II
Egypt	Ptolemy XII — Berenice IV & Cleop. V & VI — Ptolemy XII Auletes
Rome	Pompey & Crassus & Caesar — Pompey
Japan	Shujin-Tenno
China	Han Xuan Di

60	59	58	57	56	55	54	53	52	51

ROMAN EMPIRE

In the winter of 50-49, Caesar left the province of Gaul and crossed the frontier river, the Rubicon to settle accounts with Pompey and the senate with whom he was at odds. He quickly overran Italy, defeated the forces of Pompey in Spain and then crossed over to the Balkan peninsula where his adversary was assembling a large army and fleet. The decisive battle took place at Pharsalus in Thessaly where Pompey was vanquished. He fled to Egypt but was murdered on his arrival there. Caesar also visited Egypt and formed an alliance with the young queen Cleopatra who was quarrelling with her brother and her husband. The troops of the latter attacked Caesar's force and there was bitter fighting in various areas, including the Pharos lighthouse, but Caesar succeeded in holding out until reinforcements arrived. Ptolemy XIII was expelled and killed and his young brother Ptolemy XIV became consort to Cleopatra and co-regent. In due course, however, Cleopatra bore a son to Caesar. Casear won several more victories and established himself as sole ruler of his huge Mediterranean empire.

The Julian calendar, introduced by Caesar in his capacity as the Roman pontifex maximus, was effective from the year 46 BC. This created an orderly chronology after a long period of confusion. Since the Romans wished the New Year of 46 to be on the first full moon after the shortest day of the year, it became necessary to increase the duration of the previous year by ninety days, so that the year 47 lasted 455 days. In future, however, the full moon played no part in the Julian calendar. This determined the year's duration at 365 days and corrected the divergence from the true solar year by adding an intercalary day once every fourth year.

Cleopatra soon disposed of Ptolemy XIV with poison. Caesarion, her son by Julius Caesar, became Ptolemy XV.

Latin literary production from this period included the beautiful but not always decorous love poems of Catullus, Caesar's diaries described the Gallic wars and the civil war, Lucretius's great didactic poem *De rerum natura* (*On the Nature of Things*), and a number of papers by Cicero. During Caesar's dictatorship, when Cicero was compelled to abandon all political activity, he wrote a number of philosophical works. These were compilations of Greek thinking and though not particularly profound, left to posterity many of those terms and abstract words that form an integral part of every philosophical work.

On 15 March 44, Caesar was murdered and his death was followed by civil war in which the protagonists were Marcus Antonius (Antony), Marcus Junius Brutus, Gaius Cassius and Caesar's nephew and heir Gaius Octavianus (Octavian). In due course Antony, Octavian and a general named Lepidus formed the Second Triumvirate. They announced extensive proscriptions and had Cicero, among others, executed. The Triumvirate then defeated Brutus and Cassius at the battle of Philippi in 42 and divided up the Roman world among them. Antony took over the eastern part of the empire where he met Cleopatra, while Octavian ruled Italy and the western lands.

From 110 there exists a list of the Nabataean kings of Arabian Petra: Atetas II 110-96, Obodas I 95-87, Rabilus I 87, Aretas III 87-62, Obodas II 62-47 and Malchus I 47-30. The Nabataeans worshipped a mountain god called Dusares; he appears to have had some connection with the morning star and was the particular protector of the dynasty. King Obodas I was regarded as a saint and groups of pilgrims visited his tomb. Other interesting tombs for less important individuals were built in Petra from this time.

Gaius Julius Caesar, antique bronze statue in Rome.

Hyrcanus II	**Israel**
Orodes II	**Parthia**
Cleopatra VII & Ptolemy XIII — Cleopatra VII & Ptolemy XIV — Cleopatra VII & Ptolemy XV	**Egypt**
Julius Caesar — Antonius & Octavianus	**Rome**
Shujin-Tenno	**Japan**
Han Xuan Di — Han Yuan Di	**China**

50	49	48	47	46	45	44	43	42	41

40-31 BC

ROMANS
PERSIANS

In 40 BC the Parthians invaded Syria and Palestine. The high priest, Hyrcanus, was taken prisoner and fell into the clutches of his hostile nephew Antigonus who cut off his ears, thereby rendering him incapable of further clerical duties. A certain Herod, who was engaged to Hyrcanus' granddaughter Mariamne, managed to flee to Rome where he inveigled himself into the good graces of Antony, Octavian and the senate, and became recognized as king of Judaea. In 37 after a very bloody campaign Herod entered Jerusalem and asserted his kingship.
The ill-famed Herod was undoubtedly a vicious individual. He had a rare capacity for retaining the confidence of all those holding power in Rome, while ridding himself, almost without exception, of those close to him. The leaders of the aristocratic Sadducees were executed immediately and after a brief period of office by a certain Anael, he appointed his young brother-in-law Aristobulus high priest. But when Aristobulus proved to be popular he too was eliminated: under the pretext of fun and horse-play, his head was held under the water while bathing. Herod then disposed of his elderly father-in-law Hyrcanus, and because this, naturally enough, horrified Mariamne, he despatched her as well. Apparently he later regretted this action, and in his remorse had Mariamne's mother executed as well. In the latter part of his life he executed at least three sons from his nine unions. Herod, nevertheless, did make some constructive contributions. He had a palace built in Jerusalem and another one in Samaria; and his new city of Caesarea with its harbour was a major undertaking. He likewise embarked on a large-scale remodelling of the temple in Jerusalem, a project which was to continue throughout his life.

Cleopatra, who was the seventh of that name in Egypt's complicated table of rulers, was not, in fact, of Egyptian but of Macedonian descent, like the entire Ptolemaean dynasty, in which marriage between siblings was not uncommon.

The story of Antony and Cleopatra is endlessly facinating. Their love affair was described brilliantly by the Greek biographer Plutarch and the theme recurs frequently throughout literary history, including Shakespeare's great tragedy. Plutarch says that Cleopatra was irresistibly charming, and intelligent; she could converse with Egyptians, Troglodytes, Hebrews, Arabs, Medes and Parthians without using an interpreter, and when Antony first met her he fell hopelessly in love with her. Blaise Pascal made the hypothetical reflection in the 17th century: "If Cleopatra's nose had been shorter then the destiny of the world would have been otherwise."

The rule of Emperor Yuan Di had not been a success. He had permitted himself to be guided by his concubines and eunuchs, none of whom were statesmen. But when he died power was seized by the family of the dowager empress which included a number of able individuals. Six of the dowager empress's brothers rose swiftly to the summits of power and her nephew Wang Mang became supreme commander. Twenty years hence he was to become China's mightiest ruler.

In terms of world history the principal factor in this decade was the state of tension between the Romans Antony and Octavian. Sometimes they were on reasonably good terms, especially when they had a common enemy in Pompey' son Sextus, ruler of Sicily and master of the high seas, but having disposed of him, their interests clashed irreconcilably. Open war occurred in 32 when Antony left his wife Octavia, sister to Octavian, and officially married Cleopatra. In the decisive naval battle of Actium in 31, Antony and Cleopatra were put to flight and deserted by the governors of the Egyptian provinces. The following year they committed suicide together. Egypt was made a Roman province but was granted a special status directly subordinate to the emperor.

In Ceylon, at this time, the sacred writings of the Buddhist faith were codified in a collection known as the *Tripitaka*, the 'Three Baskets'. This was a fundamental aspect of that form of Buddhism which was to dominate Japan and China. It was known as Mahayana (The Great Vehicle).

Roman portrait of Cleopatra, British Museum, London. Latin and Greek authors have praised her charm and talents. But in the Talmud, the Jewish law, it is indignantly recorded that Cleopatra questioned the learned Pharisees as to their views on the resurrection, and whether one could expect to rise again with or without clothes.

Palestine — Antigonus — Herod
Parthia — Pacorus I — Phraates IV
Egypt — Cleopatra VII & Ptolemy XV (Caesarion)
Rome — Antonius + Octavianus
Japan — Shujin-Tenno
China — Han Yuan Di — Han Cheng Di

40	39	38	37	36	35	34	33	32	31

ROMANS

On 16 January 27 BC Octavian changed his name and went down in history as the Emperor Augustus, the Noble One, an honorary title respectfully conferred upon the emperor by the senate on this date.

Augustus was a conservative man. He believed in the dignity of Rome's traditions and institutions and he had strengthened his personal authority, like his adoptive father Caesar, by assuming as many offices and titles as possible. He was the senate speaker– princeps senatus – dictator for life, consul, tribune, and pontifex maximus. He treated the senate with the utmost consideration and he also maintained the fictitious idea of a power-wielding, popular assembly, using this from time to time as a manifestation of the popularity that he, the emperor, unquestionably enjoyed. The Romans celebrated his birthday for two successive days.

The Emperor Augustus had the good fortune to be the contemporary of a number of prominent authors who more or less shared his views. One of his immediate colleagues was Maecenas, an exceptionally rich man who generously supported poets such as Virgil, Horace and Propertius. These poets all extolled the goodness of their patron and emperor.

Virgil was probably the most brilliant figure in the circle of Maecenas. In addition to his great epic, the *Aeneid*, he is renowned for *Bucolica,* which was modelled on Theocritus' Greek pastorals, though it had its individual character. Virgil's other work is the poetic cycle *Georgics*, four songs dedicated to agriculture and surely the most charming tribute ever paid to this vocation. The poet Horace was a very good friend of Virgil. He was a chubby little man who has endowed the Western world with more words than any secular writer through the ages. It is Horace who has taught us to speak, for example, of the golden middle way, *aurea mediocritas,* and the naked truth, *nuda veritas.*

A census dated 29 BC revealed that there were 4,063,000 Roman citizens. In this same year the doors of the Janus temple remained closed, as evidence of the state of peace which officially existed.

In the year 30 BC the Emperor Cheng Di an insignificant individual whose rule was conducted by his uncles in the Wang family, received a deputation from King Hermaeus in north-eastern India beseeching help against the Yuechi people: the Tochari. But Cheng Di did nothing to help and Hermaeus' Hellenic kingdom was never heard of again.

The Roman empire was divided up into senatorial and imperial provinces. The senatorial provinces, whose governors had no troops at their disposal, were Africa, Asia, Achaea, Illyricum, Macedonia, Sicilia, Crete, Cyrenaica, Bithynia and Sardinia. The imperial provinces, apart from Egypt, were the three Spanish and the four Gaul provinces including Germania, and furthermore Syria, Cilicia and Cyprus. In military matters the emperor had command over all these provinces.

The citadel in Jerusalem is mediaeval but contains remnants of Herod's palace. Many human dramas have been enacted in its courtyard.

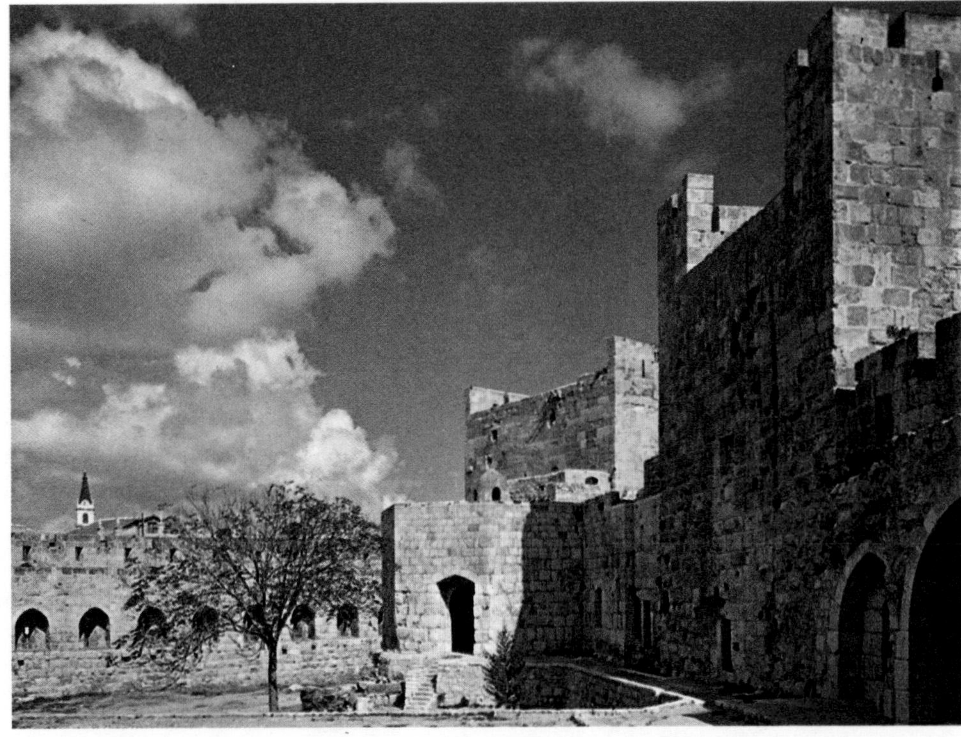

Herod — Palestine
Tiridates II — Parthia
Egypt
Octavianus — Augustus — Rome
Suinin — Japan
Han Cheng Di — China

30	29	28	27	26	25	24	23	22	21

20-11 BC

ROME

The poet Virgil died in 19 BC. The *Aeneid*, his great work on the Trojan origins of the Romans, was not complete and on his deathbed he decreed that is should be burned. But the emperor, who had heard him read several parts of the poem aloud, appointed a commission to edit and publish it.

Following the death of his former colleague Lepidus in 12 BC, Emperor Augustus now also assumed the title of pontifex maximus. He was a great believer in the Roman traditions. He had no wish to be worshipped directly as a god, except in the provinces, and a cult was devoted to his genius.

Colonial wars continued around the periphery of the empire, but in Rome the peace altar, Ara Pacis, was erected. This project commenced in 13 BC and took four years to complete.

Long processions of people are shown in the Ara Pacis reliefs and it is usually claimed that the central figure is Augustus as pontifex maximus. The Swedish sculptor Henning Malmström, who has spent a lot of time identifying the relief characters, believes that the entire frieze is a sort of illustration for the seventh song in Virgil's *Aeneid* where Rome's yet unborn heroes and celebrities appear before Aeneas during his visit to the underworld. Thus, according to Malmström, from the left the procession depicts Camillus, Gracchus, Torquatus, Pompeius, Caesar, Cato the elder, Cossus, Caesarion, Julia, Gracchus and Scipio Africanus.

A great deal of building work was taking place in Italy, particularly in Rome, where, under the command of Marcus Vispanius Agrippa, water conduits were repaired and temples and basilicas built or renovated. All this activity was good both for employment and for the appearance of the city. A whole year was spent on Via Flaminia, which, with its multitude of bridges, led from the capital to Arminium, later Rimini. The Greek geographer Strabo was most impressed.

During the reign of Augustus the northern frontier of the Roman empire was adjusted to embrace lands that would one day become Switzerland, Austria, Hungary, Yugoslavia, Belgium, Holland and southern Germany. A number of towns and support points were established here; Augusta Vindelicorum, Castellum Moguntiacum, Aqua Mattiacae and Augusta Praetoria, etc. These places are nowadays known respectively as Augsburg, Mainz, Wiesbaden and Aosta.

Augustus, who, in fact, had seized more foreign territory than any other Roman leader, contrived nevertheless to create an image for himself as a prince of peace. This was because his dictatorship had put an end to the harrowing party conflicts and the individual's lack of rights in the empire. In the capital, where the poets lived, tranquility reigned.

The poet Horace and his patron Maecenas both died in 8 BC. The former, as he assures us in the introduction to his *Odes*, had in these poems raised a monument to them both that was more enduring than bronze and taller than the royal pyramids. Augustus established another, even more lasting monument when in that same year he ensured that Caesar's calendar was reintroduced and graciously permitted the month of *sextilis* to be renamed August after himself. The seventh month, formerly known as *quintilis*, had already received its current name of July in 44 BC, in honour of Julius Caesar.

Ara Pacis in Rome; the eastern entrance.

Palestine	Herod
Parthia	
Rome	Augustus
Japan	Suinin
China	Han Cheng Di

20	19	18	17	16	15	14	13	12	11

ROME
AUGUSTUS

The Old Testament was completed. Nearly 2000 years later some of the manuscripts were to be found in caves near the Dead Sea.

Only one Latin work on architecture and related subjects, probably dating from this decade, was to survive into modern times: *De architectura* by Vitruvius. The author was an engineering officer, but this is all we know about him.

Emperor Cheng Di died of a heart attack while visiting his wife's younger sister. Emperor Ai Di was only a child, and China was ruled by the Wang family.

King Herod died in 4 BC, according to reliable and unanimous sources. Thus the year zero in our calendar cannot be correct, at least not to biblicists. The originator of our calendar was Dionysius Exiguus, a monk, who, with the help of information in Luke 2 and 3, pinpointed the birth of Christ to 25 December, 754 years after the foundation of Rome. It is remarkable that the calendar now used in most parts of the world, including non-Christian countries, should rest on such slender evidence. Incidentally, the New Year should really begin on Christmas Day.

Herod was succeeded by his sons, Archelaus and Herod Antipas. The former was given Judaea and Samaria by the Romans to rule, whereas the latter ruled over Galilee and Peraea. They were given the title tetrarch and were only tributary princes. The reason for their inclusion in the table below is that they feature in the Bible and are therefore of special interest.

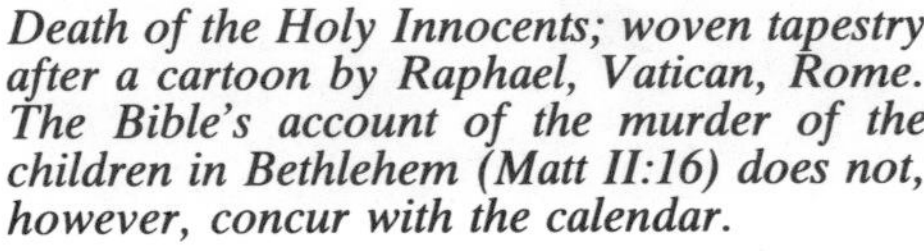
Death of the Holy Innocents; woven tapestry after a cartoon by Raphael, Vatican, Rome. The Bible's account of the murder of the children in Bethlehem (Matt II:16) does not, however, concur with the calendar.

Herod (10–4); Archelaus (4–1)	**Judaea**
Herod (10–4); Herod Antipas (4–1)	**Galilee**
Phraates V	**Parthia**
Augustus	**Rome**
Suinin	**Japan**
Han Cheng Di (10–7); Han Ai Di (7–1)	**China**

10	9	8	7	6	5	4	3	2	1

AD 1-10

ROMANS

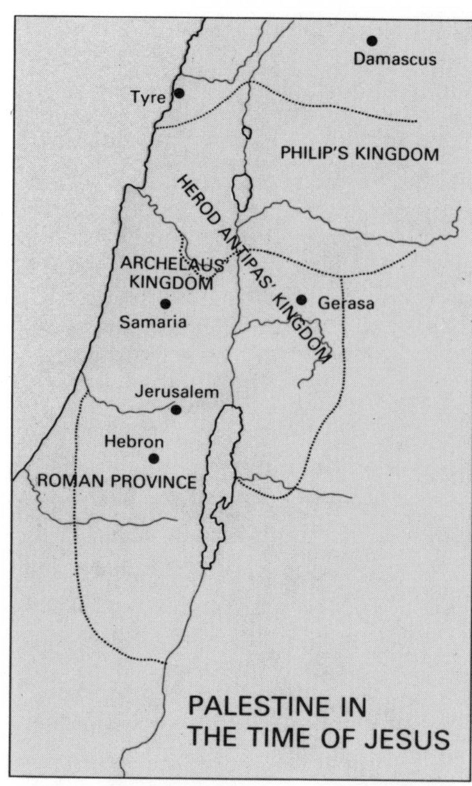
Damascus
Tyre
PHILIP'S KINGDOM
HEROD ANTIPAS' KINGDOM
ARCHELAUS' KINGDOM
Gerasa
Samaria
Jerusalem
Hebron
ROMAN PROVINCE
PALESTINE IN THE TIME OF JESUS

There was, of course, no such period as the year 0. The birth of Christ and New Year were assigned to different days in the new calendar; but prior to this, Christmas Day and New Year's Day had been reckoned as one and the same day in many Christian countries. This had simplified matters; the birth of Christ could be fixed at the midnight hour of the turn of the year. Modern calendar specialists seeking to clarify this would have to regard the year 1 BC as one week longer than usual and the year AD 1 as one week shorter. In practical terms, nobody was aware of the beginning of a new calendar.

Wang Mang, nephew of the old dowager empress, was the *de facto* ruler of China throughout this decade. He reckoned his Xin dynasty, however, from the year AD 9 when the child in whose name he ruled was killed.

Wang Mang is a widely debated figure in Chinese history. This emperor was regarded primarily as a cruel usurper and his name is not even included in the list of rulers. Radicals nowadays judge his political conduct more approvingly, even though it was clearly based on the old Confucian concept that all land belonged to the emperor. Wang Mang forced the new plutocracy to hand over their domains, forbade land-dealing and slave-trading, and introduced a state monopoly on salt, alcoholic liquors, iron and other commodities. A form of state bank was established and income tax was introduced, probably for the first time in history. This was set at ten per cent and affected almost every businessman. Those who tried to pretend they were penniless were subjected instead to an indolence tax. There was such fierce opposition to all this that Wang Mang was forced to repeal the land laws and the ban on slave-trading; and there were revolts by such colourfully named rebel groups as the Red Eyebrows or the Green Woodsmen.

The Emperor Augustus was greatly concerned about population trends in Italy where many people were emigrating and many slaves being imported, while the Roman birthrate was declining. He had a proclamation, *De prole augenda*, read in the senate, and tried to encourage marriage and fertility by introducing a bonus system for children and also by denying certain social rights to married, childless people. The people of Rome continued to be provided with free grain. There were now a quarter of a million Romans drawing public assistance.

Archelaus had been made ruler of Judaea, Samaria and Idumea. Herod Antipas controlled Galilee and Peraea, and Philip ruled Trachonitis, Batanea and Aurinitis. Decapolis was a Hellenic city league; nothing is known of its organization, but it was held together mainly by the common struggle against the desert Bedouins. There is hardly any information concerning the political situation in Palestine at the time of Christ.

Judaea and Samaria were placed under direct Roman administration in AD 7, after the tetrarch, Archelaus had been removed and deported to Gaul. Among the Roman procurators who subsequently governed here, the only one of interest to later generations was Pontius Pilate. He did not, however, assume this office until the 20s.

Wheat measure as depicted in a mural at Ostia where Rome's grain was stored.

Judaea	Archelaus (to 7)
Galilee	Herod Antipas
Parthia	Phraates V (to 4) — Orodes III (4–8) — Vonones I
Rome	Augustus
Japan	Suinin
China	Wang Mang (to 9) — (Xin)

1	2	3	4	5	6	7	8	9	10

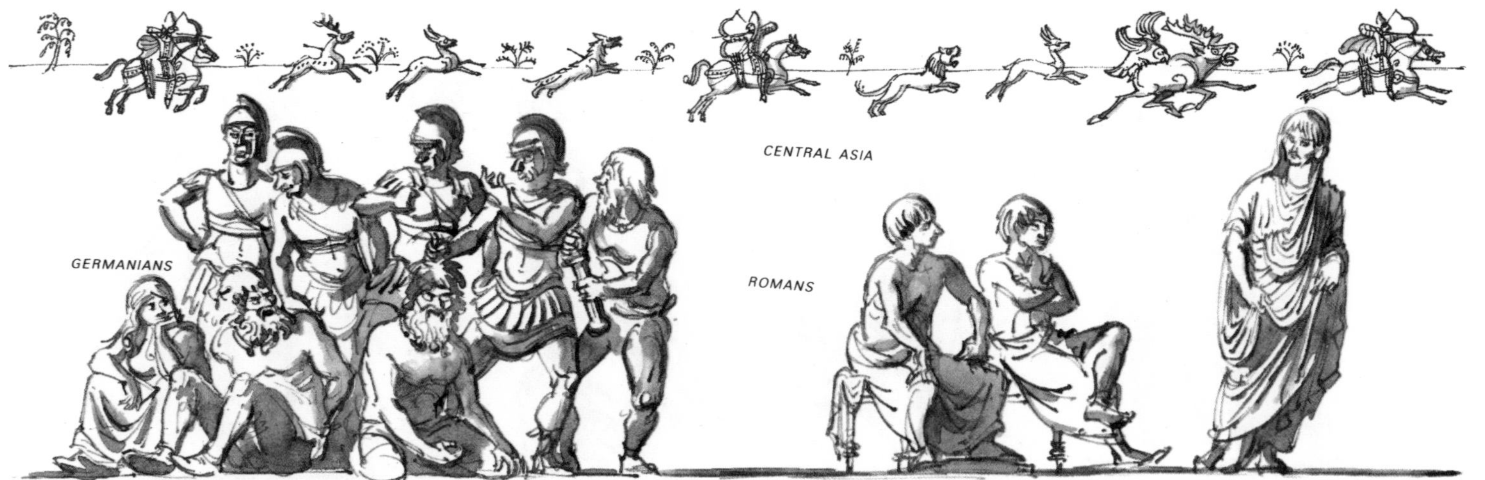
CENTRAL ASIA
GERMANIANS
ROMANS

The Emperor Augustus faced problems over the succession. Finally, almost in desperation, he chose his stepson Tiberius to succeed him. The behaviour of his own kin failed to measure up to his standards and ideals, and in his will he declared that neither his only daughter Julia nor his granddaughter of the same name should be buried in his tomb, which was being erected in Campus Martius.

Augustus died in Nola, east of Naples. After a long talk with his successor, he called for a mirror, adjusted his aged features and then admitted his relations. He asked them if they thought he had performed his part well in the Comedy of Life, and finally recited a Greek poem containing the much-quoted phrase: "*Acta est fabula, plaudite!*" ("The play has ended, applaud!")

Roman expansion northward was halted in AD 9 when three legions were suddenly annihilated in the Germanic Teutoburg Forest. The following year a Germanic tribe called the Marcomanni invaded Bohemia and established a kingdom there.

The victor of the battle in the Teutoburg Forest was Arminius (Hermann) chieftain of the Cherusci. The leader of the Marcomanni was Maroboduus (Marbod). Shortly afterwards hostilities broke out between them, causing Marbod to retreat into Roman territory so that the Marcomanni became dependent upon the Romans. Arminius was eventually murdered by his own people. He was praised as a general by Tacitus and in the 19th century was transformed by the Germans into a national hero.

There was much literary activity in the Roman empire. In about the year AD 18 Strabo's *Geography* appeared. This work, seventeen volumes in Greek, describes the entire known world, including the recently entered wilderness of Britannia and Germania. Strabo was from Pontus and he had travelled in Asia and Egypt. He also wrote a major historical work on various countries, but only his *Geography* was to survive.

At about the same time Titus Livius (Livy) wrote his Roman history, in Latin. When he died in AD 17, this work was complete, and of its 132 volumes a few have survived. Livy was born in Padua and he spent most of his time here, though he was on good terms with the authorities in Rome and wrote patriotically in the spirit of the Emperor Augustus. This was not true of the poet Ovid, who in AD 8 was banished by the emperor to spend the rest of his days at Tomis on the Black Sea. The reason for this banishment is said to be his *Ars Amatoria*, a shrewd, entertaining though undeniably licentious work. After Ovid's banishment his *Metamorphoses* made the rounds of Rome. The emperor could hardly have objected to this since it was splendid poetry in hexameters which dealt with mythological transformations and so preserved many ancient fables and tales for generations to come.

Nothing is known of events in the North. The plough had been invented quite recently, and nomadic burn-beating was being abandoned in favour of established fields on the clay lowlands. Villages were established here which were to survive until the redistribution of land in the 19th century.

Mausoleum of Augustus, from the south. This large circular stone building is located in the Campus Martius, Rome. Inside is a magnificent natural burial mound, surmounted by a statue of the emperor. According to the classical geographer Strabo, this tomb was the first building the traveller encountered when approaching Rome from the north.

Herod Antipas — Galilee
Artabanus II — Parthia
Augustus | Tiberius — Rome
Suinin — Japan
Wang Mang (Xin) — China

11	12	13	14	15	16	17	18	19	20

AD 21-30

ROMANS
PALMYRA
ROMANS

In China revolts were erupting everywhere against Wang Mang, who seemed unable to recruit many followers for his new dynasty and his socialistic policy. He met his death at the hand of an assassin and his rule became a mere incident in the long line of dynasties in Chinese history.

Guang Wu Di a posthumous name meaning The Illustrious Warrior Emperor, was known in his life time as Liu Xiu and was a devout Confucian. Although he restored the old Han dynasty, from his reign onwards this is frequently called the Eastern or Later Han because Liu Xiu moved the seat of the government from Changan, which had been badly damaged during the civil war, to Loyang farther east.

The Huns had by now recovered from their defeat and were again harrying China's northern frontier; in places they even crossed the Great Wall. The central Asian countries slipped out of China's grip during the reign of Wang Mang and the first decade of Guang Wu Di's rule.

Various Latin authors, chiefly Tacitus, have written about the Emperor Tiberius. He emerges as a dutiful, hard, cautious and reserved man, evidently possessing little charm. We know that he fought against prostitution, detested popular spectacles and the theatre, forbade public kissing on New Year's Day and was very thrifty with his own finances and state funds, which hardly enhanced his popularity. He was already fifty-four when he became emperor so that he no longer had much time or energy for major enterprises or exploits. In due course he retired to Capri.

It is impossible to establish dates for the Gospels' accounts of the life and death of Christ. Some theologians, basing themselves on accounts of darkness and the earthquake in Matthew 27:51 and Luke 23:45-45, claim that the crucifixion took place either on 7 April AD 30 or 3 April 33, while the appearance of John the Baptist at the Jordan is set, for some reason, at AD 27. Nobody can disprove these dates.

Pontius Pilate, who played a major role in the biblical accounts of the crucifixion of Christ, was the fifth Roman governor in Judaea. These governors resided in Caesarea and only occasionally came into Jerusalem. Pilate held this office between 26 and 36. He does not seem to have been a particularly tactful politician, for he permitted his soldiers to march into Jerusalem at night carrying standards bearing the emperor's portrait, which the devout Jews regarded as idolatry; and he then used temple treasures to finance the construction of water conduits – an action that led to a bloody uprising. After a massacre of Samaritans who had assembled on Mount Gerizim, Pilate was summoned to Rome for an explanation. By the time he arrived, however, Tiberius had already died and we know nothing of the subsequent fate of the fifth governor of Judaea.

Roman calendar on marble for the months of January, February and March, now in Veroli. They are reckoned on the basis of 8-day weeks between Thursdays (mundinae).

Parthia	Artabanus II
Judaea	Pontius Pilate (from 26)
Galilee	Herod Antipas
Rome	Tiberius
Japan	Suinin
China	Wang Mang (Xin) (21–23); 23–25; Han Guang Wu Di (from 25)

21	22	23	24	25	26	27	28	29	30

ROME

Caligula, successor to Tiberius, built a large racecourse among the Vatican hills and in the centre of this he raised an obelisk which was brought from Egypt in an immense ship. This obelisk remained on the site long after the racecourse had disappeared and the area had been occupied by the Vatican.

In AD 39 Herod Antipas was deposed by the Romans and his territory incorporated in the Roman empire; but this arrangement lasted only a couple of years.

Caligula, who was really named Caius, is generally depicted as an incompetent, evil monster. It was Caligula who is reputed to have said: "Oderint dum metuant" (let them hate, so long as they fear:), and who seriously considered appointing his horse a consul. Most of the anecdotes about Caligula – none of them much to his credit – are derived from the author Suetonius, a good writer but hardly a disciple of the truth.

The total population of Jerusalem was at least 55,000, including 18,000 priests and Levites, and from 4000 to 5000 Pharisees. The latter were members of several devout societies all of which required their members to live strictly according to the laws. Many were laymen, often with considerable political influence. They were not necessarily scribes.

The Goths are said to have emigrated at about this time from the island of Scandza, or possibly Gotland, in three ships: one each for the Ostrogoths and the Visigoths and one for a tribe called the Gepidae, the stragglers. Led by a King Beric, they all landed on the southern Baltic Sea coast where for some generations they inhabited a district around the mouth of the Vistula.

The conversion of the Pharisee Saul into the apostle Paul is sometimes dated at AD 33; in any event, it is certain that the conversion took place during this decade. The account is given in the ninth chapter of the Acts of the Apostles, although this is hardly a dispassionate and impartial source.

Artabanus II was a prominent general under whose command the Parthians expelled the Alani from Parthian territories in the north, and also defeated a Roman army in the west. But Artabanus had problems with his own subjects. In AD 30 the principality of Adiabene embraced Judaism without seeking his permission and other vassal states also showed independent leanings.

There was always rebellion somewhere in the Roman empire. A Numidian, Tacfarinas, led a seven-year war of liberation at Syrtis Minor in Africa and this ended in a Roman victory in AD 24. In Gaul, in AD 21, a certain Julius Sacrovir struggled in vain against a stronger power; in AD 26 a revolt was suppressed in Thracia; and in AD 36 yet another uprising was quelled in Cappadocia. The only really successful insurrection was in Frisia which the Romans were compelled to evacuate.

Paul came from Tarsus in Cilicia. His native tongue was doubtless Armenian but he wrote excellent Greek, even though experts claimed that his Greek contains certain peculiarities.

The official list of Roman popes begins with the apostle Peter. Although this early chronology is not taken too seriously even by devout Catholics, they do, nevertheless, insist that the papal chair is the chair of St Peter.

A temple of Isis was built on the Campus Martius, Rome, in AD 38, indicating that Christianity was not the only alien religion making inroads here. The later Christian worship of the Virgin Mary in Mediterranean lands was in a sense an extension of the much older cult of the Egyptian mother goddess and her oriental counterpart Cybele. Belief in the supernatural found alternative outlets in astrology and fortune-telling, both of which became more popular than ever in Italy.

Discovered at the ancient city of Caesarea on the coast of Palestine in 1961, this fragment is inscribed with not only the emperor's but also Pontius Pilate's name. The latter calls himself praefectus Iudeae, *prefect of Judaea. Har Quesari (Caesarea) Museum.*

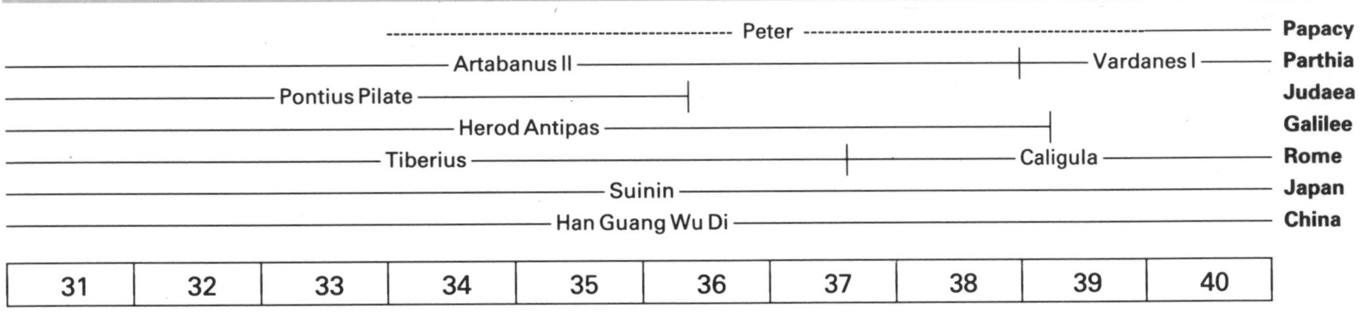
Peter
Papacy
Artabanus II
Vardanes I
Parthia
Pontius Pilate
Judaea
Herod Antipas
Galilee
Tiberius
Caligula
Rome
Suinin
Japan
Han Guang Wu Di
China
31
32
33
34
35
36
37
38
39
40

AD 41-50

CHINA

Caligula was murdered while still young. His uncle Claudius was over fifty when he succeeded his nephew as emperor, and he is described as a scholarly, absent-minded, somewhat ridiculous individual of whose family life Tacitus had some remarkable things to tell. Yet not even Tacitus could deny that there were a number of worthwhile achievements during his reign. Among other things, Claudius regulated state finances by reorganizing the taxation system. At the same time the imperial treasury, the fiscus, was transformed into a kind of bank.

Herod Agrippa I, stepson of the recently deposed Herod Antipas, was in Caligula's good graces and was therefore entrusted with the rule of all Palestine for a number of years. His son Herod Agrippa II became king of the northern part of the country only, though had charge, too, of the high priests in Jerusalem. After his death, towards the close of the century, the Herodian dynasty died out.

The most ancient of all Christian writings known to posterity are the Epistles of Saint Paul. The account of his travels in the Acts of the Apostles is of somewhat later date.

Around the middle of the 1st century AD the population of the Roman empire was approximately 54 million, excluding slaves.

In his domestic policy, Guang Wu Di, followed the Confucian doctrine, whereby successful rule of a country depends on ruling oneself. His foreign policy, however, was conducted with rather more vigour. Annam, which had been lost during the reign of the preceding monarchs, returned to imperial control, and the Chinese also tightened their hold on the semi-barbarian border provinces in the west and north-west.

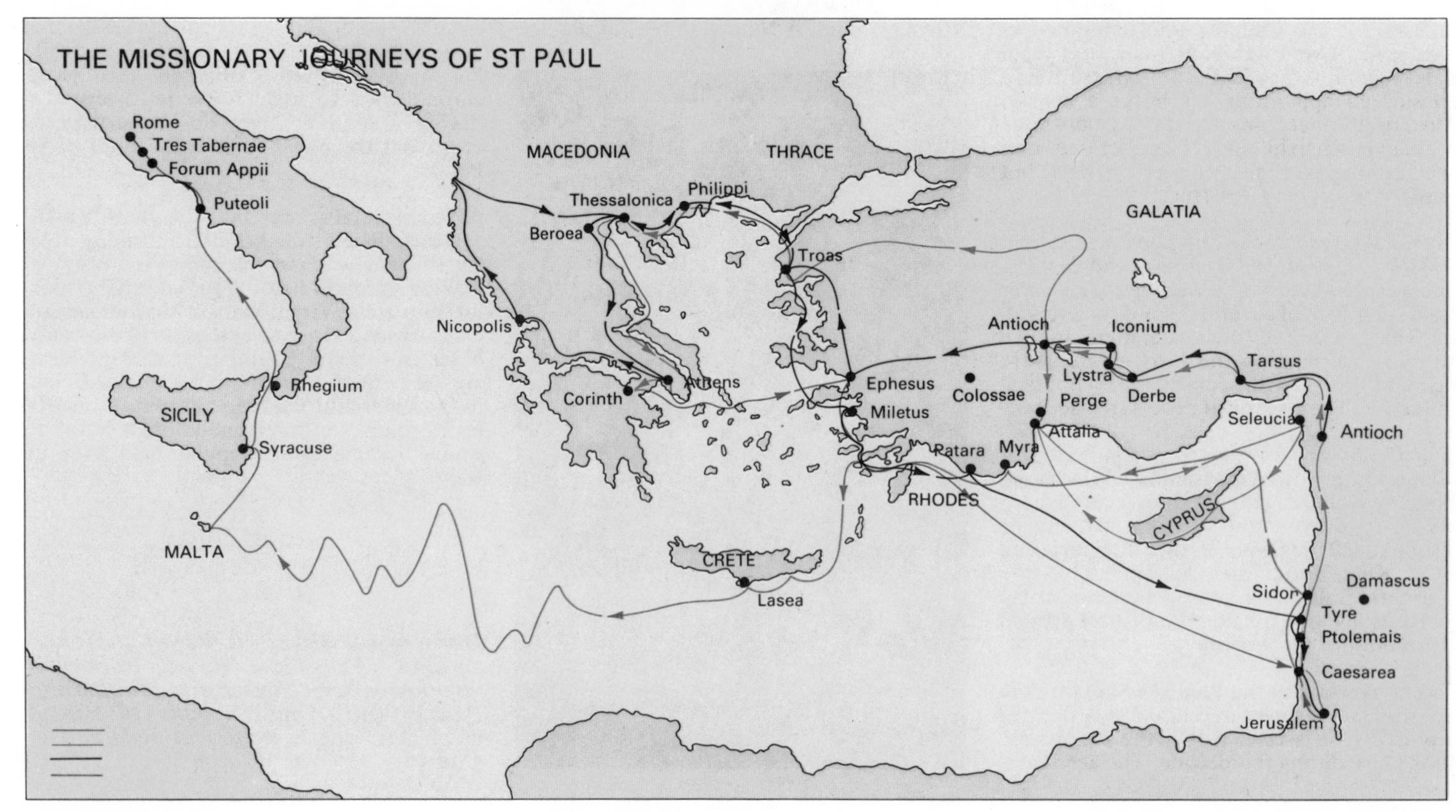
THE MISSIONARY JOURNEYS OF ST PAUL
Rome
Tres Tabernae
Forum Appii
Puteoli
MACEDONIA
THRACE
Thessalonica
Philippi
Beroea
Troas
GALATIA
Nicopolis
Antioch
Iconium
Lystra
Derbe
Tarsus
Rhegium
SICILY
Syracuse
Corinth
Athens
Ephesus
Miletus
Colossae
Perge
Attalia
Seleucia
Antioch
Patara
Myra
RHODES
CYPRUS
MALTA
CRETE
Lasea
Sidon
Damascus
Tyre
Ptolemais
Caesarea
Jerusalem

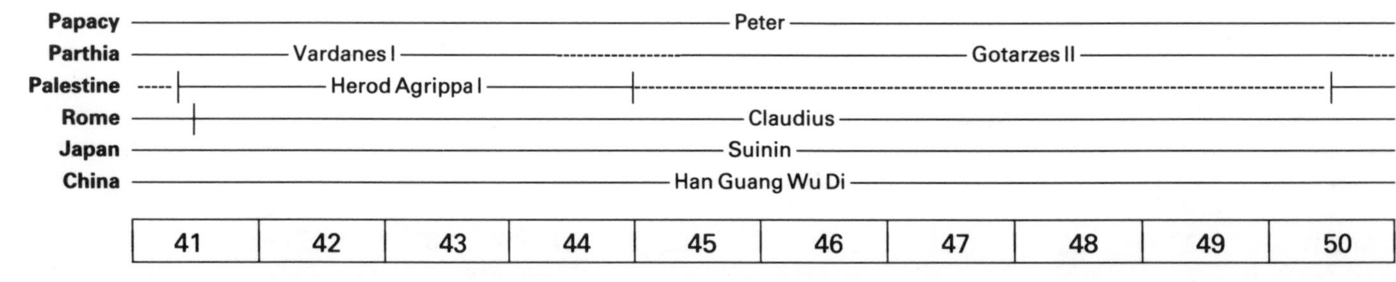
Papacy
Peter
Parthia
Vardanes I
Gotarzes II
Palestine
Herod Agrippa I
Rome
Claudius
Japan
Suinin
China
Han Guang Wu Di
41
42
43
44
45
46
47
48
49
50

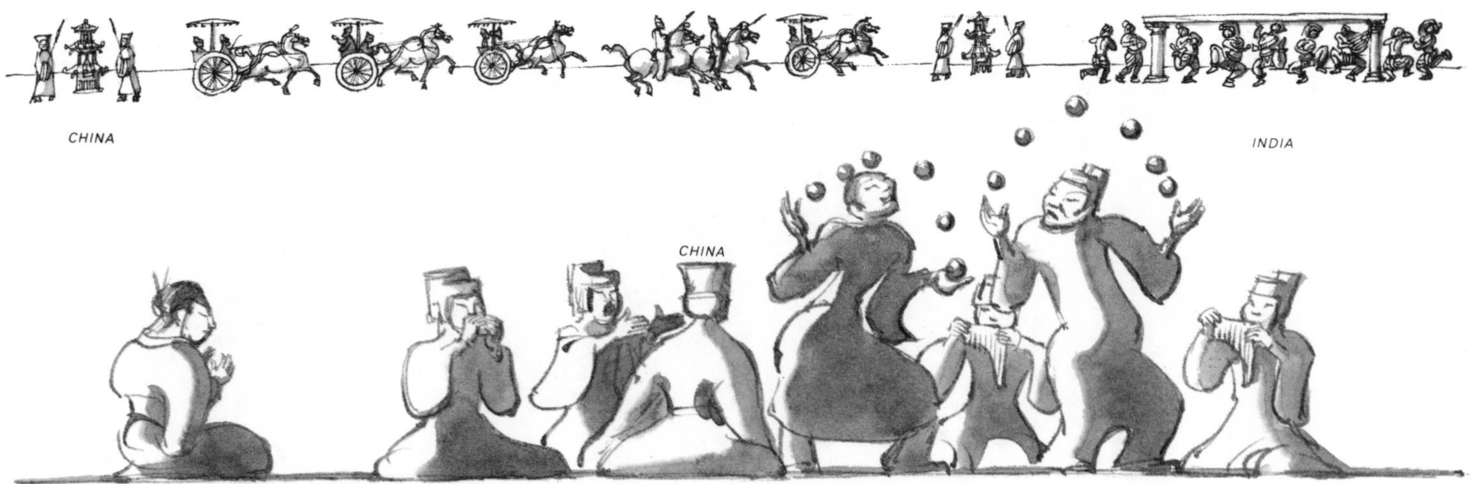
CHINA
CHINA
INDIA

In AD 48 a meeting of the apostles was held in Jerusalem, where Paul's views on international Christianity were heard and sanctioned. The mission among the Jews was restricted, however, to the original congregation in Palestine who observed the laws of Moses. Some persecution had already occurred there. In AD 41 Herod Agrippa I, who had been raised in Rome but had adopted the Jewish faith after becoming king of Judaea, gave orders for the apostle James, brother of John, to be executed.

In AD 41 the king of Yarkand broke openly with China and created his own large kingdom in the heart of Asia. His neighbours now appealed to Emperor Guang Wu Di for protection and aid, but the latter was busy with his own domestic affairs, so they turned instead to the Huns. The general from Hotan who defeated the king of Yarkand and destroyed his kingdom, was himself a vassal of the Huns.

At Pentecost AD 58 the apostle Paul entered the temple in Jerusalem and his presence there caused a tumult. The Roman garrison saved him from being lynched and despatched him to Caesarea where he was held in protective custody for several years in the interests of law and order. In the spring of AD 61 he was sent on to Rome, after which there are no records of him, though the ancient tradition that he died a martyr's death during Nero's persecution is quite credible. Apart from these, there are no reliable facts concerning the life and actions of Paul. It has been suggested that his first missionary journey took place in the mid-40s and that he spent the years AD 55-57 in Ephesus. The Epistle to the Romans is believed to have been written in 54 and the epistles to the Corinthians in AD 57. Otherwise there are conflicting opinions on the dates of his works, though it is generally agreed that the New Testament writings attributed to him, namely 2 Thessalonians, Colossians, Timothy and Titus were, in fact, written after his time.

It is said that the Emperor Claudius was poisoned by his wife Agrippina to make way for her son Nero. The popular belief that Nero set fire to Rome, blaming the Christians and exacting terrible retribution for their crime, is based on information from Tacitus, who made a habit of defaming the emperors. However, later generations of Christian authors denounced Nero as an Antichrist, so that there is probably some truth in the accounts of his persecutions. All sources agree, nevertheless, that affairs went smoothly at the beginning of Nero's reign.

Greek and Latin were equally acceptable administrative languages in the Roman provinces, but all officials were Roman citizens and were required to write documents in Latin, especially their wills. The Greek language was predominant, of course, in the eastern part of the empire but was also widely used in the western part, particularly in Gaul where for many generations Massilia had been a Greek centre.

Many of the ancient local languages within the frontiers of the Empire were extinct or rapidly disappearing. But there was still some literature in both the Syrian and Coptic tongues and this was gaining ground with the progress of Christianity.

The Parthian kingdom, which for several centuries played a major role in world politics, appears not to have had its own historian. The Parthian kings minted many coins through the ages, and these are at least helpful in sorting out the list of rulers. From accounts by Greek, Roman and Chinese writers, it would seem that Parthian history largely consisted of wars against these three powers. At this moment, however, all was apparently quiet.

Election propaganda on a wall in Pompeii, a 'poster' for the local authorities.

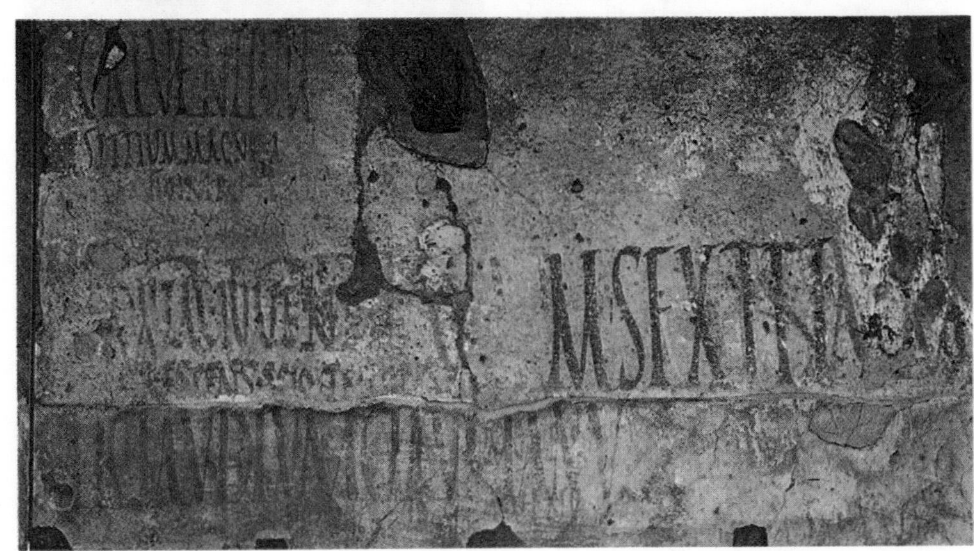

Peter — Papacy
Vonones II | Vologases I — Parthia
Herod Agrippa II — Palestine
Claudius | Nero — Rome
Suinin — Japan
Han Guang Wu Di | Han Ming Di — China

51	52	53	54	55	56	57	58	59	60

ROME
DURA-EUROPUS

Emperor Nero's enjoyment of singing and acting, was regarded as disgraceful by his biographers, who described his life, after the first few years of benevolent rule, as being depraved and bloodthirsty. He killed his virtuous wife Octavia and marrried a certain Poppaea Savina, whom he subsequently kicked to death. He had his mother murdered, set Rome on fire to make way for his golden palace, and burned Christians alive. Indeed, according to the authors his villainy knew no bounds. When his subjects could stand no more, and the revolution came, he died mouthing the familiar words: *"Qualis artifex perio!"* (What an artist is lost in me!)

Three leading literary figures were compelled to commit suicide after an unsuccessful conspiracy against Nero – the philosopher Seneca, the author Petronius and the poet Lucan. Seneca wrote Latin tragedies of great literary merit, and fine prose dialogues. Petronius main work is the *Satyricon* and contains, among other things, the entertaining story of the feast arranged by the upstart Trimalchio. Lucan's great poem is *Pharsalia* in which he praises the mighty Pompey; this in itself was practically treason.

Emperor Ming Di was a scholar who personally delivered lectures to large audiences on Confucian classics; learning and education became fashionable and not only court dignitaries and concubines but soldiers and peasants too discovered the pleasure of philosophy. Ming Di also sent out an army to repel the Huns who were blocking the way through central Asia. A young man named Ban Chao succeeded in restoring China's authority and opened the silk route right through to Persia.

Legend claims very precisely that in AD 61 Emperor Ming Di had a strange dream: he saw in the sky a golden figure which came down over the palace and swept backwards and forwards, illuminated by both the sun and moon. A learned court official informed the emperor that what he had seen was a celestial reflection of the holy Buddha in India, whereupon the emperor sent an expedition of scholars to the banks of the Ganges to learn more about this god. Two Indian missionaries accompanied them back to China and one of these, Gobharana, or Zhu-fa-lan, worked there for a long time and translated the holy scriptures of Buddhism into Chinese.

Whatever the truth of this story, Buddhism did reach China at about this time and soon spread extensively.

In AD 70 Jerusalem was destroyed and the Jews were dispersed, the consequences of a Jewish revolt which had begun as early as AD 66. There is a detailed account of this by the Pharisee Flavius Josephus who was actually in command in Galilee but who contrived, nevertheless, to ingratiate himself with the Emperor Vespasian after all his colleagues had committed suicide in the beleaguered fortress of Jotapata.

Three Roman emperors followed each other in rapid succession between the reigns of Nero and Vespasian. These were Galba, Otho and Vitellius. Vitellius was renowned for his love of food. He is said to have kept the Roman fleet busy bringing home delicacies for a vast table named Minerva's shield. Vespasian, on the other hand, was a simple and practical man, noted, among other things, for his comment on income from taxes on public conveniences: *'Non olet'* (It doesn't smell).

Above: Nero's profile on a Roman coin. He is said to have been very handsome as a young man. He was short-sighted and used a polished emerald as a sort of monocle at the arena.
Below: figure on a column in Verona, erected in honour of Jupiter during Nero's reign.

Papacy	Peter ---- Linus
Parthia	Vologases I
Palestine	Herod Agrippa II
Rome	Nero | Galba Oth. Vit. | Vesp.
Japan	Suinin
China	Han Ming Di

61	62	63	64	65	66	67	68	69	70

ROME
TITUS
TITUS

In AD 79 the volcano Vesuvius erupted and buried the cities of Pompeii and Herculaneum. Two remarkable letters to the historian Tacitus from his friend Pliny the Younger describe this great disaster in detail. Pliny's maternal uncle and adoptive father, Pliny the Elder, died in the volcanic ash and sulphur fumes when in his capacity as admiral he attempted to save the citizens, including a personal friend, by taking them out to sea. In this way antiquity lost a singularly industrious writer who had produced many books on different subjects, including the celebrated *Natural History*, in thirty-seven volumes, the only one of his works to survive.

Modern excavations in Pompeii have produced invaluable information on everyday life in the lst century AD, besides bearing tragic witness to the fate of the citizens. Innumerable tools and utensils have come to light, and it is possible to walk in their streets, enter their homes and places of work, even see graffiti scrawled by their schoolboys on the walls.

In AD 61 a British princess named Boadicea, or possibly Boudicca, initiated a war of liberation against the Romans when they entered her kingdom following the death of her royal father. The enemy fortresses of Londinium, Camulodunum (Colchester) and Verulamium (St. Albans) were destroyed, but the Romans eventually gained the upper hand and took terrible retribution. Ten years later the Romans moved into the north-west and took new territories.

According to dependable sources, the apostles Peter and Paul were executed in Rome in AD 67. The Gospel of Mark appeared in the 60s. The author is believed to have been the interpreter of the apostle Peter, though some claim he was the bishop of Alexandria. In any event, his Gospel describes the life of Christ for a period of less than one year. The language is crude, popular, but very effective.

In AD 68 a division of the tenth Roman legion, marched down to Qumran on the Dead Sea and seized a place that had been inhabited by a devout Jewish community for at least a century and a half. These people now concealed in ten or more caves an immense wealth of Hebrew manuscripts which were not rediscovered until the 1940s. The Dead Sea Scrolls are the oldest biblical manuscript ever to have been found. Some of them date from as early as 100 BC and none of them can have been written after AD 68.

In Rome, where the Colosseum was finally completed after some ten years of unemployment relief work, Europe's first professor was living and working. His name was Quintilian and he received a state salary for instruction in the subject of rhetoric, which included the science of literature.

In late antiquity the Colosseum was regarded as one of the seven wonders of the world, and this amphitheatre was unquestionably an enormous feat even by modern standards. The seven-metre-deep substructure beneath the arena provided a space for a water system, animal cages, etc.

In Pompeii compact layers of volcanic ash formed moulds round the bodies of the dead. These models have since been used to recreate their figures and postures.

Linus — Anacletus I	**Papacy**
Vologases I — Vologases II — Pacorus II	**Parthia**
Herod Agrippa II	**Palestine**
Vespasianus — Titus	**Rome**
Keiko-Tenno	**Japan**
Han Ming Di — Han Zhang Di	**China**

71	72	73	74	75	76	77	78	79	80

INDIA
CHINA

Britain, originally invaded during Caesar's day, was systematically exploited from the reign of the Emperor Claudius onwards. The principal Roman military settlement in the North was at Eburacum (York) where a legion was stationed. There was battle in AD 84 at a place which the victorious Romans called Mons Graupius. They had now reached the Scottish border and never advanced farther north than this.

The Emperor Titus, who reigned only for a couple of years, had an exceptionally good reputation among Roman historians, unlike his brother Domitian. Titus had one aim in life, to do good; on one occasion when several hours had passed without his performing any useful action, he exclaimed: *"Amici, diem perdidi"* (My friends, I have lost a day). Domitian, on the other hand, is remembered for sentencing unchaste vestal virgins to death and persecuting Christians. Although considered cruel and ineffectual, some modern scholars point to an improvement in the coinage and in provincial administration during Domitian's reign, and suggest that the malicious accounts could have been spread by the party which eventually assassinated him.

All the New Testament texts of any significance had been completed by this time. No exact dates exist for any of them but modern scholars think that the three first Gospels were written in the 70s, John's Gospel sometime between AD 70 and AD 90, and Revelations perhaps around AD 100. The Acts of the Apostles stemmed from the same period as St Luke's Gospel. The final editing of the biblical texts occurred mainly during the 4th century.

In the 80s occupied Germany was organized into two Roman provinces known as Germania Superior and Germania Inferior.

The historian Tacitus attained honour during his lifetime as an official: the Emperor Nerva conferred a consulship on him, and under Trajan he was for a time proconsul in Asia. Nevertheless, his views on life and mankind were pessimistic, and his greatest work, the *Annals*, is an imposing, wholly successful attempt to interpret everything in the worst possible light. This deals mainly with Tiberius, Claudius and Nero. His *Historiae* describe Roman lives and events from Galba until Domitian. Unfortunately,most of this work is lost. The author was now aged about thirty but had already served as a quaestor under Titus and as praestor under Domitian. Another great author, Plutarch, lived in Chaeroneia in Boeotia. Successful in his lifetime, and long to be remembered, Plutarch left two major works in Greek, one of them a series of biographies of great men, which was to prove of immeasurable significance to Western literature.

The early popes were obscure figures. However, an important letter to the Corinthians was written by Clement I, which deals with the structure of the hierarchy. Like all his colleagues prior to the 4th century, Clement was canonized.

The triumphal Arch of Titus in Rome commemorates the defeat of the Jews and the destruction of Jerusalem. This seven-armed candelabrum is one of the spoils of victory.

Papacy	Anacletus I ---------- Clement I
Parthia	Pacorus II ---------- Osroes
Palestine	Herod Agrippa II
Rome	Titus | Domitian
Japan	Keiko-Tenno
China	Han Zhang Di | Han He Di

81	82	83	84	85	86	87	88	89	90

INDIA
PARTHIANS
CHINA

Along the northern frontier of the Roman empire the first section of the fortification system, known as *limes*, was constructed. This consisted of a line of timber lookout-towers, each within good view of the next. Citadels for accommodating troops were built on the Main and on the Neckar.

In Roman Britain, a fortification system was gradually built right across the country in the north. It has become known as Hadrian's Wall and it marks the northern most limit of Roman expansion in Britain.

A considerable number of Buddhist missionaries were now successfully at work in China. Most of them came from Hotan, Kuchan, Kashgar and other central Asiatic regions, but this group also included a Persian prince, who had turned monk and made a valuable contribution as a translator into Chinese. Buddhism was the first religion to be introduced in China which gave some form of answer to the question of the purpose and meaning of life. Confucius and Laozi left these questions open and the Taoist philosopher Wang Zhong, who was active at this time, did not believe that Heaven was in the least concerned with human existence. "Man is like a little flea in our clothes or an ant in an underground nest. How can puny man hope to influence the immensity of the heavens? This is indeed vainglory."

The list of rulers in the Parthian kingdom was very complicated in this and the attendant decades. Vologases II, Pacorus II and Osroes vanish and reappear several times, and several other names turn up in certain years. A state of great political unrest appears to have prevailed.

In north-west India a major power was flourishing around its capital Peshawar. As elsewhere in India, the history of this state is very confused. A Scythian tribe, the Pahlava, had secured its independence in the easternmost part of the Parthian realm around the close of the previous century and at about the same time a chieftain known as Kūjula Kadphises had united the five Tochari, or Yuechi tribes in Bactria. He had seized power from the Pahlava in the Kabul valley, after which he and his son Vīma Kadphises consolidated the kingdom and made north-west India into a vassal state. Around AD 80 the Kadphises family was succeeded in this huge country by a certain Kaniska who initiated a new dynasty. His realm extended from Benares and Kabul right down to the Vindhya mountains.

In Peshawar, Kaniska erected a large stupa over the relics of Buddha, but his interest was in unification. A council with representatives of several sects was held in his reign and this supervised the translation of canonical writings from Prakrit to Sanskrit.

In China the Han dynasty was in decline, as a continuous struggle for power raged between royalty, officials and conniving eunuchs. The eunuchs played a major role throughout Chinese history though they had never been more vicious than in the circles around the Emperor He Di. The senior eunuch had put to death the dowager empress and all her family, thereby establishing power over the young emperor. He now conferred upon himself all manner of titles and offices, which was greatly resented by the Confucian scholars who had taken extensive academic courses in order to achieve such distinctions.

Almost without assistance from his native land, a Chinese officer named Ban Chao recovered almost the whole of central Asia from the Huns who had blocked the trans-Asian trade routes and assured authority in many of the central Asian principalities. With thirty-six men and an adjutant, Ban Chao arrived at the border state of Shanshan in the neighbourhood of Lop Nur. Here he found a large Hun embassy which he attacked and destroyed almost to the last man. This so horrified and impressed the king of Shanshan that shortly afterwards he swore an oath of allegiance and obedience to the emperor of China. Ban Chao and his little contingent rode on into Hotan, which he seized in the same audacious fashion. For some years he continued this hazardous stategy, playing off a series of small states against one another and recruiting local armies wherever he could gather support. The Chinese emperor finally sent him reinforcements and proclaimed him viceroy of the western region. But by this time his task had virtually been fulfilled, the trading routes to the Near East had been opened and there were Chinese garrisons established as far west as the Oxus. One of Ban Chao's colleagues had even penetrated as far as the Black Sea; but he halted here when the Persians insisted that it would take three years to sail across this ocean.

Lacquered boxes in bronze or wood, exquisitely decorated with figure compositions, were made in China. The lid of the one shown here represents the mountain of paradise in the ocean.

Ruler(s)	Realm
Clement I ---- Evaristus	Papacy
Pacorus II ----	Parthia
Herod Agrippa II	Palestine
Domitian — Nerva — Trajan	Rome
Keiko-Tenno	Japan
Han He Di	China

91	92	93	94	95	96	97	98	99	100

AD 101-110

ROME

Christianity was by no means restricted to the Roman Empire. It also had its disciples beyond the Tigris in the land of the Parthians. Communities emerged in Arbela and soon afterwards in Susa as well, probably because Judaism was already the national religion in the principality of Adiabene.

A war of succession was raging in the Parthian kingdom.

The Emperor Trajan was a professional soldier. In two campaigns he overran Dacia north of the lower Danube and seized a part of Arabian territory south and east of Palestine. The last of the vassal states, except for certain areas in Armenia and the Crimea, were directly incorporated in the Roman Empire. Towards the end of his reign, Trajan engaged the Parthians and occupied the whole of Mesopotamia including the provincial capital Ctesiphon.

No more is known of Pope Evaristus except that he was Greek, born in Bethlehem. His successors, Alexander I and Sixtus I, are even more shadowy.

Sextus Julius Frontinus died in 103. He had been a consul, governor of Britain, and an augur. Among other official posts, he managed the water conduits in Rome and wrote a book on the subject, *De acquae ductu*. Although the aqueducts were solidly built, the farmers along the routes were able to steal some of the water for their fields.

The Roman province of Arabia was identical with the Kingdom of the Nabataeans, whose last king, Nabilus, died in 105 after a thirty-year reign. The Romans gave the country a new capital, Bostra, in place of Petra, but the latter continued to flourish.

In an effort to overcome the declining birthrate in Italy and remedy the poor state of agriculture Rome introduced the alimentary system. The state allocated considerable sums for low-interest mortgage loans to the farmer and the interest gained from these was distributed to the children of poor Roman citizens. These funds were administered by the local authorities, though the whole system was superintended by imperial prefects. In addition, 5000 Roman children were given a free allocation of grain. The organization of these charitable arrangements was a large-scale undertaking.

The old philosopher Epictetus lived in Nicopolis. In his youth he had been a slave in Rome, but he now had a school in his native province where one of his pupils was a talented youngster named Arrian. Arrian compiled the stoic teachings of Epictetus in two extensive collections, presenting them as devout, undogmatic Christian doctrines which still make agreeable reading today.

The eunuch Zai Lun, overseer of public works in China, soaked and beat into a pulp a mixture of mulberry bark, hemp shoots, rags and old fishing nets, and thereby invented paper. This discovery, which occurred in the year 105, was especially timely because of the increasing interest in literature and the scarcity of books.

The first dictionary of the Chinese language was put together by a certain Xiu Xin, whose principles were the foundation for all future lexicography. He began with the radicals, which represent the fundamental features of the language. Chinese has no alphabet in the Western sense of the term.

Above: A bridge over the Danube in the Roman province of Pannonia. Roman bronze coin from Trajan's time. Below: Bust of Trajan in the Vatican. The citizens of Rome, who enjoyed comparative peace and quiet since he conducted his wars in distant parts, honoured the emperor with the title Optimus: 'The Best.' His reputation endured, for future emperors were exhorted officially to be happier than Augustus and better than Trajan: felicior Augusto, melior Traiano.

Papacy — Evaristus — Alexander I

Parthia — Osroes (Chosroes)

Rome — Trajan

Japan — Keiko-Tenno

China — Han He Di — Shang Di — Han An Di

101	102	103	104	105	106	107	108	109	110

ROME

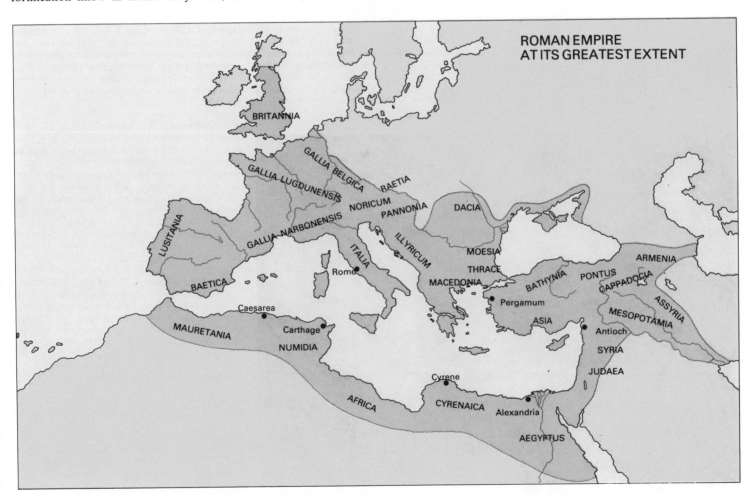

The Roman empire reached its greatest territorial limits in the time of the Emperor Trajan. In many areas, these frontiers were only vaguely defined. Probably the most definite boundaries were in central Europe where early in his career the Emperor himself had helped to establish the long lines of fortification know as *limes*. They were, of course, less well-defined in Dacia, the newly acquired area north of the lower Danube. In 119 this was divided into two provinces and peopled with colonists whose Latin tongue was in time to become Romanian.

Both Trajan and Hadrian were born in Spain. Hadrian, who assumed office in the middle of the war, established peaceful conditions by relinquishing Trajan's conquests in Mesopotamia. He then devoted himself to consolidating the Roman empire within existing frontiers. His tours of inspection included Gaul, Germania, Spain, Africa, Greece, Egypt, Syria, Asia Minor and the Danube Provinces.

ROMAN EMPIRE
AT ITS GREATEST EXTENT

BRITANNIA
GALLIA BELGICA
GALLIA LUGDUNENSIS
RAETIA
NORICUM
PANNONIA
DACIA
LUSITANIA
GALLIA NARBONENSIS
ITALIA
ILLYRICUM
MOESIA
THRACE
MACEDONIA
BAETICA
Rome
ARMENIA
BATHYNIA
PONTUS
CAPPADOCIA
ASSYRIA
Pergamum
ASIA
MESOPOTAMIA
Antioch
SYRIA
JUDAEA
Caesarea
MAURETANIA
Carthage
NUMIDIA
Cyrene
AFRICA
CYRENAICA
Alexandria
AEGYPTUS

Alexander I — Sixtus I	**Papacy**
Osroes (Chosroes)	**Parthia**
Trajan — Hadrian	**Rome**
Keiko-Tenno	**Japan**
Han An Di	**China**

111	112	113	114	115	116	117	118	119	120

AD 121-130

ARABS
DURA-EUROPUS

The Emperor Hadrian, whose right to succeed Trajan had not been undisputed, established his position through various popular measures. He abandoned Trajan's policy of conquest and doubled the soldiers' allowances, restored the privileges of the senate and annulled landowners' taxation debts of about 900 million sesterces.

In Britain, the Roman conquest had reached a line that could not be pushed any farther northward. There was continuous heavy fighting in this area, nor was it always the Britons who took the offensive. In the 120s the Romans began fortifying their frontier in earnest. Hadrian's Wall was an extensive fortification with forts and many watch-towers; it was not completed before the 180s.

During Trajan's reign the Romans were able to learn something of the people and conditions beyond their northern frontier from the latest work of the historian Tacitus, entitled *Germania*. Here Tacitus describes the clean living habits of the Germanic peoples, implicitly denouncing his own degenerate countrymen. Despite its tendentious nature, *Germania* is invaluable as the earliest such record we possess. According to Tacitus the Germanic landscape is made up of vast forests and dreadful swamps. It is inhabited by many tribes and in the far north on an island in the sea dwell the powerful Suiones, with weapons and ships, who are ruled by a single leader and in peacetime keep all their arms locked and guarded. Other Germanic tribes, however, usually carry their weapons with them and more important matters are discussed frankly by all the people during bouts of drinking and revelry, though decisions are postponed until the following day, after they have become sober. They worship gods whom Tacitus identifies with Mars and Hercules, and the earth goddess Nerthus, Hertha or Terra Mater, who dwells in a carriage on an island in the sea and who on ceremonial occasions consorts with the dead. From time to time her carriage and vestments are washed by slaves who are drowned the moment they have completed their task. More recent investigations indicate that in due course Nerthus changed sex and became known as Njord on Iceland.

The emperors An Di and Shun Di were unpopular with Confucian officials in China, because of their habit of appointing court eunuchs to the leading offices. These eunuchs were often high-born, capable individuals rather than simple harem guards, but they were awarded titles and dignities that had been reserved previously for the academically qualified. Open conflicts erupted between these groups in the imperial palace, culminating in victory for the eunuchs who arrested and executed thousands of their rivals.

After Keiko-Tenno, who was certainly a legendary figure even though the years of his reign are very precisely documented, there appears to have been a gap in Japan's traditional list of rulers. It does not become chronologically reliable until the 6th century, though a continuous series of more or less mythical emperors is listed from about AD 200 onwards.

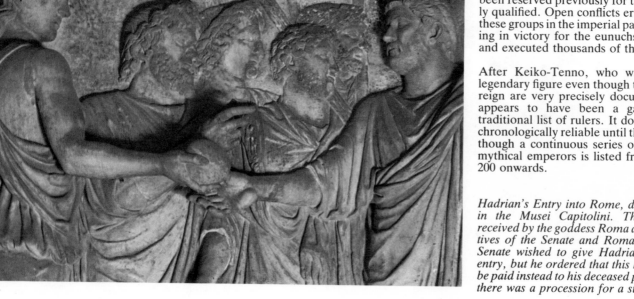

Hadrian's Entry into Rome, detail of a relief in the Musei Capitolini. The emperor is received by the goddess Roma and representatives of the Senate and Roman people. The Senate wished to give Hadrian a triumphal entry, but he ordered that this honour should be paid instead to his deceased predecessor, so there was a procession for a statue.

Papacy — Sixtus I ---- Telesphorus
Parthia — Osroes (Chosroes) ---- Vologases III
Rome — Hadrian
Japan — Keiko-Tenno
China — Han An Di | Han Shun Di

121	122	123	124	125	126	127	128	129	130

INDIA
ROME
PALMYRA

The Emperor Hadrian travelled almost continuously and needed to consult maps. A type widely used during imperial Roman times was the *itineraria picta*. Only one of these has survived, the Peutinger Table though, in fact, it is a 10th-century copy.

Hadrian moved about at a remarkable rate and managed to visit all corners of his vast empire; from distant Arabia in the east to remote Britain in the west. There were post-houses, each with a reserve of forty horses, at regular intervals all along the main highways of the empire.

In the 130s a Roman city was built on the ruins of Jerusalem. This was named Aelia Capitolina in homage to Hadrian, whose surname was Aelius. A Jewish revolt then erupted, led by Bar Kokhba. In the long run his struggle was hopeless, of course, but it lasted four years (132-136) and ended with the almost complete annihilation of the Jews in Palestine.

Little or nothing is known about the popes Sixtus I, Telesphorus and Hyginus. The last two were Greeks. Telesphorus was a hermit until elevated to the office of pope, and he is said to have introduced midnight mass on Christmas Eve.

A religious charlatan named Zhang Ling set himself up as a prophet and healer on Mt Guming in China, having been informed that the simple, honest people of the district were easy to sway. He wrote a work in twenty-four parts on Tao and conducted successful alchemical experiments with the rejuvenation elixirs of the Dragon and the Tiger, which enabled him to halve his age at will. He also dug up supernatural books from the ground and studied these until he was so accomplished that he could be present in four different places at one and the same time. Zhan Ling is credited with having founded Taoism as an established religion, which it could not claim to be according to the obscure philosophy of Laozi or the blithe mysticism of Zhuangzi.

Detail of the Peutinger Table. Paris is shown in the upper right hand corner. National Library, Vienna.

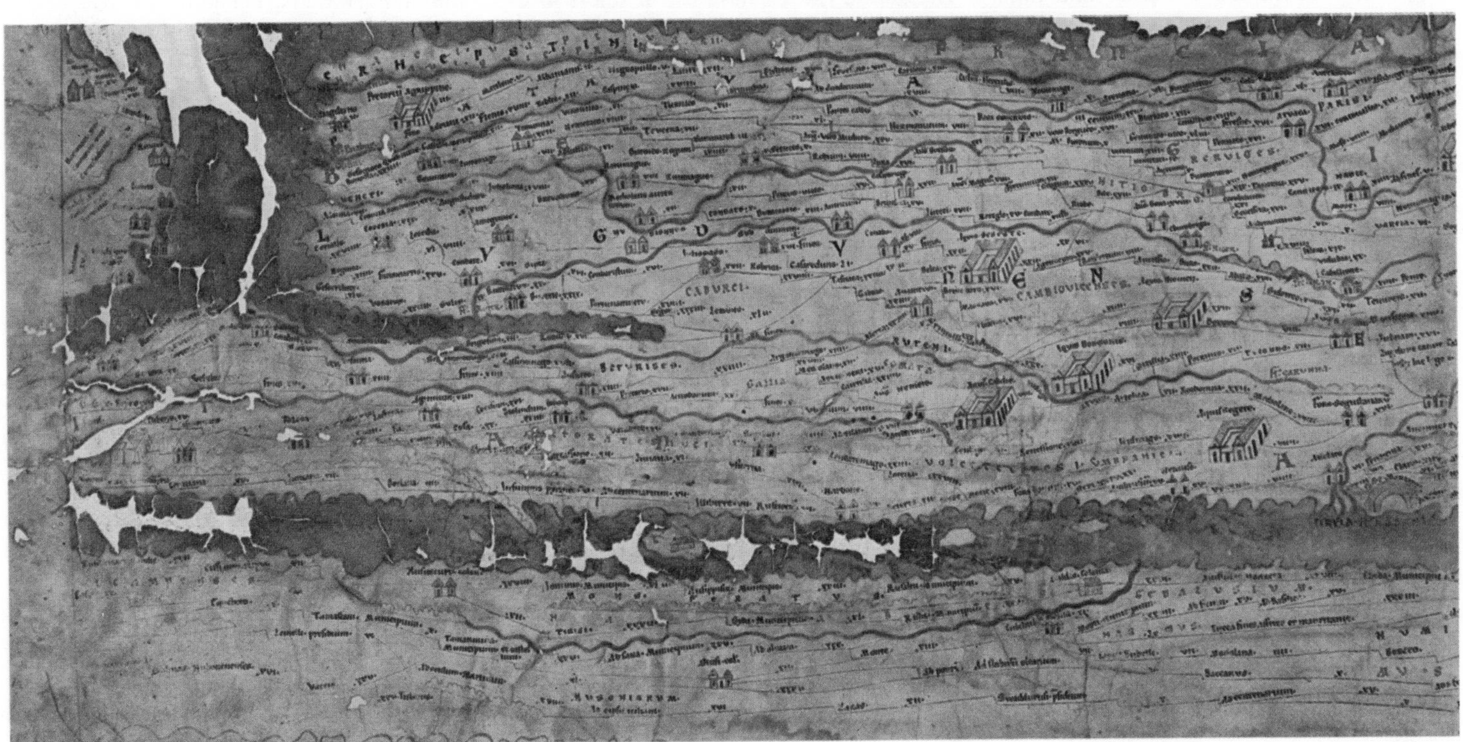

Telesphorus — Hyginus	Papacy
Mithradates IV	Parthia
Hadrian | Antoninus Pius	Rome
	Japan
Han Shun Di	China

131	132	133	134	135	136	137	138	139	140

AD 141-150

INDIA
CHINA

It is strange that despite the very long reign of the Emperor Antoninus Pius, there is practically nothing to relate of him. He is described in the records as a paragon of virtue though he neither said nor achieved anything remarkable, apart perhaps from gorging himself to death on Swiss cheese.

During his reign there was peace in the empire, and Romanization continued in the provinces where every local aristocrat usually held Roman citizenship and even acquired a Latin name, a *nomen gentile*. The soldiers, seldom Italians by birth, usually served in the legions for twenty to twenty-five years, naturally learning the language fluently. At the end of their service when they were given pensions and sent out as colonists to Africa or Gaul, they continued to speak and think largely in Latin.

In material terms, too, the empire became increasingly uniform. The cities looked much alike with temples, theatres, schools, public baths and squares all laid out according to the same pattern. Many of them were old military camps or veteran colonies where the town plan was already established, though now embellished with columns and marble statues. One very modern metropolis was Carthage, rebuilt after a fire in 145. This general state of peace did not, of course, rule out dissatisfaction in various places. Between 144 and 152 there was unrest in Mauretania, in 153 in Egypt, in 155 in Judaea, and in 160 in Africa. In Egypt the trouble was related to taxation demands. These led the peasants to abandon their villages and they had to be returned forcibly by the army since the authorities refused to have taxable land standing idle. Economically, Egypt was in a decline, due, to some extent, to the wealthy families of Alexandria who had appropriated too much land.

The gap in the Chinese list of rulers in the year 145 arises from an attempt by the empress's brother to end the courtly power of the eunuchs. But the latter poisoned the emperor, Shun Di, and seized power themselves. Shun Di's son, Huan Di, was still only a child and was entirely in the hands of the court eunuchs throughout this and much of the following decade. When the dowager empress died in 159, the young Huan Di instigated a palace revolution with the aid of the eunuchs and got rid of her family. After this, the political influence of the chief eunuch became greater than ever.

The shipping magnate Marcion of Sinope joined the Christian congregation in Rome, donated his fortune to it and began preaching an unconventional doctrine. He proclaimed God is pure love. The Old Testament God was thus of an inferior order. Christ came down to earth to save mankind as a messenger of the true God, who has nothing to do with the creation of man but takes the latter's part out of sheer goodness. In 144 Marcion was expelled from the congregation and was afterwards harshly attacked by all the church fathers. Yet his heretical teachings nevertheless won a large following for several generations to come.

Surya, the Indian Sun god (left), often mentioned in the Veda. Sandstone statue in the Mathura Museum. Centre: Indian relief from Amarvati. Below: Antoninus Pius. Museo delle Terme, Rome.

Papacy	Pius I
Parthia	Mithradates IV — (147) Vologases IV
Rome	Antoninus Pius
Japan	
China	Han Shun Di — (145) Chong Di — Zhi Di — (146) Han Huan Di

141	142	143	144	145	146	147	148	149	150

ROME
CHINA

An advanced culture, or more properly a series of cultures, had long been flourishing in Mexico; the only common factor between them was the cultivation of Indian corn. Each successive race had replaced the aesthetic ideals of its predecessor with its own over the space of several millennia. There were forty-two unrelated languages, though twenty-two of these formed a group known as Maya. One anonymous race built a temple known as Teotihuacán. Nobody knows where these people came from or what language they spoke, but there is no disputing their administration, mathematical and artistic talents. The Sun pyramid in Teotihuacán was an immense structure: millions of cubic metres of sun-dried bricks had to be carried manually to the site, for this preceded the arrival of the wheel and there were no beasts of burden. The Mayas, for their part, had a hieroglyphic script and also a number system which was superior to that of the Romans. They could make advanced astronomical calculations and determine the orbits of certain celestial bodies, while their calendar was about as exact as the Julian version. Their years consisted of eighteen months, each of twenty days, plus five or six extra days not on the calendar.

Polycarp, bishop of Smyrna and disciple of no less a person than the apostle John, came to Rome during the pontificate of Anicetus to discuss matters pertaining to Easter; there were divided opinions on the date and religious significance of this feast. The Jewish Passover related to the exodus from Egypt and the Christian version of the festival also related to this event, so that Christ's death and resurrection were associated with the march through the Red Sea as a symbol of the people's fall and salvation. The whole concept was very complicated and it is not clear what views Polycarp held on the matter. Easter was also connected with the full moon and the spring equinox, and there was discussion as to whether it should be celebrated on a specific date or a particular day of the week: the one alternative automatically ruled out the other, since the seven-day week is not an exact part of the year. It was to be another century and a half or more before agreement was reached on this issue in Christian circles.

At about this time the Goths are said to have reached the north coast of the Black Sea, after having lived for some time in the Weichsel region south of the Baltic Sea. They had come here from Scandinavia. Practically everything known about the early history of the Goths in the West derives from a Byzantine priest name Jordanes. The Scandinavian origin of the Goths is generally accepted by western historians.

Below: Mayan numerical system. Bottom: the 60-metre high Sun pyramid in Teotihuacán.

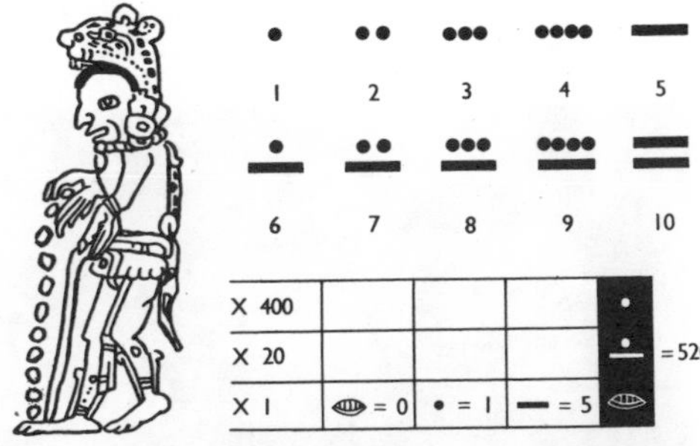
1
2
3
4
5
6
7
8
9
10
X 400
X 20
X 1
= 0
= 1
= 5
= 520

Pius I ---------- Anicetus — Papacy
Vologases IV — Parthia
Antoninus Pius — Rome
---------- Japan
Han Huan Di — China

151	152	153	154	155	156	157	158	159	160

AD 161-170

CHINA
PARTHIANS

In the quiet university town of Athens lived Herodes Atticus, a rich man keenly interested in culture. He made large donations and built the beautiful Stadium in Delphi and the Athenian Odeion.

On the death of Antoninus Pius, the Roman empire acquired two emperors – Marcus Aurelius and Lucius Verus – and officially they held equal authority. Fortunately, however, Lucius Verus was an amenable individual who never hampered his more talented colleague. Marcus Aurelius was a philosopher of the Stoic school and his *Meditations*, a remarkable little volume, give us a profound insight into his character.

There was a series of major wars during the reign of Marcus Aurelius. The first was in Armenia where the Parthians annihilated a Roman Legion and defeated the governor of Syria. Lucius Verus and his generals promptly expelled the enemy from Armenia and retook Ctesiphon. On their return journey the troops were afflicted with the plague and this continued to rage throughout the Roman empire for some years to come.

Lucius Verus' campaign greatly weakened the Parthian kingdom which entered a new period of decline. All the available knowledge of Parthia is still derived from the Greek, Roman and Chinese accounts, and from interpretation of the Parthian coinage. The kingdom was feudal in structure, the language and religion were Iranian, but there was Hellenic influence, for the Seleucid administration system had been preserved and there were Greek towns with special status.

A scribe from Samaria known as Justin the Martyr addressed two *Apologia* on Christianity to Marcus Aurelius. Among other things, he deplored the philosophy of the Cynics that competed with him for souls and which made false accusations against the Christians. Under Marcus Aurelius many Christians were executed for refusing to show proper respect for the Roman gods; they were branded as atheists who refused even to tolerate what others held sacred.

A rhetorician named Lucian came from Mesopotamian Samosata on the periphery of the Roman empire. He had travelled widely before settling in Athens where he established himself as an author and rapidly produced a series of fictional works in Attic Greek – the same language that Socrates had used 500 years earlier. But Lucian's writing, full of ideas and inventions that his contemporaries found unpalatable, brought him no profit, and he soon abandoned Athens and literature for a more prosaic official job in Alexandria. Posterity was to read Lucian more than his contemporaries had done, however, for his writing was full of ideas and inventions that nowadays might well be described as science fiction.

One martyr from this period was Saint Polycarp of Smyrna, an account of whom is given in one of the very earliest Acts of the Martyrs.

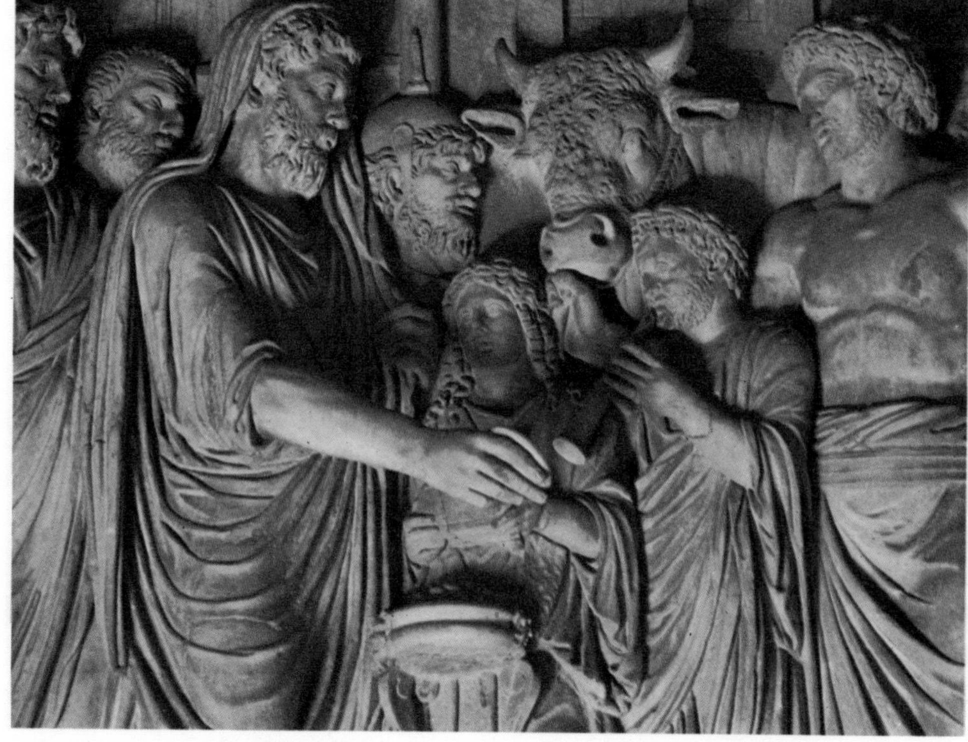

Marcus Aurelius attending a sacrifice to Jupiter. Detail of a column relief in Rome.

Papacy — Anicetus — Soter
Parthia — Vologases IV
Rome — Marcus Aurelius
Japan ----------
China — Han Huan Di — Han Ling Di

161	162	163	164	165	166	167	168	169	170

CHINA
INDIA
ROME

The astronomer and geographer Claudius Ptolemaeus (Ptolemy) lived in Alexandria. Ptolemy propounded what came to be known as the Ptolemaic system, in which the spherical Earth is the centre of the universe and the Sun, Moon and planets revolve around it. Ptolemy also left a number of maps which were to be reproduced in historical atlases throughout the ages.

Life in the North continued in comparative obscurity. Iron had been in use for several centuries, however, and glass and ceramics were imported from the Roman regions.

The Quadi and the Marcomanni, two Germanic tribes who had long dwelt in Bohemia and Mähren, crossed the Danube frontier of the Roman empire, plundered Dacia and then passed over the Alps towards Italy to attack the large city of Aquileia on the Adriatic. But Marcus Aurelius managed to expel them. He then pursued the Quadi into their own country, intercepted the Marcomanni who were on a plundering expedition in the province of Noricum, and also defeated the Sarmatae, who had allied themselves with the Germanic tribes. The fighting soon erupted again, however, and was still in progress when one day in March 180 Marcus Aurelius died of the plague in his camp at Vindobona, the future Vienna.

The physician Galen, a Greek from Pergamum, had been working in Rome for some years, writing on medicine and attendant subjects. He produced twenty-two volumes that encompassed all the medical knowledge of antiquity. The future significance of this work was immense, even though it was not always of practical benefit to the sick. It was Galen who presented the theory of the four body fluids and the four temperaments:

Yellow bile–hot and dry–fire–choleric
Black bile–cold and dry–earth–melancholy
Blood–hot and moist–air–sanguine
Phlegm–cold and moist–water–phlegmatic

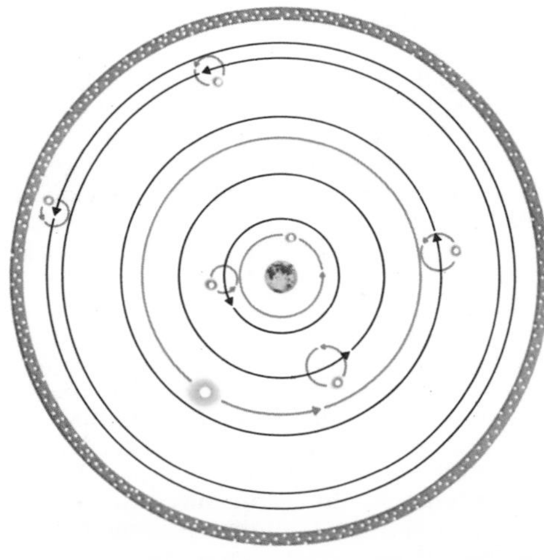

Above: The Ptolemaic concept of the universe endured until the 16th century when Copernicus removed the world from the centre of the planetary system and Kepler changed the circles into ellipses. Below: from a 15th-century edition of Ptolemy's work, best known under its Arabic name of Almagest.

Both the character and the health of the individual were determined by the mixture of these fluids.

From 177 onwards a man from Asia Minor named Irenaeus held the office of bishop of Lugdunum, the future Lyons. He was the most distinguished theologian of his day, expounding that in Christ, who is the Word, God became man and vanquished sin and death; thereby man's communion with God, lost through the flood, is restored. With these new tenets Irenaeus greatly influenced the future development of the Christian faith, and earned himself the title Father of the Church.

Irenaeus compiled the oldest existing list of Roman bishops. It closes with Eleutherus, a Greek who fought against Montanism, an ecstatic revivalist movement which awaited the return of Christ at a place named Pepuza in Phrygia. The year of Eleutherus' death is the first certain date in the list of popes. From then on it is very exact.

A group of Christians were killed in the Gallic cities of Lugdunum and Vindobona. Fanatical crowds were guilty of bestial cruelties and also induced the authorities to carry out brutal executions by burning.

Pausanias from Magnesia made a round trip of Greece and wrote a fairly detailed guide to the country. This work has been of invaluable assistance to archaeologists and art historians.

In the year 168 the Emperor Ling Di was only twelve years old. In this same year the court eunuchs instigated a palace revolution, arrested all members of the regency including the young emperor's mother, and sentenced and executed every Confucian official of any consequence. The eunuchs, a well organized body, now governed China as they thought fit through a decade and a half of growing crisis and disorder.

Soter — Eleutherius — **Papacy**
Vologases IV — **Parthia**
Marcus Aurelius — **Rome**
Japan
Han Ling Di — **China**

171	172	173	174	175	176	177	178	179	180

AD 181-190

CHINA

In 184 the revolt of the Yellow Turbans took place in China. The members of this sect were the followers of a healer name Zhang Zhue who cured all ailments by exorcism and pure water. He had organized his converted patients into an army that was to deliver the mother country from the prevailing misrule. In a short time the rebels took over the whole of eastern China. Government forces were mobilized to meet this threat, but official corruption and incompetence led to rebellion in the ranks. When Emperor Ling Di died, the chief eunuchs murdered a brother of the empress, but the palace was stormed by elite troops and everyone was killed except the heir to the throne, a child name Xian Di, who was seized by the commanding general. The young emperor was then passed from one revolutionary leader to another, none of whom was strong enough to become master of the entire nation. In the following decade, therefore, China dissolved into a number of small independent states.

Although the Han dynasty declined, Chinese art did not falter. A general who died at this time in Kansu took with him to his grave several hundred exquisite works in gold, silver, bronze, iron and jade. These included a number of bronze horses, including the superb "flying horse". The point of balance is centred on one hoof, and this hoof is touching a swallow.

The Emperor Commodus, a great sportsman who could crush a goblet with his bare hands and enjoyed shooting down wild animals at the circus, was assassinated and succeeded by the senior imperial marshal Pertinax. Pertinax attempted to reorganize the state finances and other matters but immediately fell foul of the Praetorian guard and was himself murdered after reigning only three months. The Praetorians then put up the office of emperor for auction. A wealthy senator named Julianus made the highest bid: 6250 drachmas to each member of the guard. He thus became emperor, but the armies in the provinces were angered by this and proclaimed their own generals emperor instead. Consequently there were suddenly four competing emperors, of whom Septimius Severus emerged victorious. As Severus advanced on Rome, the Praetorian guard murdered Julianus in the hope of saving their own skins, but were ordered to await the new emperor in dress uniform outside the city. They were at once surrounded by Illyrian cavalry and their punishment was pronounced–to be dismissed, and stripped of their arms and honours. From this time on, Rome ceased to be a military city.

Left: the bronze 'flying horse' from China. Below: portrait of the Emperor Commodus, from Lambesi in Numidia.

Papacy — Eleutherius — Victor I
Parthia — Vologases IV
Rome — Commodus
Japan - - - - -
China — Han Ling Di

181	182	183	184	185	186	187	188	189	190

ROME

A Roman campaign against Parthia was wholly successful. The emperor took the Mesopotamian capital of Ctesiphon and pushed on to the Persian Gulf where the Euphrates was declared the frontier. This was a great loss of prestige to the Parthian royal house and its days were numbered; a revolutionary, religious and nationalistic movement had also flourished in Iran. The campaign had little effect on the empire, though Roman rule in the area left its mark. The fortified frontier city of Dura-Europus was a garrison but also had a large civil population, and archaeologists were to find remarkable examples of Graeco-Roman art here.

The first Roman bishop whose office can be dated was Victor I. He was an African and he excommunicated the congregations in Asia because their views differed from those of Rome concerning the celebration of Easter. However, Irenaeus, bishop of Lugdunum, interceded and had this edict revoked.

Like their predecessors Sujin-Tenno, Suinin and Keiko-Tenno in the 2nd century BC, the Japanese rulers Chuai-Tenno, Ojin-Tenno and Nintoku-Tenno were certainly legendary. This is apparent from the preposterously long reigns claimed for the last two kings. But the traditional Japanese list of rulers is complete from this time onwards.

In 197 Septimius Severus led a punitive expedition against the city of Byzantium which earlier had chosen the wrong side in internal conflicts. The city was razed to the ground but the emperor, later regretting his action, had a part of it, including a large stadium, rebuilt.

Emigration from Hindustan to Sumatra, Java and other islands in the Sunda archipelago had been in progress for several centuries and was continuing. The people concerned were pious Buddhists or Hindus.

The reign of Septimius Severus was a time of great political change in Roman society. The bureaucracy was expanded and militarized, and the labour and property of the citizens were increasingly appropriated by the state. Guilds of craftsmen and merchants were turned into compulsory corporations which were organized and run by the authorities. Local self-government gradually disappeared and the local officials became instead tax-collectors and supervisors for the state.

Septimius Severus' triumphal arch at the Forum in Rome commemorates the emperor's victories over Parthians and Arabs. Such monumental architecture had become increasingly common in the western parts of the empire. The rural towns of Gaul and Italy boasted them, while in Africa fifty or more triumphal arches have survived. The arch commemorating Severus was probably the most magnificent of them all.

Victor I — Zephyrinus — **Papacy**

Vologases V — **Parthia**

Commodus — Pertinax — Jul. — Septimius Severus — **Rome**

Chuai-Tenno — **Japan**

Han Xian Di — **China**

191	192	193	194	195	196	197	198	199	200

AD 201-210

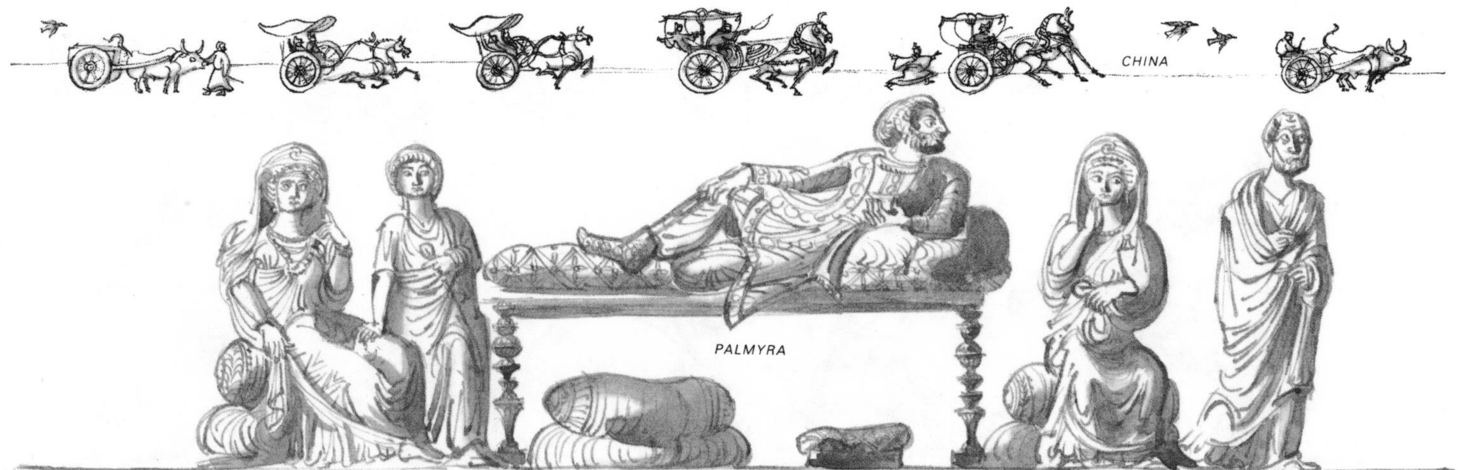
CHINA
PALMYRA

Judah ha-Nasi was a Jewish scholar who had recently codified the oral doctrine, the Mishna, which complemented the Torah, the law of Moses. The commentaries to this, in the form of interminable discussions between scholarly Jews, was called Talmud, a term now used to embrace all the accepted and authoritative Jewish theology of antiquity. Judah ha-Nasi's work was important in establishing the borderline with Christianity, the significance of which was rapidly becoming evident to Jewish congregations.

Septimius Severus ended his days in the British town of Eburacum. He was an African from Leptis Magna in Libya and his wife, Julia Domna, was from Syria, daughter of a high priest in the Temple of the Sun at Emesa. Neither of them had Latin as a native language, and spoke it with a pronounced foreign accent. Clearly, by this time Latin had become international.

Caracalla and Geta were made joint emperors by their father, but after the latter's death Caracalla murdered Geta in the arms of their mother. Nevertheless Julia Domna continued to be influential during Caracalla's reign. Finally he, too, was murdered in the neighbourhood of Edessa by his chief-of-staff Macrinus. Julia Domna now committed suicide, but her sister, niece and niece's son took up the struggle against Macrinus and won a great battle, in which they all took part. The niece's son was still very young but, like his maternal grandfather, he had since childhood been a high priest in the Temple of the Sun at Emesa, in Syria. He now became Roman emperor and his first act was to have the sacred black stone moved from Emesa to Rome. His name was Varius Avitus but he went down in history as Elagabalus or Heliogabalus, from the name of the god to whom he had been priest. Roman historians describe him as a monster who incorporated all the vices of East and West.

Around the year 200, a tribe known as the Rugi left their home district in Pomerania and began marching southward. The Burgundians, too, are mentioned for the first time. They seem to have come from the island of Bornholm in the Baltic, but nothing more is known about this migration.

In 202 Christian martyrs were created in Alexandria, Lyons and Carthage – death sentences being decreed by the authorities bowing to the fanatical accusations of adherents of rival religious sects. That such occurrences had a propaganda value was recognised by the theologian and apologist Tertullian, who pronounced that the blood of the martyrs was the seed of Christianity. Tertullian was born in Carthage and had been a lawyer. His writings resound with polemic passion. The cornerstone of his theology was requital – a thoroughly legal approach. As the advocate of Trinitarianism and Christology, certain of his tenets had a decisive influence on western Christianity.

The large Indo-Cytheran kingdom continued to prosper and the Kaniska dynasty survived. The king at this time was named Huvuska and he ruled for a long time, though little more is known of him than is revealed by his coins. These depict a hook-nosed, sharp-featured man, in addition to portraits of Hercules, Scapis and various Persian and Indian gods, though, strangely enough, not Buddha. The kingdom perhaps reached its temporal peak during Huvuska's reign.

The first decade of the 3rd century was important for Roman law, with some of its most authoritative jurists at work. The most renowned of these were Papinian and Ulpian, whose writings and views were cited throughout the Byzantine era. They both met violent deaths: Ulpian is said to have been cut down by Emperor Caracalla himself for refusing to defend the latter's fratricide before the senate.

Incredibly, Malta had all this while contrived to maintain its independence. But, in 218, it was incorporated in the Roman empire.

Septimius Severus retained his interest in his native city of Leptis Magna in Africa. The city was supplied with water and a polygonal harbour basin was built. In the new forum, replacing an earlier one, a basilica was erected, the magnificence of which is reflected in this photograph.

Papacy — Zephyrinus
Parthia — Vologases V (201–206) | Vologases VI (207–210)
Rome — Septimius Severus
Japan — Ojin-Tenno
China — Han Xian Di

201	202	203	204	205	206	207	208	209	210

ROME
CHINA

Several Eastern mystical religions gained ground in the Mediterranean region. The Egyptian cult of Isis, which had recruited so many followers in the previous century, had now passed its heyday. More enduring were the ecstatic cults of Attis, and of Cybele, the Great Mother (Magna Mater) with its blood baptism. Taurobolium was a centre of the latter religion, in which the principal deity was the Persian Mithras, the Sun god (Sol invictus) born on earth from a rock on 25 December and worshipped by shepherds. The Mithras cult gained many disciples, especially in the Roman armies; it was rooted in astrology and had sacraments not unlike those of Christianity, including mystical sacrificial meals and confirmation.

Christianity, still in its youth, encountered many difficulties from rival religions; but theologians had additional internal problems arising from a dualistic doctrine which created insurmountable barriers between spirit and matter, between the world of light and the world of darkness. This was known as Gnosticism and it claimed a greater knowledge than all the authors of the Old Testament scriptures and the three first Gospels. On the other hand, the Gnostics strongly supported the Gospel of St John. They believed that many eternal beings, known as aeons, served as intermediaries between the God of light and the material world. One of the lower aeons, Demiurge, had created the world and claimed to be the Supreme Being, and as such he sent his Son to the world in the image of man. The Son's suffering and death was thus a mere pretence. The Gnostic scriptures survived the purges of victorious Christianity. They include an apocalypse, the Apocrypha of John, the Gospels of Mary, Philip and Thomas, and the Gospel of Truth. All these were discovered in Egypt in the 1940s.

In 212 the Alemanni, a Germanic tribe, launched an attack in the Main valley and reached the Rhine. But in the following year a counter-attack by Caracalla secured the Roman *limes*.

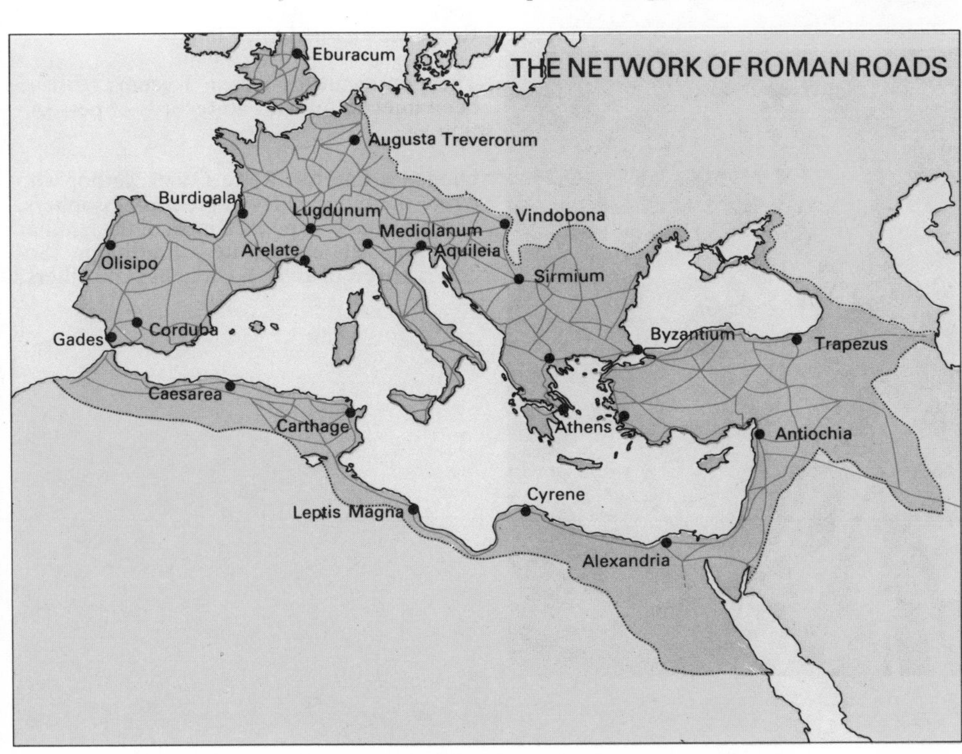
THE NETWORK OF ROMAN ROADS
Eburacum
Augusta Treverorum
Burdigala
Lugdunum
Vindobona
Mediolanum
Arelate
Aquileia
Olisipo
Sirmium
Corduba
Gades
Byzantium
Trapezus
Caesarea
Carthage
Athens
Antiochia
Cyrene
Leptis Magna
Alexandria

There are many good portraits of Caracalla. This one is in the Louvre, Paris.

Zephyrinus (211–217) — Calixtus I (217–220)	Papacy
Vologases VI	Parthia
Caracalla (211–217) — Macrinus (217–218) — Elagabalus (218–220)	Rome
Ojin-Tenno	Japan
Han Xian Di	China

211	212	213	214	215	216	217	218	219	220

AD 221-230

CHINA
ROME
SASSANIDS PERSIA

Xian Di, the last emperor of the Han dynasty, had long been the tool of an artful general named Cao Cao who created for himself the northern Chinese kingdom of Wei. In 220 he let it be known at court that he had imperial ambitions and after the young emperor had three times offered to abdicate and even handed over his seal to Cao Cao, the latter finally made a great ceremony of acceptance. Cao Cao was not recognized as emperor farther south, however, where the ruling potentates in the states of Shu-Han and Wu themselves both claimed imperial office.

The period 221-265 is known in China as Sanguo, the three kingdoms. It has come to be regarded as a singularly romantic era which featured many tales of adventure, legendary events and theatrical works. The three kingdoms were Wei, Shu-Han and Wu, the first in the north, the other two farther south. They warred constantly with one another in the mountains around the River Yangtze, and legend and song tell of a famous battle at a place known as the Red Rock. There are no true accounts of these feuds, which must have taken a heavy toll of lives, nor did they play a significant role in history.

Emperor Wen Di, known as Cao Pei, was the son of Cao Cao who wielded the real power behind the throne and did not interfere with the Han dynasty. In addition to their political activities, both father and son were good poets, as was another brother, Cao Chi. Chinese anthologies were to include poems by all three men.

The *Historia Augusta* (a collection of biographies of the Roman Emperors) describes Elagabalus as little less than a monster. He was grossly profligate, and is said to have used his shoes and linen only once before throwing them away. He had a bed made of solid silver and a chamber pot of pure gold. He gave his dogs goose liver to eat, appointed one of his horses consul, and once ordered a number of ships to be sunk, just to show that he was a large-minded man. Fortunately he was murdered at the age of eighteen, together with his mother, and succeeded by his fourteen-year-old cousin Alexander Severus, evidently his absolute antithesis.

In his private temple Alexander Severus worshipped Abraham, Orpheus, Jesus Christ and Apollonius of Thyana. The latter, who had lived some time in the previous century, was a Pythagorean ascetic who exorcised demons, resurrected the dead, foretold the future and walked straight through prison walls.

Pope Calixtus I is said to have been a liberated slave. One of the catacombs of Rome was named after him.

The pontificate of Urban I seems to have been uneventful with no records of persecution.

Diogenes Laertius was a Greek author who wrote the biographies of great philosophers, and it was he who penned most of the familiar anecdotes about Socrates, Xanthippe (Socrates' shrew of a wife), Diogenes and others.

THE THREE KINGDOMS IN CHINA
Yellow River (Huang He)
WEI
Loyang
SHU
Changan
Nanking
R. Yangtze
WU

Elagabalus. Bust in the Valladolid Museum.

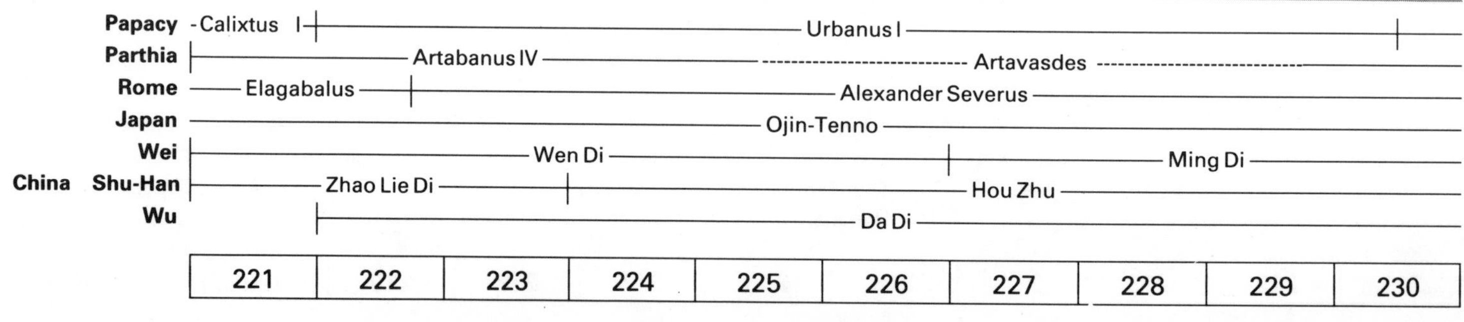

Papacy
Calixtus I
Urbanus I
Parthia
Artabanus IV
Artavasdes
Rome
Elagabalus
Alexander Severus
Japan
Ojin-Tenno
China
Wei
Wen Di
Ming Di
Shu-Han
Zhao Lie Di
Hou Zhu
Wu
Da Di
221
222
223
224
225
226
227
228
229
230

CHINA
ARDASHIR I
SASSANIDS, PERSIA
ROME

The Parthian Arsacid dynasty was overthrown in the 220s by the Persian Sassanids and this introduced a new era for the countries beyond the Euphrates. The Parthian empire had been a loosely organized feudal system largely impervious to cultural influences from east to west. The Sassanids now established a solid organization and built up an efficient bureaucracy.

The Sassanids regarded themselves as the restorer of ancient Persian power and did all they could to exclude Hellenism which had taken hold here under the Parthian regents. For the first time the teachings of Zoroaster became a national religion. The Sassanids worshipped fire, which is depicted on coins from the time of Shapur I.

Pope Pontianus was banished to Sardinia during a persecution of the Christians. There he resigned his office and never again returned to Rome.

A pope named Anterus is not included in the list since he was in office only for a few weeks (21 November 235 to 3 January 236).

In 231, the first Sassanid, Ardashir, crossed the border of the Roman empire and made an easy conquest of Syria. Emperor Alexander Severus personally led an army against Ardashir and repulsed him, but at the same time the Roman empire was attacked on its northern frontier by the Teutones. The emperor now made for the Rhineland but he made no military progress and attempted instead to bribe his adversaries. His troops mutinied and assassinated both him and his mother at the camp in Moguntiacum (modern Mainz). The leader of the mutiny, Maximinus Thrax of Thrace, was proclaimed emperor. He was a soldier who had risen through the ranks and had never set foot in Rome. He began well by driving the Teutones back to their own territory; but when he raised taxes and confiscated property, the people rebelled, and a certain Gordian and his son were proclaimed emperors against their will. Maximinus quickly disposed of them both, but shortly after that was murdered by his own soldiers. A fourteen-year-old boy now became Emperor Gordian III.

The Sassanid empire developed, under Shapur I, into a well organized society with four distinct classes: the priesthood, the military, the officials and the proletariat. The bureaucracy quickly became a very complex organization and the regular army underwent the same fate. The nobles established their own armoured cavalry and a troop of elephants.

From about this time onward, Latin became the language of the Christian church, replacing Greek.

San Callisto is one of Rome's catacombs, named after Pope Calixtus. This picture of the Good Shepherd, a popular motif of the time, is from San Callisto.

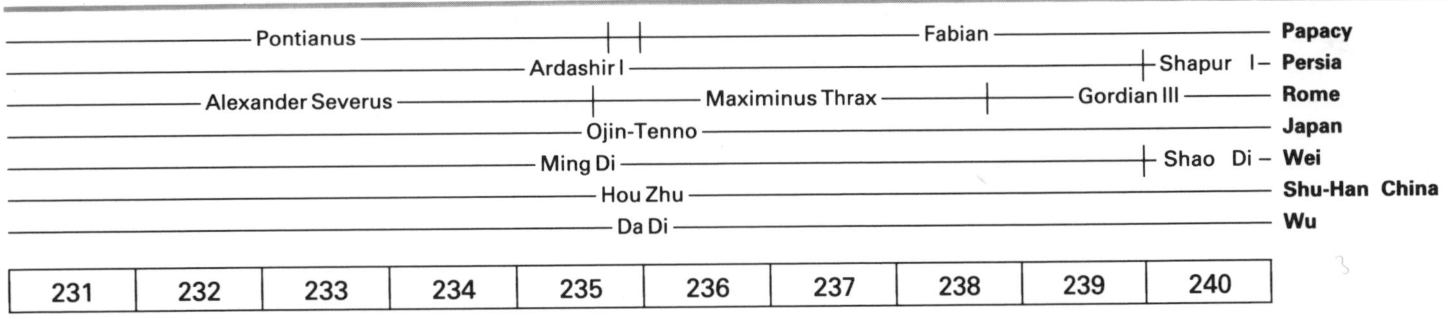
Pontianus
Fabian
Papacy
Ardashir I
Shapur I
Persia
Alexander Severus
Maximinus Thrax
Gordian III
Rome
Ojin-Tenno
Japan
Ming Di
Shao Di
Wei
Hou Zhu
Shu-Han China
Da Di
Wu
231
232
233
234
235
236
237
238
239
240

SASSANIDS PERSIA
DURA-EUROPUS

Bishop Cyprian of Carthage resolutely asserted that the universal Christian church was essential for salvation: *'Extra ecclesiam nulla salus'* (outside the church there is no salvation). His views were approved by Christians in Rome. There was more opposition to the Greek-speaking theologian Origen who claimed in Alexandria that salvation lay in the gradual spiritualization of the soul and that in time all souls were reunited with God.

Although many synods later branded Origen as a heretic, he nevertheless exerted a lasting influence on Christianity. He was a philosophical and literary scholar who composed thousands of papers in Greek and who also compiled the Old Testament work *Hexapla*: five texts parallel to the Hebrew, each with three words in a line. This he did in Caesarea after leaving Alexandria following a dispute with two bishops who had him expelled from the congregation.

Another resident of Alexandria was the mathematician Diophantus. Unlike most other Greeks, he worked with algebra rather than geometry. He introduced a symbol for the unknown quantity and could solve first and second degree equations. Much of his surviving work deals with what he calls indeterminate problems, i.e. equation systems where there are more unknown quantities than there are equations.

The abbreviation Aem. in the next decade stands for Aemilian.

The Emperor Decius provoked a large-scale persecution of Christians by decreeing that every person living and working in the empire should devoutly attend the temple and make sacrifices to the gods for the welfare of the realm. Those who refused were threatened with the death penalty, so that less ardent Christians abandoned their faith in large numbers. But the edict also produced many martyrs, including Pope Fabian. Afterwards the papal chair remained vacant for some years.

The Roman emperors tended to be a short-lived breed; either they were slain in civil wars or were murdered by their own soldiers. Decius at least had the dubious honour of dying in a major battle against the Goths who, led by a king named Cniva, had crossed the Dniester and the Danube.

Pope Sixtus II is featured in Raphael's renowned portrayal of the Sistine Madonna. Sixtus worked for peace and conciliation, endeavouring to settle the heresy dispute in Africa. He was martyred in August 258, yet despite his virtues tended to be regarded later as secondary to Lawrence the deacon, martyred at the same time. This detail from a series of scenes in the Vatican shows them together. Here Sixtus hands taxes to Lawrence for distribution among the poor.

Papacy		Fabian (to 250; then vacant)
Persia		Shapur I
Rome		Gordian III (241–244) – Philip the Arabian (244–249) – Decius (249–250)
Japan		Ojin-Tenno
China	Wei	Shao Di
	Shu-Han	Hou Zhu
	Wu	Da Di

241	242	243	244	245	246	247	248	249	250

SASSANIDS, PERSIA
DURA-EUROPUS

When he assumed the throne, Emperor Valerian was already an elderly man, and he thus appointed his son Gallienus joint-emperor. In 260 the Persian king, Shapur, invaded Syria with a large army, ravaged the country, and seized the town of Antioch, profiting from the fact that many of the citizens happened then to be attending the theatre. Valerian himself led an army against the invaders but was manoeuvred into an indefensible position at the fortified town of Edessa. Every attempt to break out failed and every appeal for negotiations was contemptuously rejected; finally the emperor and his entire force were taken prisoner by the Persian king. Shapur now put Valerian in chains, declared him an exile from all the cities of the east and set his foot on his neck whenever he mounted his horse. Never before in the history of the empire had a Roman emperor been so humiliated. Valerian died in Persian captivity.

In the 250s the Alemanni and the Franks crossed the Rhine and advanced through Gaul as far as the Spanish frontier. They also reached the area of Milan, but were defeated here in 256. In time, a governor named Postumus drove the invaders out of Gaul again, and in recognition of this feat he was, despite Valerian and Gallienus, proclaimed emperor. This in effect created an emperor of Gaul, a situation which lasted for several decades, even though the various emperors concerned did not reign long. Roman historians refer to the thirty tyrants, namely individuals who set themselves up as emperor in different parts of the empire, and among these were Postumus and his successors in Gaul.

In 256-259 the Kabyles of Africa rebelled. At the same time the Gothic Heruli were ravaging the north and west coasts of Asia Minor while the war with the Persians was still raging in the east. In 257 a Frankish force moved into Spain and the provincial capital of Tarraco was destroyed in 260. As a result of this invasion the town of Barcino (Barcelona) assumed Tarraco's role as the administrative centre. Thus the Roman empire was being attacked virtually from all quarters during the reign of Gallienus.

In America and on the Pacific islands numerous communities were flourishing, some with advanced cultures. But all are anonymous and there are no historical records of them.

Further religious persecution in 257-258 resulted in the death of, among others, the Carthaginian bishop Cyprian. In 260, however, Gallienus, left alone to make decisions, issued an edict of toleration, and the confiscated possessions of religious congregations were restored.

In the middle of the 3rd century invading Goths seized the Greek towns of Olbia and Tyras on the Black Sea, after which they raided and plundered the Aegean region.

Shapur I's triumph. Persian relief from below the rock tomb of Darius I at Naqsh-e-Rostam.

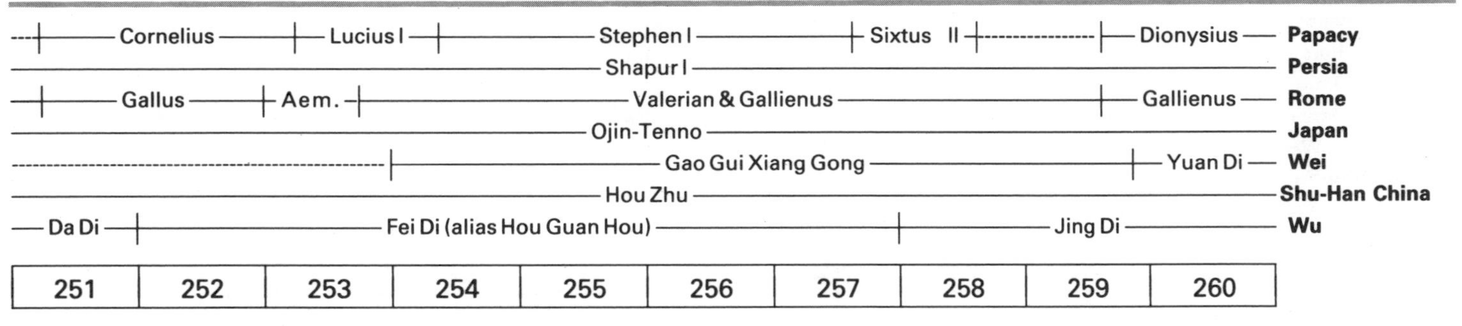
Cornelius
Lucius I
Stephen I
Sixtus II
Dionysius
Papacy
Shapur I
Persia
Gallus
Aem.
Valerian & Gallienus
Gallienus
Rome
Ojin-Tenno
Japan
Gao Gui Xiang Gong
Yuan Di
Wei
Hou Zhu
Shu-Han China
Da Di
Fei Di (alias Hou Guan Hou)
Jing Di
Wu
251
252
253
254
255
256
257
258
259
260

AD 261-270

ROME
CHINA
INDIA
PERSIA

The long reign of Emperor Gallienus was a lamentable era for the Roman empire. War and plunder had impoverished the provinces and there was no longer any solidarity among them. Prices increased without restraint, the coinage deteriorated and inflation rendered savings and credits useless, reducing the regular income of the state to an absolute minimum. Arbitrary taxes were then levied and as a result many peasants preferred to abandon their land.

Gallienus also had to contend with the problem of usurpers who, in various parts of the empire, were proclaiming themselves emperor. Some were successfully deposed, others contrived to maintain their independence throughout his reign.

The emperor was an educated man, interested in the philosophy of the Neo-Platonist Plotinus, who had rejected the iniquities of the material world, seeking instead the inner light through asceticism and self-denial. Plotinus' teachings gained ground among the Christians, too, and gave sustenance to the heresy of Gnosticism. Last of the great philosophers of antiquity, Plotinus died in 270. For the Gnostics Christ was an aeon who had descended into the darkness of the world to recover and return the sparks of light to their proper home.

The Syrian town of Palmyra, no longer under imperial authority, was ruled by a certain Odaenathus and his wife Zenobia. They held their own effectively against the Persian armies and in gratitude Gallienus appointed Odaenathus joint-emperor. The latter died soon afterwards but Zenobia continued to rule over what was, in fact, an independent Syrian state.

Sima Yan deposed the last of the Cao kings in Wei and also annexed the kingdom of Shu-Han. In due course his armies crossed the River Yangtze and occupied the whole of China. The new dynasty was known as Jin (Chin) and emperor Sima Yan was called Wu Di. He was evidently a reasonable and talented ruler, and he kept no less than 10,000 women in his harem. It was his custom to drive through his grounds in a small chariot drawn by sheep; the ladies competed in luring the sheep their way with salt, and the first to succeed was honoured with the services of the emperor that night.

The Goths crossed the Black Sea in their flat-bottomed, deckless boats with hide canopies. They made a surprise attack on the large town of Trapezus, seizing immense booty, and in a second expedition they moved through the Bosporus and the Hellespont, plundering their way along the shores. Finally they destroyed the famous temple of Artemis in Ephesus and also made an assault on Athens. Here, however, the historian Dexippus gathered a corps of volunteers and conducted a fairly successful operation against the invaders. Then, on the west coast of Greece, the Goths encountered an army led by Gallienus himself, and were at last compelled to withdraw.

Rome, undisturbed by enemy armies for centuries, was no longer quite so secure after recent events. Its fortifications were old and out-of-date. Consequently the emperor Aurelian began to build a new wall around the city.

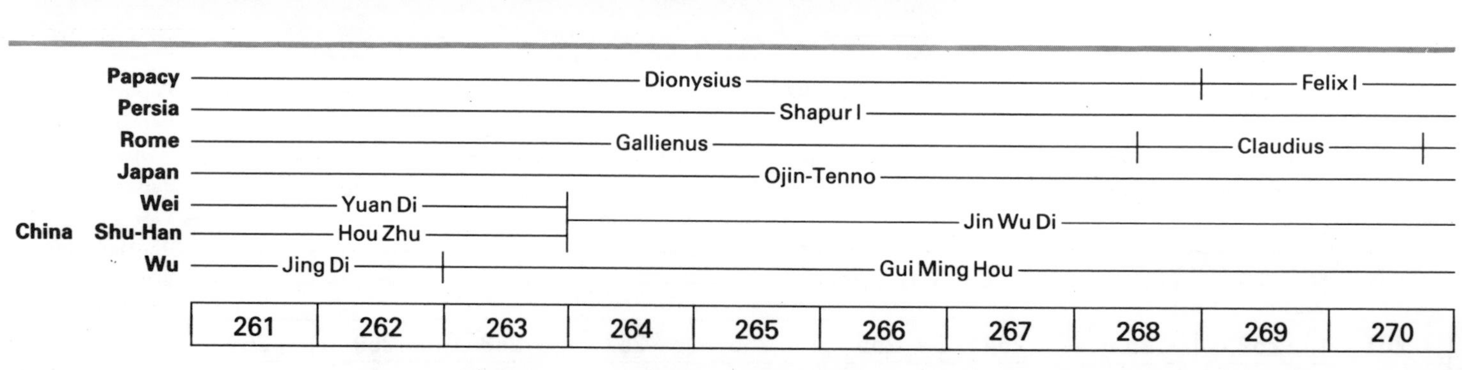
Papacy
Dionysius
Felix I
Persia
Shapur I
Rome
Gallienus
Claudius
Japan
Ojin-Tenno
China
Wei
Yuan Di
Shu-Han
Hou Zhu
Jin Wu Di
Wu
Jing Di
Gui Ming Hou
261
262
263
264
265
266
267
268
269
270

ROME

Philostratus was a Greek author, reputedly from Lemnos. He left a series of biographies on various orators and philosophers, descriptions of certain pictures he claimed to have seen and, in particular, an account of a strange figure named Apollonius of Tyana who had lived at about the time of Christ and who performed amazing deeds. Apollonius was apparently a wandering Pythagorean philosopher of exceptional moral virtue and with supernatural powers, so much so that he had a divine reputation and to some extent rivalled Christ himself. A number of eminent people actually worshipped Apollonius, including the Emperor Aurelian himself. During one of his military campaigns Aurelian occupied the defiant town of Tyana but refrained from plundering it out of respect for its famous son Apollonius.

Aurelian drove out the plundering Goths and Alemanni and used military power to reunite the Roman provinces. He captured Queen Zenobia and totally destroyed Palmyra. Shortly afterwards, however, he was assassinated by one of his own officers.

Evidently the popes Dionysius, Felix I and Eutychianus did not suffer martyrdom. We know practically nothing about them, though during Dionysius' pontificate there were apparently many spiritual disputes with another Dionysius, bishop of Alexandria and disciple of Origen. The pope attempted to amend matters in a Christological doctrinal debate, but Dionysius of Alexandria would not recognize Rome's supremacy and thus laid the foundation for the Alexandrian patriarchate.

In 271 Emperor Aurelian abandoned the empire's two Dacian provinces north of the lower Danube and thereby stabilized this front. Prior to this, he had assured the safe withdrawal of the Roman inhabitants by a temporary victory over the importunate Visigoths. These now settled in Dacia and became firm allies of the Romans.

Emperor Tacitus was an elderly senator who soon died a natural death. Emperor Probus, on the other hand, was an energetic general who immortalized his name by such undertakings as planting olive trees in Africa and establishing vineyards in Gaul – it had earlier been regarded as impossible to grow grapes anywhere north of the Cevennes.

In Persia, with the approval of King Bahram I, the priests of Mani of Zoroaster were crucified in 276. During the long reign of Shapur I, Mani had enjoyed the right to preach his particular religion and had won many followers. This creed was known as Manichaeism and its central precept was the eternal struggle between the powers of light and darkness. Moses, Zoroaster, Buddha and Christ were all, in fact, prophets of Manichaeism, but Mani himself was the last of them. This somewhat hybrid religion also embraced Neo-Platonic concepts. It spread to Spain and as far east as China at an astonishing rate; and probably had its greatest success in Mongolia where in time it became the Uighur national religion. In the Mediterranean world Manichaeism was a serious rival to Christianity for some centuries to come.

The *Historia Augusta* contains anecdotes about the emperors Gallienus and Aurelian. The former probably defended the empire capably enough, but is said to have led a dissipated life: it is claimed that he took a bath seven times a day, sprinkled gold dust in his hair and built castles of apples, grapes and melons! His greatest treat was to watch a *phago* or professional glutton; and he was the first Roman emperor to wear a tiara.

The *Historia Augusta* gives no impression of social and economic continuity. Wars and invasions had all but ruined the state. The imperial armies drained the treasury. Prices rose uncontrollably; savings and loans became worthless. Silver coins devalued rapidly; they were soon worth so little that people would put about 3,000 double-denarii into a *follis* (cloth pouch), and use this for payment without opening it.

Emperor Gallienus. Museo delle Terme, Rome.

Felix I — Eutychianus — **Papacy**

Shapur I — Hormizd I — Bahram I — Bahram II — **Persia**

Aurelian — Tacitus — Probus — **Rome**

Ojin-Tenno — **Japan**

Jin Wu Di — **Jin**

Gui Ming Hou — **Wu**

China

271	272	273	274	275	276	277	278	279	280

ROMAN EMPIRE

There were holy men in the deserts of Egypt and the most renowned of these was Anthony, still in his prime and constantly tempted by the devil who solicited him in vain with visions of beautiful women and other enticing luxuries.

In Armenia, with the approval of King Tiridates, Christianity was introduced by a missionary named Gregory the Illuminator: Gregory's first action was to destroy a fire-temple dedicated to Zoroaster.

In India someone had discovered how to extract sugar from cane.

In Mexico the Maya civilization and what is known as the Old Empire were flourishing.

While supervising the draining of a swamp at Sava, Emperor Probus was murdered by his resentful soldiers. He was succeeded by an old warrior named Carus who was struck dead by lightning during a campaign in Mesopotamia. The next emperor was an army commander named Diocletian who created a new national organization that assured the continued existence of the Roman empire. After Diocletian, no emperor was ever again murdered or chosen by the army. Diocletian's first important measure was to name his colleague and brother officer Maximian joint-emperor and master of Italy and the western provinces, while he himself ruled the eastern half of the empire. Deciding, however, that two emperors were insufficient he duly bestowed the title of Caesar upon two dependable generals, Galerius and Constantius Chlorus. He and Maximian assumed the title Augustus, and each adopted one of the generals, thereby making them their legal successors. The four men now divided the empire, each with a portion to rule, but agreeing to joint overall control of the empire. Thanks to Diocletian's determination, this system functioned surprisingly well. Law and order were established, though personal liberty was curtailed; thus citizens were prohibited from emigrating, dissenters were persecuted, arbitrary taxation was enforced and elaborate price controls were introduced.

There was unrest among the Germanic tribes of central Europe. In 288 the Franks invaded and occupied the former territories of the Batavi on the islands at the mouth of the Rhine, the Angles were on the move around the Elbe, and the Saxons were committing acts of piracy along the coasts of the North Sea and the English Channel.

Emperor Wu Di left twenty-five sons, only one of whom, of course, should have assumed the title of emperor. Yet the empire was divided up among all twenty-five sons.

Diocletian came from a small, remote place in Illyria and in time he returned there. He then built himself a retirement palace in Salona (future Split) on the Dalmatian coast. This incorporated walls, gates, mausoleums and temples and was a magnificent building.

Needless to say, there was continual discord and strife, and no semblance of national unity.

In 286 a certain Aurelius Carausius instigated a rebellion in Britain, seeking to establish an independent Roman state there. This was suppressed, with some difficulty, by Constantius Chlorus.

There were also threats to Roman Britain from outside, and defences were erected on the south coast to provide protection against seafaring Saxons.

Diocletian had reached his position, not through bravery – like Augustus he was often accused of being somewhat of a coward on the battlefield – but through wisdom, energy and leadership. He instilled respect and was able to make good use of people.

Papacy — Eutychianus — | — Gaius
Persia — Bahram II
Rome — Probus — | — Carus — | — Numerian — | — Diocletian
Japan — Ojin-Tenno
China — Jin Wu Di — |

281	282	283	284	285	286	287	288	289	290

ROMAN EMPIRE
ROMAN EMPIRE
MIRAN

The final and cruellest persecution of the Christians in the Roman empire began in the year 297 when Emperor Diocletian decreed that civil servants should make compulsory sacrifices to the emperor, with the result that all observing Christians were forced to leave the army and the administration. A few years later an edict was issued closing all the churches and dissolving all congregations. But the Christians openly and courageously defied this decree; and when mysterious fires broke out in the imperial palace at Nicomedia, Diocletian had the leaders of the congregations imprisoned and adopted violent measures against all who refused to recognize the deities and symbols of the state. Many submitted, of course, but there were also many martyrs. Although the emperor had initially not intended to shed blood, his frustration was such that persecution continued throughout the rest of his reign.

Diocletian's repressive measures were not restricted to Christianity. The first victims, in fact, were the Manichaeans, the adherents of the martyred Mani's new Persian religion, which had already won many supporters, even in Rome. The Manichaeans believed in two opposing worlds of light and darkness where cosmic beings were in everlasting conflict; and man's task was to become worthy of acceptance in the world of light through an ascetic and virtuous life. The Manichaeans also believed in transmigration of souls, but in Christian regions, at least, they regarded Jesus as one of their prophets, though they made a clear distinction between Jesus and Christ.

Both Diocletian and his colleague Maximian were provincials by birth and upbringing, and they had always disapproved of urban Rome and its privileges. Diocletian had never set foot in the city and lived mainly in Bythinian Nicomedia which was then the fourth largest city in the empire. Maximian usually kept court in Milan, never in Rome. He now called himself Herculius, while Diocletian had assumed the name Jovius.

One edict relating to the whole of the Roman empire has survived. This prescribed the maximum prices for oil, salt, meat, vegetables, fruit, clothing, wine, beer, and so on, and it also fixed the wages for various craftsmen, artists, teachers, etc. This was much resented in Roman, Greek, Syrian and Gallic trading circles and evidently they did not abide by the terms of the edict because inflation continued to rise.

Tibetan hordes began to appear on Chinese territory and the Tungus from the more northern regions reached the Chinese frontier at the great bend of the Yellow River, after having passed through the former heartland of the Huns. The Tungus established states in Manchuria while other forces moved westward and created a kingdom around Lake Kuku-nor in central Asia. The Huns were now divided into two kingdoms which were not to last much longer.

In 298 the Persian king, Narses, was severely defeated by the Romans under Galerius, and the upper Tigris region once again became a Roman province.

Early Christian fresco in the Peter and Marcellinus catacomb in Rome; the Madonna and the Wise Men Worship Christ.

Gaius — Marcellinus — **Papacy**
Bahram II — Bahram III — Narses — **Persia**
Diocletian & Maximian — **Rome**
Ojin-Tenno — **Japan**
Jin Hui Di — **China**

291	292	293	294	295	296	297	298	299	300

ROME

Emperor Diocletian abdicated voluntarily and compelled his colleague Maximian to do likewise, whereupon the two Caesars, Galerius and Constantius Chlorus, duly assumed the title of Augustus and each appointed a Caesar to succeed themselves. Constantius Chlorus died a few years later, and his son Constantine at once proclaimed himself successor to his father, though according to the constitution it was the surviving Augustus who should have made such an appointment. Galerius saw fit to accept the young Constantine as Caesar, but then Maximians' son Maxentius proclaimed himself emperor, causing his elderly father to come out of retirement and reassume the dignity of Augustus. However, Diocletian persuaded his old friend Maximian to abdicate yet again. A new figure, Licinius, was now made Augustus in the western part of the empire. Galerius died, after which war broke out between Constantine and Maxentius. The decisive battle here took place north of Rome. It was a prominent event in Church history since it was on this occasion that Constantine saw in the sky the sign of a cross and the legend: *'In hoc signo vinces'* (In this sign thou shallt be victorious). Maxentius was killed, other pretenders suffered the same fate and soon the only Caesars left (at one point there were six) were Licinius and Constantine. They divided the empire into two parts, proclaimed their sons Caesars and managed to remain on equitable terms until the following decade. In the New Year of 313 they jointly issued an edict of tolerance which recognized all religions as equal. This at last brought to an end the persecution of the Manichaeans and Christians.

The Holy Anthony who had moved from the desert to Fayum and thence to Pispir, became in time the central figure in an Egyptian colony of hermits which assembled at Pispir. This in fact constituted the beginning of a Christian monastic movement.

From the autumn of 304 until the spring of 308 the papal chair remained unoccupied, for this was the time of the Diocletian persecution of the Christians. It was the longest such vacancy in papal history. Marcellus I, who eventually assumed the office of pope, dealt harshly with those who had defected during the persecution period, but this led to general unrest within the Church and finally caused his resignation.

In Central America at this time, the advanced civilizations which modern archaeologists have named after the places La Venta and Izapa, were, for some unknown reason, suddenly extinguished: in Peru a metropolis called Paracas simultaneously disappeared. Mummies in painted or embroidered textiles have been found at this site.

In about the year 300 an immigrant tribe led by a chieftain named Kayamaga founded a kingdom in Africa known as Ghana. In due course this tribe merged with the peoples it had subjugated around the Niger. Ghana, with its salt mines in the north and gold mines in the south-west, became a prosperous state intersected by trading routes between central Africa and the countries north of the Sahara.

Maxentius, the only warrior emperor who truly cared about Rome, found time to build an immense basilica there (right); half of this survives. It was completed by Constantine who raised an enormous statue of himself inside and in time found its way into the courtyard of the Musei dei Conservatori.

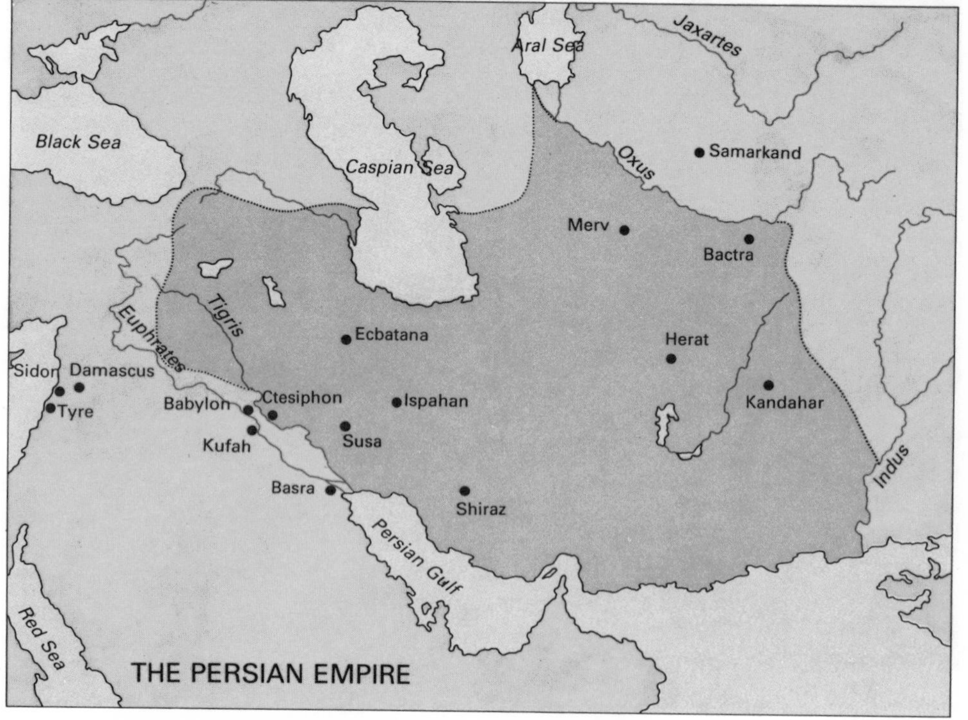

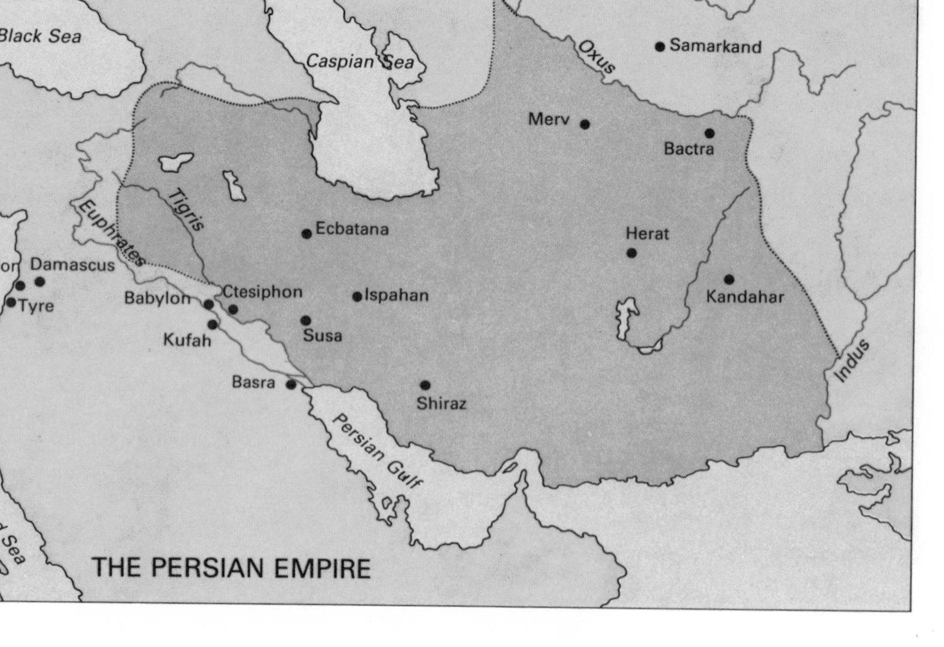
Aral Sea
Jaxartes
Black Sea
Caspian Sea
Oxus
Samarkand
Merv
Bactra
Tigris
Euphrates
Ecbatana
Herat
Sidon
Damascus
Tyre
Babylon
Ctesiphon
Ispahan
Kandahar
Kufah
Susa
Basra
Shiraz
Indus
Persian Gulf
Red Sea
THE PERSIAN EMPIRE

Papacy	Marcellinus — (vacant) — Marcellus I — Eusebius — (vacant)
Persia	Narses — Hormizd II — Shapur II
Rome	Diocletian & Maximian — Galerius + Constantius + Maxentius
Japan	Ojin-Tenno
China	Jin Hui Di — Jin Huai Di

301	302	303	304	305	306	307	308	309	310

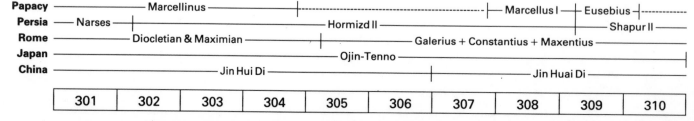

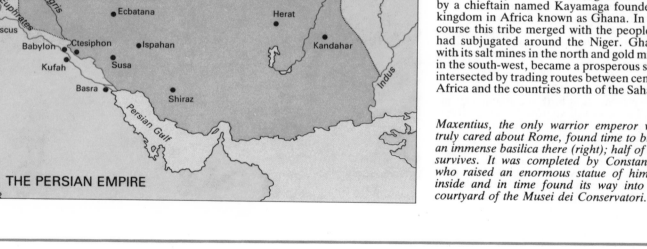

ROME

In Persia Narses abdicated after a severe defeat by the Romans. His son and successor, Hormizd II, was an enthusiastic builder and law-maker, but his reign was brief and when he died his heir had not yet been born: the child was not due for several months, but the regalia of the Persian empire was ceremoniously placed on the widowed queen's stomach. The newborn infant, already king, was named Shapur or Sapor II.

Hardly had the persecutions ended before grave doctrinal disputes broke out among the Christians. The most significant of these was the controversy between the Arians and the Athanasians over the godhead of Christ. Arius, a Presbyterian in Alexandria, claimed on philosophical grounds that the Son could not belong to and issue from God, for this would imply two and not one. His episcopal superior and his successor, Athanasius, were convinced, however, that the Son was of the same essence as the Father, born not created. This conflict between the prelates of Alexandria gave rise to an empire-wide doctrinal dispute, which disturbed Emperor Constantine. He exhorted the priests to reach a satisfactory solution as quickly as possible.

In Shapur II's reign the Persian empire was fairly securely organized, though there is some doubt as to the accuracy of the given boundaries. Because of poor communications and an almost constant state of war, the central government was never fully in control of the situation along the imperial frontiers.

There were ferocious conflicts within China's imperial house of Jin. Emperor Hui Di's wife murdered both her mother-in-law, the dowager empress, and her stepson, the successor, who was in fact the son of one of her rivals in the harem. She was then herself murdered, unleashing full-scale war among the different family factions, which cost hundreds of thousands of lives. Emperor Hui Di was poisoned and supplanted by his brother Huai Di. The capital was plundered time and time again, the heirs to the throne diminished steadily and in Shansi the Huns sat watching events with profound interest. In the end it occurred to one of the princes involved to call upon the Huns for help, and they were only too willing to oblige. In 311 the Huns simply seized the capital Loyang. Three years later they likewise took Changan where the emperor's successor resided. The whole of northern China had now been lost to the Jin dynasty. However, the court contrived to flee south to Nanjing (Nanking) where a new emperor was proclaimed and another kingdom established. The political power of this new state was negligible, but it was of immense importance as the repository of Chinese culture at a time when other parts of China were repeatedly subjected to foreign invasion. In the list of rulers the southern dynasties are particularly significant.

The conquest of northern China by the Khan of the Huns, Liu Cong, was not a major disaster. Huns had lived on Chinese territory since the days of their great emperors and had adopted a Chinese style of life; they had Chinese names and probably spoke Chinese. But Liu Cong died as early as 318. A revolution broke out in the palace, his whole family was killed, and after bitter internal fighting the Hun empire split into two. Meanwhile, aggressive Tungus dominions nearby were growing stronger and preparing to intervene.

Papacy	-------- Miltiades — Sylvester I
Persia	Shapur II
Rome	Licinius + Constantine
Japan	Nintoku-Tenno
China	Jin Min Di — Jin Yuan Di

311	312	313	314	315	316	317	318	319	320

AD 321-330

INDIA
GANDHARA, INDIA
ROME

In a great battle at Adrianople in 324, Constantine defeated Licinius and thereby became sole ruler of the entire Roman empire. This also ensured the ultimate victory of Christianity. Constantine immediately summoned 318 Church dignitaries from Asia, Africa and Europe to the Council of Nicaea; the first ecumenical synod. The purpose of this was to draw up the guidelines of the new state religion.

The Council of Nicaea determined in 325 by a majority decision that the Son was identical in essence with the Father; born and not created. Arius and his supporters, who thought otherwise, were condemned and exiled. The Council also decreed that Easter should be celebrated annually on the first Sunday following the first full moon after the vernal equinox.

The doctrine of Arius questioned the nature of Christ. It was based on Plato's Logos, the Word of God. 'In the beginning was the Word, and the Word was with God, and the Word was God' (John I.1). For Christians this Word was incarnated in Jesus the man, but then the problem arose as to whether it was he who should be worshipped as God or whether such worship should be confined solely to the invisible, almighty power that sent him. This question had been debated even earlier. The confessor Praxeas of Asia, who confused Father and Son to such an extent that it became the Father who was born of the Virgin Mary and suffered under Pontius Pilate, had been indignantly censured by the theologian Tertullian more than a hundred years previously.

Arius, then, did not accept the official doctrine of Jesus as the true God, born of the eternal Father, and likewise true man born of the Virgin Mary. He did not directly repudiate Christ the Godhead but he argued on philosophical grounds that the Son could not belong to and issue from God's essence, because this would mean two and not one. He had broadcast his news far and wide to Christian theologians, and the matter was not settled merely because he had been outvoted at Nicaea. The arguments of Arius and his followers were to cause much dissent in the Christian world for centuries to come.

Eusebius, Bishop of Caesarea, wrote a very flattering biography of Emperor Constantine I and an ecclesiastical history which is unquestionably the most important source of insight into the earliest history of the Christian church.

The emperor, subsequently known as Constantine the Great, decreed that Sunday should be a national holy day. Thus Sunday as a day of rest was not originally a Church innovation.

In India Chandra Gupta I, founded the Gupta dynasty which created an empire from a union of politically insignificant small states. Samudra Gupta expanded the empire by marrying into an ancient princely family and absorbing its territory. His son Chandra Gupta II was a great warrior who extracted tribute from south-east Bengal, Assam, Nepal, the Kabul region, and even Ceylon, to which he made an expedition; he accepted Vedic offerings and established himself as a divine, absolute ruler. He also had musical and literary talents, and was a patron of culture.

An Egyptian ascetic named Pachomius converted a colony of hermits into a monastery by initiating a system of communal living. He was thus a pioneer of Christian monastic life.

Rome had long since been adandoned as an administrative centre and in 326 work began on the building of a new imperial capital. The emperors had preferred to live in Nicomedia or Milan, or even in Trier or York. The new city was located on the Bosporus and was officially named New Rome, but it became better known as Constantinople, after its founder. During the next few years the emperor was passionately involved in the building activity, which made such rapid progress that walls, gates and the most important monuments were completed within only a few years. A considerable part of the city was built of timber from the forests around the Black Sea, and marble was fetched from the island of Proconesus in the Sea of Marmara. Many monuments were transported to the Bosporus from the ancient cities of Asia and Greece, especially from Delphi.

Head of Constantine. Musei Capitolini, Rome.

	321	322	323	324	325	326	327	328	329	330
India	Chandra Gupta I									
Papacy	Sylvester I									
Persia	Shapur II									
Rome				Constantine I						
Japan	Nintoku-Tenno									
China	Jin Yuan Di		Jin Min Di			Jin Cheng Di				

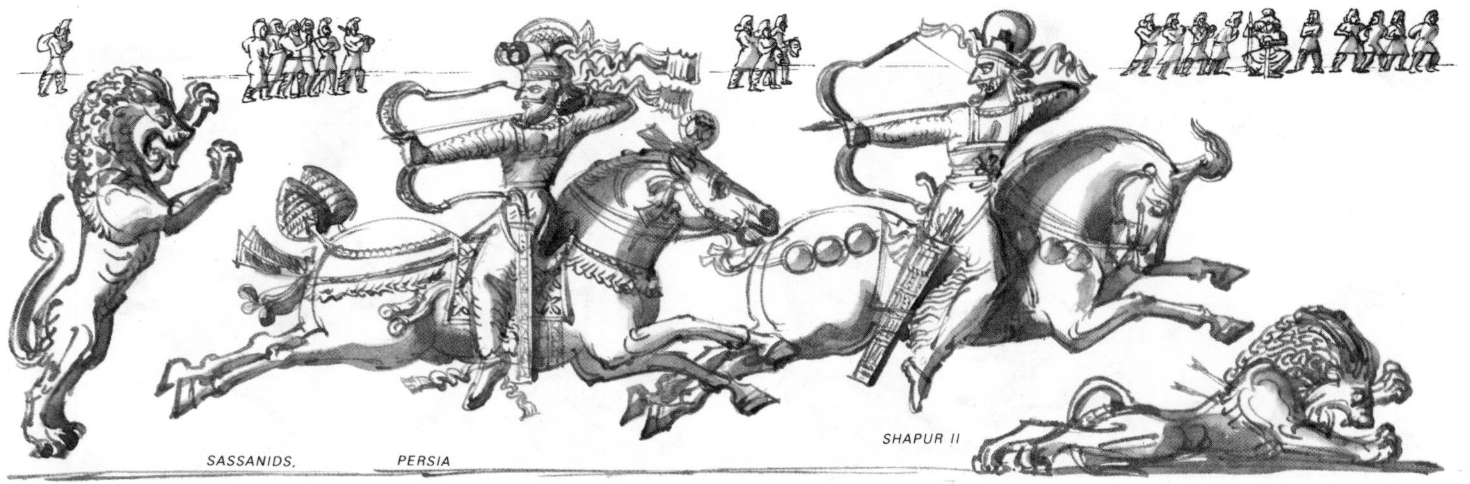
SASSANIDS. PERSIA
SHAPUR II

In 325 King Ezana of Aksum in Ethiopia shipped an army to southern Arabia and made himself master of the Yemen.

The faith of the first Christian Roman emperor was defined in the vaguest and most ambiguous terms; and he took great care to avoid offending the beliefs of other religions. Throughout his life he maintained his position as priest of the Capitoline Jupiter, *pontifex maximus*, and he issued coins with a portrait of Mithras the Sun god and the inscription *'Soli invicto comiti'* (to the unvanquished Sun, my companion). His armies included many devout worshippers of Mithras. Temples and altars to the old gods were still erected in many places with the support and approval of the emperor, who simultaneously mollified the Christians by building the Lateran in Rome as well as the first St Peter's, a five-bayed basilica above the tomb of the apostle. Not until Constantine was on his deathbed did he have himself baptised.

The kingdom of Kaniska and Huvuska, so great and powerful a century before, had lost all its Indian provinces and was now confined to the Kabul valley. But its Scythian culture had wide influence. There is later evidence of this in the ruined city of Crorainna on Lake Lop Nur which was destroyed at about this time.

A number of prominent theologians lived at this time. St Anthony, the ancient Egyptian hermit, left no works of his own, but his biography, written by Bishop Athanasius of Alexandria, is considered a landmark of religious literature and of great significance in the development of monasticism. Athanasius was the principal exponent of the doctrine of Christ's dual nature, which had recently triumphed in Nicaea and was subsequently to become the creed of all European churches. This victory was not achieved, however, while Athanasius lived; in fact, his antagonist Arius was gaining favour with the authorities, so much so that when the Goths were felt to be in need of a Christian missionary, Ulfilas was despatched to convert them to Arianism.

As usual, war raged between the Romans and Persians. In 339 Shapur II began a major persecution of the Christians, which doubtless had some connection with the successful advance of Christianity in the neighbouring empire.

In the table of rulers there is a Constantius II and a Constantine II, both sons of Constantine I. The reason is that the former's grandfather, Constantius Chlorus, held the title of Caesar Augustus for some months.

The first St Peter's Church. Fresco in the Vatican grottoes, Rome.

Samudra Gupta	India
Sylvester I — Mark — Julius I	Papacy
Shapur II	Persia
Constantine I — Constantius II, Constantine II & Constans	Rome
Nintoku-Tenno	Japan
Jin Cheng Di	China

331	332	333	334	335	336	337	338	339	340

AD 341-350

ROMAN
EMPIRE

The Arian dispute continued in the Christian world and the imperial brothers Constans and Constantius were divided in their beliefs. The latter expelled the inflexibly orthodox bishop Athanasius from his congregation in Alexandria.

In 350 Emperor Constans lost his life through an intrigue. A general named Magnentius immediately assumed the vacant office, but was defeated and deposed by Constantius II who thereby united the entire Roman empire under his own rule.

In 355 the Salian Franks – from Salland on the Ijssel – penetrated the Roman fortification in the land of the Batavians. They temporarily occupied a number of towns, known today as Xanten, Cologne and Bonn.

A number of Maya cities in Central America date from the 4th century. These were grouped around a lake (Petén) in what is now Guatemala. The largest of these cities were Copán, Palenque, Piedras Negras, Tikal, Uaxactún and Quiriquá, and it is from these jungle sites that Maya monuments from various centuries have been discovered.

Ulfilas, the Arian missionary to the Goths north of the Black Sea in the reign of Constantine II, translated the Bible into Gothic and thereby preserved that language long after it had ceased to be spoken. To do this Ulfilas actually invented a Gothic alphabet, and his work survives thanks to a magnificent transcript by his Gothic kinsmen some centuries later in Italy. In due course this *Codex Argenteus* or Silver Bible found its way to the library of the university of Uppsala.

Constantius II was practically the last of his dynasty, having disposed of his brothers and all but one of his cousins. The latter's name was Julian, a scholarly young man who was studying philosophy in Athens when he was suddenly summoned to the court in Milan, attired as an emperor, presented to the troops and sent to rule Gaul, which had been invaded by Germanic tribes. Remarkably enough, Julian succeeded in driving them back over the Rhine, recovering the future Cologne, capturing the king of the Alemanni at the town later to be called Strasburg, and then crossing the river to dictate his peace terms.

According to the historian Jordanes, the Ostrogoths had now established a large empire extending from the Baltic to the Black Sea and the Volga; this was ruled by a king named Ermanaric. Although nothing is known about his real life, except that he eventually committed suicide, he appears as a powerful king in several Norse sagas. His name in the Völsunga Saga is Jörmunrek.

These two clay figures of women with rings in their ears are from Jalisco in Mexico, and have been dated at about this time. Private collection.

India	Samudra Gupta
Papacy	Julius I
Persia	Shapur II
Rome	Constantius II & Constans
Japan	Nintoku-Tenno
China	Jin Cheng Di – Jin Kang Di – Jin Mu Di

341	342	343	344	345	346	347	348	349	350

AD 351-360

ROMAN
EMPIRE
PERSIA

The popes Julius I and Liberius were inextricably involved in the question of Christ's divine and human nature, an issue which the Arians and Athanasians were disputing with intense fervour. It had been decreed at the Council of Nicaea in 325 that the Son was of the same essence as the Father, but Emperor Constantius II was more inclined to the Arian view, that the Son was created by the Father, in other words that Jesus was man, not God. Julius I sought to mediate between the antagonists at a council in Serdica (modern Sofia), but failed entirely. Liberius was of a less conciliatory nature and when Constantius II tried to persuade him to support a denunciation of the Athanasian doctrine he resolutely refused, even though his papal legates had already endorsed the document. The emperor then banished him to Thrace and appointed an anti-pope named Felix II. During his exile, however, Liberius appears to have relented and, agreeing to a compromise formula on the nature of the Son, was permitted to return to Rome.

In 356 the holy Anthony died in Egypt at the age of 105. He had presided over a colony of hermits at Fayum and had thereby laid the foundations for the Christian monastic system. He had also performed many wonders, resisted severe temptations, and even travelled to Alexandria where he had preached against the Arians and given great support to his friend and fellow-believer, Bishop Athanasius.

In the 4th century China's political geography was confused. Since 319 the Jin dynasty in Nanking had ruled over a southern empire extending as far as the River Yangtze. In the north the Huns were predominant, though they were gradually adopting the superior culture of the Chinese and were also becoming acquainted with Buddhism.

An Indian missionary named Fo Tu Cheng won the confidence of the ruling house through prophecy and invocation and thereby created a sound foundation for his religion in northern China, even though the Confucian officials strongly opposed this. To the west and north of the Hun kingdom there were five more states on Chinese territory, including a Tungus kingdom in the north-east. The latter was ruled over by a dynasty known as Mu Rong which had Chinese advisers. This was a well-organized and fairly civilized society. In 350 it declared war on the Hun kingdom which for some years had been suffering from internal unrest and where there had been appalling massacres related to the succession. The Tungus captured and executed the king of the Huns and moved their government to his capital, Ye.

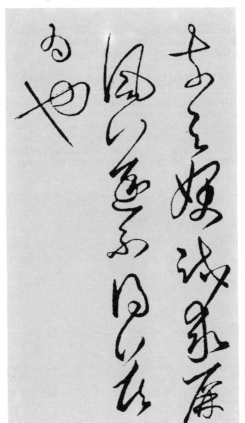

The true Chinese empire in the south took advantage of this opportunity to retake some of its lost provinces. In 365 Chinese troops attacked the Huns and advanced as far as the former capital Loyang. But they were unable to sustain their position here and were forced back to the Yangtze valley again. Although the empire of the Jin dynasty remained fairly small, it was here and here alone that the continuity of Chinese culture was preserved.

Emperor Jin Mu Di was immortalized by one of China's greatest calligraphers: Wang Xizhi. Otherwise, however, in his peaceful Nanking empire Emperor Jin Mu Di achieved nothing notable.

It was said of this example of Wang Xizhi's work: 'His brush moves like floating clouds, like rocks falling from on high, like strong bows drawn and quivering, like a serpent coiling in excitement'. While Wang Xizhi was still a young artist, a monk was reputed to have offered him 300 geese as payment if he would make a copy of Laozi's document on Tao; Wang produced a calligraphic masterpiece which was to be admired for centuries. Even more famous is a text which he composed himself later in life. This is entitled Pavilion of the Orchids, *inscribed on silk with a mouse-whisker brush. Wang Xizhi never surpassed this work.*

Samudra Gupta — India
Julius I — Liberius (+ Felix II) — Papacy
Shapur II — Persia
Constantius II — Rome
Nintoku-Tenno — Japan
Jin Mu Di — China

351	352	353	354	355	356	357	358	359	360

AD 361-370

The Alani, a Scythian tribe with an Indo-European language, had established a kingdom between the Don and the Caspian Sea. They were driven out in the mid-4th century, however, by the Huns who, having long harassed the Chinese, now appeared on the European horizon for the first time. Most of the Alani retreated westward where they joined up with the Germanic Vandals.

Constantius II had been an ardent Arian, but his cousin Julian, last of the dynasty, was a Neo-Platonist and openly embraced what is known as heathenism. He systematically weeded out the Christians from the administration, opened up the temples of the ancient gods and restored their properties to them, and attempted to create a heathen hierarchy. Julian's reign was brief, however, and his successor restored the Christian church to its position of power. Julian went down in history as 'the Apostate'.

Julian was careful never to use the word Christ or Christian. He talked instead of the Galileans, perhaps with a hint of contempt but very likely as a prudent paraphrase. The Neo-Platonists whom he supported had a mystical belief in the power of words and names. He was thus no mere sceptic or rationalist; his loathing for Christianity stemmed from firm convictions. The Neo-Platonic ideas which he had put into writing abounded in mystical allegory. He believed in a supreme being and a host of demigods and demons who sometimes visited the human world.

The Persian war in which Julian was killed had gone badly for the Romans and ended with their losing Christian Armenia.

The apostolic fathers St Basil, his brother St Gregory of Nyssa, and St Gregory of Nazianzus were industrious scribes who upheld the doctrine of the Trinity and combatted both Arian heresy and heathenism. St Basil, who was more interested in practice than theory, introduced and administered the monastic order on Greek territory.

Yemen, which had been under Ethiopian sovereignty for some decades, secured its freedom again at this time.

In Britain the Scots and Picts succeeded in crossing Hadrian's Wall in 367. The wall was extensively repaired however, in 370, and continued to serve as an effective defence line for several centuries.

The Tungus empire in northern China was torn by inner conflicts within the Mu Rong dynasty. To the west, the neighbouring Tangut, a people related to the Tibetans, took this opportunity to seize territory and soon controlled an immense area extending from Korea to central Asia.

The Tangut also conquered a number of small central Asian states along the caravan route to Iran. At Kucha, in the Tarim basin, they captured a Tocharian or Turkish military band whose performances pleased them. This band was taken to China and played an important role in the development of music there. Meanwhile, by the River Yangtze the Nanking empire continued its peaceful and prosperous existence, nurturing its poetic, quietist and very conservative culture.

The Emperor Valentinian, formerly a general, called on his brother Valens for assistance. The latter was sent to rule in Constantinople while Valentinian reigned from Milan. The head of Valens is shown on the left, Valentinian to the right. British Museum, London.

	361	362	363	364	365	366	367	368	369	370
India	Samudra Gupta									
Papacy	Liberius (+ Felix II)					Damasus I				
Persia	Shapur II									
Eastern Rome	Julian the Apostate		Jovian		Valens					
Western Rome					Valentinian I					
Japan	Nintoku-Tenno									
China	Jin Mu Di	Jin Ai Di				Jin Hai Xi Gong				

ROME
ARDASHIR II.
PERSIA

In 372 the Huns crossed the Volga into the large kingdom of the Ostrogoths, whose king, Ermanaric, committed suicide; after this defeat, vast numbers of Ostrogoth refugees fled westward. The victorious Huns now turned their attention to the Visigoth kingdom beyond the Danube border of the Roman empire. The panic-stricken Visigoths made for the Roman border, begging asylum. The Romans could scarcely reject them since the Visigoths were Arian Christians, like Emperor Valens, ruler of the eastern half of the empire. The Visigoths were permitted to cross the Danube and assembled in enormous refugee camps where the problem of supplies soon became insuperable. Consequently the Visigoths began to move southward. This the Roman authorities obviously could not tolerate. Valens himself led a large army into the field and met the Visigoths at Adrianople. Here on an August day of 378 the Romans were soundly defeated and the emperor killed. It marked the beginning of the Goths' long-lasting conquest of the Roman empire. The dead emperor's nephews in the west despatched the Spanish general Theodosius eastward to restore the situation and he proved temporarily successful. After several military encounters the entire Gothic force entered Roman service.

A citizen of Kucha, captured by the Tangut, was the famous Indian prophet Kumarajiva, leader of that branch of the Buddhist faith known as Mahayana, the Great Vehicle. The Tangut took Kumarajiva with them to China where he subsequently worked as a missionary for thirty years and recruited 5000 disciples. He translated into Chinese 98 sacred writings totalling 420 chapters.

In 380 Emperor Theodosius I issued a religious edict to the effect that all inhabitants of the Roman empire should embrace the apostle Peter's creed of the three-in-one godhead. Anyone who believed otherwise should be regarded as insane and heretical, and would have to reckon not only with the eternal wrath of God but also with temporal punishment. This edict was directed not merely at heathenism but against the Arian Christian faith as well.

Aurelius Ambrosius, Roman governor in northern Italy, was appointed bishop in 374. As such he continued to live in Milan where he drew up ordinances and provisions which were to become permanent. He introduced the mass and church singing, and he composed sermons and treatises against heathenism and Arian heresy. When the dowager Empress Justina requested that a local church be made over to herself and her Arian fellow-believers, he flatly refused; and when an edict of tolerance on their behalf was issued in the name of the young emperor Valentinian II, Aurelius Ambrosius (Ambrose) condemned this as a wicked and blasphemous outrage. He was now banished from Milan, but refused to go, knowing his own strength. His faithful congregation, including many beggars and poor people, stood constant guard around his residence and his cathedral. As they stood there they are said to have sung in unison, so giving rise to the melodious, rhythmic form of plainsong known as Ambrosian Chant.

Under the leadership of a sheik named Malikarrib Yuhan'im, the small states of southern Arabia were united into a single kingdom in 378.

Left: Valentinian II. Right: Shapur II, who defeated Julian. Coins in the British Museum, London.

Frithigern — **Visigoths**
Samudra Gupta — **India**
Damasus I — **Papacy**
Shapur II | Ardashir II — **Persia**
Valens | Theodosius I — **Eastern Rome**
Valentinian I | Gratian & Valentinian II — **Western Rome**
Nintoku-Tenno — **Japan**
Jin Jian Wen Di | Jin Xiao Wu Di — **China**

371	372	373	374	375	376	377	378	379	380

AD 381-390

ROME
EAST ROMAN
EMPIRE

In 381 the Council of Constantinople confirmed the Trinity and prepared for the admission of the Holy Spirit, the position of the Father and the Son having already been agreed upon at Nicaea in 325.

Militant Christians persecuted dissidents and tore down heathen temples in many parts of the Roman empire. They were particularly active in Alexandria where the temple of Sarapis and its attendant library were completely destroyed. One particular zealot was St Martin of Tours who demolished sacred groves and trees in his domains. It is said that when Martin was appointed bishop in Tours he tried to evade this task by concealing himself in a goose-pen, but the cackling of the birds betrayed him.

The Tangut in northern China organized a major campaign to invade the Nanjing empire as well, but they were repulsed at a decisive battle in 387. This defeat had far-reaching consequences, for the many peoples oppressed by the Tangut now rose in revolt; and the Tangut were then attacked from the north and crushed by a new master-race known as the Wei. These were Tungus, and unlike the Tangut they quickly assimilated Chinese ideas. Their dynasty, the Bei Wei or Northern Wei, which in future did much to preserve and promote Chinese culture, ruled over northern China from the 380s to 557.

After a Roman synod had prescribed which Christian scriptures should be regarded as canonical, Jerome, secretary to Pope Damasus I, set about translating these into Latin. Jerome's biblical text, entitled *Versio Vulgata*, survived ever after.

The task of making an authoritative selection from the Christian literature of the time could not have been easy. There were innumerable gospels and epistles to sort through. Jerome himself mentions the Hebrew gospel and Origen refers to the gospels of the twelve apostles; then there were the Egyptian gospels, a Nicodemus gospel, gospels on the childhood of Jesus by James and Thomas, and other gospels by Matthias, Philip, Judas, Bartholomew and Peter. There were also many different accounts of the acts of the apostles, besides various apocalypses and large numbers of letters. The synod of Rome would appear to have made a sensible selection from this mass of material. Judging from fragments of the others, Matthew, Mark, Luke and John seem to be in a class on their own. As early as the 4th century they were furnished with their attributes, which were to recur constantly in Church art through the ages: an angel for Matthew, a lion for Mark, a bull for Luke and an eagle for John.

The popes Damasus and Siricius prepared the way for the Roman bishopric's demand for right of authority over other sees. Siricius was the author of the earliest known papal letter which was an ordinance and not a private admonition. This concerned ecclesiastical discipline.

From Milan the apostolic father Ambrose exerted great influence on the authorities throughout the Roman empire. At his request Emperor Gratian had the Nike altar removed from the Curia in Rome, and in 382 he drove the Vestal virgins out of their temple where the fire had been kept alive ever since the time of Numa.

St Ambrose. Mosaic in Sant'Ambrogio, Milan.

Visigoths	----------
India	Chandra Gupta II
Papacy	Damasus I | ---------- | Siricius
Persia	Ardashir II | Shapur III | Bahram IV
Eastern Rome	Theodosius I
Western Rome	Gratian & Valentinian II | Valentinian II
Japan	Nintoku-Tenno
Nanking	Jin Xiao Wu Di
Northern China	| Bei Wei Dao Wu Di

381	382	383	384	385	386	387	388	389	390

THEODOSIUS I
WITH HIS BODY GUARD
ROME
CHINA

Chandra Gupta II assumed the title of Vikramaditya and appears in Indian tales under this name. During his reign the Gupta empire expanded to the west at the expense of a number of Scythian satraps who had thus far ruled under Persian sovereignty. With his own hand, according to legend, he slew the last of these after having disguised himself as a woman and lured the hapless satrap into a private chamber.

An imperial decree in 393 forbade the Olympic Games, which had been conducted every fourth year since 776 BC. The Games were now banned because they were related to the Zeus cult in Olympia.

For a few months, during the period 394-95, the Roman empire was for the last time united under one and the same ruler. Emperor Theodosius had defeated the Frankish general, Arbogast, and had killed the latter's puppet emperor, Eugenius. Theodosius now made a triumphant entry into Rome, appeared in the Curia before the assembled senate and demanded an answer to a simple question: Should the Romans accept the teachings of Christ or the worship of Jupiter? The senate obediently condemned the latter alternative, augurs and pontifices reluctantly adopted the new religion, and the great poet Prudentius acclaimed the event in jubilant song. Finally Rome, too, had become a city with Christian leadership.

The pontificate of Anastasius I was so brief that not even his full name is entered in the list of popes; nevertheless it was at this time that Rome repudiated the Neo-Platonic theology of Origen.

Emperor Arcadius and his wife Eudoxia became involved in a dispute with the patriarch John Chrysostom, who accused them of sinful behaviour. He was a dangerous adversary because he had the ear of the people. At the beginning of the next decade they contrived to have him exiled but this failed to silence him and he left many important works to posterity.

St Ambrose proclaimed that the worship of idols could anger God who might respond by punishing the authorities and the entire community. Paganism, non-Christian mystery religions and Ariansim were decreed to be crimes by Theodosius. Detail of obelisk in honour of Theodosius, Constantinople.

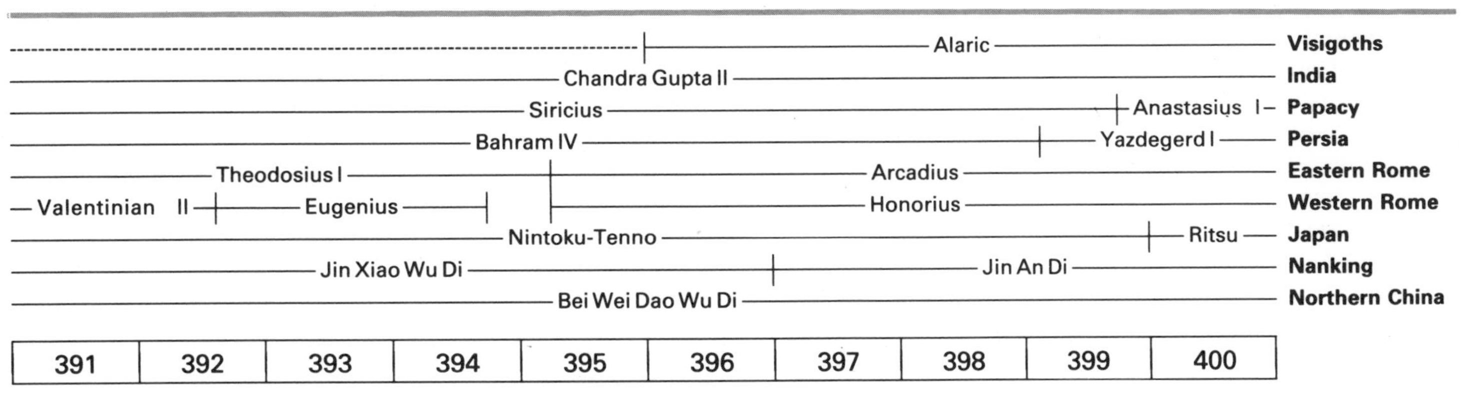
Alaric
Visigoths
Chandra Gupta II
India
Siricius
Anastasius I
Papacy
Bahram IV
Yazdegerd I
Persia
Theodosius I
Arcadius
Eastern Rome
Valentinian II
Eugenius
Honorius
Western Rome
Nintoku-Tenno
Ritsu
Japan
Jin Xiao Wu Di
Jin An Di
Nanking
Bei Wei Dao Wu Di
Northern China
391
392
393
394
395
396
397
398
399
400

AD 401-410

MOSHI, PERU
THE EASTERN EMPIRE
SERENA
STILICHO
CHINA

Once the Rhine frontier of the Roman empire had been breached, various Germanic hordes surged in through western Europe. As early as 407 three such tribes reached Spain: the Alani, the Suebi and the Vandals.

In 413 a Burgundian kingdom was established with its capital at Worms. At the same time the Salian Franks, who for some generations had inhabited the islands in the mouth of the Rhine, moved out through northern Gaul.

The great events of the early 5th century include the roving expeditions of the Visigoths and the incursions of the Alani, Vandals, Alemanni and Burgundians into the Roman empire, the two halves of which were no longer linked nor even able to maintain a state of amity. The West was governed in the name of the young emperor, Honorius, by a general named Stilicho. Stilicho was a Vandal by origin but was married to a cousin of the emperor. The authorities in the East were on strained terms with Stilicho while at the same time they had problems with the Goths who constituted a state within a state. These Goths had arrived in Italy in 401, and Stilicho only held them in check by withdrawing all his troops from the Rhine frontier,with the result that the whole of Gaul was quickly overrun by Germanic immigrants. Meanwhile Stilicho himself was deposed and killed on the orders of Honorius. From his impregnable residence in Ravenna, Honorius rejected the Goths' demands for a homeland and a livelihood. In this situation, under their king, Alaric, the Goths marched on Rome which they occupied and plundered. The fall of this ancient city aroused alarm and consternation, and the Church Father Augustine wrote much of this in his *De civitate Dei*.

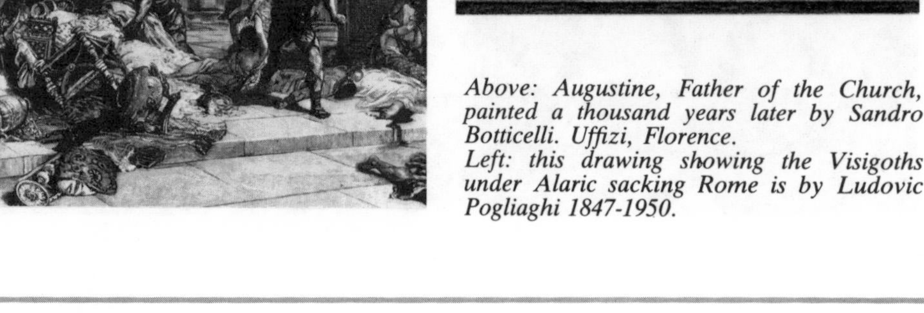

Above: Augustine, Father of the Church, painted a thousand years later by Sandro Botticelli. Uffizi, Florence.
Left: this drawing showing the Visigoths under Alaric sacking Rome is by Ludovic Pogliaghi 1847-1950.

The sack of Rome took place in 410. Alaric then moved on southward, intending to cross over to Africa with his Goths. But he suddenly died of a disease and was buried with all his treasures in the bed of a southern Italian river, the waters of which were diverted for the purpose and afterwards allowed to flow back again along their original course.

Chandra Gupta II was lauded in tale and song as a wise and brave monarch who well deserved his title of Vikramaditya, the poets' patron. The Gupta epoch was the classical age of Indian culture and Sanskrit literature. In addition to the many Buddhist writings this period also produced such works as the dramas *Sakuntala* by Kalidasa and *Mrccha-katika* (The Little Clay Cart) by Sudraka.

Yazdegerd I is known in history as 'The Sinner'. In 409 he issued an edict of tolerance permitting the Christian Persians to rebuild their churches and conduct their services publicly. A Church council was now held at which the prelates recognized the principles of faith decreed at Nicaea and repudiated Arian and other such doctrines. Yazdegerd I initially condemned the local fire-worshipping religion, but suddenly reversed his policy and proceeded to persecute the Christians. This campaign lasted four years and cost many lives.

	401	402	403	404	405	406	407	408	409	410
Visigoths					Alaric					
India					Chandra Gupta II					
Papacy						Innocent I				
Persia					Yazdegerd I					
Eastern Rome				Arcadius					Theodosius II	
Western Rome					Honorius					
Japan			Ritsu					Hansho		
Nanking					Jin An Di					
Northern China				Bei Wei Dao Wu Di					Bei Wei Ming Yuan Di	

MOSHI PERU

The year 420 witnessed the fall of the East Jin dynasty in Nanking and this was followed by the short-lived Liu Song dynasty, whose emperor was a member of the Liu family. This dynasty is also known as Pre-Song, in distinction to the later (10th century) and more renowned Song (Sung) dynasty.

The Visigoths left Italy and made for southern Gaul under the leadership of Alaric's brother-in-law Ataulphus. In Narbo the latter married the sister of Emperor Honorius, Galla Placidia, whom the Visigoths had taken prisoner in Rome. In her honour the Gauls dressed for the occasion in Roman attire. They then crossed the Pyrenees and occupied the Spanish Mediterranean coast all the way down to the Ebro. In 415 Ataulphus was assassinated in Barcelona by a certain Sigeric, who himself met the same fate a few weeks later and was succeeded by a soldier named Wallia. Wallia preferred to reside in Toulouse and reached an agreement with the Roman authorities whereby the Goths were granted the land and domiciliary rights of the region they now held, on condition that they helped drive the recently established Germanic Vandals and Suebi out of Spain. Galla Placidia was also released and shortly afterwards married a Roman general. Their son was to become Emperor Valentinian III. The Vandals soon made way for the Visigoths in Spain but Toulouse remained their capital.

Bei Wei, the northern Chinese empire of the Tungus, was a centre of culture where Chinese statesmen, authors and artists assisted the emperor and held high positions. For the next century all significant developments in Chinese literature and art took place in Bei Wei, while the Nanking empire continued to preserve traditions.

According to all early sources, the Visigoths had come originally from Scandinavia, though at the dawn of their verifiable history they dwelt by the Black Sea. They brought about great changes within the Roman Empire, but with no enduring results.
Below: a Visigoth warrior, according to a medieval manuscript.

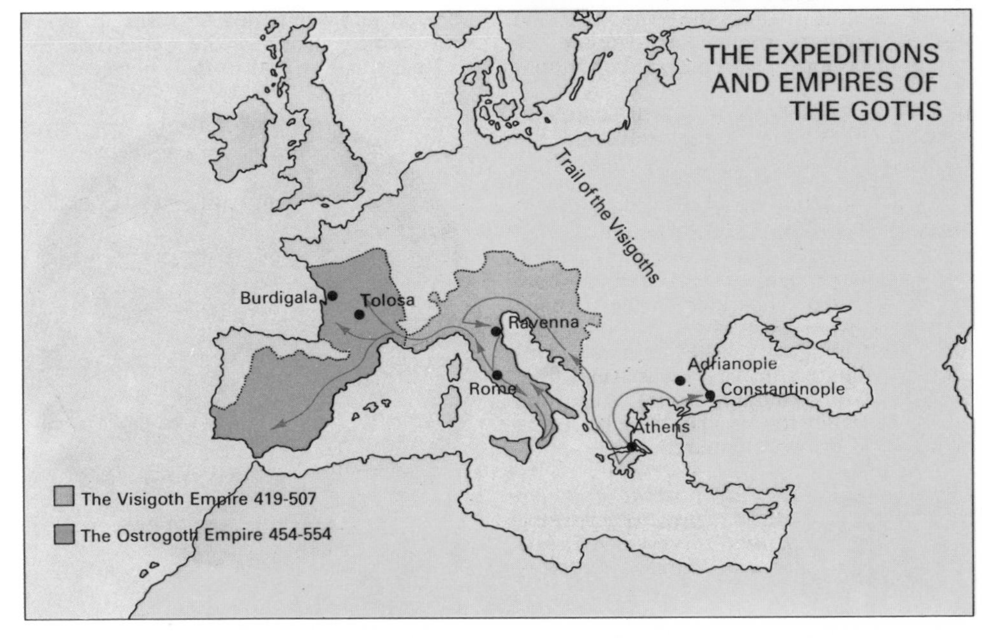
THE EXPEDITIONS AND EMPIRES OF THE GOTHS
Trail of the Visigoths
Burdigala
Tolosa
Ravenna
Rome
Adrianople
Constantinople
Athens
The Visigoth Empire 419-507
The Ostrogoth Empire 454-554

Ataulphus — --- — Wallia	**Visigoths**
Chandra Gupta II — Kumara Gupta	**India**
Innocent I — Zosimus — Boniface I	**Papacy**
Yazdegerd I	**Persia**
Theodosius II	**Eastern Rome**
Honorius	**Western Rome**
Ingyo	**Japan**
Jin An Di — Jin Gong Di — Liu Song Wu Di	**Nanking**
Bei Wei Ming Yuan Di	**Northern China**

411	412	413	414	415	416	417	418	419	420

PERSIANS
MOSHI, PERU

At this time the holy writings of Buddhism were being translated into Chinese. The quality of craftsmanship was unsurpassed by anything subsequently produced by Christianity.

In China, too, migratory movements had begun. Imperial power remained fairly secure south of the River Yangtze after a recent, unsuccessful assault by the Tangut. The defeat of the Tangut had been total and resulted in the disintegration of their power. Now, after interminable wars, northern China was split up into about a dozen independent states. The most vital of these was Tungus Bei Wei, the princes of which soon settled in the old imperial town of Loyang.

A number of the Bei Wei emperors were ardent Buddhists and during their time there emerged wonderful sculpture modelled on Indian and even Greek examples.

According to Matt. 16:18-19 Jesus says to the apostle Peter: '....thou art Peter, and upon this rock I will build my church; and the gates of hell shall not prevail against it.'
'And I will give unto thee the keys of the kingdom of heaven: and whatsoever thou shalt bind on earth shall be bound in heaven: and whatsoever thou shalt loose on earth shall be loosed in heaven'.

Pope Celestine I forcefully insisted that Peter, in his capacity as Rome's first bishop, had passed on the keys to the kingdom of heaven to each and every one of his successors. Celestine claimed that by virtue of this apostolic privilege the bishop of Rome was no ordinary prelate, but rather the bishop of bishops: *episcopus episcoporum.*

In 429 the Vandals crossed from Spain into Africa and established themselves in the Roman province there; it was to take them another ten years to gain control of the fortified capital, Carthage. The Vandal king, Gaiseric, was a prominent admiral and an accomplished politician. He and his people were Arians, probably recently baptized, and they were hailed as liberators by the Donatist sectarians who were also at odds with orthodox Christianity. The principal advocate of orthodoxy in Africa was Augustine, bishop of Hippo (modern Bône). Augustine died in 430 while the Vandals were besieging his city, but his work endured.

Left: Emperor Honorius, portrait on a coin from Antioch. Right: the Persian king Bahram V on a lion hunt, engraved on a silver goblet now in the British Museum, London.

For some decades cavalry hordes of Huns had been raiding western Asia, and Europe, too, along the Danube. But their political organization appears to have been desultory and they were always prepared to serve as mercenaries in foreign armies. Attila, however, was a great organizer and a brilliant general, uniting all the Hun forces.

Bahram V was the son of Yazdegerd I. He had been raised in the southern Arabian state of Hira, whose king, Mundhir, helped him seize power in Persia after the nobles had deposed his father and appointed his cousin Shah. Bahram continued the persecution of the Christians, who then sought refuge in Roman territory. This in turn led him to declare war on Rome in 420, but he was defeated and compelled to agree to peace terms which included the return of the Christians and an end to their persecution.

Huns	Vidin — Rugila
Vandals	Gunderic — Gaiseric
Visigoths	Theodoric I
India	Kumara Gupta
Papacy	Boniface I — Celestine I
Persia	Bahram V
Eastern Rome	Theodosius II
Western Rome	Honorius — Constantius — Valentinian III
Japan	Ingyo
Nanking	Liu Song Wu Di — Shao Di — Liu Song Wen Di
Northern China	Bei Wei Ming Yuan Di — Bei Wei Tai Wu Di

421	422	423	424	425	426	427	428	429	430

AD 431-440

PERSIANS
HUNS
MOSHI, PERU

Emperor Tai Wu Di and his advisers were persuaded by Kou Qianzhi, a Taoist, to found an organised religion in northern Wei. Prior to this the rulers here had favoured Buddhism, but suddenly, on the pretext that the emperor had recently learned of concealed arms in a monastery, a policy of persecution was initiated. Innumerable monks were killed and many temples destroyed. The survivors, who traditionally had refused to acknowledge temporal rulers, were now ordered to behave, if not to think, like the emperor's other subjects.

In 431 the Council of Ephesus censured the Constantinople patriarch, Nestorius, who claimed that the Jesus born in Bethlehem was a human being and not a god. He added that through his baptism in the River Jordan in the presence of the Holy Spirit, Jesus became the Son of God, and that the Virgin Mary had nothing to do with this latter phase. Nestorius was driven into exile and his teachings were suppressed in the Roman empire, but he then moved eastward and secured a large following in central Asia.

This same council also condemned the followers of the heretic Pelagius who twenty years earlier had denied the existence of original sin, claiming that by virtue of his own strength man could refrain from becoming a sinner. By the terms of this doctrine divine mercy was reduced to little more than modest encouragement.

Roman diptych–a foldable writing tablet waxed on the inside–dating from AD 428. Sculptured diptychs in ivory were greatly appreciated presents. Louvre, Paris.

Rulers	
Rugila — Attila	**Huns**
Gaiseric	**Vandals**
Theodoric I	**Visigoths**
Kumara Gupta	**India**
Celestine I — Sixtus III	**Papacy**
Bahram V — Yazdegerd II	**Persia**
Theodosius II	**Eastern Rome**
Valentinian III	**Western Rome**
Ingyo	**Japan**
Liu Song Wen Di	**Nanking**
Bei Wei Tai Wu Di	**Northern China**

431	432	433	434	435	436	437	438	439	440

AD 441-450

EAST ROMAN EMPIRE
ROME

The so-called Robber synod took place in Ephesus in 449. The subject of this assembly was the complex question of the dual nature of Christ. Egyptian and other theologists maintained that the Virgin Mary gave birth to a god and not a human being: Christ has thus only one nature, the divine. This doctrine was known as Monophysitism. But in Rome and Constantinople it was widely believed that Christ had a dual nature - divine and human. Before this question could be debated at Ephesus, however, the Monophysites physically attacked their opponents and drove them out. After this incident the synod decreed that Christ had but one nature.

Angles, Saxons and Jutes invaded England, the last of the Roman garrisons having departed in 407.

Tribes using a Slavic language moved into territories recently abandoned by the Teutones, between the Black Sea and the Baltic.

Galla Placidia, as guardian of her son Valentinian, ruled over the West Roman empire from Ravenna. Sister of the late emperors Arcadius and Honorius, she had been abducted by the Visigoths and forced into marriage with their king, Ataulphus; subsequently she was ill-treated by her husband's assassin and successor, and again forcibly married to a Roman general who was presumably the father of her son, Valentinian. Galla Placidia died in 450.

Galla Placidia built a small church in Ravenna, the ceiling of which is covered by splendid mosaics that have withstood the ravages of time and constitute a unique example of classical craftsmanship in this sphere. Shown below is a detail of a dome decoration with a picture of the Good Shepherd in a lunette. Other domes have different scenes and patterns.

Huns	Attila
Vandals	Gaiseric
Visigoths	Theodoric I
India	Kumara Gupta
Papacy	Leo I
Persia	Yazdegerd II
Eastern Rome	Theodosius II
Western Rome	Valentinian III
Japan	Ingyo
Nanking	Liu Song Wen Di
Northern China	Bei Wei Tai Wu Di

441	442	443	444	445	446	447	448	449	450

EAST ROMAN EMPIRE
KOREA
MEXICO
PERSIA

The mid-5th century was dominated by the brief ascendancy of the Huns. Attila twice thrust into the East Roman empire until the government there bought him off with a huge tribute. After this he moved westward instead.

A coalition of Romans and Visigoths confronted the Huns at the Marne. The so-called battle of the Catalaunian Plains was a very bloody affair and among those who died in it was the old king, Theodoric I. Afterwards Attila withdrew eastward again, but the following spring he reassembled his cavalry and made for Italy where fugitives from the conquered city of Aquileia sought refuge on certain Adriatic islands and laid the foundations of Venice. Outside Rome, Attila encountered Pope Leo I, above whose head, says legend, hovered the figure of Peter the apostle, wielding his sword against the hostile Huns. In any event Leo I and Attila reached an agreement and Rome was spared assault and destruction. Attila died in his nuptial bed in 453 and this terminated the Huns' short-lived era of greatness. Not only their empire but also the people themselves disappeared abruptly from history.

In 445 Emperor Valentinian officially authorized the ecclesiastical legislation of Leo I, pope and bishop of Rome. This gave Rome a superior status to other bishoprics and cemented the universal influence of the Papal See. When the male line of Theodosius the Great's dynasty died out, Leo I was ceremoniously crowned emperor by the patriarch of Constantinople; this was the first time that an emperor had been installed by the Church.

While the battle of the Catalaunian Plains was being fought, the Council of Chalcedon took place on the Bosporus and agreed upon the dual nature of Christ.

Christian Armenia, which had become a Persian province without any autonomy in the 420s, was compelled to adopt the Persian state religion in 456. The Christians were likewise severely persecuted in Mesopotamia during the reign of Yazdegerd II.

When they first appeared, the Franks were divided into two tribes. For half a century the Ripuarian Franks had lived between the Rhine and the Meuse; the Salian Franks between the Meuse and the Schelde. The latter had now invaded northern Gaul and a detachment took part in the battle of the Catalaunian Plains. The name of their chieftain was Merovec or Merovech, and his successors became known as Merovingians.

Valentinian III on a Roman gold coin. This son of Galla Placidia was somewhat maligned in the chronicles though his reign was comparatively short. He died at the age of 36.

Under Valentinian II the West Roman empire was governed primarily by General Aetius. In 454 the emperor had the general murdered; the following year he himself suffered the same fate and was succeeded by a Roman aristocrat named Petronius Maximus who forcibly wed Valentinian's widow Eudoxia and likewise ordered the marriage of his son and her daughter. This girl, however, was betrothed to the son and successor of the Vandal king Gaiseric, who responded by despatching a fleet which landed an army at the mouth of the Tiber. This caused dissension in Rome and Petronius Maximus was stoned; the city was occupied by the Vandals and plundered for two weeks.

There was then a rapid succession of West Roman emperors. Avitus, who came from Gaul, was deposed by a general of Suebian origin named Ricimer who shortly became the empire's *de facto* ruler. Emperor Majorian was not appointed by Ricimer, however, but by Leo I of Eastern Rome.

In Western history books the Persian king Peroz or Perozes is sometimes referred to as Firuz. But since this is a simple matter of transcription, both versions are equally acceptable.

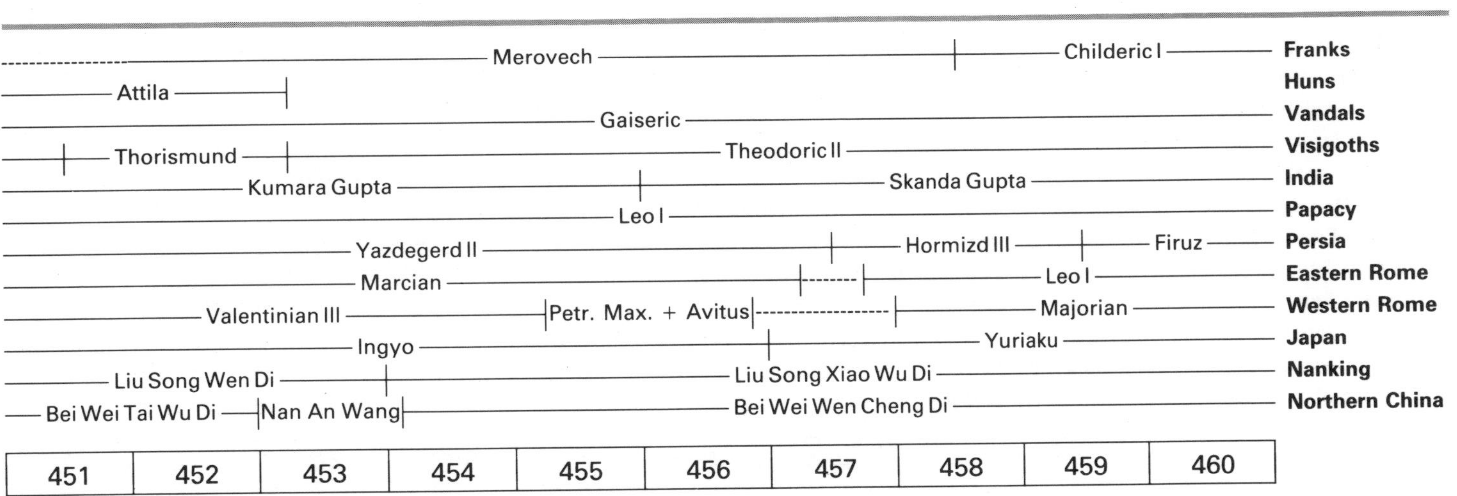
Merovech — Childeric I — Franks
Attila — Huns
Gaiseric — Vandals
Thorismund — Theodoric II — Visigoths
Kumara Gupta — Skanda Gupta — India
Leo I — Papacy
Yazdegerd II — Hormizd III — Firuz — Persia
Marcian — Leo I — Eastern Rome
Valentinian III — Petr. Max. + Avitus — Majorian — Western Rome
Ingyo — Yuriaku — Japan
Liu Song Wen Di — Liu Song Xiao Wu Di — Nanking
Bei Wei Tai Wu Di — Nan An Wang — Bei Wei Wen Cheng Di — Northern China
451
452
453
454
455
456
457
458
459
460

AD 461-470

EAST ROMAN EMPIRE

The last West Roman emperors were mere puppets. Severus, appointed by the Germanic general, Ricimer, died a natural death, whereupon the East Roman emperor, Leo I, became formal ruler of the West Roman empire as well. In due course, however, Leo despatched Anthemius to assume this office; Anthemius was promptly assassinated and supplanted by a certain Olybrius, who was a supporter of Ricimer. The latter died in 472, followed shortly afterwards by Olybrius. Emperor Glycerius was appointed by Ricimer's successor but he in turn was imprisoned by Julius Nepos, whom Leo I proclaimed emperor. Nepos was expelled by a general named Orestes, whose son, Romulus Augustulus or Augustus, became the ultimate ruler of the West Roman empire. Orestes himself was defeated and slain in a battle with the Germanic commander, Odoacer, who promptly dismissed the young emperor Romulus Augustus with a substantial pension and returned the imperial signet ring to Leo in Constantinople. Odoacer then proclaimed himself king of Italy, awarding land to his countrymen in the army.

Thus, with Romulus Augustulus, the history of the West Roman empire came to an end. It was not recognized at the time. Successive generations continued to regard the Roman Empire as eternal and the new order as a mere interlude. Nor was it only in Constantinople that the situation was viewed in this light.

The crowning of Leo I by the patriarch of Constantinople clearly denoted for the first time, the Church's position of power in relation to temporal authority; in future all Byzantine emperors were to be crowned by the Church.

Emperor Leo was himself a religious man. He often sought political advice from the stylite Daniel, who for many years stood on the Gothic pillar on the point at Constantinople.

The Ostrogoths, established in Pannonia, were allies of the Romans. Theoderic, who was a civilized Roman even though he had spent his youth as a hostage in Constantinople, was elected king of the Ostrogoths and led a march on the Balkan peninsula, securing from Leo I a promise of land for his people and a military position for himself.

The empire of the Visigoths, with its capital at Tolosa (Toulouse) extended from the Loire to the southern point of Spain; in other words a considerable proportion of southern and western Europe. In King Euric's time the Visigoths were at the peak of their power. Their principal domestic achievement was the codification of the Visigoth laws. This, the *Codex Euricianus,* is the earliest register of German law in existence, written in Latin. There does not appear to have been any literature in the Gothic language.

Leo I was succeeded by his young grandson Leo II, whose father and guardian, Zeno, thus took command in Constantinople. The child emperor died shortly afterwards, however, and Zeno was ejected, only to return some years later after it had emerged that the more highly born Basiliscus was a failure as an emperor.

In the Indian Gupta kingdom, now about to decline, Buddhist art flourished, as in the frescoes of the rock temples at Ajanta, Hyderabad. Shown here is a bodhisattva with a lotus flower, before a background of female figures, monkeys and dwarfs.

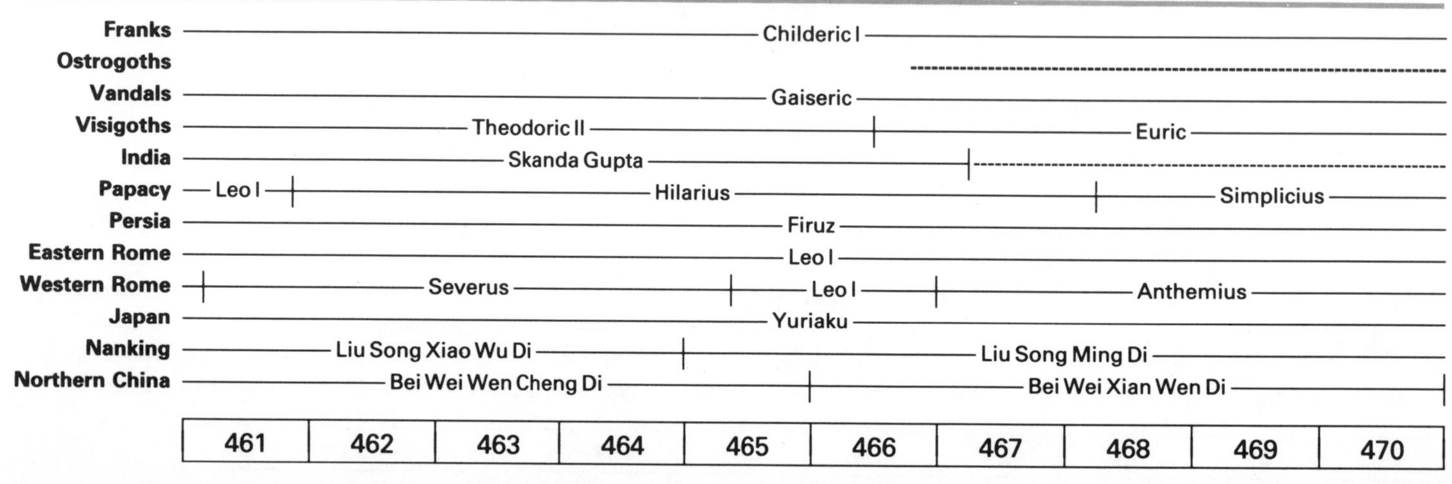
Franks
Childeric I
Ostrogoths
Vandals
Gaiseric
Visigoths
Theodoric II
Euric
India
Skanda Gupta
Papacy
Leo I
Hilarius
Simplicius
Persia
Firuz
Eastern Rome
Leo I
Western Rome
Severus
Leo I
Anthemius
Japan
Yuriaku
Nanking
Liu Song Xiao Wu Di
Liu Song Ming Di
Northern China
Bei Wei Wen Cheng Di
Bei Wei Xian Wen Di
461
462
463
464
465
466
467
468
469
470

EAST ROMAN EMPIRE

Prior to the great age of the Incas which occurred sometime after AD 1000, the regions around Lake Titicaca, in what later became Peru, were dominated by the Aymara people. With larger than normal chests and lungs, the Aymaras adapted to life in the rarified atmosphere of the high plateaus. Today they still inhabit this area and travel the waterways in reed boats, the design of which may well be unaltered. There are similarities between these craft and much earlier vessels that plied the Nile and the Euphrates, though admittedly there is only limited scope for building boats of reeds. Otherwise little or nothing is known about the earliest history of the Aymara people.

In 468, after repeated appeals for aid from West Rome, a large East Roman expedition was organized against the Vandals in Africa. The intention was to destroy the piratical Arian realm of Gaiseric. Some 1100 Byzantine ships carrying 100,000 men set sail for Carthage, while at the same time a West Roman force drove the Vandals out of Sardinia. The entire operation came to a sad end, however, when the resourceful Gaiseric won a great sea battle and put the enemy's superior armada to flight. Emperor Leo had placed his son-in-law Basiliscus in command of the Byzantine fleet, and he was clearly not the man for the job.

In northern Wei, Emperor Xiao Wen Di abolished his native tongue, Tungusic, as the official language of the administration in his large empire. He is also said to have condemned his own son to death because the latter preferred to wear Tungus dress and demonstrate his nationalist sentiments in other ways. It was mainly due to the measures of Xiao Wen Di that the Tungus race assimilated with the Chinese and, as a people, disappeared without trace.

In Korea the kingdom of Koguryo grew both in power and size. A king by the name of Changsu transferred the capital southward from the shore of the Yalu river to Pyongyang. The spiritual climate in northern Wei had changed again and the leaders were once more zealous Buddhists. They did not, however, persecute other religions.

Since the beginning of the century a central Asian people known as Hephtalites, or White Huns, had been threatening the realm of the Sassanid Persians. This had kept the Persians occupied, while their traditional East Roman enemies were hard pressed by other Huns. Around 460 the Hephtalites launched an attack on the Gupta kingdom in India and throughout his entire reign King Skanda Gupta was engaged in coping with this invasion. Although he succeeded, the effort sapped the strength of his country.

We know almost nothing about the final phase of Gupta's history. One of the last monarchs was called Budha Gupta and he appears to have reigned from 477 until at least 495. Members of the main line of the dynasty continued to reign as minor princes in Magadha for several hundred years, but they had no appreciable history.

In south China the Liu Song dynasty was supplanted by Nan Qi, South Qi.

All current and future Indian art emanates from Gupta art, but Buddhism, which characterizes the paintings at Ajanta, was already on the decline in the country of its origin. This statue of Vishnu is in the National Museum, Delhi.

Childeric I	**Franks**
Theodoric	**Ostrogoths**
Gaiseric — Huneric	**Vandals**
Euric	**Visigoths**
	India
Simplicius	**Papacy**
Firuz	**Persia**
Leo I — Leo II — Zeno — Basiliscus — Zeno	**Eastern Rome**
Anthemius — Olybr. — Glycerius — Nepos — Romul. Aug.	**Western Rome**
Yuriaku — Seinei	**Japan**
Liu Song Ming Di — Liu Song Cang Wu Wang — Liu Song Shun Di — Nan Qi Gao Di	**Nanking**
Bei Wei Xiao Wen Di	**Northern China**

471	472	473	474	475	476	477	478	479	480

AD 481-490

PERSIA
EAST ROMAN EMPIRE
ARIADNE
MANCHURIA

Ever since the time of Yazdegerd II, Armenia had been the scene of ruthless Christian persecution, by reason of the teachings of Zoroaster which constituted the state religion of Persia. However, an edict of tolerance was issued by Balash in the 480s.

With the approval of the East Roman emperor, the Ostrogoth chieftain, Theodoric, led his men into Italy and put an end to Odoacer's rule there. Having besieged Odoacer for three years in Ravenna, Theodoric finally enticed him out and then slew him with his own hand. Theodoric now proclaimed himself king and claimed the whole of Italy, plus Illyria and the coast of Gaul, as his territory. He was unquestionably a great statesman who sought to restore the administrative and cultural standards of the Roman era and who refused to allow his Goths to lord it over the local Latin-speaking inhabitants.

When Emperor Zeno died in Constantinople there was no successor, but his widow Ariadne was equal to the occasion: entering the royal box at the circus, she announced to the people that she would appoint as emperor a person who possessed all the virtues and no vices. The people jubilantly invited her to give the empire a ruler. Although it was customary for the senate and the army to make such a decision, Ariadne offended nobody when in due course she married a pious courtier named Anastasius. A sound organizer and excellent economist, Emperor Anastasius I put the affairs of state into good order, even though war and unrest prevailed throughout his reign. But his policy incurred heavy tax burdens, and popular discontent was expressed in almost daily demonstrations, riots and violence. Anastasius had to contend with both temporal and spiritual opponents. The circus in Constantinople was not only a racecourse and entertainment arena, but also a popular assembly point and debating site of the two major political parties: the Greens and the Blues. Popular spectacles, including tortures and executions, inflamed the passions of the crowd, and it was not surprising that so many riots and rebellions were sparked off here. Emperor Anastasius was once stoned as he entered the royal box. On another occasion, during a religious uproar, he showed true demagogic flair as, with white hair flying, he publicly offered to stand down if that was the people's wish, and whereupon the crowd turned indignantly on the troublemakers and resoundingly applauded their emperor.

Mediolanum
Arelate
Ravenna
Rome
Barcino
Neapolis
Lilybaeum
Hippo
Carthage

VANDAL TERRITORY

Coins above and below respectively portray the emperor Zeno and King Theodoric.

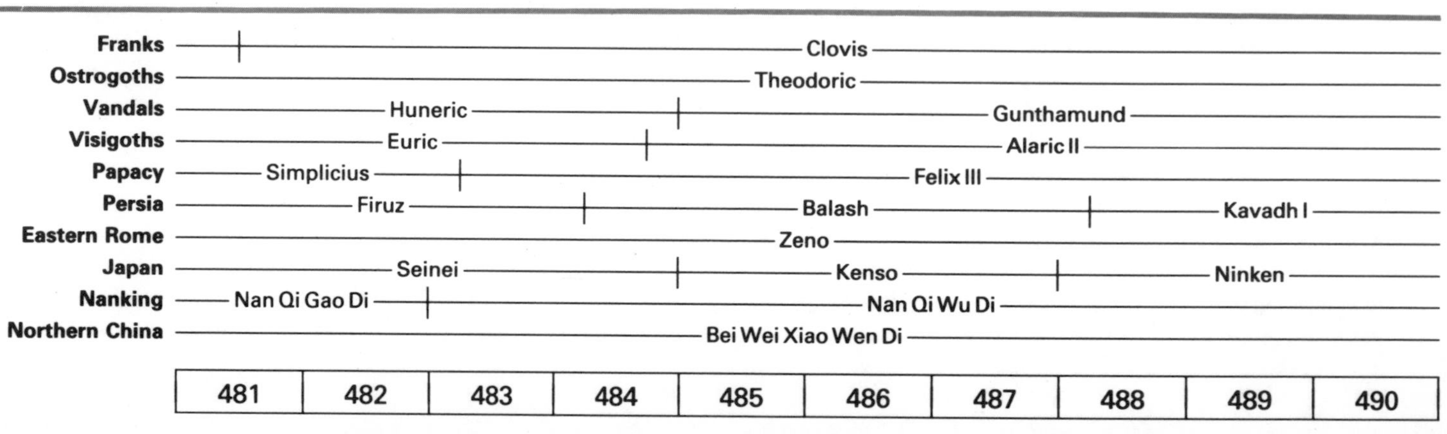
Franks — Clovis
Ostrogoths — Theodoric
Vandals — Huneric — Gunthamund
Visigoths — Euric — Alaric II
Papacy — Simplicius — Felix III
Persia — Firuz — Balash — Kavadh I
Eastern Rome — Zeno
Japan — Seinei — Kenso — Ninken
Nanking — Nan Qi Gao Di — Nan Qi Wu Di
Northern China — Bei Wei Xiao Wen Di
481 482 483 484 485 486 487 488 489 490

AD 491-500

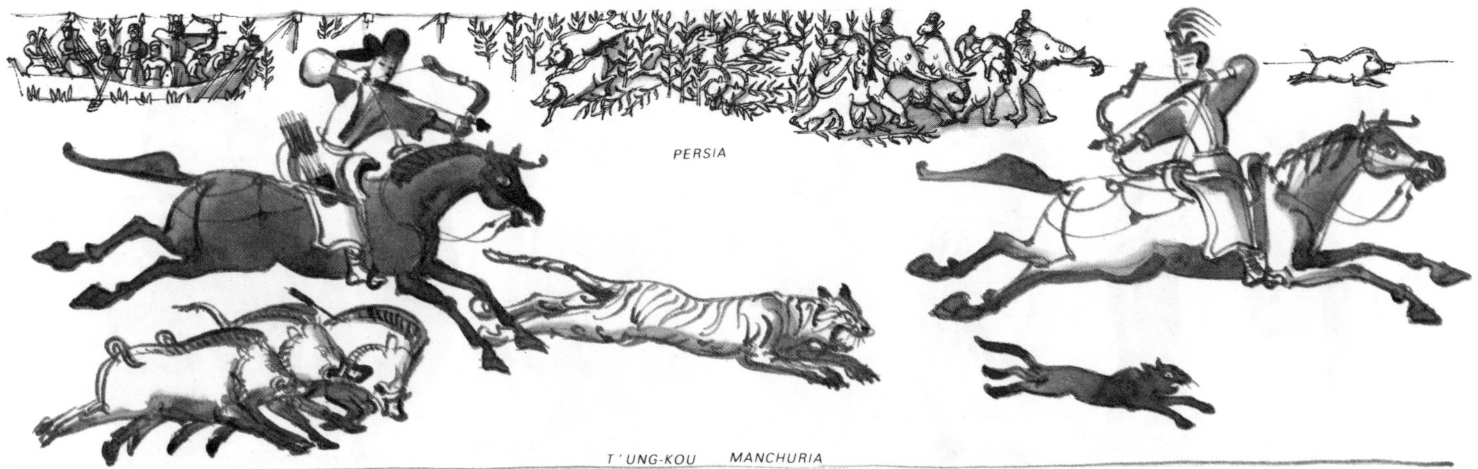
PERSIA
T'UNG-KOU
MANCHURIA

The Persian king Kavadh, or Kobad, was an interesting figure. In his youth he was influenced by an equally young philosopher and champion of liberty named Mazdak, and when Kavadh attempted to put Mazdak's 'communist' ideas into practice, the nobles and priests chased him out of the country and supplanted him by his brother Jamasb. Aided by the Huns, Kavadh returned and attempted to remedy social problems by less radical means. This policy failed, and when he also encountered opposition from Mazdak's growing host of followers, he became increasingly conservative; finally, in alliance with the nobles, he adopted brutally oppressive measures to suppress 'communism'.

In the kingdom of Southern Arabia, ruled by the Lakhmidian dynasty, Nestorian Christianity was encouraged; this antagonized not only the orthodox East Roman government but also the Monophysite prelates of Syria and Egypt.

In 486 Clovis, Choldovech or Klodwig, king of the Franks, defeated Syagrius, last of the Roman governors of Rome, and seized the province. This marked the final demise of the West Roman empire.

In 496, at Reims, Bishop Remigius baptized King Clovis and 3000 other Franks, receiving them into the true faith which decreed that the Son was of the same essence as the Father, born and not created.Thus, unlike the other Germanic tribes, the Franks did not become Arians, a factor of major historical significance. The chronicler Gregory of Tours described the campaigns of Clovis against the Burgundian and Visigoth heretics: a long series of misdeeds by which, politically at least, he won great acclaim.

494 was a year of unrest for the Nan Qi dynasty in southern China: three emperors are recorded for this year, Ming Di, Yu Ling Wang and Hai Ling Wang.

The doctrine established at the Council of Chalcedon in 451 on the dual nature of Christ had divided Christianity throughout the East Roman empire. The Monophysites in Syria and Egypt, who supported the doctrine of the single, divine, nature of Christ, had even gone so far as to reject the Greek language, conducting services instead in their own tongues. Emperor Zeno saw this schism as so profound and serious as to threaten the political solidarity of the realm. In consultation with the patriarch, Acacius, he issued the Henotikon or Union edict forbidding all further conflicts on the nature of Christ. On points of issue he referred to various conciliar resolutions, though not that of the Council of Chalcedon. The differences in opinion were deliberately smoothed over.

The Henotikon did not, as hoped, produce concord. First to express his disapproval was Pope Felix III in Rome, who not only condemned the substance of the edict but also criticized the emperor for presuming to interfere in Church affairs. At the same time he renounced the existing ecclesiastical fellowship with the patriarch, Acacius. The Nestorians now began to stir; they crossed the Persian frontier and disassociated themselves officially from Catholic Christianity at a council in Ctesiphon in 499. The Monophysites were not entirely satisfied, and the Henotikon gave rise to violent resentment among the orthodox believers in Constantinople. Nevertheless, the edict remained in force throughout Zeno's reign.

There was unrest at home and abroad during the reign of Anastasius I. The emperor was probably a Monophysite, and his economic policy was directed against the landowners who were mostly of the orthodox faith. On this ivory relief he is shown triumphant over the Sarmatae.

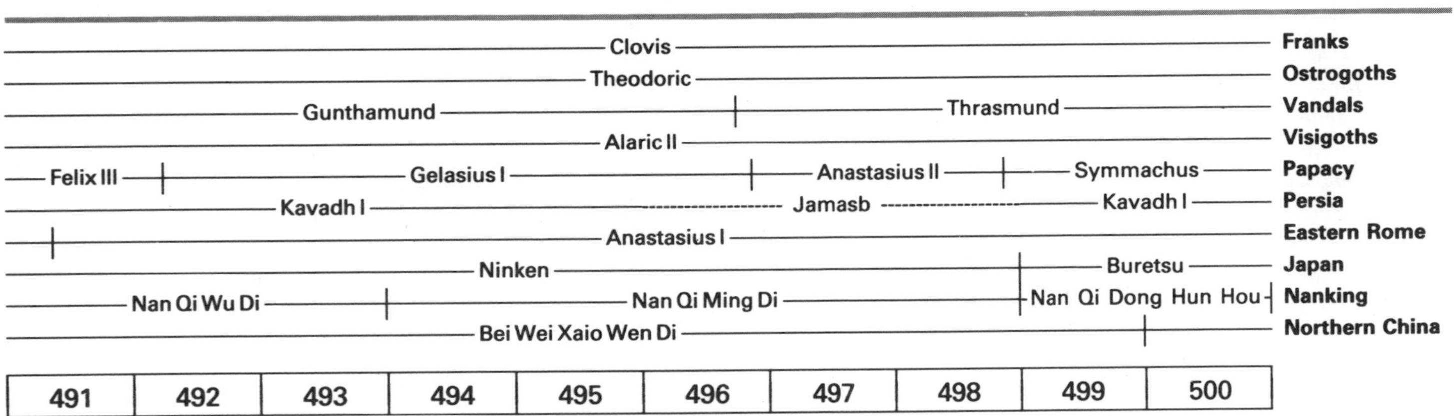
Clovis
Franks
Theodoric
Ostrogoths
Gunthamund
Thrasmund
Vandals
Alaric II
Visigoths
Felix III
Gelasius I
Anastasius II
Symmachus
Papacy
Kavadh I
Jamasb
Kavadh I
Persia
Anastasius I
Eastern Rome
Ninken
Buretsu
Japan
Nan Qi Wu Di
Nan Qi Ming Di
Nan Qi Dong Hun Hou
Nanking
Bei Wei Xaio Wen Di
Northern China
491
492
493
494
495
496
497
498
499
500

AD 501-510

INDIA
CHINA
LUNG-MEN, CHINA

The Liang dynasty, which succeeded the Nan Qi dynasty in southern China, fervently supported the Buddhist creed. The founder of the dynasty, Wu Di, was a deeply religious man who personally preached Buddhism before vast audiences. There were 700 monasteries in Nanking in his day, and occasionally he would himself temporarily become a monk. At his command, all the holy writings of Buddhism, collectively known as the Tripitaka, were published for the first time in Chinese, a task completed in 517. He also received the high-born Indian patriarch Bodhidharma, which was a gesture of major significance since the focal point of Buddhism was hereby formally shifted to China. The emperor was somewhat disappointed, however, to be informed by Bodhidharma that salvation from the torments of life could be attained only by meditation and contemplation and not through the ways of the Church.

SCA PELAGIA

Around the year 500, the White Huns acquired a competent leader called Toramana. The Gupta kingdom, was disrupted by domestic discord, and Toramana quickly overran the Punjab, Kashmir and various other Indian regions.

In 507 Clovis led his Frankish army across the Loire and into the kingdom of the Visigoths. In a very bloody encounter the Visigoths were defeated, their king slain and their entire Gallic territory occupied by the Franks. King Theodoric of the Ostrogoths intervened, however, on behalf of the Visigoths and reclaimed the territory south of the Garonne for the Visigoths, or perhaps more properly for his ward and grandson, Amalaric. Clovis, in 508, made Paris the capital of his expanded realm.

Theodoric the Great could neither read nor write. Nevertheless, the culture of late antiquity found a sanctuary in his Ostrogoth kingdom. The mosaics of Ravenna, especially in the church of San Apollinare Nuovo, Theodoric's chapel royal, bear witness for all time to a period of particular artistic achievement. Theodoric's Italian kingdom was a somewhat curious organization. The Ostrogoths had claimed for themselves one-third of all Italian farmland, including resident farmers, slaves and livestock. Segregation was very strict, religious distinction was clearly marked - the masters, after all, were Arians - and mixed marriages were not permitted. The Goths, being comparatively few, only controlled military matters, leaving civil administration and trade to the Romans. The king's associates in domestic policy matters used Latin as their native language and were Roman senators.

The wise virgins. Mosaic in Ravenna.

Franks	Clovis
Ostrogoths	Theodoric
Vandals	Thrasamund
Visigoths	Alaric II ┼ Amalaric
Papacy	Symmachus
Persia	Kavadh I
Eastern Rome	Anastasius I
Japan	Buretsu ┼ Keitai
Nanking	Qi He Di ┼ Liang Wu Di
Northern China	Bei Wei Xuan Wu Di

501	502	503	504	505	506	507	508	509	510

CHINA
EAST ROMAN EMPIRE
LUNG-MEN, CHINA

A Swedish rune-stone at Rök in Östergötland possibly alludes to the greatness of Theodoric in the following lines:

'Then Tjodrik the bold
chief of the sea warriors
was master of the Red Sea shores
Now, armed, he sits astride
his Gothic horse
with his shield over his shoulder,
principal among the Moravians'.

This stone is believed to date from the 9th century. On the other hand, mounds in Old Uppsala have been found to be early 6th century and thus contemporary with Theodoric.

Following the death of Clovis, the Frankish empire was divided up among his four sons: Thierry or Theuderic, Chlodomer, Childebert and Chlotar. These all held the title 'King of the Franks', squabbled constantly among themselves, but pursued the imperialist policies of their father.

Emperor Anastasius I was a Monophysite and in his latter days in Constantinople the Sanctus was modified to indirectly deny the human nature of Christ: 'Holy, holy, holy is the Lord Zebaoth - crucified for us'. Justin I, a practical military man who was feeble in both Greek and theology, had this addition to the Sanctus removed immediately after assuming office, exhorting his subjects to embrace the Chalcedonic doctrine of the dual natures of the Son. This resolved the grave dispute which had now existed for some decades between the patriarch in Constantinople and the pope in Rome. The new-found accord of Constantinople and Rome caused a rupture between Constantinople and the Monophysite world, i.e. the Christian majorities in Egypt, Syria and other eastern provinces.

In 515 the chieftain of the White Huns, Toramana, was succeeded by his son Mihirakula and there are accounts of the latter's cruelty. He won great military success against the Gupta kingdom, but not against Persia which reasserted itself in the reign of Kavadh and soon began to strike back. The north-western province was retaken in 513, after which the Persians gradually conquered the territory of modern Afghanistan.

The Uppsala mounds date from about the period when the kingdoms of the Goths and the Sveas were united. Old Uppsala church was built much later, in the 12th century. It was erected on the site of an ancient Aesir temple said to be the burial place of the kings Aun, Engil and Adil. All the Sveas' assemblies were once held here and elected kings were also ceremonially initiated here before possessing their domains.

Theuderic 1 + Chlodomer + Childebert + Clotar I	**Franks**
Theodoric	**Ostrogoths**
Thrasamund	**Vandals**
Amalaric	**Visigoths**
Symmachus — Hormisdas	**Papacy**
Kavadh I	**Persia**
Anastasius I — Justin I	**Eastern Rome**
Keitai	**Japan**
Liang Wu Di	**Nanking**
Bei Wei Xuan Wu Di — Bei Wei Xiao Ming Di	**Northern China**

511	512	513	514	515	516	517	518	519	520

AD 521-530

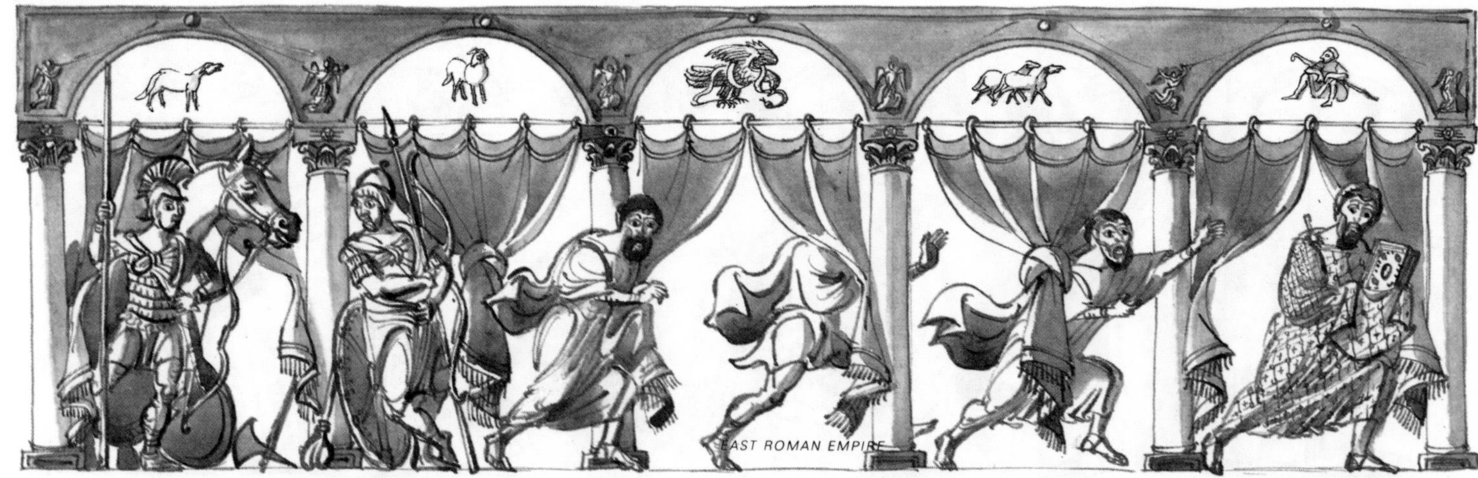
EAST ROMAN EMPIRE

The end of the Bei Wei dynasty in northern China included too many reigns to be listed here. Thus in 528 there was not only Xiao Zhuang Di but also Ling Dao Wang and in 531 both Jie Min Di and An Ding Wang were ruling. This dynasty ended in 532 and was succeeded by Zi Wei, meaning West Wei. Parallel with this, between 534-543 there was the Dong Wei, or East Wei dynasty, represented by one emperor only.

The philosopher Boethius, who had held high offices in the Ostrogoths' Italian kingdom, was arrested and sentenced to death for high treason by Theodoric. While awaiting execution in prison he wrote a treatise entitled *De consolatione philosophiae.* This contains Platonic notions to the effect that the world is a pretence and that evil and suffering do not really exist: there is no reference in this work to Christian principles.

King Theodoric sent Pope John I to Emperor Justin I in Constantinople to protest against a decree whereby the orthodox emperor prohibited Arian services in his realm. The pope was ceremoniously received by the emperor but achieved nothing of consequence; it is unlikely, in fact, that he even tried. When Pope John returned to Italy the dissatisfied Theodoric threw him into gaol where shortly afterwards he died. He was subsequently canonized.

The Vandal king, Thrasamund, was married to Amalafrida, a sister of Theodoric and had a political alliance with the king of the Ostrogoths. Thrasamund's successor, Hilderic, was, however, pro-Byzantine and he had the Goths at his court executed while the widowed Amalafrida died in prison.

Theodoric was planning an expedition of revenge when he died in Ravenna. His daughter Amalasuntha now assumed power, as guardian of her son; but the latter died in 534 and since female succession was ruled out among the Goths, Amalasuntha was compelled to accept her cousin Theodahad as co-regent.

The Frankish king Chlodomer was killed in 524 and his brothers divided his domains among themselves, and then proceeded to overrun and share out Burgundy. This was completed by 534. One brother, Theuderic, died and was succeeded by his son Theudebert, who brought the Bavarians under his dominion.

In the spring of 529 the great legal work, *Codex Justinianeus*, was presented by ten prominent jurists in Constantinople. A new commission of sixteen members was immediately appointed to sort out this enormous conglomeration of legal decrees and case reports left behind by the classical Roman law-makers. Remarkably enough they completed this complicated task in only a few years. This laid the foundations for what is known as the *Corpus Juris Civilis* which summarized Roman law and became a fundamental feature in the legislation of most European nations.

The Scythian monk, Dionysius Exiguus, working in Rome on the editing of the first ecclesiastical law book in Latin, proposed in 525 that modern time should be reckoned from the date of the birth of Christ, which he set at 753 *ab urbe condita*. For the moment, this suggestion was ignored.

In 519 the Academy at Athens, last stronghold of non-Christian learning, was closed by Emperor Justinian.

The great mausoleum of Theodoric in Ravenna is roofed by a single piece of stone 11 metres in diameter and 3 metres thick. It is estimated to weigh some 300 tons. It is probable that the twelve decorative chambers around the outside were originally built to carry the supports when the roof-piece was lifted into place.

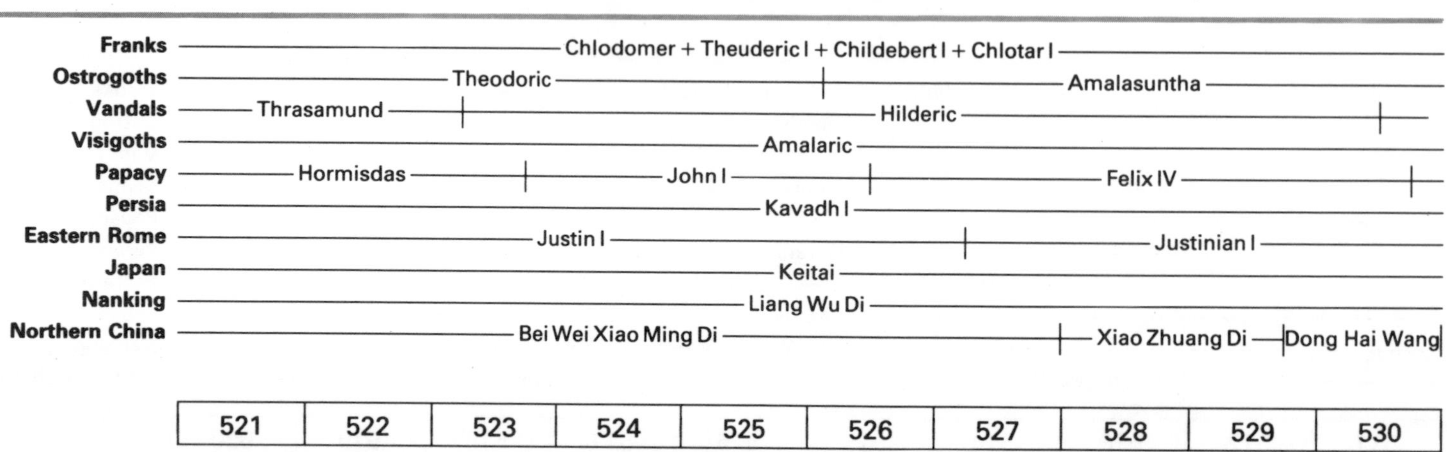
Franks
Chlodomer + Theuderic I + Childebert I + Chlotar I
Ostrogoths
Theodoric
Amalasuntha
Vandals
Thrasamund
Hilderic
Visigoths
Amalaric
Papacy
Hormisdas
John I
Felix IV
Persia
Kavadh I
Eastern Rome
Justin I
Justinian I
Japan
Keitai
Nanking
Liang Wu Di
Northern China
Bei Wei Xiao Ming Di
Xiao Zhuang Di
Dong Hai Wang
521
522
523
524
525
526
527
528
529
530

AD 531-540

EAST ROMAN EMPIRE

In the summer of 533, Emperor Justinian, who regarded it as his mission to restore the former glory of the Roman empire, despatched a military expedition under the command of General Belisarius to subdue the Vandals' African kingdom. Gelimer, the Vandal king, was taken prisoner, the territory became a Roman province once more and the Vandals were deprived both of their land and their Arian churches. Several years later, Belisarius was sent with a Byzantine army into Italy, where the Ostrogoth queen, Amalasuntha, had recently been imprisoned and murdered by her cousin Theodahad. Soon afterwards, however, Theodahad was deposed by his own people and replaced by a valiant officer named Witigis who held off the Byzantine army for four years. In 540 he was captured in Ravenna, so apparently bringing Germanic domination of Italy to an end.

The hermit Benedict of Nursia, a man of great practical and organizational ability, founded the Monte Cassino monastery in southern Italy and thereby created the basis for an organized monastic system in the West.

The so-called Nika insurrection in Constantinople was ruthlessly suppressed when two imperial regiments entered the circus and cut down the assembled revolutionary parties. Much of the city had been burned down during the unrest and Justinian began at once to build the Hagia Sophia church on a burned-out site.

In Spain the Visigoths made Toledo their capital.

A woman of considerable interest was the Byzantine empress Theodora, daughter of a bear-tamer at the circus in Constantinople, and evidently herself an entertainer and courtesan before she came to the attention of Justinian. A singularly malicious biography of this royal couple by a certain Procopius cannot conceal the fact that both were remarkable people.

Theodora and her court ladies, mosaic in San Vitale, Ravenna. The empress had great influence. She issued laws, for example, prohibiting the forcible recruitment of young girls into the theatres.

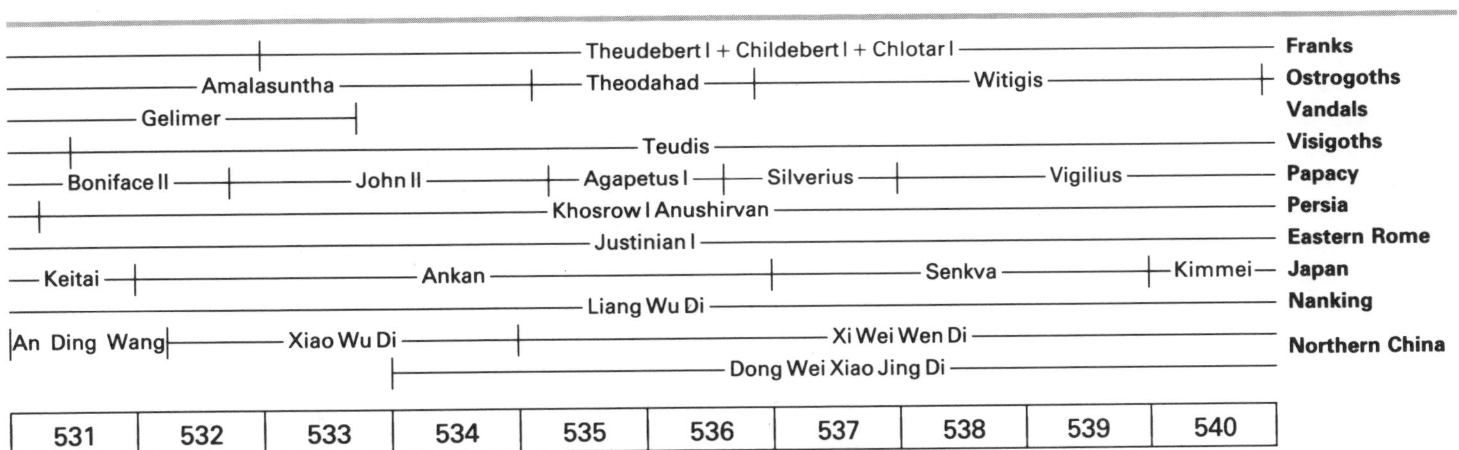
Theudebert I + Childebert I + Chlotar I
Franks
Amalasuntha
Theodahad
Witigis
Ostrogoths
Gelimer
Vandals
Teudis
Visigoths
Boniface II
John II
Agapetus I
Silverius
Vigilius
Papacy
Khosrow I Anushirvan
Persia
Justinian I
Eastern Rome
Keitai
Ankan
Senkva
Kimmei
Japan
Liang Wu Di
Nanking
An Ding Wang
Xiao Wu Di
Xi Wei Wen Di
Dong Wei Xiao Jing Di
Northern China
531
532
533
534
535
536
537
538
539
540

AD 541-550

CHINA

Chlotar, or Lothar, the youngest son of Clovis, survived his brothers and nephews, and thus the Frankish empire once again had a sole ruler. Chlotar, however, had four sons, which was to have unfortunate consequences in the next decade.

The last emperors in the Liang dynasty follow so swiftly on one another's heels that there is no room for their names in the records. In 555, for example, Yu Shang ruled immediately before Jing Di, who was succeeded by the founder of the Chen dynasty.

Throughout the 540s and 550s Persia and the East Roman empire were almost continuously at war. The Persian armies initially overran Syria and the Byzantine vassal state of Lazica south-east of the Black Sea. But the Byzantine counter-offensives were successful, so that, by and large, the fighting changed little in terms of frontiers and power status. Loss of life, nevertheless, was very heavy, especially since plague was rife among the troops.

The Ostrogoths had not been crushed in Italy. Their new leader, Totila, struck back at the Byzantine forces in several battles and reclaimed most of the country.

The last Hephtalite kingdom in West Turkestan was destroyed in 560 by the Persian king Khosrow in alliance with a Turkish khan. This eliminated all support from the north for the White Huns in India. Their enemies in the Gupta kingdom were exhausted, however, and India split up into innumerable small states under various dynasties. For the moment the most powerful of these was the Rastrakuta dynasty in the country's central region. Among the principal rulers here were Pulakesin I (550-566) and Pulakesin II (608-642).

MAXIMIAN

Justinian I, central section of the mosaic in San Vitale, Ravenna. The emperor is handing to the Church a liturgical dish and a patten. This illustration is a companion to the one on the previous page where the empress passes on the chalice. Apart from the emperor and Bishop Maximian, far right, the figures seen here are anonymous. The historian Procopius wrote much about Justinian. He hated the emperor and was convinced he had demonic powers. Despite his bias, Procopius creates the image of an ingenious and diligent politician with informal, simple habits.

Franks	Theudebert I + Childebert I + Chlotar I — Childebert I + Chlotar I + Theudebald
Ostrogoths	--- Totila
Visigoths	Teudis — ------- — Agila
Papacy	Vigilius
Persia	Khosrow I Anushirvan
Eastern Rome	Justinian I
Japan	Kimmei
Nanking	Liang Wu Di — Jian Wen Di
Northern China	Xi Wei Wen Di
	Dong Wei Xiao Jing Di

541	542	543	544	545	546	547	548	549	550

EAST ROMAN EMPIRE
CHINA
PERSIA
EAST ROMAN EMPIRE

A new, very large Byzantine army attacked the Ostrogoths in Italy, inflicting a disastrous defeat on them in the decisive battle. King Totila was killed in this encounter and his successor Teja died in a final battle the following year. The once-powerful Ostrogoths now disappeared from history. Their numbers in Italy could never have been large, but specific information is lacking.

In northern China the Bei Qi, North Qi, dynasty had a rival in the Bei Zhou, North Zhou, dynasty. The latter list of rulers begins with Emperor Zhoa Ming Di, who reigned only for a few months in 557.

Jordanes was an East Roman scribe who recorded in Latin the history of the Goths. Though not notable as a writer, he gave later historians reason to ponder by claiming that the Goths, divided into eastern and western tribes, had come originally from Scandinavia.

The Slavs were moving towards the west and the south.

In 552 Justinian received two monks who had smuggled silk worms out of China.

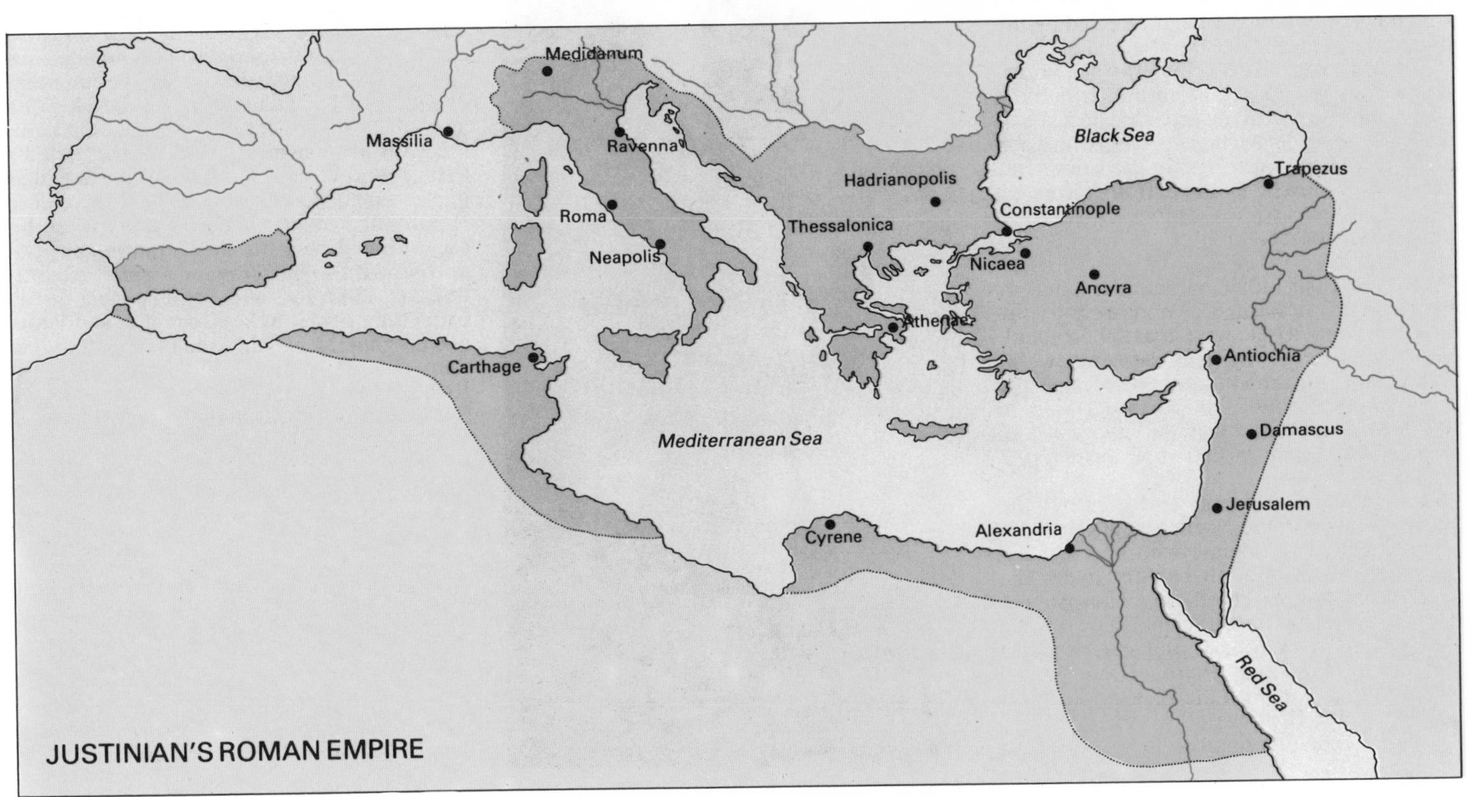
Medidanum
Massilia
Ravenna
Black Sea
Trapezus
Hadrianopolis
Roma
Constantinople
Thessalonica
Neapolis
Nicaea
Ancyra
Athenae
Carthage
Antiochia
Damascus
Mediterranean Sea
Jerusalem
Cyrene
Alexandria
Red Sea
JUSTINIAN'S ROMAN EMPIRE

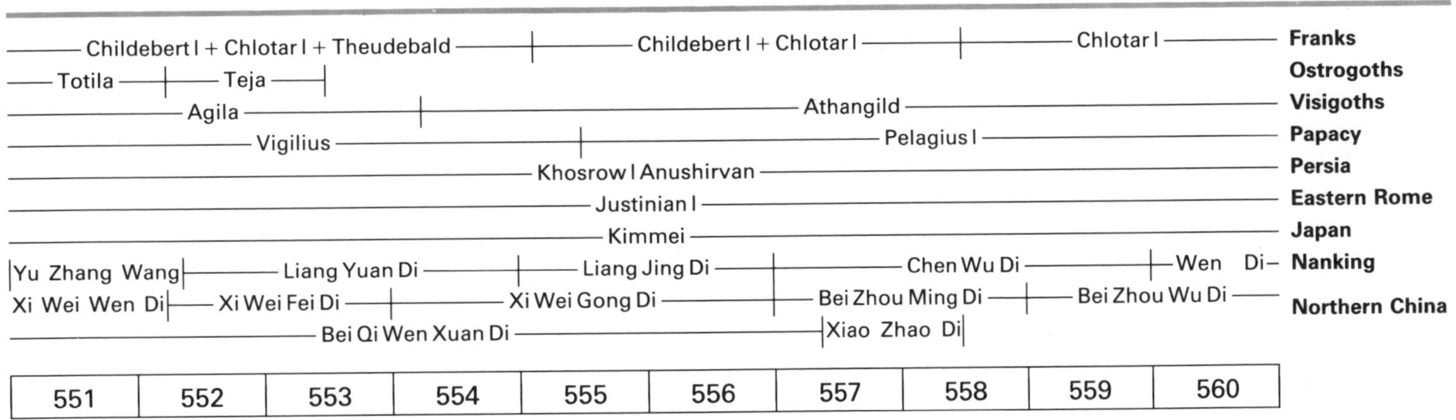
Childebert I + Chlotar I + Theudebald
Childebert I + Chlotar I
Chlotar I
Franks
Totila
Teja
Ostrogoths
Agila
Athangild
Visigoths
Vigilius
Pelagius I
Papacy
Khosrow I Anushirvan
Persia
Justinian I
Eastern Rome
Kimmei
Japan
Yu Zhang Wang
Liang Yuan Di
Liang Jing Di
Chen Wu Di
Wen Di
Nanking
Xi Wei Wen Di
Xi Wei Fei Di
Xi Wei Gong Di
Bei Zhou Ming Di
Bei Zhou Wu Di
Northern China
Bei Qi Wen Xuan Di
Xiao Zhao Di
551
552
553
554
555
556
557
558
559
560

AD 561-570

CHINA
EAST ROMAN EMPIRE
MEXICO
MOSHI, PERU
EAST ROMAN EMPIRE

Hardly had Emperor Justinian been buried before his newly restored Roman empire began to disintegrate again. As early as 565 Italy was invaded by yet another Germanic people, the Langobardi (Lombards); and a stretch of coast in south-east Spain, which had recently been retaken in the emperor's name, was quickly cleared of Byzantines by the Visigoth king, Leovigild.

An advanced Latin culture flourished in Ireland, which had not been affected by the Germanic migrations. Ireland, uniquely in Western Europe, also retained some knowledge of ancient Greek literature. Irish book craftsmanship was of unsurpassed beauty and scholarly monks were preparing a mission among the heathen tribes on the Continent. The Irish Church, isolated from Rome by heathens and Arians, pursued its own purposeful course.

In 563 an Irish monk named Columba, or Columcille, established a monastery on the island of Iona off the west coast of Scotland. This monastery, originally housing twelve monks and the abbot, quickly became the most famous establishment of its kind in Western Europe and was the nucleus of an immensely significant Christian mission.

Little is known of people and events in the countries around the North Sea at this time. The Angles and Saxons, who had invaded England in the mid-5th century under the leadership of two chieftains, Hengist and Horsa, were now well established in the eastern part of the country and had founded a number of kingdoms there. These people were often at war with the Picts in the north and the Celtic Britons in the west, and were gradually expelling them.

In 562 the Korean kingdom of Silla ridded itself of Japanese influence on the peninsula. The Japanese were now ejected from a coastal area which they had held for 200 years.

The Lombards, a singularly unprepossessing tribe, had dwelt for some time in Pannonia on the central Danube and when they left this region they handed it over to the Avars, an Asiatic people. Under their king, Alboin, the Lombards moved into Italy from the north-east seizing land and property at will. The king of the Lombards, Alboin, plays a major role in the story of Rosamunda, which in time was to become of considerable literary importance. One of the earliest and most successful dramas in the Swedish language is based upon this. Alboin becomes enamoured of the beautiful Rosamunda, daughter of King Cunimund of the Gepidae and when she rejects his advances Alboin leads his army against the Gepidae, defeats them roundly, slays Cunimund, has a gilded goblet made of his skull and forces Rosamunda to marry him. Later, when he succeeds in driving out the Byzantinians from northern Italy, he arranges a great celebration at Verona and orders the grisly Cunimund goblet to be brought in so that he and his generals can drink to their victory. He then has it refilled and proffers it to Rosamunda so that she, as he puts it, may share their pleasure along with her father. Rosamunda drinks as commanded, but then proceeds to plan her revenge. Disguised, she lures a senior officer to a secret assignation and then at the crucial moment reveals her identity to her hapless suitor. He is now confronted with the choice either of murdering Alboin or risking execution when the king learns of what has happened. The officer, needless to say chooses the former alternative.

Bodhisattva, northern Chinese dynasty Bei Zhou. Museum of Fine Arts, Boston.

	Rulers 561–570
Lombards	Alboin
Franks	Sigebert I + Chilperic I + Guntram
Visigoths	Athanagild — Liuva I — Leovigild
Papacy	John III
Persia	Khosrow I Anushirvan
Eastern Rome	Justinian I — Justin II
Japan	Kimmei
Nanking	Chen Wen Di — Chen Lin Hai Wang — Chen Xuan Di
Northern China	Bei Zhou Wu Di
	Bei Qi Wu Cheng Di — Bei Qi Wen Gong

561	562	563	564	565	566	567	568	569	570

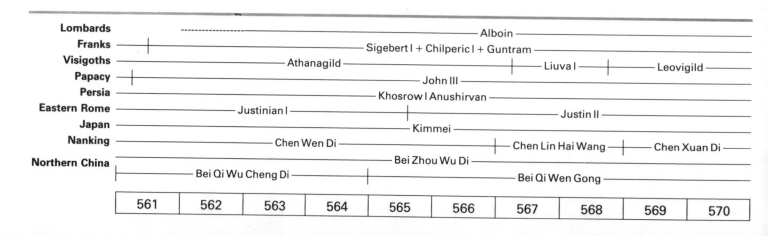

AD 571-580

INDIA
CHINA
CEYLON
CHINA
EAST ROMAN EMPIRE
PERSIA

The account of the Frankish kings, as told by the chronicler Gregory of Tours, is terrifying. After the death of Chlotar the kingdom was divided among three of his sons - the fourth died young – so that Sigebert ruled from Reims over Austrasia, Chilperic had his seat in Soissons and reigned over Neustria, while Gontran, or Guntram, ruled Southern Gaul and Burgundy from Orléans. King Sigebert was married to the beautiful Visigoth princess Brunhilda, and her elder sister Galswintha was queen to Chilperic. The latter, however, had a mistress named Fredegund and to please her had his wife strangled. This resulted in an inter-family war. Sigebert and Brunhilda managed to seize a large part of Chilperic's kingdom, though in his moment of triumph Sigebert was stabbed to death with a poisoned dagger by one of Fredegund's hired underlings. Brunhilda was captured and held prisoner in Neustria with her daughters, but her son Childebert was adopted by his uncle, Guntram, in Burgundy. Eluding her guards, Brunhilda came to her son's rescue. A few years later it was the turn of Chilperic to fall to a hired assassin's dagger. King Guntram now acted as the protector of Fredegund, and ensured that her young son Chlotar II was recognized as king of Neustria.

The prefect, Longinus, who was ruling Italy in the emperor's name, had no field force at his disposal when in 568 the Lombards invaded. He thus retired to fortified Ravenna and left the other towns to manage as best they could. The Lombards quickly seized one town after another and in 572 made Pavia the capital of their kingdom. Prior to this, Alboin had already taken Tuscany and many Roman lives. Two of his companions, Faroald and Zotto, continued southward and founded the Lombard duchies of Spoleto and Benevento. The former soon extended over most of Umbria and the coast between Ancona and Pescara; the latter embraced all of southern Italy except the peninsulas of Apulia and Calabria, where the Byzantines held out. The Byzantines also managed to retain a strip of coastland which became the East Roman duchy of Naples.

The national organization of the Lombards was somewhat loose. After the death of King Cleph no new ruler was appointed; instead, thirty-five dukes ruled individually or collectively for some ten years. They considered their conquest of Italy complete.

Khosrow I is regarded as the greatest ruler of the Persian Sassanids. His surname, Anushirvan, is said to mean 'The Just'. Khosrow administered justice wisely, combated poverty and promoted education. His portrait is seen here in the centre of an inlaid dish of gold.

The Bei Qi dynasty fell to the Bei Zhou dynasty. The latter had long controlled one half of northern China and it now took command of the other half as well.

In 575 the Sassanids overran Ethiopian Aksum, a Christian state supported by the Byzantines.

Slav tribes moved quietly into the Balkan peninsula. This invasion had actually begun during the early years of Justinianus's reign, causing him to set up an imposing ring of fortifications along the Danube frontier, but during the major operations in the west there had not been enough troops available to keep these defences manned. Consequently the foreigners poured unimpeded across the peninsula, reaching the Bay of Corinth and the north coast of the Aegean Sea.

In company with the Slavs came the Bulgars, who were unrelated to them and spoke a Turkish or a Hun language. The Bulgars' kinsmen, the Kotriguri and the Utriguri, came from a region north of the Black Sea; the former plundered and pillaged Illyria. The Byzantines then formed an alliance with the Utriguri, launched a joint attack on the Kotriguri from the rear, and expelled them.

In 572 the Visigoths retook the large town of Córdoba which had been the nucleus of the Byzantine Spanish realm.

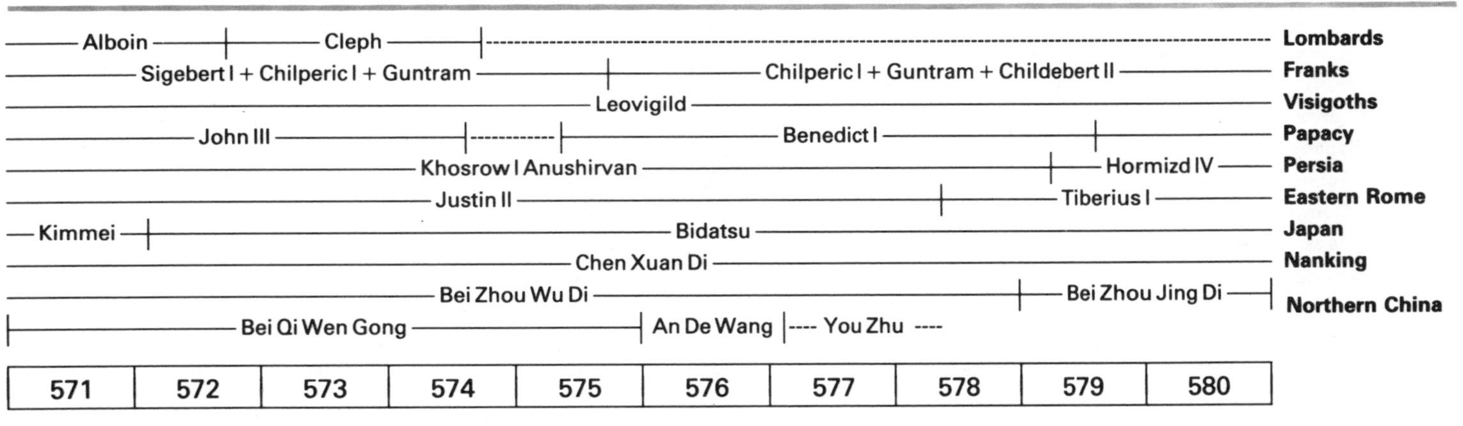
Alboin | Cleph | Lombards
Sigebert I + Chilperic I + Guntram | Chilperic I + Guntram + Childebert II | Franks
Leovigild | Visigoths
John III | Benedict I | Papacy
Khosrow I Anushirvan | Hormizd IV | Persia
Justin II | Tiberius I | Eastern Rome
Kimmei | Bidatsu | Japan
Chen Xuan Di | Nanking
Bei Zhou Wu Di | Bei Zhou Jing Di | Northern China
Bei Qi Wen Gong | An De Wang | You Zhu
571 572 573 574 575 576 577 578 579 580

AD 581-590

CHINA
CENTRAL ASIA
BYZANTIUM
MAYA, MEXICO
BYZANTIUM

In 580 a dowager queen in north China appointed her brother Yang Jian guardian and virtual regent. Yang Jian proceeded to execute all the Bei Zhou princes and proclaimed himself Emperor Wen Di, founder of the Sui dynasty. A few years later he led a military expedition against the south Chinese empire, destroyed the Chen dynasty and placed all China under his rule.

The Visigoth king, Leovigild, enjoyed major military successes against the Byzantines and Suebi in Spain (the latter had long maintained their own little kingdom in the north-west corner); but in his last years he became involved in a domestic tragedy. Goswinda, his second wife, was a devoted Arian, but his son Hermenegild was married to a Frankish princess, Ingunza, an orthodox Catholic with a strong influence on her husband. The tension between the two ladies was unbearable and Leovigild tried to intercede by sending the crown prince and his family south to take control of the Seville region. But Hermenegild, bowing to the spiritual coercion of the Catholics, renounced the Arian faith of the Visigoths and instigated a revolt against his heretical father. Although defeated, he was treated leniently, and soon initiated yet another religious war, this time starting from Valencia. When this, too, failed he was imprisoned and executed in gaol, either by or against the wishes of his father.

The name of Hermenegild still appears in modern Catholic calendars, though there is much debate as to whether or not he deserves his sainthood.

It is possible that religion was not the key factor in this conflict. King Leovigild had recently lifted the ban on mixed marriages between Arian, Gothic and Catholic subjects; and in 587 his younger son and successor, Reccared, took the decisive step towards peaceful coexistence and consolidation among the different peoples in Spain. In that year the Visigoths officially renounced their Arian faith and embraced the Nicaean doctrine. Dowager Queen Goswinda and other staunch Arians protested, but to no avail.

At a synod in Macon the Church claimed one-tenth (tithe) from all Christians. This appears to be the first time that such a demand had been expressly formulated.

CHILPERICVS·FRANCORVM·REX·
CHILPERIC·ROY·DE·FRANCE·
IX·
Tiré sur sa sepulture qui est a
St Germain des pres·

In the 580s the first Buddhist monastery was founded in Japan.

Pope Gregory I went down in history as Gregory the Great. He reformed the divine service, favouring the Roman *Schola Cantorum* and thereby lending his name to the Gregorian chant. His instructions to the priesthood, *Liber regulae pastoralis*, were also of lasting importance. Furthermore he was an accomplished diplomat who, in the 590s, brought about an armistice between the Lombards and the Byzantine authorities in Ravenna.

In 590 Gregory the Great saw an angel standing over Hadrian's tomb in Rome. The angel sheathed his sword as a sign that there would now be an end to the plague which had lately ravaged the city. The pope celebrated this miracle by replacing the tree-clad mound over the mausoleum with a chapel - the embryo of the San Angelo fortress.

In 592 Gregory the Great concluded a separate peace with the Lombard Duke Ariulf of Spoleto. From the Byzantine viewpoint this was a singularly provocative gesture since formally the pope held no temporal power, but was merely a servant of the emperor.

Chilperic, according to Gregory of Tours, was the Nero and Herod of his day, but later historians judged him to be a shrewd politician. He also wrote Latin poetry. This Baroque portrait is said to be taken from his tomb.

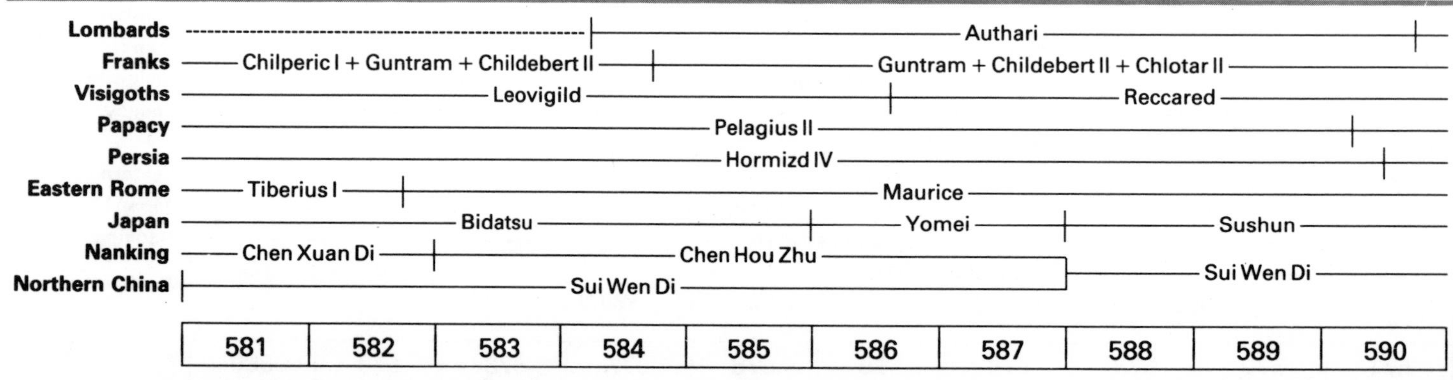
Lombards
Authari
Franks
Chilperic I + Guntram + Childebert II
Guntram + Childebert II + Chlotar II
Visigoths
Leovigild
Reccared
Papacy
Pelagius II
Persia
Hormizd IV
Eastern Rome
Tiberius I
Maurice
Japan
Bidatsu
Yomei
Sushun
Nanking
Chen Xuan Di
Chen Hou Zhu
Sui Wen Di
Northern China
Sui Wen Di
581
582
583
584
585
586
587
588
589
590

INDIA
BYZANTIUM
PERSIA

Migrations were in progress on the American continent as well, though little is known about them. It is evident, however, that new tribes were moving down from north to south, at a time when Maya culture continued to flourish on the isthmus between the two parts of the great continent.

For several conturies the temple city of Teotihuacán in Mexico had prospered. It boasted a Sun and Moon pyramid, a citadel and homes for some 50,000 people. The rain god Tlaloc was the principal deity. The region was peaceful, the city as such was not fortified and the political power of the controlling priesthood extended all the way to the sea both east and west of the highlands, and as far south as modern Guatemala. But a migratory people were on the move from the north-west and within barely a generation these would totally destroy Teotihuacán.

In south-eastern Europe the incursions of the Slavs continued. They settled in large numbers in Thrace and in Greece during the reign of Emperor Tiberius.

In Central Asia, the immense Kök-Turkish empire, though divided within itself, had managed nevertheless to sever the Chinese and Byzantine trading routes through Asia.

The Lombards' former territories on the Danube had been taken over by the Avars who subdued the neighbouring Slav and Bulgar tribes and then established a large kingdom under a khan known as Bayan. Bayan then began a series of punitive expeditions against East Roman territories and in 581 took the town of Sirmium, an important Byzantine fortified frontier post close to modern Belgrade. In 584 and 586 Bayan and his Avars went on to attack Thessalia and also penetrated Thrace, finally halting before the walls of Constantinople. In the 590s Emperor Maurice sent out a powerful army to meet these invaders and in various bloody encounters the latter were repeatedly defeated. But Maurice was unable to achieve peace and his own army became increasingly bitter and dissatisfied as the cruel war dragged on. In 599, with a maximum of publicity, the Avars ruthlessly executed 12,000 Byzantine prisoners-of-war, after failure to agree on terms for repatriation.

Suiko was Japan's first empress, though her son Shotoku ruled the nation for her.

Educated in China, he organized administration on Chinese lines, introduced the Chinese calendar and promoted Chinese culture in every possible way.

The so-called Barranca culture of South America flourished around the mouth of the Orinoco river. This civilization is notable for its sculptured ceramics. At the same time another people living in western Venezuela were producing painted ceramics, especially statuettes with flattened heads and eyes of black beans. In southern Peru artists of the Nazca culture were creating polychromatic ceramics with stylized animal and floral decorations.

In the Frankish Merovingian royal house Brunhilda and Fredegund continued their struggle for power. When King Guntram died in 593, Austrasia and Burgundy were merged under the young Childebert II. At his death two years later, his two small sons, Theudebert II and Theuderic II had received a realm under the guardianship of Brunhilda. Soon afterwards, Fredegund's army moved against Brunhilda, with some initial success; but when she died in 597 Brunhilda seized most of her son's kingdom; all that was left to Chlotar II was a small region north of the Seine.

In 597 the King of Kent and thousands of his subjects were baptized into the true Christian church by the missionary Augustine at Canterbury.

There exists no proper portrait of Muhammad who was now in his twenties. This is a Persian miniature from the 11th century. Bibliothèque Nationale, Paris.

—— Agilulf —— **Lombards**
Gun. + Child. II + Chl. II |—— Childebert II + Chlotar II ——|—— Chlotar II + Theudebert + Theuderic II —— **Franks**
—— Reccared —— **Visigoths**
—— Gregory I —— **Papacy**
—— Khosrow II Parviz —— **Persia**
—— Maurice —— **Eastern Rome**
– Sushun –|—— Suiko —— **Japan**
—— Sui Wen Di —— **China**

591	592	593	594	595	596	597	598	599	600

AD 601-610

JAPAN
CHINA
KOREA

The East Roman empire was constantly warring with the Persians in Mesopotamia and the Slavs who were invading the Balkan peninsula. On the latter front, the army mutinied under the leadership of an officer named Phocas who, with appalling cruelty, liquidated Emperor Maurice and his large family and proclaimed himself emperor. Phocas's reign was a period of disaster for the Slavs, and Avars now poured in across the unguarded Balkan frontier. The Persian king, Khosrow II, also decided to avenge the murdered emperor and family, despatching his armies westward through Armenia and Asia Minor. At this juncture the young admiral Heraclius sailed in from Carthage, which was still Byzantine, to Constantinople. Here he seized and killed Emperor Phocas, assumed the throne himself and attempted to avert the impending cataclysm.

The empire was in a state of despair. Slavs and Avars had occupied the Balkan peninsula right up to the walls of Constantinople, and from the other direction the Persians marched in, unopposed, seizing Antioch, Damascus and Cappadocian Caesarea, and occupying all the territory east of this. In 614 the Persians also took Jerusalem which was stormed by 24,000 determined Jews under the banner of the Persian king. The defenders were slaughtered wholesale, a number of Christian sanctuaries were plundered and destroyed, and the patriarch was taken prisoner and conveyed in triumph to Persia. The Persians also took with them the Calvary cross which had been discovered and set up by the devout mother of Emperor Constantine. From Palestine the Persians continued into Egypt where they occupied the Nile valley and also captured Alexandria, to the great alarm of Constantinople, which depended upon Egypt for its grain deliveries. In Africa, the Persians advanced as far west as the ancient Greek town of Cyrene which was completely destroyed.

In 619, after all this had been lost, Emperor Heraclius signed a costly peace treaty with the Khan of the Avars and finally secured his western flank. He had spent these disastrous years attempting to build up a type of military-tenure system as a basis for a new Byzantine army.

The Irish monk Columba had been preaching repentance and confession to the Franks, and his disciple Gallus now founded a monastery, St. Gallen, in accordance with these teachings. At the same time the papacy was pursuing a determined missionary campaign in Europe.

Theodolinda's first meeting with Agilulf, duke of Turin. Painting in the cathedral at Monza, made in 1444 by the Zavaretti family as one of several scenes from the life of this pious queen.

The Lombard queen Theodolinda, married first to Authari and then to Agilulf, was herself a Bavarian princess and inflexibly orthodox in her faith. When Pope Gregory sent her a nail from the Calvary cross, she had the relic made into the renowned iron crown of Lombardy. She spent all her time attempting to convert her husband, Agilulf, to the true faith though it is doubtful whether she succeeded, for there was no official announcement of his conversion. But her son Adaloald was raised as a devout Catholic, which incidentally was to cost him his crown in the following decade. The Lombard kings retained their Arian faith until the 660s.

In the year 610 Muhammad, son of Abdullah, was visited in his home at Mecca by the Angel Gabriel who exhorted him to proclaim a new religion. He immediately set about this task, though he found but few willing followers. He did, however, succeed in convincing his wealthy wife Khadija and his cousin Ali.

In 607 a Japanese ambassador named Omo Imoko arrived at the court of Emperor Yang Di in Loyang. He brought greetings from Queen Suiko and the crown prince, Shotoku, the latter being the real ruler of Japan until he died in the early 620s. Omo Imoko was followed by other ambassadors and by Japanese nobles, many of whom remained for a long time in China. In this way Chinese learning and culture flowed into Japan on a broad front and Buddhism became firmly established during Suiko's reign.

Prince Shotoku was clearly very strongly influenced by Chinese philosophy. As early as 604 he issued a moral treatise on the government of the state: this reflected not only his Buddhist faith but also his Confucian knowledge. In the same year he introduced a list of official rankings based on the Chinese pattern.

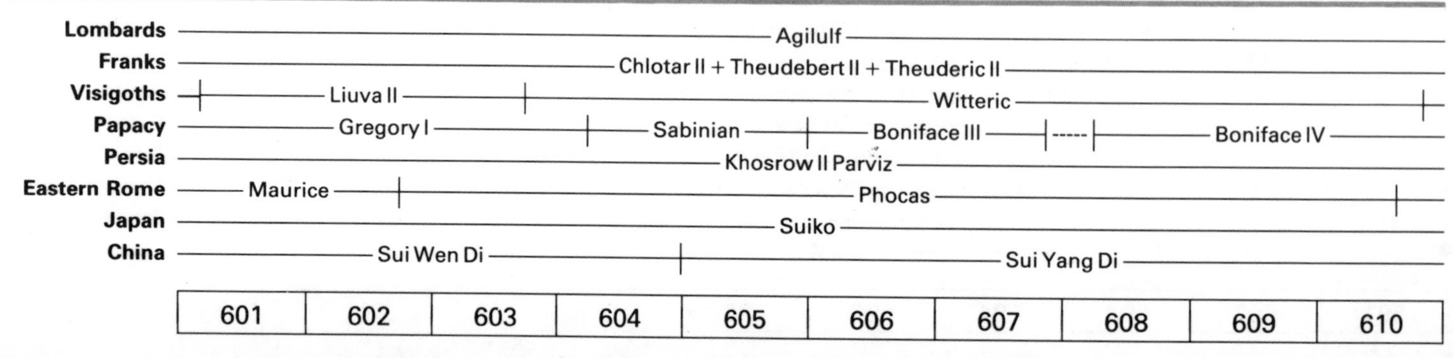

Lombards
Agilulf
Franks
Chlotar II + Theudebert II + Theuderic II
Visigoths
Liuva II
Witteric
Papacy
Gregory I
Sabinian
Boniface III
Boniface IV
Persia
Khosrow II Parviz
Eastern Rome
Maurice
Phocas
Japan
Suiko
China
Sui Wen Di
Sui Yang Di
601
602
603
604
605
606
607
608
609
610

JAPAN
KOREA
CHINA
INDIA
CHINA

The population of China more than doubled during the reign of Emperor Wen Di. The 400-year division of the country had now ended, the interminable wars were over and agriculture and other trades were beginning to flourish once more. At the death of Wen Di the overall population was something like 50 million. Wen Di himself was killed by his own son who, as emperor, became known as Yang Di. Yang Di had progressive ideas, built cities and palaces, and had a canal constructed from his capital Loyang south to the River Yangtze and beyond the river to Hangzhou. This immense project, known as the Sui Canal in honour of the dynasty, was a favourite route of the emperor himself who gazed down with satisfaction from his four-decked vessel on the busy water traffic.

The Chinese did have problems with their waterways. In 602, eight years before the Sui Canal was opened, another great river, the Yellow River, suddenly changed course, flooding this thickly populated country, to devastating effect. This was the first record in history of the Yellow River flooding its banks.

A scribe of some significance was Isidore of Seville, bishop in this Visigoth city until his death in 636. Isidore was a great compiler and thanks to him much ancient literature was preserved for posterity.

Emperor Yang Di attempted to enlarge his domains even further. An attack on Korea was unsuccessful, and as a result the Turkic hordes in Mongolia began to march. Yang Di, having lost his prestige, was eventually assassinated by one of his own generals. This was followed by some years of political chaos and warfare, until an able young man from the north-western province of Shansi contrived to reach an agreement with the Turks and took command of China. His name was Li Shimin, and in due course he became Emperor Tai Zong. For the time being he made his father Emperor Gao Zu; the latter was the first representative of the famous Tang (T'ang) dynasty.

The Visigoth king, Sisebert, was a religious man who initiated a harsh persecution of the Jews in Spain.

In 610, during the pontificate of Pope Boniface, the Pantheon in Rome was transformed into a memorial church and the bones of Christian martyrs were gathered and interred here. All Saints' Day was instituted in their memory and honour.

Left: Buddhist vase from the Sui dynasty, now in Tokyo. Right: Queen Theodolinda's Bible.

The Merovingian family tragedy continued remorselessly. In 612 Theuderic II murdered his brother Theudebert and seized the latter's realm, Austrasia. The following year he himself died, whereupon the elderly and sorely tried queen, Brunhilda, elected one of her grandsons, Sigebert, as king of the Franks and prepared to take over in his name as guardian. At this juncture the Austrasian and Burgundian aristocracy rebelled and offered their allegiance instead to Chlotar II in Neustria. Brunhilda was executed with barbaric cruelty, as were her grandchildren. Chlotar II, left in supreme power, saw his authority immediately challenged at a meeting of the nobles in Paris, where the liberty of the Church and the temporal aristocracy was proclaimed. The king pledged himself always to select his advisors from among the big landowners.

Agilulf — Adaloald	**Lombards**
Chlotar II	**Franks**
Gundemar — Sisebert	**Visigoths**
Boniface IV — Deusdedit — Boniface V	**Papacy**
Khosrow II Parviz	**Persia**
Heraclius	**Eastern Rome**
Suiko	**Japan**
Sui Yang Di — Sui Gong Di — Tang Gao Zu	**China**

611	612	613	614	615	616	617	618	619	620

AD 621-630

WEND
SWEDEN
BACTRIA
BYZANTIUM

By far the most important event from this period was the emergence of the prophet Muhammad. 16 July 662 is the date when his followers began reckoning their calendar. It commemorates the prophet's flight from Mecca to Medina and is the first day in the Arabian lunar year. In the 620s, Muhammad, who had first appeared publicly in 610, wrote letters to various princes and potentates exhorting them to embrace his teachings. Emperor Heraclius was one of those who replied in a friendly tone, even sending the prophet a modest gift as well.

From 606 to 647 an ardent Buddhist named Harsavardhana ruled over a kingdom between Dehli and Simla. He extended his country's frontiers and achieved the historic feat of establishing an eastern bulwark against threats from the West during this era of tremendous turmoil and upheaval. Harsatvardhana's realm did not long survive his death but his deeds were commemorated in a biography by the court poet Banabhatta, and also by the remarkable Chinese pilgrim Xuan Zhuang, who in an entertaining book on his travels in the West enthusiastically praised King Harsa.

A Nestorian missionary known by the Chinese as A Le Ben preached Christianity in China with great success.

On the threshold of the 620s Persia had established supremacy in all the Byzantine empire's oriental provinces, and the Avars and the Slavs were largely masters of the Balkans. Emperor Heraclius apparently offered a large tribute as a peace-keeping bribe to the khan of the Avars, while assembling an army in Armenia and in the north to attack the Persians. On a winter day in 627 there was a decisive battle at Nineveh where King Khosrow was put to flight. A few weeks later Khosrow was deposed, sentenced to death and crucified by his own people. All territory which had once belonged to the Roman empire was then restored.

On 14 December 630 Emperor Heraclius celebrated a triumph that was to be lastingly recorded in the calendars of the Christian world. This, the first day of the year in the Greek Church, commemorates the resurrection in Jerusalem of the Calvary cross, the sacred relic having been returned to the holy city in a ceremonial procession led by Heraclius himself.

A large Bulgarian realm led by a chieftain named Kovrat or Kubrat had emerged north of the Black Sea. The Bulgars were a Turkic people who still used the Turko-Tartar language, though in due course they abandoned this for the tongue of their Slav neighbours. In an alliance with the Byzantines Kubrat had managed to shake off the yoke of the Avars.

Muhammad and Abu Bakr on their way to Medina from Mecca. Bibliothèque Nationale, Paris. The journey to Medina is of central significance in the Islamic faith.

Farther to the west in Europe the Slavs were also rebelling against the Avars. Headed by a merchant named Samo, a Slav state was established in Moravia. An attempt by the Frankish king, Dagobert, to suppress this state in its infancy failed, for in 631 or 632 he was totally defeated by Samo. The Slav kingdom, however, was short-lived. Samo died in the 650s and his state vanished.

Emperor Heraclius was well aware of the political implications of the controversy concerning the nature of Christ and supported the patriarch, Sergius, in his attempt to end this theological dispute by proposing a compromise whereby the dual natures of Christ were united by a single will. Even Pope Honorius I saw fit to accept this. In the long term, however, the compromise was unsuccessful. It was opposed particularly in the West where the doctrine of Pope Honorius on the will of God was officially condemned – a unique occurrence in papal history.

Dagobert was the last of the Frankish Merovingians to hold any real political power. In all the Frankish states *de facto* authority was wielded by an official known as the major domus, who controlled the entire administration. The long-haired, long-bearded kings were of little individual importance.

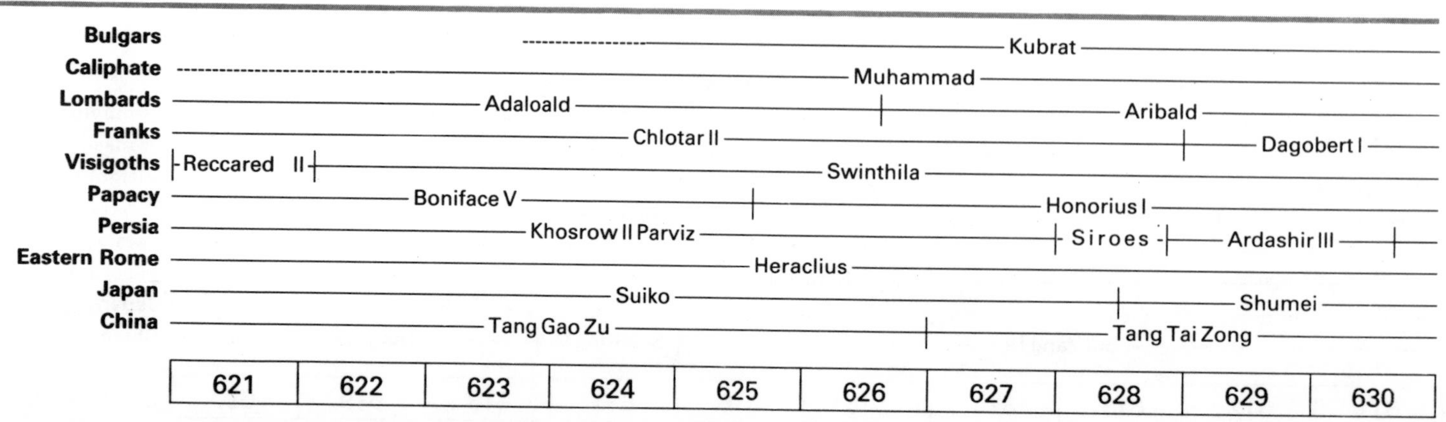

Bulgars
Kubrat
Caliphate
Muhammad
Lombards
Adaloald
Aribald
Franks
Chlotar II
Dagobert I
Visigoths
Reccared II
Swinthila
Papacy
Boniface V
Honorius I
Persia
Khosrow II Parviz
Siroes
Ardashir III
Eastern Rome
Heraclius
Japan
Suiko
Shumei
China
Tang Gao Zu
Tang Tai Zong
621
622
623
624
625
626
627
628
629
630

CHINA
PERSIA
CHINA

On 8 June 632 the prophet Muhammmad died. His followers were by this time so numerous and dedicated that Muhammad had been able to carry out full-scale military campaigns against cities, seizing, among others, his own birthplace of Mecca. Muhammad's spiritual and temporal heir was his father-in-law Abu Bakr, who became the first caliph. Abu Bakr placed the military command in the hands of Khalid ibn al-walid, a very able general who, within the space of this decade, defeated a number of Bedouin tribes and conquered Bahrein and Yemen, Persian Mesopotamia, and the East Roman imperial provinces of Palestine and Syria. The success and ease of these conquests may be explained by the fact that the countries in question were exhausted by the protracted war between the Persians and the Byzantines, and also by the lack of genuine loyalty shown by the people to their respective rulers. Furthermore, there was the religious antagonism within Christianity. Byzantine theologians of the 7th century regarded Islam as a form of Arianism, but the millions of Eastern Monophysites found an affinity with the Muhammadan faith which, like themselves, rejected the dogma of the Trinity. There is no surviving portrait of Muhammad, chiefly because the religion he created was hostile to any form of image-making. Of all the Islamic countries, Persia was virtually the only one to produce any pictorial art.

The Tang dynasty had come to power with the assistance of Turkic troops from Shansi and other provinces far off in the north-west, and subsequently these states demanded recompense in the form of annual tributes. But Emperor Tai Zong managed to ease them out of his capital, Changan, and several years later was strong enough to take the offensive himself, abetted by internal conflicts among the tribes of central Asia. In 630 the leader of the most easterly of the Turkic states, which covered much of Central Asia, was captured. The West Turkic kingdom, extending to Persia and northern India, was simultaneously rent by divisions and the Chinese generals promptly took possession of the Tarim basin. Tibet, farther south, was ruled by Srong-brtsan-sgam-po who had a Chinese wife. A devout Buddhist, she initiated a mission which ensured the continuing pacificism of Tibet.

China was once again a major power with a secure western frontier. One of Emperor Tai Zong's first measures was to re-establish a university in Changan. This soon became a very important seat of learning. Scholars from all over the empire were appointed as professors and these created an examination system which with only minor modifications was to remain in use throughout the history of imperial China until 1905. This examination system turned the nation's intellectuals into servants of the state. The system was democratic to the extent that it permitted everyone of any talent at all, irrespective of background, to compete on fairly equal terms, but at the same time it forced them all into public service since the nucleus of their studies consisted of the Confucian classics. These related almost exclusively to governmental administration and affairs of state, and the scope for using such training beyond the offices of the emperor was very limited. On one occasion Emperor Tai Zong was present at one of these examination sittings and when the large group of successful candidates surged out of the examination hall the emperor exclaimed jubilantly: 'Now they are my prisoners, these brilliant minds from all over the empire'.

Himself a convinced Confucian, Emperor Tai Zong was sceptical of Buddhism whose followers were often dull, unproductive citizens. Many monks and nuns were expelled from their temples and cloisters and set to work as being unworthy of spiritual peace. But there was no real religious persecution. This bodhisattva from Dunhuang is from Tai Zong's time. Fogg Art Museum, Harvard.

Kubrat	**Bulgars**
Abu Bakr | Umar	**Caliphate**
Aribald | Rothari	**Lombards**
Dagobert I | Sigebert III + Clovis II	**Franks**
Sisenand | Sinthila	**Visigoths**
Honorius I | ---- | Severinus	**Papacy**
Hormizd V ---- | Yazdegerd III	**Persia**
Heraclius	**Eastern Rome**
Shumei	**Japan**
Tang Tai Zong	**China**

631	632	633	634	635	636	637	638	639	640

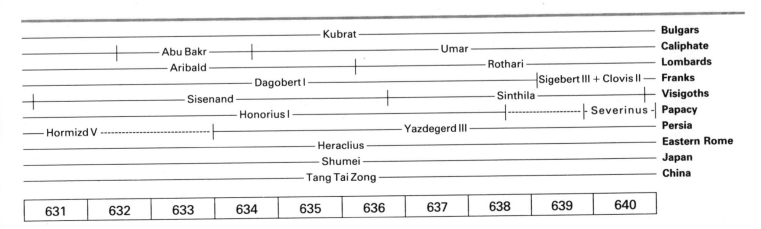

AD 641-650

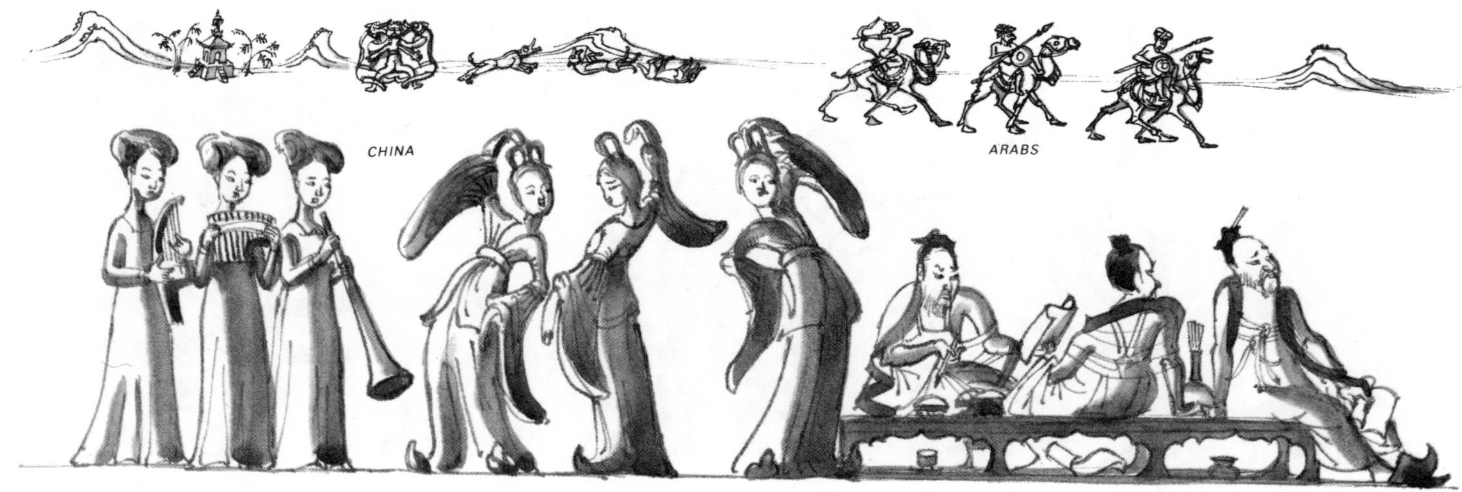
CHINA
ARABS

The Arabs continued their victorious progress. In 642 they invaded Egypt and in the same year decisively defeated the Persians at Nahavand. King Yazdegerd fled eastward and in due course was assassinated in Khorasan. Caliph Umar was an able and reasonably open-minded ruler who established a modus vivendi among Muslims, Christians and Jews in the countries he conquered. Nevertheless, he suffered a violent death, being struck down while at worship by a dissatisfied subject.

Emperor Heraclius witnessed the loss of all his conquests and the disintegration of his life's work. His son Constantine III was an epileptic and survived his father by only a few months. His half-brother Heraclonas was then deposed and butchered along with their unfortunate and unpopular mother. The next emperor was Constantine III's small son Constans II, in whose day the very existence of the East Roman empire was threatened. The Arabian governor in Syria, Mu'awiyah, made repeated puntive expeditions through Asia Minor and also seized Cyprus.

In Central America the first of the Nahua tribes invaded from the north-west. These people destroyed Teotihuacan but adopted its culture.

Calligraphy and the art of miniature painting was flourishing in Ireland where the cultural inheritance of antiquity had found a sanctuary. The Greek language, by now extinct elsewhere in the West, also survived in the Irish monasteries. The Celtic church in Ireland and in Scotland was independent of Rome and was gaining ground: Saint Cuthbert led a successful mission to convert the heathens on Britain's North Sea Coast.

Caliph Uthman favoured the Umayyads, of which he was himself a member, and dissatisfaction was thus rife in Medina where the prophet Muhammad's widow and also his cousin and son-in-law Ali led a revolt which resulted in the death of Uthman. Ali was elected to succeed him as caliph, but the Umayyad, Mu'awiyah, felt committed to revenge and refused to recognize the appointment. The Arab civil war which resulted from this dispute lasted for several years and Ali maintained his headquarters in the Mesopotamian town of Kufa. Mu'awiyah proved victorious, and allowed himself to be proclaimed caliph in Jerusalem in 660. The following New Year Ali was assassinated in the mosque at Kufa. The conflict between the two men split the Islamic world thereafter into two faiths: the Shi'ites swore eternal allegiance to Ali and renounced the Umayyads, who moved their caliphate from Medina to Damascus.

A page from the Lombardian law, codified in 388. Chapter by King Rothari, 643.

The Koran was codified during the reign of Uthman. It consists of 114 chapters, or suras, in rhyming prose.

The Bulgar kingdom in southern Germany vanished around 650. Kubrat, who for a long time had been its leader, had been dead for some years. The kingdom itself was destroyed by the Khazars who had recently emerged from the interior of Asia and now inhabited the lower Volga region. The Bulgarian tribes were dispersed, but one of them established a state in the central Volga region, choosing an important trading junction for their capital, which they called Bulgar. Another tribe went into Pannonia where they already had kinsmen under Avar sovereignty; while a third group, led by Asparukh, crossed the Danube in the following decade.

In 645 the so-called Taika reform was introduced in Japan, whereby the entire administration was reorganized on the Chinese model. The dignitaries of the ancient feudal system were now replaced by bureaucrats who were answerable only to the emperor - the mikado. The chancellor of the realm, known as the daidaishin, and a number of ministers managed the central government; and the provinces were administered by imperial governors specially appointed to these posts and endowed with estates to provide them with a livelihood.

The British king, Oswald of Northumbria became a saint when he died in battle with the heathen king Penda in Mercia in 641. From this point onwards the list of rulers in Northumbria is complete for some decades. During Oswald's reign Irish monks were summoned from Hebridean Iona and founded the monastery at Lindisfarne.

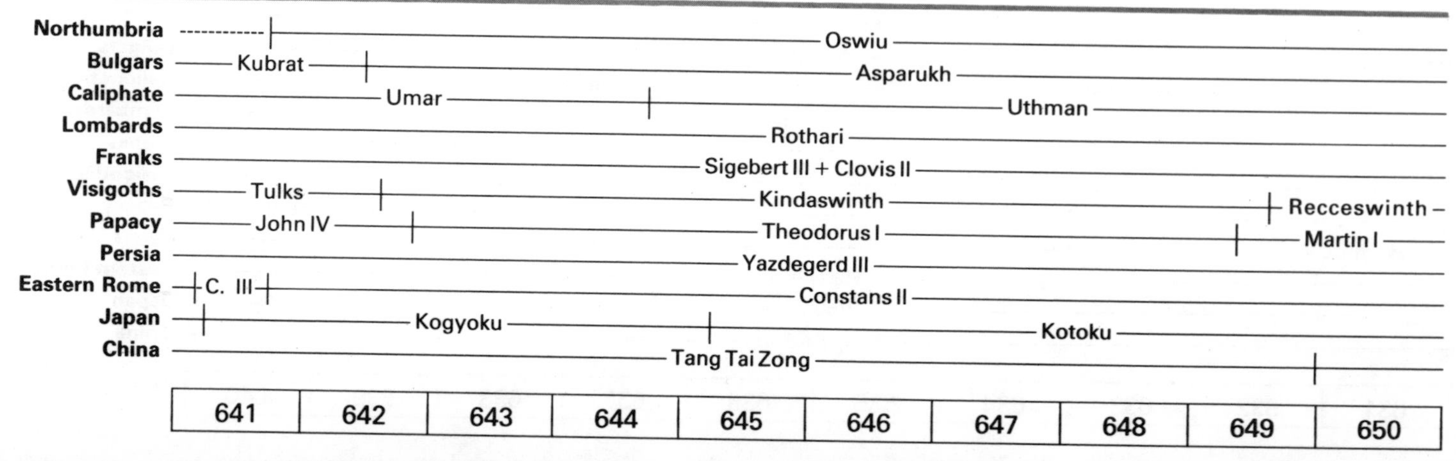
Northumbria
Oswiu
Bulgars
Kubrat
Asparukh
Caliphate
Umar
Uthman
Lombards
Rothari
Franks
Sigebert III + Clovis II
Visigoths
Tulks
Kindaswinth
Recceswinth
Papacy
John IV
Theodorus I
Martin I
Persia
Yazdegerd III
Eastern Rome
C. III
Constans II
Japan
Kogyoku
Kotoku
China
Tang Tai Zong
641
642
643
644
645
646
647
648
649
650

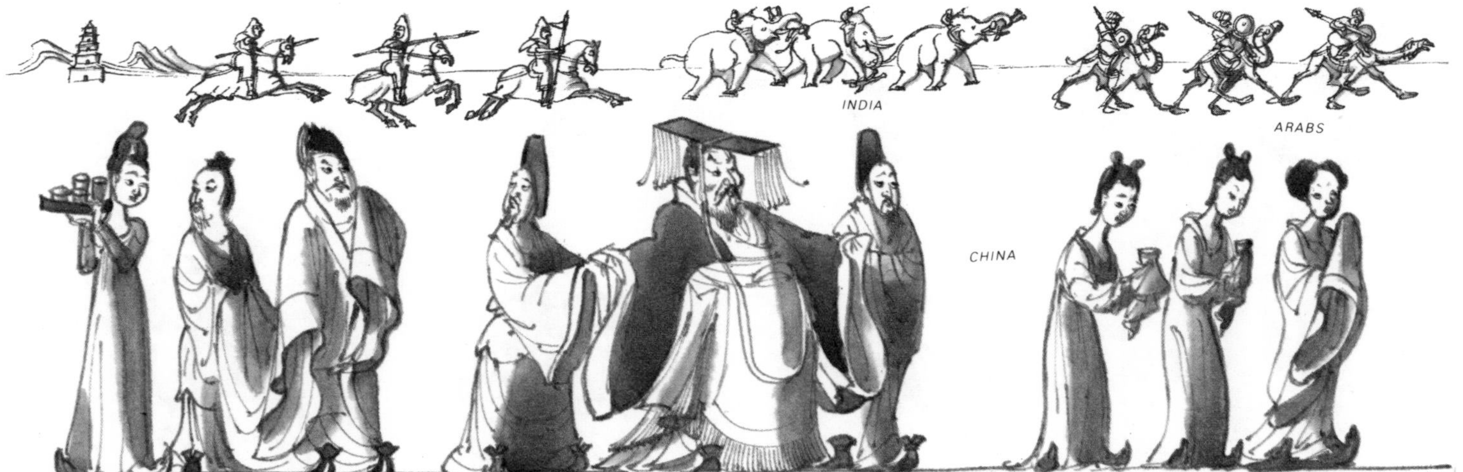
INDIA
ARABS
CHINA

Pope Martin I assembled a Lateran council which formally denounced several imperial decrees on religious issues. Emperor Constans II had the pope arrested and condemned for high treason. Martin was publically humiliated and deported to the Crimea where he died in misery a few years later.

In 657 the Chinese seized the most westerly of the large Turkic states in Central Asia. They had now reached the Persian frontier and shortly afterwards were confronted with the Arabs who had moved in from the opposite direction.

The flow of Buddhist pilgrims to and from India influenced both the art and literature of China. These pilgrims were treated with respect by the authorities and were never persecuted, especially as Emperor Tai Zong in his old age had become amicably disposed towards them. Generally, there was tolerance in China towards all religions, while in the West, Christians and Muslims were fighting bloody battles. There was already an Arab mosque in Canton, Christianity in its Nestorian form was preached freely and was gaining converts. From the west one or two other religions crept in, ancient Persian Mazdakism and its offshoot, Manichaeism. For a time they were successful.

Kogyoku and Saimei were one and the same person: an empress who ruled Japan at two different periods under two different names.

Tang Tai Zong's long rule was one of the most brilliant in the history of China. In the mid-7th century his empire extended from the east coast of Korea and the Tongking Gulf to Lake Aral. Indo-Chinese and Japanese students also attended the newly founded university at Changan, thereby bringing more Chinese culture into their native countries.

The Arabs conquered Rhodes and made a profitable deal out of selling the earthquake-stricken Colossus, one of the seven Wonders of the World, to a Jewish merchant who conveyed all this bronze scrap home to Edessa on 900 camels. The Arabs then won a large naval battle and the road to Constantinople appeared to be open. But Mu'awiyah who needed his forces elsewhere, made peace with the Greeks. Emperor Constans II used this opportunity to secure his rear and fought a successful engagement against the intruding Slavs in the Balkans. After this, however, he joined the Byzantine fleet and proceeded westward by stages. He passed through Thessalonica, Athens, Tarentum and Rome, and finally settled in Syracuse.

Extract from an early edition of the Koran. There is an enormous quantity of comments to these longitudinally arranged revelations.

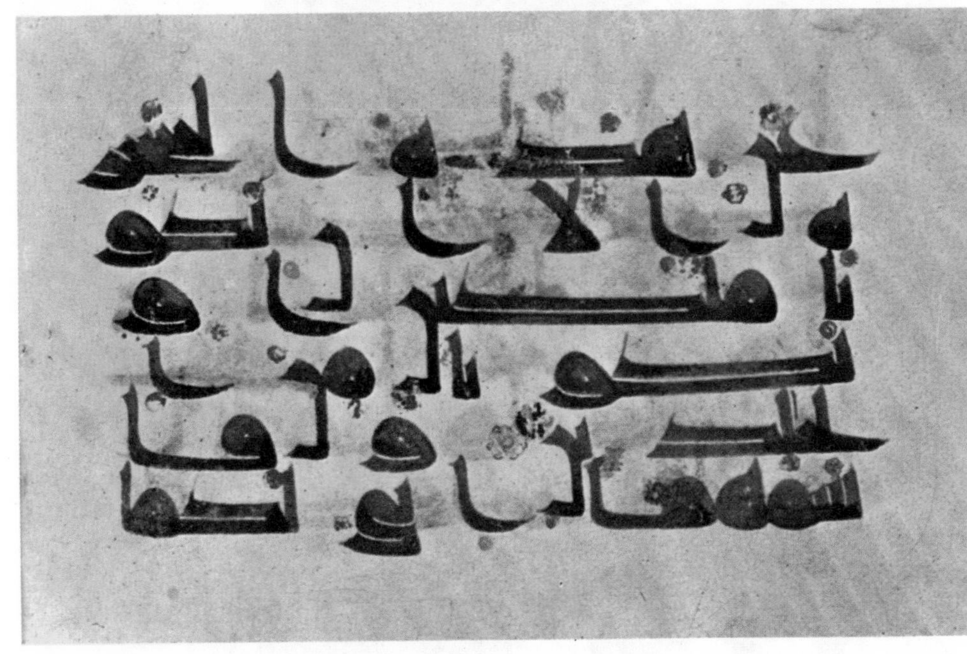

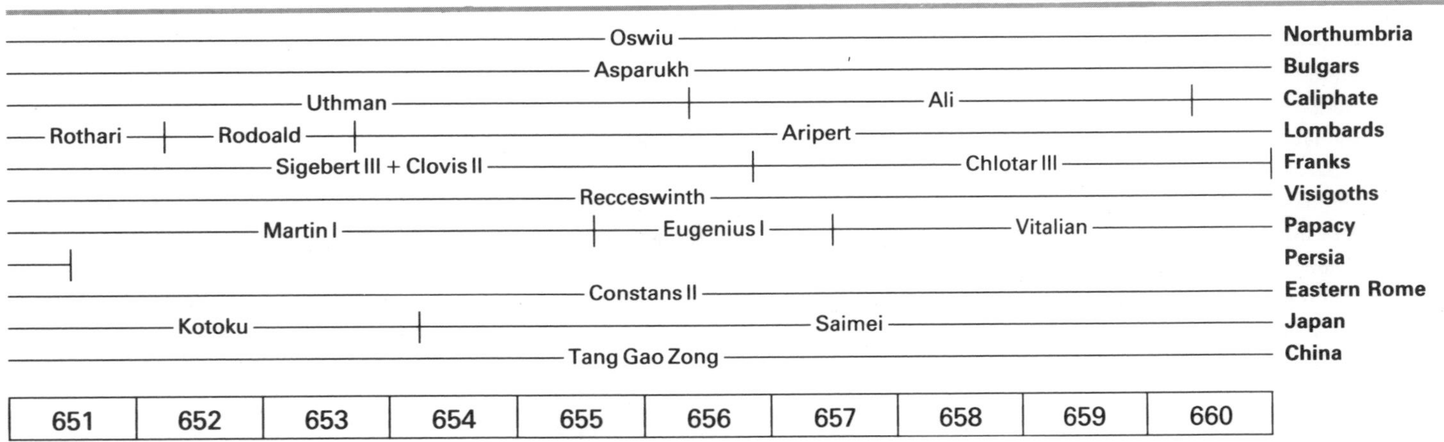
Oswiu
Northumbria
Asparukh
Bulgars
Uthman
Ali
Caliphate
Rothari
Rodoald
Aripert
Lombards
Sigebert III + Clovis II
Chlotar III
Franks
Recceswinth
Visigoths
Martin I
Eugenius I
Vitalian
Papacy
Persia
Constans II
Eastern Rome
Kotoku
Saimei
Japan
Tang Gao Zong
China
651
652
653
654
655
656
657
658
659
660

AD 661-670

CHINA
MAYA, MEXICO
CHINA
MEXICO

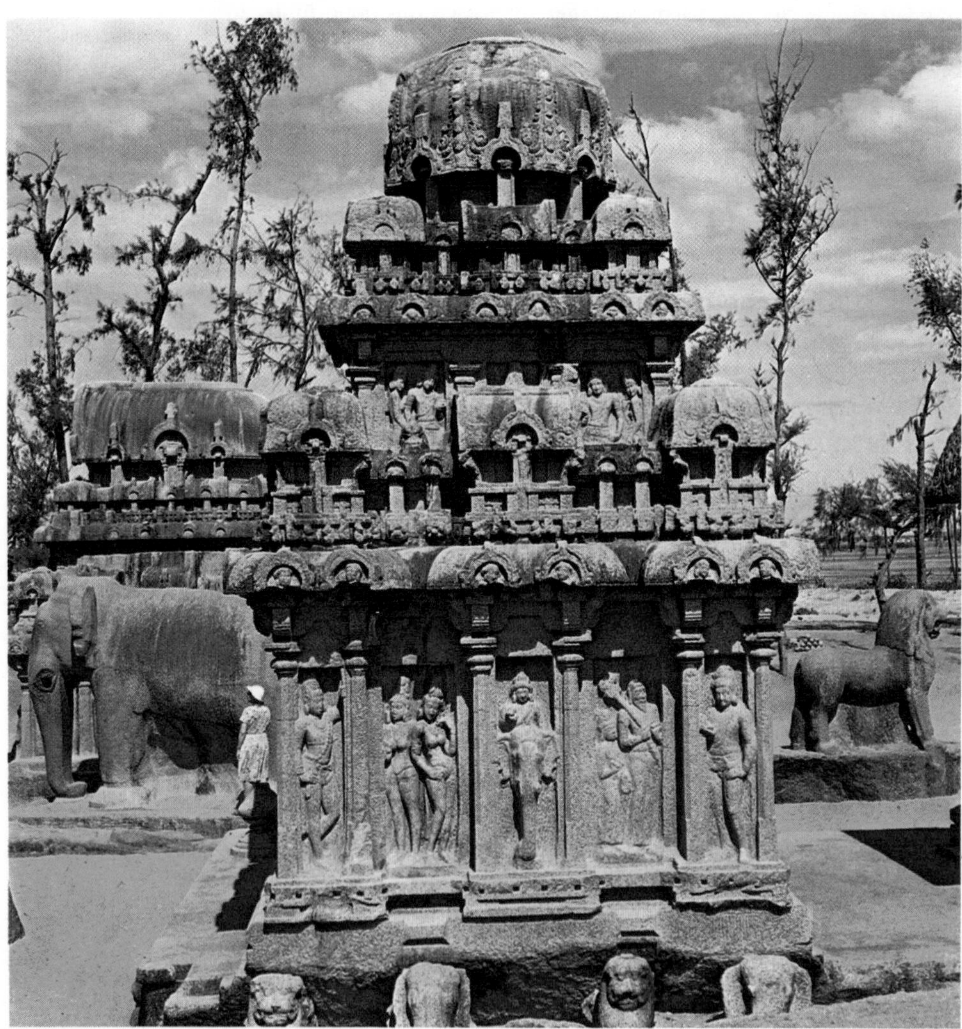

Lombardy was a kingdom divided by religious issues, but during the reign of Grimoald there was an end to Arianism in Italy where the Lombards gradually became absorbed by the Latin world. The position of the Lombard kings was also strengthened as the popular assembly lost its significance.

In Syracuse Emperor Constans II was murdered by his valet who poured a vessel of boiling water over his master and then battered him over the head with the empty pitcher. The emperor had not yet fulfilled his intention of moving his government and family to Syracuse. His son Constantine IV and the latter's brother were still in Constantinople, which thus remained the Byzantine capital.

In England a synod was held in 664 in the monastery at Whitby, and the newly formed church organized according to the Roman pattern. Hitherto it had been controlled by a Scottish-Irish missionary movement promoted by King Oswald of Northumberland, who had died in 641. The English Church fathers who now set matters to rights were Wilfred, Bishop of York, and Theodore, Archbishop of Canterbury. The former was a native Englishman while the latter was a Greek. They were not always in agreement.

In 670 the Arab military colony of Kairouan was founded in Tunisia.

In India Buddhism was on the decline and Gupta art developed Dravidian offshoots. In Mavalipuram, in Madras province, there were five monolithic temples called rathas. The one shown here is Arjuna ratha, with the elephant Airavata. India was now the promised land for sculptors.

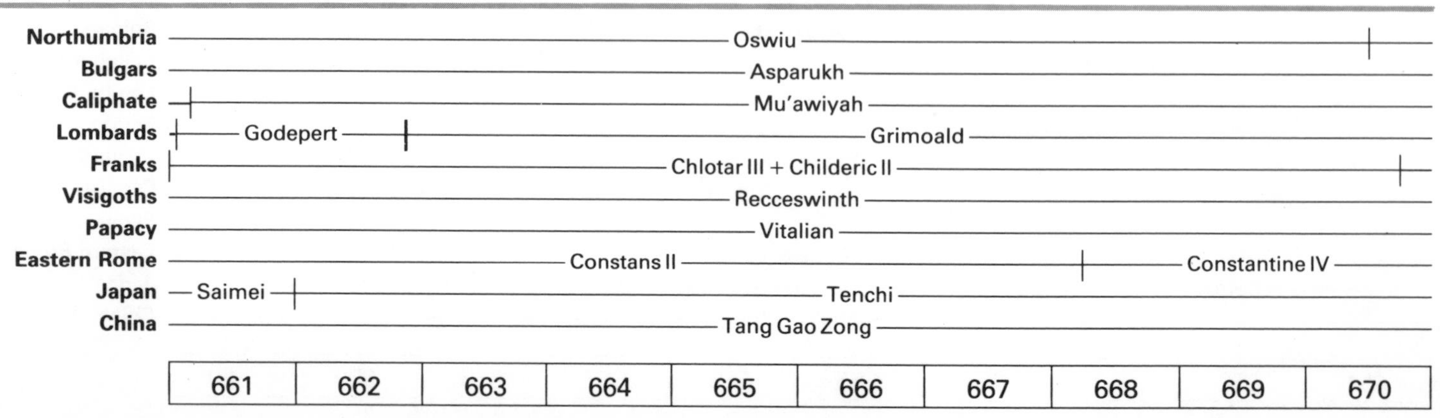
Northumbria
Oswiu
Bulgars
Asparukh
Caliphate
Mu'awiyah
Lombards
Godepert
Grimoald
Franks
Chlotar III + Childeric II
Visigoths
Recceswinth
Papacy
Vitalian
Eastern Rome
Constans II
Constantine IV
Japan
Saimei
Tenchi
China
Tang Gao Zong
661
662
663
664
665
666
667
668
669
670

INDIA
CHINA
KIZIL. CENTRAL ASIA
BYZANTIUM
CHINA

By the 660s the Chinese kingdom under the Tang dynasty had reached its greatest dimensions and had also become the biggest empire the world had ever known. For the first time in history its armies had succeeded in subjugating several Korean states so that not only Korea itself but also Japan, never yet invaded, was within reach of Chinese spiritual influence. City plans, administrative institutions and, above all, Chinese writings were copied in Japan, through the medium of Japanese students who came early to the new university in imperial Changan. There was a similar trend in Indo-China where the Chinese language was already gaining ascendancy in the protectorate of Annam. Westward, too, the Chinese had made great territorial gains, so that the frontier had now touched Lake Baikal and Lake Aral.

China's political hold on Korea began to slacken as early as the 670s, while at the same time the Tibetans of Central Asia again began to assert themselves and seized the western part of the Tarim basin. This was partly due to the fact that the Chinese princess Wencheng had recently died. But the Buddhist mission established in Tibet by this devout princess was allowed to continue and exercised lasting influence on religious and political affairs in Central Asia.

A great deal has been written of Emperor Tenchi. During his reign the Japanese administration was reorganized on Chinese lines, there was a redistribution of land, slaves were liberated and laws were codified. He himself designed a water clock with the chimes of bells and the blast of trumpets recording the time.

A Chinese named Tao Yu was reputed to have invented porcelain.

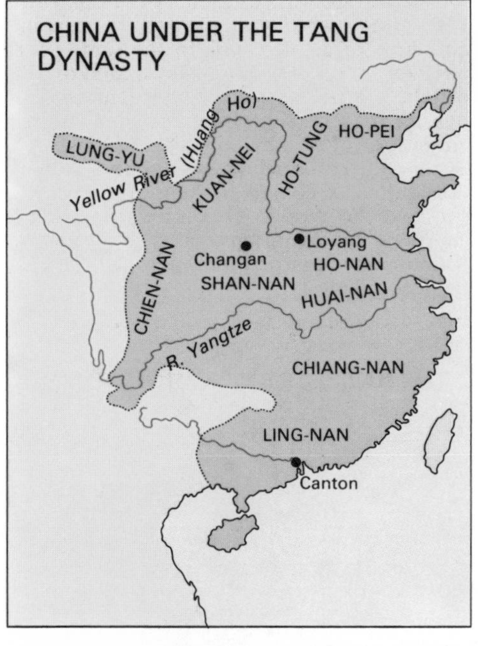
CHINA UNDER THE TANG DYNASTY
LUNG-YU
Yellow River (Huang Ho)
KUAN-NEI
HO-TUNG
HO-PEI
Changan
Loyang
HO-NAN
CHIEN-NAN
SHAN-NAN
HUAI-NAN
R. Yangtze
CHIANG-NAN
LING-NAN
Canton

Korea, which had thus far been partitioned into three separate states of more or less equal power, was now united as a single realm – Silla. Its authority was to survive until the mid-10th century. Politically and culturally, however, Silla remained entirely under Chinese influence.

In the 670s the Arabs reached the Indus and even crossed swords with the Chinese in Turkestan. Mu'awiyah made several attacks on Constantinople, which held firm, thanks largely to Greek Fire, a military device invented by the Syrian architect Callinicus. It was also known as wet fire, since it burned in water and could not be extinguished by normal methods. Although the chemical composition of Greek Fire was a secret, it was some form of explosive agent shot out through tubes known as syphons. Not much is known about this war, but the Arab losses were apparently disastrous for in 679 Mu'awiyah agreed to a thirty-year peace treaty and pledged himself to pay an annual tribute to the Byzantines of 3000 gold coins, fifty prisoners and fifty horses.

The migrating Bulgars had brought their main force uncomfortably close to the East Roman frontier on the Danube, and in the summer of 680 Constantine IV moved out against them with a large fleet and numerous cavalry. This expedition was a total failure, however, and when the Byzantines were finally compelled to withdraw from the marshlands of the Danube delta they were pursued into their own territory by the Bulgars, who settled there permanently. The Slav tribes in this area submitted to the invaders and merged with them in time, adopting their Slav language. The kingdom that the Bulgars established on the Balkan peninsula quickly gained stability and repute. The capital was Pliska.

On 10 October 680, 10 Muharram in Muslim chronology, the murdered caliph Ali's son Husayn, the head of the Prophet's family was slain at Mesopotamian Kerbala. The Shi'ites in Persia were never to forget that Husayn had been slain by an Ummayad sword and henceforth made regular pilgrimages to his grave at Euphrat.

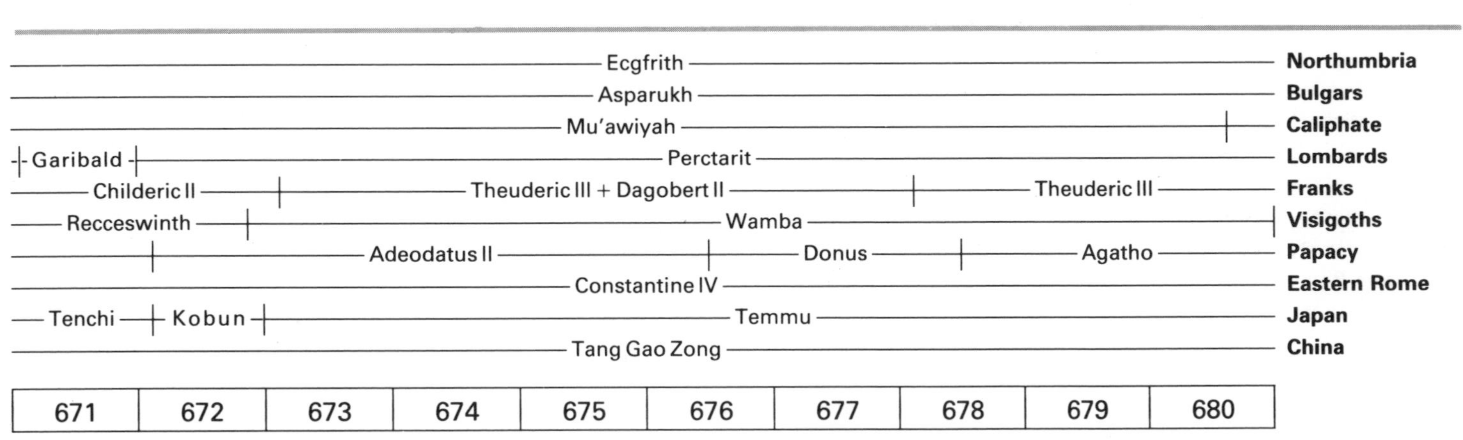
Ecgfrith — Northumbria
Asparukh — Bulgars
Mu'awiyah — Caliphate
Garibald — Perctarit — Lombards
Childeric II — Theuderic III + Dagobert II — Theuderic III — Franks
Recceswinth — Wamba — Visigoths
Adeodatus II — Donus — Agatho — Papacy
Constantine IV — Eastern Rome
Tenchi — Kobun — Temmu — Japan
Tang Gao Zong — China
671 672 673 674 675 676 677 678 679 680

AD 681-690

WEND,
SWEDEN
HORNHAUSEN
PERSIA
MAYA, GUATEMALA

At the close of the 7th century Mercia held the leading position among the small Anglo-Saxon kingdoms, while Northumbria had diminished in prominence. Two of the Mercian kings were Wulfhere and Aethelred, but little is known about them.

The greatest author of this period lived in Northumbria: Beda Venerabilis, the Venerable Bede. Bede left twelve volumes containing, first and foremost, a history of the early English church. He was, moreover, the first historian to use a calendar beginning from the birth of Christ.

Very large numbers of Greeks moved into Italy during the 7th century, especially into those provinces still held by Byzantium: Sicily, Calabria, the Naples area, the Otranto peninsula, but also Rome and the exarchate of Ravenna. The Greek language regained ground in many quarters and for the moment, indeed, the Greek-Oriental element predominated. From 685, for some thirty years the popes were either Greek or Syrian.

Wu Hou, or Empress Wu, was a remarkable woman who commenced her career as a fourteen-year-old concubine in the harem of Emperor Tai Zong. When he died, Wu, along with all the other harem women, was sent to a convent, but soon emerged to become a concubine of the new emperor, Gao Zong. She then proceeded to take control of both Gao Zong and his family. In her quest for power, she eliminated the empress, the emperor's other wives and various people besides, including some of her own children. When Emperor Gao Zong died and was formally succeeded by his son Chong Zong, Wu had the latter deposed and interned at the first sign of his independence. The same fate was suffered by the other son Rui Zong, who was allowed to become emperor for a short time in the same year, 684. After this Wu ruled undisputed and in 690 she put the final touch to her achievement by having herself officially proclaimed 'emperor' of a new dynasty: Zhou. She assumed a name which was neither female nor male, the characters being those of the sun and the moon. This ancestry was not accepted by historians, and Wu Hou is traditionally regarded as a mere interlude in the Tang dynasty.

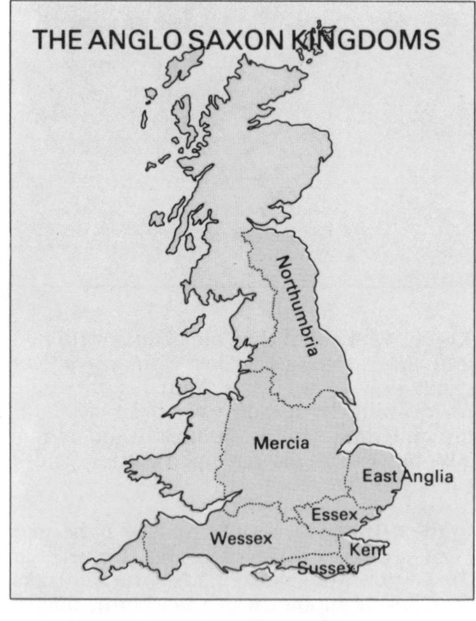
THE ANGLO SAXON KINGDOMS
Northumbria
Mercia
East Anglia
Essex
Wessex
Kent
Sussex

The frontiers of the British kingdoms were still ill-defined, but becoming clearer.

The Frankish Merovingians had long been shadow rulers in the three states of Austrasia, Neustria and Burgundy, where power lay in the hands of a royal major domus. In 687 the Austrasian major domus, Pepin, won a great military victory over his Neustrian counterpart and thereby secured supreme power in the Frankish empire.

Caliph Abd-al-Malik, whose authority was contested by his Arab kinsmen throughout his reign, established a mint between Basra and Kufa and produced coins carrying the image of Allah. The Byzantine emperor, Justinian II, was a devout Christian and this gesture angered him for he regarded it as a denunciation of the Trinity. He thus decided to go to war.

In 685 Buddhism became the national religion in Japan.

While the vast empire of the Tang dynasty flourished, the Arabs went from victory to victory and the Merovingians combed their long hair, there existed in Scandinavia something which modern archeologists have called the Wendel period. An aristocratic, artistically imposing culture was flourishing on Gotland, and also in Uppland where the navigable sea channels still penetrated deep into the province and where Lake Mälar was as yet a Baltic bay. The chieftains who died in Wendel and Valsgärde took magnificent weapons with them to their graves, while feats and events on Gotland were recorded in petroglyphics which have never been fully interpreted.

The Visigoths in Spain persecuted the Jews fanatically, and for this reason, apparently, the Jews sought contact with the Arabs in Africa.

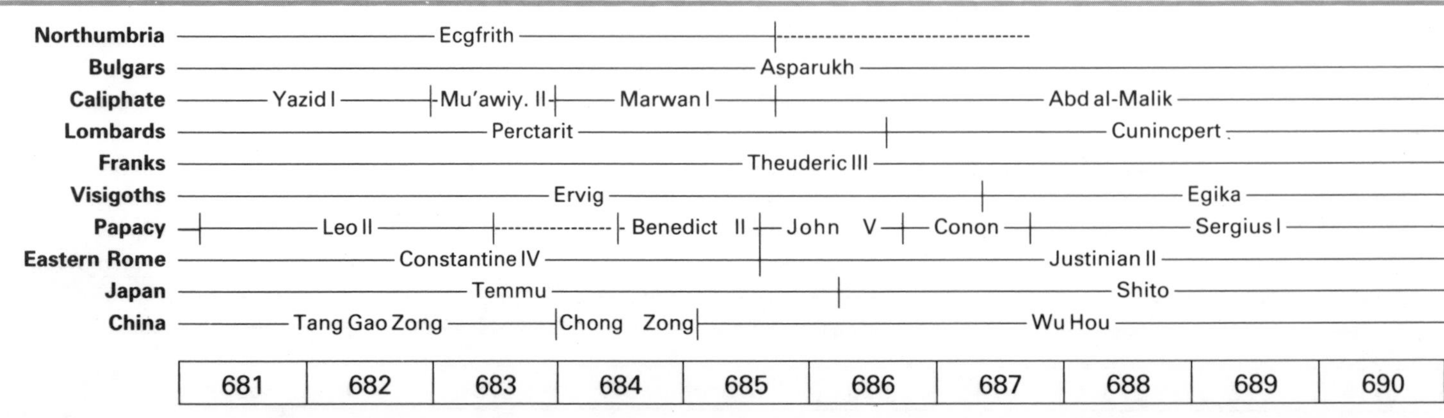
Northumbria — Ecgfrith
Bulgars — Asparukh
Caliphate — Yazid I — Mu'awiy. II — Marwan I — Abd al-Malik
Lombards — Perctarit — Cunincpert
Franks — Theuderic III
Visigoths — Ervig — Egika
Papacy — Leo II — Benedict II — John V — Conon — Sergius I
Eastern Rome — Constantine IV — Justinian II
Japan — Temmu — Shito
China — Tang Gao Zong — Chong Zong — Wu Hou
681 682 683 684 685 686 687 688 689 690

AD 691-700

PERSIA
KAZAKSTAN
VERA CRUZ
MAYA, MEXICO
KIZIL
CENTRAL ASIA

The council of Trullo, held in Constantinople in 692, explicitly authorized the marriage of priests and abolished the Roman Saturday fast. Pope Sergius, of course, did not recognize these decisions.

Pictorial stone from Lärbro, Sweden, with ships and mythological scenes. Bunge Museum, Gotland.

Following a military defeat by the Arabs, Emperor Justinian II was deposed by a military revolt, had his nose cut off and was deported to the Crimea. His successor, too, was deposed and suffered similar mutilation.

In 696 an English monk named Willibrord was appointed Bishop of Utrecht. He became the Frisians' apostle.

Carthage, until recently a Byzantine exarchate, and Algeria too, were incorporated in the Arab caliphate in 698. The triumphant progress of the Arabs continued unchecked.

The mosque of Omar in Jerusalem, named after the caliph who seized Jerusalem for Islam, was completed in 691. Jerusalem was also a holy city to the Muslims.

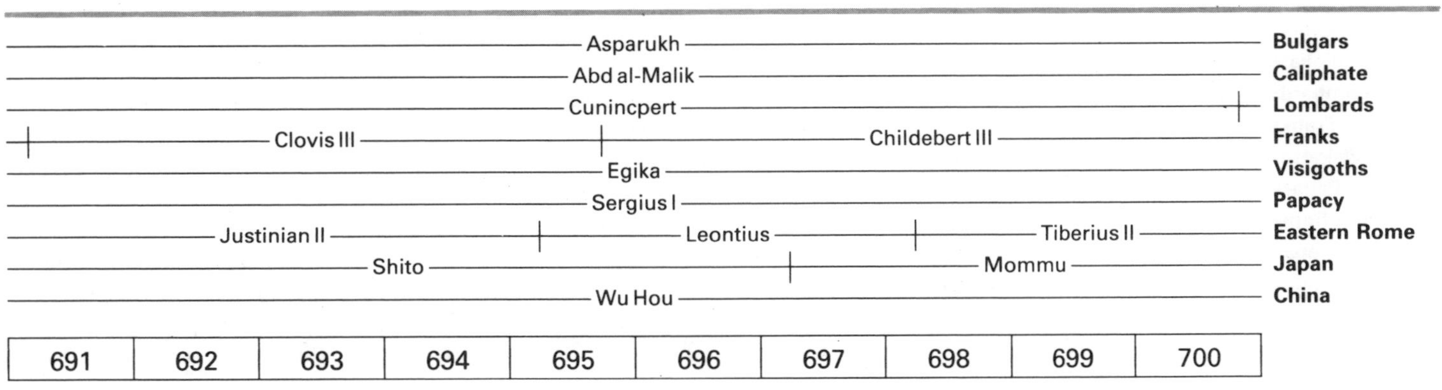
Asparukh
Bulgars
Abd al-Malik
Caliphate
Cunincpert
Lombards
Clovis III
Childebert III
Franks
Egika
Visigoths
Sergius I
Papacy
Justinian II
Leontius
Tiberius II
Eastern Rome
Shito
Mommu
Japan
Wu Hou
China
691
692
693
694
695
696
697
698
699
700

AD 701-710

CHINA

The Khazars were a Turko-Tartar people who had established a powerful kingdom around the Volga and the Don; and the Bulgars, whose ruling class still spoke a Turkic language, were settled on the west coast of the Black Sea. Justinian II had endowed the Bulgar khan, Tervel, with the title of Caesar, which the Bulgars turned into Czar.

The name of some of the rulers of Anglo-Saxon Mercia have survived. King Aethelbald is known to have exempted all clergy from tribute.

In China, the Empress Wu withdrew at the age of eighty-one to make way for her son Zhong Zong who, like his brother Rui Zong, had long been idle. A few years later Zhong Zong was poisoned by his wife who wished to see her own family rule the empire; this was thwarted by a new palace revolution led by a grandson of Wu, the future Emperor Xuan Zong. Prior to this, the latter's father, Rui Zong, ascended the throne for the second time.

Gemmyo and Gensho were reigning empresses in Japan.

The reign of Tiberius II was a sorry interlude for the East Roman empire, which four years previously had lost the exarchate of Carthage to the Arabs and now continued to surrender territory to them. The Arabs reached the Atlantic coast in 704 and even reached Asia, establishing a foothold in Cilicia.

Justinian II was in exile in the Crimea and on good terms with the khan of the Khazars. He also established friendly relations with the Bulgar khan, Tervel, and with the help of these two Justinian contrived to regain the Byzantine imperial throne. He now took revenge on all those who had opposed him. The former emperors Leontius and Tiberius II were cruelly put to death; the patriarch, Callinicus, who had crowned Leontius, lost his eyes; and the leaders in Ravenna, who ten years earlier had supported the revolution, were sent to Constantinope to die, after witnessing the plunder of their city by the emperor's army. A similar fate was intended for Cherson in the Crimea, but when Justinian's punitive expedition arrived here the people of Cherson elected to fight. The imperial admiral, Bardanes, decided to change sides and turned instead against Constantinople where Justinian II was abandoned by his guards and killed.

Bardanes, who became Emperor Philippicus, was quickly deposed and had his eyes put out. Both his successors abdicated, and Leo III, a powerful Asiatic general, inaugurated the remarkable Isaurian dynasty.

A pope name Sisinnius whose pontificate lasted only a couple of weeks in 708, is not listed here.

Caliph Abd al-Malik, eager for peace, had come to an agreement with the Byzantines. Armenia and Cyprus were to be ruled jointly and taxes shared equally between the parties. The arrangement for Cyprus lasted for some time; in spite of disunity, it was controlled by the Empire and Caliphate for several centuries to come. The two powers also agreed that the Nardites, a martial Christian tribe, should be removed from Lebanon to Peloponnesus, the island of Cephalonia and other places.

An Arab general named Musa had conquered the entire North African coastal area for the caliph and now his immediate subordinate, Tariq, crossed to Spain; his name was to be perpetually commemorated by the rock Gibr-al-Tarik. The Visigoth kingdom in Spain was shaken by conflicts over succession and by internal dissent, particularly as a result of barbaric persecution of the Jews, which reached its peak under King Witiza. Witiza's successor Roderick met the invading Arabs on a battlefield called Vejer de la Frontera. On a June day in 711 the Visigoths were totally defeated, their king died in the battle and the Gothic state ceased to exist.

By 720 the Arabs' realm in Spain was so well consolidated that they could cross the Pyrenees into Gaul. Narbonne fell into their hands in this same year. But there still remained a pocket of resistance on the Spanish side where a Visigoth warrior named Pelayo was trying to set up a small Christian state in the Asturias mountains.

Further east, however, the Arabs were not so successful. Although they seized the Indian province of Sind in 712 their major campaign against Constantinople in the same year failed. After besieging the city for a whole year the caliph's troops were forced to withdraw, having suffered great losses. A large part of the Muslim navy was sunk in stormy seas. The Byzantines celebrated the Arabs departure by offering thanks to the patron saint of the city, Blachernitissa.

The greater part of the army that conquered Spain consisted of Muslim Berbers, who were not always obedient to their Arab officers.

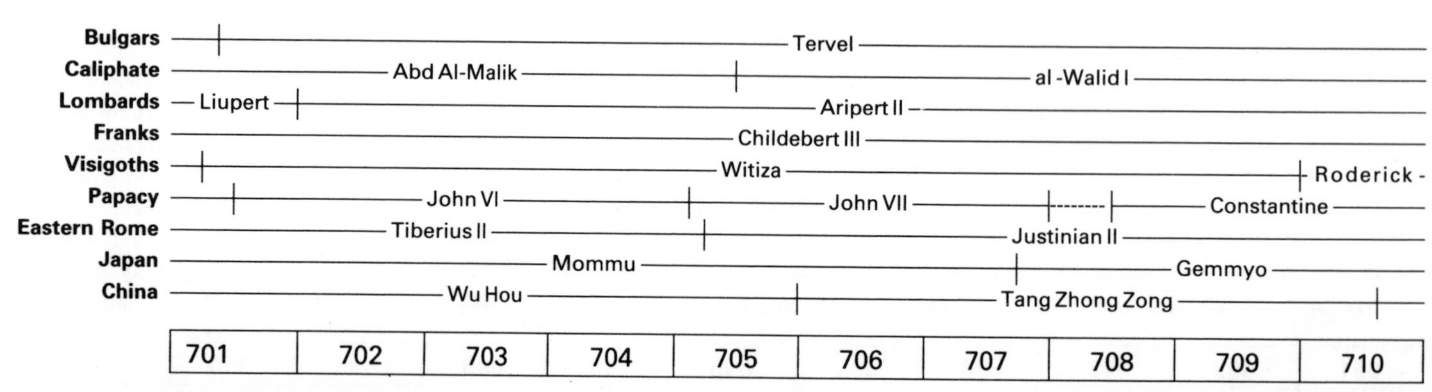
Bulgars
Tervel
Caliphate
Abd Al-Malik
al-Walid I
Lombards
Liupert
Aripert II
Franks
Childebert III
Visigoths
Witiza
Roderick
Papacy
John VI
John VII
Constantine
Eastern Rome
Tiberius II
Justinian II
Japan
Mommu
Gemmyo
China
Wu Hou
Tang Zhong Zong
701
702
703
704
705
706
707
708
709
710

CHINA

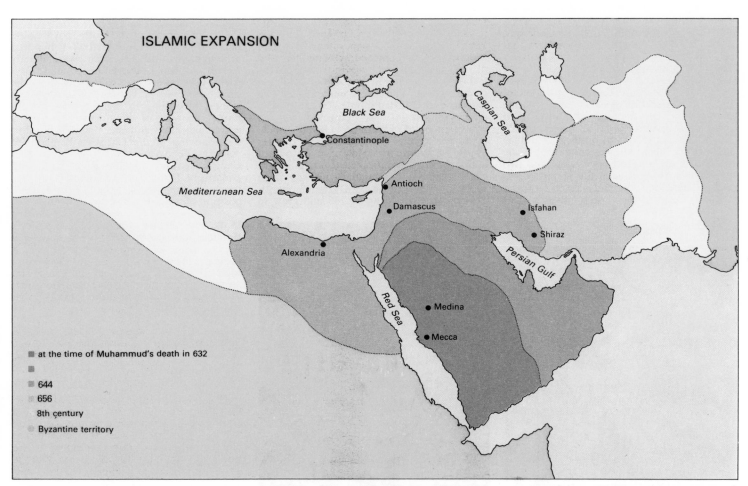

ISLAMIC EXPANSION

Black Sea
Caspian Sea
Constantinople
Mediterranean Sea
Antioch
Damascus
Isfahan
Shiraz
Alexandria
Persian Gulf
Red Sea
Medina
Mecca

- at the time of Muhammud's death in 632
-
- 644
- 656
- 8th century
- Byzantine territory

In less than 100 years Islam had overrun all the old civilizations south and east of the Mediterranean, but religious zeal had not been the only reasons for its expansion. To some extent there had also been a general migration movement of the Arab populations.

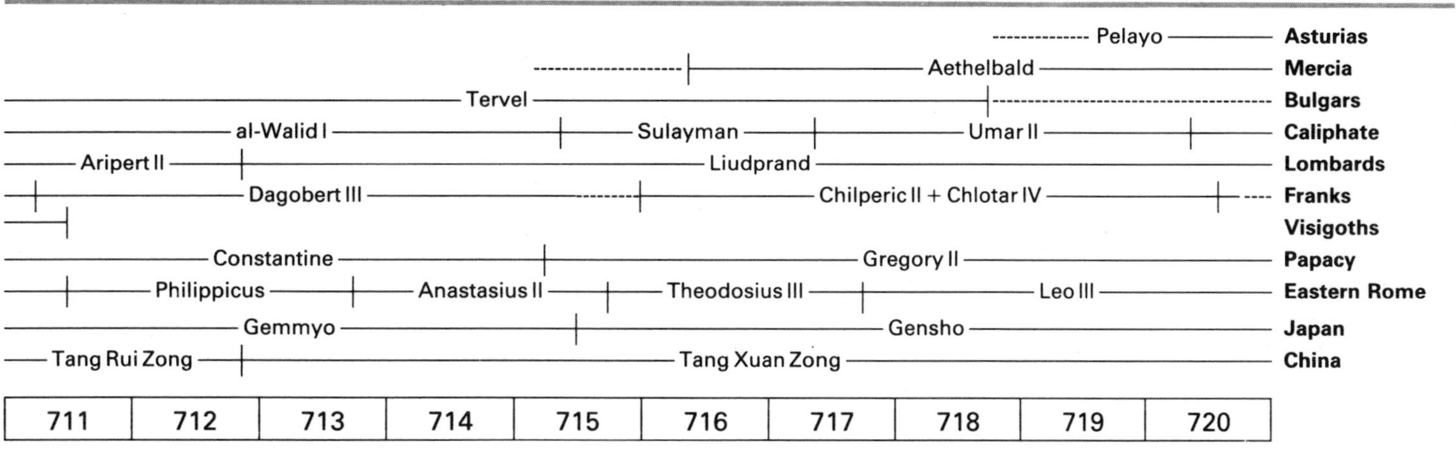
Pelayo
Asturias
Aethelbald
Mercia
Tervel
Bulgars
al-Walid I
Sulayman
Umar II
Caliphate
Aripert II
Liudprand
Lombards
Dagobert III
Chilperic II + Chlotar IV
Franks
Visigoths
Constantine
Gregory II
Papacy
Philippicus
Anastasius II
Theodosius III
Leo III
Eastern Rome
Gemmyo
Gensho
Japan
Tang Rui Zong
Tang Xuan Zong
China
711
712
713
714
715
716
717
718
719
720

AD 721-730

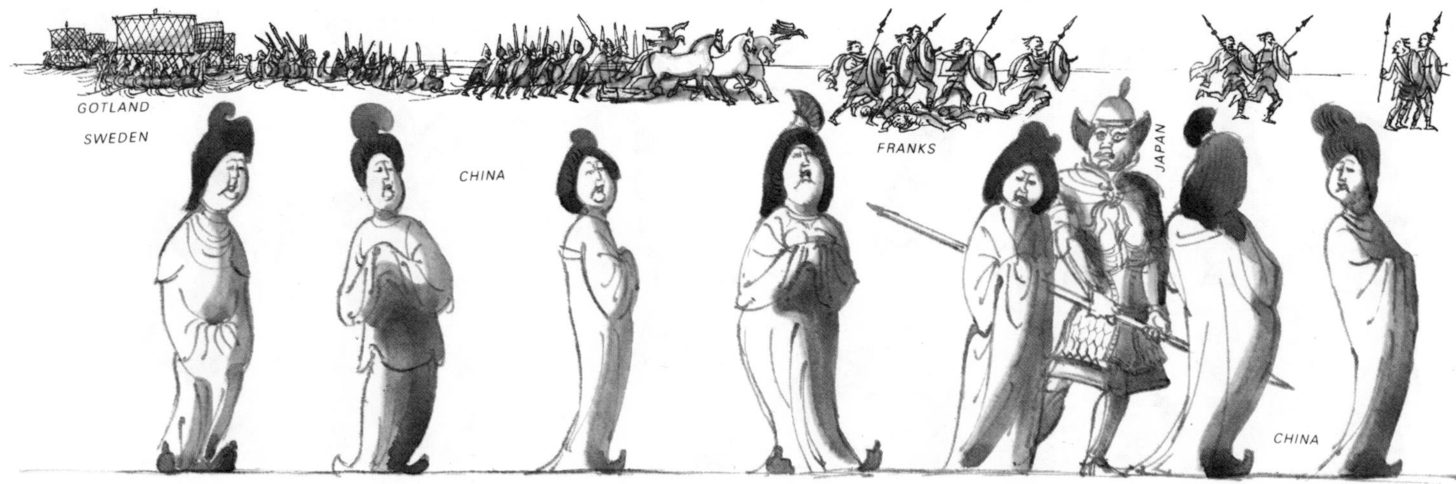
GOTLAND
SWEDEN
CHINA
FRANKS
JAPAN
CHINA

Emperor Leo III, born in Asia, was steeped in the eastern concepts of divinity: God was a spirit and could not be portrayed, so that worshipping the image of God was idolatry. But the Christian Mediterranean world abounded in pictures of Christ and images of the saints. Leo regarded this as an abomination; and he also recognized the persuasive powers of the monks who attributed miraculous qualities to these images. In 726 he ordered his troops to remove all statues and pictures from churches and other places. This naturally aroused opposition, and two theologians from outside the empire vehemently defended the holy images of the Church. One was the church father John of Damascus, who lived and worked in the tolerant court of the caliph; the other was Pope Gregory II, who summoned a council of protest and was punished by being deprived of his ecclesiastical provinces of Sicily, Calabria, Crete and Illyria. At the command of the emperor these were made over to the patriarch in Constantinople. Gregory, who now saw himself as relegated to the equivalent of a Lombard court bishop, made overtures to the Frankish regent Charles Martel – a gesture which later proved to be of major political significance. Leo III meanwhile continued to conduct his campaign against religious art in the Byzantine world. This iconoclasm began in 730 and grew in intensity until 775.

Pelayo, a member of the Gothic royal house deposed in Spain, assembled a few hundred men to combat the Arabs who were already masters of almost the entire country. In a rocky, precipitous place called Covadonga he succeeded with a barrage of arrows and stones, in putting to flight a force twenty times the size of his own. This was a psychologically significant feat which led to the founding of the Christian kingdom of Asturias. Pelayo then established his court at Cangas de Onis on the River Sella and effectively fended off the enemy. At his death, his son Fafila assumed his father's position of authority and royal dignities.

In the mid-720s the Anglo-Saxon missionary Boniface, the apostle of Germany, destroyed the sacred oak of Donnar or Thor at Fritzlar in Hesse. He preached with great success and soon afterwards the pope appointed him Archbishop of Mainz. In conjunction with Gregory II, Boniface organized the German church under Roman supremacy.

The Arabs had conquered the provinces of Sind and Multan in 712 and now Islam was beginning to gain ground in India. Buddhism, formerly very strong here, gradually gave way to the advance of Brahmanism.

In Ireland and at the Irish-founded monastery of Lindisfarne on the English coast, the art of book illustration was unsurpassed. The finest achievement was the magnificent illuminated Latin manuscript known as The Book of Kells. This treasure is today in the possession of Trinity College, Dublin.

Left: an illuminated initial from the Book of Kells. Right: Emperor Xuan Zong marching on a city, 11th century painting from an earlier original.

	721–724	724–730
Bulgars	-----	Sevar
Asturias	Pelayo	
Mercia	Aethelbald	
Caliphate	Yazid II	Hisham
Lombards	Liudpraud	
Franks	Theuderic IV	
Papacy	Gregory II	
Eastern Rome	Leo III	
Japan	Gensho	Shomu
China	Tang Xuan Zong	

721	722	723	724	725	726	727	728	729	730

CENTRAL ASIA
ARABS
CHINA

In Japanese history the years 710-784 are known as the Nara period, after the capital city at this time. The culture was Chinese-influenced and the administration was carefully and very successfully organized on the Chinese model. Buddhist architecture, sculpture and painting flourished and a national literature emerged in Japan, though this was still written in Chinese.

The Frankish regent, Charles Martel, or Carolus Martellus, ruled in the name of the Merovingian king, Theuderic IV. Although Martel omitted to appoint a successor after Theuderic's death, he did not immediately assume power in his own name, dating his documents by the years following the death of the king, not his own reign.

The 8th century was the great age of Chinese lyrical poetry. Li Bo, Du Fu, Wang Wei and Meng Haoran were among those poets who were to achieve lasting fame in the West for their impressionistic verse. Although two subjects, love and honour, were conspicuously absent, this wonderful poetry from the Tang period celebrated friendship and depicted nature in innumerable forms.

The art of the Tang period was also outstanding and some of the great poets, particularly Wang Wei, were equally accomplished calligraphers and painters, though their works have only survived in copy. More enduring was the sculpture of the period; many figurines, as of horses and girls, continue to enchant to this day.

In 733 Charles Martel defeated the Arabs in a great battle at Poitiers, thereby halting their advance into western Europe.

Left: Battle of Poiters, detail from an anonymous painting. Versailles Museum. Below: Tang figurines. Many of these have survived and the quality of the work is remarkable. Horses and camels were popular subjects.

Sevar — Kormisosh	**Bulgars**
Pelayo — Fafila — Alfonso I	**Asturias**
Aethelbald	**Mercia**
Hisham	**Caliphate**
Liudprand	**Lombards**
Theuderic IV — Charles Martel	**Franks**
Gregory III	**Papacy**
Leo III	**Eastern Rome**
Shomu	**Japan**
Tang Xuan Zong	**China**

731	732	733	734	735	736	737	738	739	740

AD 741-750

MAYA, MEXICO

In 746-47 the world was ravaged by bubonic plague. This had originated some years earlier in the Orient and reached the Byzantine empire via Egypt. In Constantinople people died in their thousands, and to maintain authority in the capital the emperor was compelled to call in large numbers of Greeks. These were brought mainly from Peloponnesus and the gap they left was filled by the Slavs. The last remnants of Constantinople's Roman inheritance disappeared and it now became a wholly Greek city.

Emperor Constantine V was an expert in mass deportation. He transferred vast numbers of people from northern Syria to the frontiers of Europe, and he likewise sent large detachments of civilian prisoners-of-war from Armenia and Mesopotamia to the same frontier region as a bulwark against the Bulgars. The Arab threat had passed and the menace to the Byzantine empire now came from this direction.

There was no Bulgarian state in the geographic sense. The frontiers of the Bulgars' sphere of power and settlements were undefined and inconstant.

In 741 Charles Martel divided the Frankish kingdom between his two sons Carloman and Pepin. When he died shortly afterwards they were faced with a revolt and after this demoralizing experience appointed a Merovingian shadow-king, while wielding power themselves in the wings. Their joint rule ended in 747 when Carloman handed over everything to Pepin and himself entered a monastery. Pepin was to be known as Le Bref, the Short.

744 was a year of unrest in the caliphate. Two caliphs, Yazid III and Ibrahim each reigned for a few weeks only and were succeeded by Marwan II who was confronted with insurrections in Damascus and elsewhere. He quelled these risings, but five years later faced a revolution in Kufa where Abu al 'Abbas as-Saffah had proclaimed himself caliph. Marwan II was defeated and killed in Egypt, thereby bringing an end to the Ummayad caliphate in the Orient. The first caliph of the new dynasty, the Abbasids, was as-Saffah, who resided in newly established Baghdad.

A battle of world significance took place in 751 by the River Talas to the north of Tashkent. Here the Arabs, in coalition with various small central Asian states, destroyed a Chinese army, so that China's hold over central Asia rapidly disintegrated. There was now an insurrection in China itself, led by a general named An Lushan. Emperor Xuan Zong was forced to flee, the royal guards lynched his prime minister, and he himself was compelled to kill his favourite concubine Gui Fei. Gui Fei's tragic fate remained a popular theme in Chinese literature through the centuries, for she had been the patron of the Changan court poets and writers who, until the battle of Talas, enjoyed favour and prosperity. They now lived in poverty.

A census conducted in 754 showed that at this time there were 9,069,154 families in China, totalling 52,880,488 people. The corresponding figures ten years later were 2,900,000 families and 16,900,000 people. The reason for this decline was the An Lushan insurrection which lasted eight years and caused political chaos and starvation.

Zacharias was the last of the Greek popes. He was a prudent politician who retained good relations with the real rulers of the Frankish kingdom.

Musicians and dancers on an elephant, Tang painting on a musical instrument. National Museum, Tokyo.

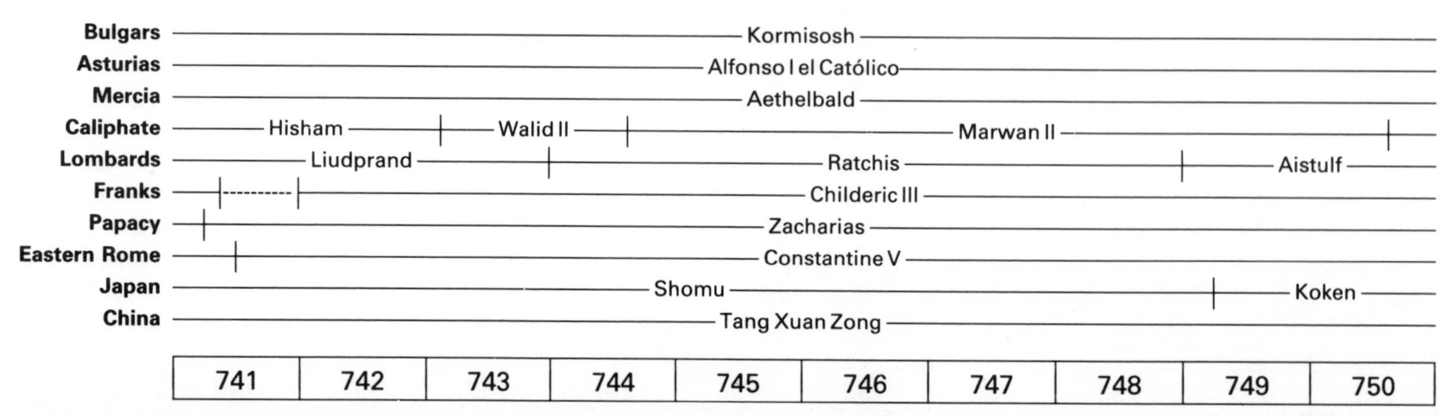
Bulgars
Kormisosh
Asturias
Alfonso I el Católico
Mercia
Aethelbald
Caliphate
Hisham
Walid II
Marwan II
Lombards
Liudprand
Ratchis
Aistulf
Franks
Childeric III
Papacy
Zacharias
Eastern Rome
Constantine V
Japan
Shomu
Koken
China
Tang Xuan Zong
741
742
743
744
745
746
747
748
749
750

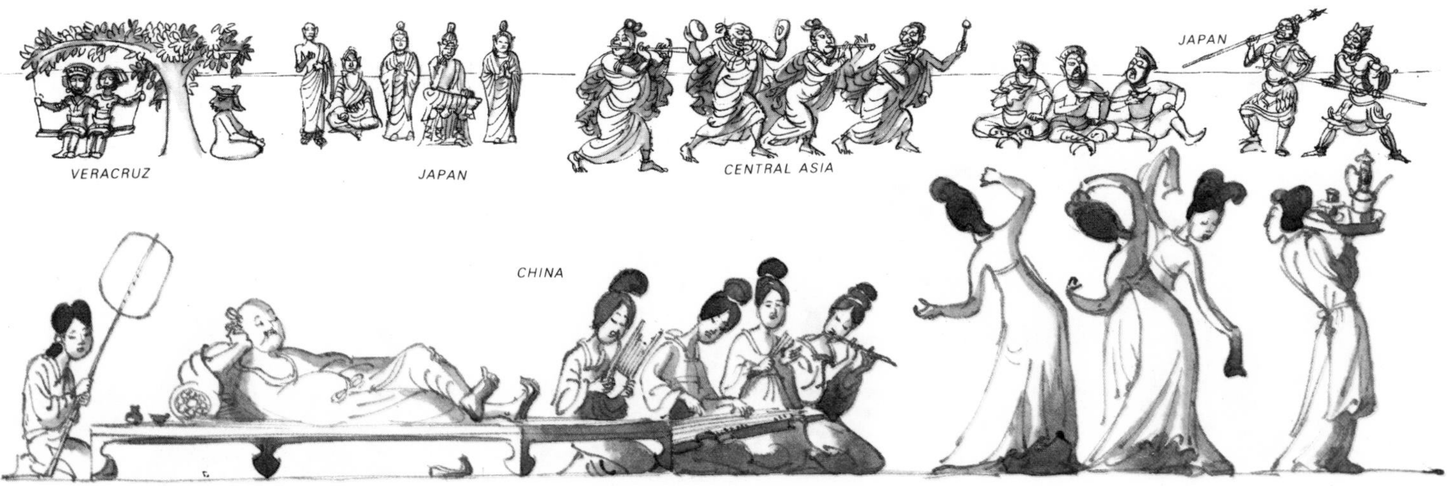
VERACRUZ
JAPAN
CENTRAL ASIA
JAPAN
CHINA

In 751 the Lombards seized the Byzantine exarchate of Ravenna and in the same year the last Merovingian was deposed by the major domus Pepin the Short, who then formally proclaimed himself head of the Frankish realm. Pepin received a visit from Pope Stephen II, seeking aid against the Lombards besieging Rome. Pepin was eager to help and after a series of defeats the Lombards were compelled to sue for peace. They now had to surrender Ravenna and the adjoining provinces, all of which Pepin handed over to the pope, on condition that he himself was named Roman patricius and overall protector. This gave rise to the temporal Papal State.

Raiatea, in the Society Islands, is reputed to have been the starting point for extensive voyages of discovery and colonizing expeditions in the South Seas. In their very seaworthy, twin-hulled canoes, some of which could carry over 100 men, the Polynesians spread out eastward, northward and southward. The names of some of these seafarers have survived: a certain Rata discovered the Paumotu islands while a leader named Rangiora sailed southward from Raratonga right down to the Antarctic.

Alfonso the Catholic was an important name in Spanish history. With patience and determination he expanded his little Asturian kingdom in the north and created a kind of no-man's-land between this and the Arabs' caliphate.

An Ummayad prince name 'Abd ar-Rahman survived the Abbasid revolution and fled to Spain. He naturally refused to recognize as-Saffah, and proclaimed himself caliph. This disrupted the Arab empire, but the Ummayads' Spanish kingdom became an important power. Nevertheless, 'Abd ar-Rahman was compelled to cede the province of Narbonne to the Franks to ensure peace in this quarter. 'Abd ar-Rahman settled in Cordoba which became the centre of a new caliphate, in addition to that of Baghdad.

The so-called Azandian culture was flourishing in the interior of East Africa. The Azandes were not a homogenous people but the artefacts in this region had common characteristics. The Azandes had discovered iron, and were competent smiths, stonemasons, road-builders and farmers.

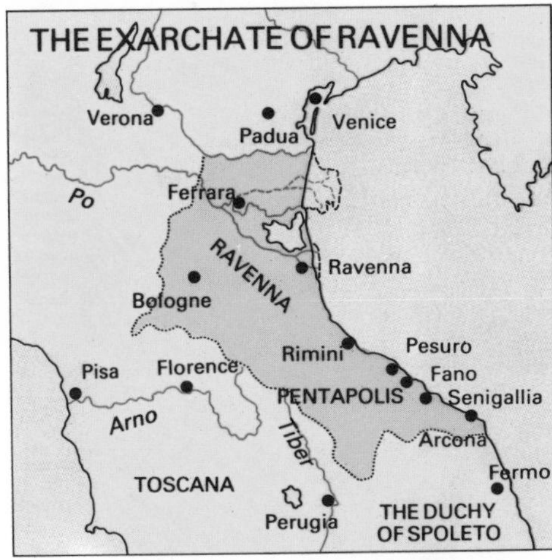
THE EXARCHATE OF RAVENNA
Verona
Padua
Venice
Po
Ferrara
RAVENNA
Ravenna
Bologne
Rimini
Pesuro
Pisa
Florence
Fano
PENTAPOLIS
Senigallia
Arno
Tiber
Arcona
Fermo
TOSCANA
Perugia
THE DUCHY OF SPOLETO

Left: Pepin the Short, illustration in a medieval manuscript. Through Pepin III the Lombard king, Aistulf, was compelled to surrender to Pope Stephen II the cities of Ravenna, Rimini, Urbino, Ancona, Faenza, Imola, Ferrara and Bologna, along with their adjoining lands. In this way most of the ancient Byzantine exarchate passed into the possession of the papacy and formed the foundation of the future Papal State. The political relationship between the papal realm and Pepin the Short's successors survived until 1870.

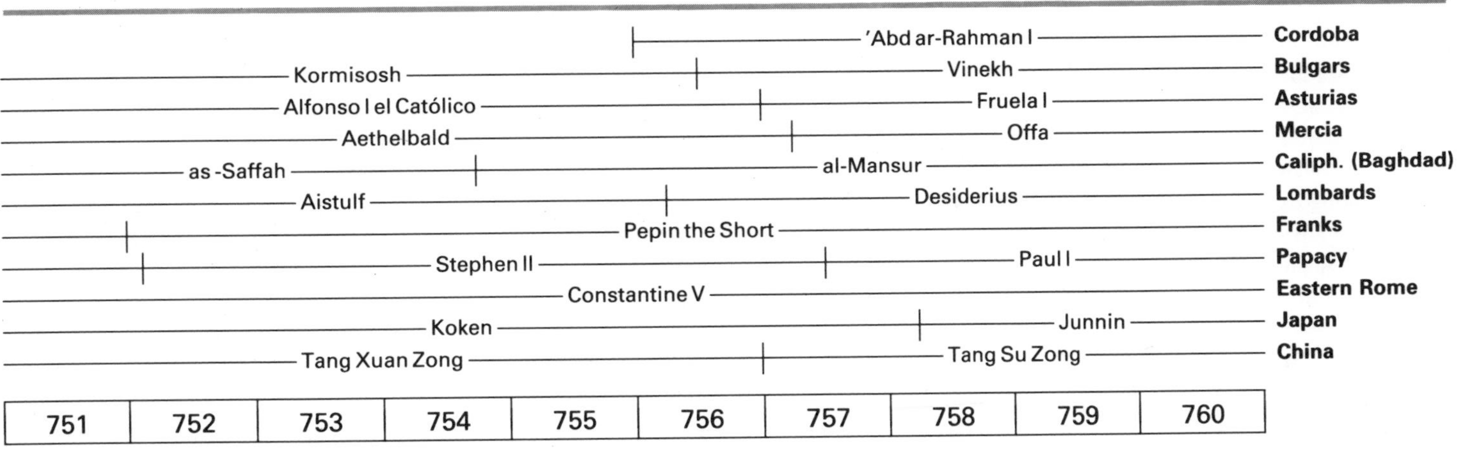
'Abd ar-Rahman I — Cordoba
Kormisosh — Vinekh — Bulgars
Alfonso I el Católico — Fruela I — Asturias
Aethelbald — Offa — Mercia
as-Saffah — al-Mansur — Caliph. (Baghdad)
Aistulf — Desiderius — Lombards
Pepin the Short — Franks
Stephen II — Paul I — Papacy
Constantine V — Eastern Rome
Koken — Junnin — Japan
Tang Xuan Zong — Tang Su Zong — China
751 752 753 754 755 756 757 758 759 760

AD 761-770

ENGLAND
CHINA
JAPAN

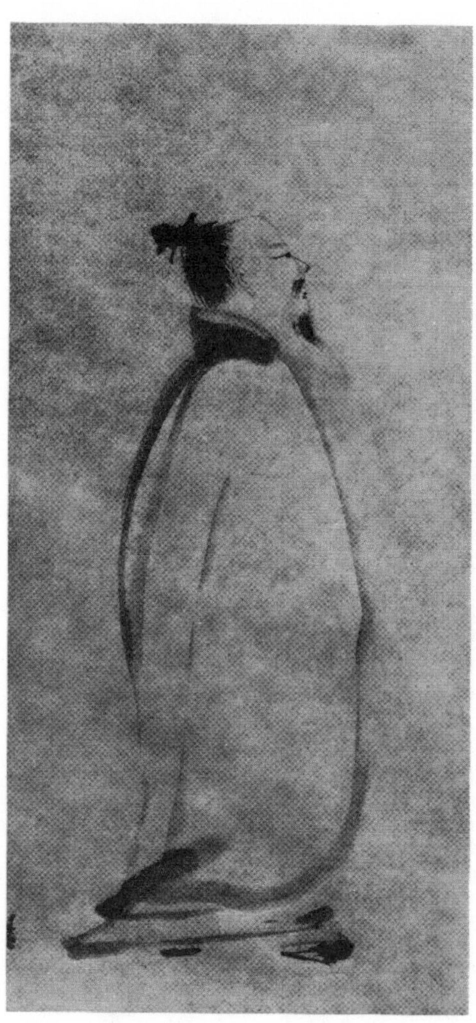

The poet Li Bo died in 762, his colleague Du Fu in 770. An Lushan's insurrection, ill-fated for both these poets, was finally suppressed in 766. This was achieved with the aid of a Turkic tribe known as the Uighurs, whose national religion, oddly enough, was Manichaeism. The Tang dynasty was thus restored, though it lacked its former power and splendour, for the administration had disintegrated and commerce was slack. Moreover the Uighurs demanded ample repayment for their services. Tibetan hordes had also run riot in China during these calamitous years and in 763 they entered and plundered the capital Changan.

At the begining of the 18th century, the collected works of the Tang poets were published in China. These comprised 48,900 poems in 900 volumes by at least 3000 authors, the majority of whom had done their best work after the An Lushan revolt. Little of the contemporary political drama was reflected in this writing, though there was one exception, Du Fu, whose verse tells of devastated villages, broken families and bleached bones on distant battlefields, loneliness and homesickness. It is said that Du Fu was found starving by his friends; he was set at a table filled with good food and proceeded to eat himself to death.

In 766 the most faithful followers of Zoroaster in Persia, persecuted by the Muslims, fled to India.

Shotoku was identical with the empress, Koken, who ruled Japan in the 750s. For her second reign she changed her name.

Following the death of Pope Paul I, an Italian duke named Toto interfered in the papal elections and arbitrarily appointed his brother pope as Constantine II. This impelled Desiderius, the Lombard king, to intervene and he also appointed a pope, Philip. War broke out on this issue and Constantine was captured and blinded while his supporters were ruthlessly pursued. Philip then resigned voluntarily and a new papal election took place, in accordance with the prescribed rules.

Left, the poet Li Bo painted by Liang Gai (14th century). Right, a relief from the Kailasa temple in Ellora, dedicated to Vishnu.

Bulgars - Vinekh | Telets | Sabin | Pagan -------- Umor | Tokt --------
Cordoba — 'Abd ar-Rahman I —
Asturias — Fruela I — | Aurelio —
Mercia — Offa —
Baghdad — al-Mansur —
Lombards — Desiderius —
Franks — Pepin the Short — | Charles & Carloman —
Papacy — Paul I — | -------- | Stephen III —
Eastern Rome — Constantine V —
Japan — Junnin — | Shotoku — |
China — Tang Su Zong — | Tang Dai Zong —

761	762	763	764	765	766	767	768	769	770

AD 771-780

FRANCE
JAVA
CHINA
MAYA

Charlemagne (Carlus Magnus or Charles the Great) was originally king of Neustria only, but when his brother Carloman died in 771 he took control of the entire Frankish empire.

In 774 Charlemagne finally defeated the Lombards, crowned himself with their famous iron crown in Pavia and seized their territory. This was the end of Lombards as an independent kingdom.

Four years later, Charlemagne went to war against the Arabs in Spain. He incorporated all the country between the Pyrenees and the Ebro into his own empire, but in the Basque pass of Roncesvalles his forces were attacked by the enemy and almost destroyed. Among those who died here was the Breton knight, Roland, best known in literature as the hero of Ariosto's long epic poem, *Orlando Furioso*.

In the Byzantine empire the iconoclasts were more active than ever. Emperor Constantine V made resolute efforts to free the realm of detested monks and idolators. All resistance was ruthlessly suppressed, many people died, and the images of the saints and in particular those of Christ disappeared entirely from the churches.

This conflict separated the Eastern church from the Roman church.

The essential features of the Papal State were established during this decade. A product of the alliance between the pope and the Frankish king against the Byzantines and the Lombards, it was to survive for 1100 years.

Durga is the spouse of the god Shiva in Indian mythology. She is also known as Parvati, Kali, etc., sometimes depicted as a terrifying creature, sometimes as a propitiatory spirit. She was worshipped with both animal and human sacrifices. This head of Durga, part of a large sculptural group, is from the Tapa Sardar temple in Ghazni, Afghanistan.

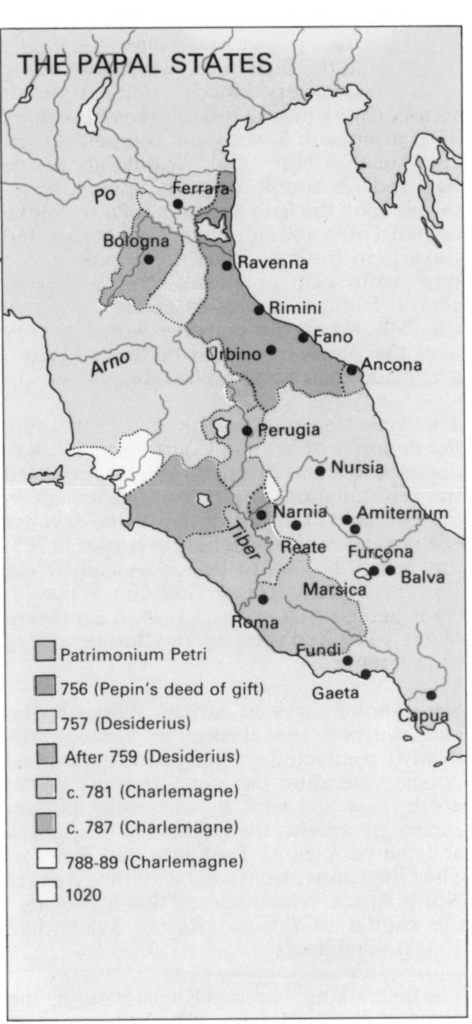
THE PAPAL STATES
Po
Ferrara
Bologna
Ravenna
Rimini
Fano
Urbino
Ancona
Arno
Perugia
Nursia
Narnia
Amiternum
Tiber
Reate
Furcona
Balva
Marsica
Roma
Fundi
Gaeta
Capua
Patrimonium Petri
756 (Pepin's deed of gift)
757 (Desiderius)
After 759 (Desiderius)
c. 781 (Charlemagne)
c. 787 (Charlemagne)
788-89 (Charlemagne)
1020

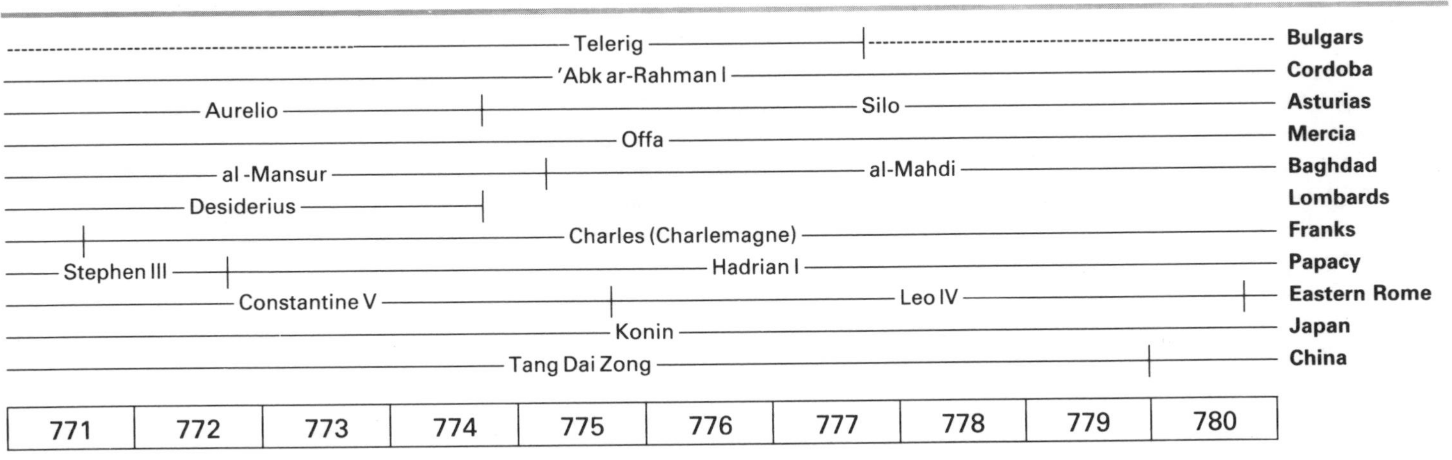
Telerig
Bulgars
'Abk ar-Rahman I
Cordoba
Aurelio
Silo
Asturias
Offa
Mercia
al-Mansur
al-Mahdi
Baghdad
Desiderius
Lombards
Charles (Charlemagne)
Franks
Stephen III
Hadrian I
Papacy
Constantine V
Leo IV
Eastern Rome
Konin
Japan
Tang Dai Zong
China
771
772
773
774
775
776
777
778
779
780

AD 781-790

BYZANTIUM
SCANDINAVIA
CHINA
MAYA, MEXICO
CHARLEMAGNE

For thirty-two years Charlemagne fought the Saxons and the final battle which took place in 763 was a very bloody affair. After his victory Charlemagne is said to have executed 4500 prominent Saxons and compelled their chieftains Alboin and Widukind to be baptized. A couple of years later, Charlemagne took the field against a Bavarian duke named Totila and subsequently incorporated Bavaria in the vast Frankish empire, which now embraced practically the whole of central Europe. It was extended farther in the 790s, when the emperor won a victory over the Avars in a great battle at Theisss, and made their khan his vassal.

The Byzantine empress, Irene, regent during the minority of her son Constantine IV, was opposed to iconoclasm and quietly permitted the reinstallation of pictures and images in the churches. On her initiative the seventh ecumenical council was held in Nicaea in 787, this being the last to be recognized by the Eastern church. Roman and Greek theologians agreed that ecclesiastical images were divinely inspired symbols and thus deserving of reverence.

Sisse Tunkare was an African politician who had usurped the throne in Ghana. His dynasty conducted an energetic expansionist policy, extending the state frontiers to the north, east and west by successful military campaigns against the Berbers in the Sahara and the peoples of Timbuktu and Senegal. The Ghanaians also traded with the Arabs in North Africa, who disclosed that at this time the capital of Ghana, Kumbi Saleh, had 30,000 inhabitants.

The first Vikings reached England during the reign of King Offa, in 793. The monks of Lindisfarne were harvesting their hay when they suddenly observed ships approaching their small island. An armed band rushed ashore, demanding booty, and when the monks resisted they were at once cut down. The invaders plundered the monastery and then destroyed it totally.

The caliph Harun ar-Rashid, principal character in *'A Thousand and One Nights'*, ruled, in fact, over a crumbling kingdom. Although he enjoyed some military success against the Byzantines whose empire was in temporary decline, the governor of Kairouan simultaneously set up his own caliphate in Tunisia and no longer accepted orders from Baghdad. He was beset by domestic problems. One day, for some unknown reason, Harun ordered the execution of the grand vizier, Ja'far and continued to persecute his entire family.

The Chinese art of making paper reached Baghdad in 793, almost 700 years after its discovery in the East.

A considerable body of Latin literature was available at Charlemagne's court in Aachen and elsewhere in the kingdom. The man responsible for assembling this was the emperor's English-born adviser Alcuin, who not only headed the court's official school but also established schools in all the large towns of the empire. Carolingian literature consisted of theological texts and chronicles, as well as a very readable biography of Charlemagne and his family by Einhard.

In 781 Charlemagne went to Rome where he made his son Pepin king of Italy.

Sculptured column at Copan, Central America, dated 782.

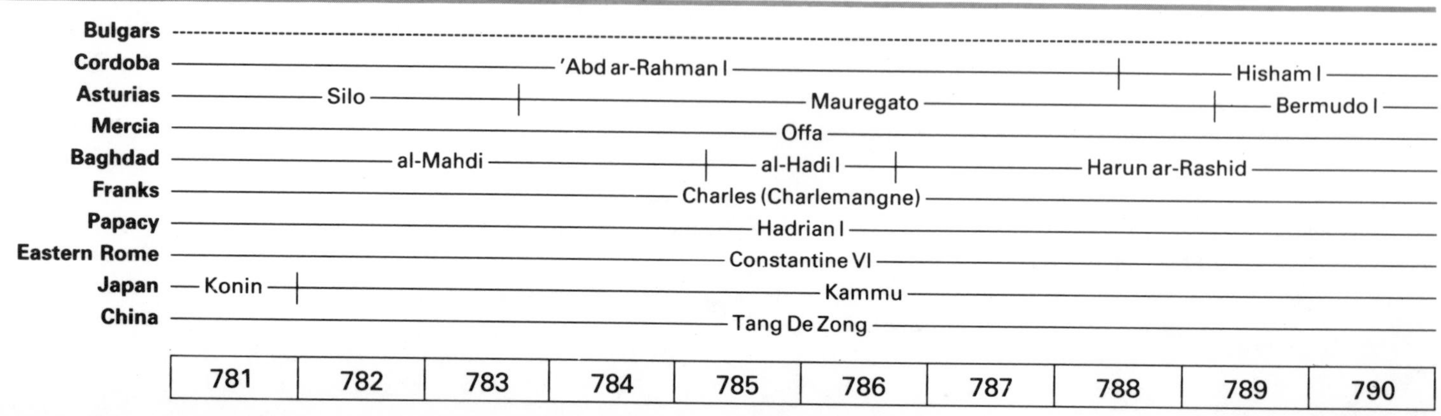
Bulgars
Cordoba
'Abd ar-Rahman I
Hisham I
Asturias
Silo
Mauregato
Bermudo I
Mercia
Offa
Baghdad
al-Mahdi
al-Hadi I
Harun ar-Rashid
Franks
Charles (Charlemangne)
Papacy
Hadrian I
Eastern Rome
Constantine VI
Japan
Konin
Kammu
China
Tang De Zong
781
782
783
784
785
786
787
788
789
790

MAYA, MEXICO

When he came of age, Emperor Constantine VI endeavoured to throw off the overbearing authority of his mother, but events conspired against his popularity. After being defeated by the Bulgars and forced to flee home, he fell in love with a lady of the court and duly celebrated a boisterous wedding with her directly after securing a separation from his former wife. Thus when his mother decided to depose him and reassume power, not a hand was raised in his defence. Arrested and bound, his eyes were put out at his mother's order in the same purple state-room where she had given birth to him twenty-seven years earlier.

Shortly afterwards, following a ceremonious Te Deum, Empress Irene appeared in imperial attire in a vehicle drawn by four white horses, tossing coronation coins to the obediently cheering crowds. She also assumed the masculine titles autocrator and basileus, dictator and king, which no reigning empress had ever dared do before. Although it was generally accepted at this time that there could be but one Christian imperial representative, the Frankish Charlemagne chose in these bizarre circumstances to regard the imperial throne as vacant.

In 795 the so-called Spanish March was founded on the frontier with the Arab empire. Here Frankish and Gothic counts ruled an area which extended from Pamplona and the upper Ebro to the district of Barcelona, though the latter city was not conquered until early in the next century.

The fall of the Lombard kingdom did not affect the duchy of Benevento in southern Italy, and a Frankish expedition in this area achieved no lasting effect.

Leo III's first gesture after being appointed pope was to send to the Frankish king the keys of St Peter's tomb and the standard of Rome. He also ordered a mosaic, in which the apostle was portrayed between the king and himself, for the Lateran. But Leo III had enemies in Rome; in 799 they attempted to assassinate him and, severely mauled, he fled to his royal patron in Paderborn. Envoys of the opposing party followed him and accused him, apparently with some justification, of loose living. In the autumn of 800 both the pope and the king were in Rome. The latter initiated an enquiry into the matter, while in St. Peter's the pope publicly took an oath of innocence. Two days later, on Christmas Day 800, he crowned Charlemagne emperor and knelt before him. The emperor is said to have been taken by surprise, having no wish to receive his crown from an obsequious pope.

The coronation of Charlemagne was significant insomuch as it conflicted with the political concept of a single Christian imperial authority. Hitherto any such division of power had been regarded as merely temporary, but clearly this was no longer the case.

The Byzantine chronicler Theophanes, basically a supporter of Irene's policy, was nevertheless appalled by the empress's treatment of her son. He claimed that the Sun did not shine for seventeen days after her accession to supreme power as a sign of disapproval. He also alleged that marriage was considered between Irene and Charlemagne with a view to the reunification of east and west. This is a contemporary portrait of the Empress Irene, carved in ivory. Museo Nazionale del Bargello, Florence.

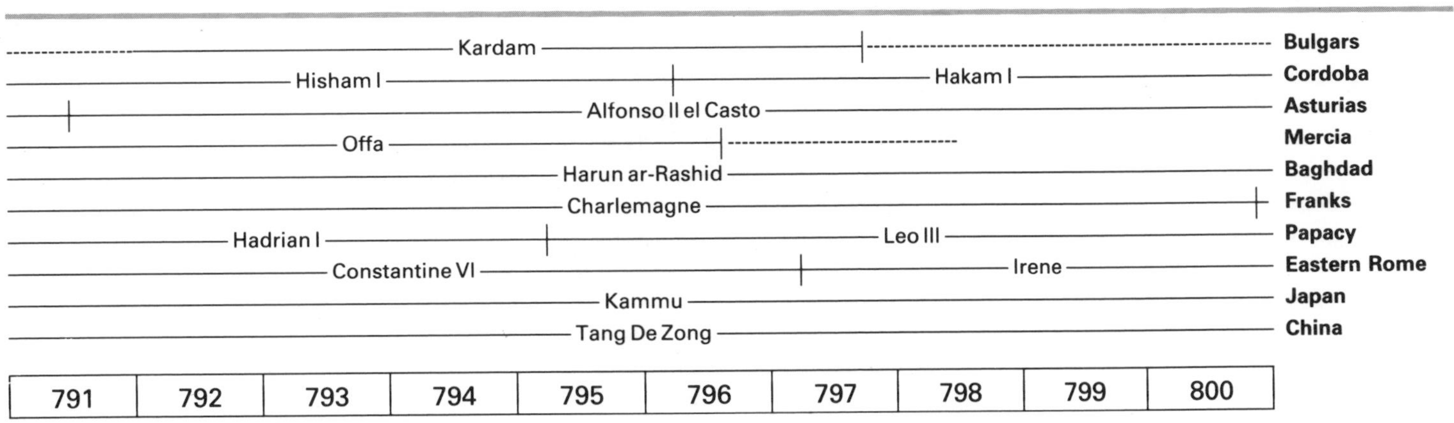
Kardam
Bulgars
Hisham I
Hakam I
Cordoba
Alfonso II el Casto
Asturias
Offa
Mercia
Harun ar-Rashid
Baghdad
Charlemagne
Franks
Hadrian I
Leo III
Papacy
Constantine VI
Irene
Eastern Rome
Kammu
Japan
Tang De Zong
China
791
792
793
794
795
796
797
798
799
800

SCANDINAVIA

In 801 the Spanish caliphate lost Barcelona to the Franks.

Charlemagne's seal bore the Latin Legend *Renovatio Romani Imperii,* Restoration of the Roman Empire. The abbreviation Imp. Rom. which was to appear among the lists of rulers right through until the 19th century, can be interpreted either as *Imperium Romanum* or *Imperator Romanus*. In general the latter was probably more apt, for it was really no more than a title.

In 808 Charlemagne became involved in a war with the Danish king Godfred who had assisted the Saxons, and here, one might claim, Nordic history began.

The famous monastery on the island of Iona off the west coast of Scotland was plundered by the Vikings in 802. The religious centre of the Scottish clans was now moved to the mainland, thereby facilitating their unification.

In 810 the Persian mathematician Muhammad ibn Musa al-Khwarizmi produced an equation system which gave the world the term 'algebra'.

Emperor Nicephorus I in Constantinople did not, of course, recognize Charlemagne's imperial accession and also challenged him over more practical issues, especially concerning influence in Venice, a city that was now becoming politically important. Nicephorus was likewise on bad terms with the caliph, Harun ar - Rashid who, on the pretext of a revolt in Asia, invaded Cyprus, Rhodes and numerous Byzantine towns and fortresses on the mainland. Under the terms of the subsequent peace treaty Byzantium was required to pay tribute to the caliphate, and the emperor compelled personally to pay a humiliating tax of three gold coins annually to the caliph.

Charlemagne's spiritual adivser, Alcuin, was a considerable poet, an eminent theologian and an experienced teacher whose ideas and institutions were to be of major significance to coming generations. Various of his pupils also achieved renown, one example being Rabanus Maurus who in time became principal of the school and subsequently abbot of Fulda and Archbishop of Mainz. Maurus was also an accomplished Latin poet.

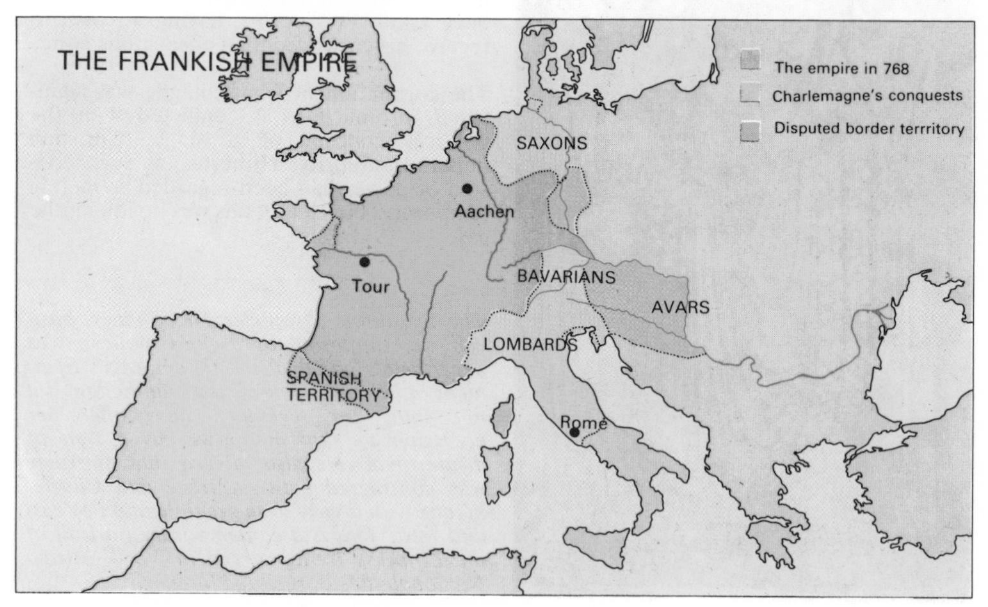
THE FRANKISH EMPIRE
The empire in 768
Charlemagne's conquests
Disputed border terrritory
SAXONS
Aachen
Tour
BAVARIANS
AVARS
LOMBARDS
SPANISH TERRITORY
Rome

The Frankish empire was a conglomerate of many countries and peoples and not even Charlemagne himself believed it could be unified. Thus in 806 he presented a plan to divide the empire up among his sons. There were no real officials nor proper state administration, while counts and margraves were given arbitrary feudal powers.

Denmark	Godfred
Bulgars	Krum
Cordoba	Hakam I
Asturias	Alfonso II el Casto
Baghdad	Harun ar-Rashid — al-Amin
Holy Rom. Emp.	Charlemagne
Papacy	Leo III
Eastern Rome	Irene — Nicephorus
Japan	Kammu — Heijo — Saga
China	Tang De Zong — Tang Xian Zong

801	802	803	804	805	806	807	808	809	810

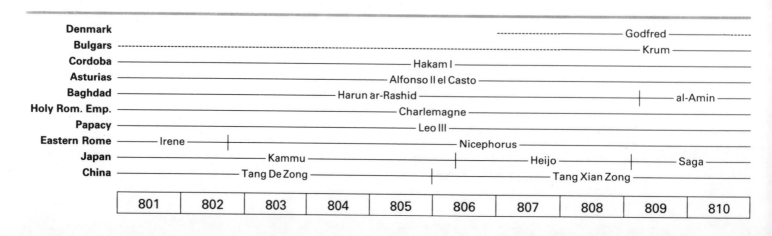

CAROLINGIAN EMPIRE
SCANDINAVIA

When Charlemagne destroyed the Avar kingdom, the tributary Bulgars joined their kinsmen in the Balkan peninsula where a chieftain named Krum became ruler of a new state. In the spring of 809 Krum conducted a successful surprise attack on Serdica, modern Sofia, one of the most important points in the Byzantine fortification line against the West. Emperor Nicephorus personally led his army against Krum, routed him and pursued him into the Balkan mountains. Here, however, he rashly entered a mountain pass which the Bulgars promptly sealed off at each end and then proceeded to annihilate the entire Byzantine army. Emperor Nicephorus was slain and Krum made a wine goblet of his skull.

In 809 or 810 the inhabitants of the Venetian islands turned Rivoalto into a naval base and the capital of their confederation.

Godfred's nephew and successor Hemming made peace with Charlemagne in 811. The Eidar was fixed as Denmark's southern boundary.

In Swedish Emperor Ludovicus or Louis I was known as Louis the Pious. At a diet in Aachen in 817 he divided the vast Frankish empire between his three sons so that the youngest, Louis or Ludvig, received Bavaria, the middle son, Pepin, got Aquitaine, i.e. the territory between the Loire and the Pyrenees, and the oldest Lotharius, Lothaire or Lothar became co-emperor and co-regent of the entire empire. This arrangement was resented by many, particularly Bernard who was the son Louis's elder brother and king of the Italian provinces. Bernard led a revolt but was seized and slain by having his eyes put out. The Italian provinces were then added to Lothar's realm.

Led by their war-like monarch Khri-srong-ide-bean, the Tibetans had made conquests both eastward and westward in central Asia, but in 802 they were severely defeated by the Chinese, who had formed an alliance with the caliph of Baghdad against their common enemy. During the forthcoming decades peace was established on both fronts, and thereafter Tibet became Buddhist and its policy increasingly pacific.

Emperor Xian Zong, a fervent Buddhist, had acquired one of the finger-bones of Buddha from an Indian monastery and exhibited this relic in the capital; it caused the Confucian philosopher Han Yu to compose an address of protest against this alien superstition. Han Yu was the founder of a doctrine embracing a number of Gnostic ideas but which related above all to the Mencian concept of the inherent faculties of human nature. By presenting Mencius as the only true successor of Confucius, he invested Confucianism with the authoritative substance it had formerly lacked.

The Bulgar khan, Krum, at the head of an enormous army and with a column of Byzantine prisoners whom he proposed using as a live battering ram, was about to storm Constantinople when he died of a haemorrhage. His son Omurtag concluded a peace treaty with the Byzantines and Emperor Leo V could now devote himself to other matters. He renewed the ban on idol-worship and once again had his churches cleared of these images.

During a war in Japan between 802-812, the Ainu people were totally suppressed.

A more or less contemporary statue of Charlemagne, in the Louvre, Paris. His biographer Einhard lists his many merits. His eating and drinking habits were modest, but he enjoyed reading at table. He never learned how to write, but was an excellent speaker, even in Latin.

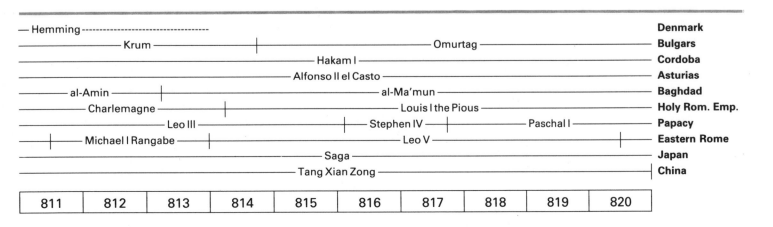

— Hemming ---------------------------------- **Denmark**
——— Krum ———|——— Omurtag ——— **Bulgars**
——— Hakam I ——— **Cordoba**
——— Alfonso II el Casto ——— **Asturias**
——— al-Amin ———|——— al-Ma'mun ——— **Baghdad**
——— Charlemagne ———|——— Louis I the Pious ——— **Holy Rom. Emp.**
——— Leo III ———|——— Stephen IV ———|——— Paschal I ——— **Papacy**
———|——— Michael I Rangabe ———|——— Leo V ———|——— **Eastern Rome**
——— Saga ——— **Japan**
——— Tang Xian Zong ———| **China**

811	812	813	814	815	816	817	818	819	820

An admiral named Euphemius led a revolt against Byzantine authority in Sicily and proclaimed himself emperor. When he encountered resistance, however, he turned for help to the Aghlabite Emir of Tunis, offering him Sicily as a tax-paying province on condition that he himself was allowed to remain emperor and rule the country. The emir agreed and sent over a professional army of 10,000 men. Palermo fell in 831 and the Arabs thereby established a foodhold in Sicily.

Paschal I was an exacting, energetic pope who succeeded in compelling Louis the Pious to recognize papal sovereignty over the Papal State.

A Danish prince name Harald Klak fled the kingdom in 826 and came to the court of Louis the Pious where he was baptized. The following year he returned home, bringing with him the Frankish monk Ansgar to preach Christianity in Denmark. But at home Harald Klak's authority was insecure and short-lived; King Godfred's son, Haarik, who drove him out, was uninterested in Ansgar's Christian message. Ansgar then turned to the Sveas around Lake Mälar in Central Sweden. In 830 he visited the town of Birka and was received by a king named Björn. Ansgar's mission had no enduring effect in this region even though he was to go down in history as the apostle of the North. He appears to have been a competent organizer and ended his days as Archbishop of Hamburg-Bremen, a diocese and mission centre which also embraced the Nordic countries.

In 826 an Arab fleet reached Crete and put ashore a force which quickly conquered the island. They had sailed from Egypt, having secured a foothold there after being expelled from the Spanish caliphate of Cordoba. In the following year these Arabs attacked and occupied Sicily, and also seized Sardinia.

Emperor Louis the Pious, Louis le Debonnaire, receives messengers from the iconoclast, Emperor Leo V, who was murdered on Christmas morning 799 in Hagia Sophia.

Pope Paschal I between St Praxedes and St Paul. Mosaic in the 9th century St Prassede Church, Rome.

A Croatian state was being formed following a revolt by a certain Lyudevit led against the Franks shortly before 823. Croatia was ruled by the margraves of Friuli and the patriarch of Aquileia. In 823-838 the Bulgars intervened; after their previous successes against by Byzantines, their prestige was high among the Balkan Slavs. The Serbs also showed a temporary interest in some form of union.

Emperor Theophilus was the last of the Byzantine iconoclasts. He was a highly educated man who had been influenced by Arab art and culture as developed under the Baghdad caliphs.

A pope name Valentine held office for a few weeks in 827.

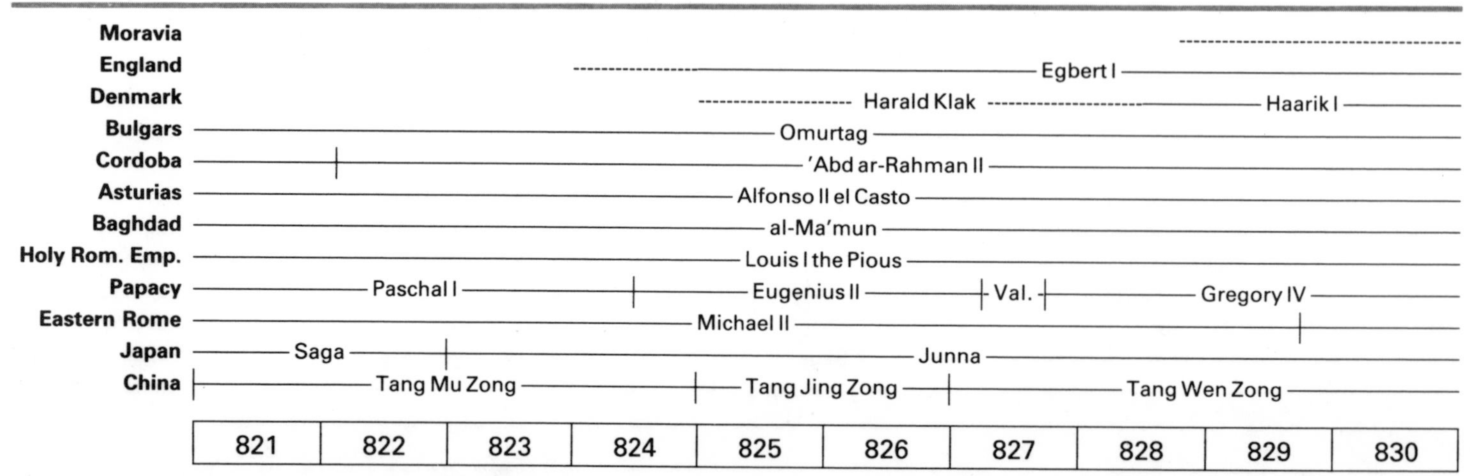
Moravia
England
Egbert I
Denmark
Harald Klak
Haarik I
Bulgars
Omurtag
Cordoba
'Abd ar-Rahman II
Asturias
Alfonso II el Casto
Baghdad
al-Ma'mun
Holy Rom. Emp.
Louis I the Pious
Papacy
Paschal I
Eugenius II
Val.
Gregory IV
Eastern Rome
Michael II
Japan
Saga
Junna
China
Tang Mu Zong
Tang Jing Zong
Tang Wen Zong
821
822
823
824
825
826
827
828
829
830

CAROLINGIANS
CENTRAL ASIA
IRAQ

The history of the Frankish empire became increasingly complicated. In 829 Emperor Louis created a new kingdom, Alamannia, for his six-year-old son Charles, but this angered the child's half-brothers Pepin and Lothair. They took up arms against their father who was supported by his next to youngest son, known in history as Louis le Germanique (Louis the German). In this first round the emperor was victorious. Lothair was deprived of his joint-imperial dignity and continued merely as king of Italy. A few years later, however, these three sons resolved their differences and jointly made war on their father and young brother Charles - later to be know as Charles le Chauve (Charles the Bald) The rebel sons were aided in their cause by Pope Gregory IV who was supposed to act as a peace mediator. By the time the armies were drawn up for battle, almost all the emperor's knights had deserted him for the other side. Emperor Louis was defeated and deposed; but soon afterwards the brothers fell out again, so that their father was released from captivity and restored to the imperial throne. Then Pepin died, his two sons were barred from the succession, Louis the German had his kingdom reduced to Bavaria alone, and the rest of the Frankish empire was divided up between Lothair and Charles. Louis the German now prepared for war with his father and brothers, but before the campaign could begin the old emperor died.

By the 830s the kingdom of Moravia, founded sometime in the late 8th century, was an important power both politically and culturally. Its kings, who had been vassals of Charlemagne, gained their independence during the reign of his successor and established contact instead with both the Byzantine and Bulgar empires. Moravia covered quite a large area from the Oder to the Tatra mountains.

Caliph al-Ma'mun, a man of culture, arranged for the systematic translation of Greek writings into Arabic. In this manner the scientific inheritance of antiquity, forsaken in western Europe, survived and progressed.

In 825 Egbert of Wessex in England defeated the king of Mercia and annexed the latter's kingdom. Two years later he likewise defeated Northumbria, thereby unifying the seven small English kingdoms. Egbert now called himself King of Angelland.

During the 820s the Vikings had formed a state around Dublin in Ireland. In the 830s they began invading the east coast of England in earnest.

The great poet Bo Juyi (772-846) was at work in China.

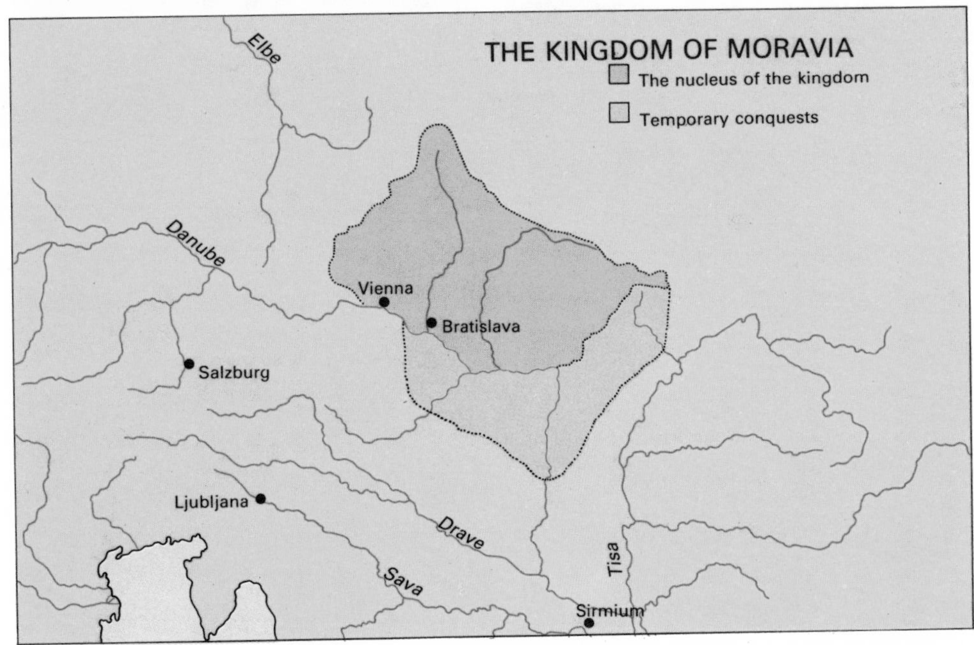
THE KINGDOM OF MORAVIA
The nucleus of the kingdom
Temporary conquests
Elbe
Danube
Vienna
Bratislava
Salzburg
Ljubljana
Drave
Sava
Tisa
Sirmium

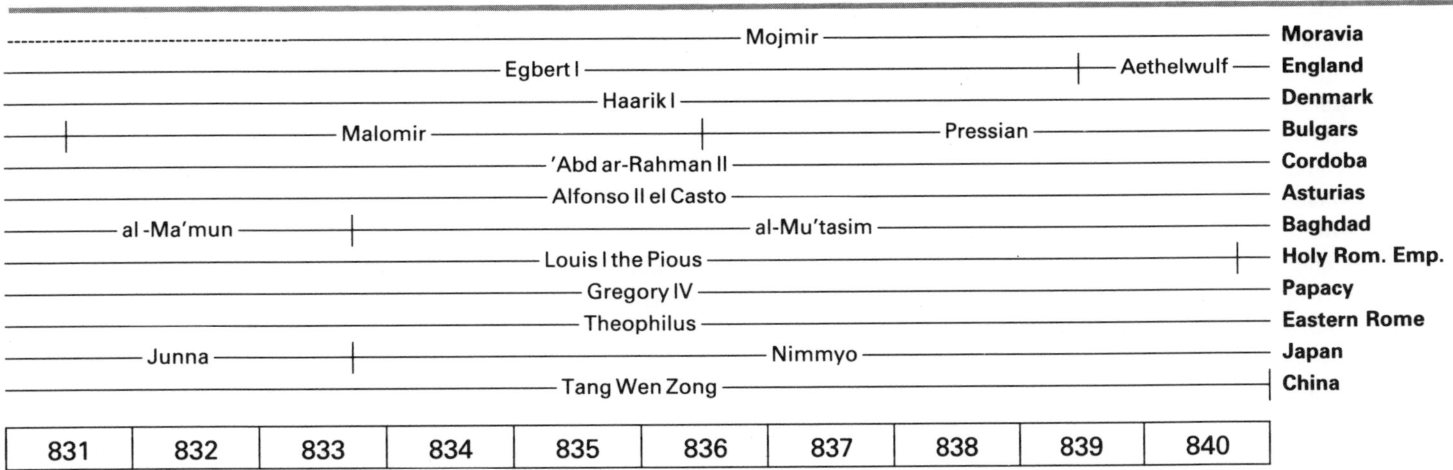
Mojmir — Moravia
Egbert I — Aethelwulf — England
Haarik I — Denmark
Malomir — Pressian — Bulgars
'Abd ar-Rahman II — Cordoba
Alfonso II el Casto — Asturias
al-Ma'mun — al-Mu'tasim — Baghdad
Louis I the Pious — Holy Rom. Emp.
Gregory IV — Papacy
Theophilus — Eastern Rome
Junna — Nimmyo — Japan
Tang Wen Zong — China
831
832
833
834
835
836
837
838
839
840

AD 841-850

FRANKS

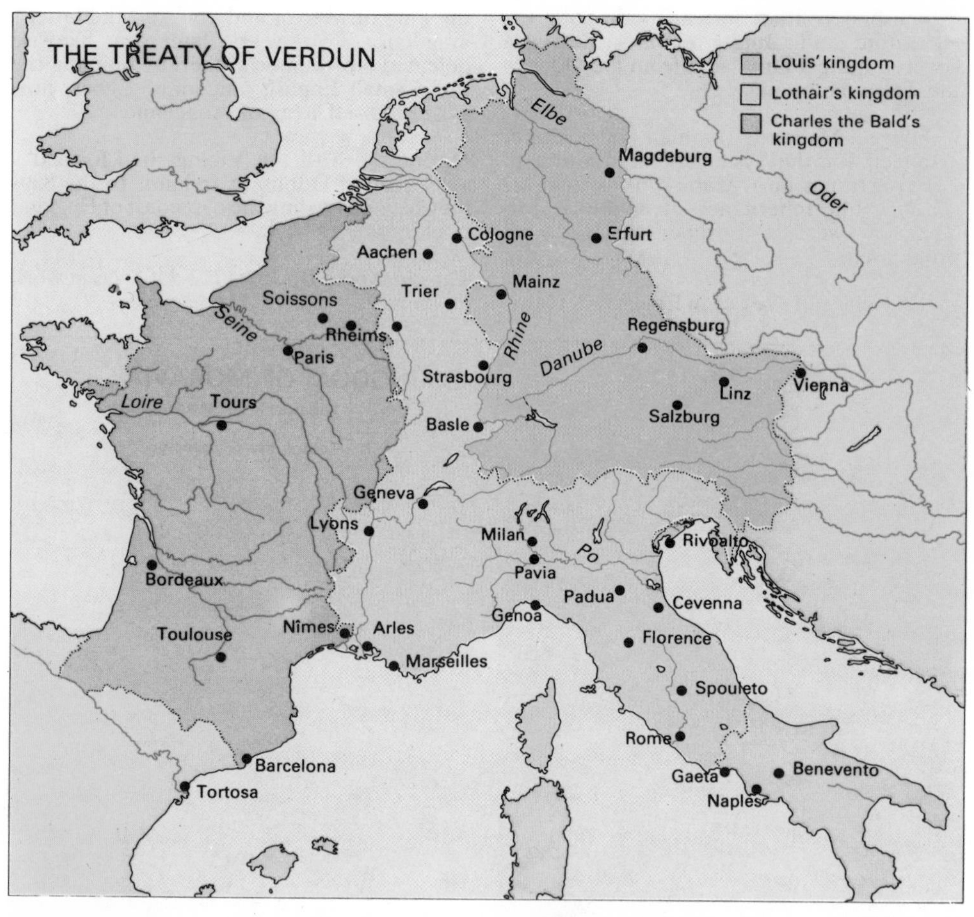
THE TREATY OF VERDUN
Louis' kingdom
Lothair's kingdom
Charles the Bald's kingdom
Elbe
Oder
Magdeburg
Cologne
Erfurt
Aachen
Mainz
Trier
Soissons
Seine
Rheims
Paris
Rhine
Regensburg
Danube
Strasbourg
Linz
Vienna
Loire
Tours
Basle
Salzburg
Geneva
Lyons
Milan
Po
Rivoalto
Pavia
Bordeaux
Padua
Cevenna
Genoa
Toulouse
Nîmes
Arles
Florence
Marseilles
Spouleto
Rome
Barcelona
Benevento
Gaeta
Naples
Tortosa

The Frankish fraternal war ended at last with the Treaty of Verdun (14 February 843) when the empire was divided among the sons of Louis the Pious. Charles the Bald received the western part of the empire, hereafter known as France, while Louis the German took the territory east of the Rhine, which became Germany. Lothair had merely become emperor of a stretch of country adjoining Germany, with no authority at all over his brothers' kingdoms. The Treaty of Verdun was an event of paramount significance in that it laid the foundations for demarcating the boundaries of modern Europe.

Kenneth MacAlpin was a Scottish chieftain who in 844 formed a union between the Scots and the Picts. The details are not known but it is generally agreed the union constituted the basis of a Scottish state. Other tribes in the country, however, remained independent for some centuries to come.

Various parts of Europe were intermittently harried by the Vikings. In 845, 857 and 861 they sailed up the Seine and plundered Paris. They are also reported to have made landings in Spain and other Mediterranean countries.

The last of the great Tang poets, Bo Juyi died in China in 846. He left a legacy of 3,800 poems, many of which, in translation, were later to delight western readers as well.

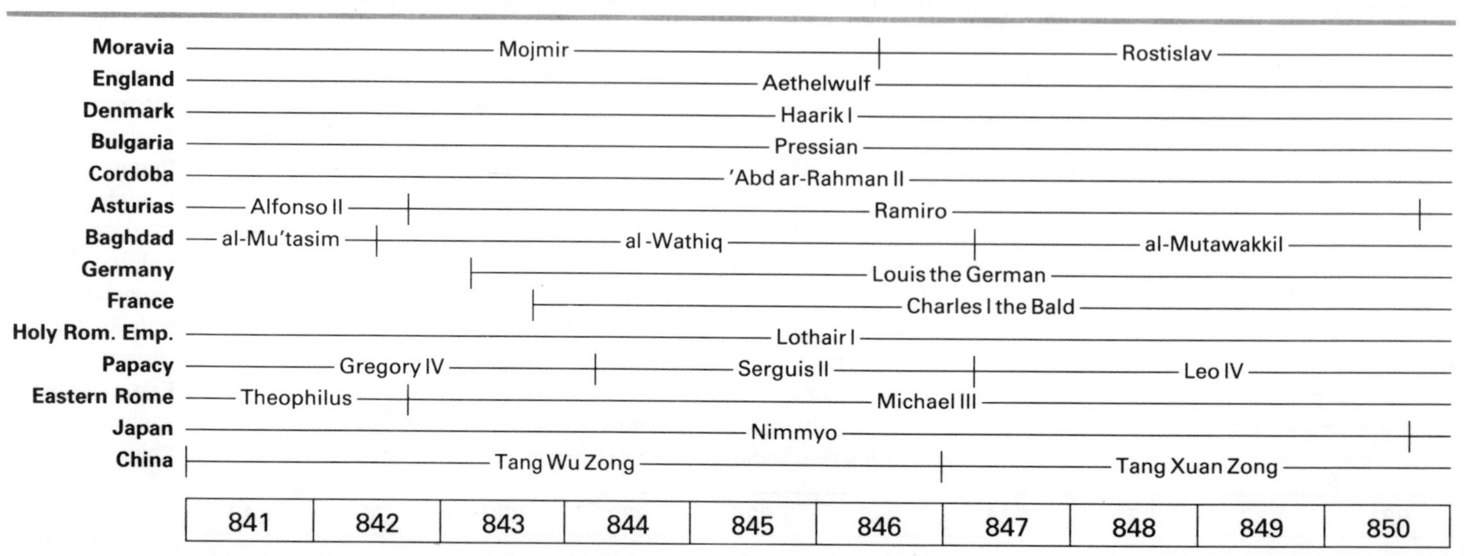
Moravia — Mojmir — Rostislav
England — Aethelwulf
Denmark — Haarik I
Bulgaria — Pressian
Cordoba — 'Abd ar-Rahman II
Asturias — Alfonso II — Ramiro
Baghdad — al-Mu'tasim — al-Wathiq — al-Mutawakkil
Germany — Louis the German
France — Charles I the Bald
Holy Rom. Emp. — Lothair I
Papacy — Gregory IV — Serguis II — Leo IV
Eastern Rome — Theophilus — Michael III
Japan — Nimmyo
China — Tang Wu Zong — Tang Xuan Zong
841 842 843 844 845 846 847 848 849 850

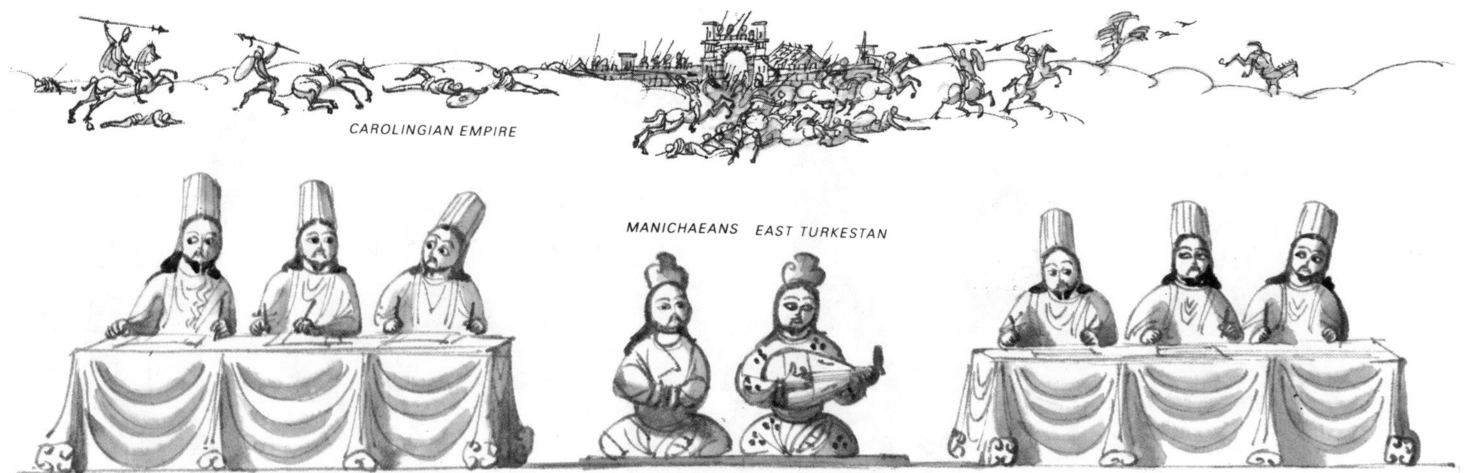
CAROLINGIAN EMPIRE
MANICHAEANS EAST TURKESTAN

A Breton governor named Nominoe led a revolt against Frankish rule, defeated Charles the Bald in a battle at Ballon, had himself annointed king and organized an independent Breton kingdom. Nominoe died in 851 but Charles the Bald recognized the royal status of his son Erispoe, provided the latter swore an oath of allegiance. After this Brittany remained *de facto* an independent state until the 13th century.

There were momentous events in central Asia during the 840s. The Uighur realm, disrupted by internal conflict, was overrun by Khirghis invaders and the Uighurs were dispersed, some settling in China, others in the Tarim basin region.

Easter Island in the Pacific is said to have been inhabited for the first time by people from the Marquesas Islands, in 858.

In China, the dissolution of the Uighur kingdom led to widespread religious persecution. Emperor Wu Zong was a devout Taoist and was opposed to Manichaeism, which had been the principal religion of the Uighurs, with a strong following in China. All Manichaean temples were closed, the priests were exiled to remote provinces and seventy Manichaean nuns were put to death in Changan. A few years later the emperor attacked other religions. Muslims and Jews were left in peace but Christianity was totally eliminated and all the Nestorian churches were plundered. Buddhism suffered worst, however: a quarter of a million monks and nuns were expelled from their monasteries and convents, and thousands of temples were destroyed.

Emperor Lothair, a portrait in his evangel, a book of Biblical texts and prayers produced in Tours in 851, now in the Bibliothèque Nationale, Paris.

The brilliant reign of 'Abd ar-Rahman II, when the Spanish caliphate of Cordoba represented a cultural oasis in an otherwise violent and barbaric Europe, was followed by the unrest of Muhammad I's reign, with repeated uprisings among both Muslims and Christians. Amid mounting religious tolerance, Archbishop Eulogius was martyred during an insurrection in Toledo.

The long, narrow realm of Emperor Lothair I embraced northern Italy and a stretch of territory from the North Sea to the Mediterranean, between the Rhine and the Alps in the east, and between the Maas, the Saône and the Rhône in the west. But after his death in 855 this was divided between his three sons Louis II, Lothair II and Charles. Louis had the title of emperor and held the northern Italian part. Charles received Provence and Lothair II ruled the region named after him as Lotharingia or Lorraine.

In the Byzantine empire iconoclasm finally came to an end.

In 858 the first Franco-German war broke out. Louis the German invaded French territory, and Charles the Bald launched a counter-offensive. Peace was settled at Koblenz without any changes in the boundaries.

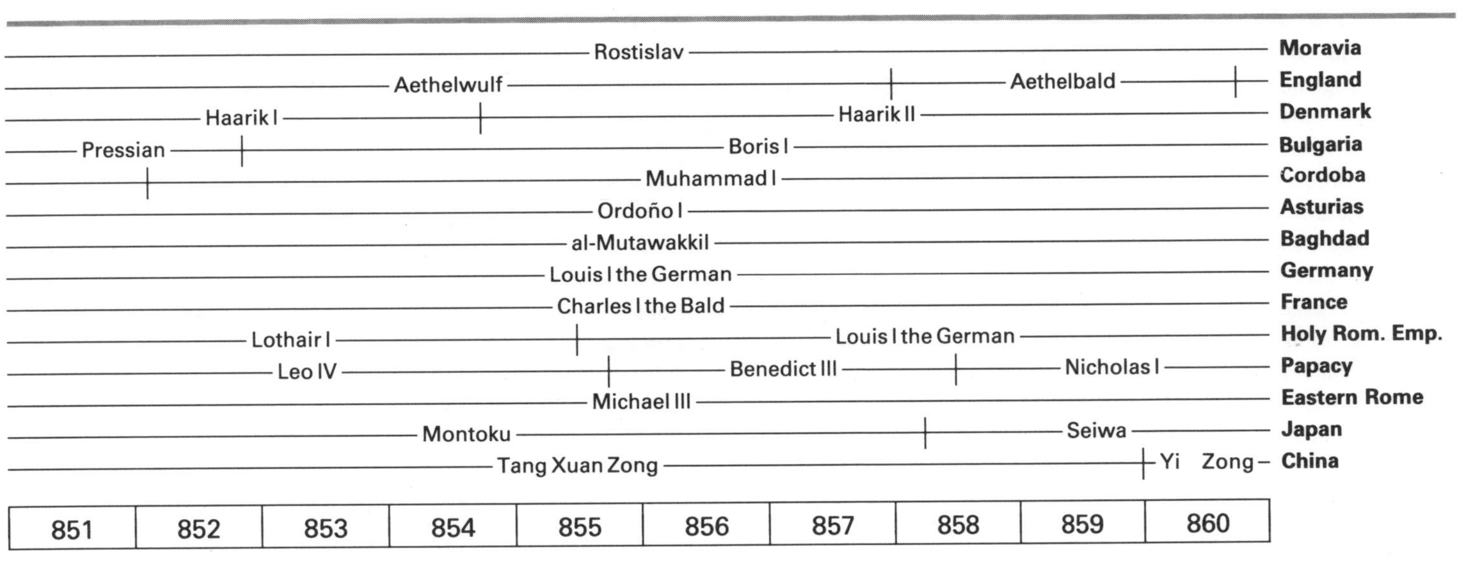
Rostislav — Moravia
Aethelwulf — Aethelbald — England
Haarik I — Haarik II — Denmark
Pressian — Boris I — Bulgaria
Muhammad I — Cordoba
Ordoño I — Asturias
al-Mutawakkil — Baghdad
Louis I the German — Germany
Charles I the Bald — France
Lothair I — Louis I the German — Holy Rom. Emp.
Leo IV — Benedict III — Nicholas I — Papacy
Michael III — Eastern Rome
Montoku — Seiwa — Japan
Tang Xuan Zong — Yi Zong — China
851 852 853 854 855 856 857 858 859 860

AD 861-870

VIKINGS
CHINA

According to the Russian Nestor chronicle in 862, a prince named Rurik came from the other side of the sea and founded a kingdom with Novgorod as its centre. Two of his companions, Askild and Dir, continued southward to Kiev and settled there, after which they made an unsuccessful expedition to Constantinople. This chronicle, which calls Rurik's people the Russ and the invading Vikings Varjager, claims that these invaders originated the Russian empire.

In 867 at a council in Constantinople, the patriarch Photius had the pope and all his western followers denounced as heretics, for having made an addition to the creed whereby the Holy Spirit was not only *ex patre* but also *filioque*. A list of the Roman Church's false rites and decrees was now circulated to all Eastern bishops, and this led to the final division of Catholic Christianity into a Roman and a Greek Church.

The 9th century was the great age of the European Christian missions. East of the Alps, the recently arrived Slav and Finno-Ugrian peoples were the concern not only of the pope and the patriarch but also of Muslim and Jewish theologians. North of the Black Sea, the Khazars appealed to Constantinople for a Christian teacher and Photius sent them a young man subsequently known as Cyril. His mission proved unsuccessful, and the Khazars, who wished to remain independent of both caliph and emperor, decided to embrace the Jewish religion.

Cyril became instead the apostle of the Slavs. With his elder brother Methodius, he converted the powerful Moravian realm to Christianity and created an alphabet for the Slavs whose speech sounds were not easy to express in Greek letters. The script devised by Cyril (Cyrillic) became the basis of the Russian, Bulgar and Yugoslavian alphabet. Cyril died in 869.

In China the army mutinied on the Annam frontier and then seized Canton and massacred the entire population. After this the rebels quickly took Changan and the emperor was put to flight.

Vikings at sea, English 12th century miniature, now in the Pierpoint Morgan Library, New York. There are some fine original examples of Viking ships, particularly in Norway. Literature, too, mentions various types of craft. The largest were the trading vessels, knarrs, *while the warships were known as longships or dragon-ships, with thirty or more oarsmen.*

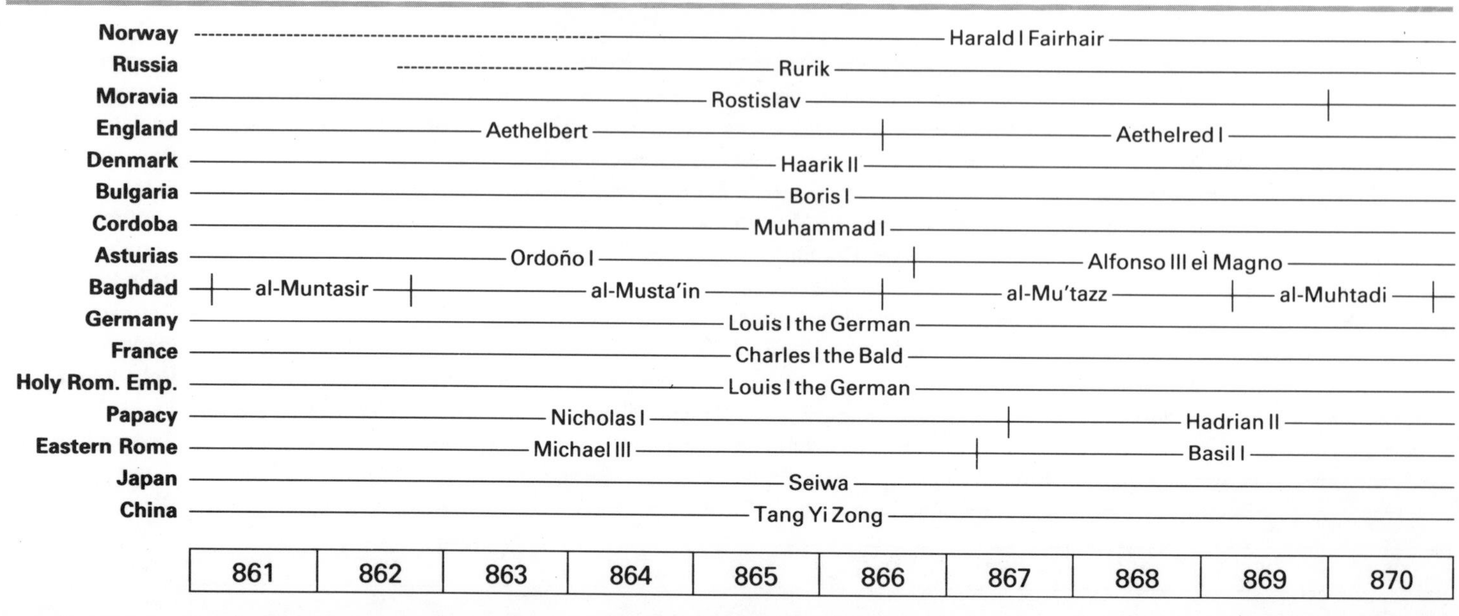
Norway
Harald I Fairhair
Russia
Rurik
Moravia
Rostislav
England
Aethelbert
Aethelred I
Denmark
Haarik II
Bulgaria
Boris I
Cordoba
Muhammad I
Asturias
Ordoño I
Alfonso III el Magno
Baghdad
al-Muntasir
al-Musta'in
al-Mu'tazz
al-Muhtadi
Germany
Louis I the German
France
Charles I the Bald
Holy Rom. Emp.
Louis I the German
Papacy
Nicholas I
Hadrian II
Eastern Rome
Michael III
Basil I
Japan
Seiwa
China
Tang Yi Zong
861
862
863
864
865
866
867
868
869
870

VIKINGS
KOCHI EAST TURKESTAN
MANICHAEANS

In 877 Paris was besieged by Danish Vikings. Charles the Bald bought them off.

The sea battle of Hafrsfjord took place in 872. Here Harald Fairhair, King of Vestfold on the Oslo fjord, defeated a coalition of other minor kings and united Norway under his rule. Many of his adversaries left the country rather than submit to Harald and in this way the Swedish province of Jämtland, and, above all, Iceland became populated.

Oleg, who succeeded Rurik, was foster-parent to the latter's son Igor. Oleg defeated his kinsmen at Kiev and moved his administration to that city.

The Anglo-Saxon king, Alfred, was the hero in many engagements with the Danes who had established themselves on England's east coast during the reign of Alfred's two predecessors. In 878 he won a major victory against the Danes which for a few years brought peace to England. Other groups of Vikings were subsequently driven off as well by Alfred. There is a more or less contemporary account of Alfred, besides two volumes of his own writings. He emerges as a wise, good and courageous man with liberal cultural interests.

Louis the German's three sons became the kings of Bavaria, Saxony and Swabia respectively. Charles the Fat, king of Swabia, was made emperor in 880. The German territory was still named Regnum Fracorum, Frankland.

King Svatopluk of Moravia had deposed his uncle Rostislav with German aid, and consequently during his reign German influence was very pronounced. In due course it embraced Christianity. Svatopluk expanded Moravia to include Bohemia, Silesia and parts of Pannonia.

In 880 Prince Branimir of Croatia freed himself from Byzantine sovereignty and put his country under the protection of the Roman popes.

The Viking era lasted for more than two centuries. Gradually these northern seafarers were assimilated with the populations of the lands in which they settled.

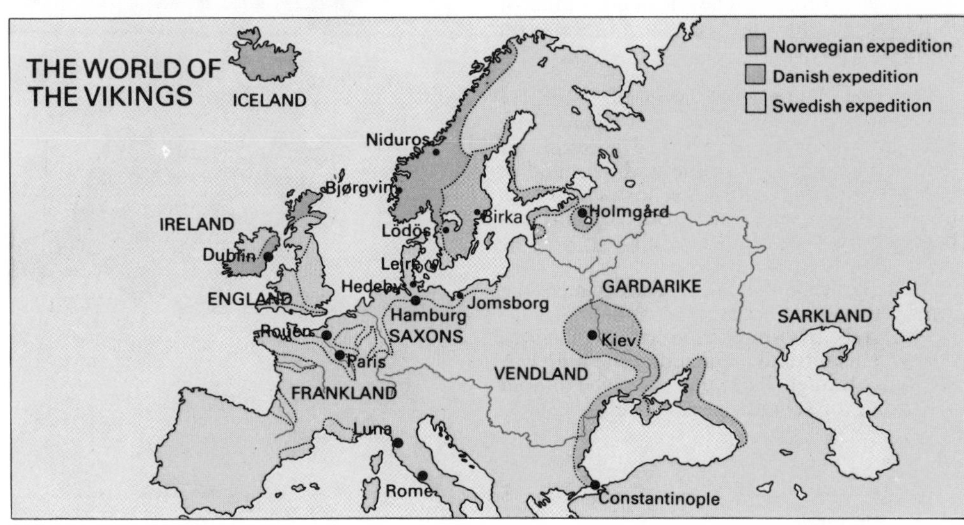
THE WORLD OF THE VIKINGS
Norwegian expedition
Danish expedition
Swedish expedition
ICELAND
Niduros
Bjørgvin
IRELAND
Dublin
ENGLAND
Lodös
Birka
Holmgård
Hedeby
Jomsborg
GARDARIKE
Hamburg
SAXONS
Rouen
Paris
SARKLAND
Kiev
VENDLAND
FRANKLAND
Luna
Rome
Constantinople

Harald I Fairhair	Norway
Rurik — Oleg	Russia
Svatopluk	Moravia
Alfred	England
	Denmark
Boris I	Bulgaria
Muhammad I	Cordoba
Alfonso III el Magno	Asturias
al-Mutamid	Baghdad
Louis I the German — Carloman + Louis II + Charles the Fat	Germany
Charles I the Bald — Louis II the Stammerer — Louis III + Carloman -	France
Louis I the German — Carolus II (Charles the Bald)	Holy Rom. Emp.
Hadrian II — John VIII	Papacy
Basil I	Eastern Rome
Seiwa — Yozei	Japan
Tang Yi Zong — Tang Xi Zong	China

871	872	873	874	875	876	877	878	879	880

AD 881-890

CHINA
CENTRAL EUROPE

A Finno-Ugrian people, the Magyars or Hungarians, had recently reached an area on the lower Danube, pursued from the east by the nomadic Pechenegs. The Byzantines immediately persuaded the Hungarians to attack the Bulgars in the rear. After a series of defeats the Bulgar khan, Symeon, requested an armistice and surrendered certain territories he had formerly seized. He now used this respite to form an alliance with the Pechenegs against the Hungarians, and the latter were driven up the Danube valley to the region which subsequently became known as Hungary. They formed a kind of linguistic island amid a sea of Slavs on Moravian territory.

After the death of Svatopluk, Moravia disintegrated never to recover again. The German emperor, Arnulf, led a couple of successful campaigns in the mid-890s and at about the same time Czechoslovakia was united under a ruler name Borivoj who was baptized by Methodius himself.

In 878 Syracuse fell into Arab hands, the inhabitants were massacred and the victorious Arab troops carried off a fabulous booty. This virtually concluded the long war on Sicily, though Taormina managed to hold out alone for several more decades.

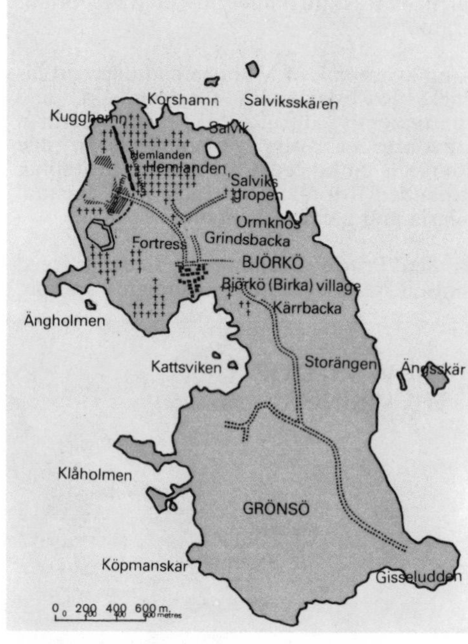
Korshamn
Salviksskären
Kugghamn
Salvik
Hemlanden
Salviks
Ormknös
Fortress
Grindsbacka
BJÖRKÖ
Björkö (Birka) village
Kärrbacka
Ängholmen
Kattsviken
Storängen
Ängsskär
Klåholmen
GRÖNSÖ
Köpmanskär
Gisseludden
0 200 400 600 m

Little is known of what was going on in Sweden at this time. Mälaren was still a Baltic bay and the channels between the islands on which Stockholm was one day to be built, were open and freely navigable. The town of Birka or Björkö on what was later Lake Mälar, was flourishing; a trading centre not only with western Eurpoe but also with the Arab world to the east, via the Russian rivers. Modern archaeologists have made remarkable finds in Birka with its extensive grave-fields and housing areas still black from burned-out dwellings. The name Birka is Latin, deriving from the monk Rimbert's biography of Bishop Ansgar who came to the town in 830 as a young missionary and organized a Christian community there. It did not last long, for when Ansgar as Archbishop of Hamburg sent a missionary named Gautbert to the Sveas he was expelled and his relative Nithard, who accompanied him, was killed. Ansgar himself returned to Birka in the 850s, endeavouring to reinstate the mission by means of gifts and banquets, but he appears not to have succeeded. The town had probably by now reverted to the Aesir cult.

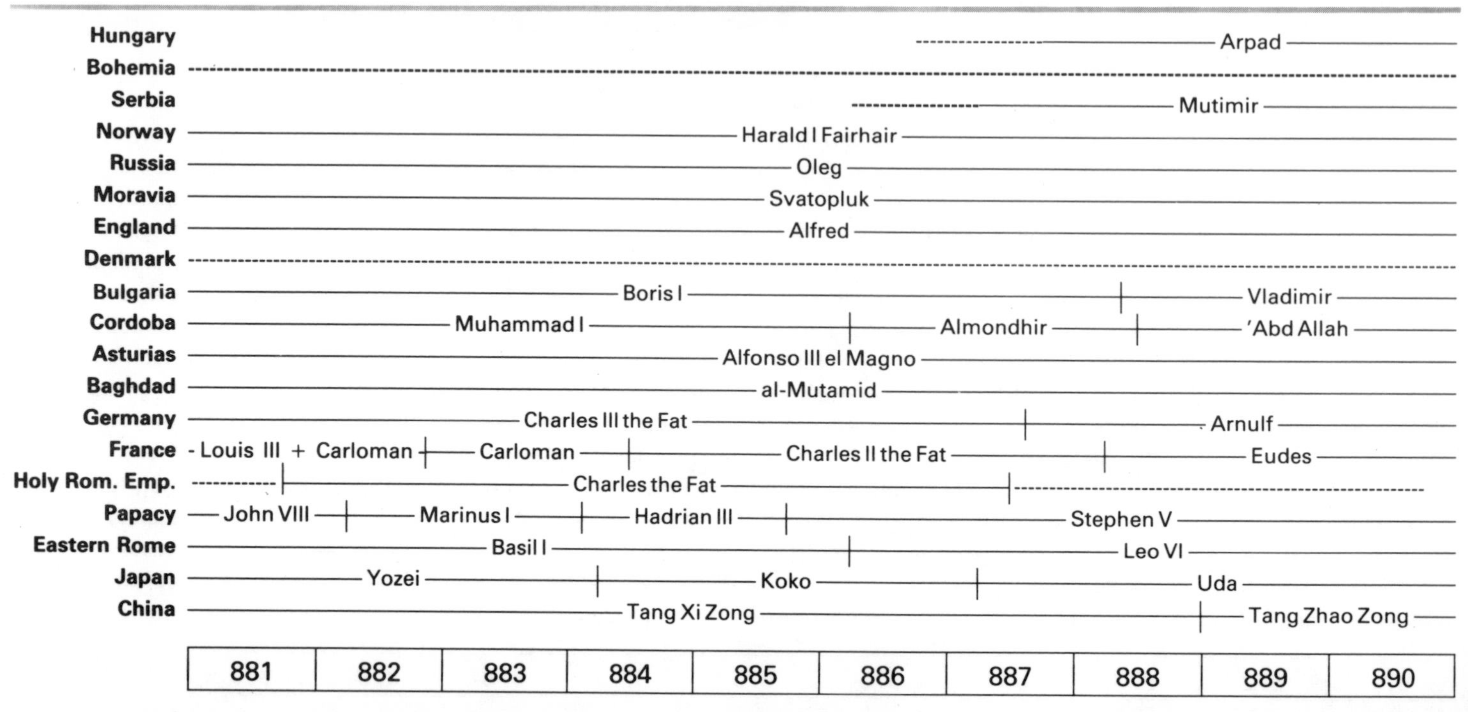
Hungary — Arpad
Bohemia
Serbia — Mutimir
Norway — Harald I Fairhair
Russia — Oleg
Moravia — Svatopluk
England — Alfred
Denmark
Bulgaria — Boris I — Vladimir
Cordoba — Muhammad I — Almondhir — 'Abd Allah
Asturias — Alfonso III el Magno
Baghdad — al-Mutamid
Germany — Charles III the Fat — Arnulf
France — Louis III + Carloman — Carloman — Charles II the Fat — Eudes
Holy Rom. Emp. — Charles the Fat
Papacy — John VIII — Marinus I — Hadrian III — Stephen V
Eastern Rome — Basil I — Leo VI
Japan — Yozei — Koko — Uda
China — Tang Xi Zong — Tang Zhao Zong
881 882 883 884 885 886 887 888 889 890

AD 891-900

CHINA
JAPAN

The Czar of the Bulgars, Boris I, entered a monastery in his old age. He was baptized during the 860s in Constantinople in the presence of both the emperor and the patriarch, yet a few years later he approached the pope with a view to making Bulgaria Roman Catholic. He was evidently dissuaded or disillusioned, for he eventually let in Greek missionaries. They were not wholly successful, since in the reign of his son there was a heathen counter-offensive.

Although the tribe was of course much older, the Serbs are first mentioned by name in the 9th century. The sovereignty of the Byzantine emperors over the Serbs had been little more than nominal.

The popes in the 890s were so numerous that it is impossible to list them all. Boniface VI came and went in 896, as did Romanus and Theodorus in 897.

Charles II le Gros was the German king Karl der Dicke (Charles the Fat). During Charles' reign most of Charlemagne's Frankish empire was reunited, since of the latter's legitimate descendants in France there remained only a two-year old child, the future Charles the Simple, posthumous son of Louis le Begue, Louis the Stammerer. Charles the Fat was weak both in body and mind. In 887 he was deposed as king and emperor of Germany, whereupon France and Italy each elected their own regent.

Emperor Arnulf also reigned in Italy, where he was challenged by two nobles, Guy and Lambert, who called themselves emperor. After the death of Arnulf, a prince named Berengarö claimed the position of sole ruler of northern Italy, but in 900 the Hungarians invaded and expelled Berengar. The latter's Italian vassals now called in a Burgundian candidate who as Roman emperor became Louis III. The succession struggle between Louis III and Berengar I continued for a number of years until Louis was finally taken prisoner and had his eyes put out.

Emperor Xi Zong secured help against the rebels from a Turkic general named Li Ke-Yung and the Chinese general Zhu Wen. These two suppressed the revolt and then competed with each other for power. Zhu Wen brought about a palace revolution, imprisoned the emperor and a year or two later had him put to death, along with practically all his family, except for a small boy who was appointed emperor; the last of the renowned Tang dynasty.

The domestic history of Denmark during the Viking era is largely unknown. There have been a great many archaeological finds, particularly coins, which give a good idea of the destinations and profitability of the Viking voyages, but there is no dependable information about people and names. According to legend, the 9th century Viking expeditions to England were led by Ragnar Lodbrok's sons and a couple of these are legendarily included in the Danish and Swedish lists of rulers. Sigurd Ormiöga is said to have been a ruler of Denmark and Björn Järnsida a ruler of Sweden. An important trade centre in the southern Baltic was Hedeby by Slienfjord in Schleswig. Vikings had also settled around the mouth of the Rhine and were in control of a considerable part of England. The slave trade with Byzantine territories was flourishing and commerce with the Khazars on the lower Volga brought in large quantities of Kufic coins, which were to be found by the barrel-load a thousand years later in Gotland, Öland and Uppland. There are linguistic traces of the Vikings to this day, chiefly in England, where towns such as Derby, Whitby and Grimsby have kept their names from the Viking era. In Normandy there are names such as Dalbec and Borgebu.

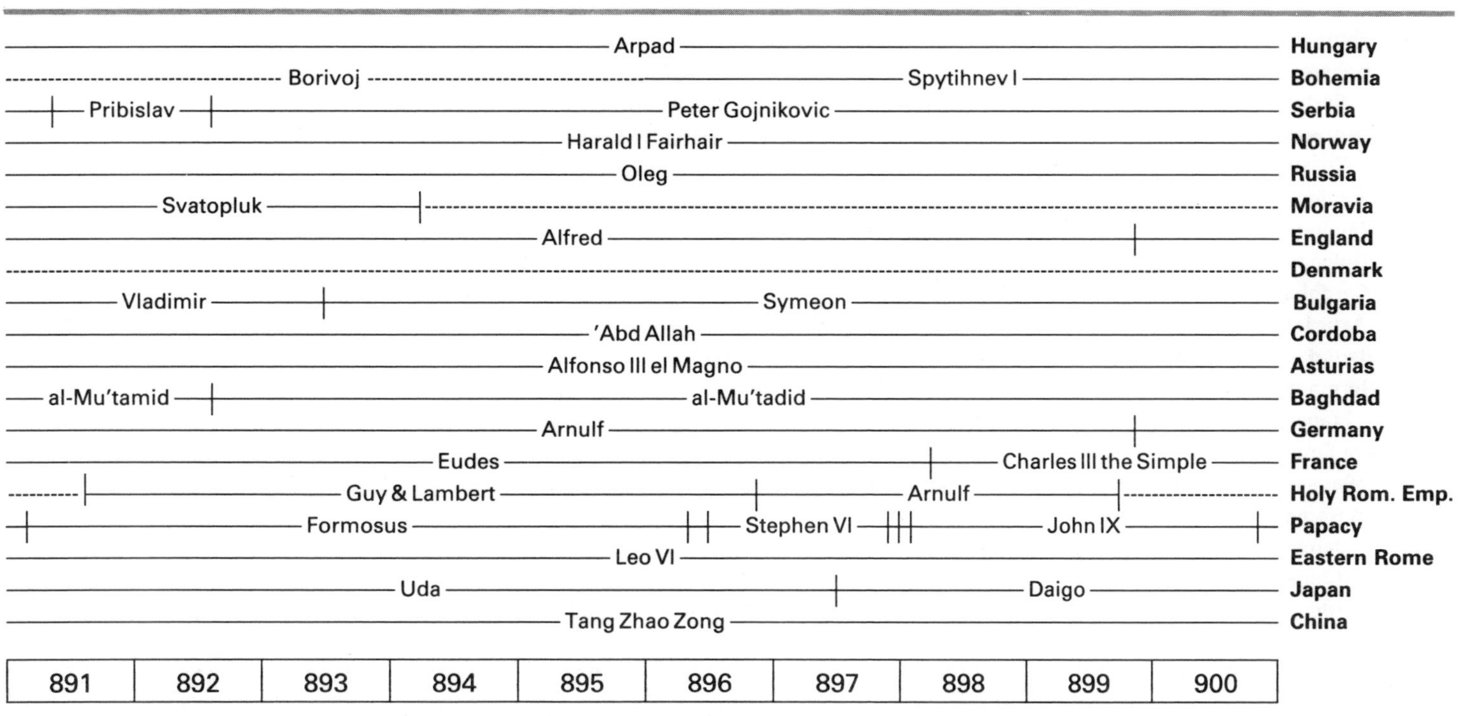

Arpad — Hungary
Borivoj — Spytihnev I — Bohemia
Pribislav — Peter Gojnikovic — Serbia
Harald I Fairhair — Norway
Oleg — Russia
Svatopluk — Moravia
Alfred — England
Denmark
Vladimir — Symeon — Bulgaria
'Abd Allah — Cordoba
Alfonso III el Magno — Asturias
al-Mu'tamid — al-Mu'tadid — Baghdad
Arnulf — Germany
Eudes — Charles III the Simple — France
Guy & Lambert — Arnulf — Holy Rom. Emp.
Formosus — Stephen VI — John IX — Papacy
Leo VI — Eastern Rome
Uda — Daigo — Japan
Tang Zhao Zong — China
891
892
893
894
895
896
897
898
899
900

AD 901-910

BYZANTIU
QI-TAN
CHINESE

China was politically divided from the beginning of the 10th to the close of the 13th century. Zhu Wen, who deposed the last of the Tang emperors in 907, created his own dynasty, Hou Liang, while at the same time a son of his Turkic rival founded the Hou Tang dynasty in another part of China. In Chinese history the first half of the 10th century is known as Wu Dai, the five dynasties, the other three being Hou Jin, Hou Han and Hou Zhou (the word Hou means Younger). But by the middle of this century there were at least ten dynasties in central China. The north was ruled by an alien tribe known in Chinese as Qitan. These were Tungus though they organized their realm according to the Chinese pattern and quickly assumed Chinese characteristics. One of their principal cities was Beijing (Peking).

A Croatian state emerged in 903-928 under a chieftain named Tomislav.

In 906 Moravia was completely overrun by the Hungarians.

The German, Louis VI, began his rule at six years of age and was only eighteen at his death. He is thus known as *das Kind,* the Child. He was the last German king of the house of Charlemagne. The Frankish Duke Conrad, who was elected as Louis' successor, spent most of his time in combat with encroaching Hungarian hordes. Henry of Saxony, who succeeded Conrad became known as *der Finkler,* the Fowler. He was out bird-shooting when he received a message that King Conrad, with whom he had long feuded, had nevertheless named him his successor. Henry the Fowler united all the German tribes under his rule and overwhelmed the Hungarians, the Slavs and the Danes, compelled Bohemia to pay taxes to him and repulsed the Swedish king, Gnupa, who had established himself in Schleswig.

A band of Saracens had seized the fortress of Fraxinetum overlooking the future Saint Tropez on the French Mediterranean coast. In this way they controlled part of the traffic through the Alpine passes and made frequent raids on the Ligurian towns. They remained secure here until the latter half of the 10th century. In 903 the Saracens seized Taormina, which was the last Byzantine foothold in Sicily. After this the island remained under Arab rule for several centuries.

The Bulgar czar, Symeon, had a Greek education and had dreams of power. He caused the Byzantines a great deal of trouble, and after a war-like demonstration of his strength, was actually admitted into Constantinople and crowned emperor. But when this coronation was declared invalid, he proceeded to devastate the land in all directions. For a while he mastered the Balkans.

The Fujiwara culture was flourishing in Japan. This took its name from the dynasty that ruled 895-1192. Here the emperors published official anthologies of their poems.

The great mosque in Cordoba is one of the most magnificent examples of Islamic architecture.

Country	Rulers (901–910)
Hungary	Arpad; Soltan
Bohemia	Spytihnev I
Serbia	Peter Gojnikovic
Norway	Harald I Fairhair
Russia	Oleg
England	Edward the Elder
Denmark	------
Bulgaria	Symeon
Cordoba	'Abd Allah
Asturias	Alfonso III el Magno
Baghdad	al-Mu'tadid; al-Muktafi; al-Muqtadir
Germany	Louis IV the Child
France	Charles III the Simple
Holy Rom.Emp.	Louis III; ------
Papacy	Benedict IV; Leo V; Christopher; Sergius III
Eastern Rome	Leo VI
Japan	Daigo
North China	Liao Tai Zu
South China	Tang Zhao Zong; Tang Ai Di; Hou Liang dyn.

901	902	903	904	905	906	907	908	909	910

BYZANTIUM
MAYA

The caliphate of Cordoba enjoyed a new era of greatness under 'Abd ar-Rahman II who once more brought the whole of Spain, apart from Leon and Catalonia, under Arab rule.

At the court of 'Abd ar-Rahman III in Cordoba there were 3750 slaves in outside service and 6300 in the harem. They were engaged in all types of professions and occupations. The white slaves came mostly from eastern Europe by way of the slave markets in Prague and Koblenz, and the Christian trading houses in Pamplona and Barcelona. The black slaves, supplied by the Berbers, were brought in directly from Africa across the Gibraltar strait. Both types were also exported in large numbers eastward across the Mediterranean to Byzantium, Syria and Egypt, the slave trade being a vital element of the caliphate's economy.

The great mosque in Cordoba, with its nineteen rows of columns and double arches, also originates from this time.

Pope Leo V was thrown into prison and tortured by a priest named Christopher who made himself pope, but was himself imprisoned, murdered and succeeded by Sergius, count of Tusculum. Sergius was closely connected with a Roman family which was to play a particular role in papal history. The youngest daughter, Marozia, was Sergius' mistress and they had a son who grew up to become Pope John XI. His predecessor was John X, the lover of Marozia's mother. John X was an energetic politician and a brave soldier who personally led the storming of a Saracen robber stronghold in southern Italy in 915.

Charles the Simple had dealings with the Vikings, paying them to go home and leave him in peace. In 911, he came to an agreement with a Danish or Norwegian chieftain, Rollo or Rolf. According to Norse accounts, he was so enormous that no horse could carry him. Charles presented Rollo with Normandy on condition that he defended it against the incursions of other Vikings.

ΑΛΕ
ΞΑΝ
ΔΡΟϹ

Garcia I was the son of Alfonso III of Asturia, though he was called King of Leon. Thus the dynasty was the same. The Asturian kingdom had grown in size during Alfonso's reign.

Gorm the Old, who apparently died in 936, was said to have ruled Denmark for one hundred winters. This is impossible, of course, but the beginning of his reign may reasonably be dated from this decade.

Portrait in the St. Sophia church, Istanbul, of the Byzantine emperor Alexander. He holds a globe, symbol of world power, and a silken pouch. On his way from the coronation ceremony to the festivities at the arena, every emperor received such a pouch called acacia ('no evil'), and was also met by grimacing figures proffering marble motifs for his sarcophagus. The purpose of this ritual was to propitiate jealous fate in the moment of triumph.

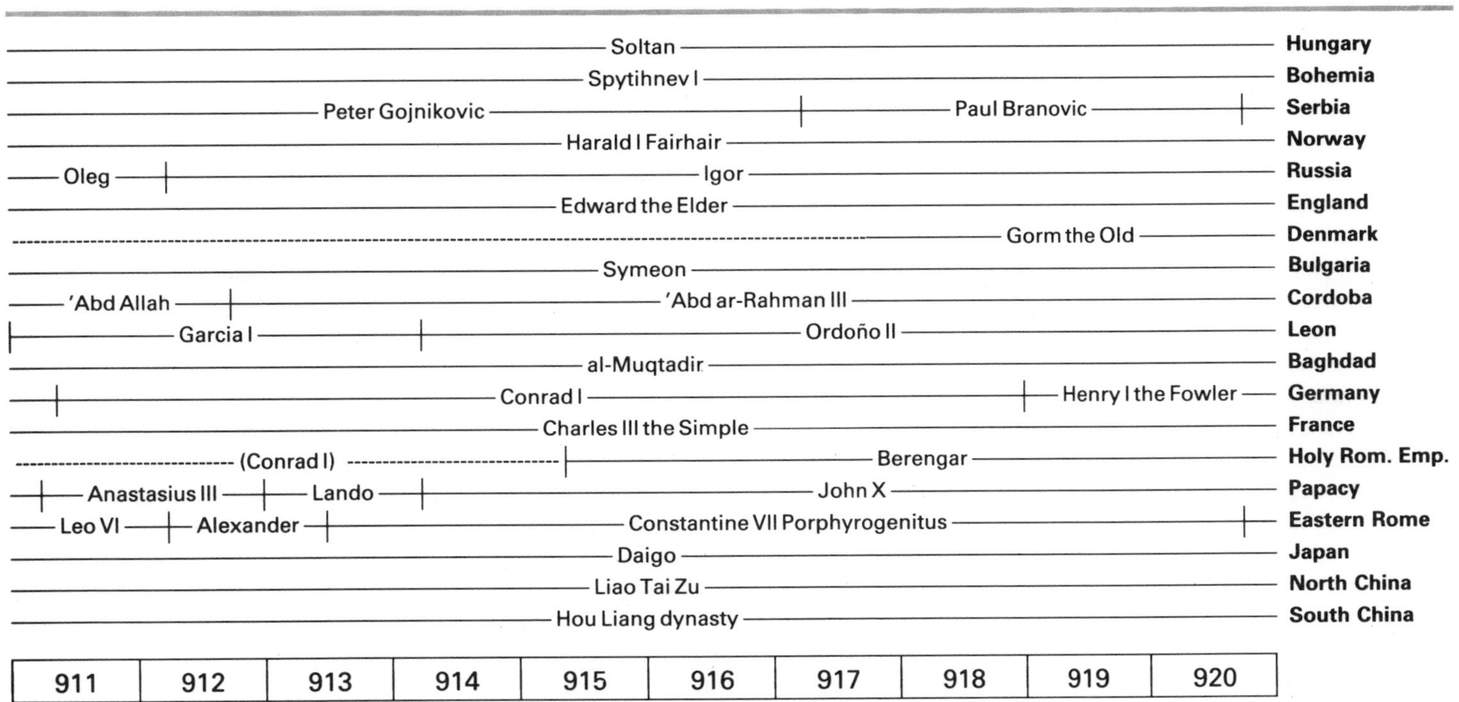
Soltan — Hungary
Spytihnev I — Bohemia
Peter Gojnikovic — Paul Branovic — Serbia
Harald I Fairhair — Norway
Oleg — Igor — Russia
Edward the Elder — England
Gorm the Old — Denmark
Symeon — Bulgaria
'Abd Allah — 'Abd ar-Rahman III — Cordoba
Garcia I — Ordoño II — Leon
al-Muqtadir — Baghdad
Conrad I — Henry I the Fowler — Germany
Charles III the Simple — France
(Conrad I) — Berengar — Holy Rom. Emp.
Anastasius III — Lando — John X — Papacy
Leo VI — Alexander — Constantine VII Porphyrogenitus — Eastern Rome
Daigo — Japan
Liao Tai Zu — North China
Hou Liang dynasty — South China
911 912 913 914 915 916 917 918 919 920

BYZANTIUM
CHINA
BYZANTIUM

Russia's relations with Byzantium improved during Igor's reign. When Igor reached the mouth of the Danube with a Viking fleet and an army of Russians and Pechenegs, an envoy arrived from Emperor Romanus Lecapenus with gifts and assurances of esteem. The result was an agreement which was economically advantageous to the Russians, while they in their turn pledged never to attack the Greek towns in the Crimea.

The Magyars, who in Arpad's time had established themselves on the Pannonian plain around the Danube, made repeated forays into the adjoining countries, plundering northern Italy, Bavaria, Saxony and Lorraine. In 933, however, they were decisively defeated by Henry the Fowler who thereby put an end to this threat.

A dynasty named Gurjara-Pratihara had ruled over a large kingdom in northern India for a century or two, but its days were now numbered.

Duke Vaclav, or Wenceslas, is the Czech national saint. He abolished capital punishment, built churches and supported Roman Catholicism; but he was murdered in a church by his brother Boleslav who, like their mother Drahomira, was a heathen.

In China books were printed on paper, using a form of lithographic technique, 500 years before Gutenberg.

In 930 a certain Ulfliótr established Iceland's *althing* and became its first legal spokesman. This brought to an end the immigration period in Icelandic history.

The Abbasid caliphate was wavering. The governor in Egypt had already declared his independence in the 870s. His family now died out and the country was reclaimed by the caliphate; yet only a few years later, in 936, a new Egyptian governor also proclaimed his independence. In 933 Persia likewise secured her freedom.

The Bulgar czar, Symeon, was at war with Serbia. His first campaign was disastrous but the following one was more successful and for a while he managed to subjugate the whole country. This, however, brought him up against the new state of Croatia, which, under its energetic King Tomislav, defeated him. The pope, who feared that the Byzantines and their Greek church would benefit from this, hastened to bring about peace. Later, the Serbian chieftain Caslav asserted his nation's independence, but Byzantium quickly reasserted its sovereignty. Not until the 12th century did Serbia once more become a significant power.

Bulgaria enjoyed a period of peace during the long reign of Czar Peter but was nevertheless weakened by inner conflicts. An anti-church sect known as the Bogomils gained ground. The Bogomils were contemptuous of worldly things: they abstained as much as possible from food, from love and even from work. They conducted a campaign of passive resistance against the authorities and for this they were persecuted, though with little effect, spreading the doctrine westwards.

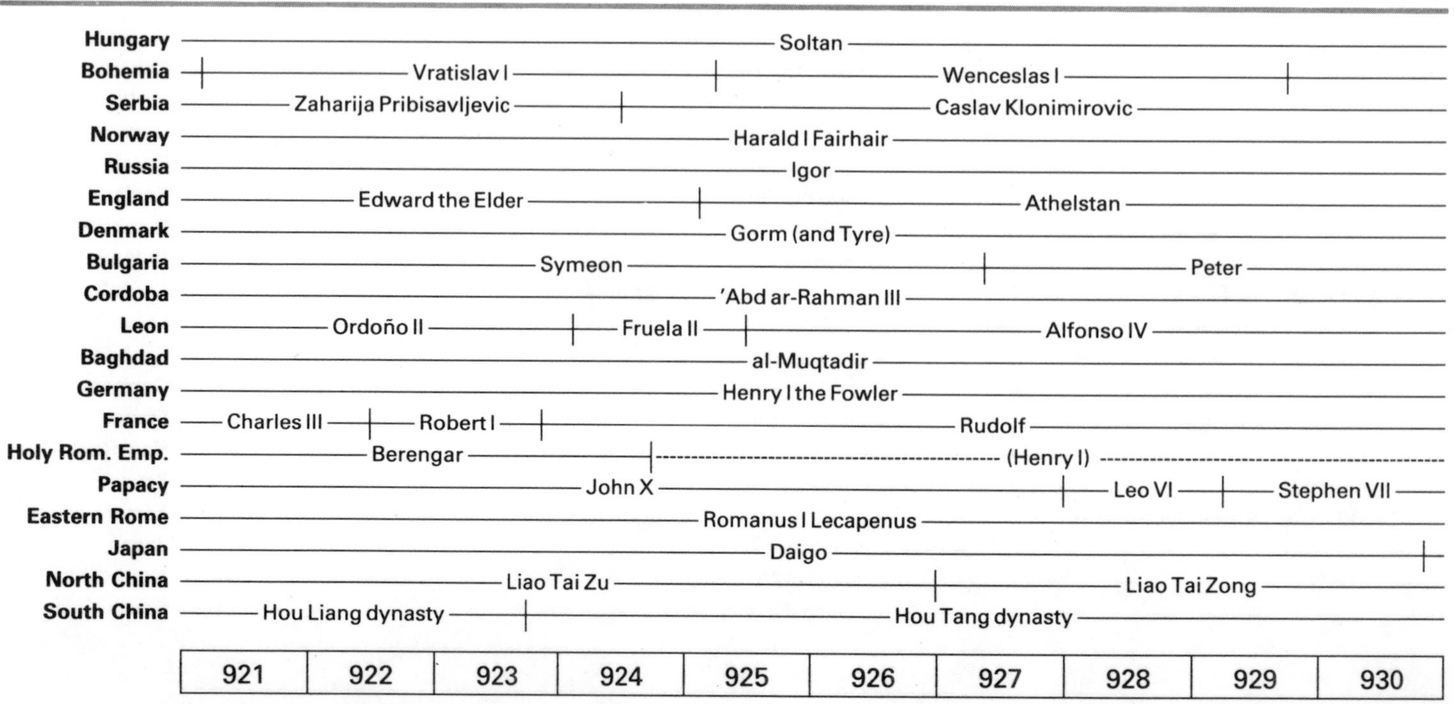
Hungary — Soltan
Bohemia — Vratislav I — Wenceslas I
Serbia — Zaharija Pribisavljevic — Caslav Klonimirovic
Norway — Harald I Fairhair
Russia — Igor
England — Edward the Elder — Athelstan
Denmark — Gorm (and Tyre)
Bulgaria — Symeon — Peter
Cordoba — 'Abd ar-Rahman III
Leon — Ordoño II — Fruela II — Alfonso IV
Baghdad — al-Muqtadir
Germany — Henry I the Fowler
France — Charles III — Robert I — Rudolf
Holy Rom. Emp. — Berengar — (Henry I)
Papacy — John X — Leo VI — Stephen VII
Eastern Rome — Romanus I Lecapenus
Japan — Daigo
North China — Liao Tai Zu — Liao Tai Zong
South China — Hou Liang dynasty — Hou Tang dynasty
921 922 923 924 925 926 927 928 929 930

AD 931-940

BYZANTIUM
CHINA
SCANDINAVIA

In France Louis the Simple was expelled by a group of vassal princes. Duke Robert, who first succeeded him on the throne, was killed shortly afterwards in a civil war. The next candidate was Duke Rudolf of Burgundy, a determined regent who successfully repulsed an invading Hungarian horde. When Rudolf died, however, Louis the Simple's son was brought home from exile in England. He became known as Louis d'Outremer, Louis from Across the Sea.

In 933 two Burgundian kings came to a significant agreement. A distinction was in future to be made between Cisjurane Burgundy, embracing Provence and other southerly regions, Transjurane Burgundy, comprising Savoy and Switzerland, and the Duchy of Burgundy which more or less corresponded to the modern province of Burgundy. The two former realms were now merged into the kingdom of Burgundy or Arelate with its capital at Arles.

The Norse sagas of the kings, the only medieval Scandinavian literature of any consequence apart from the laws, condemn the banished Erik Bloodaxe but refer to his brother Haakon as "the Good", by virtue of the fact that as a child he had been sent to England and grew up at the court of King Athelstan. He was thus Christian, though he failed totally to persuade his countrymen to be baptized. Indeed, he was himself compelled to play an official part in the Aesir sacrificial rites.

According to legend, the Danish queen, Tyre, built Danevirke, a line of fortifications which extended across southern Jutland at the narrowest point. The son of Gorm and Tyre, Harald Bluetooth (there is no explanation for the nickname), was a Christian, or in any event was tolerant of Christianity. Harald seized southern Sweden and Norway, but lost control of northern Germany where a duke named Palnatoke made himself independent and built the Viking fortification of Jornsborg.

By the church in Jelling, a rural district in Jutland, Denmark, there are two runestones, one raised by Gorm for his wife, Tyre, the other put up by their son Harald Bluetooth in their honour. This photograph shows one side of the latter, a triple-sided stone which stands on a burial mound, which may have been Gorm's. Gorm ruled the heathen kingdom of Jutland from his residence in Jelling. There were evidently other kingdoms in Denmark as well.

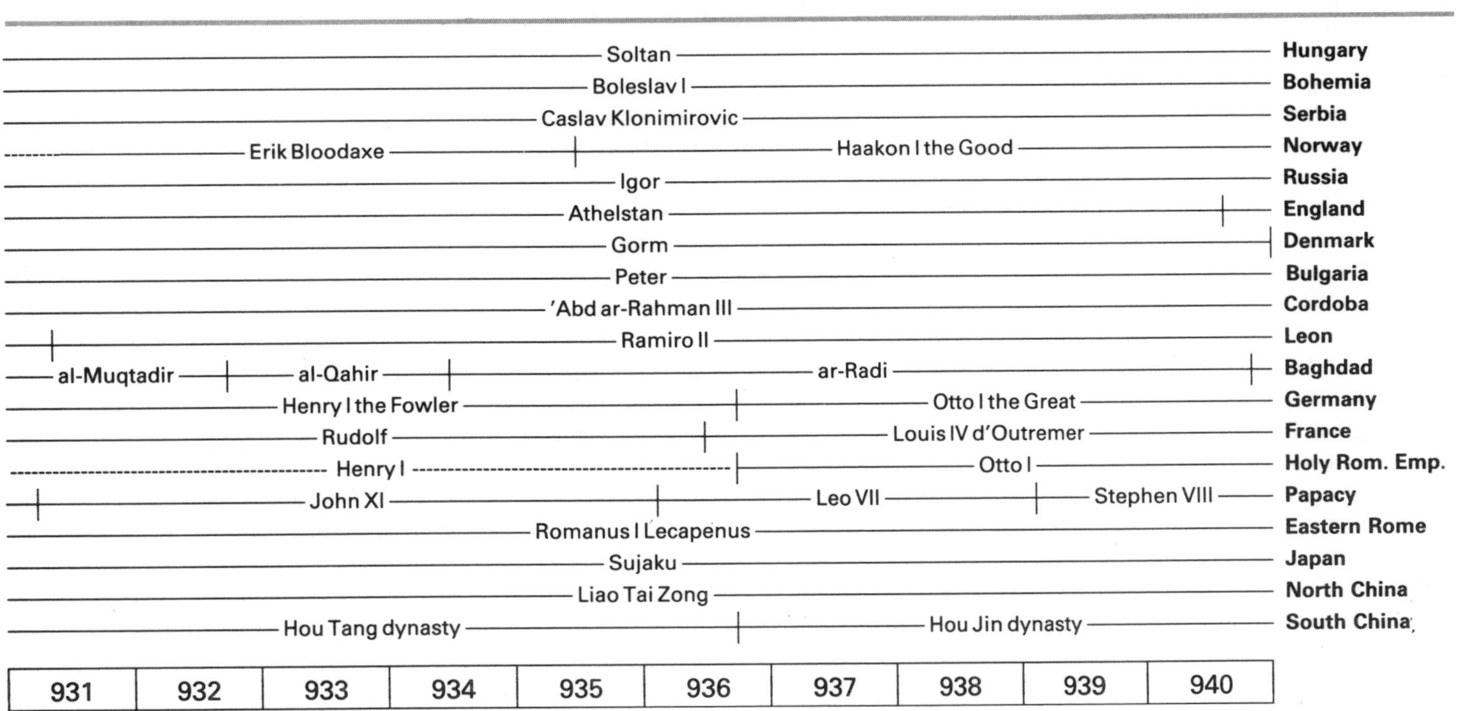
Soltan — Hungary
Boleslav I — Bohemia
Caslav Klonimirovic — Serbia
Erik Bloodaxe — Haakon I the Good — Norway
Igor — Russia
Athelstan — England
Gorm — Denmark
Peter — Bulgaria
'Abd ar-Rahman III — Cordoba
Ramiro II — Leon
al-Muqtadir — al-Qahir — ar-Radi — Baghdad
Henry I the Fowler — Otto I the Great — Germany
Rudolf — Louis IV d'Outremer — France
Henry I — Otto I — Holy Rom. Emp.
John XI — Leo VII — Stephen VIII — Papacy
Romanus I Lecapenus — Eastern Rome
Sujaku — Japan
Liao Tai Zong — North China
Hou Tang dynasty — Hou Jin dynasty — South China
931 932 933 934 935 936 937 938 939 940

AD 941-950

EAST TURKESTAN
BYZANTIUM

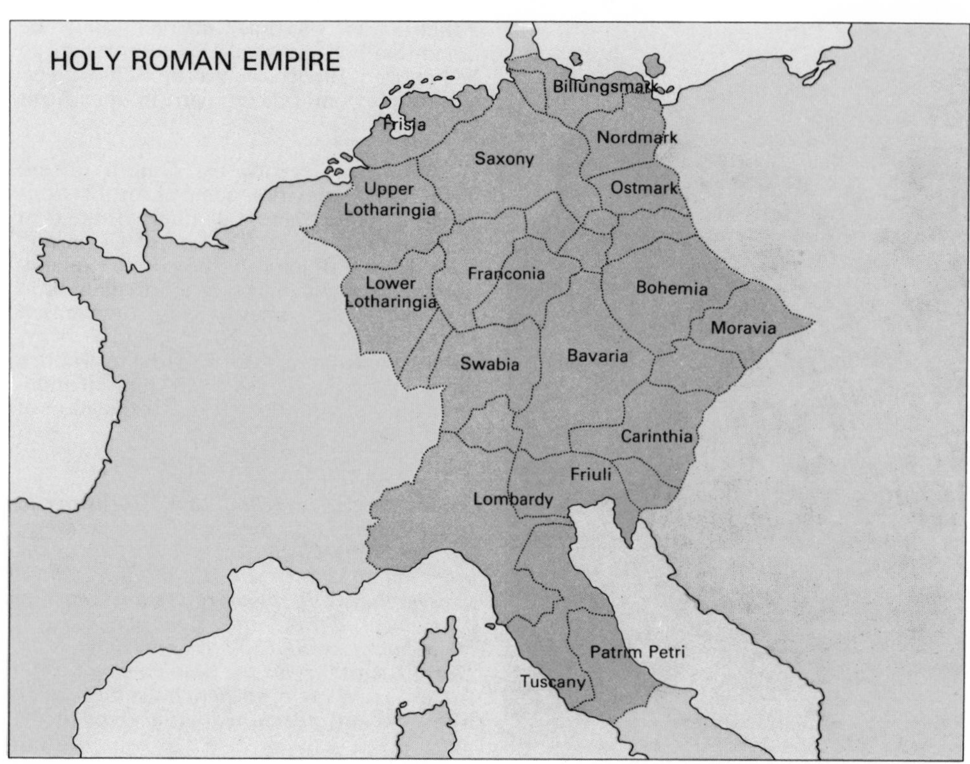

HOLY ROMAN EMPIRE
Billungsmark
Frisia
Nordmark
Saxony
Upper Lotharingia
Ostmark
Lower Lotharingia
Franconia
Bohemia
Moravia
Swabia
Bavaria
Carinthia
Friuli
Lombardy
Patrim Petri
Tuscany

During the reign of Otto I the Slavs in northern Germany were attacked and largely exterminated. After the warriors came the missionaries. Many new dioceses were established; a bishop was appointed to Meissen, another to Brandenburg and an archbishop to Magdeburg. Despite his many victories Otto I continued to fight battles throughout his reign. In the early 940s he was in France where he took Lorraine from Louis d'Outremer. In 946 he was back, advancing all the way to Rouen, seizing Rheims and other places. In 950 he defeated King Boleslav I in Bohemia and subsequently led three expeditions into Italy. In the north and east of his kingdom he set up a number of frontier defence areas known as marks: Ostermark and Nordmark, on the Oder and Herman Billungsmark, after a general of the same name, on the Danish border. A minor king in Sweden, Gnupa, ruled Schleswig Hedeby in the 930s and was then defeated and forcibly baptized; but by now this region had been seized by the heathen Danes.

Adelheid was the name of a beautiful widow with claims to the Italian throne. She was courted by Berengar, duke of Ivrea, but locked herself away in the castle of Canossa. Pope Agapetus then called in Otto I, who married Adelheid.

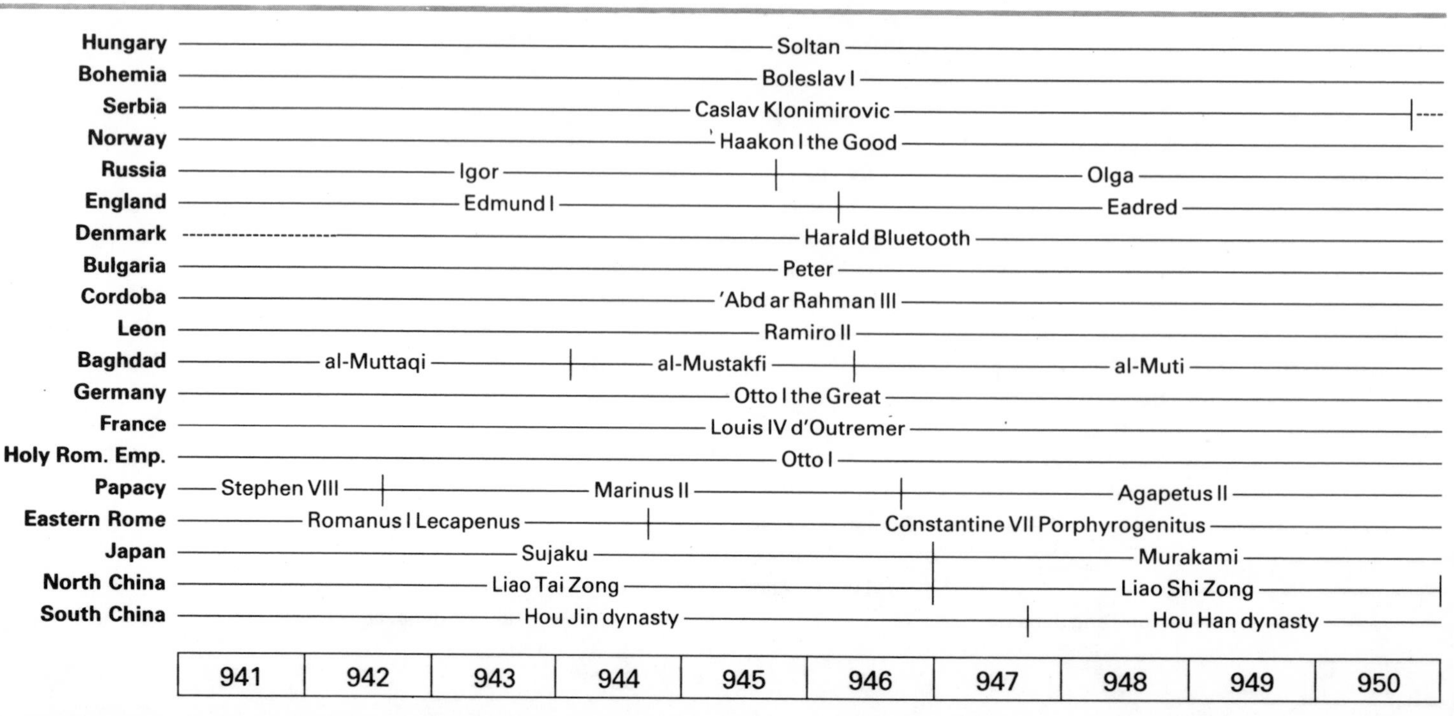

Hungary Soltan
Bohemia Boleslav I
Serbia Caslav Klonimirovic
Norway Haakon I the Good
Russia Igor Olga
England Edmund I Eadred
Denmark Harald Bluetooth
Bulgaria Peter
Cordoba 'Abd ar Rahman III
Leon Ramiro II
Baghdad al-Muttaqi al-Mustakfi al-Muti
Germany Otto I the Great
France Louis IV d'Outremer
Holy Rom. Emp. Otto I
Papacy Stephen VIII Marinus II Agapetus II
Eastern Rome Romanus I Lecapenus Constantine VII Porphyrogenitus
Japan Sujaku Murakami
North China Liao Tai Zong Liao Shi Zong
South China Hou Jin dynasty Hou Han dynasty
941 942 943 944 945 946 947 948 949 950

AD 951-960

BYZANTIUM
CONSTANTINE VII PORPHYROGENITUS
ROMANUS II
EUDOXIA

In 955 Otto I thoroughly defeated the Hungarians at a place called Lechfeld, finally putting an end to their raids, the last of which had occurred in the previous year.

The Grand Duchess Olga was the widow of Igor who, near the end of his life, had plundered the shores of the Bosporus with a Viking fleet. Olga paid a prolonged visit to Byzantium, having first been baptized and changed her name to Helena in honour of the Byzantine empress. Her meetings with priests and other representatives of the church were to have some influence on the destiny of the Russian kingdom.

In Persia during the previous century various dynasties in different provinces had thrown off the sovereignty of the Caliph of Baghdad. In 945 a member of the reigning Buyid dynasty named Mu'izz ad-Dawlah made himself emir of Baghdad and assumed all the temporal power of the caliph. From now on the caliph was no more than a religious dignitary.

In 959 Lorraine, which from the 9th century onward was a bone of contention between Germany and France, was divided into two duchies: Mosel and Brabant, as vassal states under the German crown.

In 945 the Norseman Erik Bloodaxe was ejected from York where he had ruled over a Viking kingdom ever since being expelled from Norway. The English now took control of all Scandinavian settlements on the island.

During Ramiro II's reign Count Fernan Gonzales made himself independent of Leon and established the kingdom of Castile.

Two Tahitian voyagers, Kupe and Ngahue, are said to have discovered New Zealand in 950 and become the first Polynesian emigrants there. It is aslo claimed that in 957 Society Island natives began occupying the Hawaiian archipelago.

In 960 China proper was reunited under a new dynasty named Song. The founder of this dynasty was a general who was later known as Emperor Tai Zu, the Great Founder. The capital now became Kaifeng on the Yellow River. It heralded a peaceful era with a sharp increase in population and a flourishing culture. The printing of the Confucian records was completed in 953, having taken twenty years, and a contemporary illustration shows that the people were now furnishing their rooms with chairs.

By now the Qitan Tungus had become so assimilated that their imperial dynasty was known as Liao. The Liao dynasty is reckoned from 947 and survived until 1173.

In 960 the Byzantine general Nicephorus Phocas retook Crete from the Arabs. The Cretan emir's appeals for help were ignored by his fellow believers in Cordoba and Baghdad, where the caliphs had inadequate resources at their disposal.

Above left: Under the Saxon ruler Otto I, Germany emerged as a leading power in Europe. This coin with his portrait is in the Mansell Collection, London.

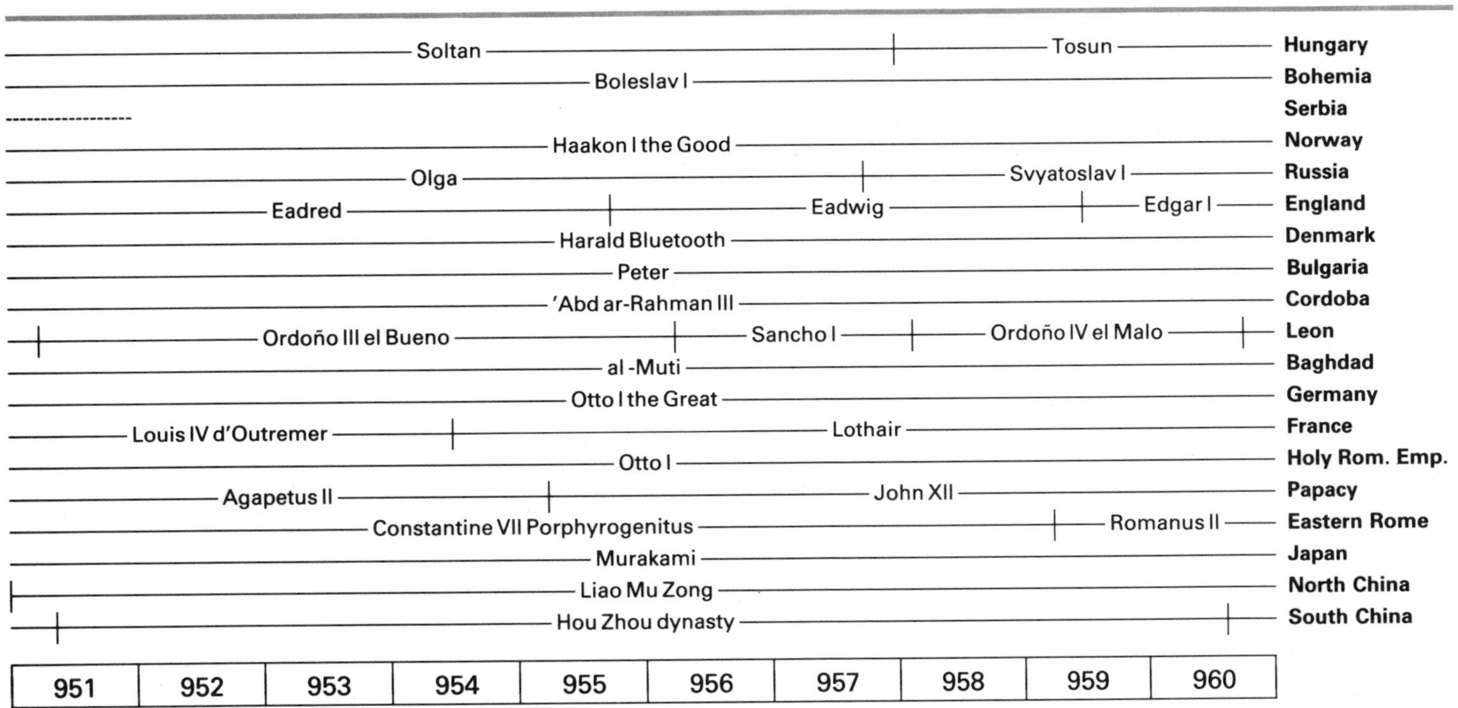
Soltan — Tosun — Hungary
Boleslav I — Bohemia
Serbia
Haakon I the Good — Norway
Olga — Svyatoslav I — Russia
Eadred — Eadwig — Edgar I — England
Harald Bluetooth — Denmark
Peter — Bulgaria
'Abd ar-Rahman III — Cordoba
Ordoño III el Bueno — Sancho I — Ordoño IV el Malo — Leon
al-Muti — Baghdad
Otto I the Great — Germany
Louis IV d'Outremer — Lothair — France
Otto I — Holy Rom. Emp.
Agapetus II — John XII — Papacy
Constantine VII Porphyrogenitus — Romanus II — Eastern Rome
Murakami — Japan
Liao Mu Zong — North China
Hou Zhou dynasty — South China
951 952 953 954 955 956 957 958 959 960

AD 961-970

ENGLAND
KING EDGAR I
BYZANTIUM
CHINA

Otto I, the first emperor of the Holy Roman empire, was crowned in Rome in 962. He soon encountered problems with the popes, however, and had to remove two of these from office. 964 was a particularly confusing year in papal history: at one point there were no less than three popes simultaneously: John XII, Leo VIII and Benedict V. Otto I was particularly concerned with Italy where he fought a king named Berengar and also turned on the Byzantine possessions in the south. He took Bari and various other towns, though he later gave them up when the Byzantines at length agreed to despatch one of their princesses to become his son's wife. Her name was Theophano and among her attendants were certain Greek artists who settled and taught in Cologne.

In 969 a warrior from Tripoli named al-Mu'izz invaded Egypt. His Fatimid dynasty represented a Muslim sect which claimed to be descended from Muhammad's daughter Fatima. The Fatimids founded Cairo and ruled as caliphs in Egypt for several centuries.

During Edgar I's reign, England was, formally, a united Anglo-Saxon kingdom with Celtic vassal states in the north and west. There was no common law, however, and feudal authority was, if anything, stronger than ever.

In Czech history Boleslav I and Boleslav II are known respectively as The Cruel and the Pious. The latter favoured Christianity which permeated Bohemia totally during his reign.

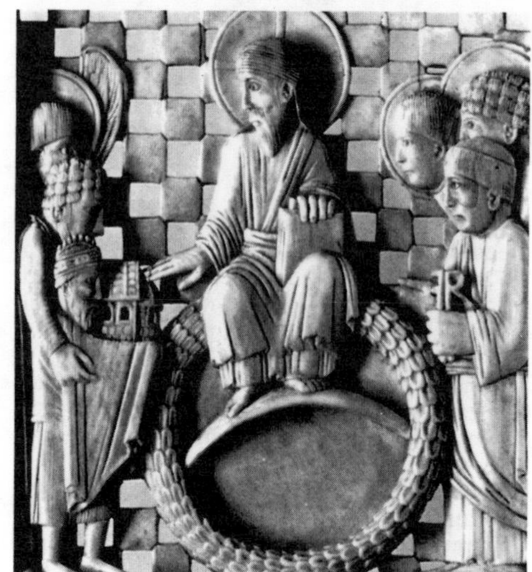

The Byzantine emperor, Nicephorus Phocas had agreed with the Russian Grand Duke Svyatoslav that the latter should make war on the Bulgars. Svyatoslav successfully occupied the whole of Bulgaria and imprisoned King Boris II. But the Byzantines had greater ambitions, and in the summer of 971 Emperor John Tzimisces took the field against the Russians in the Balkans. This expedition was a military masterpiece in which the Russians were surrounded and forced to pledge that they would never again invade the Balkan peninsula. Boris II was then taken into Byzantine custody and interned in Constantinople while his kingdom became a Byzantine province. In a bid for independence, however, a young man named Samuel appointed himself Bulgarian czar and seized almost the whole peninsula, from the Danube to central Greece. The Byzantines, under their new emperor Basil II, were for the moment engaged in other matters.

Otto I (the Great) presents Magdeburg Cathedral to Christ. Contemporary relief in ivory. The emperor had chosen Magdeburg as an unofficial German imperial capital.

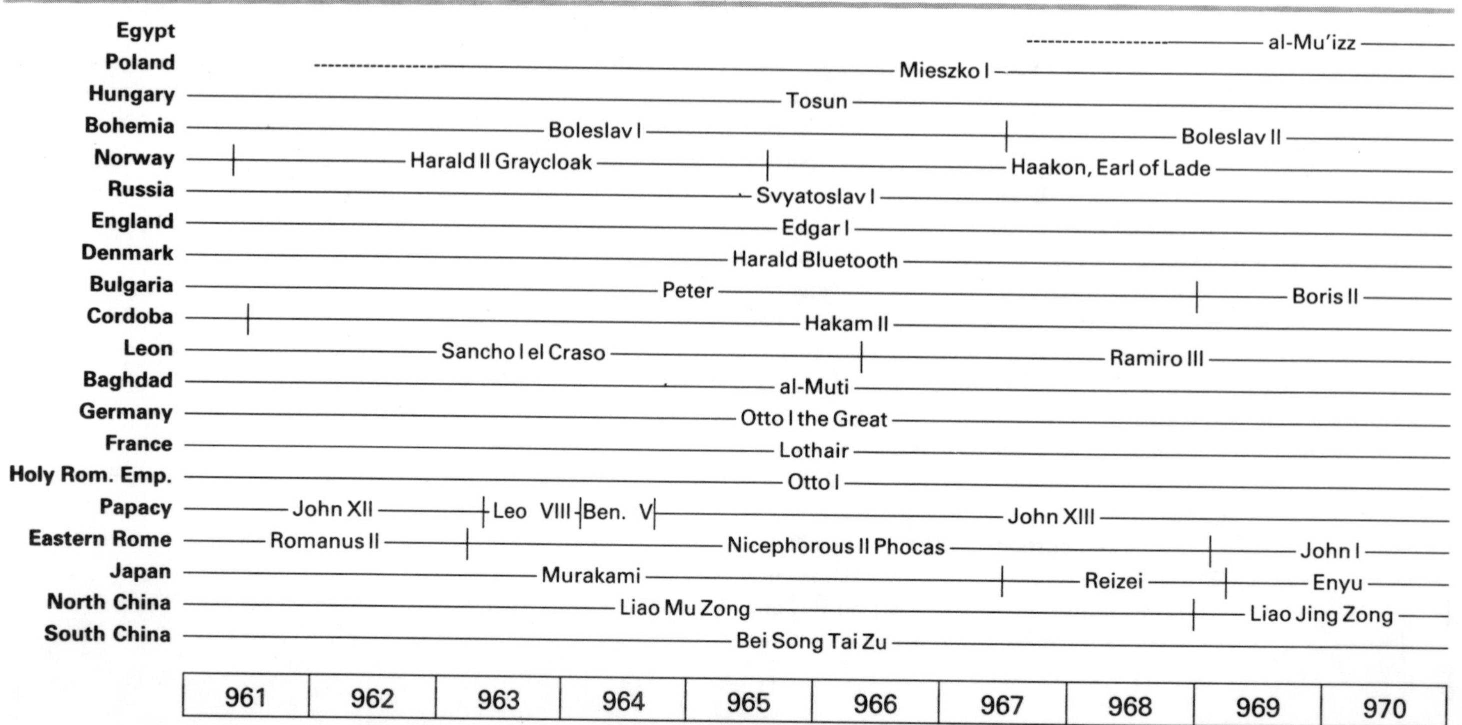
Egypt — al-Mu'izz
Poland — Mieszko I
Hungary — Tosun
Bohemia — Boleslav I — Boleslav II
Norway — Harald II Graycloak — Haakon, Earl of Lade
Russia — Svyatoslav I
England — Edgar I
Denmark — Harald Bluetooth
Bulgaria — Peter — Boris II
Cordoba — Hakam II
Leon — Sancho I el Craso — Ramiro III
Baghdad — al-Muti
Germany — Otto I the Great
France — Lothair
Holy Rom. Emp. — Otto I
Papacy — John XII — Leo VIII — Ben. V — John XIII
Eastern Rome — Romanus II — Nicephorous II Phocas — John I
Japan — Murakami — Reizei — Enyu
North China — Liao Mu Zong — Liao Jing Zong
South China — Bei Song Tai Zu
961 962 963 964 965 966 967 968 969 970

SPAIN
KHMERS.
CAMBODIA
CHINA

The first known Polish dynasty was the Piastic, said to have been established in the 9th century by a peasant named Piast. The first dependably historical member of this dynasty was Mieszko, who was baptized in 966. He was reputed to have become such a devout Christian that he neglected to govern his country properly and failed to defend it, as he had done very effectively prior to baptism, against the Russians.

Leo VIII held office from 4 December 963 to 1 March 965, though Benedict V enjoyed a brief period of power from 22 May 964 to 23 June 964. Both appear in the recognized papal lists, though the latter might more properly be reckoned as an anti-pope. John XIII, the emperor's protégé, assumed office officially on 1 October 965. It is hardly possible to present this graphically below.

A considerable body of literature developed in the court of Otto the Great and in some Western monasteries. Liutprand of Cremona, whom the emperor used for diplomatic missions in Constantinople, left a naive and hence very readable report on his meeting with Emperor Nicephorus Phocas and also wrote a *Historia Ottonis*. Widuking of Corvey composed *Res gestae Saxonicae,* and the work of a nun named Roswitha or Hrotswitha in Gandersheim included six scholarly Latin prose comedies in praise of chastity. Ekhard of St Gallen skilfully put into Latin hexameters a heroic saga relating to Waltharius from Aquitania and Hildegunda who fled home from the land of the Huns. The monastery at St Gallen in Switzerland was both a centre and a refuge of learning and literature. Living here at this time was Notker Labeo (Big Lips), as distinct from Notker Balbulus (the Stammerer) who lived in the district at the beginning of the century. One of these authors had written tracts on the mensurable music of the pipe organ, and Notker Labeo also translated the Psalter and Aristotle into the High German of his time.

Norse Vikings had established themselves in Ireland which was split up into seven small kingdoms. From 977 onwards these were united to some extent by a local chieftain called Brian, known as Brian Boru.

India. where Buddhism was beginning to be supplanted by Brahmanism, was, as always, broken up into innumerable small states, the histories of which are obscure. In nearby Afghanistan, from the 960s, an energetic Muslim dynasty appeared, represented at this time by Sebuktigin I. In 977 Sebuktigin overran Indian Peshawar, so initiating a long series of victorious expeditions in India, led by his son and successor.

An attempt by the Song dynasty to retake northern China from the Tungus' Liao dynasty failed. China thus remained divided into two states, the southern one being culturally the more significant. Its economy was so well developed that there were notes of two denominations, issued by a banking house in Szechwan in the south-west. Emperor Tai Zu also built up a very complex civil administration apparatus. There is an anecdote of how he disarmed his generals in preparation for this policy. At a banquet he mentioned to the generals that he often lay awake at night, worrying about who would depose him. He himself had become an emperor through revolution, and he feared that others were plotting against him in the same way. When the guests swore that this was not the case, the emperor announced that in order to thank them for their loyalty he would free them of all hardship, by giving them extensive properties where they could live a comfortable life with their families. There was no objection to this decision.

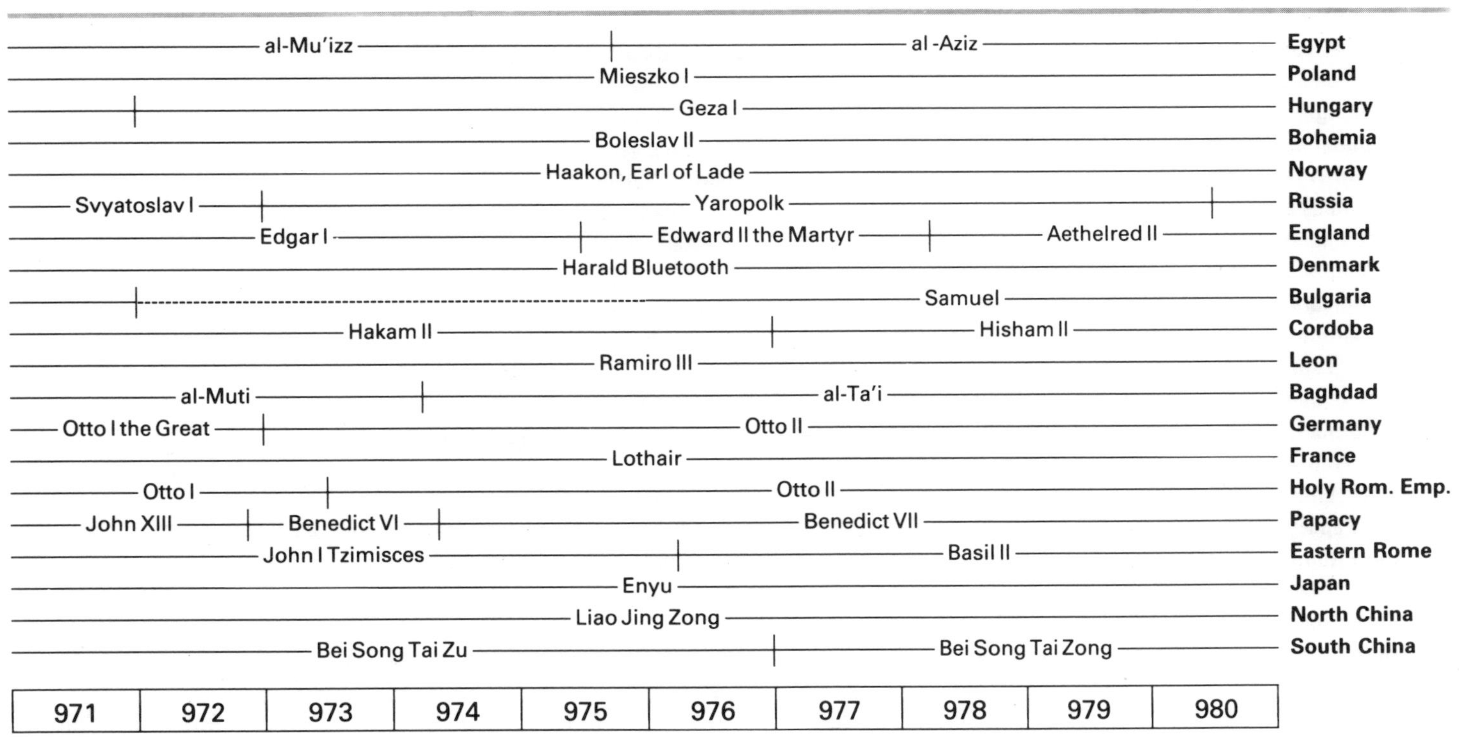
al-Mu'izz
al -Aziz
Egypt
Mieszko I
Poland
Geza I
Hungary
Boleslav II
Bohemia
Haakon, Earl of Lade
Norway
Svyatoslav I
Yaropolk
Russia
Edgar I
Edward II the Martyr
Aethelred II
England
Harald Bluetooth
Denmark
Samuel
Bulgaria
Hakam II
Hisham II
Cordoba
Ramiro III
Leon
al-Muti
al-Ta'i
Baghdad
Otto I the Great
Otto II
Germany
Lothair
France
Otto I
Otto II
Holy Rom. Emp.
John XIII
Benedict VI
Benedict VII
Papacy
John I Tzimisces
Basil II
Eastern Rome
Enyu
Japan
Liao Jing Zong
North China
Bei Song Tai Zu
Bei Song Tai Zong
South China
971
972
973
974
975
976
977
978
979
980

HOLY ROMAN
EMPIRE
BYZANTIUM

Grand Duke Vladimir, who had fought his brothers as well as Poles, Bulgars, Lithuanians and Pechenegs, became a Christian in 989. He dismissed his four wives and 800 concubines before his ceremonial wedding to the Byzantine emperor's sister, Anna. Then he ordered all the inhabitants of Kiev to wade out into the Dnieper and undergo baptism. The Nestorian chronicle describes Vladimir's conversion: first he considered Islam but the Koran's prohibition of alcohol was too much of a stumbling block; after much vacillation he finally decided upon the Greek version of Christianity. He appears in history both as Vladimir the Great and Saint Vladimir.

In the year 1000 Christianity was legally adopted in religion of Iceland. The debate that had preceded this decision appears to have been concerned mainly with the subject of eating horse-flesh.

The battle of Fyrisvallarna, in which Styrbjörn the Strong and his Joms' Vikings were defeated and slain, is said to have taken place (if it is not altogether legendary) in 988. The Swedish king, Erik the Victorious, was in any event a genuine historical figure. Although not the first Svea king whose existence can be verified - the Uppsala kings Ottar Vendelkråka, Egil and Adils had preceded him several centuries earlier - Erik the Victorious heads the first sequential list of rulers and chronological records.

The last of the Carolingians in France was Louis le Fainéant, Louis Do-Nothing, and this is all that can be said of him. Hugh Capet, who was elected to succeed him, had been Duke of Paris, which he now made the capital of the French monarchy. There was nothing particularly remarkable about Hugh Capet, but his dynasty was to be long-lived.

An interesting incident in papal history occurred in the reign of Emperor Otto III when a certain Crescentius proclaimed the resurrection of the Roman republic. He then appointed himself consul, expelled Pope Gregory V and replaced him with an anti-pope called John XVI, who subsequently had his rival blinded and ordered his ears, nose and tongue to be cut off.

From 977 to 999 a priestly king from Tula in Mexico reigned over a group who had left their native district and settled in the more southerly Yucatan beyond the reach of the warrior caste which was at this time ruling the Toltecs. The peaceful corn gods previously worshipped by the Toltecs were now supplanted by new, terrifying deities who took the guise of plumed serpents and demanded human sacrifices.

Two of the Icelandic sagas relate to Vinland, but only one of them names Leif Eriksson as its discoverer. From an original manuscript.

Sweden	Erik the Victorious
Egypt	al-Aziz
Poland	Mieszko I
Hungary	Geza I
Bohemia	Boleslav II
Norway	Haakon, Earl of Lade
Russia	Vladimir
England	Aethelred II
Denmark	Harald Bluetooth; Sweyn Forkbeard
Bulgaria	Samuel
Cordoba	Hisham II
Leon	Ramiro III; Bermudo II el Gotoso
Baghdad	al-Ta'i
Germany	Otto II; (Theophano)
France	Lothair; Louis V; Hugh Capet
Holy Rom. Emp.	Otto II; Otto III
Papacy	Benedict VII; John XIV; Bonif. VII; John XV
Eastern Rome	Basil II
Japan	Enyu; Kazan; Ichijo
North China	Liao Jing Zong; Liao Sheng zóng
South China	Bei Song Tai Zong

981	982	983	984	985	986	987	988	989	990

AD 991-1000

OTTO III
HOLY ROMAN EMPIRE

In the year 1000 the newly discovered mainland of North America was visited by Leif Eriksson from Greenland. He called this country Vinland and reported that grape vines grew wild in the place where he spent the winter. Leif Eriksson was the son of Greenland's first leader, Erik the Red. He succeeded him as chieftain of Greenland and on the orders of Olaf Tryggvason established Christianity here.

Stephen I, or Holy Stefan, is the national saint of the Hungarians. He presented himself to his heathen countrymen and was awarded the title of apostolic majesty by the pope.

The sea battle at Svolder is dated at the year 1000. Here the Norwegian king, Olaf Tryggvason was slain by the Dane Sweyn Forkbeard and the Swede Olof Skötkonung in alliance with several Norwegian jarls.

The Bulgarian Czar Samuel achieved great successes at the expense of the Byzantines. He liberated Bulgaria itself and conquered a large portion of the Bosnian and Serbian territories.

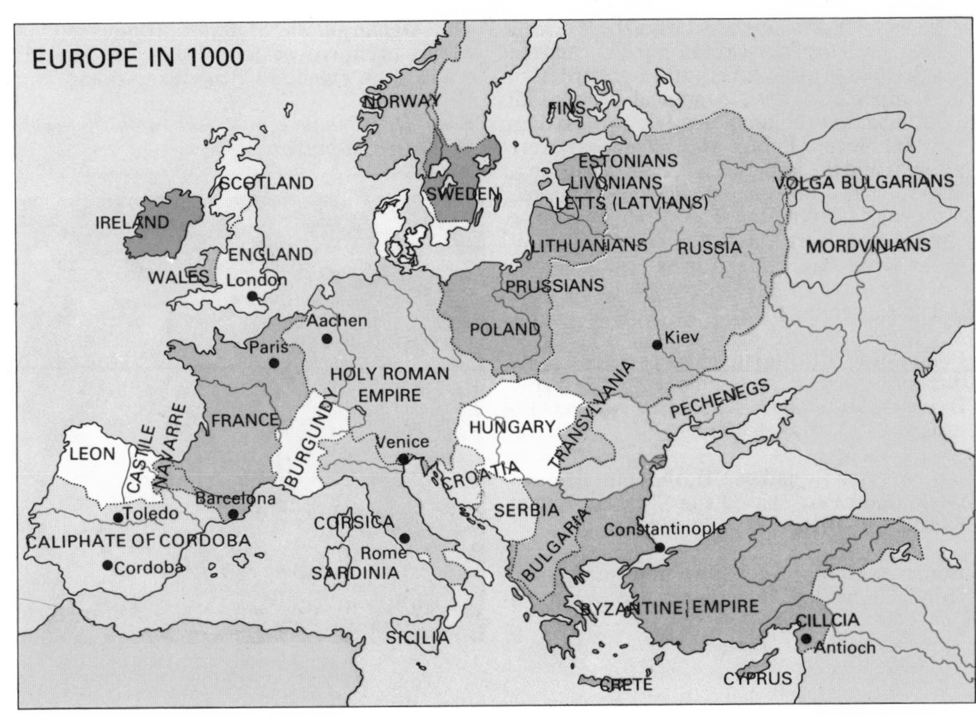
EUROPE IN 1000
NORWAY
FINS
ESTONIANS
LIVONIANS
LETTS (LATVIANS)
VOLGA BULGARIANS
SCOTLAND
SWEDEN
IRELAND
ENGLAND
LITHUANIANS
RUSSIA
MORDVINIANS
WALES
London
PRUSSIANS
Aachen
POLAND
Kiev
Paris
HOLY ROMAN EMPIRE
PECHENEGS
TRANSYLVANIA
HUNGARY
FRANCE
LEON
CASTILE
NAVARRE
BURGUNDY
Venice
CROATIA
SERBIA
Barcelona
Toledo
CORSICA
BULGARIA
Constantinople
CALIPHATE OF CORDOBA
Rome
Cordoba
SARDINIA
BYZANTINE EMPIRE
CILLCIA
Antioch
SICILIA
CRETE
CYPRUS

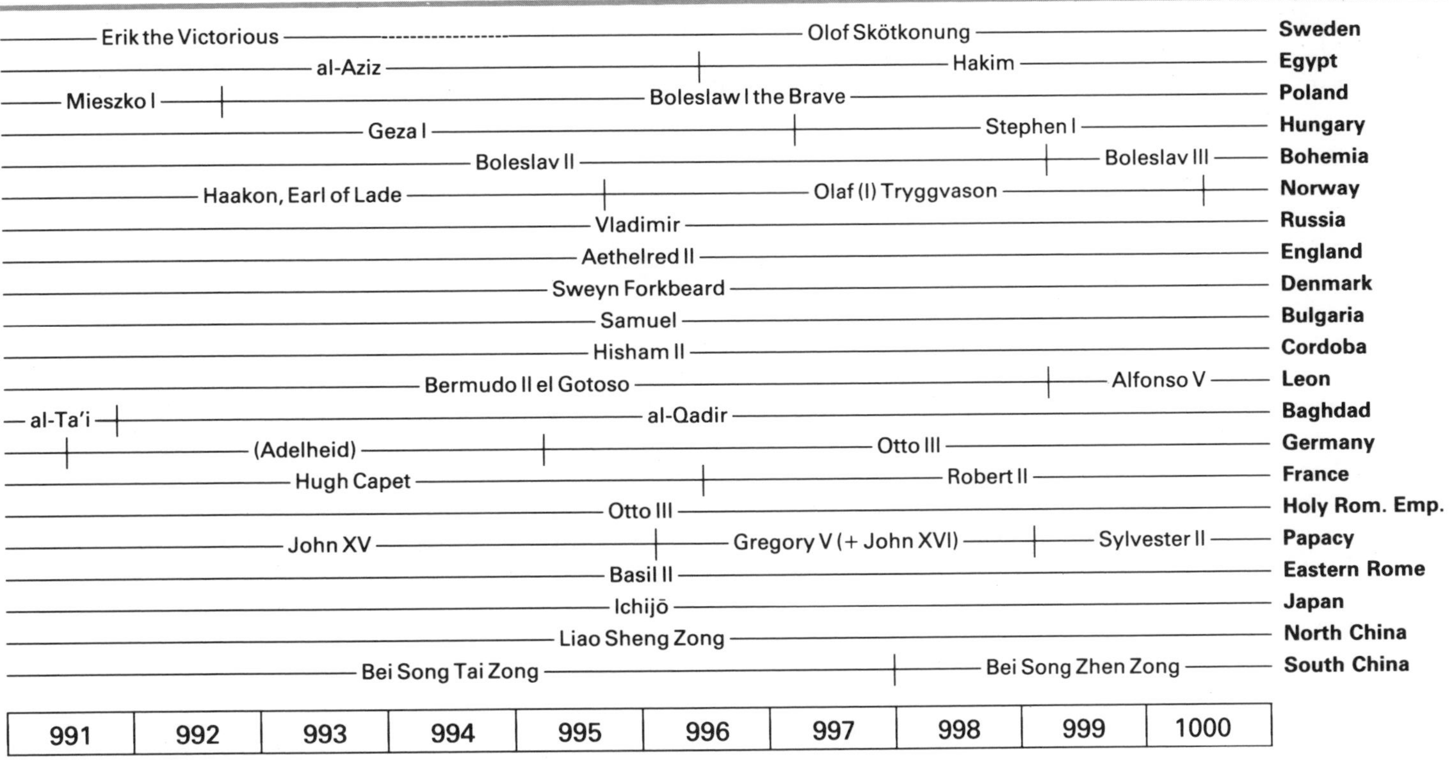
Erik the Victorious — Olof Skötkonung — Sweden
al-Aziz — Hakim — Egypt
Mieszko I — Boleslaw I the Brave — Poland
Geza I — Stephen I — Hungary
Boleslav II — Boleslav III — Bohemia
Haakon, Earl of Lade — Olaf (I) Tryggvason — Norway
Vladimir — Russia
Aethelred II — England
Sweyn Forkbeard — Denmark
Samuel — Bulgaria
Hisham II — Cordoba
Bermudo II el Gotoso — Alfonso V — Leon
al-Ta'i — al-Qadir — Baghdad
(Adelheid) — Otto III — Germany
Hugh Capet — Robert II — France
Otto III — Holy Rom. Emp.
John XV — Gregory V (+ John XVI) — Sylvester II — Papacy
Basil II — Eastern Rome
Ichijō — Japan
Liao Sheng Zong — North China
Bei Song Tai Zong — Bei Song Zhen Zong — South China
991 992 993 994 995 996 997 998 999 1000

AD 1001-1010

MAYA
CHINA

Art and science flourished during the Bei Song (Northern Song) dynasty in China. During the last decades of the 10th century, at the orders of the emperor, all the canonical writings of Buddhism were printed, involving no less than 130,000 blocks. Poetry and calligraphy were popular and the imperial academy of painting, Han Lin (the Forest of Brushes), was founded in the capital of Kaifeng. The whole of northern China, however, was ruled by the Tungus Qitan dynasty; although it had adopted the Chinese name of Liao, it showed very little interest in culture.

Poland was consolidated and extended in all directions during the reign of Boleslaw I (the Brave). An archiepiscopal see was established at Gniezno in 1000.

Led by Pope Benedict VII, the joint fleets of Genoa and Pisa chased the Saracens out of Sardinia in 1016.

Emperor Henry II is known in history as the Holy. His wife, Cunegunda, also became a saint.

The Afghan sultan, Mahmud, conquered the whole of north-western India so that his realm now extended from Samarkand and Bochara all the way to the upper Ganges. He also made himself independent of the Persians when in the next decade he deposed the last of the Buyid shahs and seized Iran.

Basil II, miniature in a Byzantine hymnal. Biblioteca Marcians, Venice.

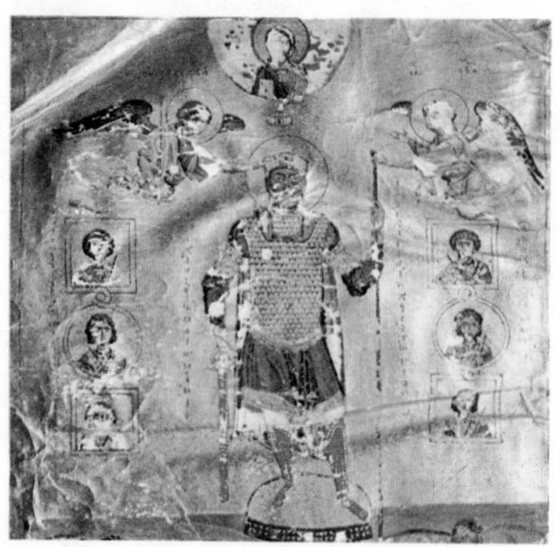

The Irish king, Brian Boru, was killed in the battle of Clontarf in 1014, after which Ireland was once more split into seven small kingdoms, in addition to the independent Viking states of Dublin, Cork, Limerick, etc.

A band of Normandy pilgrims arrived in southern Italy in 1003 and were accidentally involved in helping to repulse a Saracen raid on Salerno. In gratitude, the Lombard Duke of Salerno took them into his service. Other groups subsequently arrived from Normandy, even though the region was under Byzantine sovereignty.

Scottish history proper can be said to have begun with Malcolm II, king of a small realm named Alba. By defeating Northumbria Malcolm also gained control of the lowlands north of the Tweed.

	1001–1010
Scotland	---- | Malcolm II
Sweden	Olof Skötkonung
Egypt	Hakim
Poland	Boleslaw I the Brave
Hungary	Stephen I
Bohemia	---- | Vladivoj | Jaromir
Norway	Erik and Sweyn ----
Russia	Vladimir
England	Aethelred II
Denmark	Sweyn Forkbeard
Bulgaria	Samuel
Cordoba	Hisham II | Muhammad II |
Leon	Alfonso V el Noble
Baghdad	al-Qadir
Germany	Otto III | Henry II
France	Robert II the Pious
Holy Rom. Emp	Otto III | Henry II
Papacy	Sylvester II | John XVII | John XVIII | Sergius IV
Eastern Rome	Basil II
Japan	Ichijō
North China	Liao Sheng Zong
South China	Bei Song Zhen Zong

1001	1002	1003	1004	1005	1006	1007	1008	1009	1010

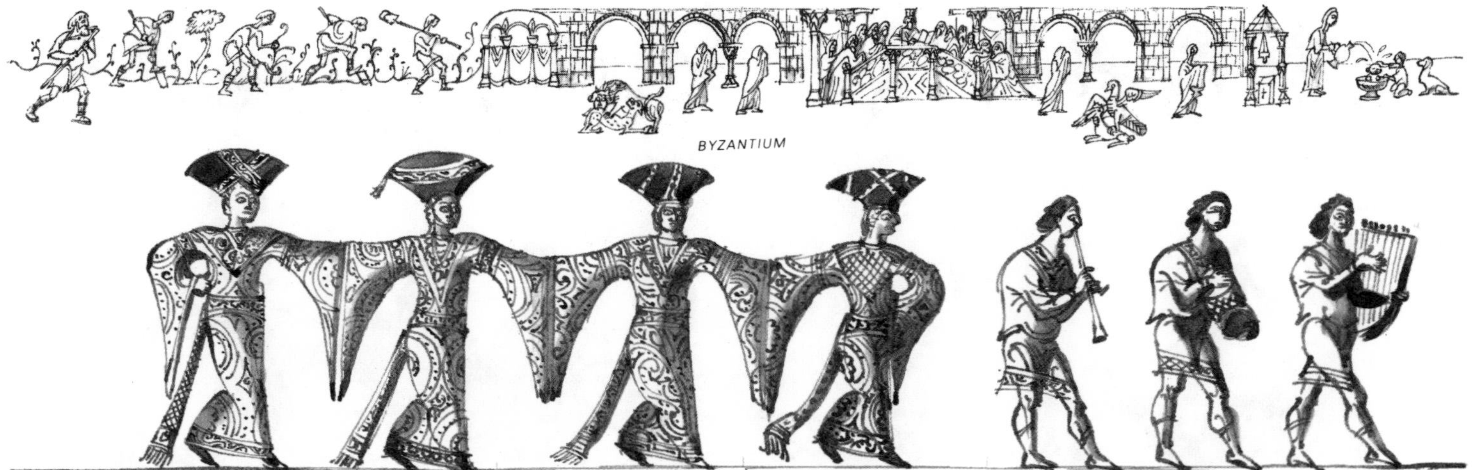
BYZANTIUM

The caliphate of Cordoba was approaching its demise. A general named al-Mansur continued to win impressive victories over the Christians even during this decade, but a series of revolutions and counter-revolutions brought about a constant succession of caliphs and completely disrupted organized rule. A slave revolt and a prolonged siege of the city of Cordoba from 1011 to 1012 created a desperate situation. For a brief period there was a republican-style administration. Some of the last caliphs were rather colourful figures. 'Abd ar-Rahman V, who appears in the next decade, was one of the principal poets in the Arab world, twenty-two years old and brimming with lyrical fervour. He used other poets as his political advisers yet managed to retain power for several months.

A southern Indian king named Rajaraja took Ceylon. His dynasty, the Chola, ruled southern India for a couple of centuries.

Canute of Denmark completed the conquest of England begun by his father Sweyn Forkbeard. At the father's death Canute's brother Harald became king of Denmark and when in due course he died as well Canute became king of both realms.

The Mayas, whose ancient Mexican empire had been dissolved some centuries ago, created a new state on the Yucatan peninsula. This was achieved under the influence of the immigrant Toltecs who were politically more advanced than the Mayas.

In Russia, after the death of Vladimir, there were fierce fraternal wars among his many sons and the country was divided between several of them. Finally, however, Russia was reunited under Yaroslav and remained intact during this time. Olof Skötkonung was baptized in 1010.

The Byzantine emperor, Basil II, finally defeated the Bulgar armies and put out the eyes of 14,000 prisoners: one man in every hundred was permitted to retain one eye so that he could lead his companions home. Czar Samuel swooned at the sight of his returning army and died two days later. Shortly afterwards the kingdom of Bulgaria ceased to exist.

Under Doge Pietro Oresolo, Venice had become a considerable power and had incorporated many towns on the eastern shore of the Adriatic.

Byzantine cavalry pursuing Vikings from Kiev, miniature in Scylitzes' chronicle for the period 811-1079. A number of Byzantine chroniclers recounted the history of Byzantium. Manuscript in the Biblioteca Nacional, Madrid.

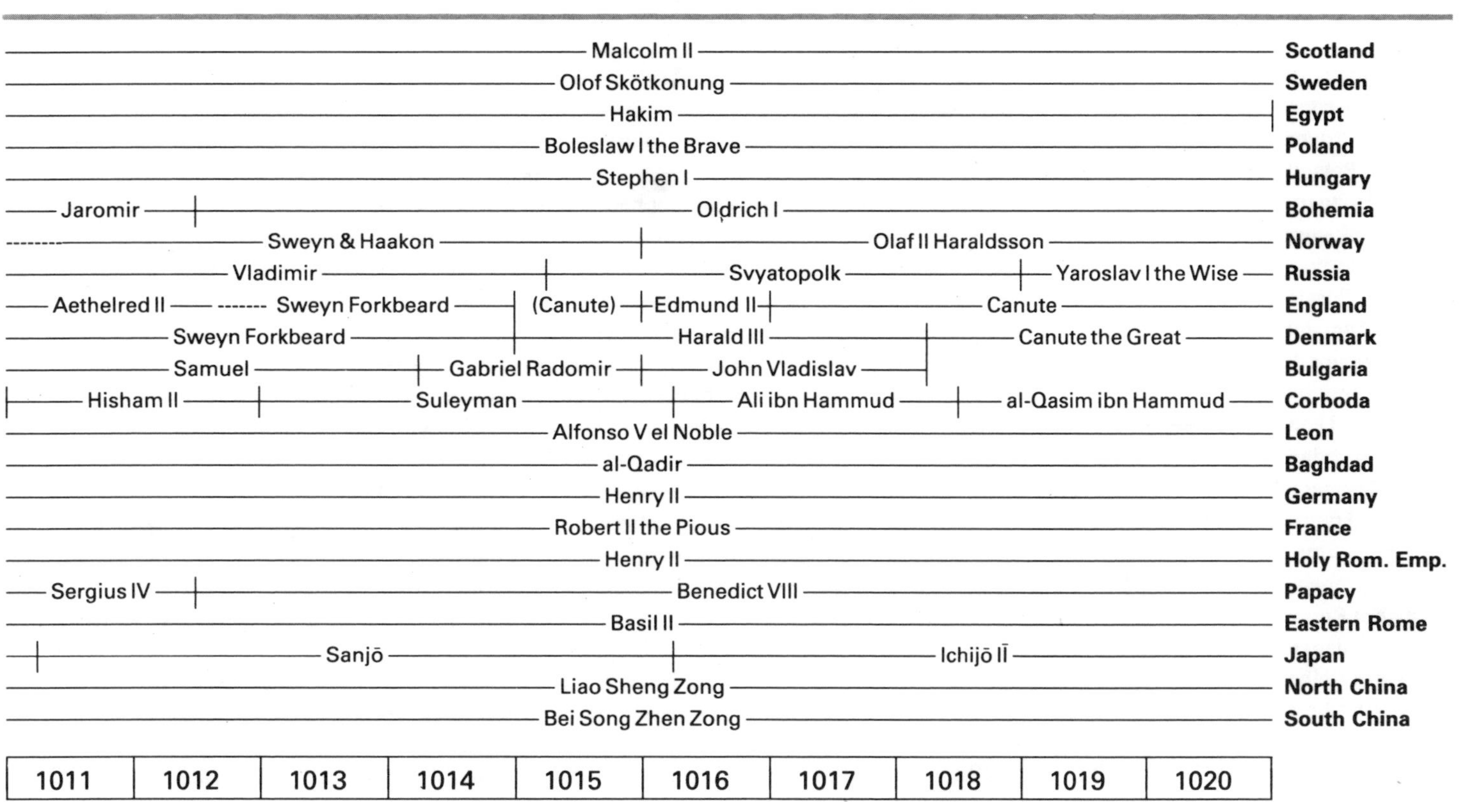
Malcolm II — Scotland
Olof Skötkonung — Sweden
Hakim — Egypt
Boleslaw I the Brave — Poland
Stephen I — Hungary
Jaromir — Oldrich I — Bohemia
Sweyn & Haakon — Olaf II Haraldsson — Norway
Vladimir — Svyatopolk — Yaroslav I the Wise — Russia
Aethelred II — Sweyn Forkbeard — (Canute) — Edmund II — Canute — England
Sweyn Forkbeard — Harald III — Canute the Great — Denmark
Samuel — Gabriel Radomir — John Vladislav — Bulgaria
Hisham II — Suleyman — Ali ibn Hammud — al-Qasim ibn Hammud — Corboda
Alfonso V el Noble — Leon
al-Qadir — Baghdad
Henry II — Germany
Robert II the Pious — France
Henry II — Holy Rom. Emp.
Sergius IV — Benedict VIII — Papacy
Basil II — Eastern Rome
Sanjō — Ichijō II — Japan
Liao Sheng Zong — North China
Bei Song Zhen Zong — South China
1011 1012 1013 1014 1015 1016 1017 1018 1019 1020

BYZANTIUM
CHINA

In 1025 Sancho III of Navarre, a small Christian kingdom whose monarchs had been called either Sancho or Garcia ever since the 9th century, also became reigning Count of Castile in succession to his brother-in-law, who was the last male member of his line. The Spanish kingdoms of Navarre and Castile were thus now united. Sancho's son Ferdinand married Princess Sancha of Leon whose family on the male side was also dying out. In this way the whole of Christian Spain was united under one and the same dynasty in the following decade. But when Sancho died in 1035, his realm was divided up between his sons Ferdinand and Ramiro. Ramiro inherited Aragon while Ferdinand became king of Castile and two years later also of Leon, which from then on declined.

1031 was the last year of the Spanish caliphate in Cordoba. By this time the caliphate had become divided up into a number of small states: Toledo, Saragossa, Valencia, Murcia, Seville and others. Cordoba itself lost its independence, the greater part of its territory going to Seville.

The question of succession had become a problem in Byzantium. Basil was unmarried and childless, and his brother Constantine VIII had only two young daughters, the elder of whom, Zoe, was quickly married off to an elderly aristocrat who became emperor when Constantine died in 1028. There was, however, no heir. The newly widowed Zoe hastened to marry a younger man who was immediately made Emperor Michael IV. There was no issue of this marriage either, perhaps just as well since Michael suffered from epilepsy and died young.

Olaf Haraldsson, who had forcibly made himself ruler of Norway in 1010, was expelled in 1028 and sought refuge with his brother-in-law Yaroslav in Russia. Shortly afterwards he returned with an army by way of Sweden, but was met by his Norwegian foes at Stiklastad in Tröndelagen, where he was slain. Miracles occurred at his grave, however, and within a few decades he had become St Olaf, Scandinavia's principal medieval saint.

Pope Benedict VIII was a prominent regent in the now influential Papal State, though his interest in spiritual affairs was limited. Benedict was also an able general and, in alliance with the states of Pisa and Genoa, led a campaign against the Saracens in southern Italy and defeated them decisively. He also made a pact with Emperor Henry II and led an unsuccessful operation against the Byzantines. Only at the request of his emperor did Benedict concern himself with certain church affairs, arranging, for example, a council in Pavia where clerical marriage, which was still very common, was prohibited on pain of excommunication.

Boleslaw I of Poland had overrun Pomerania, Silesia, Moravia, the Kiev region and various other areas, but his son Mieszko II managed to lose most of this territory. The Danes captured Pomerania, the Russians took Kiev and the Czechs regained their independence.

Russian law was codified in this decade for the first time with the appearance in Novgorod of a document entitled *Pravda*.

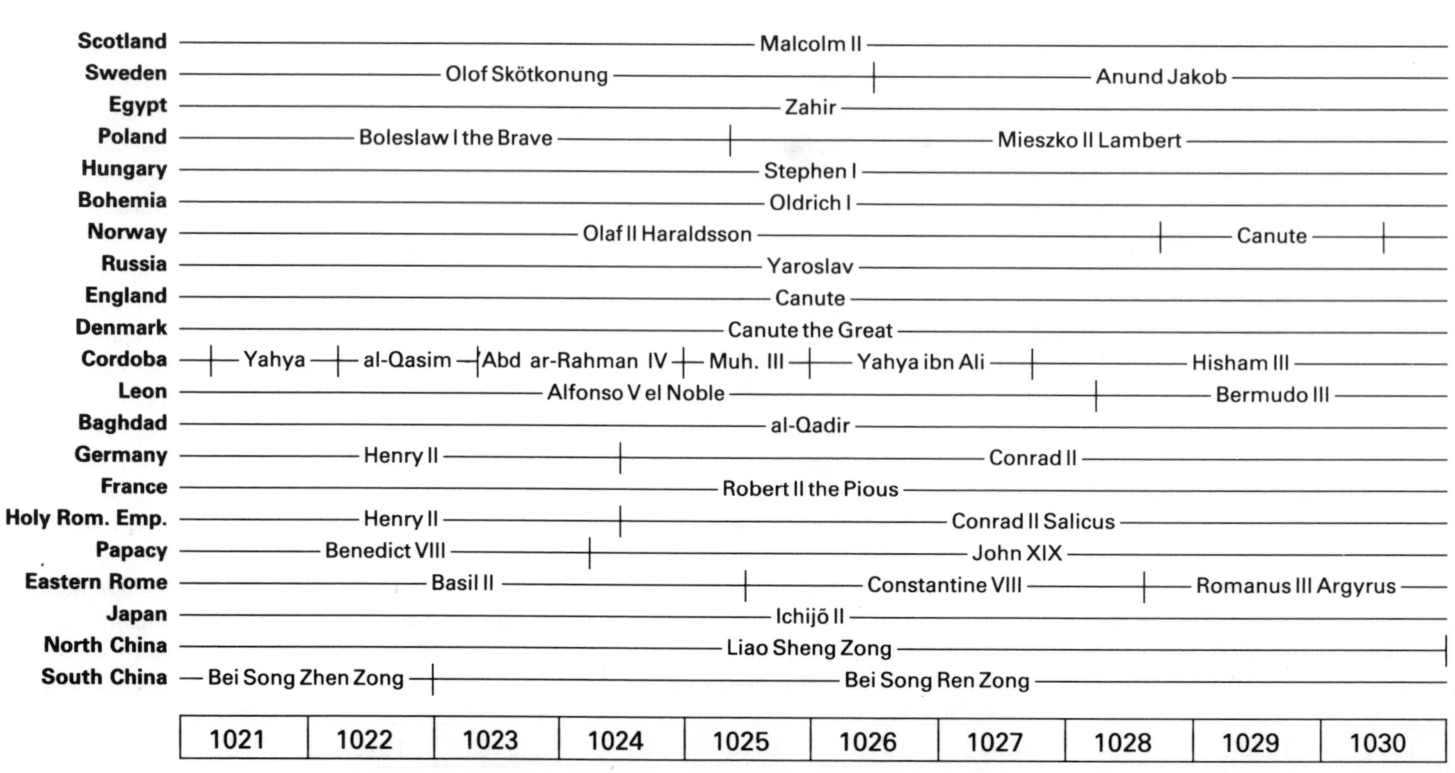
Scotland
Malcolm II
Sweden
Olof Skötkonung
Anund Jakob
Egypt
Zahir
Poland
Boleslaw I the Brave
Mieszko II Lambert
Hungary
Stephen I
Bohemia
Oldrich I
Norway
Olaf II Haraldsson
Canute
Russia
Yaroslav
England
Canute
Denmark
Canute the Great
Cordoba
Yahya
al-Qasim
Abd ar-Rahman IV
Muh. III
Yahya ibn Ali
Hisham III
Leon
Alfonso V el Noble
Bermudo III
Baghdad
al-Qadir
Germany
Henry II
Conrad II
France
Robert II the Pious
Holy Rom. Emp.
Henry II
Conrad II Salicus
Papacy
Benedict VIII
John XIX
Eastern Rome
Basil II
Constantine VIII
Romanus III Argyrus
Japan
Ichijō II
North China
Liao Sheng Zong
South China
Bei Song Zhen Zong
Bei Song Ren Zong
1021
1022
1023
1024
1025
1026
1027
1028
1029
1030

BYZANTIUM
CANUTE THE GREAT

In America the Maya people continued to live in anonymity. There was a stone column engraved with calendaric data at a cult site called Copan in the future Honduras.

Emperor Henry II's line, which died with him, was known as the Saxon dynasty. It was succeeded by the Salian dynasty.

Poland was rent by anarchy and political disruption in the mid 1030s. Casimir I who was not of age on his father's death, fled the country but returned with the support of Henry III to assert his authority. He retrieved Silesia and other lost territory.

In Scotland the murder of Duncan in 1040 by Macbeth was to be immortalized by Shakespeare.

The Seljuks were a Turkish tribe who began to invade the disintegrating caliphate from areas east of the Caspian Sea. They had already conquered northern Persia.

Immediately after his death, King Canute's large realm was dissolved. His son Sweyn was expelled from Norway in favour of St Olaf's son Magnus. England was taken over by Canute's son Harold, whose mother was English, while his half-brother Hardecanute claimed Denmark. Subsequently these monarchs warred among themselves. Hardecanute and Magnus reached an agreement whereby the one who lived longer should inherit the other's kingdom. Hardecanute then set sail for England to fight Harold who died, however, before he landed. Hardecanute, having thrown his brother's corpse into the Thames, became king of England.

Until about the 9th century, the Khazar kingdom north of the Black Sea had been a strong power. Gradually, however, it had lost ground to the Grand Dukes of Kiev and in 1016 it was finally destroyed by a Russian-Byzantine alliance.

King Canute thanking Providence for England. British Museum, London.

Ramiro I	**Aragon**
Toghril Beg	**Seljuks**
Malcolm II — Duncan I	**Scotland**
Anund Jakob	**Sweden**
Zahir — Mustansir	**Egypt**
Mieszko II — Casimir	**Poland**
Stephen I — Peter	**Hungary**
Oldrich I — Bretislav I	**Bohemia**
Sweyn Alfivason (Knutsson) — Magnus (I) the Good	**Norway**
Yaroslav	**Russia**
Canute — Harold Harefoot — Hardecanute	**England**
Canute the Great — Hardecanute	**Denmark**
	Cordoba
Bermudo III — Sancha & Ferdinand I	**Leon (Castile)**
al-Qa'im	**Baghdad**
Conrad II — Henry III	**Germany**
Henry I	**France**
Conrad II Salicus — Henry III	**Holy Rom. Emp.**
John XIX — Benedict IX	**Papacy**
Romanus III Argyrus — Michael IV	**Eastern Rome**
Ichijō II — Sujaku II	**Japan**
Laio Xing Zong	**North China**
Bei Song Ren Zong	**South China**

1031	1032	1033	1034	1035	1036	1037	1038	1039	1040

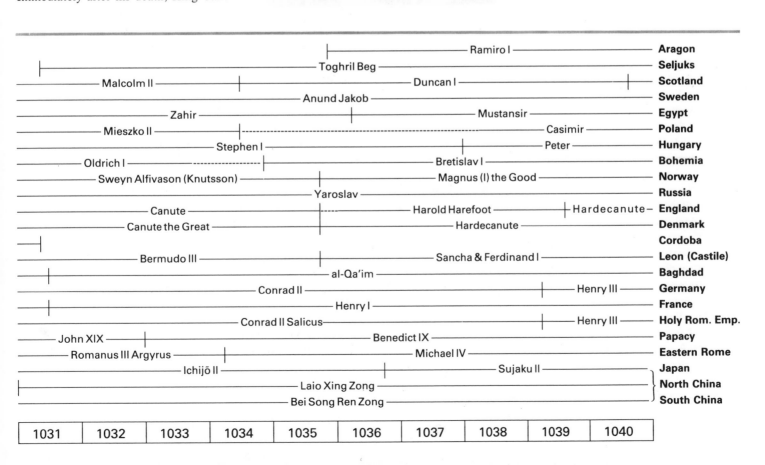

AD 1041-1050

INDIA
BYZANTIUM
CONSTANTINE IX
MONOMACHUS
BYZANTIUM
ZOE

Ferdinand I of Castile and Leon conquered Toledo, Saragossa and, in due course, Seville, and thereby became ruler of the greater part of Spain. In his battles with the Arabs he was aided by a captain named Rodrigo Diaz, known in legend as el Cid.

A curious episode in Byzantine history occurred in 1042 when Michael V was deposed and blinded, and the elderly sisters Zoe and Theodora reigned jointly. Zoe was then married to Constantine IX Monomachus, who thereby assumed power. Zoe did not survive her husband, so that Theodora again became empress in 1055.

Edward the Confessor was the half-brother of Hardecanute on his mother's side. But the real ruler of England in his day was Earl Godwin and afterwards the latter's son Harold Godwinson.

Guido of Arezzo was a monk who improved music notation by using four lines instead of only two, and also by introducing intervals. He likewise invented the system of solmization-mnemonic verse where each phrase brings in higher melodic tone than the immediately preceding one:

Ut queant laxis *re*sonare fibris
*m*ira gestorum *fa*muli tuorum
*so*lve polluti *la*bii reatum
*sa*ncte *Io*hanne.

The years 1045-1048 make up a complex period in papal history, Benedict IX, said to have been an excitable, immoral individual, sold his papal office to Gregory VI. He was deposed and succeeded by Sylvester III, himself no great theologian. In addition, Emperor Henry III appointed two popes, known as Clement II and Damasus II.

Sweyn Estridsson, son of Canute the Great's sister Estrid, squabbled constantly with the Norwegian Harald Hardraade over Denmark.

The Arabs' realm in the Mediterranean region diminished steadily. The city of Pisa captured Sardinia in 1052 while Corsica had already been retaken in the 1020s.

St Sophia in Constantinople, which had lost all its mosaics during the iconoclastic movement of the 8th century, had now acquired some new ones. Constantine IX and Zoe are seen here with the Saviour.

Aragon	Ramiro I
Seljuks	Toghril Beg
Scotland	Macbeth
Sweden	Anund Jakob
Egypt	Mustansir
Poland	Casimir I the Restorer
Hungary	Samuel Aba | Peter | Andrew I
Bohemia	Bretislav I
Norway	Magnus (I) the Good | Harald (III) Hardraade
Russia	Yaroslav
England	Hardecanute | Edward the Confessor
Denmark	Hardecanute | Magnus I | Sweyn Estridsson
Castile	Ferdinand I the Great
Baghdad	al-Qa'im
Germany	Henry III
France	Henry I
Holy Rom.Emp.	Henry III Niger
Papacy	Benedict IX | Sylv. III | Greg. VI | Clem. II | Dam. II | ----- | Leo IX
Eastern Rome	Michael V | Zoe | Constantine IX Monomachus
Japan	Sujaku II | Reizei II
North China	Liao Xing Zong
South China	Bei Song Ren Zong

1041	1042	1043	1044	1045	1046	1047	1048	1049	1050

AD 1051-1060

BYZANTIUM

During the reign of Yaroslav Russia had been much in contact with Scandinavia and Western Europe. After his death the country was split up into many small states, making it impossible to draw up a sequential list of rulers. Yarolsav's eldest son was repeatedly expelled by his relatives and the various families and their descendants remained in a state of unrest and turmoil for centuries to come. At the same time Russia became increasingly isolated from the West, partly because the Seljuks' inroads on the caliphate had curtailed trade down the Volga, and partly because of the decisive rupture between the Greek and Roman churches, and increasing intolerance between East and West.

In Sweden Erik the Victorious's line died out in 1056 and was succeeded by the Stenkils from Västergötland.

Reports of the discovery of Vinland were gradually reaching Europe. The new country was mentioned by Adam of Bremen in his chronicle.

Manco Capac was the name of a king in South America who is thought to have founded the Inca state in Peru.

In 1053 Robert Guiscard, descended from the Vikings, founded the Norman kingdom in southern Italy. Pope Nicholas II recognized him as Count of Calabria and Apulia on condition that he pledged to defend the Holy See.

In 1054 the Roman cardinal, Humbert, deposited a bull of excommunication against the patriarch, Cerularius, on the altar in Hagia Sophia. The latter immediately assembled a council which drew up a list of all the false papal doctrines and heresies, including *filioque* in the Creed. This list was then placed on the same altar as the bull and the bull itself was publically burned while its author was fiercely condemned. This incident resulted in the separation of the Greek and Roman churches.

In Sweden runestones were being erected; most of those in central Sweden are from the first half of the 11th century. The inscriptions have little literary merit compared with Byzantine, Roman and Chinese writings from the same time, but they are often concise and succinct. The stone shown here is from Ågersta in Uppland.

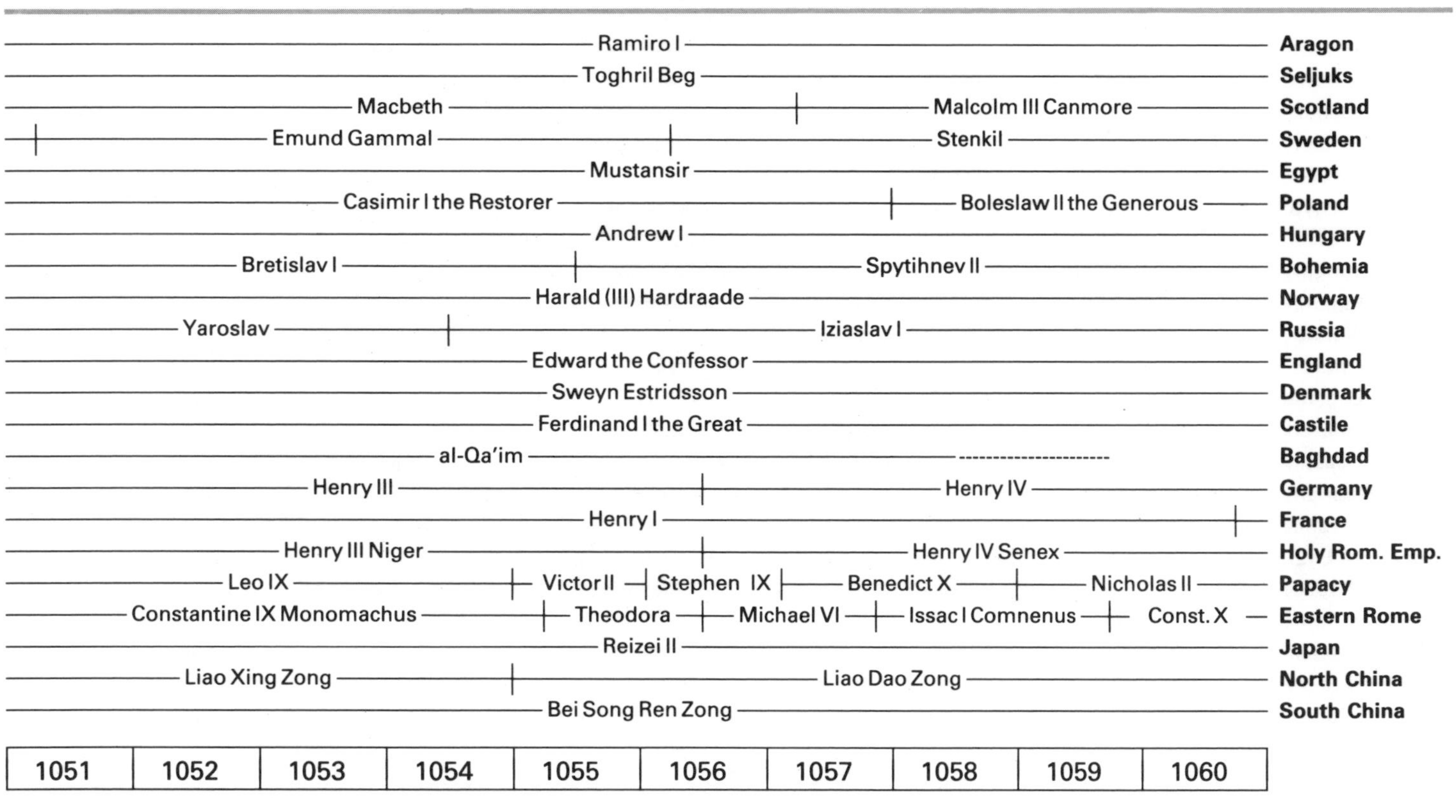
Ramiro I — Aragon
Toghril Beg — Seljuks
Macbeth | Malcolm III Canmore — Scotland
Emund Gammal | Stenkil — Sweden
Mustansir — Egypt
Casimir I the Restorer | Boleslaw II the Generous — Poland
Andrew I — Hungary
Bretislav I | Spytihnev II — Bohemia
Harald (III) Hardraade — Norway
Yaroslav | Iziaslav I — Russia
Edward the Confessor — England
Sweyn Estridsson — Denmark
Ferdinand I the Great — Castile
al-Qa'im ---------------------- Baghdad
Henry III | Henry IV — Germany
Henry I — France
Henry III Niger | Henry IV Senex — Holy Rom. Emp.
Leo IX | Victor II | Stephen IX | Benedict X | Nicholas II — Papacy
Constantine IX Monomachus | Theodora | Michael VI | Issac I Comnenus | Const. X — Eastern Rome
Reizei II — Japan
Liao Xing Zong | Liao Dao Zong — North China
Bei Song Ren Zong — South China
1051 1052 1053 1054 1055 1056 1057 1058 1059 1060

AD 1061-1070

NORMANS
ARABS
NORMANS

In 1062 Toghril Beg, chieftain of the Seljuks, made himself emir in Baghdad, claiming all the temporal power of the caliphate. The powerless caliph, al-Kaim, lived on until 1075 and was then succeeded by other Abbasid descendants for several more centuries. These were no longer of any political significance and their names are of no historical interest. At this time Toghril Beg also conquered Persia, which hitherto had been held by the Afghan Ghaznavids.

The great event in European history at this time was the Norman conquest of England in 1066. Earlier in the year the Norwegian Harald Hardraade had made an attempt to seize England but was defeated at the battle of Stamford Bridge by Harold Godwinson. Harold died a few weeks later when his army was defeated at the battle of Hastings by the Duke of Normandy who subsequently became known as William the Conqueror. He probably referred to himself as Guillaume since his language was French, which was to be of considerable significance to the future development of the English language.

In August 1071 the Byzantines were routed by the Seljuks at Manzikert in Armenia; the emperor was taken prisoner and the army destroyed. Within a very short time the Seljuks had seized control of Asia Minor almost all the way to the Hellespont. They turned this region, once the heart of Byzantium, into the Sultanate of Rum, which is the Turkish version of Rome. The capital was Iconium, modern Konya.

The Norman successes in southern Italy continued. In 1071 Robert Guiscard took Bari, the last of the Byzantine strongholds here. At the same time his younger brother Roger was making himself master of Sicily; he had come here in 1060 but it took him thirty years to conquer the entire island. He captured the capital, Palermo, in 1072.

MAR E
TRAN

The Normans on their way to England. Detail from the Bayeux tapestry which describes the entire conquest.

	Rulers
Sicily	Roger I
Aragon	Ramiro I — Sancho I
Seljuks	Toghril Beg — Alp-Arslan
Scotland	Malcolm III Canmore
Sweden	Stenkil — Erik VII and VIII — Haakan the Red
Egypt	Mustansir
Poland	Boleslaw II the Generous
Hungary	Bela I Leventa — Salamon
Bohemia	Vratislav II
Norway	Harald (III) Hardraade — Magnus II & Olaf III the Quiet — Olaf the Quiet -
Russia	Iziaslav I
England	Edward the Confessor — ---------- — William I the Conqueror
Denmark	Sweyn Estridsson
Castile	Ferdinand I — Sancho II
Germany	Henry IV
France	Philip I
Holy Rom.Emp.	Henry IV Senex
Papacy	Alexander II
Eastern Rome	Constantine X Ducas — Romanus IV Diogenes
Japan	Reizi II — Sanjō II
North China	Liao Dao Zong
South China	Bei Song Ren Zong — Bei Song Ying Zong — Bei Song Shen Zong

1061	1062	1063	1064	1065	1066	1067	1068	1069	1070

NORMANS
NICEPHORUS III
BYZANTIUM
MARIA

The renowned climax of the controversy between Emperor Henry IV and Pope Gregory VII took place in 1077. Three years earlier Gregory had decreed that priests of the church should be celibate and shortly afterwards he prohibited all investiture by laymen, which meant that the temporal authorities could not appoint bishops or abbots, even though certain temporal fiefs accompanied these offices. When the emperor appointed a bishop in Milan and also tried to invoke the support of the Normans in southern Italy, he was excommunicated by the pope. He then assembled a synod that pronounced the dismissal of the pope. Meanwhile the German princes decided to look for a new emperor in case Henry was not absolved within a year. The emperor then made a journey of penance to the Italian palace of Canossa where the pope was residing. Henry stood for three cold January days in humble supplication in the courtyard until the pope revoked the excommunication. Some historians see this as a shrewd political move on the part of the emperor, and indeed Henry not only asserted his authority but in due course rid himself of Pope Gregory VII. By and large, however, Henry's journey to Canossa has to be regarded as a gesture of humiliation.

The ecclesiastical history of Adam of Bremen entitled *Gesta Hammaburgensis ecclesiae pontificum* is the principal source of information relating to people and events in the Baltic region at this time. This history, dealing with affairs up to the year 1072, was completed in 1075. Adam of Bremen personally knew King Sweyn Estridsson.

In China, during the reign of Emperor Shen Zong, a radical but undemocratic reformer named Wang Anshi introduced a steeply graduated taxation system based on tax returns, national conscription, state loans for farming with built-in price controls, and a new practical education system. The conservative Confucian civil servants were horrified, but Wang Anshi also had many supporters who carried through his programme when, on account of ill health, he had to retire in the following decade.

The Polish king, Boleslaw, personally assassinated the archbishop of Krakow and was then condemned by the pope and driven into exile.

Henry IV, the pope and the margravine Matilda at Canossa. Biblioteca Vaticana, Rome.

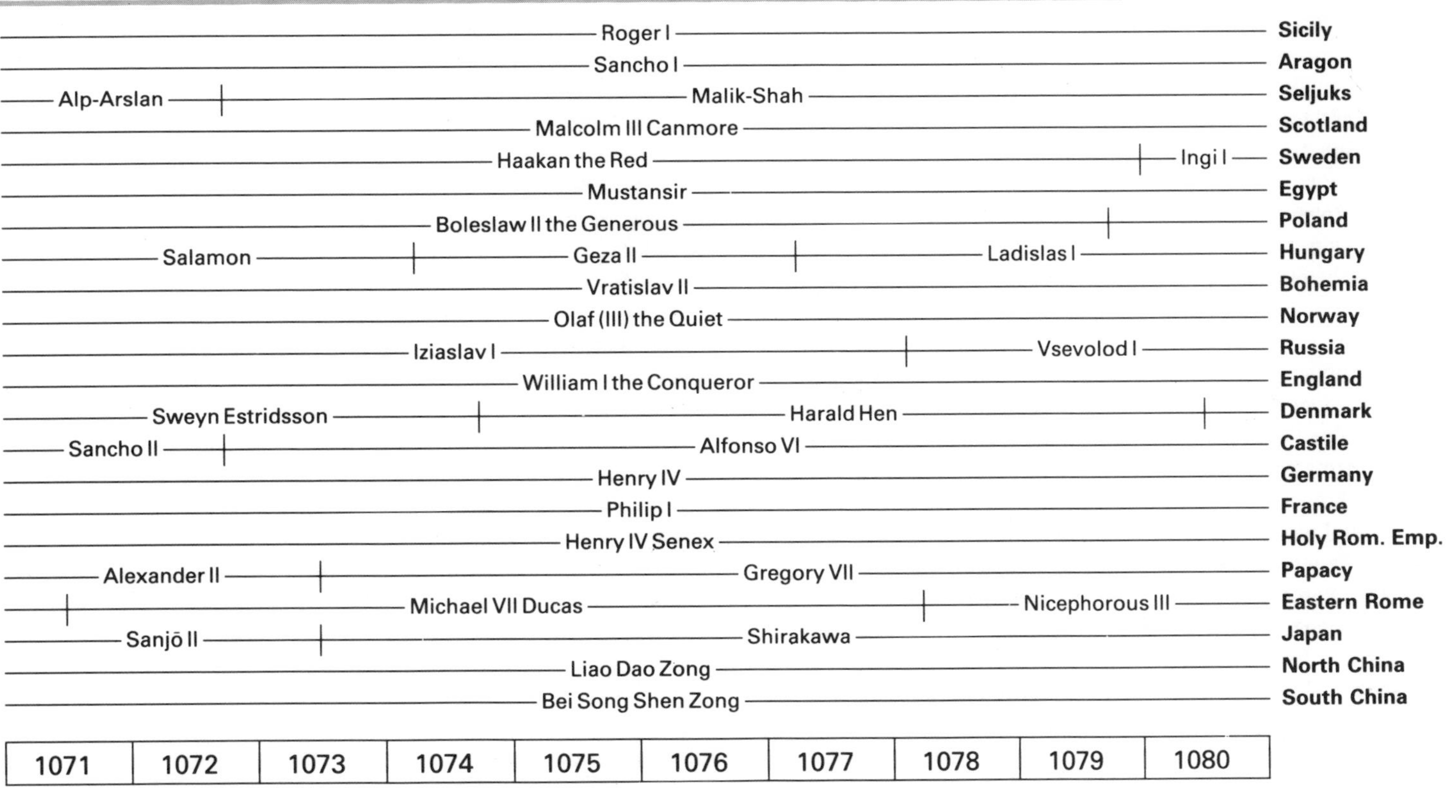
Roger I Sicily
Sancho I Aragon
Alp-Arslan Malik-Shah Seljuks
Malcolm III Canmore Scotland
Haakan the Red Ingi I Sweden
Mustansir Egypt
Boleslaw II the Generous Poland
Salamon Geza II Ladislas I Hungary
Vratislav II Bohemia
Olaf (III) the Quiet Norway
Iziaslav I Vsevolod I Russia
William I the Conqueror England
Sweyn Estridsson Harald Hen Denmark
Sancho II Alfonso VI Castile
Henry IV Germany
Philip I France
Henry IV Senex Holy Rom. Emp.
Alexander II Gregory VII Papacy
Michael VII Ducas Nicephorous III Eastern Rome
Sanjō II Shirakawa Japan
Liao Dao Zong North China
Bei Song Shen Zong South China
1071 1072 1073 1074 1075 1076 1077 1078 1079 1080

AD 1081-1090

CHINA
EGYPT
SWEDEN

Under Malik the Seljuk realm embraced much the same area as did the Abbasid caliphate at its peak, but on Malik's death it was divided into various small kingdoms among his brothers and sons, who quarrelled continuously between themselves. The Sultanate of Rum, founded under Malik's sovereignty in the 1070s by his relative Suleyman I, survived for several centuries, and was in no sense a barbarian state.

The southern Italian Normans also attacked Byzantine territory on the Balkan peninsula, but with Venetian help they were repulsed. The Venetians, demanding a reward for their services, secured the right to trade throughout the Byzantine empire without being liable to pay duties or taxes. They were thus more privileged than the Byzantines themselves.

In 1083 there were 17,211,713 families, i.e. about ninety million people, in the region of China ruled by the Song dynasty.

Henry of Burgundy, great grandson of the French king, Robert II, and son-in-law of Alfonso VI of Castile, was named reigning Count of Portugal in 1090. This state now emerged for the first time.

Clement III was an anti-pope who held office from 1080 to 1100. In the list below the line indicates the period when he was sole incumbent.

The Slavic Prussians were subjugated by German colonizers.

King Halsten, who reigned jointly with his brother Ingi the Elder, died in 1090, after which Ingi ruled alone. An undated episode from this time concerns Ingi's brother-in-law Sweyn who undertook to conduct an Aesir sacrifice in Uppsala. Ingi refused and was immediately expelled, but he soon returned with a Christian force from Västergötland and slew "Sacrificial Sven".

The last significant monarch of the independent Croatian kingdom was Zvonimir, who died in 1089. Two years later Croatia was occupied by the Hungarian King Laszlo or Ladislas I. The Croats rebelled but this was bloodily repressed in the late 1090s. Peter, the last Croatian king, was taken prisoner and put to death in 1097. Croatia and Dalmatia were now merged with Hungary – a decision that was to have far-reaching consequences.

The Danish King Canute (the Holy), who relied heavily on spiritual advisers but who was unpopular because of his tax demands, faced an insurrection and was killed in a church. His brother Olaf succeeded him.

Nizam al-Mulk was Malik-Shah's grand vizier. He was an able administrator and an educated man who established an academy in Baghdad. During his time the poet and mathematician Omar Khayyam composed a calendar.

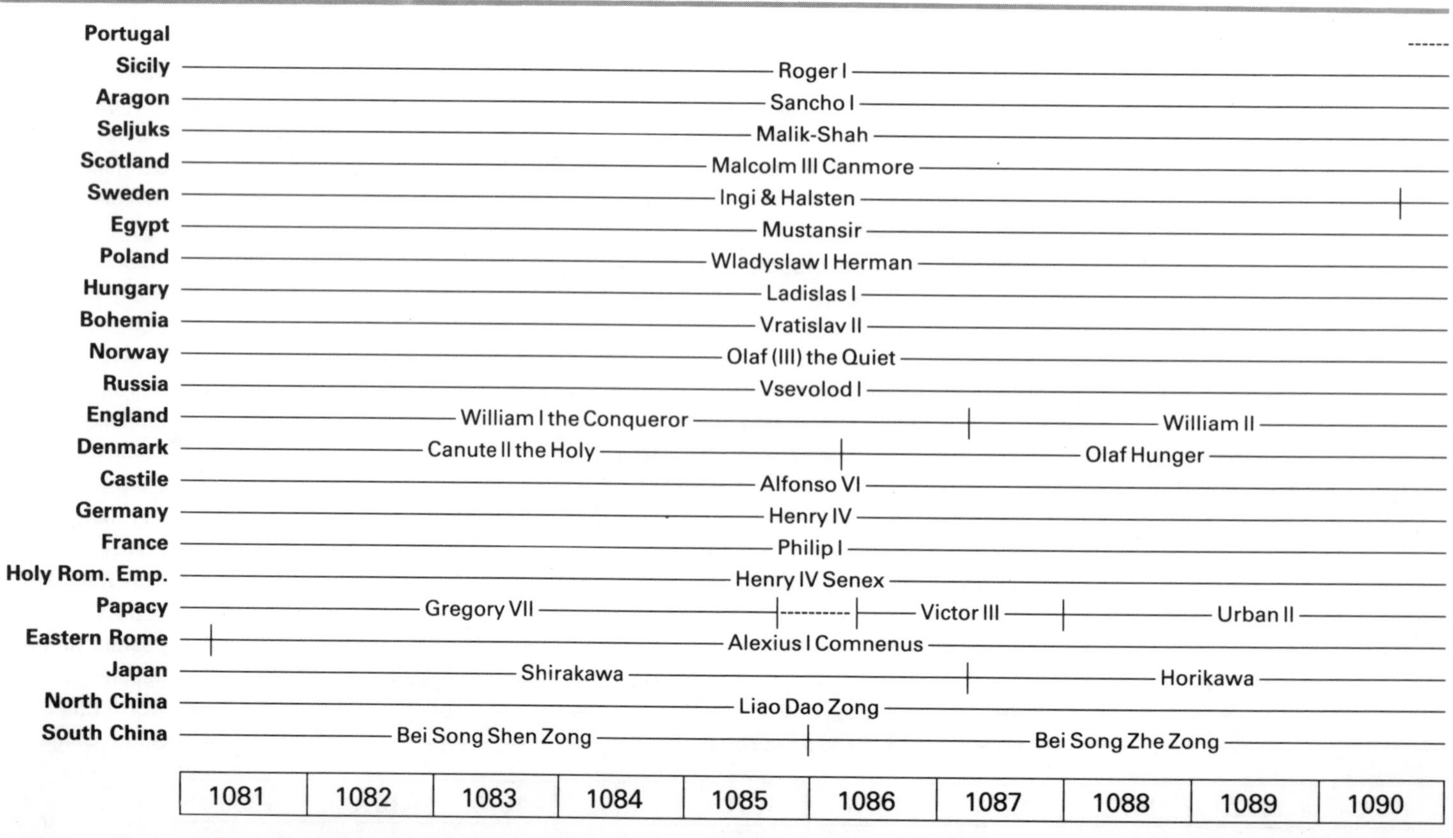
Portugal
Sicily — Roger I
Aragon — Sancho I
Seljuks — Malik-Shah
Scotland — Malcolm III Canmore
Sweden — Ingi & Halsten
Egypt — Mustansir
Poland — Wladyslaw I Herman
Hungary — Ladislas I
Bohemia — Vratislav II
Norway — Olaf (III) the Quiet
Russia — Vsevolod I
England — William I the Conqueror — William II
Denmark — Canute II the Holy — Olaf Hunger
Castile — Alfonso VI
Germany — Henry IV
France — Philip I
Holy Rom. Emp. — Henry IV Senex
Papacy — Gregory VII — Victor III — Urban II
Eastern Rome — Alexius I Comnenus
Japan — Shirakawa — Horikawa
North China — Liao Dao Zong
South China — Bei Song Shen Zong — Bei Song Zhe Zong
1081 1082 1083 1084 1085 1086 1087 1088 1089 1090

ARAGON
JEWS
BYZANTIUM
CHINA

In 1094 Valencia was overrun by the Moorish troops of Rodrigo Diaz, el Cid, who created his own kingdom.

A contributory factor to the fall of the Seljuk realm was the emergence of an assassins' fraternity which established a bloodthirsty state in the Syrian mountains.

In 1095, at a church council held in Clermont, Pope Urban II addressed the people and exhorted them to embark upon a war against the faithless who had overrun the Holy Land. This appeal met with enthusiastic response and led to the first crusade. Zealous mobs moved eastward, forcibly baptizing and massacring Jews in the central European towns, plundering to sustain their needs, and often being butchered themselves by enraged Hungarians and Bulgars. But these were followed by detachments with more military experience and the Byzantine emperor, Alexius, was considerably alarmed by the arrival in Constantinople of so many knights and their large retinues. Alexius promised to provide them with supplies and also to support their cause with his own armies, but in return he demanded an oath of allegiance whereby they pledged to place all their forthcoming conquests under his sovereignty. Accompanied by a Byzantine force, the crusaders moved on Nicaea which fell in the spring of 1097. Emir Qilich Arslan was defeated and thereby the most westerly of the Seljuk states ceased to be of any further importance. The following year Antioch was taken and here the Norman, Bohemond of Taranto, set himself up as ruler. In 1099 the rest of the crusade entered Jerusalem and established a Frankish kingdom.

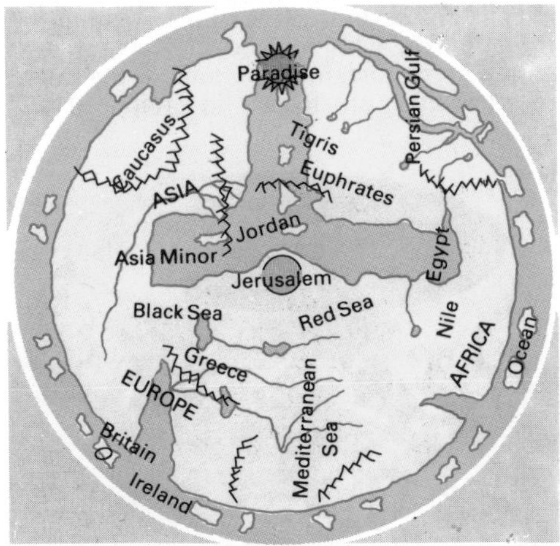
Paradise
Caucasus
ASIA
Tigris
Euphrates
Persian Gulf
Jordan
Asia Minor
Jerusalem
Egypt
Black Sea
Red Sea
Nile
AFRICA
Ocean
Greece
EUROPE
Mediterranean Sea
Britain
Ireland

The long reign of al-Mustansir was a period of decline in the Fatimid caliphate. The holy cities of Mecca and Medina had been lost and when al-Mustansir died there was civil war in Egypt between his sons. The victor, al-Musta'li, lost Syrian territories to the crusaders.

Jerusalem is the central point in medieval European maps of the world. The one shown here is relatively late, signed Andrea Bianco 1435; crusaders' maps the earlier were doubtless no more accurate.

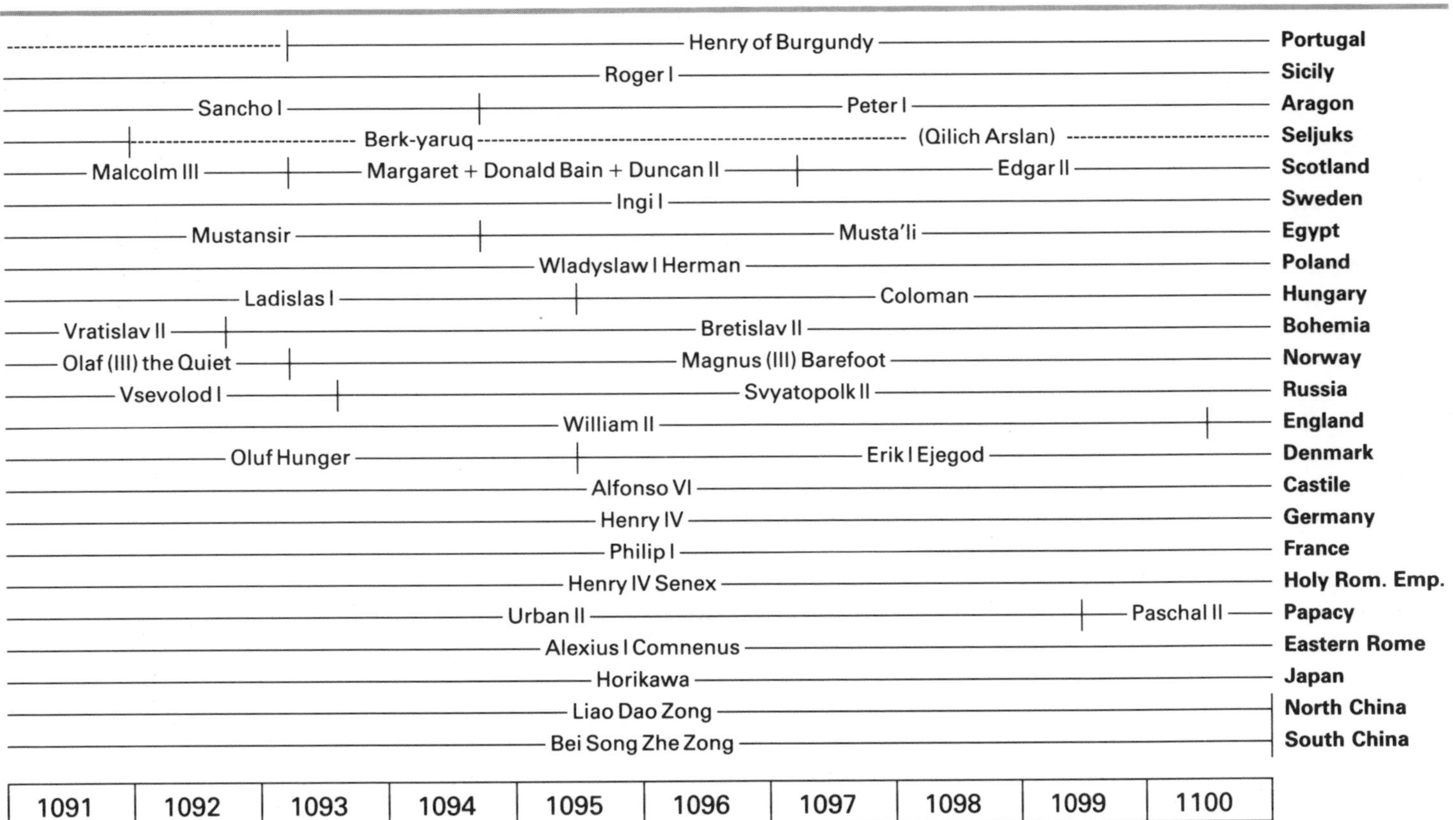
Henry of Burgundy — Portugal
Roger I — Sicily
Sancho I — Peter I — Aragon
Berk-yaruq — (Qilich Arslan) — Seljuks
Malcolm III — Margaret + Donald Bain + Duncan II — Edgar II — Scotland
Ingi I — Sweden
Mustansir — Musta'li — Egypt
Wladyslaw I Herman — Poland
Ladislas I — Coloman — Hungary
Vratislav II — Bretislav II — Bohemia
Olaf (III) the Quiet — Magnus (III) Barefoot — Norway
Vsevolod I — Svyatopolk II — Russia
William II — England
Oluf Hunger — Erik I Ejegod — Denmark
Alfonso VI — Castile
Henry IV — Germany
Philip I — France
Henry IV Senex — Holy Rom. Emp.
Urban II — Paschal II — Papacy
Alexius I Comnenus — Eastern Rome
Horikawa — Japan
Liao Dao Zong — North China
Bei Song Zhe Zong — South China
1091 1092 1093 1094 1095 1096 1097 1098 1099 1100

AD 1101-1110

BYZANTIUM
GERMANY
SPAIN

Archbishop Anselm of Canterbury, who was in fact an Italian from Aosta, formulated the ontological evidence of God's existence–God exists because the concept of God exists–and is memorable for his motto: *"Credo ut intelligam"* (I believe in that which I can understand).

The crusader states of Jerusalem, Antioch, Tripoli and Edessa were formed during the first decades of the 12th century. Conditions were unstable, due to periodic conflicts with Egypt, the Seljuks and also Byzantium. In 1104 the Byzantines seized Tarsus and occupied the Cilician pass, to protect themselves against the southern Italian Normans who now also held Antioch. In Jerusalem the elected Frankish kings were Baldwin I (1100-1118) and Baldwin II (1118-1131).

In 1104 the Nordic countries were separated from the Hamburg-Bremen see and given their own archbishop at Lund in southern Sweden. In Europe, Russian and Byzantine territories were invaded by the Pechenegs, who plundered widely but were later thoroughly defeated. At the beginning of the next decade their last army was annihilated in the Balkans by Emperor John II, but they continued to make their presence felt in Russia for several generations. Vladimir II Monomakh, who reigned in Kiev, was an eminent politician, who united the many descendants of Rurik in joint action.

Vladimir was also a literary man whose autobiographical will is one of the earliest documents in Russian secular literature.

In 1115 the Cistercian monk Bernard was appointed abbot of the newly founded monastery of Clara vallis or Clairvaux. For several decades his influence was very great, even in political affairs, since popes and princes sought his advice and often accepted his injunctions. Bernard became a saint.

In Portugal Henry of Burgundy died and left a small son named Afonso Henriques. The dowager queen had an affair with Count Pereș of Trava, who thus became the most important man in the country. In the next decade there was a revolt: Queen Teresa was deposed and imprisoned and Afonso Henriques commenced his reign.

The people who lived in inner Asia were evidently not barbarians. This gilded bowl found its way to Russia. Hermitage, Leningrad.

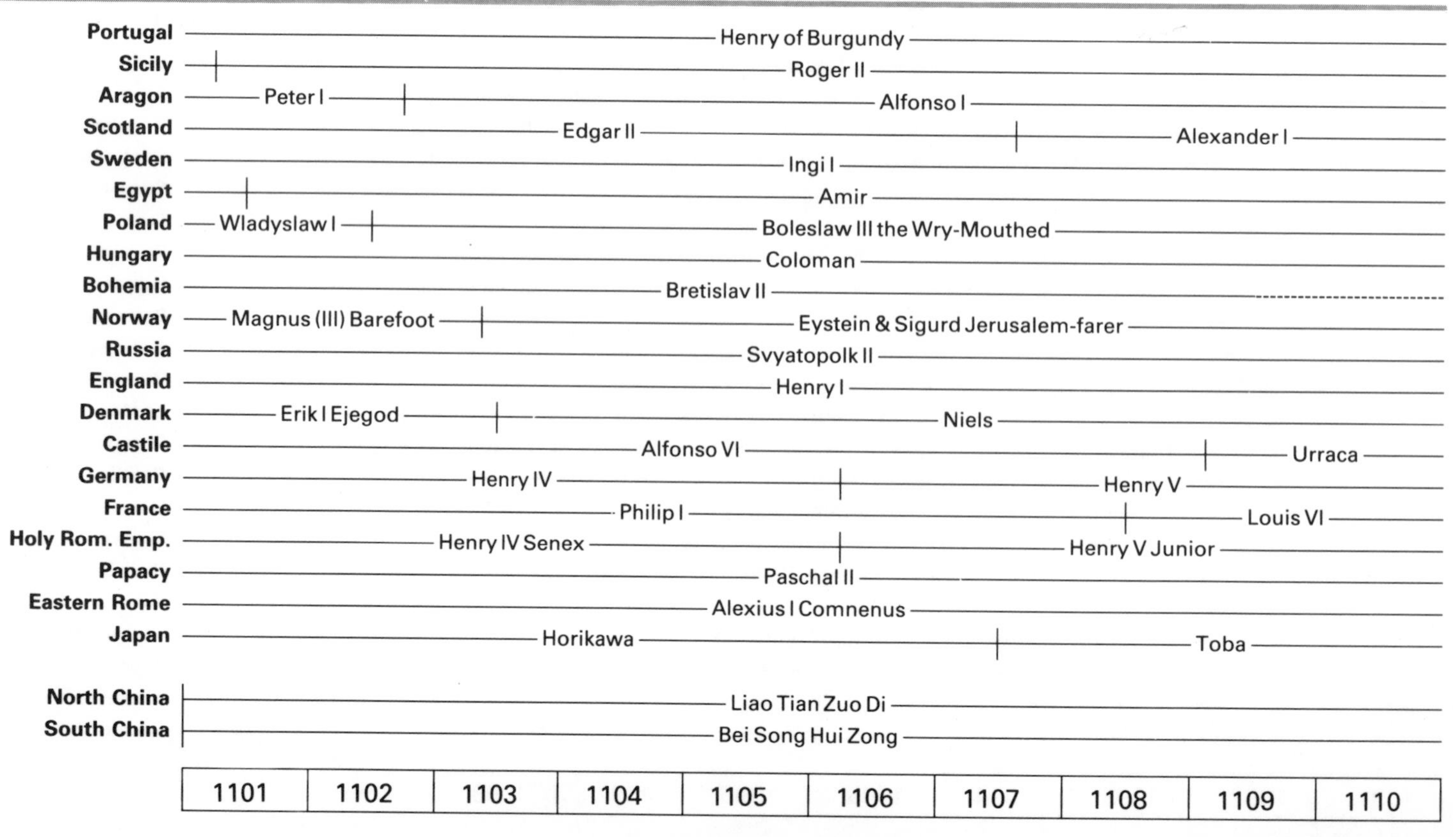
Portugal
Henry of Burgundy
Sicily
Roger II
Aragon
Peter I
Alfonso I
Scotland
Edgar II
Alexander I
Sweden
Ingi I
Egypt
Amir
Poland
Wladyslaw I
Boleslaw III the Wry-Mouthed
Hungary
Coloman
Bohemia
Bretislav II
Norway
Magnus (III) Barefoot
Eystein & Sigurd Jerusalem-farer
Russia
Svyatopolk II
England
Henry I
Denmark
Erik I Ejegod
Niels
Castile
Alfonso VI
Urraca
Germany
Henry IV
Henry V
France
Philip I
Louis VI
Holy Rom. Emp.
Henry IV Senex
Henry V Junior
Papacy
Paschal II
Eastern Rome
Alexius I Comnenus
Japan
Horikawa
Toba
North China
Liao Tian Zuo Di
South China
Bei Song Hui Zong
1101
1102
1103
1104
1105
1106
1107
1108
1109
1110

EGYPT
CHINA

In 1114 a Tungus tribe called the Juchen attacked the Liao dynasty's northern Chinese empire. The Song dynasty immediately joined the Juchen assault but were hopelessly defeated on their front, whereas the Tungus won one victory after another.

Emperor Hui Zong was himself a prominent artist and patron of the arts. He installed a porcelain factory in his palace at Kaifeng and assembled an academy of brilliant painters and calligraphers whose names and works have survived: Mi Fei, Li Dang, Su Dongpo, Zhang Ze Duang. The emperor was less interested in affairs of state, however, and during his reign much of the authority was vested in the radical followers of Wang Anshi.

A law school emerged in Bologna and this became the law faculty when the university was founded a few decades later. The principal subject was Roman law, which was associated with the fact that the Digest of Justinian had recently been rediscovered. This was very important. The Holy Roman emperors eagerly embraced the Roman law, as many other Europeans monarchs were to do in due course.

In 1114 a fleet from Pisa seized the Balearic Islands. Pisa was by this time a considerable power, both commercially and militarily.

In Kiev the monk Nestor composed a chronicle on the Viking Rurik from Roslagen and his descendants. This account is our only source of information concerning the origins of the Russian empire, and even this is not entirely credible.

In Iceland Saemundr the Wise had established a private seat of learning on his estate at Oddi which was to have great influence on Icelandic literature. Saemundr himself wrote a history of the Norwegian kings in Latin, though this has not survived. Saemundr's name is also associated, perhaps unwarrantably, with the poetic work, *Saemund's Edda*.

The Countess Matilda of Tuscany was a remarkable woman who had ruled a large part of Italy and faithfully supported the popes in their long struggle for power with the Holy Roman emperors. Matilda died in 1115 and left her extensive domains to the Church. But she did not distinguish between crown lands and so-called allodial property over which she had undisputed rights of disposal. Consequently the countess's will remained a subject of dispute between popes and emperors for several centuries to come. This controversy related largely to the towns, which took advantage of the opportunity to secure their individual freedom. Thus the emergence of the Italian city states was directly connected with Countess Matilda of Tuscany's controversial will.

In Mexico the kingdom of the Toltecs was on the verge of destruction, threatened by the Chichimec tribe.

Slav communities south of the Baltic Sea were forcibly baptized by devout Germans.

Henry of Burg. — Teresa	Portugal
Roger II	Sicily
Alfonso I	Aragon
Alexander I	Scotland
Ingi I — Philip & Ingi II — Ingi II	Sweden
Amir	Egypt
Boleslaw III the Wry-Mouthed	Poland
Coloman — Stephen II	Hungary
Vladislav I	Bohemia
Eystein & Sigurd Jerusalem-farer	Norway
Svyatopolk II — Vladimir II Monomakh	Russia
Henry I	England
Niels	Denmark
Urraca	Castile
Henry V	Germany
Louis VI the Fat	France
Henry V	Holy Rom. Emp.
Paschal II — Gelasius II — Calixtus II	Papacy
Alexius I Comnenus — John II	Eastern Rome
Toba	Japan
Jin Tai Zu; Liao Tian Zuo Di	North China
Bei Song Hui Zong	South China

1111	1112	1113	1114	1115	1116	1117	1118	1119	1120

AD 1121-1130

CHINA

By the beginning of the 1120s the Juchen Tungus had conquered most of northern China and imprisoned the Liao emperor's family and harem. The emperor himself had managed to flee to the Tangut kingdom in the north-west and thus the Liao dynasty survived, at least formally, for a few more decades.

After the collapse in northern China the Song emperor sent in his own occupation troops which were immediately expelled by the Tungus. Instead of sharing their conquests with their southern neighbours, the Tungus demanded a huge tribute as a guarantee against continuing their advance southward through Song territory. In 1125, with the Tungus at the gates of his capital Kaifeng, Emperor Hui Zong abdicated in favour of his son Qin Zong, who at once paid the required tribute. But this led to revolution; the radical administration was replaced by conservatives who persuaded the emperor to break the agreement and fight instead. The Tungus were prepared, however, and their cavalry routed Qin Zong's army. Kaifeng was captured, and the emperor, his father, his family, his court and more than 3000 other people were transported to Manchuria, never to return. In Nanking, meanwhile, beyond the reach of the Tungus, was a young prince of the imperial blood. He was now proclaimed emperor with the name Gao Zong, and through him the Song dynasty survived. In due course the Tungus took Nanjing as well, but the young emperor moved south to Hangzhou which, in a densely populated region with a network of canals around the Yangtze, was inaccessible to the enemy cavalry. The Hangzhou empire, records of which commence in 1127, is called South Song and became noted for its cultural achievements. A census taken in 1124, relating, in fact, to the Song empire prior to its collapse revealed that there were then 20,822,258 families, i.e. something like one hundred million people in China.

Anna Comnena, daughter of Alexius I, wrote a chronicle which, among other things, discussed the pilgrims in Byzantium.

Roger II became king of Apulia as well in 1130, though his kingdom was still simply called Sicily. A remarkable culture evolved here. The island had belonged to the Arabs for 300 years and most of the people were Arabs. On the mainland lived Greeks who had shared the fate of the Byzantines. The Norman conquerors spoke French and probably still retained something of their Viking traditions. These three elements combined to produce an astonishing artistic heritage.

Sigurd Jerusalem-farer became the sole ruler of Norway when his brother Eystein died in 1121. In his time Swedish Jämtland was made a Norwegian province. In 1123 Sigurd led a kind of crusade to Sweden's east coast, exacted a tribute of 1500 head of cattle and forcibly baptized a number of local Smålanders.

Ghen Guei was the Chinese inventor of gunpowder. He made himself a kind of fire-thrower of bamboo reed, but it never occurred to him to put a projectile into it.

Portugal	Teresa — Afonso I
Sicily	Roger II
Aragon	Alfonso I
Scotland	Alexander I — David I
Sweden	Ingi II — (Ragnvald Knaphövde)
Egypt	Amir —
Poland	Boleslaw III the Wry-Mouthed
Hungary	Stephen II
Bohemia	Vladislav I — Sobeslav I
Norway	Sigurd Jerusalem-farer —
Russia	Vladimir II — Mstislav
England	Henry I
Denmark	Niels
Castile	Urraca — Alfonso VII
Germany	Henry V — Lothair II the Saxon
France	Louis VI the Fat
Holy Rom Emp.	Henry V — Lothair II
Papacy	Calixtus II — Honorius II —
Eastern Rome	John II Comnenus
Japan	Toba — Sutoku
North China	Jin Tai Zu — Jin Tai Zong
	Liao Tian Zuo Di — Liao De Zong
South China	Bei Song Hui Zong — Qin Zong — Nan Song Gao Zong

1121	1122	1123	1124	1125	1126	1127	1128	1129	1130

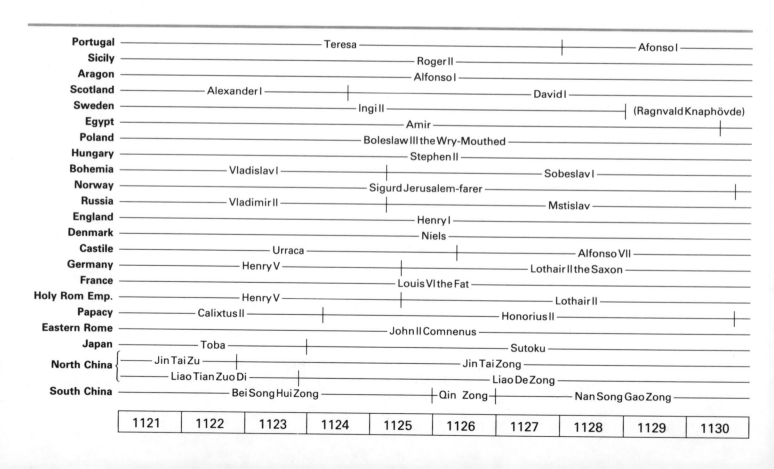

CHINA

German expansion to the north-east began in the reign of Emperor Lothair II. The Slavic tribes in Pomerania were baptized by Bishop Otto of Bamberg and in 1135 Boleslaw III of Poland, who was also involved in this mission, was awarded Pomerania and Rugen as provinces by Lothair.

The Concordat of Worms was concluded in 1122, thus ending the investiture controversy between emperor and pope. This agreement concerned matters which appear to us little more than meaningless formalities: i.e. the emperor now ceased to hand the bishops their ring and pastoral staff; in Germany he was to touch them with his sceptre before their consecration, but in Italy and Burgundy after their consecration; and in Burgundy the presence of the monarch was not even necessary. At the time, however, these were all very important decisions. In Germany the agreement strengthened the position of the temporal princes, but in Italy it benefitted the towns at the expense of imperial power.

Mid-12th century Norwegian history makes involved and somewhat hair-raising reading. Magnus, son and successor of Sigurd Jerusalem-farer, was taken prisoner and blinded by a certain Harald Gille. Harald in his turn was assassinated by a pretender named Sigurd Slembi, but in 1139 Sigurd was himself captured and slain near Strömstad on the west coast of Sweden after a battle with Harald's three jointly-reigning sons, Sigurd Mund, Ingi Krokrygg and Eystein.

In 1136 the great scholar Peter Abelard wrote his *Historia calamitatum meorum,* (Story of my Misfortunes) which was an account of his love affair with the young Héloïse that ended with Abelard being seized and castrated by her uncle. Abelard was a rationalist philosopher. As such he became involved in a dispute with Bernard of Clairvaux who saw to it that Abelard's views on the Trinity were condemned by two church councils. Bernard of Clairvaux was the religious oracle of his day, with great political power.

The Polish king Boleslaw III's surname means Wry-Mouthed. He was an active politician who retrieved practically all of Pomerania for Poland.

There was much literary activity in western Europe during the 12th century. France produced the *Chanson de Roland* and the Provençal troubadours' poems, while in Ireland the Ossianic cycle was assembled for the first time. Wandering scholars, some of them Irish, were responsible for perpetuating many fine Latin lyrical ballads, including the celebrated *Carmina Burana* collection. In Toledo, Spain many Arabic works were being translated into Latin.

Russia was divided into small states and it is not possible to draw up a comprehensive list of rulers. For the next few decades the selection of names is necessarily rather arbitrary.

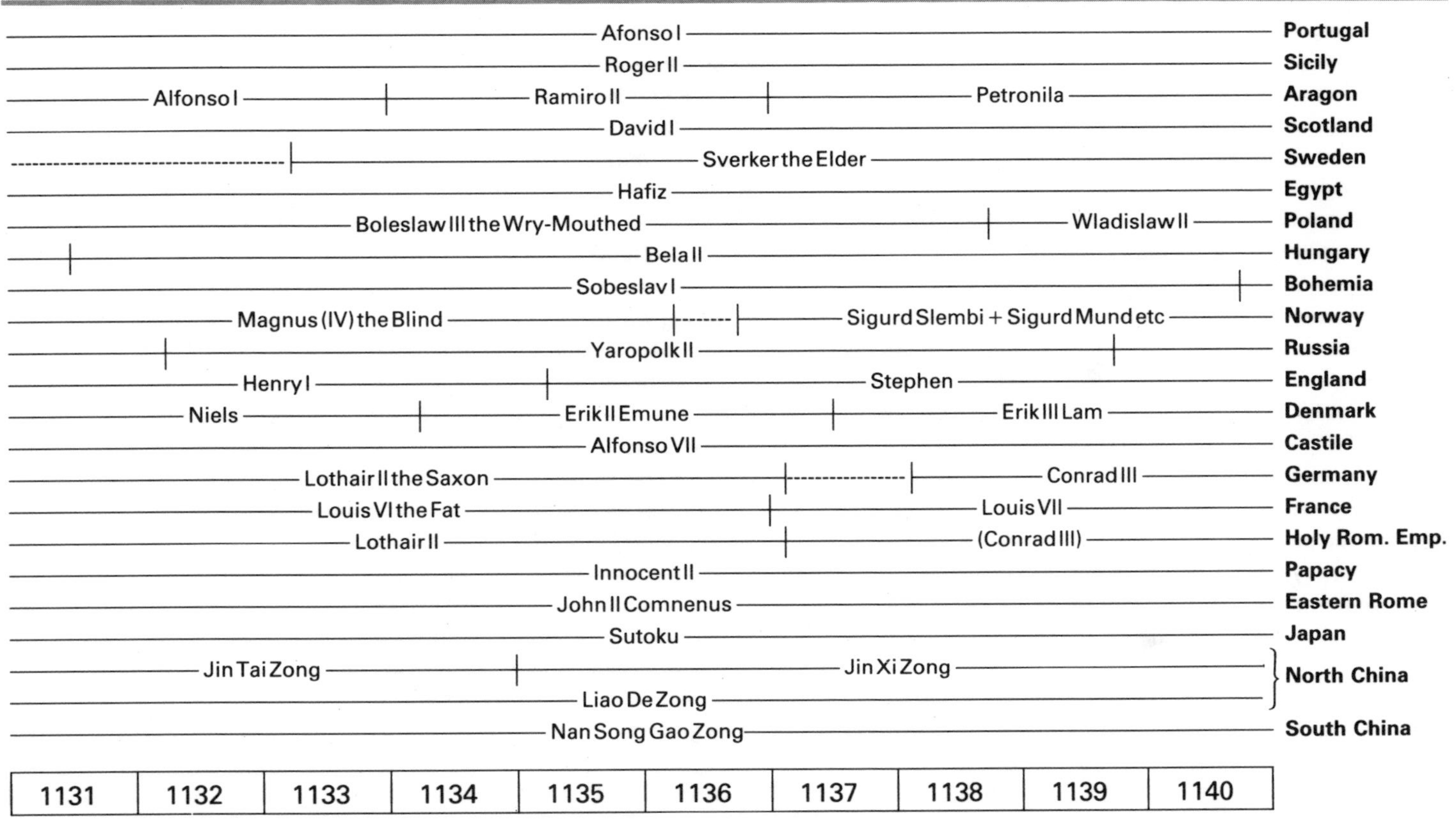
Afonso I — Portugal
Roger II — Sicily
Alfonso I — Ramiro II — Petronila — Aragon
David I — Scotland
Sverker the Elder — Sweden
Hafiz — Egypt
Boleslaw III the Wry-Mouthed — Wladislaw II — Poland
Bela II — Hungary
Sobeslav I — Bohemia
Magnus (IV) the Blind — Sigurd Slembi + Sigurd Mund etc — Norway
Yaropolk II — Russia
Henry I — Stephen — England
Niels — Erik II Emune — Erik III Lam — Denmark
Alfonso VII — Castile
Lothair II the Saxon — Conrad III — Germany
Louis VI the Fat — Louis VII — France
Lothair II — (Conrad III) — Holy Rom. Emp.
Innocent II — Papacy
John II Comnenus — Eastern Rome
Sutoku — Japan
Jin Tai Zong — Jin Xi Zong
Liao De Zong
North China
Nan Song Gao Zong — South China
1131 1132 1133 1134 1135 1136 1137 1138 1139 1140

AD 1141-1150

SICILY
ENGLAND
FRANCE
JAPAN

In 1146 the Grand Duke Iziaslav II briefly became ruler of Russia and called himself czar, apparently the first time the title was used here. This in no way alleviated the political discord.

Among the many descendants of Rurik, one of the most interesting was Yury I, youngest son of Vladimir Monomakh, who was entrusted by his father with the unsettled regions around the central Volga. Yury Dolgorusky (Longhand), founded the city of Moscow here in the 1150s and soon gained supremacy, too, in the Dnieper region, which provided large numbers of colonists for his new town. He himself was content to live as Grand Duke in the recently captured town of Kiev. Yury's son and successor, Andrew Bogolyubsky, remained in the north, though he resided not in Moscow but in the older town of Vladimir, which gave the name to his grand duchy.

In Scandinavia, relations between the three countries were fairly chaotic and the imperial government was weak and ineffective.

The Japanese Fukiwara dynasty, whose inviolable right to the imperial throne was undisputed, had lost most of its real power to other wealthy and war-like families, the best known of which included the Taira and the Minamoto. These were rivals, however, so that some of the more enterprising emperors were able to assert themselves, though first obliged by court etiquette to abdicate formally and substitute a minor on the throne. Just such an individual was Shirakawa II, who played an important part in a civil war which lasted several decades and was a recurrent subject in Japanese tale and song. Initially the Taira had the upper hand under a tyrant known as Kiyomori who, in 1159, secured almost dictatorial power and cruelly persecuted the Minamoto. But twenty years later the Minamoto were able to strike back.

In 1147 Afonso I of Portugal took Lisbon from the Arabs, thereby securing a new capital for his realm. Castile recognized Portugal as an independent state in 1143. Afonso I put it under the suzerainty of the pope.

The pope sent out Bernard of Clairvaux to raise a new crusade in 1146, the Muslims having recently retaken Edessa and put an end to the Christian Frankish regime there. St Bernard's proclamation was very effective, leading immediately to massacres of European Jews and persuading the French king Louis VII of France and Conrad III of Germany to set out with their armies. But the second crusade was a total failure. The Germans were defeated and the French king had to abandon his army in the Alps.

The dynasty of the Juchen Tungus, which unlike earlier invaders never assimilated Chinese manners and ideas, was for some reason known as Gyllne Jin. It resided in Beijing which now for the first time became the capital of a large kingdom.

At the death of Boleslaw III in 1138, Poland was split up among his four sons. Boleslaw IV the Curly was not content with his share, however, for he ejected his brother Wladislaw II and united the two kingdoms under his own crown.

Portugal	Afonso I
Sicily	Roger II
Aragon	Petronila
Scotland	David I
Sweden	Sverker the Elder
Egypt	Hafiz – Zafir
Poland	Wladislaw II – Boleslaw IV the Curly
Hungary	Geza III
Bohemia	Vladislav II
Norway	Sigurd Mund, Ingi Krokrygg & Eystein
Russia	Vsevolod II + Igor II + Iziaslav II + Yuruy Dolgorusky etc
England	Stephen
Denmark	Erik III Lam – Svend + Canute + Valdemar
Castile	Alfonso VII
Germany	Conrad III
France	Louis VII
Holy Rom. Emp.	(Conrad III)
Papacy	Innocent II – Celestine II – Lucius II – Eugenius III
Eastern Rome	John II – Manuel I Comnenus
Japan	Sutoku – Konoe
North China	Jin Xi Zong – Jin Hai Ling Wang
	Liao De Zong – Liao Gan Tian Hou
South China	Nan Song Gao Zong

1141	1142	1143	1144	1145	1146	1147	1148	1149	1150

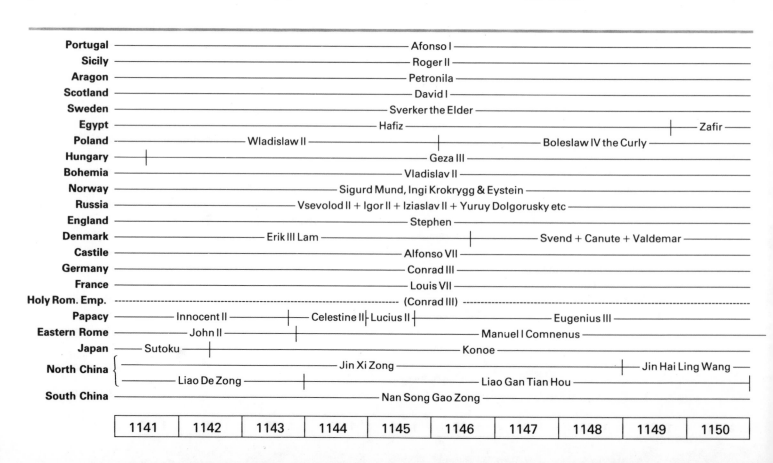

ENGLAND
FRANCE
BYZANTIUM
GERMANY
NORMANS,
SICILY

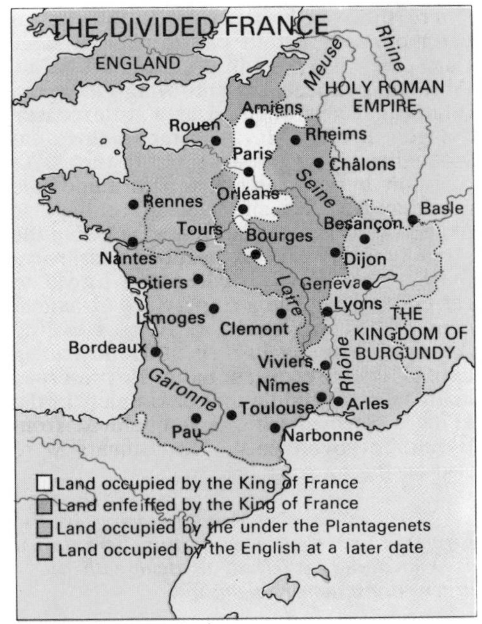
THE DIVIDED FRANCE
ENGLAND
Meuse
Rhine
HOLY ROMAN EMPIRE
Amiens
Rouen
Rheims
Paris
Châlons
Orléans
Seine
Rennes
Basle
Tours
Besançon
Bourges
Nantes
Dijon
Poitiers
Loire
Geneva
Lyons
Limoges
THE KINGDOM OF BURGUNDY
Clemont
Bordeaux
Viviers
Rhône
Nîmes
Garonne
Toulouse
Arles
Pau
Narbonne
Land occupied by the King of France
Land enfeiffed by the King of France
Land occupied by the under the Plantagenets
Land occupied by the English at a later date

Medieval feudalism developed initially in France where the political picture was somewhat bewildering. The male line of the reigning family in the Duchy of Aquitaine died out in 1137. The heir, Eleanor, first married the king of France but separated from him in 1152 and wed the future Henry II of England. This led to a war which was to last a long time. The counts of Toulouse, (all named Raymond), were compelled to recognize Henry as their sovereign. Brittany was *de facto* independent and the Duke of Burgundy conducted his own policy.

The city of Lübeck was founded in 1143, Munich in 1158. Banking was becoming a thriving business in Italian cities, most of which had been founded earlier.

Norway acquired an archbishop in 1152. Sweden, where Uppsala and Linköping were vying for the site of the archdiocese, was still under the archbishop of Lund, at that time part of Denmark.

Legend has it that Sweden's St Erik led a crusade to Finland, accompanied by a certain Bishop Henrik. Detail of an altar-piece. Statens historiska museum, Stockholm.

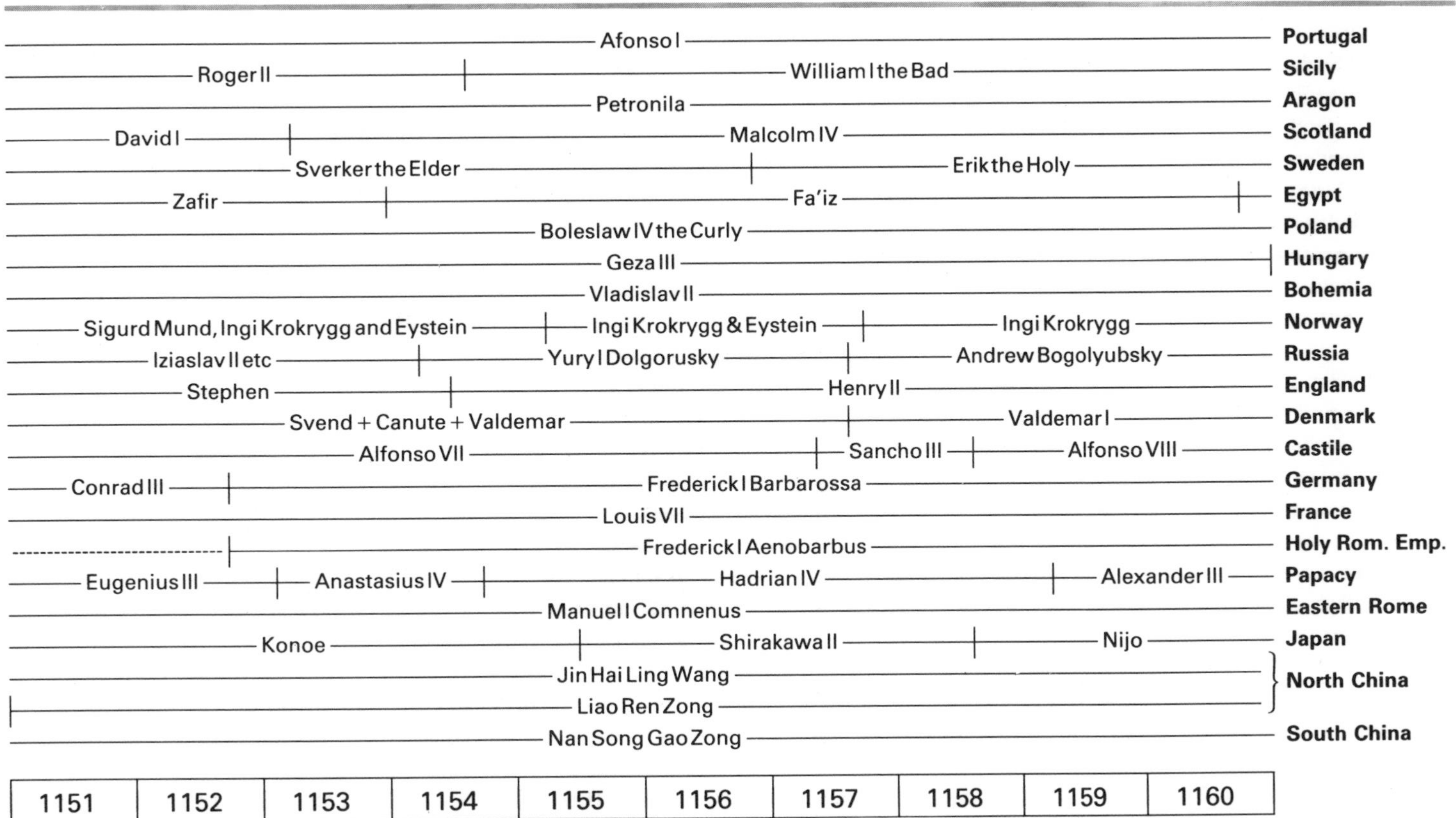
Afonso I — Portugal
Roger II | William I the Bad — Sicily
Petronila — Aragon
David I | Malcolm IV — Scotland
Sverker the Elder | Erik the Holy — Sweden
Zafir | Fa'iz | — Egypt
Boleslaw IV the Curly — Poland
Geza III | — Hungary
Vladislav II — Bohemia
Sigurd Mund, Ingi Krokrygg and Eystein | Ingi Krokrygg & Eystein | Ingi Krokrygg — Norway
Iziaslav II etc | Yury I Dolgorusky | Andrew Bogolyubsky — Russia
Stephen | Henry II — England
Svend + Canute + Valdemar | Valdemar I — Denmark
Alfonso VII | Sancho III | Alfonso VIII — Castile
Conrad III | Frederick I Barbarossa — Germany
Louis VII — France
Frederick I Aenobarbus — Holy Rom. Emp.
Eugenius III | Anastasius IV | Hadrian IV | Alexander III — Papacy
Manuel I Comnenus — Eastern Rome
Konoe | Shirakawa II | Nijo — Japan
Jin Hai Ling Wang — North China
Liao Ren Zong — North China
Nan Song Gao Zong — South China
1151 1152 1153 1154 1155 1156 1157 1158 1159 1160

AD 1161-1170

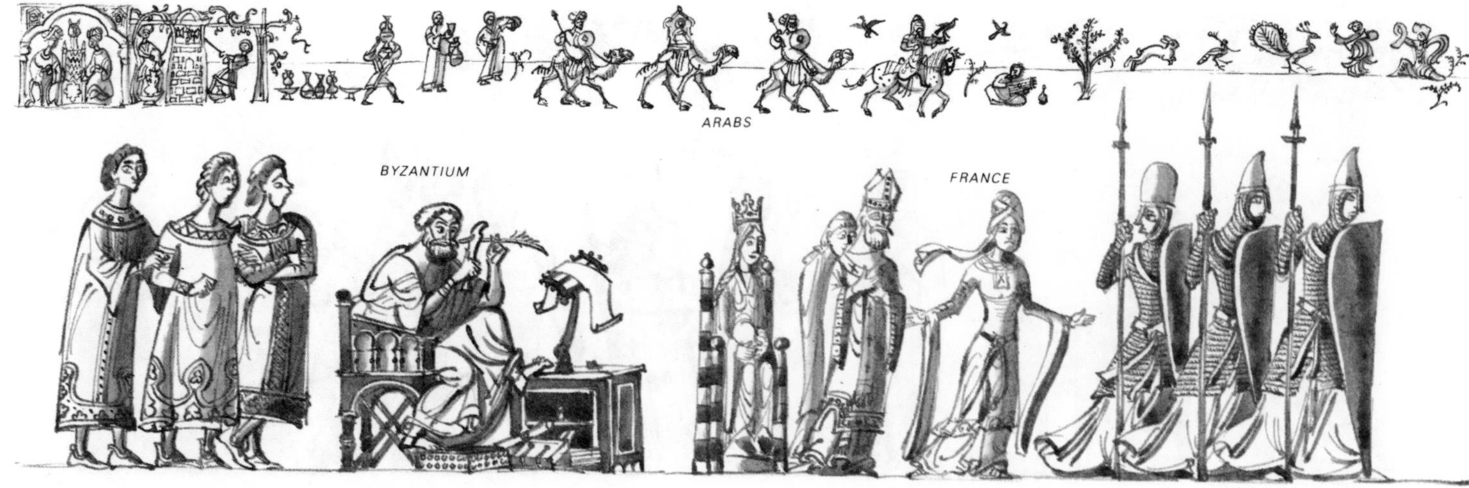
ARABS
BYZANTIUM
FRANCE

Queen Petronila of Aragon was married to the reigning count of Barcelona and in due course their son Alfonso the Chaste became ruler of both realms. In this simple manner Catalonia became Spanish after having previously been part of Provence.

For the years 1161-1163 the Hungarian list of rulers was somewhat confused when Geza III's son Stephen III was ejected by his paternal uncles Ladislas and Stephen IV, who were supported by the Byzantines. Shortly afterwards, however, Stephen III returned.

In Lyons, in 1176, a merchant named Pierre Valdes gave away his large fortune, set about translating the gospels and gathered about him a group of ascetic preachers. They soon fell foul of the Church, however, for they recognized only three sacraments; baptism, holy communion and confession, while they denounced the swearing of oaths and capital punishment. The result was a great wave of persecution which lasted 500 years and scattered the Waldenses across southern and central Europe. Despite the appalling massacres, the Waldensian movement survived.

The Danish kingdom was now establishing a Baltic empire. In the 1160s the Danes took Rügen and the Wendish fortress of Arcona where the four-headed idol Svantevit was ceremoniously cut to pieces. At the same time the warrior bishop of Roskilde, Absalon, political adviser to King Valdemar, established a stronghold at a little coastal village named Havn, later known as Köbenhavn or Copenhagen. In the 1170s Absalon became archbishop in Lund and introduced tythes and clerical celibacy to Skåne, which led to an insurrection. On the Dysie bridge, near the town of Landskrona, the Scanians were defeated and forced to surrender. The young cleric, Saxo Grammaticus, who was probably very close to Absalon, wrote a history of Denmark up until his day, in excellent Latin. He preserved many tales, including that of Hamlet. In the 1170s a Serbian state was liberated from Byzantine sovereignty. The Bulgars were also on the move.

Emperor Frederick Aenobarbus, here shown as a crusader, still had to deal with many urgent domestic problems.

Realm	Rulers 1161–1170
Serbia	Stephen Nemanja
Portugal	Afonso I
Sicily	William I the Bad; William II the Good
Aragon	Petronila; Alfonso II the Chaste
Scotland	Malcolm IV; William
Sweden	Karl Sverkersson; Knut Eriksson
Egypt	Adid; Saladin (Salah ad-Din)
Poland	Boleslaw IV the Curly
Hungary	Stephen III; Ladislas II & Stephen IV; Stephen III
Bohemia	Vladislav II
Norway	Haakon II Herdebred; Magnus (V) Erlingsson
Russia	Andrew Bogolyubsky
England	Henry II
Denmark	Valdemar I the Great
Castile	Alfonso VIII
Germany	Frederick I Barbarossa
France	Louis VII
Holy Rom. Emp.	Frederick I Aenobarbus
Papacy	Alexander III
Eastern Rome	Manuel I Comnenus
Japan	Nijo; Rokujo; Takakura
North China	Jin Shi Zong
North China	Liao Ren Zong; Liao Cheng Tian Hou
South China	Nan Song Gao Zong; Nan Song Xiao Zong

1161	1162	1163	1164	1165	1166	1167	1168	1169	1170

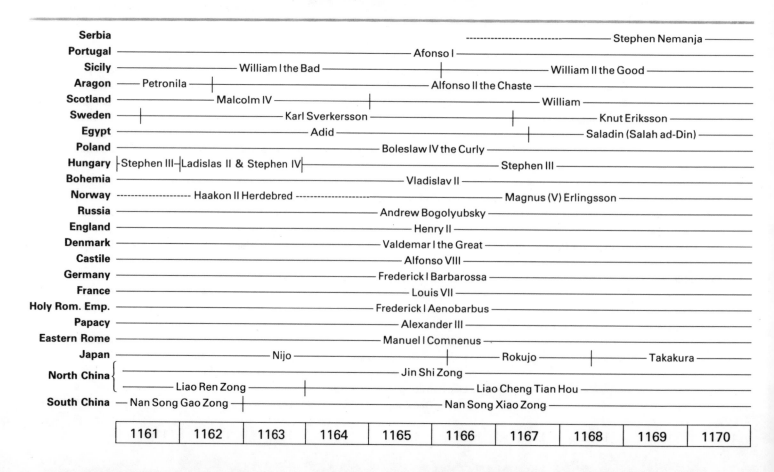

KHMERS, CAMBODIA
KHMERS, CAMBODIA
CHINA

In Norway Sigurd Mund's son Haakon Herdebred did battle with his paternal uncle Ingi Krokrygg who was slain, but Ingi's men continued the fight, led by Jarl Erling the Crooked, who proclaimed his five-year old son king. Haakon Herdebred, only fourteen, was soon crushed, but he was swiftly succeeded by other pretenders. The most important of these was the Faroe Islander Sverrir who also claimed to be the son of Sigurd Mund. Sverrir emerged the victor from this long struggle; Erling the Crooked and his son Magnus both died in 1179.

In 1171 Henry II of England landed on Ireland and was duly recognized by the pope as sovereign of that island; the local version of Christianity conflicted to some extent with that of the Roman church.

The Byzantine emperor, Manuel, sought contact with Genoa in order to free himself form the economic domination of the Venetians. In the spring of 1171 he ordered the arrest of all the Venetians in his empire and confiscated their property. This resulted in a war in which the emperor was the loser.

Zhu Xi, greatest of the confucian theologists, lived and worked in South Song. He commented upon and interpreted the classical texts with boundless energy and uncompromising consistency, tolerating no contradictions in the records. He elaborated on Zhou Tunyi's Taoist-influenced metaphysics, from the 11th century, producing a satisfying system and a dualistic cosmology.

The Fatimid dynasty in Egypt was deposed by Saladin (Salah ad-Din) whose own Ayyubid dynasty was Kurdic. Initially Saladin ruled Egypt as the viceroy of King Nureddin of Damascus, but he soon declared his independence and shortly afterwards made himself master of Syria as well.

The Toltec kingdom in Mexico was overrun in 1168 and the capital, Tula, destroyed by a barbarian people form the north, the Chichimecs. Under a chieftain named Zolotl the latter occupied the Toltec's lands, though they readily absorbed the Toltecs' advanced culture.

The Grand Duke Andrew Bogolyubsky of Vladimir defeated and killed the Grand Duke of Kiev, plundered his capital and transferred the focal point of the Russian states to the Moscow region.

Splendid cathedrals were being built in Europe especially in France and Italy.

Emperor Frederick Barbarossa led five campaigns into Italy, where Pope Alexander III and a number of Guelph cities (named after Welf, the rival imperial family) offered resistance. In Germany Frederick clashed with his Guelph cousin Henry, the Lion of Saxony, who was outlawed and banished after other grand dukes joined the emperor's side.

Rulers	Country
Stephen Nemanja	Serbia
Afonso I	Portugal
William II the Good	Sicily
Alfonso II the Chaste	Aragon
William	Scotland
Knut Eriksson	Sweden
Saladin	Egypt
Boleslaw IV – Mieszko III the Old – Casimir II	Poland
Stephen III – Bela III	Hungary
Vladislav II – Bedrich Cesky – Sobeslav II – Bedrich Cesky + Conrad II Ota	Bohemia
Magnus (V) Erlingsson – Sverrir	Norway
Andrew Bogolyubsky – Vsevolod III	Russia
Henry II	England
Valdemar I the Great	Denmark
Alfonso VIII	Castile
Frederick I Barbarossa	Germany
Louis VII	France
Frederick I Aenobarbus	Holy Rom. Emp.
Alexander III	Papacy
Manuel I Comnenus	Eastern Rome
Takakura	Japan
Jin Shi Zong	North China
Liao Cheng Tian Hou – Liao Mo Zhu	North China
Nan Song Xiao Zong	South China

1171	1172	1173	1174	1175	1176	1177	1178	1179	1180

AD 1181-1190

IRAQ
PERSIA

The Kurdic sultan, Saladin, ruler of Egypt and Syria, seized the kingdom of Jerusalem in 1187. This caused great consternation in the western Christian world and gave rise to the third crusade. The German emperor Frederick Barbarossa, the French king Philip Augustus and the English king Richard the Lion-Heart set out by different routes against Saladin. Frederick was drowned while crossing the Salef near Tarsus, but Philip Augustus and Richard, who travelled by sea, secured for the Christians a coastal stretch from Tyre to Jaffa, and received permission to send small unarmed groups to visit the Holy Sepulchre.
A secondary effect of this expedition was that the crusaders put an end to the Seljuk realm in Konya.

The German emperor, Henry VI, by marrying the Sicilian heiress Constance, became ruler of her island as Henry I.
The brothers, Ivan and Peter Asen, led a revolt against the Byzantines and organized an independent Bulgaria. In 1187 a new archbishop crowned Asen czar in a church dedicated to St Demetrius. Demetrius had hitherto been the patron saint of Greek Thessalonica but apparently moved to Bulgarian Trnovo when, a few years earlier, Thessalonica was cruelly plundered by the southern Italian Normans.

Coronation of Henry VI in Rome. Book illustration by Pietro da Eboli.

Pomerania, formerly part of Poland, became a duchy under German sovereignty.

Canute of Denmark was traditionally known at this time as Canute VI, since two Hardecanutes were included in this series. Nowadays, however, he is often referred to as Canute IV.

In 1187 a foreign fleet entered Lake Mälar, surprised and murdered Archbishop Johan in his citadel at Stäket, and went on to plunder and burn Sigtuna.

Bulgaria	Ivan Asen I
Serbia	Stephen Nemanja
Portugal	Afonso I — Sancho I
Sicily	William II the Good — Tancred
Aragon	Alfonso II the Chaste
Scotland	William
Sweden	Knut Eriksson
Egypt	Saladin
Poland	Casimir II the Just
Hungary	Bela III
Bohemia	Conrad II Ota
Norway	Sverrir
Russia	Vsevolod III
England	Henry II — Richard I
Denmark	Valdemar I — Canute VI
Castile	Alfonso VIII
Germany	Frederick I Barbarossa
France	Philip II Augustus
Holy Rom. Emp.	Frederick I Aenobarbus
Papacy	Lucius III — Urban III — Greg. VIII — Clement III
Eastern Rome	Alexius II — Andronicus I — Isaac II Angelus
Japan	Antoku — Toba II
North China	Jin Shi Zong; Liao Mo Zhu
South China	Nan Song Xiao Zong

1181	1182	1183	1184	1185	1186	1187	1188	1189	1190

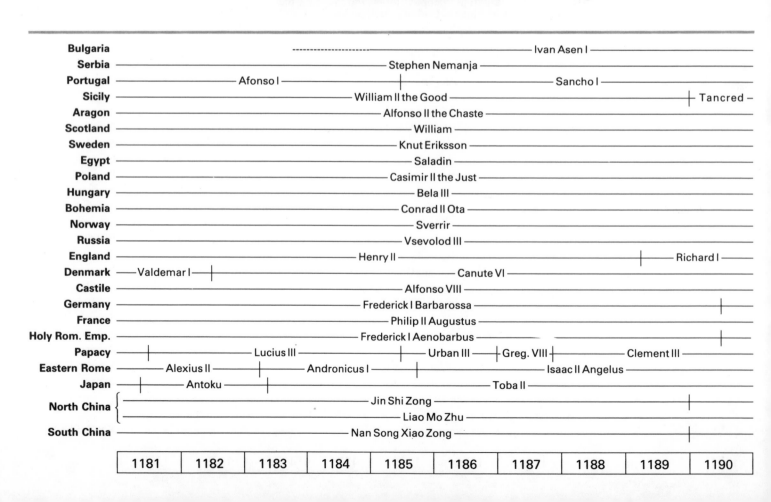

FRANCE
CHINA
KHMERS, CAMBODIA
JAPAN

In Japan the persecuted Minamoto clan rose up and drove out the dictator Kiyomori's son Munemori. The Minamoto leader, Yoshinaka, now established himself as regent in Kyoto and was invested by the emperor with the title sei-i-tai-shogun, supreme commander or military governor. Shortly afterwards, however, he became involved in a conflict with his cousins Yoritomo and Yoshitsune, the latter a prominent general. Yoshinaka was defeated and killed, and Yoshitsune turned on the Taira clan which had reassembled its forces. In a big sea battle Munemori was taken prisoner and his mother, the widow of the dictator Kiyomori, leaped into the sea with her eight-year old son, the emperor Antoku, in her arms. Yoshitsune in his turn aroused the enmity of his brother Yoritomo – there are many tales of how he was driven to his death – after which Yoritomo, now unchallenged, consolidated his realm. He moved the seat of government from Kyoto to Kamakura, site of the future Tokyo. Here in 1192 he received an imperial mission which invested him with the high office originally created for his cousin Yoshinaka: sei-i-tai-shogun. This is the origin of the curious Japanese constitution whereby the real power rested with the hereditary shogunate under the divine yet impotent emperor. The long-enduring Japanese form of feudalism also evolved in Yoritomo's time.

The Serbian Stephen Nemanja, who in the previous decade had overrun Dalmatia, Herzegovina, Montenegro and Serbia proper on the Danube, abdicated in 1196 and entered the monastery on Athos. The brothers Stephen and Vukan of Serbia quarrelled with each other but both sought the good graces of the pope and abandoned the Greek church. Bosnia, where the Bogomil heresy had been the national religion, likewise embraced the Roman church at this time.

Yoritomo of the house of Minamoto, shogun in Japan. Jingo-ji, Kyoto.

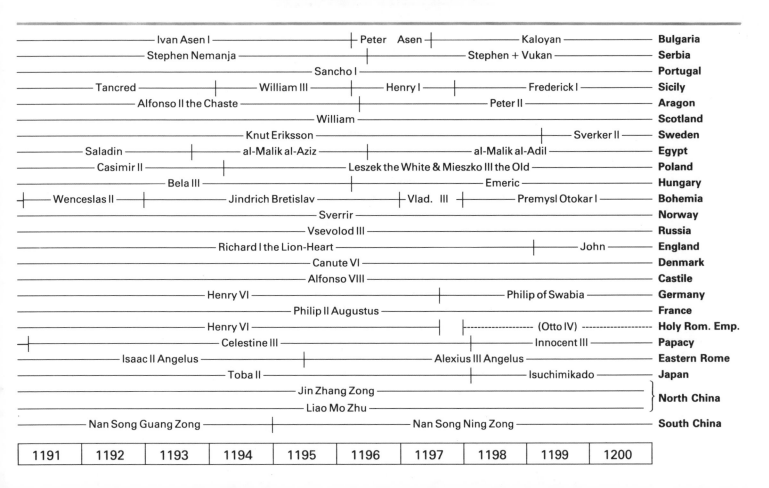

Ivan Asen I – Peter Asen – Kaloyan	**Bulgaria**
Stephen Nemanja – Stephen + Vukan	**Serbia**
Sancho I	**Portugal**
Tancred – William III – Henry I – Frederick I	**Sicily**
Alfonso II the Chaste – Peter II	**Aragon**
William	**Scotland**
Knut Eriksson – Sverker II	**Sweden**
Saladin – al-Malik al-Aziz – al-Malik al-Adil	**Egypt**
Casimir II – Leszek the White & Mieszko III the Old	**Poland**
Bela III – Emeric	**Hungary**
Wenceslas II – Jindrich Bretislav – Vlad. III – Premysl Otokar I	**Bohemia**
Sverrir	**Norway**
Vsevolod III	**Russia**
Richard I the Lion-Heart – John	**England**
Canute VI	**Denmark**
Alfonso VIII	**Castile**
Henry VI – Philip of Swabia	**Germany**
Philip II Augustus	**France**
Henry VI – (Otto IV)	**Holy Rom. Emp.**
Celestine III – Innocent III	**Papacy**
Isaac II Angelus – Alexius III Angelus	**Eastern Rome**
Toba II – Isuchimikado	**Japan**
Jin Zhang Zong; Liao Mo Zhu	**North China**
Nan Song Guang Zong – Nan Song Ning Zong	**South China**

1191	1192	1193	1194	1195	1196	1197	1198	1199	1200

AD 1201-1210

MONGOLS
CHINESE

St Francis and St Dominic each founded their own mendicant order, which were to be of fundamental importance to Western Christianity. Unlike the earlier monastic orders, the Franciscans and Dominicans established their monasteries in the towns.

When Stephen of Serbia became sole ruler of his country, he was crowned by a papal legate. Later he received a crown from Nicaea in a second coronation, thereby turning Serbia again towards the Eastern church.

Pope Innocent III called for a crusade against the Moors in Spain and likewise against the heretical Albigenses in southern France. He thus instigated a twenty-year war that was even more cruel and bloody than usual.

The fourth crusade took place in 1203-1204

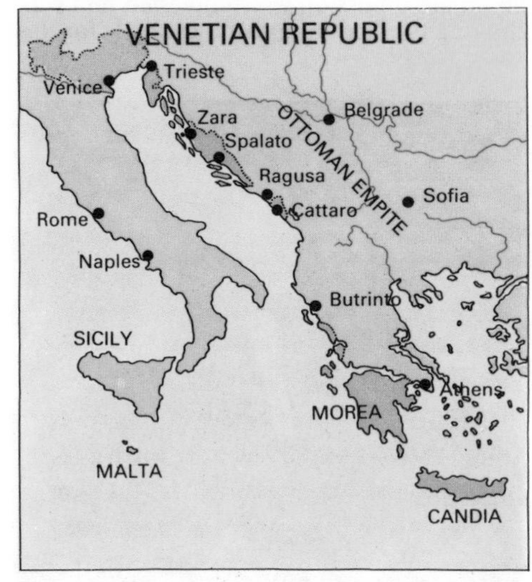
VENETIAN REPUBLIC
Venice
Trieste
Zara
Spalato
Ragusa
Cattaro
Belgrade
Sofia
OTTOMAN EMPIRE
Rome
Naples
Butrinto
SICILY
MOREA
Athens
MALTA
CANDIA

when Venetians and French barons plundered Constantinople and seized power. As a result the Eastern Roman empire was broken up into a number of small states. French and Italian nobles established feudal states of the Western type in Greece and the archipelago, Greek princes became rulers in such places as Epirus and Trebizond, the Byzantine empire survived in Nicaea, a Latin emperor named Baldwin was crowned in Constantinople. Baldwin was killed in 1205, however, in a battle at Adrianople where the Western crusaders were decisively defeated by the Bulgars under Czar Kaloyan. Their imperial power was thus shattered, though the Greek empire in Nicaea rapidly became both more stable and more prosperous.

Venice, was still a major power, ruling over Crete and a considerable part of the archipelago.

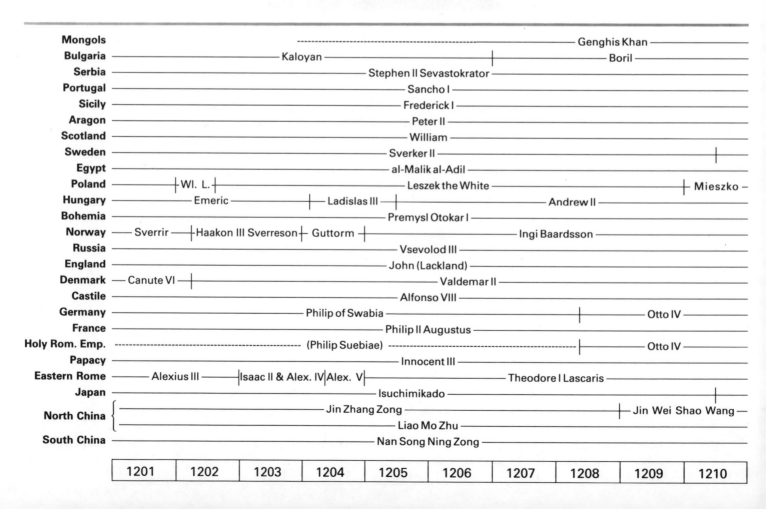

	1201–1210
Mongols	Genghis Khan
Bulgaria	Kaloyan | Boril
Serbia	Stephen II Sevastokrator
Portugal	Sancho I
Sicily	Frederick I
Aragon	Peter II
Scotland	William
Sweden	Sverker II |
Egypt	al-Malik al-Adil
Poland	| Wl. L. | Leszek the White | Mieszko
Hungary	Emeric | Ladislas III | Andrew II
Bohemia	Premysl Otokar I
Norway	Sverrir | Haakon III Sverreson | Guttorm | Ingi Baardsson
Russia	Vsevolod III
England	John (Lackland)
Denmark	Canute VI | Valdemar II
Castile	Alfonso VIII
Germany	Philip of Swabia | Otto IV
France	Philip II Augustus
Holy Rom. Emp.	(Philip Suebiae) | Otto IV
Papacy	Innocent III
Eastern Rome	Alexius III | Isaac II & Alex. IV | Alex. V | Theodore I Lascaris
Japan	Isuchimikado |
North China	Jin Zhang Zong | Jin Wei Shao Wang
	Liao Mo Zhu
South China	Nan Song Ning Zong

1201	1202	1203	1204	1205	1206	1207	1208	1209	1210

JEWS
GERMANS
CRUSADERS

The great event of the early 13th century was the rise of the Mongols. The young chieftain Temujin was a vassal of the khan of Kerait, a Christian Nestorian kingdom and a major power in central Asai. In due course Temujin attacked and destroyed the Kerait army and then conquered all the neighbouring states. In 1206 he proclaimed himself khagan, khan of all khans and assumed a new name which in Chinese is Jing Si, Consummate Warrior. Temujin was to go down in history under this name, in one version or another: Genghis, Jingis, Djingis or Jenghiz Khan. In 1209 he overran the Tanguts' empire to the north-west and then invaded the empire of the Juchen-Tungus in northern China. When Beijing (Peking) fell in 1215, Genghis Khan sent his forces east against the Golden Yin realm, and himself rode westward towards Turkestan, Persia and India. Samarkand and Bukhara were stormed and sacked before the close of the 1210s.

The Magna Carta was drawn up in England in 1215 after the nobles and clerics had defeated King John and secured various assurances from him, notably that there would be no interference with the power and property of the Church and the barons. A commission of twenty-five barons was appointed with the right to call the people to arms if the king violated the principles of the charter. This situation quickly arose although John died before full-scale war could break out. His son Henry, who succeeded him without opposition, was only nine years old.

On 15 June 1219 King Valdemar II won the battle of Reval and brought Estonia under Danish rule.

Genghis Khan. Persian miniature, Tehran.

Rulers (1211–1220)	
Genghis Khan	**Mongols**
Boril — Ivan Asen II	**Bulgaria**
Stephen II Sevastokrator	**Serbia**
— Afonso II	**Portugal**
Frederick I	**Sicily**
Peter II — James I the Conqueror	**Aragon**
William — Alexander II	**Scotland**
Erik Knutsson — John I Sverkersson	**Sweden**
al-Malik al-Adil — Kamil	**Egypt**
Plat. — Leszek the White	**Poland**
Andrew II	**Hungary**
Premysl Otokar I	**Bohemia**
Ingi Baardsson — Haakon IV Haakonsson	**Norway**
Vsevolod III — Yury II — Constantine — Yury II	**Russia**
John (Lackland) — Henry III	**England**
Valdemar II	**Denmark**
Alfonso VIII — Henry I — Ferdinand III	**Castile**
Otto IV — Frederick II Hohenstaufen	**Germany**
Philip II Augustus	**France**
Otto IV — Frederick II	**Holy Rom. Emp.**
Innocent III — Honorius III	**Papacy**
Theodore I Lascaris	**Eastern Rome**
Juntoku —	**Japan**
Jin Wei Shao Wang — Jin Xuan Zong	**North China**
Nan Song Ning Zong	**South China**

1211	1212	1213	1214	1215	1216	1217	1218	1219	1220

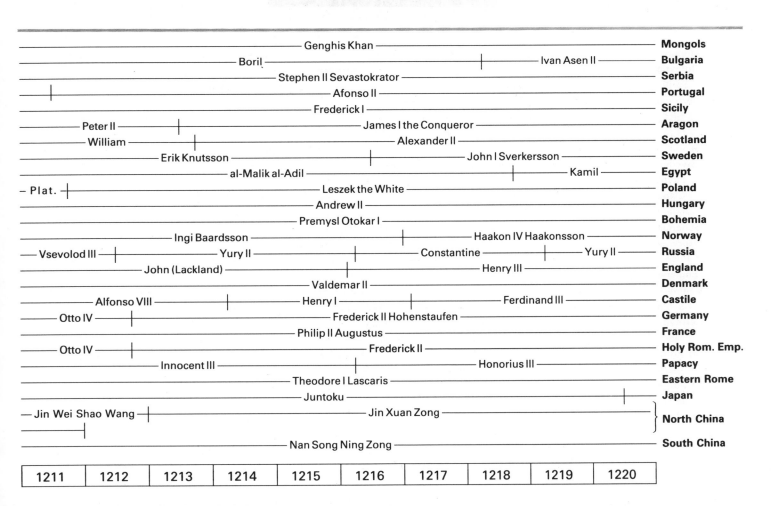

FRANCE
JAPAN

Premysl Otokar I assumed the title of king and made Bohemia an hereditary kingdom.

The German emperor Frederick II Hohenstaufen is the same Frederick I who preferred to reside at Palermo in Sicily, which he had inherited from his Norman mother. A remarkable mixed Arabic, Latin, Greek and Norman culture flourished on Sicily. Frederick was less hostile than most other western princes to the Muslims. When for various reasons he was compelled to undertake a crusade, he succeeded in winning the city of Jerusalem by peaceful negotiations alone, though ten years later, in 1239, it was again lost of by the Christians.

The Japanese emperors were in most instances children who were manipulated by their fathers or other close relations, and at this time there was some confusion as to which of two boys should be regarded as emperor. In fact, no less than three former emperors conspired to do away with the shogunate and restore the real power to the mikado. But the shogun Yoshitoki suppressed the attempted uprising and confiscated large areas of land from the conspirators.

King Valdemar II was taken prisoner by his north German vassals and by the time he managed to buy his freedom several years later, Denmark had lost all its conquests south of the Baltic. During the 1230s, however, Valdemar recaptured Rügen and a coastal strip in Estonia.

Stupor Mundi, (*The amazement of the world), was the title given to Frederick II by Matthew Paris, though the pope and the Guelphs in Italy poured abuse upon him. This portrait is from a book that he wrote himself,* De arte vanandi cum avibus (*The Art of Hunting with Birds).*

Country	Rulers (1221–1230)
Mongols	Genghis Khan — Tolui — Ögödei
Bulgaria	Ivan Asen II
Serbia	Stephen II Sevastokrator - - - Stephen Radoslav
Portugal	Afonso II — Sancho II
Sicily	Frederick I
Aragon	James I the Conqueror
Scotland	Alexander II
Sweden	John I — Erik Laaspe - - - (Knut Laange)
Egypt	Kamil
Poland	Leszek the White — Wladyslaw Laskonogi — Conrad I
Hungary	Andrew II
Bohemia	Premysl Otokar I
Norway	Haakon IV Haakonsson
Russia	Yury II
England	Henry III
Denmark	Valdemar II
Castile	Ferdinand III the Saint
Germany	Frederick II Hohenstaufen
France	Philip II Augustus — Louis VIII — Louis IX the Saint
Holy Rom. Emp.	Frederick II
Papacy	Honorius III — Gregory IX
Eastern Rome	Theodore I — John III Vatatzes
Japan	Chukyo + Horikawa II
North China	Jin Xuan Zong — Jin Ai Zong
South China	Nan Song Ning Zong — Nan Song Li Zong

1221	1222	1223	1224	1225	1226	1227	1228	1229	1230

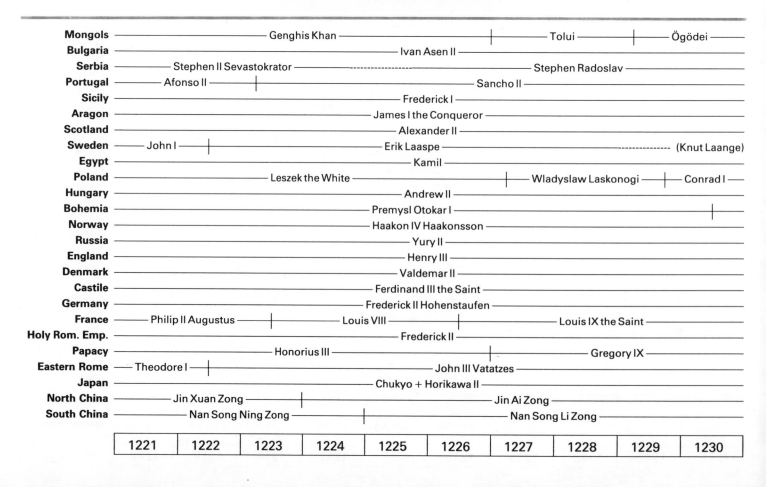

AD 1231-1240

IRAQ

In 1223 a southern Russian coalition was defeated by the Mongols on the river Kalka. After a brief respite the Mongols returned in the 1230s. The Golden Horde, as it was known, overran all the Russian duchies and then pushed on westwards through Poland, Bohemia and Hungary. Shortly afterwards, however, they were driven back from these regions.

The Mongol conquests in the east and south were no less spectacular. In 1233 Kaifeng, the last capital of the Juchen-Tungus realm in northern China, fell. The Song (Sung) dynasty in southern China, delighted with this development, promptly attempted to retrieve its former territories. This infuriated the Mongol khagan Ögödei, who drove out the southern Chinese.

Pope Gregory canonized Francis and Dominic and also organized an inquisition which was implemented by the Dominican Order.

Louis IX, also known as St Louis, was a very pious and orthodox man who led two crusades. The first was to Egypt where he was taken prisoner and had to pay a vast ransom for his freedom; the other was to Tunisia where he died of the plague.

In 1229-1235 King James of Aragon took the Balearic Islands from Pisa and in 1238 he also seized Valencia. A few years later the Arabs lost the kingdoms of Cordoba, Murcia and Seville to Castile. Of their Spanish empire little more was now left to them than the small realm of Granada, and even Granada had to recognize Castilian sovereignty in the following decade. The emirs, nevertheless, completed the building of the Alcazar (palace) of Alhambra between 1250 and 1350.

St Francis preaching to the birds, fresco by Giotto in Assisi. St Francis died in 1226. Dominic, who founded another order, died in 1221.

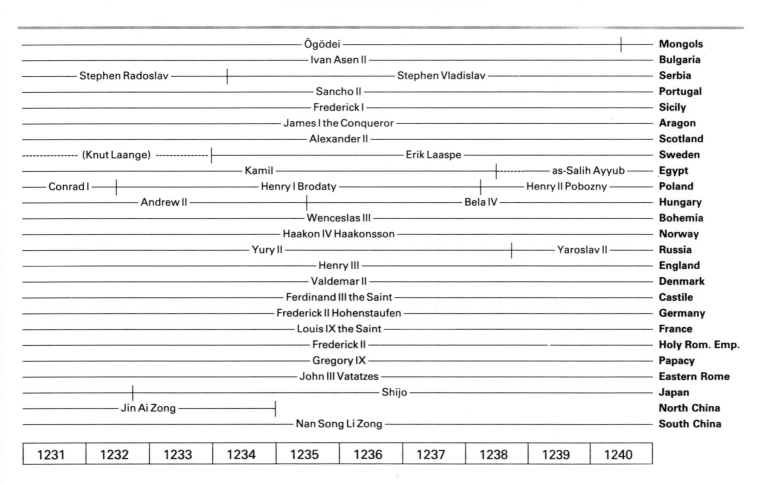

Ögödei	**Mongols**
Ivan Asen II	**Bulgaria**
Stephen Radoslav / Stephen Vladislav	**Serbia**
Sancho II	**Portugal**
Frederick I	**Sicily**
James I the Conqueror	**Aragon**
Alexander II	**Scotland**
(Knut Laange) / Erik Laaspe	**Sweden**
Kamil / as-Salih Ayyub	**Egypt**
Conrad I / Henry I Brodaty / Henry II Pobozny	**Poland**
Andrew II / Bela IV	**Hungary**
Wenceslas III	**Bohemia**
Haakon IV Haakonsson	**Norway**
Yury II / Yaroslav II	**Russia**
Henry III	**England**
Valdemar II	**Denmark**
Ferdinand III the Saint	**Castile**
Frederick II Hohenstaufen	**Germany**
Louis IX the Saint	**France**
Frederick II	**Holy Rom. Emp.**
Gregory IX	**Papacy**
John III Vatatzes	**Eastern Rome**
Shijo	**Japan**
Jin Ai Zong	**North China**
Nan Song Li Zong	**South China**

1231	1232	1233	1234	1235	1236	1237	1238	1239	1240

AD 1241-1250

FRANCE
GERMANY
GERMANY

In 1252 the Arabs lost the province of Algarve to Portugal, the frontiers of which were now finally established.

A Lithuanian kingdom emerged for the first time, its heathen population ruled by a king named Mindaugas. He had defeated the German crusaders and was extending his empire as far as the Black Sea.

The most important of the Russian small states now and in the future was Suzdal-Vladimir, near modern Moscow. In 1253 Alexander Nevsky became its grand duke. He was also ruler of Novgorod and in this capacity he defeated a Swedish-Finnish-Norwegian crusade at Neva, (hence his cognomen) in 1240. Two years later he also routed the Teutonic Knights on the frozen Lake Peipus.

In 1241 Ferdinand III of Castile took Murcia from the Arabs. This closed the route southward to James I of Aragon, national hero of the Catalonians, who had recently seized Valencia.

The kingdom of Jeruslaem ceased to exist in 1244.

The somewhat chaotic Swedish church adopted the universal principles of Catholic Christianity at a council in Skänninge in 1248, when clerical celibacy was also enforced.

The advances of the Mongols in China drove the Thai people farther to the south. The great Mongol conquest continued. After the death of Ögödei his widow, Töregene, took control of the dynasty for a few years until her son came of age; but he died soon afterwards and the authority then passed to another branch of the family. Ögödei's nephews Möngke, Kublai and Hülagü divided the leadership. Möngke became khagan in central Asia. Kublai was supreme in China where, during the 1250s, the Song (Sung) empire was largely overrun, even though the imperial dynasty continued officially to reign for another twenty years. Hülagü moved westward and took Baghdad in 1258, thereby delivering the *coup de grace* to the Abbasid caliphate. Hülagü also made himself ruler of Damascus, Aleppo and the Seljuk sultanate of Konya. His cousin Batu was made master of Russia and went on to ravage Poland, Hungary and Silesia. He suffered a defeat here, however, and retreated. All the Russian duchies were now under the rule of the Mongol Golden Horde from its headquarters in Kazan.

Golden Horde	Batu
Lithuania	Mindaugas
Mongols	Töregene; Güyük; Ogulkaimich
Bulgaria	Kaliman Asen; Michael Asen
Serbia	Stephen Vladislav; Stephen Uros I
Portugal	Sancho II; Afonso III
Sicily	Frederick I
Aragon	James I the Conqueror
Scotland	Alexander II; Alexander III
Sweden	Erik Laaspe
Egypt	as-Salih Ayyub; Turan-Shah
Poland	Conrad I Mazowiecki; Boleslaw V Wstydliwy
Hungary	Bela IV
Bohemia	Wenceslas III
Norway	Haakon IV Haakonsson
Russia	Yaroslav II; Svyatoslav
England	Henry III
Denmark	Erik Plovpenning
Castile	Ferdinand III the Saint
Germany	Frederick II Hohenstaufen
France	Louis IX the Saint
Holy Rom. Emp.	Frederick II
Papacy	Cel. IV; Innocent IV
Eastern Rome	John III Vatatzes
Japan	Shijo; Saka II; Fukakusa II
China	Nan Song Li Zong

1241	1242	1243	1244	1245	1246	1247	1248	1249	1250

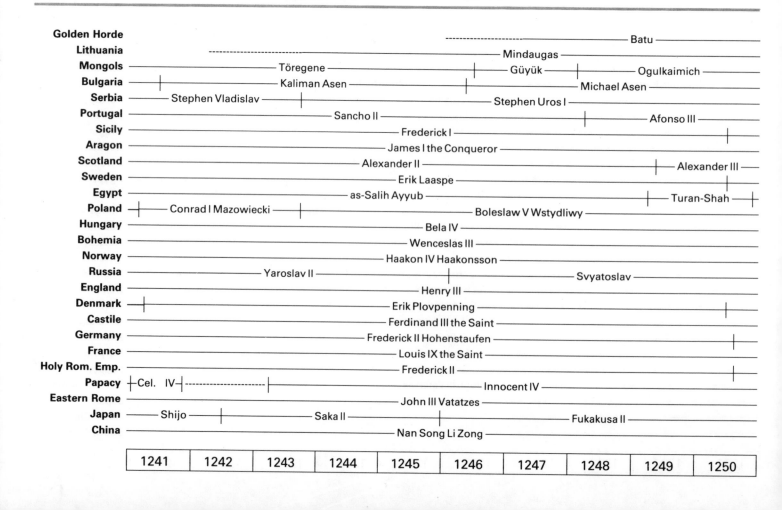

AD 1251-1260

FRANCE

Birger Jarl had ruled Sweden for a couple of decades on behalf of Erik Laaspe and after the latter's death he continued to do so as guardian of his own son Valdemar, whose mother was the sister of Erik Laaspe. Birger is generally regarded as the founder of the state of Sweden. A crusade to Finland which he organized resulted in the large-scale immigration of Swedes into Finland's coastal regions, hitherto largely unpopulated.

Premysl Otokar II encouraged the immigration of Germans into Bohemia. He also led a crusade against the Slavic Prussians who were not yet Christians. As a consequence, the city of Königsberg was founded.

The South Sea island of Raiatea emerged as the centre of a Polynesian cult featuring a war god known as Oro.

Louis IX, St Louis. Detail of a painting by El Greco. Louvre, Paris.

A Ukrainian state briefly flourished under a king named Danylo, who resided in Halicz. Pope Innocent IV was eager to enrol this kingdom in Christendom.

In 1250 Egypt's last Ayyubid sultan was dismissed and the Mamelukes took control. These were Turkish mercenaries and they continued to rule Egypt until 1811.

Serbia was enjoying a period of greatness and held most of the Balkan peninsula. There was political unrest in Bulgaria.

The period 1254-73 is known in German history as the great interregnum. None of the elected emperors secured universal recognition and Spain's Alfonso X, who was named emperor in 1257, failed even to make an appearance.

Hülagü	**Persia**
Batu — Berke	**Golden Horde**
Mindaugas	**Lithuania**
Möngke — Kublai	**Mongols**
Michael Asen — Kalimen II — Constantine Tich	**Bulgaria**
Stephen Uros I	**Serbia**
Afonso III	**Portugal**
Conrad I — Conradin — Manfred	**Sicily**
James I the Conqueror	**Aragon**
Alexander III	**Scotland**
Birger Jarl	**Sweden**
Eybek — Ali — Kutuz	**Egypt**
Boleslaw V Wstydliwy	**Poland**
Bela IV	**Hungary**
Wenceslas III — Premysl Otokar II	**Bohemia**
Haakon IV Haakonsson	**Norway**
Alexander Nevsky	**Russia**
Henry III	**England**
Abel — Christopher I — Erik Glipping	**Denmark**
Ferdinand III — Alfonso X the Wise	**Castile**
Conrad IV — William of Holland — Richard of Cornwall	**Germany**
Louis IX the Saint	**France**
Conrad IV	**Holy Rom. Emp.**
Innocent IV — Alexander IV	**Papacy**
John III Vatatzes — Theodore II Lascaris — John IV & Michael VIII	**Eastern Rome**
Go-Fukakusa — Kameyama	**Japan**
Nan Song Li Zong	**China**

1251	1252	1253	1254	1255	1256	1257	1258	1259	1260

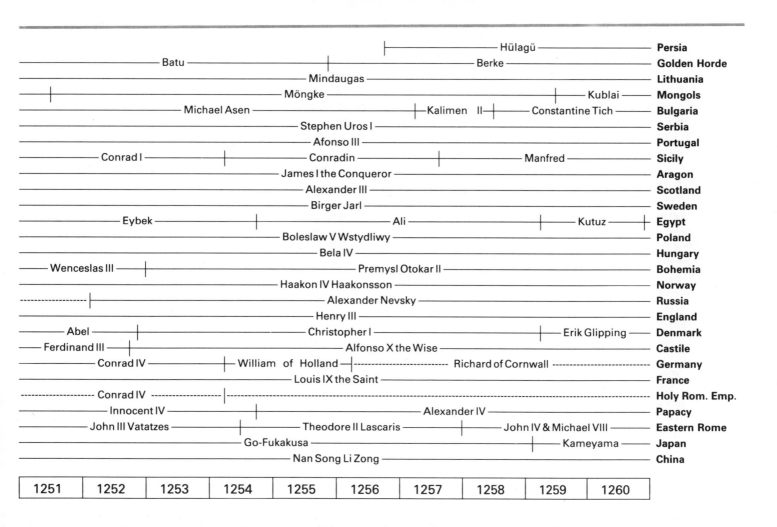

AD 1261-1270

INDIA
CASTILE

With the assistance of Genoa, Emperor Michael VIII Palaeologus took Constantinople in 1261 and put an end to Latin imperial power there. Genoa thereby gained an advantage over Venice regarding trade in Asia and the Black Sea countries.

Charles of Anjou, brother to Louis IX of France, appropriated Naples and Sicily in 1266 after having defeated and killed Manfred, ruler of these two kingdoms.

Two popes, Innocent V and Hadrian V, and also an anti-pope, all held office in 1276. There is no space for these below.

During the course of the 13th century, the Icelandic free state was continuously disrupted by family conflicts, as is so graphically described in the sagas. One of the most aggressive politicians involved was the great author Snorri Sturluson who was assassinated in 1241 on the orders of Norway's King Haakon Haakansson. His executioner, a jarl named Gissur, induced the Icelandic peasants to accept the rule of the Norwegian crown; an arrangement which was implemented in 1262-64.

Kublai, who had been khagan of all the Mongols for some years, moved his residence from Karakorum to Beijing (Peking) in 1263. His brother, Hülagü, meanwhile ruled all the lands from the Oxus to the Mediterranean and was the founder of a Persian dynasty. The distances involved in the Mongol empire were so immense that the various rulers were influenced by different cultures and soon ceased to have much in common. The dying struggle of the Song dynasty was long, arduous and bloody. The Mongols set an example by massacring the entire population of Changan, said to have contained a million inhabitants, because it refused to surrender. After this the capital, Hangzhou, opened its gates without demur and the infant emperor was taken prisoner. The whole of China was now under the Mongols.

The Venetian Marco Polo spent a long time in China during Kublai Khan's reign. In his famous book he describes, among other things, the paper currency of the Chinese.

The long interregnum of the German Empire came to an end in 1273 when Count Rudolf of Habsburg was elected king, for no better reason than that he was too insignificant a man to provoke dissent. His dynasty endured in Europe until the 20th century.

Persia	Hülagü — Abagha Khan
Golden Horde	Berke — Mangu Timur
Lithuania	Mindaugas — Troynat — Wolstinik — Svintorog
Mongols	Kublai Khan
Bulgaria	Constantine Tich
Serbia	Stephen Uros I
Portugal	Afonso III
Sicily	Manfred — Charles of Anjou
Aragon	James I the Conqueror
Scotland	Alexander III
Sweden	Birger Jarl — Valdemar
Egypt	Baybars
Poland	Boleslaw V Wstydliwy
Hungary	Bela IV
Bohemia	Premysl Otokar II
Norway	Haakon (VI) Haakonsson — Magnus VI Law-mender
Russia	Alexander Nevsky — Yaroslav III
England	Henry III
Denmark	Erik Glipping
Castile	Alfonso X the Wise
Germany	(Richard of Cornwall, Alfonso X of Castile)
France	Louis IX the Saint
Holy Rom. Emp.	
Papacy	Urban IV — Clement IV
Eastern Rome	Micahel VIII Palaeologus
Japan	Kameyama
China	Nan Song Li Zong — Nan Song Du Zong

1261	1262	1263	1264	1265	1266	1267	1268	1269	1270

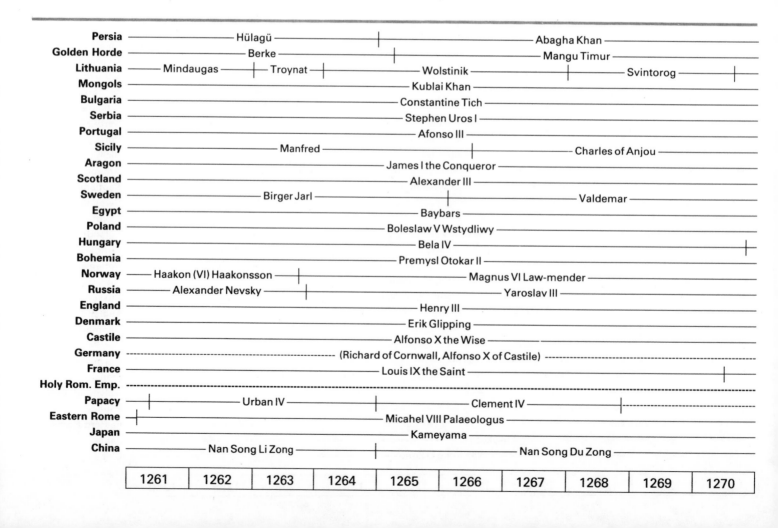

KHMERS, CAMBODIA
JAPAN

As early as 1274, when the fighting was still going on in China, Kublai Khan attempted also to capture Japan by way of Korea, the latter having been part of the Mongol empire since the 1230s. With heavy catapults and other war machines the large army crossed to the southernmost of the Japanese islands where the young shogun Tokimune had assembled his defensive forces. The subsequent battle was one of the bloodiest actions in world history: the Japanese losses were enormous, but the Mongols, too, suffered so many casualties that they were forced to abandon the operation. Under cover of darkness they reboarded their ships and then, on the return crossing to Korea, encountered a typhoon in which part of the fleet foundered.

In Egypt the Mameluke sultan Baybars successfully repulsed the Mongols who had just taken Baghdad. Baybars then established an Abbasid shadow-caliphate in Cairo after the last of the Baghdad caliphs had fled there. Thereafter, Mameluke history is of little general interest, consisting as it does mainly of internal squabbles.

In 1278 Premysl Otokar II of Bohemia suffered a severe defeat at the hands of the German emperor Rudolf. As a result, Otokar had to surrender the archduchy of Austria, so that the poverty-stricken Habsburg imperial family was now encumbered with its own hereditary state.

Kublai Khan, leader of the vast Mongolian empire, was educated in China. He was himself a Buddhist but showed great religious tolerance. Hulton Picture Library, London.

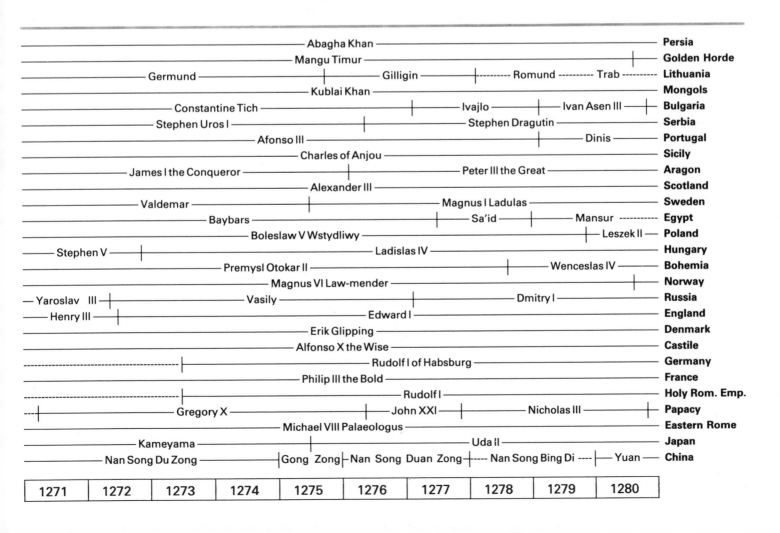

Abagha Khan	Persia
Mangu Timur	Golden Horde
Germund — Gilligin — Romund — Trab	Lithuania
Kublai Khan	Mongols
Constantine Tich — Ivajlo — Ivan Asen III	Bulgaria
Stephen Uros I — Stephen Dragutin	Serbia
Afonso III — Dinis	Portugal
Charles of Anjou	Sicily
James I the Conqueror — Peter III the Great	Aragon
Alexander III	Scotland
Valdemar — Magnus I Ladulas	Sweden
Baybars — Sa'id — Mansur	Egypt
Boleslaw V Wstydliwy — Leszek II	Poland
Stephen V — Ladislas IV	Hungary
Premysl Otokar II — Wenceslas IV	Bohemia
Magnus VI Law-mender	Norway
Yaroslav III — Vasily — Dmitry I	Russia
Henry III — Edward I	England
Erik Glipping	Denmark
Alfonso X the Wise	Castile
Rudolf I of Habsburg	Germany
Philip III the Bold	France
Rudolf I	Holy Rom. Emp.
Gregory X — John XXI — Nicholas III	Papacy
Michael VIII Palaeologus	Eastern Rome
Kameyama — Uda II	Japan
Nan Song Du Zong — Gong Zong — Nan Song Duan Zong — Nan Song Bing Di — Yuan	China

1271	1272	1273	1274	1275	1276	1277	1278	1279	1280

AD 1281-1290

KUBLAI KHAN HUNTING
FRANCE
CASTILE
ITALY
MONGOLIA

In 1282 a bloodbath took place in Palermo which has become known as the Sicilian Vespers; the ringing of the vesper bell on Easter Monday signalled the beginning of the revolt. The uprising was directed against the French who were ruling on behalf of Charles of Anjou; it was initiated by Peter III of Aragon, who was married to the late King Manfred's daughter. The political outcome of this incident was that the island of Sicily was joined with Aragon while the house of Anjou retained the kingdom of Naples. On Peter III's death, however, Sicily went to his brother James, while his son Alfonso III received Aragon. When after Alfonso's death James became king of Aragon, he relinquished Sicily to the Anjous of Naples, but the Sicilians refused to accept this and turned instead to James's brother Frederick.

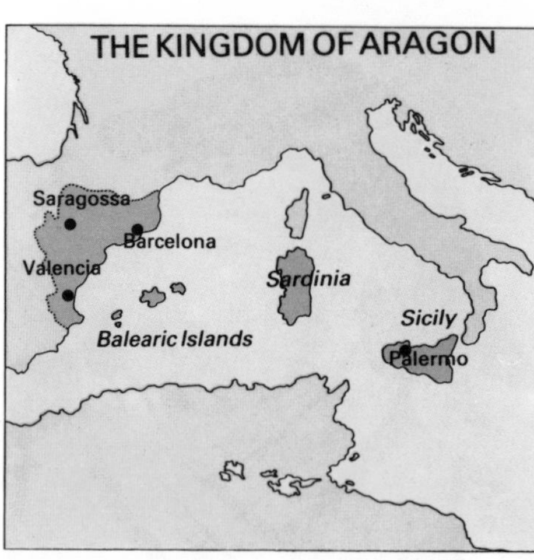
THE KINGDOM OF ARAGON
Saragossa
Barcelona
Valencia
Sardinia
Balearic Islands
Sicily
Palermo

In 1281 Emperor Rudolf of Habsburg made

over recently conquered Austria to his son Albert, who also ruled the Habsburg possessions west of Lake Boden. Albert failed to subjugate Switzerland, and the legend of William Tell may be related to this.

A Seljuk chieftain named Osman became the regent of a Turkish tribe, to whom he gave his name, in 1288. Osman made his residence in Eskisehir and resolutely expanded his kingdom westward, at Byzantine expense, as far as the outskirts of Nicaea. There in the 1290s he founded his new capital, Yenisehir. The Byzantines, exhausted by inflation and war on their territory between Genoa and Venice, were powerless to intervene.

	Rulers
Naples	Charles of Anjou — Charles II
Ottomans	Ertegrul — Osman I
Austria	Albert I
Persia	Abagha Khan — Takudar — Argun
Golden Horde	Toktu
Lithuania	Troyden — Vytenis
Bulgaria	George I Terter
Serbia	Stephen Uros II Milutin
Portugal	Dinis
Sicily	Charles of Anjou — Peter I of Aragon — James of Aragon
Aragon	Peter III the Great — Alfonso III the Liberal
Scotland	Alexander III — Margaret
Sweden	Magnus I Ladulas
Poland	Leszek II Czarny — Henry IV Probus
Hungary	Ladislas IV
Bohemia	Wenceslas IV
Norway	Erik II Priest-hater
Russia	Dmitry I
England	Edward I
Denmark	Erik Glipping — Erik Menved
Castile	Alfonso X the Wise — Sancho IV the Bold
Germany	Rudolf I of Habsburg
France	Philip III the Bold — Philip IV the Fair
Holy Rom. Emp.	Rudolf I
Papacy	Martin IV — Honorius IV — Nicholas IV
Eastern Rome	Michael VIII — Andronicus II Palaeologus
Japan	Uda II — Fushimi
China	Yuan dynasty: Kublai Khan

1281	1282	1283	1284	1285	1286	1287	1288	1289	1290

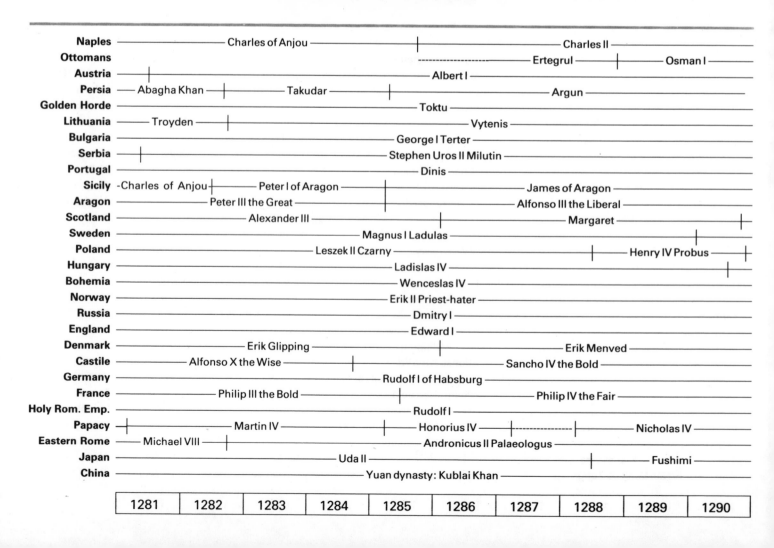

JAPAN
JAPAN
INDIA
EGYPT

Margaret (the "Maid of Norway"), heir to the throne of Scotland, was the granddaughter of Alexander III and daughter of King Erik of Norway. She was summoned home to to Scotland but died on board during the voyage. No less than twelve pretenders now presented themselves and Edward I of England became the arbitrator. Edward selected John de Balliol who became his vassal. A national uprising occurred, led by a noble named William Wallace who became protector of the realm.

In the North there was discord and disruption: the dukes Erik and Valdemar each held parts of Sweden, and in Denmark Erik Menved fought bitterly with a certain Stig and other powerful individuals who had been involved in the murder of Erik's father.

To obtain money for his campaigns he had to lease off Danish provinces so that the crown steadily lost control of the country.

The Hanseatic League was formed in 1294 on the initiative of the city of Lübeck.

The Mongols' world empire disintegrated after the death of Kublai Khan. In Persia the khan and his court were converted to Islam. After Kublai Khan, seven Mongol emperors with Chinese names represented the Yuan dynasty in Beijing (Peking). Most of these were victims of palace revolutions.

By the close of the 13th century Poland had become divided into sixteen different duchies, all fighting among themselves. King Wenceslas IV of Bohemia now intervened and made himself ruler of the entire country in 1300.

Rare Nordic portrait of Erik Glipping, in a law book from Tallinn.

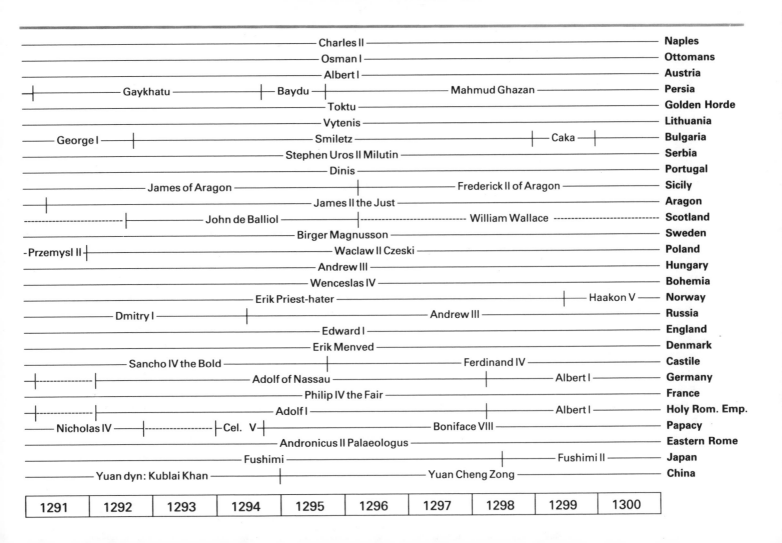

Rulers (1291–1300)	Country
Charles II	Naples
Osman I	Ottomans
Albert I	Austria
Gaykhatu — Baydu — Mahmud Ghazan	Persia
Toktu	Golden Horde
Vytenis	Lithuania
George I — Smiletz — Caka	Bulgaria
Stephen Uros II Milutin	Serbia
Dinis	Portugal
James of Aragon — Frederick II of Aragon	Sicily
James II the Just	Aragon
John de Balliol — William Wallace	Scotland
Birger Magnusson	Sweden
Przemysl II — Waclaw II Czeski	Poland
Andrew III	Hungary
Wenceslas IV	Bohemia
Erik Priest-hater — Haakon V	Norway
Dmitry I — Andrew III	Russia
Edward I	England
Erik Menved	Denmark
Sancho IV the Bold — Ferdinand IV	Castile
Adolf of Nassau — Albert I	Germany
Philip IV the Fair	France
Adolf I — Albert I	Holy Rom. Emp.
Nicholas IV — Cel. V — Boniface VIII	Papacy
Andronicus II Palaeologus	Eastern Rome
Fushimi — Fushimi II	Japan
Yuan dyn: Kublai Khan — Yuan Cheng Zong	China

1291	1292	1293	1294	1295	1296	1297	1298	1299	1300

AD 1301-1310

GERMANY
BYZANTIUM
DANTE
ITALY

In the Middle Ages Italy was disrupted by conflicts among Guelphs and Ghibellines. Initially, this concerned the dispute between the pope and the imperial Hohenstaufen house but now it was more a matter of rivalry between the nobles and middle classes in the Italian towns. The great Florentine writer Dante belonged to the Guelphs who were in power in Florence, but then they split into two factions, and Dante's was the loser. He was exiled in 1302 and never again returned to the city of his birth, spending most of his time instead in Verona with the Ghibelline regent Cangrande della Scala. Most of Dante's work, including the *Divine Comedy*, was written in exile.

A battle of immense importance was fought in July 1302 at Courtrai where a French cavalry force was annihilated by Flemish foot soldiers. Free Flanders served as an English bridgehead for several centuries to come and at the same time a form of middle-class capitalism developed here.

In Rome, where there was fierce fighting between Guelphs and Ghibellines, the French-born pope, Clement V, was persuaded to establish his residence in Avignon. The popes subsequently lived in Avignon until the close of this century.

In Hungary the Arpad dynasty died out in 1301. The throne was then taken over successfully by a Bohemian prince named Wenceslas and by Otto of Belgium, both of whom were descendants of Hungarian princesses. They, in their turn, were succeeded, in the same right, by Charles Robert of Anjou.

The Scot William Wallace was taken prisoner and executed by the English. But Scotland's struggle for freedom was quickly resumed, led now by Robert the Bruce.

The Order of the Knights Templars, which had almost 20,000 members and was extremely wealthy, served as an international bank, but many rulers coveted its funds. In 1307 the King of France suddenly imprisoned its grand masters and a number of its knights, who were accused of heresy. They were tortured until they confessed and then had their property confiscated. Other countries soon followed suit. In 1312 the order was dissolved by the pope; the knights were sentenced by the inquisition and executed in vast numbers.

Naples	Charles II
Ottomans	Osman I
Austria	Albert I — Frederick I the Fair
Persia	Mahmud Ghazan — Oljeitu
Golden Horde	Toktu
Lithuania	Vytenis
Bulgaria	Theodor Svetoslav
Serbia	Stephen Uros II Milutin
Portugal	Dinis
Sicily	Frederick II of Aragon
Aragon	James II the Just
Scotland	William Wallace — ---------------- — Robert I Bruce
Sweden	Birger Magnusson
Poland	Waclaw II Czeski — Waclaw III — Wladyslaw I the Short
Hungary	Wenceslas — Otto — ------------------------------
Bohemia	Wenceslas IV — Wenceslas V — Rudolf — Jindrich Korutansky
Norway	Haakon (V) Magnusson (Haalegg)
Russia	Andrew III — Michael
England	Edward I — Edward II
Denmark	Erik Menved
Castile	Ferdinand IV
Germany	Albert I — Henry VII
France	Philip IV the Fair
Holy Rom. Emp.	Albert I — Henry VII
Papacy	Boniface VIII — Benedict XI — Clement V
Eastern Rome	Andronicus II Palaeologus
Japan	Fushimi II — Nijo II — Hanazono
China	Yuan Cheng Zong — Yuan Wu Zong

1301	1302	1303	1304	1305	1306	1307	1308	1309	1310

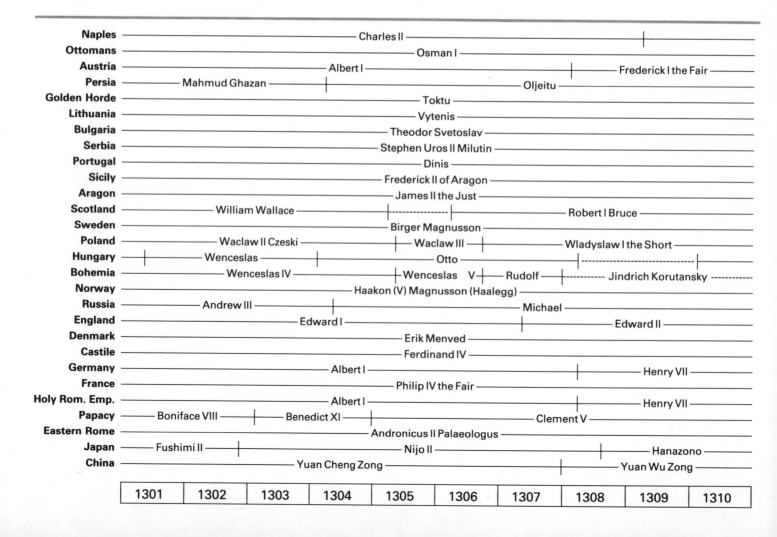

AD 1311-1320

GERMANY
FRANCE

In Sweden this period was dominated by a long struggle for power between the sons of Magnus Ladulås. In 1306 the dukes Erik and Valdemar imprisoned their brother Birger on the Håtuna estate but eleven years later Birger took both their lives following what is known as the Nyköping Banquet. Yet their supporters gained the upper hand after all, expelling Birger and electing instead his three-year old son Magnus Eriksson. Only a few months earlier this infant had inherited the throne of Norway from his maternal grandfather who died without male issue.

About 100,000 French Jews were deported in 1306.

In 1312 the Canary Islands were rediscovered by a Genoese voyager.
The Teutonic Order, clad in white cloaks with black crosses, was a major economic power with a firm footing in Slavic Prussia since 1230. In 1309 the grand master of the order, Siegfried von Feuchtwangen, moved from Venice to Prussian Marienburg with a view to building up a large state on the Baltic.

Gediminas of Lithuania, first of a new dynasty, extended the frontiers of his kingdom beyond Kiev to the Black Sea.

During the reign of Haakon Haalegg, the centre of the Norwegian kingdom was moved to the east. He made Oslo his principal centre and built the Akershus fortress there. Norway was now by far the best organized of the Nordic countries.

The numbering of the Polish Wladyslaws is puzzling. Evidently they began all over again with Wladyslaw the Short.

In Bohemia the dynasty was terminated when Wenceslas V died young. After some confusion Henry VII had his son John elected king of Bohemia. Since he was actually sightless, he was known as John the Blind.

Waclaw II Czeski of Poland and Wenceslas IV of Bohemia were one and the same person. Hungary's Wenceslas – the future Wenceslas V of Bohemia – was his son.

The Order of St John, recently expelled from Palestine and Cyprus, took possession of Rhodes in 1310.

Rulers	Country
Robert	**Naples**
Osman I	**Ottomans**
Frederick I the Fair	**Austria**
Oljeitu – Abu-Sa'id	**Persia**
Toktu – Oz Beg (Uzbek)	**Golden Horde**
Vytenis – Gediminas	**Lithuania**
Theodor Svetoslav	**Bulgaria**
Stephen Uros II Milutin	**Serbia**
Dinis	**Portugal**
Frederick II of Aragon	**Sicily**
James II the Just	**Aragon**
Robert I Bruce	**Scotland**
Birger Magnusson – ----- – Magnus Eriksson	**Sweden**
Wladyslaw I the Short	**Poland**
Charles Robert	**Hungary**
John of Luxemburg	**Bohemia**
Haakon (V) Magnusson (Haalegg) – Magnus (VI) Eriksson	**Norway**
Michael – Yury III	**Russia**
Edward II	**England**
Erik Menved – ----- –	**Denmark**
Ferdinand IV – Alfonso XI the Just	**Castile**
Henry VII – ----- – Louis of Bavaria	**Germany**
Philip IV the Fair – Louis X the Stubborn – John I – Philip V the Tall	**France**
Henry VII of Luxemburg – ----- – Louis IV	**Holy Rom. Emp.**
Clement V – ----- – John XXII	**Papacy**
Andronicus II Palaeologus	**Eastern Rome**
Hanazono – Daigo II	**Japan**
Yuan Ren Zong	**China**

1311	1312	1313	1314	1315	1316	1317	1318	1319	1320

AD 1321-1330

ENGLAND
ITALY

Denmark was in a sorry state as the crown was compelled to mortgage province after province, so that all Christopher II had left was a small part of Lolland. When Christopher died, the Holstein counts Gerhard and John became formal rulers of the country. There were insurrections, especially in the provinces of Skåne and Blekinge, which sought the support of Sweden. But Magnus Eriksson was obliged to reimburse Count John for Skåne, leaving him with insoluble economic problems.

From 1328 there was a new dynasty in France: the Valois. This, however, descended from Hugh Capet as well. Edward III of England also had claims to the throne and assumed the title King of France.

The Mongol khan Oz Beg, who was still a feudal lord under Ivan I Danilovich, recognized the latter as Grand Duke of Moscow in 1328. Two years earlier Ivan had persuaded the metropolitan St Peter to move here from Kiev. The dynasty in the Ukraine had recently died out and its realm disintegrated, Poland, Lithuania and Hungary each taking their share.

In Persia, after the death of Abu-Sa'id, various pretenders struggled for power and there was widespread confusion for almost a decade. Abu-Sa'id, incidentally, was the last member of the Mongols' dynasty.

The Solomonid dynasty, claiming to be descended from the Queen of Sheba, had just assumed power in Ethiopia. Little is known of it but it did slightly expand the frontiers of the ancient kingdom.

At this time seafarers form Genoa discovered Madeira and the Azores.

In 1328 John XXII banished five archbishops, thirty bishops and forty-six abbots for not having punctually paid their dues to Avignon. John XXII himself was an unpretentious, thrifty man who had organized the papal taxation and financial systems efficiently. Cast-iron cannons were mentioned in Italy, and cannons were in use in Europe from 1320 onwards.

Some members of the French court had taken to using a fork, but this implement did not become widely used for another century.

Naples	Robert
Ottomans	Osman I — Orhan
Austria	Frederick I the Fair
Persia	Abu-Sa'id
Golden Horde	Oz Beg (Uzbek)
Lithuania	Gediminas — Kestutis
Bulgaria	Theodor Svetoslav — George II — Michael Sisman — Ivan Stefan-
Serbia	Stephen Uros III Decansk
Portugal	Dinis — Afonso IV
Sicily	Frederick II of Aragon
Aragon	James II the Just — Alfonso IV the Benign
Scotland	Robert I Bruce — David II Bruce
Sweden	Magnus Eriksson
Poland	Wladyslaw I the Short
Hungary	Charles Robert
Bohemia	John I of Luxemburg
Norway	Magnus VI Eriksson
Russia	Yury III Danilovich — Ivan I Danilovich
England	Edward II — Edward III
Denmark	Christopher II
Castile	Alfonso XI the Just
Germany	Louis of Bavaria
France	Philip V — Charles IV the Fair — Philip VI
Holy Rom. Emp.	Louis IV
Papacy	John XXII
Eastern Rome	Andronicus II Palaeologus — Andronicus III
Japan	Daigo II
China	Yuan Ying Zong — Yuan Tai Ding Di — Yuan Ming Zong

1321	1322	1323	1324	1325	1326	1327	1328	1329	1330

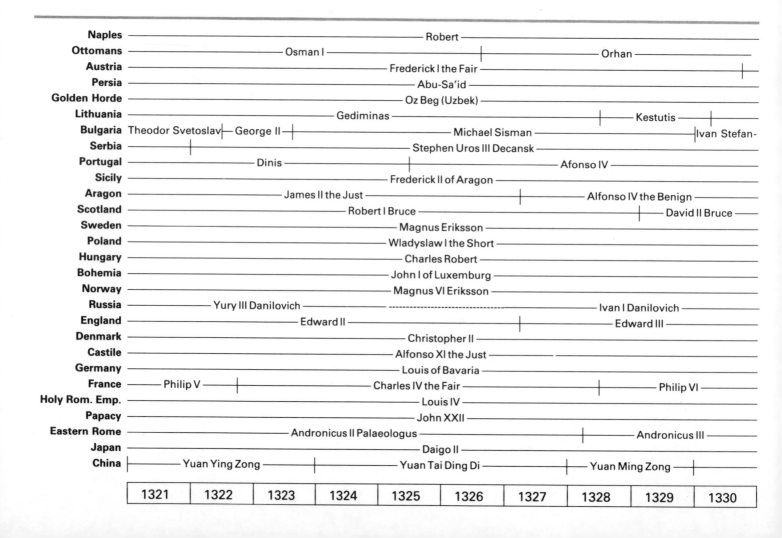

AD 1331-1340

ENGLAND

ITALY
ENGLAND

In 1336 Japan was partitioned into a northern and a southern state, a situation that continued until 1393. The country was in a state of confusion with numerous chieftains fighting among themselves under two branches of the imperial dynasty.

Casimir II, known as the Great, opened his country to the Jews who were being persecuted practically everwhere throughout Christendom.

In 1333 Edward III of England was recognized as feudal lord of Scotland, where Edward de Balliol became his vassal. Edward's hereditary claim to the French crown began a war in 1337 that was to last 100 years. In part it concerned Flanders and its vital textile industry.

The papal palace in Avignon. The popes who resided here were all Frenchmen. The acoustics of this building were magnificent.

In the reign of Stefan Dusan, Serbia was at the peak of its power. It now extended from the Danube to the Bay of Corinth and from the Aegean Sea to the Adriatic. Stefan Dusan heaped privileges and donations on the virtually inaccessible monasteries of Mount Athos, part of his domain. He also had himself crowned czar abandoning his former, national title of Kral. This created a new empire, larger than the Byzantine empire and almost equally Greek in character.

The Ottomans took Nicaea in 1331.

Giotto, founder of Renaissance Italian painting, was made surveyor, of the cathedral of Florence and architect to the city in 1334. He had also worked in other places, including Padua and Naples.

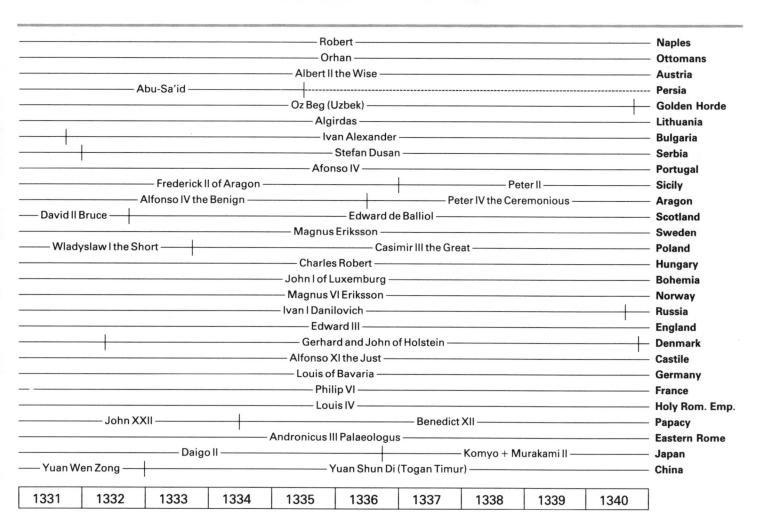

Robert	**Naples**
Orhan	**Ottomans**
Albert II the Wise	**Austria**
Abu-Sa'id	**Persia**
Oz Beg (Uzbek)	**Golden Horde**
Algirdas	**Lithuania**
Ivan Alexander	**Bulgaria**
Stefan Dusan	**Serbia**
Afonso IV	**Portugal**
Frederick II of Aragon — Peter II	**Sicily**
Alfonso IV the Benign — Peter IV the Ceremonious	**Aragon**
David II Bruce — Edward de Balliol	**Scotland**
Magnus Eriksson	**Sweden**
Wladyslaw I the Short — Casimir III the Great	**Poland**
Charles Robert	**Hungary**
John I of Luxemburg	**Bohemia**
Magnus VI Eriksson	**Norway**
Ivan I Danilovich	**Russia**
Edward III	**England**
Gerhard and John of Holstein	**Denmark**
Alfonso XI the Just	**Castile**
Louis of Bavaria	**Germany**
Philip VI	**France**
Louis IV	**Holy Rom. Emp.**
John XXII — Benedict XII	**Papacy**
Andronicus III Palaeologus	**Eastern Rome**
Daigo II — Komyo + Murakami II	**Japan**
Yuan Wen Zong — Yuan Shun Di (Togan Timur)	**China**

1331	1332	1333	1334	1335	1336	1337	1338	1339	1340

AD 1341-1350

DENMARK
ITALY
BOHEMIA
GRANADA
ENGLAND
ENGLAND

At the close of the 1340s the entire world from China to Ireland was struck by a plague, known as the Black Death. This had far-reaching political effects, too, since many prominent leaders died. In Norway, the tremendous population decline left the country economically crippled for a long time.

An emir named Yusuf I reigned in Granada from 1333 to 1354. Belying the modest influence of the realm, the magnificent Alhambra was built during the reigns of Yusuf and his son Muhammad V.

In Mexico the kingdom and culture of the Aztecs flourished around the capital Tenochtitlán built on islands in a lake on the high plateau. Their society was rigidly divided into classes.

In 1346 the English won a great victory at Crécy and took possession of Calais. Crécy is said to have been the first battle in which firearms were used, indicating that gunpowder had now been discovered. A German by the name of Berhold Schwarz was long credited with having invented gunpowder, yet in fact this was a Chinese discovery which had probably been brought to Europe by the Mongols, so that it must have been used in warfare long before the battle of Crécy.

David II Bruce was expelled from Scotland in 1332 but returned ten years later.

There was social unrest in various parts of western Europe. The weavers in Ghent, Bruges and Konstanz rebelled, as did craftsmen in Nürnberg and peasants in France. These uprisings were suppressed.

In 1346 the Teutonic Order purchased the Duchy of Estonia from Valdemar Atterdag for 19,000 marks.

Two large banks in Florence collapsed in 1348 after Edward III of England stopped payments to them, and the resultant economic crisis was felt all over Europe.

Sweden and Norway had been united for over twenty years, but the relationship was clearly not destined to last, because Magnus Eriksson had prudently given his two sons the Norwegian national names Erik and Haaton. The latter took over Norway in 1343. Unlike Sweden, it was a hereditary kingdom.

Naples	Robert | Andrew | Joan I
Ottomans	Orhan
Austria	Albert II the Wise
Persia	Nushirwan
Golden Horde	Berdibek
Lithuania	Algirdas
Bulgaria	Ivan Alexander
Serbia	Stefan Dusan
Portugal	Afonso IV
Sicily	Peter II | Louis of Aragon
Aragon	Peter IV the Ceremonious
Scotland	Edw. Ball. | David II Bruce
Sweden	Magnus Eriksson
Poland	Casimir III the Great
Hungary	Charles Robert | Louis I (Louis of Anjou)
Bohemia	John I of Luxemburg | Charles I
Norway	Magnus (VI) Eriksson | Haakon VI Magnusson
Russia	Simeon
England	Edward III
Denmark	Valdemar Atterdag
Castile	Alfonso XI the Just |
Germany	Louis of Bavaria | Charles IV
France	Philip VI |
Holy Rom. Emp.	Louis IV | Charles IV
Papacy	Benedict XII | Clement VI
Eastern Rome	| John V Palaeologus | John VI Cantacuzenus
Japan	Komyo + Murakami II | Suko + Murakami II
China	Yuan Shun Di (Togan Timur)

1341	1342	1343	1344	1345	1346	1347	1348	1349	1350

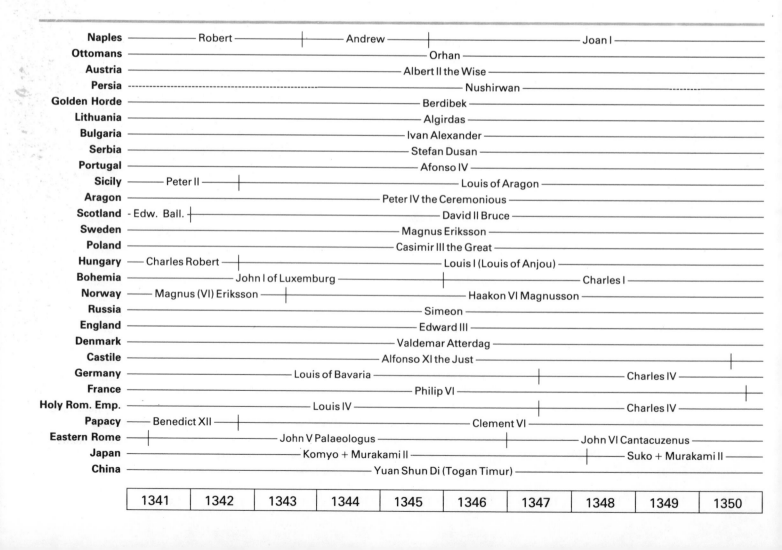

AD 1351-1360

ITALY
ENGLAND
ITALY
ENGLAND

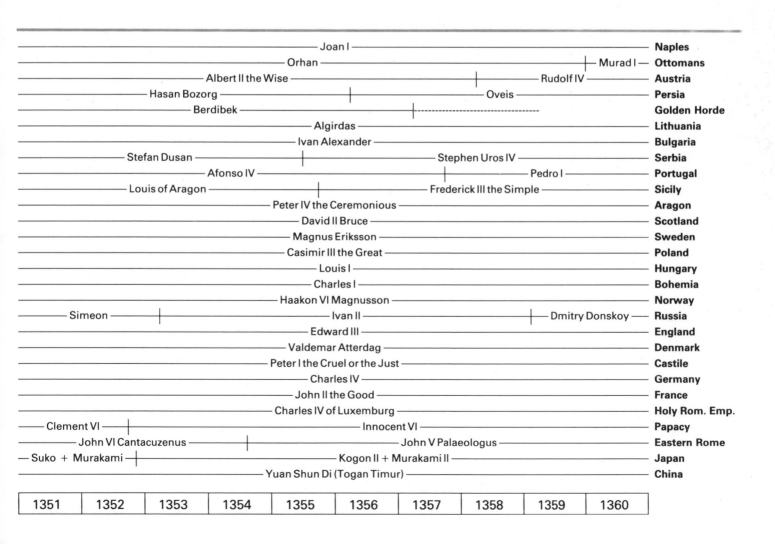

King Charles I of Bohemia and the German emperor Charles IV were one and the same individual.

Petrarch's *Il canzoniere* (which includes the sonnets to Laura) and Boccaccio's *Decameron* appeared during this decade.

King Peter of Castile's cognomen, the Cruel or the Just, clearly indicates that there were divergent opinions of him. In due course he was assassinated by his half-brother and successor Henry, known as the Benevolent.

The Tyrol became part of Austria in Rudolf IV's reign.

A local politician in Rome, Cola di Rienzo, proclaimed himself people's tribune, and set up a Roman republic on the classical model. He was quickly expelled but returned with the blessing of Pope Innocent VI and was subsequently killed in a riot.

After the death of the khan, Berdibek, the Golden Horde was disrupted by internal struggles for power.

There was chaos in the moribund Byzantine empire. The first minister, John Cantacuzenus, proclaimed himself emperor when the mother of nine-year-old John V dismissed him from his post. Civil war broke out, whereupon John VI Cantacuzenus called upon the Turkish sultan, Orhan, who despatched an army of 10,000 men, while John V was supported by a force of 4,000 knights sent by Stefan Dusan. The Turks won decisively but then refused to leave; in fact, following an earthquake which dispersed the inhabitants, they occupied the important town of Gallipoli. John VI begged the Turks to return the town and even offered a large ransom for it, but the sultan refused. John VI Cantacuzenus then abdicated and left John V Palaeologus to bear alone the honour and torment of the office of Byzantine emperor.

The Serbian empire barely survived its ruler Stefan Dusan.

The leaning tower of Pisa was completed in 1350. The city, however, no longer ranked as a great power.

Rulers	Country
Joan I	**Naples**
Orhan — Murad I	**Ottomans**
Albert II the Wise — Rudolf IV	**Austria**
Hasan Bozorg — Oveis	**Persia**
Berdibek — ----------	**Golden Horde**
Algirdas	**Lithuania**
Ivan Alexander	**Bulgaria**
Stefan Dusan — Stephen Uros IV	**Serbia**
Afonso IV — Pedro I	**Portugal**
Louis of Aragon — Frederick III the Simple	**Sicily**
Peter IV the Ceremonious	**Aragon**
David II Bruce	**Scotland**
Magnus Eriksson	**Sweden**
Casimir III the Great	**Poland**
Louis I	**Hungary**
Charles I	**Bohemia**
Haakon VI Magnusson	**Norway**
Simeon — Ivan II — Dmitry Donskoy	**Russia**
Edward III	**England**
Valdemar Atterdag	**Denmark**
Peter I the Cruel or the Just	**Castile**
Charles IV	**Germany**
John II the Good	**France**
Charles IV of Luxemburg	**Holy Rom. Emp.**
Clement VI — Innocent VI	**Papacy**
John VI Cantacuzenus — John V Palaeologus	**Eastern Rome**
Suko + Murakami — Kogon II + Murakami II	**Japan**
Yuan Shun Di (Togan Timur)	**China**

1351	1352	1353	1354	1355	1356	1357	1358	1359	1360

AD 1361-1370

CHINA
ENGLAND
CHINA

The situation in the French duchy of Burgundy had an important bearing on European political history. In 1361 the established dynasty died out, and the French king, having appropriated the duchy under the crown, made it over as a hereditary province to his younger son Philip the Bold. The latter married the heiress of Flanders and Antwerp and thereby enlarged his realm. This type of marriage became something of a feature of Burgundian policy, although the duchy was already powerful.

In 1370 Hungary and Poland were unified: the Hungarian king Louis or Louis of Anjou was the nephew of Poland's Wladyslaw IV the Short, whose son and successor died without heir. German influence had decreased during the latter's reign.

In China a new national dynasty, the Ming (the Luminous), assumed power in 1368. The revolution against the Mongols had begun twenty years earlier, in 1348, led by an able young peasant who was later known as Emperor Hong Wu. Togan Timur, last of the Mongol Yuan dynasty emperors, was a weak, voluptuous individual who reluctantly fled Beijing for the steppelands of his ancestors. The imperial porcelain factory at Jingdezhen began production in the 1360s.

Valdemar Atterdag plundered Visby in 1361.

The archbishop of Paris gives his blessing at the annual market in St Denis. Miniature, Bibliothèque Nationale.

	Rulers (1361–1370)
Naples	Joan I
Burgundy	Philip I the Bold
Ottomans	Murad I
Austria	Rudolf IV – Albert III
Persia	Oveis
Lithuania	Algirdas
Bulgaria	Ivan Alexander
Serbia	Stephen Uros IV
Portugal	Pedro I – Ferdinand I
Sicily	Frederick III the Simple
Aragon	Peter IV the Ceremonious
Scotland	David II Bruce
Sweden	Magnus Eriksson – Albert of Mecklenburg
Poland	Casimir III the Great
Hungary	Louis I
Bohemia	Charles I
Norway	Haakon VI Magnusson
Russia	Dmitry Ivanovich Donskoy
England	Edward III
Denmark	Valdemar Atterdag
Castile	Peter I the Cruel – Henry II
Germany	Charles IV
France	John II the Good – Charles V
Holy Rom. Emp.	Charles IV of Luxemburg
Papacy	Innocent VI – Urban V
Eastern Rome	John V Palaeologus
Japan	Kogon II + Murakami II – Kogon II + Chokei
China	Yuan Shun Di (Togan Timur) – Ming Hong Wu

1361	1362	1363	1364	1365	1366	1367	1368	1369	1370

AD 1371-1380

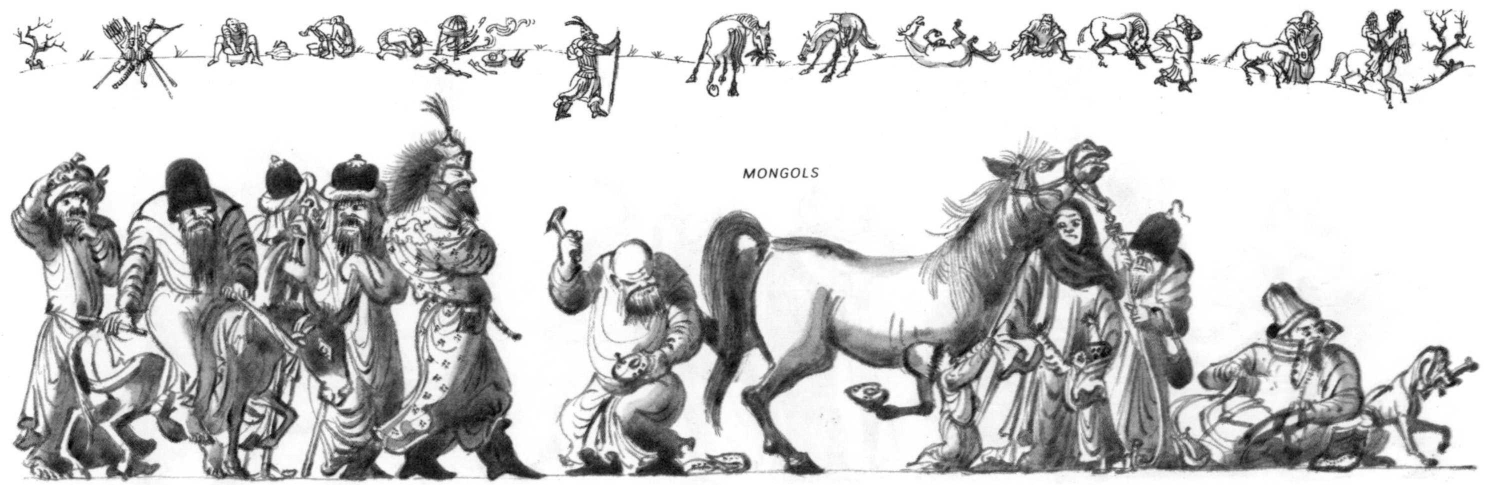
MONGOLS

Andronicus IV, son of John V, succeeded with Genoese help, in displacing his father for a few years; but the Venetians found it expedient to expel him and reinstate John. The Byzantine empire was now a mere toy in the hands of more powerful states. John V ruled Constantinople alone. In 1373 he was forced to accept the role of vassal under the Ottoman sultan, Murad I, and to accompany him on an expediton into Asia Minor.

In 1378 a Genoese admiral named Chioggia entered the Laguna Veneta with his fleet and blockaded Venice; but the Venetians sealed off the Genoese navy and starved it into surrender. In terms of foreign policy, Genoa never recovered from this debacle.

In 1372 the Mongol capital of Karakorum was taken by the Chinese, who thereby restored China's former rule in central Asia.

At the time of Louis I, Hungary was an important country, and Louis himself was also king of Poland where he was known as Ludwig of Hungary.

In the 1370s the English theologian John Wycliffe composed an ecclesiastical-political treatise demanding apostolic poverty and the renouncing of temporal dominion in accordance with the Word of God.

In 1377 parts of this were condemned by the pope, but Wycliffe was supported by Parliament and the people of London.

The Turks, who had secured a foothold in Europe under the Byzantine emperor John VI Cantacuzenus, continued their triumphant progress in the Balkans. In 1369 they forced the Bulgar czar, Sisman, to become the sultan's vassal. A few years later the Serbian brothers Uglesya and Vukasin were decisively defeated at a battle by the River Maritsa.

In 1377 the Papal Chair was moved back to Rome, but antipopes continued to reside in Avignon for some time to come. The schism was to last for over fifty years.

New literature included William Langland's *Piers Plowman* and Hafez's *Divan*.

In Japan the classical heroic Nō drama had emerged.

Joan I	**Naples**
Philip I the Bold	**Burgundy**
Murad I	**Ottomans**
Albert III & Leopold III	**Austria**
Oveis – Husayn – Ahmed	**Persia**
Algirdas – Jagiello	**Lithuania**
Ivan Sisman	**Bulgaria**
Lazar I	**Serbia**
Ferdinand I	**Portugal**
Frederick III the Simple – Maria	**Sicily**
Peter IV the Ceremonious	**Aragon**
Robert II Stuart	**Scotland**
Albert of Mecklenburg	**Sweden**
Ludwig I of Hungary	**Poland**
Louis I	**Hungary**
Charles I – Wenceslas VI	**Bohemia**
Haakon VI Magnusson	**Norway**
Dmitry Ivanovich Donskoy	**Russia**
Edward III – Richard II	**England**
Valdemar Atterdag – Olaf Haakonsson	**Denmark**
Henry II of Trastamara – John I	**Castile**
Charles IV – Wenceslas	**Germany**
Charles V	**France**
Charles IV of Luxemburg – Wenceslas	**Holy Rom. Emp.**
Gregory XI – Urban VI (+ Clement VII)	**Papacy**
John V Palaeologus – Andronicus IV – John V	**Eastern Rome**
Chokei + Ennyu II – Ennyu II + Kameyama II	**Japan**
Ming Hong Wu	**China**

1371	1372	1373	1374	1375	1376	1377	1378	1379	1380

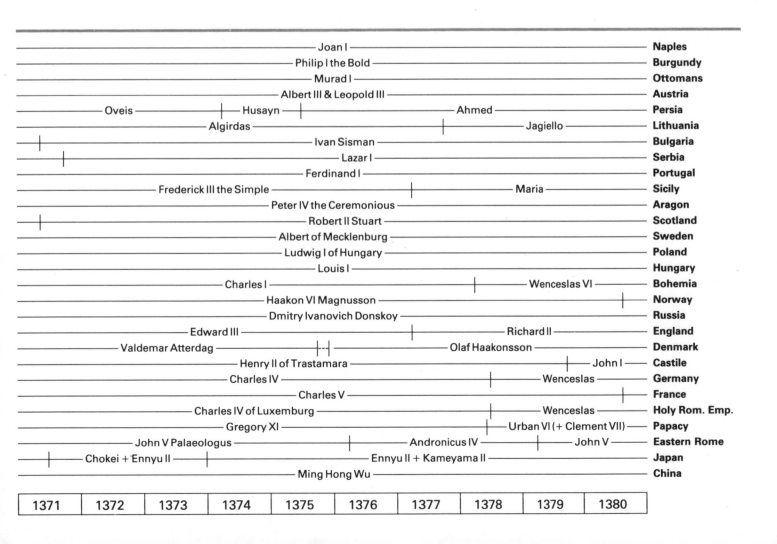

AD 1381-1390

PERSIA
BOHEMIA
BURGUNDY
PERSIA

When King Louis of Hungary died, his own people turned to his eldest daughter Maria while the Poles supported his younger daughter Jadwiga. Maria married Sigismund of Luxemburg who became her joint regent in Hungary in 1388, and also in time German emperor and king of Bohemia. Jadwig married the Grand Duke Jagiello of Lithuania who was crowned in 1381 and baptized, assuming the name of Wladyslaw. The marriage implied a Polish-Lithuanian union, though shortly afterwards Jagiello was compelled to make his cousin Vytautas grand duke of Lithuania, with a considerable degree of independence.

Olaf Haakonsson was the last male descendant of the royal houses of the three Nordic countries, but he was still a child and Denmark was thus ruled by his mother Margaret, daughter of Valdemar Atterdag and wife of Norway's King Haakon. When the latter died ten-year-old Olaf Haakonsson became king of Norway as well. Sweden, which was an electoral kingdom, had taken another course.

In the 1380s the Turks seized most of the Bulgar and Byzantine territories in the Balkans. In 1380 they defeated the Serbs in a major battle where both the Serbian prince Lazar and the Turkish sultan, Murad, died.

During the previous decade a minor prince from the Samarkand area had overrun a large part of central Asia and was to go down in history as Timur Lenk, last of the great Mongol conquerors. In the 1380s he subdued Persia, Armenia, Georgia and Kashgar; and in the 1390s he pushed all the way through to Moscow and subsequently took a large part of India. He advanced with relentless ferocity and wanton cruelty, burning down such towns as Isfahan, Delhi, Baghdad and Damascus, slaughtering the male population and ruining vast areas for ever by deliberately destroying the irrigation systems.

There was a revolt in England in 1381. Nearly 100,000 peasants marched to London and killed several landowners, lawyers and civil servants, including the archbishop. Their leader Wat Tyler was soon murdered and Richard II dispersed the peasants with false promises, later punishing them.

Naples	Joan I – Charles III – Ladislas
Burgundy	Philip I the Bold
Ottomans	Murad I – Bayezid I
Austria	Albert III + Leopold III – Albert III + William
Persia	Ahmed
Lithuania	Jagiello (Wladyslaw)
Bulgaria	Ivan Sisman
Serbia	Lazar I
Portugal	Ferdinand I – John I, Master of Aviz
Sicily	Maria
Aragon	Peter IV the Ceremonious – John I
Scotland	Robert II Stuart
Sweden	Albert of Mecklenburg – Margaret
Poland	Ludwig – Jadwiga – Jagiello (Wladyslaw II)
Hungary	Louis I – Maria I – Charles II – Maria I & Sigismund I
Bohemia	Wenceslas VI
Norway	Olaf IV Haakonsson – Margaret
Russia	Dmitry Ivanovich Donskoy – Vasily I
England	Richard II
Denmark	Olaf Haakonsson – Margaret
Castile	John I
Germany	Wenceslas
France	Charles VI
Holy Rom. Emp.	Wenceslas
Papacy	(Clement VII +) Urban VI
Eastern Rome	John V Palaeologus – John VII
Japan	Kameyama II + Komatsu II
China	Ming Hong Wu

1381	1382	1383	1384	1385	1386	1387	1388	1389	1390

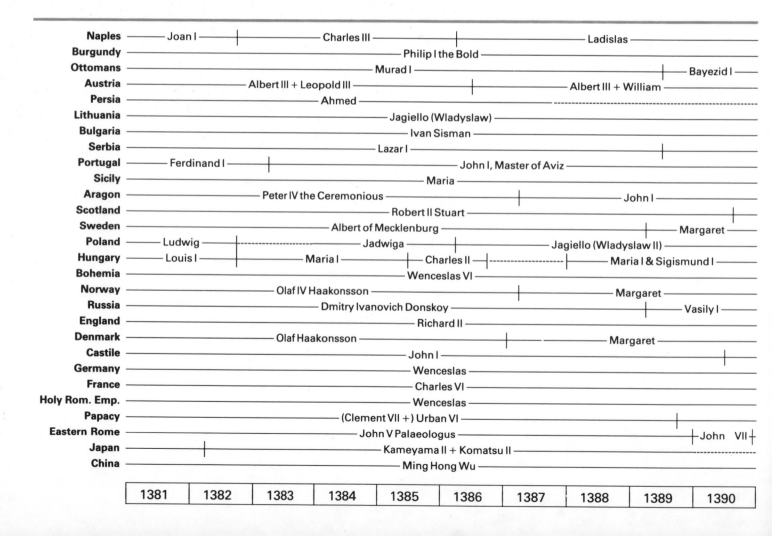

AD 1391-1400

ITALY
BURGUNDY
DENMARK

A shogun named Yoshimitsu made himself all-powerful in Japan. From 1392 there was only one imperial court here, but from the time of Yoshimitsu it is more realistic to list the names of the shoguns rather than the emperors. This situation was not to alter again until the 1860s.

The real name of Emperor Hong Wu of China, founder of the famous Ming dynasty, was Zhu Yuan-zhang. Hong Wu was, in fact, the reign title, a *nienhao*. Having begun his career as a Buddhist, he realized that Buddhism was a subversive religion and to be resisted, whereas Confuciansim was useful to those in power and should be promoted. By fair means or foul, he consolidated the traditional social system by appointing an upper class administration which safe-guarded the interests of those in power and obtained recruits from the ranks of the ordinary people by a carefully regulated examination scheme. The established Chinese examination system, with its literature courses and scholarly degrees, was formulated during Hong Wu's time.

In 1398 the Teutonic Order took Gotland from the Vitalians who were adherents of King Albert.

The Avignon epoch in papal history was approaching its close. But the return to Rome was not without its problems; during a period of transition there were rival popes in both places. Not until the second decade of the next century was the situation resolved and order restored to the papal chronology.

John VII Palaeologus appeared as Byzantine emperor around 1370. He was the son of Andronicus IV and the grandson of John V whom he attempted to depose.

In 1397 Denmark, Norway and Sweden were united in the Kalmar union. The common heir, Olaf Haakonsson had died young but Queen Margaret saw to it that her great-nephew Erik was elected king.

The Turks now conquered the entire Balkans, and the East Roman Empire was limited to the city of Constantinople, which was supported via the sea route by the Venetians. A Franco-German army of crusaders who came to their aid was totally annihilated. Emperor Manuel set off to western Europe in December 1399.

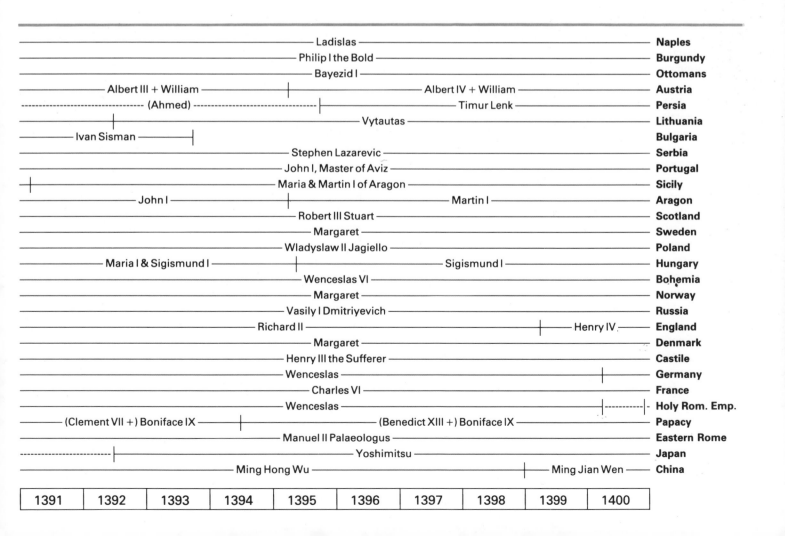

Ladislas	**Naples**
Philip I the Bold	**Burgundy**
Bayezid I	**Ottomans**
Albert III + William | Albert IV + William	**Austria**
(Ahmed) | Timur Lenk	**Persia**
| Vytautas	**Lithuania**
Ivan Sisman |	**Bulgaria**
Stephen Lazarevic	**Serbia**
John I, Master of Aviz	**Portugal**
| Maria & Martin I of Aragon	**Sicily**
John I | Martin I	**Aragon**
Robert III Stuart	**Scotland**
Margaret	**Sweden**
Wladyslaw II Jagiello	**Poland**
Maria I & Sigismund I | Sigismund I	**Hungary**
Wenceslas VI	**Bohemia**
Margaret	**Norway**
Vasily I Dmitriyevich	**Russia**
Richard II | Henry IV	**England**
Margaret	**Denmark**
Henry III the Sufferer	**Castile**
Wenceslas |	**Germany**
Charles VI	**France**
Wenceslas |	**Holy Rom. Emp.**
(Clement VII +) Boniface IX | (Benedict XIII +) Boniface IX	**Papacy**
Manuel II Palaeologus	**Eastern Rome**
| Yoshimitsu	**Japan**
Ming Hong Wu | Ming Jian Wen	**China**

1391	1392	1393	1394	1395	1396	1397	1398	1399	1400

FRANCE
FRANCE
ENGLAND
FLANDERS

Sultan Bayezid, who had made the Byzantine emperors his vassals, was defeated and taken prisoner by Timur Lenk, and Emperor Manuel II returned from western Europe in triumph to Constantinople. The Turkish empire, however, quickly recovered.

Between 1400 and 1410 there were three rival German-Roman kings, recently dismissed for drunkenness and general incompetence, an elector named Rupert the Palatine and Wenceslas's cousin Jost. When Jost died, Wenceslas's brother Sigismund was made king instead. By marriage Sigismund was also king of Hungary and was to become king of Bohemia as well.

In 1405 Venice seized power in Padua, Bassano, Vicenza and Verona. Florence took possession of Pisa in 1406.

When Timur Lenk died in Samarkand, his vast empire was divided. One son took possession of Baghdad and western Iran but was soon expelled by a Turkoman horde known as the Black Sheep. One of the younger sons was Shah Rokh who made himself master of Herat, Khorazan and other areas to the east. Under his dynasty, Persian art and literature flourished as never before.

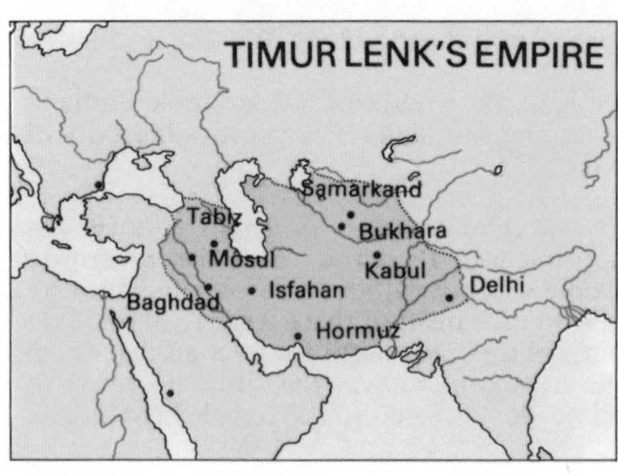
TIMUR LENK'S EMPIRE
Samarkand
Bukhara
Tabiz
Mosul
Kabul
Delhi
Isfahan
Baghdad
Hormuz

The Hundred Years' War between England and France continued. After the battle of Agincourt in 1415 the English occupied Normandy and Paris, and Burgundy then formed an alliance with England. This was a very profitable arrangement for the dukes of Burgundy, and in Philip II's time their domains were expanded to include Namur, Limburg, Holland and Friesland.

Erik of Pomerania had been formal sovereign of the three Nordic countries since 1397, though in actual fact Queen Margaret continued to rule here until her death in 1412.

Naples	Ladislas
Burgundy	Philip I the Bold — John the Fearless
Ottomans	Bayezid I — Mehmed I
Austria	Albert IV + William — Albert V + William — Albert V + Ernest
Persia	Timur Lenk — Khalil Shah — Shah Rokh
Lithuania	Vytautas
Serbia	Stephen Lazarevic
Portugal	John I, Master of Aviz
Sicily	Martin I of Aragon — Martin II
Aragon	Martin I
Scotland	Robert III Stuart
Sweden	Margaret
Poland	Wladyslaw II Jagiello
Hungary	Sigismund I
Bohemia	Wenceslas VI
Norway	Margaret
Russia	Vasily I Dmitriyevich
England	Henry IV
Denmark	Margaret
Castile	Henry III the Sufferer — John II
Germany	Rupert of the Palatinate
France	Charles VI
Holy Rom. Emp.	Rupert of the Palatinate
Papacy	Boniface IX — Innocent VII — Gregory XII
Eastern Rome	Manuel II Palaeologus
Japan	Yoshimitsu — Yoshimochi
China	Ming Jian Wen — Ming Yong Le

1401	1402	1403	1404	1405	1406	1407	1408	1409	1410

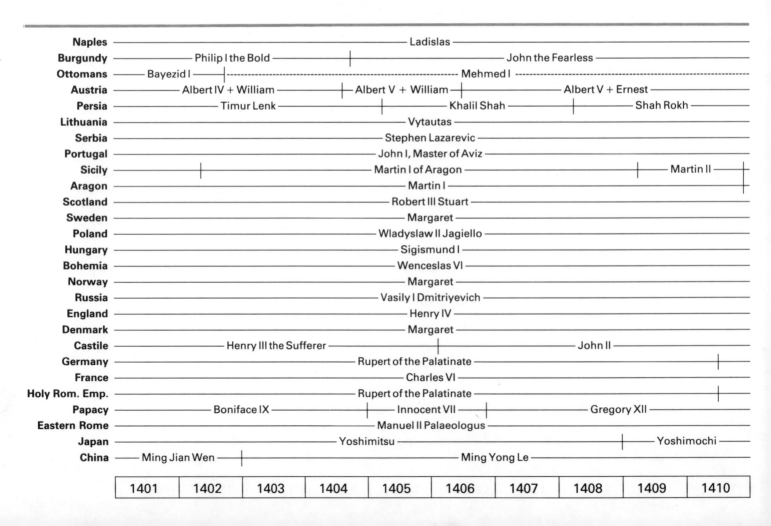

FRANCE
ITALY

Vytautas of Lithuania, formally a vassal under his cousin Jagiello of Poland, extended his power to the east where the Russians were hard pressed by Timur Lenk's hordes. The Polish-Lithuanian kingdom extended from the Baltic to the Black Sea and embraced Ukraine, White Russia and the areas around Smolensk and the Upper Oka. In the summer of 1410 Jagiello and Vytautas jointly defeated the Teutonic Knights who for a century and a half had ruled the Baltic region from East Prussia to Estonia.

Martin II of Sicily was identical with Martin I, el Humano, of Aragon and was also father of the Sicilian Martin I, whom he succeeded.

A professor in Prague, Jan Hus, had been agitating for the reformation of the Church and also for Czech emancipation from German rule. At a council in Konstanz in 1415 he was condemned as a heretic and burned at the stake. This led to a Czech war of liberation which lasted several decades.

After the death of Martin II, Sicily sought to break away from Aragon and secure the protection of the pope. But the attempt failed and thereafter the island could no longer be regarded as an independent state.

Literary activity included Thomas à Kempis's *De imitatione Christi*. In Cairo the final touches were being put to the *Thousand and One Nights* tales.

In Italian cities art flourished under the protection of various tyrants. This coin by Pisanello carries a portrait of Filippo Maria Visconti, ruler of Milan

Ladislas — Joan II	**Naples**
John the Fearless — Philip II	**Burgundy**
Mehmed I	**Ottomans**
Albert V + Ernest	**Austria**
Shah Rokh	**Persia**
Vytautas	**Lithuania**
Stephen Lazarevic	**Serbia**
John I, Master of Aviz	**Portugal**
Blanche of Navarre ---- Ferdinand of Castile — Alfonso of Aragon	**Sicily**
Blanche — Ferdinand I de Anteguera — Alfonso V	**Aragon**
Robert III Stuart	**Scotland**
Margaret — Erik of Pomerania	**Sweden**
Wladyslaw II Jagiello	**Poland**
Sigismund I	**Hungary**
Wenceslas VI — Sigismund	**Bohemia**
Margaret — Erik of Pomerania	**Norway**
Vasily I Dmitriyevich	**Russia**
Henry IV — Henry V	**England**
Margaret — Erik of Pomerania	**Denmark**
John II	**Castile**
Jost — Sigismund	**Germany**
Charles VI	**France**
Jost — Sigismund of Luxemburg	**Holy Rom. Emp.**
Gregory XII ---- Martin V	**Papacy**
Manuel II Palaeologus	**Eastern Rome**
Yoshimochi	**Japan**
Ming Yong Le	**China**

1411	1412	1413	1414	1415	1416	1417	1418	1419	1420

AD 1421-1430

AZTECS, MEXICO
FLANDERS
FRANCE
JAPAN

Joan of Arc, the French peasant girl who led the troops of Charles VII to victory at Orléans and elsewhere, was captured in the spring of 1430 by the Burgundians and burned for heresy and sorcery by the English a year later.

Shogun Yoshimochi retired in 1423 but resumed office when his son Yoshikazu died.

The Lithuanian duke, Vytautas, was succeeded by Svidrigaila, but Jagiello of Poland quickly disposed of him and thereby put an end to Lithuania as an independent state. The Polish empire, on the other hand, reached from the Oder to the upper Don and from the Baltic to the Black Sea.

The Japanese painter Josetsu formed a school, painting impressionistic landscapes reminiscent of the great Chinese artists from the Song (Sung) period.

Filippo Brunelleschi was a Florentine architect and sculptor. He made a scientific study of the laws of perspective. Some of his buildings in Florence were important to the development of architecture especially the Palazzo Pitti and the cathedral dome.

The Court Eunuch, Zheng He, or San Bao, was interested in geography and as grand admiral made seven long voyages of discovery with the Chinese fleet. He visited Borneo, Malacca, Sumatra, Calcutta, Ceylon, Ormuz on the Persian Gulf, Zanzibar, and the island of Timor not far from the Australian coast. After his death, however, the Confucian bureaucrats at Beijing (Peking) managed to stop any further expeditions, thereby leaving the field free for Columbus, Vasco da Gama and Magellan.

The Aztecs of Mexico, revolted against the Tepanecs in 1428. The insurrection was successful, the power of the Tepanecs was destroyed and their capital Atzcapotzalco was laid in ruins. The Aztecs had already established their own capital, Tenochtitlán, a hundred years earlier, and between 1428 and 1440 they were ruled from here by a certain Itzcoatl.

Henrique o Navegador, Henry the Navigator, was a Portugese prince who sent explorers to the south. Madeira was reached in 1420, the Azores in 1431. The Canary Islands already belonged to Castile.

	Rulers
Naples	Joan II
Burgundy	Philip II the Good
Austria	Murad II
Ottomans	Albert V + Ernest – Albert V + Frederick V
Persia	Shah Rokh
Lithuania	Vytautas
Serbia	Stephen Lazarevic – Djuradj Brankovic
Portugal	John I, Master of Aviz
Aragon	Alfonso V
Scotland	Robert III Stuart – James I Stuart
Sweden	Erik of Pomerania
Poland	Wladyslaw II Jagiello
Hungary	Sigismund I
Bohemia	Sigismund of Luxemburg
Norway	Erik of Pomerania
Russia	Vasily I Dmitriyevich – Vasily II Vasilyevich
England	Henry V – Henry VI
Denmark	Erik of Pomerania
Castile	John II
Germany	Sigismund
France	Charles VI – Charles VII
Holy Rom. Emp.	Sigismund of Luxemburg
Papacy	Martin V
Eastern Rome	Manuel II Palaeologus – John VIII Palaeologus
Japan	Yoshimochi – Yoshikazu – Yoshimochi – Yoshinori
China	Ming Yong Le – Hong Xi – Ming Xuan De

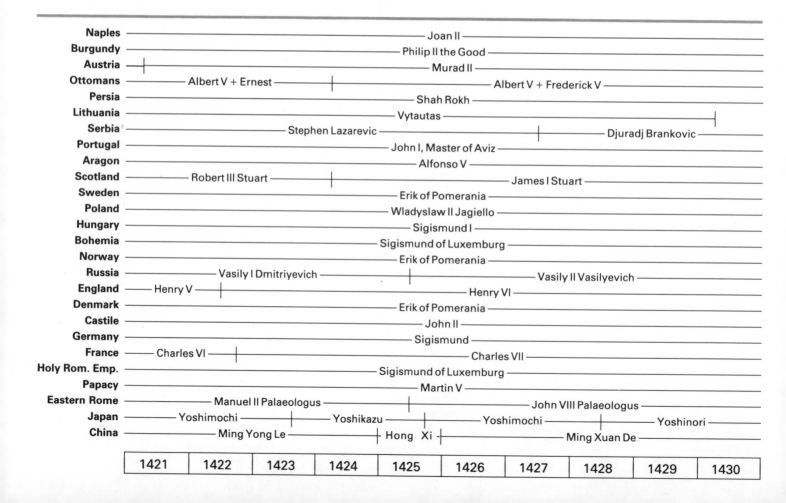

1421	1422	1423	1424	1425	1426	1427	1428	1429	1430

SWEDEN

The House of Luxemburg died out in Hungary and Bohemia in 1437, and the crown of these two countries passed to the Habsburg Albert of Austria, who also became German emperor. Albert died shortly afterwards, however, and the guardian of his unborn son Ladislas Posthumus, was his second cousin Frederick V who was to become Emperor Frederick III. Ladislas died young but appears as Ladislas IV.

Joan II was the last of the Anjou dynasty in Naples. The history of this family had been bloody and spectacular, especially under the two queens named Joan. Joan I had her first husband strangled and despite several remarriages failed to produce an heir. Eventually she was deposed and likewise strangled. Joan II was an equally domineering woman who drove her prince consort into exile and took on many lovers, though again without issue.

In the Netherlands two great artists, the brothers Hubert and Jan van Eyck, were at work. Hubert died in 1426 and is remembered solely for his Ghent Altar, which was completed by his younger brother in 1432. It heralded a new epoch in Western art, since, for the first time, full use was made of oil paints. Jan van Eyck also painted portraits and devotional pictures with a superb disposition of figures and spatial treatment.

In 1435 Philip the Good of Burgundy broke his alliance with the English and made a separate peace with the French crown. He was now exempted from all fealty and also gained territory. During Philip's reign Burgundy was a power of some economic, political and cultural significance.

The Nordic union began to founder in the 1430s when Engelbrekt, a rebel of considerable military prowess, quickly seized all the most important fortifications in Sweden. His success was short-lived, for he was assassinated and replaced as regent by a nobleman named Karl Knutsson Bonde. When in due course Erik of Pomerania relinquished his rule in Denmark and Norway, the union was renewed under Christopher of Bavaria.

The ruling families in some of the small states in northern Italy were important for the history of art. They included the Visconti and Sforza in Milan, della Scala in Verona, Gonzaga in Mantua and d'Este in Ferrara. Most notable of all, however, were the Medicis who controlled Florence.

Rulers	
Cosimo de'Medici	Florence
Joan II | Alfonso (V) of Aragon	Naples
Philip II the Good	Burgundy
Murad II	Ottomans
Albert V + Frederick V | Frederick V	Austria
Shah Rokh	Persia
Djuradj Brankovic	Serbia
John I | Edward | Afonso V	Portugal
Alfonso V	Aragon
James I Stuart | James II Stuart	Scotland
Erik of Pomerania ---- Engelbrekt ---- Karl Knutsson Bonde ---- |	Sweden
Wladyslaw II Jagiello | Wladyslaw III	Poland
Sigisimund I | Albert I | Ladislas V	Hungary
Sigismund of Luxemburg | Albert I | Ladislas IV	Bohemia
Erik of Pomerania	Norway
Vasily II Vasilyevich	Russia
Henry VI	England
Erik of Pomerania |	Denmark
John II	Castile
Sigismund | Albert II | Frederick III	Germany
Charles VII	France
Sigismund of Luxemburg | ---- Albert II | ---- |	Holy Rom. Emp.
| Eugenius IV	Papacy
John VIII Palaeologus	Eastern Rome
Yoshinori	Japan
Ming Xuan De | Ming Zheng Tong	China

1431	1432	1433	1434	1435	1436	1437	1438	1439	1440

AD 1441-1450

ITALY
ITALY
SWEDEN
CHRISTOPHER OF
BAVARIA

The Byzantine emperor John VIII had brought about an offical reunion between the Greek and the Roman church and in the 1440s a crusade was organized against the Turks who had occupied large areas in the northern Balkans. Wladyslaw VI, or Ladislas V, king of Poland and Hungary, took command and met the Turks at Varna. Here his army was defeated and he himself was killed. Sultan Murad II now seized Greece and shortly afterwards made himself master of Serbia as well. The vaivode (ruler) of Siebenbürgen, Janos Hunyadi, who succeeded LadislasV as king of Hungary, nevertheless managed to maintain his kingdom's independence.

The union of the Roman and Byzantine churches was of no significance other than that the Greek metropolitan in Russia was ousted by the grand duke, after which the Russians appointed their own metropolitans.

At this time universities were established. Among other places, at Basle, Freiburg and Greifswald. Eton College was founded in 1441 and in the same year a public library was opened in Florence. Florence also set up an academy for the study of Plato's works in 1459 and Greek scholars who had come to the city after the union of churches, became teachers here.

The brief reign of Ulugh Beg in Persia was interesting inasmuch as he was the patron of poets and artists, and built an observatory in Samarkand which has survived until today. Ulugh Beg was deposed and murdered by his own son, after which Persia was wracked by anarchy and civil war for several decades.

The Bohemian Hussites were victorious in their religious and national war. In 1448 Prague was taken by their leader, George of Podebrady, who a few years later became regent, and in 1458 king of Bohemia.

Ulaszlo is the Hungarian form of the Polish Wladyslaw. Only the kings of the Jagiellon dynasty, however, were known by the former name. Normally Vladislav or Ladislas became Laszlo.

Duke Philip of Burgundy also ruled over Flanders, Artois, Brabant, Luxemburg, Holland, Zeeland and Frisia – an extensive empire. He exerted considerable cultural and political influence, and his banquets at the court in Dijon were famous for their opulence.

Florence	Cosimo de' Medici
Naples	Alfonso V of Aragon
Burgundy	Philip II the Good
Ottomans	Murad II
Austria	Ladislas Posthumus + Frederick V (= Frederick III)
Persia	Shah Rokh | Ulugh Beg |
Serbia	Djuradj Brankovic
Portugal	Alfonso V of Africa
Aragon	Alfonso V
Scotland	James II Stuart
Sweden	Christopher of Bavaria | Karl Knutsson
Poland	Wladyslaw III | | Casimir IV
Hungary	Ladislas V (= Ulaszlo I) | Janos Hunyadi
Bohemia	Ladislas IV (Posthumus)
Norway	Erik of Pomerania | Christopher | Karl Knutsson |
Russia	Vasily II Vasilyevich
England	Henry VI
Denmark	Christopher of Bavaria | | Christian I
Castile	John II
Germany	Frederick III
France	Charles VII
Holy Rom. Emp.	Frederick III
Papacy	Eugenius IV | Nicholas V
Eastern Rome	John VIII Palaeologus | Constantine XI
Japan	| Yoshikatsu | Yoshimasa
China	Ming Zheng Tong |

1441	1442	1443	1444	1445	1446	1447	1448	1449	1450

ITALY
FRANCE

The Nordic union was again disrupted following the sudden death of King Christopher. Karl Knutsson Bonde now became king of Sweden and for a short time of Norway as well, while the Danes elected the German Duke Christian who was heir to Holstein. Soon afterwards Christian was also recognized as king of Norway as well.

As Duke of Austria, Emperor Frederick III was Frederick V.

The most glorious years of the Ming dynasty were now over, although porcelain art continued to flourish.

King Afonso V is known as the African because during his time a great part of Morocco had recently been explored under the leadership of his grandfather's brother Henry the Navigator, who lived until 1460. In 1452 the pope recognized the right of the Spaniards and Portuguese to enslave the peoples of newly discovered heathen lands.

The first large bronze sculpture to be cast in Europe since antiquity was Donatello's equestrian statue of the condottierre Gattamelata, erected in Padua in 1453.

In China, Zheng Tong and Tian Shun were the same person or, to be more precise, the titles of two periods of the same emperor's reign. This emperor was imprisoned by the Mongols and his brother proclaimed emperor in his place. The Mongols then released their prisoner in the hope that this would lead to civil war in China, but since the brother became seriously ill at that time, the ex-emperor was reinstated without opposition.

The Aztecs in Mexico expanded their empire at the expense of the allied tribes. Their king at this time, 1440-69, was Ilhuacamina.

On May 29th, 1453 Constantinople fell into the hands of the Turks. This marked the end of the thousand-year-old Eastern Roman empire. After the victory the soldiers ran amok, but eventually the conquerors showed good sense and moderation. Full religious freedom was proclaimed and the patriarch was granted an official position as head of the entire Osman empire. Constantinople remained largely a Christian city, where the principal language was Greek until the beginning of the 20th century.

The invention of the printing press by Johannes Gutenberg is traditionally dated at 1453.

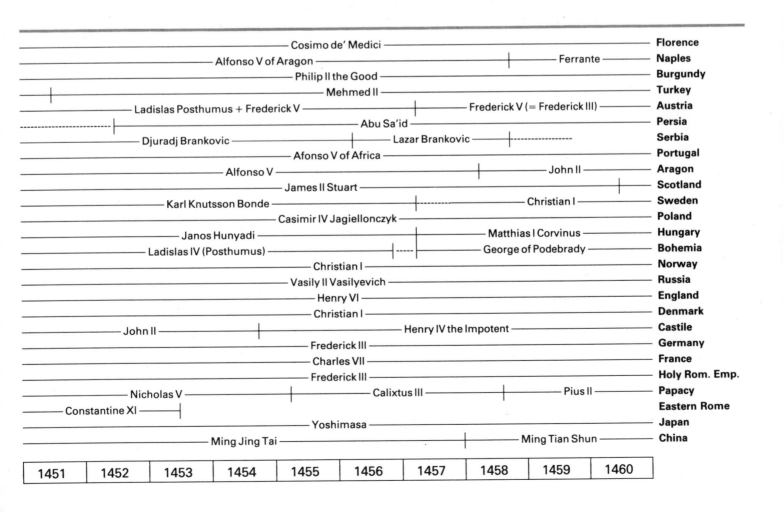

Rulers (1451–1460)	Country
Cosimo de' Medici	Florence
Alfonso V of Aragon – Ferrante	Naples
Philip II the Good	Burgundy
Mehmed II	Turkey
Ladislas Posthumus + Frederick V – Frederick V (= Frederick III)	Austria
Abu Sa'id	Persia
Djuradj Brankovic – Lazar Brankovic	Serbia
Afonso V of Africa	Portugal
Alfonso V – John II	Aragon
James II Stuart	Scotland
Karl Knutsson Bonde – Christian I	Sweden
Casimir IV Jagiellonczyk	Poland
Janos Hunyadi – Matthias I Corvinus	Hungary
Ladislas IV (Posthumus) – George of Podebrady	Bohemia
Christian I	Norway
Vasily II Vasilyevich	Russia
Henry VI	England
Christian I	Denmark
John II – Henry IV the Impotent	Castile
Frederick III	Germany
Charles VII	France
Frederick III	Holy Rom. Emp.
Nicholas V – Calixtus III – Pius II	Papacy
Constantine XI	Eastern Rome
Yoshimasa	Japan
Ming Jing Tai – Ming Tian Shun	China

1451	1452	1453	1454	1455	1456	1457	1458	1459	1460

AD 1461-1470

AZTEC,
MEXICO
BENIN,
AFRICA
NETHERLANDS
ITALY

The Castilians took Gibraltar from the Arabs in 1462 and in 1471 the Portuguese occupied Tangier.

The art of printing was progressing. Gutenberg, who had been compelled to give up his printing shop, died in 1468, poverty-stricken and unheeded. but in Venice and elsewhere new printing works were being set up. Around 1470 the Dutchman Nicolaus Janson reproduced a famous Roman print. This was significant for book publishers: the vast body of ancient literature, Latin and Greek, was now available to them. Printing led not only to a wider distribution of these works but also to a fairly correct presentation, since manuscript variants were critically studied and prepared before going to press. New publications included François Villon's *Le Petit Testament* and *Le Grand Testament.*

Between 1469 and 1483 the Aztecs in Mexico were ruled by King Axayacatl, though the leading politician in the kingdom was named Tlacaelel. He infused a religious element into Aztec power policy and changed the god of war Huitzilopochtli into a sun god requiring human sacrifices, the victims coming from subordinate tribes.

In England the Wars of the Roses between the houses of York and Lancaster continued to take a heavy toll of lives. Temporary victors were the York faction, to which Edward IV belonged. Parallel with this, intermittently, the Hundred Years' War continued between England and France, with Louis XI also engaged against the new duke of Burgundy, Charles the Bold. The latter, who also controlled the Netherlands, sought to expand his realm towards the Alps but then became involved in war with the Swiss cantons and with a duke of Lorraine who was, of course, supported by Louis XI.

The Duchy of Burgundy was a major power in the reigns of Philip the Good and Charles the Bold. All the arts flourished in their court at Dijon, including that of cuisine.

Ivan III Vasilyevich, first czar of Russia.

Florence	Cosimo de' Medici | Piero de' Medici |
Naples	Ferrante
Burgundy	Philip II the Good | Charles the Bold
Turkey	Mehmed II
Austria	Frederick V (=Frederick III)
Persia	Abu Sa'id ------- | Uzun Hasan
Portugal	Afonso V of Africa
Aragon	John II
Scotland	James III Stuart
Sweden	Christian I | Karl Knutsson | ------- | Karl Knutsson |
Poland	Casimir IV Jagiellonczyk
Hungary	Matthias I Corvinus
Bohemia	George of Podebrady
Norway	Christian I
Russia	Vasily II | Ivan III Vasilyevich (the Great)
England	| Edward IV
Denmark	Christian I
Castile	Henry IV the Impotent
Germany	Frederick III
France	| Louis XI
Holy Rom. Emp.	Frederick III
Papacy	Pius II | Paul II
Japan	Yoshimasa
China	Ming Tian Shun | Ming Cheng Hua

1461	1462	1463	1464	1465	1466	1467	1468	1469	1470

BURGUNDY
FRANCE
GERMANY
ITALY
SPAIN

In Sweden the battle of Brunkeberg took place outside Stockholm in October 1471. Here the king of the Nordic union, Christian, was defeated by Sten Sture, the elder, who then became ruler of Sweden. In the same year the city and realm of Novgorod were overrun by the Muscovite grand duke Ivan Vasilyevich. The latter subsequently liberated his own country from its dependence upon the Golden Horde, married a Byzantine princess and made claim to be the successor of the Eastern Roman emperors. Russia now emerged as a major power and at the same time established contact with both Swedes and Baltic peoples.

In 1477 Charles the Bold died in battle. His only child was a daughter named Maria and Louis XI was not slow in restoring the leaderless duchy of Burgundy to the French crown. The Netherlands, however, went to Maria. This made her a very eligible candidate for marriage and she soon became the wife of the Habsburg Maximilian, son of the Emperor Frederick, and in due course his successor. This was a union of great consequence, destined to influence European political history for centuries to come.

In the 1460s Timur's dynasty in Persia was annihilated and succeeded by a Turkoman dynasty known as the White Sheep.

Ferrante of Naples, illegitimate son of Alfonso V of Aragon, was a Renaissance figure who had gained power with the assistance of Cosimo de' Medici in Florence and Francesco Sforza in Milan.

Pope Sixtus IV, hardly notable for his ecclesiastical achievements, was a patron of culture who established the Vatican library and provided work for numerous artists: Verrocchio, Botticelli, Ghirlandajo, Perugino, Signorelli and others. He is renowned for having sponsored the building of the Sistine Chapel and for initiating the Feast of the Immaculate Conception. He also appointed the Spanish Dominican monk Tomas de Torquemada to the office of grand inquisitor.

The two Spanish states were united in 1479 when Ferdinand II succeeded his father as king of Aragon. Prior to this he had reigned jointly since 1474 with his wife Isabella in her hereditary kingdom of Castile.

The Turks who had taken most of Albania from the Venetians and who now ruled most of the Balkans, turned their attention to Italy and occupied Otranto in 1480.

The Orkney and Shetland Islands, which had hitherto belonged to Norway, were handed over in 1472 to King James III of Scotland as dowry on his marriage to Christian I's daughter.

Uppsala University was founded in 1477. It is the oldest university in Scandinavia. The University of Copenhagen was founded two years later.

Maximilian I	**Netherlands**
Lorenzo & Giuliano de' Medici – Lorenzo de' Medici	**Florence**
Ferrante	**Naples**
Charles the Bold	**Burgundy**
Mehmed II	**Turkey**
Frederick V (= Frederick III)	**Austria**
Uzun Hasan – Ya'qub	**Persia**
Afonso V the African	**Portugal**
John II – Ferdinand & Isabella	**Aragon**
James III Stuart	**Scotland**
Sten Sture the Elder	**Sweden**
Casimir IV Jagiellonczyk	**Poland**
Matthias I Corvinus	**Hungary**
Vladislav V	**Bohemia**
Christian I	**Norway**
Ivan III Vasilyevich	**Russia**
Edward IV	**England**
Christian I	**Denmark**
Henry IV the Impotent – Isabella & Ferdinand, Catholic Kings	**Castile**
Frederick III	**Germany**
Louis XI	**France**
Frederick III	**Holy Rom. Emp.**
Sixtus IV	**Papacy**
Yoshimasa – Yoshihisa	**Japan**
Ming Cheng Hua	**China**

1471	1472	1473	1474	1475	1476	1477	1478	1479	1480

AD 1481-1490

ENGLAND
GERMANY

The dynastic confusion was resolved in England when in 1485 Henry Tudor, a Lancastrian on his mother's side, defeated Richard III, last of the Yorkists. This terminated the Wars of the Roses. Not long afterwards the Hundred Years' War between England and France also ended, the formal peace treaty being signed in 1492.

The history of the Scottish kings during the 15th century had been no less dramatic than that of their English counterparts. None of the first four James Stuarts died a natural death.

There was a union between Hungary and Bohemia: thus Ulaszlo II and Vladislav V were the same person.

In Scandinavia the Kalmar Union continued. King Hans, who ruled over Norway and Denmark, was also recognized in Sweden.

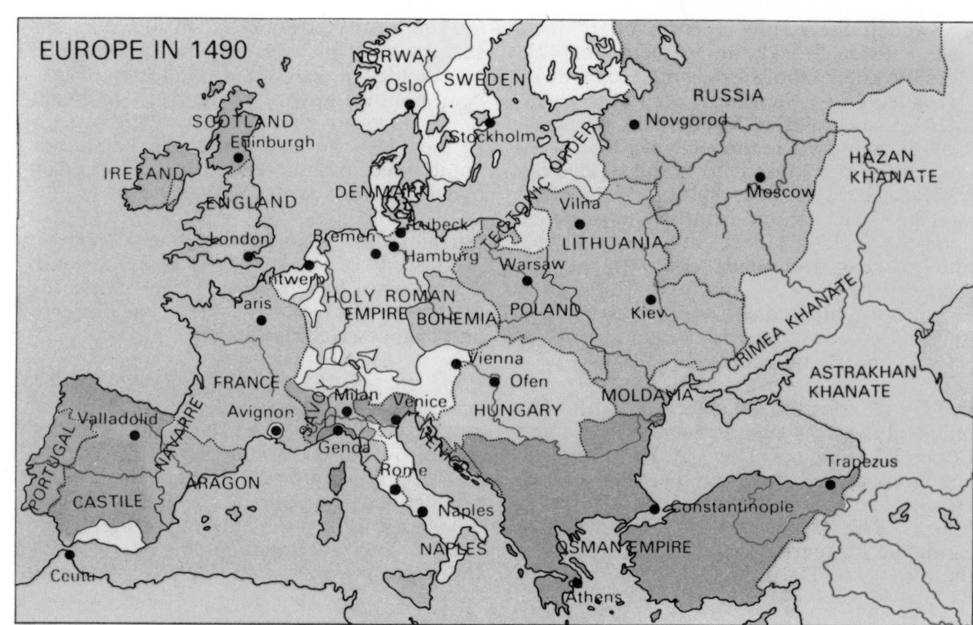

EUROPE IN 1490
NORWAY
Oslo
SWEDEN
Stockholm
RUSSIA
Novgorod
TEUTONIC ORDER
SCOTLAND
Edinburgh
IRELAND
ENGLAND
London
DENMARK
Lubeck
Bremen
Hamburg
Moscow
KAZAN KHANATE
Vilna
LITHUANIA
Warsaw
POLAND
Antwerp
Paris
HOLY ROMAN EMPIRE
BOHEMIA
Kiev
CRIMEA KHANATE
Vienna
Ofen
HUNGARY
ASTRAKHAN KHANATE
FRANCE
MOLDAVIA
Valladolid
NAVARRE
Avignon
SAVOY
Milan
Venice
PORTUGAL
CASTILE
ARAGON
Genoa
Rome
Naples
NAPLES
Trapezus
Constantinople
OSMAN EMPIRE
Ceuta
Athens

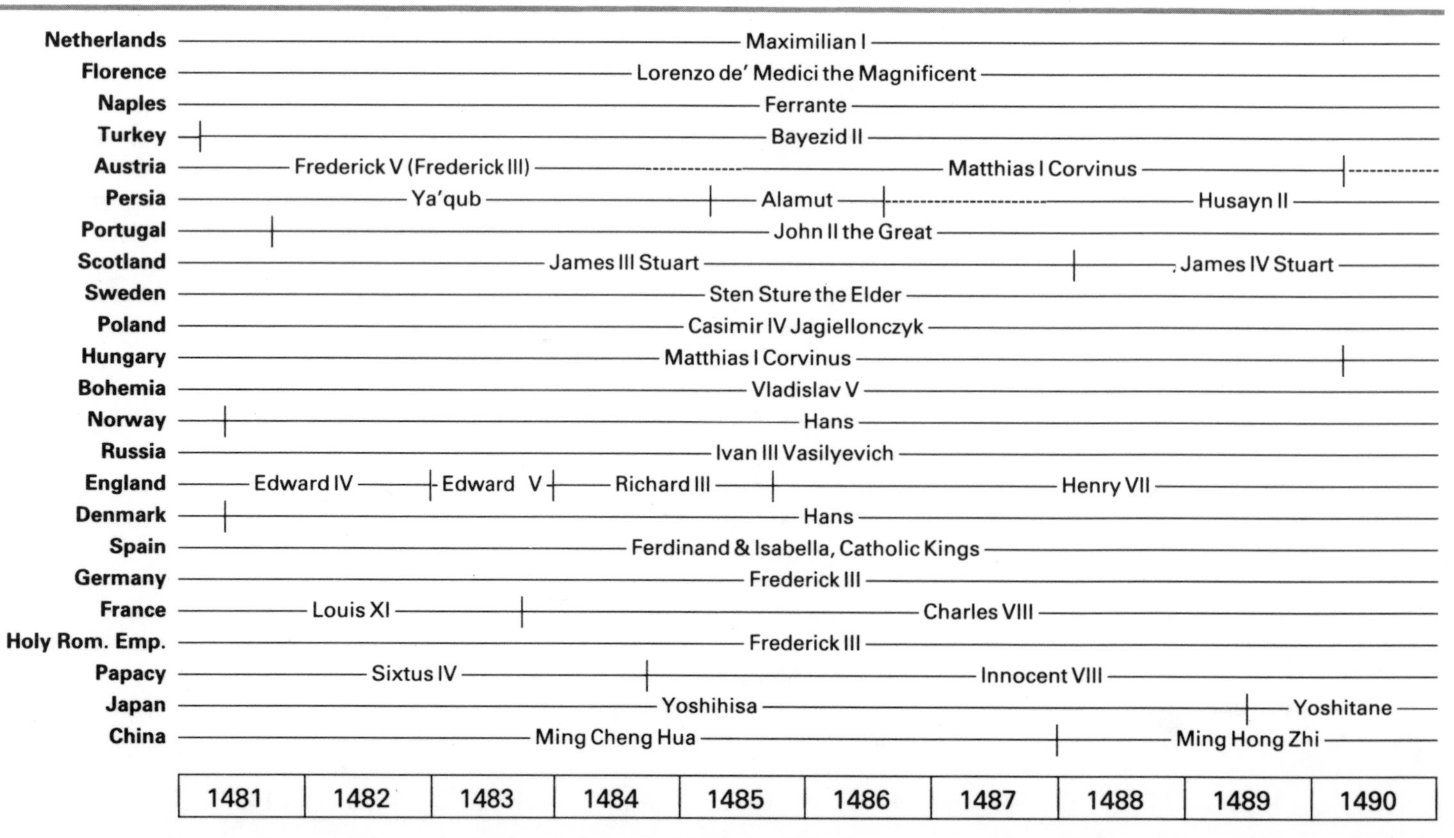

Netherlands — Maximilian I
Florence — Lorenzo de' Medici the Magnificent
Naples — Ferrante
Turkey — Bayezid II
Austria — Frederick V (Frederick III) — Matthias I Corvinus
Persia — Ya'qub — Alamut — Husayn II
Portugal — John II the Great
Scotland — James III Stuart — James IV Stuart
Sweden — Sten Sture the Elder
Poland — Casimir IV Jagiellonczyk
Hungary — Matthias I Corvinus
Bohemia — Vladislav V
Norway — Hans
Russia — Ivan III Vasilyevich
England — Edward IV — Edward V — Richard III — Henry VII
Denmark — Hans
Spain — Ferdinand & Isabella, Catholic Kings
Germany — Frederick III
France — Louis XI — Charles VIII
Holy Rom. Emp. — Frederick III
Papacy — Sixtus IV — Innocent VIII
Japan — Yoshihisa — Yoshitane
China — Ming Cheng Hua — Ming Hong Zhi
1481 1482 1483 1484 1485 1486 1487 1488 1489 1490

AD 1491-1500

SWEDEN
NETHERLANDS
FRANCE
PERSIA
AZTEC,
MEXICO

In 1492 the small emirate of Granada, the last Moorish state on Spanish territory, fell. This news was jubilantly acclaimed throughout Western Christendom. At about the same time their Catholic majesties Ferdinand and Isabella approved Christopher Columbus's request to be appointed admiral and viceroy of all those lands he hoped to discover. He was also granted the necessary revenue to fit out three ships for his voyage.

Frederick III was the last of the Holy Roman emperors to be crowned by the pope. Maximilian I assumed the title emperor-elect and sought to restore unity within the German empire; the Burgundian inheritance of the Netherlands had created new opportunities for this.

In Europe, artists such as Botticelli, Mantegna and Dürer were now at work. The Japanese artist Sesshu, influenced by Chinese southern Song (Sung) painters, was creating impressionist landscapes.
In the 1490s the French king, Charles VII, led a military expedition into Italy and this had far-reaching consequences. In Florence there was a revolution, led by the Dominican monk Savonarola, who was excommunicated by the pope and burned at the stake. In Naples Alfonso II fled the advancing French and shortly afterwards it fell under Spanish rule. Milan was later taken by Louis XII. soon there were only two independent states left in Italy: Venice and the Papal State. Naples, where Alfonso's brother had installed himself with the blessing of the pope, became a Spanish province in the next decade.

A young Persian named Esma'il Safi led an insurrection against the ruling Turkoman dynasty and made himself shah. His family, the Safavids, ruled for several centuries.

In Sweden for a while Sten Sture was forced to allow the Nordic union to operate. King Hans made his grand entry into Stockholm in the autumn of 1497.

In Europe the last decades of the 15th century constituted the great age of geographical exploration. In 1486 the Portuguese admiral Bartolomeu Dias reached the Cape of Good Hope, in 1492 America was discovered by the Genoese Christopher Columbus, who was in the service of Spain, and in 1498 Portugal's Vasco da Gama landed at Calcutta, having sailed around the southern tip of Africa. In 1493 Pope Alexander VI issued a bull on the division of the world between Spain and Portugal whereby Spain was to own all newly discovered lands west of a meridian set at 100 leagues west of the Azores and Cape Verde. In the following year, according to the Treaty of Tordesillas, this demarcation line was moved considerabale farther west, an important factor when in 1500 the Portuguese Cabral discovered the east coast of Brazil.

In 1499 the Swiss broke away from the German empire. Peace was declared in Basle with the emperor. The members of the confederation were freed from imperial taxes and laws.

Rulers	Country
Maximillian I	Netherlands
Piero de' Medici — (Savonarola)	Florence
Ferrante — Alfonso II — Ferdinand I — Frederick II of Aragon	Naples
Bayezid II	Turkey
Maximilian I	Austria
Rustam Shah	Persia
John II the Great — Manuel I the Fortunate	Portugal
James IV Stuart	Scotland
Sten Sture the Elder — Hans	Sweden
John I Albert	Poland
Ulaszlo II	Hungary
Vladislav V	Bohemia
Hans	Norway
Ivan III Vasilyevich	Russia
Henry VII	England
Hans	Denmark
Ferdinand & Isabella, Catholic Kings	Spain
Frederick III — Maximilian I	Germany
Charles VIII — Louis XII	France
Frederick III — Maximilian I	Holy Rom. Emp.
Alexander VI (de Borgia)	Papacy
Yoshitane — Yoshizume	Japan
Ming Hong Zhi	China

1491	1492	1493	1494	1495	1496	1497	1498	1499	1500

AD 1501-1510

SPAIN
AZTECS, MEXICO

His Catholic Majesty Ferdinand, king of Castile since 1474, of Aragon and Sicily since 1479 and of Granada since 1492, made himself king of Naples in 1501 and conquered Navarre in 1512. During the early years of the 16th century Spanish explorers and generals added vast areas of American territory to the empire. Ferdinand and Isabella's children were not so fortunate. Two daughters lived to become adults; the younger of these, Catherine, was married off to the future Henry VIII of England, while the older one, Joan, was mentally deficient but was nevertheless considered to be of some value in the dynastic stakes. She married Maximilian I's son, Philip of Austria, and bore him a son, Charles, in 1500. Charles acceded to his Burgundian inheritance as early as 1506 when his father died. In his teens he became ruler of Spain and Austria, and Holy Roman emperor. Furthermore, he subsequently married the Portuguese princess Isabella, heir to the world's other great colonial empire. It was said, with some truth, that the sun never set on his domains.

The Golden Horde was dissolved in 1502.

The Muscovite realm expanded southward and westward, Pskov was taken in 1510, Smolensk in 1514 and Rjazan in 1517. The Polish-Lithuanian kingdom and the realm of the Teutonic Order were in decline.

In Japan there was political unrest. Shogun Yoshitane, expelled in 1493, returned fifteen years later but was later compelled to abdicate. His four immediate successors were equally insecure in office.

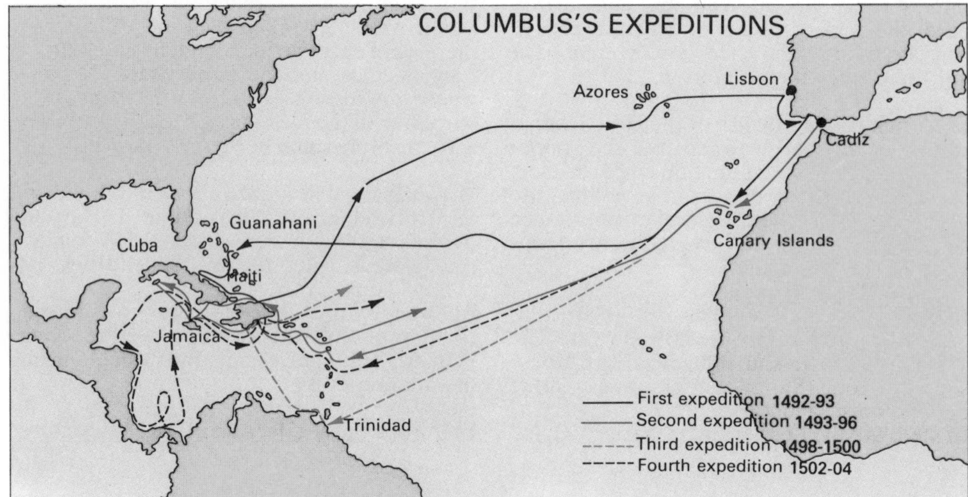
COLUMBUS'S EXPEDITIONS
Azores
Lisbon
Cadiz
Guanahani
Cuba
Haiti
Canary Islands
Jamaica
Trinidad
First expedition 1492-93
Second expedition 1493-96
Third expedition 1498-1500
Fourth expedition 1502-04

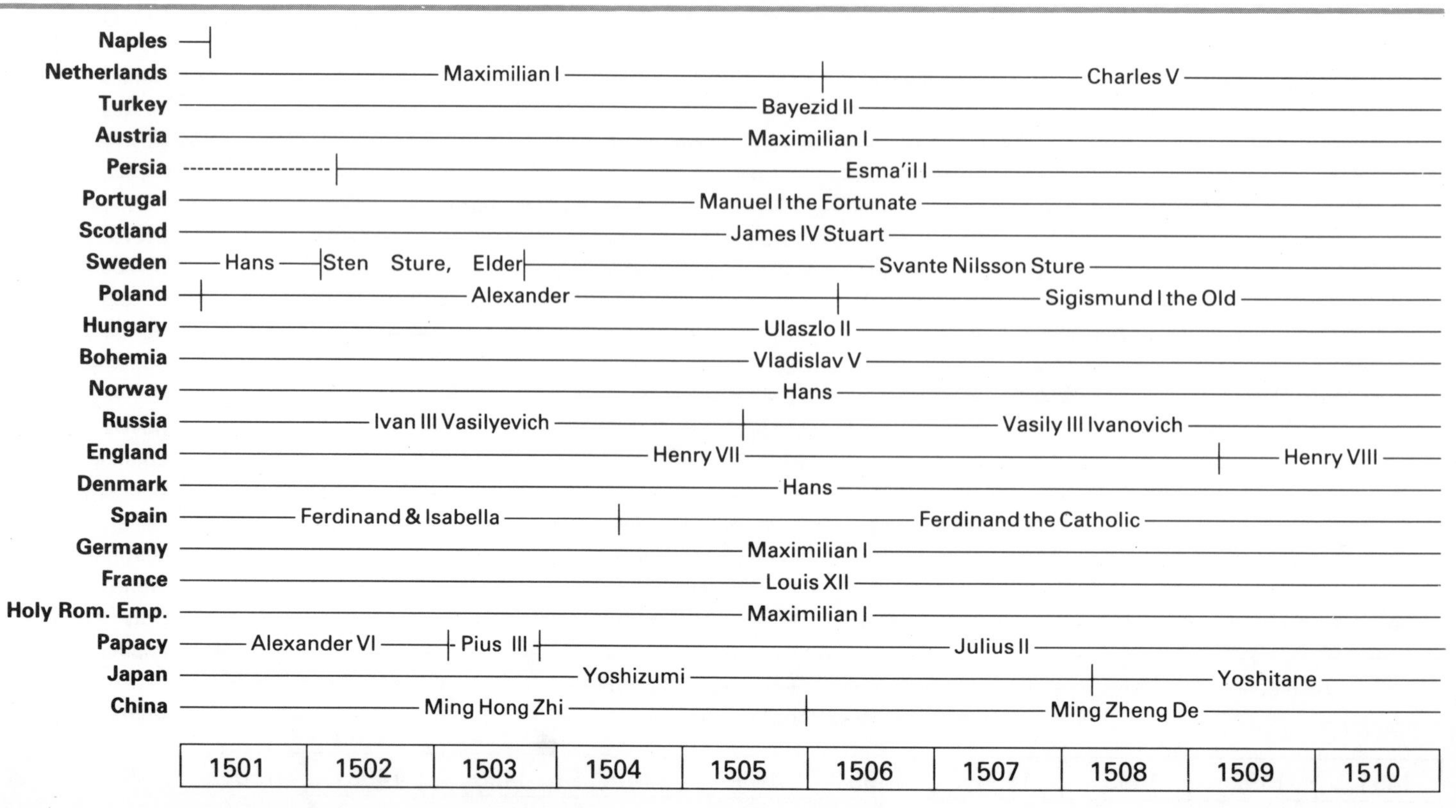
Naples
Netherlands — Maximilian I — Charles V
Turkey — Bayezid II
Austria — Maximilian I
Persia — Esma'il I
Portugal — Manuel I the Fortunate
Scotland — James IV Stuart
Sweden — Hans — Sten Sture, Elder — Svante Nilsson Sture
Poland — Alexander — Sigismund I the Old
Hungary — Ulaszlo II
Bohemia — Vladislav V
Norway — Hans
Russia — Ivan III Vasilyevich — Vasily III Ivanovich
England — Henry VII — Henry VIII
Denmark — Hans
Spain — Ferdinand & Isabella — Ferdinand the Catholic
Germany — Maximilian I
France — Louis XII
Holy Rom. Emp. — Maximilian I
Papacy — Alexander VI — Pius III — Julius II
Japan — Yoshizumi — Yoshitane
China — Ming Hong Zhi — Ming Zheng De
1501 1502 1503 1504 1505 1506 1507 1508 1509 1510

AD 1511-1520

GERMANY
AFONSO
D'ALBUQUERQUE
PORTUGAL
SWEDEN

Admiral Afonso d'Albuquerque, the principal figure in Portugal's violent colonial history, took Goa in 1510 and Malacca in 1511. A few years later Portuguese ships entered Canton in China. Their crews behaved so brutally, however, that the local inhabitants drove them out, after which China was spared visits from the West for several decades.

In the New Year 1520 the Swedish regent Sten Sture the younger was fatally wounded when he attempted to halt the advance of a large professional army in the pay of the union king, Christian II. By the autumn of this year the whole of Sweden had been conquered and in November the so-called Stockholm Bloodbath took place. Several hundreds of people, including two bishops, a number of nobles, the mayor, aldermen and ordinary citizens were executed.

Peasants' revolts flared up in several places in Central Europe. They were all stamped out.

Amerigo Vespucci reached Brazil in 1501. Balboa crossed the Panama isthmus in 1513.

In the autumn of 1519 Ferdinand Magellan sailed from Seville on what was to be the first circumnavigation of the globe. Magellan never came back, but his ship, with eighteen survivors, returned three years later.

The German Peter Henlein made the first pocket-watch.

New literature included Rechlin's *De Rudimentis Hebraicis*, Melanchthon's Greek Grammar, Erasmus's Greek edition of the New Testament, Thomas More's *Utopia* and Machiavelli's *Il Principe*.

The artists Albrecht Dürer, Leonardo da Vinci, Michelangelo, Raphael, Cranach, Matthias Grunewald, and Signorelli were all at the height of their powers.

The Spaniards took possession of Cuba and founded the city of Havana. With a force of only a few hundred men Hernán Cortés defeated the powerful Aztec kingdom in Mexico after having seized and imprisoned their king Montezuma. Setting out in 1519, the entire undertaking took two years to complete.

On 31 October 1517 Martin Luther posted his 95 theses against the sale of indulgences on the church door at Wittenberg. Portrait by Lucas Cranach, the elder.

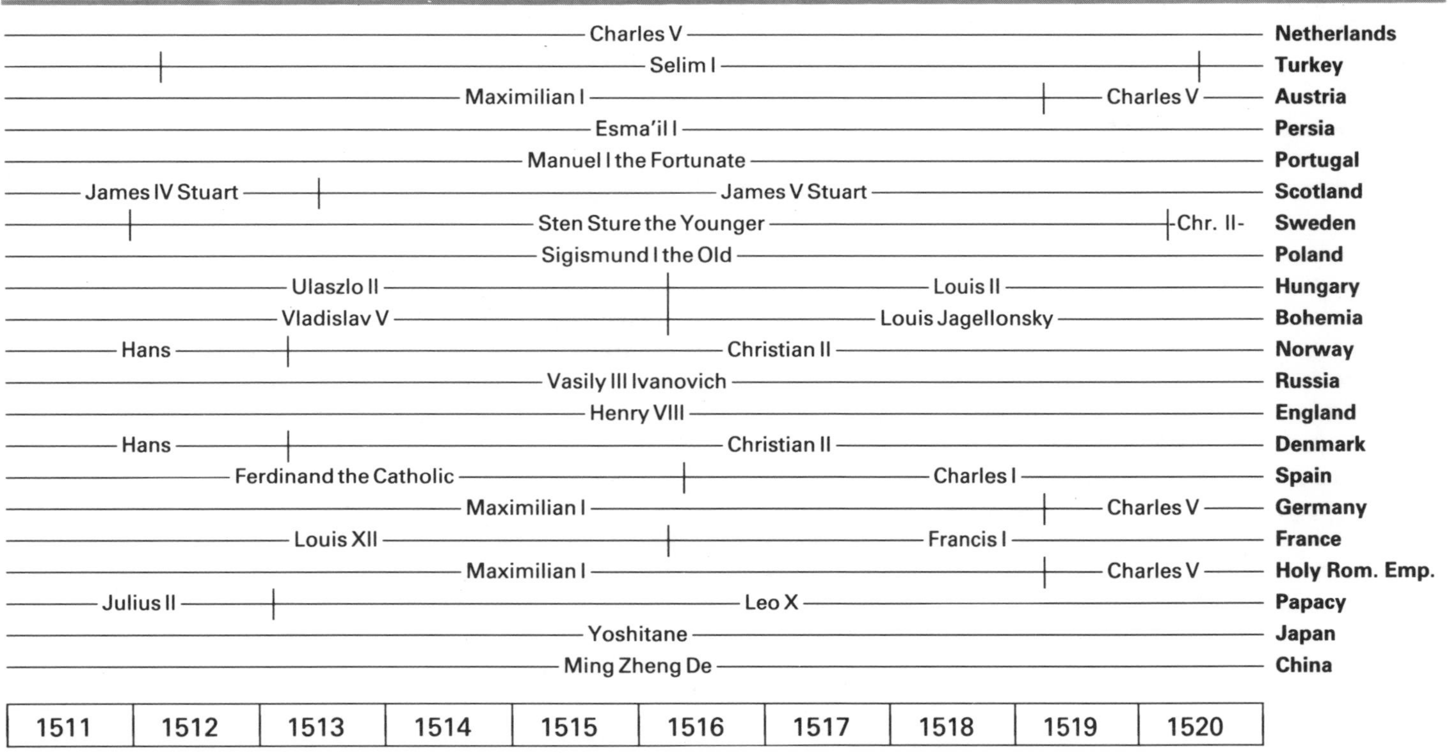
Charles V — Netherlands
Selim I — Turkey
Maximilian I — Charles V — Austria
Esma'il I — Persia
Manuel I the Fortunate — Portugal
James IV Stuart — James V Stuart — Scotland
Sten Sture the Younger — Chr. II — Sweden
Sigismund I the Old — Poland
Ulaszlo II — Louis II — Hungary
Vladislav V — Louis Jagellonsky — Bohemia
Hans — Christian II — Norway
Vasily III Ivanovich — Russia
Henry VIII — England
Hans — Christian II — Denmark
Ferdinand the Catholic — Charles I — Spain
Maximilian I — Charles V — Germany
Louis XII — Francis I — France
Maximilian I — Charles V — Holy Rom. Emp.
Julius II — Leo X — Papacy
Yoshitane — Japan
Ming Zheng De — China
1511 1512 1513 1514 1515 1516 1517 1518 1519 1520

AD 1521-1530

THE SIEGE OF BELGRADE
GERMANY

In the imperial election of 1519 Habsburg's Charles V of Spain became emperor in competition, among others, with Francis I of France. Charles V was the last great advocate of the medieval concept of a united Christian empire; but a ruler of many disparate areas in various parts of Europe he was also compelled to promote a Habsburg dynastic policy. The title of Holy Roman Emperor soon became a mere formality. Thus for our purposes there is no longer any reason to treat Germany as a political entity; it makes more sense to list the rulers of various other constituent states in addition to the emperor's own hereditary kingdom of Austria. Here Charles V delegated authority to his brother Ferdinand who shortly afterwards became king of Hungary and Bohemia as well. These countries were thereby united with Austria for several centuries to come and thus have no separate lists of rulers. The events leading up to this were associated with the Turkish offensives against the West. Sultan Suleyman drove the Knights of St John out of Rhodes, stormed Belgrade and in 1526 forced his way into Hungary where King Louis or Louis Jagiello confronted him at a place named Mohacs. Louis was slain here, his entire army was annihilated and the closest heir to the vacant throne was the Habsburg regent. The eastern part of Hungary, however, was taken over by prince Janos Zapolya who lived in Siedenbürgen.

During the reign of Charles V the Netherlands were ruled by his aunt Margaret of Habsburg, despite the fact that Charles felt more at home here than elsewhere in his empire. His native tongues were French and Flemish, and in time he learned Spanish, but never German.

In the wake of Martin Luther's Reformation, Protestant churches were established in various countries, for example, the Anglican church in England. In Germany the fervid Anabaptist sect was suppressed.

European seamen discovered the Philippines, New Guinea, the Hawaiian islands, California and many more places long since discovered and taken by other races.

At the battle of Pavia in 1525, the French king, Francis I, was defeated and taken prisoner by Charles V. This made Charles master of Italy as well.

There were major changes in the relations of the Nordic countries during the 1520s and 1530s. In 1521 the union was finally shattered by Gustav Vasa's war of liberation in Sweden and the deposing of Christian II in Denmark. By degrees the Lutheran Reformation was implemented in all three counries, so that the international church lost its hold.

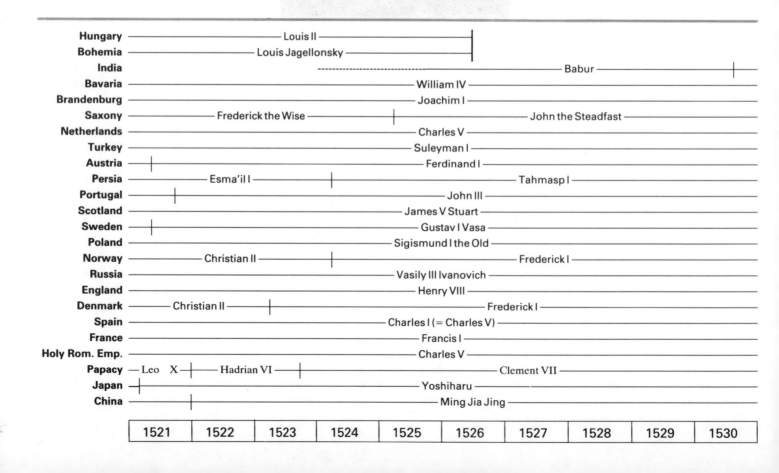

Hungary	Louis II
Bohemia	Louis Jagellonsky
India	Babur
Bavaria	William IV
Brandenburg	Joachim I
Saxony	Frederick the Wise – John the Steadfast
Netherlands	Charles V
Turkey	Suleyman I
Austria	Ferdinand I
Persia	Esma'il I – Tahmasp I
Portugal	John III
Scotland	James V Stuart
Sweden	Gustav I Vasa
Poland	Sigismund I the Old
Norway	Christian II – Frederick I
Russia	Vasily III Ivanovich
England	Henry VIII
Denmark	Christian II – Frederick I
Spain	Charles I (= Charles V)
France	Francis I
Holy Rom. Emp.	Charles V
Papacy	Leo X – Hadrian VI – Clement VII
Japan	Yoshiharu
China	Ming Jia Jing

1521	1522	1523	1524	1525	1526	1527	1528	1529	1530

AD 1531-1540

GERMANY
CHARLES V
SPAIN
INCA, PERU
TURKEY
SWEDEN

The so-called Count's Feud took place in 1533-36. As a result of this the Danish peasantry lost their freedom while Sweden's Gustav Vasa was freed from the obligation of his debts to Lübeck. Norway also lost its political independence and became a province under the Danish crown.

In Germany, with Luther's blessing, a large peasant revolt was quelled.

In India Babur, a young descendant of both Timur and Genghis Khan, established the Mogul empire. Exiled from his Turkish kingdom in Ferghana, he eventually made himself master of Kabul, the Punjab, Delhi, Agra and large areas of Hindustan and Bengal. Civil war and crisis during the reign of his son and successor, Humayun, could not prevent the consolidation of this empire.

Literary works included Luther's German translations of the Bible, psalms and catechism, Paracelsus's medical papers, Ariosto's *Orlando Furioso*, Rabelais's *Pantagruel* (1532) and *Gargantua* (1534).

Coffee, cocoa and tobacco had now reached Europe.

Shown below is the title page of Luther's German translation of the New Testament, 1522. The printer was Melchior Lotter. This work had immense linguistic and literary significance.

For a long time this protrait of Gustav Vasa could be found on Swedish ten and hundred kronor bank notes. In his later years the Swedish king shed his fringe and dressed in contemporary fashion.

Rulers 1531–1540	Country
Humayun ----------	India
William IV	Bavaria
Joachim I | Joachim II	Brandenburg
| John Frederick the Magnanimous	Saxony
Charles V	Netherlands
Suleyman I	Turkey
Ferdinand I	Austria
Tahmasp I	Persia
John III	Portugal
James V Stuart	Scotland
Gustav I Vasa	Sweden
Sigismund I the Old	Poland
Frederick I | ---------- | Christian III	Norway
Vasily III | Ivan IV the Terrible	Russia
Henry VIII	England
Frederick I | ---------- | Christian III	Denmark
Charles I (= Charles V)	Spain
Francis I	France
Charles V	Holy Rom. Emp.
Clement VII | Paul III	Papacy
Yoshiharu	Japan
Ming Jia Jing	China

1531	1532	1533	1534	1535	1536	1537	1538	1539	1540

AD 1541-1550

GERMANY
SWEDEN
GERMANY
NETHERLANDS

Nicolaus Copernicus died in 1543, having lived just long enough to see the publication of his book on the movements of the celestial bodies. This was one of the most significant works ever published, even though the Catholic church quickly banned the book and Protestant theologians also rejected it. In the same year, 1543, the Belgian physician Andreas Vesalius presented his great work *De humani corporis fabrica*, the first complete text book on the human anatomy.

The Tridentine Council was held in Trent in 1545-47, when the Catholic Counter-Reformation took shape. The Jesuit Order, founded by the Spaniard Ignatius Loyola and recently sanctioned by the pope, influenced the decisions made at this assembly.

In 1541 John Calvin entered Geneva and began to set up a theocratic republic. His rigid ecclesiastical doctrine spread swiftly across Europe.

There are actually twin lists of rulers for Saxony, because the country was split along two branches of the same dynasty. Elector John Frederic backed the losing side in the Schmalkaldic religious conflict and in 1547 had to surrender his electoral dignity to Maurice, representing the other branch of the dynasty. Maurice was the regent of the only Saxon state of any future consequence.

In 1557 the Portuguese, who had begun visiting China and Japan in the 1540s, established themselves at Macao, near Guangzhou (Canton). Formerly they had been permitted to trade in Ningbo on China's east coast, but had been expelled for their harsh treatment of the local population.

The Turks continued to advance westward into central Europe. By 1541 they had taken a large part of Hungary, including the future Budapest.

A Swedish translation of the Bible was completed in 1542. It is possible that Olaus Petri and his brother Laurentius were responsible for this achievement.

Potatoes reached Europe around 1550 and at about the same time a French diplomat named Nicot sent home tobacco from his own plantations in Lisbon.

The craft of knitting stockings had just been invented and immediately influenced clothing fashions.

Henry VIII of England by Hans Holbein the younger, Galleria Nazionale, Rome.

India	Sher Shah — Islam Shah
Bavaria	William IV
Brandenburg	Joachim II
Saxony	John Frederick the Magnanimous
Netherlands	Charles V
Turkey	Suleyman I
Austria	Ferdinand I
Persia	Tahmasp I
Portugal	John III
Scotland	James V Stuart — Mary Stuart
Sweden	Gustav I Vasa
Poland	Sigismund I the Old — Sigismund II Augustus
Russia	Ivan IV the Terrible
England	Henry VIII — Edward VI
Denmark-Norway	Christian III
Spain	Charles I (V)
France	Francis I — Henry II
Holy Rom. Emp.	Charles V
Papacy	Paul III — -----
Japan	Yoshiharu — Yoshiteru
China	Ming Jia Jing

1541	1542	1543	1544	1545	1546	1547	1548	1549	1550

AD 1551-1560

SPAIN
PERSIA
PERSIA
SWEDEN
RUSSIA

Russia continued to expand. They overran the Tartar khanates of Kazan and Astrakhan in 1552 and 1556 respectively, thus making all the territories around the Volga Russian. Even earlier than this, the Siberian khan, Yediger, had submitted to the czar and agreed to pay a tribute of 1000 sable skins; but Yediger was soon afterwards deposed and the tribute was not paid for several decades.

In 1551 the Turks occupied Tripoli in Africa and incorporated this in the Ottoman empire.

In Europe the religious strife worsened. Emperor Charles V was successful in his campaigns against the Protestant princes but was far less so in respect to his own ecclesiastical policy. The Lutherans became accepted after the Peace of Augsburg in 1555.

The Reformation in England mainly revolved around the divorces and marriages of Henry VIII. One of the king's daughters, Mary, was a Catholic while the other, Elizabeth, became a Protestant.

England's last continental possession, Calais, was lost to the French in 1557.

Michelangelo built St Peter's Church in Rome. In France, Ronsard wrote sonnets. The Flemish artist Pieter Bruegel, the elder, painted unconventional pictures.

Emperor Charles V, weary of imperial responsibilities, surrendered one crown after another. His son Philip was given the Netherlands and Spain, while his brother Ferdinand assumed the office of emperor. Charles himself settled in Spanish Estremadura.

Chile became a Spanish possession.

Pope Marcellus II held office for three weeks in April 1555. His name was to be commomorated in the famous *Missa Papae Marcelli* by Palestrina.

One of the first Westerners to enter Japan was the Jesuit missionary Francis Xavier who in the 1540s had made hundreds of thousands of converts, including provincial princes with their families and courts. Xavier died in 1557 on a small island off Macao, though he had never succeeded in penetrating China itself.

Charles V, last representative of the concept of the universal empire. Portrait by Titian, Prado, Madrid.

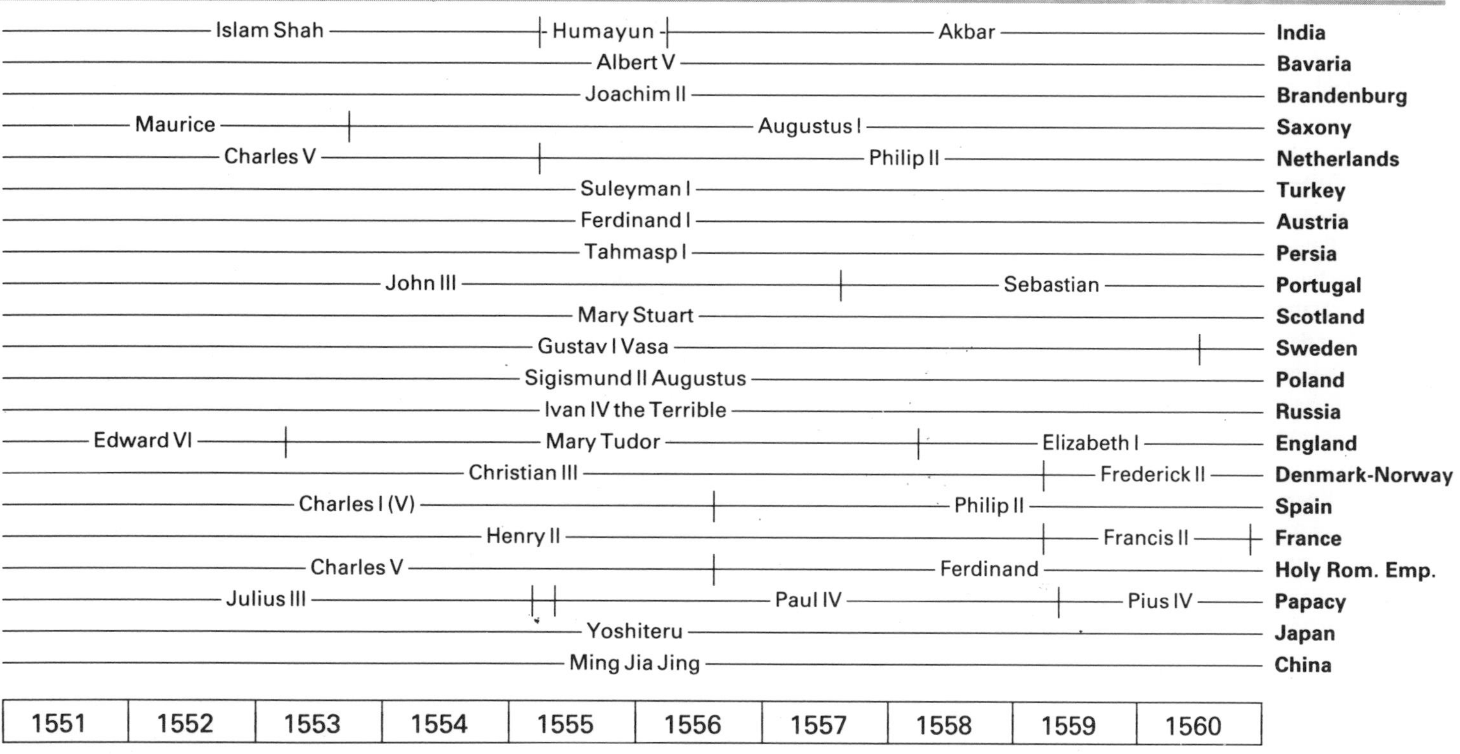

Islam Shah — Humayun — Akbar — India
Albert V — Bavaria
Joachim II — Brandenburg
Maurice — Augustus I — Saxony
Charles V — Philip II — Netherlands
Suleyman I — Turkey
Ferdinand I — Austria
Tahmasp I — Persia
John III — Sebastian — Portugal
Mary Stuart — Scotland
Gustav I Vasa — Sweden
Sigismund II Augustus — Poland
Ivan IV the Terrible — Russia
Edward VI — Mary Tudor — Elizabeth I — England
Christian III — Frederick II — Denmark-Norway
Charles I (V) — Philip II — Spain
Henry II — Francis II — France
Charles V — Ferdinand — Holy Rom. Emp.
Julius III — Paul IV — Pius IV — Papacy
Yoshiteru — Japan
Ming Jia Jing — China
1551 1552 1553 1554 1555 1556 1557 1558 1559 1560

BATTLE OF LEPANTO
NETHERLANDS

In 1561 the nineteen-year-old Mary Stuart, widow of the recently deceased Francis II, returned from France to her hereditary kingdom of Scotland. In Scotland, where her French mother had headed the regency, the puritanical John Knox had recently brought about a Protestant a revolution, declaring Catholicism illegal and making his own church a state within the state. Mary herself was a Catholic. In 1565 she married a catholic nobleman named Darnley, had him murdered in 1567 so that she might marry another named Bothwell, and found herself confronted with a rebellion. After abdicating, in favour of her small son, she fled to England where she was imprisoned and in due course condemned to death for political intrigue.

The city of Reval fell under Swedish rule in 1561, thereby giving Sweden a foothold in Estonia where the Teutonic Order was no longer capable of asserting itself. At the same time the order ceded Livonia to Poland, its last grand-master being the Duke of Courland. Shortly afterwards Sweden, Poland and Denmark became involved in war.

In 1569 the Flemish geographer Mercator completed his world map, using the projection which bears his name.

Left: Philip II of Spain. Detail of a painting by the Flemish artist Hans Eworth. Right: Elizabeth I of England. Both portraits belong to the Bedford Collection, Woburn Abbey, England.

The South American cities of Caracas and Rio de Janeiro were founded in 1567.

The early years of Elizabeth I's reign saw considerable activity at sea, but England's real age of power was still to come.

India	Akbar
Bavaria	Albert V
Brandenburg	Joachim II
Saxony	Augustus I
Netherlands	Philip II
Turkey	Suleyman I — Selim II
Austria	Ferdinand I — Maximilian II
Persia	Tahmasp I
Portugal	Sebastian
Scotland	Mary Stuart — James VI Stuart
Sweden	Erik XIV — John III
Poland	Sigismund II Augustus
Russia	Ivan IV the Terrible
England	Elizabeth I
Denmark-Norway	Frederick II
Spain	Philip II
France	Charles IX
Holy Rom. Emp.	Ferdinand I — Maximilian II
Papacy	Pius IV — Pius V
Japan	Yoshiteru — Yoshihide — Yoshiaki
China	Ming Jia Jing — Ming Long Qing

1561	1562	1563	1564	1565	1566	1567	1568	1569	1570

AD 1571-1580

INDIA
SWEDEN
SPAIN
INDIA

The Turks took Cyprus from Venice in 1571, but in the autumn of the same year the entire Turkish fleet was destroyed at Lepanto by a Western Armada under the command of John of Austria.

Revolt against Spanish rule in the Netherlands erupted when William of Orange became Stadholder in 1572. In the same year Spain occupied the Philippines, naming the island group after Philip II.

In 1580 Philip became king of Portugal as well and two vast colonial empires were united under one crown. Philip II had been married to Queen Mary of England and after her death he proposed to her successor Elizabeth. It is interesting to speculate what the world might have looked like if this union had come about.

The male line of the Jagiello dynasty died out in Poland. After a prolonged political struggle Henry of Valois was elected king of France and when he died Henryk Walezy returned home and became Henry III.

War had raged between Sweden and Denmark for seven years in the 1560s. Ivan IV Grozny was to go down in history as Ivan the Terrible.

Akbar was the most renowned ruler of the Mogul dynasty in India. He seized Kandahar and other places, initiated remarkable administrative reforms and cherished ambitions to bring about the unification of Islam, Christendom and other Persian and Indian faiths.

The Japanese shogun Yoshiaki was deposed by a provincial soldier named Nobunaga, who had already settled persistent internal conflicts between various noble families. But his relations with Yoshiaki had never been good. According to the chronicles, when the shogun presented a thirteen-act No drama in in Nobunaga's honour the latter lost patience after only five acts. No new shogun was appointed in place of Yoshiaki.

On 24 August, St Bartholomew's Day, 1572, there was a bloodbath in France when several thousand Huguenots were slain and even more were exiled.

Literary works included Camoes' *Os Lusiadas* and Tasso's *Gerusalemme Liberta*.

Erik XIV of Sweden, by an unknown artist. National Museum, Stockholm. Erik was well-educated and artistically gifted. During his later years, however, he evidently suffered from schizophrenia.

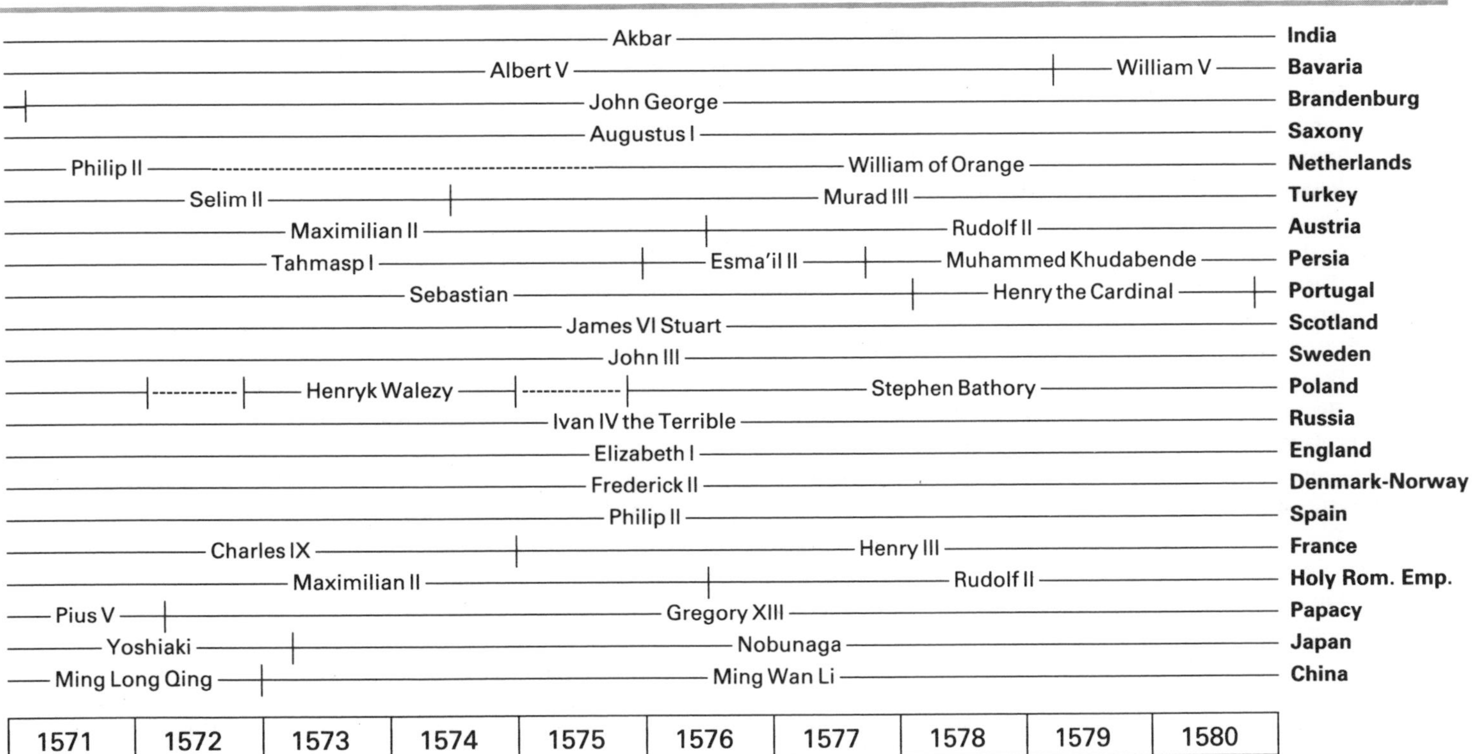
Akbar — India
Albert V — William V — Bavaria
John George — Brandenburg
Augustus I — Saxony
Philip II — William of Orange — Netherlands
Selim II — Murad III — Turkey
Maximilian II — Rudolf II — Austria
Tahmasp I — Esma'il II — Muhammed Khudabende — Persia
Sebastian — Henry the Cardinal — Portugal
James VI Stuart — Scotland
John III — Sweden
Henryk Walezy — Stephen Bathory — Poland
Ivan IV the Terrible — Russia
Elizabeth I — England
Frederick II — Denmark-Norway
Philip II — Spain
Charles IX — Henry III — France
Maximilian II — Rudolf II — Holy Rom. Emp.
Pius V — Gregory XIII — Papacy
Yoshiaki — Nobunaga — Japan
Ming Long Qing — Ming Wan Li — China
1571
1572
1573
1574
1575
1576
1577
1578
1579
1580

AD 1581-1590

ENGLAND
ELIZABETH I
PERSIA
HOLLAND
SPANISH ARMADA
SPAIN

The Gregorian calendar was introduced in the Roman Catholic world in 1582. The date of the spring equinox was fixed at 21 March by removing the intercalary days in three century years out of four. The calendar was regulated by omitting the accumulated deficit of ten days and making the day after 4 October become 15 October. The Protestant and Greek Orthodox countries, however, retained the original system.

The first English colonies were established in America in 1583 and 1584.

The Cossack Yermak and a few thousand of his men had been hired by the Stroganov merchant family for protection against the Tartars on the other side of the Urals. In 1581 Yermak seized the Tartar khan's capital Sibir and this was placed under Russian sovereignty. With the support of the czar the Cossacks then continued eastward. The first deportation of Russians to Siberia took place as early as 1582.

Songhai was an African state which had long flourished around the upper reaches of the Niger. This country now succumbed to its Moroccan neighbours, who seized the capital Timbuktu in 1591.

Under the rule of Abbas I, Persia again became a major power. He defeated the Uzbeks and the Turks and governed well.

Narva, which was Russia's only port on the Baltic, was taken by the Swedes in 1583 and formally ceded to Sweden in 1595 at the peace of Teusina.

The southern part of the modern Netherlands remained loyal to Spain while the northern provinces united as one state, known from now on by the inhabitants as Nederland. Abroad it was usually referred to as Holland.

The offices of popes Urban VII, Gregory XIV and Innocent IX were all so short – 1590-91 – that they are not shown.

Czar Fyodor Ivanovich, the last of Rurik's dynasty, was both mentally and physically deficient. Russia was therefore effectively ruled by his brother-in-law Boris Godunov, and after his death Boris continued to reign, albeit insecurely, under another name. Fyodor's younger brother, Dmitry, died at the age of ten in 1591.

In 1595 the third and last part of Gerhard Mercator's atlas of maps appeared, a year after his death. His work marked a new era, through his use of cylindrical projection.

The Spanish Armada, despatched by Philip II to crush England, was destroyed in 1588. Painting by P. de Loutherberg. National Maritime Museum, Greenwich, England.

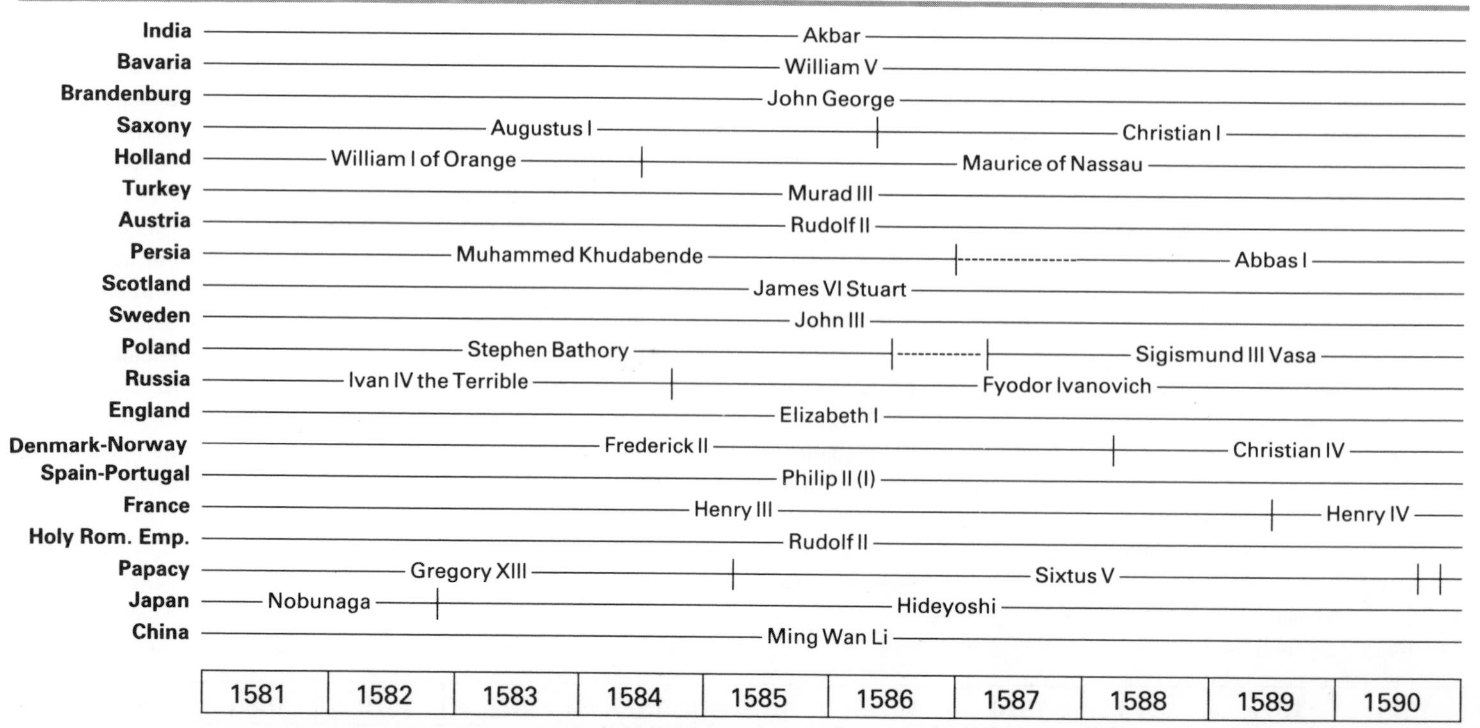
India — Akbar
Bavaria — William V
Brandenburg — John George
Saxony — Augustus I — Christian I
Holland — William I of Orange — Maurice of Nassau
Turkey — Murad III
Austria — Rudolf II
Persia — Muhammed Khudabende — Abbas I
Scotland — James VI Stuart
Sweden — John III
Poland — Stephen Bathory — Sigismund III Vasa
Russia — Ivan IV the Terrible — Fyodor Ivanovich
England — Elizabeth I
Denmark-Norway — Frederick II — Christian IV
Spain-Portugal — Philip II (I)
France — Henry III — Henry IV
Holy Rom. Emp. — Rudolf II
Papacy — Gregory XIII — Sixtus V
Japan — Nobunaga — Hideyoshi
China — Ming Wan Li
1581
1582
1583
1584
1585
1586
1587
1588
1589
1590

SPAIN
SWEDEN
JOHN III
JAPAN
INDIA

In 1593 Henry IV, leader of the French Huguenots, adopted Catholicism which was the principal religion of the people in France. 'Paris is surely worth a Mass' – the capital was still occupied by troops of the Catholic League when this statement was allegedly made.

Sigismund of Sweden and Poland's Sigismund III Vasa were one and the same person.

The Japanese dictator Hideyoshi led an invasion of Korea in 1592, and this resulted in a six-year war with China. Ultimately the Japanese were forced to retreat after a Korean admiral named Yi Sun-shin sank one of their fleets after another.

In 1596 the Dutch occupied Sumatra and part of Java, while in 1597 the Portuguese took Ceylon.

Giordano Bruno proclaimed that everything had a soul and that the number of worlds was infinite. He was burned as an heretic in Rome in 1600.

A lasting chronological system had been created in the 1580s by the Frenchman Joseph Scaliger. He numbered the days in unbroken succession from 1 January 4713 BC. This date was the zero point in the 28-year solar cycle, the 19-year lunar cycle and the 15-year indiction cycle; three periods of the utmost importance in early chronology. When multiplied these create an epoch of 7980 years which is called the Julian period, representing the time that has to elapse before the indictions and all factors regulating Easter recur in the same order.

Abbas King of Persia

The Dutchman Barents discovers Spitzbergen in 1596.

Montaigne wrote essays in France. Cervantes and Lope de Vega were at work in Spain. In England Shakespeare wrote over twenty plays during this decade.

The Linköping bloodbath took place in Sweden in 1600. A number of counsellors who had supported King Sigismund in his struggle against Duke Charles, the future Charles IX of Sweden, were murdered.

History's first opera, Peri's *Daphne*, was performed in Florence in 1594, and Palestrina died in Rome in the same year. Orlando di Lasso, formerly conductor of the orchestra royal in Munich, also died at this time.

Abbas I, English book illustration. He defeated the Turks and the Portuguese with English help and was an excellent administrator.

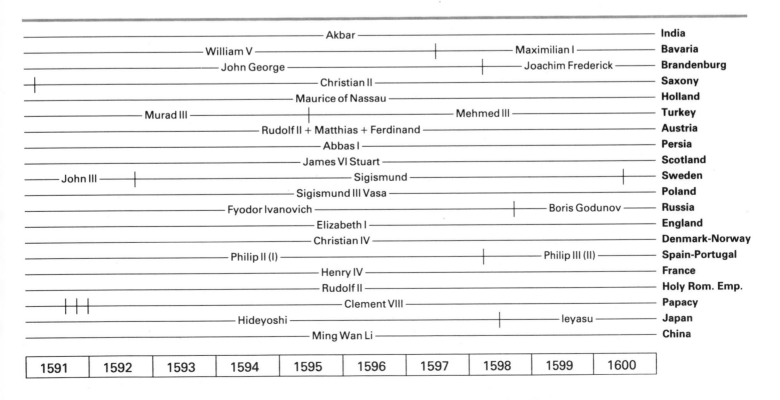

Akbar	India
William V | Maximilian I	Bavaria
John George | Joachim Frederick	Brandenburg
| Christian II	Saxony
Maurice of Nassau	Holland
Murad III | Mehmed III	Turkey
Rudolf II + Matthias + Ferdinand	Austria
Abbas I	Persia
James VI Stuart	Scotland
John III | Sigismund |	Sweden
Sigismund III Vasa	Poland
Fyodor Ivanovich | Boris Godunov	Russia
Elizabeth I	England
Christian IV	Denmark-Norway
Philip II (I) | Philip III (II)	Spain-Portugal
Henry IV	France
Rudolf II	Holy Rom. Emp.
| | | Clement VIII	Papacy
Hideyoshi | Ieyasu	Japan
Ming Wan Li	China

1591	1592	1593	1594	1595	1596	1597	1598	1599	1600

AD 1601-1610

SWEDEN
POLAND
HOLLAND
SWEDEN
CHARLES IX

The Mogul dynasty was disrupted by family conflicts. The first English traders came to India during the reign of King Jahangir. The English East India Company was founded in 1600.

In 1601 the Jesuit missionary Matteo Ricci arrived in Beijing (Peking) where he won the confidence of the emperor through his personal charm and knowledge of the natural sciences. The Christianity he preached was tolerant and easy for the Confucians to digest. Many senior officials agreed to baptism.

England's occupation of Ireland, concurrently with the Spanish war, was now more or less completed.

Queen Elizabeth I was succeeded by the Scottish king, James VI, Mary Stuart's son by Darnley. In England he was crowned as James I and the two realms were henceforth jointly known as Great Britain, though the union was not made formal for another century.

In 1606 William Jansz was the first European to sight land in Australia.

Ianuar. Anno Chr.
DC. XXVII

Kepler, imperial mathematician in Prague.

Kepler's laws were formulated in 1609. These state that the planets, including the Earth, pursue an elliptical orbit with the centre of the Sun as one focus; also that the radius vector of a planet moves over equal areas of the ellipse in equal intervals of time.

The first decades of the 17th century in Russia are referred to as "the time of troubles". Boris Godunov was not regarded as the legitimate czar and his son and successor Fyodor was swiftly despatched. With Polish aid, a pretender who claimed to be Ivan IV's son Dmitry (and may have been genuine) now made himself master of Russia; he appears to have been an able ruler, but Prince Vasily Shuysky soon had him assassinated, appointed himself czar and sought the support of the Swedes. Another Dmitry now appeared on the scene and the entire country became involved in a confusion of revolts and military expeditions until Michael Romanov, a young man related to the family of Ivan the Terrible, was finally elected czar. Poland and Sweden meanwhile seized the opportunity to appropriate considerable areas of Russian territory. Thus the Stolbova peace in 1617 gave Sweden Ingermanland and the Carelian province of Keksholm, while Poland took Smolensk and Severski.

In 1619 a Manchurian chieftain named Nurhachi defeated a large Chinese army, conquered Korea and established a realm which extended from the Amur river to the Yellow Sea and the Great Wall.

Shakespeare's *Hamlet* appeared around 1601, Cervantes' *Don Quixote* was published in 1605 and Monteverdi's *Orfeo* was performed in 1607. Both Shakespeare and Cervantes died in 1616.

India	Akbar | Jahangir
Bavaria	Maximilian I
Brandenburg	Joachim Frederick | John Sigismund
Saxony	Christian II
Holland	Maurice of Nassau
Turkey	Mehmed III | Ahmed I
Austria	Rudolf II + Mattias + Ferdinand
Persia	Abbas I
Scotland	James VI Stuart
Sweden	Charles IX
Poland	Sigismund III Vasa
Russia	Boris Godunov || Dmitry | Vasily Shuysky |
England	Elizabeth I | James I
Denmark-Norway	Christian IV
Spain-Portugal	Philip III (II)
France	Henry IV |
Holy Rom. Emp.	Rudolf II
Papacy	Clement VIII | Leo XI | Paul V
Japan	Ieyasu
China	Ming Wan Li

1601	1602	1603	1604	1605	1606	1607	1608	1609	1610

AD 1611-1620

PERSIA
JAPAN

In 1611 John Sigismund, elector of Brandenburg, married Anna heir to the Duchy of Prussia. This was an event of major importance to world history. Her grandfather, who had been grand-master of the Teutonic Order, had created this state for himself and his family.

In 1606 the Spaniards discovered Tahiti and the French founded Quebec in 1608. The Dutch were establishing themselves along the coasts of India.

In Prague the Protestant nobles had been debarred from all important offices and here in 1618 the Thirty Years' War began. The imperial counsellors Martinic and Slavata were thrown from a window, and though they were not killed, the incident led to a rebellion against the emperor. The Bohemians elected themselves a Protestant king, Frederick of the Palatine, and were attacked by the emperor and his Catholic League, headed by Maximilian of Bavaria. The League's troops, commanded by General Tilly, won a decisive victory at White Mountain not far from Prague. Frederick of the Palatine fled, Bohemia was subjugated and the Protestant population persecuted.

Tilly then turned on the Palatine, other Protestant states became involved and in the next decade this developed into a general European conflict.

Galileo Galilei discovered the solar spots in 1611 and also Jupiter's moons. Brigg published his logarithms in 1617 and Harvey discovered the blood circulation system in 1618.

Political confusion in Europe did not prevent Russia from expanding eastward. In Siberia Tomsk was founded in 1604 and Yeniseisk in 1618.

Spain continued to America. There was a Spanish viceroy in Peru and another in Mexico, and serving these were a number of audiencias each governing a particular district. The church and the religious orders played a leading part in the social, cultural and political organization of these vast territories. In 1610 the Jesuits were granted unrestricted authority to convert the Indians of Paraguary. They thereupon established a series of mission stations across Paraná and created an efficient state, though this was subjected to intermittent slave raids from the Portuguese territories.

The Englishman Henry Hudson discovered the Hudson river and Manhattan island in 1609. This region was colonized by the Dutch in 1613. The English colonisation of North America began a few years later when the Pilgrim Fathers landed in Massachusetts from the *Mayflower*.

Gustavus II Adolphus of Sweden, portrait by Heinrich Bollandt, now in Berlin.

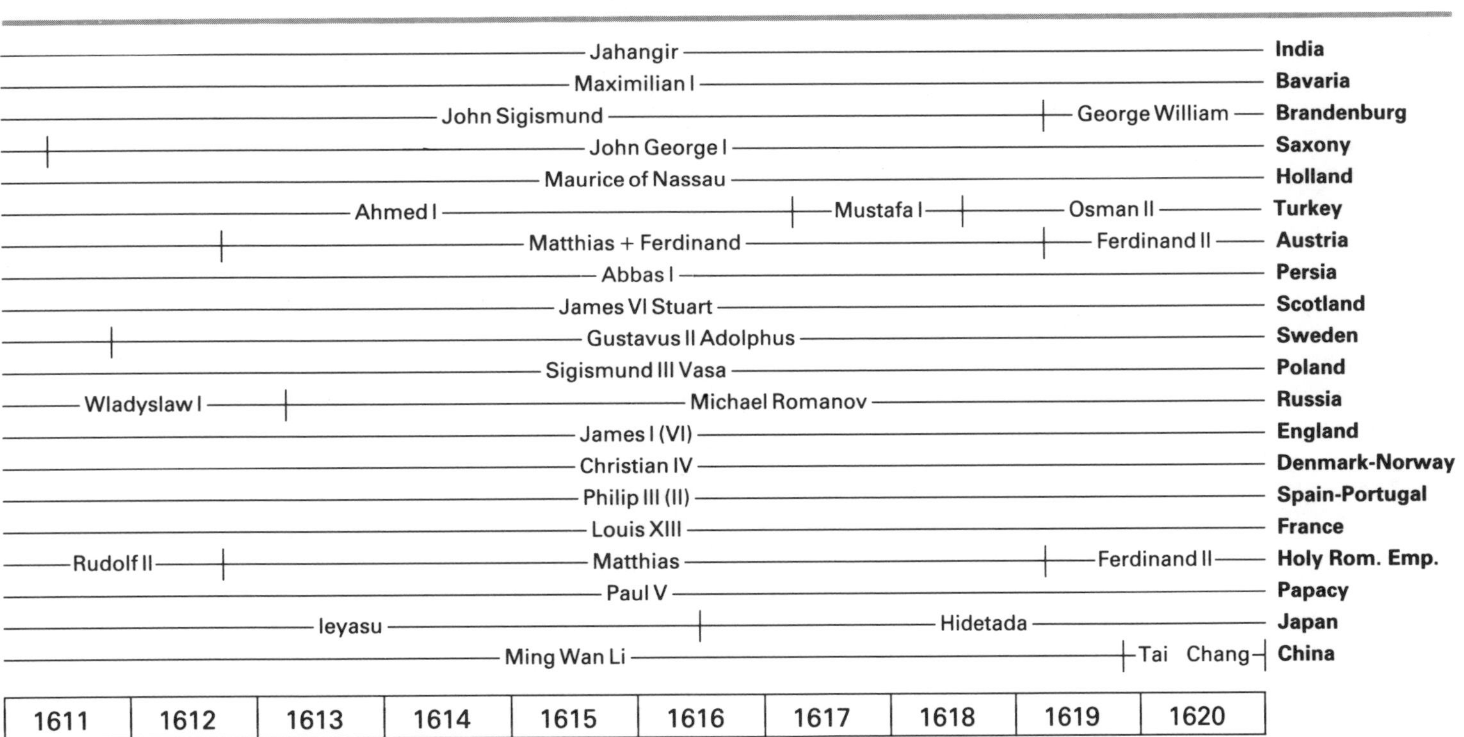
Jahangir — India
Maximilian I — Bavaria
John Sigismund — George William — Brandenburg
John George I — Saxony
Maurice of Nassau — Holland
Ahmed I — Mustafa I — Osman II — Turkey
Matthias + Ferdinand — Ferdinand II — Austria
Abbas I — Persia
James VI Stuart — Scotland
Gustavus II Adolphus — Sweden
Sigismund III Vasa — Poland
Wladyslaw I — Michael Romanov — Russia
James I (VI) — England
Christian IV — Denmark-Norway
Philip III (II) — Spain-Portugal
Louis XIII — France
Rudolf II — Matthias — Ferdinand II — Holy Rom. Emp.
Paul V — Papacy
Ieyasu — Hidetada — Japan
Ming Wan Li — Tai Chang — China
1611 1612 1613 1614 1615 1616 1617 1618 1619 1620

AD 1621-1630

FRANCE
GUSTAVUS II ADOLPHUS
SWEDEN

Galileo Galilei, professor of mathematics in Pisa and Padua and court philospher to the Duke of Tuscany since 1610, formulated the laws of falling bodies and inertia, created the parallelogram of forces, and constructed a telescope. This led to many astonishing celestial discoveries. Realizing that Copernicus was right, he did not hesitate to say so in a clever and spirited paper entitled *Dialogo sopra i due massimi sistemi del mondo*. The Church, which had recently condemned the ideas of Copernicus as heretical, reacted immediately, summoned Galileo before the Inquisition and forced him to recant and denounce his own theories. It is said that after recanting, Galileo was heard to mumble: *Eppur si muove* - (she moves anyway), referring to the Earth's orbit around the Sun.

Colonisation of Africa, America and Asia continued, as did the squabbling among the colonial powers. The Dutch founded their Guyana in 1625, nine years later the French established themselves in Cayenne and also occupied some of the West Indies, as did the English (for example, Bermuda and the Bahamas). The English also took control of the Guinea coast in Africa - valuable territory for slave trading purposes. At the same time French slave traders settled in Senegal. The French first set foot on Madagascar in 1626.

The Dutch took Ceylon from the Portuguese and secured a temporary footing in Brazil. The Portuguese also lost Hormuz on the Persian Gulf and English merchants collaborating with Abbas I's army gained certain advantages here. In North America Dutch colonists bought the island of Manhattan for 60 gulden in 1626.

In 1624 Christian IV of Denmark intervened in the Thirty Years' War but was defeated. In the following year the whole of Jutland was occupied and in 1629 Denmark was forced to conclude a separate peace with the Catholic powers, whose occupation troops were sent eastward against the Swedes. Gustavus II Adolphus had taken Riga in 1621 and occupied the mouth of the Vistula in 1625. In the summer of 1630 he landed in Pomerania and compelled the elector of Brandenburg to enter into an alliance. In 1631 Gustavus II Adolphus won his great victory against the Habsburg army at Breitenfeld and in November 1632 he died at the battle of Lützen. The Thirty Years' War continued, involving different combinations of powers. Sweden embarked on war with the Catholic League, and with Protestant Saxony and Brandenburg, simultaneously forming an alliance with Catholic France.

Reconstruction of the Pilgrim Fathers' settlement in Plymouth, Massachusetts, 1627. Friendly Indians showed them how to grow maize, but one-half of the 102 English colonists died during the first winter.

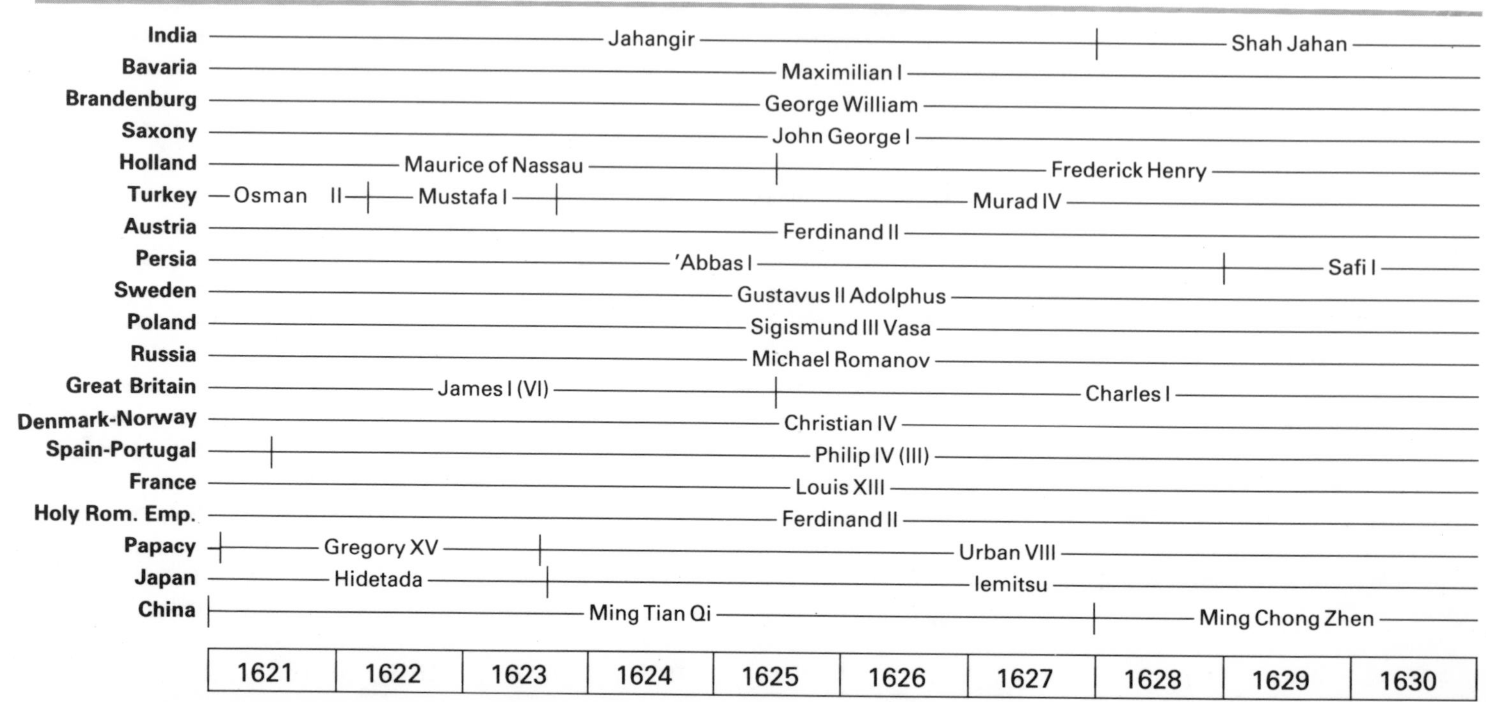
India
Jahangir
Shah Jahan
Bavaria
Maximilian I
Brandenburg
George William
Saxony
John George I
Holland
Maurice of Nassau
Frederick Henry
Turkey
Osman II
Mustafa I
Murad IV
Austria
Ferdinand II
Persia
'Abbas I
Safi I
Sweden
Gustavus II Adolphus
Poland
Sigismund III Vasa
Russia
Michael Romanov
Great Britain
James I (VI)
Charles I
Denmark-Norway
Christian IV
Spain-Portugal
Philip IV (III)
France
Louis XIII
Holy Rom. Emp.
Ferdinand II
Papacy
Gregory XV
Urban VIII
Japan
Hidetada
Iemitsu
China
Ming Tian Qi
Ming Chong Zhen
1621
1622
1623
1624
1625
1626
1627
1628
1629
1630

AD 1631-1640

FRANCE
CHARLES I
CHINA
RICHELIEU
PERSIA
JAPAN
ENGLAND
FRANCE

China was stricken by a succession of crop failures and years of famine. This disaster reached its peak in 1628 when hundreds of thousands of people starved to death and the government was unable even to supply provisions for its soldiers. In these conditions revolutionary bands ran rife across the country and in due course these disparate groups were organized into a disciplined insurrection force by a competent individual named Li Zicheng. This revolt was partially successful, however, because the imperial army was occupied on the northern frontier where the Manchurians were forcing their way in.

Turkey was in a state of political decline, with a succession of cruel and incompetent sultans. Mustafa I was slow-witted, and the young Osman II, who seized power from Mustafa, was assassinated by the Janissary guard. In the following decade, the epileptic Murad IV managed to discipline the Janissaries and others with terrible severity and cruelty, but Murad's brother and successor Ibrahim, was the slave of his harem and had little time for affairs of state.

In 1637 Descartes presented his geometry as a supplement to his *Discours de la méthode*. He was the founder of analytical geometry and thereby engendered the concept of infinitesimal calculus. He also conceived the method of expressing unknown quantities as x, y and z, while using a, b, c, etc. to express known quantities.

The French cardinal Richelieu, whose policy was expressly aimed at undermining Habsburgian Spain, was not without blame for the outbreak of a revolt in Portugal in 1640. The insignificant Duke of Braganza became king here and the union with Spain was dissolved.

British infiltration in India began in earnest during the reign of the Mogul emperors Jahangir and Shah Jahan. The latter defeated Golconda and Bijapur and was now engaged in building the Taj Mahal as a mausoleum for his favourite wife.

After Abbas I, a resourceful but merciless ruler, Persia entered a decline. The Turks took Tabriz and Baghdad. Safi I distinguished himself – like his Turkish adversary Murad IV – as an executioner.

The Spaniard Calderón wrote *La Vida es Sueño* in 1635 and in France Corneille's *Le Cid* appeared in 1636. At this time Rembrandt was about thirty years old and working on his first self-portrait. Heinrich Schütz was composing. Rubens, Frans Hals, Velasquez and Claude Lorrain were painting. St Peter's Church in Rome had been completed. The Moravian reformer Comenius wrote on education.

Armand Emmanuel du Plessis de Richelieu, portrait by Philippe de Champaigne, Louvre.

Shah Jahan	**India**
Maximilian I	**Bavaria**
George William	**Brandenburg**
John George I	**Saxony**
Frederick Henry	**Holland**
Murad IV – Ibrahim	**Turkey**
Ferdinand II – Ferdinand III	**Austria**
Safi I	**Persia**
Gustavus II Adolphus – Christina's regency	**Sweden**
Sigismund III – Wladyslaw IV Vasa	**Poland**
Michael Romanov	**Russia**
Charles I	**Great Britain**
Christian IV	**Denmark-Norway**
Philip IV (III)	**Spain-Portugal**
Louis XIII	**France**
Ferdinand II – Ferdinand III	**Holy Rom. Emp.**
Urban VIII	**Papacy**
Iemitsu	**Japan**
Ming Chong Zhen	**China**

1631	1632	1633	1634	1635	1636	1637	1638	1639	1640

ENGLAND
HOLLAND

In 1644 the Chinese rebels under Li Zicheng took Beijing, and the last of the Ming emperors hanged himself behind his palace. But General Wu Sangui, who commanded the troops on the northern frontier, preferred not to submit to Li Zicheng and let in the Manchurians instead. In a tremendous battle north of Beijing (Peking) the latter routed Li Zicheng's army, whereupon the young monarch of the Manchurians moved down from Mukden and established himself as emperor of China, with the reign title Shun Zhi. His dynasty, Qing (Ch'ing), was the final imperial dynasty in China and continued to rule there until 1911. The Manchurians quickly became Chinese-oriented.

In Europe the Thirty Years' War continued until 1648, ending with the peace of Westphalia. This resulted in major changes, especially in Germany, where Pomerania, Wismar, Bremen, Verden and other territories became Swedish. France took the towns of Metz, Toul and Verdun and likewise the Habsburg holdings in Alsace. Brandenburg extended its territory to include a number of dioceses, while Holland and Switzerland were now recognized as independent states.

In England, Puritan discontent over the king's wilful and intolerant high-church policy led to revolution. Oliver Cromwell was victorious and Charles I was seized and beheaded. The Scottish covenanters recognized his son, Charles, as king, which led Cromwell to attack and defeat the Scots. He also turned on Catholic Ireland, brutally suppressing all resistance here. In 1653 Cromwell made himself lord-protector of England and continued to rule the country in dictatorial fashion until his death in 1658. His son was unable to cope with the opposition of the army and Parliament, and after a year and a half of anarchy Charles Stuart restored the monarchy as Charles II.

The French seized Madagascar in 1643, the Dutch established the Cape colony in 1652 and the English took Jamaica from Spain in 1655.

A bishop in Ypres named Cornelius Jansen left behind him a critical work *Augustinus*, published in 1640. This was denounced by Pope Innocent X in 1654, which resulted in a prolonged and bitter controversy within the Catholic church. Innocent X also condemned the peace of Westphalia and with the aid of a brother-in-law contrived to bring about a financial collapse in the Papal State.

A serious uprising in Moscow in 1647 was followed by a new Russian code of laws in 1649. The intention was to improve the administration and put an end to various malpractices. These legislators were well-meaning but in time their laws resulted in serfdom and the loss of personal liberty. Most of Siberia was by now Russian territory.

The Turks laid claims to Crete and began a war with Venice on this issue, but the Venetians proved much stronger than anticipated; they won a number of victories and sent a fleet into the Dardanelles. The Janissaries in Constantinople now instigated a revolt, deposed Ibrahim I and made the ten-year old Mehmed IV sultan. After a period of anarchy the realm acquired an able grand vizier in the person of Mehmed Köprülü who restored discipline among the Janissaries and put the national finances in order.

Shah Jahan's reign in India was a period of great progress for the Mogul empire, but he had difficulty with his rebellious sons.

During the 1640s the Dutchman Tasman discovered Tasmania, the southern island of New Zealand and the Fiji islands.

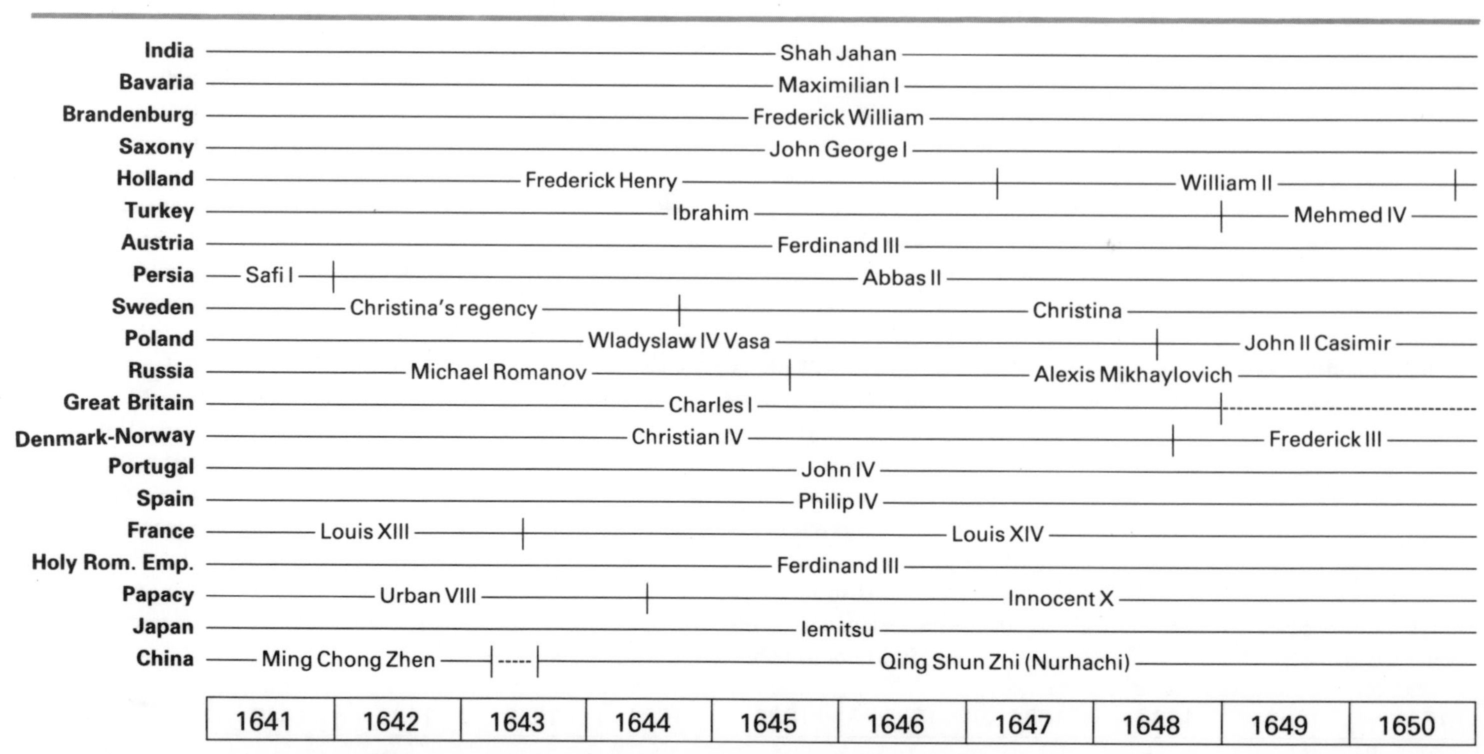
India — Shah Jahan
Bavaria — Maximilian I
Brandenburg — Frederick William
Saxony — John George I
Holland — Frederick Henry — William II
Turkey — Ibrahim — Mehmed IV
Austria — Ferdinand III
Persia — Safi I — Abbas II
Sweden — Christina's regency — Christina
Poland — Wladyslaw IV Vasa — John II Casimir
Russia — Michael Romanov — Alexis Mikhaylovich
Great Britain — Charles I
Denmark-Norway — Christian IV — Frederick III
Portugal — John IV
Spain — Philip IV
France — Louis XIII — Louis XIV
Holy Rom. Emp. — Ferdinand III
Papacy — Urban VIII — Innocent X
Japan — Iemitsu
China — Ming Chong Zhen — Qing Shun Zhi (Nurhachi)
1641 1642 1643 1644 1645 1646 1647 1648 1649 1650

AD 1651-1660

SWEDEN
BENIN, AFRICA
FRANCE
DENMARK
SPAIN
BENIN, AFRICA

Two Swedish-Danish wars ended with the peace of Brömsebo in 1645 and the peace of Roskilde in 1658. The former gave Sweden the provinces of Jemtland, Herjedalen, Götland and Halland and the latter added Scania, Blekinge, and Bohuslan. These wars were conducted mainly from the south by the Swedes who had armies on German territory. The second conflict was notable for the famous march by the Swedish army across the frozen Belt – a unique event in military history – but Charles X Gustav, who led this march, failed in the following year when he attempted to force the Danes to make further concessions. There was now a revolution in Denmark where the power of the nobles was replaced by an absolute monarchy.

Louis XIV of France was still a child and the country was ruled chiefly by the dowager queen Anna's lover Cardinal Mazarin. The latter was twice exiled but eventually triumphed.

The Peace of the Pyrenees in 1659 between the Bourbons and the Habsburgs constituted a milestone in the political domination of Europe by France and Spain. Under the treaty France acquired Roussillon and part of Flanders.

In 1658 the kingdom of Sweden reached its farthest limits. Two years later the Bornholm and Trondheim provinces were lost again. The Russian empire now extended to the Pacific coast.

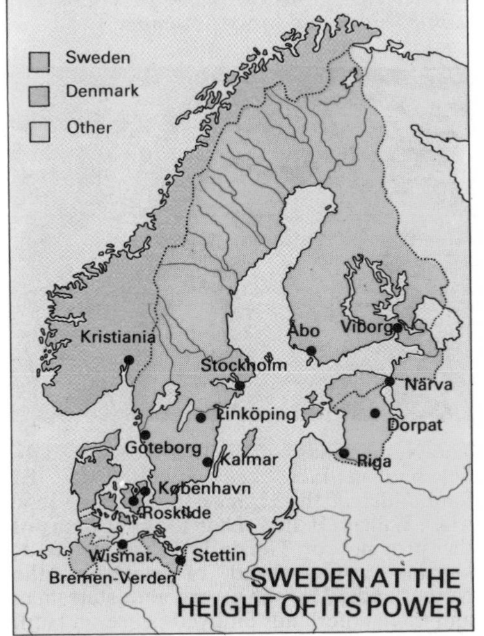
Sweden
Denmark
Other
Kristiania
Stockholm
Åbo
Viborg
Narva
Linköping
Dorpat
Göteborg
Kalmar
Riga
København
Roskilde
Wismar
Stettin
Bremen-Verden
SWEDEN AT THE
HEIGHT OF ITS POWER

An important academy of science, the Royal Society in London, was formed in 1660. Among recent major discoveries and inventions were Torricelli's mercury barometer, Guericke's air pump and his Magdeburg hemispheres, Huygen's pendulum clock, Pascal and Fermat's development of the calculus of probability, and Swammerdam's discovery of the red corpuscles in frog's blood.

The magic lantern invented in Germany was a new and very popular toy; and in Italy Procopio had discovered how to make ice-cream.

Notable works of literature included Thomas Hobbes *Leviathan* (1631), Isaac Walton's *The Compleat Angler* (1653), Molière's *Les précieuses ridicules* (1659).

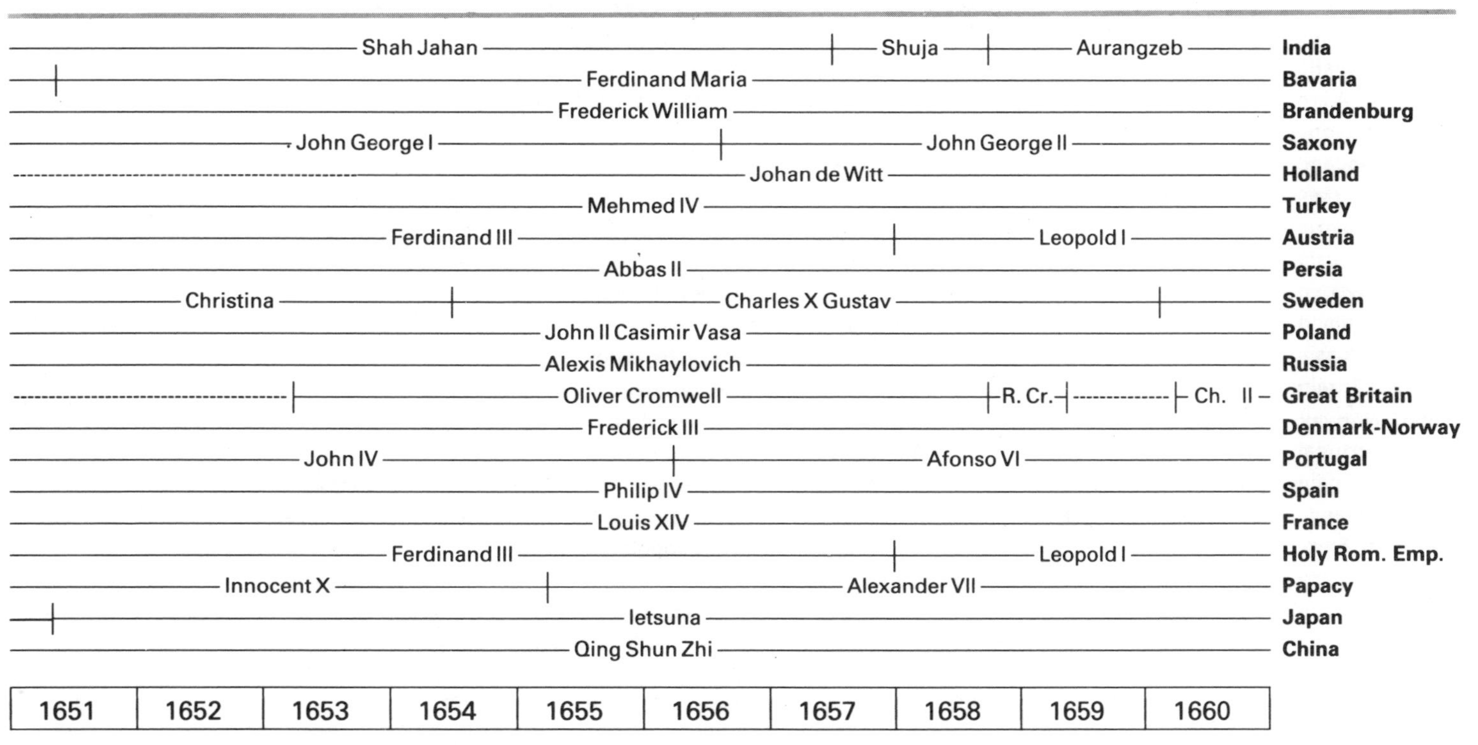
Shah Jahan – Shuja – Aurangzeb – India
Ferdinand Maria – Bavaria
Frederick William – Brandenburg
John George I – John George II – Saxony
Johan de Witt – Holland
Mehmed IV – Turkey
Ferdinand III – Leopold I – Austria
Abbas II – Persia
Christina – Charles X Gustav – Sweden
John II Casimir Vasa – Poland
Alexis Mikhaylovich – Russia
Oliver Cromwell – R. Cr. – Ch. II – Great Britain
Frederick III – Denmark-Norway
John IV – Afonso VI – Portugal
Philip IV – Spain
Louis XIV – France
Ferdinand III – Leopold I – Holy Rom. Emp.
Innocent X – Alexander VII – Papacy
Ietsuna – Japan
Qing Shun Zhi – China
1651 1652 1653 1654 1655 1656 1657 1658 1659 1660

AD 1661-1670

HOLLAND
RUSSIA

There was an almost annual succession of wars and peace settlements in Europe. Poland surrendered Smolensk, Kiev and other places to Russia in 1667, and the peace treaty in Breda in the same year gave the English New Amsterdam, or New York, while Holland received Surinam in South America instead. In 1676 the Turks deprived Poland of various areas and the following year there was unrest in Hungary. There was a peace treaty involving different countries at Nijmegen in 1678 when the French appropriated Franche-Comté, Alsace and other territories. An an ally of France, Sweden was at war with Denmark and Brandenburg in the 1670s and became an absolute monarchy under Charles Xi in 1680.

The Manchurian empire in China was stabilized during the reign of Kang Xi, who also tightened his hold on his central Asian territories. The administration was cruelly dictatorial, books were burned and opponents were executed together with their families. In religious matters, however, the emperor showed tolerance and was particularly gracious to the Jesuit missionaries. He also established a factory which began to manufacture porcelain that was known in Europe as *famille verte*.

Pirates from North Africa had menaced shipping in the 16th century and 17th century buccaneers made raids from the West Indies. In 1671 Henry Morgan sailed from England with 37 ships and sacked Panama.

The Netherlands, officially a federal republic, had in fact been governed by the Stadholder of the Orange family until 1650 when William II died. Then the pensionary of the province of Holland, Johan de Witt, became virtual head of state in the Netherlands. He was a very able statesman and the Netherlands enjoyed peace on land, though at sea they were involved in a number of conflicts. In 1667 the office of stadholder was abolished, but in 1672, when Louis XIV attacked Holland, it was reinstated for William III of Orange. Johan de Witt and his brother were then murdered by a mob and it is possible that William III was implicated. William's defence of his country was very effective; the French were halted opening the dams and letting in the sea.

King Charles II of England acquired the town of Bombay as a dowry when he married the Portuguese princess Catharine of Braganza. In 1668 he let the town to the East India Company for an annual rent ten pounds.

In 1669 the Turks took Crete, except for three fortified sites which the Venetians were permitted to retain.

New literature included Molière's *Tartuffe* (1664) and *Le Misanthrope* (1666); Racine's *Andromaque* (1667) and *Bérénice* (1670); Milton's *Paradise Lost* (1667); La Fontaine's Fables (1668); Pascal's *Pensées* (1670); Spinoza's *Tractatus theologico-politicus* (1670); and La Rochefoucauld's *Maximes* (1664). John Bunyan was in prison writing his *Pilgrim's Progress* (published 1678).

India	Aurangzeb
Bavaria	Ferdinand Maria
Brandenburg	Frederick William
Saxony	John George II
Holland	Johan de Witt
Turkey	Mehmed IV
Austria	Leopold I
Persia	Abbas II | Suleyman (Safi)
Sweden	Charles XI's regency
Poland	John II Casimir Vasa | ---- | Michael Korybut
Russia	Alexis Mikhaylovich
Great Britain	Charles II
Denmark-Norway	Frederick III |
Portugal	Afonso VI | Pedro II
Spain	Philip IV | Charles II
France	Louis XIV
Holy Rom. Emp.	Leopold I
Papacy	Alexander VII | Clement IX | - | Clem. X
Japan	Ietsuna
China	Shun Zhi | Qing Kang Xi

1661	1662	1663	1664	1665	1666	1667	1668	1669	1670

AD 1671-1680

ENGLAND
FRANCE
SWEDEN
LAPPLAND

Newton announced his law of gravity in 1666, having created infinitesimal calculus in the previous year. Independently of Newton, however, Leibniz made the same mathematical achievement in 1676 and it was his version that was later adopted. Ole Rømer calculated the speed of light in 1676 and in the same year the Greenwich observatory was founded. Leeuwenhoek first discovered microscopic life in 1675 and in 1679 Papin designed his autoclave, a type of pressure cooker. Huygens presented his wave theory of light in 1678.

The republic of Venice, until recently a major power, was now on the decline. World trade was seeking other routes, and the military power of Venice was beginning to diminish.

Frederick William of Brandenburg was known as "the Great Elector". During his time Brandenburg, with East Prussia, became an important power with an efficient central administration and a powerful army.

By 1672 the Ottoman empire had reached its greatest limits ever. It had won a victory over Poland and thereby secured Podolia and also sovereignty over the Ukraine. The real rulers of Turkey during the latter half of the 17th century were the grand viziers of the Köprülü family. Several were energetic and able politicians, but even though they took Crete from the Venetians in 1669 and in the 1670s, and almost succeeded in subjugating the Cossacks in the Ukraine, Turkish power declined. The turning point came in the next decade with the attack on Vienna.

The Indian king, Aurangzeb, who killed his father and his brothers, was an ascetic Muslim, strictly opposed to all forms of heresy and frivolity in his kingdom, and enjoyed great political success during the first decades of his reign. He took control of several large, formerly independent states, including Bijapur and Golconda. At the same time he committed many imprudent acts and atrocities. Thus he introduced a special tax to be paid by all infidels, and had his elephants trample down a Hindu deputation that tried to contest it. He also ordered the execution of a Sikh guru in the Punjab. Aurangzeb never quelled the dissatisfaction and opposition engendered by his misguided policies.

Stradivarius made violins in Cremona. Buxtehude played the organ in Lübeck. Corelli composed the first concerto grosso.

According to Voltaire, a falling apple led Isaac Newton to deduce his law of gravity. Newton also revealed the dispersion of light into a coloured spectrum. Portrait by G. Kneller, London.

Aurangzeb	**India**
Ferdinand Maria ┼	**Bavaria**
Frederick William	**Brandenburg**
John George II ┼	**Saxony**
Johan de Witt ┼ William III of Orange	**Holland**
Mehmed IV	**Turkey**
Leopold I	**Austria**
Suleyman	**Persia**
Charles XI's regency ┼ Charles XI	**Sweden**
Michael ┼ Korybut Wisniowiecki ┼ ┼ John III Sobieski	**Poland**
Alexis Mikhaylovich ┼ Fyodor Alexeyevich	**Russia**
Charles II	**Great Britain**
Christian V	**Denmark-Norway**
Pedro II	**Portugal**
Charles II	**Spain**
Louis XIV	**France**
Leopold I	**Holy Rom. Emp.**
Clement X ┼ Innocent XI	**Papacy**
Ietsuna ┼	**Japan**
Qing Kang Xi	**China**

1671	1672	1673	1674	1675	1676	1677	1678	1679	1680

AD 1681-1690

THE SIEGE OF VIENNA
JAPAN

Vienna was besieged by the Turks in 1683, though after a few months they were put to flight by a coalition army led by the Polish king, John Sobieski. A few years later imperial troops seized a considerable part of Hungary, including the capital Buda, from the Turks, whereupon the Hungarian crown was proclaimed hereditary within the house of Habsburg. As a result of further military actions in the 1690s when the Austrian general, Eugene of Savoy won a number of major victories, the peace of Carlowitz was signed and the Turks surrendered something like half their European possessions. Austria now acquired Hungary, Transylvania and Croatia, Venice took Dalmatia and Peloponnesus in Greece, while Russia, under peace terms concluded elswhere, retained Azov on the Black Sea. Sultan Mehmed IV was deposed after an insurrection in Turkey.

Koxinga, a general of mixed Chinese and Japanese parentage had expelled the Dutch from Formosa in 1661, dying the following year. Chinese imperial expeditionary forces recaptured the island in 1683.

In England the political follies of the Catholic James II led to negotiations between the English opposition and William III of Orange, who was married to James's eldest daughter Mary. In November 1688 William landed on the south coast of England and gained overwhelming support. James, with his queen and newly born son, fled to the court of Louis XIV in France. On the accession of the new monarch, Parliament issued the Declaration of Rights. William became William III in England.

Religious orthodoxy and bigotry became increasingly pronounced in many countries towards the close of the 17th century. In France the government imprudently drove out the Huguenots, which was disastrous for the French economy but of great benefit to other countries. French Huguenots set up a textile industry in Germany and began planting vineyards in South Africa.

Newton's famous *Principia* appeared in 1687.

In 1682 the Quaker William Penn founded the colony of Pennsylvania with its captial Philadelphia, on the east coast of America.

More English colonists land in Virginia. Mansel Collection, London.

Country	Rulers 1681–1690
India	Aurangzeb
Bavaria	Maximilian II Emanuel
Brandenburg	Frederick William – Frederick III (I)
Saxony	John George III
Holland	William III of Orange
Turkey	Mehmed IV – Suleyman II
Austria	Leopold I
Persia	Suleyman
Sweden	Charles XI
Poland	John III Sobieski
Russia	Fyodor – Peter I – Sophia & Golitsyn – Peter I
Great Britain	Charles II – James II – William III and Mary II
Denmark-Norway	Christian V
Portugal	Pedro II
Spain	Charles II
France	Louis XIV
Holy Rom. Emp.	Leopold I
Papacy	Innocent XI – Alex. VIII
Japan	Tsunayoshi
China	Qing Kang Xi

1681	1682	1683	1684	1685	1686	1687	1688	1689	1690

AD 1691-1700

SWEDEN
INDIA
FRANCE

In Russia Fyodor Alexeyevich died childless and his ten-year old brother Peter was proclaimed czar. Peter's elder half-brother Ivan was mentally defective, but an opposition party nevertheless placed him, together with his strong-willed sister Sophia, on the throne in preference to Peter, whose support was whittled away. The real power was wielded by Sophia's lover Prince Golitsyn, and Peter was banished to a suburb of Moscow. But in 1689 a successful coup was organized on Peter's behalf, Golitsyn was driven into exile and Sophia was placed in a convent. When Ivan died in 1695, Peter became sole ruler.

In 1697-98 Czar Peter made his celebrated tour abroad. In Holland he studied shipbuilding in Zaandam and on his way home visited Polands's newly elected Augustus II, the Strong. On his return he resolutely and ruthlessly destroyed the undisciplined *Streltsy* military corps and set about reorganizing Russia on Western lines. In August 1700 Peter declared war on Sweden and suffered a major defeat at Narva in the same year.

Charles II of Spain was the last of his line and the question of the succession was of paramount concern for the European powers. Charles died in the autumn of 1700 and in his will named a grandson of France's Louis XIV as the next ruler of the Spanish empire with all its dependencies and possessions. This conflicted, however, with an earlier agreement between France on the one hand and England and Holland on the other, and led to the outbreak of the War of the Spanish Succession in 1701.

The Russians had now completed their conquest of Siberia and in 1699 they crossed the straits between Asia and America to take possession of Alaska as well, unaware that they had set foot on another continent. Ten years earlier, in 1689, in the town of Nerchinsk they had reached an agreement with China on a boundary line in the Amur region. This was China's first agreement with a foreign power.

Louis XIV and his family. Painting by Nicolas de Largillière, Wallace collection, London. The king's family life was far from idyllic.

Frederick Augustus I of Saxony was the same person as Augustus II, the Strong, of Poland.

Louis XIV was now an old man and his long reign had also been a period of cultural and political prominence in France.

In 1697 Perrault's *Contes de ma mère l'oye* (Mother Goose) appeared, with the earliest stories of Red Riding Hood, Tom Thumb, Cinderella and others.

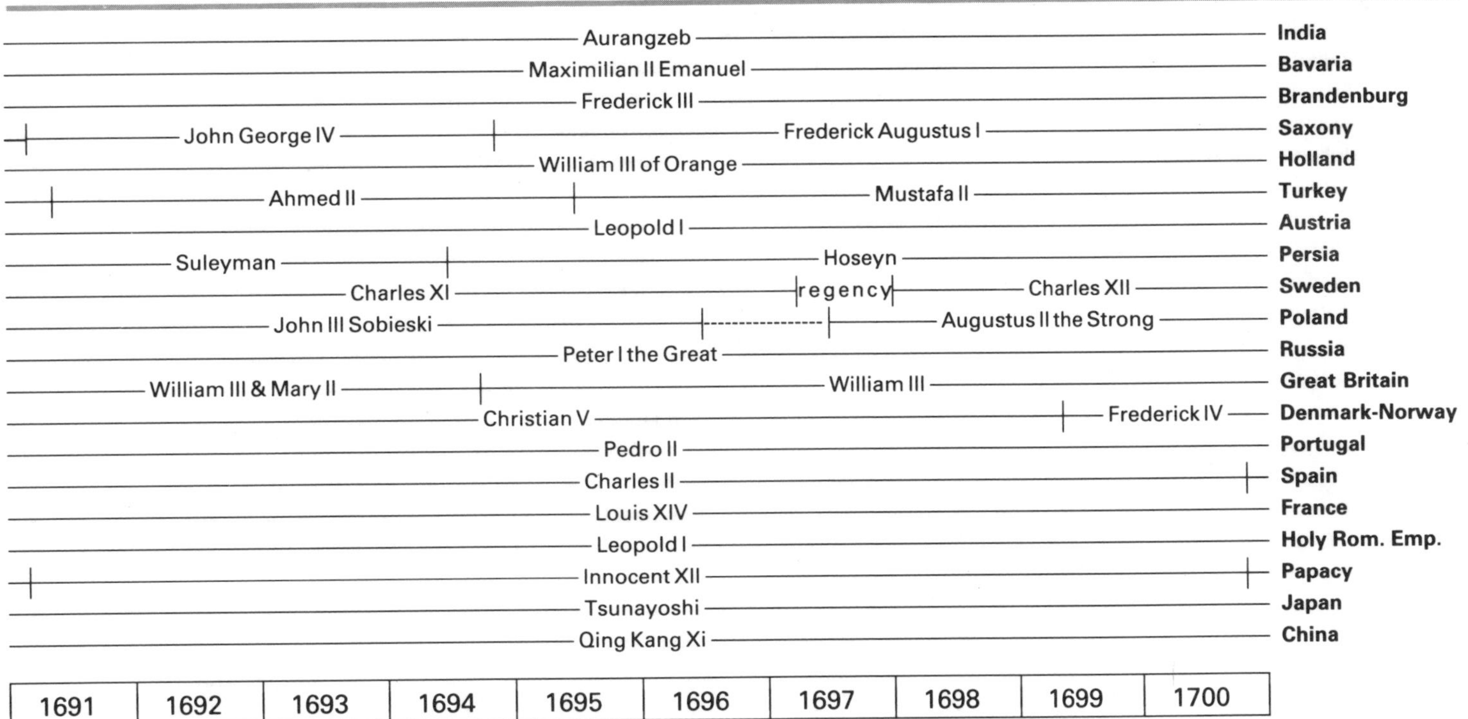
Aurangzeb — India
Maximilian II Emanuel — Bavaria
Frederick III — Brandenburg
John George IV — Frederick Augustus I — Saxony
William III of Orange — Holland
Ahmed II — Mustafa II — Turkey
Leopold I — Austria
Suleyman — Hoseyn — Persia
Charles XI — regency — Charles XII — Sweden
John III Sobieski — Augustus II the Strong — Poland
Peter I the Great — Russia
William III & Mary II — William III — Great Britain
Christian V — Frederick IV — Denmark-Norway
Pedro II — Portugal
Charles II — Spain
Louis XIV — France
Leopold I — Holy Rom. Emp.
Innocent XII — Papacy
Tsunayoshi — Japan
Qing Kang Xi — China
1691
1692
1693
1694
1695
1696
1697
1698
1699
1700

AD 1701-1710

SWEDEN
DENMARK
RUSSIA
POLAND
PRUSSIA
SAXONY
ENGLAND
SPAIN
FRANCE
SCOTLAND

In Europe the two first decades of the 18th century were dominated by wars which resulted in widespread changes in frontiers and shifts in the balance of power. In the north Sweden lost her status as a major power: the Russians took Narva in 1704, defeated Charles XII at Poltava in 1709, captured Riga, Reval and Viborg in 1710, and Finland and the Åland islands in 1711. In 1712 the new Russian capital of St Petersburg was founded on land that still formally belonged to Sweden. The greater part of Swedish Pomerania, with Stettin, was taken by Brandenburg which had changed its name after the elector, Frederick, had become king of Prussia in 1701.

There was an earthquake in Tokyo in 1703 where 200,000 people are reputed to have perished.

When Aurangzeb died the Mogul empire was already in a state of dissolution. Sikhs, Rajputs, Marathas and others had rebelled and the emperor had been at war with his own sons, who were now quarrelling among themselves. The empire survived for a few more decades, but its list of rulers is no longer of much interest.

Stanislaw Leszczynski was Charles XIII's protegé and when, after the battle of Poltava, Stanislaw fled to Turkey, Augustus II reclaimed the Polish crown.

The official Act of Union between England and Scotland, creating Great Britain, with a single Parliament at Westminister, took place in 1707.

In 1705 Halley calculated the orbit and period of revolution of the comet which bears his name. At about the same time a German named Böttger discovered how to make porcelain, an art hitherto exclusive to the Chinese. Watteau painted pictures in France, Fahrenheit devised his thermometer, Stradivarius made violins in Cremona, a Frenchman translated *A Thousand and One Nights* from the Arabic and an English journalist, Daniel Defoe, wrote *Robinson Crusoe*, which appeared in 1719.

Peter the Great founds St Petersburg. The city was the capital of Russia from 1712 to 1918. Painting in the Tretyakovskaya Gallery, Moscow.

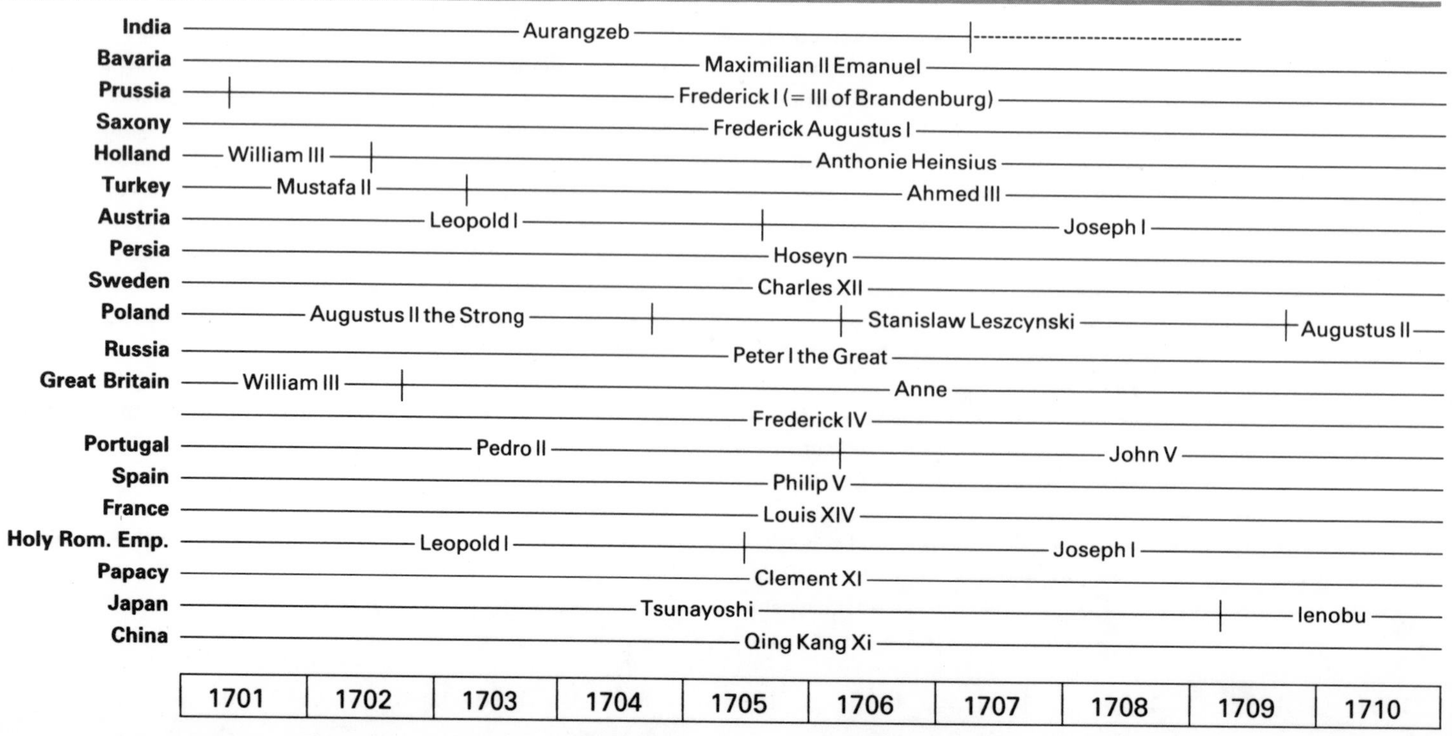
India — Aurangzeb
Bavaria — Maximilian II Emanuel
Prussia — Frederick I (= III of Brandenburg)
Saxony — Frederick Augustus I
Holland — William III — Anthonie Heinsius
Turkey — Mustafa II — Ahmed III
Austria — Leopold I — Joseph I
Persia — Hoseyn
Sweden — Charles XII
Poland — Augustus II the Strong — Stanislaw Leszcynski — Augustus II
Russia — Peter I the Great
Great Britain — William III — Anne
Frederick IV
Portugal — Pedro II — John V
Spain — Philip V
France — Louis XIV
Holy Rom. Emp. — Leopold I — Joseph I
Papacy — Clement XI
Japan — Tsunayoshi — Ienobu
China — Qing Kang Xi
1701 1702 1703 1704 1705 1706 1707 1708 1709 1710

AD 1711-1720

JAPAN
FRANCE
CHINA

Russia was now politically dominant in Europe as never before, Peter the Great having brought about widespread changes in many fields. Prussia, too, was a power of growing significance as a result of the part played in the War of the Spanish Succession. This conflict ended in 1713 with the peace of Utrecht: the Spanish empire was divided up so that the French-born Philip V continued to reign as king of Spain itself, while the Habsburg emperor Charles VI became ruler of the Italian possessions of Milan, Naples, Tuscany and Sardinia, and likewise of the Spanish Netherlands, roughly the area which was later to become Belgium. The principal beneficiary of the war, however, was Britain which now acquired Gibraltar, Minorca and north-east Canada, and secured a monopoly of the Negro slave trade to Spain's American colonies.

Louis XV of France was still only a child and the country was ruled by Philippe, duke of Orléans.

The kingdom of Sardinia was formed in 1720. the capital, curiously enough, was Turin and the kingdom also included Piedmont, Nice and Savoy. The nucleus of this new realm was Savoy, whose duke now became king of Sardinia.

The Catalans in Spain, who had defended their in dependence in the War of the Spanish Succession, were subsequently abandoned by their foreign allies, defeated and cruelly oppressed.

A Scotsman, John Law, founded a bank in Paris with the right to issue notes, and used it to back a trading company which had a monopoly to exploit the French territories of Louisiana in North America. The scheme, known as the "Mississippi Bubble", collapsed and caused a major financial crisis in France, ruining many people.

The English fleet, cruising in the Baltic from 1719 to 1721, was unable to prevent a large fleet of Russian galleys ravaging and burning the mainland and islands of Sweden's east coast. Stockholm alone managed to avoid this destruction.

Absolute monarchy was abolished in Sweden from 1719. The power was now put in the hands of the estates, especially the nobles.

In 1718 the Turks lost Serbia, Wallachia and what was known at the Banat, to Austria.

Kang Xi ruled China with a firm hand for sixty years and was probably the most powerful monarch of his day. He had set up a new Dalai Lama in Lhasa, Tibet, and curtailed all freedom of speech in his country. On the other hand, he was well disposed towards the Christian Jesuit missionaries. However, when the Pope's emissaries began to question the Jesuits' liberal attitudes towards Chinese ancestor cults Kang Xi was enraged, for he did not recognize the right of foreign priests to meddle in his nation's religious affairs. The missionary work was subsequently prohibited, but the emperor's personal friends in Beijing (Peking) were allowed to continue preaching.

Tibet became a tributary of China in 1720.

The Protestant branch of the English royal family terminated with the death of Queen Anne. The closest heir to the throne was now George, elector of Hanover, and Britain thereby entered into a untion with this country. George knew no English and was altogether most at home in Germany.

Victor Amadeus II	**Savoy**
Maximilian II Emanuel	**Bavaria**
Frederick I — Frederick William I	**Prussia**
Frederick Augustus I	**Saxony**
Anthonie Heinsius	**Holland**
Ahmed III	**Turkey**
Charles VI	**Austria**
Hoseyn	**Persia**
Charles XII — Ulrika Eleonora	**Sweden**
Augustus II the Strong	**Poland**
Peter I the Great	**Russia**
Anne — George I	**Great Britain**
Frederick IV	**Denmark-Norway**
John V	**Portugal**
Philip V	**Spain**
Louis XIV — Philippe, Duke of Orléans	**France**
Charles VI	**Holy Rom. Emp.**
Clement XI	**Papacy**
Ienobu — Ietsugu — Yoshimune	**Japan**
Qing Kang Xi	**China**

1711	1712	1713	1714	1715	1716	1717	1718	1719	1720

AD 1721-1730

FRANCE
INDIA

Charles VI of Sicily and Naples and Emperor Charles VI in Vienna were the same man, who, through the peace of Utrecht, had acquired Spain's southern Italian possessions.

The peace of Nystad in 1721 ended Sweden's era as a great power. She now lost the Baltic provinces. also Carelia, Bremen, Verden and part of Pomerania.

The Russians took Baku from Persia in 1723.

In Austria in 1724 a succession decree was issued by Charles VI which was known as the Pragmatic Sanction. By the terms of this, after the emperor's death the entire Hapsburg empire was to go to his daughter Maria Theresa, instead of being divided up among the related princely families. Various European courts took exception to this settlement.

With the death of the 15 year-old Peter II, the male line of the Romanovs died out in Russia. On the accession of the new monarch, the council, led by Dmitry Golitsyn, attempted to established an aristocratic constitution similar to the one just introduced in Sweden. This was opposed by the army, clergy and others, with the result that the new empress, Anna, rejected the covenant that had been forced upon her. Russia's absolute monarchy thus continued.

The Turks were largely successful in a war with Russia and Austria in the 1730s. This ended with the Russians retaining Azov but otherwise being cut off from the Black Sea, while Austria was forced to return Serbia and certain other territories.

Johann Sebastian Bach composed his *St John's Passion*, *St Mathew's Passion* and *Well Tempered Clavier* in the 1720s. John Gay's *Beggars' Opera* was dated 1728. Pergolesi's *La serva padrona* appeared in 1733.

Réaumur designed his thermometer. The first cuckoo clock appeared in Switzerland. Jonathan Swift wrote *Gulliver's Travels*.

Maria Theresa. Portrait by Marten Wiytens, Vienna.

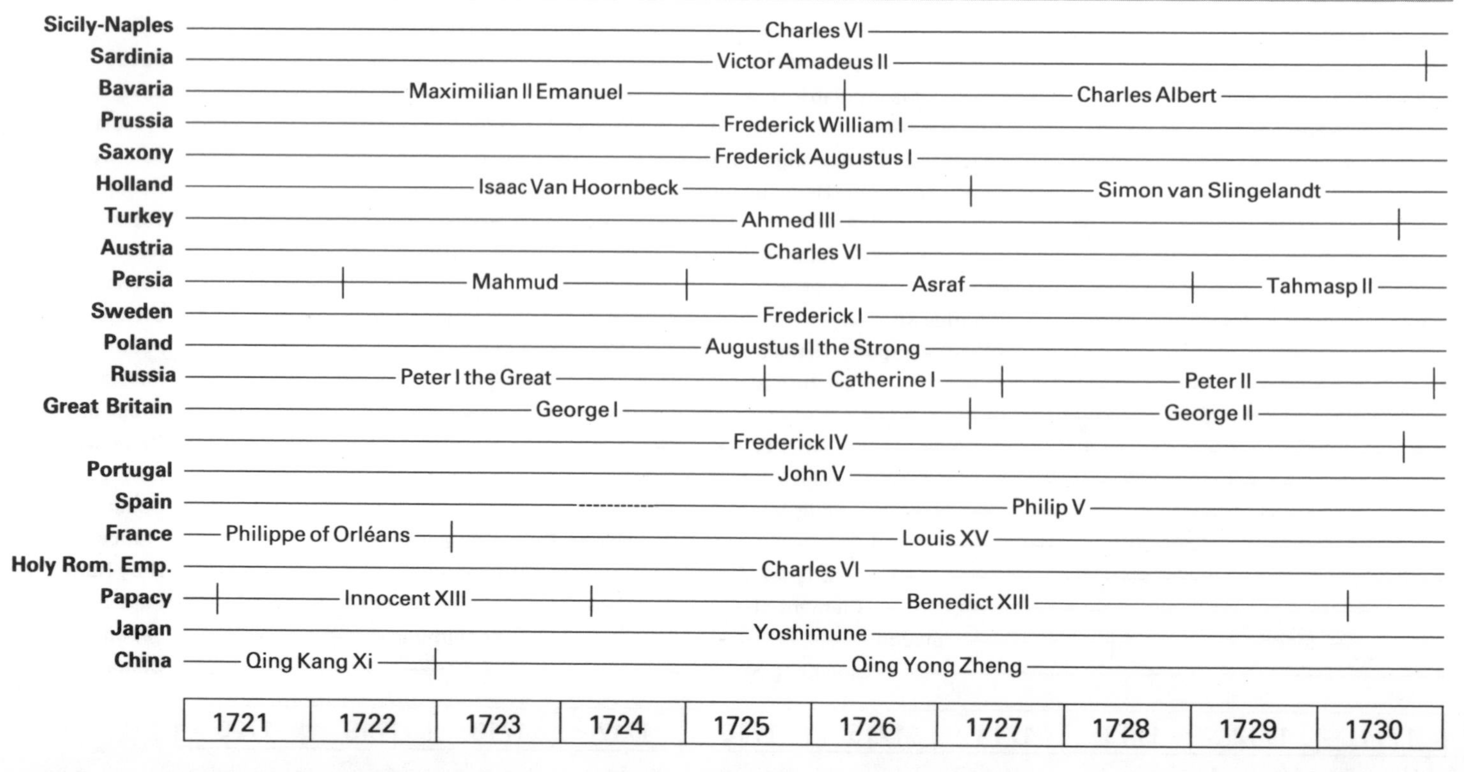
Sicily-Naples — Charles VI
Sardinia — Victor Amadeus II
Bavaria — Maximilian II Emanuel — Charles Albert
Prussia — Frederick William I
Saxony — Frederick Augustus I
Holland — Isaac Van Hoornbeck — Simon van Slingelandt
Turkey — Ahmed III
Austria — Charles VI
Persia — Mahmud — Asraf — Tahmasp II
Sweden — Frederick I
Poland — Augustus II the Strong
Russia — Peter I the Great — Catherine I — Peter II
Great Britain — George I — George II
Frederick IV
Portugal — John V
Spain — Philip V
France — Philippe of Orléans — Louis XV
Holy Rom. Emp. — Charles VI
Papacy — Innocent XIII — Benedict XIII
Japan — Yoshimune
China — Qing Kang Xi — Qing Yong Zheng
1721 1722 1723 1724 1725 1726 1727 1728 1729 1730

AD 1731-1740

CHINA
KOREA
CHINA

In Poland there were rival kings in 1733-36: the son of Augustus the Strong and Stanislaw Leszczynski. The latter was expelled by the Russians and the Austrians and became duke of Lorraine instead, since he happened to be the father of Louis XV. Spain and Sardinia were also involved in this conflict which was known as the War of the Polish Succession (1733-35).

In 1732 a Turkish robber chieftain, Nader Qoli, deposed the last Safavid shah and made himself ruler of the country. In the east the weakened Mogul empire was ripe for plunder and in 1738 Nader Qoli attacked and took, among other places, Kabul and Lahore in the Punjab. He then advanced to Delhi which was totally plundered, the Koh-i-noor diamond and a famous peacock throne being among the spoils. Kabul and the country to the west of the Indus became part of Persia, and Nader also conducted successful campaigns farther west, defeating the Ottoman sultan's troops in Mesopotamia and taking certain Armenian regions from the Turks.

Augustus III of Poland was the same person as Frederick Augustus II of Saxony.

The Englishman John Wesley founded Methodism in 1739.

Victus Bering, Danish sea captain in Russian service, made various discoveries in those waters which were to bear his name.

The three Manchurian emperors, Kang Xi, Yong Zheng and Qian Long, ruled China with a firm hand for more than 100 years. China now flourished politically and economically, and the three emperors left a good reputation which the Western Jesuit missionaries had also helped to reinforce. These missionaries had been particularly well received during the first part of Emperor Kang Xi's reign. Now however, Kang Xi was involved in a conflict with the pope in Rome who had forbidden Christians to take part in Confucian ceremonies and rituals, and consequently the missionaries were ousted. Kang Xi was also at odds with the Tibetan pontificate, having executed a number of monks and appointed a new Dalai Lama. Yong Zheng, his successor, completed this by appointing a Chinese resident alongside the Lama priesthood.

These three emperors, particularly Qian Long, promoted some of the greatest publishing ventures of the age. Huge encyclopaedias and many other works were carefully written out and printed in their Beijing (Peking) printing office.

All China's ports were closed to foreign ships except Guangzhou (Canton) where Western merchants collected porcelain and other cargoes, paid for in hard cash.

In 1732 the newly formed Swedish East India Company sent its first ship to China and this returned to Gothenburg after two years with a profit to the company of more than twice its initial outlay.

In 1740 there were fateful changes of ruler in Russia, Austria and Prussia. In the first two instances the succession was by no means clear.

Charles VI — Charles VII	**Sicily-Naples**
Charles Emmanuel I	**Sardinia**
Charles Albert	**Bavaria**
Frederick William I	**Prussia**
Frederick Augustus I — Frederick Augustus II	**Saxony**
Simon van Slingelandt — Anthonie van der Helm	**Holland**
Mahmud I	**Turkey**
Charles VI	**Austria**
Abbas III — Nader Shah	**Persia**
Frederick I	**Sweden**
Augustus II the Strong — Augustus III	**Poland**
Anna Ivanovna	**Russia**
George II	**Great Britain**
Christian VI	**Denmark-Norway**
John V	**Portugal**
Philip V	**Spain**
Louis XV	**France**
Charles VI	**Holy Rom. Emp.**
Clement XII	**Papacy**
Yoshimune	**Japan**
Qing Yong Zheng — Qing Qian Long	**China**

1731	1732	1733	1734	1735	1736	1737	1738	1739	1740

AD 1741-1750

SWEDEN
ENGLAND

Italy was still a divided and ill-managed country. Benedict XIV, however, was a scholarly and enlightened pope who admired Montesquieu and Voltaire and did a great deal to promote agriculture and other industries in the Papal State.

In Charles VII's reign attempts were made in Naples and Sicily to reduce the privileges of the nobles as well as the power and wealth of the Church. At about this time Herculaneum was being uncovered and the Doric temples in Paestum were becoming renowned. Although Venice was in political decline her culture still flourished; Goldoni was writing his comedies and Canaletto painting his incomparable views of the city and its canals.

Montesquieu's *L'Esprit des lois* appeared in 1748. This work had great influence on European political theory.

When Charles VI died in 1740 Charles Albert of Bavaria claimed the Austrian crown. Frederick II of Prussia wanted Silesia, which belonged to Austria, and the French and Spanish Bourbons came to an agreement with Charles Albert and Frederick on the partitioning of the Danubian realm. The ensuing War of the Austrian Succession lasted for eight years; eventually the Prussians took Silesia while the Bavarian claims were rejected. Although Charles Albert of Bavaria became German emperor in 1742 – and was then known as Charles VII – he soon lost his own country, and when he died in 1745, Francis Stephen of Lorraine, husband of Maria Theresa, became emperor instead as Francis I.

The Swedish war with Russia in 1741, which ended disastrously for Sweden, was associated with the War of the Austrian Succession. The accession of Peter the Great's daughter, Elizabeth, in that same year, had major foreign political consequences. Sweden was granted a fairly lenient peace settlement, the condition being that Elizabeth's protegé sovereign bishop Adolf Frederick became successor to the Swedish throne.

In 1741 Vitus Bering completed his map of Siberia. In the same year Handel composed the *Messiah*. Celsius constructed his thermometer in 1742 and Franklin invented the lightning conductor ten years later. Swedenborg was writing and publishing his scientific and theological works in the 1740s and 1750s, at about the same time as Diderot, d'Alembert and other enlightened Frenchmen were compiling their famous encyclopaedia.

China was now at the peak of her power, both politically and culturally. The Mongols were totally subjugated and the princes of Ferghana and north-east Afghanistan paid tribute to Beijing (Peking). Burma became a Chinese tributory kingdom. Exports from Guangzhou (Canton) to western Europe were paid for in silver, one of the few things which the Chinese did not produce themselves.

In France Madame de Pompadour had been enjoying considerable influence since 1745.

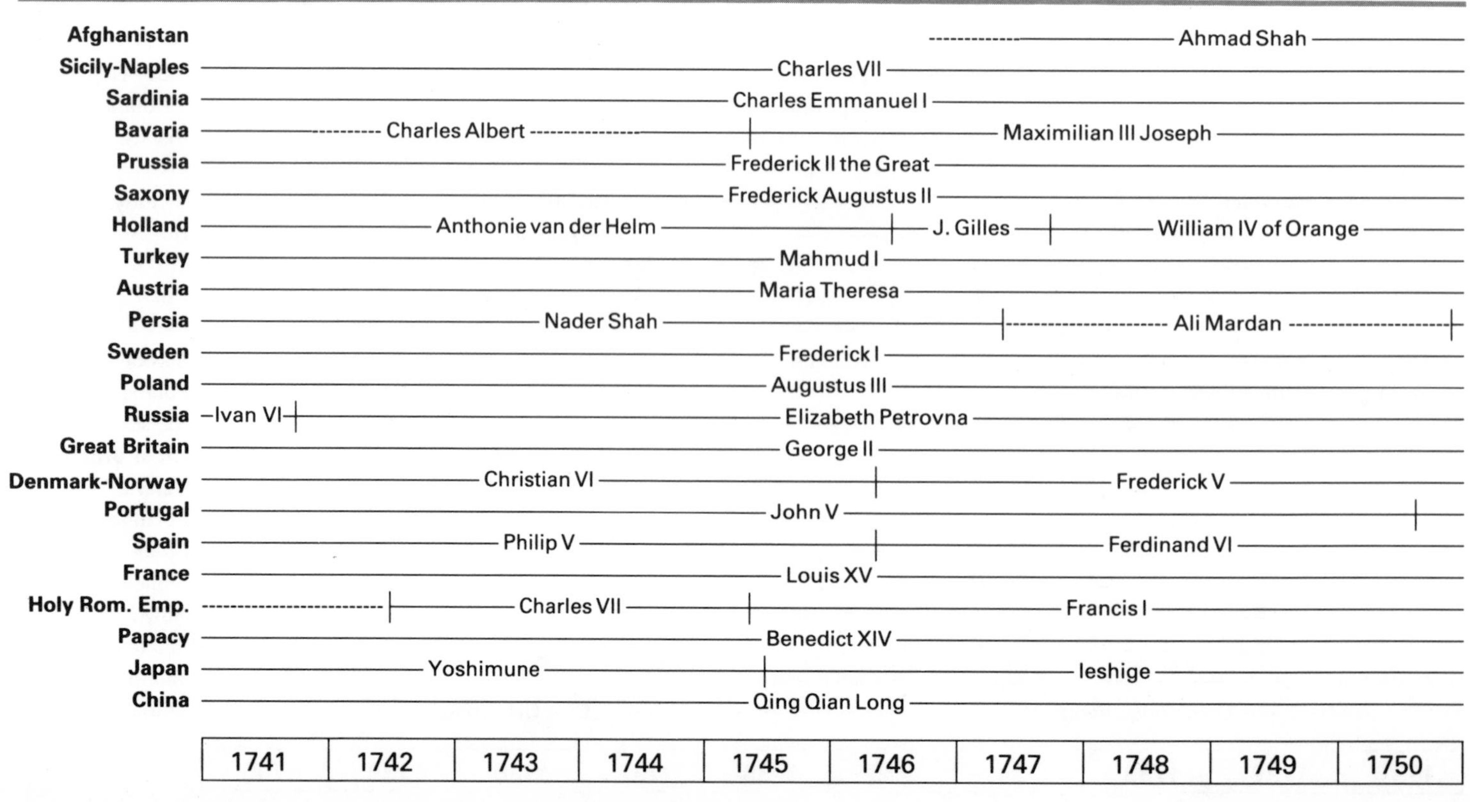
Afghanistan — Ahmad Shah
Sicily-Naples — Charles VII
Sardinia — Charles Emmanuel I
Bavaria — Charles Albert — Maximilian III Joseph
Prussia — Frederick II the Great
Saxony — Frederick Augustus II
Holland — Anthonie van der Helm — J. Gilles — William IV of Orange
Turkey — Mahmud I
Austria — Maria Theresa
Persia — Nader Shah — Ali Mardan
Sweden — Frederick I
Poland — Augustus III
Russia — Ivan VI — Elizabeth Petrovna
Great Britain — George II
Denmark-Norway — Christian VI — Frederick V
Portugal — John V
Spain — Philip V — Ferdinand VI
France — Louis XV
Holy Rom. Emp. — Charles VII — Francis I
Papacy — Benedict XIV
Japan — Yoshimune — Ieshige
China — Qing Qian Long
1741 1742 1743 1744 1745 1746 1747 1748 1749 1750

INDIA
SWEDEN
FRANCE
INDIA
AHMAD SHAH

In 1756 the Seven Years' War broke out in Europe between Austria, Russia, France, Sweden, Saxony, etc. on the one hand, Prussia, supported Britain, on the other and Prussia, thanks to military skill and a change of rulers in Russia at precisely the right time, dealt successfully with this formidable hostile alliance. More important than the battles in Europe were the overseas consequences of the war. Most of France's colonial possessions were taken over by Britain: Quebec fell in 1758, Montreal and the route to the Great Lakes in 1760, and Senegambia in West Africa in 1760. In India French colonial plans were ruined by the defeat at Plassey where the young Robert Clive, in the service of the East India Company, managed to defeat a far larger enemy force with the loss of only ten of his own soldiers.

Clive was the founder of British power in India. Titles and honours were heaped upon him but he was later accused of brutal behaviour, and subsequently committed suicide.

In Persia Nader Shah was assassinated by an Afghan officer named Ahmad Khan Abdali. Ahmad then created a kingdom in his own country and this initiated Afghanistan's history as an independent state. Ahmad also took Delhi, the Mogul emperor's capital, and fought bloody battles with Marathas and other Indian peoples, thereby exhausting both his own and their strength. This was the main reason why during the next few decades, the Europeans established themselves fairly easily in India.

In Persia, after the death of Nader, there was widespread anarchy and sporadic fighting among various potentates. Ali Mardan, who must be regarded as Nader's successor, enjoyed authority only in the capital, Isfahan.

The wealthy Jesuit Order was expelled from many countries during the course of the 18th century and was finally dissolved by the pope. This process began in South America where the Jesuits had Indian colonies which resisted Portuguese troops. The Portuguese government took advantage of this situation to confiscate all Jesuit property at home, to execute their leaders as heretics and to transport all the other Jesuits in Portugal to the Papal State. During the 1760s several countries undertook similar campaigns against the Jesuits.

In Russia capital punishment was generally replaced by deportation to Siberia from 1753 onwards. In 1751 negro slavery was abolished in Pennsylvania.

In the tenth edition of his *Systema natura*, Carl von Linne (Linnaeus) catalogued all the known flora and fauna, including mankind, with a family and species name in Latin, thereby bringing system and order into the vast multitude of living organisms.

Chippendale was making furniture in England during the 1750s.

Ahmad Shah	**Afghanistan**
Charles VII — Ferdinand IV	**Sicily-Naples**
Charles Emmanuel I	**Sardinia**
Maximilian III Joseph	**Bavaria**
Frederick II the Great	**Prussia**
Frederick Augustus II	**Saxony**
William V of Orange	**Holland**
Mahmud I — Osman III — Mustafa III	**Turkey**
Maria Theresa	**Austria**
Karim Khan	**Persia**
Adolf Frederick	**Sweden**
Augustus III	**Poland**
Elizabeth Petrovna	**Russia**
George II	**Great Britain**
Frederick V	**Denmark-Norway**
Joseph I	**Portugal**
Ferdinand VI — Charles III	**Spain**
Louis XV	**France**
Francis I	**Holy Rom. Emp.**
Benedict XIV — Clement XIII	**Papacy**
Ieshige	**Japan**
Qing Qian Long	**China**

1751	1752	1753	1754	1755	1756	1757	1758	1759	1760

ENGLAND
FRANCE

In 1769 the Frenchman Joseph Cugnot constructed a steam-powered vehicle. This had three wheels and reached a speed of about seven kilometres an hour.

Between 1769 and 1779 Captain James Cook made a number of voyages in the Pacific. He sighted the east coast of Australia in 1770 and landed at Botany Bay. He also discovered New Caledonia, Tonga, the Sandwich Islands and many other places. He was murdered by natives on Hawaii.

Karim Khan put an end to the anarchy in Persia. Karim was a Kurd from the Zend tribe and he managed to unite the country for a couple of decades, but when he died in 1779 it disintegrated once more.

Frederick Christian was an elector of Saxony, but only ruled for a few months in 1763.

The Franco-British colonial war ended in 1763 with the peace of Paris whereby Britain acquired Canada and Senegambia from France and Florida from Spain. But the British foothold elsewhere in North America was in jeopardy. The London government's centralistic policy and the duties it imposed on the colonies led to revolt, the Continental Congress and the War of Independence. On 4 July 1776 the thirteen United States issued their Declaration of Independence, which enunciated the principles of human rights.
In 1769 James Watt constructed a steam engine in which the steam was condensed in a special container rather than in a cylinder. This meant that the fuel consumption was halved. In the 1770s and later, Watt managed to attain a rotational movement with a crank and a kind of epicyclic gear. He had great influence on industrial development but was by no means the first man to construct a steam engine. An engine based on a model by Newcomen was already operating in 1728 at the Dannemora iron mines.

Louis XV, king of France for 59 years. Portrait by F.H. Drouaisse, Versailles.

Afghanistan	Ahmad Shah
Sicily-Naples	Ferdinand IV
Sardinia	Charles Emmanuel I
Bavaria	Maximilian III Joseph
Prussia	Frederick II the Great
Saxony	Frederick Augustus II — F.C. — Frederick Augustus III
Holland	William V
Turkey	Mustafa III
Austria	Maria Theresa
Persia	Karim Khan
Sweden	Adolf Frederick
Poland	Augustus III — ---- — Stanislaw August Poniatowski
Russia	Elizabeth — Peter III — Catherine II
Great Britain	George III
Denmark-Norway	Frederick V — Christian VII
Portugal	Joseph I
Spain	Charles III
France	Louis XV
Holy Rom. Emp.	Francis I — Joseph II
Papacy	Clement XIII — Clement XIV
Japan	Ieharu
China	Qing Qian Long

1761	1762	1763	1764	1765	1766	1767	1768	1769	1770

AD 1771-1780

NORTH
AMERICA
GERMANY

Gustav III brought about a coup d'etat in Sweden in 1772; the Age of Freedom constitution was abolished and more power was invested in the crown. The king was, however,unable to have people arrested at will, nor could he declare war on his own authority.

The first partition of Poland took place in 1772. The neighbouring countries of Prussia, Austria and Russia respectively acquired the West Prussian, Galician and White Russian regions.

Beaumarchais' *Le Mariage de Figaro* was publicly performed in 1778. This was revolutionary in that it ended happily for the servants at the expense of the masters.

Pedro III of Portugal was titular monarch, married to the legitimate queen, Maria I.

Independently of each other, Scheele and Priestley both discovered oxygen in 1771. Four years later Lavoisier clarified the process of combustion.

Galvani discovered electric current in 1780. He was an anatomist and happened to notice that newly prepared frogs' legs showed muscular contraction when connected by two metals in contact with each other. Galvani explained this as a demonstration of the frog's inherent life-force. In the following decade, however, his countryman, Volta, showed that there was quite another explanation.

Captain Cook is murdered on Hawaii. Painting in the National Maritime Museum, Greenwich, London.

New music: Rameau: *Abaris ou Les Boréales* (1764), Telemann: *Tag des Gerichts* (1762), C.P.E. Bach: *Sonaten für Klavier* (1763), Gluck: *Orpheus and Eurydice* (1762), *Alcestis* (1767), *Iphigenia in Aulis* (1764), Haydn: numerous string quartets and symphonies, for example the "Farewell" symphony (1772) and "La chasse" (1780), Mozart: *Bastien et Bastienne* (1768), numerous piano sonatas and the Symphony in D major.

New literature: Rousseau: *Contrat social* and *Emile* (both in 1762), Winckelmann: *Geschichte der Kunst des Altertums* (1764), Sterne: *Sentimental Journey* (1764), Goldsmith: *Vicar of Wakefield* (1765), Lessing: *Minna von Barnheim* (1763) and *Nathan der Weise* (1779), Goethe: *Goetz von Berlichingen* (1771) and *Leiden des jungen Werther* (1774), Schiller: *Die Räuber* (1779), Alfieri: *Filippo II* (1775).

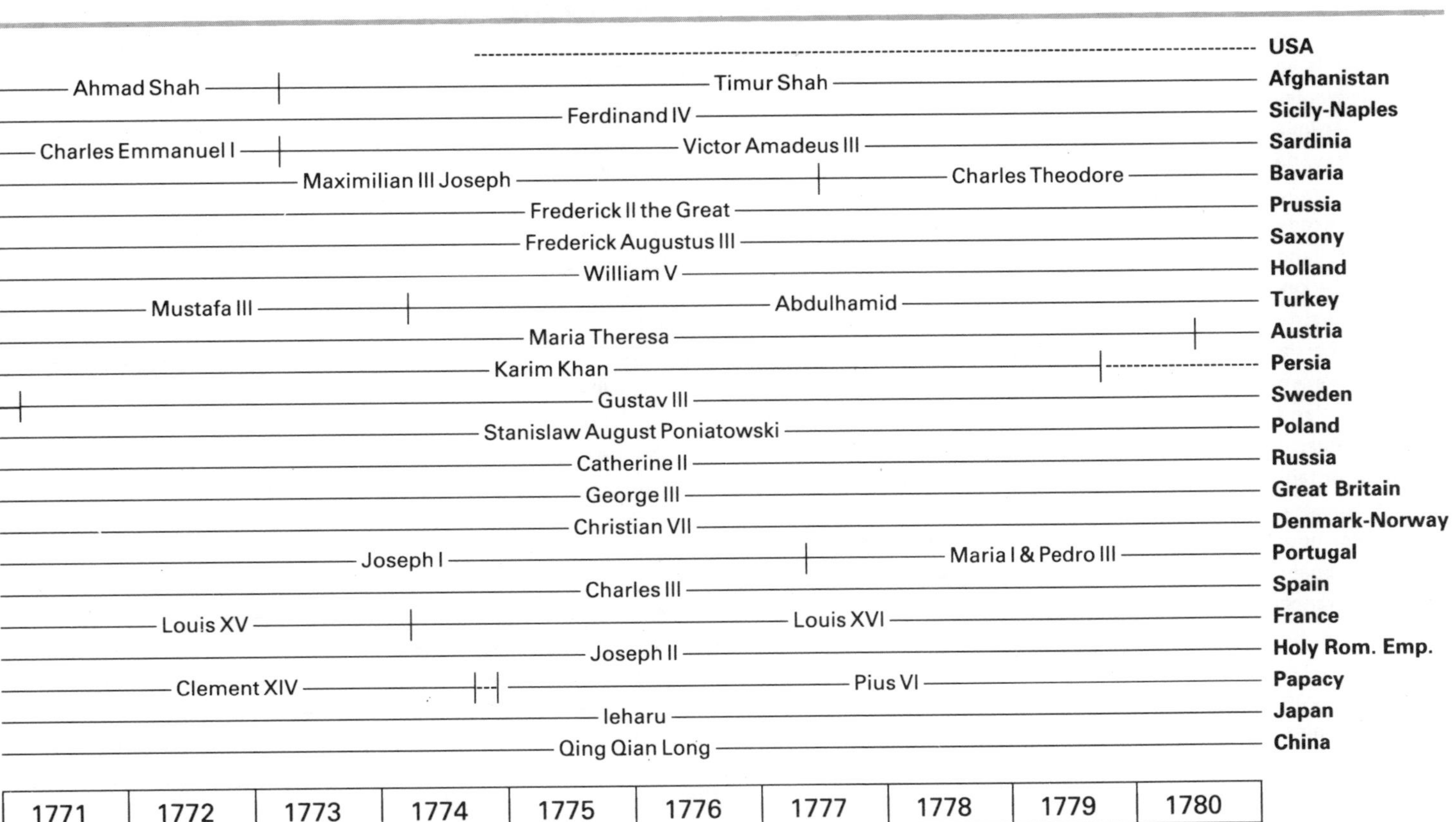
USA
Ahmad Shah
Timur Shah
Afghanistan
Ferdinand IV
Sicily-Naples
Charles Emmanuel I
Victor Amadeus III
Sardinia
Maximilian III Joseph
Charles Theodore
Bavaria
Frederick II the Great
Prussia
Frederick Augustus III
Saxony
William V
Holland
Mustafa III
Abdulhamid
Turkey
Maria Theresa
Austria
Karim Khan
Persia
Gustav III
Sweden
Stanislaw August Poniatowski
Poland
Catherine II
Russia
George III
Great Britain
Christian VII
Denmark-Norway
Joseph I
Maria I & Pedro III
Portugal
Charles III
Spain
Louis XV
Louis XVI
France
Joseph II
Holy Rom. Emp.
Clement XIV
Pius VI
Papacy
Ieharu
Japan
Qing Qian Long
China
1771
1772
1773
1774
1775
1776
1777
1778
1779
1780

AD 1781-1790

TURKEY
FRANCE

In their war with the rebellious United States in America the British mainly used German mercenaries who, after a number of defeats, notably Princeton and Saratoga, finally laid down their arms at Yorktown in 1781. French troops also took part in this war and on the American side, commanded by George Washington, there were several European celebrities, including La Fayette and the Polish national hero Kosciuszko. Among the prisoners at the Yorktown surrender was Gneisenau, the future organizer of the Prussian army.

The peace of Versailles was signed in 1783. By the terms of this treaty the British recognized the independence of the North American colonies and also returned Senegambia to France and Florida to Spain. The United States constitution was drawn up in 1787; this was the first democratic constitution in the modern sense of the term. The USA's first presidential election took place two years later.

Russia annexed the Crimea in 1783. The Russo-Turkish war ended in 1792 with the peace of Jassy. The stretch of territory between the Dniester and the Bug became Russian.

In Siam a new dynasty took power. Siam had been a Burmese tributary for a number of decades following internal conflicts.

The French Revolution was the major event in Europe in the late 18th century. This erupted in the summer of 1789 with the Tennis Court Oath declaring the National Assembly, followed by the storming of the Bastille on 14 July. In August, following the American model, the Declaration of the Rights of Man was proclaimed, demanding liberty, equality and fraternity. The properties of the Church and of the nobles who had fled the country were then confiscated. In 1791 the French National Assembly adopted a new measurement system. The length of a ten millionth of the Earth's quadrant was called a metre, and this was to form the basis of surface, volume and weight. Later it became apparent that the quadrant had been slightly underestimated, but the metre remained unchanged. A decimal system for time by creating a calendar with a ten-hour day and a ten-day week never gained acceptance.

Anarchy in Persia was terminated with the dynasty of Agha Mohammad Khan.

In Denmark, which was still an absolute monarchy despite the insanity of Christian VII, peasant serfdom was abolished in 1788. In Sweden, in the spring of 1789, Gustav III instigated his second revolution which gave him almost absolute authority.

Mozart presented *Le Nozze di Figaro* in 1785, *Don Giovanni* in 1787 and in the year of his death, 1790, *Die Zauberflöte*.

Siam	Rama I (Chao Phraya Chakkri)
USA	Washington
Afghanistan	Timur Shah
Sicily-Naples	Ferdinand IV
Sardinia	Victor Amadeus III
Bavaria	Charles Theodore
Prussia	Frederick II the Great; Frederick William II
Saxony	Frederick Augustus III
Holland	William V
Turkey	Abdulhamid I; Selim III
Austria	Joseph II
Persia	Ali Murad Shah; Jafar Shah; Lotf Ali Khan
Sweden	Gustav III
Poland	Stanislaw August Poniatowski
Russia	Catherine II
Great Britain	George III
Denmark-Norway	Christian VII; (Crown Prince Frederick)
Portugal	Maria I & Pedro III; Maria I
Spain	Charles III; Charles IV
France	Louis XVI
Holy Rom. Emp.	Joseph II
Papacy	Pius VI
Japan	Ieharu; Ienari
China	Qing Qian Long

1781	1782	1783	1784	1785	1786	1787	1788	1789	1790

FRANCE
ENGLAND
SPAIN

In 1791 the King and Queen of France attempted to escape abroad but they were seized and returned to Paris. Louis XVI was sentenced to death and guillotined on New Year's Day 1793. France was now at war with a coalition of foreign states and the reign of terror was in force. The newly invented guillotine was working unceasingly.

The reign of terror ended in France in 1794 when the revolutionary leader Robespierre and his adherents were overthrown and executed. In 1795 a new constitution was introduced whereby a Directory consisting of five individuals wielded executive power. Already, however, the most powerful man in the nation was the general, Napoleon Bonaparte, who had won the war in Italy. In 1798 Napoleon led an unsuccessful expedition to Egypt and Russian operations in Switzerland and an Anglo-Russian invasion of Holland also failed. In 1799 Napoleon was back in France where he established a military dictatorship and had himself elected first consul.

The French military campaigns against Austrians, Prussians and others were generally successful; the new military organization was based on national conscription providing an army of a million men, which for the moment was more than the enemy was able to mobilize. Hapsburg Belgium was conquered in 1793 and in 1794 the Netherlands were occupied and turned into the Batavian Republic. The Italian mainland was overrun during the 1790s and converted into a series of republics: the Cisalpine Republic with Milan as its capital, the Ligurian Republic around Genoa, the Parthenopean Republic around Naples and the Roman Republic where the pope was imprisoned and deprived of all his power. The French also appropriated Savoy and Nice. Entry into Austrian Carinthia resulted in the peace of Campo Formio in 1797 when the French frontier was moved out to the Rhine and the Austrians acquired Venice in exchange for Belgium and Milan. This marked the end of the 1000-year-old Venetian republic.

In 1793 and 1795 Poland was partitioned for the second and third time and thereby ceased to exist as an independent state. Nevertheless, the language and national spirit survived.

There was a rebellion against French rule in Haiti.

A British penal colony was established near Sydney in in Australia in 1798. Britain also took Ceylon from Holland.

Goethe and Schiller composed drama, Senefelder invented lithography. Volta described the nature of electricity and made batteries. Cartwright invented the power loom, and Malthus presented his gloomy theory on the population explosion. Other works appearing were Kant's *Kritik der reinen Vernuft* (1788) and Schelling's *Von der Weltseele* (1798).

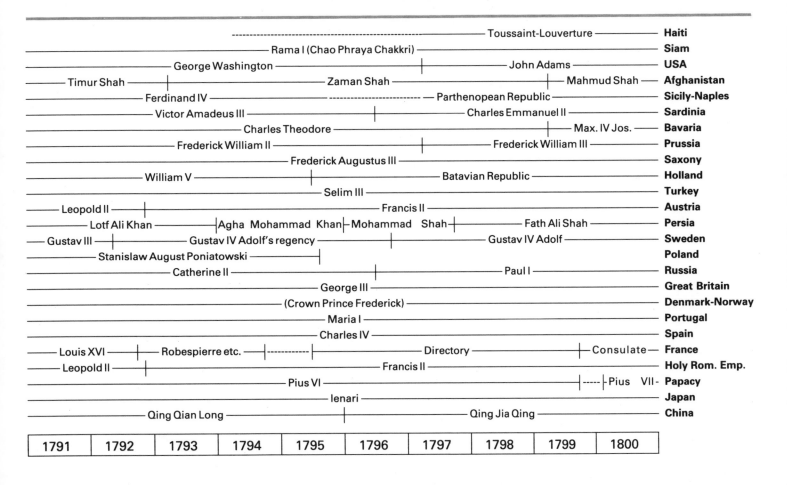

------ Toussaint-Louverture	**Haiti**
Rama I (Chao Phraya Chakkri)	**Siam**
George Washington | John Adams	**USA**
Timur Shah | Zaman Shah | Mahmud Shah	**Afghanistan**
Ferdinand IV ------ Parthenopean Republic	**Sicily-Naples**
Victor Amadeus III | Charles Emmanuel II	**Sardinia**
Charles Theodore | Max. IV Jos.	**Bavaria**
Frederick William II | Frederick William III	**Prussia**
Frederick Augustus III	**Saxony**
William V | Batavian Republic	**Holland**
Selim III	**Turkey**
Leopold II | Francis II	**Austria**
Lotf Ali Khan | Agha Mohammad Khan | Mohammad Shah | Fath Ali Shah	**Persia**
Gustav III | Gustav IV Adolf's regency | Gustav IV Adolf	**Sweden**
Stanislaw August Poniatowski |	**Poland**
Catherine II | Paul I	**Russia**
George III	**Great Britain**
(Crown Prince Frederick)	**Denmark-Norway**
Maria I	**Portugal**
Charles IV	**Spain**
Louis XVI | Robespierre etc. | ------ | Directory | Consulate	**France**
Leopold II | Francis II	**Holy Rom. Emp.**
Pius VI | ----- | Pius VII	**Papacy**
Ienari	**Japan**
Qing Qian Long | Qing Jia Qing	**China**

1791	1792	1793	1794	1795	1796	1797	1798	1799	1800

AD 1801-1810

FRANCE
NAPOLEON I
BAVARIA
AUSTRIA
SPAIN
RUSSIA
SWEDEN
PRUSSIA
ENGLAND

Napoleon made himself emperor in 1804, created 31 dukes, 451 counts and 1500 barons, besides placing his brothers and relatives on various thrones. Napoleon's victories and subsequent political arrangements resulted in tremendous changes in the map of Europe. The German empire was dissolved formally in 1806, whereupon Francis II became Francis I and called himself emperor of Austria instead. Liberal and nationalistic ideas gained ground through Napoleon's advances.

Toussaint-Louverture, who led the uprising on Haiti, was captured by the French, but his followers defeated an army sent there by Napoleon. The slaves were set free and the whites were killed or expelled. Two revolutionary leaders then successively made themselves emperor of the island.

In 1803 USA purchased Louisiana from France for fifteen million dollars, and in 1819 likewise bought Florida from Spain.

In the early 1880s, Mathew Flinders sailed completely round Australia, proving it to be one large land mass.

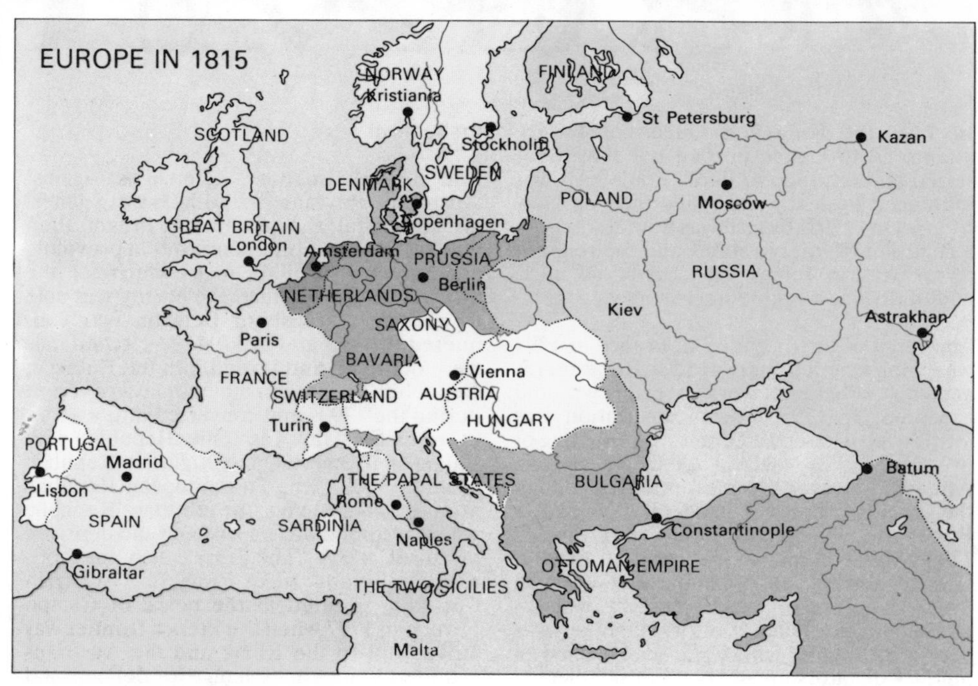

EUROPE IN 1815
NORWAY
Kristiania
FINLAND
St Petersburg
Kazan
SCOTLAND
Stockholm
SWEDEN
DENMARK
POLAND
Moscow
Copenhagen
GREAT BRITAIN
London
Amsterdam
PRUSSIA
Berlin
RUSSIA
NETHERLANDS
Kiev
SAXONY
Astrakhan
Paris
BAVARIA
Vienna
FRANCE
SWITZERLAND
AUSTRIA
HUNGARY
Turin
PORTUGAL
Madrid
Lisbon
THE PAPAL STATES
BULGARIA
Batum
Rome
SPAIN
SARDINIA
Constantinople
Naples
Gibraltar
OTTOMAN EMPIRE
THE TWO SICILIES
Malta

	1801–1810
Haiti	Louverture ┤ ------ ├ Jacques I ┤ Henry I
Siam	Rama I (Chao Phraya Chakkri) ┤ Rama II
USA	┤ Thomas Jefferson ┤ James Madison
Afghanistan	Mahmud Shah ┤ Shah Shoja ┤
Sicily	Ferdinand IV
Naples	Ferdinand IV ┤ Joseph Bonaparte ┤ Joachim Murat
Sardinia	Charles Emm. II ┤ Victor Emmanuel I
Bavaria	Maximilian IV Joseph
Prussia	Frederick William III
Saxony	Frederick Augustus III (I)
Holland	Batavian Republic ┤ Louis Napoleon ┤
Turkey	Selim III ┤ Mustafa IV ┤ Mahmud II
Austria	Francis II (I)
Persia	Fath Ali Shah
Sweden	Gustav IV Adolf ┤ Charles XIII
Russia	┤ Alexander I
Great Britain	George III
Denmark-Norway	Crown Prince Frederick ┤ Frederick VI
Portugal	Maria I
Spain	Charles IV ┤ Ferd. VII ┤ Joseph Bonaparte
France	Consulate ┤ Napoleon I
Holy Rom. Emp.	Francis II ┤
Papacy	Pius VII
Japan	Ienari
China	Qing Jia Qing

1801	1802	1803	1804	1805	1806	1807	1808	1809	1810

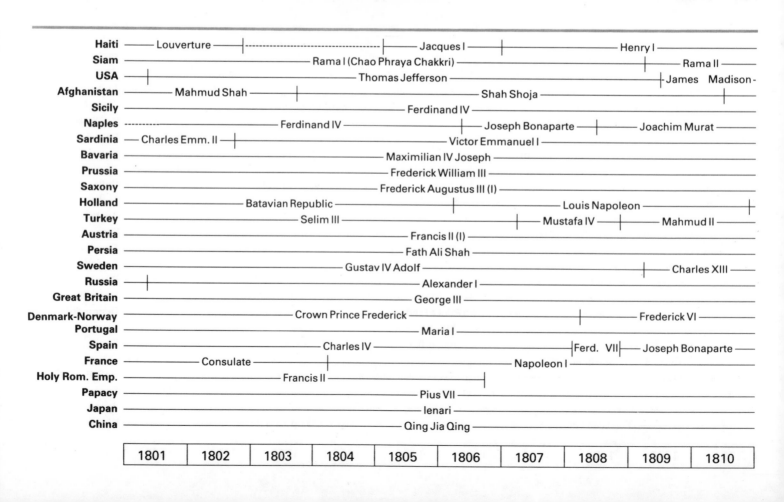

FRANCE
ENGLAND
JAPAN

A free Serbia began to emerge during internal rivalry between two patriot families. Karageorgeor George Petrovic Karageorgevic led the first insurrection against the Turks, Milos Obrenovic led the second.

The most important of the frontier changes surviving from the Napoleonic wars related to northern Europe. The Russians were Napoleon's allies in 1808-09 when they took Finland from Sweden and turned it into a grand duchy under the czar. Denmark, whose capital was bombarded by the British fleet, was thereby forced to side with Napoleon and thus lost Norway, long a Danish province, to Sweden. But the Napoleonic general, Bernadotte, who, oddly enough, had been elected king of Sweden in 1810, encountered strong opoosition from the Norwegians; they refused to accept the Swedish-Danish peace settlement and instead created their own constitution and elected their own king. Bernadotte found it wisest to compromise and the Swedish-Norwegian union of 1814 thus became little more than a formality.

The Spanish colonies in South America began to liberate themselves. In 1811 a junta proclaimed Paraguay independent and there was a similar uprising in Venezuela, though Spanish troops suppressed this rebellion in 1812. Simon Bolivar assembled an army in Haiti (where a native emperor had maintained his independence of France since 1804). Bolivar liberated the northern part of the continent and established the state of Colombia, which also embraced the future territories of Ecuador and Venezuela. In Argentina the war of liberation was led by a Spanish officer named San Martin, who helped a Chilean named O'Higgins to become dictator of Chile; and in 1820 the British adventurer Lord Cochrane transported troops to Peru, where San Martin joined up with Bolivar.

In 1816 Sicily and Naples were merged to form the kingdom of the Two Sicilies and the monarch, Ferdinand, changed his numerical title. There was the same type of numerical revision in Saxony and the Netherlands, both of which had become kingdoms in 1806.

In 1806 the British took the Cape Colony from the Dutch and in 1819 they established themselves in Singapore.

Beethoven composed symphonies, Schubert *lieder*. Goya portrayed the horrors of war. Grotefend deciphered cuneiform characters in 1802. Ampère distinguished between tension and current in 1820. Fulton's steamship set out in 1807 and Stephenson's locomotive ran in 1814. Ørsted discovered electro-magnetism in 1819 and Hahnemann advocated homeopathy in 1805. Berzelius's chemistry textbook appeared in 1808, the same year as the first part of Goethe's *Faust*. Rossini's *Il Barbiere di Siviglia* was completed in 1816 and Schopenhauer's main work was published in 1819.

Bernardo O' Higgins	**Chile**
Bolivar	**Gt. Colombia**
Karageorge – Milos Obrenovic	**Serbia**
Henry I	**Haiti**
Rama II	**Siam**
James Madison – James Monroe	**USA**
Mahmud Shah	**Afghanistan**
Ferdinand IV – Ferdinand I	**Sicily**
Joachim Murat – Ferdinand I	**Naples**
Victor Emmanuel I	**Sardinia**
Maximilian IV Joseph	**Bavaria**
Frederick William III	**Prussia**
Frederick Augustus I	**Saxony**
Napoleon I – William I	**Holland**
Mahmud II	**Turkey**
Francis I	**Austria**
Fath Ali Shah	**Persia**
Charles XIII – Charles XIV John	**Sweden**
Alexander I	**Russia**
George IV (Prince of Wales)	**Great Britain**
Frederick VI	**Denmark**
Maria I – John VI	**Portugal**
Joseph Bonaparte – Ferdinand VII	**Spain**
Napoleon I – Louis XVIII	**France**
Frederick VI – Charles XIII – Charles John	**Norway**
Pius VII	**Papacy**
Ienari	**Japan**
Qing Jia Qing	**China**

1811	1812	1813	1814	1815	1816	1817	1818	1819	1820

AD 1821-1830

MEXICO
NORTH AMERICA
MANDAN INDIANS

Peru became independent in 1821 and Bolivia separated from Peru in 1825. Uruguay became an independent state in 1828, following a war among the neighbouring states over her territory. Brazil achieved freedom in 1822 without a revolution. The Portuguese royal family, which fled to Brazil during the Napoleonic wars, was in no hurry to return home: John VI who became king of Portugal in 1816, finally returned in 1821, leaving his son Pedro in Brazil. Pedro then proclaimed himself constitutional emperor of a free Brazil when the politicians in Portugal attempted to assert their authority over his colony. Greater Colombia broke up during Bolivar's last years, when Venezuela and Ecuador both seceded. Francisco do Paula Santander became president of what remained in 1832. He is regarded as the creator of the new Colombia, but after his death in 1840 a major civil conflict erupted again.

The liberation of Mexico was a prolonged and terrible affair, involving decades of bloody guerrilla warfare between the various social classes and races. News then arrived of a military revolt in the mother country, Spain, where Ferdinand VII had been compelled to reinstate the liberal constitution from Napoleon's time. The conservative general, Iturbide, agreed with the leader of the insurgents to set up an independent Mexican kingdom ruled by a Spanish prince. In Madrid Ferdinand refused to accept this and Iturbide proclaimed himself Emperor Agustín I of Mexico in 1821. But he was forced to abdicate only two years later, after which Central America went its own way, broke with Mexico and formed a federal republic which was further subdivided into numerous small states in 1839.

There had been political strife in Afghanistan since 1818 when Mahmud Shah had lost all his provinces except Herat. However, he continued to reign until 1829. Independent power was wielded by various brothers of his dismissed vizier, Fath Ali; eventually one of them, Dost Mohammad, reunited the kingdom by force of arms. For a while Dost Mohammad was superseded by Shah Shoja, Majmud Shah's brother, who was supported by the British in India.

In 1822 philanthropic white Americans founded Monrovia, future capital of Liberia.

A conflict between the British, Argentinians and Brazilians led to the creation of the state of Uruguay in 1828.

Country	Rulers (1821–1830)
Brazil	Dom Pedro I
Mexico	Agustín I; Guadalupe Victoria; Guerrero
Argentina	Rivadavia; de Rosas
Venezuela	
Peru	Bolivar; José de Lamar
Bolivia	Antonio José de Sucre; A. Santa Cruz
Chile	Bernardo O' Higgins; Ramón Freire; Francisco Antonio Pinto
Colombia	Simón Bolivar
Serbia	Milos Obrenovic
Haiti	Jean-Pierre Boyer
Siam	Rama II; Rama III
USA	James Monroe; John Quincy Adams; Andrew Jackson
Afghanistan	
Two Sicilies	Ferdinand I; Francis I
Sardinia	Charles Felix
Bavaria	Maximilian IV Joseph; Louis I
Prussia	Frederick William III
Saxony	Frederick Augustus I; Antony I
Holland	William I
Turkey	Mahmud II
Austria	Francis I
Persia	Fath Ali Shah
Sweden-Norway	Charles John
Russia	Alexander I; Nicholas I
Great Britain	George IV
Denmark	Frederick VI
Portugal	John VI; Miguel I; John VI; P. IV; Maria da Gloria; Miguel I
Spain	Ferdinand VII
France	Louis XVIII; Charles X
Papacy	Pius VII; Leo XII; Pius VIII
Japan	Ienari
China	Qing Dao Guang

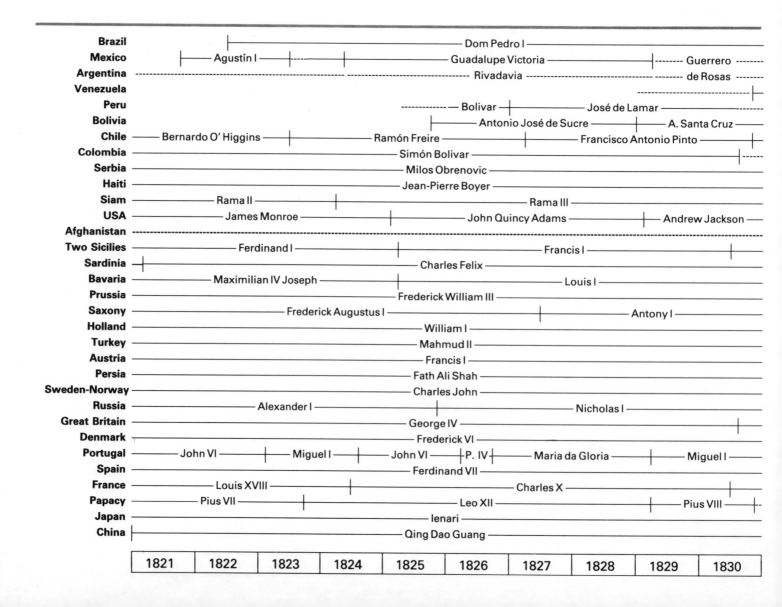

1821	1822	1823	1824	1825	1826	1827	1828	1829	1830

AD 1831-1840

GERMANY
ENGLAND
FRANCE
TURKEY

In France, as a result of the Revolution of July 1830, the Bourbons were deposed and a bourgeois kingdom was established under Louis-Philippe of Orléans. Inspired by this, Belgium, which had been united with Holland since the fall of Napoleon, now asserted her independence. Poland, which had enjoyed some autonomy in Napoleon's time, also rose in national revolt, but this was brutally suppressed by Russian military and police units, and Poland now became a Russian province.

Ferdinand VII of Spain, who with French aid had regained power in 1823, astonished the world in 1831 by introducing female succession so as to exclude his even more reactionary brother Don Carlos. The outcome of this was a terrible civil war that went on for years and had a lasting influence on Spanish politics. A similar though somewhat shorter conflict took place in Portugal at about the same time.

The Greek war of independence against Turkey began in 1821 and raged savagely for the rest of the decade. Following English, French and, in particular, Russian intervention the small kingdom of Greece was established in 1830. the Greeks themselves, whose leader Kapodistrias had been elected dictator in 1827, were not satisfied with this outcome.

Peru and Bolivia were united for a time under the same rule, but Chile divided them again by armed force in 1839.

In the famous locomotive race in 1829 Englishman George Stephenson's "Rocket" defeated Swedish John Ericsson's entry. The Manchester-Liverpool railway was opened in the following year.

Ohm's Law originated in 1827, aluminium was discovered in 1828, and the magnetic north pole in 1831. Liebig produced an artificial fertilizer in 1839 and the first postage stamp was issued in 1840. Daguerre began developing pictures in 1837. Victor Hugo wrote *Notre Dame de Paris* in 1831 and Dickens *Pickwick Papers* in 1836.

The game of football, which is said to have existed in England since the 12th century, was revived in 1831 at Eton and other British schools. It soon became popular all over the world.

Leopold I	**Belgium**
Otho I	**Greece**
Dom Pedro II	**Brazil**
Antonio López de Santa Ana	**Mexico**
Manuel de Rosas	**Argentina**
José Páez	**Venezuela**
Luis Orbegosa — Andrés Santa Cruz — Gamarra	**Peru**
Andrés Santa Cruz — J. Ballivián	**Bolivia**
Portales — Joaquín Prieto	**Chile**
Francisco de Paula Santander — José de Márquez	**Colombia**
Milos Obrenovic — Milan — Michael	**Serbia**
Jean-Pierre Boyer	**Haiti**
Rama III	**Siam**
Andrew Jackson — Martin Van Buren	**USA**
Dost Mohammad — Shah Shoja	**Afghanistan**
Ferdinand II	**Two Sicilies**
Charles Albert I	**Sardinia**
Louis I	**Bavaria**
Frederick William III	**Prussia**
Antony I — Frederick Augustus II	**Saxony**
William I	**Holland**
Mahmud II — Abdulmecid	**Turkey**
Francis I — Ferdinand I	**Austria**
Fath Ali Shah — Ali — Mohammad Shah	**Persia**
Charles John	**Sweden-Norway**
Nicholas I	**Russia**
William IV — Victoria	**Great Britain**
Frederick VI — Christian VIII	**Denmark**
Miguel I — Maria da Gloria	**Portugal**
Ferdinand VII — Isabella II	**Spain**
Louis-Philippe	**France**
Gregory XVI	**Papacy**
Ienari — Ieyoshi	**Japan**
Qing Dao Guang	**China**

1831	1832	1833	1834	1835	1836	1837	1838	1839	1840

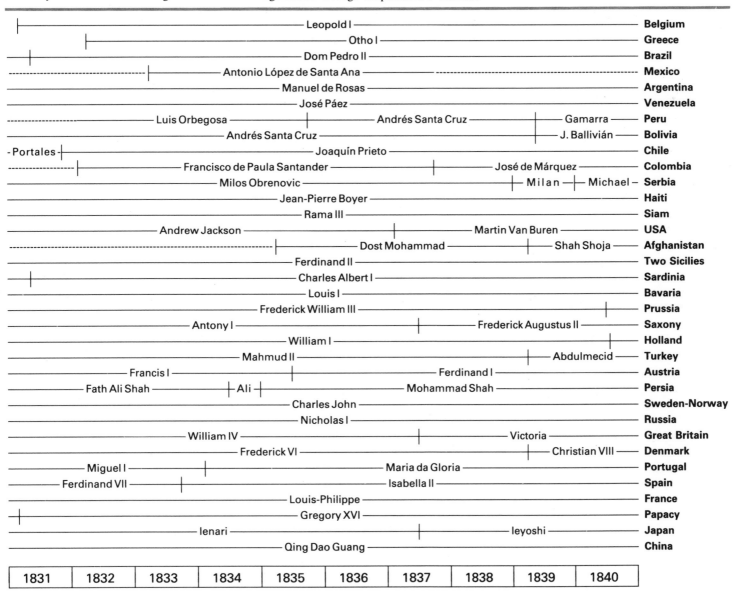

AD 1841-1850

SWEDEN
FRANCE
ENGLAND

In China Britain was victorious in the opium war of 1839-42, and in a further campaign in the 1850s Britain and France together opened up China for Western trade and virtually turned her into a colonial territory. At the same time the Russians took over the Amur province and founded Vladivostok.

In Africa in 1847 the state of Liberia was formed as a home for released American slaves. In South Africa the Boers, moving inland, founded the Orange Free State in 1842 and the Transvaal in 1853.

War broke out between Mexico and the USA when Texas was incorporated in the union. The USA now seized California, among other places. The Gold Rush began in 1850.

In the Revolution of February 1848 in France Louis-Philippe was dismissed; the president elect of the new republic was none less than Prince Louis Napoleon, who as early as 1852 made himself emperor. This revolution inspired uprisings in many other countries where the power of the monarchy was curtailed. Prussia thus acquired a new constitution with a certain degree of democratic representation. There was full-scale war in the Austrian empire where Czechs, Poles and Hungarians were fighting for their ideals. There was a new order in Switzerland, with a federal diet and a central government; and the canton of Neuchâtel was no longer attached to Prussia. In Denmark absolute monarchy was abolished through the 1849 constitution.

A US president named Henry Harrison came and went in the same year of 1841.

Santo Domingo had rebelled repeatedly against the state of Haiti on the same island and proclaimed its independence in 1844.

In 1845 there was terrible famine in Ireland when the potato crop failed.

The Crimean War took place in 1855-56. Russia gave up the Danube estuary. Romania emerged in 1859.

Prince Danilo of Montenegro was recognized in 1858. He was succeeded in 1860 by Nikita.

A cooperative consumers' association came into existence in the 1840s, together with Reuter's telegraphic agency and Cook's travel agency.

Karl Marx and Friedrich Engels published *Communist Manifesto,* the workers's Declaration of Independence, in 1847.

Country	Rulers 1841–1850
Belgium	Leopold I
Greece	Otho I
Brazil	Dom Pedro II
Mexico	de Santa Ana – de Santa Ana – Joaquín de Herrera
Argentina	Manuel de Rosas
Venezuela	José Páez – José Tadeo Monagas
Peru	– Ramón Castilla
Bolivia	José Ballivián – Manuel Belzú
Chile	Manuel Búlnes
Colombia	J. Márquez – Pedro Herrán – Tomás Mosquera – José López
Serbia	Michael Obr. – Alexander Karageorgevic
Haiti	J-P. Boyer – Faustin Soulouque – Faustin I
Siam	Rama III
USA	Har. – John Tyler – James Polk – Z. Taylor
Afghanistan	Shah Shoja – Dost Mohammad
Two Sicilies	Ferdinand II
Sardinia	Charles Albert I – Victor Emmanuel II
Bavaria	Louis I – Maximilian II
Prussia	Frederick William IV
Saxony	Frederick Augustus II
Holland	William II – William III
Turkey	Abdulmecid
Austria	Ferdinand I – Francis Joseph I
Persia	Mohammad Shah – Naser od-Din
Sweden-Norway	Charles John – Oscar I
Russia	Nicholas I
Great Britain	Victoria
Denmark	Christian VIII – Frederick VII
Portugal	Maria da Gloria
Spain	Isabella II
France	Louis-Philippe – Louis-Napoleon
Papacy	Gregory XVI – Pius IX
Japan	Ieyoshi
China	Qing Dao Guang

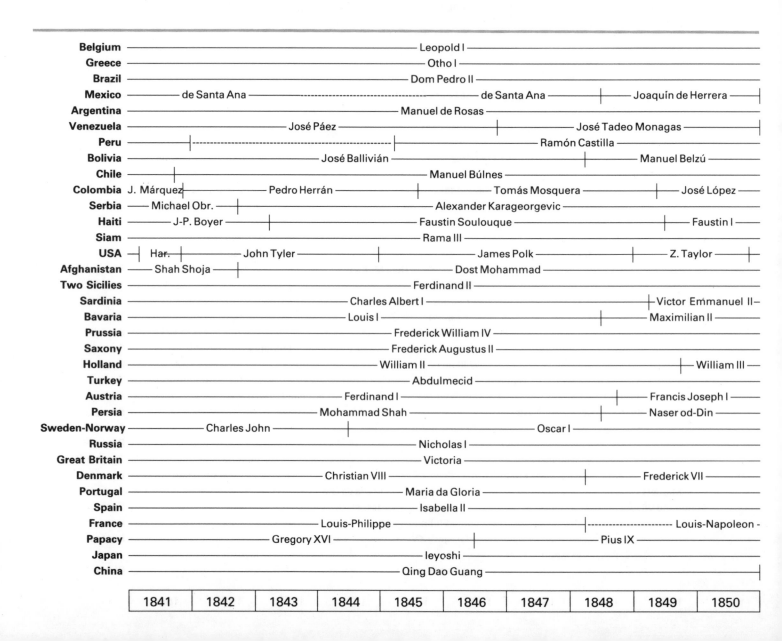

1841	1842	1843	1844	1845	1846	1847	1848	1849	1850

ENGLAND
FRANCE
ENGLAND

In Italy where the Sicilians had been in revolt since January 1848, the civil war in Austria encouraged Venice and Lombardy to rebel and King Charles Albert of Sardinia took the lead in an Italian war of independence. There was a revolution, too, in the Papal State; a republic was proclaimed and Pope Pius IX fled to the Neapolitan fortress of Gaeta. Pius was restored with French help in 1850. The northern Italians were quickly defeated and the revolution in the south was suppressed. It was Cavour, the premier of Sardinia, who finally engineered Italian unity. At the close of the 1850s this brilliant statesman persuaded Napoleon III to declare war on Austria and in the summer of 1859 Austria was defeated at the two bloody battles of Magenta and Solferino. The terrible spectacle of the Solferino battlefield inspired the Swiss philanthropist Jean Henri Dunant to create the Red Cross. France then concluded peace, handed over Lombardy to Sardinia, but appropriated Savoy and Nice, which caused great bitterness in Italy. It was now no longer possible to halt the movement for unification. Garibaldi landed in Sicily and overcame the kingdom of the Two Sicilies. Central Italy was likewise occupied, although French troops protected the pope.

Ethiopia, divided into numerous small states since 1706, was now unified by a bandit chieftain named Kassa. He had himself crowned king of kings under the name Tewodros (Theodor).

Algeria was now completely subjugated by France which was also undertaking the conquest of Morocco.

The first Atlantic cable was laid in 1858.

The Taiping uprising in China and the Sepoy rebellion, or Indian Mutiny, were both suppressed. In 1854 a US naval force compelled Japan to open its ports to trade.

New literature: Gogol's *Dead Souls* (1842), Dumas the Elder's *The Three Musketeers* (1844), Dumas the Younger's *La Dame aux Camélias* (1848), Harriet Stowe's *Uncle Tom's Cabin* (1852), Flaubert's *Madame Bovary* (1857), and Baudelaire's *Les Fleurs du mal* (1857).

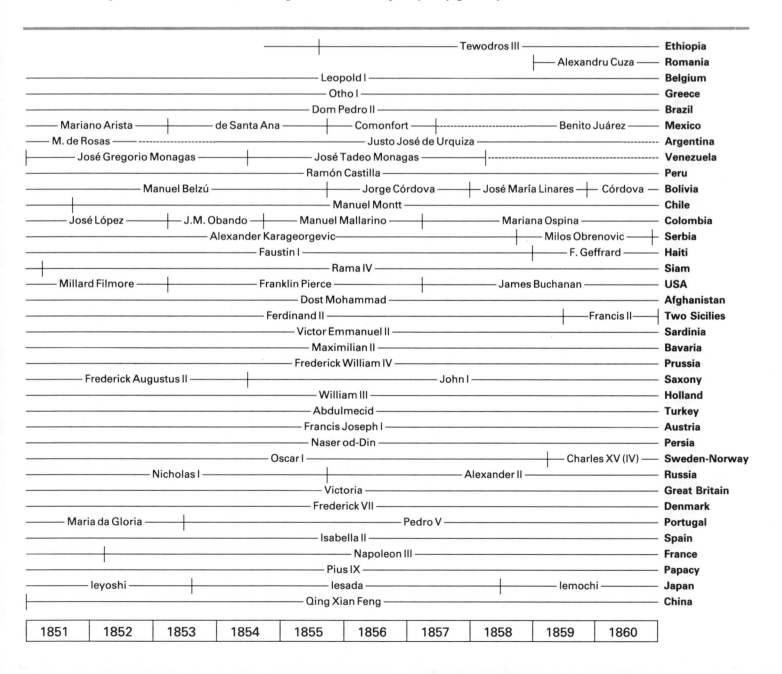

Rulers	Country
Tewodros III	Ethiopia
Alexandru Cuza	Romania
Leopold I	Belgium
Otho I	Greece
Dom Pedro II	Brazil
Mariano Arista — de Santa Ana — Comonfort — Benito Juárez	Mexico
M. de Rosas — Justo José de Urquiza	Argentina
José Gregorio Monagas — José Tadeo Monagas	Venezuela
Ramón Castilla	Peru
Manuel Belzú — Jorge Córdova — José María Linares — Córdova	Bolivia
Manuel Montt	Chile
José López — J.M. Obando — Manuel Mallarino — Mariana Ospina	Colombia
Alexander Karageorgevic — Milos Obrenovic	Serbia
Faustin I — F. Geffrard	Haiti
Rama IV	Siam
Millard Filmore — Franklin Pierce — James Buchanan	USA
Dost Mohammad	Afghanistan
Ferdinand II — Francis II	Two Sicilies
Victor Emmanuel II	Sardinia
Maximilian II	Bavaria
Frederick William IV	Prussia
Frederick Augustus II — John I	Saxony
William III	Holland
Abdulmecid	Turkey
Francis Joseph I	Austria
Naser od-Din	Persia
Oscar I — Charles XV (IV)	Sweden-Norway
Nicholas I — Alexander II	Russia
Victoria	Great Britain
Frederick VII	Denmark
Maria da Gloria — Pedro V	Portugal
Isabella II	Spain
Napoleon III	France
Pius IX	Papacy
Ieyoshi — Iesada — Iemochi	Japan
Qing Xian Feng	China

1851	1852	1853	1854	1855	1856	1857	1858	1859	1860

AD 1861-1870

FRANCE
USA
PRUSSIA
DENMARK
FRANCE
ENGLAND

Serfdom was abolished in Russia in 1861.

The dogma of the infallibility of the pope was proclaimed in 1870.

The republics of Haiti and Santo Domingo were confused and unstable.

The American civil war (1861-65) was fought between the northern states and the slave-holding southern states. Victory for the North meant the survival of the union and the formal abolishment of slavery. President Lincoln was assassinated by a Southerner while the war was still in progress. In 1867 the USA enlarged her territory by buying Alaska from Russia for a pittance.

Revolution, directed almost personally at the queen, broke out in Spain in 1869. Don Carlos was still alive and his Basque supporters soon joined the movement, yet amid tremendous turmoil an Italian was briefly elected king. A republic was then proclaimed, but after further unrest and violence Isabella's son was put on the Spanish throne.

In Prussia Bismarck became minister-president in 1862. In 1863 he concluded a friendship pact with the Russians who were suppressing an uprising in Poland. In 1864 Prussia declared war on Denmark and took Schleswig-Holstein. This was followed by the Austro-Prussian war of 1866 after which Prussia annexed the losing lands. Italy, Prussia's ally, took Venice and four years later Rome as well, which the French fled. The time was ripe in 1870 for the Franco-Prussian war, the southern German states supporting Prussia. This was disastrous for France. Napoleon and his entire army were captured and in 1871 the German empire was proclaimed with Prussia's king, William, as emperor. In the peace settlement Germany appropriated Alsace-Lorraine.

New literature: Hugo's *Les Misérables* (1862), Carroll's *Alice in Wonderland* (1865), Ibsen's *Brand* (1866), Verne's *From the Earth to the Moon* (1866), Tolstoy's *War and Peace* (1869), Twain's *Tom Sawyer* (1876), Dostoyevsky's *The Brothers Karamazov* (1879).

Ethiopia	Tewodros III
Romania	Alexandru Cuza — Carol I
Belgium	Leopold I — Leopold II
Greece	Otho I — George I
Brazil	Dom Pedro II
Mexico	Benito Juárez — Maximilian I — Juárez
Argentina	Bartolomé Mitre — Domingo Sarmiento
Venezuela	José Páez — Juan Falcón
Peru	R. Castilla — Juan Antonio Pezet — Mariano Prado — Campero — José Balta
Bolivia	José de Achá — Mariano Melgarejo
Chile	José Joaquin Pérez
Colombia	Tomás Mosquera
Serbia	Michael Obrenovic — Milan II Obrenovic
Haiti	Fabre Geffrard
Siam	Rama IV — Rama V
USA	Abraham Lincoln — Andrew Jackson — Ulysses Grant
Afghanistan	Dost Mohammad — Shir Ali
Italy	Victor Emmanuel II
Bavaria	Maximilian II — Louis II
Prussia	William I
Saxony	John I
Holland	William III
Turkey	Abdulaziz
Austria	Francis Joseph I
Persia	Naser od-Din
Sweden-Norway	Charles XV
Russia	Alexander II
Great Britain	Victoria
Denmark	Frederick VII — Christian IX
Portugal	Luis I
Spain	Isabella II — Francisco Serrano
France	Napoleon III
Papacy	Pius IX
Japan	Iemochi — Hitotsubashi Keiki — Mutsuhito
China	Qing Tong Zhi

1861	1862	1863	1864	1865	1866	1867	1868	1869	1870

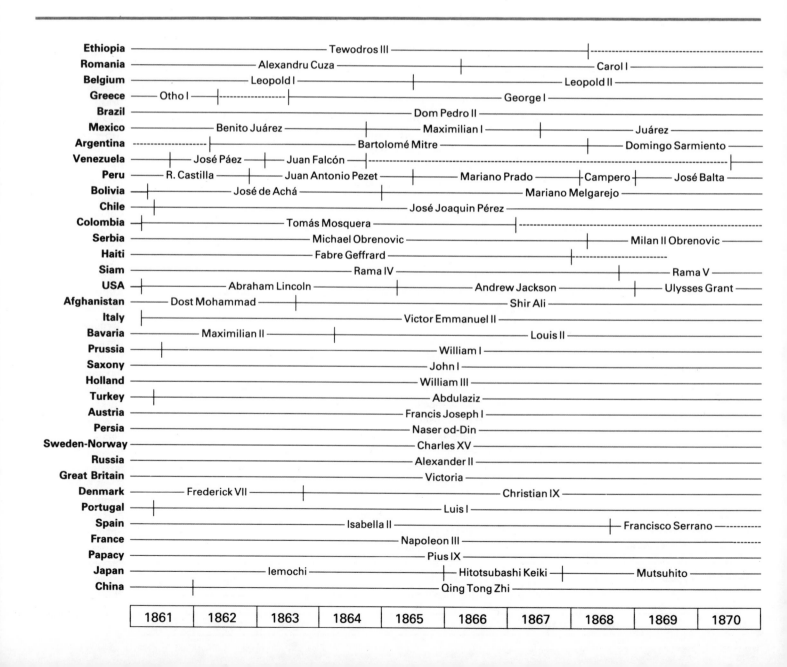

AD 1871-1880

USA
GERMANY
ENGLAND

A socialist revolution broke out in Paris in the spring of 1871 and was put down by government troops. There were terrible crimes on both sides during and after the second Paris Commune.

In 1876 Queen Victoria was proclaimed empress of India. In 1877 the Boer republic of Transvaal was occupied by the British, and the Zulu War took place in the same year.

A Bulgarian state emerged from a Russian-Turkish war on the Balkan peninsula in 1877-78. A Congress of the major powers in Berlin drew up a peace settlement whereby the Russians acquired Bessarabia and part of Armenia from Turkey. Britain now seized the opportunity to take Cyprus while Austria took Bosnia and Herzegovina.

The so-called Saltpetre War was fought between Chile and Bolivia in 1879-83 and as a result Bolivia lost its entire coastline.

Political conditions in Colombia were chaotic and there was practically no national unity for well over a decade.

The last of Japan's shoguns was ousted in 1876 and the mikado instead assumed central power. Mutsuhito, who now became emperor, was only fourteen years old. During his reign Japan evolved from a medieval samurai state into a capitalist industrial nation.

In 1878-79 the British fought their second Afghan war. Ya'qub abdicated and submitted, but his brother Abdorrahman returned from Russia and assumed control. During his long reign the two big powers were balanced off against each other and Afghanistan managed to retain its independence.

Pasteur and Koch developed the science of bacteriology.

In 1875 England bought a majority of the shares in the Suez Canal, completed in 1869.

The Universal Postal Union was established in 1874. The phonograph was invented in 1877. In 1879 Edison's electric lamp lit up and Siemens' electric tram began running.

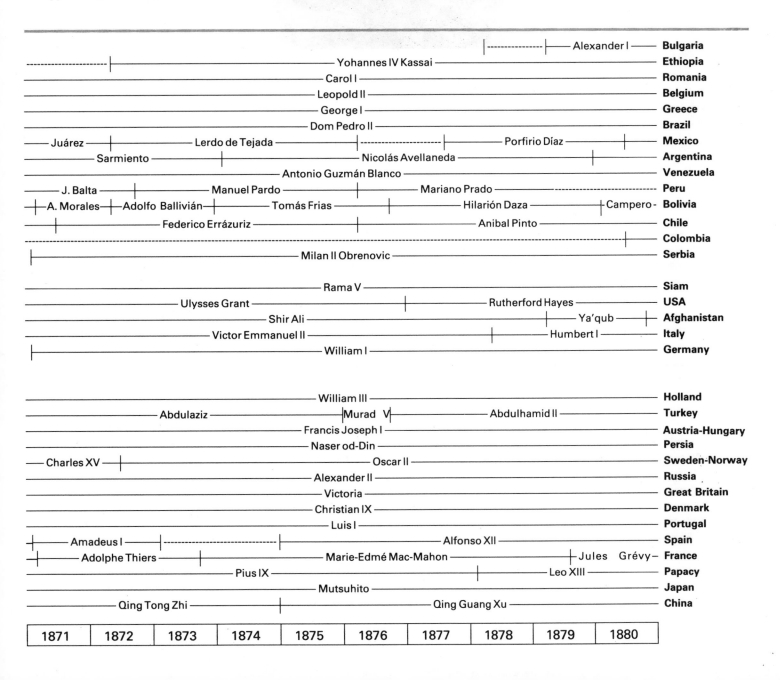

Alexander I	**Bulgaria**
Yohannes IV Kassai	**Ethiopia**
Carol I	**Romania**
Leopold II	**Belgium**
George I	**Greece**
Dom Pedro II	**Brazil**
Juárez — Lerdo de Tejada — Porfirio Díaz	**Mexico**
Sarmiento — Nicolás Avellaneda	**Argentina**
Antonio Guzmán Blanco	**Venezuela**
J. Balta — Manuel Pardo — Mariano Prado	**Peru**
A. Morales — Adolfo Ballivián — Tomás Frias — Hilarión Daza — Campero	**Bolivia**
Federico Errázuriz — Anibal Pinto	**Chile**
	Colombia
Milan II Obrenovic	**Serbia**
Rama V	**Siam**
Ulysses Grant — Rutherford Hayes	**USA**
Shir Ali — Ya'qub	**Afghanistan**
Victor Emmanuel II — Humbert I	**Italy**
William I	**Germany**
William III	**Holland**
Abdulaziz — Murad V — Abdulhamid II	**Turkey**
Francis Joseph I	**Austria-Hungary**
Naser od-Din	**Persia**
Charles XV — Oscar II	**Sweden-Norway**
Alexander II	**Russia**
Victoria	**Great Britain**
Christian IX	**Denmark**
Luis I	**Portugal**
Amadeus I — Alfonso XII	**Spain**
Adolphe Thiers — Marie-Edmé Mac-Mahon — Jules Grévy	**France**
Pius IX — Leo XIII	**Papacy**
Mutsuhito	**Japan**
Qing Tong Zhi — Qing Guang Xu	**China**

1871	1872	1873	1874	1875	1876	1877	1878	1879	1880

AD 1881-1890

ENGLAND
GERMANY

The policy of imperialism continued. Tunisia went to France in 1881, Egypt to Britain in 1882, the Cameroons and South-west Africa to Germany in 1884 and Eritrea to Italy in the late 1880s. Burma became British in 1885 and Japan seized Formosa, among other territories, from China in 1895. The death of General Gordon at Khartoum was avenged through the Sudan War of 1897-98 and as a result Equatorial Africa became a British colony. Italy made an unsuccessful attempt to appropriate Abyssinia in 1894-96 while the French acquired Madagascar and strengthened their Indo-China protectorate.

Alfonso XIII was born after the death of his father Alfonso XII. His mother, Maria Christina, headed the regency.

Serbia became a kingdom in 1882 whereupon Milan II Obrenovic called himself Milan I.

1837
1887
VR

The causes of consumption and diphtheria were discovered, and there was some understanding of the function of vitamins.

The St Gotthard tunnel was opened in 1881. In 1882 Koch isolated the tuberculosis bacillus and in 1883 Daimler designed a motor-car. Edison made his film camera in 1891 and Röntgen discovered his X-ray in 1895. Marconi transmitted a wireless signal in 1897 and the freewheel hub for velocipedes was devised in 1898.

New literature: Nietzche's *Also sprach Zarathustra* (1883), Strindberg's *Giftas* (1884), Samenhof's *Text book in Esperanto* (1887), Selma Lagerlöf's *Gösta Berlings Saga* (1891), Kipling's *Jungle Book* (1894).

Queen Victoria, Empress of India.

Country	Rulers (1881–1890)
Bulgaria	Alexander I — Ferdinand I
Romania	Carol I
Ethiopia	Yohannes IV Kassai
Belgium	Leopold II
Greece	George I
Brazil	Dom Pedro II — Deodoro da Fonseca -
Mexico	Gonzalez — Porfirio Díaz
Argentina	Julio Roca — M. Juárez Celmán —
Venezuela	Antonio Guzmán Blanco — Hermógenes López — Rojas Paúl —
Peru	Miguel Iglesias — Andres Cáceres —
Bolivia	Narciso Campero — Aniceto Arce
Chile	— Domingo Santa María — José Manuel Balmaceda
Colombia	R. Núñez — F.J. Zaldúa — Rafael Núñez
Serbia	Milan Obrenovic — Milan I — Alexander I
Siam	Rama V
USA	Garfield — Chester Arthur — Grover Cleveland — B. Harrison
Afghanistan	Abdorrahman
Italy	Humbert I
Germany	William I — Freder. III — William II
Holland	William III —
Turkey	Abdulhamid II
	Francis Joseph I
Persia	Naser od-Din
Sweden-Norway	Oscar II
Russia	— Alexander III
Great Britain	Victoria
Denmark	Christian IX
Portugal	Luis I — Carlos I
Spain	Alfonso XII — Maria Christina
France	Jules Grévy — Sadi Carnot
Papacy	Leo XIII
Japan	Mutsuhito
China	Qing Guang Xu

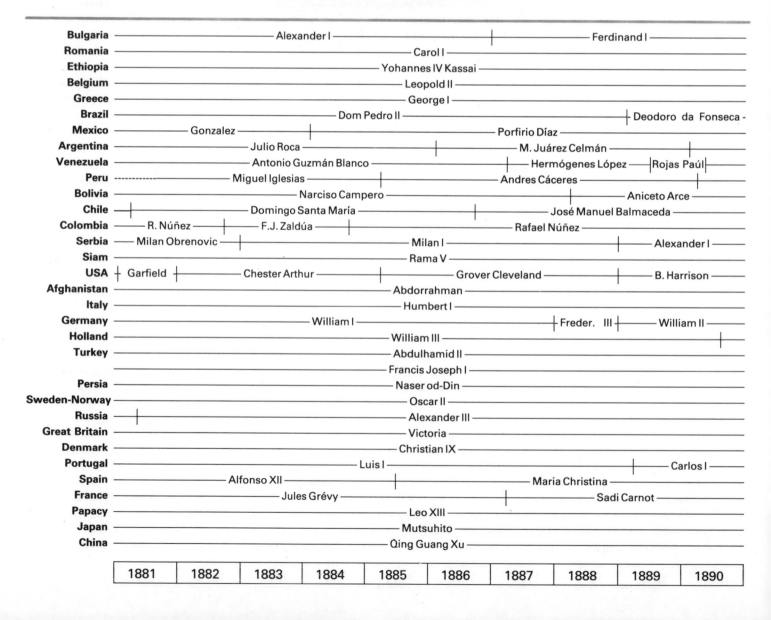

1881	1882	1883	1884	1885	1886	1887	1888	1889	1890

ENGLAND
CHINA
FRANCE
ENGLAND

In 1898 the Confucian Utopian, Kang Youwei, became adviser to the young emperor Guang Xu and set about reforming a disorganized China. He encountered opposition from the conservative officials and especially from the old dowager empress Zu Xi, who initiated a revolution which threw out the government and imprisoned the emperor. The latter was thereafter treated with extreme contempt and Zu Xi, who had previously ruled as his guardian, resumed authority. With or without her approval, there now emerged in China a secret organization named Yihequan, known to the West as the Boxers. This group was responsible for many atrocities against Christian Chinese and foreign missionaries and in the end they attacked the foreign legations in Beijing, besieging and bombarding them for several months. Aninternational army went to the legations' relief in the late summer of 1900, whereupon the old empress and her court fled westward and all the responsible dignitaries committed suicide. The Russians took advantage of this opportunity to occupy Manchuria but this created a conflict with Japan and Britain.

The Spanish-American war broke out in 1898 and resulted in Cuba's formal independence and the acquisition by the USA of the Philippines and Hawaii. In Africa the Boer War began in 1899.

The Olympic Games were resumed in 1896. This year they were held in Athens, though there were not many competitors. A group of American students won most of the events.

An unknown Austrian monk named Gregor Mendel died in 1884. But his discoveries in genetics were to be of immense importance in the following century.

With the invention of the paraffin lamp, oil became an international commodity. In the USA, Standard Oil was established by Rockefeller as early as 1870, and this quickly made him a millionaire.

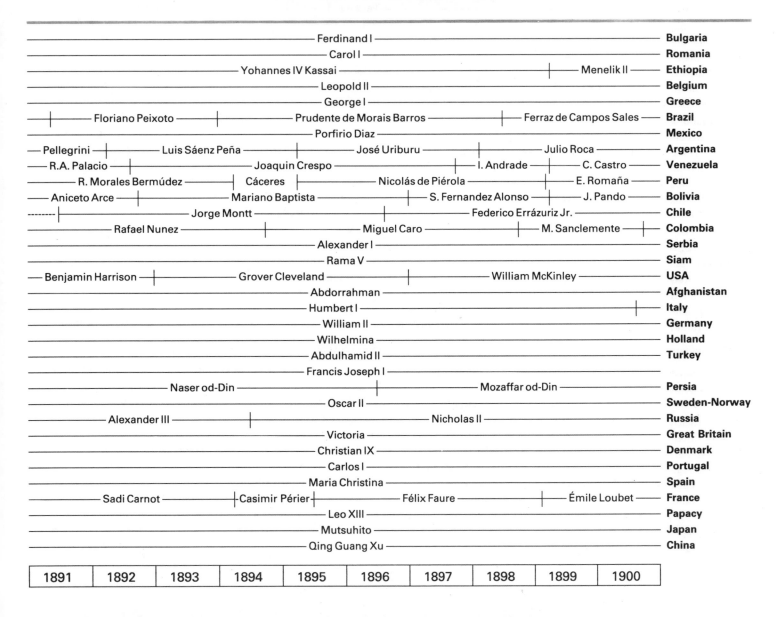

Bulgaria	Ferdinand I
Romania	Carol I
Ethiopia	Yohannes IV Kassai – Menelik II
Belgium	Leopold II
Greece	George I
Brazil	Floriano Peixoto – Prudente de Morais Barros – Ferraz de Campos Sales
Mexico	Porfirio Diaz
Argentina	Pellegrini – Luis Sáenz Peña – José Uriburu – Julio Roca
Venezuela	R.A. Palacio – Joaquin Crespo – I. Andrade – C. Castro
Peru	R. Morales Bermúdez – Cáceres – Nicolás de Piérola – E. Romaña
Bolivia	Aniceto Arce – Mariano Baptista – S. Fernandez Alonso – J. Pando
Chile	Jorge Montt – Federico Errázuriz Jr.
Colombia	Rafael Nunez – Miguel Caro – M. Sanclemente
Serbia	Alexander I
Siam	Rama V
USA	Benjamin Harrison – Grover Cleveland – William McKinley
Afghanistan	Abdorrahman
Italy	Humbert I
Germany	William II
Holland	Wilhelmina
Turkey	Abdulhamid II
	Francis Joseph I
Persia	Naser od-Din – Mozaffar od-Din
Sweden-Norway	Oscar II
Russia	Alexander III – Nicholas II
Great Britain	Victoria
Denmark	Christian IX
Portugal	Carlos I
Spain	Maria Christina
France	Sadi Carnot – Casimir Périer – Félix Faure – Émile Loubet
Papacy	Leo XIII
Japan	Mutsuhito
China	Qing Guang Xu

1891	1892	1893	1894	1895	1896	1897	1898	1899	1900

AD 1901-1910

ENGLAND
FRANCE
SWEDEN

Although Britain won the Boer War at the turn of the century, the Boers obtained local self-government and established Afrikaans as the official language. The Union of South Africa was formed in 1910 and was granted dominion status. This had already been granted to Australia, New Zealand and Newfoundland in 1901, and to Canada in 1867.

As a result of the Russian-Japanese war in 1904-05, Russia withdrew from Manchuria. Korea became a Japanese province in 1910.

Cuba secured formal independence in 1902 after North American military rule. During the period 1906-08, however, the island was again under American administration.

Congo became a Belgian colony in 1908.

Portugal abolished the monarchy in 1910.

Italy took Libya from the Turks in 1912 and at the same time Turkey lost most of its European territories to Greece and Bulgaria. The Serbs beat the Bulgarians but the new state of Albania emerged in 1913 because Austria wished to block Serbia's access to the sea. A few months later, in June 1914, Archduke Ferdinand was assassinated in Sarajevo. Austria's declaration of war on Serbia in July put the European alliance system to the test and precipitated World War I. This lasted from 1914-18 and changed Europe immensely.

In the wake of the Great War there was revolution in Russia, which was thereby transformed into the Soviet Union. A number of individual states now emerged. Serbia expanded to become Yugoslavia, Romania was enlarged, Germany dwindled and the Danube monarchy and the Turkish empire were split up.

In 1905 Einstein published his relativity theory. The cinema industry was established in Hollywood in 1910. Cosmic radiation was discovered in 1912. Rutherford's model atom was presented in 1911 and Bohr's atomic theory in 1913. The first radio broadcasting station opened in Pittsburgh in 1920.

Cuba	Tomás Estrada Palma — José M. Gómez
Bulgaria	Ferdinand I
Romania	Carol I
Ethiopia	Menelik II
Belgium	Leopold II — Albert I
Greece	George I
Brazil	Campos Sales — Rodigues Alves — Affonso Pena — Nilo Peçanha
Mexico	Porfirio Díaz
Argentina	Julio Roca — M. Quintana — Figueroa Alcorta
Venezuela	Cipriano Castro — J.V. Gómez
Peru	Eduardo de Romaña — M. Candano — José Pardo y Barreda — Augustus Leguia
Bolivia	José Pando — Ismael Montes — E. Villazón
Chile	Germán Riesco — Pedro Montt
Colombia	José Marraquín — Rafael Reyes — I.C. Restrepo
Serbia	Alexander I — Peter I Karageorgevic
Siam	Rama V
USA	Theodore Roosevelt — William Taft
Afghanistan	Habibollah
Italy	Victor Emmanuel III
Germany	William II
Holland	Wilhelmina
Turkey	Abdulhamid II — Mehmed V
Austria-Hungary	Francis Joseph I
Persia	Mozaffar od-Din — Mohammad Ali — Ahmad Mirza
Norway	Oscar II — Haakon VII
Sweden	Oscar II — Gustav V
Russia	Nicholas II
Great Britain	Edward VII
Denmark	Christian IX — Frederick VIII
Portugal	Carlos I — Manuel II
Spain	Maria Christina — Alfonso XIII
France	Émile Loubet — Armand Fallières
Papacy	Leo XIII — Pius X
Japan	Mutsuhito
China	Qing Guang Xu — Qing Xuan Tong

1901	1902	1903	1904	1905	1906	1907	1908	1909	1910

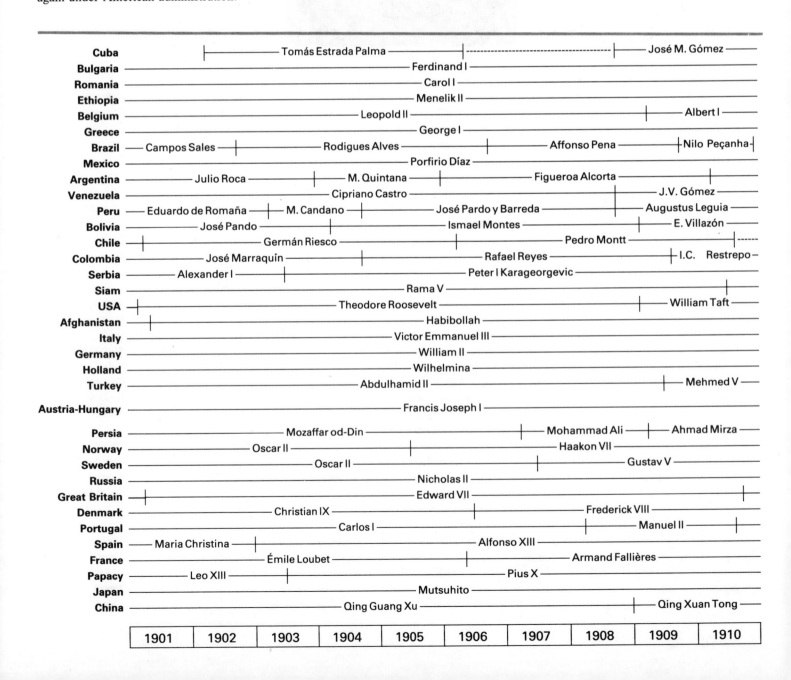

ENGLAND
SWEDEN
USA

The last Manchurian emperor in China was deposed in 1911 and a republic was proclaimed. General Yuan Shikai, who became president, made himself emperor in 1916 but was deposed in the same year. China was divided into two realms, the southern one being the more stable. This was governed by Sun Yat-sen, the founder of the national Kuomintang party.

In 1909 Peary reached the North Pole, while Amundsen got to the South Pole two years later. The Panama Canal was completed in 1913 after the state of Panama had been detached from Colombia.

The League of Nations was formed in 1919 on the initiative of President Wilson, though the USA never became a member, and neither did the Soviet Union.

Poland had arisen anew. Czechoslovakia was created from what was medieval Bohemia. Finland, Estonia, Latvia and Lithuania were now independent states, but they had gained their liberty through bloody internal conflict. This was particularly true of Finland.

After the Great War and widespread revolution only a dozen or so of Europe's many monarchies remained.

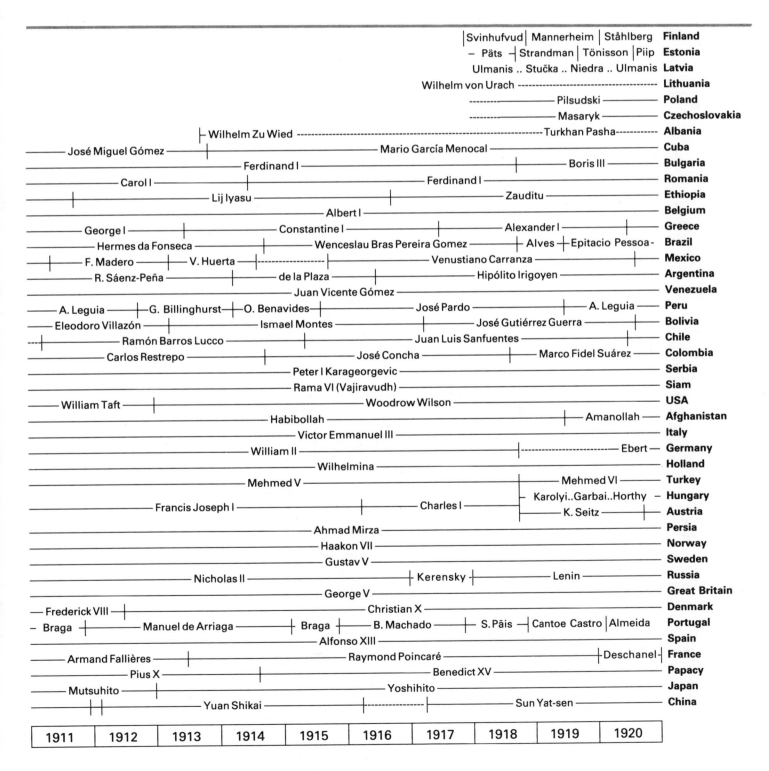

Svinhufvud | Mannerheim | Ståhlberg	Finland
Päts | Strandman | Tönisson | Piip	Estonia
Ulmanis .. Stučka .. Niedra .. Ulmanis	Latvia
Wilhelm von Urach	Lithuania
Pilsudski	Poland
Masaryk	Czechoslovakia
Wilhelm Zu Wied ... Turkhan Pasha	Albania
José Miguel Gómez | Mario García Menocal	Cuba
Ferdinand I | Boris III	Bulgaria
Carol I | Ferdinand I	Romania
Lij Iyasu | Zauditu	Ethiopia
Albert I	Belgium
George I | Constantine I | Alexander I	Greece
Hermes da Fonseca | Wenceslau Bras Pereira Gomez | Alves | Epitacio Pessoa	Brazil
F. Madero | V. Huerta | ... | Venustiano Carranza	Mexico
R. Sáenz-Peña | de la Plaza | Hipólito Irigoyen	Argentina
Juan Vicente Gómez	Venezuela
A. Leguia | G. Billinghurst | O. Benavides | José Pardo | A. Leguia	Peru
Eleodoro Villazón | Ismael Montes | José Gutiérrez Guerra	Bolivia
Ramón Barros Lucco | Juan Luis Sanfuentes	Chile
Carlos Restrepo | José Concha | Marco Fidel Suárez	Colombia
Peter I Karageorgevic	Serbia
Rama VI (Vajiravudh)	Siam
William Taft | Woodrow Wilson	USA
Habibollah | Amanollah	Afghanistan
Victor Emmanuel III	Italy
William II | ... Ebert	Germany
Wilhelmina	Holland
Mehmed V | Mehmed VI	Turkey
Francis Joseph I | Charles I | Karolyi..Garbai..Horthy	Hungary
Francis Joseph I | Charles I | K. Seitz	Austria
Ahmad Mirza	Persia
Haakon VII	Norway
Gustav V	Sweden
Nicholas II | Kerensky | Lenin	Russia
George V	Great Britain
Frederick VIII | Christian X	Denmark
Braga | Manuel de Arriaga | Braga | B. Machado | S. Päis | Cantoe Castro | Almeida	Portugal
Alfonso XIII	Spain
Armand Fallières | Raymond Poincaré | Deschanel	France
Pius X | Benedict XV	Papacy
Mutsuhito | Yoshihito	Japan
Yuan Shikai | ... | Sun Yat-sen	China

1911	1912	1913	1914	1915	1916	1917	1918	1919	1920

AD 1921-1930

ENGLAND
USA
SPAIN
FRANCE
GERMANY
SWEDEN

A Turkish national state emerged in 1923. Spain was made a republic in 1931; civil war broke out in 1936. Franco became its dictator. Italy gained Ethiopia in 1936. The Japanese occupied much of China in 1937-38.

Iraq	Faysal I
Saudi Arabia	Abd al-Aziz ibn Sa'ud
Transjordan	Abdullah ibn Hussein
Ireland	Griffith | William Cosgrave
Egypt	Fu'ad I
Finland	Kaarlo Ståhlberg | Lauri Relander
Estonia	Piip | Päts | Kukk | Pats | Akel | Jaakson | Teemant | Tönisson | Rei | Strandman
Latvia	K. Ulmanis | Cakste | Gustavs Zemgals |
Lithuania	Antanas Stulgenskis | Antanas Smetona
Poland	Pilsudski | Narutowicz | Stanislaw Wojciechowski | I. Moscicki
Czechoslovakia	Tomas Masaryk
Albania	Noli | Ahmed Zogu (1928 Zog I)
Cuba	Alfredo Zayas | Gerardo Machado
Bulgaria	Boris III
Romania	Ferdinand I | Michael I |
Ethiopia	Zauditu |
Belgium	Albert I
Greece	Constantine I | George II | Kondouriotis | Pangal. | Kondouriotis | Zaimis
Brazil	Pessoa | Artur Bernardes | W.L. Pereira de Souza | Vargas
Mexico	Alvaro Obregón | Plutarco Calles | Emilio Portes Gil |
Argentina	Irigoyen | Marcelo Alvear | Irigoyen | Uriburu
Venezuela	Juan Vicente Gómez
Peru	Augusto Leguia |
Bolivia	Juan Bautista Saavedra | Villanueva | Hernando Siles |
Chile	Arturo Alessandri | E. Figueroa | Carlos Ibáñez
Colombia	Pedro Nel Ospina | Miguel Arada Méndez |
Yugoslavia	Alexander I
Siam	Rama VI (Vajiravudh) | Rama VII (Prajadhipok)
USA	Warren Harding | Calvin Coolidge | Herbert Hoover
Afghanistan	Amanollah | Nader
Italy	Victor Emmanuel III
Germany	Friedrich Ebert | Paul von Hindenburg
Holland	Wilhelmina
Turkey	Mehmed VI | Mustafa Kemal
Hungary	Miklos Horthy
Austria	Michael Hainisch | Wilhelm Miklas
Persia	Ahmad Mirza | Reza Shah Pahlavi
Norway	Haakon VII
Sweden	Gustav V
Soviet Union	Lenin | (Rykon, Molotov) | Stalin
Great Britain	George V
Denmark	Christian X
Portugal	Almeida | Tixeira Gomes | Machado | Guimarães | Fragoso Carmona
Spain	Alfonso XIII
France	Alexandre Millerand | Gaston Doumergue
Papacy	Bened. XV | Pius XI
Japan	Yoshihito | Hirohito
China	Sun Yat-sen | Wan Jing wei | Jiang Jieshi (Chiang Kai-shek)

1921	1922	1923	1924	1925	1926	1927	1928	1929	1930

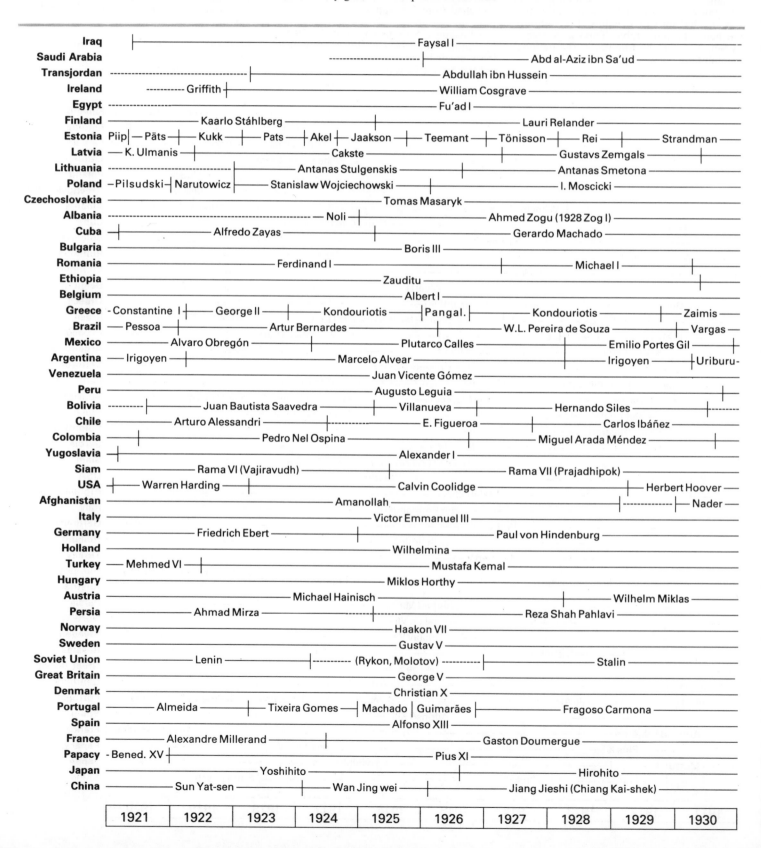

AD 1931-1940

ENGLAND
USA
ENGLAND

The German-Russian treaty of 1938 heralded the end of the Baltic states and led to the Second World War. Poland was divided. Finland lost Carelia. Denmark, Norway, Holland, Belgium and France were occupied by Germany. Italy allied with Germany.

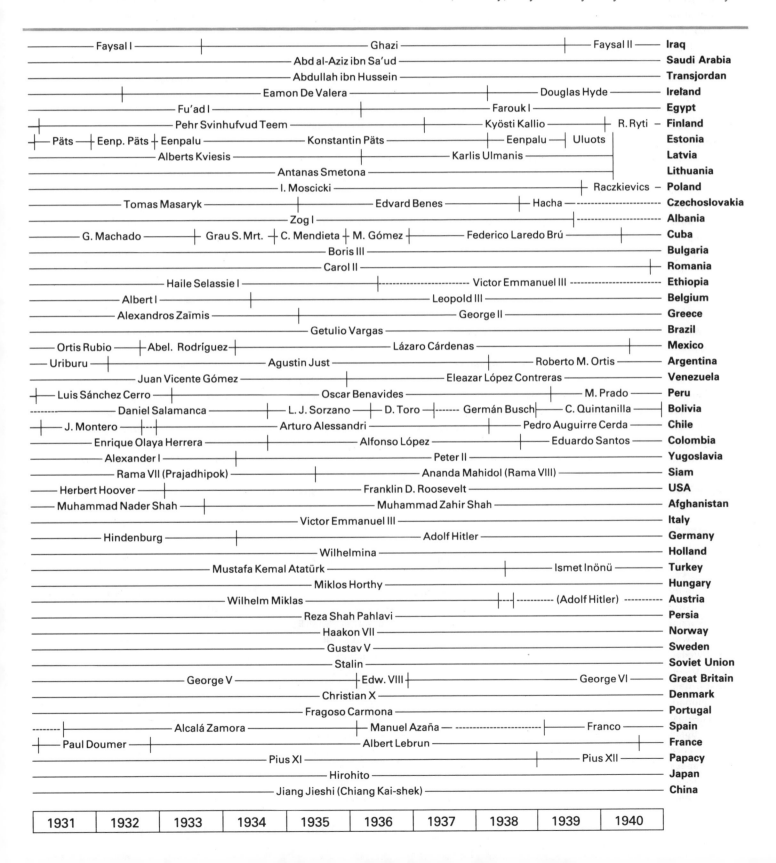

Rulers (1931–1940)	Country
Faysal I – Ghazi – Faysal II	Iraq
Abd al-Aziz ibn Sa'ud	Saudi Arabia
Abdullah ibn Hussein	Transjordan
Eamon De Valera – Douglas Hyde	Ireland
Fu'ad I – Farouk I	Egypt
Pehr Svinhufvud Teem – Kyösti Kallio – R. Ryti	Finland
Päts – Eenp. Päts – Eenpalu – Konstantin Päts – Eenpalu – Uluots	Estonia
Alberts Kviesis – Karlis Ulmanis	Latvia
Antanas Smetona	Lithuania
I. Moscicki – Raczkievics	Poland
Tomas Masaryk – Edvard Benes – Hacha	Czechoslovakia
Zog I	Albania
G. Machado – Grau S. Mrt. – C. Mendieta – M. Gómez – Federico Laredo Brú	Cuba
Boris III	Bulgaria
Carol II	Romania
Haile Selassie I – Victor Emmanuel III	Ethiopia
Albert I – Leopold III	Belgium
Alexandros Zaïmis – George II	Greece
Getulio Vargas	Brazil
Ortis Rubio – Abel. Rodríguez – Lázaro Cárdenas	Mexico
Uriburu – Agustin Just – Roberto M. Ortis	Argentina
Juan Vicente Gómez – Eleazar López Contreras	Venezuela
Luis Sánchez Cerro – Oscar Benavides – M. Prado	Peru
Daniel Salamanca – L. J. Sorzano – D. Toro – Germán Busch – C. Quintanilla	Bolivia
J. Montero – Arturo Alessandri – Pedro Auguirre Cerda	Chile
Enrique Olaya Herrera – Alfonso López – Eduardo Santos	Colombia
Alexander I – Peter II	Yugoslavia
Rama VII (Prajadhipok) – Ananda Mahidol (Rama VIII)	Siam
Herbert Hoover – Franklin D. Roosevelt	USA
Muhammad Nader Shah – Muhammad Zahir Shah	Afghanistan
Victor Emmanuel III	Italy
Hindenburg – Adolf Hitler	Germany
Wilhelmina	Holland
Mustafa Kemal Atatürk – Ismet Inönü	Turkey
Miklos Horthy	Hungary
Wilhelm Miklas – (Adolf Hitler)	Austria
Reza Shah Pahlavi	Persia
Haakon VII	Norway
Gustav V	Sweden
Stalin	Soviet Union
George V – Edw. VIII – George VI	Great Britain
Christian X	Denmark
Fragoso Carmona	Portugal
Alcalá Zamora – Manuel Azaña – Franco	Spain
Paul Doumer – Albert Lebrun	France
Pius XI – Pius XII	Papacy
Hirohito	Japan
Jiang Jieshi (Chiang Kai-shek)	China

1931	1932	1933	1934	1935	1936	1937	1938	1939	1940

AD 1941-1950

Vietnam	Ho Chi Minh
Libya	
Israel	Chaim Weizmann
Indonesia	Sukarno
Pakistan	
India	
Iceland	Sveinn Björnsson
Ireland	Douglas Hyde – Sean O' Kelly (Ceallaigh)
Egypt	Farouk I
Iraq	Faysal II
Saudi Arabia	Abd al-Aziz ibn Sa'ud
Transjordan	Abdullah ibn Hussein
Finland	Risto Ryti – Mannerheim – Juho Paasikivi
Poland	Boleslaw Bierut
Czechoslovakia	Edvard Benes – Klement Gottwald
Albania	Enver Hoxha
Cuba	Fulgencio Batista – Ramón Grau San Martín – C. Prio Socarrás
Bulgaria	Boris III – Symeon II – Georgi Dimitrov – Damianov-
Romania	Michael I – C.J. Parhon
Ethiopia	Haile Selassie I
Belgium	Leopold III
Greece	Damaskinos – George II – Paul I
Brazil	Getulio Vargas – José Linhares – Eurico Dutra
Mexico	Avila Camacho – Miguel Alemán
Argentina	Ortiz – Castillo – Pedro Ramírez – E. Farrell – Juan Perón
Venezuela	Isaias Medina – Rómulo Betancourt – Gallegos – C. Delgado Chalbaud
Peru	Manuel Prado y Ugarteche – José Luis Bustamante – (Manuel Odria)
Bolivia	Enrique Peñaranda – Gualberto Villaroel – Gui. – Gut. – Enrique Hertzog – Urriolangoitia
Chile	Cerda – Méndez – Juan Antonio Ríos Morales – Duhalde – Gabriel González Videla
Colombia	E. Santos – A. López Pumarejo – Camargo – Mariano Ospina Pérez
Yugoslavia	Tito (Josip Broz)
Thailand (Siam)	Ananda Mahidol (Rama VIII) – Bhumibol Adulyadej (Rama IX)
USA	Franklin D. Roosevelt – Harry Truman
Afghanistan	Muhammad Zafir Shah
Italy	Victor Emmanuel III – Humbert II – E. Nicola – L. Einaudi
Germany	Aldolf Hitler – Pieck / Heuss
Holland	Wilhelmina – Juliana
Turkey	Inönü
Hungary	Horthy – Szalasi – Z. Tildy – A. Szakasits
Austria	(Adolf Hitler) – Karl Renner
Iran (Persia)	Mohammad Reza Shah Pahlavi
Norway	Haakon VII
Sweden	Gustav V
Soviet Union	Josef Stalin (de facto)
Great Britain	George VI
Denmark	Christian X – Frederick IX
Portugal	Fragoso Carmona
Spain	Francisco Franco
France	Philippe Pétain – de Gaulle, Gouin, Bidault, Blum – Vincent Auriol
Papacy	Pius XII
Japan	Hirohito
China	Jiang Jieshi (Chiang Kai-shek) – Mao

1941	1942	1943	1944	1945	1946	1947	1948	1949	1950

After Germany had invaded the Soviet Union and Japan had attacked the United States, the Axis powers were forced back, and victory for the Allies came in 1945. After the war all the East European states became so-called Peoples' Republics under the influence of the Soviet Union. Germany was divided. There was continuing tension between East and West.

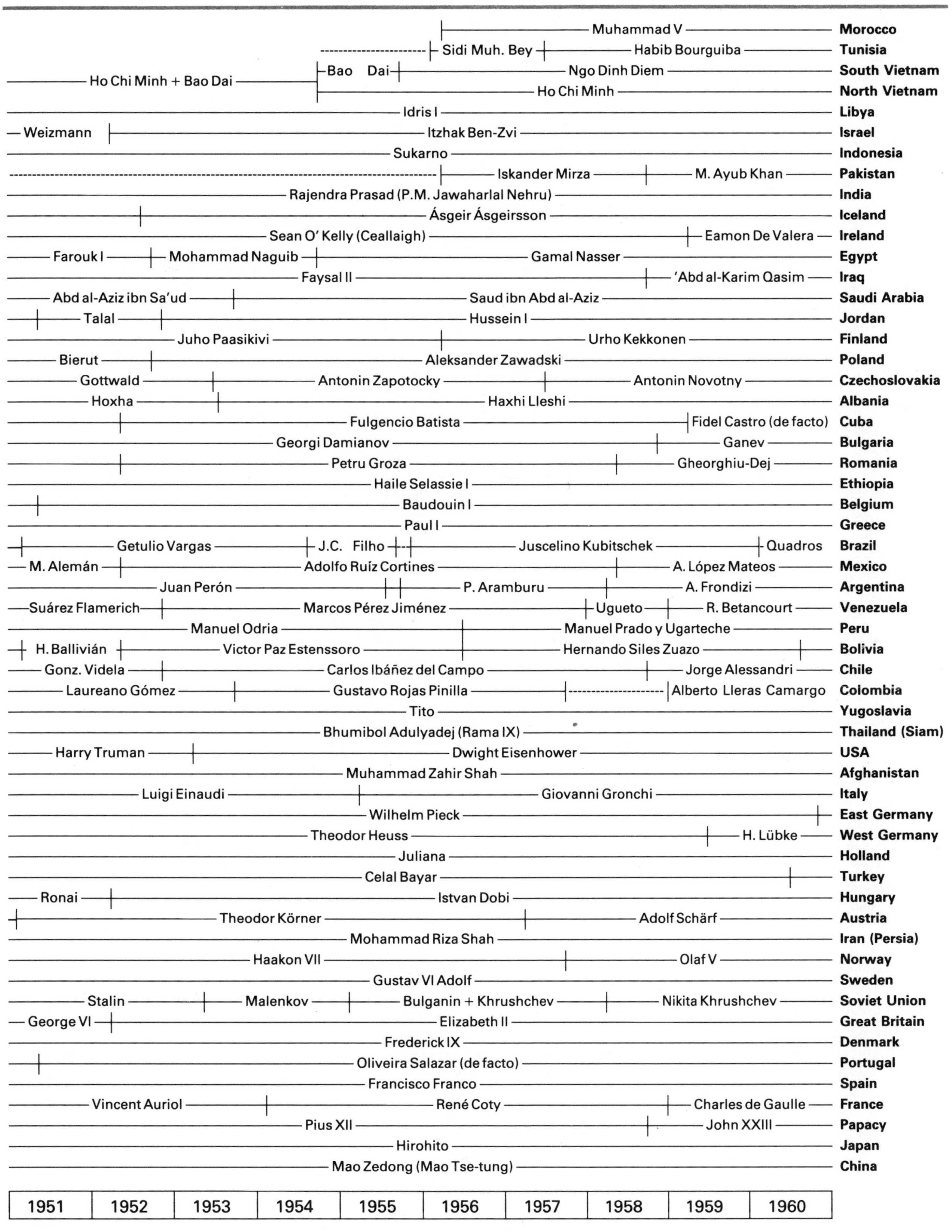
Muhammad V Morocco
Sidi Muh. Bey Habib Bourguiba Tunisia
Ho Chi Minh + Bao Dai
Bao Dai Ngo Dinh Diem South Vietnam
Ho Chi Minh North Vietnam
Idris I Libya
Weizmann Itzhak Ben-Zvi Israel
Sukarno Indonesia
Iskander Mirza M. Ayub Khan Pakistan
Rajendra Prasad (P.M. Jawaharlal Nehru) India
Ásgeir Ásgeirsson Iceland
Sean O' Kelly (Ceallaigh) Eamon De Valera Ireland
Farouk I Mohammad Naguib Gamal Nasser Egypt
Faysal II 'Abd al-Karim Qasim Iraq
Abd al-Aziz ibn Sa'ud Saud ibn Abd al-Aziz Saudi Arabia
Talal Hussein I Jordan
Juho Paasikivi Urho Kekkonen Finland
Bierut Aleksander Zawadski Poland
Gottwald Antonin Zapotocky Antonin Novotny Czechoslovakia
Hoxha Haxhi Lleshi Albania
Fulgencio Batista Fidel Castro (de facto) Cuba
Georgi Damianov Ganev Bulgaria
Petru Groza Gheorghiu-Dej Romania
Haile Selassie I Ethiopia
Baudouin I Belgium
Paul I Greece
Getulio Vargas J.C. Filho Juscelino Kubitschek Quadros Brazil
M. Alemán Adolfo Ruíz Cortines A. López Mateos Mexico
Juan Perón P. Aramburu A. Frondizi Argentina
Suárez Flamerich Marcos Pérez Jiménez Ugueto R. Betancourt Venezuela
Manuel Odria Manuel Prado y Ugarteche Peru
H. Ballivián Victor Paz Estenssoro Hernando Siles Zuazo Bolivia
Gonz. Videla Carlos Ibáñez del Campo Jorge Alessandri Chile
Laureano Gómez Gustavo Rojas Pinilla Alberto Lleras Camargo Colombia
Tito Yugoslavia
Bhumibol Adulyadej (Rama IX) Thailand (Siam)
Harry Truman Dwight Eisenhower USA
Muhammad Zahir Shah Afghanistan
Luigi Einaudi Giovanni Gronchi Italy
Wilhelm Pieck East Germany
Theodor Heuss H. Lübke West Germany
Juliana Holland
Celal Bayar Turkey
Ronai Istvan Dobi Hungary
Theodor Körner Adolf Schärf Austria
Mohammad Riza Shah Iran (Persia)
Haakon VII Olaf V Norway
Gustav VI Adolf Sweden
Stalin Malenkov Bulganin + Khrushchev Nikita Khrushchev Soviet Union
George VI Elizabeth II Great Britain
Frederick IX Denmark
Oliveira Salazar (de facto) Portugal
Francisco Franco Spain
Vincent Auriol René Coty Charles de Gaulle France
Pius XII John XXIII Papacy
Hirohito Japan
Mao Zedong (Mao Tse-tung) China
1951 1952 1953 1954 1955 1956 1957 1958 1959 1960

AD 1961-1970

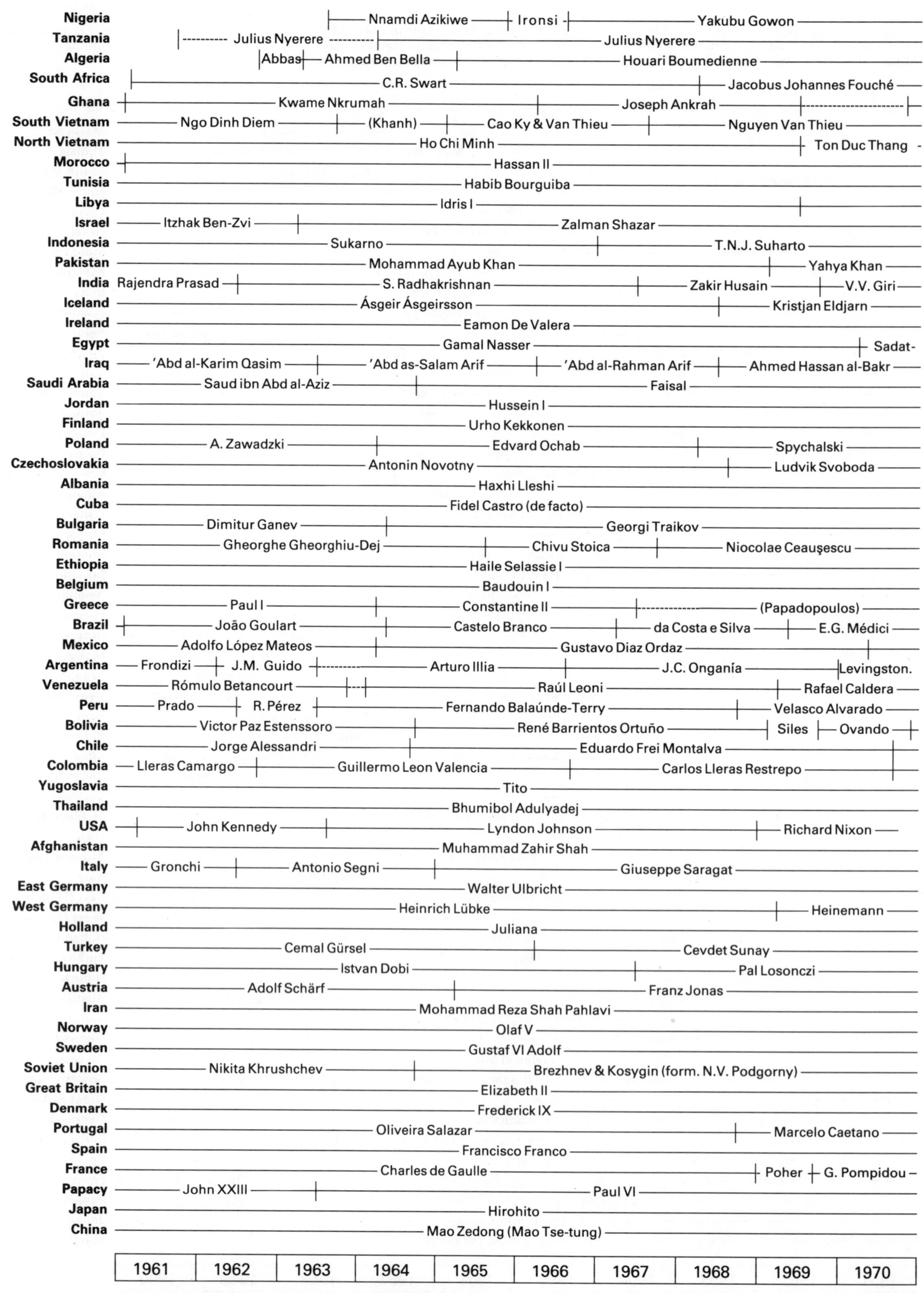

Nigeria Nnamdi Azikiwe Ironsi Yakubu Gowon
Tanzania Julius Nyerere Julius Nyerere
Algeria Abbas Ahmed Ben Bella Houari Boumedienne
South Africa C.R. Swart Jacobus Johannes Fouché
Ghana Kwame Nkrumah Joseph Ankrah
South Vietnam Ngo Dinh Diem (Khanh) Cao Ky & Van Thieu Nguyen Van Thieu
North Vietnam Ho Chi Minh Ton Duc Thang
Morocco Hassan II
Tunisia Habib Bourguiba
Libya Idris I
Israel Itzhak Ben-Zvi Zalman Shazar
Indonesia Sukarno T.N.J. Suharto
Pakistan Mohammad Ayub Khan Yahya Khan
India Rajendra Prasad S. Radhakrishnan Zakir Husain V.V. Giri
Iceland Ásgeir Ásgeirsson Kristjan Eldjarn
Ireland Eamon De Valera
Egypt Gamal Nasser Sadat-
Iraq 'Abd al-Karim Qasim 'Abd as-Salam Arif 'Abd al-Rahman Arif Ahmed Hassan al-Bakr
Saudi Arabia Saud ibn Abd al-Aziz Faisal
Jordan Hussein I
Finland Urho Kekkonen
Poland A. Zawadzki Edvard Ochab Spychalski
Czechoslovakia Antonin Novotny Ludvik Svoboda
Albania Haxhi Lleshi
Cuba Fidel Castro (de facto)
Bulgaria Dimitur Ganev Georgi Traikov
Romania Gheorghe Gheorghiu-Dej Chivu Stoica Niocolae Ceauşescu
Ethiopia Haile Selassie I
Belgium Baudouin I
Greece Paul I Constantine II (Papadopoulos)
Brazil João Goulart Castelo Branco da Costa e Silva E.G. Médici
Mexico Adolfo López Mateos Gustavo Diaz Ordaz
Argentina Frondizi J.M. Guido Arturo Illia J.C. Onganía Levingston.
Venezuela Rómulo Betancourt Raúl Leoni Rafael Caldera
Peru Prado R. Pérez Fernando Balaúnde-Terry Velasco Alvarado
Bolivia Victor Paz Estenssoro René Barrientos Ortuño Siles Ovando
Chile Jorge Alessandri Eduardo Frei Montalva
Colombia Lleras Camargo Guillermo Leon Valencia Carlos Lleras Restrepo
Yugoslavia Tito
Thailand Bhumibol Adulyadej
USA John Kennedy Lyndon Johnson Richard Nixon
Afghanistan Muhammad Zahir Shah
Italy Gronchi Antonio Segni Giuseppe Saragat
East Germany Walter Ulbricht
West Germany Heinrich Lübke Heinemann
Holland Juliana
Turkey Cemal Gürsel Cevdet Sunay
Hungary Istvan Dobi Pal Losonczi
Austria Adolf Schärf Franz Jonas
Iran Mohammad Reza Shah Pahlavi
Norway Olaf V
Sweden Gustaf VI Adolf
Soviet Union Nikita Khrushchev Brezhnev & Kosygin (form. N.V. Podgorny)
Great Britain Elizabeth II
Denmark Frederick IX
Portugal Oliveira Salazar Marcelo Caetano
Spain Francisco Franco
France Charles de Gaulle Poher G. Pompidou
Papacy John XXIII Paul VI
Japan Hirohito
China Mao Zedong (Mao Tse-tung)
1961 1962 1963 1964 1965 1966 1967 1968 1969 1970

AD 1971-1980

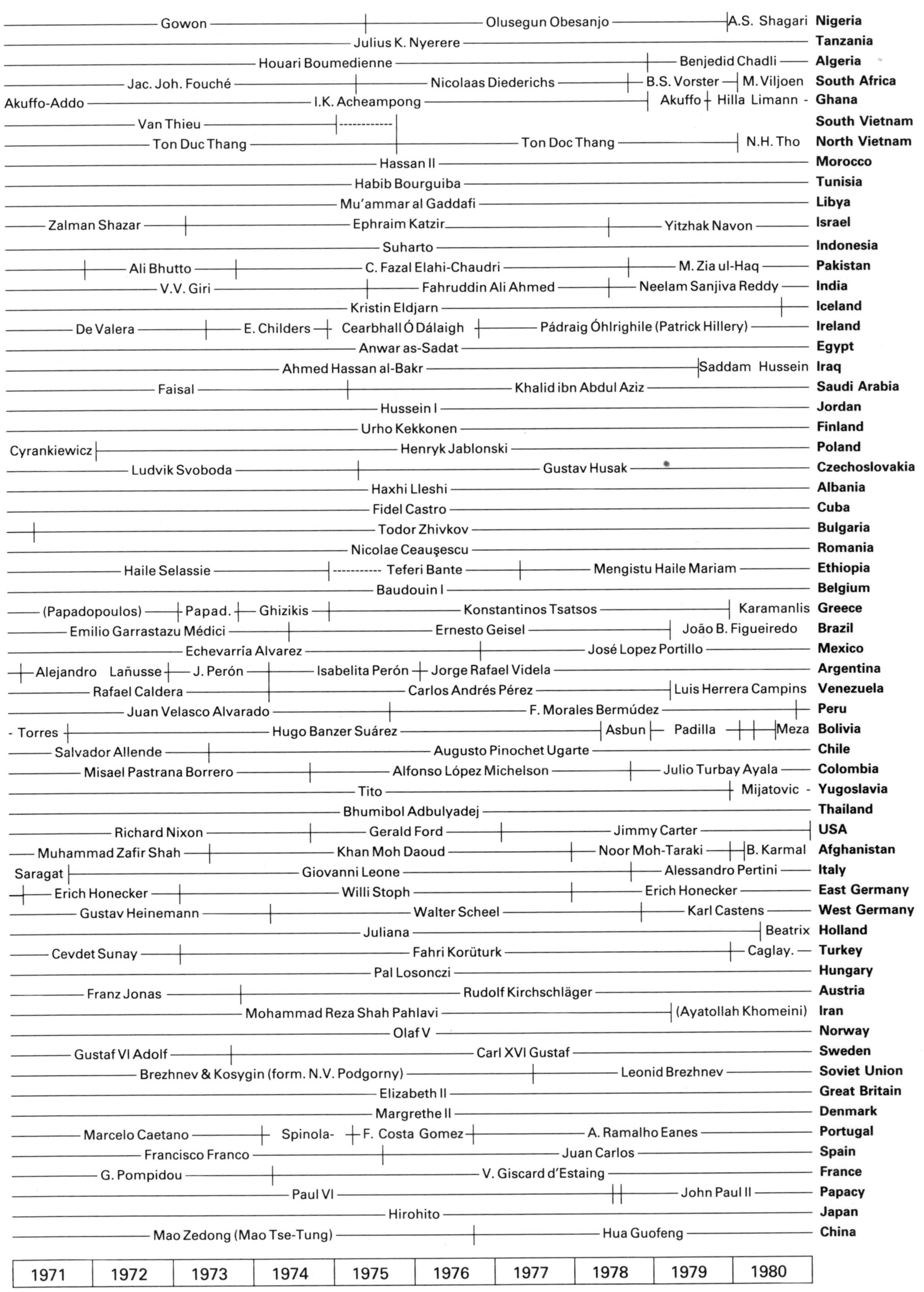
Gowon Olusegun Obesanjo A.S. Shagari Nigeria
Julius K. Nyerere Tanzania
Houari Boumedienne Benjedid Chadli Algeria
Jac. Joh. Fouché Nicolaas Diederichs B.S. Vorster M. Viljoen South Africa
Akuffo-Addo I.K. Acheampong Akuffo Hilla Limann - Ghana
Van Thieu South Vietnam
Ton Duc Thang Ton Doc Thang N.H. Tho North Vietnam
Hassan II Morocco
Habib Bourguiba Tunisia
Mu'ammar al Gaddafi Libya
Zalman Shazar Ephraim Katzir Yitzhak Navon Israel
Suharto Indonesia
Ali Bhutto C. Fazal Elahi-Chaudri M. Zia ul-Haq Pakistan
V.V. Giri Fahruddin Ali Ahmed Neelam Sanjiva Reddy India
Kristin Eldjarn Iceland
De Valera E. Childers Cearbhall Ó Dálaigh Pádraig Óhlrighile (Patrick Hillery) Ireland
Anwar as-Sadat Egypt
Ahmed Hassan al-Bakr Saddam Hussein Iraq
Faisal Khalid ibn Abdul Aziz Saudi Arabia
Hussein I Jordan
Urho Kekkonen Finland
Cyrankiewicz Henryk Jablonski Poland
Ludvik Svoboda Gustav Husak Czechoslovakia
Haxhi Lleshi Albania
Fidel Castro Cuba
Todor Zhivkov Bulgaria
Nicolae Ceauşescu Romania
Haile Selassie Teferi Bante Mengistu Haile Mariam Ethiopia
Baudouin I Belgium
(Papadopoulos) Papad. Ghizikis Konstantinos Tsatsos Karamanlis Greece
Emilio Garrastazu Médici Ernesto Geisel João B. Figueiredo Brazil
Echevarría Alvarez José Lopez Portillo Mexico
Alejandro Lañusse J. Perón Isabelita Perón Jorge Rafael Videla Argentina
Rafael Caldera Carlos Andrés Pérez Luis Herrera Campins Venezuela
Juan Velasco Alvarado F. Morales Bermúdez Peru
- Torres Hugo Banzer Suárez Asbun Padilla Meza Bolivia
Salvador Allende Augusto Pinochet Ugarte Chile
Misael Pastrana Borrero Alfonso López Michelson Julio Turbay Ayala Colombia
Tito Mijatovic - Yugoslavia
Bhumibol Adbulyadej Thailand
Richard Nixon Gerald Ford Jimmy Carter USA
Muhammad Zafir Shah Khan Moh Daoud Noor Moh-Taraki B. Karmal Afghanistan
Saragat Giovanni Leone Alessandro Pertini Italy
Erich Honecker Willi Stoph Erich Honecker East Germany
Gustav Heinemann Walter Scheel Karl Castens West Germany
Juliana Beatrix Holland
Cevdet Sunay Fahri Korüturk Caglay. Turkey
Pal Losonczi Hungary
Franz Jonas Rudolf Kirchschläger Austria
Mohammad Reza Shah Pahlavi (Ayatollah Khomeini) Iran
Olaf V Norway
Gustaf VI Adolf Carl XVI Gustaf Sweden
Brezhnev & Kosygin (form. N.V. Podgorny) Leonid Brezhnev Soviet Union
Elizabeth II Great Britain
Margrethe II Denmark
Marcelo Caetano Spinola- F. Costa Gomez A. Ramalho Eanes Portugal
Francisco Franco Juan Carlos Spain
G. Pompidou V. Giscard d'Estaing France
Paul VI John Paul II Papacy
Hirohito Japan
Mao Zedong (Mao Tse-Tung) Hua Guofeng China
1971 1972 1973 1974 1975 1976 1977 1978 1979 1980

AD 1981-1990

Nigeria	Alhaji S. Shagari
Tanzania	J.K. Nyerere
Algeria	Bendjedid Chadli
South Africa	Marais Viljoen
Ghana	Hilla Limann
Sri Lanka	J.R. Jayawardene
Vietnam	Nguyen Huu Tho
Morocco	Hassan II
Tunisia	Habib Bourguiba
Libya	Mu'ammar al Gaddafi
Israel	Yitzhak Navon
Indonesia	Suharto
Pakistan	M. Zia ul-Haq
India	Neelam Sanjiva Reddy
Iceland	Vigdis Finnbogadottir
Ireland	Pádraig Óhlrighile
Egypt	Sadat — Hosni Mubarak
Iraq	Sadam Hussein
Saudi Arabia	Khalid ibn Abdul Aziz
Jordan	Hussein I
Finland	Kekkonen — Mauno Koivisto
Poland	Henryk Jablonski
Czechoslovakia	Gustav Husak
Albania	Haxhi Lleshi
Cuba	Fidel Castro
Bulgaria	Todor Zhivkov
Romania	Nicolae Ceauşescu
Ethiopia	Mengistu Haile Mariam
Belgium	Baudouin I
Greece	Konstantinos Karamanlis
Brazil	João B. Figueiredo
Mexico	José Lopez Portillo
Argentina	Viola — Galtieri
Venezuela	Luis Herrera Campins
Peru	Fernando Relaúnde-Terry
Bolivia	Celso Torrelio Villa
Chile	Augusto Pinochet Ugarte
Colombia	Julio César Turbay Ayala
Yugoslavia	Petar Stambolic
Thailand	Bhumibol Adulyadej
USA	Ronald Reagan
Afghanistan	Babrak Karmal
Italy	Alessandro Pertini
East Germany	Erich Honecker
West Germany	Karl Castens
Holland	Beatrix
Turkey	Ihsan Sabri Caglayangli
Hungary	Pal Losonczi
Austria	Rudolf Kirchschläger
Iran	(Ayatollah Khomeini)
Norway	Olaf V
Sweden	Carl XVI Gustaf
Soviet Union	L. Brezhnev — Y. Andropov
Great Britain	Elizabeth II
Denmark	Margrethe II
Portugal	A. dos Santos Ramalho Eanes
Spain	Juan Carlos
France	François Mitterand
Papacy	John Paul II
Japan	Hirohito
China	Hu Yaobang

1981	1982	1983	1984	1985	1986	1987	1988	1989	1990

AD 1991-2000

Nigeria
Tanzania
Algeria
South Africa
Ghana
Sri Lanka
Vietnam
Morocco
Tunisia
Libya
Israel
Indonesia
Pakistan
India
Iceland
Ireland
Egypt
Iraq
Saudi Arabia
Jordan
Finland
Poland
Czechoslovakia
Albania
Cuba
Bulgaria
Romania
Ethiopia
Belgium
Greece
Brazil
Mexico
Argentina
Venezuela
Peru
Bolivia
Chile
Colombia
Yugoslavia
Thailand
USA
Afghanistan
Italy
East Germany
West Germany
Holland
Turkey
Hungary
Austria
Iran
Norway
Sweden
Soviet Union
Great Britain
Denmark
Portugal
Spain
France
Papacy
Japan
China

1991	1992	1993	1994	1995	1996	1997	1998	1999	2000

NOTES ON THE 20th CENTURY

The history of the present century is divided by the two World Wars into three separate eras. The first was a period of monarchy, colonialism and Christian missionary expansion. The First World War of 1914-18 altered the political map of Europe and Western Asia, and brought about radical changes in constitution and attitudes in many countries. The Soviet Union withdrew behind its shield of satellites, the position of Great Britain weakened, while in the United States life was lived to the full until 1929, when the country gradually descended into economic crisis. Depression and unemployment prevailed in Europe during the greater part of the inter-war period, which was probably one reason why several countries turned from democracy to dictatorship: Italy in 1922 under Mussolini, Bulgaria in 1923 under Zankoff, Spain 1923-30 under Primo de Rivera and 1939 under Franco, Poland in 1926 under Pilsudski, Portugal in 1926 under Carmona and his successor Salazar, Germany in 1933 under Hitler. Romania, Austria, Albania, Greece and the three Baltic States were also governed by authoritarian regimes during the 1930s, as were Brazil and several Asian states. From the mid-1920s, Stalin ruled in the Soviet Union.

The Second World War of 1939-45 led to the collapse of Germany and the defeat of Japan and Italy, but above all to the disintegration of European colonialism. Most of the dictatorships disappeared; the East European states became People's Republics under Soviet protection and/or administration, while American investment and enterprise created a different kind of dependence in other parts of the world. Air traffic and telecommunications developed rapidly, the Earth shrank, the Moon was suddenly within reach, but the two super-powers kept their distance, each on their own half of the planet.

The Irish Free State was created in 1921 after a long and painful birth. However, the association with the British monarchy remained formally until 1949. Six mainly Protestant Northern Irish counties remained under British rule. No peaceful political solution has thus far been found.

There was prohibition against alcohol in the 1920s in the United States as well as in Finland, Iceland and Norway.

Outer Mongolia, which belonged to the Emperors of China until 1911, became a Soviet satellite state in 1926.

In China in the 1920s private wars raged between various military factions. Sun Yat-sen, who is considered the founder of the Chinese republic, was the leader of a Southern Chinese government until his death in 1925. With the help of Russian advisers he built up the ruling Kuomintang party. In 1926 an army marched northwards under Jiang Jieshi (Chiang Kai-shek) capturing Beijing in 1928. Thus the country was brought under one government but the Communists were excluded from the Kuomintang and a new civil war broke out. In 1934 a campaign by Jiang Jieshi against the Communist south eastern provinces resulted in the long march to Yenan to the far north-west, where the Communist leader Mao Zedong set up his headquarters and resumed power.

The Japanese, who in 1931 had occupied Manchuria, thereby creating the tributary state of Manchukuo, with the last of the Chinese Qing emperors as head of state, went on to occupy China proper in 1937. For a time Chinese Nationalists and Communists united in the face of this threat, but after the collapse of Japan in August 1945 (see below) civil war broke out in China. It continued until spring 1949, when Jiang Jieshi, together with loyal supporters, took refuge in Taiwan. The birth of the People's Republic of China was proclaimed on 1 October 1949.

As a result of the Japanese occupation of Manchuria, the League of Nations branded Japan as an aggressor, which caused Japan to resign from the organization in March 1933. Germany followed suit in the autumn of the same year. The Soviet Union, on the other hand, joined the League in 1934. Two years later Italy attacked and subjugated Abyssinia, or Ethiopia; the League of Nations decided to impose economic sanctions against Italy, but this had no effect. Consequently the role of the League was largely played out. Its final show of strength was directed against the Soviet Union, which was expelled after attacking Finland in 1939.

In Germany the National Socialist (Nazi) Party came into power in 1933 with swift and far-reaching consequences for the world. Rearmament, the Aryan proclamation and the persecution of minorities soon transformed this cultured nation into a highly disciplined, technically advanced, yet barbarian state, arousing justified anxiety in neighbouring countries. In the spring of 1936 the National Socialist government felt confident enough to breach the Versailles Treaty by reintroducing conscription and occupying the demilitarized Rhineland. Chancellor Adolf Hitler and the Fascist leader Benito Mussolini, whose relationship had originally been strained because of Austria and the German-speaking South Tyrol which was under Italian rule, now joined forces. They endorsed Franco's rebel government in Spain and henceforth supplied him with military aid in the Spanish Civil War, which broke out in the summer of 1936 and lasted for three years.

In March 1938 Austria was absorbed into Nazi Germany. In September of the same year the Germans also occupied Sudetenland following an international crisis which culminated in Czechoslovakia being sacrificed to Germany, ostensibly to avoid a world war. However, the sacrifice was in vain, and in March 1939 the Germans marched into the remaining part of the Czech state, which was made a German protectorate. It was now clear that Poland was next in line. Negotiations between the West and the Soviet Union concerning military countermeasures broke down as a result of Polish opposition to the Russians marching through Poland. The Soviet Union then suddenly changed sides and signed an agreement with Germany, which led to the annihilation of the Baltic States and the outbreak of the Second World War following the division of Poland between the Soviet Union and Germany.

Finland was invaded by the Russians in December 1939 and fought the fierce Winter War which ended with the loss of Carelia. In April 1940 the Germans turned to Scandinavia, where they quickly occupied Denmark and Norway. This caused the British to occupy Iceland as a precautionary measure. In May of the same year Holland and Belgium were invaded by German troops, and in June Fance collapsed. Most of the country was occupied by the Germans, a self-governing part being left, with Vichy as the capital. Most of the British troops in Europe were able to retreat from Dunkirk. A German-Italian attack against the British in Egypt failed.

The Soviet-German alliance was short-lived, and did not survive the division of Poland. In midsummer 1941 the Germans marched eastwards on a broad front after Romania, Bulgaria and an embittered Finland had been engaged on their side, and after Yugoslavia and Greece had been invaded. The German offensive was rapid at first but was arrested by the arrival of winter. The critical turning-point came in November 1942, when a great German army was forced to surrender at Stalingrad.

By this time two other great powers had entered the fray. Japan, which had been allied to Germany and Italy ever since the autumn of 1940, found itself in an increasingly uneasy relationship with the United States, and in December 1941 it attacked the American naval base at Pearl Harbor. Japan subsequently conducted a successful campaign in the Pacific and South-East Asia, where they occupied British and Dutch colonies. However, massive American rearmament, particularly by the Air Force forced Japan into submission. At the same time the Allied forces landed in North Africa, and subsequently invaded Italy. Mussolini was overthrown and Italy changed sides. The Allies landed on the Atlantic coast of France in 1944, and the war in Europe came to an end in May 1945 with Hitler's suicide and Germany's unconditional surrender. The war against Japan, which continued for another few months, was brought to a close by the two atom bombs dropped over the two cities of Hiroshima and Nagasaki in August 1945.

Terror of the atom bomb and nuclear missiles, both invented in the 1940s, left its stamp on the victorious powers after the end of the war, leading to an incessant armaments race. Local but devastating wars in which the super-powers were involved in varying degrees of intensity were fought in Korea, Vietnam and the Middle East. A large number of independent new states were created after the war: Syria as early as 1944, Jordan in 1946, India and Pakistan in 1947, Israel in 1948, Indonesia in 1949, Libya in 1951, Morocco and Tunisia in 1956, Congo, Ghana, Mali and Cyprus in 1960, Kuwait in 1961, Jamaica, Algeria and Samoa in 1962, Kenya and Malaysia in 1963, Malta in 1964, the Falkland Islands in 1965, Barbados in 1966, Yemen in 1967, Mauritius and Swaziland in 1968, Fiji and Tonga in 1970, Bahrein in 1971.
Liberation movements in Africa also caused tension in the western world; the South African Union ruled by a Nationalist government withdrew formally from the British Commonwealth in 1961.

Cuba, which in the 1950s shed its semi-colonial relationship with the United States, was for a long time an outlying Soviet base in the western hemisphere. Advanced Russian plans to build a missile base there almost led to a new war between the super-powers in 1962. Since then, Cuban mercenary troops have been engaged in various military conflicts, mainly in Africa, where the collapse of the last of the European colonial powers, Portugal, left behind it a legacy of political unrest.

Israel, which has existed as a modern independent state since 1948, has never been recognized by its Arabic neighbours, which house a large number of Palestinian refugees. Time and time again the constant tension has erupted into bitter fighting. Israel has generally been superior in military capability, and has captured considerable parts of Jordanian, Egyptian, Syrian and Lebanese territories.

Countless scientific discoveries and technical inventions have changed life during the 20th century. At the turn of the century there were almost no cars, aeroplanes, tractors, refrigerators, electric trains, radios, artificial fibres or plastics.

Telephones were rare and there were not many electric power stations, nor, of course, any television sets or computers. Insulin and penicillin were invented in the 1930s, saving or prolonging the life of many people. In the 1940s nuclear power was used for the first time. There are always new feats of science; progress continues, and space rockets probe farther and farther into the unknown.

POST SCRIPTUM

Those of us who live long enough to know the names of the heads of state in the 1980s and 1990s may wish to complete the charts in this book. No one knows how many new names will appear, but let us hope that there will not be too many; frequent changes tend to indicate civil war or other unrest. Some countries will probably retain the same head of state for the next two decades. A glance at the charts will confirm that this is the rule rather than the exception.

The record of historical events, moving from left to right in our time-charts, does not, of course, end with this book. Children born today will themselves be parents in the 21st century; decisions made this year will affect the shape of the third millennium AD. By that time, life on our planet will certainly be different in many ways but there will probably be some continuity. So often things said and done today are remarkably similar to things said and done in the past. History moves forward in waves, which may have something to do with the succession of generations; there are always youngsters ready to reject the views of their parents, who, when they were young, grew up to reject the values of *their* parents. This can be seen clearly, for example, in fluctuations of taste and fashion, particularly in hair and dress fashion, forever changing from one extreme to another.

I would not claim, however, that history is only repetition, a mere reshuffle of the unchanging. Each generation has probably contributed *something* new under the sun despite the Bible's insistence to the contrary, and some of these innovations may have brought lasting advantages. Today we know about atoms and genes and solar energy, about the vastness of space and the mechanics of genetics, subjects which were cloaked in mystery before our time. But we are all aware, for this very reason, of being exposed to greater dangers than our ancestors. Our descendants in the next two or generations will know the price to be paid for our repletion, our leisure and our longevity.

Their planet may be small and over-crowded; distances already dramatically shortened are bound to shrink even further. Distances in time are different. The rate of our heart-beat is the same as in the age of the Pharaohs, measuring out the days of human life at a steady tempo through the centuries. To remind people of this is one of my reasons for writing this book.

Guy Henrikson

Key to drawings at the top of the pages

The dates above the notes on the following pages show a period of two decades at a time, representing each double-page spread in the book. The information does not refer primarily to the vignettes above the notes, except where indicated, but to the whole sequence of illustrations on each double-page spread in the main position of the book.

1000-981
The game of draughts, among many more important activities, had long been known in Egypt.

980-961
The climate in Northern Europe was still mild. An oval cloak, pieces of cloth for shoes, a skirt made from woollen cords were adequate – nothing was worn underneath.

960-941
Dress fashion did not change significantly in Egypt, only hair styles. Wigs were protection against the sun. The sea-faring Phoenicians were more clothes-conscious.

940-921
'Good Shepherd' figures were common during the Classical Period. The oldest one known is Egyptian.

920-901
Hittites drinking out of cups; on a crumbling relief. Rock carvings of hunting scenes tell us of life in Africa.

900-881
A Hittite 'Good Shepherd' was likely to be making for a place of sacrifice with his lamb.

880-861.
Ashurnasirpal II, dressed in a cloth wrapped diagonally over his tunic. His beard has been carefully curled.

860-841
Riding was new in Mesopotamia. Assyrian horsemen sat far back on their leather-clad horses.

840-821
Inflated animal skins were used as swimming floats and pontoons in the Euphrates and Tigris.

820-801
The Assyrians had now learned to sit further forward on their horses. They had also acquired boots.

800-781
The parasol was invented long before the umbrella.

780-761
Greeks engaged in sport are depicted on vases.

760-741
Syrio-Hittites playing with spinning tops. Olmec acrobats worshipped strange gods.

740-721
Syrio-Hittite men wore ear-rings. The women were more simply dressed. War dances were performed in Attica.

720-701
The original of the picture of Sargon's palace came from Dur-Shaarukin, Khorsabad, together with the strange Greek animals and the Assyrian ships transporting wooden boards. The Assyrians pictured above are wearing rings on their big toes.

700-681
Hebrews, in contrast with Assyrians, were dressed in open wool kaftans with four purple tassels.

680-661
Greek women wore the *peplos* and male Greek civilians wore the *himation*. Greek foot-soldiers, the Hoplites, were heavily armed, but spurned the bow-and-arrow.

660-641
King Ashurbanirpal and his soldiers trapping lions in hunting nets. Greek women wore Egyptian hair-styles.

640-621
In Mesopotamia, for practical reasons, animals were usually slaughtered under a tree, a custom which has remained unchanged through the centuries.

620-601
Eastern Greeks transported their horses by ship. The Dorian *peplos* was fashionable among women. The upper part was folded down over the shoulders, forming a kind of bodice; the folded part was called an *apotygma*.

600-581
Poultry-farming, which originated in India, had by now spread westward and was practised by the Etruscans. Phrygians played to Cybele. Medes hunted lions around the Oxus.

580-561.
The *himation*, or Greek cloak, had weights in the corners. The hat was called a *petasus*. Women plaited their hair and wore tunics seamed at the shoulders. Their hands were usually hidden.

560-541
It had become the custom to recline at table. Greek women had now sewn together their *peplos* into a kind of frock.

540-521
The Etruscans called their cloak a *tebenna*; it was wrapped half a turn under the right arm. They wore pointed shoes in the Oriental style. The Greeks, on the other hand, went barefoot.

520-501
Greek horsemen held their horses' heads high. Lion hunts still took place in Hellas.

500-481
Persian warriors might wear leather costumes and a short sword held in place with a strap at the bottom. Their hair-style was borrowed from Assyria. The Greeks wore their hair shorter.

480-461.
The Etruscans shaved carefully; the women had short hair with curls framing their faces. The *dinton* worn by Greek women had false sleeves of loose cloth which covered the arms like a shawl.

460-441
Phrygian hats and trousers were occasionally worn, though the Greeks and Romans considered trousers ludicrous. The *chiton* was pleated, wider than a *peplos*, and was belted rather than fastened at the shoulders. The 'skirt' at the hips was called a *kolpos*.

440-421
A Greek with a *petasus* on his back wears a *chlamys* over his short *chiton*. Only coachmen and actors wore a long *chiton*. Scythians of the Altai region were always elegantly dressed.

420-401
A dancer at a Dionysus festival depicted on a vase. Her skirt swirls as she moves. Many Greek men wore a pointed hat called a *pilos*.

400-381.
Scythians, sketched from pictures on gold plate from Russia, are seen pulling out a tooth, stringing a bow, and attempting to milk a mare – being very partial to mare's milk. Greek vase painters gave more emphasis to women's breasts.

380-361
This was the time of the Chinese feudal period known as the Warring States – a most suitable title. Egyptian styles changed very little through the years.

360-341
The original of this sketch of a Persian satrap may have depicted Mausolus, who ruled over Greek Halicarnassus and gained immortality through his monumental tomb, Mausolleion or Mausoleum.

340-321
There is a well-known anecdote about the philosopher Diogenes, who lived in Corinth in a barrel. One day he was visited by Alexander the Great, who offered him any favour he might request; Diogenes merely asked Alexander to move a little so as not to block the sun.

320-301
Figurines from Tanagra in Boeotia give us a good idea of Greek clothing, particularly women's fashion which often featured a straw hat. Lightly armed Roman foot-soldiers, *Velites*, wear wolf-skin hats.

300-281
Chinese musicians had a chromatic twelve-tone scale and used this to construct a system of fifths, on the same lines as Pythagoras in the West.

280-261
The Romans gradually overcame their fear of King Pyrrhus' war elephants. Greek art was influential in India.

260-241
The courtesan Thaïs was probably an old lady by now, because she was in Persepolis with Alexander the Great and then accompanied Ptolemy Soter to Egypt. This marble statue of Thaïs as a young woman was perhaps done after her death.

240-221
The first sedan chair was seen in Chinese art. Also depicted here are wooden figures from Changsha.

220-201
The Great Wall of China was built while the Romans were fighting against Hannibal.

200-181
Fashion-conscious men in the West were clean-shaven. Women's hair-styles were complex but restrained.

180-161
In China mulberry leaves were picked for the silk worms. The silk route to the West was not yet open.

160-141
The loincloth on the figure above was called a *dhoti*. Buddhism was well established in India.

140-121
A Persian prince from Shami carrying a sword in his trousers pocket. The five chaste Chinese women show quite a different attitude to life from the two bosomy Indian girls.

120-101
Hellenic art under the Romans showed pronounced baroque features, as seen here in the Laocoön group.

100-81
The horses imported into China from the West were larger than those the Chinese had traditionally known.

80-61
Europe was still dominated by the Celts. The Gundestrup Bowl in Copenhagen shows their helmets, horns and other objects.

60-41
These were troubled times in Rome, but there were still opportunities for relaxation, as can be seen in mosaics and paintings.

40-21
A Roman census is represented on Domitius Ahenobarbus' altar in the Louvre, Paris.

20-1
Solemn men dressed in togas are grouped in a marble relief on Augustus' Altar of Peace in Rome. The men and women depicted here have evidently been caught in a storm!

1-20
There was more than one road leading to Rome, but Roman chariots were still unsprung. The group of Germans is taken from a cameo, Gemma Augustea, in the Kunsthistorisches Museum, Vienna.

21-40
Roman centurions might carry a vine-wood stick to keep order. The upper classes still were a semi-circular toga out of doors over their tunic. The women wore a full-length stole and a cloak called a *palla*.

41-60
Large horses from the West were now common in China. Hatra was a small kingdom in northern Mesopotamia; the picture of Hatra women can be found in the Museum in Baghdad.

TITUS

61-80
These figures are taken from paintings in Dura-Europos and Pompeii and from reliefs on Titus' Triumphal Arch in Rome, which glorifies the destruction of Jerusalem. Above, Emperor Titus himself.

81-100
The Chinese pictured in the foreground are taken from paintings on hollow bricks, now in Boston. The Parthians shown here are from a Persian sculpture; note their hair-style.

101-120
Trajan's column in Rome contains a mass of reliefs which provide detailed information on Roman military tactics.

121-140
Roman banquet according to a mural in Pompeii; Arabic and other horsemen, from pictures in Dura-Europos; reclining woman, from a relief in Berlin; Palmyra gentleman, based on a high relief in Palmyra. Above, an Indian picture from Mathura.

141-160
The Chinese figures in the foreground are partly taken from a relief in Shandong. The Indian musicians were also originally pictured on a relief.

161-180.
When storming a stronghold, Roman foot-soldiers used to form a so-called *tortuga* or tortoise. The Parthians – note their trousers above – are drawn from sculptures in Persia; the Indians from a Greek-influenced relief in Lahore. The Chinese in the background are taken from a relief in Shandong.

181-200
Carriage-borne Chinese had long been powerless against mounted nomads, if there were enough of them. Koreans, after a lacquered painting on a basket from Seoul; Roman gladiators from a relief; the Chinese in the background are also from a relief.

201-220
The birth-rate in Rome might be lower than desired, but babies were lovingly tended. The Chinese scene in the background with carriages drawn by buffaloes and horses is sketched from a stone fragment from Sichuan.

221-240
A Roman huntsman lacing his puttees (mosaic in Carthage); Sassanid horsemen from a Persian relief. In the background, Chinese bird-shooting and rice-planting on a stone fragment from Sichuan.

241-260
In the foreground, Jewish figures based on paintings from Dura-Europos, now in a museum in Damascus. The Sassanid assault is modelled on Persian reliefs.

261-280
Indians from Gandhara in western dress show the influence of Alexander the Great. The Good Shepherd, a motif in heathen art since prehistoric times, was still popular. This particular picture is from Rome.

281-300
Miram was situated on the silk trail in Central Asia. Buddhist art was flourishing there.

301-320
Piazza Armerina in Sicily is a patrician villa with extensive floor mosaics depicting Roman life. The toga was not as popular as previously.

321-340
Indian soldiers from Gandhara, wearing turban, armour and *dhoti*. Their feet are bare. Shapur II's aide-de-camp riding behind him is sitting back-to-front on his horse, perhaps so that he can see whether his master, aiming backwards, has hit the target. The Persian horsemen are well dressed, trailing a miscellany of cloth, tassels, braids and plaits behind them.

341-360
The Roman architecture is drawn from reliefs on Junius Bassus' marble sarcophagus in the Vatican. The other pictures, appear on mosaics in the Piazza Armerina. The solitary Persian on the right is taken from a relief.

361-380
Indian art in Peru was going through a naturalistic stage. The Moshi warrior above is equipped with a club, a shield, a sleeveless, poncho-like garment and a loincloth. The axe-shaped object behind him is a brass bell. The mounted Korean is believed to display the first stirrup depicted in Far Eastern art. In Central Asia, however, stirrups had been in existence for some 500 years, and cavalry men stood up in them to use their bows-and-arrows.

381-400
Bikini-clad girls from Piazza Armerina. The Frankish life-guards of Theodosius the Great wore torques round their necks as a sign of rank. The Chinese people on the right are sketched from Gu Kaizhi's Pictures of Court Ceremonial, a hand-scroll in the British Museum.

401-420
Stilicho is wearing a short tunic, a *sagum*, fastened on one shoulder with a *fibula*. The Chinese of North Wei are drawn from earthenware burial figurines. The Moshi Indians from Peru are sketched from surprisingly realistic paintings on ceramics. Above, Moshi Indians with sedan chain.

421-440.
Moshi from northern Peru. The Indian culture was as old as the European, but completely different. Moshi warriors were heavily armed with clubs, slings and broad-bladed weapons to cut out the victims' hearts. They appear to be wearing leather armour, and their stockings seem to have an opening for the big toe. In the background, Persians on a lion hunt, and Huns, who were now at the peak of their power. Above, a group of Huns.

441-460
A Roman wearing a dalmatic, based on mosaics in Galla Placidia's Mausoleum in Ravenna. Of the two Indians, the one on the left is from Vera Cruz in east Mexico; grinning figures from this area are common, tongue between their teeth, or whistle in mouth. These Indians made a large number of toys, including animals on wheels; this is quite remarkable considering they had not invented wheeled vehicles, since they had no beasts of burden. The Indian on the right comes from Colima in west Mexico, where they bred short-haired dogs for eating. In the background, figures include pillar-saints of the Eastern Empire. Above, a Roman soldier dressed in a *lorica*, consisting of a leather waistcoat, knee-high boots and a broadcloth cloak or *sagum*.

461-480
Figures and scenes from the Eastern Empire mainly taken from an ivory triptych in Milan and mosaics in Ravenna and Rome. The toga has definitely been discarded and has been replaced by the dalmatic. The upper classes wore stripes, *clavi*.

481-500
Empress Ariadne's portrait is found on an ivory relief in Florence. The other Byzantine women are drawn from a manuscript in Vienna.

501-520
A number of Buddhist sculptures and reliefs from rock temples in Longmen have been used as material for these drawings of Chinese people. On the right, Byzantines from reliefs in ivory and from a mural in St Demetrius, Thessalonica. The consul in the middle – and above – is wearing a dalmatic and a long sash or *pallium* wrapped round his body; this was how the Classical cloak had evolved. The square on the dress of the right hand figure is the *tablion*, denoting rank; this remained fashionable for a long time.

521-540
Figures and scenes from the Eastern Empire, based on the Codex Purpureus in Rossano and an ivory diptych in Berlin. The architect advising Emperor Justinian is drawn from a mosaic in St Cosimo e Damiano, Rome. Avove, a Byzantine foot-soldier with a large bow and a club.

541-560
The Chinese figures are taken from, among others, a fresco named "The Story of 500 Thieves" and from a fragment of a stone sarcophagus, now in Kansas City. Above, Empress Theodora's ladies-in-waiting, from a mosaic in Ravenna.

561-580
Ball-game in Jalisco, Mexico, with a heavy ball made of solid rubber. Next to the ball player is a Moshi Indian from Peru with his man-shaped pot. To the right of the Indians and in the background are pictures from floor mosaics in the former Imperial Palace in Constantinople; to a modern viewer they do not look typically Byzantine. The demonic drawings in the background come from reliefs on stone sarcophagi, now in Toronto. On the right-hand side, an Indian woman with a young boy, three Singalese from Ceylon, Chinese and Persians with a mouth organ (a Chinese invention) – all from paintings and sculptures in rock temples. The Chinese mouth organ – above – was later developed in the West as the harmonium.

581-600
The Chinese procession is taken from sculptures from Longmen; the Byzantine figures are from pictures in the Codex Purpureus, Rossano, and from a manuscript in Florence. The Maya Indians playing ball wear guards on the right foot, knee and arm. The ball might be hit with back or knees only; it was solid and therefore extremely dangerous. Above, stallion-baiting, from a carved stone.

601-620
The Chinese from Sui, and the figures at the top, are sketched from small sculptures and from Yan Liben's painting "The Thirteen Emperors", now in Boston. At the back, Japanese, a Korean, Africans and Indians.

621-640
Swedes from Vendel, illustration in Statens historiska museum, Stockholm. Their trousers might be shaggy and they wore horns on their helmets, which was not the case during the true Viking Age, although modern illustrators of our day often think otherwise. Bearded Byzantines from pictures in St Demetrius, Thessalonica; woman from a mosaic in Angeloctistus. Indo-Scythians of the Bokhara area, on the right hand page, from murals. Chinese man with a horse, from a relief in Philadelphia.

641-660
Chinese people from paintings by Yan Liben, now in Boston, and from burial figurines. The paintings in question are titled "Learned Men Studying Classical Texts" and "The Thirteen Emperors". In the background, and also above, Arabs on the march.

661-680
Chinese women from clay figurines and from Yan Liben's painting of the emperors. Two Maya Indians and one Zapotec – the figure above – drumming on a tortoise shell; the Indians never made stringed instruments from these. The three Nestorian men originate from Kizil in Central Asia, sketched from a painting from the Kusha area.

681-700
Maya Indians from Chama in Guatemala had long smoked tobacco as part of a ritual. Other customs were less innocent; in Veracruz, Mexico, for instance, they sacrificed defeated football players to the gods – see above. These drawings are loosely copied from pictures on stone reliefs. In the background a Vendel warrior, a pair of horsemen from Hornhausen in Germany, a number of Persians and two soldiers from Kazakhstan in battle, from a silver plate from the area beyond the Ural Mountains. The plate also shows weapons strewn on the ground.

701-720
Chinese fashions during the Tang dynasty. The women wore dresses of Central Asian style, with a high waist, tight sleeves and a stole over their shoulders. Men from the inner part of Asia wore belted coats with lapels and puffed trousers. The sequence on silk production is from a painting by Zhang Xuan, later copied by the Emperor of the Song dynasty Hui Zong, now in Boston. The scenery in the background to the right is based on a mosaic in the Great Mosque in Damascus. Above, Chinese resting by the Silk Route.

721-740
Seven Chinese women from burial figurines: their hair is in a bun on top of the head, and they are wearing long skirts, rounded collars and stoles. The Chinese writer on the right-hand page is a poet, from a painting by Wang Wei. The Japanese is one of four Celestial Kings in Nara, while the Caliphate figures are from a floor fresco from Qasr al-Hayr al-Gharbi, Syria, now in the National Musuem, Damascus. At the back, figures from a carved stone in Lärbro, Gotland; Frankish cavalry from the Utrecht Psalter, Bibliothèque Nationale, Paris; Persian polo players -also above- and Central Asian scenes from a Dun Huang fresco.

741-760
Mayas carrying their chief in a hammock, an Indian invention Tame jaguars were worshipped as deities. (From a painted frieze on an earthenware vessel). Right-hand page, entertainment at court of Emperor Xuan Zong in Changan. Above, a swing from Veracruz; group of Japanese; musicians from Central Asia.

761-780
Chinese women, from a painting by Zhou Fang. Three Japanese, from wooden sculptures. Frankish chair; woman from East Turkestan, from fragments of a cave painting in Sorcuq, Mayas. Background, Anglo-Saxon scenes, from stone reliefs in Meigle Church, Scotland ; life in Java, from pictures in the Temple of Borobudur. Above, a Javanese ship.

781-800
Charlemagne was 6′ 4″ tall. He is dressed in a short tunic, a cloak fastened on one shoulder and laced shoes. The Indian priest sitting on a table is called Amoghavajra; the picture, painted by Li Zhen, is now in Kyoto. Many architectural relics of the Maya culture, including instructive frescoes, have been uncovered in Bonampak. One custom was to hang a tiny ball on the forehead on a lock of hair to encourage squinting, which was considered attractive – see above. Maya art was aristocratic and comparatively life-like.

801-820
Viking life, from finds in Oseberg and a picture on a piece of wood in Bergen, including, above, a realistic representation of a fleet in port. Right hand page, background, Carolingian farming with iron-tipped plough and shod horses, from an illustrated manuscript.

821-840
More Viking life, mainly from Oseberg finds. Curtains were brought back from Byzantium by the Varangians. Right hand page, Carolingian warriors and scholars; Nestorians, from murals in a Christian temple in Qarakhocho, Central Asia; a Tartar huntsman; an Arabic prince from the Jawsaq Palace in Samarra, Iraq. Above, a Carolingian horseman.

841-860
Franks dressed in clothes from the time of Charles the Bald – see above – from a fresco in St Benedetto, Malles, from the Codex Aureus in Munich and the Utrecht Psalter in Paris. Right-hand page, Manichaeians from East Turkestan, miniature painting now in Berlin.

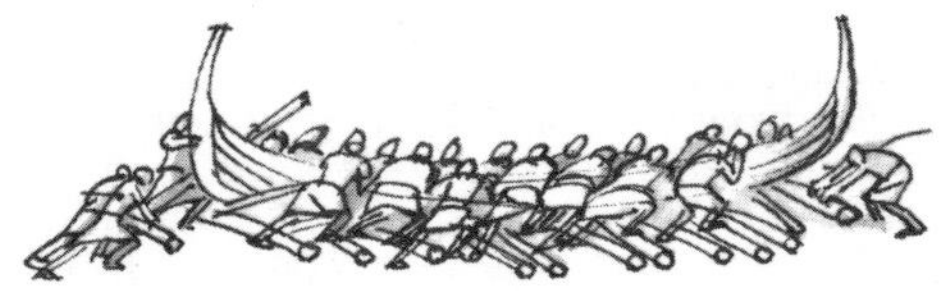

861-880
The Vikings are wearing puffed trousers and

plaited beards; they had learnt this in the East. Right-hand page, Uighurs, from a fresco in Koco, East Turkestan. A Chinese Tang horse remains aloof to the ravages of the Vikings. Above, a Viking ship is rolled into the Dnieper.

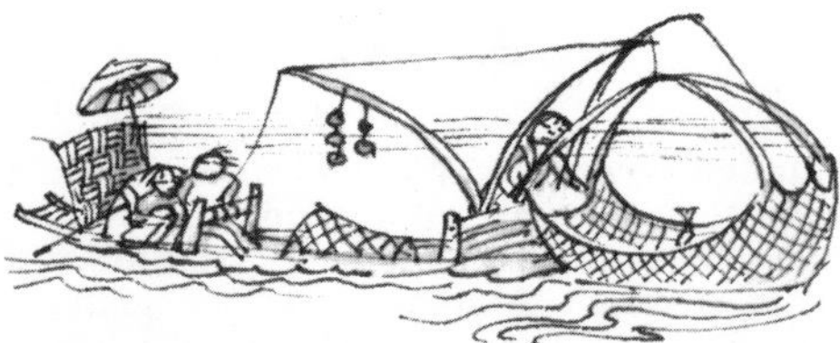

881-900
Europeans at the close of the Carolingian period were dressed in a short tunic and were often bare-headed. Four Chinese Buddhists, stone engraving from Hangzhou; solitary Japanese, from painted wooden sculpture. Background and above, Chinese fishermen with scoop-nets.

901-920
Quitan Tungus with horses and hounds. Two Chinese with fighting-cocks. Right, Byzantine family, from manuscript in Paris. Mayas, from small earthenware sculptures; note the tall hat, and also the weaving women with the warp round her waist. Background, Byzantine scenes. Above, a Byzantine wearing a dalmatic with edging (*clavi*), finished with ornamental circles (*orbiculi*).

921-940
Byzantine woman in an easy chair with cushions – see above – from a picture of the Madonna. Chinese women musicians, from painting on silk, now in Chicago. Far right, rear view of Harold Bluetooth. Background, Byzantines.

941-960
Two figures from East Turkestan, from Chinese painting on silk, Dun-huang. Interior from Constantinople, from portrait of St Luke (miniature on parchment), British Museum. Far right, Emperor Constantine VII Porphyrogenitus with Romanus II and Eudoxia, from an ivory relief. The right-hand page is completely Byzantine, while the background on the left-hand page shows medieval India. Above, a Byzantine water-organ.

961-980
Chinese women, from paintings by Zhou Wenju: "Women and Children on a Terrace" and "Ladies in the Palace", both now in London. Far right, Khmers in Cambodia fighting over a girl, in fact, a flying deity called an *apsara*. Background, Edgar I of England – also above – from miniature on parchment, British Museum; Christians from León, Spain.

981-1000
Otto III's subjects and surroundings, from ivory reliefs in Vienna and painting in Trier. Centre of right-hand page, the Emperor himself, from miniature in Munich. Background, characters from the Eastern Empire and Varangians. Above, Byzantine teacher and pupil with a slate.

1001-1020
Chinese scholars, Byzantine women and musicians, from songbook in the Vatican. Background, left, Maya Indians from Chichén Itzá – also above – and right, Byzantine scenes.

1021-1040
Chinese family life, North Song. Russian princesses in Kiev, Canute the Great in Denmark. Byzantine royal couple, from picture in Monte Cassino. Benedictine friars – above. Byzantines in background also from Monte Cassino.

1041-1060
Byzantine women wearing hooded cloaks -also above. Centurion. Constantine IX Monomachus and Empress Zoë, from mosaic in St Sophia. Right, Byzantine building workers wearing a short *chiton*; these were the same for both sexes. Indian and Byzantine scenes in background.

1061-1080
Far left, three Arabs; far right, Emperor Nicephorus III with Empress Maria. The rest of the illustration shows people and activities from the Bayeux Tapestry, which depicts the Norman Conquest. The Normans – see also above – carry short bows fired from chest height; they are wearing coats of mail, slit at the bottom to enable them to ride a horse. At the battle of Hastings, the Normans used heavily armed horsemen against Britain's foot-soldiers; this decided the day, and settled the history of Europe for several centuries to come. For some reason the Normans shaved their heads at the back, but after they established themselves in England they adopted the fashion there, and grew their hair long.

1081-1100
Arabic wrestling in Cairo. Swedes in a church pew. A high-born Chinese couple; two Byzantine women with children; three Aragonese soldiers with shields and spears; two Jews from Verona, and a group of Byzantines led by a bishop dressed in a long tunic braided in gold. In the background, one Chinese, and crusaders. The agricultural scene above, with a woman at the plough, comes from a bronze relief on the gateway of St Zeno, Verona.

1101-1120
Four unmarried German women – see also above: their hair is long and parted in the middle. Two armed Germans; European civilian in a tunic; two Spaniards sawing wood and four more Spanish figures. Right-hand page, a Coptic priest with incense; a one-wheeled Chinese cart; a Central Asian on horseback. Background, Spanish, Byzantine, Nordic and Chinese scenes.

1121-1140
Chinese characters and activities. Left, people on their way to the Spring Festival in Kaifeng, picture scroll by Chang Zhang Zeduan, far right, a barber.

1141-1160
Two high-born Japanese from Kyoto. Two scythe grinders from Notre Dame, Paris – see also above. French crusader from Nancy returning home. Geoffrey of Anjou with Phrygian helmet and heraldic shield covering his entire body. Only gentlemen like himself were allowed to wear a cloak. Right-hand page, five French people from Chartres; a Christian Byzantine; four German citizens. The then-fashionable turbans worn by the women were 'borrowed' from Persia. Right, two Sicilian Normans, from Capella Palatina in Palermo; baptismal font from Löderup, Skåne, Sweden. In the background, *mureri* in Sicily; miscellaneous activities in England.

1161-1180
Four Byzantines, one with a quill – also pictured above. Madonna from Viklau, Gotland, Sweden, now at Statens Historiska Museum, Stockholm. French bishop wearing a mitre. French gentlewoman with long sleeves. Three French knights wearing a full-length tunic under their armour – a highly impractical fashion! Right-hand page, Khmers in Cambodia with elongated ear-lobes, a Buddhist custom. Far right, two Chinese women, from painting by Su Hanchen. Background, Muslims and Khmers.

1181-1200
Three gardeners, a food carrier and a dancer from North Iraq. A Persian Shah with two attendants. Right-hand page, a French crusader; Khmers setting up a cock-fight – also above; Japanese wearing platform shoes. Background, left, medieval Europe; right, Chinese with carts, pulling a barge.

1201-1220
Six Mongols and a Chinese beggarman, from painting by Zhorue Jichiang. Fisherman with a type of spinning rod, from painting by Ma Yuan. Right-hand page, a Franciscan; a Dominican; a pilgrim wearing a *petasus*; two Jews – also above – wearing yellow pointed hats, imposed by the Lateran Council of 1215.

Far right, a group of crusaders: German on the left, French, Venetian and others on the right; the Germans are wearing surcoats over their armour. Background, Mongols and Chinese in battle; crusaders in the West.

1221-1240
Two French women – also above – with elongated sleeves and collars, a fashion novelty. Married European women wore a barbette, covering the hair and part of the chin, whereas unmarried women wore their hair freely falling. Eight Japanese, including a Samurai in black headgear called an *eboshi*. Right, and background, people from Iraq.

1241-1260
German and French Gothic figures and architecture, from sculptures in Naumburg Cathedral, Bible illustrations and other sources. According to the fashion, men are clean-shaven and both men and women have long hair and wear full-length garments. Helmets were now brimmed, a surcoat was worn over the armour, and the hood which originally formed part of the cloak was now a separate garment. The woman above is wearing a sleeveless surcoat similar to that of the knights.

1261-1280
Spanish Castilians – including those pictured above – from a chess manual by Alfonso X the Wise. Japanese with swords and bows-and-arrows, from a painting entitled "Heiji Monogatari Emaki". In the background, Indians and Khmers.

1281-1300
Two French wine-harvesters, from the cathedral in Reims; Spaniard from Castile wearing a cloak with a cone-shaped hood; Italian thrown off his horse; Mongolian bowman. Right-hand page, a Japanese wearing puffed trousers, see also above. Indian with his horse, from Konarak, Orissa; a group of Arabs. In the background, Kublai Khan hunting, from painting by Lin Guandao; Japanese scenes from the painting "Heiji Monogatari Emaki".

1301-1320
A church founder in Constantinople; four Syrian musicians; Dante and other Italians, from frescoes by Giotto in Padua; woman from Erfurt; German huntsman with falcon and helpers; three German Minnesinger, from Manesse Codex – also pictured above. The dress was bicoloured and hugged the contour of the body. Far right, a French couple: beards were now fashionable again; the woman is wearing a barbette. In the background, scenes from the German court.

1321-1340
Italian people – including the figure above – from frescoes by Ambrogio Lorenzetti in Siena. It appears from these that the well-bred never went outdoors without hats and that buttons were now common – formerly, ribbons were used to fasten the clothes. Gloves were fashionable. Far right, an English knight dressing, assisted by two squires. Background, English scenes.

1341-1360
Italian monk with striped cloak; two English jesters; two Bohemian women with pleated frills round their bonnets; two aged Moors from Granada; two English bowmen, one with a longbow – these had to wear their hair short so as not to get entangled in the string. Right-hand page, three more jesters from England – also pictured above. Note the extreme lengthening of the hood used as a receptacle or as a scarf. Two English women; four Italians, including a couple of swells dressed in sleeved cloaks or *houppelandes*; another English woman; an English civilian and an English soldier in tin armour. In the background, dancing Danes, Orlev Church, Sjaelland, Denmark; right-hand side, Italian scenes.

1361-1380
Four Englishmen dressed in light shoes with cut-away tops; three Chinese; a group of nomads from Central Asia, from Siyah Kalem. Background, Chinese on the left, Mongols on the right.

1381-1400
Bathing-women in Bohemia; two Burgundian monks, from sculpture by Claus Sluter; Persian with armour-clad horse. Two women wearing *hennin* headdresses, a man with bells on his belt, and a woman wearing a hood, fastened at the neck with buttons, all from Burgundy. Right-hand page, four Danes from Holbaek, Tirsted and Maribo – including an offender sitting in the stocks. Background, Persian soldiers, and Italian Guelphs and Ghibellines.

1401-1420
Three French women with trains on their dresses and folded-down collars. Three English people, including a knight in full armour. Flemish couple – note the man's sleeves. Right-hand page, French country people, from miniatures in *Les tres riches heures du duc de Berry*; Frenchman with a dog, from a hunting manual by Gaston Phebus; two Italians, from illustrations in *Decameron* – see also above. The figure on the right is wearing a *houppelande*. Background, from French miniatures.

1421-1440
A Japanese; Flemish people sitting on a sofa; a French gentleman and three French gentlewomen, who may show their ears but not their hair; women plucked their hairline to look almost bald. Right-hand page, Swedish scenes, from pictures in Magnus Eriksson's Law Code – see also above – and from paintings in Tensta Church. Bells and *houppelandes* were fashionable. The waistline was high on women's garments, low on men's. Background, left, Aztecs on the move; right, daily life in Sweden according to the illustrated Law Code.

1441-1440
Christopher of Bavaria wearing a tabard and excessively pointed shoes – also pictured above; Swedish carpenter, Vendel Church; five Italian gentlemen from the court in Ferrara, accompanying a lady (on the right).

The fashion focused on hats and hair. Right-hand page, two Italian soldiers, based on Piero della Francesca; a French beggar; a group of French people wearing very tall hennins and trains which had to be carried; a Swiss-German wearing wooden galoshes and with the left sleeve longer than the right. Background, Italian scenes, based on Paolo Uccello.

1461-1480
An Aztec; an African from Benin; a group of Dutchwomen, depicted by Hans Memling; two Italian women; two Capuchins from Burgundy; two bishops from Flanders armed for war; a group of Germans, from Hausbuchmeister; an Italian woman with a handkerchief – also pictured above; a heretic and a Dominican friar. Background, mainly German scenes, from Hausbuchmeister.

1481-1500
An English knight; a German knight wearing boots and with a double-handed sword, after Dürer; Germans, from Hausbuchmeister. Right-hand page, three Swedes from Härkeberga, one with a bagpipe; three Flemish people, depicted by Hieronymus Bosch, one of them a skater – also pictured above; a Frenchman, from a tapestry; three Persians, including a high-born prisoner having his picture drawn; an Aztec, from Codex Mendoza. Background includes St Erik in combat with a unicorn and a dragon.

1501-1520
Spaniards and Indians in Mexico, from Codex Mendoza – above, one of the Indians. Right-hand page, four German *landsknechts*; the Portugese admiral Afonso d'Albuquerque, viceroy of India; a group of Swedish soldiers with pike, halberd and crossbows, from drawings by Paul Dolnstein, himself a *landsknecht*. In the background, Mexican scenes.

1521-1540
German people, based on Dürer, among others. Right-hand page, a crossbowman; a German couple; Emperor Charles V; a Spaniard wearing stockings – the art of knitting stockings had just been invented and was to revolutionize men's fashions; two Incas; a Turkish soldier; a Swede – also pictured above – from Gripsholm Castle, a good source of information on fashion at the court of Gustav Vasa. In the background, Belgrade besieged by the Turks; the Spanish taking Peru from the Incas.

1541-1560
Life in the Netherlands, after Pieter Brueghel the elder; the picture above is derived from his painting on games. Right-hand page, a Russian with a knout; a gentleman in Spanish dress; two Persians, one with heels on the shoes; two Swedes drinking – note the drinking vessel. Background, left-hand page, European scenes, from Albrecht Dürer – who drew the knight – and illustrations of Olaus Magnus and Agricola. Background, right-hand page, Persian scenes.

1561-1580
Dutch peasants, from Pieter Brueghel the elder. Right-hand page, a Swedish lady named Elsa Trolle – also pictured above; three soldiers, from charcoal drawings by Erik XIV of Sweden; a cardinal, as depicted by El Greco; the Spanish Queen Elizabeth of Valois; King Charles IX in France; a royal child; four Indians from the Great Mogul Empire. Background, the Battle of Lepanto; Indian cavalry.

1581-1600
Two British courtiers in Spanish dress, one wearing a ruff and garters; Queen Elizabeth of England; a Persian huntsman, from Riza-i-Abbasi; two Dutch sailors; two Spanish musketeers; a Spaniard, after Hendrik Goltzius; King John III of Sweden in Spanish dress; a group of Japanese, as depicted in a series of paintings from Kyoto. Background, the sinking of the Spanish Armada; Akbar hunting in India with a leopard.

1601-1620
Five Dutch people, after Adriaen Brouwer and others. Tobacco-smoking (cf 681-700)

had reached Europe; Charles IX of Sweden wearing a falling collar; three Polish guards; Right-hand page, Japanese pipe-smoker, tea-drinkers, carpenter, transport workers. Swedish background on the left, Persian on the right.

1621-1640
Two officers, after Jacques Callot; three characters from Commedia dell'arte, Venice; two street vendors in Paris with a wheelbarrow, a Chinese invention which had just reached the West; King Gustavus II Adolphus of Sweden. Right-hand page, four French people – the European climate had become colder, and furs were worn. Charles I of England, after Van Dyck; three Persians, from Riza-i-Abbasi; three Japanese – also above. Card games were introduced to Japan from the West. Far right, Cardinal Richelieu. Background, the Thirty Years' War raged in Europe; life in China.

1641-1660
Three English people, including a woman with a hairstyle *à la Sévigné*; Dutch people, from Wenzel Hollar. Right-hand page, Magnus Gabriel de la Gardie with wife and attendant; three French aristocrats – one of them permanently masked; three Danish people; a little Spanish princess, from Velasquez – also pictured above – children were still wearing adult dress; three figures from Benin, Nigeria. Background, left, the coronation of Queen Christina of Sweden; right, scenes from Benin.

1661-1680
Dutch people, based on Vermeer and Frans Hals, among others; three Russians. To the right, three English academics, after David Loggan; a French dandy in winter clothes and a Swedish dandy, after Magalotti – also above. Far right, a Laplander in his sledge, from Ehrenstrahl and Schefferus. Background, left, the four-day battle between the English and Dutch in 1666; right, the hard life of the Lapps.

1681-1700
Japanese with sedan and parasols – the woman above is wearing stilt shoes; Indian man and woman; French people wearing full-bottomed wig, fontange and bustle, after Jean Berain. Pockets were becoming more common. Background left, Vienna besieged by the Turks; right, the long, muddy roads in Sweden.

1701-1720
Swedish horseman; Danish grenadier; two Russians; Polish horseman; Saxon life-guard; English grenadier; Spanish guard; French horseman; Scottish bagpiper. Right-hand page, young Japanese gentleman; European figures, from Antoine Watteau. The man pictured above is wearing knee-breeches, *culottes*, buckled shoes, powdered full-bottomed wig and a three-cornered hat to be held under the arm. Background, left, Swedish-Russian War; right, Chinese dredging.

1721-1740
Washerwoman, based on Chardin; French grinder; two Frenchwomen – note the pleat running right down the back of the dress, the fan and the hurdy-gurdy; whirling dervishes. Right-hand page, four Koreans; a china-carrier from Jingdezhen; two coolies with a mandarin in a sedan; Chinese playing a *sanxian*. Background, left – and above – whaling. Whalebones were in great demand as stiffeners for ladies' skirts. Background, right, Chinese porcelain making, an art which fascinated the West.

1741-1760
English man and women, as depicted by Hogarth and Gainsborough; three Swedes, including a soldier with powdered hair, from a drawing by J.E. Rehn; French soldier; French woman playing battledore and shuttlecock, from Chardin; people from India and Afghanistan; Emperor Ahmed of Great Mogul smoking a water-pipe with a long tube. Background, left, Swedish countryside – above, a manor house from Linnaeus' day; right, Indian hunt.

1761-1780
English and French rococo fashions, as seen by John Zoffany and Moreau le jeune, among others. Women's hairstyles had increased in height, eyebrows were darkened and skirts were so wide that women had to walk through doors sideways. Right-hand page, figures from the American Civil War: Fox Indian; Sioux Indian; American scout; French grenadier; English musketeer; Hessian grenadier. Far right, three Europeans. Background, hawkers in Paris; American Civil War.

1781-1800
Three Turks, including a janissary on the left. A group of people from France, where cats had become domestic pets and special children's clothes had been introduced. The French Revolution brought an instant change to fashion, as can be seen on the right-hand page. Pantaloons were worn and Paris was taken over by fashion-conscious fops, nicknamed "incroyables". A woman with a yoyo was a common sight at this time. Dresses were inspired by Ancient Greece. The four figures on the right – also pictured above – are two Frenchwomen, an Englishman wearing a redingote, and a Spanish woman, after Goya. The background shows Parisian scenes; the hot-air balloon and the guillotine were new inventions.

1801-1820
French soldier, after Goya; French cavalryman, from Géricault; Napoleon I; Bavarian gunner; Austrian hussar; Spanish infantry soldier; Russian gunner; Russian Guards officer; Swedish infantry soldier; Prussian grenadier; English colonel. The French people on the right-hand page are wearing : redingote: tails and top hat; chemise dress; Spencer jacket and reticule; dress with a redingote cut; feminine Garrick. Fashion accessories worn by the English trio include a turban, cut-throat collar and poke bonnet –

see above. Far right, Japanese wrestlers with referee, from Hokusai.

1821-1840
Ten Mexicans; two Mandan Indians, after George Catlin. Right-hand page, a line-up of Europeans dressed respectively in fur-edged pelerine; havelock; Biedermayer shoulders; winter redingote fringed shawl; another pelerine; pantaloons – the last three also pictured above. Far right, four Ottoman Turks in formal pose.

1841-1860
Four Swedes, from Fritz von Dardel; groups of French and English people, including one woman in an American Bloomer dress – also pictured above; the children are playing with hoops and a skipping rope; one of the Englishmen rides a bicycle.

1861-1880
Three French labourers, after Daumier; two Americans, one from the North and one from the South; Prussian hussar; two Danish children in military dress; Frenchwoman in a crinoline with her daughter; Englishman in a frock-coat; Englishwoman in a Garibaldi dress; Englishman in a lounge coat. Right-hand page, four Americans bathing in the sea, after Fritz von Dardel; eight Germans – note hairstyles with false plaits, also bustles; English salvationist – also pictured above.

1881-1900
English and German leisure activities. Right-hand page, English painting scene, after Caldecott; three Chinese, including a Mandarin; French and English fashions.

1901-1920
Fashion scenes from England, France, Sweden and USA.

1921-1940
Three English characters, from *Punch*; Charlie Chaplin – above – and an assortment of contemporary figures from USA, Britain, Spain, France, Germany and Sweden.

THE FOLLOWING INSTITUTES AND PHOTOGRAPHERS HAVE CONTRIBUTED ILLUSTRATIONS:

Alinari, Florence: 710 BC, 80 AD, 280 AD + Frederico Arborio Mella, Milan; 320 AD, 640 AD, 750 AD, 1220 AD + Archives Photographiques: 140 AD, 840 BC + Archivio Mondadori, Milan: 980 BC, 790 BC, 740 BC, 690 BC, 610 BC, 500 BC, 450 BC, 100 AD, 160 AD, 230 AD, 250 AD, 270 AD, 280 AD, 400 AD, 470 AD, 480 AD, 570 AD, 580 AD, 610 AD, 650 AD, 790 AD, 1160 AD, 1180 AD, 1330 AD, 1410 AD, 1460 AD, 1510 AD, 1660 AD, 1670 AD, 1700 AD, 1880 AD + Archivi Vaticani, Rome 820 AD, 1070 AD + Archivio il libro del mondo; 470 AD + Artia; 1100 AD + Bayeux, Musee de: 1060 AD + Bevilacqua 700 BC, 900 AD + Biblioteca Marciana, Venice; 1000 AD + (Hirmer): Biblioteca Nacional, Madrid: 1010 AD + Bibliothèque Nationale, Paris: 430 AD, 730 AD, 820 AD, 850 AD, 1360 AD + Roberto Bosi: 280 AD + British Museum, London: 620 BC, 1030 AD + Carpinecci: 180 AD, 200 AD, 220 AD + Colombo: 590 AD + Nationalmuséet, Copenhagen: 970 BC + Dimt: 610 BC + Editorial Herrero, Mexico City: 340 AD + Fogg Art Museum, Harvard University, Cambridge: 630 AD + Foundation Saint-Thomas, Strasbourg: 1600 AD + Werner Forman: 420 BC, 980 AD, + John Freeman: 1690 AD, 770 AD + Freer Gallery, Washington DC; 860 BC + Giraudon, Paris: 680 BC, 1760 AD + Ian Graham: 1590 AD + Green Studio, Dublin: 720 AD + Ara Güler, Ankara: 910 AD, 1040 AD + Hachette (Michel Cabaud): 810 AD + Hamlyn Group Picture Library, London: 670 BC + David Harris: 690 AD + André Heldford: 290 AD + Michael Holford, London: 550 BC + Holle Verlag, Munich: 490 AD, 720 AD + Imperial Library, Teheran (Mandel): 1210 Ad + Kodansha, Tokyo: 780 BC, 660 BC, 580 BC, 460 BC, 440 BC, 90 AD, 140 AD, 240 AD, 260 AD, 300 AD, 420 AD, 560 AD, 610 AD, 660 AD, 760 AD, 770 AD, 780 AD, 1250 AD + Öffentliche Kunstsammlung, Basle: 920 BC + Laffont Collection: 410 AD + Louvre, Paris: 730 BC, 210 AD + Madanjeet Singh, New Delhi: 460 AD + Mansell Collection, London: 950 AD, 1680 AD + Marzari: 930 BC, 1540 AD + Mercurio, Milan: 490 BC + Metropolitan Museum of Art, New York: 960 AD + Meyer: 1720 AD + Cecilia Moessner Collection, Staatliche Antikensammlungen und Glyptothek, Munich, 540 BC + Musuem of Fine Art, Boston: 870 BC + Museum of the University of Pennsylvania; 910 BC + Nationalmuseum, Stockholm: 1570 AD + New York Public Library, Spencer Collection: 620 AD Ö stasiatiska museet, Stockholm: 440 BC, 70 BC, 180 AD, 350 AD, 730 AD, 760 AD + R. Pellegrini: 760 BC + Pictor, Milan: 830 BC + Pierpont Morgan Library, New York: 860 AD + Pilgrim's Hall, Plymouth Plantation: 1620 AD + Plimpton Collection Columbia University Libraries: 920 AD + Pucciarelli, Rome: 390 AD + Radio Times Hulton Picture Library, London: 1270 AD + Konstantino Reyes-Valerio, Mexico City: 150 AD + Ricciarini, Milan: 560 BC, (Bevilacqua), 170 AD, (Tomsich) Fulvio Roiter, Venice: 950 BC + John Ross: 990 BC + Sant' Ambrogio, Milan: 380 AD + Scala, Florence; 530 BC, 140 AD, 330 AD, 360 AD, 370 AD, 400 AD, 420 AD, 440 AD, 450 AD, 480 AD, 600 AD, 1230 AD, 1550 AD + Scarnati, Milan 130 AD 1630 AD + Sovrintendenza alle antichitá della Calabria: 640 BC + Standard Oil of New Jersey Collection, University of Louisville: 1890 AD + Staatliche Museen, Berlin: 590 BC, 1610 AD + Stanford University Press: 150 AD + Statens historiska museum, Stockholm: 1150 AD + Tourist Association, Japan: 1100 AD + Ullstein Bilderdienst, Berlin: 1530 AD + Walter, Milan: 170 AD + Willemin, Paris: 740 AD + Vitterhetsakademien, Stockholm: 1050 BC + Woburn Abbey Collection: 1560 AD + Zampieri: 770 BC.

INDEX

KEY TO INDEX

I have used the international code for car numberplates to denote the nationality of people listed in the index. This code is used for kings and presidents of all existing states as well as of other states which ceased to exist long ago. Thus the heads of state of Ancient Egypt, Ancient Persia, Ancient Israel, Ancient Bulgaria and Great Moravia (codes ET, IR, IL, BG and CS respectively) are also indicated by modern car registration codes. RC signifies China throughout its history: R may be interpreted as "Royal" during the long periods when it could not possibly mean "Republic". However, I found it unbearably anachronistic to use the code SU for Russians of the past, such as Rurik and Ivan the Terrible: instead I have given the code RU to Russians before 1918.

When it comes to states which have been absorbed by other states or expired without heirs in the past, long before the car era, new codes had to be invented. It seemed vital not to have too many codes, however: whenever possible I have used new combinations of existing codes. The purpose of the codes after all is to bring order into the myriad of names in the index.

In the index, the sign – means BC; + stands for AD.

THE COUNTRIES OF THE CODES

A = Austria
AFG = Afghanistan
AL = Albania
ARA = Aragon
ASS = Assyria
AST = Asturia, León
ATH = Athens

B = Belgium
BAB = Babylonia
BACT = Bactria
BAY = Bavaria
BG = Bulgaria
BOSP = Greek Crimea
BR = Brazil
BRAN = Brandenburg
BURG = Burgundy, Bourgogne
BYZ = Byzantium = Eastern Empire after Justinian

C = Cuba
CAL = Caliphate (in Medina, Damascus and Bhagdad)
CAPP = Cappadocia
CART = Carthage
CAST = Castile
CO = Colombia, Gran Colombia
CORD = Cordoba, the Spanish Caliphate
CS = Great Moravia, Bohemia, Czechoslovakia

D = Germany
DK = Denmark
DZ = Algeria

E = Spain
EAT = Tanzania
EIR = Ireland
EST = Estonia
ET = Egypt
ETH = Ethiopia

F = Franks, France
FEN = Phoenicians
FIR = Florence

GB = England, Great Britain
GH = Ghana
GR = Greece

H = Hungarians, Hungary
HAT = Hittites, Hatti
HKJ = Jordan
HUN = Huns

I = Italy
IL = Israel, Palestine
IMP = Imperium Romanum = Frankish Empire, Holy Roman Empire
IN = Indonesia
IND = India
IR = Persia, Parthia, Iran
IRQ = Iraq
IS = Iceland

J = Japan
JU = Judaea

LAR = Libya
LET = Lettland
LIT = Lithuania
LONG = Lombards
LYD = Lydia

MA = Morocco
MAC = Macedonia
MED = Media
MEX = Mexico
MIT = Mitanni, the Hurrian Empire
MONG = Mongols, the Golden Horde

N = Norway
NA = Naples, the Two Sicilies
NIG = Nigeria
NL = Netherlands, Holland

OGO = Ostrogoths

P = Portugal
PAK = Pakistan
PE = Peru
PERG = Pergamon
PHRY = Phrygia
PL = Poland
PONT = Pontus
PREU = Prussia

R = Romania
RA = Argentina
RB = Bolivia
RC = China
RH = Haiti
ROM = Rome, Roman Empire
RU = Russia, Soviet Union

S = Sweden
SARD = Sardinia
SAVO = Savoy
SAX = Saxony
SCOT = Scotland
SCYT = Scythians
SELD = Seljuks
SF = Finland
SIC = Sicily
SM = Saudi Arabia
SU = Soviet Union
SYA = Syracuse, Siracusa
SYR = Syria

T = Siam, Thailand
THEB = Thebes
THRA = Thrace
TN = Tunisia
TO = Teutonic Order
TR = Ottomans, Turkey

USA = United States of America

V = the Vatican, the Papal Chair
VAND = Vandals
VEN = Venice
VIGO = Visigoths
VN = Vietnam

YU = Serbia, Yugoslavia
YV = Venezuela

ZA = South African Union

THE CODES OF THE COUNTRIES

Afghanistan = AFG
Albania = AL
Algeria = DZ
Aragon = ARA
Argentina = RA
Assyria = ASS
Asturia = AST
Athens = ATH
Austria = A

Babylonia = BAB
Bactria = BACT
Bavaria = BAY
Belgium = B
Bohemia = CS
Bolivia = RB
Brandenburg = BRAN
Brazil = BR
Bulgaria = BG
Burgundy = BURG

Caliphate (in Medina, Damascus and Bhagdad) = CAL
Caliphate (in Cordoba) = CORD
Cappadocia = CAPP
Carthage = CART
Castile = CAST
China = RC
Colombia = CO
Cordoba = CORD
Cuba = C
Czechoslovakia = CS

Denmark = DK

Eastern Empire = BYZ (Justiniano mortuo)
Egypt = ET
England = GB
Estonia = EST
Ethiopia = ETH

Finland = SF
Florence = FIR
France = F
Franks = F
Frankish Empire = IMP

Germany = D
Ghana = GH
Golden Horde = MONG
Gran Colombia = CO
Great Britain = GB
Great Moravia = CS
Greece = GR

Haiti = RH
Hittites = HAT
Holland = NL
Holy Roman Empire = IMP
Huns = HUN
Hungary = H

Iceland = IS
India = IND
Indonesia = IN
Iran = IR
Iraq = IRQ
Ireland = EIR
Israel = IL
Italy = I

Japan = J
Jordan = HKJ
Judaea = JU

León = AST
Lettland = LET
Libya = LAR
Lithuania = LIT
Lombards = LONG
Lydia = LYD

Macedonia = MAC
Media = MED
Mexico = MEX
Mitanni = MIT
Mongols = MONG
Morocco = MA

Naples = NA
Netherlands = NL
Nigeria = NIG
Norway = N

Ottomans = TR
Ostrogoths = OGO

Pakistan = PAK
Papal Chair = V
Papal States = V
Parthia = IR
Pergamon = PERG
Persia = IR
Peru = PE
Phoenicia = FEN
Phrygia = PHRY
Poland = PL
Pontus = PONT
Portugal = P

Prussia = PREU

Roman Empire = ROM
Romania = R
Russia = RU

Sardinia = SARD
Saudi Arabia = SM
Savoy = SAVO
Saxony = SAX
Scotland = SCOT
Scythians = SCYT
Seljuks = SELD
Serbia = YU
Siam = T
Sicily = SIC
South African Union = ZA
Soviet Union = SU
Spain = E
Sweden = S
Syracuse = SYA
Syria = SYR

Tanzania = EAT
Teutonic Order = TO
Thailand = T
Thebes = THEB
Thrace = THRA
Tunisia = TN
Turkey = TR
Two Sicilies = TO

United States of America = USA
Vandals = VAND
Vatican = V
Venice = VEN
Venezuela = YV
Vietnam = VN
Visigoths = VIGO

Yugoslavia = YU

A Le Ben (RC) +630
Abagha Khan (IR) 1265-1282
Abbas (DZ) 1962-1963
'Abbas I (IR) 1588-1628
'Abbas II (IR) 1642-1666
'Abbas III (IR) 1732-1736
'Abd Allah (CORD) 889-912
Abd al-Aziz ibn Sa'ud (SM) 1926-1953
Abdalmik = Abd al-Malik (CAL) 685-705
'Abd ar-Rahman I (CORD) 756-788
'Abd ar-Rahman II (CORD) 822-852
'Abd ar-Rahman III (CORD) 912-961
'Abd ar-Rahman IV (CORD) 1023-1024
Abdera (GR) -650
Abdon (IL) ca 1080-1070
Abdorrahman (AFG) 1880-1901
Abdulaziz (TR) 1861-1876
Abdulhamid I (TR) 1774-1789
Abdulhamid II (TR) 1876-1909
Abdullah ibn Hussein (HKJ) 1923-1951
Abdulmecid (TR) 1839-1861
Abel (DK) 1250-1252
Abelard, Peter (F) +1136
Abieshu (BAB) 1647-1620
Abijah (JU) 909-907
Abimelech (IL) ca 1120-1110
Abirattash (BAB) ca 1500-1491
Abishag (IL) -970
Absalon (DK) +1170
Abu Bakr (CAL) 632-634
ab urbe condita (ROM) -753
Abu-Sa'id (IR) 1316-1335
Abu Sa'id (IR) 1452-1467
Abu Simbel (ET) -1270, 600
Acacius (BYZ) +500
Achà, José de (RB) 1861-1864
Acheampong, I (GH) 1972-78
Achoris (ET) ca 392-381
Acragas (SIC) -580, 560, 480, 470
Actium (ROM) -31
Adad-apal-iddin (BAB) 1083-1062
Adad-nirari I (ASS) 1308-1281
Adad-nirari II (ASS) 911-891
Adad-nirari III (ASS) 811-784
Adad-nirari IV (ASS) 763-755
Adad-shum-iddin (BAB) ca 1240-1233
Adad-shum-nasir (BAB) 1232-1203
Adaloald (LONG) 616-626
Adam of Bremen (DK,S) +1060, 1080
Adams, John (USA) 1797-1801
Adams, John Quincy (USA) 1825-1829
Adelheid (D) 991-995
Adeodatus (V) 672-676
Adid (ET) 1160-1167
Adolf Frederick (S) 1751-1771
Adolf of Nassau (D) 1292-1298 = Adolf I (IMP)
Adonijah (IL) -970
Aegeus (ATH) -690
Aegina -440
Aemilian (ROM) +253
Aemilius Paullus, L (ROM) 167-164
Aeschylus (ATH,SIC) -480, -460, -420
Aesop (GR) -610
Aethelbald (I) (GB) 716-757
Aethelbald (GB) 858-860
Aethelbert (GB) 860-866
Aethelred I (GB) 866-871
Aethelred II (GB) 978-1012
Aethelwulf (GB) 839-858
Aetius (ROM) +460
Afghanistan +980, 1760, 1830
Afonso I (P) 1128-1185
Afonso II (P) 1211-1223
Afonso III (P) 1248-1279
Afonso IV (P) 1325-1357
Afonso V the African (P) 1438-1481
Afonso VI (P) 1656-1667
Agapetus I (V) 535-536
Agapetus II (V) 946-955
Agatho (V) 678-681
Agathocles (SYA) 317-289
Agha Mohammad Khan (IR) 1794-1795
Agila (VIGO) 549-554
Agilulf (LONG) 590-616
Agincourt (F,GB) +1415
Agrippa, Marcus (ROM) -20
Agrippina (ROM) +60
Aguirre Cerda, Pedro (RCH) 1938-1941
Agum I (BAB) ca 1516-1515
Agum II (BAB) ca 1460-1441
Agustín I (MEX) 1821-1823
Ahab (IL) 869-851
Ahaz (JU) 742-725
Ahaziah (IL) 851-850
Ahaziah (JU) 845-844
Ahijah (IL) -920
Ahmad Mirza (IR) 1909-1925
Ahmad Shah (AFG) 1747-1773
Ahmed Zogu (AL) 1925-1939
Ahmed Ben Bella (DZ) 1963-1965
Ahmed (IR) 1375-1395
Ahmed I (TR) 1603-1617
Ahmed II (TR) 1691-1695
Ahmed III (TR) 1703-1730
Ahmose (ET) ca 1577-1557
Ahmose (ET) 569-527
Ainu (J) +812
Aistulf (LONG) 749-756
Ajātaśatru (IND) 554-527
Akbar (IND) 554-527
Akbar (IND) 1556-1605
Akel (EST) +1924
Akhenaton (ET) 1378-1362
Aksum (ETH) +575
Akuffo (GH) +1978
Akufo-Addo (GH) 1970-1972
al-Amīn (CAL) 809-813
Alamut (IR) 1485-1486
Alani -120, +370, +407
Alaric (VIGO) 396-410
Alaric II (VIGO) 484-506
al-Aziz (ET) 975-996
Alba (SCOT) +1010
al-Bakr, Ahmad Hassan (IRQ) 1968-1979
Albert I (A) 1281-1308
Albert II the Wise (A) 1329-1358
Albert III (A) 1356-1395
Albert IV (A) 1395-1404
Albert V (A) 1404-1439
Albert I (B) 1909-1934
Albert V (BAY) 1550-1579
Albert I (D) 1298-1308
Albert II (D) 1437-1439 = Albert I (H) = Albert I (CS) = Albert II (IMP)
Albert I (H) 1437-1439 = Albert I (CS) = Albert II (D) = Albert II (IMP)
Albert I (IMP) 1298-1308 = Albert I (D)
Albert II (IMP) 1437-1439 = Albert I (H) = Albert I (CS) = Albert II (D)
Albert of Mecklenburg (S) 1363-1389
Albigensians (F.V) +1210
Alboin (LONG) 562-572
Alboin (SAX) +763
Albrecht (A,BAY,D) = Albert
Alcaeus (GR) -570
Alcibiades (ATH) ca 418-417, 409-408
Alcorta, José Figueroa (RA) 1906-1910
Alcuin (F) +790, 810
Alemán, Miguel (MEX) 1946-1952
Alemanni +210, 220, 260, 350, 410
d'Alembert (F) +1750
Alessandri, Arturo (RCH) 1920-1924, 1932-1938
Alessandri, Jorge (RCH) 1958-1964
Alexander I (BG) 1879-1886
Alexander (BYZ) 912-913
Alexander I (GR) 1917-1920
Alexander Jannaeus (IL) 104-77
Alexander II (MAC) 370-369
Alexander III (MAC) 336-323 = Alexander the Great
Alexander (PL) 1501-1506
Alexander Severus (ROM) 222-235
Alexander Nevsky (RU) 1252-1263
Alexander I (RU) 1801-1825
Alexander II (RU) 1855-1881
Alexander III (RU) 1881-1894
Alexander I (SCOT) 1107-1124
Alexander II (SCOT) 1213-1249
Alexander III (SCOT) 1249-1286
Alexander Balas (SYR) 150-145
Alexander I (V) 105-115
Alexander II (V) 1061-1073
Alexander III (V) 1159-1181
Alexander IV (V) 1254-1261
Alexander V (V,contra) 1409-1410
Alexander VI de Borgia (V) 1492-1503
Alexander VII (V) 1655-1667
Alexander VIII (V) 1689-1691
Alexander Karageorgevic (YU) 1842-1858
Alexander I (Serbia, YU) 1889-1903
Alexander I (YU,II Serbia) 1921-1934
Alexandru Cuza (R) 1859-1866
Alexis Mikhaylovich (RU) 1645-1676
Alexius Comnenus (BYZ) 1081-1118
Alexius II (BYZ) 1180-1183
Alexius III Angelus (BYZ) 1195-1202
Alexius IV (BYZ) 1203-1204
Alexius V (BYZ) +1204
Alfonso I (ARA) 1102-1134
Alfonso II the Chaste (ARA) 1162-1196
Alfonso III the Liberal (ARA) 1285-1291
Alfonso IV the Benign (ARA) 1327-1336
Alfonso V (ARA) 1416-1458 = Alfonso of Aragon (SIC)
Alfonso I the Catholic (AST) 739-757
Alfonso II the Chaste (AST) 791-842
Alfonso III the Great (AST) 866-910
Alfonso IV (AST,León) 925-931
Alfonso V the Noble (AST,León) 999-1028
Alfonso VI (CAST) 1072-1109
Alfonso VII (CAST) 1126-1157
Alfonso VIII (CAST) 1158-1214
Alfonso IX (CAST,León) 1217-1230
Alfonso X the Wise (CAST) 1252-1284
Alfonso XI the Just (CAST) 1312-1350
Alfonso of Castile (D) ca +1267 = Alfonso X the Wise (CAST)
Alfonso XII (E) 1875-1885
Alfonso XIII (E) 1885-1931
Alfonso II (NA) 1494-1495
Alfonso (V) of Aragon (NA) 1435-1458
Alfonso of Aragon (SIC) 1416-1458 = Alfonso V (ARA)
Alfred (GB) 871-899
Algarve (P) +1252
Algirdas (LIT) 1330-1377
Alhambra (E) +1350
Alī (CAL) 656-660
Ali (ET) 1254-1259
Ali (IR) +1834
Ali ibn Hammūd (CORD) 1016-1018
Ali Mardan (IR) 1749-1750
Ali Murad Shah (IR) 1782-1783
Alice in Wonderland +1865
Allende Gossens, Salvador (RCH) 1970-1973
Alluwamnas (HAT) ca 1498-1493
al-Mamun (CAL) 813-833
al-Mansūr (CORD) +1020
Almeida, Antonio José de (P) 1919-1923
Almondhir (CORD) 886-888
al-Muhtadi (CAL) 869-870
al-Mu'izz (ET) 869-975
al-Muktafi (CAL) 902-908
al-Muntasir (CAL) 861-862
al-Muqtadir (CAL) 908-932
al-Musta'in (CAL) 862-866
al-Mustakfī (CAL) 944-946
al-Mustasir (CAL) 861-862
al-Mu'tadid (CAL) 892-902
al-Mutakki (CAL) 940-944
al-Mu'tamid (CAL) 870-892
al-Mu'tasim (CAL) 833-842
al-Mutawakkil (CAL) 847-861
al-Mu'tazz (CAL) 866-869
al-Muti (CAL) 946-974
al-Muttaqī (CAL) 940-944
Alonso, S. Fernandez (RB) 1896-1899
Alp-Arslan (SELD) 1063-1072
alphabet -900,410
al-Qādir (CAL) 991-1031
al-Qāhir (CAL) 932-934
al-Qā'im (CAL) 1031-1058
al-Qāsim ibn Hammūd (CORD) 1018-1021, 1022-1063
al-Ta'i (CAL) 974-991
Alvarado, Juan Velasco (PE) 1968-1975
Alvarez, Echeverrīa (MEX) 1970-1976
al-Wāthiq (CAL) 842-847
Alvear, Marcelo (RA) 1922-1928
Alves, Rodrigues (BR) 1902-1906, 1918-1919
Alyattes (LYD) ca. 585-561
Amadeus I (E) 1871-1873
Amalaric (VIGO) 507-531
Amalasuntha (OGO) 526-535
Amanollah (AFG) 1919-1929
Amaziah (JU) 799-782
Ambrose +374, 382
Amenemhet I (ET) 1991-1962
Amenemhet II (ET) 1927-1895
Amenemhet III (ET) 1849-1801
Amenemhet IV (ET) 1800-1792
Amenemope (ET) ca 985-973
Amenhotep I (ET) 1555-1531
Amenhotep II (ET) 1447-1420
Amenhotep III (ET) 1411-1379
Amenhotep IV (ET) 1378-1362
Amir (ET) 1101-1130
Ammiditana (BAB) 1619-1583
Ammisaduqa (BAB) 1582-1562
Amon (JU) 642-640
Amos (IL) -770
Ampère, André-Marie 1775-1836
Amundsen, Roald (N) +1911
Amyntas III (MAC) 380-371
Amyrtaeus (ET) 404-399
Amytis (BAB) -570
Anabasis (ATH) -400
Anacletus I (V) 77-87
Ananda Mahidol (T) 1935-1946
Anastasius I (ROM,BYZ) 491-518
Anastasius II (BYZ) 713-715
Anastasius I (V) 399-401
Anastasius II (V) 496-498
Anastasius III (V) 911-913
Anastasius IV (V) 1153-1154
Anaxagoras -430
Ancus Marcius (ROM) 640-617
Andrade, I. (YV) 1897-8

Andrew I (H) 1046-1060
Andrew II (H) 1205-1235
Andrew III (H) 1290-1301
Andrew (NA) 1343-1345
Andrew Bogolyubsky (RU) 1157-1175
Andrew III (RU) 1294-1304
Andronicus I (BYZ) 1183-1185
Andronicus II Palaeologus (BYZ) 1282-1328
Andronicus III Palaeologus (BYZ) 1328-1341
Andronicus IV (BYZ) 1376-1379
Andropov, Y (RU) 1982-
Angelico, Fra Giovanni 1387-1455
Angles +290, 450, 570
Anicetus (V) 156-166
Ankan (J) 532-536
Ankrah, Joseph (GH) 1966-1970
An Lu-shan (RC) ⅛ 750, 766
Anna Comnena (BYZ) +1130
Anna (RU) +989
Anna Ivanovna (RU) 1730-1740
Anne (GB) 1702-1714
Anselm of Canterbury (GB) +1110
Ansgar (DK,S) +830
Anterus (V) +236
Anthemius (ROM) 467-472
Anthony, St. +290, 310, 340, 356
Antigonus (IL) 40-39
Antigonus II Gonatus (MAC) 285-239
Antigonus III Doson (MAC) 229-221
Antigonus (PHRY) 323-301
Antiochus I Soter (SYR) 280-261
Antiochus II Theos (SYR) 261-246
Antiochus III (SYR) 223-187
Antiochus IV Epiphanes (SYR) 175-164
Antiochus V (SYR) 163-162
Antiochus VI (SYR) 145-142
Antiochus VII Sidetes (SYR) 139-129
Antiochus VIII Grypus (SYR) 125-113, 112-95
Antiochus IX Cyzicenus (SYR) 112-95
Antiochus X (SYR) –95
Antiochus XI (SYR) –94
Antiochus XII (SYR) 88-84
Antiochus XIII Asiaticus (SYR) 69-67
Antipater (MAC) 323-319
Antoku (J) 1181-1183
Antoninus Pius (ROM) 138-161
Antonius, M, (ROM) 44-31
Antony I (SAX) 1827-1837
Anund Jakob (S) 1026-1051
Apilsin (BAB) 1766-1749
Apollonius of Perga –180
Apollonius of Tyana +230, 280
Apopi I (ET) ca 1720-1710
Apopi II (ET) ca 1710-1700
Apopi III (ET) ca 1699-1680
Appius Claudius (ROM) –450
Appius Claudius Caecus (ROM) 304-302
Apries (ET) 588-564
Aquitaine (F) +1152
Arada Mendez, Miguel (CO) 1926-1930
Aramburu, Pedro (RA) 1955-1958
Arame (URARTU) –860
Ara pacis (ROM) –13
Arbogast (ROM) +394
Arcadius (ROM) 395-408
Arce, Anicete (RB) 1888-1892
Archelaus (JU) –4 - +7
Archilochus (GR) –680
Archimedes (SYA) –210
Archons (ATH) –690, –490
Ardashīr I (IR) 230-239
Ardashīr II (IR) 379-383
Ardashīr III (IR) 628-630
Ardys (LYD) –660
Aretas I (Petra) –160
Aretas II (Petra) 110-96
Aretas III (Petra) 87-62
Argishti I (URARTU) –770
Argun (IR) 1285-1291
Ariadne (ROM,BYZ) +490
Arians (IND) –910, +320
Ariarathes Eusebes (CAPP) –260
Aribald (LONG) 626-636
Arif, 'Abd al-Rahman (IRQ) 1966-1968
Arif, 'Abd as-Salam (IRQ) 1963-1966
Arik-den-ili (ASS) 1325-1309
Ariosto, Ludovico 1474-1533
Ariovistus (D) –70
Aripert (LONG) 653-661
Aripert II (LONG) 701-712
Arista, Mariano (MEX) 1851-1853
Aristagoras (Miletus, GR) –500
Aristarchus (GR) –270
Aristides (ATH) ca. 486-485
Aristophanes (ATH) –430
Aristotle (ATH) –360
Ariulf of Spoleto (LONG) +592
Arius +320, 330, 340
Arminius (D) +11
Arnulf (D) 887-899
Arnuwandas I (HAT) ca 1446-1423
Arnuwandas II (HAT) 1385-1375
Arnuwandas III (HAT) 1340-1338
Arnuwandas IV (HAT) 1219-1191
Árpád (H) 888-907
ar-Radi (CAL) 934-940
Arrhidaeus (MAC) –330
Arriaga, Manuel de (P) 1911-1915
Arrian (GR) +110
Arsaces I (IR) 247-212
Arsaces II Tiridates (IR) 212-191
Arsaces III Priapatius (IR) 189-176
Arses (IR) 338-336
Arslan, Alp (SELD) 1063-1072
Arslan, Qilich (SELD) ca 1098
Artabanus I (IR) 127-124
Artabanus II (IR) 10-38
Artabanus IV (IR) 221-225
Artasumara (MIT) ca 1396-1394
Artatama I (MIT) ca 1426-1414
Artavasdes (IR) 226-229
Artaxerxes I (IR) 465-424
Artaxerxes II (IR) 404-359
Artaxerxes III (IR) 358-338
Arthur, Chester (USA) 1881-1885
Asa (JU) 907-867
Asbun, Juan Pereda (RB) +1978
Asgeirsson, Asgeir (IS) 1952-1968
Ashurbanipal (ASS) 668-635
Ashur-bel-kala I (ASS) 1092-1076
Ashur-bel-kala II (ASS) 1068-1062
Ashur-bel-nisheshu (ASS) 1450-1431
Ashur-dan I (ASS) 1175-1141
Ashur-dan II (ASS) 934-912
Ashur-dan III (ASS) 773-764
Ashur-etel-ilani (ASS) ca 635-627
Ashur-nadin-akhe (ASS) 1410-1393
Ashur-nadin-apli (ASS) 1231-1214
Ashur-nadin-shum (BAB) 700 – ca 694
Ashurnasirpal I (ASS) 1049-1031
Ashurnasirpal II (ASS) 885-860
Ashur-nirari II (ASS) ca 1460-1451
Ashurnirari III (ASS) 1213-1208
Ashur-nirari IV (ASS) 1018-1013
Ashur-nirari V (ASS) 755-746
Ashur-rabi (ASS) ca 1480-1460
Ashur-rabi II (ASS) 1012 – ca 995
Ashur-resh-ishi (ASS) 1127-1116
Ashur-resh-ishi II (ASS) ca 995-967
Ashur-rim-nisheshu (ASS) 1430-1411
Ashur-uballit I (ASS) 1380-1331
Aśoka (IND) 274-238
Asparukh (BG) 642-701
Asraf (IR) 1725-1728
as-Saffah (CAL) 750-754
as-Salih, Ayyub (ET) 1239-1249
Astyages (MED) 585 – ca. 560
Atahuallpa (Inca) +1533
Atatürk, Mustafa Kemal (TR) 1922-1938
Ataulphus (VIGO) 410-415
Athaliah (IL) –830
Athaliah (JU) 844-837
Athanagild (VIGO) 554-567
Athanasius +320, 340, 360
Athelstan (GB) 925-940
Athens (GR) –440, –430, +270, 530
Atilius Regulus, C. (ROM) 254-252
Atlantis –370
Attalus I Soter (PERG) 241-197
Attalus II (PERG) 159-138
Attalus III (PERG) 138-133
Attila (HUN) 434-453
Augustine +410, 430
Augustine of Canterbury (GB) +597
Augustus the Strong = Augustus II the Strong (PL) 1697-1706, 1709-1733 = Frederick Augustus I (SAX)
August III (PL) 1736-1763 = Frederick Augustus II (SAX)
Augustus (ROM) –27 - +14
August I (SAX) 1553-1586
Aurangzeb (IND) 1658-1707
Aurelian (ROM) 270-275
Aurelio (AST) 768-774
Auriol, Vincent (F) 1947-1954
Australia +1606, 1770, 1810, 1851, 1901
Authari (LONG) 584-590
Avars +570, 600, 610, 630, 790
Avellaneda, Nicolas (RA) 1874-1880
Avignon (V) +1309, 1400
Avila Camacho, Manuel (MEX) 1940-1946
Avitus (ROM) 455-456
Awil-Marduk (BAB) 562-559
Ay (ET) 1351-1348
Aymaras (PE) +480
Ayub Khan, Mohammed (PAK) 1958-1969
Azaña, Manuel (E) 1936-1939
Azandian culture +760
Azikiwe, Nnamdi (NIG) 1963-1965
Azov +1696
Aztecs (MEX) +1350, 1428, 1460, 1470, 1520

Baal (IL) –860
Baasha (IL) 905-883
Baba-aha-iddina (BAB) 814-811
Babur (IND) 1525-1530
Babylon (BAB,IR) –620, –540, –312
Bach, Johann Sebastian 1685-1750
Bactria –280, –190, –150
Bahrām I (IR) 273-275
Bahrām II (IR) 276-293
Bahrām III (IR) 293-294
Bahrām IV (IR) 388-399
Bahrām V (IR) 421-438
al-Bakr, Ahmad Hassan (IRQ) 1968-1979
Balāsh (IR) 484-488
Baldwin (BYZ) +1205
Baldwin I (Jerusalem) 1100-1118
Baldwin II (Jerusalem) 1118-1131
Balearic Islands (E) +1113, +1240
Balliviān, Adolfo (RB) 1872-1874
Balliviān, Hugo (RB) 1951-1952
Balliviān, José (RB) 1839-1847
Balmaceda, José Manuel (RCH) 1886-1891
Balta, José (PE) 1869-1872
Ban Chao (RC) +70, +100
Banābhatta (IND) +630
Bante, Teferi (ETH) 1974-1977
Banzer-Suārez, Hugo (RB) 1971-1978
Bao Dai (VN) 1954-1955
Baptista, Mariano (RB) 1892-1896
Barcelona +801
Bar Kokhba (IL) +136
Barrancas (YV) –940, +600
Barrientos Ortuno, René (RB) 1964-1969
Barros Lucco, Ramón (RCH) 1911-1915
Bartholomew's Day +1572
Basil I (BYZ) 867-886
Basil II (BYZ) 976-1025
Basil, St. +370
Basiliscus (ROM) 475-476
Batavian Republic (NL) 1795-1806
Batista, Fulgencio (C) 1940-1944, 1952-1959
Battus (GR) –640
Batu (MONG) 1247-1255
Baudelaire (F) +1857
Baudouin I (B) 1951-
Bayan, Avar Khan, +600
Bayar, Celāl (TR) 1950-1960
Baybars (ET) 1260-1277
Baydu (IR) 1294-1295
Bayezid I (TR) 1389-1402
Bayezid II (TR) 1481-1512
Bazi (BAB,dyn) 1017-996
Beatrix (NL) 1980-
Beaumarchais (F) +1778
Bede the Venerable (GB) +690
Bedřich Cesky (CS) 1173-1174, 1178-1179
Beethoven, Ludwig van 1770-1827
Bei Qi An De Wang (RC) +576
Bei Qi Wen Gong (RC) 565-575
Bei Qi Wen Xuan Di (RC) 550-559
Bei Qi Wu Cheng Di (RC) 561-564
Bei Qi Xiao Zhao Di (RC) +560
Bei Qi You Zhu (RC) +577
Bei Song Hui Zong (RC) 1101-1125
Bei Song Qin Zong (RC) +1126
Bei Song Ren Zong (RC) 1023-1063
Bei Song Shen Zong (RC) 1068-1085
Bei Song Tai Zong (RC) 977-997
Bei Song Tai Zu (RC) 960-976
Bei Song Ying Zong (RC) 1064-1067
Bei Song Zhe Zong (RC) 1086-1100
Bei Song Zhen Zong (RC) 998-1022
Bei Wei An Ding Wang (RC) +531
Bei Wei Dao Wu Di (RC) 386-408
Bei Wei Dong Hai Wang (RC) +530
Bei Wei Ming Yuan Di (RC) 409-423
Bei Wei Nan An Wang (RC) +453
Bei Wei Tai Wu Di (RC) 424-452
Bei Wei Wen Cheng Di (RC) 454-465
Bei Wei Xian Wen Di (RC) 466-470
Bei Wei Xiao Ming Di (RC) 516-527
Bei Wei Xiao Wen Di (RC) 471-499
Bei Wei Xiao Wu Di (RC) 532-534
Bei Wei Xiao Zhuang Di (RC) 528-529
Bei Wei Xuan Wu Di (RC) 500-515
Bei Zhou Jing Di (RC) 579-580
Bei Zhou Ming Di (RC) 557-558
Bei Zhou Wu Di (RC) 559-578
Beijing (RC) +910, 1150, 1215, 1644
Béla I Leventa (H) 1061-1063
Béla II (H) 1131-1141
Béla III (H) 1173-1196
Béla IV (H) 1235-1270
Belaúnde-Terry, Fernando (PE) 1963-1968, 1980-
Belisarius (ROM) +533
Bella, Ahmed ben (DZ) 1963-1965
Belzú, Manuel (RB) 1847-1855
Benavides, Oscar (PE) 1914-1915, 1933-1939
Benedict of Nursia (I) +540
Benedict I (V) 575-579
Benedict II (V) 684-685
Benedict III (V) 855-858
Benedict IV (V) 900-903
Benedict V (V) +964
Benedict VI (V) 973-974
Benedict VII (V) 974-983
Benedict VIII (V) 1012-1024
Benedict IX (V) 1032-1045

Benedict X (V) +1058
Benedict XI (V) 1303-1304
Benedict XII (V) 1334-1342
Benedict XIII (V,Avignon) 1394-1400
Benedict XIII (V) 1724-1730
Benedict XIV (V) 1740-1758
Benedict XV (V) 1914-1922
Benes, Eduard (CS) 1935-1938, 1945-1948
Benevento (LONG) +800
Ben-Hadad II (DAMASCUS) -860
Ben Zvi, Itzhak (IL) 1952-1963
Berdibek (MONG) 1340-1357
Berengar (IMP) 915-924
Berenice IV (ET) 58-55
Beric (VIGO,OGO,S) +40
Bering, Vitus (DK) +1740, 1741
Berke (MONG) 1255-1265
Berk-yaruq (SELD) ca. 1094
Bermudez, F. Morales (PE) 1975-1980
Bermudo I (AST) 789-791
Bermudo II el Gotoso (AST,León) 984-999
Bermudo III (AST,León) 1028-1035
Bernard of Clairvaux +1115, +1136, +1146
Bernardes, Artur (BR) 1922-1926
Berzelius, Jöns Jakob 1779-1848
Betancourt, Rómulo (YV) 1945-1947, 1959-1963
Bhumibol Adulyadej (T) 1946-
Bhutto, Ali (PAK) 1971-1973
Bidatsu (J) 572-585
Bidault, Georges (F) +1946
Bierut, Bolesław (PL) 1945-1952
Billinghurst, Guillermo (PE) 1912-1914
Bimbisāra (IND) 582-554
Birger Jarl (S) 1250-1266
Birger Magnusson (S) 1290-1318
Birka +890
Bismarck (D) +1862
Bithynia -300, -70
Björn of Birka (S) +830
Björn Järnsida (S) +900
Björnsson, Sveinn (IS) 1941-1952
Blanche (ARA) 1410-1412 = Blanche of Navarre (SIC)
Blanco, Antonio Guzmàn (YV) 1870-1888
Blum, Léon (F) 1946-1947
Bo Juyi (RC) +840, 850
Boadicea (GB) = Boudicca
Boccaccio, Giovanni 1313-1375
Bocchoris (ET) ca. 720-712
Bodhidharma (RC) +510
Boerhaave, Hermann 1668-1738
Boethius (OGO) +530
Bogomils (BG) +930
Bohemond of Taranto +1100
Bohr, Niels (DK) +1913
Boii -70
Boileau +1675
Boleslav I (CS) 929-967
Boleslav II (CS) 967-999
Boleslav III (CS) 999-1000
Bolesław I the Brave (PL) 992-1025
Bolesław II the Generous (PL) 1058-1079
Bolesław III the Wry-Mouthed (PL) 1102-1138
Bolesław IV the Curly (PL) 1146-1173
Bolesław V Wstydliwy (PL) 1243-1279
Bolivar, Simon (CO) 1819-1830
Boniface, missionary (D) +725
Boniface I (V) 418-422
Boniface II (V) 530-532
Boniface III (V) 606-607
Boniface IV (V) 608-615
Boniface V (V) 619-625
Boniface VI (V) +876
Boniface VII (V) 987-985
Boniface VIII (V) 1294-1303
Boniface IX (V) 1389-1404
Book of Death (ET) -630
Boril (BG) 1207-1218
Boris I (BG) 852-888
Boris II (BG) 969-971
Boris III (BG) 1918-1943
Boris Godunov (RU) 1598-1605
Bořivoj (CS) +893
Borrero, Misael Pastrana (CO) 1970-1974
Bosporus, Kingdom of -430, -370, -107
Botticelli +1480, 1500
Boudicca (GB) +61
Boumedienne, Houari (DZ) 1965-1979
Bourguiba, Habib (TN) 1957-
Boyer, Jean-Pierre (RH) 1820-1843
Boxers (RC) +1900
Braga, Theofilo (P) 1910-1911, 1915
Brahmanism (IND) +730, 980
Branco, Castelo (BR) 1964-1967
Branimir (Croat) +880
Bras Pereira Gomez, Wenceslau (BR) 1914-1918
Breitenfeld (S) +1631
Brennus (ROM) -390
Bretislav I (CS) 1034-1055
Bretislav II (CS) 1092-1109
Brezhnev, Leonid (SU) 1964-1982
Brian (EIR) +977, +1014
Brittany +851
Brömsebo +1645
Broz, Josip (YV) = Tito 1944-1981
Brú, Federico Laredo (C) 1937-1940
Bruegel, Pieter, the elder +1560
Brunelleschi, Filippo ca 1377-1446
Brunhilda (F) +580, +600
Bruno, Giordano +1600
Brutus, Junius (ROM) 509-505
Brutus, Marcus (ROM) -44
Buchanan, James (USA) 1857-1861
Buddha (IND) -570, -530
Budha Gupta (IND) ca. 477-495
Bulganin, Nikolai (SU) 1954-1958
Bulgars +580, 630, 650, 680, 750, 930
Búlnes, Manuel (RCH) 1841-1851
Bunyan, John +1670
Burebistas (CS) -70
Buretsu (J) 499-506
Burgundy, Burgundians +210, 413, 940, 1361, 1470
Burnaburiash I (BAB) 1440-1431
Burnaburiash II ca (BAB) 1369-1345
Bur-Sin (BAB) 1994-1986
Busch, Germàn (RB) 1937-1939
Bustamente, José Luis (PE) 1945-1948
Buxtehude +1670
Byzantium (GR) -650, +200

Cabral (P) +1500
Cáceres, Andres (PE) 1885-1890
Caesar, Julius (ROM) 60-53, 47-44
Caesarion (Ptolemy XV, ET) 44-30
Caetano, Marcello (P) 1968-1974
Çaglayangli, Ihsan Sabri (TR) 1980-
Čaka (BG) +1299
Cakste (LET) 1922-1927
Calais (GB) +1557
Caldera, Rafael (YV) 1969-1974
Calderon +1635
calendar -960 238, 153, 46, 8, +1, 160, 325, 1470, 1582
California +1850
Caligula (ROM) 37-41
Calixtus I (V) 217-221
Calixtus II (V) 1119-1124
Calixtus III (V) 1455-1458
Calles, Plutarco (MEX) 1924-1928
Callinicus (BYZ) +678, 710
Calvin, John +1541
Camacho, Avila (MEX) 1940-1946
Camargo, Alberto Lleras (CO) 1945-1946, 1958-1962
Cambyses (IR) 529-522
Camillus (ROM) ca 395-393, 383-382
Camões, Luis Vaz +1580
Campero, Pedro Diaz (PE) +1868
Campero, Narciso (RB) 1880-1888
Campins, Luis Herrera (YV) 1979-
Campora (RA) +1973
Campos Sales, Ferraz de (BR) 1898-1902
Canada +1763
Canary Islands +1312
Candano, M. (PE) 1903-1904
Candaules (LYD) -690
Canossa (IMP,V) +1077
Canto e Castro, Joã de (P) 1918-1919
Canton (RC) -111, +1520
Canute the Great (DK) 1018-1035
Canute II the Holy (DK) 1080-1086
Canute III (DK) 1146-1157
Canute IV or VI (DK) 1182-1202
Canute (N) 1028-1030 = Canute the Great (DK)
Cao Cao (RC) +230
Cao Chi (RC) +230
Cao Ky, Nguyen (VN) 1965-1967
Cape Colony +1652, 1806
Capet, Hugh (F) 987-996
Caracalla (ROM) 211-217
Carausius, Aurelius (GB) +286
Carchemish (ET,BAB) -610
Cárdenas, Lázaro (MEX) 1934-1940
Carl XVI Gustaf (S) 1973-
Carlo (NA,SA) = Charles
Carloman (D) 876-880
Carloman I (F) 768-771
Carloman II (F) 879-884
Carlos (E) = Charles
Carlos I (P) 1889-1908
Carmina Burana (EIR) +1140
Carmona, Fragoso (P) 1926-1951
Carnot, Sadi (F) 1887-1894
Caro, Miguel (CO) 1894-1898
Carol I (R) 1866-1914
Carol II (R) 1930-1940
Carolus (IMP) = Charles
Carranza, Venustiano (MEX) 1915-1920
Carter, Jim (USA) 1977-1981
Cartesius = Descartes, René
Carus (ROM) 282-283
Casimir I the Restorer (PL) 1038-1058
Casimir II the Just (PL) 1177-1194
Casimir III the Great (PL) 1333-1370
Casimir IV Jagiellończyk (PL) 1447-1492
Casimir-Perier, Jean (F) 1894-1895
Časlav Klonimirović (YU) 924-950
Cassander (MAC) 316-298
Cassius, Spurius (ROM) ca 476-475
Cassius, L. (ROM) -44
Castelo Branco (BR) 1965-1966
Castens, Karl (D) 1979-
Castilla, Rámon (PE) 1845-1862
Castillo, Ramón (RA) 1942-1943
Castro, Cipriano (YV) 1899-1908
Castro, Fidel (C) 1959-
Catalans +1720
Catherine I (RU) 1725-1727
Catherine II (RU) 1762-1796
Catholic Kings (E) 1474-1504
Catilina (ROM) -62
Cato, Marcus Porcius (ROM) -200, 186-183
Catullus (ROM) -50
Cavour (I) +1860
Ceallaigh, Sean (EIR) = O'Kelly 1945-1959
Ceausescu, Nicolae (R) 1967-
Celestine I (V) 422-432
Celestine II (V) 1143-1144
Celestine III (V) 1191-1198
Celestine IV (V) +1241
Celestine V (V) +1294
celibacy (V) +1030, 1074
Celmán, M. Juárez (RA) 1886-1890
Celsius, Anders (S) +1742
Celts -420
Cerularius (BYZ) +1054
Cerda, Pedro Aguirre (RCH) 1938-1941
Cervantes +1605
Ceylon +1020, 1597, 1798,
Chadli, Bendjedid (DZ) 1978-
Chaeronea (GR) -338
Chalbaud, Carlos Delgado (YV) 1948-1950
Chalcedon, Council of +460
Chalcis (GR) -690
Chandra Gupta Maurya (IND) 321-297
Chandra Gupta I (IND) 320-330
Chandra Gupta II (IND) 380-415
Chang (RC) = Zhang
Ch'ang (RC) = Chang
Chao (RC) = Zhao
Ch'ao (RC) = Chao
Chao Phraya Chakkri (T) = Rama I
Charlemagne (F) 768-800, (IMP) 800-814
Charles V (A) 1519-1521 = Charles V (IMP) = Charles I (E) = Charles V (NL) = Charles V (D)
Charles VI (A) 1711-1740 = Charles VI (IMP) = Charles VI (SIC & NA)
Charles I (A) 1916-1918
Charles Albert (BAY) 1726-1745
Charles Theodore (BAY) 1777-1799
Charles the Bold (BURG) 1467-1477
Charles I (CS) 1346-1378
Charles IV (D) 1347-1378 = Charles IV (IMP)
Charles I (E) 1516-1556 (= Charles V)
Charles II (E) 1665-1700
Charles III (E) 1759-1788 = Charles VII (SIC & NA)
Charles IV (E) 1788-1808
Charles Martel (F) 737-741
Charles I (F) = Charlemagne 768-814
Charles II the Fat (F) 884-888 = Charles the Fat (D) 876-887
Charles III the Simple (F) 898-922
Charles IV the Fair (F) 1322-1328
Charles V (F) 1364-1380
Charles VI (F) 1380-1422
Charles VII (F) 1422-1461
Charles VIII (F) 1483-1498
Charles IX (F) 1560-1574
Charles X (F) 1824-1830
Charles I (GB) 1625-1649
Charles II (GB) 1660-1685
Charles Robert of Anjou (H) 1310-1342
Charles II (H) 1385-1386
Charles I (IMP) 800-814 = Charlemagne (F)
Charles II (IMP) 875-877 = Charles the Bald (F)
Charles III (IMP) 881-887 = Charles the Fat
Charles IV of Luxemburg (IMP) 1347-1378 = Charles IV (D)
Charles V (IMP) 1519-1556
Charles VI (IMP) 1711-1740 = Charles VI (A)
Charles VII (IMP) 1742-1745 = Charles Albert (BAY)
Charles (II) (N) 1814-1818 = Charles XIII (S)
Charles (III) John (N) 1818-1844 = Charles XIV John (S)
Charles (IV) (N) 1859-1872 = Charles XV (S)
Charles II (NA) 1285-1309
Charles III (NA) 1382-1386

Charles V (NL) 1506-1555 = Charles V (A & D) = Charles V (IMP) = Charles I (E)
Charles IX (S) 1600-1611
Charles X Gustav (S) 1654-1660
Charles XI (S) 1672-1697
Charles XI's regency (S) 1660-1672
Charles XII (S) 1697-1718
Charles XIII (S) 1809-1818, (N) 1814-1818
Charles XIV John (S & N) 1818-1844
Charles XV (S) 1859-1872 = Charles IV (N)
Charles Albert I (SARD) 1831-1849
Charles Emmanuel I (SARD) 1730-1773
Charles Emmanuel II (SARD) 1706-1802
Charles Felix (SARD) 1821-1831
Charles VI (SIC & NA) 1720-1735 = Charles VI (IMP) = Charles VI (A)
Charles VII (SIC & NA) 1736-1759 = Charles III (E)
Chatauire Ugafa (ET) 1785-1782
Chaudri, Fazal Elahi (PAK) 1973-1978
Chavin (PER) -940
Cheng (RC) = Zhen
Ch'en (RC) = Chen
Chen Hou Zhu (RC) 583-587
Chen Lin Hai Wang (RC) 567-568
Chen Wen Di (RC) 560-566
Chen Wu Di (RC) 557-559
Chen Xuan Di (RC) 569-582
Cheng (RC) = Zheng
Ch'eng (RC) = Cheng
Ch'i (RC) = Qi
Chia (RC) = Jia
Chiang Kai-shek (RC) = Jiang Jieshi 1926-(1949)
Chichimecs (MEX) +1120
Chien (RC) = Jian
Ch'ien (RC) = Qian
Childebert I (F) 511-558
Childebert II (F) 575-595
Childebert III (F) 695-711
Childeric I (F) 458-481
Childeric II (F) 660-673
Childeric III (F) 742-751
Childers, Erskine (EIR) 1973-1974
Chile +1560
Chilperic I (F) 561-584
Chilperic II (F) 716-720
Chin (RC) = Jin
Ch'in (RC) = Qin
China, Great Wall of -250
Ching (RC) = Jing
Ch'ing (RC) = Qing
Chiripa (PE) -940
Chiung (RC) = Qiong
Chlodomer (F) 511-524
Chlodovech = Clovis (F) 481-511
Chlotar I (F) 511-561
Chlotar II (F) 584-629
Chlotar III (F) 657-670
Chlotar IV (F) 716-720
Chokei (J) 1368-1373
Chosroes (IR) = Osroes
Chou (RC) = Zhou
Christian I (DK) 1448-1481, (N) 1450-1481, (S) 1457-1464
Christian II (DK) 1513-1523, (N) 1513-1524, (S) 1520-1521
Christian III (DK) 1534-1559, (N) 1536-1559
Christian IV (DK & N) 1588-1648
Christian V (DK & N) 1670-1699
Christian VI (DK & N) 1730-1746
Christian VII (DK & N) 1766-1785, (-1808)
Christian VIII (DK) 1839-1848
Christian IX (DK) 1863-1906
Christian X (DK) 1912-1947
Christian I (SAX) 1586-1591
Christian II (SAX) 1591-1611
Christina (S) 1644-1654
Christina's regency (S) 1632-1644
Christopher I (DK) 1252-1259
Christopher II (DK) 1320-1332
Christopher of Bavaria (DK & S) 1440-1448, (N) 1442-1448
Christopher (V) 903-904
Chrysostom, John +400
Chu (RC) = Zhu
Chu Hsi (RC) = Zhu Xi
Chü Yüan (RC) = Qu Yuan
Chuai-Tenno (J) 192-200
Chuang (RC) = Zhuang
Chukyo (J) 1220-1252
Chulalongkorn (T) = Rama V
Ch'un Ch'iu (RC) = Qun Qiu
Chün (RC) = Jun
Chung-kuo (RC) = Zhongguo
Cicero, M. Tullius (ROM) 63-61, -80, -60, -50
Cid (E) +1050, 1094
Cimbri -110
Cimmerians -700
Cimon (ATH) ca. 474-473, 468-467
Cincinnatus (ROM) ca. 466-465
Claudius (ROM) 41-54
Claudius (ROM) 268-270
Claudius Pulcher, P. (ROM) 245-242
Cleisthenes (ATH) 510-509
Clement I (V) 88-97
Clement II (V) 1046-1047
Clement III (V) 1187-1191
Clement IV (V) 1265-1268
Clement V (V) 1305-1314
Clement VI (V) 1342-1352
Clement VII (V) 1523-1534
Clement VIII (V) 1592-1605
Clement IX (V) 1667-1669
Clement X (V) 1670-1676
Clement XI (V) 1700-1721
Clement XII (V) 1730-1740
Clement XIII (V) 1758-1769
Clement XIV (V) 1769-1774
Cleomenes (SPARTA) -226
Cleon (ATH) 430-422
Cleopatra I (ET) 181-176
Cleopatra II (ET) 170-145, 116-107
Cleopatra III (ET) 145-116, 107-101
Cleopatra (IV) Berenice (ET) 101-88
Cleopatra V (ET) 58-55
Cleopatra VI (ET) 58-55
Cleopatra VII (ET) 51-30
Cleophon (ATH) ca 406-404
Cleph (LONG) 572-574
Clepsydra (ET) -90
Clermont (V) +1095
Cleveland, Grover (USA) 1885-1889, 1893-1897
Clive, Robert (GB) +1760
Clontarf (EIR) +1014
Clotaire = Chlotar
Clovis (F) 481-511
Clovis II (F) 639-657
Clovis III (F) 691-695
Cniva (VIGO) +250
Codex Euricianus (VIGO) +470
Codrus (ATH) -690
Cola di Rienzi (V) +1360
Coloman (H) 1095-1114
Colophon (LYD) -660
Colosseum (ROM) +80
Colossus of Rhodes (GR) -280, +660
Columba (EIR) +563, 610
Columbus, Christopher (E) +1498
Commodus (ROM) 180-192
Comonfort (MEX) 1855-1856
Concha, José (CO) 1914-1918
Confucius (RC) -520, -480
Congo +1908
Conon (V) 686-687
Conrad II Ota (CS) 1179-1191
Conrad I (D) 911-918
Conrad II (D) 1024-1039 = Conrad II (IMP)
Conrad III (D) 1138-1152 = Conrad III (IMP)
Conrad IV (IMP) = Conrad I (SIC)
Conrad IV (D) 1250-1254 = Conrad I (IMP) 911-915
Conrad II (IMP) 1024-1039 = Conrad II (D)
Conrad III (IMP) 1138-1152 = Conrad III (D)
Conrad I Mazowiecki (PL) 1229-1232, 1241-1243
Conrad I (SIC) 1250-1254 = Conrad IV (D) = Conrad IV (IMP)
Conradino (SIC) 1254-1257
Constance (SIC) +1190
Constans (ROM) 337-350
Constans II (BYZ) 641-668
Constantine Tich (BG) 1258-1277
Constantine I-II (BYZ) = Constantine I-II (ROM)
Constantine III (BYZ) +641
Constantine IV (BYZ) 668-685
Constantine V (BYZ) 741-775
Constantine VI (BYZ) 780-797
Constantine VII Porphyrogenitus (BYZ) 913-920, 944-959
Constantine VIII (BYZ) 1025-1028
Constantine IX Monomachus (BYZ) 1042-1055
Constantine X Ducas (BYZ) 1059-1067
Constantine XI (BYZ) 1449-1453
Constantine I (GR) 1913-1917, 1920-1922
Constantine II (GR) 1964-1973
Constantine I (ROM) 305-337
Constantine II (ROM) 337-340
Constantine (RU) 1216-1219
Constantine (V) 708-715
Constantinople +330, 867, 1261
Constantius (ROM) 423-425
Constantius II (ROM) 337-361
Constantius Chlorus (ROM) 305-312
Consulate, the (F) 1799-1804
Contreras, Eleazar López (YV) 1936-1941
Cook, James (GB) +1770
Coolidge, Calvin (USA) 1923-1929
Copernicus, Nicolaus 1473-1543
Córdova, Jorge (RB) 1855-1857
Corelli, Arcangelo +1670
Corinth (GR) -640 -146
Coriolanus (ROM) ca 490-488
Corneille, Pierre 1606-1684
Cornelius (V) 251-253
Corrado (SIC) = Conrad
Corsica +1050, 1768
Cortes, Hernan (E) +1520
Cosgrave, William (EIR) 1922-1932
Cosimo de'Medici (FIR) 1435-1464
Costae Silva, Arthur da (BR) 1967-1969
Costa Gómez, F. da (P) 1975-1976
Coty, René (F) 1954-1959
Counts' Feud (DK,N,S) +1536
Cranach, Lucas 1472-1553
Crassus, M. (ROM) 74-73, 60-53
Crécy (F,GB) +1346
Crespo, Joaquin (YV) 1892-1897
Crete +830, 1650, 1669
Crimea (RU) +1783
Croats, Croatia +823, 880, 910, 1090
Croesus (LYD) 561-547
Cromwell, Oliver (GB) 1653-1658
Cromwell, Richard (GB) 1658-1659
Croton -520
Crusades +1100, 1110, 1146, 1190, 1210, 1450
Ctesibius (ET) -90,
Cuba +1520, 1898, 1902
Cugno, Joseph +1769
Cumae (ROM) -580, -540
Cunaxa (IR) -400
Cunegunda (IMP) +1010
Cunincpert (LONG) 686-700
Curiatii (ROM) -680
Curius Dentatus, M. (ROM) 285-282
Cuthbert, St. (GB) +650
Cyaxares (MED) 625-585
Cybele (FRY) -770, +40, 220
Cynoscephalae (GR) -198
Cyprian, Church Father +250, 260
Cypselus (GR) -640
Cyrankiewicz (PL) 1970-1971
Cyrene (GR) -640, -570, +619
Cyril (CS) +869
Cyrus (IR) 559-529

Dagobert I (F) 629-639
Dagobert II (F) 673-678
Dagobert III (F) 711-715
Daguerre (F) +1837
Daigo (J) 897-930
Daigo II (J) 1319-1336
Daimler (D) +1883
Dálaigh, C.O. (EIR) 1974-1976
Damaskinos (GR) 1944-1945
Damasus I (V) 366-383
Damasus II (V) 1047-1048
Damianov (BG) 1950-1958
Damocles (SYA) -390
Daniel, stylite +470
Dante, Alighieri, 1265-1321
Danylo (Ukraine) +1260
Daoud, Kahn Muhammed (AFG) 1973-1978
Darius I (IR) 522-486
Darius II (IR) 423-404
Darius III (IR) 336-331
David (IL) 1003- ca 965
David I (SCOT) 1124-1153
David II Bruce (SCOT) 1329-1332, 1341-1371
Daza, Hilarión (RB) 1876-1880
Dead Sea Scrolls (IL) +68
Deborah (IL) ca. 1200-1190
Decemvirate (ROM) ca. 453-448
Decius (ROM) 249-251
Decius Mus, P. (ROM) 297-294
Defoe, Daniel +1719
Deioces (MED) -650
Delgado Chalbaud, Carlos (YV) 1948-1950
Delian League (GR) -480
Delphi -590
Demetrius, St. (BG) +1187
Demetrius I (MAC) 294-285
Demetrius II (MAC) 239-229
Demetrius I Soter (SYR) 162-150
Demetrius II Nicator (SYR) 145-140, 129-125
Demetrius III Philopator (SYR) 95-88
Democritus (GR) -430
Demosthenes (ATH) -350
Descartes, René 1596-1650
Desiderius (LONG) 756-774
Deusdedit (V) 615-618
De Valera, Eamon (EIR) 1932-1938, 1959-1973
Dexippus (ATH) +270
Dias, Bartolomeu (P) +1486
Diaz, Ordas, Gustavo (MEX) 1964-1970
Diaz, Porfirio (MEX) 1877-1880, 1884-1911
Dickens, Charles (GB) +1836
Diderot (F) +1750
Dido (CART) -820
Diederichs, N. (ZA) 1975-1978
Dimitrov, Georgi (BG) 1946-1949
Dinh Diem, Ngo (VN) 1955-1963

Frederick III (D) 1439-1493 = Frederick V (A) = Frederick III (IMP)
Frederick I (DK) 1523-1533, (N) 1524-1533
Frederick II (DK & N) 1559-1588
Frederick III (DK & N) 1648-1670
Frederick IV (DK & N) 1699-1730
Frederick V (DK & N) 1746-1766
Frederick VI (DK) 1808-1839, (N) 1808-1814 Frederick VII (DK) 1848-1863
Frederick VIII (DK) 1906-1912
Frederick IX (DK) 1947-1972
Frederick I (IMP) = Frederick Barbarossa (D) 1152-1190
Frederick II (IMP) 1212-1250 = Frederick II Hohenstaufen (D)
Frederick III (IMP) 1440-1493
Frederick II of Aragon (NA) 1296-1337
Frederick I (PREU) 1701-1713 = Frederick III (BRAN)
Frederick II the Great (PREU) 1740-1786
Frederick III (D & PREU) +1888
Frederick I (S) 1720-1751
Frederick the Wise (SAX) 1486-1525
Frederick I (SIC) 1197-1250 = Frederick II Hohenstaufen (D) = Frederick II (IMP)
Frederick II of Aragon (SIC) 1296-1337
Frederick III the Simple (SIC) 1355-1377
Frederick Augustus I (SAX) 1694-1733 = Augustus II the Strong (PL) = Augustus the Strong
Frederick Augustus II (SAX) 1733-1763 = Augustus III (PL)
Frederick Augustus III (SAX) 1763-1827 = (King) Frederick Augustus I (1806-1827)
Frederick Augustus II (SAX, King) 1837-1854
Frederick Christian (SAX) +1763
Frederick Henry (NL) 1625-1647
Frederick William (BRAN) 1640-1688
Frederick William I (PREU) 1713-1740
Frederick William II (PREU) 1786-1797
Frederick William III (PREU) 1797-1840
Frederick William IV (PREU) 1840-1861
Frederik (DK,NL) = Frederick
Fredrik (S) = Frederick
Frei Montalva, Eduardo (RCH) 1964-1970
Freire, Ramon (RCH) 1823-1827
Frias, Thomás (RB) 1874-1876
Friedrich (A,BRAN,D,PREU,SAX) = Frederick
Friesland +1410
Frithigern (VIGO) 377-380
Frondizi, Arturo (RA) 1958-1962
Frontinus, Sextus J. (ROM) +103
Fruela I (AST) 757-768
Fruela II (AST, León) 924-925
Fu'ad I (ET) 1922-1936
Fujiwara culture (J) +910, 1150
Fukakusa II (J) 1246-1259
Fulton (USA) +1820
Fulvius Nobilior, L. (ROM) 176-174
Fushimi (J) 1288-1298
Fushimi II (J) 1298-1302
Fyodor Ivanovich (RU) 1584-1598
Fyodor Alexyevich (RU) 1676-1682

G

Gabriel Radomir (BG) 1014-1015
Gaddafi, Mu'ammar al (LAR) 1969-
Gaiseric (VAND) 428-477
Gaius (V) 284-296
Galatians -280
Galba (ROM) +68
Galen (ROM) +180
Galerius (ROM) 305-311
Galileo, Galilei 1564-1642
Galla Placidia (ROM) +420, 450
Gallegos, Romulo (YV) 1947-1948
Gallienus (ROM) 253-268
Gallus (ROM) 251-253
Galswintha (F) +580
Galtieri, Leopoldo (RA) 1981-
Galvani, Luigi 1737-1798
Gamarra, Agustin (PE) 1839-1841
Gandza (BAB) ca 1525-1522
Ganev, Dimitur (BG) 1958-1964
Garbai, Alexander (H) 1919-1920
Garcia I (AST, León) 911-914
Garfield, James A (USA) +1881
Garibald (LONG) 671-672
Garibaldi (I) +1860
Garrastazu, E. (BR) 1969-1974
Gaulle, Charles de (F) 1944-1946, 1959-1969
Gauss, Carl Friedrich 1777-1855
Gautama Buddha (IND) -520
Gay, John (GB) +1728
Gaykhatu (IR) 1291-1294
Gay-Lussac, Joseph 1778-1850
Gediminas (LIT) 1316-1328
Geffrard, Fabre (RH) 1859-1867
Geisel, Ernesto (BR) 1974-1979
Gelasius I (V) 492-496
Gelasius II (V) 1118-1119
Gelimer (VAND) 530-533
Gelon I (SYA) 485-478
Gemmyo (J) 707-715
Genghis Khan (MONG) = Ghengis Khan 1206-1226
Gensho (J) 715-724
Georg (BG,CS) = George
George I Terter (BG) 1280-1292
George II (BG) 1322-1323
George of Podiebrady (CA) 1458-1471
George I (GB) 1714-1727
George II (GB) 1727-1760
George III (GB) 1760-1811 (-1820)
George IV (GB) (1811-) 1820-1830
George V (GB) 1910-1936
George VI (GB) 1936-1952
George I (GR) 1863-1913
George II (GR) 1922-1923, 1935-1941, 1945-1947
George William (BRAN) 1619-1640
Georgios (GR) = George
Gepidae +40
Gerhard of Holstein (DK) 1332-1340
Gerizim (IL) -400
Germund (LIT) 1270-1275
Geta (ROM) +210
Géza I (H) 972-997
Géza II (H) 1074-1077
Géza III (H) 1141-1161
Ghana +301
Ghazan Mahmūd (IR) 1295-1304
Ghazi (IRQ) 1933-1939
Ghen Guei (RC) +1130
Ghengis Khan (MONG) 1206-1226
Gheorghiu-Dej, Gheorghe (R) 1958-1965
Ghizikis, Faidon (GR) 1973-1974
Giacomo (SIC) = James
Gibraltar +1462, 1713
Gideon (IL) ca. 1150-1140
Gilgamesh (BAB) -890
Gilles, J (NL) 1746-1747
Gilligin (LIT) 1275-1278
Giotto +1334
Giovanna (NA) = Joan
Giri, V.V. (IND) 1969-1974
Giscard d'Estaing (F) 1974-1981
Gissur (IS) +1262
Glipping, Erik (DK) 1259-1286
Gluck, Christoph Willibald von, 1714-1787
Glycerius (ROM) +473
Gneisenau (D) +1790
Gnosticism +220, 270
Gnupa (S) +910, 950
Godepert (LONG) 661-662
Godfred (DK) 808-809
Godwin (GB) +1050
Godwinson, Harold (GB) +1050, 1066
Goethe, Johann Wolfgang von, 1749-1832
Gogol, Nikolai, 1809-1852
Golden Horde (MONG) +1223, 1246-1357, 1502
Goldoni, Carlo 1707-1793
Golitsyn, Vasily (RU) 1686-1689
Golitsyn, Dmitry (RU) +1700, 1730
Gómez, José, Miguel (C) 1908-1913
Gomez, Juan Vicente (YV) 1908-1935
Gómez, Laureano (C) 1950-1953
Gomez, Manoel Texeira (P) 1923-1925
Gómez, Miguel Mariano (C) +1936
Gontran (F) = Guntram
Gonzaga +1440
Gonzales Videla, Gabriel (RCH) 1946-1952
Gonzalez (MEX) 1880-1884
Gordian III (ROM) 238-244
Gordian knot (PHRY) -770
Gordius (PHRY) -770
Gorm the Old (DK) 917-940
Gospels +390
Gotarzes I (IR) 88-81
Gotarzes II (IR) 45-50
Goths +40, 160, 250, 260, 270, 401
Gottwald, Klement (CS) 1948-1953
Goulart, João (BR) 1961-1964
Gouin, Félix (F) +1946
Gowon, Yakubu (NIG) 1966-1975
Goya (E) +1820
Gracchus, Caius (ROM) 126-123
Gracchus, Tiberius (ROM) 137-133
Granada (E) +1240, 1492
Grant, Ulysses (USA) 1869-1877
Gratian (ROM) 375-383
Grau San Martin, Ramón (C) 1933-1934, 1944-1948
Great Wall of China -250
Gregory I (V) 590-604
Gregory II (V) 715-731
Gregory III (V) 731-741
Gregory IV (V) 827-844
Gregory V (V) 996-999
Gregory VI (V) 1045-1046
Gregory VII (V) 1073-1085
Gregory VIII (V) +1187
Gregory IX (V) 1227-1241
Gregory X (V) 1271-1275
Gregory XI (V) 1370-1378
Gregory XII (V) 1406-1415
Gregory XIII (V) 1572-1585
Gregory XIV (V) 1590-1591
Gregory XV (V) 1621-1623
Gregory XVI (V) 1831-1846
Gregory, Armenian missionary +290
Gregory of Nazianzus, St. +370
Gregory of Nyssa, St. +370
Greek Fire (BYZ) +678
Grévy, Jules (F) 1879-1887
Griffith, Arthur (EIR) +1922
Grimoald (LONG) 662-671
Gronchi, Giovanni (I) 1955-1962
Grotefend (D) +1820
Groza, Petru (R) 1952-1958
Guericke +1660
Guerra, José Gutiérrez (RB) 1917-1920
Guerrero, Vicente (MEX) 1829-1930
Guglielmo (SIC) = William
Gui Fei (RC) +750
Guido (IMP) = Guy
Guido, J.M. (RA) 1962-1963
Guido of Arezzo (V) +1050
Guillén, Nestor (RB) +1946
Guimarães (P) +1926
Gundemar (VIGO) 610-612
Gunderic (VAND) 425-428
Gunthamund (VAND) 485-496
Guntram (F) 561-592
Gurjara-Pratihara (IND) +930
Gürsel, Cemal (TR) 1960-1966
Gustav I Vasa (S) 1521-1560
Gustav III (S) 1771-1792
Gustav IV Adolf (S) 1796-1809
Gustav IV Adolf's regency (S) 1792-1796
Gustav V (S) 1907-1950
Gustav VI Adolf (S) 1950-1973
Gustavus II Adolphus (S) 1611-1632
Gutenberg, Johannes ca. 1395-1468
Gutiérrez, Monje (RB) 1946-1947
Guttorm (N) +1204
Guy (IMP) 891-896
Gûyük (MONG) 1246-1248
Gyges (LYD) -690, -660, -650

Haakon I the Good (N) 935-961
Haakon II Herdebred (N) 1161-1162
Haakon (III) Sverreson (N) 1202-1204
Haakon (IV) Haakonsson (N) 1217-1263
Haakon V Magnusson (N) 1299-1319
Haakon VI Magnusson (N) 1343-1380
Haakon VII (N) 1905-1957
Haakon, Duke (N) 1011-1016
Haakon, Duke of Lade (N) 965-995
Haakon the Red (S) 1067-1079
Haarik I (DK) 828-854
Haarik II (DK) 854-869
Habibollah (AFG) 1901-1919
Hacha (CS) 1938-1939
Hadad (IL) -940
Hadad II (DAMASCUS) -810
al-Hādī (CAL) 785-786
Hadrian (ROM) 117-138
Hadrian I (V) 772-795
Hadrian II (V) 867-872
Hadrian III (V) 884-885
Hadrian IV (V) 1154-1159
Hadrian V (V) +1276
Hadrian VI (V) 1521-1523
Hafiz (ET) 1130-1149
Hafrsfjord (N) +872
Haggai (IL) -520
Hahnemann (D) +1820
Haile Selassie (ETH) 1930-1974
Hainsch, Michael (A) 1920-1928
Hakam I (CORD) 796-822
Hakam II (CORD) 961-976
Hākim (ET) 996-1020

Håkon (N,S) = Haakon
Halley + 1705
Halsten (S) 1080-1090
Halys (LYD) – 600
Hamilcar the Elder (CART) – 480
Hamilcar (CART) 243-229
Hammurabi (BAB) 1728-1686
Han Ai Di (RC) 6-1
Han An Di (RC) 107-125
Han Cheng Di (RC) – 32- + 7
Han Chong Di (RC) + 145
Han Gao Zu (RC) 204-195
Han Guang Wu Di (RC) 25-57
Han He Di (RC) 89-105
Han Huan Di (RC) 147-167
Han Hui Di (RC) 194-188
Han Jing Di (RC) 156-141
Han Ling Di (RC) 168-189
Han Ming Di (RC) 58-75
Han Shang Di (RC) + 106
Han Shun Di (RC) 126-144
Han Wen Di (RC) 179-157
Han Wu Di (RC) 140-87
Han Xian Di (RC) 190-220
Han Xuan Di (RC) 73-49
Han Yu (RC) + 810
Han Yuan Di (RC) 48-33
Han Zhang Di (RC) 76-88
Han Zhao Di (RC) 86-74
Han Zhi Di (RC) + 146
Hanazono (J) 1308-1318
Handel + 1741
Hannibal (CART) 221-203
Hans (DK & N) 1481-1513,
(S) 1497-1501
Hansan + 1294
Hanseatic League + 1294
Hansho (J) 406-410
Harald Klak (DK) 826-827
Harald Bluetooth (DK) 942-985
Harald Hen (DK) 1074-1080
Harald III (DK) 1014-1018
Harald Fairhair (N) 864-930
Harald (II) Graycloak (N) 961-965
Harald (III) Hardraade (N) 1047-1066
Harbashipak (BAB) ca 1480-1471
Hardecanute (DK) 1036-1042
Hardecanute (GB) 1039-1042 =
Hardecanute (DK)
Harding, Warren (USA) 1921-1923
Hårik (DK) = Haarik
Harmodius & Aristogiton (ATH)
– 510
Harold I Harefoot (GB) 1035-1039
Harold II Godwinson (GB) + 1050,
1066
Harrison, Benjamin (USA) 1889-1893
Harrison, William Henry (USA)
+ 1841
Harsavardhana (IND) + 630
Hārūn ar-Rashid (CAL) 786-809
Harvey, William 1578-1657
Hasan Bozorg (IR) 1349-1356
Hasdrubal (CART) 229-221
Hasmaneans (JU) – 120, – 80
Hassan II (MA) 1961-
Hastings (GB) + 1066
Hatshepsut (ET) 1519-1482
Hattusilis II (HAT) ca 1419-1402
Hattusilis III (HAT) 1274-1250
Hautilis II (HAT) ca 1487-1484
Hawaii + 960, 1898
Haydn, Joseph 1732-1809
Hayes, Rutherford (USA) 1877-1881
Hazael (DAMASCUS) – 810
Hedeby (S) + 950
Heijō (H) 806-809
Heinemann, Gustav (D) 1969-1974
Heinrich (D) = Henry
Heinsius, Anthonie (NL) 1702-1720
Heliocles (BACT) – 150
Heliogabalus (ROM) = Elagabalus
Helm, Anthonie van der (NL)
1736-1745
Héloïse (F) + 1136
Hemming (DK) 811-812
Hengist (GB) + 570
Henlein, Peter + 1520
Henotikón (BYZ) + 500
Henri (F,RH) = Henry
Henry I (CAST) 1214-1217
Henry II of Trastamara (CAST)
1369-1379
Henry III the Sufferer (CAST)
1390-1406
Henry IV the Impotent (CAST)
1454-1474
Henry the Fowler (D) 919-936
Henry II (D) 1002-1024 =
Henry II (IMP)
Henry III (D) 1039-1056 =
Henry III (IMP)
Henry IV (D) 1056-1106 =
Henry IV (IMP)
Henry V (D) 1106-1125 =
Henry V (IMP)
Henry VI (D) 1190-1197 =
Henry VI (IMP) = Henry I (SIC)
Henry VII (D) 1308-1313
Henry I (F) 1031-1060
Henry II (F) 1547-1559
Henry III (F) 1574-1589 =
Henry of Valois (PL)
Henry IV (F) 1589-1610
Henry I (GB) 1100-1135
Henry II (GB) 1154-1189
Henry III (GB) 1216-1272
Henry IV (GB) 1399-1413
Henry V (GB) 1413-1422
Henry VI (GB) 1422-1461
Henry VII (GB) 1485-1509
Henry VIII (GB) 1509-1547
Henry I (IMP) =
Henry the Fowler (D) 924-936
Henry II (IMP) 1002-1024 =
Henry II (D)
Henry III (IMP) 1039-1056 =
Henry III (D)
Henry IV (IMP) 1056-1106 =
Henry IV (D)
Henry V (IMP) 1106-1125 =
Henry V (D)
Henry VI (IMP) 1190-1197 =
Henry VI (D) = Henry I (SIC)
Henry VII of Luxemburg (IMP)
1308-1313 = Henry VII (D)
Henry of Burgundy (P) 1093-1112
Henry the Cardinal (P) 1578-1580
Henry I Brodaty (PL) 1232-1238
Henry II Pobozny (PL) 1238-1241
Henry IV Probus (PL) 1288-1290
Henry of Valois (PL) 1572-1574 =
Henry III (F)
Henry I (RH) 1806-1820
Henry I (SIC) 1196-1197 =
Henry VI (IMP) = Henry VI (D)
Henryk (PL) = Henry
Hephtalites + 480, 500, 550
Heraclius (BYZ) 610-641
Heraclitus – 520
Herculaneum + 79, 1750
Herihor (ET) ca. 1086-1062
Hermaeus (IND) – 30
Hermenegila (VIGO) + 590
Hero (ET) – 90
Herod (IL) 37-4
Herod Agrippa I (IL) 41-44
Herod Agrippa II (IL) 50-100
Herod Antipas (IL) – 4- + 39
Herodes Atticus (ATH) + 170
Herodotus (ATH) – 770, – 700, – 500,
– 490, – 460
Herostratus (GR) – 360
Herrán, Pedro (CO) 1842-1845
Herrera, Enrique Olaya (CO)
1930-1934
Herrera, Joaquín de (MEX)
1848-1850
Hertzog, Enrique (RB) 1946-1949
Heruli + 260
Hesiod (GR) – 680
Heuss, Theodor (D) 1949-1959
Hezekiah (JU) 725-697
Hidetada (J) 1616-1623
Hideyoshi (J) 1582-1598
Hieron I (SYA) 478-466
Hieron II (SYA) 270-215
Hilarius (V) 461-468
Hilderic (VAND) 523-530
Hilkiah (JU) – 630
Hillery, Patrick (EIR) 1976-
Himera (GR) – 480
Hindenburg, Paul von (D) 1925-1934
Hipparchus (ATH) 527-514
Hippias (ATH) 527-510, – 500
Hippocrates (GR) – 430
Hiram (SYR) - 960, – 910
Hirohito (J) 1926-
Hisham (CAL) 724-743
Hishām I (CORD) 788-796
Hishām II (CORD) 977-1009,
1011-1012
Hishām III (CORD) 1027-1031
Hitler, Adolf (D & A) 1934-1945
Hitotsubashi Keiki (J) 1866-1867
Hittites, – 890, – 970
Ho (RC) = He
Ho Chi Minh (VN) 1946-1969
Ho Guang (RC) – 80
Hobbes, Thomas, 1588-1679
Homer (GR) – 800
Honecker, Erich (D) 1971-1973, 1976-
Honorius (ROM) 395-423
Honorius I (V) 625-638
Honorius II (V) 1124-1130
Honorius III (V) 1216-1227
Honorius IV (V) 1285-1287
Hoornbeek, Isaac van (NL) 1720-1727
Hoover, Herbert (USA) 1929-1933
Hopewell culture (USA) – 400
Horace (ROM) = Horatius Flaccus, Q
Horatii (ROM) – 680
Horatius Cocles (ROM) – 510
Horatius Flaccus, Q. (ROM) – 30, – 20
Horemheb (ET) 1347- ca 1319
Horikawa (J) 1087-1107
Horikawa II (J) 1224-1232
Hormisdas (V) 514-523
Hormizd I (IR) 272-273
Hormizd II (IR) 302-309
Hormizd III (IR) 457-459
Hormizd IV (IR) 579-590
Hormizd V (IR) + 631
Horsa (GB) + 570
Horthy, Miklos (H) 1920-1944
Hosea (IL) prophet – 750, – 730
Hoseyn (IR) = Husayn
Hoshea (IL) 732-723
Hou Han (RC,dyn) 947-951
Hou Jin (RC,dyn) 936-947
Hou Liang (RC,dyn) 907-923
Hou Tang (RC,dyn) 923-936
Hou Zhou (RC,dyn) 951-960
Hoxha, Enver (AL) 1945-1953
Hroswitha (IMP) + 980
Hsi = Xi
Hsia (RC) = Xia
Hsin (RC) = Xin
Hsiu (RC) = Xiu
Hsüan (RC) = Xuan
Hu Yaobang (RC) 1981-
Hua Guofeng (RC) 1976-1981
Huai Nan Zi (RC) – 100
Hudson, Henry + 1609
Huerta, V (MEX) 1913-1914
Huguenots (F) + 1690
Hugo, Victor (F) + 1831, 1862
Hugues Capet (F) 987-996
Hülagü (IR) 1256-1264
Humayun (IND) 1530-1539,
1555-1556
Humbert I (I) 1878-1900
Humbert II (I) + 1946
Humbert, Cardinal (V) + 1054
Huneric (VAND) 477-484
Hung (RC) = Hong
Huns – 180, – 130, – 90, + 30, 60, 100,
300, 320, 360, 372, 430, 460
Hus, Jan (CS) + 1415
Husain, Zakir (IND) 1967-1969
Husak, Gustav (CS) 1975-
Husayn I (IR) 1374-1375
Husayn II (IR) 1487-1490
Husayn III (IR) 1694-1722
Huss, Johan (CS) + 1415
Hussein I (HKJ) 1952-
Hussein, Saddam (IR) 1979-
Huvuska (IND) + 210
Huygens, Christiaan 1629-1695
Huzziyas II (HAT) ca 1467-1463
Hyde, Douglas (EIR) 1938-1945
Hyginus (V) 136-140
Hyksos (ET) ca. 1730-1680
Hyrcanus I, John (IL) 134-104
Hyrcanus II (IL) 63-40

I (RC) = Yi
Ibáñez, Carlos (RCH) 1927-1931
1952-1958
Ibbi-Sin (BAB) 1976-1952
ibn Saud, Ab al-Aziz (SM) 1926-1953
Ibrahim (TR) 1640-1648
Ibsen, Henrik, 1828-1906
Iceland + 880, 930, 990, 1120, 1270
Ichijō (J) 986-1011
Ichijō II (J) 1016-1036
iconoclasm (BYZ) + 730, 780, 820,
860
Iddin-Dagan (BAB) 1910-1890
Idris I (LAR) 1950-1969
Ieharu (J) 1760-1786
Iemitsu (J) 1623-1651
Iemochi (J) 1858-1866
Ienari (J) 1786-1837
Ienobu (J) 1709-1713
Iesada (J) 1853-1858
Ieshige (J) 1745-1760
Ietsugu (J) 1713-1716
Ietsuna (J) 1651-1680
Ieyasu (J) 1598-1616
Ieyoshi (J) 1837-1853
Iglesias, Miguel (PE) 1882-1885
Igor (RU) 912-945
Igor II (RU) 1139-1147
Iliad – 990, – 800
Illi (MED) – 650
Illia, Arturo (RA) 1964-1966
Incas + 1060, 1533
Ingi Krokrygg (N) 1139-1161
Ingi Baardsson (N) 1205-1217
Ingi I (S) 1079-1112
Ingi II (S) 1112-1129
Ingyo (J) 411-456
Innocent I (V) 401-417
Innocent II (V) 1130-1143
Innocent III (V) 1198-1216
Innocent IV (V) 1243-1254
Innocent V (V) + 1276
Innocent VI (V) 1352-1362
Innocent VII (V) 1004-1406
Innocent VII (V) 1484-1492
Innocent IX (V) + 1591
Innocent X (V) 1644-1655
Innocent XI (V) 1676-1689
Innocent XII (V) 1691-1700
Innocent XIII (V) 1721-1724
Inönü, Ismet (TR) 1938-1950
Iona (SCOT) + 563, 802
Iphicrates (ATH) 394-392
Ireland + 570, 650, 730, 840, 980,

1010, 1171, 1610, 1845
Irenaeus, Church Father +177, 200
Irene (BYZ) 797-802
Irigoyen, Hipólito (RA) 1916-1922, 1928-1930
Ironsi, Aguiyi (NIG) +1966
Isaac I Comnenus (BYZ) 1057-1059
Isaac II Angelus (BYZ) 1185-1195, 1203-1204
Isabella I (E) 1474-1504
Isabella II (E) 1833-1868
Isaiah (IL) -740, -710, -600, -540
Ishbi-Erra (BAB) 1951-1921
Ishme-Dagan (BAB) 1889-1871
Ishpakai (SCYT) -680
Isidore of Seville (E) +636
Iskander Mirza (PAK) 1956-1958
Islam Shah (IND) 1545-1555
Ismail (IR) = Esma'il
Istvan (H) = Stephen
Isuchimikado (J) 1198-1210
Itti-Marduk-balatu (BAB) 1100-1092
Itzcoatl (MEX) +1430
Ivajlo (BG) 1277-1279
Ivan Alexander (BG) 1331-1371
Ivan Asen I (BG) 1185-1196
Ivan Asen II (BG) 1218-1241
Ivan Asen III (BG) 1279-1280
Ivan Šišman (BG) 1371-1393
Ivan Stefan (BG) 1330-1331
Ivan I Danilovich (RU) 1327-1340
Ivan II (RU) 1353-1359
Ivan III Vasilyevich (RU) 1462-1505
Ivan IV the Terrible (RU) 1533-1584
Ivan V (RU sub Sophia) 1682-1689
Ivan VI (RU) 1740-1741
Izban (IL) ca 1100-1090
Iziaslav I (RU) 1054-1078
Iziaslav II (RU) 1146-1154

Jaakson (EST) 1924-1925
Jablonski, Henry (PL) 1971-
Jackson, Andrew (USA) 1829-1837
Jacques I (RH) 1804-1806
Jadwiga (PL) 1384-1386
Ja'far (CAL) +790
Jafar Shah (IR) 1785-1786
Jagiello (LIT) 1377-1392
Jahan Shah (IND) 1628-1657
Jahangir (IND) 1605-1627
Jaime (ARA) = James
Jamaica +1655
Jāmāsb (IR) 496-497
James I the Conqueror (ARA) 1213-1276
James II the Just (ARA) 1291-1327
James I (GB) 1603-1652 = James VI Stuart (SCOT)
James II (GB) 1685-1688
James I Stuart (SCOT) 1424-1437
James II Stuart (SCOT) 1437-1460
James III Stuart (SCOT) 1460-1488
James IV Stuart (SCOT) 1488-1513
James V Stuart (SCOT) 1513-1542
James VI Stuart (SCOT) 1567-1625 = James I (GB)
James of Aragon (SIC) 1285-1296
James, Apostle (JU) +41
Jämtland (N,S) +880, 1125
Jan (CS, PL) = John
Jannai, Alexander (IL) 104-77
Janós Hunyadi (H) 1446-1457
Jansz, William +1606
Janus (ROM) -720
Jaromir (CS) 1003-1012
Java +1596
Jayawardene, J.R. (SRI LANKA) 1980-
Jean (F) = John
Jeanne d'Arc = Joan of Arc
Jefferson, Thomas (USA) 1801-1809
Jehoahaz (IL) 817-802
Jehoahaz (JU) -609
Jehoiachin (JU) 598-597
Jehoiada (IL) -830
Jehoiakim (JU) 609-598
Jehoram (IL) 850-844
Jehoram (JU) 849-845
Jehoshaphat (JU) 867-850
Jehu (IL) 844-817
Jelling (DK) +940
Jen (RC) = Ren
Jephthah (IL) ca 1110-1100
Jeremiah (IL) -610, -570, -560
Jeroboam (IL) 923-906
Jeroboam II (IL) 786-748
Jerome, Church Father +390
Jerusalem -996, -740, -700, -600, -520, +40, 70, 140, 614, 1099, 1187, 1229, 1239, 1244
Jesuits (V) +1550, 1620, 1740, 1760
Jezebel (IL) -870
Jiang Jie-shi (RC) 1926- (1949) = Chiang Kai-shek
Jimenez, Marcos Pérez (YV) 1954-1958
Jimmu-Tenno (J) -650
Jin Ai Di (RC) 362-365
Jin Ai Zong (RC) 1224-1234
Jin An Di (RC) 397-418
Jin Cheng Di (RC) 326-342
Jin Gong Di (RC) +419
Jin Hai Ling Wang (RC) 1149-1160
Jin Hai Xi Gong (RC) 366-370
Jin Huai Di (RC) 307-312
Jin Hui Di (RC) 291-306
Jin Jian Wen Di (RC) 371-372
Jin Kang Di (RC) 343-344
Jin Min Di (RC) 313-316
Jin Ming Di (RC) 323-325
Jin Mu Di (RC) 345-361
Jin Shi Zong (RC) 1161-1189
Jin Tai Zong (RC) 1123-1134
Jin Tai Zu (RC) 1115-1122
Jin Wei Shao Wang (RC) 1209-1212
Jin Wu Di (RC) 264-290
Jin Xi Zong (RC) 1135-1148
Jin Xiao Wu Di (RC) 373-397
Jin Xuan Zong (RC) 1213-1223
Jin Yan Di (RC) 317-322
Jin Zhang Zong (RC) 1190-1208
Jindřich Břetislav (CS) 1193-1197
Jindřich Korutanský (CS) 1307-1310
Jiri (CS) = George
Joachim I (BRAN) (1449)-1535
Joachim II (BRAN) 1535-1571
Joachim Frederick (BRAN) 1598-1608
Joan the Mad (E,A,BURG) +1501
Joan I (NA) 1345-1382
Joan II (NA) 1414-1435
Joan of Arc (F) +1430
Joao (P) = John
Joash (JU) 836-799
Joash (IL) 801-786
Job (IL) -520
Johan (DK,S) = John
Johan, Archbishop (S) +1187
Johan de Witt (NL) 1653-1672
Johann (BRAN, SAX) = John
Johannes (BG,BYZ IL,V) = John
John I (ARA) 1387-1395
John II (ARA) 1458-1479
John the Fearless (BURG) 1404-1419
John Chrysostomus (BYZ) +390
John I Tzimisces (BYZ) 969-976
John II Comnenus (BYZ) 1118-1143
John III Vatatzes (BYZ) 1222-1254
John IV (BYZ) 1258-1261
John V Palaeologus (BYZ) 1341-1347, 1354-1376, 1379-1390
John VI Cantacuzenus (BYZ) 1347-1354
John VII (BYZ) +1390
John VIII Palaeologus (BYZ) 1425-1448
John I (CAST) 1379-1390
John II (CAST) 1406-1454
John I of Luxemburg (CS) 1311-1345
John of Holstein (DK) 1332-1340
John I (F) +1316
John II the Good (F) 1350-1364
John (Lackland) (GB) 1199-1216
John Hyrcanus (IL) 134-104
John I, Master of Aviz (P) 1383-1433
John II the Great (P) 1481-1495
John III (P) 1521-1557
John IV (P) 1640-1656
John V (P) 1706-1750
John VI (P) 1816-1823, 1824-1826
John I Albert (PL) 1492-1501
John II Casimir Vasa (PL) 1648-1668
John III Sobieski (PL) 1674-1696
John (I) Sverkersson (S) 1216-1222
John II (S) = Hans
John III (S) 1569-1692
John I (SAX) 1854-(1873)
John the Steadfast (SAX) 1525-1532
John de Balliol (SCOT) 1292-1296
John I (V) 523-526
John II (V) 532-535
John III (V) 561-574
John IV (V) 640-642
John V (V) 685-686
John VI (V) 701-705
John VII (V) 705-707
John VIII (V) 787-882
John IX (V) 897-900
John X (V) 914-928
John XI (V) 931-936
John XII (V) 955-963
John XIII (V) 965-972
John XIV (V) 983-984
John XV (V) 985-996
John XVI (V) 996-998
John XVII (V) +1003
John XVIII (V) 1003-1009
John XIX (V) 1024-1032
John XX (V) non est.
John XXI (V) 1276-1277
John XXII (V) 1316-1334
John XXIII (V) 1958-1963
John of Damascus +730
John Frederick the Magnanimous (SAX) 1532-1547
John George (BRAN) 1571-1598
John George I (SAX) 1611-1656
John George II (SAX) 1656-1680
John George III (SAX) 1680-1691
John George IV (SAX) 1691-1694
John Paul I (V) +1978
John Paul II (V) 1978-
John Sigismund (BRAN) 1608-1619
John Vladislav (BG) 1016-1018
Johnson, Andrew (USA) 1865-1869
Johnson, Lyndon (USA) 1963-1969
Jonas, Franz (A) 1965-1973
Jordanes +160, 350, 560
Joretsu (J) +1430
José (P) = Joseph
José Linhares (BR) 1945-1947
Joseph I (A) 1705-1711 = Joseph I (IMP)
Joseph II (A) 1780-1790 = Joseph II (IMP)
Joseph Bonaparte (E) 1808-1813
Joseph I (IMP) 1705-1711 = Joseph I (A)
Joseph II (IMP) 1765-1790
Joseph I (P) 1750-1777
Josephus, Flavius (IL) +70
Joshua (IL) ca 1240-1220
Josiah (JU) 639-609
Jost (D) 1410-1411
Jotham (JU) 746-742
Jovian (ROM) 363-364
Juan (CAST) = John
Juan Carlos (E) 1975-
Juana (E) = Joan
Juárez, Benito (MEX) 1858-1864, 1867-1872
Juchen (RC) +1114, 1125, 1150, 1240
Judah ha-Nasi (JU) +210
Judith (ETH) = Zauditu
Jugurtha (ROM) -120
Jui (RC) = Rui
Julia Donna (ROM) +210
Julian the Apostate (ROM) +350, 361-363
Juliana (NL) 1948-80
Julianus (ROM) +193
Julius Nepos (ROM) 474-475
Julius I (V) 336-352
Julius II (V) 1503-1513
Julius III (V) 1550-1555
Julius Sacrovir (ROM) +21
Junius Brutus (ROM) 509-505
Junna (J) 823-833
Junnin (J) 758-764
Juntoku (J) 1210-1220
Justin I (ROM) 518-527
Justin II (BYZ) 565-578
Justin the Martyr +170
Justinian I (ROM) 527-565
Justinian II (BYZ) 685-695, 705-711
Justo, Agustin (RA) 1932-1938
Jutes +450

Kabyles 256-259
Kadashman-Enlil I (BAB) ca 1374-1370
Kadashman-Enlil II (BAB) 1276-1271
Kadashman-Harbe I (BAB) ca 1383-1380
Kadashman-Harbe II (BAB) ca 1250-1241
Kadashman-Turgu (BAB) 1293-1277
Kadphises (IND) +100
Kagemaya (GH) +301
Kaikhatu (IR) 1291-1292
Kairouan (TN) +670
Kālidāsa (IND) +410
Kaliman Asen (BG) 1241-1246
Kaliman II (BG) 1257-1258
Kalinin, Michael (SU) +1923
Kallio, Kyösti (SF) 1937-1940
Kalmar Union (DK,N,S) +1397
Kaloyan (BG) 1197-1207
Kameyama (J) 1259-1275
Kameyama II (J) 1373-1389
Kamil (ET) 1218-1238
Kammu (J) 781-806
Kamose (ET) ca. 1620-1592
Kang (RC) = Gang
Kang Youwei (RC) +1898
K'ang (RC) = Kang
Kaniska (IND) +100
Kant, Immanuel 1724-1804
Kao (RC) = Gao
K'ao (RC) = Kao
Kapodistrias (GR) +1827
Karageorge (YU) 1811-1812
Karaindash (BAB) ca 1387-1384
Karamanlis, Konstantinos (GR) 1980-
Kardam (BG) 792-797
Karel (CS,NL) = Charles

Karim al-Kassem, Abdul (IRQ) 1958-1963
Karim Khan (IR) 1750-1779
Karl (A,BAY,D) = Charles
Karl (I) Knutsson (N) 1448-1450 see also Charles (N)
Karl VII Sverkersson (S) 1161-1167
Karl (VIII) Knutsson Bonde (S) 1437-1440, 1448-1457, 1464-1465, 1467-1470, see also Charles (S)
Karmal, Babrak (AFG) 1979-
Karobert (H) = Charles Robert
Karoly (H) = Charles
Károlyi, Michael (H) 1918-1919
Kashtariti (ASS) – 700, – 680
Kashtiliash I (BAB) ca 1510-1507
Kashtiliash II (BAB) ca 1430-1421
Kashu-nadin-akhe (BAB) 1021-1017
Kasimierz (PL) = Casimir
Katzir, Ephraim (IL) 1973-1978
Kavadh I (IR) 488-495, 498-531
Kayamaga (GH) + 300
Kazan (J) 984-986
Keiko Tenno (J) 71-130
Keitai (J) 507-531
Kekkonen, Urho (SF) 1956-1981
Kemal, Mustafa (TR) 1922-1938
Kennedy, John (JSA) 1961-1963
Kenso (J) 485-487
Kepler, Johannes 1571-1630
Kerensky Alexander (RU) + 1917
Kestutis (LIT) 1328-1330
Khalid (SM) 1975-
Khalid ibn al-walid-(CAL) + 640
Khalil Shah (IR) 1405-1408
Khan Liu Cong (RC) + 320
Khanh, Nguyen (VN) 1963-1965
Khazars + 650, 710, 1040
Khirgis + 860
Khomeini, Ayatollah (IR) 1979-
Khosrow I Anushirvan (IR) 531-579
Khosrow II Parviz (IR) 590-628
Khri-srong-lde-bean (Tibet) + 802
Khrushchev, Nikita (SU) 1955-1964
Khubushkia (ASS) – 700
Khwarizmi, Muhammad ibn Musa al-(CAL) + 810
Kiev + 1030, 1667
Kimmei (J) 540-571
Kindaswinth (VIGO) 642-649
Kirchschläger, Rudolf (A) 1973-
Kivik (S) – 980, – 840
Kiyomori (J) + 1159
Kizikis (GR) 1973-1974
Knud (DK) = Canute
Knut Eriksson (S) 1167-1199
Knut Laange (S) 1228-1233
Kobad = Kavadh (IR)
Kobun (J) + 672
Koch, Robert 1843-1910
Kogon II (J) 1352-1371
Koguryo + 480
Kogyoku (J) 641-645
Koivisto, Mauno (SF) 1981-
Koken (J) 749-758
Koko (J) 884-887
Kök-Turkish Empire + 600
Komatsu II (J) 1382-1389
Komyo (J) 1336-1348
Kon Qianzhi (RC) + 440
Kondouriotis, Paulos (GR) 1924-1925, 1926-1929
Kongfuzu (RC) – 520
Konin (J) 770-781
Konoe (J) 1142-1155
Konrad (CS,D,PL) = Conrad
Konya (SELD) + 1070
Köprülü, Mehmed (TR) + 1650
Koran + 650, 660
Korea + 680, 1592
Kormisosh (BG) 739-756
Körner, Theodor (A) 1951-1957
Korüturk, Fahri (TR) 1973-1980
Korybut Wiśniowecki, Michael (PL) 1669-1673
Kosciuszko (PL) + 1790
Kosygin, Alexey (SU) + 1964
Kotoku (J) 645-654
Kotriguri + 580
Kovrat (BG) + 630
Kristian (DK,N,S,SAX) = Christian
Kristina (S) = Christina
Kristoffer (DK & N,S) = Christopher
Kuang (RC) = Guang
Kubitschek, Juscelino (BR) 1955-1960
Kublai Khan (MONG) 1259-1294, (RC) 1280-1294
Kubrat (BG) 624-642
Kudur-Enlil (BAB) 1270-1263
Kukk (EST) 1922-1923
Kumara Gupta (IND) 415-455
Kumārajīva (RC) + 380
Kung (RC) = Gong
K'ung (RC) = Kung
Kupe (Tahiti) + 960
Kurigalzu I (BAB) 1411-1391
Kurigalzu II (BAB) ca 1380-1376
Kurigalzu III (BAB) ca 1344-1320
Kutuz (ET) 1259-1260
Kviesis, Alberts (LET) 1930-1936

Ladislas I (H) 1077-1095
Ladislas II (H) 1162-1163
Ladislas III (H) 1204-1205
Ladislas IV (H) 1272-1290
Ladislas V (H) 1439-1444 = Vladislav IV (CS)
Ladislas (NA) 1386-1414
Ladislas Posthumus (A) 1439-1457
Laenas, Publ. Pompillius (ROM) 157-154
La Fayette (F) + 1790
La Fontaine + 1668
Lajos (H) = Louis
Lamar, José de (PE) 1827-1830
Lamarck, Jean-Baptiste 1744-1829
Lambert (IMP) 891-896
Lando (V) 913-914
Lañusse (RA) 1971-1973
Laozi (RC) – 450
Laredo Bru, Federico (C) 1937-1940
Lars Porsena (ROM) – 510
Laszlo (H) = Ladislas
Laviosier, Antoine 1743-1794
Law, John (F) + 1720
Lawrence, the Deacon + 250
Lazar I (YU) 1371-1389
Lazar Brancović (YU) 1456-1458
Lebrun, Albert (F) 1932-1940
Leeuwenhoek, Antony van + 1675
Leguia, Augusto (PE) 1908-1912, 1919-1930
Leibniz, Gottfried Wilhelm 1646-1716
Leif Eriksson (N,IS,USA) + 1000
Lenin (SU) 1917-1924
Leo I (ROM,BYZ) 457-474
Leo II (ROM,BYZ) + 474
Leo III BYZ) 717-741
Leo IV (BYZ) 775-780
Leo V (BYZ) 813-820
Leo VI (BYZ) 886-912
Leo I (V) 440-461
Leo II (V) 681-683
Leo III (V) 795-816
Leo IV (V) 847-855
Leo V (V) + 903
Leo VI (V) 928-929
Leo VII (V) 936-939
Leo VIII (V) 963-964
Leo IX (V) 1049-1054
Leo X (V) 1513-1521
Leo XI (V) + 1605
Leo XII (V) 1823-1829
Leo XIII (V) 1878-1903
Leon Valencia, Guillermo (CO) 1962-1966
Leonardo da Vinci 1452-1519
Leone, Giovanni (I) 1971-1978
Leoni, Raúl (YV) 1964-1969
Leontius (BYZ) 695-698
Leopold I (A,IMP) 1658-1705
Leopold II (A,IMP) 1790-1792
Leopold I (B) 1831-1865
Leopold II (B) 1865-1909
Leopold III (B) 1934-1951
Leopold I (IMP) 1658-1705 = Leopold I (A)
Leopold II (IMP) 1790-1792 = Leopold II (A)
Leovigild (VIGO) 568-586
Lepidus, M. Aemilius (ROM) 77-75
Lepidus (ROM) – 12
Lessing, Gotthold Ephraim 1729-1781
Leszek the White (PL) 1202-1210, 1211-1227
Leszek II Czarny (PL) 1279-1288
Leucon I (BOSP) 389-349
Leuctra (THEB) – 380
Levingston, R.M. (RA) 1970-1971
Li Bo (RC) + 740, 762
Li Dang (RC) + 1120
Li Zicheng (RC) + 1640, 1650
Liang Jian Wen Di (RC) + 550
Liang Jing Di (RC) 555-556
Liang Wu Di (RC) 502-549
Liang Yu Zhang Wang (RC) 551-552
Liang Yuan Di (RC) 552-554
Liao Cheng Tian Hou (RC) 1164-1177
Liao Dao Zong (RC) 1055-1100
Liao De Zong (RC) 1124-1143
Liao Gan Tian Hou (RC) 1144-1150
Liao Jing Zong (RC) 969-982
Liao Mo Zhu (RC) 1178-1211
Liao Mu Zong (RC) 951-968
Liao Ren Zong (RC) 1151-1163
Liao Sheng Zong (RC) 983-1030
Liao Shi Zong (RC) 947-950
Liao Tai Zong (RC) 927-946
Liao Tai Zu (RC) 907-926
Liao Tian Zuo Di (RC) 1101-1123
Liao Xing Zong (RC) 1031-1054
Liberia + 1822, 1847
Liberius (V) 352-366
Licinius, C (ROM) ca 376-375
Licinius, Val. (ROM) 311-324
Lieh (RC) = Lie
Lij Iyasu (ETH) 1911-1916
Limann, Hilla (GH) 1978-1981
Limes (ROM) + 100, 120
Linares, José Maria (RB) 1858-1861
Lincoln, Abraham (USA) 1861-1865
Lindisfarne (GB) + 730, 793
Lindley, Nicolás (PE) + 1963
Linhares, José (BR) 1945-1946
Linné, Carl von 1707-1778
Linus (V) 68-76
Lipit-Ishtar (BAB) 1870-1860
Lithuania + 1245
Litorin period – 970
Liu Cong (RC) + 320
Liu Sheng – 120
Liu Song Cang Wu Wang (RC) 473-476
Liu Song Ming Di (RC) 465-472
Liu Song Shao Di (RC) + 423
Liu Song Shun Di (RC) 477-478
Liu Song Wen Di (RC) 424-453
Liu Song Wu Di (RC) 420-422
Liu Song Xiao Wu Di (RC) 454-464
Liudpert (LONG) 700-701
Liudprand (LONG) 712-744
Liutprand of Cremona (IMP) + 980
Liuva I (VIGO) 567-568
Liuva II (VIGO) 601-603
Livius Drusus, M (ROM) 97-94
Livy (ROM) – 430, – 290, + 17
Lleras Camargo, Alberto (CO) 1958-1962
Lleras Restrepo, Carlos (CO) 1966-1970
Lleshi, Haxhi (AL) 1953-
Lo (RC) = Le
Locri (I) – 664
Lodbrok's sons (DK,S) + 900
Lodewijk (NL) = Louis
Lombards + 570, 580, 670, 760, 780
Lonardi, Eduardo (RA) + 1955
Longinus (exarch. Ravenna) + 568
Lope de Vega + 1600
López, Alfonso (CO) 1934-1938
López, Hermógenes (YV) 1887-1889
López, José (CO) 1849-1853
López Contreras, Eleazar (YV) 1936-1941
López Mateos, Adolfo (MEX) 1958-1964
López Michelson, A. (CO) 1974-
López Pumarejo, A. (CO) 1942-1945
Lorenzo de' Medici, il Magnifico (FIR) 1469-1492
Losonczi, Pal (H) 1967-
Lotf Ali Khan (IR) 1789-1793
Lothair (F) 954-986
Lothair the Saxon (D) 1125-1137 = Lothair II (IMP)
Lothair I (IMP) 840-855
Lothair II (IMP) 1125-1137 = Lothair the Saxon (D)
Lothar (F) 511-561 = Clothar
Loubet, Emile (F) 1899-1906
Louis I (BAY) 1825-1848
Louis II (BAY) 1864-1886
Louis I the German (D) 843-876
Louis II the Stammerer (D) 877-879
Louis III (D) + 879
Louis IV the Child (D) 899-911
Louis of Bavaria (D) 1313-1347
Louis (I) the Pious (F) 814-840
Louis II the Stammerer (F) 877-879
Louis III (F) 879-882
Louis IV d'Outremer (F) 936-954
Louis V (F) 986-987
Louis VI the Fat (F) 1108-1137
Louis VII (F) 1137-1180
Louis VIII (F) 1223-1226
Louis IX the Saint (F) 1226-1270
Louis X the Stubborn (F) 1314-1316
Louis XI (F) 1461-1483
Louis XII (F) 1498-1515
Louis XIII (F) 1610-1643
Louis XIV (F) 1643-1715
Louis XV (F) 1723-1774
Louis XVI (F) 1774-1792
Louis XVIII (F) 1814-1824
Louis Napoleon (F) 1848-1852 = Napoleon III
Louis-Philippe (F) 1830-1848
Louis I (H) 1342-1382 = Louis of Anjou
Louis II (H) 1516-1526 = Louis Jagellonský (CS)
Louis I (IMP) 814-840
Louis II (IMP) 855-875 = Louis the German
Louis III (IMP) 901-905
Louis IV (IMP) 1314-1347 = Louis of Bavaria (D) Louis Napoleon (NL) 1806-1810
Louis of Aragon (SIC) 1342-1355
Louisiana (USA) + 1803
Louverture, Toussaint (RH) 1794-1802
Loyola, Ignatius + 1545
Lü Hou (RC) 187-180
Lübeck + 1143, + 1294
Lübke Heinrich (D) 1959-1969
Lucan (ROM) + 70
Lucian (ATH) + 170
Lucius I (V) 253-254
Lucius II (V) 1144-1145

Lucius III (V) 1181-1185
Lucius Verus (ROM) +170
Lucretius (ROM) -50
Lucullus, L. Licinius (ROM) 69-67
Ludvik Jagellonský (CS) 1516-1526 = Louis II (H)
Ludwig (D) = Louis
Ludwik Węgierski (PL) 1370-1382 = Louis I (H)
Luigi (SIC) = Louis
Luis I (P) 1861-1889
Luis Orbegosa (PE) 1832-1835
Lund (DK,S) +1104
Lung (RC) = Long
Luther, Martin +1517, 1540
Lützen (S) +1632
Lycurgus (GR) -710
Lydia -690, -650
Lysander (Sparta, GR) -410
Lysimachus (THRA) 323-281
Lysistrata (ATH) -411
Lyudevit, Croat +823

Macbeth (SCOT) 1040-1057
Maccabeus, Jonathan (IL) 153-142
Maccabeus, Judas (IL) 166-160
Machado, Bernardino (P) 1915-1917, 1925
Machado, Gerardo (C) 1925-1933
Machiavelli, Nicolò 1469-1527
Mac-Mahon, Marie-Edmé (F) 1873-1879
Macrinus (ROM) 217-218
Madagascar +1643
Madeira +1330, 1430
Madero, F (MEX) 1911-1913
Madison, James (USA) 1809-1817
Maecenas (ROM) -30, -8
Magellan, Ferdinand (P) +1519
magic Lantern +1660
Magna carta (GB) +1215
Magna mater +220
Magnentius (ROM) +350
Magnus I (DK) 1024-1047 = Magnus the Good (N)
Magnus (I) the Good (N) 1035-1047
Magnus II (N) 1066-1069
Magnus (III) Barefoot (N) 1093-1103
Magnus (IV) the Blind (N) 1130-1136
Magnus V Erlingsson (N) 1165-1176
Magnus VI Lawmender (N) 1263-1280
Magnus VII (N) 1319-1343 = Magnus Eriksson (S)
Magnus I Laduås (S) 1275-1290
Magnus Eriksson (S) 1319-1363
Magyars +890, 930
al-Mahdī (CAL) 775-785
Mahmūd (AFG) +1010
Mahmud Shah (AFG) 1799-1803, 1810-1818
Mahmud (IR) 1722-1724
Mahmud I (TR) 1730-1754
Mahmud II (TR) 1808-1839
Majorian (ROM) 457-461
Malchus I (PETRA) 47-30
Malcolm II (SCOT) 1005-1034
Malcolm III Canmore (SCOT) 1057-1093
Malcolm IV (SCOT) 1153-1165
Malenkov, Georgi (SU) 1953-1954
Malik al Adil, al- (ET) 1196-1218
Malik al-Aziz, al- (ET) 1193-1196
Malik-shah (SELD) 1072-1092
Mallarino, Manuel (CO) 1854-1857
Malomir (BG) 831-836
Malta -400, +218
Malthus, Thomas 1766-1834
Mamitiarshu (MED) -700
Mamlūks (ET) 1250-1811
al-Ma'mūn (CAL) 813-833
Manasseh (JU) 697-742
Manco Capac (INC) +1060
Manetho (ET) -900, -300
Manfred (SIC) 1257-1266
Mangu Timur (MONG) 1265-1280
Mani (IR) +276
Manichaeism +280, 297, 660
Manlius Capitolinus, M (ROM) ca. 388-384
Manlius Imperiosus, Cn. (ROM) ca. 359-356
Manlius Torquatus, Tit. (I) (ROM) 349-346
Manlius Torquatus, Tit. (II) (ROM) 237-233
Mannerheim, Karl Gustaf (SF) 1918-1919, 1944-1946
Mannians -700
Manoel (P) = Manuel
Mansur (ET) +1279
al-Mansūr (CAL) 754-775
Mantegna +1500
Mantinea (THEB) -370
Manuel I Comnenus (BYZ) 1143-1180
Manuel II Palaeologus (BYZ) 1391-1425
Manuel I the Fortunate (P) 1495-1521
Manuel II (P) 1908-1910
Manzikert (BYZ,SELD) +1071
Mao Dun (HUN) -180
Mao Tse-tung (RC) = Mao Zedong 1950-1976
Marathon (ATH) -500
Marbiti-akhe-iddin (BAB) 953-942
Marbiti-apal-usur (BAB) 995-991
Marbod +11
Marcellinus (V) 296-304
Marcellus, M. Claudius (ROM) -220
Marcellus I (V) 308-309
Marcellus II (V) +1555
Marcian (ROM) 450-457
Marcion of Sinope +150
Marco Polo +1270
Marcomanni +20, 190
Marconi, Guglielmo, 1874-1937
Marcus Aurelius (ROM) 161-180
Marduk-balassu-iqbi (BAB) 827-815
Marduk-nadin-akhe (BAB) 1116-1101
Marduk-shapik-zeri (BAB) 1091-1084
Marduk-shapir-zeri (BAB) 1170-1153
Marduk-zakir-shumi (BAB) 851-828
Margaret (DK & N) 1387-1412
Margaret (S) 1389-1412 = Margaret (DK & N)
Margaret (SCOT) +1093
Margaret (SCOT) 1286-1290
Marggraf (D) +1747
Margrete (DK & N) = Margaret
Margrethe II (DK) 1972-
Maria I (H) 1382-1385, 1388-1395
Maria I (P) 1777-1816
Maria da Gloria (P) 1826-1829, 1834-1853
Maria (SIC) 1377-1402
Maria Christina (E) 1885-1902
Maria Theresa (A) 1740-1780
Mariamne (IL) -40
Marinus I (V) 882-884
Marinus II (V) 942-946
Marius, Caius (ROM) -110, 100, 86
Mark (V) 335-336
Mark, St. +80
Mark Twain +1876
Marozia (V) +920
Márquez, José de (CA) 1837-1841
Martin I (ARA) 1395-1410
Martin of Tours, St. (F) +390
Martin I of Aragon (SIC) 1391-1409
Martin II (SIC) 1409-1410
Martin I (V) 649-655
Martin II-III (V) = Marinus I-II
Martin IV (V) 1281-1285
Martin V (V) 1417-1431
Marwān I (CAL) 684-685
Marwān II (CAL) 744-750
Mary Tudor (GB) 1553-1558
Mary II (GB) 1688-1694
Mary Stuart (SCOT) 1542-1567
Marquez, José de (CO) 1837-1842
Marraquin, José (CO) 1900-1904
Martel, Charles (F) 737-741
Marx, Karl 1818-1883
Masaryk, Tomas (CS) 1918-1935
Massilia -580, -300, -110, +60
Mateos, A. López (MEX) 1958-1964
Matilda (I) +1115
Matthias I Corvinus (A) 1485-1490
Matthias (A) 1593-1619 = Matthias (IMP)
Matthias (IMP) 1612-1619 = Matthias (A)
Mattiwaza (MIT) ca. 1370-1362
Mauregato (AST) 783-789
Maurice (BYZ) 582-602
Maurice of Nassau (NL) 1584-1625
Maurice (SAX) 1549-1553
Mausaeus Carausius (GB) +286
Mausolus (GR) -380
Maxentius (ROM) 305-312
Maximian (ROM) 285-305
Maximilian I (A) 1493-1519 = Maximilian I (NL & D) = Maximilian I (IMP)
Maximilian II (A) 1564-1576 = Maximilian II (IMP)
Maximilian I (BAY) 1597-1651
Maximilian II (BAY) 1848-1864
Maximilian II Emanuel (BAY) 1679-1726
Maximilian III Joseph (BAY) 1745-1777
Maximilian IV Joseph (BAY) 1799-1825
Maximilian I (MEX) 1864-1867
Maximilian I (NL) 1477-1506
Maximinus Thrax (ROM) 235-238
Maximus, Petronius (ROM) +455
Maya (MEX) +160, 290, 350, 600, 990, 1020, 1040
Mazarin (F) +1660
Mazdak (IR) +500
McAlpin, Kenneth (SCOT) +844
McKinley, William (USA) 1897-1901
Medes -700, -650
Médici, E.G. (BR) 1969-1974
Medici, Giuliano de' (FIR) 1469-1478
Medici, Lorenzo de', il Magnifico (FIR) 1469-1492
Medici, Piero de' (FIR) 1464-1469
Medina, Isaias (YV) 1941-1945
Megiddo (JU) -610
Mehmed I (TR) 1405-1421
Mehmed II (TR) 1451-1481
Mehmed III (TR) 1595-1603
Mehmed IV (TR) 1649-1687
Mehmed V (TR) 1909-1918
Mehmed VI (TR) 1918-1922
Melanchthon, Philipp 1497-1560
Melgarejo, Mariano (RB) 1864-1870
Melishipak (BAB) ca 1390-1388
Melishipak II (BAB) 1202-1188
Memling, Hans, 1433-1494
Memnon's colossi (ET) -1420
Menahem (IL) 746-736
Mencius (RC) -300, +820
Mendel, Gregor 1822-1884
Mēndez, Geronimo (RCH) 1941-1942
Mendez, Miguel Arada (CO) 1926-1930
Mendieta, Carlos (C) 1934-1935
Menelik (ETH) -940
Menelik II (ETH) 1899-1911
Menenius Agrippa (ROM) -430
Meng Hao-jan (RC) +740
Mengistu Haile Mariam (ETH) 1977-
Mengzi (RC) -300
Menocal, Mario Garcia (C) 1913-1921
Mentuhotep II (ET) 2000-1992
Mercator +1569, 1590
Merneptah (ET) 1232- ca 1220
Merodach-Baladan I (BAB) 1187-1175
Merodach-Baladan II (BAB) 721-710 705-701
Meroë (ETH) -300
Merovech, Mérovée (F) 452-458
Mesha (IL) -850
Metellus, Q. Caecilius (ROM) 117-115
Methodius (CS) +870
Meton (ATH) -440
Mexico 151-160
Meza, Luis Garcia (RB) 1980-1981
Mi Fei, artist (RC) +1120
Michael Asen (BG) 1246-1257
Michael Šišman (BG) 1323-1329
Michael I Rangabe (BYZ) 811-813
Michael II (BYZ) 820-829
Michael III (BYZ) 842-867
Michael IV (BYZ) 1034-1041
Michael V (BYZ) 1041-1042
Michael VI (BYZ) 1056-1057
Michael VII Ducas (BYZ) 1171-1178
Michael VIII Palaeologus (BYZ) 1261-1282
Michael Korybut Wiśniowiecki (PL) 1669-1673
Michael I (R) 1927-1930, 1940-1947
Michael (RU) 1304-1319
Michael Romanov (RU) 1613-1645
Michael Obrenović (YU) 1839-1842, 1860-1868
Michelangelo 1475-1564
Michelson, A. López (CO) 1974-1978
Midas (PHRY) -770, -740, -690
Mieszko I (PL) 962-992
Mieszko II Lambert (PL) 1025-1034
Mieszko III the Old (PL) 1173-1177
Mieszko IV Plątonogi (PL) 1210-1211
Miguel I (P) 1823-1824, 1829-1834
Mihail (R) = Michael
Mihailo (YU) = Michael
Mihirakula (IND) +515
Mijatović, Cvijetin (YU) 1980-1981
Miklas, Wilhelm (A) 1928-1938
Milan Obrenovic (YU) +1839
Milan I (= II Obrenovic (YU) (1868-) 1883-1889
Miletus -960, -570, -550, -500
Millerand, Alexandre (F) 1920-1924
Milos Obrenovic (YU) 1816-1839, 1858-1860
Miltiades (ATH) ca. 490-489
Miltiades (V) 311-313
Milton, John +1667
Minamoto (J) +1150, 1200
Mindaugas (LIT) 1243-1263
Mindove (LIT) = Mindaugas
Ming Cheng Hua (RC) 1465-1487
Ming Chong Zhen (RC) 1626-1643
Ming Hong Wu (RC) 1368-1398
Ming Hong Xi (RC) +1425
Ming Hong Zhi (RC) 1488-1505
Ming Jia Jing (RC) 1522-1566
Ming Jian Wen (RC) 1399-1402
Ming Jing Tai (RC) 1450-1457
Ming Long Qing (RC) 1567-1572
Ming Tai Chang (RC) +1620
Ming Tian Qi (RC) 1621-1627
Ming Tian Shun (RC) 1458-1464
Ming Wan Li (RC) 1573-1619
Ming Xuan De (RC) 1426-1435
Ming Yong Le (RC) 1403-1424
Ming Zheng De (RC) 1506-1521
Ming Zheng Tong (RC) 1436-1449
Minotaur (GR) -690
Mithradates, I (IR) 170-138
Mithradates II (IR) 124-88, -90
Mithradates IV (IR) 131-147
Mithradates VI (PONT) -107

Mithras +220, 340
Mitre, Bartolomé (RA) 1862-1868
Mitterrand, François (F) 1981-
Moabites -850
Mogul Empire (IND) +1540
Mohammad Ali (IR) 1907-1909
Mohammad Reza Shah Pahlavi (IR) 1941-1979
Mohammed (AFG,CORD,IR,KHA, MA) = Muhammad
Mohammed (TR) = Mehmed
Mojimír (CS) 833-846
Molech -940
Molière 1622-1673
Molotov, Vyacheslav (SU) 1925-1926
Mommu (J) 697-707
Monagas, José Gregorio (YV) 1851-1854
Monagas, José Tadeo (YV) 1846-1850, 1854-1858
Möngke (MONG) 1251-1259
Mongkut (T) = Rama IV
Monophysites +449, 500, 520
Monroe, James (USA) 1817-1825
Montaigne +1600
Montalva, Eduardo Frei (RCH) 1964-1970
Montenegro +1858
Montero, Juan (RCH) 1931-1932
Montes, Ismael (RB) 1904-1909, 1913-1917
Montesquieu, Louis de 1689-1755
Monteverdi +1607
Montoku (J) 850-858
Montt, Jorge (RCH) 1891-1896
Montt, Manuel (RCH) 1851-1861
Montt, Pedro (RCH) 1906-1911
Morais Barros, Prudente de (BR) 1894-1898
Morales, Agustin (RB) 1870-1872
Moravia +840, 880, 890, 906
Morgan, Thomas H. 1866-1945
Moritz (SAX) = Maurice
Moscicki I (PL) 1926-1939
Moscow +1155, 1326
Moses (IL) ca. 1300-1240
Mosquera, Tomás (CO) 1845-1849, 1861-1867
Mozaffar od-Din (IR) 1896-1907
Mozart, Wolfgang Amadeus 1756-1791
Mo Zu (RC) -430
Mstislav (RU) 1125-1132
Mu'āwiyah (CAL) 661-680
Mu'āwiyah II (CAL) +683
Mubarak, Hosni (ET) 1981-
Mucius Scaevola (ROM) -510
Muhammad +610, 630, 640
Muhammad Nader Shah (AFG) 1929-1933
Muhammad Zahir Shah (AFG) 1933-1973
Muhammad (CAL) 622-632
Muhammad ibn Mūsā al Khwarizmi (CAL) +810
Muhammad I (CORD) 852-886
Muhammad II (CORD) 1009-1010
Muhammad III (CORD) 1024-1025
Muhammad Khudabende (IR) 1577-1586
Muhammad Shah (IR) 1796-1797
Muhammad Shah (IR) 1835-1848
Muhammad V (MA) 1956-1961
Muhammad I-IV (TR) = Mehmed I-IV
Muhtadi, al- (CAL) 869-870
Mu'izz ad-Dawlah (IR) +945
Mu'izz, al- (ET) 968-975
Muktafi, al- (CAL) 902-908
Mundhir (Arabia) +430
Munemori (J) +1200
Muqtadir, al- (CAL) 908-932
Murad I (TR) 1360-1389
Murad II (TR) 1421-1451
Murad III (TR) 1574-1595
Murad IV (TR) 1623-1639
Murad V (TR) +1876
Murakami (J) 947-967
Murakami II (J) 1336-1368
Mursilis I (HAT) -1530
Mursilis II (HAT) 1337-1306
Musa (CAL) +711
Mustafa I (TR) 1617-1618, 1622-1623
Mustafa II (TR) 1695-1703
Mustafa III (TR) 1757-1774
Mustafa IV (TR) 1807-1808
Musta'in, al- (CAL) 862-866
Mustakfi, al- (CAL) 944-946
Musta'li (ET) 1094-1101
Mustansir (ET) 1036-1094
Mustasir, al- (CAL) 861-862
Mu'tadid, al- (CAL) 892-902
Mutakki, al- (CAL) 940-944
Mutakkil-Nusku (ASS) 1137-1128
Mu'tamid, al- (CAL) 870-892
al-Mu'tasim (CAL) 833-842
Mutawakkil, al- (CAL) 847-861
Mu'tazz, al- (CAL) 866-869
Muti, al- (CAL) 946-974
Mutimir (YU) 887-891
Mutsuhito (J) 1867-1912
Muwatallis (HAT) 1305-1282
Mycenae -920
Mystical religions +220

Nabataeans (PETRA) -160, -50
Nabilus (PETRA) +105
Nabonassar (BAB) 747-735
Nabonidus (BAB) 555-539
Nabopolassar (BAB) 626-605
Nabonassar (BAB) 747-735
Nabu-apal-iddin (BAB) 885-852
Nabu-mukin-apli (BAB) 990-955
Nabu-shum-libur (BAB) 1061-1039
Nabu-shum-ukin (BAB) 900-886
Nadab (IL) 906-905
Nader Shah, Muhammad (AFG) 1929-1933
Nader Shah (IR) 1736-1747
Nadinu (BAB) 734-733
Naguib, Mohammad (ET) 1952-1954
Nahua (MEX) +650
Nahum (IL) -640, -620
Nan Qi Dong Hun Hou (RC) 499-500
Nan Qi Gao Di (RC) 479-482
Nan Qi He Di (RC) +501
Nan Qi Ming Di (RC) 494-498
Nan Qi Wu Di (RC) 483-493
Nan Song Bing Di (RC) 1278-1279
Nan Song Du Zong (RC) 1265-1274
Nan Song Duan Zong (RC) 1276-1277
Nan Song Gao Zong (RC) 1127-1162
Nan Song Gong Zong (RC) +1275
Nan Song Guang Zong (RC) 1190-1194
Nan Song Li Zong (RC) 1225-1264
Nan Song Ning Zong (RC) 1195-1224
Nan Song Xiao Zong (RC) 1163-1189
Napoleon I (F) 1804-1814, (NL) 1810-1812
Napoleon III (F) (1848-) 1852-1870
Nara period (J) +740
Narbo (F) -118
Narses (IR) 299-302
Narutowicz (PL) +1922
Naser od-Din (IR) 1848-1896
Nasser, Gamal (ET) 1954-1970
Naucratis (ET) -560
Navigare necesse est -70
Navon, Yitzhak (IL) 1978-
Nazima-ruttash (BAB) ca 1320-1294
Nazca culture (PE) +600
Nebuchadrezzar I (BAB) 1146-1123
Nebuchadrezzar II (BAB) 605-562
Necho (ET) 609-594
Nectanebo I (ET) 380-363
Nektanebos II (ET) 360-346
Nefelkheres (ET) ca. 990-985
Neferhotep (ET) ca. 1770-1750
Nefertite (ET) -1360
Nehemiah (IL) -540, -430
Nehru, Jawaharlal (IND) 1947-1964
Nemanja, Stevan (YU) 1168-1196
Nepherites I (ET) 399- ca 395
Nepos (ROM) 474-5
Nergal-ushesib (BAB) ca 694-691
Neriglissar (BAB) 559-556
Nero (ROM) 54-68
Nerva (ROM) 96-98
Nestor (RU) +1120
Nestorians +500
Nestorius +431
Nestors chronicle (RU) +870, 990, 1120
Nevsky Alexander (RU) 1252-1263
New York +1667
New Zealand +960
Newton, Isaac 1642-1727
Ngahue (Tahiti) +960
Ngo Dinh Diem (VN) 1955-1963
Nicephorus I (BYZ) 802-811
Nicephorus II Phocas (BYZ) 963-969
Nicephorus III (BYZ) 1078-1081
Nicias (ATH) 422-421, 414-413
Nicholas I (RU) 1825-1855
Nicholas II (RU) 1894-1917
Nicholas I (V) 858-867
Nicholas II (V) 1059-1061
Nicholas III (V) 1277-1280
Nicholas IV (V) 1288-1292
Nicholas V (V) 1447-1455
Nicola, Enrico (I) 1946-1948
Nicot +1550
Niedra (LET) +119
Niels (DK) 1103-1134
Nietzsche, Friedrich 1844-1900
Nijo (J) 1158-1165
Nijo II (J) 1302-1308
Nimmyo (J) 833-850
Nineveh (ASS) -890, -660, -620, +630
Ninken (J) 488-498
Nintoku-Tenno (J) 313-399
Ninurta-apal-ekur I (ASS) 1201-1176
Ninurta -apal-ekur II (ASS) 1102-1093
Ninurta-kudur-usur (BAB) 955-953
Ninurta-nadin-shumi (BAB) 1152-1147
Ninurta-tukulti-Ashur (ASS) 1140-1138
Nixon, Richard (USA) 1969-1974
Nizām al-Mulk (CAL) +1090
Nkrumah, Kwame (GH) 1961-1966
Nobunaga (J) 1573-1582
Noli (AL) +1924
Nominoe (F) +851
Norra Sung (RC) = Bei Song
Notger Balbulus (IMP) +980
Notger Labeo (IMP) +980
Novotny, Antonin (CS) 1957-1968
Numa Pompilius (ROM) 720-673
Numantia (E) -133
Numerian (ROM) 283-284
Núñez, Rafael (CO) 1880-1882, 1884-1894
Nurhachi (RC) 1643-1661
Nushirwan (IR) 1344-1349
Nyerere, Julius (EAT) 1964-
Nyköping Banquet +1317

Obando, José Maria (CO) 1853-1854
Obesanjo, Olusegun (NIG) 1975-1979
Obodas I (PETRA) 95-87
Obodas II (PETRA) 62-47
Obregón, Alvaro (MEX) 1920-1924
Ochab, Edvard (PL) 1964-1968
Octavianus (ROM) 44-27 = Augustus -27- +14
Odaenathus (SYR) +270
Odoacer (ROM) +476, 490
Odria, Manuel (PE) 1948-1950, 1959-1956
Odyssey -790
Offa (GB) 757-796
Ögödei (MONG) 1229-1240
Ogulkaimich (MONG) 1248-1251
O'Higgins, Bernardo (RCH) 1818-1823
Ohlrighile, Pádraig (EIR) 1976-
Ohm, George 1789-1854
Ojin-Tenno (J) 201-312
O'Kelly, Sean (EIR) 1945-1959 = Ceallaigh
Olaf (I) Tryggvason (N) 995-1000
Olaf (II) Haraldsson (N) 1016-1028 = Olav den helige
Olaf (III) the Queit (N) 1066-1093
Olaf IV Haakansson (N) 1380-1387
Olaf V (N) 1957-
Olaus Petri (S) 1493-1552
Olav (N) = Olaf
Olaya Herrera, Enrique (CO) 1930-1934
Olbia +260
Oldřich I (CS) 1012-1034
Oleg (RU) 879-912
Olga (RU) 945-957
Öljeitü (IR) 1304-1315
Olmecs -670, -300
Olof Haakansson (DK) 1376-1387
Olof Skötkonung (S) 994-1026
Oluf Hunger (DK) 1086-1095
Olybrius (ROM) +472
Olympia (GR) -780
Olympic Games -780, +393, 1896
Omar Khayyam (CAL) +1090
Omo Imoko (J) +607
Omri (IL) ca 877-870
Omurtag (BG) 814-831
Onganía, J.C. (RA) 1966-1970
Orange Free State +1842
Ordaz, Gustavo Diaz (MEX) 1964-1970
Ordoño I (AST) 850-866
Ordoño II (AST) 914-924
Ordoño III the Good (AST, León) 951-956
Ordoño IV the Bad (AST, León) 958-960
Oresolo, Pietro (VEN) +1020
Orestes (ROM) +476
Orhan (TR) 1326-1359
Origen +250
Orkney Isles +1472
Orlando furioso (F) +778
Orlando de Lasso +1594
Orodes I (IR) 81-78
Orodes II (IR) 57-41
Orodes III (IR) 4-7
Ortiz, Roberto (RA) 1938-1942
Ortuño, René Barrientos (RB)

1964-1969
Oscar I (N,S) 1844-1859
Oscar II (N) 1872-1905 (S) 1872-1907
Osokhor (ET) ca. 973-965
Osorkon I (ET) ca. 913-874
Osorkon II (ET) ca. 860-835
Osorkon III (ET) ca. 730-720
Ospina, Mariano (CO) 1857-1861
Ospina, Pedro Nel (CO) 1921-1926
Ospina Pérez, Mario (CO) 1946-1950
Osman (CAL) = Uthmān 644-656
Osman I (TR) 1288-1326
Osman II (TR) 1618-1622
Osman III (TR) 1754-1757
Osroes (IR) 109-126
Ossian (EIR) +1140
Ostrogoths +40, 350, 372, 470, 550, 560
Oswald of Northumbria (GB) +641
Oswiu (GB) 641-670
Otho I (GR) 1832-1862
Otho (ROM) +69
Otto I, II, III (D) = Otto I, II, III (IMP)
Otto I (IMP) = Otto the Great (D) 936-973
Otto II (IMP) 973-983 = Otto II (D)
Otto III (IMP) 983-1002 = Otto III (D)
Otto IV (IMP) 1198-1200, 1208-1212
Otto of Bavaria (H) 1304-1308
Ouverture, Toussaint L' (RH) = Louverture
Ovando Candia, Alfredo (RB) 1969-1970
Oveis (IR) 1356-1374
Ovid (ROM) +20
Øystein (N) = Eystein
Öz Beg (MONG) 1312-1340

Paasikivi, Juho (SF) 1946-1956
Pachomius (ET) +320
Pacorus I (IR) 40-39
Pacorus II (IR) 79-86, 92-95
Padilla, David (RB) 1978-1980
Paestum -650, +1750
Páez, José (YV) 1830-1846, 1861-1863
Pagan (BG) 764-765
Pairisades I (BOSP) 349-311
Pairisades II (BOSP) -107
Pāis, Sidonio (P) 1917-1918
Palacio, Raimundo Anduza (YV) 1890-1892
Palermo -580
Palestrina +1594
Palmyra (SYR) +270
Palnatoke (DK) +940
Panama +1913
Panathenaia (ATH) -570
Pando, José (RB) 1899-1904
Pangalos, Theodores (GR) 1925-1926
Panticapaeum (BOSP) -430
Pantheon +620
Papadopoulos (GR) 1967-1973
Papal State +760
paper (RC) +105, (CAL) +793
Papinian (ROM) +210
Papirius Cursor, L. (ROM) 314-312
Pardo, José (PE) 1915-1919
Pardo, Manuel (PE) 1872-1876
Parhon, C.J. (R) 1947-1952
Parsua (MED) -650
Partatua (SCYT) -700
Parthenopean republ. (NA) 1798-1801
Parthians -260, -180, -140, +40, 60, 100, 110, 170, 200, 240
Pascal, Blaise 1623-1662
Paschal I (V) 817-824
Paschal II (V) 1099-1118
Pasteur, Louis 1822-1895
Pastrana Borrero, Misael (CO) 1970-1974
Päts, Konstantin (EST) 1918-1919, 1921-1922, 1923-1924, 1931-1932, 1932-1933, 1933-1938
Paul I (GR) 1947-1964
Paul I (RU) 1796-1801
Paul I (V) 757-767
Paul II (V) 1464-1471
Paul III (V) 1534-1549
Paul IV (V) 1555-1559
Paul V (V) 1605-1621
Paul VI (V) 1963-1978
Paul Branović (YU) 917-920
Paul, apostle +33, 58, 67
Paul the Deacon (LONG) +570
Paula Santander, Francisco (CO) 1832-1837
Pausanias (Sparta) -480
Pausanias (the younger) (Sparta) -400
Pausanias (of Magnesia) +180
Pavle (YU) = Paul
Paz Estenssoro, Victor (RB) 1952-1956, 1960-1964
Peary, Robert E. (USA) +1920
Peçanha, Nilo (BR) 1909-1910
Pechenegs +89, 1110
Pedro (ARA,CAST) = Peter
Pedro I (BR) 1822-1831
Pedro II (BR) 1831-1889
Pedro I (P) 1357-1367
Pedro II (P) 1667-1706
Pedro III (P) 1777-1786
Pedro IV (P) +1826 = Pedro I (BR)
Pedro V (P) 1853-1861
Pei Ch'i = Bei Qi
Pei Chou = Bei Zhou
Pei Sung = Bei Song
Pei Wei = Bei Wei
Peistratus (ATH) ca. 560-528
Peixoto, Floriano (BR) 1891-1894
Pekah (IL) 734-732
Pekahiah (IL) 736-734
Peking (RC) = Beijing
Pelagius, theologian +431
Pelagius I (V) 555-561
Pelagius II (V) 579-590
Pelayo (AST) 719-736
Pellegrini, Carlos (RA) 1890-1892
Pelopidas (THEB) ca. 378-376
Peloponnesian War -420, 400
Pena, Alfonso (BR) 1906-1909
Peñaranda, Enrique (RB) 1940-1943
Penda (GB) +641
Penn, William +1682
People's Tribunes (ROM) -500
Pepin (F) 752-768
Perctarit (LONG) 672-686
Perdiccas (BAB & IR) 323-321
Perdiccas III (MAC) 365-359
Pereira de Souza, W.L. (BR) 1926-1930
Pérez, Carlós Andrés (YV) 1974-1979
Pérez, José Joaquin (RCH) 1861-1871
Perez, Mario Ospina (CO) 1946-1949
Pérez Godoy, Ricardo (PE) 1962-1963
Pérez Jiménez, Marcos (YV) 1954-1958
Pergamum -290, -190, -140
Pergolesi +1733
Periander (GR) -640
Pericles (ATH) 463-430
Perón, Isabelita (RA) 1974-1976
Perón, Juan (RA) 1946-1955, 1973-1974
Peroz (IR) = Firuz
Perrault +1697
Perseus (MAC) 179-168
Pertinax (ROM) 192-193
Pertine Alessandro (I) 1978-
Pessoa, Epitacio (BR) 1919-1922
Pétain, Philippe (F) 1940-1944
Petar (YU) = Peter
Peter I (ARA) 1094-1102
Peter II (ARA) 1196-1213
Peter III the Great (ARA) 1276-1285
Peter IV the Ceremonious (ARA) 1336-1387
Peter (BG) 927-969
Peter Asen (BG) 1196-1197
Peter I the Cruel or the Just (CAST) 1350-1369
Peter (Croat) +1090
Peter (H) 1038-1041, 1044-1046
Peter I (RU) 1682-1686, 1698-1725
Peter II (RU) 1727-1730
Peter III (RU) +1762
Peter I of Aragon (SIC) 1282-1285 = Peter III the Great (ARA)
Peter II (SIC) 1337-1342
Peter (V) ca. 36-66
Peter Gojniković (YU) 892-917
Peter I Karageorgevic (YU) 1903-1921
Peter II (YU) 1934-1941
Petrarch, Francesco, 1304-1374
petroglyphs (S) -980, -870, -840
Petronila (ARA) 1137-1162
Petronius (ROM) +70
Petronius Maximus (ROM) +455
Petubastis (ET) 745- ca. 730
Pezet, Juan Antonio (PE) 1862-1865
Phalaris (SIC) -560
Pharisees (JU) -140, +40
Pharos (ET) -280
Pharsalus -50
Pheidippides (ATH) -500
Pheidon (GR) -680
Phidias (ATH) -460, -440
Philetaerus (PERG) 281-263
Philip I the Bold (BURG) 1363-1404
Philip II the Good (BURG) 1419-1467
Philip of Swabia (D) 1197-1208
Philip II (E) 1556-1598 = Philip II (NL) = Philip I (P)
Philip III (E) 1598-1621 = Philip II (P)
Philip IV (E) 1621-1665 = Philip III (P)
Philip V (E) 1700-1746
Philip I (F) 1060-1108
Philip II Augustus (F) 1180-1223
Philip III the Bold (F) 1270-1285
Philip IV the Fair (F) 1285-1314
Philip V the Tall (F) 1316-1322
Philip VI (F) 1328-1350
Philip of Swabia (IMP) 1198-1208
Philip II (MAC) 359-336
Philip V (MAC) 221-179
Philip II (NL) 1555-1572 = Philip II (E)
Philip I (P) 1580-1598 = Philip II (E)
Philip II (P) 1598-1621 = Philip III (E)
Philip III (P) 1621-1640 = Philip IV (E)
Philip the Arabian (ROM) 244-249
Philip (S) 1112-1118
Philip I (SYR) 84-83
Philippe (Burg F) = Philip
Philippe of Orleans (F) 1715-1723
Philippicus (BYZ) 711-713
Philippines +1572, 1898
Philopaemen (GR) -183
Philostratus +280
Phocas (BYZ) 602-610
Phocis (GR) -540 -350
Phoenicians -960, -940, -540
Photius (BYZ) +867
Phraates I (IR) 175-171
Phraates II (IR) 138-128
Phraates III (IR) 69-58
Phraates IV (IR) 38-30
Phraates V (IR) -3- +3
Phraortes ca 628-625
Phrygians -770, -690
Phrynicus (ATH) -500
Piankhi (ET) ca 1053-1051
Piankhi (ET) -750, -740
Picts (GB) +367, 570
Pieck, Wilhelm (D) 1949-1960
Pierce, Franklin (USA) 1853-1857
Piero I de' Medici (FIR) 1464-1469
Piero (II) de' Medici (T-IR) 1492-1494
Pierola, Nicolas de (PE) 1895-1899
Pietro (SIC) = Peter
Piip (EST) 1920-1921
Pilate, Pontius (JU) 26-36
Pitsudski (PL) 1919-1922
Pimai (ET) ca 770-765
Pindar (GR) = 480
* Ping (RC) = Bing
* P' ing (RC) = Ping
Pinilla, Gustavo Rojas (CO) 1953-1957
Pinochet Ugarte, Augusto (RCA) 1973-
Pinto, Anibal (RCH) 1876-1881
Pinto, Francisco Antonio (RCH) 1827-1830
Pius I (V) 141-155
Pius II (V) 1458-1464
Pius III (V) +1503
Pius IV (V) 1559-1565
Pius V (V) 1566-1572
Pius VI (V) 1775-1799
Pius VII (V) 1800-1823
Pius VIII (V) 1829-1830
Pius IX (V) 1846-1878
Pius X (V) 1903-1914
Pius XI (V) 1922-1939
Pius XII (V) 1939-1958
plague -430, +170, 750, 1270, 1350
Plato (ATH) -400, -370
Plautus (ROM) -200
Plaza, de la (RA) 1914-1916
Pliny the Elder (ROM) +80
Pliny the Younger (ROM) +80
Plotinus, Gnostic philosopher +270
Plutarch -40, +90
Po Chü-i (RC) = Bo Juyi
Podgorny, N.V. (SU) 1965-
Poher, Alain (F) +1969
Poincaré, Raymond (F) 1913-1920
Poitiers (F) +733
Polk, James (USA) 1845-1849
Polycarp +160, 170
Polycrates (GR) -530
Polynesians -500 +1250
Polyperchon (MAC) 319-316
Pomerania +1140, 1190, 1648
Pompeii +79
Pompey, Cn. (ROM) 73-71, 65-64, 60-49
Pompidou, Georges (F) 1969-1974
Poniatowski, Stanislav August (PL) 1764-1795
Pontianus (V) 230-235
Pontius Pilate (IL) 26-36
Porsena, Lars (ROM) -510
Portales, Diego José Victor (RCH) 1830-1831
Portes Gil, Emilio (MEX) 1928-1930
Portillo, J.L. (MEX) 1976-
Portugal +1110
Postumus (ROM) +260
potatoes +1550
Prado, Mariano (PE) 1865-1868, 1876-1879
Prado y Ugarteche, Manuel (PE) 1939-1944, 1956-1962
Prague +1618
Prajadhipok (T) 1925-1935
Prasad, Rajendra (IND) 1950-1962
Přemysl Otokar I (CS) 1198-1230
Přemysl Otokar II (CS) 1253-1278
Pressian (BG) 836-852
Pribislav (YU) 891-892
Priestley, Joseph, 1733-1804
Prieto, Joaquin (RCH) 1831-1841
Prio Socarras, Carlos (C) 1948-1952
Probus (ROM) 276-282
Procopius (BYZ) +540

Propertius (ROM) –30
Prudentius +400
Prussia +1611
Przemysl II (PL) 1290-1291
Psamtik I (ET) ca 662-610
Psamtik II (ET) 594-589
Psamtik III (ET) 526-525
Psammuthis (ET) ca. 395-392
Psusennes I (ET) ca. 1040-990
Psusennes II (ET) ca. 960-945
Ptolemaeus (MAC) 369-365
Ptolemaic system +180
Ptolemy, Claudius (ET) +180
Ptolemy I Soter (ET) 323-282
Ptolemy II Philadelphus (ET) 282-247
Ptolemy III Euergetes (ET) 246-222
Ptolemy IV Philopator (ET) 222-204
Ptolemy V Epiphanes (ET) 203-181
Ptolemy VI Philometor (ET) 181-145
Ptolemy VII (ET) –145
Ptolemy VIII Physcon (ET) 164, 145-116
Ptolemy IX Lathyrus (ET) 116-107, 88-80
Ptolemy X Alexander (ET) 107-88
Ptolemy XI (ET) –80
Ptolemy XII Auletes (ET) 80-58, 55-51
Ptolemy XIII (ET) 51-47
Ptolemy XIV (ET) 47-44
Ptolemy XV (Caesarion) (ET) 44-30
Puakeśin (IND) +550
Pulu (BAB) 730-728
Pumarejo, A. López (C) 1942-1945
Pu'myaton (FEN) –820
Punic Wars –270, –260, –220, –150
Pydna (MAC) –168
pyr hygron (BYZ) +678
Pyrrhus (ROM) –280
Pythagoras –520
Pytheas of Massilia (GR) –310

Qadir, al- (CAL) 991-1031
Qahir, al- (CAL) 932-934
Qa'im, al (CAL) 1031-1058
Qaluyu (PE) –940
Qasim, 'Abd al-Karim, al- (IRQ) 1958-1963
Qasim ibn Hammud, al- (CORD) 1018-1021, 1022-1063
Qilich Arslan (SELD) 210-217
Qin Er Shi (RC) 210-217
Qin Shi Huang Di (RC) 246-210
Qing Dao Guang (RC) 1821-1850
Qing Guang Xu (RC) 1875-1908
Qing Jia Qing (RC) 1796-1820
Qing Kang Xi (RC) 1662-1722
Qing Qian Long (RC) 1736-1795
Qing Shun Zhi (RC) 1643-1661
Qing Tong Zhi (RC) 1862-1874
Qing Xian Feng (RC) 1851-1861
Qing Xuan Tong (RC) 1909-1911
Qing Yong Zheng (RC) 1723-1735
Qitan (RC) +910, 947, 1010
Qu Yuan (RC) –310
Quadi +180
Quadros, Janio da Silva (BR) 1960-1961
Quebec +1608, 1758
Quinctius Flaminius, T. (ROM) 197-194
Quintanilla, Carlos (RB) 1939-1940
Quintana, Manuel (RA) 1904-1906
Quintilian (ROM) +80
Qumran (IL) +68
Qun Qiu (RC) –730
Quosque tandem –63

Rabanus Maurus (F) +810
Rabelais, François ca. 1444-1553
Rabilus I (PETRA) –87
Racine, Jean +1670
Radi, ar- (CAL) 934-940
Raczkievics (PL) 1939-1945
Radhakrishnan, S. (IND) 1962-1967
Ragnvald Knaphövde (S) 1129-1130
Raiatea +760, 1260
Rajagopalachari, Chakravarti (IND) 1948-1950
Rājarāja (IND) +1020
Rama I (T) 1782-1809
Rama II (T) 1809-1824
Rama III (T) 1824-1851
Rama IV (T) 1851-1868
Rama V (T) 1868-1910
Rama VI (T) 1910-1925
Rama VII (T) 1925-1935
Rama VIII (T) 1935-1946
Rama IX (T) 1946-
Ramalho Eanes, A. (P) 1976-
Rameau, Jean Philippe, 1683-1764
Ramírez, Pedro (RA) 1943-1944
Ramiro I (ARA) 1035-1062
Ramiro II (ARA) 1134-1137
Ramiro I (AST) 842-850
Ramiro II (AST, León) 931-951
Ramiro III (AST, León) 966-984
Ramses I (ET) ca 1319-1318
Ramses II (ET) 1303-1233
Ramses III (ET) ca 1198-1157
Ramses IV (ET) ca 1155-1150
Ramses V (ET) ca 1150-1140
Ramses VI (ET) ca 1140-1130
Ramses VII (ET) 1130-1125
Ramses VIII (ET) 1125-1120
Ramses IX (ET) ca 1120-1115
Ramses X (ET) ca 1115-1110
Ramses XI (ET) ca 1110-1090
Raoul (F) = Rudolf
Raphael 1483-1520
Ratchis (LB) 744-749
Ravenna +450, 540, 760
Rawlings, Jerry (GH) 1981-
Reagan, Ronald (USA) 1981-
Réaumur (F) +1730
Reccared I (VIGO) 586-601
Reccared II (VIGO) +621
Recceswinth (VIGO) 649-672
Reddy, Neelam Sanjiva (IND) 1977-
Rehoboam (JU) 923-909
Rei (EST) 1928-1929
Reizei (J) 967-969
Reizei II (J) 1045-1068
Relander, Lauri (SF) 1925-1931
Rembrandt +1640
Remigius (F) +496
Renner, Karl (A) 1945-1951
Restrepo, Carlos (CO) 1909-1914
Restrepo, Carlos Lleres (CO) 1966-1970
Reval +1561
Reyes Católicos, los (E) 1474-1504
Reyes, Rafael (CO) 1904-1909
Reza Shah Pahlavi (IR) 1925-1941
Richard of Cornwall (D) 1256-1269
Richard I the Lion-Heart (GB) 1189-1199
Richard II (GB) 1377-1399
Richard III (GB) 1483-1485
Richelieu +1640
Ricimer +460
Riesco, Germán (RCH) 1901-1906
Rio de Janeiro +1567
Ríos Morales, Juan Antonio (RCH) 1942-1946
Ritsu (J) 400-405
Rivadavia (RA) 1826-1827
Robert I (F) 922-923
Robert II the Pious (F) 996-1031
Robert Guiscard (I) +1053, 1070
Robert (NA) 1309-1343
Robert I Bruce (SCOT) 1306-1329
Robert II Stuart (SCOT) 1371-1390
Robert III Stuart (SCOT) 1390-1424
Roberto (NA) = Robert
Robespierre (F) 1792-1794
Robinson Crusoe +1719
Roca, Júlio (RA) 1880-1886, 1898-1904
Rochefoucauld +1670
Roderick (VIGO) 710-711
Rodoald (LONG) 652-653
Rodríguez, Abelardo (MEX) 1932-1934
Roger I (SIC) 1062-1101
Roger II (SIC) 1101-1154
Rojas Pinilla, Gustavo (CO) 1953-1957
Rojas Paul (YV) 1889-90
Rokujo (J) 1165-1168
Roland (o furioso) (F) +778
Rollo (F) +920
Romaña, Edúardo de (PE) 1899-1903
Romano, Giulio, 1499-1546
Romanus I Lacapenus (BYZ) 920-944
Romanus II (BYZ) 959-963
Romanus III Argyrus (BYZ) 1028-1034
Romanus IV Diogenes (BYZ) 1067-1071
Romanus (V) +897
Romer, Ole, 1644-1710
Romulus (ROM) 753-721
Romulus Augustulus (ROM) 475-476
Romund (LIT) 1278-1279
Ronai (H) 1950-1952
Ronceval (F) +778
Ronsard +1560
Röntgen, Wilhelm, 1845-1923
Roosevelt, Franklin D (USA) 1933-1945
Roosevelt, Theodore (USA) 1901-1909
Rosamunda (LONG) +570
Rosas, Manuel de (RA) 1829-1852
Roskilde +1658
Rossini, Gioacchino, 1792-1868
Rostislav (CS) 846-869
Roswitha (IMP) +980
Rothari (LONG) 636-652
Rou-ma (RC) = Sima
Rousseau, Jean Jacques, 1712-1778
Rubio, Ortiz (MEX) 1930-1932
Rudolf IV (A) 1358-1365
Rudolf II (A) 1576-1612 = Rudolf II (IMP)
Rudolf (CS) 1306-1307
Rudolf I of Habsburg (D) 1273-1291
Rudolf (F) 923-936
Rudolf I (IMP) 1273-1291 = Rudolf I of Habsburg (D)
Rudolf II (IMP) 1576-1612 = Rudolf II (A)
Ruggiero (SIC) = Roger
Rugi +210
Rugila (HUN) 427-434
Ruíz Cortines, Adolfo (MEX) 1952-1958
Rukh, shah (IR) 1408-1446
Rum (SELD) +1070, 1090
runestones +520
Rupert of the Palatine (D) 1400-1410 = Rupert of the Palatine (IMP)
Rurik (RU) 864-879
Rustam Shah (IR) 1491-1497
Rutherford, Ernest 1871-1937
Rykov, Alexei (SU) 1924-1925
Ryti, Risto (SF) 1940-1944

Saavedra, Juan Bautista (RB) 1921-1925
Sabin (BG) +764
Sabinian (V) 604-606
Sabium (BAB) 1780-1767
Sadat, Anwar as- (ET) 1970-1981
Sæmundr the Wise (IS) +1120, 1133
Saenz Peña, Luis (RA) 1892-1895
Sáenz Peña, Roque (RA) 1910-1914
Safavids +1500
as-Saffāh (CAL) 750-754
Safi I (IR) 1629-1641
Safi II alias Suleyman (IR) 1667-1694
Saga (J) 809-823
Sa'id (ET) 1277-1278
Saimei (J) 654-661
Saint John, Knights of +1521
Saisunaga (IND) –570
Saka II (J) 1242-1245
Sakuntala (IND) +410
Saladero (PE) –940
Salahad-Din (ET) 1167-1193 (Saladin)
Salamanca, Daniel (RB) 1931-1934
Salamis (GR) –480
Salamon (H) 1063-1074
Salazar, Oliveira (P) 1951-1968
Salitis (ET) ca. 1730-1720
Sallust (ROM) –120
Salma Alexandra (JU) –80
Salome (IL) 76-67
Saltpetre War (PE & RCH) +1879
Samaria (IL) –870, –740
Samnites (ROM) –350, –340, –290
Samo (CS) +630
Samoa +1721
Samson (IL) ca 1070-1060
Samsuiluna (BAB) 1685-1648
Samudra Gupta (IND) 330-380
Samuel (BG) 976-1014
Samuel (IL) ca 1040-1020
Sámuel Aba (H) 1041-1044
San Bao, Admiral (RC) +1430
San Martin, Ramón Grau (C) 1933-1934, 1944-1948
Sanatruces (IR) 77-70
Sancha (CAST) 1035- ca 1040
Sánchez Cerro, Luis (PE) 1931-1933
Sancho I (ARA) 1063-1094
Sancho I (AST,León) 956-958, 960-966
Sancho II (CAST) 1065-1072
Sancho III (CAST) 1157-1158
Sancho IV the Bold (CAST) 1284-1295
Sancho I (P) 1185-1211
Sancho II (P) 1223-1248
Sanclemente, Miguel (CO) 1898-1900
Sanfuentes, Juan Luis (RCH) 1915-1920
Sang Hongyang (RC) –120
Sanguo (RC) 221-265
Sanjō (J) 1011-1016

Sanjō II (J) 1068-1073
Santa Ana, Antonio López de (MEX) 1833-1837, 1840-1844, 1846-1848, 1853-1855
Santa Cruz, Andrés (RB) 1830-1839, (PE) 1835-1839
Santa María, Domingo (RCH) 1881-1886
Santander, Fransisco de Paula (CO) 1832-1837
Santos, Eduardo (CO) 1938-1942
Sappho (GR) –570
Saracens (SIC) +910, 1016
Saragat, Guiseppe (I) 1964-1971
Saratoga (USA) +1790
Sardanapalus = Ashurbanipal (ASS) –670
Sardar Mohammed Daud (AFG) 1973-1978
Sardinia +1016, 1052, 1720
Sardis (LYD) –550, –500
Sarduri (URARTU) –840
Sargon II (ASS) 721-706, (BAB) 709-706
Sarmatians –260, +180
Sarmiento, Domingo (RA) 1868-1874
Sassanids (IR) +240, 575
Satrapies (IR) –500
Satyrus I (BOSP) –430
Saud ibn Abd al-Aziz (SM) 1953-1964
Saul (IL) 1020-1005
Saustator (MIT) ca. 1478-1444
Savonarola (FIR) 1495-1498
Saxo Grammaticus (DK) +1170
Saxons +290, 450, 570, 763
Scala, della +1310, 1440
Scaliger, Joseph, 1540-1609
Scipio, Cn. & P. Cornelius (ROM) 227-223
Scipio, Publ. Cornelius (ROM) 207-203
Scipio Aemilianus, P. Corn. (ROM) 147-144 – 130
Schärf, Adolf (A) 1957-1965
Scheel, Walter (D) 1974-1979
Scheele, Carl, 1742-1786
Schiller, Friedrich von, 1759-1805
Schliemann –790
Schopenhauer, Arthur, 1788-1860
Schubert, Franz, 1797-1828
Schütz, Heinrich, 1585-1672
Schwarz, Berthold +1350
Scots (GB) +367
Scythians –770, –620
Sebastian (P) 1557-1758
Sebekhotep (ET) ca. 1750-1730
Sebeknefru (ET) ca. –1788
Sebüktigin I (AFG) +980
Segni, Antonio (I) 1962-1964
Seinei (J) 479-484
Seitz, Karl (A) 1919-1920
Seiwa (J) 858-876
Sekemkheres (ET) ca. 1780-1770
Seleucus I Nicator (IR,SYR) 312-281
Seleucus II Callinicus (SYR) 246-226
Seleucus III Soter (SYR) 226-223
Seleucus IV Philopator (SYR) 187-175
Selim I (TR) 1512-1520
Selim II (TR) 1566-1574
Selim III (TR) 1789-1807
Seljuks +1040, 1070, 1090, 1100, 1190
Semiramis (BAB) –830
Seneca (ROM) +70
Senechtenre (ET) ca. 1591-1581
Senefelder, Aloys, 1771-1834
Senkva (J) 537-539
Sennacherib (ASS) 705-683
Septimius Severus (ROM) 193-211
Seqenenre I (ET) ca. 1680-1660
Seqenenre II (ET) ca. 1660-1640
Seqenenre III (ET) ca. 1640-1620
Serbs +900, 930, 1170, 1260, 1360
Sergius I (V) 687-701
Sergius II (V) 844-847
Sergius III (V) 904-911
Sergius IV (V) 1009-1012
Serrano, Francisco (E) 1868-1869
Sertorius, Q. (E) –70
Servius Tullius (ROM) 576-534
Sesostris I (ET) 1961-1928
Sesostris II (ET) 1894-1879
Sesostris III (ET) 1878-1850
Sesshu (J) +1500
Seti I (ET) ca. 1317-1304
Seti II (ET) ca 1210-1200
Sevar (BG) 724-739
Severinus (V) +640
Severus (ROM) 461-465
Sextius, Lucius (ROM) ca. 368-367
Sforza +1440
Shabaka (ET) 712-700
Shagerakhti-Shuriash (BAB) 1262-1250
Shagari, A.S. (NIG) 1979-
Shah Jahan (IND) 1628-1657
Shah Rokh (IR) 1408-1446
Shakespeare, William, 1564-1616
Shallum (IL) 747-746
Shalmaneser I (ASS) 1280-1261
Shalmaneser II (ASS) 1030-1019
Shalmaneser III (ASS) 859-825
Shalmaneser IV (ASS) 783-774
Shalmaneser V (ASS) ca. 726-722
Shamash-mudammiq (BAB) 941-901
Shamshi-Adad IV (ASS) 1055-1050
Shamshi-Adad V (ASS) 824-812
Shamshuditana (BAB) 1561-1531
Shanabushumma (ASS) –700
Shang, dyn (RC) 1783-1401
Shang Yang (RC) –360
Shāpūr I (IR) 240-272
Shāpūr II (IR) 309-379
Shāpūr III (IR) 383-388
Shastri, Lal (IND) 1964-1966
Shazar, Zalman (IL) 1963-1973
Sheba –940, –80
Shebitku (ET) 700-688
Sher Shah (IND) 1541-1545
Sheshonk I (ET) ca. 940-915
Sheshonk II (ET) non est
Sheshonk III (ET) ca. 823-772
Sheshonk IV (ET) ca. 765-745
Shih (RC) = Shi
Shijo (J) 1232-1242
Shimmash-Shipak (BAB) 1038-1030
Shir Ali (AFG) 1863-1879
Shirakawa (J) 1073-1087
Shirakawa II (J) 1155-1158
Shishak = Sheshonk I (ET) –930
Shito (J) 686-697
Shogun (J) +1181
Shoja, Shah (AFG) 1803-1810, 1839-1842
Shōmu (J) 724-749
Shotoku (J) 764-770
Shu-Han Hou Zhu (RC) 224-264
Shu-Han Zhao Lie Di 221-223
Shu-ilishu (BAB) 1920-1911
Shuja (IND) 1657-1658
Shulgi (BAB) (2000) -1995
Shumei (J) 628-641
Shu-Sin (BAB) 1985-1977
Shuttarna I (MIT) ca. 1499-1493
Shuttarna II (MIT) ca. 1408-1398
Shuttarna III (MIT) ca. 1373-1370
Siamon (ET) ca. 965-960
Siberia + 1581
Sibylene books (ROM) –540
Sicilian vespers (SIC) +1282
Siddharta Buddha (IND) – 574,-530
Sidi Muhammad Bey (TN) 1956-1957
Siebenbürgen (H) +1526
Siemens (D) +1879
Sigebert I (F) 561-575
Sigebert II (F) +613
Sigebert III (F) 639-656
Sigismund of Luxemburg (CS) 1419-1437
Sigismund (D) 1411-1437 = Sigismund of Luxemburg (IMP)
Sigismund of Luxemburg (IMP) 1411-1437
Sigismund I (H) 1388-1437
Sigismund I the Old (PL) 1506-1548
Sigismund II Augustus (PL) 1548-1572
Sigismund III Vasa (PL) 1587-1632 = Sigismund (S)
Sigismund (S) 1592-1600
Signorelli, Luca, ca. 1441-1523
Sigurd Ormiöga (DK) +900
Sigurd Jerusalemfarer (N) 1103-1130
Sigurd Mund (N) 1139-1155
Sigurd Slembi (N) 1136-1139
Siles, Hernando (RB) 1926-1930
Siles Salinas, Adolfo (RB) 1969-1970
Siles Zuazo, Herman (RB) 1956-1960, 1969
Silk route (RC) –130, –100, +70
Silla (Korea) +562, 680
Silo (AST) 774-783
Silverius (V) 536-537
Sima Qian (RC) –100
Sima Yan (RC) +270
Simeon (RU) 1340-1353
Simon (IL) 142-134
Simplicius (V) 468-483
Singapore (GB) +1819
Sinnuballit (BAB) 1748-1729
Sin-shar-ishkun (ASS) ca. 626-612
Sinthila (VIGO) 636-640
Siptah (ET) 1215-ca 1210
Siraks –120
Siricius (V) 384-399
Siroes (IR) +628
Sisebert (VIGO) 612-620
Sisenand (VIGO) 631-636
Sisinnius (V) +708
Sisse Tunkare (GH) +790
Sixtus I (V) 116-125
Sixtus II (V) 257-258
Sixtus III (V) 432-440
Sixtus IV (V) 1471-1484
Sixtus V (V) 1585-1590
Skanda Gupta (IND) 455-467
Slavs +560, 580, 600, 610, 630
Slingelandt, Simon van (NL) 1727-1736
Smendes (ET) ca 1050-1040
Smenkhkare (ET) 1362-ca 1360
Smetona, Antanas (LIT) 1926-1940
Smiletz (BG) 1292-1299
Snorri Sturluson (IS) +1241
Soběslav I (CS) 1125-1140
Soběslav II (CS) 1174-1178
Sobieski, Jan (PL) 1674-1696
Socarrás, Carlos Prio (C) 1948-1952
Socrates (ATH) –450, –400, –370
Sol invictus +220
Solomon (IL) ca. 963-923
Solon (ATH) –600
Sóltan (H) 907-957
Sophia (RU) 1686-1689
Sophocles (ATH) –460, –440, –420
Sorzano, Luis Tejada (RB) 1934-1936
Soter (V) 166-175
Soulouque, Faustin (= Faustin I) (RH) 1843-1859
South Pacific –490
South Sung (RC) = Nan Song
Spanish Armada (E,GB) +1588
Spanish March, +800
Spanish War of Succession +1701, 1713
Sparta –935, –750, –710, –660, –550, –480, –390, –290
Spartacus I (BOSP) –430
Spartacus III (BOS) –304
Spartacus (ROM) –71
Spinola (P) 1974-1975
Spinoza +1670
Spitzbergen +1596
Spurius Postumius (ROM) 323-322
Spychalski (PL) 1968-1970
Spytihněv I (CS) 896-921
Spytihněv II (CS) 1055-1061
Srong-brtsan-sgam-po (Tibet) +640
Ståhlberg, Kaarlo (SF) 1919-1925
Stalin, Josef (SU) 1927-1953
Stambolic, Petar (YU) 1981-
Stanfordbridge (GB) +1066
Stanisław Leszczyński (PL) 1704-1709
Stanisław August Poniatowski (PL) 1764-1795
Stefan (PL) = Stephen
Stenkil (S) 1056-1066
Stephen (GB) 1135-1154
Stephen I (H) 997-1038
Stephen II (H) 1114-1131
Stephen III (H) 1161-1162, 1163-1173
Stephen IV (H) 1162-1163
Stephen V (H) 1270-1272
Stephen Bathory (PL) 1576-1586
Stephen I (V) 254-257
Stephen II (V) 752-757
Stephen III (V) 767-772
Stephen IV (V) 816-817
Stephen V (V) 885-891
Stephen VI (V) 896-897
Stephen VII (V) 929-931
Stephen VIII (V) 939-942
Stephen IX (V) 1057-1058
Stephen Dragutin (YU) 1276-1281
Stephen Dušan (YU) 1332-1355
Stephen Lazarević (YU) 1389-1427
Stephen Nemanja (YU) 1168-1196
Stephen Radoslav (YU) 1225-1234
Stephen II Sevastokrator (YU) 1196-1224
Stephen Uroš I (YU) 1243-1276
Stephen Uroš II Milutin (YU) 1281-1321
Stephen Uroš III Dečansk (YU) 1322-1331
Stephen Uroš IV (YU) 1355-1371
Stephen Vladislav (YU) 1234-1243
Stephenson +1814, 1840
Stiernhielm, George (S) +1650
Stiklastad (N) +1030
Stilicho (ROM) +401
Stockholm (S) +1520
Stoica, Chivu (R) 1965-1967
Stoicism (ATH) –300
Stonehenge (GB) –850
Stoph, Willi (D) 1973-1976
Stora Kopparberg (S) +1284
Strabo (GR) +18
Stradivarius +1670, 1710
Strandman (EST) 1918-1919, 1929-1931
Strindberg (S) +1879, 1884
Stroganov (RU) +1581
Stučka (LET) +1919
Stulgenskis, Antanas (LIT) 1922-1926
Sture, Sten the Elder (S) 1470-1497, 1502-1503
Sture, Sten the Younger (S) 1512-1520
Sture, Svante Nilsson (S) 1503-1512
Styrbjörn the Strong (S) +988
Su Dongpo (RC) +1120
Suárez, Hugo Banzer (RB) 1971-1978
Suárez, Marco Fidel (CO) 1918-1921
Suárez Flamerich (YV) 1950-1952
Sucre, Antonio José de (RB) 1825-1828
Sudrāka (IND) +410
Suebi +407, 590
Suez Canal +1869
Suharto, T.N.J. (IN) 1967-
Sui Canal (RC) +620
Sui Gong Di (RC) +617
Sui Wen Di (RC) 581-604
Sui Yang Di (RC) 605-616
Suiko (J) 592-628
Suinin (J) –29- +70
Suintorog (LIT) 1268-1270
Sujaku (J) 930-946
Sujaku II (J) 1036-1045
Sujin-Tenno (J) 97-30
Sukarno (IN) 1946-1966
Suko (J) 1348-1352
Sulaymān (CAL) 715-717
Suleyman (CORD) 1013-1016
Suleyman alias Safi (IR) 1667-1694

Suleyman I (TR) 1520-1566
Suleyman II (TR) 1687-1691
Sulla, L. Cornelius (ROM) 87-79
Sulpicius Galba, S. (ROM) –150
Sumu'abum (BAB) 1830-1817
Sumulael (BAB) 1816-1781
Sun Yat-sen (RC) 1917-1924
Sunay, Cevdet (TR) 1966-1973
Sung (RC) = Song
(Bei Song + Nan Song)
Suppiluliumas I (HAT) 1375-1340
Suppiluliumas II (HAT) ca 1190-1184
Sushun (J) 588-591
Sutoku (J) 1124-1142
Suzubu (BAB) ca 690-689
Svatopluk (CS) 870-894
Sven Knutsson (N) =
Sweyn Alfivason 1030-1035
Svend Tveskæg (DK) 985-1014 =
Sweyn Fork beard (GB)
Svend Grate (DK) 1146-1157
Sverker the Elder (S) 1133-1156
Sverker II (S) 1199-1210
Sverrir (N) 1176-1202
Svidrigaila (LIT) +1430
Svinhufvud, Pehr (SF) 1918, 1931, 1937
Svintorog (LIT) 1267-1270
Svoboda, Ludvik (CS) 1968-1975
Svolder (DK,N,S) +1000
Svyatopolk I (RU) 1015-1018
Svyatopolk II (RU) 1093-1113
Svyatoslav I (RU) 957-972
Svyatoslav II (RU) 1246-1250
Swammerdam +1660
Swart, C.R. (ZA) 1961-1968
Swedenborg, Emanuel, 1688-1772
Sweyn Estridsson (DK) 1047-1074
Sweyn Forkbeard (GB) 1013-1014 =
Svend Tveskåeg (DK)
Sweyn Alfivason (N) 1030-1035
Sweyn, Duke (N) 1000-1016
Sweyn (S) +1090
Swift, Jonathan (GB) +1730
Swinthila (VIGO) 621-631
Switzerland +1499
Syagrius (ROM) +486
Sybaris –650, –520, –380
Sydney +1798
Sylvester I (V) 314-335
Sylvester II (V) 999-1003
Sylvester III (V) +1045
Symeon (BG) 893-927
Symeon II (BG) 1943-1946
Symmachus (V) 498-514
Szakasits, A (H) 1948-1950
Szalasi (H) 1944-1945

Tacfarinas (ROM) +24
Tachos (ET) 363-361
Tacitus (ROM) +30, 50, 70, 90, 130
Tacitus, M. Claudius (ROM) 275-276
Taft, William (USA) 1909-1913
Taharqa (ET) 688-663
Tahiti +1606
Tahmasp I (IR) 1524-1575
Tahmasp II (IR) 1729-1731
Tai (RC) = Dai
Tai at- (CAL) 974-991
T'ai (RC) = Tai
Taira (J) +1150
Takakura (J) 1168-1181
Takelot I (ET) ca. 873-860
Takelot II (ET) 835-824
Takudar (IR) 1282-1285
Talal (HKJ) 1951-1952
Talas (RC) +751
Talmud +210
Tanaquil (ROM) –620, –580
Tancred (SIC) 1190-1194
T'ang (RC) = Tang
Tang Ai Di (RC) 904-906
Tang Chong Zong (RC) +648
Tang Dai Zong (RC) 763-779
Tang De Zong (RC) 780-805
Tang Gao Zong (RC) 640-683
Tang Gao Zu (RC) 618-626
Tang Jing Zong (RC) 825-826
Tang Mu Zong (RC) 821-824
Tang Rui Zong (RC) 710-712
Tang Su Zong (RC) 757-762
Tang Tai Zong (RC) 627-649
Tang Wen Zong (RC) 827-840
Tang Wu Zong (RC) 841-846
Tan Xi Zong (RC) 874-888
Tang Xian Zong (RC) 806-820
Tang Xuan Zong I (RC) 713-756
Tang Xuan Zong II (RC) 847-859
Tang Yi Zong (RC) 860-873
Tang Zhao Zong (RC) 889-903
Tang Zhong Zong (RC) 706-710
Tangier +1471
Tangut +370, 380, 387, 430
Tanum (S) –980
Tao (RC) = Dao
T'ao (RC) = Tao
Taoism (RC) –100, +140
Tariq (CAL) +711
Taraqi, Noor Mohammad (AFG) 1978-1979
Tarquinius Priscus (ROM) 616-576
Tarquinius Superbus (ROM) 534-509
Tarraco +260
Tarshish (E) –910
Tartessus (E) –910
Tashigurumash (BAB) ca 1490-1481
Tasman, Abel +1642
Tasso, Torquato, 1544-1595
Taurini (A) –120
Taylor, Zachary (USA) 1849-1850
Teemant (EST) 1925-1927, 1932
Tefnakhte (ET) –750, –740
Teh (RC) = De
Teja (OGO) 552-553
Tejada, Lerdo de (MEX) 1872-1876
Telemann, Georg Philip, 1681-1767
Telerig (BG) 773-777
Telesphorus (V) 125-136
Telets (BG) 761-763
Tell, William +1290
Temmu (J) 672-686
Templars, Order of Knights (F) +1310
Tenchi (J) 662-672
Tennes of Sidon (SYR) –360
Teodor (BG) = Theodor
Teotihuacán (MEX) –310, +160, 600
Terence (ROM) –160
Teresa (P) 1112-1127
Terry, Fernando Belaúnde (YV) 1963-1968
Tertullian +210
Tervel (BG) 701-718
Teudis (VIGO) 531-548
Teutoburg Forest (ROM) +9
Teutones –110, +240
Teutonic Order +1320, 1346, 1398, 1410
Tewodros III (ETH) 1855-1868
Thai people +1250
Thales (GR) –640, –600
Themistocles (ATH) ca 493-492, 482-477
Theocritus (SYRA) –270
Theodahad (OGO) 535-536
Théodebald (F) = Theudebald
Théodebert (F) = Theudebert
Théoderic (F) = Theuderic
Theoderic (OGO) 471-526
Theoderic I (VIGO) 420-451
Theoderic II (VIGO) 453-466
Theodolinda (LONG) +610
Theodor Svetoslav (BG) 1299-1322
Theodor (ETH) = Tewodros
Theodora (BYZ) +540
Theodora (BYZ) 1055-1056
Theodore I Lascaris (BYZ) 1204-1222
Theodore II Lascaris (BYZ) 1254-1258
Theodore of Canterbury (GB) +664
Theodorus I (V) 642-649
Theodorus II (V) +897
Theodosius I (ROM) 379-395
Theodosius II (ROM) 408-450
Theodosius III (BYZ) 715-717
Theophano (D) 983-991
Theophilus (BYZ) 829-842
Thermopylae (GR) –480
Theron (SIC) –480, –450
Theseus (ATH) –690
Thespis (ATH) –530
Theudebald (F) 548-555
Theudebert I (F) 534-548
Theudebert II (F) 595-612
Theuderic I (F) 511-533
Theuderic II (F) 595-612
Theuderic III (F) 673-691
Theuderic IV (F) 721-737
Thierry (F) = Theuderic
Thiers, Adolphe (F) 1871-1873
Thirty Years War 1618-1648
Tho, Nguyen Huu (YV) 1980-
Thorismund (VIGO) +451, 453
Thrasamund (VAND) 496-523
Thrasybulus (ATH) 400-399
Three Kingdoms (RC) = Sanguo
Thucydides (ATH) –430
Thusnelda (D) +11
Thutmose I (ET) 1530-1520
Thutmose II (ET) 1519-1504
Thutmose III (ET) 1519-1447
Thutmose IV (ET) 1420-1411
Ti (RC) = Di
Tibareni –600
Tiberius I (BYZ) 578-582
Tiberius II (BYZ) 698-705
Tiberius (ROM) 14-37
Tibet +802, 1720
Tibetans +300
Tich, Konstantin (BG) 1258-1277
T'ien (RC) = Tian
Tiglath-pileser I (ASS) 1115-1103
Tiglath-pileser II (ASS) 966-934
Tiglath-pileser III (ASS) 745-728
Tigranes (SYR) 82-69
Tildy, Z. (H) 1946-1948
Tilly, Tserclaes +1620
Timaeus (GR) –780
Timoleon (SYA) 343-336
Timur Lenk (IR) 1395-1405
Timur Shah (AFG) 1773-1793
Ting (RC) = Ding
Tiptakzi (BAB) ca 1470-1461
Tiridates II (IR) 30-25
Tito (YU) = Josip Broz 1944-1980
Titus (ROM) 79-81
Tixeira Gomes (P) 1923-1925
Toba (J) 1107-1123
Toba II (J) 1183-1198
Tochari –180, –150, –127 –30, +100
Tocqueville, Alexis de, 1805-1859
Togan Timur (RC) 1333-1367
Toghrïl Beg (SELD) 1031-1063
Tokimune (J) +1274
Tokt (BG) 766-767
Toktu (MONG) 1280-1312
Tolstoy, Leo +1869
Toltecs (MEX) +999, 1120, 1168
Tolui (MONG) 1227-1229
Tomislav (YU) +910
Ton Duc Thang (VN) 1969-1980
Tönisson (EST) 1919-1920, 1927-1928
Toramāna (IND) +510
Töregene (MONG) 1240-1246
Toro, David (RB) 1936-1937
Torres, Juan José (RB) 1970-1971
Torricelli +1660
Tosun (H) 958-971
Totila (BAY) +790
Totila (OGO) 541-552
Tou Wan (RC) –120
Traikov, Georgi (BG) 1964-1971
Trajan (ROM) 98-117
Transvaal +1853
Tripitaka (J,RC) –40, +517
Troy –990, –790
Troyden (LIT) 1281-1282
Troynat (LIT) 1263-1264
Trullo (BYZ) +692
Truman, Harry (USA) 1945-1953
Trundholm Mose (DK) –980
Tsao Tsao (RC) = Cao Cao
Ts'ao (RC) = Zao
Tsatsos, K. (GR) 1974-1980
Tsin (RC) = Jin
Tsu (RC) = Zu
Tsui (RC) = Zui
Tsunayoshi (J) 1680-1709
Ts'ung (CRC) = Cong
Tu (RC) = Du
Tu Fu (RC) = Du Fu
Tuan (RC) = Duan
Tudhaliyas II (HAT) ca 1457-1453
Tudhaliyas III (HAT) 1401-1385
Tudhaliyas IV (HAT) 1250-1220
Tukulti-Ninurta I (ASS) 1260-1232
Tukulti-Ninurta II (ASS) 890-885
Tulka (VIGO) 640-642
Tullus Hostilius (ROM) 673-641
Tung (RC) = Dong
T'ung (RC) = Tong
Tung-son (IND) –670
Tungus +300, 360, 370, 420, 480, 500, 910, 1125
Tūrān-Shāh (ET) 1249-1250
Turbay Ayala, J.C. (CA) 1978-
Turkhan Pasha (AL) 1918-1919
Tushratta (MIT) ca 1393-1373
Tutankhamen (ET) ca 1360-1351
Twain, Mark +1876
Tyler, John (USA) 1841-1845
Tyler, Wat (GB) +1381
Tyre (DK) ca 920-940
Tyrole (A) +1360
Tyrtaeus (GR) –660
Tyre –960, –820
Tz'u-hsi (RC) +1898

Uda (J) 887-897
Uda II (J) 1275-1288
Ugarteche, Manuel Prado y (PE) 1939-1944, 1956-1962
Ugueto, Wolfgang Larrazábal (YV) +1958
Uighurs +770, 860
Ukin-zer (BAB) 732-730
Ukraine +1260, 1330
Ulamburiash (BAB) ca 1420-1411
Ulászló I (H) 1439-1444 = Ladislas V (H) = Wladyslaw IV (PL)
Ulászló II (H) 1490-1516 =
Vladislav I (CS)
Ulbricht, Walter (D) 1960-1971
Ulfilas (VIGO) +340, 350
Ulfliótr (IS) +930
Ulmanis, Karlis (LET) 1918,

1920-1922, 1936-1940
Ulpian (ROM) +210
Ulugh Beg (IR) 1446-1449
Ululai (BAB) 728-722
Uluots (EST) 1939-1940
Ulrika Eleonora (S) 1718-1720
Umar I (CAL) 634-644
Umar II (CAL) 717-720
Umberto (I) = Humbert
Umor (BG) 756-766
universities +1120, 1450, 1477
Urach, Willhelm von (LIT) 1917-1918
Urartu -970, -830
Urban I (V) 222-230
Urban II (V) 1088-1099
Urban III (V) 1185-1187
Urban IV (V) 1261-1264
Urban V (V) 1362-1370
Urban VI (V) 1378-1389
Urban VII (V) +1590
Urban VIII (V) 1623-1644
Urhi-Teshub (HAT) 1281-1275
Uriburu, José (RA) 1895-1898
Uriburu, José (RA) 1930-1932
Ur-Ninurta (BAB) 1859-1832
Urquiza, Justo José de (RA) 1854-1860
Urraca (CAST) 1109-1126
Urriolangoitia, Mamerto (BR) 1949-1951
Urruria, Manuel (C) +1959
Usshi (BAB) ca 1504-1503
Uthmān (CAL) 644-656
Ut-Napishtim (BAB) -890
Utriguri +580
Uzbek (MONG) = Öz Beg
Uzun Hasan (IR) 1468-1477
Uzziah (JU) 781-746

Václav (CS) = Wencelas
Vajiravudh (T) = Rama VI
Valdemar I the Great (DK) 1157-1182
Valdemar (II) Sejr (DK) 1202-1241
Valdemar Atterdag (DK) 1340-1375
Valdemar (S) 1266-1275
Valdemar (S) + 1300
Valdes, Pierre (F) +1176
Valencia (E) +1094, 1238
Valencia, Guillermo Leon (CO) 1962-1966
Valens (ROM) 364-378
Valentine (V) +827
Valentinian I (ROM) 364-375
Valentinian II (ROM) 375-392
Valentinian III (ROM) 425-455
Valerian (ROM) 253-259
Valerius, Publius (ROM) ca 503-502
Van Buren, Martin (USA) 1837-1841
Van Thieu, Nguyen (YN) 1965-1975
Vandals +370, 407, 420, 429, 439, 468, 480, 540
Vardanes I (IR) 39-43
Vargas, Getulio (BR) 1930-1945, 1951-1954
Vasco da Gama (P) +1495
Vasily I Dmitriyevich (RU) 1389-1425
Vasily II Vasilyevich (RU) 1425-1462
Vasily III Ivanovich (RU) 1505-1533
Vasily (IV) Shuysky (RU) 1606-1610
Vasily (RU) 1272-1277
Västergötland (S) -900
Veda (IND) -950
Veii (ROM) -400
Vejer de la Frontera (VIGO) +711
Velasco Alvardo, Juan (PE) 1968-1975
Venice +460, 810, 1020, 1090, 1210, 1378, 1405, 1670, 1797
Verdun (F) +843
Vergil (ROM) -820, -30, -20
Vermudo (AST) = Bermudo
Verne, Jules +1866, 1873
Verrocchio +1480
Vesalius, Andreas 1514-1564
Vespasianus (ROM) 69-79
Victor I (V) 189-199
Victor II (V) 1055-1057
Victor III (V) 1086-1088
Victor Amadeus I (SAVO,SAR) (1675)-1730
Victor Amadeus II (SARD) 1773-1796
Victor Emmanuel I (SARD) 1802-1821
Victor Emmanuel II (SARD) & I) 1849-1878
Victor Emmanuel III (I) 1900-1946, (ETH) 1936-1941
Victoria (GB) 1837-1901
Victoria, Guadalupe (MEX) 1824-1829
Videla, Gabriel Gonzalez (RCH) 1946-1952
Videla, Jorge Rafael (RA) 1976-1980
Vidin (HUN) ca. 421-423
Vienna +1683
Vigilius (V) 537-555
Vihekh (BG) 756-761
Vikings +793, 802, 830, 850, 870, 880, 890, 910, 960, 980
Viksubuu (I) -280
Viljoen, Marais (ZA) 1979-
Villa, Celso Torrelio (RB) 1981-
Villanueva, José Cabino (RB) 1925-1926
Villanovan culture -910
Villaroel, Gualberto (RB) 1943-1946
Villazón, Eleodoro (RB) 1909-1913
Villon, François (F) +1470
Viola, Roberto E. (RA) 1980-1981
Virgil (ROM) -820, -30, -20
Virginia (ROM) -450
Viriatus (E) -140
Visby (DK,S) +1361
Visconti +1440
Visigoths +40, 280, 372, 410, 420, 470, 510, 540, 710
Vitalian (V) 657-672
Vitellius (ROM) +69
Vitovt (LIT) = Vytautas 1391-1430
Vitruvius (ROM) -10
Vittorio (I SARD, SAVO) = Victor
Vladimir (BG) 888-893
Vladimir I (RU) 980-1015
Vladimir II Monomakh (RU) 1113-1125
Vladislav I (CS) 1111-1125
Vladislav II (CS) 1140-1173
Vladislav III (CS) +1197
Vladislav IV Posthumus (CS) 1439-1457 = Ladislas Posthumus (A)
Vladislav V (CS) 1471-1516 = Ulászló II (H)
Vladivoj (CS) 1002-1003
Vladivostok (RU) +1850
Vologases I (IR) 54-76
Vologases II (IR) 77-78
Vologases III (IR) 127-130
Vologases IV (IR) 148-190
Vologases V (IR) 191-206
Vologases VI (IR) 207-220
Volta, Alessandro, 1745-1827
Voltaire 1694-1778
Vonones I (IR) 8-9
Vonones II (IR) 51-54
Vorster, B.J. (ZA) 1978-1979
Vratislav I (CS) 921-925
Vratislav II (CS) 1061-1092
Vsevolod I (RU) 1078-1093
Vsevolod II (RU) 1139-1146
Vsevolod III (RU) 1176-1212
Vytautas (LIT) 1392-1430 = Vitovt
Vytenis (LIT) 1282-1315

Wacław II Czeski (PL) 1291-1305 = Wenceslas IV (CS)
Wacław III (PL) 1305-1306 = Wenceslas V (CS)
Waldenses +1170
Walīd I (CAL) 705-715
Walīd II (CAL) 743-744
Wallia (VIGO) 415-419
Wamba (VIGO) 672-680
Wang Anshi (RC) +1080
Wang Jing-wei (RC) 1924-1926
Wang Mang (RC) 1-23
Wang Wei (RC) +740
Wang Xizhi (RC) +360
Wang Zhong +100
Washington, George (USA) 1789-1797
Wāthiq, al- (CAL) 842-847
Watt, James 1736-1819
Wei Gao Gui Xiang Gong (RC) 254-259
Wei Ming Di (RC) 227-239
Wei Shao Di (RC) 240-250
Wei Wen Di (RC) 221-226
Wei Yuan Di (RC) 260-264
Weizmann, Chaim (IL) 1949-1952
Wencelas I (CS) 925-929
Wencelas II (CS) 1911-1192
Wencelas III (CS) 1230-1253
Wencelas IV (CS) 1278-1305
Wencelas V (CS) 1305-1306 = Wactaw III (PL)
Wencelas VI (CS) 1378-1419
Wencelas (D) 1378-1400 = Wenceslas (IMP)
Wenceslaus (H) 1301-1304
Wendel period (S) +1690
Wenzel (D) = Wenceslas
Wesley, John (GB) +1739
Westphalia Peace of +1648
Widukind (SAX) +783
Widukind of Corvey (IMP) +980
Wied, Wilhelm zu (AL) 1913-1914
Wilfred of York (GB) +664
Wilhelm (A,BAY,D) = William
Wilhelmina (NL) 1890-1948
Willem (NL) = William
William (A) 1386-1406
William IV (BAY+ (1503)- 1550
William V (BAY) 1579-1597
William of Holland (D) 1254-1256
William I (D) 1871-1888 = William I (PREU) 1861-1888
William II (D) 1888-1918
William I the Conqueror (GB) 1066-1087
William II (GB) 1087-1100
William III (GB) 1688-1702 = William III of Orange (NL)
William IV (GB) 1830-1837
William I of Orange (NL) 1575-1584
William II of Orange (NL) 1647-1650
William III of Orange (NL) 1672-1702
William IV of Orange (NL) 1747-1751
William V of Orange (NL) 1751-1795
William I, King (NL) 1815-1840
William II, King (NL) 1840-1849
William III, King (NL) 1849-1890
William (SCOT) 1165-1214
William Wallace (SCOT) 1297-1305
William I the Bad (SIC) 1154-1166
William II the Good (SIC) 1166-1189
William III (SIC) 1194-1196
William Tell +1290
Willibrord (GB) +696
Wilson, Woodrow (USA) 1913-1921
Witigis (OGO) 536-540
Witiza, (VIGO) 701-709
Witt, Johan de (NL) 1653-1672
Witteric (VIGO) 603-610
Władysław I Herman (PL) 1079-1102
Władysław II (PL) 1138-1146
Władysław Laskonogi (PL) 1202, 1227-1229
Władysław the Short (PL) 1306-1333
Władysław (= Jagiello) (PL) 1386-1434
Władysław (III) (PL) 1434-1444
Władysław IV Vasa (PL) 1632-1648
Władysław (RU) 1610-1613 = Wladyslaw IV Vasa (PL)
Wojciechowski, Stanisław (PL) 1923-1926
Wolstinik (LIT) 1264-1267
Wstydliwy, Bolesław V (PL) 1243-1279
Wu Da Di (RC) 222-251
Wu Fei Di (RC) 252-257
Wu Gui Ming Hou (RC) 263-280
Wu Hou (RC) 685-705
Wu Hou Guan Hou (RC) 252-257
Wu Jing Di (RC) 258-263
Wu Ling (RC) -310
Wulfhere (GB) +690
Wycliffe, John, ca. 1324-1384

Xavier, Francis (JAP) +1560
Xenophon (ATH) -400
Xerxes I (IR) 486-465
Xi Wei Fei Di (RC) 552-553
Xi Wei Gong Di (RC) 554-556
Xi Wei Wen Di (RC) 535-551
Xia, dyn, (RC) (2200)-1784
Xin Wang Mang (RC) 9-23
Xiu Xin (RC) +110
Xolotl (MEX) +1168
Xuan Zhuang (RC) +630

Yahyā ben Ali (CORD) 1021-1022, 1025-1027
Yahya Khan (PAK) 1968-1971
Yamato (J) -660
Ya'qub (AFG) 1879-1880
Yaq'ub (IR) 1478-1485
Yarkand +60

Yaropolk I (RU) 973-980
Yaropolk II (RU) 1132-1139
Yaroslav I (RU) 1019-1054
Yaroslav II (RU) 1238-1246
Yaroslav III (RU) 1263-1272
Yazdegerd I (IR) 399-420
Yazdegerd II (IR) 438-457
Yazdegerd III (IR) 634-651
Yazid II (CAL) 720-724
Yellow River (RC) +620
Yellow Turbans (RC) +190
Yemen +325, 370
Yermak (RU) +1581
Yin (RC) 1401-1155
Yin Zhou (RC) 1154-1123
Yohannes IV Kassai (ETH) 1872-1899
Yōmei (J) 586-587
Yoritomo (J) +1200
Yoshiaki (J) 1568-1573
Yoshiharu (J) 1521-1545
Yoshihide (J) 1565-1568
Yoshihisa (J) 1473-1489
Yoshihito (J) 1913-1926
Yoshikatsu (J) 1441-1443
Yoshikazu (J) 1423-1425
Yoshimasa (J) 1443-1473
Yoshimitsu (J) 1392-1408
Yosimochi (J) 1409-1423, 1425-1428
Yoshimune (J) 1716-1745
Yoshinaka (J) +1200
Yoshinori (J) 1428-1441
Yoshitane (J) 1489-1493, 1508-1521
Yoshiteru (J) 1545-1565
Yoshitoki (J) +1230
Yoshitsune (J) +1200
Yoshizumi (J) 1493-1508
Yozei (J) 876-884
Yu, Emperor (RC) -2205
Yuan, dyn (RC) 1280-1367
Yuan Cheng Zong (RC) 1295-1307
Yuan Ming Zong (RC) 1328-1329
Yuan Ren Zong (RC) 1312-1320
Yuan Shikai (RC) 1912-1916
Yuan Shun Di (RC) 1333-1367
Yuan Tai Ding Di (RC) 1324-1327
Yuan Wen Zong (RC) 1330-1332
Yuan Wu Zong (RC) 1308-1311
Yuan Ying Zong (RC) 1321-1323
Yüan (RC) = Yuan
Yucatán +999, 1020
Yuechi (RC) -180, +100
Yuhan'im, Malikarrib (Arabia) +378
Yung (RC) = Yong
Yuriaku (J) 457-479
Yury I Dolgorusky (RU) 1154-1157
Yury II (RU) 1212-1216, 1219-1238
Yury III Danilovich (RU) 1319-1324

Zababa (BAB) 1174-1173
Zachariah (IL) -520
Zacharias (V) 741-752
Zafir (ET) 1149-1153
Zaharija Pribisavljević (YU) 920-924
Zahir (ET) 1020-1036
Zahir Shah, Muhammad (AFG) 1933-1973
Zai Lun (RC) +105
Zaimis, Alexandros (GR) 1929-1935
Zaldúa, F.J. (CO) 1882-1884
Zaleucus (I) -664
Zaman Shah (AFG) 1793-1799
Zamora, Alcalá (E) 1931-1936
Zápolya, Janós (H) +1526
Zapotocky, Antonin (CS) 1953-1957
Zarathustra = Zoroaster
Zauditu (Judith) (ETH) 1916-1930
Zawadzki, Aleksander (PL) 1952-1964
Zayas, Alfredo (C) 1921-1925
Zedekiah (JU) 597-587
Zemgals, Gustavs (LET) 1927-1930
Zeno (ATH) -300
Zeno (ROM) 474-475, 576-491
Zenobia (SYR) +270, 280
Zephaniah (IL) -640
Zephyrinus (V) 199-217
Zhang Ling (RC) +140
Zhang Xian (RC) -130
Zhang Ze Duang (RC) +1120
Zhang Zhue (RC) +190
Zhivkov, Todor (BG) 1971-
Zhongguo (RC) -670
Zhou An-Wang (RC) 401-376
Zhou Cheng Wang (RC) 1115-1076
Zhou Ding Wang (RC) 606-586
Zhou Dong Zhou Jun (RC) 255-251
Zhou Gong Wang (RC) 946-935
Zhou Guang Wang (RC) 612-607
Zhou Huan Wang (RC) 719-697
Zhou Hui Wang (RC) 676-652
Zhou Jian Wang (RC) 585-572
Zhou Jing Wang I (RC) 544-520
Zhou Jing Wang II (RC) 519-476
Zhou Kang Wang (RC) 1075-1053
Zhou Kao Wang (RC) 440-426
Zhou Li Wang (RC) 878-828
Zhou Lie Wang (RC) 375-369
Zhou Ling Wang (RC) 571-545
Zhou Mu Wang (RC) 1001-947
Zhou Ping Wang (RC) 770-720
Zhou Qiong Wang (RC) 618-613
Zhou She Wang (RC) 314-256
Zhou Shen Jing Wang (RC) 320-315
Zhou Wei Lie Wang (RC) 425-402
Zhou Wu Wang (RC) 1122-1116
Zhou Xian Wang (RC) 368-321
Zhou Xiang Wang (RC) 651-619
Zhou Xiao Wang (RC) 908-895
Zhou Xuan Wang (RC) 827-782
Zhou Yi Wang I (RC) 934-909
Zhou Yi Wang II (RC) 894-879
Zhou Yi Wang III (RC) 681-677
ZhouYou Wang (RC) 781-771
Zhou Yuan Wang (RC) 475-469
Zhou Zhao Wang (RC) 1052-1002
Zhou Zhen Ding Wang (RC) 468-441
Zhou Zhuang Wang (RC) 696-682
Zhu Wen (RC) +900, 907
Zhu Xi (RC) +1180
Zhuangzi (RC) -300
Zia ul-Haq (PAK) 1978-
Zidantas II (HAT) ca 1477-1473
Zikmund (CS) = Sigismund
Zimri (IL) -881
Zinzendorf (D) +1727
Zipoetes (Bithynia) 297-280
Zoe (BYZ) +1030, 1042
Zog I (AL) 1925-1939 = Ahmed Zogu
Zoroaster (IR) -630, +240, 490, 770
Zosimus (V) 417-418
Zotto (LONG) +580
Zsigmond (H) = Sigismund
Zu Xi (RC) +1898
Zuazo, Hernando Siles (RB) 1956-1960, 1969
Zvonimir (YU) +1089
Zygmunt (PL) = Sigismund